CWLA's Guide to Adoption Agencies:
A National Directory of Adoption Agencies and Adoption Resources

Julia L. Posner

with James Guilianelli, Contributing Editor

Child Welfare League of America

440 First Street, NW, Suite 310, Washington, DC 20001-2085

CHILD WELFARE LEAGUE OF AMERICA, INC.
440 First Street, NW, Suite 310
Washington, DC 20001-2085

Cover design by Anita Crouch
Text design by Eve Malakoff-Klein

Current Printing (last digit)
10 9 8 7 6 5 4 3 2

PRINTED IN THE UNITED STATES OF AMERICA

ISBN # 0-87868-345-3

To
David,
Sarah,
Meredith,
and
Rachel

CONTENTS

PREFACE

The adoption process is not difficult, but finding information about adoption can be. In spite of the information explosion, learning about adoption is still essentially a word-of-mouth process. When my husband and I decided to adopt five years ago, we found it difficult to get information about adoption. After a fruitless visit to the local bookstore, I called our local social services agency. They gave me a bleak picture of the prospect of adopting through a public agency (five year wait for a child of any race under the age of three) and sent me the names of five private agencies in New York. (I know now that there are more than 80 agencies in New York!) Finally, we found out about our agency through a chance meeting with a stranger in the grocery store. (Thank you, John!) Four months later, our daughter arrived from Korea.

This personal experience coupled with my frustration at media coverage of adoption as virtually impossible led me to begin research on this book. It seems to me that experience as a private investigator shouldn't be a prerequisite for adoption. Prospective adoptive parents shouldn't have to send out massive mailings to agencies from New York to California, from the Gulf Stream waters to the Redwood forests. They should be able to look in a book and find agencies whose programs and philosophies are in accord with their needs. They should be able to find out how much it costs and how long it takes and what the requirements are without doubling their phone bill. This book makes that possible.

As I worked on the book, it became clear that professional social workers, too, are interested in finding out more about the programs and policies of their counterparts across the country. So while I wrote the book with prospective adoptive parents in mind, I hope that it will be useful, directly or indirectly, to all whose lives are touched by adoption—adoptive parents, birthparents, social workers, and, most important, children.

Encouragement from friends and family gave me the push to get started. Three, in particular, volunteered their time and energy. I am grateful to Janine Weeks for volunteering to help with clerical work; to Dick Wagenaar for giving me the benefit of his substantial editorial skill; and especially to Jim Guilianelli, friend and contributing editor.

I am, of course, most thankful to my family; to my children—David, Sarah, Rachel, and Meredith—for putting up with my long hours at the computer and for not complaining too much ("Fish sticks again?"); to Breda Oakley for her assistance in keeping our household functioning; and most of all to my husband, Larry, not only for his love and steadfast support, but for his sound, practical guidance from beginning to end.

ACKNOWLEDGMENTS

While I am grateful to many for their encouragement and support, I am principally indebted to Jim Guilianelli, friend and contributing editor. Jim composed many of the agency descriptions, drafted the summary tables, and helped verify the accuracy of the information. His enthusiasm was a constant support. I am grateful to him for his contribution and his friendship.

This book would not have been possible without the cooperation of the professional adoption community and all the participating agencies who took the time to respond to the questionnaire. My special thanks to Suzanne D'Aversa and Deborah McCurdy at Parsons Child and Family Center for their advice and encouragement; Lori Obluck at the Adoption Information Center of Wisconsin for her support and for permission to use AIC's format for the private agency summaries; Anna Marie Merrill at International Concerns Committee for Children for reviewing part of the manuscript and offering her suggestions. I am especially grateful to Sue Brite and Eve Malakoff-Klein, Child Welfare League of America, for their editorial guidance and to David Liederman for his enthusiastic response to the project. It is consistent with CWLA's long history of innovation to welcome new ideas and to attempt what others say is impossible.

There are two factors I ask you to keep in mind as you use this resource. First, the information presented is based on data gathered between October 1987 and October 1988. Invariably, things change—addresses, phone numbers, fees, even programs. Use this guide as a starting point for your search for an agency that is right for you, and anticipate change.

Second, all agencies and organizations listed in the guide participated voluntarily and approved the accuracy of their descriptions. Agency participation was as high as 100% in some states, and as low as 50% in a few.

You may obtain a complete list of licensed agencies in a given state by sending a written request to the appropriate department in that state (see Public Adoption Program at the beginning of each chapter).

PUBLIC ADOPTION PROGRAM/COMMUNITY RESOURCES

The information on public adoption programs, general adoption resources, and special-needs adoption resources was provided by the appropriate department in each state and, in some cases, by the state's NACAC representative. Some provided voluminous descriptions of their programs and resources; others provided minimal information. Keep in mind that support groups and support services come into being to meet the needs of individuals and families in a given area and may become inactive when those needs change. In short, addresses and telephone numbers change. A number of organizations included in the last chapter ("National Child Welfare and Triad Support Organizations") provide information and referral to support groups and services across the U.S. (notably OURS, Inc.; North American Council on Adoptable Children; Committee for Single Adoptive Parents). In addition, private agencies often sponsor support groups or can refer you to a group in your area.

OUT-OF-STATE AGENCIES

Included at the beginning of each chapter is a list of agencies located in other states which provide placement services for residents of that state. In many cases, these are agencies which are located near state lines. In other cases, the out-of-state agency is located across the country but has been either licensed or approved for placement in that state by the appropriate authority.

LICENSED PRIVATE ADOPTION AGENCIES

In reading the agency descriptions, there are several factors to keep in mind.

Area of service

The agency's area of service is clearly defined in the first paragraph (The Program). In some cases, the area of service is restricted by the licensing authority in a given state, authorizing the agency to provide child placement services only to residents of a specific geographic area. In other cases, the area of service is limited by the scope of the agency's program. In any case, to request services of an agency which does not serve your area will lead to frustration and disappointment.

The Cost

Keep in mind that fees are approximate and subject to change. Adoption agencies work hard to minimize expenses, and social workers are obviously not "in it for the money." Adoption agencies have to face the same cost increases in utility bills and insurance coverage that all of us face. Fees are included in the agency's description to give you a general idea of what to anticipate.

The Wait

The time required to complete the adoption process is also approximate and subject to change. Numerous factors (many of which are not within the agency's control) impact the length of time from application to placement. If the agency you select cites an average wait of 10 months, be prepared to wait 15 months and be pleasantly surprised when placement occurs at 9 months. Keep in mind that the agency's goal is to unite children who need families with families who want children as quickly as possible.

The Requirements

In accordance with supply and demand, the requirements are generally more restrictive for people interested in adopting Caucasian infants, less restrictive for people interested in international adoption, and least restrictive for people interested in special-needs adoption. The problem with this formulation is that it sounds as though agencies arbitrarily impose restrictions to prevent prospective adoptive parents from getting what they want. Actually, the agency's primary concern is to act in the child's best interests (although your notion of what is best for the child may differ from the agency's). It may be helpful (and certainly more just) to think of it this way: People who have a lot of restrictions about the kind of child they feel they can parent will have to face a lot of restrictions in order to become parents; people who have fewer restrictions will have to face fewer restrictions. Most of us do have limitations and preconceptions about the kind of child we envision as part of our family, but we should recognize them as our limitations.

PRIVATE AGENCY SUMMARY

The tables at the end of this book summarizing services provided by the agencies included are meant to serve as a quick reference to guide you to agencies which may be appropriate for you. If you are interested in open adoption, for example, use the summary to find the agencies in your state which provide open adoption services and then read the descriptions of the agencies. In reading the agency descriptions, you will note that "open" for some agencies means an exchange of non-identifying information between birthparents and adoptive parents while for others it means ongoing communication. In short, the summary is only a summary. To get a thorough and accurate picture of the agency and its programs, read the agency's description.

Area of Service

This category indicates the geographic area served by the

agency. If the agency has branch offices in other states or across the country, the location of these branch offices is enclosed in parentheses.

Age

The age requirement cited in this category generally reflects the agency's most restrictive policy. Refer to the agency's description for exceptions to the age requirement. The age requirement for applicants pursuing older child or special-needs adoption is often flexible.

Religion

Some agencies provide services only to members of a specific faith. However, many agencies which are affiliated with a particular faith provide services to applicants of other faiths. Typically, agencies which provide services to birthparents honor the religious preferences of the birthparents whenever possible, and the requirement varies accordingly.

Types of Adoption Services

Single Parent: A "Y" in this category indicates that the agency is willing to provide services to single parents. In some cases, this means that the agency will "consider" single parents for some placements; in others, it means that single parents are eligible for some programs.

Traditional: A "Y" in this category indicates that the agency practices traditional, confidential infant adoption. This may include Caucasian, Black, Hispanic, or bi-racial infant adoption. In some cases, the program is limited to the placement of infants of a specific race (i.e., Black and bi-racial infants).

Identified: A "Y" in this category indicates that the agency will work with applicants pursuing identified adoption. An identified adoption is one in which the prospective adoptive parents locate a birthmother who is willing to specify the adoption of her child by that couple. "Designated" and "identified" are synonymous.

Open: A "Y" in this category indicates that the agency provides for "openness" in the adoption process. This may be limited to an exchange of non-identifying information or it may include agency-mediated meetings between prospective adoptive parents and birthparents and ongoing communication.

U.S. Special Needs: A "Y" in this category indicates that the agency places American-born children with special needs (children of minority race; older children; children with physical, emotional, or developmental handicaps; sibling groups). In some cases, the agency has custody of the children placed. In other cases, the agency does not have custody of the children, but works with other private or public agencies or with national or regional exchange programs to facilitate the placement of children with special needs. "Hard to place" and "waiting children" are synonymous with "special needs." Please note that "handicapped" is not synonymous with "special needs;" rather, it is one type of special need. Many children who have no significant physical or developmental problems are classified as "special needs" because of their age or racial heritage.

Foreign: A "Y" in this category indicates that the agency places healthy and/or special-needs children born in countries other than the U.S. In some cases, the agency works directly with foreign sources. In other cases, the

agency does not have custody of the children and does not have direct contacts abroad, but works with other U.S. agencies which maintain international programs to facilitate placement. "International," "intercountry," and "foreign" all refer to the placement of children born in other countries in U.S. families.

Homestudy/Post-placement: A "Y" in this category indicates that the agency will provide homestudy and post-placement services for applicants pursuing adoption through another placement source. In some cases, the agency will provide such services only for one type of adoption (i.e., U.S. special-needs adoptions). In others, the agency will provide homestudy and post-placement services for applicants pursuing a range of adoption options (i.e., domestic or international interagency adoptions, private or independent adoptions, relative or stepparent adoptions, parent-initiated international adoptions, etc.).

NATIONAL CHILD WELFARE AND TRIAD SUPPORT ORGANIZATIONS

While the list is by no means exhaustive, the organizations included in this chapter are national organizations, some of which address adoption issues exclusively and some of which address broader issues of social and child welfare. Some provide services to members of the adoption triad (adoptive parents, birthparents, adoptees) while others provide support services (training, consultation, advocacy) to the agencies themselves. The organizations described in the chapter are not adoption agencies. They are included in the directory to provide an understanding of the forces at work in the professional adoption community.

The range of adoption options and resources is astonishing. Whether you are single or married, 28 years old or 47 years old, Black or Caucasian, Catholic or Buddhist, childless or parents of five, from Arkansas or from Nebraska, rich or poor—there is an agency which will work with you. And, sadly, there are many more children who need and want families than there are families who want children. I hope this book will give them—and you—better odds.

APPENDIX A

Agencies Providing Nationwide Services: Appendix A lists agencies which provide nationwide placement services. If you wish to work with one of the agencies listed, you will need to identify an agency in your home state which will provide the homestudy and post-placement supervision (refer to Private Agency Summary to identify agencies in your state which will provide these services for inter-agency adoptions).

A FINAL THOUGHT

One final note of caution. I am an adoptive parent and a writer—not a social worker. I have attempted to describe the agencies as objectively and accurately as possible, on the basis of the information they provided. I have made no judgments about the quality of their services or the nature of their programs. My purpose was to give you sufficient information to begin your inquiry into adoption and to embark on your quest for parenthood and fulfillment.

Alabama

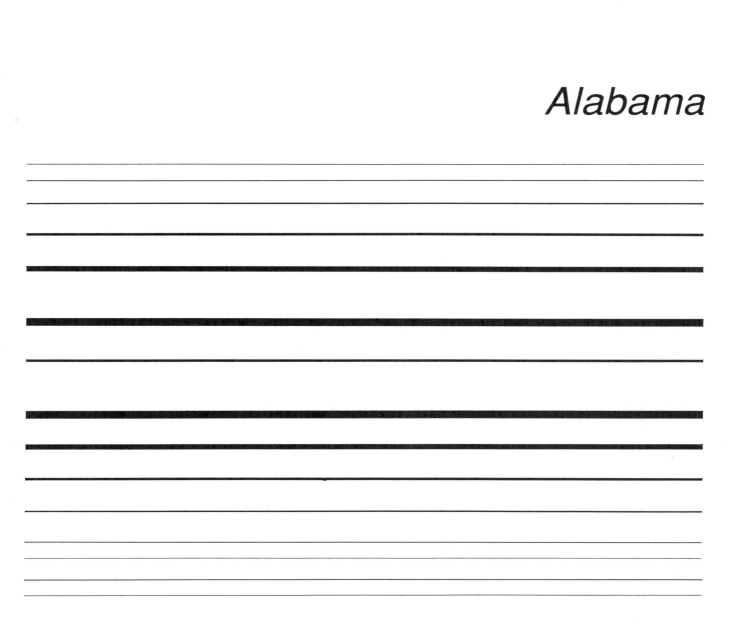

PUBLIC ADOPTION PROGRAM/ COMMUNITY RESOURCES

Department of Human Resources
Division of Family and Children's Services
Office of Adoption
64 North Union Street
Montgomery, AL 36130
(205) 261-3409
Adoption specialist: Jerry Milner

THE PROGRAM

Alabama has a centralized program of adoption; all inquiries about adoption services should be directed to the Office of Adoption (above). The Office of Adoption recruits and prepares families and supervises the placement of special-needs children (older, handicapped, and minority children and large sibling groups).

STATE EXCHANGE

Alabama Resource Book. For information, contact the Office of Adoption (above).

STATE ADOPTION REUNION REGISTRY

None.

STATE SUBSIDY

For information, contact the Office of Adoption (above).

NACAC REPRESENTATIVE

Jan Gentry
1821 Chanbury Circle
Pelham, AL 35124
(205) 663-6659

GENERAL ADOPTION RESOURCES

Alabama Friends of Adoption
4968 Springrock Road
Birmingham, AL 35223

SPECIAL-NEEDS ADOPTION RESOURCES

Dale Brantley, Director of Social Services
Sparks Center for Developmental and Learning Disorders
University of Alabama in Birmingham
P.O. Box 313
Birmingham, AL 35294
(205) 934-5471

OUT-OF-STATE AGENCIES

SEE APPENDIX A

Agencies Providing Nationwide Services

AGAPE OF CENTRAL ALABAMA

P.O. Box 230472
Montgomery, AL 36123
(205) 272-9466
Program director: Jimmy Dobbs

THE PROGRAM

Licensed in 1979 as a child placing agency, AGAPE of Central Alabama is a nonprofit agency serving central Alabama and placing 5 to 10 children annually. Seeking "to serve the best interests of children," AGAPE provides counseling and maternity services to birthmothers regardless of race or religion. In addition, AGAPE provides foster care services, adoption services, and counseling services for individuals, couples, and families.

THE COST

AGAPE's fee is 10% of the applicant's annual gross income. The fee includes all phases of the adoption procedure. In addition, prospective adoptive parents should anticipate financial responsibility for fingerprinting costs ($40).

THE WAIT

The average time from application for acceptance into the program to the homecoming of the adoptive child is 1 to 2 years.

THE CHILDREN

AGAPE places primarily healthy infants, but also some special-needs children. Children may be of Caucasian, Black, or mixed racial backgrounds.

THE REQUIREMENTS

Age: Applicants may be no more than 40 years older than the adoptive child. The requirement may vary for special-needs adoptions.
Health: Applicants must be in reasonably good health. Infertility documentation is required for healthy Caucasian infant adoption.
Religion: At least one spouse must be a practicing member of the Church of Christ.
Financial status: Applicants must demonstrate financial stability.
Marital status: For adoption of healthy Caucasian infant, applicants must be married. The requirement may vary for special-needs adoptions.
Family size: For adoption of a healthy Caucasian infant, applicants may have no more than 1 child currently in the family. The requirement may vary for special-needs adoptions.
Racial, ethnic or cultural origin: Preference for placing children in families of similar origins.

THE PROCEDURE

Participation in AGAPE's adoption program entails the following basic steps:
Application
Homestudy
Placement
Post-placement supervision

ADDITIONAL PROGRAMS/SERVICES AVAILABLE

In addition to adoption services, AGAPE provides foster care for dependent/neglected children (0–18 years of age); counseling and housing for pregnant women; individual, marital, and family counseling.

BRANCH/NETWORK OFFICES

AGAPE of Central Alabama maintains a branch office in Birmingham.

LICENSE/ACCREDITATION/PROFESSIONAL AFFILIATIONS

AGAPE of Central Alabama is licensed by the State of Alabama Department of Human Resources.

AGAPE OF SOUTH ALABAMA

6300 Airport Boulevard
P.O. Box 850663
Mobile, AL 36685
(205) 343–4875
Program director: Kenny McLeod, MSW

THE PROGRAM

Licensed in 1979 as a child placing agency, AGAPE is a nonprofit agency serving residents of south Alabama. Seeking "to serve the best interests of children," AGAPE provides counseling and maternity services to birthmothers and places infants for adoption when birthmothers in the agency's program elect adoption as the best plan for their children.

THE COST

The agency's fee for adoption services is 10% of the applicants' annual gross income, with a minimum fee of $1,700 and a maximum of $5,000. Prospective adoptive parents should anticipate financial responsibility for the cost of fingerprinting ($40).

THE WAIT

The time from application to the homecoming of the adoptive child ranges from 1 to 3 years.

THE CHILDREN

AGAPE places primarily healthy infants, but also some special-needs children. Children may be of Caucasian, Black, or mixed racial backgrounds, born in the U.S.

THE REQUIREMENTS

Age: Applicants may be no more than 40 years older than the adoptive child. The requirements may vary for special-needs adoptions.
Health: Applicants must be in reasonably good health. Infertility documentation is required for healthy Caucasian infant adoptions.
Religion: At least on spouse must be a practicing member of the Church of Christ.
Financial status: Applicants must demonstrate financial stability.
Marital status: For healthy Caucasian infant adoptions, applicants must be married. The requirement may vary for special-needs adoptions.
Family size: For healthy Caucasian infant adoption, applicants may have no more than 1 child currently in the family. The requirement may vary for special-needs adoptions.
Racial, ethnic or cultural origin: Preference for placing children in families of similar origins.

THE PROCEDURE

Participation in AGAPE's adoption program entails the following basic steps:
Orientation meeting
Application
Homestudy
Placement
Post-placement supervision

ADDITIONAL PROGRAMS/SERVICES AVAILABLE

AGAPE provides foster care for dependent/neglected children (0–18 years of age); counseling and housing for pregnant women.

BRANCH/NETWORK OFFICES

Enterprise Branch
P.O. Box 1541
Enterprise, AL 36331
(205) 393–1990

LICENSE/ACCREDITATION/PROFESSIONAL AFFILIATIONS

AGAPE of South Alabama is licensed by the State of Alabama Department of Human Resources.

CATHOLIC FAMILY SERVICES

2164 11th Avenue
Birmingham, AL 35205
(205) 324–6561
Program director: Ray Donlevy

THE PROGRAM

Catholic Family Services is a nonprofit child welfare and family services agency serving residents of the Diocese of Birmingham (39 north Alabama counties) and placing approximately 10 to 15 children annually through its adoption program. The agency provides services to birthparents and places both healthy and special-needs infants for adoption when birthparents elect adoptive placement as the best plan for their child. In addition, the agency is willing to provide homestudy and post-placement services for applicants pursuing interagency adoption (domestic and international).

THE COST

As of October 1988, the agency's fee for adoption services is based on a sliding scale and ranges from $2,000 to $5,000. Services covered by the fee include all phases of the adoption process.

THE WAIT

The time from application to placement averages 2 to 3 years.

THE CHILDREN

Catholic Family services places healthy infants (6 weeks to 1 year) of Black, Caucasian, and bi-racial backgrounds, born in the U.S.

THE REQUIREMENTS

Age: Applicants must be at least 21 and no more than 37 years of age.

Health: Applicants must be in reasonably good health. Infertility documentation is required.

Religion: Applicants must be practicing members of a Protestant or Catholic church. A reference from a priest or minister is required.

Financial status: Applicants must have sufficient income to provide adequately for the family's needs.

Marital status: Applicants must be married; the length of the marriage must be at least 3 years.

Family size: Applicants must be childless.

Racial, ethnic or cultural origin: No requirement, but preference for placing children in families of similar origins.

THE PROCEDURE

Participation in the adoption program of Catholic Family Services entails the following basic steps:
Orientation meeting
Application
Homestudy
Individual counseling sessions
Adoption preparation group
Placement
Post-placement supervision

ADDITIONAL PROGRAMS/SERVICES

Catholic Family Services provides counseling services for birthparents and foster care for infants awaiting placement.

BRANCH/NETWORK OFFICES

Catholic Family Services maintains branch offices in Huntsville and Tuscaloosa, Alabama.

LICENSE/ACCREDITATION/PROFESSIONAL AFFILIATIONS

Catholic Family Services is licensed by the state of Alabama Department of Human Resources.

CATHOLIC SOCIAL SERVICES

401 Holcombe Street
P.O. Box 454
Montgomery, AL 36101
(205) 269–2387
Program director: Sr. Geraldine Whelan

THE PROGRAM

Catholic Social Services is a private, nonprofit agency serving central and southeastern Alabama and placing 13 to 15 children annually. Founded in the 1830s, Catholic Social Services is the oldest private social service organization in Alabama and is today the only private, nonprofit agency in its region which places children with families of all religious and racial backgrounds. The agency is recognized for its contributions, direct services, and advocacy in behalf of the poor.

THE COST

The agency's fee is 8% of the applicants' annual gross income, with a minimum fee of $2,500 and a maximum of $6,000, plus an application fee of $100. The services covered by the fee include adoption services, maternity services, counseling and professional staff costs, infant hospital care, and foster care expenses. In addition, prospective adoptive parents should anticipate financial responsibility for the cost of fingerprinting ($40 per couple) and the cost of filing the adoption petition (approximately $20).

THE WAIT

The time from application to the homecoming of the adoptive child varies depending on the type of child the applicant wishes to adopt. For infant (2 years and under) adoption, the wait is approximately 3 years. For older children or sibling groups, the wait is between 6 months and 1 year.

THE CHILDREN

Catholic Social Services places both healthy and special-needs children, ranging in age from infancy to adolescence, of Black and Caucasian racial backgrounds. In addition, the agency will complete homestudies for couples waiting to receive children through foreign agencies, subject to state approval of the integrity of the source.

THE REQUIREMENTS

Age: Applicants must be at least 25 and no older than 40 years of age.

Health: Applicants must be in reasonably good health. Infertility documentation is required for healthy Caucasian infant adoption.

Religion: Applicants must be practicing members of a Christian faith. References are required.

Financial status: Applicants must demonstrate financial stability. References are required.

Marital status: For infant adoption, applicants must be married and must have been married for at least 3 years. The requirement may vary for older child or special-needs adoptions.

Residence: Applicants must reside within the 20 county area serviced by the agency. No out-of-state residents can be accepted.

Family size: For infant adoption, applicants may have no more than 1 child currently in the family. The requirement may vary for older child or special-needs adoptions.

Racial, ethnic or cultural origin: Preference for placing children in families of similar origins. Requirement may vary for older child or special-needs adoption.

THE PROCEDURE

Participation in Catholic Social Service's adoption program entails the following basic steps:
Telephone inquiry/referral
Application
Orientation
Group counseling session
Homestudy (individual and joint interviews)
Submission of references
Compliance with immigration/naturalization requirements (foreign adoptions only)
Submission of fingerprints
Completion of individual life story by applicants
Placement

Post-placement supervision (approximately 9 months)
Finalization

ADDITIONAL PROGRAMS/SERVICES AVAILABLE

In addition to adoption services, Catholic Social Services provides a 24–hour pregnancy hotline: maternity services for birthmothers; foster care program for children and expectant mothers; counseling program for children and expectant mothers; counseling program for families, couples, and individuals; direct aid and assistance for the poor.

BRANCH/NETWORK OFFICES

Southern region
Mobile Catholic Social
P.O. Box 759
Mobile, AL 36601
(205) 438–1603

South central and southeastern region
Dothan Catholic Social Services
P.O. Box 6184
Dothan, AL 36302
(205) 793–3601

LICENSE/ACCREDITATION/PROFESSIONAL AFFILIATIONS

Catholic Social Services is licensed by the State of Alabama Department of Human Resources and is a member of the United Way.

CHILDREN'S AID SOCIETY

3600 8th Avenue South, Suite 300
Birmingham, AL 35222
(205) 251–7148
Program director: Gloria King, Adoption Coordinator

THE PROGRAM

Established in 1912, Children's Aid Society is a private, nonprofit agency of the United Way, serving children and their families to assure a better quality of life through the provision of preventive and remedial services. The agency serves the counties of Jefferson, Shelby, Walker, and Blount and provides a wide range of family support services. Children's Aid Society began its adoption program in 1960 and currently places approximately 10 children annually.

THE COST

The agency fee varies depending on the type of child placed and the nature of the agency's involvement in the placement. The agency charges a flat fee for the placement of special-needs children ($350). The fee for other placements is based on a sliding scale. Agency services covered by the fee include homestudy, placement activities, follow-up supervision, and the maintenance of a permanent record for post-adoptive needs. Prospective adoptive parents should anticipate financial responsibility for legal and court fees involved in finalization of the adoption and for obtaining a new birth certificate.

THE WAIT

The time from application to the homecoming of the adoptive child varies depending on the circumstances of each case.

THE CHILDREN

Children's Aid Society places both healthy and special-needs children of all races, ranging from infancy to 19 years of age. Countries of origin include U.S., India, Taiwan, Korea, and South America.

THE REQUIREMENTS

Age: Applicants must be at least 24 years old. Other age requirements may vary depending on the best interests of the child.

Health: Applicants must be in reasonably good health; applicants with health problems or handicaps are given individual consideration. Infertility documentation is required for the adoption of Caucasian infants.

Religion: Importance is placed on providing children with the opportunity for spiritual training.

Financial status: Applicants must demonstrate the ability to manage on their income.

Marital status: Single applicants are accepted. Married couples must have been married for at least 2 years.

Family size: In order to adopt a Caucasian infant, applicants must be childless. No requirement for other types of placement.

Racial, ethnic or cultural origin: No requirement.

THE PROCEDURE

Participation in Children's Aid Society adoption program entails the following basic steps:
Orientation meeting
Preliminary interview
Application
Group preparation
Homestudy
Compliance with immigration/naturalization requirements
    (intercountry adoptions only)
Referral
Placement
Post-placement supervision

ADDITIONAL PROGRAMS/SERVICES AVAILABLE

Services provided by the Children's Aid Society include foster care; homemaker services; respite care; pregnancy counseling/single parent services; services to children in their own homes.

BRANCH/NETWORK OFFICES

None.

LICENSE/ACCREDITATION/PROFESSIONAL AFFILIATIONS

Children's Aid Society is licensed by the State of Alabama Department of Human Resources and is accredited by the Council on Accreditation of Services for Families and Children. The agency is a member of the Child Welfare League of America and the United Way of Central Alabama.

Alaska

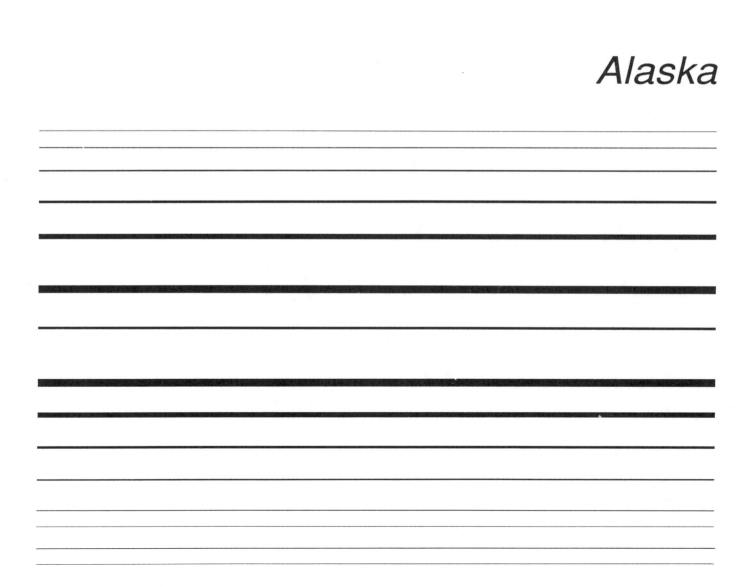

PUBLIC ADOPTION PROGRAM/ COMMUNITY RESOURCES

Department of Health and Social Services
Division of Family and Youth Services
P.O. Box H-05
Juneau, AK 99811-0630
(907) 465-3170
Adoption specialist: Karl Brimmer

THE PROGRAM

Public adoption services in Alaska are provided by the Division of Family and Youth Services. Adoptive placement of children by the Division is limited to children who are in state custody. The majority of these children have special needs due to physical handicaps or emotional problems or are Alaska Natives who fall within the purview of the Indian Child Welfare Act. The Division lists children for whom homes have not been found in Alaska with the Northwest Adoption Exchange (Seattle, Washington) and the National Adoption Network.

STATE EXCHANGE

None.

STATE ADOPTION REUNION REGISTRY

None.

STATE SUBSIDY

For information, contact the Division of Family and Youth Services (above).

NACAC REPRESENTATIVE

None at this time.

GENERAL ADOPTION RESOURCES

Adoption support services in Alaska are normally provided by private adoption agencies as a service to their clients. Contact private agencies in Alaska for information about support groups and services in your area.

SPECIAL-NEEDS ADOPTION RESOURCES

For information about resources for children with special needs, contact the Division of Family and Youth Services (above).

OUT-OF-STATE AGENCIES

SEE APPENDIX A

Agencies Providing Nationwide Services

ADOPTION SERVICES OF WACAP

P.O. Box 240741
Anchorage, AK 99524
(907) 278-3574
Program director: Janice Neilson, Executive Director

THE PROGRAM

For a full description of programs and services, refer to Washington listing:
Adoption Services of WACAP
P.O. Box 88948
Seattle, WA 98138
(206) 575-4550

CATHOLIC SOCIAL SERVICES

225 Cordova, Bldg. B
Anchorage, AK 99501
(907) 277-2554
Program director: Elaine Glaser

THE PROGRAM

Catholic Social Services is a nonprofit agency serving residents of the state of Alaska and placing approximately 15-17 children annually through its adoption program. Working directly with birthparents, with other licensed agencies (private and public), and with national and regional exchange programs, the agency places both infants and special-needs children in adoptive families. In addition, the agency will provide homestudy and supervisory services for applicants pursuing interagency adoption (domestic or international) or independent adoption.

THE COST

The agency's fees for adoption services are determined on an individual basis. The average fee is $3,000 and includes application, homestudy, placement, and supervision. In addition, applicants may anticipate possible medical and/or transportation costs for the birthmother and child.

THE WAIT

The time from application to the homecoming of the adoptive child ranges from 1 1/2 to 3 years.

THE CHILDREN

Catholic Social Services places primarily healthy infants of all racial backgrounds born in Alaska. The agency also places a limited number of special-needs children.

THE REQUIREMENTS

Age: Applicants must be at least 25 and no more than 45 years of age.
Health: Applicants should be in reasonably good health. Infertility documentation (or documentation of the number of years the couple has been unable to conceive) is required for healthy infant adoption.
Religion: No requirement.
Financial status: No requirement.
Marital status: Applicants must be married; the length of the marriage must be at least 5 years.
Family size: Applicants may have no more than 1 child currently in the family. The requirement is flexible for special-needs placements.
Racial, ethnic or cultural origin: No requirement, but preference for placing children in families of similar origins. The requirement is determined on a case-by-case basis.

THE PROCEDURE

Participation in Catholic Social Services' adoption program entails the following basis steps:
Application
Orientation meeting
Homestudy (including individual and group counseling sessions)
Placement
Post-placement supervision

ADDITIONAL PROGRAMS/SERVICES AVAILABLE

Catholic Social Services provides individual and group counseling on a number of issues; foster care services; and adoption workshops for prospective adoptive couples.

BRANCH/NETWORK OFFICES

None.

LICENSE/ACCREDITATION/PROFESSIONAL AFFILIATIONS

Catholic Social Services is licensed by the State of Alaska Department of Health and Social Services. All social work staff are professionally trained and accredited social workers.

FAIRBANKS COUNSELING AND ADOPTION

P.O. Box 1544
Fairbanks, AK 99707
(907) 456–4729
Program director: Melody Jamieson

THE PROGRAM

Fairbanks Counseling and Adoption is a nonprofit agency serving residents of northern Alaska (usually Fairbanks) and placing approximately 7 children annually through its adoption program. Founded in 1977 by the Catholic diocese "to strengthen families in stress," the agency provides a range of services to individuals and families (see Additional Programs/Services). Working with birthparents, with other private and public agencies, and with national and regional exchange programs, the agency places healthy and special-needs children born in the U.S. Working cooperatively with other U.S. Agencies which maintain international programs, the agency facilitates the placement of children from various countries. In addition, the agency will provide homestudy and supervisory services for applicants pursuing interagency adoption (domestic or international) or independent adoption. Fairbanks Counseling and Adoption believes that "all children should be in a home where they are loved and nurtured."

THE COST

For domestic adoptions, the agency's fee is $3,500; for special-needs and/or international adoptions, the agency's fee ranges from $1,400 to $1,700. Services covered by the fee include the homestudy, child search, post-placement supervision and support services. For domestic adoptions, appli-

cants should anticipate legal and medical expenses. For international adoptions, applicants should anticipate fees to the cooperating agency, possible travel, and related expenses. For all programs, applicants are responsible for legal fees connected with finalization.

THE WAIT

For domestic Caucasian infant adoption, the time from application to placement ranges from 2 to 4 years, with an average wait of 3 years. For international adoption, the wait varies depending on the country and the cooperating agency, with an average wait of 2 years.

THE CHILDREN

Fairbanks Counseling and Adoption places and facilitates the placement of both healthy and special-needs children of all ages and racial backgrounds, born in the U.S. or abroad.

THE REQUIREMENTS

Age: The age requirement is evaluated on a case-by-case basis.
Health: Applicants should be in reasonably good health. Applicants with health problems or handicaps are given individual consideration.
Religion: No requirement.
Financial status: No requirement.
Marital status: No requirement.
Family size: For domestic Caucasian infant adoption, applicants may have no more than 1 child currently in the family.
Racial, ethnic or cultural origin: No requirement, but preference for placing children in families of similar origins.

THE PROCEDURE

Participation in the adoption programs of Fairbanks Counseling and Adoption entails the following basic steps:
Orientation meeting
Application
Individual counseling sessions
Homestudy
Compliance with immigration/naturalization requirements (international adoptions only)
Referral
Placement
Post-placement supervision

ADDITIONAL PROGRAMS/SERVICES

Fairbanks Counseling and adoption provides individual, marital and family counseling; parenting education; pregnancy counseling; grief and post-relinquishment counseling; seminars on a variety of topics.

BRANCH/NETWORK OFFICES

None.

LICENSE/ACCREDITATION/PROFESSIONAL AFFILIATIONS

Fairbanks Counseling and Adoption is licensed by the State of Alaska Department of Human Resources.

LDS SOCIAL SERVICES

4020 DeBarr Street, #225A
Anchorage, AK 99508
(907) 337–6696
Program director: Terence A. Robrecht

THE PROGRAM

For a full description of programs and services, refer to
Utah listing:

LDS Social Services
50 East North Temple Street
Salt Lake City, UT 84150

Arizona

PUBLIC ADOPTION PROGRAM/ COMMUNITY RESOURCES

Department of Economic Security
1400 West Washington, 940A
Phoenix, AZ 85005
(602) 542–3981
Adoption specialist: Carol Lussier

THE PROGRAM

The public adoption program in Arizona is administered by the Department of Economic Security.

STATE EXCHANGE

Arizona Families for Children
P.O. Box 17951
(602) 327–3324

STATE ADOPTION REUNION REGISTRY

Arizona State Adoption Registry. For information, contact the Department of Economic Security (above).

STATE SUBSIDY

For information, contact the Department of Economic Security (above).

NACAC REPRESENTATIVE

Susan Iliff
131 E. Country Club Drive
Phoenix, AZ 85014
(602) 265–6155

GENERAL ADOPTION RESOURCES:

Adoption Counseling Center
2211 E. Highland Avenue, Suite 130
Phoenix, AZ 85016
(602) 224–9757

Adoption Information Center
1011 N. Craycroft, Suite 304
Tucson, AZ 85711
(602) 237–3324

Adoptive Parents Education Program
P.O. Box 32114
Phoenix, AZ 85064
(602) 957–2896

Arizona Advocates for Children
4439 E. Broadway, Suite 212
Tucson, AZ 85771
(602) 795–5437

SPECIAL-NEEDS ADOPTION RESOURCES

Aid to Adoption of Special Kids (Aask)
234 N. Central Avenue, Suite 127
Phoenix, AZ 85004
(602) 254–2275

OUT-OF-STATE AGENCIES

AGENCY

Smithlawn Maternity Home, Texas (special-needs and minority placements)

SEE APPENDIX A

Agencies Providing Nationwide Services.

ARIZONA CHILDREN'S HOME ASSOCIATION

2700 S. 8th Avenue
P.O. Box 7277
Tucson, AZ 85725–7277
(602) 622–7611
Program director: Susan Winder, Director/Permanency Planning

THE PROGRAM

Arizona Children's Home Association (ACHA) is a non-profit child welfare agency which provides a wide range of programs for children and families in Tucson and the surrounding area. Founded in 1912 for the purpose of "finding homes for homeless children," the agency has evolved in response to the changing needs of the community and today provides a continuum of care and services designed to meet the varying needs of children and their families, including residential treatment, special education programs, treatment foster home and older child adoption programs, family therapy, day treatment, unwed parent and teen parent programs, and an infant adoption program. The agency places infants for adoption (approximately 20 annually) when birthparents in the agency's counseling program elect adoptive placement as the best plan for their child. Through the treatment foster home and older child adoption program, the agency places older children (typically from 9 to 14), many of whom have emotional problems resulting from abuse or neglect. The agency places approximately 10 children annually through the older child adoption program.

THE COST

The agency's fee for infant adoption (1988 fee schedule) is $6,000. Services covered by the fee include all phases of the adoption process and all services to birthparents. Fees may be reduced for families interested in adopting a special-needs infant. For older child adoption, services are provided at no cost to the adoptive family.

THE WAIT

The time from application to the placement of the adoptive child varies depending on the program and ranges from 6 to 30 months.

THE CHILDREN

ACHA places both healthy and special-needs children, ranging in age from birth to 17 years, of all racial backgrounds, born in the U.S.

The Requirements

Age: The requirement varies depending on the age of the child.

Health: Applicants should be in reasonably good health. Applicants with health problems or handicaps are give individual consideration.

Religion: No requirement.

Financial status: Applicants must demonstrate the ability to support themselves and the child.

Marital status: The requirement varies depending on the needs and the age of the child.

Family size: The requirement varies depending on the needs and the age of the Child.

Racial, ethnic or cultural origin: Preference for placing children in families of similar origins.

The Procedure

Participation in ACHA's adoption programs entails the following basic steps:

Older Child Adoption Program
Individual counseling sessions
Application
Homestudy
Training program (8 weeks)
Placement
Post-placement supervision
Post-placement support services

Infant Adoption Program
Preliminary Information Form
Orientation meeting
Individual counseling sessions
Application
Homestudy
Waiting Parent seminars (5 weeks)
Placement
Post-placement supervision
Post-placement support services

Additional Programs/Services

ACHA provides a wide range of services in addition to adoption services, including residential treatment for emotionally handicapped children and youth; special education program; treatment foster home; family therapy; day treatment; unwed parent and teen parent programs.

Branch/Network Offices

None.

License/Accreditation/Professional Affiliations

Arizona Children's home Association is licensed by the State of Arizona Department of Economic Security and is accredited by the Council on Accreditation of Services for Families and Children and by the Joint Commission on Accreditation of Hospitals. The agency is a member of the Child Welfare League of America, the Arizona Council of Child Care Agencies, and the Arizona Association of Private Schools for Exceptional Children.

CATHOLIC FAMILY AND COMMUNITY SERVICES

1825 W. Northern Avenue
Phoenix, AZ 85021
(602) 997–6105
Program director: Sr. Sybil Bourgeois, ACSW

The Program

Catholic Family and Community Services (CFCS) is a nonprofit multi-service agency serving residents of the Diocese of Phoenix and placing approximately 46 children annually through its adoption program. Initiated by volunteers in 1933 and evolving in response to the changing needs of the community, CFCS provides a wide range of services to individuals and families designed "to serve and empower people in need, especially the poor, neglected and vulnerable, regardless of religious beliefs." The agency provides services to birthparents and places both healthy and special-needs children for adoption when birthparents elect adoptive placement as the best plan for their child. In addition, the agency will provide homestudy and supervisory services for applicants pursuing interagency adoption (domestic or international) or private adoption.

The Cost

The agency's fee for adoption services is based on a sliding scale with an average cost of $6,200. Services covered by the fee include orientation, application, homestudy and court certification, placement, and post-placement supervision. There are no additional fees which prospective adoptive parents need anticipate.

The Wait

The time from application to placement averages 15 months.

The Children

CFCS places both healthy and special-needs children (infants and older children), of all racial backgrounds, born in the U.S.

The Requirements

Age: For infant adoption, applicants must be at least 24 and no more than 45 years of age.

Health: Applicants should be in reasonably good health. Applicants with health problems or handicaps are given individual consideration. Infertility documentation is required.

Religion: The preference of the birthmother is honored.

Financial status: Applicants must demonstrate financial stability.

Marital status: Applicants must be married; the length of the marriage must be at least 3 years. Single parents are considered for special-needs adoption.

Family size: Applicants may have no more than 1 child currently in the family for healthy infant adoption. For special-needs placements, the requirement is flexible.

Racial, ethnic or cultural origin: Preference for placing children in families of similar origins. The requirement varies depending on the child's needs and the request of the birthparents.

THE PROCEDURE

Participation in the adoption program of CFCS entails the following basic steps:
Orientation meeting
Application
Homestudy
Placement
Post-placement supervision

ADDITIONAL PROGRAMS/SERVICES

CFCS provides a wide range of services including individual, marital, and family counseling; pregnancy counseling; infant foster care; outreach, immigration, legalization and refugee resettlement and assistance; refugee foster care; foster home recruitment and supervision; Spring Haven (shelter for girls aged 8 to 18 who are victims of in-home sexual abuse); Casa Linda Lodge (home for unmarried pregnant young women between 12 and 22 years of age); Aspen House (residence for unmarried pregnant women 18 years of age and older); Head Start program.

BRANCH/NETWORK OFFICES

Catholic Social Service of Phoenix
1825 W. Northern Avenue
Phoenix, AZ 85021

Catholic Social Service of Mohave
2064 Plaza Dr., Suite F
Bullhead City, AZ 86442
(602) 758–4176

East Valley Catholic Social Service
610 E. Southern
Mesa, AZ 85204
(602) 964–8771

Catholic Social Service of Yavapai
116 N. Summit
Prescott, AZ 86301
(602) 778–2531

Flagstaff Catholic Social Service
201 W. University Dr.
Flagstaff, AZ 86001–0814
(602) 774–9125

LICENSE/ACCREDITATION/PROFESSIONAL AFFILIATIONS

Catholic·Family and Community Services is licensed by the State of Arizona Department of Economic Security and is affiliated with Catholic Charities USA.

CHRISTIAN FAMILY CARE AGENCY

1105 E. Missouri
Phoenix, AZ 85014
(602) 234–1935
Program director: Dorothy Bloom, MSW, Director of Social Services

THE PROGRAM

Christian Family Care Agency (CFCA) is a nonprofit agency serving residents of Arizona (but primarily the metropolitan Phoenix area) and placing approximately 45 children annually in Christian homes. CFCA was established in 1982 by a group of Christians concerned about offering legitimate, caring alternatives to abortion. Since its inception, the agency has grown rapidly and now operates with 20 full and part-time staff members. The agency is "a Christ-centered social service agency whose goal is to strengthen family life and minister to hurting people in order to fulfill the great commandment, 'You must love and help your neighbors just as much as you love and take care of yourself.' (James 2:8) CFCA seeks to function as an extension of the local church, providing those services which are better performed outside of the church context."

THE COST

For infant adoptions, the agency's fee is $6,650. Services covered by the fee include all phases of the adoption process (adoptive parenting classes through post-placement services) and all medical costs related to the birthmother and child. The only additional fee which applicants need anticipate is a $20 court filing fee. Fees for special-needs adoptions are 5% of the adoptive couple's gross annual income, plus application and certification fees.

THE WAIT

The time from application to the placement of the adoptive child ranges from 1 to 3 years.

THE CHILDREN

CFCA places primarily healthy Caucasian infants but also older and special-needs children of all racial backgrounds. Children placed by CFCA are born in the U.S.

THE REQUIREMENTS

Age: Applicants must be at least 25 years of age and no more than 43 years older than the child being considered for placement.
Health: Applicants should be in reasonably good health. Applicants with health problems or handicaps are given individual consideration. For healthy infant adoption, either infertility documentation or undiagnosed impaired fertility is required.
Religion: Applicants must have a personal relationship with Jesus Christ.
Financial status: Applicants must be financially stable and able to manage the added expense of raising a child.
Marital status: Applicants must be married couples who have been married for at least 3 years.
Family size: Applicants may have no more than 1 child currently in the family. Exceptions are made for special-needs adoptions.
Racial, ethnic or cultural origin: No requirement.

THE PROCEDURE

Participation in CFCA's adoption program entails the following basic steps:
Orientation meeting
Application

Submission of fingerprinting, medical exams, and references
Personality test
Group education sessions
Individual counseling sessions
Homestudy
Placement
Post-placement supervision

ADDITIONAL PROGRAMS/SERVICES

CFCA provides counseling for birthparents before and after placement; post-placement support groups; post-birth parenting classes; community referral services; foster care for infants, children, teens, and pregnant women; fertility counseling; adoption counseling; adoption education classes; community education programs.

BRANCH/NETWORK OFFICES

None.

LICENSE/ACCREDITATION/PROFESSIONAL AFFILIATIONS

Christian Family Care Agency is licensed by the State of Arizona Department of Economic Security. The agency is an associate member of the Child Welfare League of America and a member of Evangelical Christians for Financial Accountability.

DILLON SOUTHWEST

P.O. Box 3535
Scottsdale, AZ 85257
(602) 945–2221
Program director: Emilie Sundie, Administrator

THE PROGRAM

Dillon Southwest (DSW) is a nonprofit agency serving families who are residents of Arizona and placing approximately 40 children annually. Dillon International, Inc. was formed in 1978 to broaden the scope of services to children and families in developing countries. The Korean adoption program included in Dillon International has been administered by Dillon Southwest (a DBA of Dillon International) in Arizona since 1984. Working directly with Eastern Child Welfare Society in Korea, DSW seeks "to fulfill the need of permanent homes for the children whose best interests would be served through intercountry adoption and to assure legal and social safeguards."

THE COST

The agency's fee for adoption services is $6,000. Services covered by the fee include homestudy, adoption service fee for Dillon Southwest and Eastern Child Welfare Society, transportation of the child from Korea to the U.S., and postplacement services. In addition, applicants should anticipate fingerprint fee ($20), immigration filing fee ($50), county attorney filing fee ($20), transportation for 1 adult from Arizona to the child's point of arrival in the U.S. (usually Los Angeles), and social worker's travel expenses if the family resides outside the Phoenix area.

THE WAIT

The time from application to the homecoming of the younger adoptive child averages 7 to 9 months. Placement of older children may take up to 2 years.

THE CHILDREN

DSW places both healthy and special-needs Korean children, primarily infants (under 1 year) but older children as well (up to 15 years of age).

THE REQUIREMENTS

Age: For infant adoption, applicants should be at least 25 and no more than 40 years of age. For older child adoption, the requirement varies depending on the age of the child. Occasional exceptions to age requirements are considered.
Health: Applicants should be in reasonably good health.
Religion: There are some restrictions. It is important that the child be taught moral principles and be provided with conventional medical care.
Financial status: No specific requirement.
Marital status: Applicants must be married couples who have been married for at least 3 years.
Family size: Applicants may have no more than 4 children currently in the home.
Racial, ethnic or cultural origin: No requirement.

THE PROCEDURE

Participation in DSW's adoption program entails the following basic steps:
Orientation meeting
Group counseling sessions
Application
Homestudy
Certification by county court
Referral
Compliance with immigration/naturalization requirements
Placement
Post-placement supervision

ADDITIONAL PROGRAMS/SERVICES

Dillon Southwest will provide homestudy and post-placement services for Arizona residents receiving placement of a child in the custody of another agency.

BRANCH/NETWORK OFFICES

None.

LICENSE/ACCREDITATION/PROFESSIONAL AFFILIATIONS

Dillon Southwest is licensed by the State of Arizona Department of Economic Security. The agency is a member of the North American Council on Adoptable Children and the Joint Council on International Children's Services.

FAMILY SERVICE AGENCY

1530 East Flower
Phoenix, AZ 85014
(602) 264–9891
Program director: Suzanne Johnson

THE PROGRAM

Family Service Agency is a nonprofit child welfare and family service agency serving residents of Maricopa County, Arizona and placing approximately 25–30 children annually. In existence for about 40 years, the agency's objectives include: "to contribute to harmonious family interrelationships; to strengthen the positive values in family life; to promote healthy personality development and satisfactory social functioning of various family members; to conserve and strengthen home life and parental care for children; and to cultivate the development of the mental, physical, and spiritual potentialities of children." The agency provides services to birthparents and places infants for adoption when birthparents in the agency's counseling program elect adoptive placement as the best plan for their child. In addition, the agency will provide homestudy and supervisory services for applicants pursuing private, interagency, or intercountry adoption.

THE COST

The agency's fee for adoption services is $5,500. Services covered by the fee include all phases of the adoption process.

THE WAIT

The time from application for acceptance into the program to the homecoming of the adoptive child averages 2 years.

THE CHILDREN

Family Service Agency places healthy infants of Caucasian, Caucasian/Hispanic, and Caucasian/Black racial backgrounds, born in the U.S.

THE REQUIREMENTS

Age: Applicants must be at least 23 years of age.
Health: Applicants with health problems or handicaps are given individual consideration. Infertility documentation is required.
Religion: No requirement.
Financial status: No requirement.
Marital status: Applicants must be married couples who have been married for at least 3 years.
Family size: Applicants may have no more than 1 child currently in the family.
Racial, ethnic or cultural origin: Preference for placing children in families of similar origins.

THE PROCEDURE

Participation in Family Service Agency's adoption program entails the following basic steps:
  Application
  Orientation meeting
  Homestudy
  Group counseling sessions
  Individual counseling sessions
  Certification
  Placement
  Post-placement supervision
  Finalization

ADDITIONAL PROGRAMS/SERVICES

Family Service Agency will do homestudies, post-placement services, reports to court, and birthparent counseling for applicants pursuing private, interagency, or intercountry adoption.

BRANCH/NETWORK OFFICES

Tempe Branch
  3030 S. Rural Rd.
  Tempe, AZ 85282
  (602) 966–0739
Paradise Valley Branch
  4202 E. Union Hills
  Phoenix, AZ 85024
  (602) 569–1524
Scottsdale Branch
  7375 E. Stetson Dr., #105
  Scottsdale, AZ 85251
  (602) 994–0187
Metrocenter Branch
  3233 W. Peoria
  Phoenix, AZ 85029
  (602) 863–1862
Mesa/Chandler Branch
  623 W. Southern
  Mesa, AZ 85202
  (602) 834–9290

LICENSE/ACCREDITATION/PROFESSIONAL AFFILIATIONS

Family Service Agency is licensed by the State of Arizona Department of Economic Security and is accredited by the Council on Accreditation of Services for Families and Children. The agency is a member of Family Service America.

GLOBE INTERNATIONAL ADOPTION, INC.

6334 West Villa Theresa Drive
Glendale, AZ 85308
(602) 843–7276
Program director: Karen Baughn

THE PROGRAM

Globe International Adoption is a nonprofit Christian adoption agency serving residents of most states and placing approximately 15 children annually in Christian homes. Founded by a group of born-again Christians, the agency's mission is "to assist and bring together orphaned children from around the world into permanent Christian homes to call their own." Globe International Adoption works with authorized sources and in cooperation with appropriate laws and requirements in both the U.S. and foreign countries to place children from Colombia, El Salvador, Philippines, Taiwan, and India. In addition, some local children are occasionally available for adoption.

THE COST

The agency's fee schedule for adoption services is as follows:

Application fee	$75.00
Homestudy fee	$700.00
Homestudy review (if homestudy is prepared by another agency)	$200.00
Homestudy update	$500.00
Post-placement fee	$350.00

In addition, applicant should anticipate international program fees as follows:

Columbia (average cost)	$3,000.00–$3,400.00
El Salvador (average cost), (plus foster care)	$5,500.00–$5,900.00
Philippines (average cost)	$3,000.00–$3,400.00
Taiwan (average cost)	$5,600.00–$6,000.00
India (average cost)	$4,000.00–$5,000.00

In addition, applicants should anticipate financial responsibility for airfare or escort expenses, immigration/naturalization fees, and legal fees connected with finalization. Finally, applicants should note that all costs are approximate and subject to change without notice.

THE WAIT

The time from application to the homecoming of the adoptive child varies depending on the program and ranges from 12 to 24 months.

THE CHILDREN

Globe International Adoption places both healthy and special-needs children, ranging in age from infancy through adolescence, of Hispanic, Asian, and Indian backgrounds. Countries of origin include Colombia, El Salvador, Philippines, Taiwan, and India.

THE REQUIREMENTS

Age: The requirement varies depending on the program. Generally applicants should be at least 25 and no more than 50, although some programs are more flexible and others more restrictive.

Health: No requirement.

Religion: Applicants must be practicing Christians.

Financial status: No requirement.

Marital status: The requirement varies depending on the program. The length of marriage requirement ranges from 2–5 years. Single applicants are accepted for some programs.

Family size: No requirement.

Racial, ethnic or cultural origin: No requirement.

THE PROCEDURE

Participation in the adoption program of Globe International Adoption entails the following basic steps:

Application
Individual counseling sessions
Homestudy
Compliance with immigration/naturalization requirements
Referral
Placement
Post-placement supervision

Out-of-state applicants must arrange for licensed agency in their home state to provide the homestudy and post-placement supervision.

ADDITIONAL PROGRAMS/SERVICES

None.

BRANCH/NETWORK OFFICES

None.

LICENSE/ACCREDITATION/PROFESSIONAL AFFILIATION

Globe International Adoption Inc. is licensed by the State of Arizona Department of Economic Security.

HOUSE OF SAMUEL CHILDREN'S SERVICES

2430 N. Sycamore
Tucson, AZ 85712
(602) 325–2662
Program director: Gary and Jennie Woods

THE PROGRAM

House of Samuel Children's Services is a nonprofit agency serving primarily residents of Arizona (but also some out-of-state residents for selected programs). The agency began in 1969 when Jennie and Gary Woods agreed to care for an Indian baby until her parents could reclaim her. They soon took in other children in severe family crisis situations. In 1973, House of Samuel was licensed by the State of Arizona as a foster placement agency. Today, the agency is also licensed to make adoptive placements. The agency placed 13 children in 1987 and has been experiencing an annual increase in the number of placements of approximately 20% since they began processing adoptions. The agency's goal is "that adults and children alike may know Jesus Christ as Lord and Savior." To that end, the agency provides Christian foster families for the voluntary and temporary placement of children whose families are experiencing crisis, with the ultimate goal of successful reunification of the family. The agency also provides permanent Christian families for infants and children who have been orphaned or abandoned or whose birthparents have elected adoptive placement as the best plan for their child. The agency also places children from Guatemala and from Peru. This program is currently limited due to political complications.

THE COST

The agency's fee varies depending on the program. For infant adoption, the fee is $5,700 and includes all phases of the adoption process, excluding long distance telephone calls and mileage for casework outside the Tucson area. The foster/adopt program involves the acceptance of a foster child who may later become free for adoption. The fee for the foster/adopt program is $1,200, including all services except long distance telephone calls and mileage for casework outside the Tucson area. For adoption from Guatemala or Peru, the agency's fee is $5,300, excluding the homestudy.

THE WAIT

The time from application to the homecoming of the adoptive child ranges from 4 months to 3 years. The agency maintains a pool of waiting parents for newborns. Birthparents select adoptive parents from the agency's file, based on nonidentifying information.

THE CHILDREN

House of Samuel places both healthy and special-needs children, ranging in age from birth to 12 years, of all racial backgrounds. Countries of origin include U.S., Guatemala, and Peru.

THE REQUIREMENTS

Age: At least one applicant must be between the ages of 23 and 45.

Health: Applicants with health problems or handicaps are given individual consideration.

Religion: Applicants must be practicing evangelical Christians.

Financial status: Applicants must demonstrate the ability to provide for the child's basic needs.

Marital status: For healthy infant adoptions, applicants must be married couples, and the length of the marriage must be at least 2 years. For foster/adopt, older child, and special-needs adoptions, single applicants are welcomed.

Family size: Family size is evaluated on an individual basis.

Racial, ethnic or cultural origin: No requirement.

THE PROCEDURE

Participation in House of Samuel's adoption program entails the following basic steps:
Registration
Submission of references
Application
Submission of autobiographies/questionnaires
Homestudy
Placement
Post-placement supervision

ADDITIONAL PROGRAMS/SERVICES

House of Samuel provides seminars, counseling services, foster care, and foster care support services. The agency maintains a lending library.

BRANCH/NETWORK OFFICES

11777 S. Old Nogales Highway (open Tuesday Only)
Tucson, AZ 85706
(602) 325–2662

LICENSE/ACCREDITATION/PROFESSIONAL AFFILIATIONS

House of Samuel Children's Services is licensed by the State of Arizona Department of Economic Security.

LDS SOCIAL SERVICES

3535 South Richey
Tucson, AZ 85713
(602) 745–6459
Program director: Barry H. Drage

THE PROGRAM

For a full description of programs and services, refer to Utah listing:
LDS Social Services
50 East North Temple Street
Salt Lake City, UT 84150

BRANCH OFFICES

LDS Social Services/Arizona:
112 Sixth Ave.
Box 3544
Page, AZ 86040
(602) 645–2489
Director: Glen G. Grygla

P.O. Box 856
Snowflake, AZ 85937
(602) 536–4117
Director: H. Larue Crockett

235 South El Dorado
Mesa, AZ 85202
(602) 968–2995
Director: Richard K. Brown

SOUTHWEST ADOPTION CENTER, INC.

4327 N. Scottsdale Road, #200
Scottsdale, AZ 85253
(602) 234–2229
Program director: Michael R. Sullivan, Administrator; James R. Medlock, Chairman of Governing Body

THE PROGRAM

Southwest Adoption Center is a for-profit agency providing nationwide services and placing approximately 80–100 children annually. The agency was founded in 1984 by Michael Sullivan, an attorney specializing in adoption law. The agency's mission is "to place newborn infants for adoption with infertile adoptive parents." However, applicants should note that infertility is not a requirement for adoption through this agency.

THE COST

For Arizona applicants, the agency's fee for adoption services is $12,000. Services covered by the fee include all phases of the adoption process. For out-of-state applicants, the agency's fee is $14,000. In addition, out-of-state applicants should anticipate financial responsibility for homestudy and supervisory services by an agency in their home state and for legal fees connected with finalization of the adoption.

THE WAIT

Applicants can anticipate a response to their application within 90 days. The time from acceptance into the program to placement is approximately 1 year.

The Children

Southwest Adoption Center places healthy children, ranging in age from birth to 2 years, primarily of Caucasian and Hispanic racial backgrounds (but others as well), born in the U.S.

The Requirements

Age: No requirement.
Health: Applicants must be in reasonably good health.
Religion: No requirement.
Financial status: No requirement.
Marital Status: Applicants must be married couples who have been married for at least 3 years.
Family size: No requirement.
Racial, ethnic or cultural origin: No requirement.

The Procedure

Participation in Southwest Adoption Center's adoption program entails the following basic steps for Arizona residents:

Application
Orientation meeting (including individual and group counseling sessions)
Homestudy
Placement
Post-placement supervision
Finalization

Out-of-state residents submit an application. If accepted into the program, applicants then arrange for homestudy and supervisory services by an agency in their home state and for legal finalization by an attorney in their home state.

Additional Programs/Services

Southwest Adoption Center provides for independent counseling of birthparents outside the agency; provides short-term (1 week or less) foster care for infants; conducts a series of seminars on adoption (required for in-state applicants).

Branch/Network Offices

5050 E. Broadway, #C–214
Tucson, AZ 85711
(602) 722–0380

License/Accreditation/Professional Affiliations

Southwest Adoption Center, Inc. is licensed by the State of Arizona Department of Economic Security. The agency is a member of Arizona Advocates for Children.

Arkansas

PUBLIC ADOPTION PROGRAM/ COMMUNITY RESOURCES

Department of Human Services
Division of Children and Family Services
Permanency Planning Unit
P.O. Box 1437
Little Rock, AR 72203–1437
(501) 682–8462
Adoption specialist: Helen M. Beard, Manager, Permanency Planning Unit

THE PROGRAM

Arkansas Children and Family Services Permanency Planning Unit provides 15 adoption specialists located throughout the state to recruit and prepare families for adoption and to provide assistance after placement. While most children available for adoptive placement through the Permanency Planning Unit are special-needs children (older children, sibling groups, minority children, children with mental and/ or physical handicaps), the agency does have an Unmarried Parents program through which a limited number of infants are referred for adoption planning each year. In 1980, the agency established the Black Family Outreach Unit to address the needs of waiting Black children.

STATE EXCHANGE

For information, contact the Permanency Planning Unit (above).

STATE ADOPTION REUNION REGISTRY

Voluntary Adoption Registry. For information, contact the Permanency Planning Unit (above).

STATE SUBSIDY

For information, contact the Permanency Planning Unit (above).

NACAC REPRESENTATIVE

Frank Street
Rt. 3, Box 240
Paragould, AR 72450
(501) 573–6466

GENERAL ADOPTION RESOURCES

Arkansas-Oklahoma Adoption Support Group
Box 386
Hartford, AR 72938
Valley Adoption Support Group
Route 1, Box 80
London, AR 72847

Adoptive Parents and Children Together
Route 1, Box 58
Winslow, AR 72959

Central Arkansas Adoptive Support Group
Route 1, Box 261
Bismark, AR 71929

Linking Intentional Families Together
Route 1, Box 110–0
Jacksonville, AR 72076

NEA-FACT
Route 2, Box 22F
Jonesboro, AR 72401
Blended Families Support Groups
Parent Center, Independence County Courthouse
192 East Main
Batesville, AR 72501
AFACT, Inc.
1903 Green Acres Road
Jacksonville, AR 72076
North Central Arkansas Adoption Group
Route 1, Box 268
Bald Knob, AR 72010

SPECIAL-NEEDS ADOPTION RESOURCES

For information concerning special-needs adoption resources, contact Permanency Planning Unit (above).

OUT-OF-STATE AGENCIES

AGENCY

Holt International Children's Service, Tennessee branch
Edna Gladney Center, Texas
Smithlawn Maternity Home, Texas, (special-needs and minority placements)

SEE APPENDIX A

Agencies Providing Nationwide Services.

BETHANY CHRISTIAN SERVICES

1501 N. University, Suite #564
Little Rock, AR 72207–5242
(501) 664–5729
Program director: James K. Haveman, Jr., Executive Director

THE PROGRAM

For a full description of programs and services, refer to Michigan listing:
Bethany Christian Services
901 Eastern Avenue, N.E.
Grand Rapids, MI 49503–1295
(616) 459–6273

FOR THE LOVE OF CHILDREN, INC. (FLOC)

217 West Second Street, Suite 250
Little Rock, AR 72201
(501) 378–0225
Program director: Lynne Flanders, LCSW, ACSW

THE PROGRAM

For the Love of Children is a for-profit agency serving

residents of Arkansas and other states who recognize Arkansas licensure and placing approximately 10 children annually. FLOC was established in October 1985, by Ray and Kaye Hartenstein, husband-and-wife attorneys in Little Rock, who have been involved in private adoptions since 1981. Their intent is "to combine the positive aspects of private adoptions with the benefits of an agency structure." The agency received permanent licensure in October, 1987. The agency's mission is "to afford all members of the adoption triangle the opportunity for a productive and meaningful life and to provide loving, stable homes for unplanned or homeless children by acting as a facilitator/liaison between biological parents who are unable to provide such homes for their children and mature, emotionally stable couples or individuals who desire to become parents."

The Cost

The agency's fee schedule for adoption services is as follows:

Preliminary application	$50.00
Final application	$900.00
Homestudy and post-placement supervision (in state)	$900.00
Placement fee (upon match between birthparents and prospective adoptive parents)	$14,500.00

Services covered by the fee include all phases of the adoption process (including finalization) and expenses incurred by the birthmother. Applicants should anticipate financial responsibility for additional medical expenses if the birthmother delivers by C-Section and for travel expenses (airfare, lodging, and meals) for 2 visits to Little Rock for agency interviews and adoption proceedings upon birth of the child.

The Wait

The time from application for acceptance into the program to the homecoming of the adoptive child averages between 6 months and 2 years.

The Children

For the Love of Children places newborn infants, both healthy and special needs, of all racial backgrounds.

The Requirements

Age: Applicants must be at least 25 years of age.
Health: Applicants must be in reasonably good health. Applicants with health problems or handicaps are given individual consideration.
Religion: No requirement.
Financial status: No requirement.
Marital status: No requirement.
Family size: No requirement.
Racial, ethnic or cultural origin: No requirement.

The Procedure

Participation in For the Love of Children adoption program entails the following basic steps:
Application
Orientation meeting
Individual counseling sessions
Homestudy
Placement
Post-placement supervision

Additional Programs/Services

For the Love of Children provides counseling and support groups; bibliography of adoption readings; community education programs; coordination with public assistance programs.

Branch/Network Offices

None.

License/Accreditation/Professional Affiliations

For the Love of Children is licensed by the State of Arkansas Department of Human Services.

California

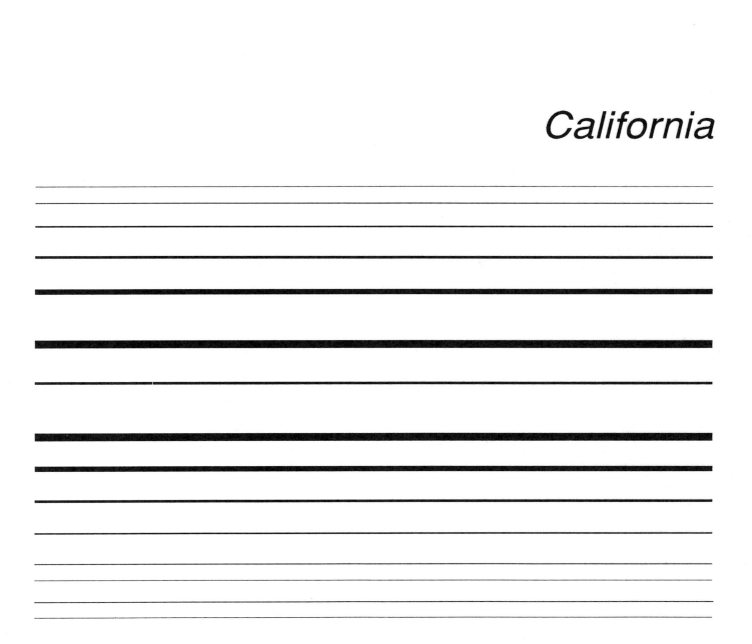

PUBLIC ADOPTION PROGRAM/ COMMUNITY RESOURCES

Department of Social Services
Adoptions Branch
744 P Street, M.S. 19/68
Sacramento, CA 95814
(916) 322–5973
Adoption specialist: Frank Sanchez, Chief, Adoptions
Recruitment Bureau

THE PROGRAM

Public adoption services in California are provided through the district offices of the Department of Social Services and through 28 licensed county welfare departments. Services vary depending on the office and may include relinquishment adoptions (placement of children relinquished by their birthparents), independent adoptions (placements in which birthparent(s) place a child directly with an adopting family), and special-needs adoptions (older, minority, and handicapped children and sibling groups).

STATE EXCHANGE

Pending (expected to be operational in 1988).

STATE ADOPTION REUNION REGISTRY

For information, contact the Adoptions Branch (above).

STATE SUBSIDY

The Adoption Assistance Program (AAP) provides financial and medical assistance to eligible special-needs children. The amount of assistance is dependent upon the needs of the child and the family's circumstances. California Children Services are also available for physically handicapped children at no cost to the adoptive parents if the physical handicap had been diagnosed at the time of the adoption. For information concerning these programs, contact the Adoptions Branch (above).

NACAC REPRESENTATIVE

Katie Miller
1214 South Gramercy Place
(213) 731–3467

GENERAL ADOPTION RESOURCES

Adoptee, Birthparent, and Search Groups:

Adoptee Identity Discovery
P.O. Box 2159
Sunnyvale, CA 94087
(408) 737–2222

Adoptees, Birthparents Assoc.
P.O. Box 039
Harbor City, CA 93010
(805) 842–8667/583–4306

Adoptees' Search Workshop
P.O. Box 039
Harbor City, CA 90710–0030
(213) 534–2547

Adoption with Truth
P.O. Box 20276
Oakland, CA 94611
(415) 848–2165

Adoption Reality
2180 Clover Street
Simi Valley, CA 93065
(805) 516–2289

ALMA—Sacramento
P.O. Box 8081
Sacramento, CA 95818
(916) 393–2562

ALMA—Bay Area
P.O. Box 2341
Alameda, CA 94501
(415) 523–4774

ALMA—Fresno Area
P.O. Box 553
Selma, CA 93662
(209) 897–4861

ALMA—Southern California
P.O. Box 44454
Panorama City, CA 91412
(818) 882–6969

ALMA—San Diego
P.O. Box 880335
San Diego, CA 92108
(619) 299–7966/443–2282

Bay Area Birth Mothers Assoc.
75 Elsie Street
San Francisco, CA 94110
(415) 528–5640

CUB—Los Angeles
11514 Ventura Blvd., Suite A–179
Studio City, CA 91604

CUB—Orange Co. Inland Empire Branch Independent Search Consultants
10801 San Paco Circle P.O. Box 638
Fountain Valley, CA 92708 Westminster, CA 92683

Los Angeles Co. Search Assoc.
11514 Ventura Blvd., Suite A–179
Studio City, CA 91604
(213) 763–9236

Search-Finders of California
P.O. Box 24595
San Jose, CA 95154
(408) 356–6711

Resources for Adoptive Parents, Adoptees, and Birthparents:

Central Coast Adoption Support Parenting Resources
Box 5165 250 El Camino Real, Suite 111
Santa Maria, CA 93456 Tustin, CA 92680
(805) 922–7251

TRIADOPTION Library
P.O. Box 638
Westminster, CA 92683
(714) 892–4098

PACER (Post Adoption Committee for Education and Research
2255 Ygnacio Valley Rd.
Walnut Creek, CA 94598
(415) 654–3099

SPECIAL-NEEDS ADOPTION RESOURCES

Aask America
450 Sansome St., Suite 210
San Francisco, CA 94111
(415) 543–2275

OUT-OF-STATE AGENCIES

AGENCY

Universal Family, Colorado
Smithlawn Maternity Home, Texas (special-needs and minority placements)

SEE APPENDIX A

Agencies Providing Nationwide Services.

ADOPTION HORIZONS

P.O. Box 247
Arcata, CA 95521
(707) 822–2660
Program director: Sherill Chand, Interim Director

THE PROGRAM

Adoption Horizons is a nonprofit adoption agency that serves the northern California counties of Humboldt, Trinity, Mendocino, and Del Norte and places about 12 to 24 children annually. Founded in 1982 by adoptive parents, Adoption Horizons is licensed to place foreign-born children and U.S. special-needs children. The emphasis of Adoption Horizons is on non-discriminatory adoption services and on pre- and post-adoptive education for all interested applicants.

THE COST

The agency's fee for adoption services is based on a sliding scale and ranges from $1,700 to $2,900. Services covered by the fee include homestudy, post-placement supervision and finalization report for the adoption. For foreign adoptions, applicants can expect to pay document fees of $150 to $200 and a liaison agency fee of $500 to $2,000. For U.S. special-needs adoptions, there is a $250 fee for search and referral services.

THE WAIT

The time from application for acceptance into the program to homecoming of the child averages from 1 to 2 years.

THE CHILDREN

Adoption Horizons places both healthy foreign infants and older children as well as special-needs American children, from birth to 16 years old, of all racial backgrounds. Many countries of origin are represented.

THE REQUIREMENTS

Age: For foreign adoptions, the requirement varies depending on the country of origin.
Health: Applicants with health problems or handicaps are given individual consideration.
Religion: No requirement.
Financial status: Applicants must demonstrate financial stability.
Marital status: No requirement. Couples should be married at least 1 year.
Family size: No requirement.
Racial, ethnic or cultural origin: No requirement.

THE PROCEDURE

Participation in Adoption Horizon's program entails the following basic steps:
  Orientation meeting
  Application
  Group counseling sessions
  Homestudy
  Compliance with immigration/naturalization requirements
    (foreign adoptions only)
  Referral
  Placement
  Post-placement report
  Finalization

ADDITIONAL PROGRAMS/SERVICES

Adoption Horizons offers educational adoption study classes and a series of lectures on adoption issues (Speakers' Bureau).

BRANCH/NETWORK OFFICES

None.

LICENSE/ACCREDITATION/PROFESSIONAL AFFILIATIONS

Adoption Horizons is licensed by the State of California Department of Social Services and is a member of the California Association of Adoption Agencies and the Joint Council on International Children's Services.

ADOPT INTERNATIONAL

3142 La Mesa Drive
San Carlos, CA 94070
(415) 593–1008
Program director: Lynne Jacobs

THE PROGRAM

Adopt International is a nonprofit agency serving residents of the San Francisco Bay area and placing approximately 20 to 30 children annually. Licensed for 4 years in California, the director has 15 years experience with domestic and inter-country adoption. The agency's mission is "to place children in homes with families wanting to become parents, maintaining professional standards and always considering the needs and specific situations of individual families." Working directly with sources in foreign countries (child welfare institutions and intermediaries) and working cooperatively with other U.S. agencies which maintain international programs, Adopt International places children from various countries in California families. In addition, the agency will provide homestudy and supervisory services for applicants pursuing international interagency or parent-initiated international adoption. The agency also provides assistance in complying with immigration and naturalization requirements.

THE COST

The agency's fee for adoption services ranges from $1,500 to $2,000. Services covered by the fee include consultation, homestudy, and liaison work with the cooperating agency or foreign source. In addition, applicants should anticipate fees to the cooperating agency or foreign source, travel/escort expenses, and other expenses related to international adoption. Applicants are responsible for legal fees connected with finalization.

THE WAIT

The time from application to completion of the homestudy is 6 to 8 weeks. After completion of the homestudy, the child is eligible to enter the U.S. within 2 to 8 months. The average time from application to placement is 4 to 6 months.

THE CHILDREN

Adopt International places primarily healthy infants and young children (birth to 2 years) of Hispanic and Asian racial backgrounds. Countries of origin include Honduras, Colombia, Peru, Mexico, Chile, Taiwan, and India.

THE REQUIREMENTS

Age: No agency requirement, but may vary depending on the country of origin.
Health: Applicants should be in reasonably good health. Applicants with health problems or handicaps are given individual consideration. Infertility documentation is required for some countries.
Religion: No agency requirement, but may vary depending on the country of origin.
Financial status: No requirement.
Marital status: No agency requirement, but may vary depending on the country of origin.
Family size: No requirement.
Racial, ethnic or cultural origin: No requirement.

THE PROCEDURE

Participation in the adoption program of Adopt International entails the following basic steps:
Application
Homestudy
Compliance with immigration/naturalization requirements
Referral
Placement
Post-placement supervision

ADDITIONAL PROGRAMS/ SERVICES

Adopt International provides counseling services which include option counseling for birthparents; counseling for birthparents and prospective adoptive parents who are making an adoption plan; counseling for prospective adoptive parents considering international adoption; advisory services to assist adoptive parents in complying with immigration and naturalization requirements.

BRANCH/NETWORK OFFICES

Adopt International maintains branch offices in Marin County and San Francisco.

LICENSE/ACCREDITATION/PROFESSIONAL AFFILIATIONS

Adopt International is licensed by the State of California Department of Social Services. The agency is a member of the California Adoption Agency Association, American Adoption Congress, and Private Adoption Agency Coalition.

ADOPTION SERVICES INTERNATIONAL

4737 Ortega Drive
Ventura, CA 93003
(805) 644–3067
Program director: Bonnie McKay, Executive Director; Robert N. Renard, Program Director

THE PROGRAM

Adoption Services International (ASI) is a nonprofit adoption agency that serves the residents of California and places from 80 to 100 children annually. Formed in 1984, ASI specializes in foreign adoptions and works with agencies overseas to place children for adoption. The agency seeks to secure "loving, permanent homes for children who have been orphaned, abandoned or freed for adoption in foreign countries."

THE COST

The agency's fee for adoption services ranges from $2,500 to $3,200 depending on the services provided. Services covered by the fee include the homestudy, post-placement liaison agency work, immigration document preparation, and child placement preparation. Applicants should anticipate fees to the overseas agency and/or attorney ranging from $2,700 to $10,000 and varying depending on the country. In addition, applicants are responsible for U.S. legal fees connected with finalization.

THE WAIT

The time from application for acceptance into the program to homecoming of the adoptive child varies depending on the country and ranges from 6 months to 2 years or more.

THE CHILDREN

ASI places both special-needs and healthy children who range in age from newborn to 16 years of age, of Asian, Latin, Filipino, and Indian backgrounds. Countries of origin include Korea, India, Mexico, Central and South American countries, Taiwan, and the Philippines. ASI also provides services for parent-initiated adoption from any country which allows immigration of a child to the U.S.

THE REQUIREMENTS

Age: The requirement varies depending on the country or source.

Health: Applicants with health problems or handicaps are given individual consideration.

Religion: No requirement.

Financial status: The requirement varies depending on the requirements of the country or source.

Marital status: ASI requires a marriage of at least 2 years for married applicants. Single applicants are considered for some programs.

Family size: The requirement varies depending on the requirements of the country or source.

Racial, ethnic or cultural origin: The requirement varies depending on the requirements of the country or source.

THE PROCEDURE

Participation in ASI's adoption program entails the following basic steps:

Orientation meeting (depending on the area)
Application
Homestudy
Compliance with immigration/naturalization requirements
Referral
Placement
Post-placement supervision

ADDITIONAL PROGRAMS/SERVICES

None.

BRANCH/NETWORK OFFICES

While the agency maintains case workers throughout the state, all inquires are processed through the main office.

LICENSE/ACCREDITATION/PROFESSIONAL AFFILIATIONS

Adoption Services International is licensed by the State of California Department of Social Services and is a member of the Southern and Northern California Council on Adoption and the Joint Council on Adoptions.

ADOPTIONS UNLIMITED, INC.

Mailing Address
P.O. Box 462
Chino, CA 91708

Office Address
4724 Brooks Street
Montclair, CA 91763
(619) 435–4114
(714) 621–5819

Program director: Jane Moss, Executive Director; Cheryl Yeamans, Program Coordinator

THE PROGRAM

Adoptions Unlimited, Inc., is a nonprofit, parent led adoption agency that serves residents of Los Angeles, Orange, San Bernardino, Riverside, and San Diego counties and places approximately 75 children annually. Licensed in 1982 by the State of California, Adoptions Unlimited provides (1) homestudies, search, cooperative placement and post-placement services for families wishing to adopt U.S. waiting children,

(2) homestudies, search, cooperative placement, post-placement and re-adoption services for families wishing to adopt internationally, and (3) assistance for families pursuing parent initiated adoptions. Adoptions Unlimited gives priority to applicants who wish to adopt special-needs waiting children. Adoptions Unlimited works cooperatively with other U.S. agencies and with national and regional exchange programs to facilitate the placement of healthy and special-needs children born in the U.S. Working directly with child welfare institutions abroad and with other U.S. agencies which maintain international programs, Adoptions Unlimited places children from countries in Central and South America and from Asia and India in American families. For applicant pursuing parent-initiated adoption abroad, Adoptions Unlimited provides resource information on over 30 countries. However, applicants are responsible for verifying the integrity of the source.

THE COST

The agency's fee schedule is as follows:

Consultation (per hour)	$35.00
Registration	$100.00
Homestudy	$1,000.00
Homestudy review	$250.00
Homestudy update (per hour)	$35.00
Child search (fee for U.S. special needs only)	$500.00
Processing (if applicable)	$1,000.00
Interstate compact (if applicable)	$250.00
Program fee(varies depending on program)	$5,000.00–$8,025.00
Post-placement supervision	$750.00
Voluntary change of program	$500.00

In addition, applicants should anticipate additional expenses which may include physicals for all family members, fingerprinting (state and federal), immigration and naturalization fees, travel and related costs, foreign attorney's fees, notarization, certifications, authentications, translations, and U.S. legal fees connected with finalization. Applicants should note that fees are subject to change.

THE WAIT

The average time from application for acceptance into the program to homecoming of the adoptive child is from 1 to 2 years. After registration, applicants wait approximately 1 month to begin the education process. Most families have had a child placed within 1 year of class attendance.

THE CHILDREN

Adoptions Unlimited places (directly and cooperatively) both healthy and special-needs children, ranging in age from birth to 15 years, of all racial backgrounds. Countries of origin include U.S., India, Central and South American countries, and Asian countries.

THE REQUIREMENTS

Age: Applicants must be at least 25 years of age. The requirement may vary depending on the country.

Health: Adoptions Unlimited requires that applicants be in reasonably good health. Additional requirements may vary depending on the country.

Religion: No requirement for Adoptions Unlimited, but the requirement may vary depending on the country.

Financial status: No requirement for Adoptions Unlimited, but the requirement may vary depending on the country.

Marital status: Applicants may be either married couples or single women. Adoptions Unlimited requires a marriage of at least 2 years for married applicants. Additional requirements may vary depending on the country.

Family size: No requirement for Adoptions Unlimited, but the requirement may vary depending on the country.

Racial, ethnic or cultural origin: No requirement for Adoptions Unlimited, but the requirement may vary depending on the country.

THE PROCEDURE

Participation in the adoption program of Adoptions Unlimited entails the following basic steps:
  Registration
  Education sessions (3 weeks; mandatory)
  Application
  Homestudy (includes individual counseling sessions)
  Compliance with immigration/naturalization requirements
  Dossier preparation
  Compliance with Interstate Compact requirements (if applicable)
  Referral
  Placement
  Post-placement supervision
  Finalization of adoption

ADDITIONAL PROGRAM/SERVICES

Adoptions Unlimited sponsors Sharing Our Love, a program established to donate food, medical supplies, and nursery items to foreign child welfare institutions. Adoptions Unlimited is opening an orphanage in southern Brazil and hopes to have several such facilities in the future. Adoptions Unlimited publishes a quarterly newsletter ($10 donation for handling and postage is appreciated) on program changes and agency events.

BRANCH/NETWORK OFFICES

None.

LICENSE/ACCREDITATION/PROFESSIONAL AFFILIATIONS

Adoptions Unlimited, Inc., is licensed by the State of California Department of Social Services.

AID TO ADOPTION OF SPECIAL KIDS (AASK)

(Northern California)
3530 Grand Avenue
Oakland, CA 94610
(415) 451–1748
Program director: Rina Baker; Pat Hanson (takes child referrals only)

THE PROGRAM

Aid to Adoption of Special Kids (Aask) of Northern California is a nonprofit adoption agency that serves residents of northern California only and facilitates the placement of approximately 35 children annually. Incorporated in 1973 by Bob and Dorothy DeBolt, Aask was licensed in 1978 to facilitate the adoption of special-needs children who are in the custody of private and public agencies throughout the United States. Over 36,000 of these special-needs children are legally free for adoption, and the agency's policy is not to exclude from consideration adoptive parents on the basis of race, ethnic background, religion, cultural heritage, physical handicap, sexual orientation, or marital status. It is Aask's mission "to find adoptive families for children with special needs, those physically, cognitively, and emotionally handicapped, older children, with siblings, and of minority race, and through cooperative placement."

THE COST

The agency charges no fee for its services; however, applicants can expect to pay a non-agency fingerprint processing fee.

THE WAIT

The time from application for acceptance into the program to homecoming of the child ranges from 4 months to 1 year.

THE CHILDREN

Aask places special-needs children of all ages and racial backgrounds. Although some children may be foreign born, all children placed must be U.S. citizens.

THE REQUIREMENTS

Age: Applicants must be at least 21 years of age.
Health: Applicants should be in reasonably good health. Applicants with health problems or handicaps are given individual consideration.
Religion: No requirement.
Financial status: Applicants should be able to demonstrate financial stability.
Marital status: No requirement.
Family size: No requirement.
Racial, ethnic or cultural origin: No requirement.

THE PROCEDURE

Participation in Aask's adoption program entails the following basic steps:
  Orientation meeting
  Group preparation sessions
  Individual screening session
  Application
  Homestudy
  Referral (matching and child search)
  Placement
  Post-placement supervision
  Parental support program

ADDITIONAL PROGRAMS/SERVICES

Aask provides an ongoing support group for adoptive parents that meets monthly.

BRANCH/NETWORK OFFICES

Aask Northern California is a branch of Aask America. For a complete description of the Aask America program and a list of Aask America branches and affiliates, refer to National Child Welfare and Triad Support Organizations.

Aask America/National Headquarters
450 Sansome Street, Suite 210
San Francisco, CA 94111
(415) 543–2275
John D. Badger, Executive Vice President

LICENSE/ACCREDITATION/PROFESSIONAL AFFILIATIONS

Aask Northern California is licensed by the State of California Department of Social Services. The agency is a member of The National Committee for Adoption and The North American Council on Adoptable Children.

BAL JAGAT—CHILDREN'S WORLD, INC.

9311 Farralone Ave.
Chatsworth, CA 91311
(818) 709–4737
Program director: Hemlata Momaya

THE PROGRAM

Bal Jagat—Children's World, Inc., is a nonprofit adoption agency serving residents of Los Angeles, Orange, San Bernardino, Ventura, and Santa Barbara Counties. Bal Jagat annually places about 16 children and conducts homestudies and supervisory services for applicants pursuing international adoptions. The goal of Bal Jagat is to provide complete, professional adoption services to its California applicants and to find homes for orphaned children throughout the world. Applicants should note that the agency requires a self-addressed stamped envelope for inquiry.

THE COST

The agency's fee is fixed at $1,350 and includes application, pre-placement, homestudy, and post-placement supervision. (An attorney is not required for finalization.) In addition, applicants can expect to pay international program fees (India, $4,500; Costa Rica, $7,000–$10,000; Peru, $7,5000; Mexico, $6,000–$7,000; Brazil, $5,500), immigration/naturalization fees, and related fees (legal documents, notaries).

THE WAIT

The time from application for acceptance into the program to homecoming of the adoptive child averages under 1 year.

THE CHILDREN

Bal Jagat places both healthy and special-needs children who range in age from 3 months to 16 years, of all racial backgrounds. Countries of origin include India, Mexico, Costa Rica, Peru, and other South American countries. Bal Jagat also is licensed to conduct homestudies for applicants pursuing adoption of children from countries other than those listed.

THE REQUIREMENTS

Age: The requirement varies according to the child's age and country of origin. Applicants may be no more than 45 years of age for Indian infants.

Health: Applicants must be in reasonably good health. Infertility documentation is required for some programs.

Religion: No requirement.

Financial status: Applicants must demonstrate financial stability.

Marital status: The requirement varies, depending on the child's country of origin. For some programs, applicants must be married and the length of the marriage must be at least 2 years.

Family size: No requirement; preference is given to childless couples.

Residence: Applicants must reside in the 5 county area served by the agency (Los Angeles, Orange, San Bernardino, Ventura, and Santa Barbara Counties).

Racial, ethnic or cultural origin: No requirement.

THE PROCEDURE

Participation in Bal Jagat's adoption program entails the following basic steps:
Orientation meeting
Application
Homestudy
Compliance with immigration/naturalization requirements
Placement
Post-placement supervision

ADDITIONAL PROGRAMS/SERVICES

Bal Jagat publishes a newsletter on adoption.

BRANCH/NETWORK OFFICES

None.

LICENSE/ACCREDITATION/PROFESSIONAL AFFILIATIONS

Bal Jagat is licensed by the State of California Department of Social Services.

BAY AREA ADOPTION SERVICES, INC.

P.O. Box 2617
Sunnyvale, CA 94087
(408) 736–2227
Program director: Pamela Ward

THE PROGRAM

Bay Area Adoption Services, Inc. (BAAS) is a nonprofit adoption agency that serves eight counties in the San Francisco area. Founded about three years ago by an attorney/adoptive parent, BAAS is the fifth parent-led adoption agency to be started in California and to date has placed about 106 children. The agency works with private and public state approved agencies or sources to place foreign-born children with adoptive families. The mission of BAAS is simple: "to find loving homes for international children in need of loving families."

THE COST

The agency's fee for adoption services currently ranges

from $1,350 to $1,750 (though applicants should note that the agency has recently sought state approval to increase fees to $1,550 to $1,950) and includes registration, supervision, and finalization of adoption if required. Additional non-agency fees for international adoptions include foreign legal, travel, medical, and foster care expenses, passport, and other U.S. legal fees. The total cost for international adoption ranges from $5,000 to $10,000, depending on the program.

THE WAIT

The time from application for acceptance in the program to homecoming of the child averages about 1 year or less.

THE CHILDREN

BAAS places primarily healthy children who range in age from birth to 16 years, primarily of Asian, Hispanic, Filipino, and Indian backgrounds. The agency also places some special-needs children. Countries of origin include mainly Asian nations, Central and South America, the Philippines, India, and anywhere else legally possible.

THE REQUIREMENTS

Applicants should note that many of the following requirements vary depending on the country or program selected.

Age: The requirement varies with the program or country of origin. Generally, the applicant must be at least 10 years older than the adopted child.

Health: Applicants should be in reasonably good health. Applicants with health problems or handicaps are given individual consideration.

Religion: No requirement.

Financial status: Applicants must demonstrate financial stability.

Marital status: No requirement; however, if married couples must be married at least 1 year. Single applicants are welcome.

Family size: No requirement.

Racial, ethnic or cultural origin: No requirement.

THE PROCEDURE

Participation in BAAS's adoption program entails the following basic steps:

Orientation meeting
Group counseling sessions (evening pre-adoption classes)
Application
Compliance with immigration/naturalization requirements
Homestudy
Individual counseling session
Referral
Placement
Post-placement supervision
Assistance with California legal finalization
Referral to other community resources (as needed)

ADDITIONAL PROGRAMS/SERVICES

Bay Area Adoption Services, Inc., is developing plans to offer post-placement support groups to adoptive parents.

BRANCH/NETWORK OFFICES

None.

LICENSE/ACCREDITATION/PROFESSIONAL AFFILIATIONS

Bay Area Adoption Services, Inc., is licensed by the State of California Department of Social Services.

BETHANY CHRISTIAN SERVICES

9556 Flower, Suite #1
Bellflower, CA 90706–5708
(213) 804–3448
Program director: James K. Haveman, Jr., Executive Director

THE PROGRAM

For a full description of programs and services, refer to Michigan listing:

Bethany Christian Services
901 Eastern Avenue, N.E.
Grand Rapids, MI 49503–1295
(616) 459–6273

BRANCH OFFICES

Bethany Christian Services/California
2937 Veneman, Suite #265C
Modesto, CA 95356–0638
(209) 522–5121

CATHOLIC CHARITIES OF SAN FRANCISCO

2045 Lawton Street
San Francisco, CA 94122
(415) 665–5100
Program director: Marcia L. Popper, LCSW

THE PROGRAM

Catholic Charities San Francisco is a nonprofit social welfare agency that serves the greater San Francisco Bay Area and places approximately 20 children annually. Licensed in 1953 as a special-needs adoption program for older and minority children, the adoption program of Catholic Charities has now expanded to offer special-needs, healthy newborn, and international adoption services. Catholic Charities mission is to place "children unable to be raised by their biological family, for whatever reason, in the most appropriate, permanent adoptive home"

THE COST

The agency's fee for adoption is based on a sliding scale and ranges from no cost to $5,000. The fee covers all adoption expenses except overseas agency fees (for foreign adoptions), legal fees connected with finalization, immigration and naturalization expenses (for foreign adoptions).

THE WAIT

The wait varies according to the needs of the child.

THE CHILDREN

The agency places both healthy and special-needs children of all ages and racial backgrounds and from many countries.

THE REQUIREMENTS

Age: The requirement varies depending on the needs of the child and cooperating agency (if any) requirements.

Health: The requirement varies depending on the needs of the child and cooperating agency (if any) requirements.

Religion: The requirement varies depending on the needs of the child and cooperating agency (if any) requirements.

Financial status: The requirement varies depending on the needs of the child and cooperating agency (if any) requirements.

Marital status: The requirement varies depending on the needs of the child and cooperating agency (if any) requirements.

Family size: The requirement varies depending on the needs of the child and cooperating agency (if any) requirements.

Racial, ethnic or cultural origin: The requirement varies depending on the needs of the child and cooperating agency (if any) requirements.

THE PROCEDURE

Participation in Catholic Charities' adoption program entails the following basic steps:
Orientation meeting
Application
Individual counseling sessions
Group counseling sessions
Homestudy
Compliance with immigration/naturalization requirements (foreign adoptions only)
Referral
Placement
Post-placement supervision
Legal completion
Post-legal counseling as needed

ADDITIONAL PROGRAMS/SERVICES

Catholic Charities of San Francisco provides referrals to a number of local support groups and services.

BRANCH/NETWORK OFFICES

None.

LICENSE/ACCREDITATION/PROFESSIONAL AFFILIATIONS

Catholic Charities of San Francisco is licensed by the State of California Department of Social Services.

CATHOLIC COMMUNITY SERVICES/ADOPTION AGENCY

349 Cedar Street
San Diego, CA 92101
(619) 231–2828
Program director: Sr. Barbara Welliver

THE PROGRAM

Catholic Community Services of the Diocese of San Diego is a nonprofit social-service organization whose adoption program serves residents of San Diego and the Imperial Counties and which places approximately 25 children annually. The adoption program began in 1984 and was designed to serve the needs of the pregnant woman in the agency's Single Pregnant Women's Program. The adoption program strives to protect all parties involved in the adoption triangle and offers "a life confirming alternative to pregnant women who do not feel prepared to raise their expected children."

THE COST

The agency's fee is based on a sliding scale and ranges from $3,000 to $5,000. Services covered by the fee include homestudy, group seminars, placement, post-placement supervision, and preparation for finalizing the adoption. Applicants can expect to pay attorney fees for finalization. Applicants occasionally pay some expenses of the birthmother.

THE WAIT

The time from application for acceptance into the program to homecoming of the adoptive child averages about 1 year for infants.

THE CHILDREN

Catholic Community Service's adoption agency places mostly healthy (about 95%) Caucasian (about 70%) children born in the U.S.

THE REQUIREMENTS

Age: The requirement varies but generally applicants should be under 40 years of age.

Health: Applicants must be in reasonably good health.

Religion: The requirement varies depending on the request of the birthmother.

Financial status: Applicants should demonstrate financial stability.

Marital status: Applicants must be married. The length of the marriage must be at least 2, preferably 3 years.

Family size: Applicants can have no more than 1 child currently in the family.

Racial, ethnic or cultural origin: Preference for placing children in families of similar origins.

THE PROCEDURE

Participation in Catholic Community Service's adoption program entails the following basic steps:
Inquiry (by telephone)
Pre-application
Orientation meeting
Application
Individual counseling sessions
Home visit
Group counseling sessions
Placement
Post-placement supervision
Finalization

ADDITIONAL PROGRAMS/SERVICES

Catholic Community Services offers a variety of social and community programs including counseling, social services, group houses for birthmothers, foster care, and various support groups.

BRANCH/NETWORK OFFICES

None.

LICENSE/ACCREDITATION/PROFESSIONAL AFFILIATIONS

Catholic Community Services is licensed by the State of California Department of Social Services and is accredited by the Council on Accreditation of Services for Families and Children.

CHILDREN'S HOME SOCIETY OF CALIFORNIA

2727 W. 6th Street
Los Angeles, CA 90057–3111
(213) 389–6750
Program director: James T. Spradley, Jr. President and Chief Executive Officer

THE PROGRAM

Children's Home Society of California is a nonprofit multi-service children's services agency serving residents of California and placing approximately 350 to 400 children annually through its adoption programs. Providing diversified child welfare services since 1891, the agency's mission is "to protect the rights of children to a secure home, loving parents, and full opportunity for healthy development." Working directly with birthparents, other private and public agencies, and national and regional exchange programs, the Society provides both traditional and open adoption services for healthy and special-needs children. Working directly with foreign sources and working cooperatively with other U.S. agencies which maintain international programs, the agency places children from various countries in California families. In addition, the agency will provide homestudy and supervisory services for applicants pursuing interagency adoption (domestic or international) or identified adoption.

THE COST

The agency's fee for adoption services is based on a sliding scale and ranges from $3,500 to $5,800. Services covered by the fee include application, homestudy, placement, and post-placement services. Applicants should anticipate additional costs which vary depending on the program and may include fees to a cooperating agency (international placements), transportation costs, medical fees for the necessary physical examinations, legal fees connected with finalization, and other incidental cost.

THE WAIT

The time from application to the homecoming of the adoptive child varies depending on the type of adoption and ranges from 6 months to 3 years.

THE CHILDREN

Children's Home Society places both healthy and special-needs children, ranging in age from birth to 17 years, of all racial backgrounds. Countries of origin include U.S., Korea, Hong Kong, the Philippines, India, several Central and South American countries, and any other country where applicants may identify a child who is available for adoption.

THE REQUIREMENTS

Age: No requirement.
Health: No requirement. Applicants with health problems or handicaps are given individual consideration.
Religion: No requirement.
Financial status: No requirement.
Marital status: No requirement.
Family size: For healthy Caucasian infant adoption, applicants may have no more than 2 children currently in the family. No requirement for other programs.
Racial, ethnic or cultural origin: Preference for placing children in families of similar origins.

THE PROCEDURE

Participation in the adoption program of Children's Home Society entails the following basic steps:
  Orientation meeting
  Application
  Homestudy (including individual and group sessions)
  Compliance with immigration/naturalization requirements
    (international adoptions only)
  Child referral
  Placement
  Post-placement supervision

ADDITIONAL PROGRAMS/SERVICES

Children's Home Society provides many services including post-adoption information and counseling; expectant parent counseling; services to children in their own homes; family day care; foster family care; group home care; public education and child advocacy; volunteer opportunities.

BRANCH/NETWORK OFFICES

2819 H St, Suite C
Bakersfield, CA 93301
(805) 324–5436

920 Atlantic Ave., #D
Long Beach, CA 90813
(213) 436–3201

4041 Saviers Rd.
Oxnard, CA 93033
(805) 486–0090

2200 21st St.
Sacramento, CA 95818
(916) 452–4672

1941 Johnson Ave.
San Luis Obispo, CA 93401
(805) 962–9191

3017 Porter St.
Soquel, CA 95073
(408) 475–3996
(408) 373–4126

1216 Sheridan Ave.
Chico, CA 95926
(916) 342–2464

1300 W. 4th St.
Los Angeles, CA 90017
(213) 482–5443

1556 Harnell Ave., #B
Redding, CA 96002
(916) 222–4141

7695 Cardinal Ct.
San Diego, CA 92123
(619) 278–7800

1010 Ruff Dr.
San Jose, CA 95110
(408) 293–8940

210–A W. Main St., #6
Santa Maria, CA 93454
(805) 925–0330

5665 N. Pershing, #B5
Stockton, CA 95207
(209) 941–4761

703 N. Fulton St., Suite E
Fresno, CA 93728
(209) 486–0355

3200 Telegraph Ave.
Oakland, CA 94609
(415) 655–7406

6900 Brockton, #102
Riverside, CA 92506
(714) 684–6810

3000 California St.
San Francisco, CA 94115
(415) 922–2803

300 S. Sycamore St.
Santa Ana, CA 92701
(714) 542–1147

1211–C College Ave.
Santa Rosa, CA 95404
(707) 523–2442

6851 Lennox Ave.
Van Nuys, CA 914–5
(818) 908–5055

670 Joy Way, #C
Yuba City, CA 95991
(916) 673–7503

LICENSE/ACCREDITATION/PROFESSIONAL AFFILIATIONS

Children's Home Society of California is licensed by the State of California Department of Social Services and is accredited by the Council on Accreditation of Services for Families and Children. The agency is a member of the Child Welfare League of America and the California Association of Services to Children.

CHILDREN'S SERVICES CENTER OF MONTEREY COUNTY

648 Pine Avenue
Pacific Grove, CA 93950
(408) 649–3033
Program director: Carol Biddle, MSW, Executive Director

THE PROGRAM

Children's Services Center is a nonprofit agency serving residents of Monterey and San Benito Counties and placing approximately 30 to 40 children annually through its adoption program. The Center was chartered in 1984 to provide counseling, adoption, specialized foster family care, and support group services to families and children in the central coast area of California. Working directly with birthparents, with other licensed private and public agencies, and with national and regional exchange programs, the agency places both healthy and special-needs children. Working cooperatively with other U.S. programs that maintain international programs, Children's Services Center facilitates the placement of foreign-born children in California families. In addition, the agency will provide homestudy and supervisory services for applicants pursuing interagency adoption (domestic or international) or private adoption.

THE COST

The agency's fee for adoption services is based on a sliding scale and ranges from $750 to $5,000. Services covered by the fee include homestudy, educational groups, placement, post-placement supervision, and support groups. For domestic infant adoption, applicants may contribute on a voluntary basis to help defray medical and housing expenses of the birthparent. Applicants pursuing international adoption should anticipate fees to the custodial agency and other costs related to international adoption. For all programs, applicants are responsible for legal fees connected with finalization of the adoption.

THE WAIT

The time from application to placement averages 1 to 2 years for Caucasian infant placements, 1 year for older child placements, and no longer than 1 year for minority placements.

THE CHILDREN

Children's Services Center places both healthy and special-needs children, ranging in age from birth to 15 years, of all racial backgrounds. In addition, the agency will provide homestudy and supervisory services to facilitate the adoption of children of any age, race, or country of origin.

THE REQUIREMENTS

Age: No requirement.
Health: Applicants should be in reasonably good health. Applicants with health problems or handicaps are given individual consideration.
Religion: No requirement.
Financial status: No requirement other than the ability to provide adequately for the child. Financial assistance is available for some domestic special-needs children.
Marital status: No requirement.
Family size: No requirement.
Racial, ethnic or cultural origin: No requirement.

THE PROCEDURE

Participation in the adoption program of Children's Services Center entails the following basic steps:
Orientation meeting

Individual counseling sessions
Application
Homestudy
Compliance with immigration/naturalization requirements
  (international adoptions only)
Placement
Post-placement supervision
Support group
Post-adoption counseling

ADDITIONAL PROGRAMS/SERVICES

Children's Services Center provides educational workshops for families and professionals; specialized foster care; pre-adoptive foster care; support groups for birthparents, adoptive parents, and foster parents; educational scholarship assistance for foster children; child passenger safety program; boarding homes for pregnant women; special events and fund raising activities.

BRANCH/NETWORK OFFICES

None.

LICENSE/ACCREDITATION/PROFESSIONAL AFFILIATIONS

Children's Services Center of Monterey County is licensed by the State of California Department of Social Services and is a member of the California Association of Adoption Agencies.

CHRISTIAN CHILDREN'S SERVICES OF CALIFORNIA

10016 Pioneer Boulevard, Suite 212
Santa Fe Springs, CA 90670
(213) 948–4441
(800) 333–5683
Program director: Glenda Jordan, ACSW, LCSW, BCCSW

THE PROGRAM

Christian Children's Services of California (CCS) is a nonprofit agency serving residents of 10 southern counties of California (and clients throughout the U.S. through cooperative arrangements with other agencies) and anticipating placement of approximately 25 to 30 children in 1988. Incorporated as a nonprofit religious corporation and licensed as an adoption and foster family agency in 1985, the agency's purpose is "to provide social services to individuals and families of all ages through placement of children in foster care and adoption, through counseling, and through all other services related there to which might become useful or necessary in meeting the needs of the church and the community." The agency provides services to birthparents and places both healthy and special-needs children for adoption in Church of Christ families when birthparents elect adoptive placement as the best plan for their child. In addition, the agency will provide homestudy and supervisory services for applicants pursuing domestic interagency adoption or private adoption.

THE COST

The agency's fee for adoption services is based on a sliding scale and ranges from $2,500 to $7,300. Services covered by the fee include the homestudy, adoption counseling, post-placement supervision, and assistance in finalizing the adoption. Applicants are responsible for legal fees connected with finalization.

THE WAIT

The time from application to the homecoming of the adoptive child averages 18 to 24 months.

THE CHILDREN

CCS places both healthy and special-needs children, ranging in age from birth to 12 years, of all racial backgrounds. While the agency extends services to children of any age or race, most children placed by the agency are healthy Caucasian infants.

THE REQUIREMENTS

Age: The requirement varies depending on the age of the child being considered for placement.
Health: Applicants with health problems or handicaps are given individual consideration. Infertility documentation is required for healthy Caucasian infant adoption.
Religion: Applicants must be practicing members of the Church of Christ.
Financial status: Applicants must have sufficient income to provide for an additional family member.
Marital status: Applicants must be married; the length of the marriage must be at least 2 years.
Family size: For healthy Caucasian infant adoption, applicants may have no more than 1 child currently in the family. For special-needs adoption, the requirement varies depending on the special needs of the child.
Racial, ethnic or cultural origin: Preference for placing children in families of similar origins.

THE PROCEDURE

Participation in CCS's adoption program entails the following basic steps:
  Application
  Group counseling sessions
  Individual counseling sessions
  Homestudy
  Placement
  Post-placement supervision
  Finalization

ADDITIONAL PROGRAMS/SERVICES

CCS provides individual, marital, and family counseling; foster care; seminars and workshops; post-adoption services.

BRANCH/NETWORK OFFICES

CCS maintains a branch office in Bakersfield (800–300–5683).

LICENSE/ACCREDITATION/PROFESSIONAL AFFILIATIONS

Christian Children's Services of California is licensed by

the State of California Department of Social Services. The agency is a member of California Association of Adoption Agencies, Coalition of Professional Pregnancy Counseling Agencies of Southern California, and Christian Adoption Resource Exchange.

CHRYSALIS HOUSE

2134 W. Alluvial Avenue
Fresno, CA 93711
(209) 432–7171
Program director: Josie-Lee Kuhlman

THE PROGRAM

Chrysalis House is a nonprofit agency serving residents of Fresno, Kings, Tulare, Kern, Madera, and Mariposa Counties and placing approximately 20 children annually. The agency's mission is "to enhance the quality of family life through family, expectant parent, and post adoption counseling; family building by adoption; pre-adoptive, respite, and long term foster care; and educative seminars and workshops." Working directly with birthparents, with other private and public agencies, and with national and regional exchange programs, the agency places both healthy and special-needs children born in the U.S. Working in cooperation with other U.S. agencies which maintain international programs, Chrysalis House facilitates the placement of children from various countries in California families. In addition, the agency will provide homestudy and supervisory services for applicants pursuing interagency adoption (domestic or international).

THE COST

The agency's fee for adoption services is $1,500 for the homestudy (4 interviews and processing) and $1,500 for postplacement supervision (4 visits and finalizing). For domestic infant adoption, applicants should also anticipate financial responsibility for maintenance of the birthmother. For international adoption, applicants should anticipate fees to the cooperating agency and possible travel expenses. For all programs, applicants are responsible for legal fees connected with finalization of the adoption.

THE WAIT

The time from application to the homecoming of the adoptive child ranges from 2 months to 2 years.

THE CHILDREN

Chrysalis House places both healthy and special-needs children, ranging in age from birth to 12 years, of all racial backgrounds. Various countries of origin are represented in the international programs.

THE REQUIREMENTS

Age: No specific requirement. The applicant's age is taken into consideration in the evaluation.
Health: Applicants should be in reasonably good health. Applicants with health problems or handicaps are given individual consideration.
Religion: The preference of the birthparents is honored.
Financial status: Applicants must demonstrate financial stability.

Marital status: No specific requirement. The applicant's marital status is taken into consideration in the evaluation.
Family size: No requirement.
Racial, ethnic or cultural origin: The requirement varies depending on the applicant's experience and values.

THE PROCEDURE

Participation in the adoption program of Chrysalis House entails the following basic steps:
  Inquiry
  Individual counseling session
  Application
  Homestudy
  Compliance with immigration/naturalization requirements
    (international adoptions only)
  Placement
  Post-placement supervision

ADDITIONAL PROGRAMS/SERVICES

Chrysalis House provides certified fos-adopt homes, counseling services and workshops on adoption issues.

BRANCH/NETWORK OFFICES

None.

LICENSE/ACCREDITATION/PROFESSIONAL AFFILIATIONS

Chrysalis house is licensed by the State of California Department of Social Services. The agency is affiliated with the National Association of Social Workers, Joint Council on International Children's Services, California Association of Adoption Agencies, Adoption Exchange Association, and American Adoption Congress.

FAMILY CONNECTIONS

1528 Oakdale Road
Modesto, CA 95351
(209) 524–8844
Program director: Audrey Foster

THE PROGRAM

Family Connections is a nonprofit agency serving residents of the State of California and placing approximately 85 children annually. Family Connections provides intercountry adoption as well as domestic adoption services.

THE COST

The agency charges a flat fee of $980 that can be reduced or waived in some circumstances. Services covered by the fee include homestudy, child search, placement, post-placement supervision, finalization, post-legal services, support groups, and quarterly newsletter. For intercountry adoption, applicants can expect to pay orphanage or foster care fees as well as transportation and escort fees that vary depending on the country.

THE WAIT

The time from application for acceptance into the program to homecoming of the adoptive child ranges from 3 months to 18 months.

THE CHILDREN

Family Connections places both healthy and special-needs children who range in age from birth to 18 years, of all racial backgrounds. Countries of origin include the U.S., Korea, India, Mexico, Thailand, Philippines, Colombia, Chile, and other South American countries.

THE REQUIREMENTS

Age: The requirement varies depending on the country of origin of the child.

Health: Applicants with health problems or handicaps are given individual consideration.

Religion: No requirement.

Financial status: Applicants must demonstrate financial stability.

Marital status: No requirement; however, if married, couples must be married at least 2 years.

Family size: No requirement.

Racial, ethnic or cultural origin: No requirement.

THE PROCEDURE

Participation in Family Connection's adoption program entails the following basic steps:
 Orientation meeting
 Group counseling sessions (with trained adoptive parents)
 Interview
 Application
 Homestudy (includes group and individual interviews and home visit)
 Compliance with immigration/naturalization requirements
 Referral
 Placement
 Post-placement supervision

ADDITIONAL PROGRAMS/SERVICES

Family Connections offers a variety of services that include adoptive parent workshops, seminars for therapists, support group activities (picnics and holiday parties), and a newsletter published quarterly.

BRANCH/NETWORK OFFICES

None.

LICENSE/ACCREDITATION/PROFESSIONAL AFFILIATIONS

Family Connections is licensed by the State of California Department of Social Services.

FUTURE FAMILIES, INC.

3233 Valencia Avenue, #A6
Aptos, CA 95003
(408) 662–0202
Program director: Graham Wright

THE PROGRAM

Future Families, Inc., is a nonprofit agency that serves the California counties of Santa Cruz, Monterey, Santa Clara, San Mateo, and San Benito and places about 20 children annually. The agency provides "treatment adoptions" for children from 2 to 18 years old. "Treatment adoption" involves extensive family training and therapy that seeks to integrate the adoptive child into the family. Begun in 1984, the program has had an 83% success rate.

THE COST

The agency fee for adoption services is based on a sliding scale: $35 for applicants with a gross annual income up to $65,000; a maximum of $800 for applicants with a gross annual income above $65,000. Services covered by the fee include all training and therapy as part of the full treatment adoption service. In addition, adoptive families receive from $625 to $650 per child while participating in the program.

THE WAIT

The time from application for acceptance into the program to homecoming of the child ranges from 2 months to 1 year.

THE CHILDREN

Future Families, Inc., places both healthy and special-needs children who range in age from 2 to 16 years, from all racial backgrounds. Children in the program are born in the U.S.

THE REQUIREMENTS

Age: No requirement.

Health: Applicants with health problem or handicap are given individual consideration.

Religion: No requirement.

Financial status: No requirement.

Family size: No requirement.

Racial, ethnic or cultural origin: Preference for placing children in families of similar origin.

THE PROCEDURE

Participation in Future Families' adoption program entails the following basic steps:
 Orientation meeting
 Application
 Homestudy
 Group counseling sessions
 Placement
 Post-placement supervision
 Individual counseling sessions
 Monthly support groups

ADDITIONAL PROGRAMS/SERVICES

Future Families offers treatment foster care and child therapy programs.

BRANCH/NETWORK OFFICES

Future Families maintains branch offices in Santa Cruz and San Jose.

LICENSE/ACCREDITATION/PROFESSIONAL AFFILIATIONS

Future Families is licensed by the State of California Department of Social Services. The agency is a member of California Association of Adoption Agencies, Bay Area Supervisors of Adoption, PACER, and American Adoption Congress.

HOLT INTERNATIONAL CHILDREN'S SERVICES, INC.

14895 East 14th, Suite 350
San Leandro, CA 94578
(415) 351–4996
Program director: David H. Kim, Executive Director

THE PROGRAM

Holt International Children's Services in San Leandro serves residents of the Bay area and Sacramento. For a full description of programs and services, refer to Oregon listing:

Holt International Children's Services, Inc.
P.O. Box 2880, 1195 City View
Eugene, OR 97402
(503) 687–2202

BRANCH OFFICE

Holt International Children's Services/Southern California
5230 Clark Avenue, Suite 32
Lakewood, CA 90713
(213) 925–0933
(Serves residents of 10 Southern California counties)

HOLY FAMILY SERVICES COUNSELING AND ADOPTION

155 N. Occidental Boulevard
Los Angeles, CA 90026
(213) 387–1600
Program director: Sr. Bertille Prus, LCSW

THE PROGRAM

Holy Family Services is a nonprofit agency serving residents of Los Angeles and Orange Counties and placing approximately 60 children annually through its adoption program. Founded in 1949 to provide professional counseling services to birthparents considering placement of their children for adoption and to couples seeking to adopt regardless of race or religion, the agency's goal is "to enable those served to make informed decisions which are in the best interests of their future as well as that of the child." Holy Family Services provides pre-and post-delivery counseling for birthparents; recruitment and certification of foster homes for the temporary care of children being considered for adoption; case work services and medical evaluation of children in foster care; homestudies, placement, and post-placement supervision; direct hospital placement and openness in adoption when possible; post-adoption counseling including services to adult adoptees and birthparents in search.

THE COST

The agency's fee for adoption services is based on a sliding scale and ranges from $2,500 to $5,000. (Fees may be reduced or waived under some circumstances.) Services covered by the fee include orientation, intake, homestudy, placement, and supervision. In addition, fees help to underwrite the cost of services to birthparents. Applicants are responsible for fees connected with fingerprinting, medical reports, and finalization.

THE WAIT

The time from application for acceptance into the program to the homecoming of the adoptive child ranges from 6 months to 2 to 3 years, depending on the number of children currently available and the adoptive couples' openness to the birthparents requests.

THE CHILDREN

Holy Family Services places both healthy and special-needs children, ranging in age from birth to 5 years, of all racial backgrounds, born in the U.S.

THE REQUIREMENTS

Age: Applicants must be at least 25 years of age. The maximum age requirement varies depending on the age of the child.

Health: Applicants should be in reasonably hood health. Applicants with health problems or handicaps are given individual consideration. Infertility documentation is required for healthy Caucasian infant adoption.

Religion: Applicants must be practicing members of the faith of their choice.

Financial status: No requirement.

Marital status: Applicants must be married; the length of the marriage must be at least 3 years.

Family size: Applicants must be either childless or have no more than 1 child currently in the family. Exceptions are made for special-needs placements.

Racial, ethnic or cultural origin: No requirement, but preference for placing children in families of similar origins.

THE PROCEDURE

Participation in the adoption program of Holy Family Services entails the following basic steps:

Orientation meeting
Adoption workshop
Application
Homestudy
Individual counseling sessions
Placement
Post-placement supervision

ADDITIONAL PROGRAMS/SERVICES

Holy Families Services provides birthparent counseling; pre-adoptive foster care; post-adoption counseling; child abuse counseling (through Santa Ana office only).

BRANCH/NETWORK OFFICES

6851 Lennox Ave.
Van Nuys, CA 91405
(818) 908–5069

1403 S. Main St.
Santa Ana, CA 92707
(714) 835–5551

LICENSE/ACCREDITATION/PROFESSIONAL AFFILIATIONS

Holy Family Services is licensed by the State of California Department of Social Services. The agency is affiliated with the National Association of Social Workers, Catholic Charities USA, National Adoption Task Force, and California Association of Adoption Agencies.

JEWISH FAMILY AND CHILDREN'S SERVICES

1600 Scott Street
San Francisco, CA 94115
(415) 567–8860
Program director: Lynne Fingerman

THE PROGRAM

Jewish Family and Children's Services (JF&CS) is a multi-service agency that serves seven counties in the San Francisco Bay Area. The agency has provided adoption services for over one hundred years but discontinued its adoption program in the 1960s. Responding to the changes that have taken place in the field of adoption, JF&CS resumed its services in 1982 by offering education and support programs for those interested in adopting a child. The agency now administers an identified adoption program in which the applicants locate a suitable birthmother who is willing to place her child for adoption with those applicants. The mission of JF&CS is "to strengthen family life and to assist children, individual adults, and families to develop and maintain their maximum human potential." To achieve this goal, the agency provides a wide range of services "to meet the needs of people in all phases of their lives."

THE COST

The agency's fee is based on a sliding scale. The maximum fee for adoption is $2,900. Services covered by this fee include homestudy, birthmother counseling, legal fees involved with relinquishment of the child, placement, and post-placement fees. In addition, applicants can expect to pay limited legal fees and certain medical and living expenses of the birthmother and child.

THE WAIT

The time from application for acceptance into the program to homecoming of the adoptive child ranges from about 6 to 20 months.

THE CHILDREN

JF&CS places primarily healthy Caucasian infants from the U.S.

THE REQUIREMENTS

Age: No requirement.
Health: Applicants must be in reasonably good health.
Religion: No requirement.
Financial status: Applicants should demonstrate financial stability.
Marital status: No requirement.
Family size: No requirement.
Racial, ethnic or cultural origin: No requirement.

THE PROCEDURE

Participation in JF&CS adoption program entails the following basic steps:
   Orientation meeting/referrals
   Application
   Homestudy
   Pre-adoption workshop
   Placement
   Post-placement supervision

ADDITIONAL PROGRAMS/SERVICES

Jewish Family and Children's Services offers workshops on introducing applicants to adoption (Introduction to the World of Adoption and Preparing for Adoption), group sessions on adoption (Adoptive Parents Group and Teen Adoptees Group) and counseling for individuals, couples, and birthparents.

BRANCH/NETWORK OFFICES

Adoption program operates only from this office.

LICENSE/ACCREDITATION/PROFESSIONAL AFFILIATIONS

Jewish Family and Children's Services is licensed by the State of California Department of Social Services and is a member of the California Association of Adoption Agencies, Bay Area Adoption Council, and American Adoption Congress.

LDS SOCIAL SERVICES

501 North Brookhurst, #300
Anaheim, CA 92801
(714) 520–0525
Program director: Dennis B. Irving

THE PROGRAM

For a full description of programs and services, refer to Utah listing:
LDS Social Services
   50 East North Temple Street
   Salt Lake City, UT 84150

BRANCH OFFICES

LDS Social Services/California
   1003 East Cooley Dr., #203
   Colton, CA 92324
   (714) 824–5191
   Director: Mark H. Glade

   3000 Auburn Blvd., Suite 1
   Sacramento, CA 95821
   (916) 971–3555
   Director: Lloyd N. Campbell

   37541 Blacow Rd.
   Fremont, CA 94536
   (415) 790–1800
   Director: Larry R. Mansell

   7100 Hayvenhurst Ave., #102
   Van Nuys, CA 91406
   (818) 781–5511
   Director: Robert G. Anderson

1885 North Fine, #102
Fresno, CA 93727
(209) 255–6556
Director: Harold Fondren

3585 Maple St., #256
Ventura, CA 93004
(805) 642–0338

5463 Grossmont Center Dr., #330
La Mesa, CA 92041
(619) 466–5558
Director: Nicholas Aste

LIFE ADOPTION SERVICES

440 W. Main Street
Tustin, CA 92680
(714) 838–5433
Program director: Joan LeJeune

THE PROGRAM

Life Adoption Services is a nonprofit agency serving residents of Orange, Riverside, Los Angeles, San Bernadino and San Diego Counties. Working directly with child welfare institutions abroad, with other U.S. Agencies which maintain international programs, and with foreign intermediaries, Life Adoption Services places children from various countries in California families. In addition, the agency will provide homestudy and supervisory services for applicants pursuing interagency adoption (international) or private adoption.

THE COST

The agency's fees for adoption services include a $75 registration fee, a fee of $1,200 for the homestudy, and a fee of $650 for post-placement supervision. In addition, applicants can expect to pay the foreign agency's fees, immigration and naturalization fees, travel and/or escort expenses, legal fees, and other expenses related to international adoption.

THE WAIT

The time from application to the homecoming of the adoptive child ranges from 6 months to 1 1/2 years.

THE CHILDREN

Life Adoption Services places both healthy and special-needs children of all ages and all racial backgrounds. Countries of origin include Korea, Taiwan, Thailand, the Philippines, Mexico, India, Japan, and various South American countries.

THE REQUIREMENTS

Age: The requirement varies depending on the country of origin.
Health: The requirement varies depending on the country of origin.
Religion: No requirement.
Financial status: No requirement, but may vary depending on the country of origin.
Marital status: The requirement varies depending on the country of origin.

Family size: The requirement varies depending on the country of origin.
Racial, ethnic or cultural origin: The requirement varies depending on the country of origin.

THE PROCEDURE

Participation in the adoption program of Life Adoption Services entails the following basic steps:
Orientation meeting
Group counseling sessions
Compliance with immigration/naturalization requirements
Application
Homestudy
Referral
Placement
Post-placement supervision

ADDITIONAL PROGRAMS/SERVICES

Life Adoption Services provides referral services to counseling if needed.

BRANCH/NETWORK OFFICES

None.

LICENSE/ACCREDITATION/PROFESSIONAL AFFILIATIONS

Life Adoption Services is licensed by the State of California Department of Social Services.

PARTNERS FOR ADOPTION

3913 Mayette Avenue
P.O. Box 2791
Santa Rosa, CA 95405
(707) 578–0212
Program director: Rose Marie Nielsen

THE PROGRAM

Partners for Adoption is a nonprofit agency serving residents of Sonoma, Marin, Napa, Lake, Mendocino, and Solano Counties and placing approximately 12 to 15 children annually. Founded by 4 adoptive parents to address the needs of children waiting for homes, the agency affirms "the right of every child to a permanent, nurturing family." Partners for Adoption does not have custody of children but works cooperatively with child placing agencies throughout the U.S. and abroad to place both healthy and special-needs children with families residing in the counties served by the agency.

THE COST

The agency's fee for adoption services is $3,500. Services covered by the fee include application, educational meeting, adoptive homestudy, search, placement, post-placement visits and reports, and consultations. Applicants should anticipate cooperating agency fees and, for international adoption, possible travel expenses and related costs. Applicants assume responsibility for the cost of fingerprinting and legal fees connected with finalization.

THE WAIT

The time from application to the homecoming of the adoptive child ranges from 6 months to 2 years, depending on the type of child applicants wish to adopt.

THE CHILDREN

Partners for Adoption places both healthy and special-needs children, ranging in age from infancy to adolescence, of all racial backgrounds. Countries of origin currently include U.S., Korea, India, and South America.

THE REQUIREMENTS

Age: No requirement.
Health: Applicants should be in reasonably good health. Applicants with health problems or handicaps are given individual consideration.
Religion: No requirement.
Financial status: Applicants must demonstrate the ability to meet the financial needs of the child.
Marital status: No requirement.
Family size: No requirement.
Racial, ethnic or cultural origin: No requirement.

THE PROCEDURE

Participation in the adoption program of Partners for Adoption entails the following basic steps:
Orientation meeting
Application
Educational seminars
Homestudy
Compliance with immigration/naturalization requirements (international adoptions only)
Referral
Placement
Post-placement visits (4)
Post-placement services (support group meetings, social events)

ADDITIONAL PROGRAMS/SERVICES

Partners for Adoption provides counseling on an individual basis; support groups which meet monthly; information and referral services; support services to orphanages in South America.

BRANCH/NETWORK OFFICES

None.

LICENSE/ACCREDITATION/PROFESSIONAL AFFILIATIONS

Partners for Adoption is licensed by the State of California Department of Social Services and is a member of the Bay Area Supervisors Association.

SIERRA ADOPTION SERVICES

P.O. Box 361
Nevada City, CA 95959
(916) 265–6959
Program director: Gail Johnson

THE PROGRAM

Sierra Adoption Services is a nonprofit agency that serves the nine California counties of Sierra, Nevada, Placer, El Dorado, Sacramento, Sutter, Butte, Yolo, and Yuba and works with a number of private and public adoption agencies to place from 20 to 30 children annually. Founded by an adoptive parent and licensed in 1983, Sierra Adoption Services is a parent-led adoption agency that recruits and trains adoptive parents for difficult-to-place and special-needs children. Sierra Adoption Services also performs home studies for applicants pursuing foreign adoption or open adoption, providing an exchange of nonidentifying information between the birthparents and adoptive parents and on-going contact if desired by all parties. Applicants should note that no applications are accepted from families wishing only to adopt a healthy U.S. infant.

For applicants wishing to adopt special-needs children, the agency promotes a fost-adopt program for children who are in the process of becoming legally free. The placement of the child in the home is initially a foster placement which converts automatically to an adoptive placement when the legal process is complete. Thus, both the child and the adoptive family have the benefit of living together before the actual termination of parental rights.

At the center of the agency's philosophy is respect for the adoptive parent. Sierra Adoption Services strives to "recruit and prepare loving homes for America's waiting children in the belief that no child is unadoptable."

THE COST

The agency charges a flat fee of $2,000. Services covered by the fee include pre-adoption classes, homestudy, matching special-needs U.S. children with families, placement, post-placement supervision, and finalization. In addition, applicants can expect to pay expenses for telephone calls, transportation costs, postage, and other miscellaneous expenses. A small "scholarship" fund exists for families adopting special-needs children who cannot afford the fee.

THE WAIT

The time from application for acceptance into the program to homecoming of the child averages from 1 to 3 years, depending on the family's openness to the variety of types and numbers of children in need of permanent families.

THE CHILDREN

Sierra Adoption Services places both healthy and special-needs children who range in age from six years (U.S.) and up, and from infant (foreign) and up, of all racial backgrounds. All placements are cooperative with other agencies. Countries of origin include the U.S., Korea, India, and several from Latin America.

THE REQUIREMENTS

Age: Applicants must be at least 21 years of age. Maximum age varies depending on the health of the applicant and the age of the child.
Health: Applicants should be in reasonably good health. Applicants with health problems or handicaps are given individual consideration.
Religion: No requirement.

Financial status: Applicants must demonstrate financial stability.

Marital status: No requirement. Couples must be married at least 1 year.

Family size: No requirement.

Racial, ethnic or cultural origin: No requirement.

THE PROCEDURE

Participation in Sierra Adoption Services' adoption program entails the following basic steps:

Orientation meeting

Application

Homestudy (group format)

Compliance with immigration/naturalization requirements (foreign adoptions only)

Referral

Placement

Post-placement supervision

Finalization

ADDITIONAL PROGRAMS/SERVICES

Sierra Adoption Services provides pregnancy counseling; open adoption services; family therapy workshops for adoptive parents, social workers, and therapists.

BRANCH/NETWORK OFFICES

None.

LICENSE/ACCREDITATION/PROFESSIONAL AFFILIATIONS

Sierra Adoption Services is licensed by the State of California Department of Social Services. The agency is also a member of the Valley Adoption Exchange, Bay Area Supervisors of Adoption Exchange, National Adoption Network, Private Adoption Agency Coalition, and California Association of Parent Led Adoption Agencies.

VISTA DEL MAR

320 Motor Avenue

Los Angeles, CA 90034

(213) 836–1223

Program director: Eli Lefferman, LCSW, Ph.D.

THE PROGRAM

Vista Del Mar is a nonprofit multi-service agency that serves Los Angeles, Orange, and Ventura Counties and places from 60 to 80 children annually. The agency promotes open adoption and provides birthparents the opportunity to choose and meet the adopting couple. Vista Del Mar believes that adoption works best when the rights and interests of all members of the "adoption triangle" are served. Adoption programs include agency adoption (traditional), identified adoption, and collaborative adoption. The agency will work collaboratively with an adoption attorney. This provides the adopting couple and the birthparents counseling through the agency as well as on-going adoption services. The agency offers pre-adoptive education for adoptive parents, pregnancy counseling for birthmothers, and post-adoption services that are crucial for a successful adoption.

THE COST

The agency charges a fee that averages from $2,000 to $2,500, depending on the services requested. Services covered by the adoption fee include pre-adoption workshops, homestudy, birthparent counseling, placement, and post-placement supervision. Applicants can expect to pay non-agency fees such as legal expenses and medical and living expenses of the birthmother and child.

THE WAIT

The time from application for acceptance into the program to homecoming of the child varies depending on the program. For agency adoptions (traditional), the wait is about 2 years. For an identified adoption (in which the applicants locate a birthmother), the wait ranges from a few weeks to 1 year. For collaborative adoptions the wait can be a few weeks to several months.

THE CHILDREN

Vista Del Mar places primarily healthy infants of all racial backgrounds. If the adoptive parents request it, the agency can also facilitate the placement of special-needs children and intercountry adoptions.

THE REQUIREMENTS

Age: No requirement.

Health: No requirement, but the agency does request health problem information to allow birthparents options.

Religion: No requirement.

Financial status: Applicants should demonstrate financial stability.

Marital status: No requirement; however, couples must be married at least 2 years. Vista Del Mar encourages single-parent adoptions.

Family size: No requirement.

Racial, ethnic or cultural origin: No requirement.

THE PROCEDURE

Participation in Vista Del Mar's adoption program entails the following basic steps:

Application

Orientation meeting

Group counseling session

Homestudy

Placement

Post-placement supervision

ADDITIONAL PROGRAMS/SERVICES

Vista Del Mar offers a variety of programs that include a residential treatment program, day treatment, group homes, foster care, infant shelter care, home-based social services, therapeutic treatment for children under the age of eight, pre- and postadoption workshops, transcultural workshops, and adoption workshops for couples and single-adoptive parents.

BRANCH/NETWORK OFFICES

West Los Angeles

3200 Motor Ave.

Los Angeles, CA 90034

(213) 836–1223

West Hills
22622 Vanowen St.
West Hills, CA 91307
(818) 884–0682

Van Nuys
6851 Lennox St.
Van Nuys, CA 91405
(818) 908–5046

License/Accreditation/Professional Affiliations

Vista Del Mar is licensed by the State of California Department of Social Services and is accredited by the Council on Accreditation of Services for Families and Children. The agency is a member of the Child Welfare League of America.

Colorado

PUBLIC ADOPTION PROGRAM/ COMMUNITY RESOURCES

DEPARTMENT OF SOCIAL SERVICES

Division of Family and Children's Services Adoption Program
1575 Sherman Street
Denver, CO 80203–1714
(303) 866–3209
Adoption specialist: Charlotte Little and Barbara Killmore

THE PROGRAM

Public adoption services in Colorado are provided by county Departments of Social Services (DSS). The focus of the DSS Adoption Program is to recruit and prepare families and to supervise the placement of both easily placeable and special-needs children who are in the custody of the State of Colorado. In addition, DSS is responsible for supervising foreign and interstate adoptions and for administering the adoption subsidy program.

STATE EXCHANGE

Colorado Adoption Resource Registry (CARR). For information, contact the Division of Family and Children's Services (above).

STATE ADOPTION REUNION REGISTRY

Colorado Voluntary Adoption Registry
Colorado State Department of Health
4210 E. 11th Ave.
Denver, CO 80220
(303) 331–4887

STATE SUBSIDY

For information contact the Division of Family and Children's Services at (303) 886–3209

NACAC REPRESENTATIVE

Violet Pierce
6630 South Race Circle West
Littleton, CO 80121
(303) 795–2890

GENERAL ADOPTION RESOURCES

Colorado Parents for All Children issues a useful booklet on adoption resources in Colorado, including support and search assistance groups for adult adoptees and birthparents; infertility support groups; support groups for adoptive parents; specialized counseling, educational, therapeutic, and recreational resources for children with special needs. To obtain a copy of the booklet, *How to Adopt in Colorado*, send $5.00 (postpaid) to:
Judie Zinsser
Colorado Parents for All Children
16739 E. Prentice Ave.
Aurora, CO 80015
For information about membership in Colorado Parents for All Children or about the chapter in your area, contact Linda Donovan at (303) 794–4838.

SPECIAL-NEEDS ADOPTION RESOURCES

See General Adoption Resources (above).

OUT-OF-STATE AGENCIES

AGENCY

Southwest Maternity Center, Texas

SEE APPENDIX A

Agencies Providing Nationwide Services

ADOPTION CONNECTION

(Jewish Family and Children's Service)
300 S. Dahlia Street, Suite 101
Denver, CO 80222
(303) 321–3829
Program director: Sandy Martin

THE PROGRAM

Adoption Connection is a nonprofit agency serving Colorado families (primarily front range) and placing approximately 25 children annually through its adoption programs. Providing adoption services for the last 36 years, Adoption Connection provides traditional and designated adoption services. A traditional adoption involves the matching of an infant who has been surrendered to the agency to a couple whose homestudy has been approved by the agency. In a designated adoption, applicants locate a specific pregnant woman who is willing to specify the adoption of her child by those parents. The agency's mission is "to help couples and birthparents connect so that they may help each other fulfill a meaningful goal: for the couple to become a family and for the birthparents to have peace of mind knowing that their child will have a bright future in a good home."

THE COST

The agency's fee for adoption services is $3,575. For traditional and designated adoptions, the fee includes all services to all parties. All applicants should anticipate financial responsibility for the medical expenses of the birthmother and child and possible living expenses which may cost $3,000 to $4,000 or more.

THE WAIT

The time from application to the homecoming of the adoptive child varies depending on the program. For the traditional program, the wait ranges from 6 to 24 months. For the designated program, the wait varies depending on the applicants' assertiveness in locating a potential birthparent.

THE CHILDREN

Adoption Connection places primarily healthy children, ranging in age from birth to 2 years, of all (but primarily Caucasian) racial backgrounds, born in the U.S.

THE REQUIREMENTS

Age: No requirement for designated adoptions. For the

traditional program, the combined age of the applicants should not exceed 85 years.

Health: Applicants should be in reasonably good health. Applicants with health problems or handicaps are given individual consideration. Infertility documentation is required for the traditional program.

Religion: No requirement for designated adoptions. For the traditional program, applicants must be practicing members of the Jewish faith.

Financial status: Applicants must be employed and must not be receiving public assistance.

Marital status: Applicants must be married couples.

Family size: No requirement for designated adoptions. For the traditional program, applicants must be childless.

Racial, ethnic or cultural origin: No requirement.

The Procedure

Participation in Adoption Connection's adoption program entails the following basic steps:

Adoptive Parents
  Application
  Feasibility counseling
  Homestudy (including educational meetings)
  Placement
  Post-placement supervision

Birthparents
  Feasibility counseling
  Hospital visit after birth
  Court proceeding (if decision is for adoption)

Additional Programs/Services

Adoption Connection provides foster care; complete services to birthparents; counseling services; annual picnic for adoptive parents and children.

Branch/Network Offices

While Adoption Connection maintains several branch offices, all adoption inquiries are processed by the Denver Office.

License/Accreditation/Professional Affiliations

Adoption Connection is licensed by the State of Colorado Department of Social Services. The agency is a member of the Colorado Association of Family and Children's Agencies.

THE ADOPTION OPTION

2600 S. Parker Rd.
Suite 2–320
Aurora, CO 80014
(303) 695–1601 (24–hour number)
Program director: Carol Foster Monaghan

The Program

The Adoption Option is a nonprofit, non-sectarian agency providing statewide services and placing between 50 to 70 children annually. Licensed in 1981, the agency's goal is "to facilitate service for special-needs and healthy infant adop-

tions through the use of the uniquely sensitive TEAM approach." The purpose of this approach is to enhance family education and support before, during and after placement. The agency's programs include a birthparent decision making counseling program, healthy infant (Anglo and minority) designated adoption program, a fledgling waiting child program, and post-legalization services (Beyond Adoption).

The Cost

The agency's fee for adoption services is approximately $7,500. The fee varies depending on the program, and some programs have sliding fee scales. Services to prospective adoptive parents covered by the fee include homestudy, placement, post-placement supervision, and court related costs. Fees also help to underwrite the cost of services to the birthparents and child. The services of an attorney in connection with finalization of the adoption are optional. If applicants elect to use an attorney, they are responsible for legal fees.

The Wait

The time from application for acceptance into the program to the homecoming of the adoptive child ranges from 3 to 5 years.

The Children

The Adoption Option places both healthy and special-needs children (primarily infants but some older children as well) of all racial backgrounds, born in the U.S.

The Requirements

Age: Applicants must be at least 25 years of age.

Health: Applicants must be in reasonably good health. Applicants with health problems or handicaps are given individual consideration. Infertility documentation is required for non special-needs infant adoption.

Religion: No requirement.

Financial status: No requirement.

Marital status: For non special-needs infant adoption, applicants must be married. For special-needs adoption, single applicants are considered.

Family size: For non special-needs infant adoption, applicants may have no children of this marriage (but may have children of a previous marriage or a previously adopted special-needs child). For special-needs adoption, the requirement is flexible.

Racial, ethnic or cultural origin: No requirement, but preference for placing children in families of similar origins. Crosscultural and cross-racial placements are made after careful screening when in the best interests of the child.

The Procedure

Participation in the adoption program of the Adoption Option entails the following basic steps:
  Registration for waiting list
  Orientation meeting (3 meetings are offered annually; attendance is optional)
  Pre-homestudy group meeting
  Individual counseling session (required for applicants interested in cross-racial, cross-cultural, or special-needs placement)
  Application

Homestudy (including group counseling sessions)
Placement
Post-placement supervision

ADDITIONAL PROGRAMS/SERVICES

The Adoption Option provides foster (cradle) care for infants; post-legalization services to adoptive families; post-legalization services to birthparents without charge for up to 2 years and seminars on parenting and adoption issues for adoptive families who have adopted through the Adoption Option or through other agencies and for professional colleagues.

BRANCH/NETWORK OFFICES

While all telephone inquiries are processed through the main office, the agency maintains satellite offices (by appointment only) at the following locations:

7625 W. 5th Ave.
Lakewood, CO 80226

2090 W. Littleton Blvd.
Littleton, CO 80120

LICENSE/ACCREDITATION/PROFESSIONAL AFFILIATIONS

The Adoption Option is licensed by the State of Colorado Department of Social Services. The agency is affiliated with the Rocky Mountain Adoption Exchange and the Colorado Coalition.

BETHANY CHRISTIAN SERVICES

2140 S. Ivanhoe, Suite 106
Denver, CO 80222
(303) 758–4484
Program director: James K. Haveman, Jr., Executive Director

THE PROGRAM

For a full description of programs and services, refer to Michigan listing:

Bethany Christian Services
901 Eastern Avenue, N.E.
Grand Rapids, MI 49503–1295
(616) 459–6273

BRANCH OFFICES

Bethany Christian Services/Colorado
2355 Heathercrest Dr.
Colorado Springs, CO 80915–1462
(719) 596–3239

CATHOLIC SOCIAL SERVICES, INC.

302 Jefferson
Pueblo, CO 81004
(317) 544–4233
Program director: Marvin J. Kapushion, MSW, ACSW, LSWII

THE PROGRAM

Catholic Social Services is a nonprofit agency serving residents of southern Colorado. Established in the early 1940s and adapting to meet the needs of changing times, the agency's mission is "to provide each child with the best possible parenting alternative." The agency provides services to birthparents and places infants for adoption when birthparents in the agency's counseling program elect adoptive placement as the best plan for their child. The agency actively recruits families for waiting children in the custody of the state or other agencies (through purchase of service contracts or subsidy). In addition, the agency will provide homestudy and supervisory services for applicants pursuing international or interagency adoption.

THE COST

The agency's fee for infant adoption services is based on a sliding scale with an average fee of $5,500. Services covered by the fee include family assessment, placement, and post-placement supervision for the adoptive family and relinquishment counseling for the birthparents. In addition, applicants should anticipate medical expenses for the birthmother and child (if uninsured), possible foster care expenses, and legal fees connected with finalization of the adoption.

For international or interagency adoptions, the agency's fee for homestudy and supervisory services is $1,800.

For waiting child adoptions, services are provided, when possible, through purchase of service contracts or subsidy at no cost to the adoptive family.

THE WAIT

For infant adoptions, the time from application to the homecoming of the adoptive child averages 3 to 4 years.

THE CHILDREN

Catholic Social Services places both healthy and special-needs children, ranging in age from birth to 15 years, of all racial backgrounds, born in the U.S. The agency will also provide homestudy and supervisory services for applicants pursuing international or interagency adoption.

THE REQUIREMENTS

Age: Applicants must be at least 21 years of age. The maximum age limit varies depending on the age and needs of the child.

Health: Applicants with health problems or handicaps are given individual consideration.

Religion: No requirement.

Financial status: Applicants must have financial resources sufficient to meet the needs of the child.

Marital status: For infant adoptions, applicants must be married and the length of the marriage must be at least 2 years. No requirement for special-needs adoptions.

Family size: The requirement varies depending on the needs of the child.

Racial, ethnic or cultural origin: Preference for placing children in families of similar origins.

THE PROCEDURE

Participation in Catholic Social Services' adoption program entails the following basic steps:

Pre-application
Application
Family assessment
Compliance with immigration/naturalization requirements
   (international adoptions only)
Presentation of child
Placement
Post-placement supervision
Post-legalization services

ADDITIONAL PROGRAMS/SERVICES

Catholic Social Services provides pregnancy and relinquishment counseling; counseling for the clinically unattached child and family: infant foster care; older child foster care (through purchase of service); search services for adult adoptees.

BRANCH/NETWORK OFFICES

While the agency maintains branch offices in La Junta and Grand Junction, all initial inquiries and requests for information concerning adoption programs are processed through the Pueblo office.

LICENSE/ACCREDITATION/PROFESSIONAL AFFILIATIONS

Catholic Social Services is licensed by the State of Colorado Department of Social Services. M.A. social workers are licensed by the State as independent practitioners.

COLORADO CHRISTIAN SERVICES

4796 S. Broadway
Englewood, CO 80110
(303) 761–7236
Program director: Andrew Bolton

THE PROGRAM

Colorado Christian Services is a nonprofit agency serving residents of the northern United States and placing between 37 and 60 children annually. Established in 1963, the agency has placed over 800 children for adoption. The agency's mission is "to provide assistance to unwed mothers of all racial and religious backgrounds and to provide homes for children with members of the Church of Christ."

THE COST

The agency's fee for adoption services is $7,000. Services covered by the fee include all phases of the adoption process, excluding legal fees connected with finalization of the adoption. A subsidy is available in some cases for low income families.

THE WAIT

The time from application to the homecoming of the adoptive child averages 3 years.

THE CHILDREN

Colorado Christian Services places both healthy and special-needs children, ranging in age from birth to 8 years, of all racial backgrounds, born in the U.S.

THE REQUIREMENTS

Age: Applicants must be at least 21 and no more than 40 years of age.
Health: Applicants must be in reasonably good health.
Religion: Applicants must be practicing members of the Church of Christ.
Financial status: No requirement.
Marital status: Applicants must be married couples.
Family size: Applicants may have no more than 1 child currently in the family.
Racial, ethnic or cultural origin: No requirement.

THE PROCEDURE

Participation in the adoption program of Colorado Christian Services entails the following basic steps:
   Application
   Orientation meeting
   Individual counseling sessions
   Homestudy
   Placement
   Post-placement supervision

ADDITIONAL PROGRAMS/SERVICES

In addition to adoption services and services to birthparents, Colorado Christian Services provides family therapy.

BRANCH/NETWORK OFFICES

Colorado Christian Services maintains branch offices in Colorado Springs and Grand Junction.

LICENSE/ACCREDITATION/PROFESSIONAL AFFILIATIONS

Colorado Christian Services is licensed by the State of Colorado Department of Social Services and is affiliated with the Colorado Association of Children's and Family Agencies.

FRIENDS OF CHILDREN OF VARIOUS NATIONS

600 Gilpin Street
Denver, CO 80218
(303) 321–8251
Program director: Cheryl Markson, Executive Director

THE PROGRAM

Friends of Children of Various Nations (FCVN) is a nonprofit agency serving primarily Colorado and New Mexico families (but nationwide placement services for adoption through India) and placing between 250 and 300 children annually. Founded in 1967 as an assistance program in Vietnam, the agency evolved into an aid and adoption program serving the children of many countries. The agency is currently providing aid and adoption services for children from Korea, East India, and Latin America. Working cooperatively with public agencies, other private agencies, and national and regional exchange programs, the agency also places Black, bi-racial, and special-needs children born in the U.S. In addition, the agency will provide homestudy and supervisory services for applicants pursuing interagency adoption (domestic or international) or independent adoption. The agency's purpose is "to promote the well-being of orphaned, abandoned, sick, injured, and otherwise needy children throughout the world and to inform the public of the needs of these children."

THE COST

The cost of adopting internationally through FCVN varies depending on the country. General cost estimates are as follows:

Homestudy/post placement supervision (based on sliding scale; possible reduction for homestudy update)	$600.00–$1,350.00
Placement	$2,570.00–$3,700.00
Single child	$2,570.00–$3,700.00
2 siblings	$2,645.00–$4,700.00
Transportation (arranged by agency)	$1,025.00–$1,500.00

(for siblings, multiply by number of children)

Additional expenses may include application fees, immigration/naturalization fees, translations, dossier preparation, current family medical exams, medical care costs for the child (for some programs). For all programs, applicants should anticipate legal fees connected with finalization of the adoption.

THE WAIT

The time from application to the completion of the homestudy process ranges from 4 to 6 months. The time from completion and approval of the homestudy to the homecoming of the adoptive child varies depending on the program. The waiting period for a child referral can often be up to 1 year. However, depending upon the child's needs, the wait can be less.

THE CHILDREN

FCVN places both healthy and special-needs children, ranging in age from birth to 16 years, of all racial backgrounds. Countries of origin include U.S. (For Black, bi-racial, and special-needs children), Korea, India, and Latin America.

THE REQUIREMENTS

Age: The requirement varies depending on the country. The general guideline is that the age difference between parent and child should be no less than 20 and no more than 40 years.

Health: Applicants should be in reasonably good health. Applicants with health problems or handicaps are given individual consideration.

Religion: No requirement.

Financial status: The requirement is evaluated individually on the basis of the applicant's ability to meet the financial needs of the family. Some programs have a minimum income requirement.

Marital status: The requirement varies depending on the country. Some options are available to single applicants. FCVN requires that, if applicants are married, the length of the marriage must be at least 2 years.

Family size: The requirement varies depending on the country.

Racial, ethnic or cultural origin: No requirement.

THE PROCEDURE

Participation in the adoption program of FCVN entails the following basic steps:

Preliminary application
Formal application
Orientation meeting
Individual and group counseling session
Adoption education classes
Homestudy (group format)
Referral
Pre-arrival meeting
Placement supervision

Families adopting older children also participate in Parents of Older Children Group Meetings and Older Child group Meetings.

ADDITIONAL PROGRAMS/SERVICES

FCVN provides adoption education classes, support groups, and foster care (in special cases). FCVN has established the Foster Orphanage Program and several other fundraising projects to assist children in foreign countries.

BRANCH/NETWORK OFFICES

Rainbow House/FCVN
19676 Highway 85
Belen, NM 87002
(505) 865–5550

LICENSE/ACCREDITATION/PROFESSIONAL AFFILIATIONS

Friends of Children of Various Nations is licensed by the State of Colorado Department of Social Services and by the State of New Mexico Department of Human Services. The agency is a member of the North American Council on Adoptable Children, the Rocky Mountain Adoption Exchange, and the Joint Council on International Children's Services.

HAND IN HAND INTERNATIONAL ADOPTION AGENCY

4965 Barnes Road
Colorado Springs, CO 80917
(303) 596–1588
Program director: MaryLee Fahrenbrink

THE PROGRAM

Hand In Hand International Adoption Agency is a non-profit agency providing services to prospective adoptive parents in most states (except Georgia, Ohio, and New Jersey) and placing approximately 65 children annually. Founded in 1974 by Mrs. MaryLee Fahrenbrink, the wife of a missionary with the Lutheran Church in the Philippines, the focus of the organization is to provide for abandoned children in the Philippines who have been left in hospitals and orphanages and who are in need of permanent families. Because of the agency's long-standing relationship with the Philippine government, it is anticipated that this program of intercountry adoption and support services will continue to be a very viable program. The agency's purpose "is to provide permanent placement in loving homes and adoption by loving parents and to provide the necessary medical, dental, emotional and nutritional care for these needy and deserving children of the world."

THE COST

For Colorado families, the agency's fee for adoption services is $5,850; for out-of-state families, $5,500. For Colorado applicants, services covered by the fee include all phases of the adoption process (application through finalization), excluding immigration/naturalization filing fee ($50), the cost of obtaining birth, marriage, death or divorce certificates, and medical exams. Out-of-state applicants should anticipate fees to a licensed agency in their home state for homestudy and supervisory services and legal fees to an attorney in their home state for finalization of the adoption.

THE WAIT

For a female child, the time from the official government approval of the family's dossier to actual placement ranges from 18 to 24 months; for a male child, from 12 to 18 months.

THE CHILDREN

Hand In Hand places both healthy and special-needs children, ranging from birth to 15 years of age, of Filipino origins.

THE REQUIREMENTS

Age: For infant adoption, at least one spouse must be at least 25 and no more than 40 years of age. The general requirement is that the age difference between the adoptive parents and the adoptive child/children should not exceed 40 years.

Health: Applicants must be in reasonably good health. Applicants with health problems or handicaps are given individual consideration.

Religion: Applicants must be practicing members of the Christian or Jewish faith.

Financial status: No requirement.

Marital status: Applicants must be married couples who have been married for at least 2 years (or at least 1 year with documented infertility).

Family size: No requirement although preference is given to childless and infertile couples.

Racial, ethnic or cultural origin: No requirement, but Filipino adoptive families are given preference.

THE PROCEDURE

Participation in Hand In Hand's adoption program entails the following basic steps for Colorado applicants:

Inquiry (telephone or letter)
Orientation meeting
Application
Group counseling sessions
Individual counseling sessions
Homestudy
Compliance with immigration/naturalization requirements

Referral
Placement
Post-placement supervision
Finalization
Naturalization

Out-of-state applicants are invited to make inquiry and application to Hand In Hand. Applicants then arrange for a licensed agency in their home state to provide homestudy and post-placement supervision.

ADDITIONAL PROGRAMS/SERVICES

Hand In Hand provides foster care services and birthparent counseling services.

BRANCH/NETWORK OFFICES

None.

LICENSE/ACCREDITATION/PROFESSIONAL AFFILIATIONS

Hand In Hand is licensed by the State of Colorado Department of Social Services and is affiliated with Lutheran International Children's Services.

LDS SOCIAL SERVICES

3263 Fraser Street, Suite 3
Aurora, CO 80011
(303) 371–1000
Program director: John F. Christensen

THE PROGRAM

For a full description of programs and services, refer to Utah listing:

LDS Social Services
50 East North Temple Street
Salt Lake City, UT 84150

UNIVERSAL FAMILY

315 S. Clay Street
Denver, CO 80219
(303) 935–3525
Program director: David B. Meacham

THE PROGRAM

Universal Family is a nonprofit non-sectarian agency serving prospective adoptive parents in Colorado, California, New York, Kansas, Missouri, and possibly other states in the near future. Universal Family places approximately 20–30 children annually. Previously known as the Adoption Program at Special Child, the agency has been in existence for more than 8 years and has been actively involved in adoption for the last 4 years. The agency's purpose is to serve poor children and families throughout the world through relief and adoption activities. The agency believes "that every human being—regardless of race, creed, or sex—is part of the same family and that each person should have the chance to develop to his/her greatest potential, mentally, physically, and spiritually." Universal Family established an affiliate agency in Mexico 4 years ago and has been placing Mexican children in American families since that time. Recently the agency began working with a licensed agency in Ecuador and expects in the near future to place children from the Dominican Republic, Chile, Colombia, Guatemala, and El Salvador.

THE COST

For Colorado residents, the agency's fee for adoption of a child from Mexico or Ecuador is $7,000. Out-of-state applicants can anticipate a fee reduction of $500–$1,000 but must also anticipate fees for homestudy and supervisory services by an agency in their home state. Services covered by the fee include all phases of the adoption process except the following: travel (Mexico—$600; Ecuador—$2,100); translation (approximately $500); legalization/authentication (approximately $250).

THE WAIT

The time from application for acceptance into the program to the homecoming of the adoptive child ranges from 1 to 2 years. For the adoption of a school-age child from Ecuador, the wait is significantly less.

THE CHILDREN

Universal Family places both healthy and special-needs children, ranging in age from birth to 16 years, of Hispanic/Indian racial background. Countries of origin currently include Mexico and Ecuador.

THE REQUIREMENTS

Age: Applicants must be at least 30 and no more than 45 years of age. For applicants interested in adopting a school age child, the upper age limit is flexible.

Health: Applicants must be in reasonably good health. Applicants with health problems or handicaps are given individual consideration.

Religion: No requirement.

Financial status: Applicants should have an income of at least approximately $30,000, but the requirement may vary depending on individual circumstances.

Marital status: Single applicants are accepted. If married, the length of the marriage must be at least 2 years for Mexico and at least 5 years for Ecuador.

Family size: Applicants may have no more than 2 children currently in the family.

Racial, ethnic or cultural origin: No requirement, but preference for placing children in families of similar origins or families with sensitivity to Latin culture, society, and language.

THE PROCEDURE

Participation in Universal Family's adoption program entails the following basic steps:
Open House
Application
Individual counseling sessions
Orientation meeting
Homestudy
Compliance with immigration/naturalization requirements
Referral
Placement
Post-placement supervision

ADDITIONAL PROGRAMS/SERVICES

Universal Family provides domestic special-needs adoption services.

BRANCH/NETWORK OFFICES

None.

LICENSE/ACCREDITATION/PROFESSIONAL AFFILIATIONS

Universal Family is licensed by the State of Colorado Department of Social Services. The agency is a member of the Rocky Mountain Adoption Exchange and the Colorado Coalition of International Adoption Agencies.

Connecticut

PUBLIC ADOPTION PROGRAM/ COMMUNITY RESOURCES

Department of Children and Youth Services
170 Sigourney Street
Hartford, CT 06105
(203) 566-8742
1-800-842-6347 (toll free in Connecticut)
Adoption specialist: Jean Watson

THE PROGRAM

Public adoption services in Connecticut are provided by regional offices throughout the state. The Department of Children and Youth Services recruits and prepares families and supervises the placement of healthy Caucasian younger children (on a limited basis) and special-needs children (older, minority, and handicapped children and sibling groups).

STATE EXCHANGE

Connecticut Adoption Resource Exchange. For information, contact the Department of Children and Youth Services (above).

STATE ADOPTION REUNION REGISTRY

For information, contact the Department of Children and Youth Services (above).

STATE SUBSIDY

For information, contact the Department of Children and Youth Services (above).

NACAC REPRESENTATIVE

Linda Cotter
73 Mather Street
Manchester, CT 06040
(203) 649-8115

GENERAL ADOPTION RESOURCES

Open Door Society of Connecticut
2 Willow Court
Cromwell, CT 06416
(203) 635-0486
Contact: Kathy Dunham

CUB (Concerned United Birthparents)
Box 526
Rocky Hill, CT 06067
Contact: Donna Mocarsky

Adoptive Parent Support Groups:
Center Congregational Church
Center and Main
Manchester, CT 06040
(203) 566-7410
Contact: Barbara Burford

Dept. of Children and Youth Svcs.
331 Main St.
Norwich, CT 06309
(203) 886-2641
Contact: Shirley Deflavis

St. Michael's Church
Bucks Hill Road
Waterbury, CT 06702
(203) 753-9541
Contact: Marion Small

SPECIAL-NEEDS ADOPTION RESOURCES

The Connecticut Council on Adoption sponsored a six-part training program for social service and mental health professionals to support the adoptive families of special-needs children. A list of professionals who completed the program and received certificates is available upon request from the Department of Children and Youth Services.

Adopting Children With Special Needs: A Resource Guidebook for Parents in Connecticut, by Patricia Wilson-Coker and Lorrie Greenhouse Gardella (Saint Joseph College Center for Child Welfare Studies, 1987), is an invaluable resource for families adopting special-needs children in Connecticut. The book contains a wealth of information concerning medical, mental health, educational, and child welfare services; parent support groups; parental advocacy; and adoption subsidies. In addition, the book contains a directory of resources (including local, state, and national organizations) and an annotated bibliography. The book is available from the Saint Joseph College Center for Child Welfare Studies, West Hartford, Connecticut, 06112 (203-232-4571, Ext. 264).

OUT OF STATE AGENCIES

AGENCY

World Child, District of Columbia
Brightside for Families and Children, Massachusetts
Harlem-Dowling Children's Services, New York
New Beginnings Family and Children's Services, New York
The Edna Gladney Center, Texas
Smithlawn Maternity Home (special-needs and minority placements), Texas

SEE APPENDIX A

Agencies Providing Nationwide Services

BETHANY CHRISTIAN SERVICES

222 Lincoln Street
Kensington, CT 06037
(203) 223-0645
Program director: James K. Haveman, Jr., Executive Director

THE PROGRAM

For a full description of programs and services, refer to Michigan listing:
Bethany Christian Services
901 Eastern Avenue, N.E.
Grand Rapids, MI 49503-1295
(616) 459-6273

CATHOLIC CHARITIES/CATHOLIC FAMILY SERVICES, INC.

896 Asylum Avenue
Hartford, CT 06105
(203) 522–8241
Program director: Aileen Garriott, Assistant Executive Director

THE PROGRAM

Catholic Charities/Catholic Family Services is a nonprofit multi-service agency which provides services on a nonsectarian basis to the communities of Hartford, New Haven, and Litchfield Counties. In keeping with its Judeo-Christian tradition, Catholic Charities/Catholic Family Services exists "to improve the physical, social, and emotional well-being of all persons." Actively involved in adoption for over 50 years, the agency has evolved in response to society's changing needs and today provides a range of special-needs adoptions. Through these various programs, the agency places approximately 50 children annually.

THE COST

The agency's fee is based on a sliding scale, the cost to the applicant ranging from $0 to $12,000. Services covered by the fee include homestudy, placement, post-placement supervision, and finalization services.

THE WAIT

The time from application to the homecoming of the adoptive child varies depending on the type of adoption and on the district.

THE CHILDREN

Catholic Charities/Catholic Family Services places both special-needs and other children of all racial backgrounds. Most children placed by the agency are infants, but the agency places older children as well. The agency works with the State Permanency Planning Program to facilitate the placement of special-needs children.

THE REQUIREMENTS

Age: No requirement.
Health: Applicants must be in reasonably good health. Applicants with health problems or handicaps are given individual consideration. Infertility documentation is required for traditional Caucasian infant adoption.
Religion: No agency requirement, but the preference of the birthparent is honored. Children are placed in homes of the same religious background as the birthparents if possible.
Financial status: No requirement beyond adequate stability to provide a secure home.
Marital status: No agency requirement, but may vary depending on the type of adoption.
Family size: No agency requirement, but may vary depending on the type of adoption.
Racial, ethnic or cultural origin: Preference for placing children in families of similar origins. The requirement may vary depending on the needs of the child.

THE PROCEDURE

The adoption procedure varies depending on the type of adoption. Contact appropriate district office for information on basic procedure.

ADDITIONAL PROGRAMS/SERVICES

Catholic Charities/Catholic Family Services offers a wide range of counseling services and family life education programs for single parents, married couples, families, and individuals.

BRANCH/NETWORK OFFICES

205 Wakelee Ave.
Ansonia, CT
(203) 735–7481

57 Whitfield St.
Guilford, CT
(203) 453–5746

90 Franklin Sq.
New Britain, CT
(203) 225–3561

132 Grove St.
Torrington, CT
(203) 482–5558

124 Main St.
Bristol, CT
(203) 589–8662

220 Colony St.
Meriden, CT
(203) 235–2507

478 Orange St.
New Haven, CT
(203) 787–2207

56 Church St.
Waterbury, CT
(203) 755–1196

109 Elm St.
Enfield, CT
(203) 745–1727

203 High St.
Milford, CT
(203) 874–6270

524 Hopmeadow St.
Simsbury, CT
(203) 651–3448

LICENSE/ACCREDITATION/PROFESSIONAL AFFILIATIONS

Catholic Charities/Catholic Family Services, Inc. is licensed by the State of Connecticut Department of Children and Youth Services and is accredited by the Council on Accreditation of Services for Families and Children. The agency is a member of the United Way, Catholic Charities USA, Family Service America, Council of Catholic Women, Child Welfare League of America, and Travelers Aid.

CATHOLIC CHARITIES/CATHOLIC FAMILY SERVICES, INC.

Diocese of Norwich
11 Bath Street
Norwich, CT 06360
(203) 889–8346
Program director: Rev. Robert E. McNulty

THE PROGRAM

Catholic Charities/Catholic Family Services, a nonprofit family and children's agency, provides counseling and assistance to families and individuals in the Diocese of Norwich. The agency provides specialized services to unwed mothers and married couples seeking to adopt, placing 20 children annually.

THE COST

The agency fee is 8% of the gross family income. The fee includes a homestudy evaluation and recommendation. In addition to the agency fee, prospective adoptive parents should anticipate financial responsibility for legal fees associated with finalization of the adoption.

THE WAIT

The time from application for acceptance into the program to the homecoming of the adoptive child ranges from 3 to 5 years.

THE CHILDREN

The children placed by Catholic Charities/Catholic Family Services are infants of Caucasian and mixed racial backgrounds. The agency places both special-needs and healthy infants.

THE REQUIREMENTS

Age: No requirement.
Health: Applicants must be in reasonably good health; infertility documentation is required.
Religion: Applicants must have a strong affiliation and practice in Christian denomination.
Financial status: No requirement.
Marital status: Applicants must be married couples who have been married for a minimum of 3 years.
Family size: Applicants must be childless.
Racial, ethnic or cultural origin: No requirement.

THE PROCEDURE

Participation in the adoption program sponsored by Catholic Charities/Catholic Family Services, Inc. entails the following basic steps:
Application
Homestudy
Individual counseling sessions
Placement

ADDITIONAL PROGRAMS/SERVICES

Catholic Charities/Catholic Family Services, Inc. provides individual, marital, and parent/child counseling as well as short-term foster care for newborns.

BRANCH/NETWORK OFFICES

Catholic Charities/Catholic Family Services, Inc.
33 St. John Square
Middletown, CT 06457
(203) 346–9611

LICENSE/ACCREDITATION/PROFESSIONAL AFFILIATIONS

Catholic Charities/Catholic Family Services, Inc. is licensed by the State of Connecticut Department of Children and Youth Services (for adoption and foster care services) and by the Department of Health Services (for psychiatric clinic and outpatient services). The agency is a member of Catholic Charities USA and the Connecticut Council on Adoption.

CATHOLIC FAMILY AND SOCIAL SERVICE OF THE DIOCESE OF BRIDGEPORT

238 Jewett Avenue
Bridgeport, CT 06606
(203) 372–4301
Program director: John Mahoney

THE PROGRAM

Serving residents of Fairfield County (Diocese of Bridgeport) for more than 50 years, Catholic Family and Social Service (CFSS) places approximately 30 children annually through its adoption program. Providing services to clients without regard to their racial or religious heritage, the agency's mission is "to serve the needs of Fairfield County residents with a Catholic (Christian) philosophy within the context of professional service." The agency provides services to birthparents and places infants for adoption when birthparents elect adoptive placement as the best plan for their child. Working in cooperation with the Department of Children and Youth Services, the agency also occasionally facilitates the adoption of older or special-needs children. In addition, the agency provides homestudy and supervisory services for applicants pursuing identified adoption and international adoption.

THE COST

The agency's fee for adoption services ranges from 17% to 19% of the applicants' combined annual gross income, with a maximum fee of $15,000. Services covered by the fee include services to the birthmother (counseling and some medical costs), foster care of the infant awaiting placement, and social services to the applicants (homestudy, placement, post-placement supervision, and legal finalization). Applicants are responsible for court costs connected with finalization of the adoption (approximately $75).

THE WAIT

The time from application for acceptance into the program to the homecoming of the adoptive child ranges from less than 1 year to 2 years.

THE CHILDREN

CFSS places both healthy and special-needs infants (birth to 1 year), of Caucasian, Black, and bi-racial backgrounds, born in the U.S. In addition, the agency facilitates international, identified, and special-needs adoptions.

THE REQUIREMENTS

Age: Applicants must be at least 25. The maximum age requirement is evaluated on a case-by-case basis.

Health: Applicants should be in reasonably good health. Applicants with health problems or handicaps are given individual consideration. Infertility documentation is required for infant adoption.

Religion: No requirement, but the preference of the birthmother is honored.

Financial status: The applicant's financial situation is evaluated on a case-by-case basis.

Marital status: For Caucasian infant adoption, applicants must be married couples, and the length of the marriage must be at least 3 years. The requirement varies for other programs. Some options are available to single parents.

Family size: For Caucasian infant adoption, applicants must be childless. For other programs, family size is evaluated on a case-by-case basis.

Racial, ethnic or cultural origin: Preference for placing children in families of similar origins. The requirement varies depending on the wishes of the birthparents.

THE PROCEDURE

Participation in the adoption program of CFSS entails the following basic steps:

Orientation meeting

Group counseling sessions

Application

Homestudy

Compliance with immigration/naturalization requirements (international adoptions only)

Placement

Post-placement supervision.

ADDITIONAL PROGRAMS/SERVICES

CFSS provides a range of community services including individual, marital, family, and group counseling; services to birthparents (counseling services and maternity home); short term infant foster care; services to senior citizens; day care; mental health clinic.

BRANCH/NETWORK OFFICES

CFSS maintains branch offices in Shelton, Norwalk, Wilton, Danbury, Ridgefield, Stamford, Stratford, Darian, and Greenwich.

LICENSE/ACCREDITATION/PROFESSIONAL AFFILIATIONS

Catholic Family and Social Service of the Diocese of Bridgeport is licensed by the State of Connecticut Department of Children and Youth Services. The agency is accredited by the Council on Accreditation of Services for Families and Children and is a member of Catholic Charities USA.

CHILD AND FAMILY AGENCY OF SOUTHEASTERN CONNECTICUT, INC.

255 Hempstead Street
New London, CT 06320
(203) 443-2896
Program director: Crystal Lebovitz, MSW, CISW

THE PROGRAM

Child and Family Agency is a nonprofit agency serving residents of New London County and the lower half of Middlesex County and placing approximately 10 children annually through its adoption program. Originally founded in 1809 as the Female Benevolent Society of Hartford, the agency has evolved in response to the changing needs of the community and today provides a wide range of services to families and children. The agency's purpose is "to promote the well-being of all children and their families, in particular to give priority to the unmet needs of children lacking physical, emotional and intellectual care and nurturing." The agency provides services to birthparents and places infants for adoption when birthparents elect adoptive placement as the best plan for their child. Working cooperatively with public agencies and with national and regional exchange programs, the agency will provide homestudy and supervisory services for applicants pursuing interagency adoption (domestic or international).

THE COST

The agency's fee for adoption services is based on a sliding scale, 10% of the combined annual gross income for applicants with an income of less than $10,000 and 12% of the combined annual gross income for applicants with an income over $10,000 and up to $100,000. Services covered by the fee include all phases of the adoption process.

THE WAIT

The time from application to the homecoming of the adoptive child averages 2 years.

THE CHILDREN

Child and Family Agency places both healthy and special-needs children, ranging in age from birth to 11 years of age, of all racial backgrounds, born in the U.S.

THE REQUIREMENTS

Age: For infant adoption, applicants must be at least 21 and no more than 40 years of age. For older special-needs children, the requirement is flexible.

Health: Applicants should be in reasonably good health. Infertility documentation is required for infant adoption.

Religion: No requirement. For older special-needs placements, applicants should be of the same religious background as the child.

Financial status: No requirement.

Marital status: For infant adoption, applicants must be married, and the length of the marriage must be at least 3 years. Single applicants are eligible for older special-needs placements.

Family size: For infant adoption, applicants may have no more than 1 child currently in the family. For older special-needs placements, the requirement is flexible.

Racial, ethnic or cultural origin: Preference for placing children in families of similar origins. However, transracial placements are made when in the child's best interests.

THE PROCEDURE

Participation in the adoption program of Child and Family Agency entails the following basic steps:
Orientation meeting
Group and individual counseling sessions
Application
Homestudy
Referral
Placement
Post-placement supervision

ADDITIONAL PROGRAMS/SERVICES

Child and Family Agency provides a wide range of services including parent/child counseling; sexual abuse counseling; pregnancy counseling; assessment and evaluation services; adolescent pregnancy services.

BRANCH/NETWORK OFFICES

All adoption inquiries are processed through the main office.

LICENSE/ACCREDITATION/PROFESSIONAL AFFILIATIONS

Child and Family Agency of Southeastern Connecticut, Inc. is licensed by the State of Connecticut Department of Children and Youth Services. The agency is a member of the Child Welfare League of America, Connecticut Association of Mental Health Clinics for Children, Connecticut Council of Family Service Agencies, Connecticut Council on Adoption, Essex Community Fund, Middlesex United Way, and United Way of Southeastern Connecticut.

CHILD AND FAMILY SERVICES, INC.

1680 Albany Avenue
Hartford, CT 06105
(203) 236-4511
Program director: Janet Jackson, CISW, Adoption Coordinator; Runa Wassermann, CISW, Intern Adoption Coordinator

THE PROGRAM

Child and Family Services (C&FS) is a private, nonprofit agency serving the state of Connecticut and placing 16 to 26 children annually. Founded in 1809 as the Female Beneficent Society of Hartford, C&FS is one of the oldest preventive and protective agencies for children in the country. Through a continuous evolution of services, the agency is committed "to providing effective remedial and preventive services" and now sponsors a wide variety of programs. Over the past 10 years, the agency's emphasis has been the placement of

special-needs children and the recruitment of minority families. Presently, the agency does not accept applications for healthy Caucasian infants.

THE COST

The agency's fee for adoption services is adjusted according to income and the number of members in the family. Services covered by the fee include homestudy, identification of child, placement, post-placement supervision until finalization of the adoption, and preparation of court papers. In addition, prospective adoptive parents should anticipate a probate court fee of $50 and the cost of psychological or psychiatric evaluation. In some cases, financial assistance is available from the State of Connecticut.

THE WAIT

The time from application to the homecoming of the adoptive child varies depending on the circumstances of each case.

THE CHILDREN

C&FS places both healthy and special-needs children, ranging in age from birth to 14 years, of Caucasian, Black, Hispanic, and mixed racial backgrounds.

THE REQUIREMENTS

Age: No requirement.

Health: No requirement. Applicants with health problems or handicaps are given individual consideration.

Religion: No requirement.

Financial status: No requirement. The agency does not accept applications from ADC families.

Marital status: No requirement. If married, applicants should have been married for at least 1 year. This requirement may be waived if the couple has lived together prior to marriage.

Family size: No requirement.

Racial, ethnic or cultural origin: Preference for placing children in families of similar origins.

THE PROCEDURE

Participation in C&FS's adoption program entails the following basic steps:
Orientation meeting
Educational series
Intake meeting and application
Homestudy
Referral
Placement
Post-placement supervision
Finalization

ADDITIONAL PROGRAMS/SERVICES

C&FS sponsors a wide variety of programs for children and families including family day care; a group home; day treatment; a child guidance clinic; individual, marital, and family counseling; specialized foster care; research; foster home care; Family Life Enrichment; Plays for Living; crisis intervention counseling; adoptive parent support group.

BRANCH/NETWORK OFFICES

Child and Family Services has branch offices in Manchester, Farmington, and Hartford.

LICENSE/ACCREDITATION/PROFESSIONAL AFFILIATIONS

Child and Family Services, Inc. is licensed by the State of Connecticut Department of Children and Youth Services and is accredited by the Council on Accreditation of Services for Families and Children. The agency is a member of Family Service America, Child Welfare League of America, Connecticut Council on Adoption, Open Door Society, and Advocates for Black Children. The agency is affiliated with the Connecticut Adoption Resource Exchange and the Massachusetts Adoption Resource Exchange.

THE CHILDREN'S CENTER

1400 Whitney Avenue
Hamden, CT 06473
(203) 248-2116
Program director: Mr. Streeter Seidell, CISW; Ms. Susan Cabranes-Saccio, CISW, Director of Outpatient Services (Adoption)

THE PROGRAM

The Children's Center is a private, nonprofit, non-sectarian, multi-function social service agency. Founded in 1833, the Center was the first child-caring agency to be chartered in the State of Connecticut. The Outpatient Services Department provides counseling during and after pregnancy, short-term infant foster care, and adoption services. The department's Center for the Adoptive Community provides information, counseling and long-term support for adoptees, adoptive families, and birthparents. The department also provides permanency planning for children in the care of the Department of Children and Youth Services. Serving New Haven County (for healthy, Caucasian infants) and the state of Connecticut and surrounding states (for special-needs infants and children), the agency places between 6 and 16 children annually. In addition, the agency will provide homestudy and supervisory services for applicants pursuing the adoption of a foreign-born child through another source, subject to state approval of the integrity of the source. The Children's Center's purpose is "to provide loving and permanent adoptive homes for infants and children of all races and religious backgrounds who are without families to care for them."

THE COST

The agency's fee is based on the applicants' adjusted gross income, ranging from $0 to $15,000. Services covered by the fee include the homestudy, support during the approved-and-waiting period, supervision of placement, and adoption finalization. In addition, prospective adoptive parents should anticipate a $50 probate court filing fee at the time of finalization.

THE WAIT

The time from application for acceptance into the program to the homecoming of the adoptive child ranges from a few months (for special-needs infants and children) to 1 to 5 years. For healthy Caucasian infants, waits have become increasingly longer, both from the time of initial inquiry to homestudy and from completion of the homestudy to placement.

THE CHILDREN

The Children's Center places both healthy and special-needs infants and children of all racial backgrounds, ranging in age from birth to 16 years, born in the U.S. In addition, homestudy and supervisory services are provided for applicants pursuing foreign adoption through another source.

THE REQUIREMENTS

Age: For healthy Caucasian infant adoption, applicants must be at least 25 and no more than 40 years of age at the time of the homestudy. The requirement varies for special-needs children depending on the best interests of the child.

Health: For healthy Caucasian infant adoption, infertility documentation is required. Applicants must be in good health. Applicants with health problems or handicaps are given individual consideration. The requirement varies for special-needs adoption depending on the best interests of the child.

Religion: No requirement unless a preference is indicated by the birthparents of the child in question.

Financial status: No requirement beyond the capacity to adequately meet the child's financial needs through income or income-support programs.

Marital status: For healthy Caucasian infant, applicants must be married and must have been married for at least 2 years. The requirement may vary for special-needs adoption depending on the best interests of the child.

Family size: For healthy Caucasian infant adoption, applicants must be childless. The requirement may vary for special-needs adoption depending on the best interests of the child.

Racial, ethnic or cultural origin: No requirement, but preference for placing children in families of similar origins when possible. The requirement may vary depending on the best interests of the child.

Residence: For healthy Caucasian infant, applicants must reside in New Haven County, Connecticut. Applicants residing in other counties or out-of-state are considered for special-needs adoptions.

THE PROCEDURE

Participation in the Children's Center's adoption program entails the following basic steps:
   Telephone inquiry
   Submission of application and homestudy fee to the agency
   Homestudy (including individual and/or group counseling sessions)
   Compliance with immigration/naturalization and/or interstate compact regulations (out-of-state and foreign adoptions only)
   Placement
   Post-placement supervision
   Finalization

ADDITIONAL PROGRAMS/SERVICES

The Children's Center provides pregnancy and birthparent counseling. Through the Center for the Adoptive Community, the agency sponsors support groups for birthparents, adoptive parents, foster parents, and adolescent or adult adoptees; arranges special workshops on issues related to adoption; provides therapy by experienced clinicians with special training in adoption issues.

BRANCH/NETWORK OFFICES

None.

LICENSE/ACCREDITATION/PROFESSIONAL AFFILIATIONS

The Children's Center is licensed by the State of Connecticut Department of Children and Youth Services and is accredited by the Joint Commission on the Accreditation of Hospitals (JCAH) and by the American Association of Children's Residential Centers. The Children's Center is a member of the Connecticut Council on Adoption.

THE CURTIS HOME CHILDREN'S PROGRAM

380 Crown Street
Meriden, CT 06450
(203) 237–9526
Program director: Michael S. Rohde

THE PROGRAM

The Curtis Home Children's Program is a small, private nonprofit multi-service child caring agency which serves children and families without regard to race, religion or ethnic origin. Founded in 1884, the Curtis Home Children's Program has evolved from a simple home for orphans to a modern facility which today offers a comprehensive range of professional services to children and families. The agency provides residential treatment services, day treatment, permanent family care and a special education program for children with special emotional and developmental needs, ranging in age from 6 to 12 years at intake. The goal of the Curtis Home Children's Program is "to provide therapeutic services to promote the child and family's growth toward normal and adequate functioning" and "to ensure that upon discharge from the program, every child has a permanent family in which to grow up."

THE COST

The agency does not charge a fee for adoption services.

THE WAIT

The time from application to the homecoming of the adoptive child varies depending on the needs of the child and the circumstances of each case.

THE CHILDREN

The Curtis Home Children's Program serves boys and girls of all racial backgrounds from 6 to 12 years of age at intake. The children have special-needs which may include emotional disturbances, behavior problems, learning disabilities, and social/emotional problems.

THE REQUIREMENTS

Age: No requirement, but may vary depending on the needs of the child.

Health: No requirement, but may vary depending on the needs of the child.

Religion: No requirement, but may vary depending on the needs of the child.

Financial status: No requirement.

Marital status: No requirement, but may vary depending on the needs of the child.

Family size: No requirement, but may vary depending on the needs of the child.

Racial, ethnic or cultural origin: No requirement, but may vary depending on the needs of the child.

THE PROCEDURE

Curtis Home recruits and trains families who have expressed interest in making a permanent commitment to an older child. Interested families should contact the agency directly for further information about the basic procedure.

ADDITIONAL PROGRAMS/SERVICES

The Curtis Home Children's Program provides a residential treatment service and a day treatment service; operates the Curtis School (a Special Education program approved by the State Board of Education); provides specialized foster care. In addition to children's services, the Curtis Home operates a comprehensive geriatric program which includes 5 levels of care for the elderly (skilled care, intermediate care, home for the aged, apartment living, and adult day care).

BRANCH/NETWORK OFFICES

None.

LICENSE/ACCREDITATION/PROFESSIONAL AFFILIATIONS

The Curtis Home Children's Program is affiliated with St. Andrew's Episcopal Church in Meriden and is licensed by State of Connecticut Department of Children and Youth Services.

FAMILY AND CHILDREN'S AID OF GREATER NORWALK

138 Main Street
Norwalk, CT 06851
(203) 846–4203
Program director: Teddi Tucci

THE PROGRAM

Family and Children's Aid of Greater Norwalk (F&CA) is a nonprofit, non-sectarian, multi-service agency serving the State of Connecticut and placing approximately 100 children annually. The mission of F&CA is "to assist families and individuals by providing professional guidance and assistance promoting harmonious family life, interpersonal relationships and healthy personal development." The agency has several domestic and foreign adoption programs, including an identified adoption program and Korean adoption program. An identified adoption is one in which the prospective adoptive parents have become aware of a specific pregnant woman who is willing to specify the adoption of her child by those parents. In rare cases, prospective adoptive parents who have undergone a homestudy but have been unable to locate a child may be placed in a pool of families to be considered for any child released to the agency by a birthmother who does not have a specific family identified. Through its Korean adoption program, the agency works with Social Welfare Society of Seoul to place Korean children (primarily infants) with families in Connecticut. In addition, F&CA will provide home study and supervisory services for families considering adoption of foreign-born children from countries other than Korea, subject to State of Connecticut approval of the integrity of the source.

THE COST

The agency fee varies depending on the program selected. For identified, Korean, and traditional agency adoptions, the cost of the homestudy, post-placement and finalization is 6% of the annual gross income with a minimum of $2,000 and a maximum of $6,000. Other costs will depend on the circumstances of each case and the extent of the services provided. Prospective adoptive parents should anticipate financial responsibility for all medical and counseling costs of the birthmother and child as well as legal fees for finalization of the adoption. For a Korean adoption, there is an additional a fee of $2,230 to the Korean agency and an escorting fee of $900. Applicants should note that these fees are subject to change.

THE WAIT

The time from application to the homecoming of the adoptive child varies depending on the program. The wait involved in identified adoptions varies widely depending on the applicants' degree of success in networking and other factors beyond the agency's control. The wait for Korean adoptions, once a home study is sent to Korea, is 6 to 8 months for an infant girl and 3 to 4 months for boys or older children. Applicants should note that these times are approximate and subject to change.

THE CHILDREN

Through identified and traditional agency adoptions, F&CA places healthy Caucasian infants as well as special-needs infants and Black children born in the U.S. Through Korean adoption, F&CA places Korean children, both healthy and special-needs, ranging in age from birth to 14 years.

THE REQUIREMENTS

Applicants should note that requirements for an identified adoption will vary depending on the preferences of the birthmother. Requirements for other adoption programs are as follows:

Age: For Korean adoption, applicants must be at least 25 and no more than 40 years older than the child.

Health: Applicants must be in reasonably good health, i.e. free of communicable and/or chronic life threatening diseases.

Religion: No requirement.

Financial status: Applicants must demonstrate financial stability.

Marital status: For Korean adoption, applicants must be married and must have been married for at least 3 years.

Family size: For Korean adoption, applicants may have no more than 1 child currently in the family.

Racial, ethnic or cultural origin: No requirement, but preference for placing children in families of similar origins.

THE PROCEDURE

Participation in F&CA adoption programs entails the following basic steps:
    Orientation meeting
    Application
    Homestudy (including individual and group counseling sessions)
    Compliance with immigration/naturalization requirements (foreign adoptions only)
    Placement
    Post-placement supervision
    Finalization

ADDITIONAL PROGRAMS/SERVICES

F&CA offers a wide range of support services for individuals and families including an extensive counseling program; Homemaker-Home Health Aide services; a Parent Aide program; Project Friendship (a volunteer, child/adult matching program). For adoptive families, F&CA offers workshops for families at various stages of development (families with 3 to 6 year olds, families with 13 year olds, families with adult adoptees).

BRANCH/NETWORK OFFICES

None.

LICENSE/ACCREDITATION/PROFESSIONAL AFFILIATIONS

Family and Children's Aid is licensed by the State of Connecticut Department of Children and Youth Services and is a member of Family Service America and the Connecticut Council on Adoption.

HALL NEIGHBORHOOD HOUSE, °INC.

Adoption and Foster Care program
52 Green Street
Bridgeport, CT 06608
(203) 334–3900 EXT. 213
Program director: Marilyn J. Lewis, MPA

THE PROGRAM

Hall Neighborhood House is a nonprofit, multi-faceted social service agency serving the greater Bridgeport community. Founded in 1886 as Associated Charities and renamed Hall Home in 1901, the agency has evolved in response to the changing needs of the community and today provides assistance for more than 28,000 individuals who are in need of basic human services. Licensed in 1985 as a child placing agency, Hall Neighborhood House is Connecticut's first licensed Black and Hispanic adoption agency and placed 9 children in its first year of service.

THE COST

There are no fees for the adoption and foster care programs. However, tax deductible donations are accepted.

THE WAIT

The average time from application for acceptance into the program to the homecoming of the adoptive child is 2 to 3 months.

THE CHILDREN

Hall Neighborhood House places both healthy and special-needs children, ranging in age from birth to 18 years, of Black, Hispanic, and bi-racial backgrounds. All children placed by the agency were born in the U.S.

THE REQUIREMENTS

Age: applicants must be at least 18 years of age.
Health: All family members must meet the health requirements of the Connecticut Department of Children and Youth Services. Physical examinations are required.
Religion: No requirement.
Financial status: Applicants must demonstrate financial stability. The state offers a subsidized adoption program for special-needs children.
Housing: Applicants' dwelling must comply with state and local building, safety, and sanitation codes.
Marital status: No requirement.
Family size: No requirement.
Racial, ethnic or cultural origin: Preference for placing children in families of similar origins.

THE PROCEDURE

Participation in Hall Neighborhood House's adoption program entails the following basic steps:
Orientation meeting
Application
Homestudy
Group counseling sessions
Individual counseling sessions
Referral
Placement
Post-placement supervision

ADDITIONAL PROGRAMS/SERVICES

Hall Neighborhood House offers a wide range of services including child development programs; senior citizens programs; social service program; employment and training program; youth and young adult services; special services for youth; community development program; volunteer opportunities.

BRANCH/NETWORK OFFICES

Hall Neighborhood House operates 28 sites for the delivery of services to the Greater Bridgeport Community. All adoption inquiries are processed through the main office.

LICENSE/ACCREDITATION/PROFESSIONAL AFFILIATIONS

Hall Neighborhood House Adoption and Foster Care Program is licensed by the State of Connecticut Department of Children and Youth Services. The agency is a member of the United Way of Eastern Fairfield County, United Neighborhood Centers of America, National Conference of Social Welfare, and Day Care and Child Development Council of America.

HIGHLAND HEIGHTS

St. Francis Home for Children, Inc.
651 Prospect Street
New Haven, CT 06505
(203) 777–5513
Program director: Adriana F. Seawright, Director/Community Based Services Program

THE PROGRAM

Highland Heights is a nonprofit agency serving the greater New Haven area and placing approximately 10 special-needs children annually. Founded as a orphanage in 1882, Highland Heights has evolved in response to the changing needs of the community. In 1962, the agency developed a residential treatment program for children with emotional problems. The Community-Based Services Department was initiated in 1983 to find permanent families for children in the residential treatment program who are ready for family life but unable to return to their biological families. The agency's mission is "to relieve the misery and suffering of children... by providing comprehensive psychological, educational, and residential care and to safeguard the dignity and value of the person, the essential nature of the community, and the special significance of the family in human development." Guided by the Sisters of Mercy, Highland Heights affirms its Catholic heritage while reaching out to serve and collaborate with people of all faiths.

THE COST

Adoption services are provided at no cost to the adoptive family.

THE WAIT

The time from application to the homecoming of the adoptive child varies depending on the number of children in need of permanent families at any given time.

THE CHILDREN

Highland Heights places special-needs children, ranging in age from 5 to 18 years, of all racial backgrounds, born in the U.S.

THE REQUIREMENTS

Age: Applicants must be at least 21 and no more than 65 years of age. The requirement may vary depending on the age of the child.
Health: Applicants must be in reasonably good health. Applicants with health problems or handicaps are given individual consideration.
Religion: No requirement.
Financial status: Applicants are evaluated individually on the basis of their ability to manage financial resources adequately.

Marital status: No requirement.
Family size: No requirement.
Racial, ethnic or cultural origin: Practice supports placing children in families of similar origins.

THE PROCEDURE

Participation in Highland Heights' adoption program entails the following basic steps:
Orientation meeting
Application
Homestudy
Group counseling sessions
Placement
Post-placement supervision

ADDITIONAL PROGRAMS/SERVICES

Highland Heights provides residential care and intensive day treatment for children experiencing emotional difficulties.

BRANCH/NETWORK OFFICES

None.

LICENSE/ACCREDITATION/PROFESSIONAL AFFILIATIONS

Highland Heights, St. Francis Home for Children, Inc. is licensed by the State of Connecticut Department of Children and Youth Services and is accredited by the State of Connecticut Department of Education and the American Association of Psychiatric Services for Children.

INTERNATIONAL ADOPTIONS, INC.

99 W. Main Street
New Britain, CT 06050
(203) 223–6172
Program director:

THE PROGRAM

For a full description of programs and services, refer to Massachusetts listing:
International Adoptions, Inc.
282 Moody Street
Waltham, MA 02154
(617) 894–5330

INTERNATIONAL ALLIANCE FOR CHILDREN, INC.

23 South Main Street
New Milford, CT 06776
(203) 354–3417
Program director: Jan Mabasa

THE PROGRAM

International Alliance for Children (IAC), a nonprofit agency, was established in 1975 with the express purpose of "aiding parentless children in the Philippine Islands by pro-

viding a variety of services to foster wholesome nutritional, medical and emotional development." IAC helps to provide a secure and permanent future for these children through adoptive placement with appropriate families in the Philippines and the United States. IAC also provides assistance for pregnant women in crisis in the U.S. through supportive counseling, medical care and foster care. IAC serves the states of Connecticut and New York and places 15 to 20 children annually.

THE COST

The agency's fee is based on a sliding scale, ranging from $1,000 to $7,500 depending on the services provided. These services are homestudy, travel for the child and escort, placement, and post-placement supervision. In addition, prospective adoptive parents should anticipate financial responsibility for physical examination by a private physician, court costs, and immigration fees.

THE WAIT

The time from approval of the applicant's homestudy by the Philippine Government to the homecoming of the adoptive child is approximately 12 months.

THE CHILDREN

IAC places healthy Filipino children, ranging in age from birth to 6 years. The agency also places a limited number of domestic infants.

THE REQUIREMENTS

Age: Applicants must be at least 25 and no more than 45 years old. Applicants over 40 years of age are not eligible for infants under 1 year.
Health: Applicants must be in reasonably good health.
Religion: No requirement.
Financial status: The primary wage earner must have an annual income of at least $20,000.
Marital status: Applicants must be married and must have been married for at least 3 years.
Family size: Applicants may have no more than 4 children currently in the family.
Racial, ethnic or cultural origin: No requirement.

THE PROCEDURE

Participation in IAC's adoption program entails the following basic steps:
Preliminary application
Orientation meeting
Formal application
Intake meeting with adoption coordinator
Homestudy (4 meetings)
Approval of homestudy by Philippine Government
Compliance with immigration/naturalization requirements
Placement
Post-placement supervision (3 visits)
Finalization proceedings

ADDITIONAL PROGRAMS/SERVICES

IAC provides a domestic adoption program, available to all pregnant women in crisis, which includes counseling, medical care, foster care for mother and child, and assistance throughout the legal process.

BRANCH/NETWORK OFFICES

None.

LICENSE/ACCREDITATION/PROFESSIONAL AFFILIATIONS

International Alliance for Children, Inc. is licensed by the State of Connecticut Department of Children and Youth Services, by the State of New York Department of Social Services, by the State of Connecticut Department of Consumer Protection, and by the Agency for International Development. The agency is also licensed as a child-caring agency by the Department of Social Welfare and Development, Republic of the Philippines.

JEWISH FAMILY SERVICE, INC.

2370 Park Avenue
Bridgeport, CT 06604
(203) 366–5438
Program director: Elaine Bluestein, ACSW, Adoption Coordinator

THE PROGRAM

Founded in 1922, Jewish Family Service is a nonprofit, multi-service agency, serving the Jewish community of Bridgeport and the surrounding area. Evolving in response to the changing times and needs of the Jewish population, the agency's purpose is "to preserve and strengthen the quality of individual and family life in accordance with basic Jewish values and precepts." Jewish Family Service's adoption program consists of traditional and identified adoptions. The agency does not at this time have children to place; consequently, the traditional adoption program consists principally of homestudy and supervisory services for applicants pursuing foreign or out-of-state adoptions. In the identified adoption program, Jewish Family Service acts as the coordinator, working with the birthparents, the adoptive couple and the referring physician or attorney.

THE COST

The agency's fee for homestudy and supervisory services (2 post-placement visits) is $800. For identified adoptions, the agency's fee is 10% of gross family income with a minimum of $3,000 and a maximum of $5,000 to the agency to hold on reserve in an escrow account for payment of scheduled allowed expenses.

THE WAIT

Not applicable.

THE CHILDREN

Jewish Family Service will provide homestudy and supervisory services for the adoption of children of any age, race, or national origin.

THE REQUIREMENTS

Age: The age requirement is determined on an individual basis.
Health: Applicants must be in reasonably good health.
Religion: Applicants of any religious affiliation are accepted.
Financial status: No requirement.
Marital status: If married, applicants must have been married for at least 5 years. Single applicants are accepted.
Family size: No requirement.
Racial, ethnic or cultural origin: No requirement.

THE PROCEDURE

Applicants interested in pursuing adoption are invited to contact the agency to arrange a meeting with the adoption coordinator to talk about their interest in and commitment to adopting and to learn more about the agency's adoption program. If the person/couple is interested in continuing, a homestudy will be initiated.

ADDITIONAL PROGRAMS/SERVICES

In addition to its adoption program, JFS provides family and individual counseling; services for older people and their families; emergency assistance; Jewish family life education; mental health programs; refugee resettlement; holiday assistance; volunteer opportunities.

BRANCH/NETWORK OFFICES

None.

LICENSE/ACCREDITATION/PROFESSIONAL AFFILIATIONS

Jewish Family Service, Inc. is licensed by the State of Connecticut Department of Health Services and Department of Children and Youth Services and is accredited by the Council on Accreditation of Services for Families and Children. JFS is a member of the United Way of Eastern Fairfield County, Jewish Federation of Greater Bridgeport, Association of Jewish Family and Children's Agencies, and the Connecticut Council of Family Service Agencies.

JEWISH FAMILY SERVICE INFERTILITY CENTER

740 N. Main Street
West Hartford, CT 06117
(203) 236–1927
Program director: Philip M. Wrener, Executive Director; Cyral A. Sheldon, Adoption Administrator

THE PROGRAM

Jewish Family Service Infertility Center is a nonprofit agency serving residents of Connecticut and placing approximately 8 to 12 children annually through its adoption program. Providing adoption services for 75 years, the agency offers direct, identified, and cooperative placements. Direct placement involves the placement of an infant located by the agency to a couple whose homestudy has been approved by the agency. Identified placement involves the placement of an infant located by an already-approved family on their own. Cooperative placements are those in which JFS works in tandem with another agency on the placement of a child, each agency providing specified services.

THE COST

The agency's fee for adoption services varies depending on the type of adoption and the circumstances of both the adoptive family and the birthparents. (Medical expenses, in particular, vary widely.) Fees range from $5,000 to $15,000. Services covered by the fee include all phases of the adoption process, excluding legal and travel expenses (if required).

THE WAIT

The time from application to placement varies depending on the program. For direct placement, the wait averages 4 to 5 years; for intercultural placement, the wait is approximately 18 months; for identified placement, the wait ranges from 12 to 18 months.

THE CHILDREN

Jewish Family Service places healthy infants of Caucasian and Hispanic (Mexican) racial backgrounds, born in the U.S.

THE REQUIREMENTS

Age: The requirement is evaluated on a case-by-case basis.
Health: Applicants should be in good health. Applicants with handicaps are given individual consideration. Infertility documentation is required.
Religion: For direct placement, applicants must be committed to raising their child in the Jewish faith. No requirement for other programs.
Financial status: Applicants must demonstrate financial stability and must have sufficient income to provide for an additional family member.
Marital status: It is preferred that applicants be married.
Family size: For direct placement, applicants who are childless or who have no more than 1 child are given preference. No requirement for other programs.
Racial, ethnic or cultural origin: No requirement.

THE PROCEDURE

Participation in the adoption program of Jewish Family Service entails the following basic steps:
Application
Homestudy (including individual counseling sessions)
Placement
Post-placement supervision

ADDITIONAL PROGRAMS/SERVICES

Jewish Family Service provides adoption/alternatives workshops (8 sessions); legal/informational seminar on adoption; assistance with search and reunion.

BRANCH/NETWORK OFFICES

None.

LICENSE/ACCREDITATION/PROFESSIONAL AFFILIATIONS

Jewish Family Service Infertility Center is licensed by the State of Connecticut Department of Children and Youth Services and is accredited by the Council on Accreditation of Services for Families and Children. The agency is a member of the Connecticut Council on Adoption.

JEWISH FAMILY SERVICE OF NEW HAVEN, INC.

152 Temple Street
New Haven, CT 06510
(203) 777–6641
Program director: Jared N. Rolsky

THE PROGRAM

Jewish Family Service of New Haven is a nonprofit agency serving residents of south central Connecticut and placing approximately 10 to 25 children annually through its adoption program. Providing adoption services for over 40 years, the agency's mission is "to enhance individual and family life." Working directly with birthparents, with other private and public agencies, and with national and regional exchange programs, the agency places both healthy and special-needs children in Connecticut families. Working directly with child welfare institutions abroad, the agency places children from Latin America. In addition, the agency provides services for interstate and intrastate identified adoptions and will provide homestudy and supervisory services for applicants pursuing interagency adoption (domestic or international).

THE COST

The agency's fee for adoption services is based on a sliding scale with a maximum fee of $7,500. Services covered by the fee include the homestudy, placement, and post-placement supervision. For homestudy only, the agency's fee is $1,100. Additional expenses which applicants should anticipate vary depending on the type of adoption.

THE WAIT

The time from application to placement varies depending on the program. For healthy domestic infant adoption, the wait averages 2 to 4 years; for domestic special-needs adoption, the wait averages up to 1 year. For international adoption, the wait ranges from less than 1 year to 1-1/2 years, depending on the country. For identified adoption, the wait varies depending on the applicants' degree of assertiveness in locating a birthparent.

THE CHILDREN

Jewish Family Services places both healthy and special-needs children, ranging in age from infancy to adolescence, of all racial backgrounds. Countries of origin include U.S. and several Latin American countries.

THE REQUIREMENTS

Age: The requirement varies depending on the age of the child being considered for placement.
Health: The requirement varies depending on the program.
Religion: No requirement, but may vary depending on the program.
Financial status: Applicants should have sufficient income to support an additional family member.
Marital status: No requirement.
Family size: No requirement.
Racial, ethnic or cultural origin: Preference for placing children in families of similar origins when possible.

THE PROCEDURE

Participation in the adoption program of Jewish Family Service entails the following basic steps:
- Orientation meeting
- Homestudy (group format)
- Search for birthparent (identified adoptions only)
- Compliance with immigration/naturalization requirements (international adoptions only)
- Placement
- Post-placement supervision

ADDITIONAL PROGRAMS/SERVICES

Jewish Family Service provides post-adoption counseling and support groups for birthmothers and for adoptive parents.

BRANCH/NETWORK OFFICES

230 Boston Post Rd.
Madison, CT 06443
(203) 245–3797

LICENSE/ACCREDITATION/PROFESSIONAL AFFILIATIONS

Jewish Family Service of New Haven is licensed by the State of Connecticut Department of Children and Youth Services and is accredited by the Council on Accreditation of Services for Families and Children.

LUTHERAN CHILD AND FAMILY SERVICES OF CONNECTICUT

74 Sherman Street
Hartford, CT 06105
(203) 236–0679
Program director: Kristina A. Backhaus, LICSW

THE PROGRAM

Lutheran Child and Family Services (LCFS) is a nonprofit agency serving residents of Connecticut and placing approximately 25 children annually through its adoption program. Providing adoption services for more than 40 years, the agency's mission is "to provide specialized services of care, shelter, counseling, guardianship and education so that the serving love of God in Christ may be made known and so that the ministry of Christians individually, in congregations and in specialized settings may grow in the New England area." The agency provides domestic and international adoption services. Domestic adoption services include identified adoptions and special-needs adoptions (in cooperation with the Department of Children and Youth Services). Working cooperatively with World Child (see District of Columbia listing), LCFS places foreign-born children (primarily from Central and South America) in Connecticut families. In addition, the agency will provide homestudy and supervisory services for applicants pursuing domestic interagency adoption.

THE COST

The agency's fee for identified adoption services is $5,000. For international adoption services, the fee is $3,500. Adoption services for special-needs children who are in the custody of the Department of Children and Youth Services are provided at no cost to the adoptive family. Services covered by the fee include homestudy, parent preparation, advocacy, and post-placement supervision. For international adoption, applicants should anticipate financial responsibility for fees to the cooperating agency, travel, and related expenses ranging from $6,000 to $10,000. For both programs, applicants are responsible for legal fees connected with finalization.

THE WAIT

The time from application for acceptance into the program to the homecoming of the adoptive child averages 18 months.

THE CHILDREN

LCFS places both healthy and special-needs children, ranging in age from infancy to adolescence, of all racial backgrounds. Countries of origin include U.S., Bolivia, Brazil, Chile, Colombia, Dominican Republic, Ecuador, El Salvador, Guatemala, Paraguay, Peru, and Thailand.

THE REQUIREMENTS

Age: Applicants must be at least 25 years of age. The maximum age requirement varies depending on the age of the child. In addition, some foreign countries have specific requirements regarding age.
Health: Applicants with health problems or handicaps are given individual consideration. Infertility documentation is required by some countries.
Religion: No requirement.
Financial status: No requirement for identified adoption. For international adoption, an annual gross income of $30,000 is recommended.
Marital status: Both married couples and single people may apply. If married, the length of the marriage must be at least 2 years. Some foreign countries have specific requirements regarding marital status.
Family size: No agency requirement, but some foreign countries have specific requirements regarding family size.
Racial, ethnic or cultural origin: No requirement for international adoption. For domestic adoption, preference for placing children in families of similar origins.

THE PROCEDURE

Participation in LCFS' adoption program entails the following basic steps:
- Application
- Group counseling sessions
- Homestudy
- Compliance with immigration/naturalization requirements (international adoptions only)
- Referral
- Placement
- Post-placement supervision

ADDITIONAL PROGRAMS/SERVICES

LCFS provides birthparent counseling and foster care services.

BRANCH/NETWORK OFFICES

None.

LICENSE/ACCREDITATION/PROFESSIONAL AFFILIATIONS

Lutheran Child and Family Services of Connecticut is licensed by the State of Connecticut Department of Children and Youth Services.

Delaware

PUBLIC ADOPTION PROGRAM/ COMMUNITY RESOURCES

Department of Services for Children, Youth and Families
Division of Child Protective Services
Division of Program Support
330 East 30th Street, 3rd Floor
Wilmington, DE 19802
(302) 571–6419
Adoption specialist: Carol W. King

THE PROGRAM

The Division of Child Protective Services (DCPS) provides foster care services for Delaware children in need of temporary foster care. DCPS contracts with Delaware adoption agencies to provide services for special-needs children in need of adoptive families. Children needing adoptive homes are identified monthly to the adoption agencies via DELA-DOPT, a listing of pertinent information concerning waiting children. In addition, the Division of Program Support provides Interstate Compact services and inter-country adoption services.

STATE EXCHANGE

None.

STATE ADOPTION REUNION REGISTRY

None.

STATE SUBSIDY

For information, contact the Division of Child Protective Services (above).

NACAC REPRESENTATIVE

Nancy Czeiner
8 Chadd Road
Newark, DE 19711
(302) 737–5530

GENERAL ADOPTION RESOURCES

Delaware Coalition for Children
23 Arthur Drive, RD #1
Hockessin, DE 19707
(302) 239–7340

Adoptive Families with Information and Support
2610 Northgate Rd.
Channin
Wilmington, DE 19810
(302) 475–1027

SPECIAL-NEEDS ADOPTION RESOURCES:

One Church/One Child Program
Rev. Leonard Clark
504 W. 5th St.
Wilmington, DE 19801
(302) 655–8563

Post-Adoption Services
Vicky Jackson-Kelley
Children's Bureau of Delaware
2005 Baynard Blvd.

Wilmington, DE 19802
(302) 658–5177

OUT-OF-STATE AGENCIES

AGENCY

Golden Cradle, New Jersey
Rainbow Christian Services, Virginia

SEE APPENDIX A

Agencies Providing Nationwide Services

THE ADOPTION AGENCY

1308 Delaware Avenue
Wilmington, DE 19806
(302) 658–8883
Program director: Maxine G. Chalker, MSW

THE PROGRAM

For a full description of programs and services, refer to Pennsylvania listing:

The Adoption Agency
76 Rittenhouse Place
Ardmore, PA 19003
(215) 643–7200

CATHOLIC SOCIAL SERVICES, INC.

1200 N. Broom Street
Wilmington, DE 19806–4297
(302) 655–9624
Program director: Naomi D. Litonjua, ACSW

THE PROGRAM

Catholic Social Services is a nonprofit, multi-service agency serving residents of Delaware and placing approximately 15 children annually through its adoption program. Originally established in 1931, Catholic Social Services "fulfills in a modern context the spiritual obligation to respond to human needs in the name of our Creator" through a wide range of services to the community (see Additional Programs/Services). Services are provided to all who seek help, regardless of race, religion, or economic status. Catholic Social Services provides services to birthparents and places infants for adoption when birthparents elect adoptive placement as the best plan for their child. The agency is also actively involved in recruiting and preparing families for the adoption of special-needs children (older and/or minority children; children with emotional, physical, and intellectual special needs; sibling groups).

THE COST

The agency's fee for adoption services is based on the

applicants' income, with fees ranging from $1,000 to $3,000. Services covered by the fee include all phases of the adoption process, excluding legal fees connected with finalization. For special-needs children who are in the custody of the State of Delaware, adoption services are provided at no cost to the adoptive family. In addition, some special-needs children are eligible for subsidy.

THE WAIT

Because the number of families desiring to adopt healthy Caucasian infants far exceeds the number of available children, the agency is unable to predict how long couples have to wait for their study to begin, and, if completed and approved, how long they will wait for placement. For special-needs adoption, the wait varies depending on the range of special needs the adoptive family can accept.

THE CHILDREN

Catholic Social Services places both healthy and special-needs children, ranging in age from infancy to adolescence, of all racial backgrounds, born in the U.S.

THE REQUIREMENTS

Age: For infant adoption, the wife must be no older than 38 and the husband no older than 43 at the initiation of the homestudy. For special-needs adoption, the age of the applicant is considered in relation to the age of the child desired.

Health: Applicants must be in good health.

Religion: Applicants must have a commitment to fostering a strong spiritual dimension in the life of the child through participation in a religious community of faith.

Financial status: Applicants must be financially secure.

Marital status: For infant adoption, applicants must be married, and the length of the marriage must be at least 2 years. Single applicants are eligible for special-needs adoption.

Family size: For infant adoption, applicants must be childless. For special-needs adoption, the requirement is flexible and varies depending on the needs of the child.

Racial, ethnic or cultural origin: No requirement.

THE PROCEDURE

Participation in the adoption program of Catholic Social Services entails the following basic steps:
Inquiry
Informational meeting
Registration
Homestudy (including group sessions, office appointments, home visit, references, and physical examination)
Placement
Post-placement supervision

ADDITIONAL PROGRAMS/SERVICES

Catholic Social Services provides a wide range of community services including individual, marital, and family counseling; pregnancy counseling; alcohol and drug abuse therapy; foster care; group care of dependent children; economic counseling; services to the elderly; refugee resettlement; fuel assistance; advocacy.

BRANCH/NETWORK OFFICES

21 Chestnut Street
Georgetown, DE 19947
(302) 856–9578
1405 Wesley Drive, Suite #36
Salisbury, MD 21801
(301) 749–1121
422 S. New Street
Dover, DE 19901
(302) 674–1600

LICENSE/ACCREDITATION/PROFESSIONAL AFFILIATIONS

Catholic Social Services, Inc. is licensed by the State of Delaware Department of Services for Children, Youth and Their Families and is Accredited by the Council on Accreditation of Services for Families and Children. The agency is a member of Catholic Charities USA and the United Way.

·CHILD AND HOME STUDY ASSOCIATES

101 Stonecrop Road
Wilmington, DE 19810
(302) 475–5433
Program director: Geraldine Carson and Helene Gumerman

THE PROGRAM

For a full description of programs and services, refer to Pennsylvania listing:
Child and Home Study Associates
31 E. Franklin Street
Media, PA 19063
(215) 565–1544

WELCOME HOUSE ADOPTION SERVICES

P.O. Box 1079
Hockessin, DE 19707
(302) 239 2102
Program director: Barbara B. Bird, Executive Director

THE PROGRAM

For a full description fo programs and services, refer to Pennsylvania listing:
Welcome House Adoption Services
P.O. Box 836
Doylestown, PA 18901
(215) 345–0430

District of Columbia

PUBLIC ADOPTION PROGRAM/ COMMUNITY RESOURCES

District of Columbia Department of Human Services
Adoption and Placement Resources Branch
500 First Street, N.W., Room 8040
Washington, D.C. 20002
(202) 724–2093
Adoption specialist: Evelyn P. Andrews

THE PROGRAM

Public adoption services in the District of Columbia are provided by the Adoption and Placement Resources Branch. The agency recruits and prepares foster and adoptive families in the D.C. metro area (within a 25 mile radius of Washington, D.C.) and supervises the placement of special-needs children (older, minority, and handicapped children and sibling groups). In addition, purchase of service is available.

STATE EXCHANGE

Register of Available Children
Director: Julia Hutcherson, Adoption Coordinator
500 First Street, N.W.
Washington, D.C. 20001
(202) 724–8768

STATE ADOPTION REUNION REGISTRY

None.

STATE SUBSIDY

Adoption Subsidy (medical and maintenance)
Director: Faye Spencer
500 First Street, N.W.
Washington, D.C. 20001
(202) 724–2025

NACAC REPRESENTATIVE

None at this time.

GENERAL ADOPTION RESOURCES

The Adoption and Placement Resources Branch sponsors support groups for single adoptive parents and adoptive parents. Call (202) 724–2093 for information.

SPECIAL-NEEDS ADOPTION RESOURCES

The Adoption and Placement Resources Branch provides a range of services for families adopting special-needs children including adoption subsidy (medical and maintenance); Medicaid for all children adopted with subsidy; support group for parents adopting special-needs children; support group for single adoptive parents; counseling services; respite care; infant stimulation and child development programs; classes and equipment for children to age 5; therapeutic horseback riding; speech therapy; day care; homemaker services; orthodontic treatment. The Adoption and Placement Resources Branch provides for all aspects of pre-existing conditions for special-needs children placed by the branch.

OUT-OF-STATE AGENCIES

AGENCY

Welcome House Adoption Services, Virginia Branch
Catholic Charities of Richmond, Virginia
Rainbow Christian Services, Virginia

SEE APPENDIX A

Agencies Providing Nationwide Services

ADOPTION SERVICE INFORMATION AGENCY INC.

7720 Alaska Avenue, N.W.
Washington, D.C. 20012
(202) 726–7193
Program director: Mrs. Mary S. Durr

THE PROGRAM

Adoption Service Information Agency (ASIA) is a non-profit agency serving residents of Washington D.C., Maryland, Virginia, and North Carolina and placing approximately 100 to 120 children annually. Incorporated in 1981, ASIA was founded on the belief that "every child has the right to have a home and a loving family." The agency provides services to birthparents and places infants for adoption when birthparents elect adoptive placement as the best plan for their child. Working directly with child welfare institutions in other countries and working cooperatively with other licensed U.S. agencies which maintain international programs, the agency places children from South Korea, India, Thailand, and Taiwan in American families.

THE COST

The agency's fee for adoption services varies depending on the program and ranges from $6,000 to $7,000. Services covered by the fee include all phases of the adoption process, excluding legal fees connected with finalization and miscellaneous fees (minimal) related to international adoption (immigration and naturalization fees).

THE WAIT

The time from application to the homecoming of the adoptive child ranges from 1 to 2 years.

THE CHILDREN

ASIA places both healthy and special-needs children, ranging in age from 3 months and up, of all racial backgrounds (but primarily of Indian, Korean, and Chinese descent). Countries of origin include South Korea, India, Thailand, Taiwan, and U.S.

THE REQUIREMENTS

Age: Applicants must be at least 25 and no more than 44 years of age.
Health: Applicants should be in reasonably good health. Specific requirements may vary depending on the country of origin.

Religion: No requirement.

Financial status: Applicants must demonstrate financial stability. Specific income requirements may vary depending on the country of origin.

Marital status: Applicants must be married; the length of the marriage must be at least 3 years.

Family size: Applicants may have no more than 4 children currently in the family.

Racial, ethnic or cultural origin: No requirement.

THE PROCEDURE

Participation in ASIA's adoption program entails the following basic steps:

Application
Orientation meeting
Group counseling sessions
Homestudy
Compliance with immigration/naturalization requirements
Referral
Placement
Post-placement supervision
Finalization
Naturalization

ADDITIONAL PROGRAMS/SERVICES

ASIA offers workshops and seminars for adoptive parents on special topics and provides foster care and counseling services. ASIA maintains Saturday Culture School for adopted children and their adoptive parents.

BRANCH/NETWORK OFFICES

12658–60A Lake Ridge Road
Woodbridge, VA 22191

LICENSE/ACCREDITATION/PROFESSIONAL AFFILIATIONS

Adoption Service Information Agency, Inc. is licensed by the District of Columbia Department of Human Services and by the Commonwealth of Virginia Department of Social Services. The agency is a member of the National Committee for Adoption.

THE AMERICAN ADOPTION AGENCY

1228 M Street, N.W.
Washington, D.C. 20005
(202) 638–1543
Program director: Martha Correa, Executive Director

THE PROGRAM

The American Adoption Agency is a nonprofit non-sectarian agency providing nationwide services and placing approximately 40 to 60 children annually. The agency works directly with foreign sources in India and Latin America to place foreign-born children in American families. In addition, the agency will provide homestudy and supervisory services for applicants pursuing interagency adoption (domestic or international) and will make placements out-of-state and overseas.

THE COST

The agency's fee for adoption services is based on a sliding scale and averages $5,000. Services covered by the fee include homestudy, child referral, document preparation, and post-placement supervision. In addition, applicants should anticipate financial responsibility for country program fees, transportation and lodging, immigration/naturalization fees, and legal fees connected with finalization of the adoption.

THE WAIT

The time from application to the homecoming of the adoptive child varies depending on the program, ranging from 12 weeks to 12 months.

THE CHILDREN

The American Adoption Agency places both healthy and special-needs children, ranging in age from infants to school age children, of Hispanic, Black, and bi-racial backgrounds. Countries of origin include Chile, Paraguay, Bolivia, India, El Salvador, Brazil, and U.S.

THE REQUIREMENTS

Age: Applicants must be in reasonably good health. Applicants with health problems or handicaps are given individual consideration. Infertility documentation is required for some programs. The requirements may vary depending on the country.

Religion: No requirement.

Financial status: Applicants must have an income of at least $16,000.

Marital status: The requirement varies depending on the requirements of the child's country of origin.

Family size: No requirement, but may vary depending on the country.

Racial, ethnic or cultural origin: No requirement.

THE PROCEDURE

Participation in The American Adoption Agency's program entails the following basic steps:

Application
Orientation meeting
Homestudy (including group and individual counseling sessions)
Referral
Placement
Post-placement supervision

ADDITIONAL PROGRAMS/SERVICES

The American Adoption Agency provides post-adoptive parent discussion groups and counseling services; out-of-state and overseas placements; homestudy and supervisory services for applicants pursuing interagency adoption (domestic or international).

BRANCH/NETWORK OFFICES

3600 Broad Street
Richmond, VA 23230
(804) 254–0411

LICENSE/ACCREDITATION/PROFESSIONAL AFFILIATIONS

The American Adoption Agency is licensed by the District

of Columbia Department of Human Services and by the Commonwealth of Virginia Department of Social Services.

ASSOCIATED CATHOLIC CHARITIES

Archdiocese of Washington
1438 Rhode Island Avenue, N.E.
Washington, D.C. 20018
(202) 526–4100
Program director: Mona Lisa Dasbach, LCSW, ACSW

THE PROGRAM

Associated Catholic Charities is a nonprofit multi-service agency serving residents of Washington, D.C. and Maryland (Calvert, Charles, Montegomery, Prince George's and St. Mary's Counties) and placing approximately 30 children annually through its adoption programs. The agency exists "to help the Catholic community of Washington reach out to the 'least among us' (Matthew 25) and respond to the pressing social and human needs of the diverse communities which make up the Archdiocese." For 65 years, Catholic Charities has worked to improve the lives of people in the District of Columbia and 5 Maryland counties. Placing children for adoption became a major service in the early 1940s, although adoption was formerly a small part of the agency's program. In addition to traditional adoption services, in the 1970s special emphasis was placed on finding families for older children with medical and/or emotional difficulties. In 1985, Associated Catholic Charities expanded its adoption services to include an international adoption program. Most children placed through the international program are born in Korea.

THE COST

For domestic adoptions, the agency's fee for adoption services is $5,000 (due in 3 installments and negotiable in certain situations). Services covered by the fee include all phases of the adoption process, excluding legal fees connected with finalization of the adoption. For Korean adoption, the transportation, placement fees, and fees to the agency in Korea are additional and change periodically according to the Korean agency. Applicants pursuing Korean adoption can also expect to pay legal fees connected with finalization and immigration and naturalization fees.

THE WAIT

For domestic adoptions, the time from application to the homecoming of the adoptive child ranges from 6 months to 4 years, depending on the needs and availability of children. For Korean adoptions, the wait averages 12 to 14 months.

THE CHILDREN

Associated Catholic Charities places both healthy and special-needs children, ranging in age from 2 months to 5 years and older, of all racial backgrounds. Countries of origin include U.S., Korea, and others.

THE REQUIREMENTS

Age: For domestic adoption, the requirement varies de-

pending on the age of the child. For healthy Korean infant adoption, applicants must be at least 25 and no more than 40 years of age. For special-needs and older Korean child adoptions, applicants must be at least 25 and no more than 45.

Health: Applicants should be in reasonably good health. Applicants with health problems or handicaps are given individual consideration.

Religion: The requirement varies depending on the religious heritage of the child.

Financial status: No specific requirement for domestic adoptions. For Korean adoptions, applicants must have an annual income of at least $15,000.

Marital status: No requirement for domestic adoptions. For Korean adoptions, applicants must be married, and the length of the marriage must be at least 3 years.

Family size: No requirement.

Racial, ethnic or cultural origin: Preference for placing children in families of similar origins.

THE PROCEDURE

Participation in the adoption programs of Associated Catholic Charities entails the following basic steps:
Application
Orientation meeting
Homestudy
Compliance with immigration/naturalization requirements (international adoptions only)
Placement
Post-placement supervision

ADDITIONAL PROGRAMS/SERVICES

Associated Catholic Charities provides a wide range of community services including counseling and social support services for single parents and their families; counseling and social support services for troubled families; shelter for the homeless; case management for the elderly; Harvest for the Hungry (food program); immigration and migrations services (job training, orientation program, unaccompanied minors program); foster care; group homes for minor children (wards of the District of Columbia).

BRANCH/NETWORK OFFICES

While the agency maintains several branch offices in the metropolitan area, all adoption inquiries are processed through the main office.

LICENSE/ACCREDITATION/PROFESSIONAL AFFILIATIONS

Associated Catholic Charities is licensed by the District of Columbia Department of Human Services and is affiliated with Catholic Charities USA.

THE BARKER FOUNDATION

4114 River Road, N.W.
Washington, D.C. 20016
(202) 363–7751
Program director: Robin B. Allen

THE PROGRAM

The Barker Foundation is a nonprofit agency serving residents of the Washington, D.C. metropolitan area and placing approximately 70 to 75 children annually. Founded in 1945, the agency's goals are "to provide full support for young women facing unplanned pregnancies, for babies requiring medical and foster care prior to adoptive placement, and for babies requiring medical and foster care prior to adoptive placement, and for couples who are hoping to build their families through adoption." The agency provides services to birthparents and places infants for adoption when birthparents elect adoptive placement as the best plan for their child. In 1978, the agency expanded its programs to include the placement of children from other countries. Working with child welfare institutions abroad and with other U.S. Agencies which maintain international programs, the agency places foreign-born children (primarily from South America).

THE COST

For domestic adoptions, the agency's fee ranges from $0 to $8,500. Services covered by the fee include all phases of the adoption process and services to the birthmother and child, excluding legal fees connected with finalization of the adoption. For international adoptions, the agency's fee is $3,000. In addition, applicants pursuing international adoption should anticipate a fee to the foreign agency (currently $3,200 to the orphanage in Bogota), travel and accommodation expenses ($2,000 to $4,000), other miscellaneous expenses related to international adoption, and legal fees for finalization.

THE WAIT

For domestic adoptions, the time from application to placement ranges from 6 months to 2 years. For international adoptions, the wait ranges from 6 to 15 months.

THE CHILDREN

The Barker Foundation places primarily healthy children (domestic infants and international children ranging from infancy to 10 years of age). Domestic children are of Caucasian, Black, Hispanic, and bi-racial backgrounds. International children are of Hispanic backgrounds. Countries of origin include U.S., Colombia, Paraguay, and Brazil (for older children).

THE REQUIREMENTS

Age: For domestic adoption, applicants must be at least 25 and no more than 40 years of age. For international adoption, there should be no more than 40 years difference between the oldest parent and the child to be adopted.
Health: Applicants should be in reasonably good health. Applicants with health problems or handicaps are given individual consideration. Infertility documentation is required for domestic adoption.
Religion: No requirement.
Financial status: No requirement.
Marital status: Applicants must be married, and the length of the marriage must be at least 2 years.
Family size: For domestic adoption, applicants may have no more than 1 child currently in the family. The requirement

is flexible for international adoption.
Racial, ethnic or cultural origin: No requirement.

THE PROCEDURE

Participation in the adoption program of The Barker Foundation entails the following basic steps:
Orientation meeting
Application
Group counseling sessions
Individual counseling sessions
Homestudy
Compliance with immigration/naturalization requirements (international adoptions only)
Referral
Placement
Post-placement supervision

ADDITIONAL PROGRAMS/SERVICES

The Barker Foundation provides foster care, post-adoptive workshops and meetings, post-adoptive counseling for birthmothers, adoptees, and adoptive families.

BRANCH/NETWORK OFFICES

While the agency maintains a branch office in Falls Church, Virginia, all adoption inquiries are processed by the main office in Washington, D.C.

LICENSE/ACCREDITATION/PROFESSIONAL AFFILIATIONS

The Barker Foundation is licensed by the District of Columbia Department of Human Services and by the Commonwealth of Virginia Department of Social Services.

HOMES FOR BLACK CHILDREN

Family and Child Services
929 L Street, N.W.
Washington, D.C. 20001
(202) 289–1510
Program director: Mae H. Best

THE PROGRAM

Family and Child Services is a nonprofit agency serving residents of the metropolitan Washington, D.C. area and placing approximately 35 to 40 Black children annually. The Homes for Black Children program was developed to find permanent homes for Black children and to encourage the active participation of the Black community in helping to meet the needs of Black children. The agency works directly with birthparents, with public and private agencies, and with national and regional exchange programs to place Black infants, older children, and special-needs children in permanent homes.

THE COST

The agency's fee for adoption services is based on a sliding scale and ranges from $0 to $2,500. Services covered by the fee include all phases of the adoption process, excluding attorney's fees connected with finalization of the adoption. Families adopting special-needs children are eligible for subsidy.

The Wait

The time from application to the homecoming of the adoptive child ranges from 1 month to 1 year, depending on the type of child requested. The wait for a female child is usually much longer than the wait for a male child.

The Children

Homes for Black Children places both healthy and special-needs children, ranging in age from birth to 17 years, of Black and bi-racial backgrounds, born in the U.S.

The Requirements

Age: No specific requirement; however, the child's age in relation to the age of the parents is taken into consideration.

Health: Applicants should be in reasonably good health. Applicants with health problems or handicaps are given individual consideration.

Religion: No requirement.

Financial status: No requirement. Families adopting special-needs children are eligible for subsidy.

Marital status: No requirement.

Family size: No requirement.

Racial, ethnic or cultural origin: Preference for placing children in families of similar origins.

The Procedure

Participation in the Homes for Black Children adoption program entails the following basic steps:
Orientation meeting
Application
Individual counseling sessions
Homestudy
Referral
Placement
Post-placement supervision

Additional Programs/Services

Family and Child Services provides a range of community services including foster care, counseling, day care, RSVP, services to seniors, and camping services.

Branch/Network Offices

None.

License/Accreditation/Professional Affiliations

Family and Child Services is licensed by District of Columbia Department of Human Services. The agency is a member of the Child Welfare League of America, Family Service America, and the United Way.

JEWISH SOCIAL SERVICE AGENCY OF METROPOLITAN WASHINGTON

2028 P St., N.W.
Washington, D.C. 20036
(202) 887–1644
Program director: Agency Executive Director

The Program

For a full description of programs and services, refer to Maryland listing:
Jewish Social Service Agency of Metropolitan Washington
6123 Montrose Road
Rockville, MD 20852
(301) 881–3700

Branch Office

Jewish Social Service Agency/District of Columbia:
619 D St., S.E.
Washington, D.C. 20003
(301) 881–3700

LUTHERAN SOCIAL SERVICES OF THE NATIONAL CAPITAL AREA, INC.

5121 Colorado Avenue, N.W.
Washington, D.C. 20011
(202) 829–7605
Program director: R. Williams

The Program

Lutheran Social Services of the National Capital Area is a nonprofit agency serving residents of northern Virginia, District of Columbia, and Maryland and placing approximately 50 children annually. Licensed under a reciprocal agreement between the District of Columbia and the State of Maryland and licensed by the Commonwealth of Virginia, the agency has been placing children for 31 years. The agency provides domestic and intercountry adoption services and strives "to provide permanent homes for all children who are waiting to be adopted in the United States and throughout the world, regardless of race, sex, religion, creed, color, or national origin."

The Cost

The agency's fee is based on a sliding scale and ranges from $2,500 to $5,000 for the Domestic Adoption Program and from 47,000 to $12,000 for the Intercountry Adoption Program. Services covered by the fee include all phases of the adoption process. There are no additional non-agency fees which prospective adoptive parents need anticipate.

The Wait

There is no wait for families interested in adopting Black infants. There is a 5–year waiting list for families interested in adopting healthy Caucasian infants. The wait for inter-country placement ranges from 12 to 15 months.

The Children

Lutheran Social Services places both healthy and special-needs children, ranging in age from infancy to adolescence, of Black, Asian, Hispanic, and Caucasian racial backgrounds. Countries of origin include the U.S. and various Latin American countries.

THE REQUIREMENTS

Age: Applicants must be in reasonably good health. Applicants with handicaps are given individual consideration. Infertility documentation is required for foreign adoption.

Religion: Applicants of any religious faith are accepted.

Financial status: Applicants must demonstrate ability to financially support a child.

Marital status: No requirement. If married, the length of the marriage must be at least 2 years.

Family size: No requirement.

Racial, ethnic or cultural origin: Preference for placing children in families of similar origins. The requirement varies for Intercountry Adoption Program.

THE PROCEDURE

Participation in Lutheran Social Services' adoption program entails the following basic steps:

Orientation meeting
Application
Group consideration and recommendation
Homestudy
Compliance with immigration/naturalization requirements (Intercountry Program only)
Referral (Intercountry Program only)
Placement
Post-placement supervision
Finalization
Naturalization (Intercountry Program only)

ADDITIONAL PROGRAMS/SERVICES

Lutheran Social Services provides birthparent pregnancy counseling, temporary foster care, and post-adoption counseling.

BRANCH/NETWORK OFFICES

While the agency maintains several branch offices, all inquiries are processed through the main office in Washington, D.C.

LICENSE/ACCREDITATION/PROFESSIONAL AFFILIATIONS

Lutheran Social Services is licensed by the Commonwealth of Virginia Department of Social Services, by the District of Columbia Department of Human Services, and under reciprocity agreement by the State of Maryland Department of Human Resources.

PAN AMERICAN ADOPTION AGENCY, INC.

3325 Garfield Street, N.W.
Washington, D.C. 20008
(202) 690–3079
Program director: Nancy Croteau, Executive Director

THE PROGRAM

For a full description of programs and services, refer to Virginia listing:

Pan American Adoption Agency, Inc.
12604 Kahns Road
Manassas, VA 22111
(703) 791–3260

SAINT SOPHIA GREEK ORTHODOX ADOPTION SERVICE

36th Street and Massachusetts Avenue, N.W.
Washington, D.C. 20007
(202) 333–4730 or (703) 971–2141
Program director: Rev. John T. Tavlarides, Director
Mrs. Janice E. Labovites, ACSW, Casework Supervisor

THE PROGRAM

Saint Sophia Greek Orthodox Adoption Service is a small, nonprofit agency serving residents of the Washington, D.C. metropolitan area (excluding Virginia residents as per Virginia law) and specializing in homestudy and post-placement supervision for international adoption. The agency was originally licensed to work with couples in the Greek Orthodox Church who planned adoption in Greece through licensed Greek agencies. When Greece stopped international adoptions, the agency continued to provide homestudy and supervisory services for applicants pursuing international adoption. Greek Orthodoxy is not a requirement for applicants requesting services. In most cases, couples complete the adoption in another country, and Saint Sophia provides the homestudy and post-placement supervision for the follow-up U.S. adoption. On a case-by-case basis, the agency will provide homestudy and supervisory services for applicants pursuing independent or interagency adoption.

THE COST

The agency's fee is $650 for the homestudy and $600 for post-placement supervision.

THE WAIT

Not applicable.

THE CHILDREN

Not applicable

THE REQUIREMENTS

There are no categorical restrictions. Each homestudy is evaluated on its own merits for the adoption being planned.

Age: No specific requirement; case-by-case evaluation.

Health: No specific requirement; case-by-case evaluation.

Religion: No specific requirement; case-by-case evaluation.

Financial status: No specific requirement; case-by-case evaluation.

Marital status: No specific requirement; case-by-case evaluation.

Family size: No specific requirement; case-by-case evaluation.

Racial, ethnic or cultural origin: No specific requirement; case-by-case evaluation.

THE PROCEDURE

Applicants pursuing international adoption who are in need of homestudy and supervisory services are invited to contact the agency to make arrangements for services.

ADDITIONAL PROGRAMS/SERVICES

None.

BRANCH/NETWORK OFFICES

None.

LICENSE/ACCREDITATION/PROFESSIONAL AFFILIATIONS

Saint Sophia Greek Orthodox Adoption Service is licensed by the District of Columbia Department of Human Services.

WORLD CHILD, INC.

5121 Colorado Avenue, N.W.
Washington, D.C. 20011
(202) 829–5244
Program director: Sherrell Goolsby

THE PROGRAM

World Child is a nonprofit agency serving residents of the District of Columbia, North Carolina, Connecticut, and Pennsylvania through its member agencies and placing approximately 80 children from Latin America annually. Founded in 1981 and licensed as a child placement agency by the District of Columbia in 1983, the agency's mission is "to promote family life through adoptive placement for homeless children abroad; to provide child welfare assistance to children abroad; to respect the primacy of a child's family of origin, seeking the adoption alternative only in order to honor every child's right to a permanent, secure, and nurturing family." World Child works directly with child welfare institutions in Latin America and with intermediaries to place both healthy and special-needs children for adoption in the U.S. and abroad.

THE COST

The agency's fee for intercountry adoption services is $1,700 plus a $100 application fee. The agency does not provide the homestudy or post-placement supervision; these services are provided by World Child member agencies (see "Branch/Network Offices"), and applicants can expect to pay a fee for the provision of these services. In addition, applicants should anticipate expenses for travel, visas, passports, immigration and naturalization fees, translations, and couriers. Applicants are responsible for legal fees connected with finalization.

THE WAIT

The time from application to the homecoming of the adoptive child ranges from 6 months to 2 years.

THE CHILDREN

World child places both healthy and special-needs children, ranging in age from infancy to 15 years. Countries of origin include most of Latin America and Thailand.

THE REQUIREMENTS

Age: Applicants must be at least 25 years of age. The maximum age requirement may vary depending on the country of origin.

Health: Applicants should be in reasonably good health and should have normal life expectancy. Applicants with health problems or handicaps are given individual consideration.

Religion: No requirement.

Financial status: No requirement other than basic financial stability.

Marital status: The requirement varies depending on the country of origin. Married applicants must be married at least 2 years.

Family size: No requirement.

Racial, ethnic or cultural origin: No requirement.

THE PROCEDURE

Participation in World Child's adoption program entails the following basic steps:
Application
Group and individual counseling (as needed)
Homestudy (provided by member agency)
Compliance with immigration/naturalization requirements
Referral
Placement
Post-placement supervision (provided by member agency)
Post-adoption reports to foreign country

ADDITIONAL PROGRAMS/SERVICES

World Child provides parent group activities and assistance services (including sponsorship) abroad.

BRANCH/NETWORK OFFICES

Lutheran Service Association of New England, Inc.
74 Sherman Street
Hartford, CT 06105
(203) 236–0679

Lutheran Family Services of North Carolina
P.O. Box 12907
Raleigh, NC 27605
(919) 832–2620

Lutheran Children and Family / Family Service of Eastern PA
2900 Queen Lane
Philadelphia, PA 19129
(215) 951–6888

Lutheran Social Services of the National Capital Area, Inc.
5121 Colorado Ave., N.W.
Washington, D.C. 20011
(202) 829–7605

LICENSE/ACCREDITATION/PROFESSIONAL AFFILIATIONS

World Child, Inc. is Licensed by the District of Columbia Department of Human Services.

Florida

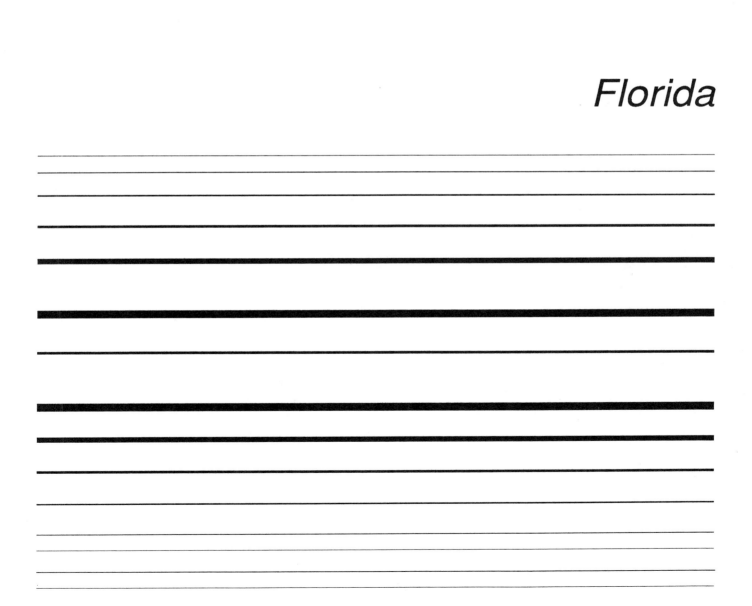

PUBLIC ADOPTION PROGRAM/ COMMUNITY RESOURCES

Department of Health and Rehabilitative Services
Children, Youth and Families Program Office
1317 Winewood Boulevard
Tallahassee, FL 32301
(904) 488–8000
Adoption specialist: Gloria Walker

THE PROGRAM

Public adoption services in Florida are provided through district offices of the Department of Health and Rehabilitative Services (HRS). HRS recruits and prepares foster and adoptive families and supervises the placement of special-needs children (toddlers to teenagers, minority children, handicapped children, children with medical, emotional, or intellectual special needs, and sibling groups).

STATE EXCHANGE

Florida Adoption Exchange. For information, contact the Children, Youth and Families Program Office (above).

STATE ADOPTION REUNION REGISTRY

Florida Adoption Registry
Vital Statistics Registry
P.O. Box 2197
Jacksonville, FL 32232
(904) 354–3961, ext. 3152 and 3153

STATE SUBSIDY

For information, contact the Children, Youth and Families Program Office (above).

NACAC REPRESENTATIVE

Gail Kreitz
P.O. Box 17184
Plantation, FL 33318
(305) 972–2735

GENERAL ADOPTION RESOURCES

Northwest Florida Adoptive Parents Support Group
Escambia County Chapter
c/o Donna Fuller
2818 B. Smith Avenue
Pensacola, FL 32507

Reaching Every Adoptable Child Today (REACT)
Santa Rosa County Chapter
769 Old High Road
Milton, FL 32570

Friends of Hillsborough County
c/o Linda McIlwain
620 Downs Avenue
Temple Terrace, FL 3361

Council on Adoptable Children of Mid Florida
c/o Eric Foxman
941 W. Morse Boulevard
Winter Park, FL 32789

Advocacy for Black Children Advisory Board

c/o Lori Richmond-Graves
1000 N.E. 16th Avenue
Gainesville, FL 32601

c/o Carrie E. Pyle
1313 N. Tampa Street
Tampa, FL 33602

c/o Cindy Morales
941 W. Morse Boulevard
Winter park, FL 32789

c/o Bette T. McLean
P.O. Box 06177
Ft. Myers, FL 33906

c/o MaryAnne Llewellyn
311 N. State Road 7
Plantation, FL 33317

c/o Lourdes C. Villalba
1150 S.W. 1st Street
Miami, FL 33130

SPECIAL-NEEDS ADOPTION RESOURCES

Parents Support for Special-Needs Children
c/o June Fountain
Project CAN
2960 Roosevelt Boulevard
Clearwater, FL 33520

One Church, One Child Program
Department of Health and Rehabilitative Services
State Coordinator: Pamela Eby
1317 Winewood Blvd.
Tallahassee, FL 32301
(904) 488–8000

OUT-OF-STATE AGENCIES

AGENCY

Smithlawn Maternity Home, (special needs and minority placements), Texas

SEE APPENDIX A

Agencies Providing Nationwide Services.

THE ADOPTION CENTRE, INC.

500 N. Maitland Ave.
Maitland, FL 32751
(305) 740–0044
Program director: Dr. Lorraine T. Boisselle

THE PROGRAM

The Adoption Centre is a nonprofit, non-sectarian agency serving the state of Florida. The agency's mission is "to find loving secure homes for children in (its) custody or in the custody of agencies with whom (it) works." The Adoption Centre offers several domestic and foreign adoption programs. Through its domestic program, the agency places (a) children (primarily infants) who have been surrendered to the agency by birthparents who have decided that adoption is in the best interests of the child and (b) children in the custody of the State of Florida (children with physical and/or emotional problems, large sibling groups, older children, Black children) who are waiting for permanent families. Through its international program, the agency places (a) waiting children (infants to school age children with medical conditions ranging from mild to moderate, older children, sibling groups from Korea, India, and the Philippines and (b) children (predominantly infants but also some older children) from Paraguay, Chile, and Guatemala.

THE COST

Agency fees vary depending on the program and the type of child placed. Adoption services for domestic waiting children are provided at no cost to the adoptive family. The fee schedule for other Adoption Centre programs is as follows:

Domestic Program

Application Fee	$1000.00
Homestudy Fee	$875.00
Placement Fee	$5,000.00

In addition, prospective adoptive parents should anticipate financial responsibility for the medical expenses of the birthmother and child, caseworker travel costs, and legal fees connected with finalization of the adoption. If applicants have a homestudy which is more than one year old, the update fee is $575.

International Adoptions/Waiting Children

The complete cost is approximately $5,000 and includes application, homestudy, placement, cooperating agency fee, travel and escort costs, and support services. Applicants should anticipate legal fees connected with finalization of the adoption.

International Adoptions/Paraguay/Guatemala/Chile

Application fee	$100.00
Homestudy	$875.00
Review Fee (if homestudy is completed by another agency)	$200.00
Dossier Preparation (record maintenance, authentication, express mail fees, translation fees)	$2,000.00
Adoption Centre Placement Fee	$500.00
Chile Placement Fee (varies depending on the age of the child)	$5,000.00—$6,500.00
Paraguay Placement Fee	$4,500.00
Guatemala Placement Fee	$2,500.00

In addition, prospective adoptive parents should anticipate financial responsibility for travel costs, immigration/naturalization fees, legal fees connected with finalization of the adoption. If applicants have a homestudy which is more than one year old, the update fee is $575.00

THE WAIT

The time from application to the homecoming of the adoptive child varies depending on the program and the type of child the applicants wish to adopt.

THE CHILDREN

The Adoption Centre places both healthy and special-needs children, ranging in age from infancy to adolescence, of all racial backgrounds. Countries of origin include U.S., Korea, Philippines, India, Paraguay, Guatemala, and Chile.

THE REQUIREMENTS

Age: The age requirement may vary depending on the program. Generally, there should be no more than 40 years difference between the child and the parents.

Health: Applicants must be in reasonably good health.

Religion: No requirement. For adoption through domestic program, the preferences of the birthparents are honored.

Financial status: Applicants must demonstrate financial stability.

Marital status: Requirements vary for international programs. For adoption through domestic program, the preferences of the birthparents are honored.

Family size: No requirement. Preference is given in some countries to childless or 1 child families.

Racial, ethnic or cultural origin: No requirement. For adoption through domestic program, preference of the birthparents is honored.

THE PROCEDURE

Participation in The Adoption Centre's adoption programs entails the following basic steps:
Orientation meeting
Application
Group counseling sessions
Individual counseling sessions
Homestudy
Compliance with immigration/naturalization requirements (international adoptions only)
Referral
Placement
Post-placement supervision

ADDITIONAL PROGRAMS/SERVICES

The Adoption Centre provides foster care services; counseling services for birthparents, adoptees, and adoptive parents; educational community outreach programs; workshops relating to Florida's Waiting Children.

BRANCH/NETWORK OFFICE

None.

LICENSE/ACCREDITATION/PROFESSIONAL AFFILIATIONS

The Adoption Centre is licensed by the State of Florida Department of Health and Rehabilitative Services and is a member of the North American Council on Adoptable Children.

CATHOLIC CHARITIES BUREAU

P.O. Box 1931
134 E. Church St.
Jacksonville, FL 32201
(904) 354–3416
Program director: Kathryn L. Strayer

THE PROGRAM

Providing child care and child placement services since 1945, Catholic Charities Bureau is a nonprofit agency serving the Diocese of St. Augustine (a 17 county area in northeastern Florida) and placing approximately 25 children annually. Providing services on a non-sectarian basis, the agency's mission is "to be a sign of the compassionate love of the Creator for His children in need."

THE COST

The agency's fee is based on a sliding scale and ranges between $1,500 and $4,000. Fees are waived or reduced in special-needs adoptions. Services covered by the fee include adoption preparation and homestudy, placement, and post-placement services. In addition, prospective adoptive parents should anticipate financial responsibility for legal fees connected with finalization of the adoption.

THE WAIT

The time from application to the homecoming of the adoptive child varies depending on the kind of child the applicant wishes to adopt. For non special-needs adoptions, the wait ranges from 3 to 5 years. For special-needs adoptions, the wait ranges from 3 to 12 months.

THE CHILDREN

Catholic Charities Bureau places both healthy and special-needs children of all racial backgrounds, ranging in age from birth to 18 years.

THE REQUIREMENTS

Age: For non special-needs adoptions, applicants must be at least 21 and no more than 42 years of age. For special-needs adoptions, applicants must be at least 21 and no more than 65 years of age.

Health: Applicants must be in reasonably hood health. Applicants with health problems or handicaps are given individual consideration.

Religion: No requirement.

Financial status: No requirement.

Marital status: For non special-needs adoptions, applicants must be married and must have been married for at least 2 years. Applications from single parents are accepted for special-needs adoptions.

Family size: No requirement for special-needs adoptions. For non special-needs adoptions, applicants may have no more than 1 child currently in the family.

Racial, ethnic or cultural origin: No requirement, but preference for placing children in families of similar origins.

THE PROCEDURE

Participation in Catholic Charities Bureau's adoption program entails the following basic steps:

Application
Orientation meeting
Homestudy
Referral
Placement
Post-placement supervision

ADDITIONAL PROGRAMS/SERVICES

Catholic Charities Bureau sponsors a parent support group and provides post-adoption counseling and referral services.

BRANCH/NETWORK OFFICES

1717 N.E. 9th Street
Gainsville, FL 32609
(904) 372-0294

40 Sanford Street
P.O. Box 543
St. Augustine, FL 32085
(904) 892-6300

LICENSE/ACCREDITATION/PROFESSIONAL AFFILIATIONS

Catholic Charities Bureau is licensed by the State of Florida Department of Health and Rehabilitative Services and is a member of Catholic Charities USA.

CATHOLIC CHARITIES BUREAU, INC.

P.O. Box 543 (40 Sanford Street)
St. Augustine, FL 32085
(904) 829-6300
Program director: Mary Dowling

THE PROGRAM

Catholic Charities Bureau, Inc. (CCB) is a nonprofit social service organization that serves the residents of St. Johns, Flagler, and Putnum Counties, Florida, and places approximately 2 children annually. Opened in 1975, the agency has expanded its social services and is dedicated to providing "effective, efficient, direct service" and acts as "an advocate for, and enabler of people in need." The agency provides services to birthparents and places infants for adoption when birthparents elect adoptive placement as the best plan for their child. The agency is involved in the placement of special-needs children and provides homestudy and post-placement supervision for those pursuing foreign adoptions.

THE COST

The agency's fee is based on a sliding scale as follows: 8.5% of the applicants' gross annual income, the total not to exceed $4,000, for non-special-needs infants. Services covered by the fee include homestudy, placement, and post-placement supervision. In addition, applicants can expect to pay legal fees associated with finalization of the adoption. Services connected with special needs placements are provided at no cost to the adoptive family.

THE WAIT

The average wait from submitting the application to home-coming of the adoptive child is 3 to 5 years for non special-needs infants; 12 to 18 months for special-needs children.

THE CHILDREN

CCB places both non special-needs infants and special-needs children who range in age from birth to 18 years, of all racial backgrounds. In addition, the agency will provide homestudy and supervisory services for applicants pursuing foreign adoption.

THE REQUIREMENTS

Age: Applicants must be at least 21 and no more than 42 years of age for non special-needs infants and no more than 65 for special-needs children.

Health: Applicants with health problems or handicaps are given individual consideration. Infertility documentation is required for non-special needs.

Religion: No requirement.

Financial status: Applicants should demonstrate financial stability.

Marital status: No requirement for special-needs children. Applicants must be married to adopt non special-needs infants; the length of the marriage must be at least 2 years.

Family size: No requirement for special-needs children. Applicants for non special-needs infant may have no more than 1 child currently in the family.

Racial, ethnic or cultural origin: Preference for placing children in families of similar races.

THE PROCEDURE

Participation in CCB's adoption program entails the following basic steps:
Orientation meeting
Application
Group counseling sessions
Individual counseling sessions
Homestudy
Compliance with immigration/naturalization requirements (foreign adoptions only)
Referral
Placement
Post-placement supervision

ADDITIONAL PROGRAMS/SERVICES

Catholic Charities Bureau, Inc., offers a foster care program utilizing Catholic Charities' homes in Jacksonville, emergency assistance services, crisis counseling, parish social ministry, and independent living programs for the elderly.

BRANCH/NETWORK OFFICES

Catholic Charities Bureau is associated with Catholic Charities offices in Jacksonville and Gainesville, Florida.

LICENSE/ACCREDITATION/PROFESSIONAL AFFILIATIONS

Catholic Charities Bureau, Inc., is licensed by the State of Florida Department of Health and Rehabilitative Services and is a member of Catholic Charities USA.

CATHOLIC CHARITIES OF THE DIOCESE OF VENICE

Catholic Social Services, Inc.
3190 Davis Boulevard
Naples, FL 33942
(813) 774–6483
Program director: Ed Ullmann, ACSW, Diplomat, Director of Professional Services

THE PROGRAM

Catholic Social Services is a nonprofit multi-service agency serving residents of the Diocese of Venice (10 counties of south west Florida) and placing approximately 6–10 children annually. The agency provides services to birthparents and places infants for adoption when birthparents in the agency's program elect adoptive placement as the best plan for their child. Working with a statewide network, the agency also recruits families for special-needs children.

THE COST

The agency's fee for adoption services is $2,000 (for homestudy and supervisory services) plus 10% of the applicants' annual gross income, with a minimum of $3,000 (for the pregnancy counseling services fund). In addition, applicants assume responsibility for legal fees connected with finalization of the adoption (approximately $150–$250).

THE WAIT

The time from application to the homecoming of the adoptive child averages 1 to 2 years.

THE CHILDREN

Catholic Social Services places both healthy and special-needs children, primarily infants (birth to 2 years) but some older children as well. Children placed by the agency are born in the U.S., of Caucasian and Hispanic racial backgrounds.

THE REQUIREMENTS

Age: Applicants must be at least 20 and no more than 40 years of age. The requirement may be flexible for special needs placements.

Health: Applicants must be in reasonably good health. Applicants with health problems or handicaps are given individual consideration. For Caucasian infant adoption, infertility documentation is required.

Religion: Applicants must be practicing members of a recognized church.

Financial status: Applicants must have sufficient income to add a new family member without significantly changing the standard of living.

Marital status: Applicants must be married. The length of the marriage must be at least 3 years. The requirement may vary for special-needs placements.

Family size: For Caucasian infant adoption, applicants must be childless. The requirement may be more flexible for special needs placements.

Racial, ethnic or cultural origin: No requirement, but preference for placing children in families of similar origins.

THE PROCEDURE

Participation in Catholic Social Services' adoption program entails the following basic steps:
Orientation meeting
Application
Homestudy (including individual and group counseling)

Placement
Post-placement supervision (3 visits)
Finalization

ADDITIONAL PROGRAMS/SERVICES

Catholic Social Services provides a wide range of community services including pregnancy counseling; infant foster care; family counseling; spouse abuse crisis intervention; post-abortion counseling; immigration/legalization services; refugee resettlement services.

BRANCH/NETWORK OFFICES

2015 S. Tuttle, Suite C
Sarasota, FL 33579
(813) 957–4496

LICENSE/ACCREDITATION/PROFESSIONAL AFFILIATIONS

Catholic Social Services, Inc. is licensed by the State of Florida Department of Health and Rehabilitative Services. The agency is a member of the Florida Association of Licensed Adoption Agencies, the United Way, and Catholic Charities USA.

CATHOLIC SOCIAL SERVICES, INC.

1771 N. Semoran Boulevard
Orlando, FL 32807
(407) 658–1818
Program director: Thomas J. Aglio

THE PROGRAM

Catholic Social Services is a nonprofit multi-service agency "responding to a variety of human needs" and serving residents of central Florida on a non-sectarian basis. Licensed as a child placing agency since 1962, the agency places approximately 70 children annually through its adoption program. Working with birthparents, with other private and public agencies, Catholic Social Services places both healthy and special-needs children.

THE COST

The agency's fee for adoption services is $5,100. Services covered by the fee include all phases of the adoption process and services to the birthmother and child, excluding legal fees connected with finalization of the adoption (approximately $200).

THE WAIT

The time from application to the homecoming of the adoptive child averages 2 years.

THE CHILDREN

Catholic Social Services places both healthy and special-needs children, ranging in age from infancy to adolescence, of all racial backgrounds.

THE REQUIREMENTS

Age: For infant adoption, applicants may be no more than 40 years of age.

Health: Applicants should be in reasonably good health. Applicants with health problems or handicaps are given individual consideration.
Religion: Applicants should be practicing members of the faith of their choice.
Financial status: No requirement.
Marital status: Applicants must be married, and the length of the marriage must be at least 3 years.
Family size: Applicants may have no more than 1 child currently in the family.
Racial, ethnic or cultural origin: No requirement.

THE PROCEDURE

Participation in the adoption program of Catholic Social Services entails the following basic steps:
Telephone inquiry and screening
Application
Group counseling sessions
Individual counseling sessions
Homestudy
Placement
Post-placement supervision

ADDITIONAL PROGRAMS/SERVICES

Catholic Social Services provides pregnancy counseling (free pregnancy tests); foster care; workshops and seminars; marital and family counseling; search assistance and counseling.

BRANCH/NETWORK OFFICES

319 Riveredge Blvd.
Cocoa, FL 32922
(305) 636–6144

803 E. Palmetto
Lakeland, FL 33801
(813) 686–7153

771 Briarwood Dr.
Daytona Beach, FL 32014
(904) 255–6521

1602 S.E. 3rd Ave.
Ocala, FL 32671
(904) 629–1738

LICENSE/ACCREDITATION/PROFESSIONAL AFFILIATIONS

Catholic Social Services, Inc. is licensed by the State of Florida Department of Health and Rehabilitative Services. All professional staff are ACSW and affiliated with the National Association of Social Workers. The agency is a member of Catholic Charities USA.

CATHOLIC SOCIAL SERVICES

218 E. Government Street
P.O. Box 285
Pensacola, FL 32592
(904) 438–8564
Program director: Sister Gail Lambert, MSW, Executive Director; Mary S. Giblin, MS, Diocesan Coordinator of Adoption Services

THE PROGRAM

Catholic Social Services is a nonprofit, multi-service organization serving the Diocese of Pensacola (18 counties in northwest Florida) and placing 20–35 children annually. Providing adoption services since 1951, the agency has evolved in response to the changing needs of the community, striving to "respect the dignity and unique personhood of the individual, their right to life, freedom of self-determination and human dignity." Catholic Social Services places primarily infants and toddlers when birthparents in the agency's unmarried parents program decide that the infant's best interests will be served by adoptive placement. The agency encourages open adoption through the exchange of non-identifying information between birthparents and adoptive parents.

THE COST

The agency's fee for adoption services is based on a sliding scale of 8% of the applicants' adjusted gross income, with a minimum fee of $600 and a maximum of $6,000. Services covered by the fee include all phases of the adoption process as well as medical and/or foster care services for birthmothers and their children. In addition, prospective adoptive parents should anticipate financial responsibility for legal fees connected with finalization of the adoption (usually between $150 and $250).

THE WAIT

The time from application for acceptance into the program to the homecoming of the adoptive child ranges from 6 months to 2 years.

THE CHILDREN

Catholic Social Services places both healthy and special-needs children, ranging in age from infancy to 4 years, of Caucasian, Black, Hispanic, and mixed racial backgrounds. All children placed by the agency are born in the U.S.

THE REQUIREMENTS

Age: Applicants must be at least 25 and no more than 40 years of age. The requirement may be flexible depending on the agency's assessment of the couple's situation.

Health: Applicants must be in reasonably good health. Applicants with health problems or handicaps are given individual consideration.

Religion: The cultural and religious background of the birthparents is taken into consideration when selecting adoptive parents. The specific requests of birthparents regarding religious preference are honored whenever possible. Although Catholic Social Services is a Catholic agency, couples of other denominations may apply.

Financial status: Applicants must demonstrate financial stability.

Residence: Applicants must reside within the Diocese of Pensacola-Tallahassee which covers 18 counties in northwest Florida.

Marital status: Applicants must be married and must have been married for at least 3 years.

Family size: Applicants may have no more than 1 child currently in the family. Requirement may be flexible in some cases, especially special-needs adoptions.

Racial, ethnic or cultural origin: Requirement varies depending on the needs of the child and the applicants' degree of openness to a child who is different from them.

THE PROCEDURE

Participation in Catholic Social Services' adoption program entails the following basic steps:
Orientation meeting
Group educational sessions
Application
Individual counseling sessions
Homestudy
Placement
Post-placement supervision

ADDITIONAL PROGRAMS/SERVICES

Catholic Social Services provides crisis pregnancy counseling; specialized foster care; individual, marital, and family counseling; refugee resettlement, and immigration services; community outreach services; direct aid to the poor.

BRANCH/NETWORK OFFICES

Ft. Walton Beach Office
40 Beal Parkway, S.W.
Ft. Walton, FL 32548
(904) 244–2825
Panama City Office
714 N. Cove Blvd.
Panama City, FL 32401
(904) 763–0475
Tallahassee Office
855 W. Carolina St.
Tallahassee, FL 32316
(904) 224–9112

LICENSE/ACCREDITATION/PROFESSIONAL AFFILIATIONS

Catholic Social Services is licensed by the State of Florida Department of Health and Rehabilitative Services. The agency is a member of Catholic Charities USA and the National Association of Social Workers.

CATHOLIC SOCIAL SERVICES

St. Petersburg Office
6533 9th Avenue, N., Suite 1–East
St. Petersburg, FL 33710
(813) 345–9126
Program director: Michael L. Cook

THE PROGRAM

Catholic Social Services is a nonprofit multi-service agency sponsored by the Catholic Diocese of St. Petersburg and serving residents of Pinellas County. The agency's mission is "to provide quality social service programs to individuals, couples, and families regardless of ethnic origin, race, sex, religion or economic condition who have experienced certain adjustment or situational problems that have an impact on their lives and to assist clients to maximize their personal and social adjustment to achieve an enhanced quality of life, thereby strengthening the family unit." Working directly with birthparents, with other private and public agencies, and with national and regional exchange programs, the agency places both healthy and special-needs children. In addition, the agency will provide post-placement supervision for applicants pursuing adoption through another Catholic Charities agency.

THE COST

The agency's fee for adoption services is $5,500. Services covered by the fee include the adoption study, placement service, post-placement supervision, and application for the amended birth certificate. In addition, applicants should anticipate financial responsibility for legal fees connected with finalization of the adoption and physician's fee for a complete physical examination.

THE WAIT

The time from application to placement averages 24 to 30 months.

THE CHILDREN

Catholic Social Services places both healthy and special-needs children, primarily infants, of all racial backgrounds, born in the U.S.

THE REQUIREMENTS

Age: Applicants must be at least 25 and no more than 39 years of age. The age requirement may be waived for special needs placements.
Health: Applicants should be in reasonably good health. Applicants with health problems or handicaps are given individual consideration. Infertility status should be explored.
Religion: No requirement.
Financial status: No requirement.
Marital status: Applicants must be married, and the length of the marriage must be at least 3 years. Single parents are considered for special-needs placements.
Family size: Applicants may have no more than 1 child currently in the family. The requirement may be waived for special-needs placements.
Racial, ethnic or cultural origin: Preference for placing children in families of similar origins when possible.

THE PROCEDURE

Participation in the adoption program of Catholic Social Services entails the following basic steps:
Inquiry or referral to agency
Orientation meeting
Application
Individual counseling sessions
Homestudy
Submission of references and medical reports
Placement
Post-placement supervision

ADDITIONAL PROGRAMS/SERVICES

Catholic Social Services provides a wide range of services including individual, marital and family counseling; services to birthparents; foster care for infants awaiting adoption; services to the elderly; refugee social services; immigration and legalization services; social ministry; consultation and training to government and private groups; income programs for poor cottage industries; small minority business development program.

BRANCH/NETWORK OFFICES

St. Cecelia's—Larkin Center
820 Jasmine
Clearwater, FL 33516
(813) 447-3494

LICENSE/ACCREDITATION/PROFESSIONAL AFFILIATIONS

Catholic Social Services is licensed by the State of Florida Department of Health and Rehabilitative Services. The agency is a member of Catholic Charities USA, Florida Association of Licensed Adoption Agencies, and Pinellas United Way.

CATHOLIC SOCIAL SERVICES

730 S. Sterling Avenue
Tampa, FL 33609
(813) 870-6220
Program director: Martha Franco

THE PROGRAM

Catholic Social Services is a nonprofit agency serving Hillsborough, Pasco, Hernando, and Citrus Counties and placing approximately 17 children annually. The Tampa office of CSS was created in 1944 under the auspices of the Bishop of St. Augustine to serve unmarried mothers and their children. Providing services on a non-sectarian basis, the agency's purpose is "to continue the mission of Christ in the world today under the direction of the Bishop so as to respond to the needs of people, especially the poor, the oppressed and those who are hurting."

THE COST

For the placement of healthy Caucasian children, the agency charges a flat fee of $5,000. For the placement of hard-to-place children (including children of Black or mixed racial backgrounds), the agency fee is based on a sliding scale, with an average cost of $950. (For placements in which a state subsidy is available, there is no fee to the adoptive parents.) Services covered by the fee include homestudy, selection and placement of the child, social study of the child, post-placement supervision, interaction with attorney throughout the legal process, and obtaining birth and baptismal certificate (if appropriate). In addition, prospective adoptive parents should anticipate financial responsibility for legal fees connected with finalization of the adoption.

THE WAIT

The average time from application for acceptance into the program to the homecoming of the adoptive child is 3 years.

THE CHILDREN

Catholic Social Services places both healthy and special-needs children, ranging in age from infancy to 6 years, of Caucasian, Black, and mixed racial backgrounds.

THE REQUIREMENTS

Age: Applicants must be at least 21 and no more than 45 years of age. The requirement may vary for special-needs adoptions.

Health: Applicants must be in reasonably good health. Applicants with health problems or handicaps are given individual consideration. For the adoption of a healthy Caucasian infant, infertility documentation is required.

Religion: No requirement, but the preference of the birthmother is honored.

Financial status: Applicants must demonstrate financial stability.

Marital status: For healthy Caucasian infant adoption, applicants must be married and must have been married for at least 3 years. Applications from single parents are accepted for hard-to-place children.

Family size: For healthy Caucasian infant adoption, applicants may have no more than 1 child currently in the family. The requirement may vary for hard- to-place children.

Racial, ethnic or cultural origin: Preference for placing children in families of similar origins.

THE PROCEDURE

Participation in Catholic Social Services' adoption program entails the following basic steps:
   Orientation meeting
   Application and orientation
   Couple counseling session
   Individual counseling sessions
   Homestudy
   Clearance with abuse registry
   Submission of references
   Submission of physical examination and fertility report
   Placement
   Post-placement supervision

ADDITIONAL PROGRAMS/SERVICES

Catholic Social Services provides counseling services to individuals, couples, and families; foster care services; refugee services.

BRANCH/NETWORK OFFICES

607 Washington Street
New Port Richey, FL 33552
(813) 845–0589

LICENSE/ACCREDITATION/PROFESSIONAL AFFILIATIONS

Catholic Social Services is licensed by the Florida Department of Health and Rehabilitative Services. All CSS social workers are Florida Licensed Clinical Social Workers and members of the National Association of Social Workers or the Academy of Certified Social Workers.

THE CHILDREN'S HOME SOCIETY OF FLORIDA

Central Administrative Office
P.O. Box 10097, 3027 San Diego Rd.
Jacksonville, FL 32247–0097

(904) 396–4084

Program director: Jean S. Price, Director of Social Services

THE PROGRAM

The Children's Home Society of Florida is a nonprofit, non-sectarian agency, providing statewide services through eleven branch offices and placing approximately 400 children annually. Providing services since 1902, the agency's mission is "to preserve and strengthen family life." The agency provides pregnancy counseling services to birthparents and places infants for adoption when birthparents in the agency's program decide that the best interests of the child will be served by adoptive placement. The agency is also actively involved in the placement of special-needs children. The agency's goal is "the best permanent placement plan for each child served."

THE COST

The agency's fee is based on the cost of providing the service, and the fee scale is reviewed annually. Fees are reduced or waived depending upon the need.

THE WAIT

The length of time prospective adoptive families wait for a placement after their assessment and preparation for adoption is completed depends upon the children needing adoptive families and the kind of child the families wish to parent.

THE CHILDREN

Children's Home Society of Florida places both healthy and special-needs children, ranging in age from birth to 18 years, of Caucasian, Black, Hispanic, and mixed racial backgrounds.

THE REQUIREMENTS

Age: Applicants must be at least 23 years of age. The requirement may be waived to meet a child's needs.

Health: Applicants must be in reasonably good health. Applicants with health problems or handicaps are given individual consideration.

Religion: No requirement, but preference of the birthparents is honored whenever possible.

Financial status: No requirement.

Marital status: No requirement, but preference of the birthparents is honored whenever possible.

Family size: No requirement.

Residence: Applicants must be Florida residents.

Racial, ethnic or cultural origin: No requirement, but preference for placing children in families of similar origins.

THE PROCEDURE

Participation in the Children's Home Society of Florida's adoption program entails the following basic steps:
   Orientation meeting
   Application
   Assessment and preparation for adoption
   Placement
   Post-placement supervision

ADDITIONAL PROGRAMS/SERVICES

The Children's Home Society of Florida provides pregnancy counseling; pre-adoption foster family care and temporary foster family care for families in crisis; post-legal adoption services; social services for persons with developmental disabilities; group care programs to prepare younger children for adoption and to make permanent living plans for teenagers; shelter care programs; family counseling; and an array of family preservation services including homemaker services, crisis intervention, and permanency planning to enable children to exit from the public foster care system.

BRANCH/NETWORK OFFICES

Buckner Division
3027 San Diego Road
P.O. Box 5616 P.O.
Jacksonville, FL 32247–5616
(904) 396–2641

North Central Division
370 Office Plaza
Box 3474
Tallahassee, FL 32315–3474
(904) 877–5176

Central Florida Division
212 Pasadena Place
Orlando, FL 32803–3828
(305) 422–4441

North Coastal Division
201 Osceola Avenue
Daytona Beach, FL 32014–6185
(904) 255–7407
Unit Office
1273 S. Florida Avenue, Suites 2 & 3
Rockledge, FL 32955–2439
(305) 636–0126

Gulf Coast Division
5700 54th Avenue, North
St. Petersburg, FL 33709–2095
(813) 546–4626

Intercoastal Division
105 N.E. 3rd Street
Fort Lauderdale, FL 33301–1094
(305) 763–6573
Unit Office
Intercoastal S.W. Area
2517 Second Street
Fort Myers, FL 33901–2598
(813) 334–2008

Rose Keller Division
842 S. Missouri Avenue
Lakeland, FL 33801–4740
(813) 688–7968

South Coastal Division
3600 Broadway
West Palm Beach, FL 33407–4844
(305) 844–9785

Mid-Florida Division
401 S.E. 19th Avenue
Ocala, FL 32671–2554
(904) 629–7597

Unit Office
605 N.E. 1st St., Suite H
Gainesville, FL 32601
(904) 376–5186

Southeastern Division
800 N.W. 15th Street
Miami, FL 33136–1495
(305) 324–1262

Western Division
5375 N. 9th Avenue
Pensacola, FL 32504–8725
(904) 476–3133

LICENSE/ACCREDITATION/PROFESSIONAL AFFILIATIONS

The Children's Home Society of Florida is licensed by the State of Florida Department of Health and Rehabilitative Services, is accredited by the Council on Accreditation of Services for Families and Children, and is a member of the Child Welfare League of America.

FAMILY SERVICE CENTERS OF PINELLAS COUNTY

(Florida Project CAN)
2960 Roosevelt Blvd.
Clearwater, FL 34620
(813) 531–0481
Program director: June R. Fountain, ACSW, LCSW

THE PROGRAM

Family Service Centers, a nonprofit agency serving west/central Florida, was chartered in 1938 to provide services to children. It has evolved into a multi-service agency providing for the needs of individuals and families from before birth to after death. Project CAN was established in 1972 as an outgrowth of a traditional adoption program because of the agency's concern for children waiting in foster care for homes and families which never materialized. Placing 15–20 children annually, Project CAN provides permanent, legal homes for children who, because of their special needs, cannot be placed by other agencies.

THE COST

There is no fee for the adoption of Project CAN children. Agency services provided at no cost to the adoptive family include adoption preparation, pre-placement, post-placement, and post-finalization services. Prospective adoptive parents should anticipate financial responsibility for required physical examinations, legal fees connected with the finalization of the adoption, law enforcement and child abuse checks (required by Florida statute), and new birth certificate.

THE WAIT

The time from initial inquiry to the placement of the adoptive child depends upon the flexibility of the applicant, ranging from 2 months to 1 year. If a year has elapsed without placement, the applicant is usually referred to an agency which places children with less severe special needs.

THE CHILDREN

All Project CAN children have special emotional, physical, and developmental needs and are considered among the most difficult to place of the "waiting children." Project CAN does not place healthy, "normal" infants and young children. Project CAN does not place foreign-born children. Children placed by Project CAN may be of any race or ethnic background and range in age to 17 years.

THE REQUIREMENTS

Age: The requirement varies depending on the needs of the child.

Health: The requirement varies depending on the needs of the child.

Religion: No requirement.

Residency: Applicants must reside in west-central Florida.

Financial status: No requirement.

Marital status: Couples living together and wishing to adopt must be married; single applicants are accepted.

Family size: No requirement.

Racial, ethnic or cultural origin: Preference for placing children in families of similar origins if practical or possible.

THE PROCEDURE

Participation in Project CAN entails the following basic steps:

Intake/return of information sheet
Orientation meeting
Application
Homestudy
Individual and/or group counseling
Educational groups
Placement
Post-placement services/counseling
Post-finalization services/counseling

ADDITIONAL PROGRAMS/SERVICES

Project CAN conducts workshops, seminars, adoption staff training programs; sponsors adoptees' support groups; provides counseling, advocacy for children/permanence.

BRANCH/NETWORK OFFICES

None.

LICENSE/ACCREDITATION/PROFESSIONAL AFFILIATIONS

Family Service Centers/Project CAN is licensed as a child placing agency by the Florida Dept. of Health and Rehabilitative Services and is a funded agency of the Juvenile Welfare Board of Pinellas County. Family Service Centers is accredited by the Council on Accreditation of Services for Families and Children. Family Service Centers is a member agency of Family Service America, the United Way of Pinellas County, Family Builders by Adoption, and Florida Association of Licensed Adoption Agencies.

FLORIDA BAPTIST CHILDREN'S HOMES

P.O. Box 8190
Lakeland, FL 33802–8190
(813) 687–8811
Program director: Richard Phillips, Executive Director

THE PROGRAM

Florida Baptist Children's Homes is a private, nonprofit organization affiliated with Florida Baptist churches and serving residents of the state of Florida through three regional offices. Founded in 1904, Children's Homes began as an orphanage and has evolved over the years into a multi-service agency providing residential care, foster care, counseling, adoption services, emergency shelter, group homes, maternity care, and continuing education. Throughout its history, the mission of Children's Homes has been "to provide creative, redemptive care for needy, dependent children." Children's Homes places older children for adoption when a child in the agency's residential care program cannot return to his/her birth family. Children's Homes places infants for adoption when birthparents in the agency's maternity care program decide that the infant's best interests will be served by adoptive placement. Children's Homes encourages the exchange of non-identifying information between birthparents and adoptive parents. On an individual basis, birthparents may choose the adoptive family for their baby from a number of approved adoptive applicants.

THE COST

The agency's fee for adoption services is $5,000. Fees are determined annually, based on current costs. For those couples who are unable to pay the adoption fee, a sliding scale based on 10% of the couple's annual gross income will be used, with a minimum fee of $2,000. Services covered by the fee include adoption preparation, homestudy, placement, post-placement supervision, and, in the case of infant adoption, pre-placement services to birthparents and child (including medical and foster care). In addition, prospective adoptive parents should anticipate financial responsibility for legal fees connected with finalization of the adoption.

THE WAIT

The time from application for acceptance into the program to the homecoming of the adoptive child varies depending on the type of child the applicants wish to adopt.

THE CHILDREN

Children's Homes places both healthy and special-needs children, ranging in age from infancy to adolescence, primarily Caucasian, but also of Black, Hispanic, and mixed racial backgrounds.

THE REQUIREMENTS

Age: At least one of the adoptive parents will not be more than 40 years older than the child they are considering for adoption.

Health: Applicants must be in reasonably good health.

Religion: Applicants must be practicing members of a Christian faith.

Financial status: Applicants must demonstrate financial stability.

Marital status: Applicants must be married couples.

Family size: For older child or special-needs adoption, no requirement.

Racial, ethnic or cultural origin: No requirement, but preference for placing children in families of similar origins.

THE PROCEDURE

Participation in Children's Homes adoption program entails the following basic steps:
Inquiry
Orientation meeting
Application
Parent training sessions
Homestudy
Placement
Post-placement supervision

ADDITIONAL PROGRAMS/SERVICES

Children's Homes provides family-style living for children through its residential care program on three campuses; foster care services; crisis care for runaway, abused and neglected teenage girls; counseling services for individuals, families, and groups; scholastic aid program; maternity care services.

BRANCH/NETWORK OFFICES

Central Florida Campus
P.O. Box 1870
Lakeland, FL 33802
(813) 688–4981

South Florida Campus
7748 S.W. 95th Terrace
Miami, FL 33156
(305) 271–4121

North Florida Campus
8415 Buck Lake Rd.
Tallahassee, FL 32301
(904) 878–1458

LICENSE/ACCREDITATION/PROFESSIONAL AFFILIATIONS

Florida Baptist Children's Homes is licensed by the Florida Department of Health and Rehabilitative Services and is an agency of the Florida Baptist Convention. The agency is a member of the National Association of Homes for Children.

JEWISH FAMILY & COMMUNITY SERVICES, INC.

1415 LaSalle Street
Jacksonville, FL 32207–3196
(904) 396–2941
Program director: Iris Young

THE PROGRAM

Jewish Family & Community Services (JF&CS) is a nonprofit agency providing services to the people of north-eastern Florida on a non-sectarian basis. Incorporated in 1929, JF&CS is one of the oldest agencies of its kind in the community and has been giving continuous service as a professional counseling agency since that date. JF&CS "is dedicated to helping people help themselves through a wide variety of services designed to enrich the quality of life by helping deal with forces that threaten the integrity of the individual and the family." JF&CS maintains a small adoption program.

THE COST

The agency fee is 8% of the gross family income. Services covered by the fee include all phases of the adoption process except for legal fees in connection with finalization of the adoption. In addition, prospective adoptive parents should anticipate financial responsibility for the medical expenses (pre-natal care, delivery, post-partum care) of the birthmother.

THE WAIT

The time from application to homecoming of the adoptive child varies depending on the circumstances of each case.

THE CHILDREN

Children placed by JF&CS are healthy Caucasian children born in the U.S., ranging in age from birth to 18 years.

THE REQUIREMENTS

Age: No requirement.

Health: Applicants must be in reasonably good health.

Religion: The requirement varies depending on needs of the child.

Financial status: Applicants must demonstrate ability to provide for the child.

Marital status: No requirement.

Family size: No requirement.

Racial, ethnic or cultural origin: Preference for placing children in families of similar origins.

THE PROCEDURE

Participation in JF&CS adoption program entails the following basic steps:
Pre-application information
Application
Orientation meeting
Individual counseling sessions
Homestudy
Placement

ADDITIONAL PROGRAMS/SERVICES

JF&CS provides foster care, counseling, workshops, adoption referral information packet.

BRANCH/NETWORK OFFICES

None.

LICENSE/ACCREDITATION/PROFESSIONAL AFFILIATIONS

Jewish Family and Community Services, Inc. is licensed by the State of Florida Department of Health and Rehabilitative Services and is a charter member of the United Way.

LDS Social Services

1020 N. Orlando Avenue, Suite F
Winter Park, FL 32789
(305) 628–8899
Program director: Dennis T. Haynes

The Program

For a full description of programs and services, refer to Utah listing:
LDS Social Services
50 East North Temple Street
Salt Lake City, UT 84150

Shepherd Care Ministries, Inc.

(d/b/a Christian Adoption Services)
5935 Taft Street
Hollywood, FL 33021
(305) 981–2060
Program director: Marian Kunz, Vice President

The Program

Shepherd Care Ministries is a private agency serving the state of Florida that provides a range of services to individuals and families. In 1985, Shepherd Care established the only evangelical Christian adoption agency in Florida, Christian Adoption Services, an affiliate of Bethany Christian Services. The agency's mission is to provide adoptive opportunities in Christian homes, striving to ensure the best arrangement for both the child and the new parents. Christian Adoption Services places approximately 40 children annually.

The Cost

The agency fee is based on a sliding scale. The average fee is $5,725. Services covered by the fee include all phases of the adoption procedure except for legal fees associated with finalization of the adoption (approximately $300).

The Wait

The time from application for acceptance into the program to the homecoming of the adoptive child ranges from 6 months to 1 year.

The Children

Christian Adoption Services places both healthy and special-needs children of any race or country of origin, ranging in age from newborn to toddler. Recently, older children and sibling groups have become available for adoption also.

The Requirements

Age: Applicants must be at least 25 and no more than 45 years of age. Exceptions may be made in cases involving special-needs children.
Health: Applicants must be in reasonably good health. Applicants with health problems or handicaps are given individual consideration. Infertility documentation is required. Exceptions may be made in cases involving special-needs children.
Religion: Applicants must be practicing members of an Evangelical Christian Church.
Financial status: Applicants must demonstrate fiscal ability to support and maintain family life.
Marital status: Applicants must be married and must have been married for at least 3 years. Exceptions may be made in cases involving special-needs children.
Family size: Applicants may have no more than 1 child currently in the family. The requirement may be waived for special-needs adoptions.
Racial, ethnic or cultural origin: Preference for placing children in families of similar origins; may vary depending on extenuating circumstances.

The Procedure

Participation in Christian Adoption Services program entails the following basic steps:
Orientation meeting
Application
Individual counseling sessions
Homestudy
Group counseling sessions
Placement

Additional Programs/Services

Shepherd Care Ministries, Inc. offers a wide range of support services including counseling services for individuals, couples, and/or families; crisis pregnancy program; foster care program; a small group maternity home and shelter homes.

Branch/Network Offices

Lake Worth
(305) 588–3649
Ft. Myers
(813) 574–3080
Labelle
(813) 675–4404
Orlando
(305) 644–2210

License/Accreditation/Professional Affiliations

Christian Adoption Services is licensed by the State of Florida Department of Health and Rehabilitative Services and has a contracted affiliation with Bethany Christian Services to provide services for Bethany in Florida. Christian Adoption Services is a member of the National Committee For Adoption.

St. Vincent Maternity and Adoption Center

717 Ponce de Leon Boulevard, Suite 235
Coral Gables, FL 33134
(305) 445–5714
Program director: Hilda A. Fluriach, MSW

THE PROGRAM

St. Vincent Maternity and Adoption Center is a nonprofit agency serving residents of Dade County and placing approximately 25 children for adoption annually. Serving the community for over 50 years, the agency's mission is "to serve the unwed pregnant population by providing counseling, residential, and referral for medical services" for relinquishing and non-relinquishing birthmothers. In addition, the agency is actively involved in domestic special-needs adoption and also works directly with child welfare institutions and other intermediaries abroad to place foreign-born children in Dade County families. In addition, the agency will provide homestudy and supervisory services for applicants pursuing interagency adoption (domestic or international).

THE COST

The agency's fee for adoption services is based on a sliding scale. As of October 1988, the agency's fees range from $1,500 for international placements up to $7,500 for domestic placements. Services covered by the fee include homestudy, placement, and post-placement supervision. Applicants pursuing domestic infant adoption need anticipate no additional expenses. Applicants pursuing international adoption should anticipate possible legal and travel expenses.

THE WAIT

The time from application to placement varies depending on the program. For domestic infant adoption, the wait averages 3 years. For international adoption, the wait ranges from 6 to 12 months.

THE CHILDREN

The agency places both healthy and special-needs children, ranging in age from birth to 18 years, of all racial backgrounds from the U.S. and various Central and South American countries.

THE REQUIREMENTS

Age: For infant adoption, applicants must be at least 25 (at the time of application) and no more than 40 years of age (at the time of finalization). The requirement for special-needs and international adoptions varies depending on the country of origin and the child's needs.

Health: Applicants must be in reasonably good health.

Religion: Applicants must be practicing members of the faith of their choice.

Financial status: Applicants must demonstrate financial stability.

Marital status: For infant adoption, applicants must be married. The requirement for special needs and international adoptions varies depending on the country of origin and the child's needs.

Family size: For infant adoption, applicants may have no more than 2 children currently in the family. For special needs and international adoptions, the requirement varies depending on the country of origin and the child's needs.

Racial, ethnic or cultural origin: Preference for placing children in families of similar origins.

THE PROCEDURE

Participation in the adoption program of St. Vincent Adoption and Maternity Center entails the following basic steps:

Application
Orientation meeting
Homestudy
Individual counseling sessions
Compliance with immigration/naturalization requirements (international adoptions only)
Referral
Placement
Post-placement supervision

ADDITIONAL PROGRAMS/SERVICES

St. Vincent Adoption and Maternity Center provides residential care for unwed pregnant teenagers.

BRANCH/NETWORK OFFICES

None.

LICENSE/ACCREDITATION/PROFESSIONAL AFFILIATIONS

St. Vincent Adoption and Maternity Center is licensed by the State of Florida Department of Health and Rehabilitative Services and is accredited by the Council on Accreditation of Services for Families and Children. The agency is a member of the Child Welfare League of America and Catholic Charities USA.

SUNCOAST INTERNATIONAL ADOPTIONS, INC.

P.O. Box 332
Indian Rocks Beach, FL 34635–0332
(813) 596–3135

Program director: Jane A. Pearce, Executive Director

THE PROGRAM

Suncoast International Adoptions, Inc. is a private, nonprofit organization, licensed by the state of Florida to provide homestudy and post-placement services to qualified Florida families wishing to adopt children from overseas. The agency was founded in 1980 by three adoptive mothers who believed that a need existed in west central Florida for an agency with expertise in providing assistance to persons interested in adopting foreign-born children. Since that time, the agency has expanded into an organization with social workers throughout the state. Facilitating the adoption of approximately 25 children annually, Suncoast International's goal is "to provide...families with the opportunity to share their love, lives and home with a child deprived of such basic necessities."

THE COST

Suncoast International charges a fee of $950 which includes an application fee, homestudy, and post-placement services. In addition, prospective adoptive parents should anticipate financial responsibility for placement fees (charged by placing agency), travel expenses, and legal fees. The total cost for an international adoption ranges between $5,000 and $9,000.

THE WAIT

The time from application for acceptance into the program to the homecoming of the adoptive child usually takes between 1 and 2 years. The wait may vary depending on the sex and age of the child requested and the child's country of origin.

THE CHILDREN

Suncoast International facilitates adoptions of foreign-born infants and toddlers of Asian and Hispanic racial backgrounds. Countries of origin include India, Thailand, Taiwan, Hong Kong, the Philippines, Belize, Bolivia, Brazil, Chile, Colombia, Costa Rica, Dominican Republic, Ecuador, El Salvador, Guatemala, Haiti, Honduras, Mexico, Paraguay, Panama, and Peru.

THE REQUIREMENTS

Age: Applicants must be at least 25 years old. Generally, applicants may not be more than 40 years older than the adoptive child.

Health: Applicants must be in reasonably good health.

Religion: No requirement.

Financial status: No requirement.

Marital status: No requirement. If married, applicants must have been married for at least 2 years.

Family size: The requirement varies depending on the child's country of origin and the requirements of the placing agency.

Racial, ethnic or cultural origin: No requirement. Applicants must be U.S. citizens.

THE PROCEDURE

Participation in Suncoast International's program entails the following basic steps:

Application
Homestudy
Compliance with immigration/naturalization requirements
Referral
Placement
Post-placement supervision

ADDITIONAL PROGRAMS/SERVICES

Suncoast International provides counseling for expectant mothers considering adoption placement.

BRANCH/NETWORK OFFICES

None.

LICENSE/ACCREDITATION/PROFESSIONAL AFFILIATIONS

Suncoast International Adoptions, Inc. is licensed by the State of Florida Department of Health and Rehabilitative Services.

Georgia

Public Adoption Program/ Community Resources

Department of Human Resources
Division of Family and Children Services
State Adoption Unit
878 Peachtree Street N.E., Suite 501
Atlanta, GA 30309
(404) 894–4454
Adoption specialist: Rosserlyn Andersen

The Program

Public adoption services in Georgia are provided by the State Adoption Unit of the Division of Family and Children Services through regional and county offices located throughout the state. The agency recruits and prepares adoptive families and supervises the placement of special-needs children (older, minority, and handicapped children and sibling groups) who are wards of the State of Georgia. In addition, regional offices provide services to applicants pursuing independent adoptions.

State Exchange

Adoption Exchange. For information, contact the State Adoption Unit (above).

State Adoption Reunion Registry

None.

State Subsidy

Adoption Assistance Program. For information, contact the State Adoption Unit (Attention: Gail Merklinger).

NACAC Representative

Kathryn Karp
c/o My Turn Now, Inc.
P.O. Box 7727
Atlanta, GA 30309
(404) 894–3748

General Adoption Resources

Adoptive parent support services in Georgia are normally provided by private adoption agencies as a service to their clients. Contact private adoption agencies in Georgia (see Georgia listing) for information on support services in your area.

Special-Needs Adoption Resources

For information, contact the State Adoption Unit (above).

Out-of-State Agencies

Agency

Catholic Charities of Tennessee, Tennessee (residents of 4 Georgia counties near Chattanooga)

See Appendix A

Agencies Providing Nationwide Services

Bethany Christian Services

682 Mulberry Street
Macon, GA 31201
(912) 742–6964
Program director: James K. Haveman, Jr.—Executive Director

The Program

For a full description of programs and services, refer to Michigan listing:

Bethany Christian Services
901 Eastern Avenue, N.E.
Grand Rapids, MI 49503–1295
(616) 459–6273

Catholic Social Services, Inc.

680 W. Peachtree Street, N.W.
Atlanta, GA 30308
(404) 881–6571
Program director: D. Jean Reiss

The Program

Catholic Social Services is a nonprofit agency serving residents of the metropolitan Atlanta area and placing approximately 12 to 15 children annually through its adoption program. The adoption program was developed as an extension of the agency's crisis pregnancy program. The mission of the agency's crisis pregnancy program is "to provide quality services on a non-discriminatory basis to the young woman whose pregnancy is creating a crisis in her life." Services to birthmothers include pre-natal care, housing, and counseling (pre- and post-delivery). The purpose of the adoption program is "to provide loving, stable homes for children where they can grow and develop physically and emotionally within a secure environment." In addition, the agency will provide homestudy and supervisory services for applicants pursuing interagency adoption (domestic or international) or private adoption.

The Cost

The agency's fee for adoption services is $9,400. Services covered by the fee include all phases of the adoption process, excluding legal fees connected with finalization of the adoption.

The Wait

The time from application for acceptance into the program to the homecoming of the adoptive child averages 4 to 5 years.

The Children

Catholic Social Services places primarily healthy infants (birth to 1 year) of all racial backgrounds, born in the U.S.

The Requirements

Age: Applicants may be no more than 37 years of age. The requirement may be waived for special-needs placements.

Health: Applicants should be in reasonably good health with normal life expectancy.

Religion: No requirement.

Financial status: Applicants must have sufficient financial resources to meet the family's needs.

Marital status: Applicants must be married. The requirement may be waived for special needs placements.

Family size: Applicants may have no more than 1 child currently in the family. The requirement may be waived for special-needs placements.

Racial, ethnic or cultural origin: No requirement.

THE PROCEDURE

Participation in the adoption program of Catholic Social Services entails the following basic steps:

Orientation meeting
Application
Group counseling sessions
Homestudy
Individual counseling sessions
Placement
Post-placement supervision
Post-adoption support/contact activities

ADDITIONAL PROGRAMS/SERVICES

None.

BRANCH/NETWORK OFFICES

None.

LICENSE/ACCREDITATION/PROFESSIONAL AFFILIATIONS

Catholic Social Services, Inc. is licensed by the State of Georgia Department of Human Resources and is a member of the Child Welfare League of America.

CHILDREN'S SERVICES INTERNATIONAL, INC.

1819 Peachtree Road, N.E.
Suite 318
Atlanta, GA 30309–1847
(404) 355–3233
Program director: Patricia Johnson

THE PROGRAM

Children's Services International is a nonprofit child welfare agency providing nationwide and international placement services and placing approximately 150 children annually through its adoption programs. Founded in 1980, the agency's mission is "to find a family for each child in need of one" and to provide support services (sponsorship, medical, and educational services) to child welfare institutions overseas. The agency provides services to birthparents and places infants for adoption when birthparents decide that the best interests of their child will be served by adoptive placement. Working directly with child welfare institutions overseas, the agency places children from Korea and Latin America. The Korean program is available only to Georgia applicants. The Latin American program is available to applicants from all over the world. In addition, the agency will provide homestudy and supervisory services for Georgia applicants pursuing inter-agency adoption (domestic or international) or private adoption.

THE COST

The agency's fee schedule (effective April 1, 1988) is as follows:

Application fee	$100.00
Homestudy fee	$1,170.00
Homestudy update fee	$900.00
Homestudy review fee	$285.00
Translations (per dossier, dossier only)	$ 400.00
Placement preparation:	
Domestic	$250.00
Korea	$350.00
Latin America	$900.00
Placement/referral services:	
Domestic	$9,000.00
Korea	$1,200.00
Latin America	$600.00
Post-placement services:	
Domestic	$750.00
Korea	$750.00
Latin America	$500.00

In addition, applicants interested in placement through Latin America should anticipate in-country costs ranging from $3,000 to $6,000 and out-of-state applicants should anticipate fees to a licensed agency in their home state for homestudy and supervisory services. For all programs, applicants are responsible for legal fees connected with finalization.

THE WAIT

The time from application to placement varies depending on the program. For domestic Caucasian infant placements, the wait ranges from 2 to 3 years. For domestic minority infant placements, the wait averages 1 year. For Korean placements, the wait averages 1 1/2 years. For Latin American placements, the wait is generally 1 year or less.

THE CHILDREN

Children's Services International places primarily healthy but also some special-needs children, ranging in age from birth to 15 years, of all racial backgrounds. Countries of origin include U.S., Korea, El Salvador, Honduras, Colombia, Ecuador, Peru, Bolivia, and Paraguay.

THE REQUIREMENTS

Age: The age requirement varies depending on the country.

Health: The requirement varies depending on the country.

Religion: The requirement varies depending on the country. The only current limitation is that Korea will not accept applications from Jehovah's Witnesses.

Financial status: No specific requirement, but applicants must have sufficient financial resources to pay program fees and to provide adequately for an additional family member.

Marital status: The requirement varies depending on the country.

Family size: The requirement varies depending on the country.

Racial, ethnic or cultural origin: No requirement.

THE PROCEDURE

For Georgia residents, participation in the adoption program of Children's Services International entails the following basic steps:
- Orientation meeting
- Application
- Group counseling sessions
- Individual counseling sessions
- Homestudy
- Compliance with immigration/naturalization requirements (international adoptions only)
- Referral
- Placement
- Post-placement supervision

Non-Georgia residents begin by submitting an application to Children's Services International. They must then identify a licensed agency in their home state which will provide services associated with the development of the homestudy, preparation for placement, and in some cases supervision until finalization.

ADDITIONAL PROGRAMS/SERVICES

Children's Services International provides a range of services including a sponsorship program (operating in Sri Lanka, the Philippines, El Salvador and Honduras) for needy children and their families; medical services program (free diagnostic and treatment opportunities to children in Third World countries); educational and material assistance to foreign governments and agencies in child welfare matters; adoptive parent organization; informational meetings on adoption; short term foster care; extensive counseling to birthparents; community education programs on adoption.

BRANCH/NETWORK OFFICES

None.

LICENSE/ACCREDITATION/PROFESSIONAL AFFILIATIONS

Children's Services International, Inc. is licensed by the State of Georgia Department of Human Resources.

FAMILIES FIRST

1105 W. Peachtree Street
Atlanta, GA 30309
(404) 873–6916
Program director: Robert M. Weaver

THE PROGRAM

Families First is a nonprofit multi-service agency serving residents of Georgia and placing approximately 24 to 30 children annually through its adoption program. Founded as an orphanage in 1890, the agency has evolved in response to the changing needs of the community and today provides a wide range of family and children's services. Working directly with birthparents, with public agencies, and with national and regional exchange programs, the agency places both healthy and special-needs children. In addition, the agency will provide homestudy and supervisory services for applicants pursuing interagency adoption (domestic or international) or independent adoption.

THE COST

The agency's fee for adoption services is based on a sliding scale and ranges from $850 to $8,500. Services covered by the fee include all phases of the adoption process.

THE WAIT

For applicants pursuing the adoption of a Caucasian child, the time from application to placement averages 2 years. For applicants pursuing the adoption of a Black child, the wait averages 6 months.

THE CHILDREN

Families First places both healthy and special-needs children, ranging in age from infancy to adolescence, of Caucasian and Black racial backgrounds, born in the U.S.

THE REQUIREMENTS

Age: No requirement.
Health: No requirement.
Religion: No requirement.
Financial status: No requirement.
Marital status: No requirement.
Family size: No requirement.
Racial, ethnic or cultural origin: Preference for placing children in families of similar origins.

THE PROCEDURE

Participation in the adoption program of Families First entails the following basic steps:
- Application
- Orientation meeting
- Individual counseling sessions
- Group counseling sessions
- Homestudy
- Referral and placement
- Post-placement supervision

ADDITIONAL PROGRAMS/SERVICES

Families First provides a wide range of services including family and individual counseling; domestic crisis intervention; services to birthparents; foster care and group homes; employee assistance program; community education; chemical dependency program.

BRANCH/NETWORK OFFICES

Cobb
997 Windy Hill Rd., SE
Smyrna, GA 30080
(404) 436–1567

Decatur
750 Commerce Dr., #104
Decatur, GA 30030
(404) 378–2543

Rockdale
1171 West Avenue
Rockdale Plaza
Conyers, GA 30207
(404) 922–7396

Gwinnett
318 W. Pike St.
Suite 450
Lawrenceville, GA 30245
(404) 882–2370

Sprayberry
1855 E. Piedmont Rd.
Suite 103
Marietta, GA 30066
(404) 977–2120

Harris-Johnston Center
25 Newcastle St., SW
Atlanta, GA 30314
(404) 755–1510

North Fulton
Roswell Summit Bldg. 200
Suite 100
1080 Holcomb Bridge Rd.
Roswell, GA 30076
(404) 993–0604

Fulton/Clayton
5538M Old National Hwy.
Suite 150/100C
College Park, GA 30349
(404) 767–7777

Douglas
6279 Fairburn Rd.
Douglasville, GA 30134
(404) 949–5200

LICENSE/ACCREDITATION/PROFESSIONAL AFFILIATIONS

Families First is licensed by the State of Georgia Department of Human Resources and is accredited by the Council on Accreditation of Services for Families and Children. The agency is a member of Family Service America and the Child Welfare League of America.

GEORGIA BAPTIST CHILDREN'S HOMES AND FAMILY MINISTRIES, INC.

Meansville Campus
P.O. Box 440
Meansville, GA 30256
(404) 567–8987
Program director: Thomas B. Dobson

THE PROGRAM

Georgia Baptist Children's Homes (GBCH) is a nonprofit agency serving residents of southwest Georgia. The agency's primary focus is to provide residential group care, foster care, and educational/preventive services to older children (10 to 16 years of age). In order to provide a continuum of care, the agency became licensed to provide adoption services in January of 1987, with the primary goal of seeking adoptive placement for older children who are in the agency's residential or foster care programs. In addition, the agency will provide homestudy and supervisory services for applicants pursuing interagency adoption.

THE COST

The agency's fee for adoption services is based on a sliding scale and ranges from $700 to $3,000. Services covered by the fee include all phases of the adoption process. For applicants pursuing interagency adoption, the agency's fee for homestudy and supervisory services is $35 per hour plus mileage and travel expenses.

THE WAIT

The time from application to placement averages 3 years or more.

THE CHILDREN

GBCH places both healthy and special-needs children, ranging in age from 10 to 16 years, of Caucasian and Black racial backgrounds, born in the U.S.

THE REQUIREMENTS

Age: Applicants must be at least 25. Generally, applicants should be no more than 35 years older than the child being considered for placement. However, the requirement varies depending on the needs of the child and the applicants' strengths.

Health: Applicants should be in reasonably good health.

Religion: The requirement varies depending on the child's religious background.

Financial status: Applicants should have sufficient financial resources to provide adequately for an additional family member.

Marital status: Applicants must be married; the length of the marriage must be at least 5 years.

Family size: No requirement.

Racial, ethnic or cultural origin: Preference for placing children in families of similar origins.

THE PROCEDURE

Participation in GBCH's adoption program entails the following basic steps:
Orientation meeting
Application
Homestudy (including group counseling sessions)
Placement
Post-placement supervision

ADDITIONAL PROGRAMS/SERVICES

GBCH provides residential group care; community based counseling; educational/preventive services; foster care; family support groups; developmental disabilities ministry for retarded adults.

BRANCH/NETWORK OFFICES

None.

Georgia Baptist Children's Homes and Family Ministries, Inc. is licensed by the State of Georgia Department of Human Resources. The agency is a member of the Georgia Residential Child Care Association and the National Association of Homes for Children.

HOMES FOR CHILDREN INTERNATIONAL, INC.

1655 Peachtree Street, N.E., Suite 1109
Atlanta, GA 30309
(404) 897–1766
Program director: Cheryl G. Stevens, MSW

THE PROGRAM

Homes for Children International is a nonprofit agency providing nationwide placement services (homestudies for Georgia families only) and placing approximately 15 children annually. The agency's purpose is "to provide assistance to needy children around the world." The agency provides food, clothing, and medical supplies to overseas child welfare institutions and provides adoption services for children who have no permanent families. The agency works directly with overseas agencies in Ecuador, El Salvador, Honduras, Paraguay and Peru and works cooperatively with other U.S.-based agencies to facilitate the placement of children from India, Korea, Mexico, Guatemala, and other countries. The agency provides homestudies for independent adoptions on a case-by-case basis. Special consideration is given to couples or singles who wish to adopt special-needs children (domestic or international).

THE COST

The cost of adopting internationally varies depending on the country. Total costs range from $4,000 to $9,000, including application, homestudy, placement, post-placement services, translations, couriers, legal services, child care, medical care, and travel. In addition, applicants should anticipate immigration and naturalization fees (approximately $200 for U.S. Visa and for filing of I-600). The cost of certifications and authentications depends upon the applicant's state of residence and the child's country of origin.

THE WAIT

The time from acceptance of the application to completion and approval of the homestudy varies depending on how quickly the applicant is able to gather the necessary documents. The time from approval of the homestudy to the referral of a child is less than a year (and usually less than 6 months). The time from referral to the child's arrival in the U.S. varies depending on the country of origin.

THE CHILDREN

Homes for Children International directly places both healthy and special-needs children, ranging in age from birth to 16 years, primarily of Hispanic (Mestizo) racial backgrounds. Countries of origin include Ecuador, El Salvador, Honduras, Paraguay, and Peru. Working cooperatively with other U.S.-based agencies, Homes for Children International facilitates the placement of children from India, Korea, Mexico, and Guatemala. In addition, the agency will provide homestudy and supervisory services on a case-by-case basis for applicants pursuing domestic special-needs adoption or independent adoption.

THE REQUIREMENTS

Age: Age requirements vary greatly from country to country.

Health: Applicants with health problems or handicaps are given individual consideration. Infertility documentation is required for adoption from Honduras.

Religion: No requirement.

Financial status: Applicants must demonstrate financial stability.

Marital status: The requirement varies depending on the country and the age of the applicant. Some options are available to single parents.

Family size: No requirement.

Racial, ethnic or cultural origin: No requirement.

THE PROCEDURE

Participation in the adoption program of Homes for Children International entails the following basic steps:
Orientation meeting
Application
Homestudy
Compliance with requirements of the child's country of origin
Compliance with immigration/naturalization requirements
Referral
Placement
Post-placement supervision

ADDITIONAL PROGRAMS/SERVICES

Homes for Children International maintains support services to overseas child welfare institutions through the provision of food, clothing, and medical supplies.

BRANCH/NETWORK OFFICES

None.

LICENSE/ACCREDITATION/PROFESSIONAL AFFILIATIONS

Homes for Children International, Inc. is licensed by the State of Georgia Department of Human Resources.

ILLIEN ADOPTIONS INTERNATIONAL, LTD

1254 Piedmont Avenue, N.E.
Atlanta, GA 30309
(404) 872–6787
Program director: Anna Belle Illien, Executive Director

THE PROGRAM

Illien Adoptions International (IAI) is a nonprofit agency providing nationwide placement services and placing approximately 85 children annually. Founded in 1982 by Anna Belle Illien who first experienced adoption as a single person trying to adopt, the agency's main objective is "to serve as the necessary administrative link between adults who are desirous of and qualified for parenting and children in need of and legally free for adoption." IAI provides domestic and foreign adoption services. The agency provides counseling services to birthparents and places infants born in Georgia for adoption when birthparents elect adoptive placement as the best plan for their child. IAI works directly with child welfare institutions in India, El Salvador, and Costa Rica to place foreign-born children in American families. Out-of-state families apply first to IAI and then to an agency in their home state which will work cooperatively with IAI and will provide homestudy and supervisory services. In addition, IAI will provide homestudy and supervisory services for applicants pursuing independent adoption (domestic or international).

THE COST

The agency's basic fee schedule is as follows:

Application fee	$ 300.00
Homestudy and post-placement supervision fee (Georgia residents only)	$ 1,700.00
Foreign adoptions processing fee	$ 1,500.00

Placement fee:

Domestic adoptions (20% of annual gross income)	$13,000.00–$16,000.00
India (10% of annual gross income)	$ 5,500.00–$ 7,000.00
El Salvador (10% of annual gross income)	$ 6,500.00–$ 8,000.00
Costa Rica (10% of annual gross income)	$ 5,500.00–$ 7,000.00

Applicants pursuing international adoption can expect to pay escort or travel expenses, immigration and naturalization fees, and related expenses. Out-of-state applicants can also expect to pay fees to an agency in their home state for homestudy and supervisory services. For all programs, applicants are responsible for legal fees connected with finalization of the adoption. Applicants should note that fees are subject to change without notice.

For a complete description of fees and services (including refund policies, exclusions, payment terms, and the like), write to IAI for an application packet (includes fee schedule and agreement).

THE WAIT

For domestic infant adoptions, no reliable estimate of the time from application to placement is available. For foreign adoption, the time from application to placement averages 15 months. However, applicants should note that wait is dependent on many variables.

THE CHILDREN

Through the domestic program, IAI places healthy and special-needs infants of all racial backgrounds, born in the U.S. Through the foreign program, IAI places both healthy and special-needs children. Most children available from India are infants. Most children available from El Salvador and Costa Rica are older waiting children and sibling groups.

THE REQUIREMENTS

Age: No IAI requirement, but may vary depending on the child's country of origin.

Health: Applicants should be in reasonably good health. Applicants with health problems or handicaps are given individual consideration.

Religion: No requirement.

Financial status: Applicants must demonstrate financial stability.

Marital status: No requirement.

Family size: No IAI requirement, but may vary depending on the child's country of origin.

Racial, ethnic or cultural origin: No requirement.

THE PROCEDURE

Participation in IAI's adoption program entails the following basic steps:

Orientation meeting
Application
Group counseling sessions (optional)
Individual counseling sessions
Homestudy
Compliance with immigration/naturalization requirements (international adoptions only)
Referral
Placement
Post-placement supervision

Out-of-state applicants first submit a completed application to IAI. If accepted, applicants then apply to an agency in their home state to provide homestudy and supervisory services in cooperation with IAI.

ADDITIONAL PROGRAMS/SERVICES

IAI provides counseling services for birthparents.

BRANCH/NETWORK OFFICES

None.

LICENSE/ACCREDITATION/PROFESSIONAL AFFILIATIONS

Illien Adoptions International is licensed by the State of Georgia Department of Human Resources.

JEWISH FAMILY SERVICES, INC.

1605 Peachtree Road, N.E.
Atlanta, GA 30309
(404) 873–2277
Program director: Irving Perlman, Executive Director

THE PROGRAM

Jewish Family Services is a nonprofit multi-service agency serving residents of metropolitan Atlanta and placing approximately 4 to 5 children annually through its adoption program. Providing adoption services for over 25 years, Jewish Family Services has a two-fold goal: "to support and perpetuate Jewish family life and to see that every child has the security of a permanent home so that he or she may develop to his or her full potential." When the child's family of origin is unable to provide permanency, the agency "feels a responsibility to seek a Jewish adoptive home to meet the individual needs of each child surrendered to the agency." The agency provides services to birthparents and places infants for adoption when birthparents elect adoptive placement as the best plan for their child. In addition, the agency will provide homestudy and supervisory services for Jewish applicants pursuing interagency adoption (domestic or international) or private adoption.

THE COST

The agency's fee for adoption services is based on a sliding scale and ranges from $8,500 to $12,000. Services covered by the fee include services to the birthparents and child (counseling, medical, and foster care) and social services to the applicants (homestudy, placement, and post- placement supervision). If the expenses associated with the birth of the child exceed the average (and if these expenses are not covered by insurance), applicants are asked to cover additional costs up to $5,000. In addition, applicants are responsible for legal fees connected with finalization.

THE WAIT

The time from application to the homecoming of the adoptive child ranges from 1 to 3 years.

THE CHILDREN

Jewish Family Services places healthy Caucasian infants, born in the U.S.

THE REQUIREMENTS

Age: No requirement.
Health: Applicants should be in reasonably good health. Applicants with health problems or handicaps are given individual consideration. Infertility documentation is required.
Religion: Applicants must be practicing members of the Jewish religion. If one spouse is non-Jewish, the spouse has to have converted and/or the couple has to be affiliated with a temple or synagogue.
Financial status: No requirement.
Marital status: Applicants must be married; the length of the marriage must be at least 3 years.
Residence: Applicants must live in the metropolitan Atlanta area.
Family size: Applicants may have no more than 1 child currently in the family.
Racial, ethnic or cultural origin: No requirement.

THE PROCEDURE

Participation in the adoption program of Jewish Family Services entails the following basic steps:
Orientation meeting
Application
Homestudy
Placement
Post-placement supervision
Post-placement services

ADDITIONAL PROGRAMS/SERVICES

Jewish Family Services sponsors Stars of David, a social and educational support group for Jewish adoptive couples. Additional services include counseling and therapy; services to the elderly; community and family life education; resettlement services; foster care for infants, pregnant mothers, and children; outreach to Jewish day schools; child diagnostic evaluation services.

BRANCH/NETWORK OFFICES

Jewish Family Services maintains branch offices in Cobb and Dunwoody (Atlanta Jewish Community Center).

LICENSE/ACCREDITATION/PROFESSIONAL AFFILIATIONS

Jewish Family Services is licensed by the State of Georgia Department of Human Resources. The agency is affiliated with the Georgia Association of Licensed Adoption Agencies, Association of Jewish Family and Children's Agencies, Family Service America, Atlanta Jewish Federation, and the United Way.

LDS SOCIAL SERVICES

4823 North Royal Atlanta Drive
Tucker, GA 30084
(404) 939–2121
Program director: K. Dean Black

THE PROGRAM

For a full description of programs and services, refer to Utah listing:
LDS Social Services
50 East North Temple Street
Salt Lake City, UT 84150

LUTHERAN MINISTRIES OF GEORGIA, INC.

756 West Peachtree Street, N.W.
Atlanta, GA 30308
(404) 875–0201
Program director: Rev. Henry K. Wohlgemuth, ACSW, Executive Director; Joyce R. Hayes, MSW, Program Director/Adoption Services

THE PROGRAM

Lutheran Ministries of Georgia is a nonprofit agency serving residents of Georgia and some out-of-state applicants as well and placing approximately 45 children annually. The adoption program began in 1983 and was founded primarily to provide international adoption services. International adoption remains the program's focus; however, the agency also has a domestic adoption program. The agency's mission is "to minister to people in need, to address and seek to remove the causes of human need on the social, economic, and political level, and to assist Lutheran congregations to carry out their mission of Christian service."

The Cost

The agency's fee and international fees for adoption services varies depending on the country of origin and ranges from $5,500 to $11,500. Services covered by the fee include all phases of the adoption process.

The Wait

The time from application to the homecoming of the adoptive child ranges from 6 months to 2 years.

The Children

Lutheran Ministries places both healthy and special-needs children, ranging in age from birth to 14 years, of various racial backgrounds. Countries of origin include Korea, India, El Salvador, Paraguay, Chile, Peru, and U.S.

The Requirements

Age: The requirement varies depending on the age of the child.

Health: Applicants should be in reasonably good health.

Religion: Applicants should be practicing members of a religious faith with active church participation.

Financial status: Applicants must demonstrate financial stability.

Marital status: The requirement varies depending on the requirements of the country of origin.

Family size: The requirement varies depending on the requirements of the country of origin.

Racial, ethnic or cultural origin: The requirement varies depending on the requirements of the country of origin.

The Procedure

Participation in the adoption program of Lutheran Ministries entails the following basic steps:

Orientation meeting
Application
Group counseling sessions
Individual counseling sessions
Homestudy
Compliance with immigration/naturalization requirements
Referral
Placement
Post-placement supervision
Post-placement support services

Additional Programs/Services

Lutheran Ministries provides a wide range of services including job employment services; sponsorship and resettlement for refugees; early delinquency intervention program; tutoring services; child care/latch key planning; services to older adults (congregational workshop and housing service planning).

Branch/Network Offices

Coastal Area Office
10 West 31st St.
Savannah, GA 31401

License/Accreditation/Professional Affiliations

Lutheran Ministries of Georgia, Inc. is licensed by the State of Georgia Department of Human Resources and is a charter member of Georgia Association of Licensed Adoption Agencies.

New Beginnings Adoption and Counseling Agency

A Ministry of Edgewood Baptist Church
P.O. Box 12143
3564 Forest Road
Columbus, GA 31907–0830
(404) 561–7954 or 563–4643
Program director: Phoebe Dawson, MSW, Executive Director

The Program

New Beginnings Adoption and Counseling Agency is a nonprofit agency providing statewide services and placing approximately 35 children annually in Christian families. Initiated to address the needs of women in crisis pregnancies, the agency's primary role "is that of advocacy for the birthmother and her child." The agency provides extensive services to both relinquishing and non-relinquishing birthmothers and places both healthy and special-needs infants (and occasionally toddlers) for adoption when the birthmother decides that the best interests of her child will be met through adoptive placement. The birthmother may participate in the selection of adoptive parents by reviewing non-identifying profiles or by developing her own profile to be matched with a couple on the agency's list. In some cases, the birthmother may have identified a couple she would like to parent her child by way of referral from a third party, prior to contacting New Beginnings. The agency has a transitional living center for birthmothers (age 18 and over) after placement who are not quite ready to be on their own.

In addition to traditional adoption services, the agency will provide homestudy and supervisory services for applicants pursuing interagency adoption (domestic or international) or independent adoption.

The Cost

The agency's fee for adoption services is $6,995. Services covered by the fee include all phases of the adoption process.

The Wait

The time from completion of the homestudy to the homecoming of the adoptive child averages 1 year.

The Children

New Beginnings places both healthy and special-needs infants and toddlers of all racial backgrounds, born in the U.S.

The Requirements

Age: Applicants must be at least 25 years of age.

Health: Applicants must be in reasonably good health.

Religion: Applicants must be practicing members of the Christian faith.

Financial status: Applicants must demonstrate the ability to provide adequately for the child.

Marital status: Applicants must be married.

Family size: No requirement.

Racial, ethnic or cultural origin: Preference for placing children in families of similar origins, but varies depending on the availability of preferred families. The agency will consider placing Black infants with Caucasian families.

THE PROCEDURE

Participation in the adoption program of New Beginnings entails the following basic steps:

Completion of Christian Maturity Questionnaire

Orientation meeting

Application

Individual counseling sessions

Homestudy

Placement

Post-placement supervision

Pictures and progress reports from the adoptive couple

ADDITIONAL PROGRAMS/SERVICES

New Beginnings provides counseling services; foster care; seminars on adoption and parenting issues; post-placement counseling for relinquishing birthmothers; social activities (Christmas parties, picnics); conferences and retreats.

BRANCH/NETWORK OFFICES

1806 Horseleg Creek Rd., S.W.
Rome, GA 30161
(404) 291–2574

3017 Angela St.
Augusta, GA 30907
(404) 860–4703

LICENSE/ACCREDITATION/PROFESSIONAL AFFILIATIONS

New Beginnings Adoption and Counseling Agency is licensed by the State of Georgia Department of Human Resources.

OPEN DOOR ADOPTION AGENCY

P.O. Box 4
Thomasville, GA 31799
(912) 228–6339
Program director: Mary H. Malone

THE PROGRAM

Open Door Adoption Agency is a nonprofit agency serving residents of Georgia for infant adoption and residents of other states as well for special-needs adoption. In its first year of service (1987), the agency placed 10 children. The agency's mission is "to promote the adoption option as a primary possibility for the unplanned pregnancy, to provide support and assistance to women choosing this option, and to build families through the adoptive placement of babies in loving and stable homes." Birthparents participate in the selection of adoptive parents through the review of non-identifying information. In order to promote mutual understanding, prospective adoptive parents are asked to provide housing for a birthmother, though not the mother of the child being considered for placement in their home.

THE COST

The agency's fee for healthy Caucasian infant adoption is $11,000; for special-needs adoption (handicapped, Black, and bi-racial children), $5,000. Services covered by the fee include all phases of the adoption process, excluding legal fees connected with finalization of the adoption and transportation costs for out-of-state applicants. In addition, fees help to underwrite the cost of services (medical, residential, and counseling) to birthparents.

THE WAIT

The time from application to the homecoming of the adoptive child ranges from 6 to 18 months.

THE CHILDREN

The Open Door Adoption Agency places healthy and special-needs infants of all racial backgrounds, born in the U.S.

THE REQUIREMENTS

Age: If single, applicants must be at least 25 years of age. No age requirement for married couples.

Health: Applicants must be in reasonably good health. Applicants with health problems or handicaps are given individual consideration.

Religion: Applicants must be practicing members of a Christian-Judeo faith.

Financial status: Applicants must demonstrate the ability to support a child financially.

Marital status: Single applicants are accepted. If married, the length of the marriage must be at least 3 years.

Family size: For healthy Caucasian infant adoption, applicants may have no more than 2 children currently in the family. No requirement for special-needs adoption.

Racial, ethnic or cultural origin: No requirement.

THE PROCEDURE

Participation in the Open Door Adoption Agency's program entails the following basic steps:

Application

Orientation meeting

Group counseling sessions

Homestudy (including individual counseling sessions)

Housing of a birthmother (not the mother of the child being considered for placement)

Placement

Post-placement supervision

ADDITIONAL PROGRAMS/SERVICES

The Open Door Adoption Agency provides extensive services to birthparents and counseling services.

BRANCH/NETWORK OFFICES

Caseworkers are located throughout the state. However, all adoption inquiries are processed through the main office in Thomasville.

LICENSE/ACCREDITATION/PROFESSIONAL AFFILIATIONS

The Open Door Adoption Agency is licensed by the State of Georgia Department of Human Resources. The agency is an associate member of the Child Welfare League of America and a member of the National Committee for Adoption.

PARENT AND CHILD DEVELOPMENT SERVICES, INC.

21 East Broad Street
Savannah, GA 31401
(912) 238–2777
Program director: Marcia Elrod

THE PROGRAM

Parent and Child Development Services (PCDS) is a nonprofit agency serving residents of 13 counties in Georgia for healthy Caucasian infant adoptions and providing nationwide services for minority and special-needs adoptions. Founded in 1947 as the first adoption program in Savannah, Georgia, the agency's mission is "to find homes for children that provide love, care, protection, and opportunities essential for a child's healthy personality growth and development." The agency provides services to birthparents and places both healthy and special-needs infants for adoption when birthparents in the agency's counseling program decide that the best interests of their child will be served by adoptive placement. The agency also places older children. PCDS places approximately 15–20 children annually.

THE COST

The agency's fee for healthy Caucasian infant adoption is $7,000. Services covered by the fee include all phases of the adoption process and all services to the birthmother and child. For minority or special-needs adoption, the agency's fee is 12% of the applicants' annual gross income, with a maximum fee of $7,000.

THE WAIT

The time from application to the homecoming of the adoptive child varies depending on the program. For healthy Caucasian infant adoption, the wait averages 4 years; for minority and special-needs adoptions, the wait averages 1 year.

THE CHILDREN

PCDS places both healthy and special-needs children, ranging in age from birth to 15 years, of Caucasian, Black, and bi-racial backgrounds, born in the U.S.

THE REQUIREMENTS

Age: Applicants must be at least 25 and no more than 45 years of age.
Health: Applicants should be in reasonably good health. Applicants with health problems or handicaps are given individual consideration. Infertility documentation is required for healthy Caucasian infant adoption.
Religion: No requirement.
Financial status: Applicants must demonstrate financial stability.
Marital status: No requirement.
Family size: No requirement for minority or special-needs adoptions. For healthy Caucasian infant adoption, applicants must be childless.
Racial, ethnic or cultural origin: Preference for placing children in families of similar origins.

THE PROCEDURE

Participation in the adoption program of PCDS entails the following basic steps:
Orientation meeting
Application
Group counseling sessions
Homestudy
Placement
Post-placement supervision

ADDITIONAL PROGRAMS/SERVICES

PCDS sponsors a wide range of programs including the Florence Crittenton Home, Gould Cottage for Boys, Savannah Home for Girls, Teen Pregnancy Project, Family Counseling Center, Youth Estate for Boys, Montessori Preschool and Day Care Services.

BRANCH/NETWORK OFFICES

None.

LICENSE/ACCREDITATION/PROFESSIONAL AFFILIATIONS

Parent and Child Development Services, Inc. is licensed by the State of Georgia Department of Human Resources and accredited by the Council on Accreditation of Services for Families and Children. The agency is a member of the Child Welfare League of America, the Georgia Association of Licensed Adoption Agencies, and the National Association of Homes for Children.

Hawaii

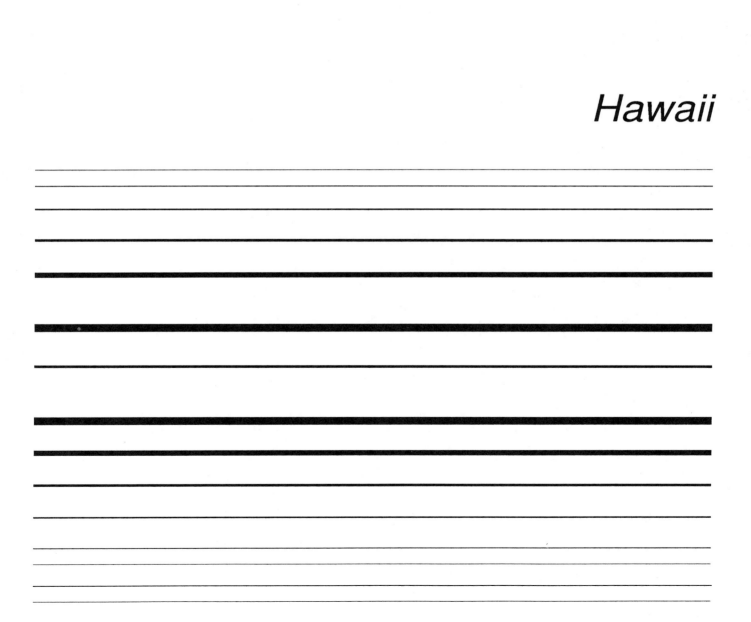

PUBLIC ADOPTION PROGRAM/ COMMUNITY RESOURCES

Department of Human Services
Adoption Program
P.O. Box 339
Honolulu, HI 96809–0339
(808) 942–9456
Adoption specialist: Beatrice C. Yuh

THE PROGRAM

Public adoption services in Hawaii are provided by the Adoption Program of the Department of Human Services through branch offices in Oahu, Hawaii, Kauai, Maui, and Molokai. Branch offices of the Adoption Program recruit and prepare adoptive families and supervise the placement of special-needs children (older, minority, and handicapped children and sibling groups) who are in the custody of the State of Hawaii.

STATE EXCHANGE

None.

STATE ADOPTION REUNION REGISTRY

Family Court, Central Registry
P.O. Box 3498
Honolulu, HI 96811
(808) 548–4601

STATE SUBSIDY

For information, contact the Department of Human Services, Adoption Program (above).

NACAC REPRESENTATIVE

Priscilla Heilveil
47–337 Iuiu Street
Kaneohe, HI 96744
(808) 239–8050

GENERAL ADOPTION RESOURCES

The Adoptive Parents League
P.O. Box 1426
Kaneohe, HI 96744
(808) 239–8050
(808) 623–6353

SPECIAL-NEEDS ADOPTION RESOURCES

For information about resources for children with special needs, contact the Department of Human Services (above).

OUT-OF-STATE AGENCIES

SEE APPENDIX A

Agencies Providing Nationwide Services

CATHOLIC SERVICES TO FAMILIES

Family Service Unit
250 South Vineyard Street
Honolulu, HI 96813
(808) 537–6321
Program director: Ana Rosal, M.Ed.

THE PROGRAM

Catholic Services to Families is a nonprofit family service agency serving residents of Hawaii (primarily the Island of Oahu) and placing approximately 20 to 25 children annually through its adoption program. First licensed as a child placing agency in 1945, the agency's mission is "to help families and individuals deal with the causes and impact of breakdown, violence, and stress, and to promote healthy growth with special concern for single parent families and the well being of children." Catholic Services to Families provides both domestic and international adoption services. The agency provides services to birthparents and places infants for adoption when birthparents elect adoptive placement as the best plan for their child. Working cooperatively with mainland U.S. agencies, the agency facilitates the placement of Black and bi-racial children. Working directly with Eastern Child Welfare Society in Korea, the agency places Korean infants in Hawaii families. The agency also provides services for the adoption of orphaned children from the Philippines who have relatives in Hawaii. In addition, the agency will provide homestudy and supervisory services for applicants pursuing either domestic or international interagency adoption and will provide homestudies for applicants pursuing private adoption.

THE COST

For applicants pursuing adoption of local, domestic infants, the agency's fee ranges from $1,212 to $3,107. For applicants pursuing the adoption of Black or bi-racial children, the fee varies depending on the cooperating agency. For applicants pursuing international adoption, the agency's fee ranges from $805 to $1,041. In addition, applicants can expect to pay a fee to the Korean agency (currently $2,400) and other costs related to international adoption. For all programs, applicants are responsible for legal fees connected with finalization of the adoption.

THE WAIT

For local, domestic infant adoption, the time from application to the homecoming of the adoptive child ranges from 1 1/2 to 3 1/2 years. For adoption from Korea, the wait ranges from 6 to 12 months.

THE CHILDREN

Catholic Services to Families places primarily healthy infants of Caucasian, Asian, Black, and bi-racial backgrounds. Countries of origin include U.S., Korea, and the Philippines.

THE REQUIREMENTS

Age: For local, domestic infant adoption, applicants must be at least 23 and no more than 40 years of age. For Korean adoption, applicants must be at least 25 and no more than 45 years of age.

Health: Applicants should be in reasonably good health.

Religion: No requirement.

Financial status: Applicants must demonstrate financial stability and must have sufficient income to support an additional family member.

Marital status: Applicants must be married couples who have been married for at least 3 years.

Family size: For local, domestic infant adoption, preference is given to applicants who are childless and unable to have children. For adoption from Korea, applicants may have no more than 5 children currently in the family.

Racial, ethnic or cultural origin: The requirement varies depending on the program.

THE PROCEDURE

Participation in the adoption program of Catholic Services to Families entails the following basic steps:

Orientation meeting

Application

Individual counseling sessions

Homestudy

Compliance with immigration/naturalization requirements (international adoptions only)

Referral

Placement

Post-placement supervision

ADDITIONAL PROGRAMS/SERVICES

Catholic Services to Families provides individual, marital, and family counseling; therapeutic foster care for troubled/troubling adolescents; services to birthparents; temporary foster care for infants awaiting placement; support group for adoptive parents of Korean children.

BRANCH/NETWORK OFFICES

None.

LICENSE/ACCREDITATION/PROFESSIONAL AFFILIATIONS

Catholic Services to Families is licensed by the State of Hawaii Department of Social Services and is a member of Catholic Charities USA and the United Way.

CHILD AND FAMILY SERVICE

200 N. Vineyard Boulevard, #20
Honolulu, HI 96817
(808) 521–2377
Program director: Clara Niimoto

THE PROGRAM

Child and Family Service (CFS) is a nonprofit agency serving residents of Hawaii and placing approximately 41 children annually. Originally established in Hawaii in 1899, foster and adoptive child placements are among the oldest services that CFS has offered to the community. Working directly with birthparents, with other licensed public and private agencies, and with national and regional exchange programs, CFS places both healthy and special-needs children in Hawaii families. Working in cooperation with Hawaii International Child Placement and Family Services, CFS places Korean children in Hawaii families. Additional international services include assistance to local families in adopting orphaned or part-orphaned children of relatives, domiciled in the Philippine Islands. CFS will also provide homestudy and supervisory services for applicants pursuing either domestic or international interagency adoption. In 1981, CFS began Fost/Adopt services, offering foster care in an approved adoptive home to the pre-adoptive child, pending termination of parental rights. Fost/Adopt parents are approved adoptive applicants who agree to care for a pre-adoptive child on a foster care basis until he/she is legally free for adoption. When the child is freed, the family goes on to complete the legal adoption process. In all of its programs, the agency's mission is "to provide quality services that are responsive to community needs."

THE COST

The agency's fee for adoption services varies depending on the program. For local, domestic infant adoption, the fee ranges from $1,100 to $3,772 and includes counseling services to birthparents and social services to adoptive parents (homestudy, placement, and post-placement supervision). For international adoption, the agency's fee ranges from $1,100 to $1,450. Applicants pursuing international adoption can also expect to pay a fee to the Korean agency (approximately $4,000) and other costs related to international adoption. For applicants pursuing interagency adoption, the fee for homestudy and supervisory services is negotiated with the cooperating agency.

THE WAIT

The time from application to the homecoming of the adoptive child varies depending on the program and ranges from 2 months to 2 years. There is no guarantee of placement. If placement does not occur within 2 years, the application is discontinued to permit families to pursue other avenues and resources.

THE CHILDREN

CFS places both healthy and special-needs children, ranging in age from birth to 16 years, of all racial backgrounds. Countries of origin include U.S., Korea, and the Philippines.

THE REQUIREMENTS

Age: No requirement.

Health: Applicants should be in reasonably good health. Applicants with health problems or handicaps are given individual consideration.

Religion: No requirement.

Financial status: No requirement.

Marital status: Applicants must be married couples who have been married for at least 3 years.

Family size: No requirement.

Racial, ethnic or cultural origin: Preference for placing children in families of similar origins.

THE PROCEDURE

Participation in the adoption program of CFS entails the following basic steps:

Orientation meeting
Application
Homestudy
Compliance with immigration/naturalization requirements
   (international adoptions only)
Referral
Placement
Post-placement supervision

ADDITIONAL PROGRAMS/SERVICES

CFS provides a wide range of services to the community including counseling services to birthparents; pre-adoptive foster care; foster parent training; post-adoption services (counseling, reunion); emergency shelter; residential treatment for adolescents; family related sex abuse treatment; employee assistance services; treatment and prevention of substance abuse; refugee acculturation and employment; family life education.

BRANCH/NETWORK OFFICES

While CFS maintains several branch offices, adoption inquiries are processed through the Honolulu office (above).

LICENSE/ACCREDITATION/PROFESSIONAL AFFILIATIONS

Child and Family Service is licensed by the State of Hawaii Department of Human Services and is accredited by the Council on Accreditation of Services for Families and Children. CFS is a member of the Child Welfare League of America and Family Service America.

HAWAII INTERNATIONAL CHILD PLACEMENT

P.O. Box 13
Hawi, HI 96719
(808) 889–5122
Program director: Monroe Woollard, MSW

THE PROGRAM

Hawaii International Child Placement is a nonprofit agency serving residents of Hawaii and placing approximately 100 children annually. Founded in 1975 by the director, following years of service in international adoption as the director of services for Holt International Children's Services, the agency provides domestic and international adoption services. The agency works directly with birthparents, public and private agencies, and national and regional exchange programs to place domestic infants and special-needs children. Working with U.S.-based and foreign-based agencies, the agency places both infants and special-needs children from a number of foreign countries. In addition, the agency will provide homestudy and supervisory services for applicants pursuing interagency adoption (international or domestic) or independent adoption.

THE COST

The agency's fee for adoption services ranges from $750 to $2,000. The fee may be decreased for special-needs

adoptions. Services covered by the fee include application, homestudy, placement, and post-placement supervision. Applicants pursuing domestic adoption should anticipate financial responsibility for the medical costs of the birthmother and child. Applicants pursuing international adoption should anticipate fees to the international agency, transportation, and related expenses. In all programs, applicants pay legal fees connected with finalization of the adoption.

THE WAIT

The time from application to the homecoming of the adoptive child ranges from 2 months to 1 year.

THE CHILDREN

Hawaii International Child Placement places both healthy and special-needs children, ranging in age from birth to 16 years, of all racial backgrounds. Countries of origin include Korea, Thailand, Taiwan, Philippines, Japan, China, South Pacific, South and Central America, and the U.S.

THE REQUIREMENTS

The agency has no requirements other than a commitment and a desire to parent. However, for international or interagency placements, the agency must work within the framework of the cooperating agency's requirements.

Age: The requirement varies depending on the requirements of the cooperating agency.

Health: The requirement varies depending on the requirements of the cooperating agency.

Religion: The requirement varies depending on the requirements of the cooperating agency.

Financial status: The requirement varies depending on the requirements of the cooperating agency.

Marital status: The requirement varies depending on the requirements of the cooperating agency.

Family size: The requirement varies depending on the requirements of the cooperating agency.

Racial, ethnic or cultural origin: The requirement varies depending on the requirements of the cooperating agency.

THE PROCEDURE

Participation in the adoption program of Hawaii International Child Placement entails the following basic steps:
Application
Homestudy
Compliance with immigration/naturalization requirements
   (international adoptions only)
Referral
Placement
Post-placement supervision
Naturalization

ADDITIONAL PROGRAMS/SERVICES

The agency provides a range of services including foster care, family counseling, educational workshops, legal programs, community education, and interagency coordination. The director is the author of *Adoption without Prejudice*, scheduled for publication in 1989.

BRANCH/NETWORK OFFICES

While the agency maintains staff at all islands of the State except Molokai, all adoption inquiries are processed through the main office.

LICENSE/ACCREDITATION/PROFESSIONAL AFFILIATIONS

Hawaii International Child Placement is licensed by the State of Hawaii Department of Social Services. The agency is a member of the Joint Council on International Children's Services.

LDS SOCIAL SERVICES

1500 South Beretania Street
Honolulu, HI 96826
(808) 945–3690
Program director: Alifeleti Malupo

THE PROGRAM

For a full description of programs and services, refer to Utah listing:

LDS Social Services
50 East North Temple Street
Salt Lake City, UT 84150

QUEEN LILI'UOKALANI CHILDREN'S CENTER

1300 Halona Street
Honolulu, HI 96817
(808) 847–1302
Program director: Margery Chapman

THE PROGRAM

Queen Lili'uokalani Children's Center is a nonprofit child welfare agency providing statewide services "to assist the orphaned and destitute Hawaiian child to become self-sufficient." Since 1946, the agency has provided child welfare services including foster care and adoption services to orphaned and destitute children of Hawaiian ancestry. Working directly with birthparents and with other private and public agencies, the agency places both healthy and special-needs children who have some Hawaiian ancestry.

THE COST

Adoption services are provided at no cost to the adoptive family. Applicants are, however, responsible for legal fees connected with finalization of the adoption.

THE WAIT

The time from application to placement varies depending on the availability of children.

THE CHILDREN

Queen Lili'uokalani Children's Center places both healthy and special-needs children, ranging in age from birth to 17 years. Agency services are limited to children who have some Hawaiian ancestry. The child must be an orphan (both parents deceased) or half-orphan (single parent, mother not married to the father, or the father deceased).

THE REQUIREMENTS

Age: The requirement varies depending on the age and the needs of the child being considered for placement.

Health: Applicants must be in reasonably good health. Applicants with health problems or handicaps are given individual consideration.

Religion: No requirement.

Financial status: Applicants must have sufficient income to provide for an additional family member.

Marital status: Married couples and single persons are considered. The requirement varies depending on the needs of the child.

Family size: No requirement.

Racial, ethnic or cultural origin: No requirement.

THE PROCEDURE

Participation in the adoption program of Queen Lili'uokalani Children's Center entails the following basic steps:

Application
Individual counseling sessions
Homestudy
Referral
Placement
Post-placement supervision
Finalization report

ADDITIONAL PROGRAMS/SERVICES

Queen Lili'uokalani Children's Center provides a range of services including workshops and seminars on child welfare services and the implementation of Hawaii State laws to protect children; financial assistance for educational tutoring services, recreation, and other enrichment activities for children; individual and family counseling; legal services; foster care; pediatric assessments.

BRANCH/NETWORK OFFICES

While Queen Lili'uokalani Children's Center maintains 9 branch offices, all adoption inquiries are processed through the office in Honolulu.

LICENSE/ACCREDITATION/PROFESSIONAL AFFILIATIONS

Queen Lili'uokalani Children's Center is licensed by the State of Hawaii Department of Social Services and is a member of the Child Welfare League of America.

Idaho

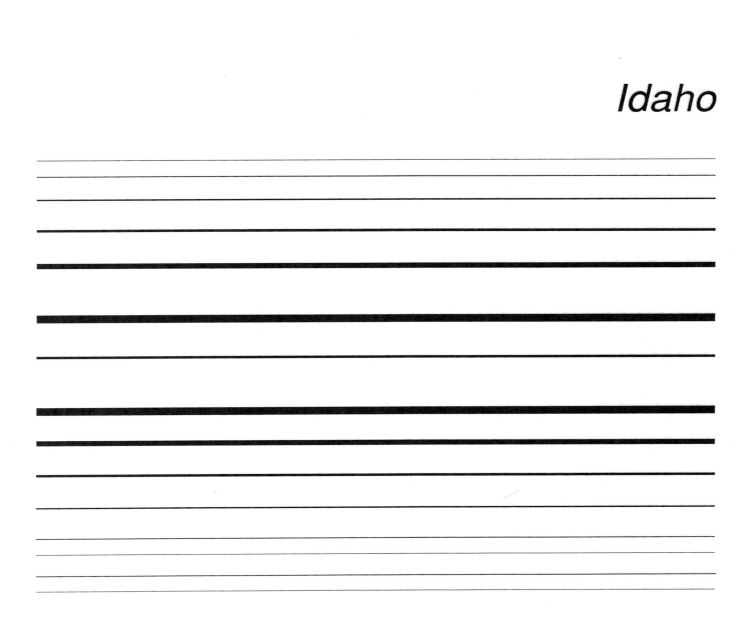

PUBLIC ADOPTION PROGRAM/ COMMUNITY RESOURCES

Department of Health and Welfare
Division of Family and Children's Services
Statehouse Mail
Boise, ID 83720
(208) 338–7000
Adoption specialist: Shirley Wheatley, State Adoptions Coordinator

THE PROGRAM

Public adoption services in Idaho are provided by the Department of Health and Welfare through regional offices located throughout the state. The agency recruits and prepares adoptive families and supervises the placement of special-needs children (older, minority, and handicapped children and sibling groups). The agency also prepares children who are in the Department's guardianship for adoption and matches them with families. Through a recent federal grant, a complete telecommunications system was installed in the central office adoption section, giving the agency access (through membership in the National Adoption Network) to the National Adoption Bulletin Board and Electronic Mail as well as adoption exchanges and other agencies throughout the country.

STATE EXCHANGE

For information, contact the Division of Family and Children's Services at (208) 334–5700.

STATE ADOPTION REUNION REGISTRY

Idaho Adoption Registry
Cooperative Center for Health Statistics
450 W. State St., 1st Floor
Boise, ID 83720
(208) 334–5084

STATE SUBSIDY

For information, contact the Division of Family and Children's Services (above).

NACAC REPRESENTATIVE

Susan Smith
P.O. Box 729
Post Falls, ID 83854
(208) 773–0526

GENERAL ADOPTION RESOURCES

Families Through Adoption
378 Roosevelt
Pocatello, ID 83201

Forever Families
899 Saratoga
Boise, ID 83706

Lewis-Clark Adoptive Families
3628 16th St.
Lewiston, ID 83501

North Idaho Adoptive Families
N. 11650 Three Forks Rd.
Post Falls, ID 83854

Parents and Children Together
7474 S. Cloverdale
Boise, ID 83709

SPECIAL-NEEDS ADOPTION RESOURCES

Department of Health and Welfare
Division of Health
450 W. State St.
Boise, ID 83720
Crippled Children's Service: (208) 334–5962
WIC Program: (208) 334–5948

Department of Health and Welfare
Division of Family and Children's Services
450 W. State St.
Boise, ID 83720
Child Protection: (208) 334–5700
Child Development Center: (208) 334–5700

Idaho School for the Deaf and Blind
202 14th Ave., E.
Gooding, ID 83330
(208) 934–4457

OUT-OF-STATE AGENCIES

SEE APPENDIX A

Agencies Providing Nationwide Services

CATHOLIC COUNSELING SERVICES

2308 N. Cole Road, Suite H
Boise, ID 83704
(208) 322–1262
Program director: Michael J. Eisenbeiss, Ph.D.

THE PROGRAM

Catholic Counseling Services is a nonprofit agency serving the state of Idaho and placing 2–4 children annually. Children placed by the agency are primarily infants whose birthparents have decided that the child's best interests will be served by adoptive placement.

THE COST

The agency's fee for adoption services is $2,400. Services covered by the fee include initial interview, attorney's fee, homestudy, psychological testing, placement, and post-placement supervision. In addition, prospective adoptive parents should anticipate financial responsibility for the medical costs of the birthmother and child.

THE WAIT

The average time from application for acceptance into the program to the homecoming of the adoptive child is 2 years.

THE CHILDREN

Catholic Counseling Services places primarily healthy

Caucasian infants (0–6 months) born in the U.S. However, the agency will provide homestudy and supervisory services for the adoption of children of any race or age if requested.

THE REQUIREMENTS

Age: Applicants may be no more than 45 years of age. Requirement may vary depending on individual circumstances.

Health: No requirement.

Religion: No requirement.

Financial status: No requirement other than ability to support a child.

Marital status: No requirement.

Family size: Applicants may have no more than 1 child currently in the family.

Racial, ethnic or cultural origin: No requirement, but may vary depending on need and availability.

THE PROCEDURE

Participation in Catholic Counseling Service's adoption program entails the following basic steps:

Orientation meeting
Application
Individual counseling sessions
Homestudy
Placement
Post-placement supervision

ADDITIONAL PROGRAMS/SERVICES

Catholic Counseling Service provides individual, marital, and family counseling.

BRANCH/NETWORK OFFICES

None.

LICENSE/ACCREDITATION/PROFESSIONAL AFFILIATIONS

Catholic Counseling Services is licensed by the State of Idaho Department of Health and Welfare.

CHRISTIAN COUNSELING SERVICES OF IDAHO, INC.

545 Shoup Avenue, Suite 230
Idaho Falls, ID 83402
(208) 529–4673
Program director: Kirk Anderson, Agency Director; Betty Lu Holland, Adoption Program Director

THE PROGRAM

Christian Counseling Services is a nonprofit agency serving residents of Idaho. Providing services to individuals of any religion, race, or nationality, the agency offers a range of family and community services designed to "enable hurting and seeking people, families and institutions to experience healing and growth in the emotional, physical, spiritual, and relational aspects of their lives." CCS places infants for adoption when birthparents in the agency's maternity counseling program decide that the infant's best interests will be served by adoptive placement. Birthparents select the adoptive family for their baby by reading profiles of a number of approved applicants. Non-identifying background information is exchanged between birthparents and adoptive parents. CCS places approximately 4–5 children annually.

THE COST

The agency's current fee schedule (1987) is as follows:

Application	$50.00
Homestudy	$300.00
Adoptive Parent Workshop	$150.00
Placement/Post-placement Fee	$1,000.00
Total*	$1,500.00

*Plus mileage and travel expenses if applicants' home is more than one hour from Idaho Falls.

In addition, prospective adoptive parents should anticipate financial responsibility for actual medical, hospital, infant foster care, and legal fees connected with finalization of the adoption. Applicants should anticipate a total cost of $4,500–$5,000.

THE WAIT

The time from application for acceptance into the program to the homecoming of the adoptive child varies depending on availability and ranges from 2 to 4 years.

THE CHILDREN

CCS places primarily healthy Caucasian infants (birth to 1 year old), born in the U.S. CCS may occasionally place children of bi-racial backgrounds.

THE REQUIREMENTS

Age: Applicants may be no more than 40 years of age at the time of application.

Health: Applicants must be in reasonably good health.

Religion: No requirement. Birthparents' preferences are honored, and many request a Christian home.

Financial status: Applicants must demonstrate financial stability.

Marital status: No requirement, but birthparents' preferences are honored.

Family size: Applicants may have no more than 1 child currently in the family.

Racial, ethnic or cultural origin: No requirement.

THE PROCEDURE

Participation in CCS' adoption program entails the following basic steps:

Intake interview
Application (including life summary questionnaire and references)
Adoptive parent workshop
Homestudy
Placement
Post-placement supervision (3–4 visits)

ADDITIONAL PROGRAMS/SERVICES

CCS sponsors a workshop twice a year for prospective adoptive families. The workshop includes a panel of adoptive parents; a talk or a film by a birthmother; a talk by a woman adoptee who has searched for and found her birthmother;

information on openness in adoption, trends in unwed pregnancy, birth, and adoption in Idaho; questions adopted children often ask at different ages; research on factors related to successful adoption outcomes. CCS maintains a small library on adoption issues. In addition to services related to adoption issues, CCS provides individual, marital, and family counseling; preventive classes and workshops on a variety of topics.

BRANCH/NETWORK OFFICES

None.

LICENSE/ACCREDITATION/PROFESSIONAL AFFILIATIONS

Christian Counseling Services is licensed by the State of Idaho Department of Health and Welfare and is sponsored by ten area churches of various denominations.

IDAHO YOUTH RANCH ADOPTION SERVICES

1416 W. Franklin Street
Boise, ID 83702
(208) 342–6805
Program director: Jeannie Swenson

THE PROGRAM

Idaho Youth Ranch Adoption Services is a private, nonprofit agency serving central and southern Idaho. Idaho Youth Ranch, a residential treatment facility for older children and adolescents, was established in 1957. In 1983, Idaho Youth Ranch developed a licensed adoption agency in order to meet a need for adoption services that resulted when the Idaho Department of Health & Welfare reduced their adoption staff. The adoption program includes the placement of infants with adoptive parents, counseling to birthparents, provision of services to families adopting children from foreign countries, and adoption education workshops. The mission of Idaho Youth Ranch Adoption Services is "to provide the best possible plan for the children in its care. This is done by providing counseling for birthmothers and fathers, adoption counseling for prospective adoptive parents, and support for parents after the adoptive placement." The agency places approximately 24 children annually.

THE COST

The agency charges a flat fee of $2,000 for adoption services. Services covered by the fee include application, orientation, homestudy, legal services (termination of parental rights of birthparents), educational workshops, and post-placement supervision. In addition to the agency fee, prospective adoptive parents should anticipate financial responsibility for exact medical expenses of the birthmother (prenatal care, delivery, and post-partum care) and legal fees associated with finalization of the adoption.

THE WAIT

The average time from application for acceptance into the program to the homecoming of the adoptive child is 2 years.

THE CHILDREN

While birthparents of any race or cultural background are accepted as clients, most are Caucasian. Consequently, most children placed by the agency are healthy Caucasian infants. The agency also provides services for foreign and special-needs adoptions (exchange books, homestudy, post-placement supervision) on a limited basis.

THE REQUIREMENTS

Age: Applicants must be at least 21 and no more than 45 years old.
Health: Applicants must be in reasonably good health and must provide infertility documentation. Applicants with health problems or handicaps are given individual consideration.
Religion: No requirement.
Financial status: Applicants must demonstrate financial stability.
Residence: Applicants must be residents of the state of Idaho.
Marital status: Applicants must be married and must have been married for at least 3 years.
Family size: Applicants must have no more than 1 child currently in the family.
Racial, ethnic or cultural origin: No requirement, but may vary depending on the needs of the child.

THE PROCEDURE

Participation in Idaho Youth Ranch Adoption Services entails the following basic steps:
Pre-application summary
Application
Orientation meeting
Submission of homestudy information
Homestudy interviews
Placement
Post-placement visits (minimum of 3)
Finalization of adoption in court

ADDITIONAL PROGRAMS/SERVICES

In addition to adoption services, Idaho Youth Ranch operates several residential facilities for older children and adolescents including the ranch (north of Rupert, Idaho), a group home for boys in Nampa, and an independent living program for boys in Boise.

BRANCH/NETWORK OFFICES

Idaho Youth Ranch
Twin Falls Office (part-time staff only)
650 Addison West, Room 306
Twin Falls, ID 83301
(208) 734–0274

LICENSE/ACCREDITATION/PROFESSIONAL AFFILIATIONS

Idaho Youth Ranch, Inc. is licensed by State of Idaho Department of Health and Welfare and is accredited by the National Association of Homes for Children.

LDS Social Services

10740 Fairview, Suite 100
Boise, ID 83704
(208) 376–0191
Program director: Caleb A. Shreeve, Jr.

The Program

For a full description of programs and services, refer to Utah listing:

LDS Social Services
50 East North Temple Street
Salt Lake City, UT 84150

Branch Offices

LDS Social Services/Idaho
1420 E. 17th St., Suite B
Idaho Falls, ID 83401
(208) 529–5276
Director: Arthur E. Finch

255 Overland Ave.
Burley, ID 83318
(208) 678–8200
Director: Garner Oleson

1070 Hiline Rd., Suite 200
Pocatello, ID 83201
(208) 232–7780
Director: Karl R. White

Illinois

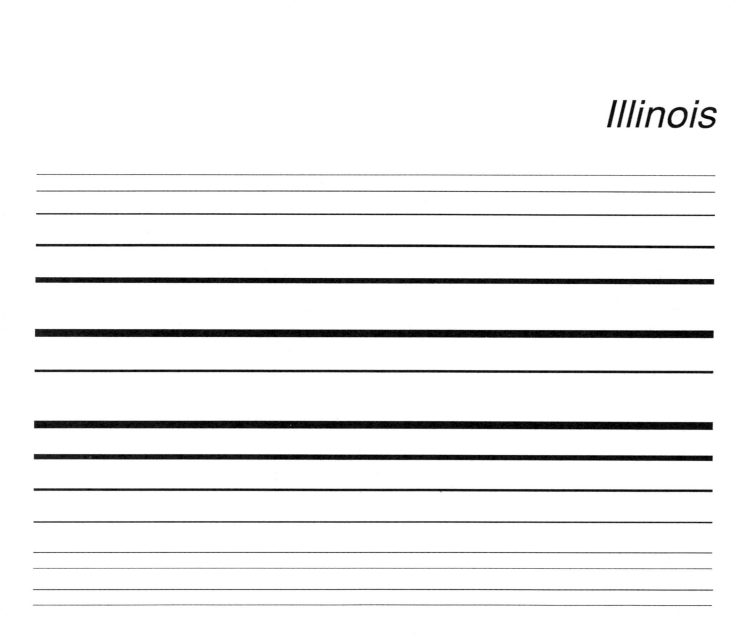

PUBLIC ADOPTION PROGRAM/ COMMUNITY RESOURCES

Department of Children and Family Services
Office of Adoptions
100 West Randolph
Chicago, IL 60601
Dept. of Children and Family Services: (312)917–6834
Adoption Information Center: (312) 346–1516
Adoption Hotline: 1–800–572–2390
Adoption specialist: Gary Morgan, Dept. of Children and Family Services; .Marilyn Panichi, Adoption Information Center

THE PROGRAM

Public adoption services in Illinois are provided by the Department of Children and Family Services through regional offices located throughout the state. Information about adoption in Illinois is provided by the Adoption Information Center of Illinois, a cooperative effort of the Child Care Association of Illinois and the Illinois Department of Children and Family Services (see State Exchange below). The Adoption Information Center is the state's central source for all inquiries, referrals, and information about adoption. While the Adoption Information Center provides information on a wide range of adoption resources (support services, private agencies, intercountry agencies), its focus is to find families for special-needs children (older children, minority children, children with physical, intellectual, or emotional special needs, and sibling groups). The Adoption Information Center provides a statewide adoption listing service of children available for adoption and families ready for adoption, a computer match/referral program that links waiting children with potential families in Illinois, a statewide adoption referral service, and a public education and recruitment program.

STATE EXCHANGE

Adoption Information Center (see The Program above)
201 North Wells Street, Suite 1342
Chicago, IL 60606
(312) 346–1516
Adoption Hotline 1–800–572–2390
Director: Marilyn Panichi

STATE ADOPTION REUNION REGISTRY

Illinois Adoption Registry
Illinois Department of Public Health
Division of Vital Records—Adoption Registry
605 W. Jefferson St.
Springfield, IL 62702
(217) 782–6553

STATE SUBSIDY

Adoption Assistance Program. For information, contact the Adoption Information Center (above).

NACAC REPRESENTATIVE

Drucilla Fair
7930 South Colfax
Chicago, IL 60617
(312) 734–2305

GENERAL ADOPTION RESOURCES

The following list represents selected adoptive parent support organizations and general adoption resources in Illinois. For a complete and current list of adoption support services, contact the Adoption Information Center (above).

Adoption Exploration and Education Resources

RESOLVE of Chicago, Inc.
30 N. Michigan Ave., #508
Chicago, IL 60602
(312) 743–1623

Dimensions in Adoption
1461 W. Glenhill Dr.
Glendale Heights, IL 60139
(312) 801–1138

ADOPT-ED
Olympia Fields Osteopathic Medical Ctr.
20201 Crawford Ave.
Olympia Fields, IL
(312) 747–4000

Adoptive Parent Support Groups

Heart of Illinois OURS
3517 N. Finnell St.
Peoria, IL 61604
(217) 682–6205

Greater Rockford OURS
804 Hollybrook Dr.
Rockford, IL 61111
(815) 633–4884

OURS—Chicago South Suburban
301 Oregon
Frankfurt, IL 60423
(217) 367–9539

OURS of East Central Illinois
1609 Willow Rd.
Urbana, IL 61801
(217) 367–9539

Kishawaukee OURS
1416 Pleasant St.
Dekalb, IL 60115
(815) 578–4275

International Families
3296 Knox Dr.
Freeport, IL 61032
(815) 232–7547

Single Adoptive Parent Support Group
5100 N. Marine Dr., Apt. 9L
Chicago, IL 60640
(312) 275–0092

Latin America Parents Assn.
P.O. Box 900
Evanston, IL 60204
(312) 369–1750

Freeport Interagency Support Group
c/o IL Dept. C&FS
1255 W. Empire
Freeport, IL 61032
(815) 235–7878

Dixon Interagency Support Group
c/o IL Dept. C&FS
102 E. Route 30
Rock Falls, IL 61071
(815) 625–7594

Rockford Interagency Support Group
c/o IL Dept. C&FS
4302 N. Main St.
Rockford, IL 61103
(815) 962–1043

IL Council on Adoptable Children
5 Park Road Ct.
Lombard, IL 60148
(312) 653–2299

Adult Adoptee Search Groups
Adoptees Liberty Movement Assn.
(ALMA)
c/o Woody Mitchell
P.O. Box 74
Lebanon, IL 62254
(618) 537–6358

Adoptees Liberty Movement Assn.
(ALMA—Central IL Chapter)
c/o Susan Lentz
P.O. Box 81
Bloomington, IL 61702
(309) 828–2217

Truth Seekers in Adoption
P.O. Box 366
Prospect Heights, IL 60070–0366
(312) 625–4476

Yesterday's Children
4323 N. Marmora
Chicago, IL 60634
(312) 545–6900

SPECIAL-NEEDS ADOPTION RESOURCES

Coordinating Council for Handicapped Children
20 E. Jackson Blvd., Room 900
Chicago, IL 60604
(312) 939–3513

Coalition of Citizens with Disabilities in Illinois
P.O. Box 5417
Springfield, IL 62705
(217) 522–7016

Alliance for the Mentally Ill
(Greater Chicago)
833 N. Orleans
Chicago, IL 60610
(312) 642–3338

Alliance for the Mentally Ill
(south suburbs of Chicago)
P.O. Box 275
Olympia Fields, IL 60461
(312) 798–4182

Community Connection
Hartgrove Hospital
520 N. Ridgeway

Chicago, IL 60624
(312) 722–3113, Ext. 230
Thresholds
2700 N. Lakeview Ave.
Chicago, IL 60614
(312) 281–3800

Of special interest to professionals involved in special-needs adoption is *After Adoption: A Manual for Professionals Working with Adoptive Families*, by Jean-Pierre Bourguignon and Kenneth Watson, published by and available from the Department of Children and Family Services. The manual addresses such issues as identification of difficulties, post-adoptive diagnostic assessment, and intervention with adoptive families.

OUT-OF-STATE AGENCIES

AGENCY

Christian Family Services, Missouri
Love Basket, Missouri
Smithlawn Maternity Home, Texas (special-needs and minority placements)

SEE APPENDIX A

Agencies Providing Nationwide Services

THE BABY FOLD

108 E. Willow Street, Box 327
Normal, IL 61761
(309) 452–1170
Program director: Mary Ann Pullin, ACSW

THE PROGRAM

The Baby Fold is a private, nonprofit adoption agency serving 54 counties in central Illinois and placing 15–20 children annually. The Baby Fold has provided adoption services since its inception in 1902, changing over the years to meet the changing needs of children. Focusing now on special-needs adoptions, the agency seeks "to recruit, study, prepare, and support adoptive families for the many children in need of adoptive placement."

THE COST

The agency's fee is based on a sliding scale and ranges from $50 to $4,350. Services covered by the fee include adoptive study and supervision of the adoptive placement. In addition, prospective adoptive parents should anticipate legal fees connected with finalization of the adoption.

THE WAIT

The time from application for acceptance into the program to the homecoming of the adoptive child ranges from 6 months to 5 years, depending on the availability of the kind of child desired by the applicants.

THE CHILDREN

The Baby Fold places primarily special-needs children of all ages and all racial backgrounds, born in the U.S. The agency also places a limited number of non-special-needs children.

THE REQUIREMENTS

Age: For non-special needs, applicants must be at least 24 and no more than 38 years of age. The age requirement may vary for special needs placement.

Health: Applicants must be in reasonably good health. Applicants with health problems or handicaps are given individual consideration.

Religion: No requirement.

Financial status: Applicants must meet state licensing requirements and adoption laws.

Marital status: No requirement. If married, applicants must have been married for at least 3 years.

Family size: No requirement for special needs. For non-special needs, applicants may have no more than 1 child currently in the family.

Racial, ethnic or cultural origin: Preference for placing children in families of similar origins.

THE PROCEDURE

Participation in The Baby Fold's adoption program entails the following basic steps:
Orientation meeting
Application
Individual counseling sessions
Group counseling sessions
Homestudy
Referral
Placement
Post-placement supervision

ADDITIONAL PROGRAMS/SERVICES

In addition to its adoption program, the agency provides post-legalization adoption services, foster care, and pregnancy counseling. The agency operates a residential treatment center and a child development center.

BRANCH/NETWORK OFFICES

1212 W. Calhoun
Macomb, IL 61455
(309) 833–2153

P.O. Box 357
Charleston, IL 61920
(217) 348–8191

LICENSE/ACCREDITATION/PROFESSIONAL AFFILIATIONS

The Baby Fold is licensed by the State of Illinois Department of Children and Family Services and is certified by the National Association of Health and Welfare Ministries of the United Methodist Church. The Baby Fold is a member of the Child Care Association of Illinois, the Association of Commerce and Industry of McLean County, the Normal Chamber of Commerce, and the United Way of McLean County.

BENSENVILLE HOME SOCIETY

A Lifelink Company
331 South York Road
Bensenville, IL 60106–2673
(312) 766–5800
Program director: Alan L. Hollis, Vice President, Child and Family Services

THE PROGRAM

Bensenville Home Society is a not-for-profit multi-service agency related to the United Church of Christ, serving residents of Illinois and placing approximately 135 children annually. Founded in 1895, the mission of the organization continues to be "in Christ's name, to meet the spiritual, physical, emotional, and social needs of children, families and aging by providing professionally effective health and human services." Bensenville Home Society was founded to provide a home for orphaned children and the aged. In 1955, the Society phased out institutional care of children and expanded its services to include adoption, counseling, foster care, and services to children in their own homes. International adoption services were begun in the Chicago area in 1984, and regional offices opened in 1985. Orphans from South Korea, India, Hong Kong, the Philippines and Latin America are now being place with families in Illinois. In addition, the agency is actively involved in special-needs adoption.

THE COST

The agency's fee for international adoption services varies depending on the child's country of origin and ranges from $5,000 to $13,000. Services covered by the fee include social services (homestudy, processing of paperwork, post-placement supervision), foreign services (child's care, medical, processing), and transportation of child and/or parents' travel. In addition, applicants should anticipate miscellaneous costs (immigration, birth and marriage documents, phone and mailing costs) and legal fees connected with finalization of the adoption.

For U.S. special-needs adoptions, the fee ranges from $0 to $1,800. If the child is a ward of the State of Illinois and meets their definition of special needs, adoption services are provided at no cost to the adoptive family.

THE WAIT

The time from application to the arrival of the adoptive child varies depending on the country and ranges from 6 months to 3 years. The wait for a special-needs child could range, after study, from 6 months to several years depending upon the type of child requested and type of children available. The wait factor for teenagers, especially boys, would be minimal compared to the wait for a school-age girl.

THE CHILDREN

Through the international program, the Society places both healthy and special-needs children, ranging in age from 2 months to 16 years, from South Korea, Hong Kong, India, the Philippines and Latin America. Through the U.S. special needs program, the agency places American-born special-needs children of all ages and racial backgrounds.

THE REQUIREMENTS

Age: For international adoption, the requirement varies from country to country. For U.S. special needs, the age of single or married parents must be between 23 and 60, depending upon the age of the child or children placed.

Health: The requirement varies depending on the country. Most require good health, ability to care for the child, and life expectancy of at least 18 years. Infertility documentation is required for some countries.

Religion: No requirement.

Financial status: For adoption through Korea, applicants must have an income of at least $20,000. For other programs, applicants must have sufficient income to support an additional family member.

Marital status: The requirement varies depending on the country. Most require that applicants be married couples, but some options are available to single parents. The length of the marriage requirement ranges from 2 to 5 years, depending on the country. The requirement for U.S. special needs program is 2 years.

Family size: The requirement varies depending on the country. Some require that applicants be childless; others allow as many as 4 children currently in the family. For U.S. special needs program, applicants may have no more than 7 children in the family.

Racial, ethnic or cultural origin: No requirement.

THE PROCEDURE

Participation in the Society's adoption program entails the following basic steps:
  Intake inquiry
  Orientation meeting
  Application
  Homestudy and licensing
  Compliance with immigration/naturalization requirements
    (international adoptions only)
  Group parent training sessions
  Child referral
  Placement
  Post-placement supervision
  Finalization
  Naturalization (international adoptions only)

ADDITIONAL PROGRAMS/SERVICES

Bensenville Home Society provides a wide range of services including nursing home care; senior housing (low and moderate income); home-delivered meals; DUI assessments, remedial education, and counseling; family and individual counseling; foster care; Head Start program; maternity services; housing for the physically handicapped; information and referral services.

BRANCH/NETWORK OFFICES

Champaign
  St. Peter's United Church of Christ
  905 S. Russell St.
  Champaign, IL 61820
Edwardsville
  Eden United Church of Christ
  903 N.Second St.

Edwardsville, IL 62025
(618) 656–8278
Moline
  First Congregational Church
  620 22nd St.
  Moline, IL 61265
  (309) 762–5645
Rockford
  Second Congregational Church
  318 N. Church St.
  Rockford, IL 61101
  (815) 965–2231

LICENSE/ACCREDITATION/PROFESSIONAL AFFILIATIONS

Bensenville Home Society is licensed by the State of Illinois Department of Children and Family Services. The Society is accredited by the Council on Accreditation of Services for Families and Children. The agency is a member of Adoption Information Service, Child Care Association of America, Child Welfare League of America, Council of Health and Human Services Ministries related to the United Church of Christ, Group for Action Planning for Services to Children, Illinois Conference Council for Health and Human Services, National Association for the Education of Young Children, and National Head Start Association.

BETHANY CHRISTIAN SERVICES

9730 S. Western Avenue, Suite 203
Evergreen Park, IL 60642
(312) 422–9626
Program director: James K. Haveman, Jr.—Executive Director

THE PROGRAM

For a full description of programs and services, refer to Michigan listing:
  Bethany Christian Services
  901 Eastern Avenue, N.E.
  Grand Rapids, MI 49503–1295
  (616) 459–6273

BETHANY HOME, INC.

P.O. Box 638
220 11th Avenue
Moline, IL 61265
1606 Brady Street
Suite 213
Davenport, IA 52803
(309) 797–7700
Program director: Marcy Bell, Judy Foote

THE PROGRAM

Bethany Home is a nonprofit agency serving the states of Illinois and Iowa. Founded in 1898, the agency initiated adoption services in 1956 and has evolved through the years to meet the changing needs of the community. The mission of Bethany Home is "to support the children in its care with love, nurture, education, and protection; to help each person in its care to develop a positive attitude and a strong sense of self-worth through counseling; to help each person or family in its care to function in society as capably and satisfactorily as possible."

THE COST

The agency's fee for adoption services is based on a sliding scale and ranges from $1,000 to $4,000 for agency adoption and $0–$1,000 for special-needs adoption. Services covered by the fee include all phases of the adoption process. In addition, prospective adoptive parents should anticipate financial responsibility for physician's fee (required medical exam), psychological evaluation, and legal fees connected with finalization of the adoption.

THE WAIT

The time from application for acceptance into the program to the homecoming of the adoptive child varies depending on the type of child the applicant wishes to adopt. The wait for a Caucasian infant ranges from 4 to 7 years. The wait for a special-needs child averages 1 to 2 years.

THE CHILDREN

Bethany Home places both infants and special-needs children of all racial backgrounds. All Bethany Home children are born in the U.S.

THE REQUIREMENTS

Age: The general requirement is that applicants must be at least 21 and no more than 35 years of age. The requirements may vary depending on the age of the child being considered for placement.
Health: A physician's examination is required.
Religion: No requirement.
Financial status: Applicants must demonstrate financial ability to meet basic needs.
Marital status: The requirement varies depending on the type of child being considered for placement. The general requirement is that the length of the marriage should be at least 2 years although single applicants are accepted for the special needs program.
Family size: No requirement.
Racial, ethnic or cultural origin: Preference for placing children in families of similar origins.

THE PROCEDURE

Participation in Bethany Homes' adoption program entails the following basic steps:
Orientation meeting
Application
Group counseling sessions
Individual counseling sessions
Homestudy
Placement
Post-placement counseling

ADDITIONAL PROGRAMS/SERVICES

Bethany Homes provides a wide range of services including residential placement; single parent services; day treatment services; foster care services; counseling for individuals, couples, and families; workshops on various topics.

BRANCH/NETWORK OFFICES

Bethany Home, Inc.
1606 Brady St., Suite 213
Davenport, IA 52803
(319) 324–9169

LICENSE/ACCREDITATION/PROFESSIONAL AFFILIATIONS

Bethany Home, Inc. is licensed by the State of Illinois Department of Children and Family Services and by the State of Iowa Department of Human Services. The agency is accredited by the Child Welfare League of America and is a member of the Child Care Association of Illinois, United Way of the Quad Cities, Council on Training, and the National Association of Homes for Children.

CATHOLIC CHARITIES OF THE ARCHDIOCESE OF CHICAGO

126 N. Desplaines Street
Chicago, IL 60606
(312) 236–5172
Program director: Mary Lou O'Brien

THE PROGRAM

Catholic Charities of the Archdiocese of Chicago is a nonprofit agency serving residents of Cook County and placing approximately 63 children annually. The goal of the adoption program is "to provide permanent placement for children by offering a range of services to assure the child's well-being and to enhance the functioning of families who desire to adopt." The agency provides services to birthparents and places both healthy and special-needs infants and young children when birthparents elect adoptive placement as the best plan for their child. The agency promotes openness in adoption. In addition, the agency will provide homestudy and supervisory services for applicants pursuing interagency adoption (domestic or international).

THE COST

The agency's fee for adoption services is based on a sliding scale with an average fee of $5,000. Services covered by the fee include adoption preparation, placement, and post-placement supervision. In addition, applicants can expect to pay an application fee of $100 as well as court costs and legal fees connected with finalization of the adoption.

THE WAIT

The time from application for acceptance into the program to the homecoming of the adoptive child ranges from 9 to 18 months for non-special-needs infants and 3 to 6 months for children with special needs.

THE CHILDREN

Catholic Charities places both healthy and special-needs children, ranging in age from infancy to 4 years, of all racial backgrounds.

THE REQUIREMENTS

Age: The age requirement varies depending on the type of child the applicants wish to adopt.

Health: Applicants should be in reasonably good health. Applicants with health problems or handicaps are given individual consideration. Infertility documentation is required for the adoption of non-special-needs infants.

Religion: The requirement varies depending on the religious preference of the birthparents.

Financial status: Applicants who are receiving public assistance are not eligible. Applicants must demonstrate sufficient income to provide for the needs of the family.

Marital status: Generally, applicants must be couples who have been married for at least 3 years. This requirement may vary depending on the preferences of the birthparents.

Family size: The requirement varies depending on the type of child the applicants wish to adopt.

Racial, ethnic or cultural origin: The requirement varies depending on the preferences of the birthparents.

THE PROCEDURE

Participation in the adoption program of Catholic Charities entails the following basic steps:
   Orientation meeting
   Application
   Group counseling sessions
   Individual counseling sessions
   Homestudy
   Placement
   Post-placement supervision

ADDITIONAL PROGRAMS/SERVICES

Additional programs related to adoption include adoption clubs; educational conferences; children's workshops; post-legal counseling; adoption registry; infant care classes; temporary infant foster care; adolescent group home; openness in adoption.

BRANCH/NETWORK OFFICES

Catholic Charities maintains regional offices throughout Cook County.

LICENSE/ACCREDITATION/PROFESSIONAL AFFILIATIONS

Catholic Charities of the Archdiocese of Chicago is licensed by the State of Illinois Department of Children and Family Services and is accredited by the Council on Accreditation of Services to Families and Children. The agency is a member of the Child Care Association, Catholic Charities USA, Catholic Charities of Illinois, and Adoption Information Service of Illinois.

CATHOLIC CHARITIES

Diocese of Springfield
108 E. Cook Street
Springfield, IL 62704
(217) 523–4551
Program director: Mary F. Stone, MSW

THE PROGRAM

Catholic Charities is a nonprofit agency serving residents of the Diocese of Springfield (28 central and southern Illinois counties) and placing approximately 30 to 40 children annually through its adoption program. Providing professional services for all members of the adoption triad, regardless of religious, racial, or ethnic backgrounds, since 1928, the agency's mission is "to administer, promote, supervise, and engage in charitable, welfare and social service work...and to aid the poor and needy, including neglected, dependent, delinquent and underprivileged children." The agency operates St. Monica's Maternity Center, a licensed residential care facility offering comprehensive services (health, social, educational, vocational and recreational) to young women faced with a problem pregnancy. Working directly with birthparents, with other private and public agencies, and with national and regional exchange programs, the agency places both healthy and special-needs infants and children for adoption. Working directly with child welfare institutions abroad and cooperatively with other U.S. agencies which maintain international programs, the agency places children from various countries in Illinois families. In addition, the agency will provide homestudy and supervisory services to applicants pursuing interagency adoption (domestic or international) or private adoption.

THE COST

The agency's fee for adoption services is based on a sliding scale and ranges from $0 to $7,300. Services include individual, group and family counseling; group educational sessions; homestudy and licensure as foster care home; post-placement supervision and court reports. Fees also help to underwrite the cost of services to the birthmother and child (legal, medical, and foster care expenses). Applicants are responsible for legal fees and court costs connected with finalization of the adoption. For international placements, applicants should anticipate travel expenses.

THE WAIT

The time from application to the homecoming of the adoptive child varies depending on the type of child the applicants wish to adopt, ranging from 3 months to 5 or 6 years.

THE CHILDREN

Catholic Charities places both healthy and special-needs children, ranging in age from birth to 18 years, of all racial backgrounds. Various countries of origin are represented in the international program.

THE REQUIREMENTS

Age: Applicants must be at least 21 years of age. There is no arbitrary maximum age limit. Generally, the age difference between the child and the adoptive parents should not exceed the usual difference between biological parents and children (approximately 40 years).

Health: Applicants should be in reasonably good health. Infertility documentation is required for healthy Caucasian infant adoption.

Religion: Applicants must be practicing members of the church or synagogue of their choice.

Financial status: Applicants must demonstrate the ability to meet the family's financial needs.

Marital status: For healthy Caucasian infant adoption, applicants must be married, and the length of the marriage must be at least 2 years. The requirement varies for other programs.

Family size: For healthy Caucasian infant adoption, applicants may have no more than 2 healthy children in the family. The requirement varies for other programs.

Racial, ethnic or cultural origin: Preference for placing children in families of similar origins.

The Procedure

Participation in the adoption program of Catholic Charities entails the following basic steps:

Orientation meeting
Application
Individual and group counseling sessions
Homestudy
Compliance with immigration/naturalization requirements (international adoptions only)
Referral
Placement
Post-placement supervision

Additional Programs/Services

Additional programs related to adoption include adoption informational meetings; family and marital counseling; annual meetings with waiting prospective adoptive parents; semi-annual newsletter; foster care services; information and referral services.

Branch/Network Offices

The Springfield office serves residents of Sangamon, Menard, Christian, and Montgomery Counties and part of Macoupin County.

Decatur Catholic Charities
247 W. Prarie
Decatur, IL 62523
(217) 428-3458
Serving Macon, Shelby, Moultrue, Douglas, Coles, and Edgar Cos.

Alton Catholic Charities
115 Jefferson
Alton, IL 62002
(618) 462-0634
Serving Calhoun, Jersey, parts of Macoupin and Madison Cos.

Effingham Catholic Charities
420 W. Jefferson
Effingham, IL 62401
(217) 342-9800

Serving Effingham, Clark, Cumberland, Jasper, and Crawford Cos.

Jacksonville Catholic Charities
P.O. Box 1252
Jacksonville, IL 62651
(217) 245-6913
Serving Morgan, Cass, Scott, Greene, and part of Macoupin Cos.

Quad-Cities Catholic Charities
2012 Delmar
(618) 877-1184
Granite City, IL 62040
Serving Bond, Fayette, and part of Madison Cos.

Catholic Social Service
926 State St.
Quincy, IL 62301
(217) 222-0958
Serving Adams, Brown, and Pike Cos.

License/Accreditation/Professional Affiliations

Catholic Charities, Diocese of Springfield, is licensed by the State of Illinois Department of Children and Family Services. The agency is affiliated with Catholic Charities USA and is a member of the United Way and Catholic Conference of Illinois.

Catholic Charities of Lake County

1 North Genesee Street, Suite 203
Waukegan, IL 60085
(312) 249-3500
Program director: Carol Wessel, Supervisor; Denice Miholic, Adoption Caseworker

The Program

Catholic Charities of Lake County is a nonprofit agency serving residents of Lake County and placing approximately 14 children annually. The agency provides services to birthparents and places Caucasian and Black infants for adoption when birthparents in the agency's counseling program elect adoptive placement as the best plan for their child. The agency also places special-needs children. Although special-needs children are not frequently available, the agency has a need for families who are willing to wait.

The Cost

For Caucasian infant adoption, the agency's fee for adoption services is $500 (homestudy fee) plus 6% of the applicants' annual gross income (with a minimum fee of $2,500). Services covered by the fee include all phases of the adoption process, excluding legal fees connected with finalization of the adoption. For Black infant and special-needs adoptions, applicants are asked to make a donation (based on applicant's discretion and ability to pay).

The Wait

The time from application to completion of the homestudy averages 4 to 6 months. The time from completion of the homestudy to placement varies depending on the program. For Caucasian infant adoption, the wait ranges from 1 month to 2 years (and sometimes longer depending on the circumstances). For Black infant adoption, the wait ranges from a few weeks to 6 months (and sometimes longer depending on the circumstances). For special-needs adoption, the wait varies depending on the current need for adoptive families and may be as long as 5 years.

The Children

Catholic Charities of Lake County places both healthy and special-needs infants and foster care conversions ranging in age from birth to adolescence, of all racial backgrounds. All children placed by the agency are born in the U.S.

The Requirements

Age: For Caucasian infant adoption, applicants must be at least 23 and no more than 40 years of age. No maximum age requirement for special needs placements.

Health: For Caucasian infant adoption, infertility documentation is required. Applicants with health problems or handicaps are given individual consideration.

Religion: No requirement.

Financial status: Applicants must demonstrate financial stability.

Marital status: For Caucasian infant adoption, applicants must be married and must have been married for at least 2 years. For special needs placements, applicants may be either single or married for at least 1 year.

Family size: For Caucasian infant adoption, applicants must be childless. No requirement for special needs placements.

Racial, ethnic or cultural origin: No requirement.

The Procedure

Participation in Catholic Charities of Lake County's adoption program entails the following basic steps:
Orientation meeting (Caucasian infant adoption only)
Individual counseling sessions
Group meetings
Homestudy (foster family licensing)
Placement
Post-placement supervision

Families wishing to adopt a Caucasian infant must attend an informational meeting in order to be eligible to be considered for a licensing study. The licensing process is begun on a new family only when a previously licensed family has had a placement. If a family is to be licensed, the study process will begin within 6 months of having attended a meeting.

For families wishing to adopt a minority or special-needs child, interviews will begin at the family's and worker's earliest convenience.

Additional Programs/Services

In addition to adoption services, the agency provides foster care services and maternity counseling services.

The adoption program has its headquarters in the Waukegan office, although appointments may be scheduled at other locations. Additional telephone numbers for information are as follows:
Mundelein(312) 949–1557
Highland Park(312) 432–4110
Deerfield(312) 945–2445

License/Accreditation/Professional Affiliations

Catholic Charities of Lake County is licensed by the State of Illinois Department of Children and Family Services and is accredited by the Council on Accreditation of Services for Families and Children.

Catholic Social Service

220 West Lincoln
Belleville, IL 62220
(618) 277–9200
Program director: Peter Cerneka

The Program

Catholic Social Service (CSS) is a private, nonprofit agency serving the 28 southern counties of Illinois which comprise the Catholic Diocese of Belleville. Serving all people regardless of religious affiliation, the mission of Catholic Social Service is, as an agency of the Catholic Church, "to promote the social mission of the church by providing assistance to children in need and their families through direct service such as counseling, foster care, day care, adoption, and refugee services; through advocacy for appropriate law and public policy; through development of volunteer efforts within local Christian communities." Catholic Social Service established its domestic adoption program (services to adoptive parents and expectant single parents) in 1947. In 1982, the services expanded to include an intercountry program and, in 1983, a waiting child program. Through the domestic program, the agency places children born in the U.S. (usually healthy Caucasian infants). There is a waiting list for this program. Through the waiting child program, the agency places (a) minority children age 3 or older without mental, emotional, or physical handicaps, (b) children of all races with severe special needs, (c) non-minority children 12 years old or older, and (d) sibling groups. These children are not in the custody of CSS; they are currently in foster or institutional care. There is no waiting list for this program. Through the intercountry program, the agency works with and through a U.S.-based child-placing agency to find families for children born in foreign countries. Catholic Social Services places between 36 and 43 children annually.

The Cost

Catholic Social Service's fee schedule is as follows: Domestic Program: The service fee for the adoption of a U.S.-born infant is $6,200 or 10% of gross family income, whichever is higher, but not to exceed $10,000. The full fee is expected to be paid by the time the child joins the family (half when the homestudy is completed and the family receives the Family Home License, half when the child joins the family). This service fee underwrites all of the agency's services to single expectant parents (including medical costs).

Intercountry Program

Catholic Social Service's fee for the adoption of a foreign-born child is $1,500. In addition, the adoptive applicant must be prepared to pay a fee to the U.S.-based child-placing agency and to the foreign agency. There are also miscellaneous government fees and traveling expenses. The total fee will vary depending upon the country and agencies involved. It is not uncommon for the total fee to range between $5,500 and $8,500.

Waiting Child Program

There is no fee for the adoption of a waiting child. Adoption of a waiting child is subsidized whole or in part by the State of Illinois. CSS does not charge a fee for its services to applicants seeking to adopt a waiting child. In addition, adoption subsidies for the waiting child include necessary and therapeutic treatment after legal finalization of the adoption.

THE WAIT

The time from application to the homecoming of the adoptive child varies depending on the program.

Domestic Program

Healthy Caucasian infant
    5 years
Healthy Black infant 6 months

Waiting Child Program

Depends on the age of the child and the severity of the handicap.

Intercountry Program

Depends on the country; 7 months to 1 1/2 years.

THE CHILDREN

Catholic Social Service places healthy and special-needs children of all races, ranging in age from birth to 17 years. Countries of origin include U.S., Korea, Philippines, Thailand, Taiwan, Guatemala, Honduras, Colombia, Bolivia, and Brazil.

THE REQUIREMENTS

Age: Applicants must be at least 21 years old. The maximum age varies depending on the age of the child. Generally, the youngest spouse must be no more than 40 years older than the child.

Health: Applicants must be in reasonably good health. Infertility documentation is required for the domestic program (healthy Caucasian infant).

Religion: Applicants must be practicing members of a religion.

Financial status: Applicants must demonstrate financial stability.

Marital status: No requirement for waiting child and intercountry. For domestic, applicants must be married and must have been married for at least 3 years.

Family size: No requirement for waiting child and intercountry. For domestic, applicants may have no more than 1 child currently in the family.

Racial, ethnic or cultural origin: No requirement for waiting child and intercountry. For domestic, preference for placing children in families of similar origins.

THE PROCEDURE

Participation in Catholic Social Service adoption programs entails the following basic steps:
    Orientation meeting (recommended but not required)
    Application
    Group preparation program
    Individual counseling sessions
    Homestudy and foster home licensing (required by State of Illinois)
    Compliance with immigration/naturalization requirements
    Placement
    Post-placement supervision

ADDITIONAL PROGRAMS/SERVICES

Catholic Social Service provides a wide range of services including foster care, day care, family counseling, refugee assistance, natural family planning, expectant single parent counseling, senior citizens employment program, and legalization of immigrants.

BRANCH/NETWORK OFFICES

100 S. Monroe
Marion, IL 62959–2559
(618) 997–9381
361 N. Main St.
Breese, IL 62230–1524
(618) 526–2287
604 N. Market St.
P.O. Box 23
Mt. Carmel, IL 62863–0023
(618) 263–3863

LICENSE/ACCREDITATION/PROFESSIONAL AFFILIATIONS

Catholic Social Service is licensed by the State of Illinois Department of Children and Family Services and is a member of the Child Care Association of Illinois, the Catholic Conference of Illinois, the Adoption Forum of Illinois, and Catholic Charities USA.

CATHOLIC SOCIAL SERVICE

Adoption Unit
413 N.E. Monroe
Peoria, IL 61603
(309) 671–5720
Program director: Betty Gilmore, Agency Director; Juanita Burdick, Program Coordinator

THE PROGRAM

Catholic Social Service is a nonprofit agency serving residents of central Illinois and placing approximately 50 children annually. Founded as an orphanage in 1890 to provide residential and adoption services for abandoned or orphaned children, the agency has evolved in response to the changing needs of the community and now offers a wide range of services. The agency provides services to birthparents and places infants for adoption when birthparents in the agency's counseling program elect adoptive placement as the best plan for their child. The agency facilitates the placement of foreign-born children and is also actively involved in the recruitment of families for special-needs children. In all of its programs, the agency's mission is to provide counseling, support, and educational services to those in need, regardless of age, ethnic or religious background, or financial status.

THE COST

For healthy infant adoptions, the agency's fee is $4,000 plus medical and foster care expenses. Services covered by the fee include all phases of the adoption process (homestudy through post-legal services), excluding legal fees connected with finalization of the adoption. For special-needs adoptions, services are provided at no cost to the adoptive family.

THE WAIT

The time from the start of the homestudy process to the homecoming of the adoptive child varies depending on the program. For an "infant in demand," the wait ranges from 1 to 2 1/2 years. For special needs placements, the wait ranges from 6 months to 3 years.

THE CHILDREN

Catholic Social Service places both healthy and special-needs children, ranging in age from birth to 10 years, of all racial backgrounds. Countries of origin include U.S., Korea, Colombia, Brazil, and India.

THE REQUIREMENTS

Age: For infant adoption, applicants must be at least 25 and no more than 40 years of age. Requirements for special-needs adoptions are flexible.

Health: Applicants with health problems or handicaps are given individual consideration. For infant adoption, infertility documentation is required.

Religion: Requirements for special-needs adoptions are flexible. For domestic infant adoptions, the preferences of the birthparents are honored.

Financial status: Applicants are evaluated individually on the basis of their ability to manage financial resources adequately.

Marital status: For infant adoptions, applicants must be married, and the length of the marriage must be at least 2 years. Single applicants are accepted for special needs placements.

Family size: For infant adoptions, applicants may have no more than 1 child currently in the family. Requirement may vary for special-needs adoptions.

Racial, ethnic or cultural origin: Requirements are flexible, but the preference is for placing children in families of similar origins. The requirement may vary depending on the needs of the child.

THE PROCEDURE

Participation in Catholic Social Service's adoption program entails the following basic steps:
Orientation meeting

Application
Group counseling sessions
Homestudy
Compliance with immigration/naturalization requirements (foreign adoptions only)
Placement
Post-placement supervision

ADDITIONAL PROGRAMS/SERVICES

Catholic Social Service provides a wide range of community services including Women-In-Need pregnancy program; residential maternity home (Cabrini Hall); foster care services; residence for unaccompanied minors (Tha Huong); refugee resettlement services; youth intervention program; school psychological testing services; residential home and school for children with behavioral problems (Gill Hall, Lawrence Hall); senior citizens services (meals-on-wheels program, counseling, friendly visitor program, adult day care); Peoria Community Service (La Casa de Santa Maria).

BRANCH/NETWORK OFFICES

CSS Administrative Office
2900 W. Heading Ave.
Peoria, IL 61604
(309) 671–5700

603 N. Center
Bloomington, IL 61764
(309) 829–6307

Adoption Program Central Office
413 N.E. Monroe
Peoria, IL 61603
(309) 671–5720

501 N. Chicago
Pontiac, IL 61764
(815) 844–3629

365 N. 3rd St.
Canton, IL 61520
(309) 647–5082

124 W. Mazon Ave.
Dwight, IL 61420
(815) 584–3110

610 1/2 E. Park
Champaign, IL 61820
(217) 352–5179

211 N. Walnut
Danville, IL 61832
(217) 443–1772

310 S. Logan
Lincoln, IL 62656
(217) 732–3771

210 S. Market, #313
Hoopeston, IL 60942
(217) 283–5544

625 W. Jackson
Macomb, IL 61455
(309) 833–1791

3053 Grand Ave.
Galesburg, IL 61401
(309) 342–1136

816 20th St.
Rock Island, IL 61201
(309) 788–9581
542 Crosat
LaSalle, IL 61301
(815) 223–4007

LICENSE/ACCREDITATION/PROFESSIONAL AFFILIATIONS

Catholic Social Service is licensed by the State of Illinois Department of Children and Family Services. The agency is a member of Central Illinois United Ways, National Association of Social Workers, Catholic Charities USA, Catholic Charities of Illinois, Adoption Forum, and OURS (local and national).

CATHOLIC SOCIAL SERVICE

Rockford Diocese
921 W. State Street
Rockford, IL 61102
(815) 965–0895
Program director: Paul R. Brandt, Director of Social Services

THE PROGRAM

Catholic Social Service is a nonprofit multi-service agency serving residents of the Diocese of Rockford and placing approximately 40 to 60 children annually through its adoption program. Founded in 1938, the agency "recognizes its call and its duty to witness to the Gospel of Jesus Christ both in word and in deed." Working directly with birthparents, with other private and public agencies, and with national and regional exchange programs, the agency places both healthy and special-needs children born in the U.S. Working cooperatively with other U.S. agencies which maintain international programs, the agency facilitates the placement of children from various countries. In addition, the agency will provide homestudy and supervisory services for applicants pursuing interagency adoption (domestic or international).

THE COST

The agency's fee for adoption services is based on a sliding scale and ranges from $0 to $7,500. Services covered by the fee include all phases of the adoption process, excluding legal fees connected with finalization. Applicants pursuing international adoption should also anticipate fees to the cooperating international agency and miscellaneous expenses related to inter- country adoption.

THE WAIT

The time from application for acceptance into the program to the homecoming of the adoptive child ranges from 2 to 5 years for domestic and international placements and from 0 to 14 months for special needs placements.

THE CHILDREN

Catholic Social Service places both healthy and special-needs children, ranging in age from infancy to adolescence, of all racial backgrounds. Various countries of origin are represented.

THE REQUIREMENTS

Age: Applicants must be at least 21 and no more than 40 years of age.
Health: Applicants should be in reasonably good health. Applicants with health problems or handicaps are given individual consideration. Infertility documentation is required for infant adoption.
Religion: Applicants must be practicing members of a Christian faith.
Financial status: Applicants must have sufficient income to support an additional family member.
Marital status: Applicants must be married.
Family size: Applicants may have no more than 2 children currently in the family. The requirement varies for special needs placements.
Racial, ethnic or cultural origin: Preference for placing children in families of similar origins when possible. However, transracial placements are made when in the child's best interests.

THE PROCEDURE

Participation in the adoption program of Catholic Social Service entails the following basic steps:
Inquiry or referral
Orientation meeting
Application
Individual and group counseling sessions
Homestudy
Compliance with immigration/naturalization requirements (international adoptions only)
Wait listing
Placement
Post-placement supervision

ADDITIONAL PROGRAMS/SERVICES

Catholic Social Service provides foster care; unplanned pregnancy counseling; home-school counseling; Parents Too Soon program; marital counseling; family counseling.

BRANCH/NETWORK OFFICES

556 W. Galena Blvd.
Aurora, IL 60506
(312) 892–4366
566 Dundee Ave.
Elgin, IL 60120
(312) 742–4525
202 Summit St.
Galena, IL 61036
(815) 777–1048
207 N. Benton
Woodstock, IL 60098
(815) 338–7220
921 W. State St.
Rockford, IL 61102
(815) 965–0623
302 E. 5th St.
Sterling, IL 61081
(815) 625–6945

Catholic Social Service is licensed by the State of Illinois Department of Children and Family Services. The agency is a member of Catholic Charities USA and the Catholic Conference of Illinois.

CHICAGO CHILD CARE SOCIETY

5467 S. University Avenue
Chicago, IL 60615
(312) 643-0452
Program director: Sylvia Ragland

THE PROGRAM

Chicago Child Care Society is a nonprofit agency serving residents of Cook County and placing approximately 40 children annually through its adoption program. Providing adoption services since 1849, the agency's mission is "to help children served by the Society to achieve their full potential, to assist their families in meeting the needs of these children, and to encourage society's recognition of the value of children and its responsibility for them." Working with birthparents, with other private and public agencies, and with national and regional exchange programs, the agency places both healthy and special-needs children. For the last 30 years, the major focus of the program has been (and continues to be) to provide adoption services for children who are the most likely to wait the longest for adoptive families (Black and biracial children, ranging in age from birth to 10 years; Caucasian children with special needs, ranging in age from birth to 10 years). In addition, the agency will provide homestudy and post-placement supervision for applicants pursuing interagency adoption (domestic or international) or private adoption.

THE COST

Adoption services are provided at no cost to the adoptive family. However, prospective adoptive parents should anticipate legal fees connected with finalization of the adoption.

THE WAIT

The time from application to the homecoming of the adoptive child averages 6 to 8 months.

THE CHILDREN

Chicago Child Care Society places both healthy and special-needs children, ranging in age from birth to 10 years, of Caucasian, Black, and bi- racial backgrounds, born in the U.S.

THE REQUIREMENTS

Age: Applicants must be at least 21. The maximum age requirement varies depending on the age of the child being considered for placement.
Health: Applicants with health problems or handicaps are given individual consideration.
Religion: No requirement.
Financial status: Applicants must be self-supporting.

Marital status: Applicants may be either married or single (never married, legally divorced, or widowed). If married, the length of the marriage must be at least 2 years.
Family size: Applicants may have no more than 7 children currently in the family.
Racial, ethnic or cultural origin: Preference for placing children in families of similar origins.

THE PROCEDURE

Participation in the adoption program of Chicago Child Care Society entails the following basic steps:
Orientation meeting
Application
Individual counseling sessions
Homestudy
Pre-placement preparation
Placement
Post-placement supervision

ADDITIONAL PROGRAMS/SERVICES

Chicago Child Care Society provides individual and family counseling; services for single or adolescent parents; foster care; day care.

BRANCH/NETWORK OFFICES

None.

LICENSE/ACCREDITATION/PROFESSIONAL AFFILIATIONS

Chicago Child Care Society is licensed by the State of Illinois Department of Children and Family Services and is accredited by the Council on Accreditation of Services for Families and Children. The agency is a member of the Child Welfare League of America, Child Care Association of Illinois, and United Way of Illinois.

CHILDREN'S HOME AND AID SOCIETY OF ILLINOIS

1122 North Dearborn
Chicago, IL 60610
(312) 944-3313
Program director: Robert Wolf

THE PROGRAM

Children's Home and Aid Society of Illinois (CHAS) is a non- profit multi-service agency serving residents of the Chicago area, Rockford area, Champaign-Urbana area, and Alton-East St. Louis area and placing approximately 150 children annually through its adoption program. Providing adoption services since 1883, the agency's mission is "to provide services to meet the needs of children and families, primarily those services related to social and emotional problems, and to inform the general public of these needs." Working directly with birthparents, with other private and public agencies, and with national and regional exchange programs, the agency places both healthy and special-needs infants and children, born in the U.S. Working in cooperation with other U.S. agencies which maintain international programs, the agency facilitates the placement of children from Korea and South America in Illinois families. In addition, the agency will provide homestudy and supervisory services for applicants pursuing interagency adoption (domestic or international) or private adoption.

THE COST

As of October 1988, the agency's fee for adoption services is based on a sliding scale and ranges from $0 to $5,000. Applicants pursuing inter- agency adoption (domestic or international) should anticipate fees to the cooperating agency. Applicants are responsible for legal fees connected with finalization of the adoption.

THE WAIT

The time from application to placement varies depending on the type of adoption and ranges from 6 months to 5 years.

THE CHILDREN

CHAS places both healthy and special-needs children, ranging in age from birth to 18 years, of all racial backgrounds. Countries of origin include the U.S.., Korea, and South America.

THE REQUIREMENTS

Age: The requirement varies depending on the age and needs of the child being considered for placement.

Health: Applicants must be in reasonably good health. Applicants with health problems or handicaps are given individual consideration.

Religion: No requirement.

Financial status: Applicants must have sufficient income to support an additional family member.

Marital status: The requirement varies depending on the age and the needs of the child being considered for placement.

Family size: The requirement varies depending on the age and the needs of the child being considered for placement.

Racial, ethnic or cultural origin: Preference for placing children in families of similar origins.

THE PROCEDURE

Participation in the adoption program of CHAS entails the following basic steps:
Orientation meeting
Application
Group-counseling sessions
Individual counseling sessions
Homestudy
Compliance with immigration/naturalization requirements (international adoptions only)
Placement
Post-placement supervision

ADDITIONAL PROGRAMS/SERVICES

CHAS provides a wide range of services including child and family counseling; foster care; day care; residential treatment; professional education and training; research; post adoptive searches; post adoptive counseling.

BRANCH/NETWORK OFFICES

Chicago Region
South Office
2151 W. 95th St.
Chicago, IL 60643
(312) 238–3203

East Central Region
Regional Office
1819 S. Neil St., Suite D
Champaign, IL 61820
(217) 359–8815

Northwest Region
Regional Office
730 N. Main St.
Rockford, IL 61101
(815) 962–1043

Southwest Region
Regional Office
1002 College Ave.
Alton, IL 62002
(618) 462–2714

DeKalb Office
2337 Sycamore Rd.
DeKalb, IL 60115
(815) 758–2980

St. Clair County Office
7623 W. Main St.
Belleville, IL 62222
(618) 398–6700

Granite City Office
1254 Niodringhaus
Granite City, IL 62040
(618) 452–0121

LICENSE/ACCREDITATION/PROFESSIONAL AFFILIATIONS

Children's Home and Aid Society of Illinois is licensed by the State of Illinois Department of Children and Family Services and is accredited by the Council on Accreditation of Services for Families and Children and the American Association of Psychiatric Services for Children. The agency is a member of the American Association of Children's Residential Centers, the Child Welfare League of America, Child Care Association of Illinois, Day Care Council of Illinois, Illinois Association of Community Mental Health Agencies, Illinois Collaboration on Youth, and National Association of Psychiatric Treatment Centers for Children.

COUNSELING AND FAMILY SERVICE

1821 North Knoxville Avenue
Peoria, IL 61603
(309) 685–5287
Program director: Robert Buss

THE PROGRAM

Counseling and Family Service is a nonprofit, non-sectarian child welfare agency serving a tri-county area (Peoria, Tazewell, and Woodford) for healthy Caucasian infant adoption and special-needs adoption and an 8 county area (Peoria, Tazewell, Woodford, Mason, McLean, Fulton, Logan and Knox) for international adoption. Founded in 1900 and providing adoption services for more than 50 years, the agency's mission is "to find families for the many children in need of loving, adoptive homes." Working directly with birthparents, with other private and public agencies, and with national and regional exchange programs, the agency places healthy and special-needs children born in the U.S. Working in cooperation with other U.S. agencies which maintain international programs, the agency facilitates the placement of foreign-born children in Illinois families. In addition, the agency will provide homestudy and supervisory services for applicants pursuing inter- agency adoption (domestic or international) or independent adoption.

THE COST

For the adoption of special needs and minority children, the agency provides services at no cost to the adoptive parents. For the adoption of healthy Caucasian infants or pre-school children, the agency's fee is based on the family's income and ranges from $5,000 to $6,500 (as of October 1988). For international adoption or independent adoption, the fee ranges from $800 to $1,300. For international adoption, applicants should also anticipate fees to the cooperating agency, possible travel and related costs. For all programs (excluding special needs placements in which the child is eligible for subsidy), applicants are responsible for legal fees connected with finalization of the adoption.

THE WAIT

The time from application to the homecoming of the adoptive child varies depending on the type of adoption. For international and special-needs adoptions, the wait ranges from 6 to 18 months. For healthy Caucasian infant adoption, the agency maintains a small waiting list. Families may be on the waiting list for 2 to 3 years before the adoption process begins and may wait for 1 to 2 years for placement after the formal application has been submitted.

THE CHILDREN

Counseling and Family Service places both healthy and special-needs children, ranging in age from birth to adolescence, of all racial backgrounds. Countries of origin include U.S., Korea, India, and South America.

THE REQUIREMENTS

Age: Applicants must be at least 25 years old. The general requirement is that there should not be a difference of more than 40 years between the applicant and the child being considered for placement.
Health: No rigid requirement. The applicant's health is evaluated on a case-by-case basis.
Religion: No requirement.
Financial status: No requirement, but applicants must be able to assume the cost of the adoption and the care of the child.

Marital status: For Caucasian infant adoption, applicants must be married. No requirement for special needs or international adoption.
Family size: For Caucasian infant adoption, applicants may have no more than 2 children currently in the family. No requirement for special needs and international adoption.
Racial, ethnic or cultural origin: No requirement for international adoption. For domestic programs, preference for placing children in families of similar origins.

THE PROCEDURE

Participation in the adoption program of Counseling and Family Service entails the following basic steps:
Inquiry
Orientation interview
Application
Fingerprinting and background check (required by State)
Group preparation
Homestudy (including individual and joint interviews)
Referral to cooperating agency (international adoptions only)
Compliance with immigration/naturalization requirements (international adoptions only)
Placement
Post-placement supervision
Finalization

ADDITIONAL PROGRAMS/SERVICES

Counseling and Family Service provides a wide range of services including individual, marital, and family counseling; services to single parents; pregnancy prevention program; family life education seminars; employment assistance program; plays for living; foster care services.

BRANCH/NETWORK OFFICES

CFS
Friendship House
800 N.E. Madison
Peoria, IL 61603
(309) 671–5200
CFS
Community United Church of Christ
300 N. Main St.
Morton, IL 61550
(309) 266–8711
CFS
First Church of the Nazarene
3514 E. Broadway
Pekin, IL 61554
(309) 346–5890
CFS
Evangelical United Methodist Church
401 Walnut
Washington, IL 61571
(309) 444–9445

LICENSE/ACCREDITATION/PROFESSIONAL AFFILIATIONS

Counseling and Family Service is licensed by the State of Illinois Department of Children and Family Services and is accredited by the Council on Accreditation of Services for Families and Children. The agency is a member of the Child Welfare League of America, Family Service America, and the United Way.

EVANGELICAL CHILD AND FAMILY AGENCY

1530 N. Main Street
Wheaton, IL 60187
(312) 653–6400
Program director: Beverly M. Ozinga, ACSW, Program Coordinator

THE PROGRAM

Evangelical Child and Family Agency (ECFA) is a non-profit child- welfare agency serving residents of Illinois and designated counties of Wisconsin (within a 50–mile radius of the agency's offices) and placing approximately 50–60 children annually in evangelical Christian homes. Providing services to children and families for the past 36 years, the agency's adoption program strives "to provide permanent, healthy homes for children who range in age from infancy to early adolescence." The agency provides services to unmarried parents and places infants for adoption when birthparents in the agency's program elect adoptive placement as the best plan for their child. The agency is also actively involved in the placement of special-needs children.

THE COST

The agency's current fee (1987) for adoption of a healthy Caucasian infant is $4,500. Services covered by the fee include all phases of the adoption process (pre-adoption counseling through post-placement services), excluding legal fees connected with finalization of the adoption. Fees help to underwrite the cost of services to birthparents (legal, medical, and foster care). The fee for placement of children with special needs is $750, but special consideration can be given.

THE WAIT

The length of time from application to placement varies depending on the flexibility of the adoptive family regarding sex, age, and needs of the child. The time ranges from several weeks to 2 years.

THE CHILDREN

ECFA places both healthy and special-needs children, ranging in age from infancy to adolescence, primarily of Caucasian but also of Black, Hispanic, and bi-racial backgrounds. Children placed by ECFA are born in the U.S.

THE REQUIREMENTS

Age: Both husband and wife should be no more than 38 years older than the child they are seeking to adopt.
Health: Applicants should be in reasonably good health. Applicants with health problems or handicaps are given individual consideration. Exploration and evaluation of infertility factors is required.

Religion: Applicants must be actively involved in a protestant, evangelical church and must have personally accepted Jesus Christ as Lord and Savior.
Residence: Applicants must reside in Illinois or Wisconsin, within a 50– mile radius of the agency's offices. In Wisconsin, services are provided to adoptive applicants of designated counties only.
Financial status: Applicants must be able to live within their income and demonstrate the ability to meet the basic financial needs of the children in their home.
Marital status: Single applicants are considered on an individual basis. Married applicants must have been married for at least 2 years.
Family size: Applicants with 2 children under 5 years of age will not be eligible for a third child in that age range. The youngest child in the home must be at least 18 months at the time of application.
Racial, ethnic or cultural origin: Preference for placing children in families of similar origins.

THE PROCEDURE

Participation in ECFA's adoption program entails the following basic steps:
  Inquiry
  Orientation
  Application
  Family study (including individual counseling sessions)
  Eligibility decision (placement recommended, postponed, or not recommended)
  Child referral (background of child presented)
  Pre-placement visits (older child adoption)
  Placement
  Post-placement supervision
  Finalization

ADDITIONAL PROGRAMS/SERVICES

ECFA provides a wide range of services including services to unmarried parents; foster care services; individual and family counseling; community outreach programs.

BRANCH/NETWORK OFFICES

Wisconsin applicants should note that services are provided only to residents of designated counties.
Chicago Office
  127 N. Dearborn St.
  Chicago, IL 60602
  (312) 372–0310
Wisconsin Office
  2401 N. Mayfair Rd.
  Milwaukee, WI 53226
  (414) 476–9550

LICENSE/ACCREDITATION/PROFESSIONAL AFFILIATIONS

Evangelical Child and Family Agency is licensed by the State of Illinois Department of Children and Family Services and by the State of Wisconsin Department of Health and Social Services. The agency is accredited by the Council on Accreditation of Services for Families and Children and is a member of the Child Care Association of Illinois, the Child Welfare League of America, and the United Way of Metropolitan Chicago. The agency is affiliated with the National Association of Evangelicals.

FAMILY CARE SERVICES

234 S. Wabash
Chicago, IL 60604
(312) 427–8790
Program director: Lois Zyks, Supervisor, Foster Care/Adoption

THE PROGRAM

Family Care Services is a nonprofit agency serving residents of Illinois. Placing children in adoptive homes since the 1930s, the agency works directly with birthparents, with other private and public agencies, and with national and regional exchange programs to place both healthy and special-needs children.

THE COST

The agency's fee for adoption services is based on a sliding scale and ranges from $0 to $1,000. Services covered by the fee include all phases of the adoption process, excluding transportation of the child.

THE WAIT

No reliable estimate of the time from application to placement is available.

THE CHILDREN

Family Care Services places both healthy and special-needs children, ranging in age from birth to 18 years, of all racial backgrounds, born in the U.S.

THE REQUIREMENTS

Age: The age requirement is evaluated on a case-by-case basis.
Health: Applicants with health problems or handicaps are given individual consideration. The requirement may vary depending on the needs of the child.
Religion: The requirement varies depending on the religion of the child.
Financial status: The requirement is evaluated on a case-by-case basis.
Marital status: Applicants may be either married or single.
Family size: No requirement.
Racial, ethnic or cultural origin: No requirement, but preference for placing children in families of similar origins.

THE PROCEDURE

Participation in the adoption program of Family Care Services entails the following basic steps:
Inquiry or referral
Orientation meeting
Application
Individual counseling sessions
Homestudy
Placement
Post-placement supervision

ADDITIONAL PROGRAMS/SERVICES

Family Care Services provides counseling, workshops, foster care, and homemaker services.

BRANCH/NETWORK OFFICES

None.

LICENSE/ACCREDITATION/PROFESSIONAL AFFILIATIONS

Family Care Services is licensed by the State of Illinois Department of Children and Family Services and is a member of the Child Welfare League of America.

FAMILY COUNSELING CLINIC, INC.

19300 W. Highway 120
Grayslake, IL 60030
(312) 223–8107
Program director: Sandra Arbit

THE PROGRAM

Family Counseling Clinic is a for-profit agency serving northeastern Illinois and placing from 20 to 40 children annually. Providing adoption services since 1970, the agency's mission is "to provide professional counseling and assistance to women with an unplanned pregnancy and to families wishing to adopt a pre-school age child." Family Counseling Clinic offers several adoption programs including a newborn infant program, a special needs program, an agency-assisted private adoption program, and a program providing homestudy and post-placement supervisory services for families adopting foreign-born children.

THE COST

The agency's fee schedule is as follows:

Newborn Infant Adoption	$2,800
Special-needs adoption	$50–$900
International Adoption:	
Homestudy	$ 850
Post-placement supervision	$ 150–$300
Agency-assisted Private Adoption:	
In-state	$600–$1,750
Interstate, Illinois family	$1,150
Interstate, Illinois birthparents	$1,000

In addition, prospective adoptive parents should anticipate financial responsibility for the medical expenses of the birthmother and child (if newborn) and for legal fees connected with finalization of the adoption.

THE WAIT

The time from application for acceptance into the program to the homecoming of the adoptive child ranges from 6 months to 2 years, depending upon the program.

THE CHILDREN

Family Counseling Clinic places both healthy and special-needs children, ranging in age from birth to 5 years, of all racial backgrounds, born in the U.S. In addition, the agency will facilitate the adoption of foreign-born children.

THE REQUIREMENTS

Age: For newborn infant program, applicants may be no more than 43 years of age. No requirement for other programs.

Health: For newborn infant program, medical exploration of infertility is required. Applicants with health problems or handicaps are given individual consideration.

Religion: No requirement.

Financial status: No requirement.

Marital status: For newborn infant program, applicants must be married and must have been married for at least 4 years. No requirement for other programs.

Family size: For newborn infant program, applicants may have no more than 1 child currently in the family. No requirement for other programs.

Racial, ethnic or cultural origin: No requirement.

THE PROCEDURE

Participation in Family Counseling Clinic's adoption programs entails the following basic steps:
Orientation meeting (newborn infant program only)
Application
Homestudy
Compliance with immigration/naturalization requirements (international adoptions only)
Referral
Placement
Post-placement supervision

ADDITIONAL PROGRAMS/SERVICES

Family Counseling Clinic is also a private mental health clinic providing therapy for individuals, couples, and families.

BRANCH/NETWORK OFFICES

Family Counseling Clinic maintains branch offices in Barrington, Deerfield, and Libertyville. To schedule an appointment at a branch office, call the main office (312–223–8107).

LICENSE/ACCREDITATION/PROFESSIONAL AFFILIATIONS

Family Counseling Clinic, Inc. is licensed by the State of Illinois Department of Children and Family Services. The agency is a member of the Adoption Information Service of Metropolitan Chicago, the Youth Service Network of Lake County, and the north suburban Committee on Pregnant Teens.

FAMILY SERVICE AGENCY

915 Vermont Street
Quincy, IL 62301
(217) 222–8254
Program director: Paula M. Brown, MA, MSW, Executive Director

THE PROGRAM

Family Service Agency, a nonprofit agency serving the state of Illinois (within a 150–175 mile radius of Quincy), provides a range of adoption services and strives to promote "Strength to Families." The agency's adoption programs include infant adoptions; older, sibling and special-needs adoptions; foreign adoptions. Through its infant adoption program, the agency directly places infants with infertile, married couples. Working with a state listing service, the agency places older and special-needs children and sibling groups. Working with several licensed cooperating agencies, the agency facilitates the placement of foreign-born children. Family Service Agency also provides infertility counseling and a peer couple counseling program for adopting couples.

THE COST

Family Service Agency's fee varies depending on the extent of the services requested and may be either a flat fee or a sliding scale fee, depending on which is the least expensive for the applicants. In addition to the agency's fee, prospective adoptive parents should anticipate financial responsibility for the medical and legal expenses of the birthparent and child, legal fees connected with finalization of the adoption, and (in foreign adoptions) cooperating agency fees.

THE WAIT

The time from application for acceptance into the program to the homecoming of the adoptive child varies depending on the program. The average wait for a Caucasian infant is 5 years. Special needs and foreign adoptions, on the other hand, usually entail no wait to initiate the homestudy licensing process.

THE CHILDREN

Family Service Agency directly places Caucasian infants and facilitates the placement of older, special needs, siblings and foreign-born children of all ages and racial backgrounds.

THE REQUIREMENTS

The requirements for the foreign adoption program vary greatly depending on the child's country of origin and the requirements of the cooperating agency. The requirements for infant adoption, too, may vary depending on the preferences of the birthparents.

Age: No requirement, but may vary depending on requirements of cooperating agency. The general guideline is that there should be no more than a 40 year difference between the youngest parent and the child being considered for placement.

Health: Infertility documentation is required for the infant adoption program.

Religion: No requirement, but may vary depending on the requirements of the cooperating agency.

Financial status: Applicants must demonstrate financial stability, must have insurance coverage and a current will.

Marital status: For infant adoption, applicants must be married. Single applicants are accepted for older, special needs, and foreign adoptions.

Family size: For infant adoption, applicants must be childless.

Racial, ethnic or cultural origin: No requirement.

THE PROCEDURE

Participation in Family Service Agency's adoption programs entails the following basic steps:
   Orientation meeting
   Application/submission of state-required fingerprinting
   Homestudy and individual counseling sessions (4–8 months)
   Compliance with immigration/naturalization requirements (foreign adoptions only)
   Placement
   Post-placement supervision

ADDITIONAL PROGRAMS/SERVICES

Family Service Agency provides a wide range of services including a peer couple counseling program for adoptive parents; marriage and family counseling; infertility counseling; biological parents counseling; group counseling for teens and pre-teens; sexual abuse counseling for victims and perpetrators; 24–hour crisis intervention services for teens and their families; short-term foster care for teens; parenting support classes and groups.

BRANCH/NETWORK OFFICES

None.

LICENSE/ACCREDITATION/PROFESSIONAL AFFILIATIONS

Family Service Agency is licensed by the State of Illinois Department of Children and Family Services to provide state, interstate, and intercountry adoption services. Family Service Agency is a member of the United Way, the Illinois Association of Family Service Agencies, and the Illinois Collaboration on Youth.

FAMILY SERVICE CENTER OF SANGAMON COUNTY

1308 S. 7th Street
Springfield, IL 62703
(217) 528–8406
Program director: Lorraine Scott

THE PROGRAM

Family Service Center of Sangamon County is a nonprofit agency serving residents of Sangamon County and placing less than 10 children annually through its adoption program. The agency's primary purpose is "to develop programs which assist low income families to become independent through short-term intervention and child care." Until the mid 1970s, the agency placed a number of healthy Caucasian infants for adoption each year. Since that time, the agency has experienced a steady decline in the availability of such children but continues to serve families who will accept special-needs children. In addition, the agency will provide homestudy and supervisory services for applicants pursuing interagency adoption (domestic or international) or independent adoption.

THE COST

The agency's fee for domestic infant placements is based on a sliding scale and ranges from $3,000 to $6,500. For applicants pursuing special needs, international, or independent adoption, the agency's fee ranges from $300 to $1,000, depending on the type of homestudy. The homestudy includes licensing of the home, post-placement supervision, and court report. Applicants pursuing these options should also anticipate travel expenses, fees to the cooperating agency (if any), and legal fees connected with finalization.

THE WAIT

The time from application to placement varies depending on the program and ranges from 1 year (for international adoptions) to 5 years (for healthy domestic infant adoptions).

THE CHILDREN

Family Service Center places both healthy and special-needs children, ranging in age from birth to school age, of Caucasian and Black racial backgrounds, born in the U.S.

THE REQUIREMENTS

Age: Applicants must be at least 21 years of age.
Health: Applicants should be in reasonably good health.
Religion: No requirement.
Financial status: No requirement.
Marital status: Applicants must be married; the length of the marriage must be at least 2 years.
Family size: No requirement.
Racial, ethnic or cultural origin: Preference for placing children in families of similar origins.

THE PROCEDURE

Participation in the adoption program of Family Service Center entails the following basic steps:
   Initial inquiry
   Orientation meeting
   Application
   Homestudy
   Individual counseling sessions
   Group counseling sessions
   Placement
   Post-placement supervision
   Adoptive parents support group (optional)

ADDITIONAL PROGRAMS/SERVICES

Family Service Center sponsors Adoptive Parents Association (support group) and hosts the Adoption Forum bi-monthly meetings for downstate adoption agencies. The agency also provides counseling services; young parent support services; day care center; foster care homes.

BRANCH/NETWORK OFFICES

None.

LICENSE/ACCREDITATION/PROFESSIONAL AFFILIATIONS

Family Service Center of Sangamon County is licensed by the State of Illinois Department of Children and Family Services and is a member of Family Service America.

FAMILY SERVICE OF DECATUR

151 East Decatur
Lower Level East
Decatur, IL 62521(217) 429–5216
Program director: Becky White

THE PROGRAM

Family Service of Decatur is a nonprofit agency serving the counties of Macon, Moultrie, Christian, Shelby, Piatt, Logan and DeWitt and placing approximately 13 children annually. The agency sponsors several adoption programs, including infant adoptions, special-needs adoptions, and foreign adoptions. Providing pregnancy counseling services and medical assistance to relinquishing and non-relinquishing birthparents, the agency places infants for adoption when birthparents in the agency's counseling program decide that the best interests of the child will be served by adoptive placement. However, the agency's focus has increasingly been the placement of special-needs children who are in the custody of the Illinois Department of Children and Family Service. Family Service of Decatur received an award in 1986 for outstanding work in finding homes for children with special needs. The agency extended its services in 1986 to include placement of foreign-born children through an agreement with Adoption World, an agency in Chicago which facilitates placement of children from South America.

THE COST

The agency's fee for adoption services varies depending on the program. The agency does not charge a fee for special-needs adoptions. For infant adoptions, the fee is 8% of the applicant's annual gross income. In addition, applicants interested in pursuing infant adoption should anticipate financial responsibility for medical expenses of the birthmother and child, with the total cost of an infant adoption ranging from $2,000 to $5,000. For foreign adoptions, the total cost ranges from $5,000 to $10,000. For all programs, applicants assume responsibility for legal fees connected with finalization of the adoption.

THE WAIT

The time from application for acceptance into the program to the homecoming of the adoptive child varies depending on the program. For infant adoptions, applicants should anticipate a wait ranging from 8 to 10 years. For foreign adoptions, the wait ranges from 12 to 15 months. There is no wait for special needs placements.

THE CHILDREN

Family Service of Decatur places both healthy and special-needs children, ranging in age from birth to adolescence, of Caucasian, Black, Hispanic, and bi-racial backgrounds. Countries of origin include U.S., South America, Korea, and Hong Kong.

THE REQUIREMENTS

Age: The age requirement is determined on an individual basis.
Health: Applicants must be in reasonably good health.
Religion: No requirement.
Financial status: Applicants must demonstrate financial stability.
Marital status: No requirement.
Family size: No requirement.
Racial, ethnic or cultural origin: No requirement.

THE PROCEDURE

Participation in Family Service of Decatur's adoption programs entails the following basic steps:
Orientation meeting
Application
Licensing (as required by Dept. of Children and Family Services)
Homestudy
Group and individual counseling sessions
Compliance with immigration/naturalization requirements (foreign adoptions only)
Referral
Placement
Post-placement supervision

ADDITIONAL PROGRAMS/SERVICES

Family Service of Decatur provides individual, marital, and family counseling; problem pregnancy counseling; community education programs; pre-school program (Self Start); senior citizens program.

BRANCH/NETWORK OFFICES

None.

LICENSE/ACCREDITATION/PROFESSIONAL AFFILIATIONS

Family Service of Decatur is licensed by the State of Illinois Department of Children and Family Services.

JEWISH CHILDREN'S BUREAU OF CHICAGO

One South Franklin Street
Chicago, IL 60606
(312) 346–6700
Program director: Lois K. Samuels, CSW, ACSW

THE PROGRAM

Jewish Children's Bureau is a nonprofit child-caring agency serving metropolitan Chicago. Founded in 1893 as the Chicago Home for Jewish Orphans, the agency has evolved in response to the changing needs of the community and today provides a wide range of services to families and children. Through its adoption program, the agency provides services for applicants pursuing traditional and identified adoptions. A traditional adoption involves the matching of an infant who has been surrendered to the agency with a couple whose homestudy has been approved by the agency. In an identified adoption, the applicants locate a specific pregnant woman who is willing to specify the adoption of her child by those parents.

THE COST

In the agency's traditional adoption program, fees are paid by the adoptive couple on a sliding scale according to income, ranging from $2,860 to $5,200. In identified adoptions, the prospective adoptive parents are obligated to pay fees covering the total costs of services to themselves, the child, and the birthparents. The homestudy fee is $760; the fee for placement and post-placement services is $1,000. Additional costs vary with each situation and may include fees for foster care, medical expenses, counseling, traveling, etc. Legal fees connected with finalization are handled directly between the adoptive parents and their attorney.

THE WAIT

The time from application to the homecoming of the adoptive child varies depending on the program. For a traditional adoption, the wait ranges from 1 to 3 years. For an identified adoption, the wait varies depending on the applicants' degree of assertiveness.

THE CHILDREN

Most children placed by Jewish Children's Bureau are healthy, Caucasian infants, born in the U.S. However, children of other races are also available, and JCB will facilitate the adoption of healthy or special-needs children of all races and ages.

THE REQUIREMENTS

The following are the requirements for JCB's traditional and identified adoption programs. The requirements for special-needs adoption are flexible and are evaluated on a case-by-case basis.

Age: For traditional adoption, applicants must be under 40 at the time of application. For identified adoption, one spouse must be under 45 years of age.

Health: Applicants must be in good health. For traditional adoption, applicants must have initiated medical diagnosis and/or treatment of their infertility.

Religion: For traditional adoption, the couple must both be Jewish. For identified adoption, one spouse must be Jewish. The couple must make a commitment to raise the child as a Jew.

Financial status: For traditional adoption, applicants must have an annual income of at least $16,000 (based on husband's income). For identified adoption, applicants must have sufficient income to cover the costs of raising a child.

Residence: Applicants must be Illinois residents or reside in the area served by the Jewish Federation of Northwest Indiana.

Marital status: Applicants must be married. The length of the marriage must be at least 3 years.

Family size: For traditional adoption, applicants must be childless. For identified adoption, applicants may have other children.

Racial, ethnic or cultural origin: No requirement.

THE PROCEDURE

Participation in the adoption program of Jewish Children's Bureau entails the following basic steps:

Orientation meeting

Application
Homestudy
Placement
Post-placement supervision

ADDITIONAL PROGRAMS/SERVICES

JCB provides a wide range of services including individual, family, and group counseling; single adolescent parent services; foster care services; residential treatment programs; therapeutic school services; in-home counseling services; information and referral services; pre-adoption services; post-placement services.

BRANCH/NETWORK OFFICES

The following branch offices offer all JCB programs. The adoption program is headquartered at the One South Franklin office.

North Side Office
2800 W. Peterson
Chicago, IL 60659
(312) 761–7404

North Suburban Office
601 Skokie Blvd.
Northbrook, IL 60062
(312) 498–4202

Northwest Suburban Office
1250 Radcliffe Rd.
Buffalo Grove, IL 60089
(312) 255–9585

Skokie Office
5050 Church St.
Skokie, IL 60077
(312) 673–3004

South Suburban Office
3649 W. 183rd St.
Hazel Crest, IL 60429
(312) 798–1859

LICENSE/ACCREDITATION/PROFESSIONAL AFFILIATIONS

Jewish Children's Bureau of Chicago is licensed by the State of Illinois Department of Children and Family Services and is accredited by the Council on Accreditation of Services for Families and Children. The agency is affiliated with the Child Welfare League of America, the Child Care Association of Illinois, the Illinois Foster Parent Association, the National Council of Jewish Communal Services, and the American Association of Children's Residential Centers.

LDS SOCIAL SERVICES

1813 Mill Street, Suite H
Naperville, IL 60540
(312) 396–0486
Program director: G. Kem Nixon

THE PROGRAM

For a full description of programs and services, refer to Utah listing:

LDS Social Services
50 East North Temple Street
Salt Lake City, UT 84150

LUTHERAN CHILD AND FAMILY SERVICES OF ILLINOIS

P.O. Box 78
7620 W. Madison Street
River Forest, IL 60305(312) 771–7180
Program director: LaNell S. Hill

THE PROGRAM

Lutheran Child and Family Services (LC&FS) is a non-profit agency serving the state of Illinois and placing 70–80 children annually. LC&FS began in 1873 as an orphanage for German Lutheran children and has evolved through the years in response to the changing needs of the community. The agency's mission, "as a witness to the Gospel of Jesus Christ and as a ministry of the Lutheran Church, is to serve people in need and to provide social services to Lutherans in cooperation with pastors and congregations of the Church." Providing adoption services on a non-sectarian basis, the agency offers two adoption programs. The first is a program for the adoption of Black infants; the second is a program for the adoption of Caucasian, Hispanic, U.S.-born Asian, and bi-racial infants.

THE COST

The agency fee varies depending on the program. For the adoption of a Black infant, the agency's fee is based on a sliding scale, with the cost ranging between $200 and $1,000. For the adoption of other minority or Caucasian infants, the agency's fee is 7% of the applicants' annual gross income, plus a medical fee (approximately $2,000), with a maximum fee of $5,000. The average fee for the second program is $4,500. Services covered by the fee include homestudy, foster care licensing, placement, and post- placement supervision. In addition, prospective adoptive parents should anticipate financial responsibility for legal fees connected with finalization of the adoption (on the average, between $550 and $600).

THE WAIT

The time from acceptance into the program to the homecoming of the adoptive child varies depending on the program and the type of child the applicants wish to adopt. The average wait for a male Black infant is less than 6 months. The average wait for a female Black infant is 6 to 12 months. The average wait for other minority or Caucasian infants is 6 to 12 months.

THE CHILDREN

LC&FS places healthy children, ranging in age from birth to 2 years, of Black, Caucasian, Hispanic, Asian, and bi-racial backgrounds. LC&FS children are born in the U.S.

THE REQUIREMENTS

Age: For the adoption of a Black infant, married applicants must be at least 21 and single applicants must be at least 27.

For the adoption of other minority or Caucasian infant, applicants must be at least 21 and no more than 40 years of age.

Health: For both programs, infertility resolution is required; applicants may not be still actively involved in fertility testing or trying to become pregnant. Applicants with health problems or handicaps are given individual consideration.

Religion: For the adoption of a Black infant, no requirement but birthmother's preferences are honored. For the adoption of other minority or Caucasian infant, applicants must be practicing Christians.

Financial status: Applicants may not be on Public Aid. Applicants must demonstrate financial stability and capacity to support a child.

Marital status: For the adoption of a Black infant, applicants may be married or single. For other minority or Caucasian infant adoption, applicants must be married. In both programs, married applicants must have been married for at least 2 years.

Family size: No requirement for the adoption of a Black infant. For other minority or Caucasian infant adoption, applicants may have no more than 1 child currently in the family.

Racial, ethnic or cultural origin: Preference for placing children in families of similar origins. Preference of the birthparents is honored.

THE PROCEDURE

Participation in LC&FS' adoption programs entails the following basic steps:

Black Infant Program
Application
Individual counseling
Homestudy
Placement
Post-placement supervision

Other Minority & Caucasian Infant Program
Application
Intake interview
Group sessions
Individual counseling sessions
Homestudy
Placement
Post-placement supervision

ADDITIONAL PROGRAMS/SERVICES

LC&FS provides infant foster care; post-legalized adoption services including counseling and search. In addition, LC&FS will provide homestudy and foster care licensing services for families who have identified a specific child or source (in-state, out-of- state, or international) subject to State approval of the integrity of the source. The average fee for homestudy, foster care licensing, and post- placement services is $1,000.

BRANCH/NETWORK OFFICES

2408 Lebanon Avenue
Belleville, IL 62221
(618) 234–8904

220 E. Cook Street
Springfield, IL 62704
(217) 544-4631

LICENSE/ACCREDITATION/PROFESSIONAL AFFILIATIONS

Lutheran Child and Family Services is licensed by the State of Illinois Department of Children and Family Services, is accredited by the Council on Accreditation of Services for Families and Children, and is a member of the Child Welfare League of America.

ST. MARY'S SERVICES

5725 North Kenmore Avenue
Chicago, IL 60660-4598
(312) 561-5288
Program director: Adrienne D. Kraft, ACSW, CSW
Hours: Monday and Thursday, 9:00 A.M.-Noon Only

THE PROGRAM

St. Mary's Services is a nonprofit specialized child welfare agency serving Cook, Lake and DuPage Counties and the Episcopal Diocese of Chicago, IL. Established in 1894 and affiliated with the Episcopal Sisters of St. Mary, the agency provides maternity counseling services to birthparents who are considering adoptive placement of their unborn child and adoption services to families seeking to adopt a child. The agency's mission is "to provide new beginnings for newborn infants of all races, their birthmothers, and adoptive parents."

THE COST

The agency's fee for adoption services is based on a sliding scale and ranges from $4,000 to $12,000. In addition, prospective adoptive parents should anticipate financial responsibility for legal fees connected with finalization of the adoption.

THE WAIT

The time from application for acceptance into the program to the homecoming of the adoptive child ranges from 2 to 9 months.

THE CHILDREN

St. Mary's Services places healthy infants of all racial backgrounds, born in the U.S.

THE REQUIREMENTS

Age: Applicants may be no more than 39 years of age.
Health: Applicants must be in excellent health. Infertility documentation is required.
Religion: Applicants must be practicing members of a Christian religion. Priority is given to Episcopal couples.
Financial status: Applicants must own their own home and must be financially secure.
Marital status: Applicants must be married couples, and the length of the marriage must be at least 3 years.
Family size: Applicants may have no more than 1 child currently in the family, and the child must be over the age of 3.

Racial, ethnic or cultural origin: No requirement.

THE PROCEDURE

Participation in St. Mary's Services' adoption program entails the following basic steps:
Intake telephone eligibility interview
Submission of infertility documentation (MD report)
Submission of autobiographical letters by both spouses
Pre-application meeting
Application and homestudy with licensing
Educational preparation
Placement
Post-placement supportive services

ADDITIONAL PROGRAMS/SERVICES

In addition to maternity counseling services and adoption services, St. Mary's Services provides clinical diagnostic evaluations and therapy for children from birth to eleven years of age; case consultation and educational services to professionals who work with children; group homes for pregnant women both under and over the age of 18.

BRANCH/NETWORK OFFICES

717 W. Kirchoff Rd.
Arlington Heights, IL 60005
(312) 870-8181
St. Helena's Church
7600 S. Wolf Rd.
Burr Ridge, IL 60525
(312) 246-5012
210 McHenry Ave.
Crystal Lake, IL 60014
(815) 459-1009
5725 N. Kenmore
Chicago, IL 60660]
(312) 561-5288

LICENSE/ACCREDITATION/PROFESSIONAL AFFILIATIONS

St. Mary's Services is licensed by the Illinois Department of Children and Family Services. St. Mary's Services is affiliated with the Episcopal Sisters of St. Mary, The Episcopal Charities, United Way, The American Association of Psychiatric Services for Children, International Association for Pediatric Social Services, National Committee For Adoption, Alternatives to Abortion, International. The agency is endorsed by the Chicago Association of Commerce and Industry.

SUNNY RIDGE FAMILY CENTER

Address: 2 S 426 Orchard Road
Wheaton, IL 60187
(312) 668-5117
Program director: Larry G. Betts, President

THE PROGRAM

Sunny Ridge Family Center is a nonprofit multi-service child and family agency serving residents of Illinois, Indiana,

Wisconsin, and Michigan. Established in 1926 as a home for needy children, the agency has responded to the changing needs of the community and today provides a variety of family-focused services to a large number of individuals and families. Between 1978 and 1983, the agency developed programs in the areas of adoption, family life education, outpatient counseling, and services to unmarried parents to complement the residential and foster care services it has provided throughout its history. Recently, the agency assumed responsibility for a major new program, HEAL THE CHILDREN (see "Additional Programs"). The agency's mission is "to provide care and shelter for children through...residential treatment, specialized medical services, foster care and adoption services" and "to provide treatment and preventative services aimed at strengthening and enhancing the functioning of individuals and families."

The agency provides services for birthparents and places infants for adoption when birthparents in the agency's counseling program elect adoptive placement as the best plan for their child. Through its domestic program, the agency places approximately 60–80 children each year. The agency also facilitates intercountry, interstate, and identified adoptions (approximately 60–80 each year) through the provision of homestudy and supervisory services. Since its inception, the intercountry program has facilitated the adoption of several hundred children from 19 different countries around the world.

THE COST

The agency's fee for the domestic program is $7,500. Services covered by the fee include all phases of the adoption process (homestudy through post-placement services), excluding legal fees connected with finalization if the adoption. Services to birthparents (medical and counseling) as well as the medical expenses of the child are included in the fee.

For applicants pursuing intercountry, interstate, or identified adoptions, the agency's fee for homestudy is $1,250 and for post-placement supervision, $600. Applicants pursuing intercountry adoption should also anticipate additional costs related to travel and fees to the placing agency.

THE WAIT

Sunny Ridge does not maintain a waiting list in the traditional sense of the term. The agency maintains approximately 300 active applicants on file. Families are chosen to match the criteria established by the birthparents and the agency. After a homestudy has been completed, placement usually occurs within 1 year. Families with fewer restrictions on the type of child they will accept (race, age, nationality, handicap) increase their chances of a placement. For intercountry, interstate, and identified adoptions, the wait varies depending on factors beyond the agency's control.

THE CHILDREN

Sunny Ridge directly places both healthy and special-needs children, ranging in age from infancy to 3 years, of Caucasian, Hispanic, Black, and bi-racial backgrounds. The agency also facilitates intercountry, interstate, and identified adoptions of children of any age, race, or country of origin.

THE REQUIREMENTS

Age: For the domestic program, applicants may have a combined age of no more than 80 years. The requirement varies for intercountry program.

Health: Applicants must be in reasonably good health. Applicants with health problems or handicaps are given individual consideration. For the domestic program, infertility documentation is required.

Religion: The requirement varies depending on the program. For the domestic program, applicants must demonstrate a personal commitment to the tenets of the Christian faith unless a religion other than Christian religion is requested by the birthparents. For interstate, the preferences of the birthparents are honored. For intercountry, the requirement varies depending on the requirements of the placing agency.

Financial status: Applicants must be financially independent.

Marital status: No requirement.

Family size: No requirement for intercountry or minority placements. For domestic program, applicants may have no more than 1 child currently in the family.

Racial, ethnic or cultural origin: No requirement, but preference for placing children in families of similar origins.

THE PROCEDURE

Participation in Sunny Ridge Family Center's adoption program entails the following basic steps:

Domestic Program
    Application
    Orientation (by invitation only)
    Individual counseling sessions
    Personality Inventory Test
    Group counseling sessions
    Homestudy
    Preparation of profile
    Placement
    Post-placement supervision

Intercountry Program
    Application
    Orientation (open to all)
    Individual counseling sessions
    Group counseling sessions
    Homestudy
    Preparation of profile
    Referral
    Compliance with immigration/naturalization requirements
    Placement (by placing agency)
    Post-placement supervision

ADDITIONAL PROGRAMS/SERVICES

Sunny Ridge Family Center provides services to birthparents (foster care; prenatal classes, counseling); out-patient counseling program; family life education seminars; consultation services to churches, schools, and community groups; residential and foster care services. In addition, Sunny Ridge Family Center has recently assumed responsibility for HEAL THE CHILDREN, a specialized foster care program for children from all over the world with life-threatening conditions who are coming to the U.S. for advanced medical treatment.

Branch/Network Offices

Illinois
Temple Baptist Church
3215 E. State St.
Rockford, IL 61108
(815) 399-2665

Wisconsin
c/o Bethel Baptist Church
1601 Libal
Green Bay, WI 54301
(414) 437-4437

Indiana
9105-A Indianapolis Blvd., Suite 301
Highland, IN 46322
(219) 838-6611

Michigan
Fairview Professional Bldg.
5675 Fairview Ave.
Stevensville, MI 49127
(616) 429-2757

License/Accreditation/ Professional Affiliations

Sunny Ridge Family Center is licensed by the appropriate state department in Illinois, Indiana, Wisconsin, and Michigan. The agency is affiliated with the National Association of Homes for Children and endorsed by the Baptist General Conference.

Indiana

PUBLIC ADOPTION PROGRAM/ COMMUNITY RESOURCES

Department of Public Welfare
Child Welfare-Social Services Division
141 South Meridian Street
Indianapolis, IN 46225
(317) 232–4444
Adoption specialist: Ruth Lambert, Adoption Consultant

THE PROGRAM

Public adoption services in Indiana are provided by the Department of Public Welfare, Child Welfare-Social Services Division through county offices. DPW recruits and prepares adoptive families and supervises the placement of special-needs children (older, minority, and handicapped children and sibling groups) who are in the custody of the State of Indiana.

STATE EXCHANGE

Indiana Adoption Resource Exchange. For information, contact the Child Welfare-Social Services Division (above).

STATE ADOPTION REUNION REGISTRY

Indiana State Board of Health
330 W. Michigan Street
Indianapolis, IN 46202
(317) 633–0274

STATE SUBSIDY

IV-E Adoption Assistance
Indiana State Department of Public Welfare
141 S. Meridian St., 6th Fl.
Indianapolis, IN 46225
(317) 232–4432
Director: Ann Fuller, Consultant

NACAC REPRESENTATIVE

Jeanine Jones
5320 Far Hall Road
Indianapolis, IN 46226
(317) 542–1256

GENERAL ADOPTION RESOURCES

ARC
P.O. Box 509
Notre Dame, IN 46556

Adoptive Families Together
1862 W. 60th St.
Indianapolis, IN 46208

ARC
3223 Bass Road
Ft. Wayne, IN 46808

COAC of Lafayette
1021 Holly Drive
Lafayette, IN 47905

Rainbow Families of OURS
61529 C.R. 127
Goshen, IN 46526

COAC of Grant County
503 East Washington Street
Fairmount, IN 46928

Families Adopting Children Today
819 North Rensselaer
Griffith, IN 46319

Adoptive Parents Together
3624 Grand
Connersville, IN 47331

Families United OUR Way
6114 O'Hara Drive]
Evansville, IN

Adoptive Parents Together
3312 Ivory Way
Indianapolis, IN 46227

Black Adoption Committee
P.O. Box 1221
Indianapolis, IN 46204

SPECIAL-NEEDS ADOPTION RESOURCES

Bonnie Henson, Liaison
Aask Midwest
Elaine P. Walters, Coordinator
P.O. Box 402
(317) 984–3128

Indiana One Church, One Child
850 N. Meridian St.
Cicero, IN 46034
Indianapolis, IN 46204
(317) 637–2553

OUT-OF-STATE AGENCIES

AGENCY

Smithlawn Maternity Home, Texas (special-needs and minority placement)

SEE APPENDIX A

Agencies Providing Nationwide Services

ADOPTION RESOURCE SERVICES, INC.

724 W. Bristol Street
Elkhart, IN 46514
(219) 262–2499
Program director: Greg R. Immel, ACSW

THE PROGRAM

Adoption Resource Services is a nonprofit non-sectarian agency providing statewide services and placing approximately 11 children annually. Incorporated in 1985, the agency's focus is to provide services to birthmothers. Services are provided at no cost to the birthmother and are not contingent upon her relinquishing her child for adoption. The agency recognizes "that each young woman who is experiencing an unwanted pregnancy is in a state of personal crisis" and is "committed to helping her achieve a positive resolution to that crisis."

THE COST

The agency's fee for adoption services is $14,950. Services covered by the fee include all phases of the adoption process (pre-adoptive counseling through finalization).

THE WAIT

The time from application for acceptance into the program to the homecoming of the adoptive child averages 5 months.

THE CHILDREN

Adoption Resource Services places healthy Caucasian children, ranging in age from birth to 2 years, born in the U.S.

THE REQUIREMENTS

Age: Applicants must be at least 28 years of age.
Health: Applicants must be in reasonably good health.
Religion: No requirement.
Financial status: Applicants must have an adequate income to provide for a child's needs.
Marital status: Applicants must be married couples who have been married for at least 3 years.
Family size: No requirement.
Racial, ethnic or cultural origin: No requirement.

THE PROCEDURE

Participation in Adoption Resource Services' program entails the following basic steps:
Referral
Application
Initial interview
Submission of autobiographical information, letters of reference, and required documents
Homestudy
Placement
Post-placement supervision
Finalization

ADDITIONAL PROGRAMS/SERVICES

Adoption Resource Services provides foster care services, boarding care for birthmothers, counseling services for birthparents and their families, and community education programs.

BRANCH/NETWORK OFFICES

None.

LICENSE/ACCREDITATION/PROFESSIONAL AFFILIATIONS

Adoption Resource Services, Inc. is licensed by the State of Indiana Department of Public Welfare.

BETHANY CHRISTIAN SERVICES

9595 Whitley Drive, Suite 210
Indianapolis, IN 46240
(317) 848–9518

Program director: James K. Haveman, Jr.—Executive Director

THE PROGRAM

For a full description of programs and services, refer to Michigan listing:
Bethany Christian Services
901 Eastern Avenue, N.E.
Grand Rapids, MI 49503–1295
(616) 459–6273

BRANCH OFFICES

Bethany Christian Services/Indiana:
7895 Broadway, Suite J-1
Merrillville, IN 46410–5529
(219) 769–0211

CATHOLIC CHARITIES BUREAU OF THE DIOCESE OF EVANSVILLE

603 Court Building
Evansville, IN 47708
(812) 423–5456
Program director: Richard C. Rust, Executive Director

THE PROGRAM

Catholic Charities Bureau is a nonprofit agency serving residents of the Diocese of Evansville (12 county area in southwestern Indiana). The agency's mission is "to improve human social conditions for all persons in Southwestern Indiana" through direct provision of comprehensive social work services, educational services, and support services. The agency provides services to birthparents and places infants for adoption when birthparents in the agency's program elect adoptive placement as the best plan for their child. The agency works cooperatively with private and public agencies and with national and regional exchange programs to facilitate the placement of special-needs children. In addition, the agency will provide homestudy and supervisory services for applicants pursuing interagency adoption (domestic or international) or independent adoption.

THE COST

The agency's fee for adoption services is 8% of the applicants' previous year's income, not to exceed $1,700. Services covered by the fee include the homestudy and post-placement supervision for 1 year. In addition, applicants assume responsibility for legal fees connected with finalization of the adoption.

THE WAIT

For infant adoptions, the time from application to placement ranges from 5 to 7 1/2 years. For special-needs adoptions, the time from approval of the homestudy to placement varies depending on the availability of children eligible for adoption through the Indiana Adoption Resource Exchange and on the type of child the family feels they can cope with financially, psychologically, and emotionally.

THE CHILDREN

Catholic Charities Bureau places both healthy and special-needs children, ranging in age from birth to 18 years, of all racial backgrounds, born in the U.S.

THE REQUIREMENTS

Age: Applicants must be at least 24 years of age.
Health: Infertility documentation is required for infant adoptions.
Religion: No requirement for special-needs adoptions. For infant adoptions, at least one spouse must be a practicing member of the Roman Catholic Church.
Financial status: No requirement.
Marital status: For infant adoptions, applicants must be married, and the length of the marriage must be at least 3 years. Single applicants are considered for special-needs adoptions.
Family size: No requirement for special-needs adoptions. For infant adoptions, applicants may have no more than 1 child currently in the family.
Racial, ethnic or cultural origin: Preference for placing children in families of similar origins.

THE PROCEDURE

Participation in the adoption program of Catholic Charities Bureau entails the following basic steps:
Referral
Orientation meeting
Application
Homestudy
Adoption education group meetings
Placement
Post-placement supervision

ADDITIONAL PROGRAMS/SERVICES

Catholic Charities Bureau provides pregnancy counseling, foster care, family/individual counseling, pre-marriage/marriage counseling.

BRANCH/NETWORK OFFICES

None.

LICENSE/ACCREDITATION/PROFESSIONAL AFFILIATIONS

Catholic Charities Bureau of the Diocese of Evansville is licensed by the State of Indiana Department of Public Welfare and is accredited by the Council on Accreditation of Services for Families and Children. The agency is affiliated with Catholic Charities USA.

CATHOLIC SOCIAL SERVICES

919 Fairfield Avenue
Fort Wayne, IN 46802
(219) 422-7511
Program director: Karen Crosley, MS

THE PROGRAM

Catholic Social Services is a nonprofit agency which places approximately 22 children annually and serves resi-dents of the following counties: Allen, Adams, Dekalb, Huntington, Noble, Steuben, Wells, Wabash, and Whitley. Catholic Social Services is a full service adoption agency providing unplanned pregnancy counseling, infant adoption, older child adoption, counseling services for adoptive and birth families (pre- and post-adoption), outreach, and advocacy. In addition, the agency will provide homestudy and supervisory services for applicants pursuing either private adoption or international adoption through a licensed U.S. agency which maintains an international program.

THE COST

The agency's fee schedule is as follows:

Application for adoption waiting list	$25
Group series	$ 90
Adoption study	$ 375
Placement fee (sliding scale)	
Minimum fee	$1,300
Maximum fee	$5,200
Placement outside of Allen County	$ 100
Interstate Compact fee (if applicable)	$ 100

Placement fees may be waived for minority placements. Services covered by the fee include all phases of the adoption process and services to the birthmother and child, excluding legal fees connected with finalization of the adoption.

THE WAIT

The time from application to the homecoming of the adoptive child averages 4 to 5 years.

THE CHILDREN

Catholic Social Services places both healthy and special-needs children, ranging in age from infancy to adolescence, of all racial backgrounds, born in the U.S.

THE REQUIREMENTS

Age: Applicants must be at least 21 years of age.
Health: Applicants with health problems or handicaps are given individual consideration. Infertility documentation is required.
Religion: No requirement.
Financial status: No requirement other than the ability to provide adequately for an additional family member.
Marital status: For healthy Caucasian infant adoption, applicants must be married, and the length of the marriage must be at least 5 years. Single applicants are considered for special-needs children and minority infants.
Family size: Applicants must either be childless or have no more than 1 child currently in the home.
Racial, ethnic or cultural origin: Preference for placing children in families of similar origins.

THE PROCEDURE

Participation in the adoption program of Catholic Social Service entails the following basic steps:
Orientation meeting
Application
Group counseling sessions
Homestudy
Placement
Post-placement supervision
Post-placement services

ADDITIONAL PROGRAMS/SERVICES

Catholic Social Service provides foster care and counseling on demand for adoptive families and birth families. The agency co-sponsors Adoption Forum (held every other year).

BRANCH/NETWORK OFFICES

None.

LICENSE/ACCREDITATION/PROFESSIONAL AFFILIATIONS

Catholic Social Service is licensed by the State of Indiana Department of Public Welfare.

CATHOLIC SOCIAL SERVICE

120 South Taylor Street
South Bend, IN 46601
(219) 234–3111
Program director: William T. Brechenser

THE PROGRAM

Catholic Social Services is a nonprofit agency serving residents of St. Joseph County, Indiana and placing approximately 15–20 Caucasian infants and 5–7 special-needs children annually. Providing services to the local community since 1947, the agency's mission is "to help childless couples to have a family and to help provide homes for waiting and special-needs children," with the welfare of the child as the primary concern. The agency provides services to unwed mothers or women with a problem pregnancy and places infants for adoption when birthmothers in the agency's counseling program elect adoptive placement as the best plan for their children.

THE COST

The agency's fee for adoption services is based on a sliding scale and ranges from $1,000 to $4,500. Services covered by the fee include all phases of the adoption process (homestudy, adoptive parents education program, placement, and supervision), excluding legal fees connected with finalization of the adoption. Fees also help to underwrite the cost of services to the birthmother and child.

THE WAIT

The time from application for acceptance into the program to the homecoming of the adoptive child averages 4 years.

THE CHILDREN

Catholic Social Service places healthy infants ranging in age from 1 week to 4 months and special-needs children ranging in age from infancy to adolescence. The children are of Caucasian and Black racial backgrounds, born in the U.S.

THE REQUIREMENTS

Age: For Caucasian infant adoption, applicants must be at least 21 and no more than 38 years of age. For special-needs adoption, the requirement is flexible.
Health: Applicants must be in reasonably good health. Applicants with health problems or handicaps are given individual consideration. Infertility documentation is required for Caucasian infant adoptions.
Religion: No requirement, but if Catholic, applicants must be practicing members of their parish.
Financial status: Applicants are evaluated individually on the basis of their ability to provide adequately for an additional family member.
Marital status: For Caucasian infant adoption, applicants must be married couples who have been married for at least 3 years. Single applicants are considered for special-needs adoption.
Family size: For Caucasian infant adoption, applicants may have no more than 1 child currently in the family.
Racial, ethnic or cultural origin: No requirement.

THE PROCEDURE

Participation in Catholic Social Service's adoption program entails the following basic steps:
Intake interview
Application
Adoptive Parent Education Program
Homestudy
Approval by adoption committee
Placement
Post-placement supervision
Finalization

ADDITIONAL PROGRAMS/SERVICES

Catholic Social Service provides family counseling services.

BRANCH/NETWORK OFFICES

None.

LICENSE/ACCREDITATION/PROFESSIONAL AFFILIATIONS

Catholic Social Service is licensed by the State of Indiana Department of Public Welfare.

CHILDPLACE

2420 Highway 62
Jeffersonville, IN 47130
(812) 282–8248 (502)
3248 Taylor Blvd.
Louisville, KY 40215
363–1633
Program director: Jo Len Janes, Director of Child Placement; Ken Samuel, Executive Director

THE PROGRAM

Childplace is a nonprofit agency serving Church of Christ families in Kentucky and Indiana and placing approximately 10–15 children annually. Initiated as a foster care agency in Indiana in 1967, the agency expanded to include adoption services in Indiana in 1979 and foster care and adoption services in Kentucky in 1980. The agency provides services to birthparents and places infants for adoption when birthparents in the agency's counseling program elect adoptive placement as the best plan for their child. Working cooperatively with national and regional exchange programs, the agency also places older and special-needs children. In addition, the agency will provide homestudy and supervisory services for applicants pursuing inter- agency adoption. The agency's mission is "to provide adoptive homes for children who are legally free for adoption, to serve the best interests of the child, and to work cooperatively with other agencies to ensure permanency for the children."

THE COST

The agency's fee for adoption services is based on a sliding scale and varies depending on the actual expenses incurred by the birthmother and child. The average fee is $7,500. Services covered by the fee include all phases of the adoption process, excluding legal fees connected with finalization of the adoption.

THE WAIT

The time from application to the homecoming of the adoptive child averages 3 to 4 years.

THE CHILDREN

Childplace places both healthy and special-needs children (primarily infants but some older children as well), of Caucasian, Black, and bi-racial backgrounds, born in the U.S.

THE REQUIREMENTS

Age: Applicants must be at least 21 years old and at least 1 of the couple may be no more than 40 years old.
Health: Applicants should be in reasonably good health. Applicants with health problems or handicaps are given individual consideration. Infertility documentation is requested.
Religion: Applicants must be practicing members of a Church of Christ.
Financial status: No requirement.
Marital status: Applicants must be married couples who have been married for at least 3 years.
Family size: For infant adoption, applicants may have no more than 2 children currently in the family. No requirement for older child adoption.
Racial, ethnic or cultural origin: Preference (though not a requirement) for placing children in families of similar origins.

THE PROCEDURE

Participation in the Childplace adoption program entails the following basic steps:
Letter of inquiry or referral
Group orientation meeting
Application
Homestudy
Individual counseling sessions (as necessary)
Placement
Post-placement supervision (6 months)

ADDITIONAL PROGRAMS/SERVICES

Childplace provides foster care services, maternity home care, and counseling services.

BRANCH/NETWORK OFFICES

3248 Taylor Blvd.
Louisville, KY 40215
(502) 363–1633

LICENSE/ACCREDITATION/PROFESSIONAL AFFILIATIONS

Childplace is licensed by the State of Indiana Department of Public Welfare and by the State of Kentucky Cabinet for Human Resources. The agency is a member of the National Committee for Adoption.

CHILDREN'S BUREAU OF INDIANAPOLIS, INC.

615 North Alabama, Room 426
Indianapolis, IN 46204
(317) 634–6481
Program director: Janet Myers, ACSW

THE PROGRAM

Children's Bureau of Indianapolis is a nonprofit agency serving residents of Marion County and 8 surrounding counties and placing approximately 50 children annually through its adoption program. Founded in 1852, the agency has evolved in response to the changing needs of the community, focusing today on recruiting families for children with special needs, with special emphasis on Black children. Working directly with birthparents, with other private and public agencies, and with national and regional exchange programs, the agency places Black infants and older children of all racial backgrounds with special needs.

THE COST

As of October 1988, the agency's fee for adoption services is based on a sliding scale and ranges from no fee to $500. Services covered by the fee include all phases of the adoption process.

THE WAIT

The time from application to placement averages 6 to 9 months.

THE CHILDREN

Children's Bureau places both healthy and special-needs children, with Caucasian children ranging in age from 2 to 16 years and Black children ranging from birth to 16 years.

THE REQUIREMENTS

Age: No requirement.
Health: Applicants must be in reasonably good health. Applicants with health problems of handicaps are given individual consideration.
Religion: No requirement.
Financial status: Applicants must have sufficient income to provide for the needs of the family.
Marital status: Applicants may be single or married. If married, the length of the marriage must be at least 2 years.

Family size: No requirement.

Racial, ethnic or cultural origin: Preference for placing children in families of similar origins.

THE PROCEDURE

Participation in the adoption program of the Children's Bureau entails the following basic steps:
Orientation meeting
Application
Group counseling sessions
Individual counseling sessions
Homestudy
Referral
Placement
Post-placement supervision

ADDITIONAL PROGRAMS/SERVICES

Children's Bureau of Indianapolis co-sponsors an adoptive parents' support group and provides counseling services.

BRANCH/NETWORK OFFICES

None.

LICENSE/ACCREDITATION/PROFESSIONAL AFFILIATIONS

Children's Bureau of Indianapolis, Inc. is licensed by the State of Indiana Department of Public Welfare and is accredited by the Council on Accreditation of Services to Families and Children. The agency is a member of the Child Welfare League of America.

CHOSEN CHILDREN ADOPTION SERVICES, INC.

305 Bank Street
New Albany, IN 47150
(812) 945–6021
Program director: Raymond G. Kalef, MSW, Executive Director

THE PROGRAM

For a full description of programs and services, refer to Kentucky listing:
Chosen Children Adoption Services, Inc.
5227 Bardstown Road
Louisville, KY 40291
(502) 591–6410

COLEMAN ADOPTION SERVICES

615 North Alabama, #419
Indianapolis, IN 46204
(317) 638–0965
Program director: Jeanine Jones, M.S.W.

THE PROGRAM

Coleman Adoption Services is a licensed nonprofit agency providing statewide service and placing approximately 20–30 children annually. Established in 1894 as a maternity home and child-placing agency, the agency has provided continuous service to young women experiencing unplanned pregnancies. The agency places infants for adoption when birthmothers in the agency's counseling program decide that the best interests of the child will be served by adoptive placement. In addition, the agency will provide homestudy and supervisory services for applicants pursuing older child adoption or adoption through another licensed agency.

THE COST

For special-needs adoption, the agency's fee is $2,000–$3,000; for healthy Caucasian infant adoption, $7,500. Services covered by the fee include all phases of the adoption process, excluding legal fees connected with finalization of the adoption. Fees help to underwrite the cost of services to birthparents.

THE WAIT

For healthy Caucasian infant adoption, the time from application to placement is approximately 4 years. For special-needs adoption, the time from application to placement ranges from 3 months to 4 years.

THE CHILDREN

Coleman Adoption Services places both healthy and special-needs children, ranging in age from newborn to toddler, of Caucasian, Black, and bi- racial backgrounds, born in the U.S.

THE REQUIREMENTS

Age: Applicants must be at least 25 years old. The maximum age for healthy Caucasian infant adoption is 38; for special-needs infant, 46.

Health: Applicants with health problems or handicaps are given individual consideration. Infertility documentation is required for healthy Caucasian infant adoption.

Religion: No requirement.

Financial status: No requirement.

Marital status: For healthy Caucasian infant adoption, applicants must be married couples who have been married for at least 3 years. No requirement for special-needs adoptions.

Family size: For healthy Caucasian infant adoption, applicants must be childless. No requirement for special-needs adoptions.

Racial, ethnic or cultural origin: The agency places minority children with families of the same race if possible. However, the agency does make transracial placements when in the best interests of the child.

THE PROCEDURE

Participation in Coleman Adoption Services' program entails the following basic steps:
Application
Group counseling sessions
Individual counseling sessions
Homestudy
Placement
Post-placement supervision (6 months)

ADDITIONAL PROGRAMS/SERVICES

Coleman Adoption Services provides foster care for pregnant clients and for infants/children. The agency provides homestudy and supervisory services for interagency adoptions and older child adoptions. The agency plans to offer seminars for families who have adopted transracially and to provide post-placement counseling for members of the adoption triangle.

BRANCH/NETWORK OFFICES

None.

LICENSE/ACCREDITATION/PROFESSIONAL AFFILIATIONS

Coleman Adoption Services, Inc. is licensed by the State of Indiana Department of Public Welfare.

LDS SOCIAL SERVICES

5151 West 84th Street
Indianapolis, IN 46268
(317) 872–1745
Program director: Ken J. Christensen

THE PROGRAM

For a full description of programs and services, refer to Utah listing:

LDS Social Services
50 East North Temple Street
Salt Lake City, UT 84150

LUTHERAN CHILD AND FAMILY SERVICES

1525 N. Ritter Avenue
Indianapolis, IN 46220
(317) 359–5467
Program director: Marlon A. Dean, ACSW

THE PROGRAM

Lutheran Child and Family Services is a nonprofit agency providing statewide services and placing approximately 25 children annually. Founded in 1883, the agency provides services regardless of the race, religion, or economic status of its clients. The agency provides services to birthparents and places infants for adoption when birthparents in the agency's counseling program elect adoptive placement as the best plan for their child. Working with the public agency and with various exchange programs, the agency also facilitates the placement of special-needs children. The agency will provide homestudy and supervisory services for applicants pursuing inter- agency adoption (international or domestic) or independent adoption.

THE COST

The agency's fee for adoption services is based on a sliding scale, with an average fee of $4,000. Services covered by the fee include the homestudy, placement, and post-placement supervision. In addition, applicants should anticipate financial responsibility for the medical expenses of the birthmother and child and legal fees connected with finalization of the adoption.

THE WAIT

For infant adoptions, the time from application to the homecoming of the adoptive child averages 3 to 4 years. For special needs or older child adoptions, the wait averages 6 months.

THE CHILDREN

Lutheran Child and Family Services places both healthy and special-needs children, ranging in age from infancy to adolescence, of all racial backgrounds, born in the U.S.

THE REQUIREMENTS

Age: For infant adoptions, applicants must be at least 21 and no more than 34 years of age. The requirement is flexible for special-needs adoptions.
Health: Infertility documentation is required for infant adoptions.
Religion: No requirement.
Financial status: No requirement.
Marital status: For infant adoption, applicants must be married. Single applicants are accepted for special-needs adoptions.
Family size: No requirement for special-needs adoptions. For infant adoptions, applicants must be childless.
Racial, ethnic or cultural origin: The requirement varies depending on the needs of the child.

THE PROCEDURE

Participation in the adoption program of Lutheran Child and Family Services entails the following basic steps:
Orientation meeting
Application
Group counseling sessions
Homestudy
Placement
Post-placement supervision

ADDITIONAL PROGRAMS/SERVICES

Lutheran Child and Family Services provides counseling services and group workshops.

BRANCH/NETWORK OFFICES

Lutheran Church of Our Redeemer
705 Southway Blvd. E.
Kokomo, IN 46901
(317) 453–0969
United Way Service Center
212 S. 9th St.
Noblesville, IN 46060
(317) 773–1308, Ext. 13
Grace Lutheran Church
3201 Central
(812) 372–4859
Columbus, IN 47201

Rev. Ed Keinath
410 S. Chestnut
Seymour, IN 47274
(812) 522–9549

King of Glory Lutheran Church
2201 E. 106th St.
Carmel, IN 46032
(317) 846–1555

LICENSE/ACCREDITATION/PROFESSIONAL AFFILIATIONS

Lutheran Child and Family Services is licensed by the State of Indiana Department of Public Welfare.

LUTHERAN FAMILY SERVICES OF NORTHWEST INDIANA, INC.

575 West 84th Drive
Merrillville, IN 46410
(219) 769–3521
Program director: Mary Ann Orban, ACSW, Director of Adoptions and Pregnancy and Parenting Support Services

THE PROGRAM

Lutheran Family Services is a nonprofit agency serving residents of Lake, Porter, LaPorte, Starke, Newton, Pulaski, and Jasper Counties and placing approximately 20 to 25 children annually. While Lutheran Family Services is "a Christian agency dedicated to sharing the mercy and love of Christ," the agency serves all people in the community, regardless of race, color, or religious affiliation. Licensed to provide adoption services since 1978, the agency initially placed newborns with childless couples. In 1980, the program expanded to include placement of infants (birth to 2 years) with couples with 1 child, placement of special-needs children in cooperation with other public and private agencies, and the provision of homestudy and supervisory services to married and single applicants pursuing international adoption. In addition, the agency provides homestudy and supervisory services to applicants pursuing private adoption.

THE COST

As of October 1988, the agency's fee schedule is as follows:

Infant adoption	$5,000
Black infant adoption	$1,800
Special-needs adoption	$3,500
International adoption	$1,500.

Services covered by the fee include all phases of the adoption process except medical fees for required physicals, legal fees connected with finalization, transportation to the child (if necessary), and psychological testing fees. In addition, applicants pursuing international adoption should anticipate fees to the cooperating agency or source and other expenses which vary depending on the agency and the country of origin.

THE WAIT

The time from application to placement varies depending on the program. For infant adoption, the wait averages 5 to 6 years. For special-needs adoption, the wait ranges from 6 months to 2 years. For Black infant adoption, the wait ranges from 2 months to 1 year. For international adoption, the wait varies depending on the cooperating agency and the country of origin.

THE CHILDREN

Lutheran Family Services places both healthy and special-needs children, ranging in age from birth to 17 years, of all racial backgrounds, born in the U.S. In addition, the agency provides homestudy and supervisory services to facilitate the placement of foreign-born children from many countries.

THE REQUIREMENTS

The following are the requirements for Lutheran Family Services infant, Black infant, and special needs programs. For international adoptions, applicants must meet the requirements of the cooperating agency.

Age: For infant adoption, 1 spouse must be 40 or younger at the time of inquiry. For special-needs adoption, the requirement varies depending on the age of the child.

Health: Applicants must be in reasonably good health. Applicants with health problems or handicaps are given individual consideration. Infertility documentation is required for infant adoption.

Religion: Applicants must be practicing members of the faith of their choice.

Financial status: Applicants must demonstrate financial stability.

Marital status: No requirement.

Family size: No requirement for Black infant, special needs, or international adoption. For infant adoption, applicants must either be childless or have no more than 1 child in the family.

Racial, ethnic or cultural origin: Preference for placing children in families of similar origins.

THE PROCEDURE

Participation in the adoption program of Lutheran Family Services entails the following basic steps:
Orientation meeting
Group counseling sessions
Homestudy
Application
Compliance with immigration/naturalization requirements (international adoptions only)
Referral
Placement
Post-placement supervision

ADDITIONAL PROGRAMS/SERVICES

Lutheran Family Services provides a wide range of services including individual, family, and group counseling; counseling and support services for birthparents; life enrichment education; foster care; workshops and seminars.

BRANCH/NETWORK OFFICES

All adoption inquiries are processed by the main office.

LICENSE/ACCREDITATION/PROFESSIONAL AFFILIATIONS

Lutheran Family Services of Northwest Indiana, Inc. is licensed by the State of Indiana Department of Public Welfare. The agency is a member of the Child Welfare League of America.

LUTHERAN SOCIAL SERVICES, INC.

P.O. Box 11329, 330 Madison Street
Fort Wayne, IN 46857–1329
(219) 426–3347
Program director: Joan Weber, M.A.; John McAhren, Director of Professional Services

THE PROGRAM

Lutheran Social Services is a nonprofit social ministry agency which serves 12 northeastern Indiana counties (Allen, Whitley, Kosciusko, Adams, Noble, LaGrange, Wells, Elkhart, Steuben, Huntington, Wabash, and Dekalb) and places approximately 15–24 children annually. In 1901, Rev. Wambsganss initiated a program of temporary and permanent foster care for homeless children. In 1927, Lutheran Social Service League founded a family service organization affiliated with the Community Chest. After mergers and reincorporation as an agency, Lutheran Social Services expanded to become a social service agency of Lutheran congregations in all of northeastern Indiana. The agency now has a complete adoption program which includes infant, older and special needs, and foreign adoption. The agency's mission is "to preserve and strengthen the individual well-being and dignity of men, women, and children, in families, communities, and institutions."

THE COST

For infant adoption, the agency's fee is 10% of the applicants' combined annual gross income, with a minimum fee of $1,500 and a maximum of $5,000. For older/special needs and foreign adoption, the fee is based on the number of direct service hours ($43 per hour) plus a homestudy fee of $400 (non-refundable). Applicants assume responsibility for legal fees connected with finalization of the adoption.

THE WAIT

For infant adoption, the time from application to placement averages 4–5 years. For older or special-needs adoption, the wait ranges from 1 to 3 years. For foreign adoption, the wait ranges from 1 to 2 years.

THE CHILDREN

Lutheran Social Services places both healthy and special-needs children (including children with correctable handicaps), ranging in age from birth to 10 years, of all racial backgrounds. Countries of origin include U.S., Philippines, South America, Central America, Korea, and India.

THE REQUIREMENTS

Age: For infant adoption, applicants must be at least 25 and no more than 45 years of age. For special needs, the requirement is flexible. For foreign adoption, the requirement varies but usually allows for an age range of 25–40.
Health: Applicants must be in reasonably good health.
Religion: No requirement.
Financial status: Applicants must demonstrate financial stability.
Marital status: Applicants must be married couples who have been married for at least 3 years. For foreign adoption, some sources require as many as 5 years of marriage.
Family size: No requirement for infant adoption. For foreign adoption, many sources require that adoptive families have no more than 1 or 2 children currently in the family.
Racial, ethnic or cultural origin: Preference for placing children in families of similar origins.

THE PROCEDURE

Participation in Lutheran Social Services' program entails the following basic steps:
    Orientation meeting
    Application
    Group counseling sessions (special-needs adoptions)
    Individual counseling sessions (infant adoptions)
    Homestudy
    Compliance with immigration/naturalization requirements
        (foreign adoptions only)
    Referral
    Placement
    Post-placement supervision

ADDITIONAL PROGRAMS/SERVICES

Lutheran Social Services', in conjunction with two other adoption agencies in Fort Wayne, offers older child adoption classes for prospective adoptive parents of older children. (The classes are also appropriate for prospective parents of infants.) Topics covered include resolution of infertility, forming attachments, adoption as a family affair, birthparents and the adopted child's biological heritage, and legal issues. The agency also participates in the Adoption Forum, held every two years in Fort Wayne, which focuses attention on the needs of waiting children but also addresses issues of concern to all members of the adoption triad.

BRANCH/NETWORK OFFICES

All adoption inquiries are processed through the central office.

LICENSE/ACCREDITATION/PROFESSIONAL AFFILIATIONS

Lutheran Social Services is licensed by the State of Indiana Department of Public Welfare and is accredited by the Council on Accreditation of Services for Families and Children. The agency is affiliated with all major denominations of the Lutheran Church through the Lutheran Social Service Systems.

ST. ELIZABETH'S HOME

2500 Churchman Avenue
Indianapolis, IN 46203
(317) 787–3412
Program director: Anthony J. Logan

THE PROGRAM

St. Elizabeth's Home is a nonprofit agency providing statewide services and placing approximately 55 children annually. Established in 1915 as a day care center for working women, St. Elizabeth's became a maternity home in 1921. Today, the agency provides residential and outreach services to birthparents, single parents, and adoptive parents. The agency provides extensive services to birthmothers, including career and life skills programs to prepare single mothers who elect to parent their children themselves for self-sufficient living and positive parenting. In addition to infant adoptions, the agency works with the public agency and with national and regional exchange programs to facilitate the placement of special-needs children. The agency works cooperatively with U.S.-based agencies to facilitate the placement of foreign-born children and will provide homestudy and supervisory services for applicants pursuing interagency adoption. In all of its programs, the agency's mission is to preserve "the worth and sanctity of life from conception onward."

THE COST

The agency's fee for adoption services is based on a sliding scale with an average fee of $4,000. Services covered by the fee include the adoption study, placement, and post-placement supervision. In addition, applicants should anticipate financial responsibility for required medical examinations and legal fees connected with finalization of the adoption. The fee for special-needs adoption ranges from $500 to $1,300. In some cases, the fee may be waived or reduced.

THE WAIT

For infant adoptions, the time from application to placement ranges from 2 to 4 years. For special-needs adoptions, the wait varies depending on the availability of children in need of adoptive families.

THE CHILDREN

St. Elizabeth's Home places both healthy and special-needs children, primarily under 6 months of age but some older children as well, of Caucasian and Black racial backgrounds, born in the U.S. In addition, the agency will work cooperatively with international agencies to facilitate the placement of foreign-born children in American homes.

THE REQUIREMENTS

Age: For infant adoptions, applicants must be at least 21 and no more than 40 years of age. The requirement is more flexible for special-needs adoptions.
Health: Applicants with health problems or handicaps are given individual consideration. Infertility consultation is required for infant adoptions.
Religion: No requirement.
Financial status: No requirement.
Marital status: For infant adoptions, applicants must be married, and the length of the marriage must be at least 3 years. Single parents are considered for special-needs adoptions.
Family size: No requirement for special-needs adoptions. For infant adoptions, applicants may have no more than 1 child currently in the family.
Racial, ethnic or cultural origin: Preference for placing children in families of similar origins.

THE PROCEDURE

Participation in the adoption program of St. Elizabeth's Home entails the following basic steps:
Application
Orientation meeting
Homestudy
Placement
Post-placement supervision

ADDITIONAL PROGRAMS/SERVICES

St. Elizabeth's Home provides short term infant foster care, counseling services, and PACT (Parent and Child Together).

BRANCH/NETWORK OFFICES

PACT
3410 W. Third St.
Bloomington, IN 47401
(812) 332–1262

LICENSE/ACCREDITATION/PROFESSIONAL AFFILIATIONS

St. Elizabeth's Home is licensed by the State of Indiana Department of Public Welfare.

SUNNY RIDGE FAMILY CENTER

9105–A Indianapolis Boulevard, Suite 301
Highland, IN 46322
(219) 838–6611
Program director: Larry G. Betts, President

THE PROGRAM

For a full description of programs and services, refer to Illinois listing:
Sunny Ridge Family Center
2 S 426 Orchard Road
Wheaton, IL 60187
(312) 668–5117

THE VILLAGES OF INDIANA, INC.

2405 N. Smith Pike
Bloomington, IN 47401
(812) 332–1245
Program director: Gina Alexander

THE PROGRAM

The Villages of Indiana is a nonprofit agency founded in 1964 by Dr. Karl Menninger to provide residential group home care for homeless children. The Villages serves special-needs children (older children, minority children, siblings, and children with special emotional, physical, and developmental needs). Most of the children come to the agency from state and county agencies serving children and youth who have been neglected, abused or abandoned. An important part of the Villages' program for the care of these children "is the possibility of permanence; no child who comes to a Villages' home need ever leave it until he or she reaches adulthood unless it is judged to be in that particular child's best interests." Though a child can find a permanent home in a Villages group home, some children are better served by adoption. Thus, The Villages has established an adoption service to provide another option of permanence for children who need it.

THE COST

Adoption services are provided at no cost to prospective adoptive parents who complete the Villages' training program. The only fees which applicants need to anticipate are legal fees connected with finalization of the adoption.

THE WAIT

The time from application to the homecoming of the adoptive child ranges from 6 months to 1 year.

THE CHILDREN

The Villages places special-needs children, often with emotional, behavioral, or learning problems, ranging in age from 6 to 17, of Caucasian, Black, and Hispanic racial backgrounds, born in the U.S.

THE REQUIREMENTS

Age: Applicants must be at least 21 years of age.
Health: Applicants must be in reasonably good health.
Religion: No requirement.
Financial status: Applicants must have sufficient resources to care for the child.
Marital status: No requirement.
Family size: No requirement.
Racial, ethnic or cultural origin: Preference for placing children in families of similar origins, as required by state law.

THE PROCEDURE

Participation in The Villages of Indiana adoption program entails the following basic steps:
Orientation meeting
Adoptive parent training sessions (20 hours)
Application
Homestudy
Placement
Family counseling sessions
Post-placement supervision and services
Post-placement workshops and seminars (recommended but not required)

ADDITIONAL PROGRAMS/SERVICES

The Villages of Indiana provides specialized foster care. The requirements for families interested in fostering are similar to the requirements for adoption except that on-going in-service training is required. Foster parents are paid per diem for the care of the child, plus a monthly training stipend.

BRANCH/NETWORK OFFICES

3050 N. Meridian
Indianapolis, IN 46205
(317) 924-1474

LICENSE/ACCREDITATION/PROFESSIONAL AFFILIATIONS

The Villages of Indiana, Inc. is licensed by the State of Indiana Department of Public Welfare. The agency is a member of the Indiana Association of Residential Child Care Agencies and the Indiana Association on Adoption and Child Care Services.

Iowa

PUBLIC ADOPTION PROGRAM/ COMMUNITY RESOURCES

Department of Human Services
Adoption Program
Hoover State Office Building
Des Moines, IA 50319–0114
(515) 281–5358
Adoption specialist: Margaret Corkery, Program Manager

THE PROGRAM

Public adoption services in Iowa are provided by the Department of Human Services through district offices located throughout the state. DHS adoption specialists recruit and prepare families and supervise the placement of special-needs children (older, minority, and handicapped children and sibling groups) who are under the guardianship of the State of Iowa.

STATE EXCHANGE

Iowa Adoption Exchange. For information, contact the DHS Adoption Program (above).

STATE ADOPTION REUNION REGISTRY

For information, contact the DHS Adoption Program (above).

STATE SUBSIDY

For information, contact the DHS Adoption Program (above).

NACAC REPRESENTATIVE

None at this time.

GENERAL ADOPTION RESOURCES

For information about adoption resources in your area, contact your DHS district office or the State Program Manager (above).

SPECIAL-NEEDS ADOPTION RESOURCES

See General Adoption Resources (above).

OUT-OF-STATE AGENCIES

AGENCY

Christian Family Service, Kansas

SEE APPENDIX A

Agencies Providing Nationwide Services

AMERICAN HOME FINDING ASSOCIATION

217 E. 5th St., Box 656
Ottumwa, IA 52501
(515) 682–3449
Program director: Tom Lazio, Executive Director

THE PROGRAM

American Home Finding Association (AHFA) is a nonprofit agency providing services for children and families in the state of Iowa. Founded in 1899 by a group of concerned citizens, the agency provides services without regard to race, color, national origin, sex, age, religion, creed, political affiliation, or handicap. Placing both infants and older children, AHFA's goal is "to find the best home for each child considering the child's age, needs, and previous experiences."

THE COST

AHFA's fee for adoption services is $3,040. Services covered by the fee include registration, homestudy, placement, and post-placement supervision. In addition, prospective adoptive parents should anticipate financial responsibility for legal fees connected with finalization.

THE WAIT

The time from application for acceptance into the program to the homecoming of the adoptive child averages 3 to 4 years.

THE CHILDREN

AHFA places both healthy and special-needs children, ranging in age from birth to 18 years, of Black and Caucasian racial backgrounds. Children placed by AHFA are born in the U.S.

THE REQUIREMENTS

Age: The general requirement is that applicants must be at least 18 and no more than 36 years of age. The requirement may vary depending on the special needs of the child.

Health: Applicants must be in reasonably good health. Applicants with health problems or handicaps are given individual consideration.

Religion: Applicants must be practicing members of some faith. The requirement may vary depending on the special needs of the child.

Financial status: Applicants must demonstrate financial stability.

Marital status: The general requirement is that applicants must be married and must have been married for at least 2 years. The requirement may vary for special-needs adoption.

Family size: For infant adoption, applicants must be childless. The requirement may vary for special-needs adoption.

Racial, ethnic or cultural origin: Preference for placing children in families of similar origins.

THE PROCEDURE

Participation in AHFA's adoption program entails the following basic steps:
 Orientation meeting
 Application
 Group counseling sessions
 Individual counseling sessions
 Homestudy
 Placement
 Post-placement supervision

ADDITIONAL PROGRAMS/SERVICES

AHFA provides a range of services for families and individuals including specialized foster care; family and individual counseling; emergency shelter care; maternal-child health program; WIC (Women, Infant & Children) program; pregnancy counseling; post-adoption services.

BRANCH/NETWORK OFFICES

None.

LICENSE/ACCREDITATION/PROFESSIONAL AFFILIATIONS

American Home Finding Association is licensed by the State of Iowa Department of Human Services. The agency is a member of the National Association of Homes for Children and the Coalition for Family and Children Services in Iowa.

BETHANY CHRISTIAN SERVICES

322 Central Avenue, Box 143
Orange City, IA 51041
(712) 737–4831
Program director: James K. Haveman, Jr., Executive Director

THE PROGRAM

For a full description of programs and services, refer to Michigan listing:
Bethany Christian Services
901 Eastern Avenue, N.E.
Grand Rapids, MI 49503–1295
(616) 459–6273

BRANCH OFFICES

Bethany Christian Services/Iowa:
712 Union St., Suite 303
Pella, IA 50219–1768
(515) 628–4606

BETHANY HOME, INC.

1606 Brady Street
Suite 213
Davenport, IA 52803
(319) 324–9169
Program director: Marcy Bell, Judy Foote

THE PROGRAM

For a full description of programs and services, refer to Illinois listing:
Bethany Home, Inc.
P.O. Box 638
220 11th Avenue
Moline, IL 61265
(309) 797–7700

BUILDING FAMILIES THROUGH ADOPTION/IA

P.O. Box 550, 7th and Chestnut
Dawson, MN 56232
(612) 769–2933
Program director: Mary Carpenter and Therese Giesen

THE PROGRAM

For current address and telephone number of BFTA Iowa branch offices, contact BFTA main office (listed above). For full description of BFTA programs and services, refer to Minnesota listing for Building Families Through Adoption.

CATHOLIC CHARITIES OF THE ARCHDIOCESE OF DUBUQUE

P.O. Box 1309
Dubuque, IA 52001
(319) 588–0558
Program director: James L. Yeast, Executive Director Joseph Featherston, Director of Professional Services; Nancy K. Copeland, Adoption Coordinator

THE PROGRAM

Catholic Charities is a nonprofit multi-service agency serving residents of the Archdiocese of Dubuque and placing approximately 25 to 30 children annually through its adoption program. The agency's mission is "to provide social services to prevent and alleviate social problems, facilitating the convening and consciousness raising of people regarding human need and justice issues in order to transform and humanize the social order." Catholic Charities' adoption program originated from St. Mary's Orphanage in 1919 and has evolved in response to societal trends. The agency provides services to birthparents and places both healthy and special-needs children (primarily infants) for adoption when birthparents elect adoptive placement as the best plan for their child. Additionally, the agency will provide homestudy and supervisory services for applicants pursuing domestic interagency adoption.

THE COST

The agency's fee for adoption services is based on a sliding scale and ranges from $4,200 to $5,000. Services covered by the fee include all phases of the adoption program (application through finalization). The only additional expense which applicants need anticipate is a Department of Human Services Criminal Record Check ($15.60).

THE WAIT

The time from application to placement averages 2 to 4 years.

THE CHILDREN

Catholic Charities places both healthy and special-needs children, ranging in age from birth to 3 years, of Caucasian and bi-racial backgrounds, born in the U.S.

THE REQUIREMENTS

Age: Applicants may be no more than 40 years of age.

Health: Applicants with health problems or handicaps are given individual consideration. Infertility documentation is required.

Religion: Applicants must be practicing Protestants or Catholics.

Financial status: Applicants must have an annual gross income of at least $15,000.

Marital status: Applicants must be married; the length of the marriage must be at least 3 years.

Family size: Applicants must be childless.

Racial, ethnic or cultural origin: Preference for placing children in families of similar origins.

THE PROCEDURE

Participation in the adoption program of Catholic Charities entails the following basic steps:

Inquiry
Application
Orientation meeting
Homestudy
Placement
Post-placement supervision

ADDITIONAL PROGRAMS/SERVICES

Catholic Charities provides a range of community services including infant foster care and services to unmarried parents; individual, marital, and family counseling; parochial school guidance and education; ministry to divorced, widowed, or separated persons; independent living program; advocacy services; housing services; information and referral services.

BRANCH/NETWORK OFFICES

1229 Mt. Loretta
Dubuque, IA 52001
(319) 556–2580 or 588–0558

1430 2nd Ave., SE
Cedar Rapids, IA 52403
(319) 364–7121

Colorado Junction Mall
113 Colorado Ave.
Ames, IA 50010
(515) 292–5305

First National Bldg.
Suite 402
Waterloo, IA 50703
(319) 235–6237

15 1st St., NE
Suite 202
Mason City, IA 50401
(515) 424–9683

LICENSE/ACCREDITATION/PROFESSIONAL AFFILIATIONS

Catholic Charities of the Archdiocese of Dubuque is licensed by the State of Iowa Department of Human Services and is a member of Catholic Charities USA.

CATHOLIC CHARITIES

P.O. Box 2025
Sioux City, IA 51104
(712) 252–2701
Program director: James K. Taylor

THE PROGRAM

Catholic Charities is a nonprofit agency serving residents of 24 counties in northwest Iowa and placing approximately 16 infants annually. Incorporated in 1942, the agency began by providing services to single parents, adoption services, and child care. Over the years, the agency has expanded to provide additional services including after-care (for single parents who choose to keep their children), residential treatment for adolescents, and individual, family, and group therapy. In all of its programs, the agency's mission is "to relieve distress and promote the well- being, whether physical or spiritual, of all people who seek its services, regardless of race, religion, or creed."

THE COST

The agency's fee for adoption services is based on a sliding scale and averages $4,500. Services covered by the fee include application, evaluation/study, placement, post-placement supervision, and preparation of documents required for finalization. Applicants assume responsibility for legal fees connected with finalization of the adoption.

THE WAIT

The time from application for acceptance into the program to the homecoming of the adoptive child averages 3 years.

THE CHILDREN

Catholic Charities places primarily healthy Caucasian infants, born in the U.S.

THE REQUIREMENTS

Age: Applicants may be no more than 40 years of age.

Health: Applicants must be in reasonably good health (physician's examination is required). Applicants with health problems or handicaps are given individual consideration. Infertility documentation is required.

Religion: Applicants must be practicing members of a recognized religion.

Financial status: Applicants must demonstrate financial stability.

Marital status: Applicants must be married couples.

Family size: Applicants must be childless.

Racial, ethnic or cultural origin: Preference for placing children in families of similar origins.

THE PROCEDURE

Participation in Catholic Charities' adoption program entails the following basic steps:

Application
Orientation meeting
Group counseling sessions
Individual counseling sessions
Homestudy
Placement
Post-placement supervision

ADDITIONAL PROGRAMS/SERVICES

Catholic Charities provides individual, family and group therapy; services to birthparents; foster care services; residential treatment for adolescents; social concerns program.

BRANCH/NETWORK OFFICES

409-1/2 W. 7th St.
P.O. Box 13
Carroll, IA 51401
(712) 792-9597

2510 9th Ave., S.
Fort Dodge, IA 50501
(515) 576-4156

LICENSE/ACCREDITATION/PROFESSIONAL AFFILIATIONS

Catholic Charities is licensed by the State of Iowa Department of Human Services.

CATHOLIC COUNCIL FOR SOCIAL CONCERN

818 Fifth Avenue
Des Moines, IA 50309
(515) 244-3761
Program director: Beverly West

THE PROGRAM

Catholic Council for Social Concern (CCSC) is a nonprofit social welfare agency that serves the Diocese of Des Moines (southwest Iowa) and places approximately 10 children annually. Established in 1925, the agency originally provided pre-adoptive infant care as the Christ Child Home. Since 1970, adoption services have been offered under the agency name CCSC. CCSC "seeks to implement the social values and teachings of the Catholic Church through advocacy, service and education on behalf of justice for the benefit of the urban and rural communities of Iowa."

THE COST

The agency fee for adoption is based on a sliding scale and ranges from $3,740 to $6,040. Services covered by the fee include (1) inquiry interview, (2) participation in Exploring Infertility group, (3) application, (4) homestudy, (5) medical fees for the birthmother and child, and (6) placement and post-placement services. In addition, applicants can expect to pay legal fees (usually under $500) associated with the finalization of the adoption.

THE WAIT

The wait from application for acceptance into the program to the homecoming of the adoptive child ranges from 3 to 6 years.

THE CHILDREN

CCSC places both healthy and special-needs infants (4 to 6 weeks), of all racial backgrounds. Children placed by CCSC are born in the U.S.

THE REQUIREMENTS

Age: Applicants must not be older than 35 years of age at time of inquiry, and 40 years of age at time of placement.

Health: Applicants with health problems or handicaps are given individual consideration. Infertility documentation is required.

Religion: Applicants must be a practicing members of a faith. Infants born to Catholic birthmothers are placed with Catholic families.

Financial status: No requirement.

Marital status: Applicants must be married. The length of the marriage must be at least 2 years.

Family size: Applicants must be childless.

Racial, ethnic or cultural origin: No requirement, but preference for placing children in families of similar origins.

THE PROCEDURE

Participation in CCSC's adoption program entails the following basic steps:
Inquiry interview
Participation in Exploring Infertility group
Application
Homestudy (office visits, home visits, and group sessions)
Placement
Post-placement supervision

ADDITIONAL PROGRAMS/SERVICES

Catholic Council for Social Concern provides a number of social welfare programs including individual, group, and marriage counseling, refugee services, Catholic Peace Ministry, and Catholic Rural Life programs.

BRANCH/NETWORK OFFICES

Catholic Council for Social Concern, Inc.
315 W. Pierce Street
Council Bluffs, IA 51501
(712) 328-3086

LICENSE/ACCREDITATION/PROFESSIONAL AFFILIATIONS

Catholic Council for Social Concern, Inc. is licensed by the State of Iowa Department of Human Services.

HILLCREST FAMILY SERVICES

1727 First Avenue, S.E.
Cedar Rapids, IA 52402
(319) 362-3149
Program director: Nancylee Ziese, MSW

THE PROGRAM

Hillcrest Family Services is a nonprofit multi-service agency serving residents of Iowa on a non-sectarian basis and placing approximately 20 to 30 children annually through its adoption programs. Founded at the turn of the century by two prominent Dubuque women, Dr. Nancy Hill and Anna B. Cook, to provide shelter and care for unwed mothers and their children, the agency has evolved in response to the changing needs of the community and today provides a wide range of services to individuals, families, and children. The agency's mission is "to provide effective services to people in need, in order to strengthen individual and family life." Hillcrest provides services to birthparents and places infants for adoption when birthparents elect adoptive placement as the best plan for their child. Working in cooperation with other U.S. agencies which maintain international programs, Hillcrest places children from India and from several Latin American countries in Iowa families. In addition, the agency will provide homestudy and supervisory services for applicants pursuing interagency adoption (domestic or international) or private adoption.

THE COST

The agency's fee for adoption services varies depending on the program. For domestic infant adoption, the agency's fee is based on a sliding scale and ranges from $5,300 to $6,300. Services covered by the fee include all phases of the adoption process, excluding legal fees connected with finalization.

For international adoption, applicants can expect to pay Hillcrest approximately $1,310 (registration, application, psychological evaluation, homestudy, case management, and post-placement supervision) and international program fees ranging from $4,500 to $8,000. In addition, applicants should anticipate expenses for the adoption trip to Latin America, miscellaneous expenses related to international adoption (notarization, certification, and translation of documents; immigration and naturalization fees; passport and visa fees; postage and long distance telephone expenses), and legal fees connected with finalization.

THE WAIT

For domestic adoption, the time from application to placement averages 1 to 2 years. For international adoption, the wait varies depending on the cooperating agency and the country.

THE CHILDREN

Hillcrest places primarily healthy children, ranging in age from birth to 16 years, of all racial backgrounds. Countries of origin include India, U.S., and several Latin American countries.

THE REQUIREMENTS

Age: For domestic infant adoption, applicants may be no more than 40 years of age. For international adoption, the requirement varies depending on the age of the child and the requirements of the country of origin.
Health: Applicants should be in reasonably good health. Infertility evaluation is required.
Religion: No requirement.
Financial status: No requirement other than sufficient income to provide for an additional family member.
Marital status: For domestic infant adoption, applicants must be married, and the length of the marriage must be at least 3 years. For international adoption, the requirement varies depending on the country.
Family size: For domestic infant adoption, applicants must be childless. For international adoption, the requirement varies depending on the country.

Racial, ethnic or cultural origin: Preference for placing children in families of similar ethnic backgrounds when possible.

THE PROCEDURE

Participation in Hillcrest's adoption program entails the following basic steps:
Registration
Application
Orientation meeting, psychological testing
Group counseling sessions
Individual counseling sessions
Homestudy
Compliance with immigration/naturalization requirements (international adoptions only)
Placement
Post-placement supervision
Post-adoptive counseling (as needed)

ADDITIONAL PROGRAMS/SERVICES

Hillcrest provides foster care for domestic infants; counseling for birthparents; psychological consultation; family planning and maternal health programs; adult group homes and supervised apartment living programs for chronically mentally ill adults; residential treatment facilities for adolescents; emergency shelter for children and adolescents; home-based counseling for families in crisis; nutritional program for women, infants, and children (WIC); individual, marital and family counseling; evaluations and counseling for people with chemical dependencies and members of their family.

BRANCH/NETWORK OFFICES

2005 Asbury Rd.
P.O. Box 1160
Dubuque, IA 52001
(319) 583–7357

LICENSE/ACCREDITATION/PROFESSIONAL AFFILIATIONS

Hillcrest Family Services is licensed by the State of Iowa Department of Human Services and is accredited by the Council on Accreditation of Services for Families and Children. Hillcrest is a ministry of the Iowa Conference of the United Methodist Church and the Synod of Lakes and Prairies, Presbyterian Church, USA. The agency is a member of the Iowa City and Dubuque Area United Ways and the Iowa Adoption Commission.

HOLT INTERNATIONAL CHILDREN'S SERVICES, INC.

2175 N.W. 86th Street, Suite 10
Des Moines, IA 50322
(515) 253–0622
Program director: David H. Kim, Executive Director

THE PROGRAM

Holt International Children's Services in Des Moines serves residents of Iowa. For a full description of programs and services, refer to Oregon listing:

Holt International Children's Services, Inc.
P.O. Box 2880, 1195 City View
Eugene, OR 97402
(503) 687–2202

Iowa Children's and Family Services

1001 Walnut
Des Moines, IA 50309
(515) 288–1981
Program director: Mildred Floyd, MSW, Contact Person

The Program

Iowa Children's and Family Services is a nonprofit multiservice agency serving families who live within 60 miles of Des Moines. The agency is "committed to maintaining an organization that cares about the developmental well-being and growth of all Iowans, particularly its children and families in crisis and transition." From 1988 to 1983, the agency provided traditional adoption services for the placement of infants and homestudy services for applicants pursuing international and special-needs adoption. The agency's adoption program was discontinued in 1983. In 1987, a new adoption program was initiated through grant funding. The focus of the agency's new program is to find homes for waiting special-needs children of Iowa, working cooperatively with the public agency and with the Iowa Adoption Exchange.

The Cost

Grant funding currently enables the agency to charge only a nominal fee of $15 for adoption services. This may change as grant funds are reduced; call for current information. Applicants should anticipate travel to visit the child, physical examinations, criminal records check (approximately $18), legal and court costs for finalization of the adoption. Adoption subsidy may be available in some cases.

The Wait

As the program is new, the agency is unable to accurately predict the time from application to the homecoming of the adoptive child. The agency expects the wait to vary significantly depending on the availability of the type of child desired. At present, the time from application to the completion of the homestudy is approximately 3 months.

The Children

Iowa Children's and Family Services places special-needs children, ranging in age from birth to 18 years, of all racial backgrounds. Most children available for placement through the agency are over the age of 8; most are physically healthy, but are classified as special needs (Black and bi-racial children, sibling groups, and children with mental or emotional disabilities).

The Requirements

Age: Applicants must be at least 21. The general guideline is that applicants should be no more than 40 years older than the child being considered for placement. The requirement may vary depending on the age of the child, the health of the applicants, and the child's specific needs.

Health: Applicants should be in reasonably good health. Applicants with health problems or handicaps are given individual consideration.

Religion: No specific requirement; however, the specific practices of the religious organization that the applicants belong to may cause denial of the application. Applicants must accept traditional medical and mental health assistance. Other beliefs and practices may also be evaluated with respect to how they effect the applicant's ability to raise a special-needs child.

Financial status: Applicants should be able to support their family on their income. Subsidy may be available to meet the special needs of the child in some cases.

Marital status: Applicants may be married or single. If married, the length of the marriage must be at least 2 years.

Family size: No specific requirement; family size is evaluated on a case-by-case basis.

Racial, ethnic or cultural origin: Preference for placing children in families of similar origins. The requirement varies depending on the child's needs. The agency will not accept applications from non-black applicants who wish to adopt a young, healthy Black child. The agency will accept such applications from Black or mixed-race couples.

The Procedure

Participation in the adoption program of Iowa Children's and Family Services entails the following basic steps:
Orientation meeting
Application
Homestudy (including individual counseling sessions)
Referral
Placement
Post-placement supervision

Additional Programs/Services

Iowa Children's and Family Services provides a range of services including foster care; counseling; residential treatment; day care; art therapy; protective payee; crisis intervention; family violence center; domestic abuse intervention; in-home counseling; workshops and seminars.

Branch/Network Offices

The adoption program is available only through the headquarters in Des Moines.

License/Accreditation/Professional Affiliations

Iowa Children's and Family Services is licensed by the State of Iowa Department of Human Services, is a member of the Child Welfare League of America, and is accredited by the Council on Accreditation of Services for Families and Children.

Lutheran Family Service

4403 1st Ave., S.E.
Suite 304, Executive Plaza
Cedar Rapids, IA 52403
(319) 393–1000
Program director: Leon Schmidt, ACSW, LSW

THE PROGRAM

Lutheran Family Service is a nonprofit agency serving members of the Lutheran Church in the state of Iowa and placing 2 to 5 children annually. Originally founded as an orphanage in 1901, the agency's mission is "to provide skilled professional services to individuals and families." Children placed by the agency are primarily infants whose birthparents have decided that the child's best interests will be served by adoptive placement.

THE COST

The agency's fee schedule is as follows:

Filing fee	$50.00
Homestudy/placement fee	$3,800.00
Medical pool	$1,000.00
Total	$4,850.00

In addition, prospective adoptive parents should anticipate financial responsibility for legal fees connected with finalization of the adoption. Applicants should note that fees are subject to change.

THE WAIT

The time from application for acceptance into the program to the homecoming of the adoptive child ranges from 5 to 6 years.

THE CHILDREN

Lutheran Family Services places healthy Caucasian infants (up to 1 year old) born in the U.S.

THE REQUIREMENTS

Age: Applicants may be no more than 36 years of age.
Health: Applicants must be in reasonably good health.
Religion: Applicants must be active members of a Lutheran church.
Financial status: Applicants must demonstrate financial stability.
Marital status: Applicants must be married and must have been married for at least 3 years.
Family size: Applicants must be childless.
Racial, ethnic or cultural origin: Preference for placing children in families of similar origins.

THE PROCEDURE

Participation in Lutheran Family Service's adoption program entails the following basic steps:
Application
Individual counseling sessions
Group counseling sessions
Homestudy
Placement
Post-placement supervision

ADDITIONAL PROGRAMS/SERVICES

Lutheran Family Service offers individual, marital, and family counseling and therapy; operates group homes for developmentally disabled; sponsors workshops and seminars on various topics.

BRANCH/NETWORK OFFICES

518 Paramount Building
305 2nd Street, S.E.
Cedar Rapids, IA 52401
(319) 365–5219

1230 32nd Street
Des Moines, IA 50311
(515) 279–8808

LICENSE/ACCREDITATION/PROFESSIONAL AFFILIATIONS

Lutheran Family Service is licensed by the State of Iowa Department of Human Services and is affiliated with the Lutheran Church Missouri Synod Board for Social Ministry Services.

LUTHERAN SOCIAL SERVICE OF IOWA

3116 University Avenue
Des Moines, IA 50311
(515) 277–4476
Program director: Lyn Lienhard

THE PROGRAM

Lutheran Social Service is a nonprofit agency serving residents of Iowa and placing approximately 13 children annually. Providing adoption services since 1939, the agency's mission is "to join and assist people in their struggle toward wholeness and empower them to achieve an improved quality of life." The agency provides services to birthparents and places infants for adoption when birthparents elect adoptive placement as the best plan for their child. Working cooperatively with the public agency and with national and regional exchange programs, the agency facilitates the placement of special-needs children. In addition, the agency will provide homestudy and supervisory services for applicants pursuing interagency adoption (domestic or international) or private adoption. The agency also provides post-legal adoption counseling.

THE COST

The agency's fee for adoption services is based on a sliding scale with an average cost of $6,400. Services covered by the fee include all phases of the adoption process (excluding legal fees connected with finalization) as well as services to the birthmother and child.

THE WAIT

The time from application for acceptance into the program to the homecoming of the adoptive child averages 4 to 5 years.

THE CHILDREN

Lutheran Social Service places both healthy and special-needs children, ranging in age from birth to 14 years, primarily of Caucasian but also of American Indian and Black racial backgrounds, born in the U.S.

THE REQUIREMENTS

Age: For healthy infant adoption, applicants may be no more than 34. No requirement for special needs.

Health: Applicants should be in reasonably good health. Applicants with health problems and handicaps are given individual consideration. Infertility documentation is required for healthy infant adoption.

Religion: Applicants must demonstrate Christian faith.

Financial status: For healthy infant adoption, applicants must have an annual gross income of at least $11,000.

Marital status: Married couples are preferred, but single applicants are considered for special-needs adoption.

Family size: For healthy infant adoption, applicants must be childless; no child of birth or adoption may be living with the couple. The requirement is flexible for special-needs adoption.

Racial, ethnic or cultural origin: Preference for placing children in families of similar origins.

THE PROCEDURE

Participation in the adoption program of Lutheran Social Service entails the following basic steps:

Letter of inquiry or intent
Orientation meeting
Application
Individual counseling sessions
Homestudy
Placement
Post-placement supervision

ADDITIONAL PROGRAMS/SERVICES

Lutheran Social Service provides a range of services including individual and family counseling; foster care; in-home, group home, and residential treatment; refugee service; chaplaincy; services to the aging; family life education.

BRANCH/NETWORK OFFICES

1323 Northwestern
Ames, IA 50010
(515) 232–7262

3125 Cottage Grove
Des Moines, IA 50311
(515) 274–4946

1510 Logan
Waterloo, IA 50703
(319) 233–3579

2000 1st Ave., NE
Cedar Rapids, IA 52402
(319) 366–2374

1312 Morningside
Sioux City, IA 51106
(712) 276–1073

1500 Sycamore
Iowa City, IA 52240
(319) 351–4880

628 First St.
Council Bluffs, IA 51501
(712) 323–1558

1327 6th St., SW
Mason City, IA 50401
(515) 423–6313

2104 Brady
Davenport, IA 52803
(319) 322–7419

550 S. Bluff 1812
Clinton, IA 52732
(319) 243–8200

24th Ave., W
Spencer, IA 51301
(712) 262–9171

LICENSE/ACCREDITATION/PROFESSIONAL AFFILIATIONS

Lutheran Social Service of Iowa is licensed by the State of Iowa Department of Human Services. The agency is accredited by the Council on Accreditation of Services for Families and Children and is affiliated with 12 United Ways in Iowa.

YOUNG HOUSE FAMILY SERVICES, INC.

105 Valley Street
Burlington, IA 52601
(319) 752–4000
Program director: Tom Richert

THE PROGRAM

Young House Family Services (YHFS) is a nonprofit organization serving southeast Iowa and providing a range of family services. Established in 1971 by Br. Bob Reinke, the initial focus of the agency was the development of community based group homes. YHFS currently operates the following programs: Woodlands Treatment Center for chemically dependent adolescents; three male adolescent group homes; in-home counseling; individual, marital, and family counseling; foster family care; big brother/big sister program; adult education/parenting classes; in-home skills training for families. Although YHFS maintains a child placing license, the agency does not offer a full range of adoptive services due to a lack of children available for placement in southeast Iowa. However, the agency will provide homestudy and post-placement supervision for families pursuing private adoption.

THE COST

The agency charges a fee of $300 for completion of a homestudy and $45 for post-placement supervision (3 visits and post-placement report).

THE WAIT

Not applicable.

THE CHILDREN

Not applicable.

THE REQUIREMENTS

Age: No requirement.
Health: No requirement.
Religion: No requirement.
Financial status: No requirement.
Marital status: No requirement.
Family size: No requirement.
Racial, ethnic or cultural origin: No requirement.

THE PROCEDURE

Families pursuing private adoption through an attorney or a physician may contact YHFS to arrange for homestudy and post-placement supervision.

ADDITIONAL PROGRAMS/SERVICES

See program description.

BRANCH/NETWORK OFFICES

None.

LICENSE/ACCREDITATION/PROFESSIONAL AFFILIATIONS

Young House Family Services is licensed by the State of Iowa Department of Human Services. The agency is a member of the National Association of Homes for Children (NAHC) and the Coalition for Family and Children's Services in Iowa.

Kansas

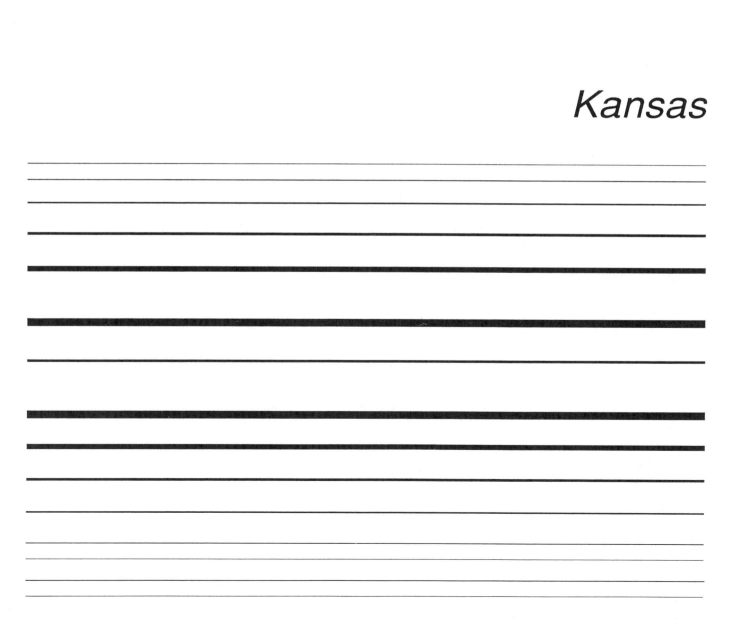

PUBLIC ADOPTION PROGRAM/ COMMUNITY RESOURCES

Department of Social and Rehabilitation Services
Permanency Planning Unit
2700 West 6th Street
Topeka, KS 66606–1861
(913) 296–3284
Adoption specialist: Barbara Stodgell

THE PROGRAM

Public adoption services in Kansas are provided by the Permanency Planning Unit of the Department of Social and Rehabilitation Services through county offices located throughout the state. The Permanency Planning Unit recruits and prepares families and supervises the placement of special-needs children (older, minority, and handicapped children and sibling groups) who are in the custody of the State of Kansas.

STATE EXCHANGE

Youth Services
2700 W. 6th St.
Topeka, KS 66606–1861
(913) 296–4661

STATE ADOPTION REUNION REGISTRY

None.

STATE SUBSIDY

For information contact Youth Services (see State Exchange above).

NACAC REPRESENTATIVE

None at this time.

GENERAL ADOPTION RESOURCES

Adoptive parent support groups in Kansas are normally formed by private adoption agencies as a service to their clients and by the Department of Social and Rehabilitation Services county branch offices in response to the needs of the local community. Contact private adoption agencies in Kansas (see Kansas listing) or DSRS branch offices for information on support services in your area.

SPECIAL-NEEDS ADOPTION RESOURCES

Counseling services for families adopting special-needs children are provided through Kansas Children's Service League, Lutheran Social Service, and The Villages (see Kansas listing). In addition, family services are available through local Social and Rehabilitation Services offices. Families who adopt special-needs children are categorically eligible for such services.

OUT-OF-STATE AGENCIES

SEE APPENDIX A

Agencies Providing Nationwide Services

BAUMANN, POWELL & STONESTREET INDEPENDENT ADOPTIONS, P.A.

5847 S.W. 29th Street
Topeka, KS 66614
(913) 273–7524

Program director: Carol Baumann, LSCSW

THE PROGRAM

Baumann, Powell & Stonestreet Independent Adoptions (BPS) is a for-profit agency serving the state of Kansas and making a limited number of out-of-state placements as well. Licensed in January, 1987, the agency was founded by three social workers who have worked with private adoptions for a number of years. BPS is a non-traditional agency in that the participating birthparents create their own adoption plan, which may or may not involve contact with the adoptive parents. The agency's mission is "to maintain a child advocacy position to insure the optimal physical and emotional care and placement of the children served" and to respond with sensitivity to the needs of all parties involved in the adoption process.

THE COST

The agency's fee for adoption services in-state is $2,000. Services covered by the fee include initial interview, homestudy, placement fee, and post-placement report. The agency's fee for out-of-state services is $1,700 and includes all arrangements through Interstate Compact. In addition, prospective adoptive parents should anticipate all medical costs of the birthmother and child not covered by insurance or medicare; occasionally limited living expenses for the birthmother during her pregnancy and recovery; legal fees connected with finalization of the adoption.

THE WAIT

Because BPS is a new agency, no reliable estimates of the time from application to the homecoming of the adoptive child are available at this time.

THE CHILDREN

BPS places both healthy and special-needs infants of Caucasian and bi-racial backgrounds, born in the U.S.

THE REQUIREMENTS

Age: Applicants may be no more than 50 years of age.
Health: Applicants must be in reasonably good health. Applicants with health problems or handicaps are given individual consideration.
Religion: No requirement.
Financial status: Applicants must demonstrate financial stability and sufficient resources to provide for a child.
Marital status: Single applicants are accepted. However, the preference of the birthparents is honored. If married, applicants must have been married for at least 2 years.
Family size: Applicants may have no more than one child currently in the family.
Racial, ethnic or cultural origin: No requirement.

THE PROCEDURE

Participation in BPS' adoption program entails the following basic steps:

Intake interview

Application

Homestudy

Agency approval, denial, or delay (If approved, applicants must furnish letter to birthparents. Approval does not guarantee placement as birth- parents select adoptive parents.)

Placement

Post-placement supervision

ADDITIONAL PROGRAMS/SERVICES

BPS provides counseling to birthparents throughout the pregnancy and following relinquishment. BPS also provides counseling and support services to adoptive parents while they are waiting to be chosen and for a year following placement.

BRANCH/NETWORK OFFICES

None.

LICENSE/ACCREDITATION/PROFESSIONAL AFFILIATIONS

Baumann, Powell & Stonestreet Independent Adoptions, P.A. is licensed by the State of Kansas Department of Health and Environment. All three social workers are LSCSW (Licensed Specialist Clinical Social Worker) and are members of the National Association of Social Workers.

CATHOLIC CHARITIES OF SALINA, INC.

137 North 9th St.
Salina, KS 67401
(913) 825–0208
Program director: Monsignor Alfred Wasinger, Executive Director; Bonnie Frey, LMSW, Director of Adoption Program

THE PROGRAM

Catholic Charities of Salina is a nonprofit agency serving residents of the Diocese of Salina (31 counties) and placing approximately 12 children annually. Founded in 1910 as a shelter for orphans, the agency has evolved in response to changing societal needs and today provides a wide range of services, based on the conviction that "the Christian owes a debt of service to his neighbor, as an expression of the love of Christ." The agency provides services to birthparents and places infants for adoption when birthparents in the agency's counseling program elect adoptive placement as the best plan for their child.

THE COST

The agency's fee for adoption services is based on a sliding scale and ranges from $2,500 to $5,000. Services covered by the fee include all phases of the adoption process (pre-adoption counseling through post-placement services), excluding legal fees connected with finalization of the adoption (approximately $150–$300). Fees help to underwrite the cost of services to the birthmother and child.

THE WAIT

Applicants should anticipate being wait-listed for approximately 2 years before the homestudy is initiated. The time from the initiation of the homestudy to the homecoming of the adoptive child is approximately 1 year.

THE CHILDREN

Catholic Charities of Salina places primarily healthy Caucasian infants (birth to several months old). Some bi-racial infants (Hispanic/Caucasian, Black/Caucasian, or Asian/Caucasian) are also placed. All children placed by the agency are born in the U.S.

THE REQUIREMENTS

Age: Applicants must be at least 22 and no more than 40 years of age.

Health: Applicants must be in reasonably good health. Applicants with health problems or handicaps are given individual consideration. Infertility documentation is required.

Religion: Applicants must be practicing members of a Catholic or Protestant faith.

Financial status: Applicants are evaluated individually on the basis of their ability to manage financial resources adequately.

Marital status: Applicants must be married couples. The length of the marriage must be sufficient to demonstrate stability.

Family size: Applicants may have no more than 1 child currently in the family. Exceptions are possible for adoptions involving a bi-racial child.

Racial, ethnic or cultural origin: When possible, preference for placing children in families of similar origins.

THE PROCEDURE

Participation in Catholic Charities' adoption program entails the following basic steps:

Orientation meeting

Application

Homestudy

Adoption workshop

Submission of autobiographies

Placement

Post-placement supervision

ADDITIONAL PROGRAMS/SERVICES

Catholic Charities of Salina provides individual, marital, and family counseling; services to birthparents; foster care services at St. Joseph's Home; emergency shelter; educational workshops; consultation services; emergency assistance; refugee resettlement services.

BRANCH/NETWORK OFFICES

Hays Outreach Office
1201 B. Fort St.
Hays, KS 67601
(913) 625–2644

LICENSE/ACCREDITATION/PROFESSIONAL AFFILIATIONS

Catholic Charities of Salina, Inc. is licensed by the State of Kansas Department of Social and Rehabilitative Services.

CATHOLIC SOCIAL SERVICE

2546 20th Street
Great Bend, KS 67530
(316) 792–1393
Program director: Rev. Ted Skalsky, Executive Director
Paula Vink, LBSW, Program Director

THE PROGRAM

Catholic Social Service is a nonprofit agency serving residents of western Kansas (28 counties) and placing approximately 12 children annually through its adoption program. Founded 22 years ago, the agency's mission is "to engage in organized charitable, welfare, and social service work for promotion of the physical, mental, and moral betterment of all persons who may come under the care of this society." Catholic Social Service provides services to birthparents and places both healthy and special-needs infants for adoption if birthparents elect adoptive placement as the best plan for their child. Catholic Social Service has implemented open adoptions if requested by the birthparents or adoptive parents. In addition, the agency will provide homestudy and supervisory services for applicants pursuing interagency adoption (domestic or international) or private adoption.

THE COST

The agency's fee for adoption services is $6,000. Services covered by the fee include all phases of the adoption process.

THE WAIT

The time from application for acceptance into the program to the homecoming of the adoptive child ranges from a few months to 2 years.

THE CHILDREN

Catholic Social Service places both healthy and special-needs infants of all racial backgrounds, born in the U.S.

THE REQUIREMENTS

Age: The requirement is evaluated on a case-by-case basis.
Health: Applicants should be in reasonably good health. Infertility documentation is required.
Religion: Applicants must be practicing members of a Catholic or Protestant faith.
Financial status: Applicants must have sufficient income to provide for an additional family member.
Marital status: Applicants must be married; the length of the marriage must be at least 3 years.
Family size: Applicants may have no more than 1 child currently in the family.
Racial, ethnic or cultural origin: No requirement, but preference for placing children in families of similar origins.

THE PROCEDURE

Participation in the adoption program of Catholic Social Service entails the following basic steps:
Application
Individual counseling sessions
Homestudy
Referral
Placement

ADDITIONAL PROGRAMS/SERVICES

Catholic Social Service provides a range of services including foster care; day care center; youth care; family crisis center; Meals on Wheels program; court-ordered pre-marital evaluations; public education and sexual prevention programs in schools.

BRANCH/NETWORK OFFICES

None.

LICENSE/ACCREDITATION/PROFESSIONAL AFFILIATIONS

Catholic Social Service is licensed by the State of Kansas Department of Social and Rehabilitation Services.

CATHOLIC SOCIAL SERVICE

229 South 8th Street
Kansas City, KS 66101
(913) 621–5058
Program director: Mary Schimberg

THE PROGRAM

Catholic Social Service is a nonprofit agency serving residents of the 14 county area of the Archdiocese of Kansas City, Kansas on a non-sectarian basis and placing approximately 23 children annually. The agency provides services for relinquishing and non-relinquishing birthparents, including counseling, medical assistance, and parenthood preparation. The agency places infants for adoption when birthparents in the agency's pregnancy counseling program decide that the best interests of the child will be served by adoptive placement. Catholic Social Service promotes open adoption through the non-identifying exchange of information between birthparents and adoptive parents.

THE COST

The agency's fee for adoption services is $7,000 and includes all phases of the adoption process and all services to the birthmother and child, excluding legal fees connected with finalization.

THE WAIT

The time from application to the homecoming of the adoptive child is approximately 3 years.

THE CHILDREN

Catholic Social Service places primarily healthy Caucasian infants born in the U.S.

THE REQUIREMENTS

Age: Applicants may be no more than 40 years old at the time of application.

Health: Applicants must be biologically unable to have children.

Religion: Applicants must be practicing members of their faith.

Financial status: No requirement.

Marital status: Applicants must be married, and the length of the marriage must be at least 3 years at the time of application.

Residence: Applicants must reside within the 14 county area of the Archdiocese of Kansas City, Kansas.

Family size: Applicants may have no more than 1 child currently in the home.

Racial, ethnic or cultural origin: No requirement.

THE PROCEDURE

Participation in Catholic Social Service's adoption program entails the following basic steps:

Intake interview (telephone)
Letter of interest
Application
Pre-waiting list
Homestudy
Placement
Post-placement supervision

ADDITIONAL PROGRAMS/SERVICES

Catholic Social Service provides a wide range of community services including individual, marital, and family counseling; pregnancy counseling; emergency foster care; refugee services; child care services; handicapped services; services to the elderly; family crisis intervention; support groups.

BRANCH/NETWORK OFFICES:

306 Van Buren
Topeka, KS 66603
(913) 233–6300

320 Main
Lawrence, KS 66044
(913) 841–0307

501 North 5th St.
Leavenworth, KS 66048
(913) 651–8060

LICENSE/ACCREDITATION/PROFESSIONAL AFFILIATIONS

Catholic Social Services is licensed by the State of Kansas Department of Social and Rehabilitative Services, is accredited by the Council on Accreditation of Services for Families and Children, and is a member of the United Way.

CHRISTIAN FAMILY SERVICES OF THE MIDWEST, INC.

10901 Granada Lane, Suite 102
Overland Park, KS 66211
(913) 491–6751
Program director: Douglas L. Mead

THE PROGRAM

Founded in 1981, Christian Family Services is a nonprofit family service agency primarily serving residents of Kansas, Missouri, Oklahoma, Nebraska, and Iowa and placing approximately 10 children annually in Church of Christ families through its adoption program. Founded in 1981, the agency's mission is "to provide professional services to help people who struggle with personal crises and troubled relationships and to enhance the quality of family life." The agency provides services to birthparents and places both healthy and special-needs infants for adoption when birthparents elect adoptive placement as the best plan for their child.

THE COST

The agency's fee for adoption services is $5,750 and includes the homestudy, placement, and post-placement supervision. Applicants who live outside the greater Kansas City area should anticipate possible travel expenses.

THE WAIT

The time from application to the homecoming of the adoptive child ranges from 1 to 2 1/2 years.

THE CHILDREN

Christian Family Services places primarily infants, both healthy and special needs, of Caucasian, Black, and bi-racial backgrounds, born in the U.S.

THE REQUIREMENTS

Age: The age requirement is evaluated on a case-by-case basis.

Health: Applicants should be in reasonably good health.

Religion: Applicants must be practicing members of the Church of Christ.

Financial status: Applicants must demonstrate financial responsibility and ability to provide for an additional child.

Marital status: Applicants must be married. Some exceptions may be made for special needs placements.

Family size: For healthy Caucasian infant adoption, applicants may have no more than 2 children currently in the home. For minority and special needs placements, no requirement.

Racial, ethnic or cultural origin: Preference for placing children in families of similar origins.

THE PROCEDURE

Participation in the adoption program of Christian Family Services entails the following basic steps:

Preliminary application
Orientation meeting
Adoption workshop
Homestudy (including individual counseling sessions)
Placement
Post-placement supervision

ADDITIONAL PROGRAMS/SERVICES

In addition to adoption services, Christian Family Services provides unplanned pregnancy counseling, foster care services, family and marital counseling, and family enrichment seminars.

BRANCH/NETWORK OFFICES

Christian Family Services maintains an office in Raytown, Missouri. However, telephone inquiries are processed through the Kansas office at (913) 491–6751.
6000 Blue Ridge Blvd.
Raytown, MO 64133

LICENSE/ACCREDITATION/PROFESSIONAL AFFILIATIONS

Christian Family Services of the Midwest, Inc. is licensed by the Kansas Department of Health and Environment and by the State of Missouri Department of Social Services.

FAMILY LIFE SERVICES ADOPTION AGENCY

115 E. Chestnut Avenue
Arkansas City, KS 67005
(316) 442–1688
Program director: Brian Feldhus, B.S.

THE PROGRAM

Family Life Services is a nonprofit agency serving the state of Kansas and placing from 6 to 8 children annually. Family Life Services began as a pregnancy crisis center offering counseling in 1984 and expanded to include child placement services in June of 1985. The agency's mission is "to focus on the pregnant woman, meeting her needs and offering her physical and spiritual support; to establish and operate a pregnancy crisis center, a residential home, and a child placing agency." Family Life Services places infants for adoption when birthparents in the agency's pregnancy crisis program decide that the infant's best interests will be served by adoptive placement.

THE COST

The agency's fee for adoption services is $2,100. Services covered by the fee include all interviews, psychological evaluation, homestudy, up- date homestudy (when needed), post-placement supervision, preparation of agency documents for finalization. In addition, prospective adoptive parents should anticipate financial responsibility for some of the living expenses of the birthmother prior to the birth of the baby, medical expenses of the birthmother and child, and legal fees connected with finalization of the adoption.

THE WAIT

The average time from application for acceptance into the program to the homecoming of the adoptive child is 16 months.

THE CHILDREN

Family Life Services places both healthy and special-needs infants. Most infants placed by FLS are Caucasian, but the agency will provide services for birthmothers and children of any race.

THE REQUIREMENTS

Age: Applicants may be no more than 43 years of age.
Health: Applicants must be in reasonably good health. Infertility documentation is requested.
Religion: Applicants must be practicing members of a Christian faith.
Financial status: Applicants must demonstrate financial stability.
Marital status: Applicants must be married and must have been married for at least 3 years.
Family size: Applicants may have no more than 1 child currently in the family.
Racial, ethnic or cultural origin: Preference for placing children in families of similar origins.

THE PROCEDURE

Participation in Family Life Services' adoption program entails the following basic steps:
Inquiry/Request for information packet
Application
Individual counseling sessions (including psychological evaluation)
Homestudy
Placement
Post-placement supervision

ADDITIONAL PROGRAMS/SERVICES

Family Life Services provides individual, marital, and family counseling and foster care services on a limited basis.

BRANCH/NETWORK OFFICES

None.

LICENSE/ACCREDITATION/PROFESSIONAL AFFILIATIONS

Family Life Services Adoption Agency is licensed by the State of Kansas Department of Social and Rehabilitative Services and is a member of the Kansas Adoption Coalition.

GENTLE SHEPHERD CHILD PLACEMENT SERVICES, INC.

304 S. Clairborne, Suite 201
Olathe, KS 66062
(913) 764–3811
Program director: Gayle Rundberg

THE PROGRAM

Gentle Shepherd Child Placement Services (GSCPS) is a nonprofit agency providing nation-wide service and placing approximately 25 children annually. The agency was founded in 1983 on the belief in "the importance of assisting women facing an unplanned pregnancy, children in need, and families who desire to adopt a child." The agency offers domestic and foreign adoption programs. Since 1983, the agency has placed over 100 healthy and special-needs children.

THE COST

The agency's fee for adoption services is based on a sliding scale and ranges between $2,500 and $10,350, depending on the program. Services covered by the fee include all phases of the adoption process; medical, foster care, and legal expenses of the birthparents and child. In addition, prospective adoptive parents should anticipate financial responsibility for legal fees connected with finalization of the adoption (approximately $500).

THE WAIT

The time from application for acceptance into the program to the homecoming of the adoptive child ranges from 1 to 2 1/2 years, depending on the type of child being considered for placement.

THE CHILDREN

GSCPS places both healthy and special-needs children, ranging in age from birth to 5 years, of all racial backgrounds. Countries of origin include the U.S. and Samoa.

THE REQUIREMENTS

Age: Applicants must be at least 21 and no more than 40 years of age.
Health: Applicants must be in reasonably good health.
Religion: Applicants must be practicing members of a Christian denomination.
Financial status: No requirement.
Marital status: Applicants must be married and must have been married for at least 3 years.
Family size: No requirement.
Racial, ethnic or cultural origin: No requirement.

THE PROCEDURE

Participation in GSCPS' adoption program entails the following basic steps:
Application
Orientation meeting
Homestudy
Placement
Post-placement supervision

ADDITIONAL PROGRAMS/SERVICES

GSCPS provides services to birthparents (counseling, medical care, housing, and birthing classes); parenting classes and support groups for adoptive parents.

BRANCH/NETWORK OFFICES

None.

LICENSE/ACCREDITATION/PROFESSIONAL AFFILIATIONS

Gentle Shepherd Child Placement Services, Inc. is licensed by the State of Kansas Department of Social and Rehabilitative Services. The agency is a member of the National Committee for Adoption and Alternatives to Abortion International.

HEART OF AMERICA FAMILY SERVICES

3217 Broadway
Kansas City, MO
(816) 753–5280
Program director: Margaret McCorkendale

THE PROGRAM

While Heart of America Family Services maintains 8 branch offices serving Kansas and Missouri, all adoption inquiries are processed through the midtown office (listed above) in Kansas City, Missouri. For a full description of Heart of America Family Services programs and services, refer to Missouri listing.

INSERCO

5120 E. Central #A
Wichita, KS 67208
(316) 681–3840
Program director: Irvin Penner, LSCSW

THE PROGRAM

INSERCO is a for-profit agency serving residents of the state of Kansas and placing approximately 7 children annually. Incorporated in 1986, INSERCO facilitates primarily foreign but also domestic adoptions. Working "to help place children in loving homes," INSERCO provides counseling, homestudy, and supervisory services for applicants pursuing foreign, interstate, and private adoptions.

THE COST

The agency's fee for homestudy/supervisory services is based on a sliding scale and averages under $1,000. For domestic adoptions, applicants should anticipate financial responsibility for legal and medical expenses of the birthmother and child. For foreign adoptions, applicants should anticipate foreign agency or source fees, overseas legal fees, travel expenses, and related costs. In all programs, applicants assume responsibility for legal fees connected with finalization of the adoption.

THE WAIT

As the agency is newly incorporated, no reliable estimate of the time from application to placement is available.

THE CHILDREN

INSERCO facilitates the placement of healthy children, ranging in age from birth to 5 years. Countries of origin include Korea, South America, India, and U.S.

THE REQUIREMENTS

Age: No specific requirement. Applicants are assessed individually.
Health: Applicants must be in reasonably good health. Applicants with health problems or handicaps are given individual consideration.

Religion: No specific requirement. Applicants are assessed individually.
Financial status: No requirement.
Marital status: Applicants must be married couples.
Family size: Applicants may have no more than 3 children currently in the family.
Racial, ethnic or cultural origin: No requirement.

THE PROCEDURE

Participation in INSERCO's adoption program entails the following basic steps:
Orientation and application
Homestudy
Compliance with immigration/naturalization requirements (foreign adoptions only)
Referral
Placement
Post-placement supervision

ADDITIONAL PROGRAMS/SERVICES

INSERCO provides infertility counseling.

BRANCH/NETWORK OFFICES

None.

LICENSE/ACCREDITATION/PROFESSIONAL AFFILIATIONS

INSERCO is licensed by the State of Kansas Department of Social and Rehabilitative Services.

KANSAS CHILDREN'S SERVICE LEAGUE

Black Adoption Program and Services
710 Minnesota
Kansas City, KS 66101
(913) 621–2016
Program director: Janice Greene, District Director

THE PROGRAM

Kansas Children's Service League is a nonprofit agency serving metropolitan Kansas City and placing approximately 24 children annually. The Black Adoption Program and Services was established in 1973 to recruit Black families to adopt Black children. The agency's mission is "to protect, enhance and promote the welfare of children through educational and social services.

THE COST

The agency's fee for adoption services is based on a sliding scale and ranges from $300 to $1,300. Services covered by the fee include all phases of the adoption process (pre-placement services through post-adoption services), excluding legal fees connected with finalization of the adoption.

THE WAIT

The time from application to the homecoming of the adoptive child ranges from 3 to 6 months, depending on the age of the child the applicants wish to parent.

THE CHILDREN

KCSL Black Adoption Program places both healthy and special needs Black children, ranging in age from infancy to adolescence.

THE REQUIREMENTS

Age: Applicants must be at least 21 years of age.
Health: Applicants must be in reasonably good health.
Religion: No requirement.
Financial status: Applicants must have sufficient income to meet the needs of the family.
Marital status: No requirement.
Family size: No requirement.
Racial, ethnic or cultural origin: Preference for placing children in families of similar origins.

THE PROCEDURE

Participation in KCSL Black Adoption Program entails the following basic steps:
Orientation meeting
Application
Homestudy
Group counseling sessions
Placement
Post-placement supervision

ADDITIONAL PROGRAMS/SERVICES

KCSL Black Adoption Program and Services provides temporary foster care; birthparent counseling; teen pregnancy prevention program.

BRANCH/NETWORK OFFICES

1601 E. 18th St.
Suite 227
Kansas City, MO 64127
(816) 283–3596

LICENSE/ACCREDITATION/PROFESSIONAL AFFILIATIONS

Kansas Children's Service League is licensed by the State of Kansas Department of Social and Rehabilitative Services and by the State of Missouri Division of Family Services. The agency is accredited by the Council on Accreditation of Services for Families and Children and is a member of the Child Welfare League of America and the United Way.

LUTHERAN SOCIAL SERVICE OF KANSAS AND OKLAHOMA

1855 N. Hillside
Wichita, KS 67214
(316) 686–6645
Program director: Virginia Rodman, LSCSW, ACSW

THE PROGRAM

Lutheran Social Service is a nonprofit agency serving the states of Kansas and Oklahoma and placing approximately 50 children annually. Founded in 1879 as two orphanages, Lutheran Social Service programs united to become a multi-service agency in 1961, providing service to persons without regard to race, color, sex, ancestry, national origin, age, creed, religion, or disability. As an agency of the church working closely with other organizations in areas of human need, the purpose of Lutheran Social Service is "to combine Christian love and service to enable individuals and families to live more abundant lives." Infant adoption (for Caucasian and minority clients), special-needs adoption (finding homes for children with handicaps, older children, and large sibling groups), and specialized foster care have long been services of the agency. The agency's One Church, One Child program recruits Black families for Black children and infants. The agency has been a member of the Family Builders Network since 1978 and has a strong commitment to permanent homes for all children. Lutheran Social Service encourages open adoption through the non-identifying exchange of information between birthparents and adoptive parents.

THE COST

The agency's fee for adoption services varies depending on the program. For special-needs adoptions, services are provided at no cost to the adoptive family. For minority infant adoption, fees are determined through a cost-share agreement between the agency and adoptive parents. For Caucasian infant adoption, the agency's fee is $4,700. For both the minority infant and Caucasian infant adoption programs, prospective adoptive parents are responsible for medical costs of the birthmother and child (average for 1987, Caucasian—$2,350; minority—$450). Services covered by agency fees include family preparation (educational workshops and homestudy), placement, and post-placement supervision and services. In addition, applicants should anticipate financial responsibility for legal fees connected with finalization of the adoption (approximately $250).

THE WAIT

The time from application for acceptance into the program to the homecoming of the adoptive child varies depending on the program selected. For special needs and minority infant adoptions, the time ranges from 6 to 18 months. For Caucasian infant adoptions, the time ranges from 6 months to 4 years.

THE CHILDREN

Lutheran Social Service places both healthy and special-needs children, ranging in age from birth to adolescence, of all racial and ethnic backgrounds.

THE REQUIREMENTS

Age: The age requirement varies depending on the age of the child. The agency prefers the child to reach maturity before the eldest parent reaches retirement age.
Health: Applicants with health problem or handicap are given individual consideration.
Religion: Applicants must be practicing members of a Christian congregation.
Financial status: No requirement.
Marital status: For Caucasian infant adoption, applicants must be married. For minority infant or special-needs adoption, single applicants are accepted.

Family size: For Caucasian infant adoption, applicants may have no more than 1 child currently in the family. No requirement for other programs.
Racial, ethnic or cultural origin: No requirement, but preference for placing children in families of similar origins.

THE PROCEDURE

Participation in Lutheran Social Service's adoption programs entails the following basic steps:
Orientation meeting (special needs program only)
Application
Group educational sessions
Individual counseling sessions (as needed)
Homestudy
Placement
Post-placement supervision

ADDITIONAL PROGRAMS/SERVICES

Lutheran Social Service offers counseling services for individuals, couples, and families; a wide variety of family life education programs; refugee resettlement services; foster care for unaccompanied refugee minors.

BRANCH/NETWORK OFFICES

Lutheran Social Service
(all services)
2901 N. Classen
Oklahoma City, OK 73106
(405) 528–3124
Lutheran Social Service
(Special-needs adoptions only)
1017 N. Washington
Hutchinson, KS 67501
(316) 669–8710

LICENSE/ACCREDITATION/PROFESSIONAL AFFILIATIONS

Lutheran Social Service of Kansas and Oklahoma is licensed by the State of Kansas Department of Social and Rehabilitative Services and by the State of Oklahoma Department of Human Services.

THE VILLAGES, INC.

Special-needs Adoption Program
2209 S.W. 29th Street
P.O. Box 1695
Topeka, KS 66601
(913) 267–5905
Program director: Peggy Henry

THE PROGRAM

The Villages, Inc. is a nonprofit organization founded in 1964 by Dr. Karl Menninger to provide residential group home care for homeless children. Though a child can find a permanent home in a Villages group home, some children are better served by adoption. Thus, The Villages established an adoption program in 1981 to provide another option or permanence for children who need it. Residents of the state of Kansas are eligible for the adoption program. The Villages provides extensive pre-placement training classes to prepare parents for special-needs adoption as well as intensive, ongoing support services, pre and post finalization. The Villages places approximately 6 to 8 children annually through its adoption program.

THE COST

Adoption services are provided at no cost to the adoptive family. The only expenses which prospective adoptive families should anticipate are legal fees connected with finalization of the adoption.

THE WAIT

The time from application to placement varies depending on the number of children currently in need of adoptive families and on the range of special needs the prospective adoptive family can accept.

THE CHILDREN

The Villages places special-needs children, ranging from 6 to 18 years of age, of all racial backgrounds.

THE REQUIREMENTS

Age: Applicants must be at least 21 years of age.
Health: Applicants should be in reasonably good health. Applicants with health problems or handicaps are given individual consideration.
Religion: No requirement.
Financial status: The requirement varies depending on the number of family members and on the special needs of the child(ren) placed.
Marital status: Applicants must be married; the length of the marriage must be at least 3 years.
Family size: No requirement.
Racial, ethnic or cultural origin: Preference for placing children in families of similar origins. The requirement may vary depending on the best interests of the child.

THE PROCEDURE

Participation in The Villages' adoption program entails the following basic steps:
Orientation meeting
Adoptive parent training sessions
Homestudy
Referral
Placement
Post-placement supervision and services

ADDITIONAL PROGRAMS/SERVICES

The Villages provides residential group home care for homeless children.

BRANCH/NETWORK OFFICES

The Villages, Inc. is affiliated with The Villages of Indiana, Inc. (see Indiana listing).

LICENSE/ACCREDITATION/PROFESSIONAL AFFILIATIONS

The Villages, Inc. is licensed by the State of Kansas Department of Social and Rehabilitation Services.

WYANDOTTE HOUSE, INC.

632 Tauromee
Kansas City, KS 66101
(913) 342–9332
Program director: B. Wayne Sims

THE PROGRAM

Wyandotte House is a nonprofit youth agency which offers a network of residential care/emergency shelter, educational programs, and treatment services to troubled youth and their families from the metropolitan Kansas City area and throughout the state. Founded in 1970 by the Junior League of Kansas City, Kansas, in conjunction with the Wyandotte County Juvenile Court, the agency serves approximately 500 youth annually through a wide range of services. Wyandotte House works cooperatively with the public agency to facilitate the placement of special-needs children who are in the custody of the State of Kansas. In addition, the agency will provide homestudy and supervisory services for applicants pursuing domestic interagency adoption or private adoption.

THE COST

Adoption services for children in the custody of the State of Kansas are provided at no cost to the adoptive parents. Adoptive parents are responsible for legal fees connected with finalization of the adoption.

THE WAIT

The time from application to placement averages 1 year.

THE CHILDREN

Wyandotte House facilitates the placement of both healthy and special-needs children, ranging in age from 1 to 18 years, of all racial backgrounds, born in the U.S. Children placed are in the custody of the State of Kansas.

THE REQUIREMENTS

Age: Applicants must be at least 18 years of age.
Health: Applicants must be in reasonably good health. Applicants with health problems or handicaps are given individual consideration.
Religion: No requirement.
Financial status: No requirement.
Marital status: No requirement.
Family size: No requirement.
Racial, ethnic or cultural origin: Preference for placing children in families of similar origins.

THE PROCEDURE

Participation in the adoption program of Wyandotte House entails the following basic steps:
Orientation meeting
Application
Homestudy
Individual counseling sessions
Referral
Placement
Post-placement supervision
Group counseling sessions

Additional Programs/Services

Wyandotte House provides a wide range of programs and services for youth including intermediate and long-term residential care; emergency/temporary shelter; Behavior Disorder Day School; Competency-Based Learning Center; satellite family foster care; drug prevention education program; independent living skills training.

Branch/Network Offices

None.

License/Accreditation/Professional Affiliations

Wyandotte House, Inc. is licensed by the State of Kansas Department of Social and Rehabilitation Services and by the Department of Health and Environment. The agency is a member of the Kansas Association of Licensed Private Child Care Agencies, Kansas Association of Foster Care, Kansas Children's Coalition, National Network of Runaway Youth, Missouri/Iowa/Nebraska/Kansas Network of Runaway Shelters, and an associate member of the Child Welfare League of America.

Kentucky

PUBLIC ADOPTION PROGRAM/ COMMUNITY RESOURCES

Cabinet for Human Resources
Department for Social Services
275 East Main Street, 6th Floor West
Frankfort, KY 40621
(502) 564–2136
Adoption specialist: Sue Howard

THE PROGRAM

Public adoption services in Kentucky are provided by the Cabinet for Human Resources, Department for Social Services. For information concerning Kentucky's Special-needs Adoption Project (SNAP), contact:

SNAP
710 West High Street
Lexington, KY 40508
(606) 252–1728

SNAP
908 West Broadway
Louisville, KY 40263
(502) 588–4303

STATE EXCHANGE

Kentucky Adoption Resource Exchange (KARE); 1–800–432–9346 (toll-free in Kentucky).

STATE ADOPTION REUNION REGISTRY

None.

STATE SUBSIDY

Adoption Subsidy
275 E. Main St., 6th Fl. W.
Frankfort, KY 40621
(502) 564–2136
Director: Gwen Winters

NACAC REPRESENTATIVE

Darlene Ogata
3832 Hidden Springs Dr.
Lexington, KY 40514
(606) 224–3085

GENERAL ADOPTION RESOURCES

Adoption support services in Kentucky are normally provided by private adoption agencies as a service to their clients. Contact private adoption agencies in Kentucky (see Kentucky listing) for information on support services in your area.

SPECIAL-NEEDS ADOPTION RESOURCES

For information concerning special-needs adoption resources, contact Kentucky Adoption Resource Exchange (above).

OUT-OF-STATE AGENCIES

AGENCY

Jewish Family Service (Cincinnati), Ohio

SEE APPENDIX A

Agencies Providing Nationwide Services

CATHOLIC SOCIAL SERVICE BUREAU

3629 Church Street
Covington, KY 41015
(606) 581–8974
Program director: Monica Kuhlman

THE PROGRAM

Catholic Social Service Bureau (CSSB) is a nonprofit multi- service agency serving residents of the Diocese of Covington regardless of color, creed or national origin and placing approximately 20 children annually through its adoption program. Founded in 1948 to provide adoption services, the agency has evolved in response to the changing needs of the community and today provides a wide range of family and community services. The agency provides services to birthparents and places infants for adoption when birthparents decide that their child's best interests will be served by adoptive placement. In addition, the agency will provide supervisory services for applicants pursuing interagency adoption.

THE COST

The agency's fee for adoption services is based on a sliding scale according to income and ranges from $5,000 to $7,000. However, the agency will not refuse anyone a child because of an inability to pay the fee. In addition, applicants can expect to pay a $100 application fee and legal fees (approximately $600) connected with finalization of the adoption. Applicants should note that fees are subject to change.

THE WAIT

The time from application to the homecoming of the adoptive child ranges from 1 1/2 to 3 1/2 years.

THE CHILDREN

CSSB places primarily healthy infants born in the U.S. Most children placed by the agency are Caucasian, but the agency also places several bi-racial children annually.

THE REQUIREMENTS

Age: At the time of application, applicants must be at least 23 and no more than 38 years of age.
Health: Applicants should be in reasonably good health. Infertility documentation is required.
Religion: No requirement.
Financial status: No requirement other than the ability to financially provide for the child.
Marital status: Applicants must be married couples who have been married for at least 3 years.

Family size: Applicants must be childless.
Racial, ethnic or cultural origin: No requirement.

THE PROCEDURE

Participation in CSSB's adoption program entails the following basic steps:
    Application
    Orientation meeting
    Group counseling sessions
    Individual counseling sessions
    Homestudy
    Referral
    Placement
    Post-placement supervision
    Finalization

ADDITIONAL PROGRAMS/SERVICES

CSSB provides a wide range of services including individual, marital, and family counseling; counseling for children and adolescents; unplanned pregnancy counseling; premarriage counseling; foster care; crisis intervention; services to the aged; outreach for Vietnamese refugees; family life education programs; parish and community organization programs.

BRANCH/NETWORK OFFICES

1310 Leestown Road
Lexington, KY 40502
(606) 253–1993

LICENSE/ACCREDITATION/PROFESSIONAL AFFILIATIONS

Catholic Social Service Bureau is licensed by the State of Kentucky Cabinet for Human Resources.

CHILDPLACE

3248 Taylor Boulevard
Louisville, KY 40215
(502) 363–1633
Program director: Jo Len Janes

THE PROGRAM

For a full description of programs and services, refer to Indiana listing:

Childplace
2420 Highway 62
Jeffersonville, IN 47130
(812) 282–8248

CHOSEN CHILDREN ADOPTION SERVICES, INC.

5227 Bardstown Road
Louisville, KY 40291
(502) 591–6410
Program director: Raymond G. Kalef, MSW, Executive Director

THE PROGRAM

Chosen Children Adoption Services is a nonprofit agency serving residents of Kentucky, Indiana, Tennessee, New York, New Jersey, and Connecticut for Caucasian infant adoptions and all states in the U.S. except Michigan for Black and bi-racial adoptions. Founded in 1979 by Ray and Barbara Kalef as a complement to already existing public and religious agencies, Chosen Children maintains a close, family relationship with birthparents, adoptive parents, and their children. Chosen Children is dedicated "to serving childless couples desiring to complete their family, young women who have chosen adoption as an alternative for an unplanned pregnancy, and infants needing a secure and loving future." In addition, Chosen Children will provide homestudy and supervisory services for applicants pursuing interagency adoption (international or domestic) or independent adoption.

THE COST

The agency's fee for adoption services is based on a sliding scale and ranges from $2,250 to $6,000. Services covered by the fee include application, homestudy, placement, post-placement supervision, reports for finalization, and support activities (reunions, newsletters, seminars, support groups). In addition, applicants should anticipate financial responsibility for living expenses of the birthmother, medical expenses for the birthmother and child, legal fees for termination of parental rights, foster care pending placement, and legal fees connected with finalization.

THE WAIT

The time from application to the homecoming of the adoptive child averages 3 1/2 years.

THE CHILDREN

Chosen Children places predominantly healthy infants, of Caucasian, Black and bi-racial backgrounds, born in the U.S.

THE REQUIREMENTS

Age: Applicants must be at least 23 years of age.
Health: Applicants must be in reasonably good health. Applicants with health problems or handicaps are given individual consideration.
Religion: No requirement.
Financial status: No requirement.
Marital status: Applicants must be married, and the length of the marriage must be at least 3 years.
Family size: Applicants must be childless.
Racial, ethnic or cultural origin: No requirement.

THE PROCEDURE

Participation in the adoption program of Chosen Children entails the following basic steps:
    Application
    Orientation meeting
    Group counseling sessions
    Homestudy
    Individual counseling sessions
    Placement
    Post-placement supervision

ADDITIONAL PROGRAMS/SERVICES

Chosen Children provides workshops and seminars; short term infant foster care; counseling on demand for adoptive parents; weekly counseling for birthparents; reunions of all placed parents and children; newsletter.

BRANCH/NETWORK OFFICES

305 Bank Street
New Albany, IN 47150
(812) 945–6021

LICENSE/ACCREDITATION/PROFESSIONAL AFFILIATIONS

Chosen Children Adoption Services is licensed by the appropriate state department in Kentucky, Indiana, Connecticut, and New Jersey and is approved for placement in New York. Placements in other states are made through the Interstate Compact.

HOLT INTERNATIONAL CHILDREN'S SERVICES, INC.

4229 Bardstown Road, Suite 234
Chrysler Building
Louisville, KY 40218–0266(502) 499–1562
Program director: David H. Kim, Executive Director

THE PROGRAM

Holt International Children's Services in Louisville serves residents of Kentucky. For a full description of programs and services, refer to Oregon listing:

Holt International Children's Services, Inc.
P.O. Box 2880
1195 City View
Eugene, OR 97402
(503) 687–2202

Louisiana

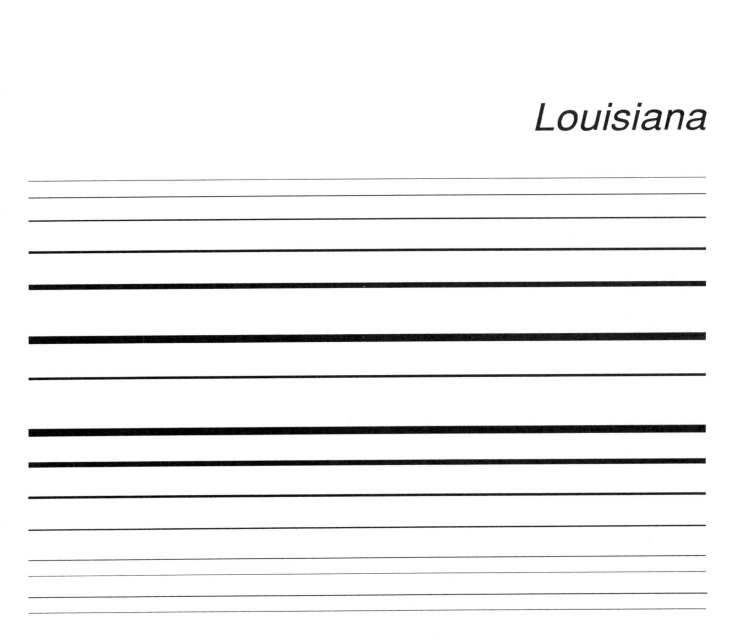

PUBLIC ADOPTION PROGRAM/ COMMUNITY RESOURCES

Department of Health and Human Resources
Division of Children, Youth, and Family Services
P.O. Box 3318
Baton Rouge, LA 70821
(504) 342–4041
Adoption specialist: Joel M. McLain

THE PROGRAM

Public adoption services in Louisiana are provided by the Department of Health and Human Resources under the jurisdiction of the Office of Human Development, Division of Children, Youth, and Family Services (OHD/DCYFS). OHD/DCYFS provides services to Louisiana families through regional offices located throughout the state. The focus of the OHD/DCYFS Adoption Program is to recruit and prepare families and to supervise the placement of special-needs children in Louisiana (primarily older, minority, and handicapped children and sibling groups) who are in the custody of the State. Related services include the administration of the Louisiana Adoption Resource Exchange (LARE), Louisiana Voluntary Registry, resource and referral services, and maintenance of security of adoption records sealed by the court and forwarded to the Department of Health and Human Resources.

STATE EXCHANGE

Louisiana Adoption Resource Exchange (LARE). For information contact the Division of Children, Youth, and Family Services (above).

STATE ADOPTION REUNION REGISTRY

Louisiana Voluntary Registry. For information contact the Division of Children, Youth, and Family Services (above).

STATE SUBSIDY ADOPTION SUBSIDY PROGRAM

For information contact the Division of Children, Youth, and Family Services (504–342–2844).

NACAC REPRESENTATIVE

None at this time.

GENERAL ADOPTION RESOURCES

Adoption Triad Network
Route 3, Box 211 AB
Lafayette, LA 70506
(318) 984–3682
Ms. Johnnie Kocurak

Adoptee's Birthright Committee
P.O. Box 7213
Metairie, LA 70010
(504) 242–0750
Ms. Mary Langhetee

SPECIAL-NEEDS ADOPTION RESOURCES

For information on special-needs adoption resources, contact the Division of Children, Youth and Family Services (above).

OUT-OF-STATE AGENCIES

AGENCY

The Edna Gladney Center, Texas
Smithlawn Maternity Home, Texas (special-needs and minority placement)
Southwest Maternity Center, Texas

SEE APPENDIX A

Agencies Providing Nationwide Services

CARING ALTERNATIVES— °VOLUNTEERS OF AMERICA

3900 N. Causeway Boulevard, Suite 700
Metairie, LA 70002
(504) 836–5225
1–800–535–9646 (toll free in Louisiana)
Program director: Paula Norris

THE PROGRAM

Licensed since 1945, Volunteers of America is a nonprofit agency which provides maternity home services as well as adoption services. Maternity home services are available to all Louisiana residents; adoption services are available to central and southern Louisiana residents. The agency places infants for adoption when birthmothers receiving maternity home services elect adoptive placement as the best plan for their child. In addition, the agency will provide homestudy and supervisory services for applicants pursuing interagency adoption (domestic or international) or private adoption. Since licensure, Volunteers of America has placed over 2,500 children in adoptive families and annually places approximately 30 children.

THE COST

The agency's fee for adoption services includes a registration fee of $100, a homestudy fee of $1,500, and a placement fee of 10% of the applicant's annual gross income. Services covered by the fee include all phases of the adoption process, excluding legal fees connected with finalization of the adoption (usually $250 to $400).

THE WAIT

The time from application for acceptance into the program to the homecoming of the adoptive child averages 1 1/2 to 2 years.

THE CHILDREN

Volunteers of America places both healthy and special-needs infants, of Caucasian, Black, and bi-racial backgrounds, born in the U.S.

THE REQUIREMENTS

Age: Applicants must be at least 25. Female applicants may be no more than 45 years of age; male applicants may be no more than 50.

Health: Applicants should be in reasonably good health.
Religion: No requirement.
Financial status: No requirement.
Marital status: Applicants may be either married or single. If married, the length of the marriage must be at least 3 years.
Family size: No requirement.
Racial, ethnic or cultural origin: No requirement.

THE PROCEDURE

Participation in the adoption program of Volunteers of America entails the following basic steps:
Submission of questionnaire
Application
Individual counseling sessions
Homestudy
Placement
Post-placement supervision

ADDITIONAL PROGRAMS/SERVICES

Volunteers of America provides foster care, counseling, and support groups.

BRANCH/NETWORK OFFICES

354 Jordan St.
Shreveport, LA 71101
(318) 221-2669

LICENSE/ACCREDITATION/PROFESSIONAL AFFILIATIONS

Volunteers of America is licensed by the State of Louisiana Department of Health and Human Resources.

CATHOLIC COMMUNITY SERVICES

Counseling, Maternity, and Adoption Department
4884 Constitution Avenue, Suite #1-B
Baton Rouge, LA 70808
(504) 927-4930
Program director: Janice D. Sapp, BCSW

THE PROGRAM

Catholic Community Services is a nonprofit agency serving only residents of the diocesan area (East Baton Rouge, West Baton Rouge, Iberville, Assumption, Ascension, Pointe Coupee, East Feliciana, West Feliciana, St. Helena, Livingston, Tangipahoa, and St. James) and placing approximately 15-20 children annually. Founded in 1964 as the Catholic Charities office for the Diocese of Baton Rouge, the agency works directly with birthparents, with other private and public agencies, and with national and regional exchange programs to place domestic infants and special-needs children. In addition, the agency provides homestudy and supervisory services, working in cooperation with other licensed agencies, to facilitate intercountry or interstate adoptions through the Interstate Compact. The agency gives a higher priority to couples/singles who wish to adopt a minority or hard-to-place child (a child with a congenital but correctable birth defect).

THE COST

The agency's fee for adoption services is based on a sliding scale and ranges from $420 to $10,000. Services covered by the fee include the homestudy, placement, and post-placement supervision.

For applicants pursuing intercountry or interstate adoptions, the agency's fee for homestudy and supervisory services is $700 plus $65 per supervisory home visit, if requested by the child placing agency.

THE WAIT

The time from application to the homecoming of the adoptive child averages 1 to 2 years.

THE CHILDREN

Catholic Community Services directly places healthy infants of all racial backgrounds, born in the Diocese of Baton Rouge. In addition, the agency will provide homestudy and supervisory services to facilitate the intercountry or interstate placement of children of any age, race, or national origin.

THE REQUIREMENTS

Age: Applicants must be at least 21 and no more than 38 years of age.
Health: Applicants must be in reasonably good health. Infertility documentation is required for infant adoptions.
Religion: No specific religious affiliation required.
Residence: Applicants must reside in the Diocese of Baton Rouge (the 12 surrounding civil parishes listed in the program description above).
Financial status: Applicants must demonstrate financial stability.
Marital status: Applicants must be married, and the length of the marriage must be at least 3 years.
Family size: Applicants may have no more than 1 child currently in the family.
Racial, ethnic or cultural origin: Preference for placing children in families of similar origins.

THE PROCEDURE

Participation in Catholic Community Services' adoption program entails the following basic steps:
Agency Adoption
Pre-application
Orientation meeting
Group counseling sessions
Application
Individual counseling sessions
Homestudy
Placement
Post-placement supervision
Finalization
Intercountry/Interstate Adoption
Pre-application
Application
Orientation meeting
Individual counseling sessions
Homestudy (Placement by cooperating agency)
Post-placement supervision
Compilation of court report for finalization (if requested by child placing agency)

ADDITIONAL PROGRAMS/SERVICES

The Counseling, Maternity, and Adoption Department (one of 3 departments of Catholic Community Services) provides individual counseling for unplanned pregnancy clients; group counseling for relinquishing clients; group counseling for non- relinquishing clients; short term infant foster care; individual, marital, and family counseling. Catholic Community Services' Family Life Department provides pre cana, engaged encounter, and natural family planning services. The Social Responsibility Department provides social justice, emergency assistance, senior employment, refugee resettlement, and foster grandparent programs.

BRANCH/NETWORK OFFICES

All adoption inquiries are processed through the main office in Baton Rouge.

LICENSE/ACCREDITATION/PROFESSIONAL AFFILIATIONS

Catholic Community Services is licensed by the State of Louisiana Department of Health and Human Resources. The agency is a member of the Louisiana Catholic Conference, Agenda for Children, Catholic Charities USA, and Louisiana Licensed Adoption Agencies.

CATHOLIC SOCIAL SERVICES

P.O. Box 883
1220 Aycock Street
Houma, LA 70361
(504) 876–0490
Program director: Sister Miriam Mitchell, SHSP.

THE PROGRAM

Catholic Social Services is a nonprofit agency serving residents of Terrebonne, Lafourche, and St. Mary Parishes and placing approximately 3 children annually. Incorporated in 1978, the agency's was organized for the purpose of "encouraging, promoting, advancing and conducting a Catholic family life" through the provision of social services. The agency provides services to birthparents and places infants for adoption when birthparents in the agency's counseling program elect adoptive placement as the best plan for their child. In addition, the agency will provide homestudy and supervisory services for applicants pursuing interagency adoption (international or domestic).

THE COST

The agency's fee for adoption services is 10% of the applicants' combined gross income, plus $200 for the homestudy. Services covered by the fee include all phases of the adoption process, excluding legal fees connected with finalization of the adoption (approximately $350).

Applicants pursuing interagency adoption (international or domestic) can expect to pay $500 for homestudy and supervisory services.

THE WAIT

The time from application to the homecoming of the adoptive child ranges from 3 to 6 years.

THE CHILDREN

Catholic Social Services places primarily healthy infants, of Caucasian, Black and bi-racial backgrounds, born in the U.S. In addition, the agency will provide homestudy and supervisory services for applicants pursuing interagency adoption of children of any age, race, or national origin.

THE REQUIREMENTS

Age: Applicants must be at least 21 and no more than 35 at the time of application.
Health: Applicants must be in reasonably good health. Infertility documentation is required.
Religion: Applicants must be practicing Catholics.
Financial status: No requirement.
Marital status: Applicants must be married, and the length of the marriage must be at least 2 years.
Family size: Applicants must be childless.
Racial, ethnic or cultural origin: Preference for placing children in families of similar origins.

THE PROCEDURE

Participation in the adoption program of Catholic Social Services entails the following basic steps:
Application
Group counseling sessions
Individual counseling sessions
Homestudy
Placement
Post-placement supervision

ADDITIONAL PROGRAMS/SERVICES

Catholic Social Services provides a range of community services including Assisi Bridge House (a home for alcoholic men); advocacy and referral; emergency financial services; budgeting and financial management services; maternity program; short term foster home care.

BRANCH/NETWORK OFFICES

None.

LICENSE/ACCREDITATION/PROFESSIONAL AFFILIATIONS

Catholic Social Services is licensed by the State of Louisiana Department of Health and Human Resources.

CATHOLIC SOCIAL SERVICES

1408 Carmel Avenue
Lafayette, LA 70506
(318) 261–5654
Program director: Sister Norma Garcia, CSJ

THE PROGRAM

Catholic Social Services is a nonprofit agency serving residents of Louisiana and placing approximately 22 children annually through its adoption program. In operation for 26 years, the agency provides extensive services to birthmothers (counseling, maternity home care, and school) and places infants for adoption when birthmothers decide that the best interests of their children will be served by adoptive placement.

THE COST

The agency's fee for adoption services is $6,000. Services covered by the fee include adoption preparation, homestudy, placement, post-placement supervision, and court report. In addition, applicants can expect to pay legal fees and court costs related to finalization of the adoption.

THE WAIT

The time from application for acceptance into the program to the homecoming of the adoptive child averages 2 years.

THE CHILDREN

Catholic Social Services places primarily healthy infants (birth to 1 month), of Black and Caucasian racial backgrounds.

THE REQUIREMENTS

Age: Applicants must be at least 25 and no more than 35 years of age.

Health: Applicants should be in reasonably good health. Applicants with health problems or handicaps are given individual consideration. Infertility documentation is required.

Religion: Applicants of all Christian faiths are eligible.

Financial status: Applicants must demonstrate financial stability.

Marital status: Applicants must be couples who have been married for at least 5 years and who display a stable marriage.

Family size: Applicants must be childless.

Racial, ethnic or cultural origin: Preference for placing children in families of similar origins.

THE PROCEDURE

Participation in the adoption program of Catholic Social Services entails the following basic steps:

Orientation meeting
Application
Group counseling sessions
Individual counseling sessions
Homestudy
Placement
Post-placement supervision

ADDITIONAL PROGRAMS/SERVICES

Catholic Social Services provides maternity home services and educational services to birthmothers, counseling services for birthparents and their families, and foster care for infants awaiting placement.

BRANCH/NETWORK OFFICES

None.

LICENSE/ACCREDITATION/PROFESSIONAL AFFILIATIONS

Catholic Social Services is licensed by the State of Louisiana Department of Health and Human Resources. The agency is an affiliate of Catholic Charities USA and a member of Licensed Louisiana Adoption Agencies Association.

CHILDREN'S BUREAU OF NEW ORLEANS

921 Canal Street, Suite 840
New Orleans, LA 70112
(504) 525–2366
Program director: Richard Zeilinger, Executive Director

THE PROGRAM

The Children's Bureau of New Orleans is a nonprofit agency serving residents of greater New Orleans and the surrounding area and placing approximately 27 children annually. Originally founded as the Louisiana Society for Prevention of Cruelty to Children in 1892, the agency has evolved in response to the changing needs of the community and today provides a range of services to children and families including adoption services, counseling services to families and children, pregnancy counseling, and other support services. Working directly with birthparents and working cooperatively with other agencies and national and regional exchange programs, the agency places domestic infants and special-needs children. Working with U.S.-based agencies with international programs, the Children's Bureau facilitates the placement of international infants and special-needs children. In addition, the agency will provide homestudy and supervisory services for applicants pursuing interagency adoption (domestic or international) or independent adoption.

THE COST

The agency's fee for adoption services is based on a sliding scale with an average fee of $2,500. Services covered by the fee include the adoption study, placement (for domestic children in the agency's custody), post-placement supervision, and post-legalization services. Applicants pursuing interagency adoption (domestic or international) should anticipate cooperating agency fees, travel expenses, and related costs. For all programs, applicants assume responsibility for legal fees connected with finalization of the adoption (approximately $400).

THE WAIT

The time from application to the homecoming of the adoptive child varies depending on the child's race, age, country of origin, and other factors. The wait could be as little as a week and as much as 4 to 5 years.

THE CHILDREN

The Children's Bureau places both healthy and special-needs children, ranging in age from infancy to adolescence, of all racial backgrounds. Countries of origin include U.S., Central and South America.

THE REQUIREMENTS

Age: Applicants must be at least 21 years of age. If married, the prospective father should be no more than 50, and the prospective mother should be no more than 45.

Health: Applicants should be in reasonably good health.

Religion: No requirement.

Financial status: No requirement other than the ability to adequately provide for the child.

Marital status: Applicants may be either married or single. If married, the length of the marriage must be at least 3 years.

Family size: No requirement.

Racial, ethnic or cultural origin: Preference for placing children in families of similar origins.

THE PROCEDURE

Participation in the adoption program of the Children's Bureau entails the following basic steps:

Application
Individual counseling sessions
Homestudy
Compliance with immigration/naturalization requirements (international adoptions only)
Placement
Post-placement supervision

ADDITIONAL PROGRAMS/SERVICES

The Children's Bureau provides family counseling and pregnancy counseling services.

BRANCH/NETWORK OFFICES

None.

LICENSE/ACCREDITATION/PROFESSIONAL AFFILIATIONS

The Children's Bureau of New Orleans is licensed by the State of Louisiana Department of Health and Human Resources and is accredited by the Council on Accreditation of Services for Families and Children. The agency is a founder member of the National Committee for Adoption.

CHRISTIAN HOMES

(A Program of Louisiana Child Care and Placement Services, Inc.)
9080 Southwood Drive
Shreveport, LA 71118
(318) 686-2243
Program director: Lynn Harms

THE PROGRAM

Christian Homes is a nonprofit agency placing approximately 10 children annually and serving residents of the state of Louisiana for healthy infant and special needs placements and serving out-of-state residents for special needs placements. Christian Homes began 20 years ago as Louisiana Child Care and Placement Services, a ministry of the Southern Hills Church of Christ in Shreveport, Louisiana, as "an effort by Christians to practice pure religion in caring for people who are vulnerable—children, families in trouble,

those who cannot care for themselves." The program began with 4 group homes and expanded to include individual foster care, adoption services, a maternity program, and counseling for families in the church and the community. Christian Homes provides services to birthparents and places infants for adoption when birthparents elect adoptive placement as the best plan for their child. Christian Homes also places special-needs children and works cooperatively with the public agency and with national and regional exchange programs to find families for waiting children. In addition, the agency will provide homestudy and supervisory services for applicants pursuing interagency adoption (domestic or international) or private adoption.

THE COST

For infant adoption, the agency's fee ranges from $6,500 to $9,000 and includes all services to the birthparents and child and all phases of the adoption process, excluding legal fees connected with finalization of the adoption. For special-needs adoption, there is no placement fee. There is, however, a minimal fee to cover incidental expenses.

THE WAIT

The time from application to the homecoming of the adoptive child averages 1 to 2 years.

THE CHILDREN

Christian Homes places both healthy and special-needs children, ranging in age from birth to 18 years, of all racial backgrounds, born in the U.S.

THE REQUIREMENTS

Age: Applicants must be at least 25.

Health: Applicants should be in reasonably good health.

Religion: Applicants must be practicing members of the Church of Christ. The requirement may be flexible for special needs placements.

Financial status: No requirement.

Marital status: For healthy infant adoption, applicants must be married, and the length of the marriage must be 3 years. The requirement is flexible for special needs placements.

Family size: For healthy infant adoption, applicants may have no more than 1 child currently in the home. The requirement is flexible for special needs placements.

Racial, ethnic or cultural origin: Preference for placing children in families of similar origins.

THE PROCEDURE

Participation in the adoption program of Christian Homes entails the following basic steps:

Application
Individual counseling sessions
Homestudy
Referral
Placement
Post-placement supervision

ADDITIONAL PROGRAMS/SERVICES

Christian Homes provides foster care, a maternity program, counseling services, and workshops on parenting and foster care.

BRANCH/NETWORK OFFICES

None.

LICENSE/ACCREDITATION/PROFESSIONAL AFFILIATIONS

Christian Homes (A Program of Louisiana Child Care and Placement Services, Inc.) is licensed by the State of Louisiana Department of Health and Human Resources. The agency is affiliated with the Louisiana Association of Child Care Agencies, Louisiana Licensed Adoption Agencies, and Christian Child Care Conference.

JEWISH CHILDREN'S REGIONAL SERVICE OF JEWISH CHILDREN'S HOME

P.O. Box 15225
New Orleans, LA 70175
(504) 899–1595
Program director: Viola W. Weiss

THE PROGRAM

Jewish Children's Regional Service is a nonprofit agency serving families who live in Alabama, Arkansas, Louisiana, Mississippi, Oklahoma, Tennessee, and Texas. Founded in 1855 as an orphanage, the agency has evolved in response to the needs of the community and today provides a range of educational and treatment services for children. While the agency does not usually have custody of children who are free for adoption, the agency maintains a small adoption program to serve families who have no other resource and provides homestudy and supervisory services for applicants pursuing domestic or international adoption through a licensed custodial agency. The agency's mission is "to enhance the well-being of Jewish children by providing care, education and treatment."

THE COST

The agency's fee for adoption services is based on a sliding scale and ranges from $0 to $2,500. Services covered by the fee include adoption counseling, homestudy, and post-placement supervision. Additional fees which applicants should anticipate include caseworker travel expenses, fees to the custodial agency, and legal fees connected with finalization of the adoption.

THE WAIT

Not applicable.

THE CHILDREN

Jewish Children's Regional Service places few children directly but will provide homestudy and supervisory services to facilitate the placement of either healthy or special-needs children of any age, race, or country of origin.

THE REQUIREMENTS

Age: The requirement varies depending on the age of the child to be placed. In general, applicants must be young enough to reasonably expect to survive until the child is 21 years old.

Health: Applicants should be in reasonably good health.

Religion: Applicants must be practicing members of the Jewish faith.

Financial status: Applicants must demonstrate financial stability.

Marital status: Applicants must be married couples.

Family size: Applicants may have no more than 1 child currently in the family. Exceptions are made for applicants adopting domestic special-needs children.

Racial, ethnic or cultural origin: No requirement.

THE PROCEDURE

Participation in Jewish Children's Regional Service adoption program entails the following basic steps:
  Application
  Individual counseling sessions
  Homestudy
  Referral
  Placement (by custodial agency)
  Post-placement supervision
  Post-adoption counseling (when requested)

ADDITIONAL PROGRAMS/SERVICES

Jewish Children's Regional Service provides financial assistance for special needs of children; education scholarships and camp scholarships; subsidy for emotionally disturbed children placed in residential treatment facilities other than hospitals; consultation and referral.

BRANCH/NETWORK OFFICES

None.

LICENSE/ACCREDITATION/PROFESSIONAL AFFILIATIONS

Jewish Children's Regional Service is licensed by the State of Louisiana Department of Health and Human Resources and is accredited by the Council on Accreditation of Services for Families and Children. The agency is a member of the Child Welfare League of America and the Jewish Family & Children's Agencies.

LDS SOCIAL SERVICES

2000 Old Spanish Trail
Pratt Center, Suite 203
Slidell, LA 70458 (504) 649–2774
Program director: Paul W. Denhalter

THE PROGRAM

For a full description of programs and services, refer to Utah listing:
  LDS Social Services
  50 East North Temple Street
  Salt Lake City, UT 84150

SELLERS BAPTIST HOME AND ADOPTION CENTER

2010 Peniston Street
New Orleans, LA 70115
(504) 895-2088
Program director: Mary Dan Kuhnle, ACSW, BCSW, Agency Director; Gisele Brown, ACSW, BCSW, Adoption Program Director

THE PROGRAM

Sellers Baptist Home and Adoption Center is a nonprofit agency owned and operated by the Home Mission Board of the Southern Baptist Convention. The agency will work with applicants from any state in the U.S., if permitted under the laws of the applicants' state of residence. Established in 1933 to provide maternity services to unmarried pregnant girls, the agency has expanded in response to the changing needs of the community. The agency's purpose is "to provide a Christian ministry" through maternity services (residential and non-residential), child care/day care, foster home care, services to birthfathers, and adoption services. In addition, on a case-by-case basis the agency will consider providing homestudy and supervisory services for applicants pursuing interagency adoption (domestic or international).

THE COST

The agency's fee for healthy Caucasian infant adoption is $5,000. Services covered by the fee include homestudy, placement, and post-placement supervision. The fee for the placement of Black, bi-racial, or special-needs children varies. (Interested applicants may contact the agency for more information on this program.) In addition, applicants can expect to pay for required reading materials and expenses incurred in completing the application (obtaining a credit report, medical exam, etc.). Out-of-state applicants can expect to pay fees to an agency in their home state for the provision of homestudy and supervisory services.

THE WAIT

The time from application to the homecoming of the adoptive child ranges from 2 to 5 years.

THE CHILDREN

Sellers Baptist Home and Adoption Center places both healthy and special-needs infants (birth to 6 months), of Caucasian, Black, and bi-racial backgrounds, born in the U.S.

THE REQUIREMENTS

Age: For healthy Caucasian infant adoption, applicants must be at least 21 and no more than 35 at the time of initial contact. The requirement is flexible for the placement of minority and special-needs children.

Health: Applicants must be in reasonably good health. Applicants with health problems or handicaps are given individual consideration. Infertility documentation is required for healthy Caucasian infant adoption.

Religion: For healthy Caucasian infant adoption, applicants must be practicing members of the Southern Baptist faith. For minority or special needs placements, applicants must be practicing Christians.

Financial status: Applicants must demonstrate the ability to provide for the child's financial needs and to pay the adoption fee.

Marital status: Applicants must be married, and the length of the marriage must be at least 2 years.

Family size: For healthy Caucasian infant adoption, applicants must be childless. The requirement is flexible for minority and special needs placements.

Racial, ethnic or cultural origin: Preference for placing children in families of similar origins.

THE PROCEDURE

Participation in the adoption program of Sellers Baptist Home and Adoption Center entails the following basic steps:
Submission of inquiry form
Submission of autobiographical information
Application
Submission of references
Homestudy (including individual interviews)
Approval/denial of approval of the homestudy
Placement
Post-placement supervision

ADDITIONAL PROGRAMS/SERVICES

Sellers Baptist Home and Adoption Center provides residential maternity care; foster care; day care; counseling and search services for adult adoptees, adoptive parents, and birthparents.

BRANCH/NETWORK OFFICES

None.

LICENSE/ACCREDITATION/PROFESSIONAL AFFILIATIONS

Sellers Baptist Home and Adoption Center is licensed by the State of Louisiana Department of Health and Human Resources.

Maine

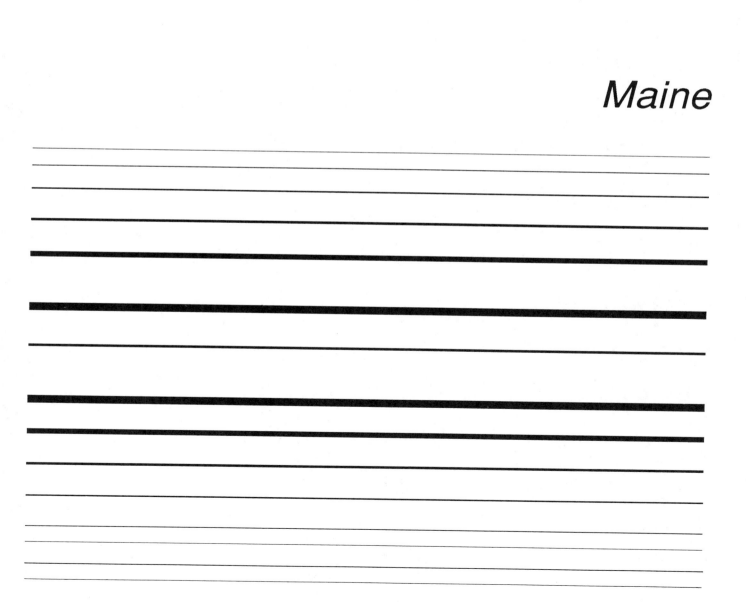

PUBLIC ADOPTION PROGRAM/ COMMUNITY RESOURCES

Department of Human Services
Bureau of Social Services
State House, Station 11
Augusta, ME 04333
(207) 289–5060
Adoption specialist: Leanore Taylor

THE PROGRAM

Public adoption services in Maine are provided by the Department of Human Services, Bureau of Social Services, through regional offices located throughout the state. While the agency does place a limited number of very young children, the primary focus of the State adoption program is to recruit and prepare adoptive families who are interested in adopting school aged and older children (8–17). Waiting children from Maine, New Hampshire, and Vermont are photo-listed in an exchange book which is available for viewing at any regional office of the Department of Human Services.

STATE EXCHANGE

Maine/Vermont/New Hampshire Exchange. For information, contact the Department of Human Services (above).

STATE ADOPTION REUNION REGISTRY

Maine State Adoption Reunion Registry
Division of Vital Records
221 State Street
Augusta, ME 04333
(207) 289–3181

STATE SUBSIDY

For information, contact the Department of Human Services (above).

NACAC REPRESENTATIVE

Judy Collier
281 Parkmur Avenue
Bangor, ME 04411
(207) 947–3178

GENERAL ADOPTION RESOURCES

Adoptive Parent Support Groups
Adoptive Families of Maine (AFM) Chapters
Sue Curran, AFM
11 Chandler Street
Calais, ME 04619
(207) 454–3675

Kitsie Claxton, AFM
445 Lake Street
Auburn, ME 04210
(207) 784–3804

Sharon Pierce, AFM
21 Glenwood Avenue
Augusta, ME 04330
(207) 622–0062

Nancy Kephart, AFM
Hancock, ME 04640
(207) 422–9555

Judy Collier, AFM
281 Parkview
Bangor, ME 04401

Edie Keller, AFM
19 Roosevelt Avenue
Waterville, ME 04901

Leslie Callahan, AFM
35 Crestview Drive
Presque Isle, ME 04769
(207) 764–4633

Infertility and Search Support Organizations
Resolve of Maine
P.O. Box 1682
Portland, ME 04104

Adoption Search Consultants of Maine (ASC-ME)
P.O. Box 2793
South Portland, ME 04106

SPECIAL-NEEDS ADOPTION RESOURCES

For information about resources for children with special needs, contact the Department of Human Services (above).

OUT-OF-STATE AGENCIES

SEE APPENDIX A

Agencies Providing Nationwide Services

COASTAL ADOPTION PLACEMENT SERVICE

Box 85
Addison, ME 04606
(207) 497–2441
Program director: Susan F. Harper

THE PROGRAM

Coastal Adoption Placement Service (CAPS) is a non-profit agency, serving the state of Maine, which began in 1983. After adopting 6 special-needs children, Lou and Sue Harper founded the agency with the belief that there must be other families, like their own, who were willing and able to adopt special-needs children. Although CAPS occasionally takes custody of an infant, the agency's focus is to provide assistance for handicapped children, older children, bi-racial or Black children, and sibling groups. Placing 20 to 25 children annually, CAPS goal is to find families who can provide for the special developmental and emotional needs of these children. CAPS emphasizes parental involvement throughout the adoption process.

THE COST

The agency's fee is based on a sliding scale. The fee

schedule is as follows:

Application fee	$75.00
Homestudy fee	
Gross family income of $30,000 or less (minimum charge)	$1,400.00

For each additional $5,000 of income, an additional $100.00 is charged.

Maximum	$2,000.00
Post-placement study	$ 500.00

In addition, prospective adoptive parents should anticipate financial responsibility for travel expenses ($.35/mile, meals) incurred by a CAPS worker traveling on the family's behalf, long distance phone calls made on behalf of the adoptive family, any outside evaluations deemed necessary by the agency in order to complete the homestudy, any costs involved in transporting the child, and legal costs connected with finalization of the adoption.

THE WAIT

The time from application for acceptance into the program to the homecoming of the adoptive child ranges from 2 to 14 months.

THE CHILDREN

CAPS places healthy and special-needs children, ranging in age from birth to 17 years, of all racial backgrounds. Children placed by CAPS are born in the U.S.

THE REQUIREMENTS

Age: Applicants must be at least 21 years old.
Health: Applicants must be in reasonably good health. Applicants with health problems or handicaps are given individual consideration.
Religion: No requirement.
Financial status: Applicants must demonstrate ability to meet the needs of the family on their income.
Marital status: Married couples must have been married for at least 2 years.
Family size: No requirement.
Racial, ethnic or cultural origin: No requirement.

THE PROCEDURE

Participation in CAPS adoption program entails the following basic steps:
Orientation meeting
Application
Interview with casework supervisor
Group counseling sessions
Homestudy
Individual counseling sessions
Attendance at support group meeting
Preparation of a lifebook or videotape of family
Referral
Placement
Post-placement supervision
Post-adoption services

ADDITIONAL PROGRAMS/SERVICES

CAPS offers a limited respite care program, a peer parenting program, counseling (mandatory monthly visits after placement), and two annual workshops concerning handicap awareness, advocacy in school and with other professionals, sexual abuse and the adoptive family, and other adoption issues.

BRANCH/NETWORK OFFICES

None.

LICENSE/ACCREDITATION/PROFESSIONAL AFFILIATIONS

CAPS is licensed by the State of Maine Department of Human Services. Casework supervisor (LCSW) and all caseworkers (LSW) are licensed by the Maine Board of Social Work Registration.

COMMUNITY COUNSELING CENTER

622 Congress Street
Portland, ME 04101
(207) 874–1030
Program director: Sylvia D. Schroeder, LCSW, Clinical Director

THE PROGRAM

Community Counseling Center is a nonprofit agency serving residents within a 40 mile radius of Portland and placing approximately 5 to 6 children annually. The agency's mission is "to provide and develop quality social work services to children, families and individuals within Cumberland County who need assistance with resolving personal, interpersonal, and environmental problems." The agency provides services to birthparents and places healthy infants for adoption when birthparents elect adoptive placement as the best plan for their child. Options available to birthparents and adoptive parents include modified, open, and traditional adoption services. In addition, the agency provides homestudy and supervisory services for applicants pursuing international adoption or private adoption.

THE COST

As of October 1988, the agency's fee for adoption services is 7% of the applicants' annual gross family income. Services covered by the fee include the homestudy, placement, and post-placement services. Applicants pursuing modified adoption should also anticipate legal expenses.

THE WAIT

The time from application to placement varies depending on the type of adoption, with an average wait of 1 to 2 years.

THE CHILDREN

Community Counseling Center places healthy infants, ranging in age from birth to 3 months, of all racial backgrounds, born in the U.S.

THE REQUIREMENTS

Age: Applicants must be at least 23 and no more than 45 years of age.

Health: Applicants must be in reasonably good health. Applicants with health problems or handicaps are given individual consideration. Infertility documentation is required.

Religion: No requirement.

Financial status: No requirement.

Marital status: No requirement.

Family size: Priority is given to childless, infertile couples. However, couples with children may be considered for hard-to-place infants.

Racial, ethnic or cultural origin: No requirement.

THE PROCEDURE

Participation in the adoption program of Community Counseling Center entails the following basic steps:

Orientation meeting

Application

Homestudy

Placement

Post-placement supervision

ADDITIONAL PROGRAMS/SERVICES

Community Counseling Center provides counseling services to birthparents and foster care for infants.

BRANCH/NETWORK OFFICES

None.

LICENSE/ACCREDITATION/PROFESSIONAL AFFILIATIONS

Community Counseling Center is licensed by the State of Maine Department of Human Services. The agency is a member of the Child Welfare League of America and Family Service America.

GOOD SAMARITAN AGENCY

P.O. Box 319
160 Broadway
Bangor, ME 05501
(207) 942–7211
Program director: James H. Clark

THE PROGRAM

Good Samaritan Agency is a nonprofit agency serving Penobscot, Piscataquis, Hancock, Washington, and Waldo Counties for infant and special-needs adoptions and serving the state of Maine for international adoptions. Since its inception in 1902, the agency has offered services to single parents. Providing counseling and educational services as well as foster home care, the goal of the agency's pregnancy counseling program is to assist birthparents in making "the most favorable plan for all concerned." The agency offers adoption placement services to birthparents who have selected adoption as the plan for their infants. The agency also facilitates the placement of special-needs children and foreign-born children, placing approximately 17 children annually.

THE COST

The agency's fees for adoption services vary depending on the program. The fee for a domestic adoption is based on a sliding scale and ranges from $1,000 to $3,000. The fee for international adoption services is $800. In addition, applicants interested in pursuing international adoption should anticipate fees to the cooperating agency and related costs, with the total cost for an international adoption ranging between $4,000 and $7,000. Services covered by the fee include information sessions, homestudy, child search and placement, post-placement supervision and consultation, and consultation during the finalization period. In addition, applicants assume responsibility for finalization of the adoption, including legal fees, if any.

THE WAIT

The time from application to the homecoming of the adoptive child varies depending on the program. For the adoption of a domestic infant or pre-school child, the wait averages 3 1/2 years following a period of up to 2 years on the application waiting list. For the adoption of a special needs or foreign-born child, the wait ranges between 12 and 18 months.

THE CHILDREN

Through its domestic program, Good Samaritan Agency places primarily newborn and pre-school (and occasionally older) children, both healthy and special needs, of various racial backgrounds. Through its international program, the agency places children ranging in age from birth to adolescence. Countries of origin include U.S., Korea, Chile, India, and Honduras.

THE REQUIREMENTS

Age: Applicants must be at least 21 years of age for domestic infant or special needs placements. For international placements, applicants must be at least 25. Maximum age requirement varies depending on the condition of the applicant's health. Generally, the age difference between the applicant and the child being considered for placement should not exceed 40 years.

Health: Applicants must be in reasonably good health. Applicants with health problem or handicap are given individual consideration.

Religion: No requirement.

Financial status: Applicants must demonstrate financial stability.

Marital status: Applicants may be either married or single. If married, the length of the marriage must be at least 2 years.

Family size: For domestic infant/pre-school age placement, the applicant couple must be childless or have no children by their marriage. The applicant couple is eligible for domestic infant/pre-school age placement if they have already adopted a special needs or international child through the Good Samaritan program. No requirement for special needs or international placement.

Racial, ethnic or cultural origin: No requirement, but preference for placing children in families of similar origins whenever possible and whenever in the best interest of the child.

THE PROCEDURE

Participation in the Good Samaritan Agency's adoption program entails the following basic steps:

Orientation meeting
Application
Group counseling sessions
Homestudy
Referral
Compliance with immigration/naturalization requirements (international adoptions only)
Placement
Post-placement supervision

ADDITIONAL PROGRAMS/SERVICES

Good Samaritan Agency offers a full range of single parent services and provides community education programs.

BRANCH/NETWORK OFFICES

None.

LICENSE/ACCREDITATION/PROFESSIONAL AFFILIATIONS

Good Samaritan Agency is licensed by the State of Maine Department of Human Services and social work staff members are licensed by the State Board of Social Worker Registration. Good Samaritan Agency is a member of the United Way, Statewide Coalition on Adolescent Pregnancy, and Public-Private Adoption Forum.

GROWING THRU ADOPTION

P.O. Box 7082
Lewiston, Maine 04240
(207) 786–2597/0325
Program director: Nora Quinn, Executive Director; Margery Goldberg, Program Director

THE PROGRAM

Growing Thru Adoption is a nonprofit adoption agency serving the state of Maine (except for Aroostock and Washington Counties), and placing approximately 35 children annually. Established in 1978, Growing Thru Adoption believes "that every child has the basic right to grow and develop in a loving and supportive family unit." Working with state-approved agencies in foreign countries, the agency places children from India, Korea, Hong Kong, Philippines, Guatemala, El Salvador, Colombia, and the U.S. The agency also provides homestudy and supervisory services fore applicants pursuing private adoption. The agency is committed to finding the resources that can bring "homeless children and loving families together."

THE COST

The agency's fee is based on a sliding scale and ranges from $1,200 to $2,500. The fee includes homestudy and post-placement services. For adoption of foreign children, applicants can expect a $5,000 to $8,000 fee to the foreign agency. In addition, applicants assume responsibility for legal fees connected with finalization of the adoption, although families can choose to finalize without the assistance of an attorney.

THE WAIT

The time from application to the homecoming of the adoptive child is approximately 1 to 2 years.

THE CHILDREN

Growing Thru Adoption places both healthy and special-needs children, ranging in age from birth to adolescence, of all racial backgrounds. Countries of origin include India, Korea, Hong Kong, Philippines, Guatemala, El Salvador, Colombia, and the United States. The Caucasian children available through the agency have special needs. The agency also provides homestudy and supervisory services for private adoptions.

THE REQUIREMENTS

Age: Applicants must be 21 years or older.
Health: Individual consideration is given to applicants with health problems or a handicap.
Religion: No requirement.
Financial status: No requirement.
Marital status: Couples should be married 2 or more years, although single applicants are also accepted.
Family size: No requirement.
Racial, ethnic or cultural origin: No requirement.

THE PROCEDURE

Participation in the Growing Thru Adoption program entails the following basic steps:
Orientation meeting
Application
Group counseling sessions (6–7)
Individual counseling sessions
Homestudy
Compliance with immigration/naturalization requirements
Referral
Placement
Post placement home visits/interviews
Assistance with finalization
Assistance with naturalization

ADDITIONAL PROGRAMS/SERVICES

Growing Thu Adoption Agency provides occasional workshops on special adoption issues with guest speakers and/or special programs.

BRANCH/NETWORK OFFICES

None.

LICENSE/ACCREDITATION/PROFESSIONAL AFFILIATIONS

Growing Thru Adoption is licensed by the state of Maine Department of Human Services.

INTERNATIONAL CHRISTIAN ADOPTION AGENCY

60 West River Road
Waterville, ME 04901 (207) 872–2156
Program director: James M. Woodward

THE PROGRAM

International Christian Adoption Agency is a nonprofit agency providing direct services for Maine residents. The agency also provides nationwide adoption placement services through the Interstate Compact for the Placement of Children for applicants working with licensed agencies in their home state who will provide homestudy, preparation for placement, and supervisory services. Incorporated in 1979, the mission of International Christian Adoption Agency is "to help provide permanency to the thousands of children living in third-world countries" who have been abandoned or orphaned. Since 1979, seven international adoption programs have been established with private and public programs in Latin America, Asia, and the Middle East. The agency places approximately 50 children annually.

THE COST

The agency's fee for adoption services is based on a sliding scale of 7% of the applicants' combined yearly income with minimum and maximum fees of $2,500 and $5,000. Additional costs include foreign agency fees, legal fees here and abroad, document authentication, and other related costs. Approximate total costs (excluding transportation, accommodations, and authentications) are as follows:

Hong Kong
$ 4,000.00
Chile
$ 9,500.00
Colombia
$ 3,600.00
Haiti
$ 5,100.00
The Philippines
$ 3,700.00
Taiwan
$ 6,100.00
Lebanon (includes escort transportation
to New York)
$10,100.00
El Salvador
$ 5,800.00

THE WAIT

The time from application for acceptance into the program to the homecoming of the adoptive child varies depending on the child's country of origin and the kind of child the applicants wish to adopt. The average wait is 1 year.

THE CHILDREN

International Christian Adoption Agency places primarily healthy children, ranging in age from birth to 15 years, of Hispanic, Asian, and Black racial backgrounds. Countries of origin include Colombia, Chile, Philippines, Haiti, Hong Kong, Taiwan, Lebanon, and El Salvador.

THE REQUIREMENTS

Age: Applicants must be at least 25 years of age. The maximum age requirement varies depending on the child's country of origin. Generally, the age difference between the applicant and the child being considered for placement should not exceed 45 years.

Health: Applicants must be in reasonably good health. For adoption of a child from Taiwan, infertility documentation is required.

Religion: Applicants must be practicing members of a Christian faith.

Financial status: Applicants must demonstrate ability to meet the on-going needs of the family.

Marital status: Single and married applicants are accepted. However, the requirement varies depending on the child's country of origin. For adoption from Taiwan, Colombia, Hong Kong, and the Philippines, applicants must be married. Generally, the length of the marriage must be at least 3 years.

Family size: For adoptions from Taiwan, applicants may have no more than 1 adopted child. For healthy infant placements from the Philippines, large families are not considered. For other programs, no requirements.

Racial, ethnic or cultural origin: No requirement.

THE PROCEDURE

For Maine residents, participation in ICAA's adoption program entails the following basic steps:
   Orientation meeting
   Application
   Individual counseling sessions
   Homestudy
   Compliance with immigration/naturalization requirements
   Referral
   Placement
   Post-placement supervision
   Finalization
   Naturalization

Non-Maine applicants must identify a licensed, child-placing agency in their home state which will provide the direct services associated with the development of the homestudy, preparation for placement, and supervision until finalization. Upon receipt of the applicant's homestudy and his anticipated approval by ICAA, the following steps will be taken by the direct service agency, ICAA and the adoptive applicants:
   Compliance with immigration/naturalization requirements
   Referral
   Placement
   Post-placement supervision
   Finalization
   Naturalization

ADDITIONAL PROGRAMS/SERVICES

International Christian Adoption Agency offers monthly workshops and semi-annual adoptive family gatherings; provides counseling and short-term foster care for women with unplanned pregnancies; supports sponsorship programs for international children not free for adoption.

BRANCH/NETWORK OFFICES

None.

LICENSE/ACCREDITATION/PROFESSIONAL AFFILIATIONS

International Christian Adoption Agency is licensed by the State of Maine Department of Human Services. The agency is a member of the Joint Council on International Children's Services and the North American Council of Adoptable Children.

MAINE ADOPTION PLACEMENT SERVICE

P.O. Box 772
Houlton, ME 04730
(207) 532–9358/4122
Program director: Dawn C. Degenhardt

THE PROGRAM

Maine Adoption Placement Service (MAPS) is a nonprofit child- placing agency, serving the state of Maine and specializing in the placement of special-needs children, which means "all children everywhere who are waiting for forever families." MAPS was established in 1977, growing out of a grassroots effort to bring children and families together with the conviction that there are many families waiting for special-needs children. Placing between 20 and 40 children annually, MAPS is committed "to adoption; to doing homestudies for prospective adoptive parents; to preparing families for adoption; to locating children for waiting families; to advocating adoption for children whose biological families are no longer willing or able to provide them with a stable and loving home; to counseling prospective parents about family planning; to educating the community; to working with birthmothers and assisting them in making good choices for themselves and their babies." In addition, MAPS works cooperatively with other U.S.-based agencies with foreign programs and provides homestudy and supervisory services for applicants who are interested in pursuing foreign adoption.

THE COST

MAPS' fee for adoption services is based on a sliding scale and averages $1,600. Services covered by the fee include parent training sessions of 16 hours, homestudy, search and placement of the child, counseling with the family before, during and after placement until finalization. In addition, prospective adoptive parents should anticipate financial responsibility for mileage, phone calls, and special postage in connection with the homestudy, fee to cooperating agency (varies greatly), travel costs to bring the child home, and legal fees connected with finalization of the adoption.

THE WAIT

The average time from application for acceptance into the program to the homecoming of the adoptive child is usually less than 1 year.

THE CHILDREN

MAPS places both healthy and special-needs children, ranging in age from birth to 12 years, of all racial backgrounds, born in the U.S. In addition, MAPS works cooperatively with other U.S.-based agencies, providing homestudy and supervisory services, to facilitate the placement of children from Korea, Bolivia, Philippines, Vietnam, and Costa Rica.

THE REQUIREMENTS

Age: The general requirement for infant adoption is that applicants must be at least 24 and no more than 45 years of age. Requirement may vary depending on the special needs of the child.

Health: Applicants must be in reasonably good health. Applicants with health problem or handicap are given individual consideration.

Religion: No requirement.

Financial status: No requirement.

Marital status: No requirement. If married, applicants must have been married for at least 2 years.

Family size: No requirement.

Racial, ethnic or cultural origin: No requirement.

THE PROCEDURE

Participation in MAPS' adoption program entails the following basic steps:

Application
Parent training sessions (16 hours)
Homestudy
Child search
Referral
Placement
Post-placement supervision (6–12 months)
Finalization

ADDITIONAL PROGRAMS/SERVICES

MAPS hosts an annual camp-out on the coast of Maine for adoptive families and professionals over Labor Day weekend. MAPS supports and encourages parent support groups throughout the state. MAPS is in the process of establishing a birthmother program and presently provides counseling services for birthparents. Future plans include establishing a residential facility for birthmothers.

BRANCH/NETWORK OFFICES

MAPS South
P.O. Box 4035, Station A
Portland, ME 04101
(207) 77–ADOPT

LICENSE/ACCREDITATION/PROFESSIONAL AFFILIATIONS

MAPS is licensed by the State of Maine Department of Human Services and is a member of several parent/adoptive groups around the country.

THE MAINE CHILDREN'S HOME FOR LITTLE WANDERERS

34 Gilman Street
Waterville, Maine 04901
(207)873–4253
Program director: Caroline Hutchinson

THE PROGRAM

The Maine Children's Home for Little Wanderers is a nonprofit organization that has extensive experience placing infants and school-age children in adoptive homes. Founded in 1899, the agency places infants with childless couples and also places special-needs children and children of mixed racial backgrounds. The agency's mission is to find "qualified couples who can provide a loving, secure and permanent home for children free for adoption." The Maine Children's Home for Little Wanderers serves the residents of the state of Maine only and places between 8 and 15 children annually.

THE COST

The fee is based on a sliding scale of 6 % of the applicants earnings for the prior year. The adoption fee covers group study and preparation sessions, home visits, placement, post-placement visits that lead to finalization, post-finalization visits and counseling (if needed), adoption information, and search if requested at a later time by the adopted child. In addition, applicants assume responsibility for legal fees connected with finalization of the adoption.

THE WAIT

The time from application to the homecoming of the adoptive child is 5 to 6 years for infants and 1 to 2 year wait for a special-needs child.

THE CHILDREN

The Maine Children's Home for Little Wanderers places both healthy and special-needs children, ranging in age from birth to adolescence, of Caucasian and mixed racial backgrounds. All children placed by the agency are born in the U.S.

THE REQUIREMENTS

Age: Applicants should be at least 21 years or older; the difference in age between an adopting couple and the child should not exceed 40 years.

Health: Applicants with health problems or a handicap are given individual consideration.

Religion: No requirement, but the preference of the birth-parents is honored.

Financial status: Applicants must have the financial ability to support an additional member of the family.

Marital status: For infant adoption, applicants must be married. The length of the marriage must be at least 3 years. Single applicants are accepted for special-needs adoptions.

Family size: For infant adoption, applicant must be childless. No requirement for special-needs adoptions.

Racial, ethnic or cultural origin: Preference for placing children in families of similar origins.

THE PROCEDURE

Participation in the Maine Children's Home for Little Wanderers adoption program entails the following basic steps:
Orientation meeting
Application
Individual counseling sessions
Homestudy
Group counseling sessions
Placement
Post-placement supervision

ADDITIONAL PROGRAMS/SERVICES

The Maine Children's Home for Little Wanderers provides foster care services as well as counseling and support services to unmarried parents and their families.

BRANCH/NETWORK OFFICES

116 State St.
Augusta, ME 04330
(207) 622–1552

LICENSE/ACCREDITATION/PROFESSIONAL AFFILIATIONS

The Maine Children's Home for Little Wanderers is licensed by the state of Maine Department of Human Services.

ST. ANDRE HOME, INC.

283 Elm Street
Biddeford, ME 04005
(207) 282–3351
Program director: Gregory C. Foltz, Ed.D., Executive Director

THE PROGRAM

St. Andre Home is a nonprofit agency serving the state of Maine and placing approximately 12 children annually. St. Andre Adoption Program was founded in 1940 in response to the needs of the unwed mother and her unborn child. In 1974, three group homes were established as a contemporary response to societal trends and client needs. St. Andre's Home is founded "on the Christian beliefs that human life is sacred, should be respected, and must be preserved and protected against injustice from the moment of conception. In its pursuit in furthering human life to its fullest development, the agency seeks to concretize the mission of Christ and ultimately to unite persons with God and with each other." St. Andre Home places infants for adoption when a birthmother in the agency's pregnancy counseling program decides that the best interests of the infant will be served by adoptive placement.

THE COST

The agency's fee schedule is as follows:

Application	$ 125.00
Homestudy	$1,035.00
Placement	$ 965.00
Supervision	$ 575.00
Total	$2,700.00

In addition, prospective adoptive parents should anticipate financial responsibility for legal fees connected with finalization of the adoption (approximately $300).

THE WAIT

The average time from application for acceptance into the program to the homecoming of the adoptive child is 2 1/2 years.

THE CHILDREN

St. Andre Home places healthy Caucasian infants (up to 12 months old), born in the U.S. The agency occasionally places a child with a correctable handicap.

THE REQUIREMENTS

Age: Applicants must be at least 22 and no more than 38 years of age.

Health: Applicants must be in reasonably good health. Infertility documentation is required.

Religion: Applicants must be practicing members of a Christian denomination.

Financial status: Applicants should have savings of at least $3,000.

Marital status: Applicants must be married and must have been married for at least 3 years.

Family size: Applicants must be childless or may have 1 child previously adopted through St. Andre Home.

Racial, ethnic or cultural origin: Preference for placing children in families of similar origins.

THE PROCEDURE

Participation in St. Andre Home adoption program entails the following basic steps:

Application
Homestudy
Placement
Post-placement supervision
Legalization

ADDITIONAL PROGRAMS/SERVICES

St. Andre Home provides foster care services; shelter programs for mothers with their infants, troubled adolescents, and unmarried mothers; non-residential adoption counseling; post-adoption services for adoptees, adoptive parents, and birthmothers.

BRANCH/NETWORK OFFICES

87 Ohio Street
Bangor, ME 04401
(207) 945-5021

188 Sabattus Street
Lewiston, ME 04240
(207) 783-8003

LICENSE/ACCREDITATION/PROFESSIONAL AFFILIATIONS

St. Andre Home, Inc. is licensed by the State of Maine Department of Human Services. The agency is a member of the National Committee For Adoption and the Maine Adoption Agencies Directors' Consortium.

Maryland

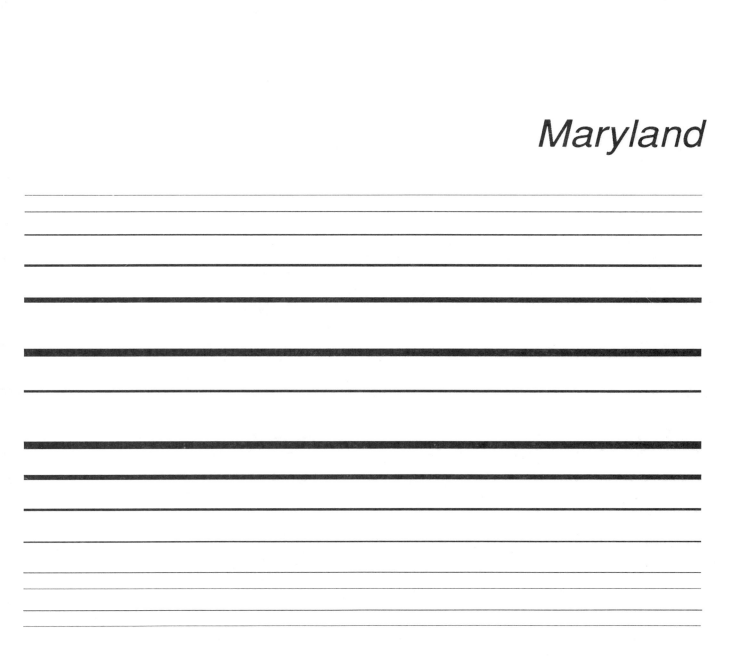

PUBLIC ADOPTION PROGRAM/ COMMUNITY RESOURCES

Department of Human Resources
Adoption Unit
311 W. Saratoga Street
Baltimore, MD 21201
(301) 333–0235
Adoption specialist: Fern Blake

THE PROGRAM

Public adoption services in Maryland are provided by the Department of Human Resources Social Services Administration through DSS branch offices located in each county. Working in cooperation with the Maryland Adoption Resource Exchange (see State Exchange below), local DSS offices recruit and prepare families and supervise the placement of special-needs children (older, minority, and handicapped children and sibling groups) who are in the guardianship of the State of Maryland.

STATE EXCHANGE

Maryland Adoption Resource Exchange (MARE) is a registry which serves as a link between children who need permanent homes and families who want to adopt. Waiting Maryland children are registered with MARE by their agencies, as are approved adoptive families. In addition to match/referral services, MARE provides information and photographs of waiting children to agencies, parent groups, and other exchanges around the country; coordinates agency referrals of children to other exchanges; provides adoption information to interested persons; and participates in community education and outreach efforts.

EXCHANGE COORDINATOR

Lillian B. Lansberry
Social Services Administration
311 W. Saratoga St.
Baltimore, MD 21201
(301) 333–0236

STATE ADOPTION REUNION REGISTRY

Mutual Consent Voluntary Adoption Registry
Social Services Administration
311 W. Saratoga St.
Baltimore, MD 21201
(301) 333–0237
Director: Susan Weigel

STATE SUBSIDY

The adoption subsidy program is administered through 24 local DSS offices. Contact the DSS office in your area for information.

NACAC REPRESENTATIVE

Chris Griffin
1046 Cockeys Mill Road
Reistertown, MD 21136
(301) 833–9229

GENERAL ADOPTION RESOURCES

Adoptive Parent Support Groups
Committee for Single Adoptive Parents
P.O. Box 15084
Chevy Chase, MD 20815
F.A.C.E. (Families Adopting Children Everywhere)
P.O. Box 28058
Northwood Station
Baltimore, MD 21239
(301) 256–0410
(Chapters located throughout the state)
BARN (Black Adoption Recruitment Network)
1510 Guilford Ave.
Baltimore, MD 21202
(301) 486–4160
IFBA (International Families By Adoption)
Box 1
Frederick, MD 21798
(301) 271–4163
LAPA (Latin America Parents Association)
Box 4403
Silver Spring, MD 20904
(301) 384–7467
Adult Adoptee Search Assistance
Adoptee-Birthparent Support Network
Box 23674, L'Enfant Plaza Station
Washington, DC 20026–0674
(301) 464–5755 (for Maryland inquiries)
Adoptees in Search, Inc.
Box 41016
Bethesda, MD 20014
(301) 656–8555

SPECIAL-NEEDS ADOPTION RESOURCES

F.A.C.E. (Families Adopting Children Everywhere)
P.O. Box 28058
Northwood Station
Baltimore, MD 21239
(301) 256–0410

OUT-OF-STATE AGENCIES

AGENCY

Adoption Service Information Agency, Washington, D.C.
Associated Catholic Charities, Washington, D.C.
Lutheran Social Services, Washington, D.C.
Welcome House Adoption Services, Delaware
Catholic Charities of Richmond, Virginia
Rainbow Christian Services, Virginia

SEE APPENDIX A

Agencies Providing Nationwide Services

BETHANY CHRISTIAN SERVICES

114–B Annapolis Street
Annapolis, MD 21401
(301) 263–7703
Program director: James K. Haveman, Jr., Executive
Director

THE PROGRAM

For a full description of programs and services, refer to
Michigan listing:
Bethany Christian Services
901 Eastern Avenue, N.E.
Grand Rapids, MI 49503–1295
(616) 459–6273

FAMILY AND CHILDREN'S SERVICES OF CENTRAL MARYLAND

204 West Lanvale Street
Baltimore, MD 21217
(301) 669–9000
Program director: Elizabeth A. Kavanagh, LCSW

THE PROGRAM

Family and Children's Services is a nonprofit, non-sectarian, multi-service agency serving residents of central Maryland and placing approximately 50 children annually through
its adoption program. The agency provides services to birthparents and places both healthy and special-needs children
for adoption when birthparents elect adoptive placement as
the best plan for their child. The agency's current focus is to
find Black adoptive families for Black infants. In addition,
the agency provides homestudy and supervisory services for
applicants pursuing either parent-initiated or interagency
international adoption and for applicants pursuing independent adoption. In all of its programs, the agency is committed
"to strengthening individual and family life by providing
high quality counseling, education and support services in
stress situations, so that each individual can find an opportunity for a happy and useful life and develop to his or her full
potential."

THE COST

As of October 1988, the agency's fee for adoption services
is based on a sliding scale and ranges from $0 to $7,500.
Services covered by the fee include the homestudy, placement, and post-placement supervision. For applicants pursuing international adoption, the agency's fee for homestudy
and post-placement supervision is $1,600. For applicants
pursuing independent adoption, the agency's fee for homestudy and post-placement supervision is $2,000. In addition,
applicants can anticipate approximately $90 in court costs
related to finalization.

THE WAIT

The time from application to placement varies depending
on the type of child the applicants wish to adopt.

THE CHILDREN

Family and Children's Services places both healthy and
special-needs children, ranging in age from birth to 1 year, of
Black and Caucasian racial backgrounds. In addition, the
agency will provide homestudy and supervisory services for
applicants pursuing international or independent adoption.

THE REQUIREMENTS

Age: Applicants must be at least 21. The maximum age
limit varies depending on the type of child requested. The
requirement is flexible for applicants interested in special
needs or international adoption.
Health: Applicants should be in reasonably good health.
Applicants with health problems or handicaps are given
individual consideration.
Religion: No requirement.
Financial status: One member of the household must be
employed.
Marital status: The requirement varies depending on the
type of child requested.*Family size*: The requirement varies
depending on the type of child requested.
Racial, ethnic or cultural origin: Preference for placing
children in families of similar origins.

THE PROCEDURE

Participation in the adoption program of Family and
Children's Services entails the following basic steps:
Application
Homestudy (including individual and group counseling
sessions)
Compliance with immigration/naturalization requirements
(international adoptions only)
Placement
Post-placement supervision

ADDITIONAL PROGRAMS/SERVICES

Family and Children's Services provides a range of services including extensive counseling services; residential treatment center for adolescent girls; treatment center for sexually
abused children; adult day care; sheltered housing; senior
aides; homemaker services.

BRANCH/NETWORK OFFICES

Family and Children's Services maintains branch offices
in Anne Arundel, Baltimore, Carroll, Harford, and Howard
Counties. All adoption inquiries are processed by the main
office in Baltimore.

LICENSE/ACCREDITATION/PROFESSIONAL AFFILIATIONS

Family and Children's Services of Central Maryland is
licensed by the State of Maryland Department of Human
Resources and is accredited by the Council on Accreditation
of Services for Families and Children. The agency is a
member of the Child Welfare League of America, Family
Service America, The United Way of Central Maryland, and
an associate member of the National Home Caring Council.

JEWISH FAMILY SERVICES

5750 Park Heights Avenue
Baltimore, MD 21215(301) 466–9200
Program director: Myra Hettleman, LCSW

THE PROGRAM

Jewish Family Services is a nonprofit agency serving Baltimore and the surrounding counties (including Baltimore, Howard, Harford, Carroll, and Anne Arundel). Providing homes for homeless children for the past 131 years, the agency's purpose is "to strengthen Jewish individual and family life, to promote Jewish identity and commitment, to enhance the quality of life, and to enable individuals and families to function as independently as possible." Considering the child to be the primary client in the adoption process, the agency offers several adoption programs including traditional, identified, and international adoptions. An increasingly small number of children are placed through the traditional program in which birthparents surrender their child to the agency for adoptive placement. Through the identified adoption program, prospective adoptive parents themselves locate a pregnant woman who is willing to specify the adoption of her child by those parents. Through the international program, the agency provides homestudy and supervisory services for adoptive parents who have located a foreign-born child who is available for adoption.

THE COST

The agency's fee for adoption services is based on a sliding scale and varies depending on the program. The maximum fee for a traditional adoption is $7,500. Services covered by the fee include homestudy, placement, post-placement supervision, and finalization report. The maximum fee for an identified adoption is $1,800. The maximum fee for an international adoption is $1,200. Services covered by fees for identified and international adoptions include homestudy, post-placement supervision, and finalization report. In addition, for identified and international adoptions, prospective adoptive parents should anticipate financial responsibility for travel costs, legal fees, and long distance telephone calls. In all programs, applicants assume responsibility for legal fees connected with finalization of the adoption.

THE WAIT

The average time from application for acceptance into the traditional program to the homecoming of the adoptive child is 4 years. The wait for other programs varies depending on the applicants' degree of assertiveness in locating a child.

THE CHILDREN

Jewish Family Services places primarily healthy infants of Caucasian and bi-racial backgrounds. However, as noted, the agency will provide homestudy and supervisory services for the adoption of healthy or special-needs children of any age, racial background, or country of origin.

THE REQUIREMENTS

Age: No requirement, but factors of age and health will be considered in assessing the applicants' eligibility.

Health: For traditional adoption, infertility documentation is required. For all programs, factors of age and health will be considered in assessing the applicants' eligibility.

Religion: At least one member of the couple must be a practicing member of Judaism.

Financial status: Applicants must demonstrate financial stability.

Marital status: Applicants must be married and must have been married for at least 2 years.

Family size: For traditional program, applicants must be childless. No requirement for other programs.

Racial, ethnic or cultural origin: Preference for placing children in families of similar origins.

THE PROCEDURE

Participation in Jewish Family Services' adoption programs entails the following basic steps:
Application
Group and individual counseling sessions
Homestudy
Referral
Placement
Post-placement supervision

ADDITIONAL PROGRAMS/SERVICES

Jewish Family Services provides short-term support groups for infertile couples; foster care services; individual, marital, and family counseling services.

BRANCH/NETWORK OFFICES

All adoption inquiries are processed through the main office in Baltimore.

LICENSE/ACCREDITATION/PROFESSIONAL AFFILIATIONS

Jewish Family Services is licensed by the State of Maryland Department of Human Resources and is accredited by the Council on Accreditation of Services for Families and Children. Jewish Family Services is an agency of the Associated Jewish Charities & Welfare Fund and is a member of Family Service America and the Association of Jewish Family & Children's Agencies.

JEWISH SOCIAL SERVICE AGENCY OF METROPOLITAN WASHINGTON

6123 Montrose Road
Rockville, MD 20852
(301) 881–3700
Program director: Joan de Pontet, LCSW

THE PROGRAM

Jewish Social Service Agency (JSSA) is a nonprofit agency serving residents of Maryland (Montgomery and Prince George's Counties), Virginia (Alexandria, Arlington, Fairfax, and Prince William Counties), and the District of Columbia and placing approximately 2 to 4 children annually (with expansion to 10 to 12 placements anticipated in 1988–89). JSSA's mission is "to prevent and relieve psychological, social and economic problems in the Jewish community and to extend appropriate services to individuals, families and groups of other faiths who can be helped through certain agency programs." JSSA offers a non-sectarian program of maternal assistance (including exploration of all options, pregnancy and post-partum counseling, and financial assistance), infant foster care, services to families seeking adoption (including counseling, homestudies, information and referral, and post-placement supervision), post-adoption counseling and workshops, and counseling and information for adult adoptees. The agency places infants for adoption when birthparents in the agency's counseling program elect adoptive placement as the best plan for their child. The agency also recruits families for older children and special-needs children who come to the agency's attention. In addition, the agency will provide homestudy and supervisory services for applicants pursuing domestic interagency adoption.

THE COST

The agency's fee for adoption services is based on a sliding scale and ranges from $1,500 to $7,500. Services covered by the fee include services to birthparents and child (counseling, medical, legal, relinquishment, and foster care) and services to the adoptive parents (counseling, homestudy, post-placement supervision, and court report). Applicants are responsible for legal fees connected with finalization.

THE WAIT

The time from application for acceptance into the program to the homecoming of the adoptive child has averaged 5 years.

THE CHILDREN

JSSA places primarily healthy Caucasian infants, born in the U.S. The agency also recruits families for older children and special-needs children who come to the agency's attention.

THE REQUIREMENTS

Age: Applicants may be no more than 40 years of age.
Health: Applicants must be in reasonably good health. Applicants with health problems or handicaps are given individual consideration. Infertility documentation is required.
Religion: For infant adoption, adoptive applicants must be Jewish. For older child or special-needs adoption, one parent must be Jewish.
Financial status: Applicants must have sufficient income to support a child.
Marital status: Applicants must be married; the length of the marriage must be at least 1 year at the time of application.
Family size: For healthy infant adoption, applicants must be childless. The requirement is flexible for special needs placements.
Racial, ethnic or cultural origin: No requirement.

THE PROCEDURE

Participation in JSSA's adoption program entails the following basic steps:
Application
Orientation meeting
Group counseling sessions
Homestudy
Referral
Placement
Post-placement supervision

ADDITIONAL PROGRAMS/SERVICES

JSSA provides a range of services to the community including individual, marital, and family counseling; services to the aging; newcomer resettlement; special services and outreach to disabled persons; children's services (child guidance clinic, infant foster care, emergency foster care); home health care; hospice care; family services; Jewish family life education; volunteer services.

BRANCH/NETWORK OFFICES

Northern Virginia
8822 Little River Turnpike
Fairfax, VA 22031
(301) 881–3700
(703) 323–1668
Prince George's County
6525 Belcrest Rd., Suite 906
Hyattsville, MD 20782
(301) 881–3700
(301) 927–2660
District of Columbia
2028 P St., NW
Washington, DC 20036
(202) 887–1644
District of Columbia
619 D St., SE
Washington, DC 20003
(301) 881–3700

LICENSE/ACCREDITATION/PROFESSIONAL AFFILIATIONS

Jewish Social Service Agency is licensed by the State of Maryland Department of Human Resources (with reciprocity in the District of Columbia) and by the Commonwealth of Virginia Department of Social Services. JSSA is accredited by the Council on Accreditation of Services for Families and Children and is a member of the Association of Jewish Family and Children's Agencies and the National Committee For Adoption.

LDS SOCIAL SERVICES

Amber Meadows Professional Building
198 Thomas Johnson Drive, #13
Frederick, MD 21701(301) 428–4988
Program director: A. Dean Byrd

The Program

For a full description of programs and services, refer to Utah listing

LDS Social Services
  50 East North Temple Street
  Salt Lake City, UT 84150

Massachusetts

PUBLIC ADOPTION PROGRAM/ COMMUNITY RESOURCES

Department of Social Services
Adoption Unit
150 Causeway Street
Boston, MA 02114
(617) 727–0900
Adoption specialist: Mary Hansen

THE PROGRAM

Public adoption services in Massachusetts are provided by the Department of Social Services through regional adoption units located throughout the state. The Department of Social Services provides funding for the Massachusetts Adoption Resource Exchange (MARE), a private, nonprofit organization which provides information/referral and listing/recruitment services for special-needs children (older children, minority children, children with emotional, intellectual, or physical special needs, and sibling groups). Working cooperatively with MARE, the Adoption Unit recruits and prepares families for special-needs adoption of children who are in the custody of the Commonwealth of Massachusetts. (For a complete description of MARE's programs and services, refer to Massachusetts listing.)

STATE EXCHANGE

Massachusetts Adoption Resource Exchange (MARE)
867 Boylston Street
Boston, MA 02116
(617) 536–0362
1–800–882–1176 (toll-free in Massachusetts)
Director: Phyllis P. Tourse

STATE ADOPTION REUNION REGISTRY

None.

STATE SUBSIDY

Adoption Subsidy Administration
Department of Social Services
150 Causeway Street
Boston, MA 02114
(617) 727–0900

NACAC REPRESENTATIVE

Mary·Lou Robinson
96 Rick Drive
Florence, MA 01060
(413) 584–8459

GENERAL ADOPTION RESOURCES

Adoptive Parent Support Groups
MARE Support Center for Adoptive Families
Massachusetts Adoption Resource Exchange, Inc.
867 Boylston Street
Boston, MA 02116
(617) 536–0362
1–800–882–1176 (toll-free in MA)

Open Door Society of Massachusetts (ODS)
c/o Massachusetts Adoption Resource Exchange, Inc.
867 Boylston Street
Boston, MA 02116
(617) 527–5660 (eastern MA)
(413) 585–9869 (western MA)
Single Parents for Adoption of Children Everywhere (SPACE)
Betsy Burch
6 Sunshine Ave.
Natick, MA 01760
(617) 655–5426 (evenings)

SPECIAL-NEEDS ADOPTION RESOURCES

Today's Children, Tomorrow's Families, prepared by Deborah Burke Henderson for the Massachusetts Adoption Resource Exchange, is an important resource for families adopting special-needs children in Massachusetts. The manual answers questions about special-needs children and the adoption process; addresses such issues as adoption subsidy, post-placement services, and parent advocacy; provides addresses and telephone numbers of local, state, and national resources for medical, mental health, educational, and child welfare services. The manual is available from the Massachusetts Adoption Resource Exchange (above).

OUT-OF-STATE AGENCIES

AGENCY

Smithlawn Maternity Home, Texas (special-needs and minority placements)

SEE APPENDIX A

Agencies Providing Nationwide Services

THE ALLIANCE FOR CHILDREN, INC.

110 Cedar Street
Wellesley, MA 02181
(617) 431–7148
Program director: Filis Casey, Executive Director; Vivian Cone, Director of Professional Services

THE PROGRAM

The Alliance for Children is a nonprofit agency serving residents of Massachusetts only (excluding western Massachusetts) and placing approximately 70 to 90 children annually. Founded in 1975, the agency's mission is "to aid in the placement of children of various racial and national backgrounds in Massachusetts homes." Working directly with foreign sources and working cooperatively with other U.S. agencies which maintain international programs, Alliance for Children places both healthy and special-needs children, principally of Latin American origin (but from other countries as well), in Massachusetts families. In addition, the agency provides services for parent-initiated or identified adoptions (both domestic and international) and will provide homestudy and post-placement supervision for applicants pursuing interagency adoption (both domestic and international). The Alliance for Children is committed to assisting children who will remain in their own country.

THE COST

The agency's fee for adoption services is based on a sliding scale and ranges from $700 to $2,000. Services covered by the fee include the homestudy, post-placement services, and finalization of the adoption. Applicants should also anticipate placement fees to the source agency (either a child welfare institution abroad or a cooperating U.S. agency), possible travel expenses, and related costs.

THE WAIT

The time from application to the homecoming of the adoptive child ranges from 1 year to 18 months.

THE CHILDREN

The Alliance for Children places primarily healthy children of Hispanic and Indian racial backgrounds. Countries of origin include Colombia, Ecuador, Chile, Guatemala, Mexico, and India. The agency also places a small number of children from other countries (Peru, Brazil, the Philippines). The agency will provide homestudy and supervisory services for applicants pursuing parent-initiated or interagency adoption of children of any age, race, or national origin.

THE REQUIREMENTS

Age: Applicants must be at least 25 years old. The maximum age for infant adoption is 45 years. The requirement may vary depending on the requirements of the source.

Health: Applicants should be in reasonably good health. Applicants with health problems or handicaps are given individual consideration.

Religion: No requirement, but may vary depending on the requirements of the source.

Financial status: Applicants must demonstrate financial stability and sufficient resources to support an additional child.

Marital status: The requirement varies depending on the requirements of the source.

Family size: The requirement varies depending on the requirements of the source.

Racial, ethnic or cultural origin:: No requirement.

THE PROCEDURE

Participation in the adoption program of the Alliance for Children entails the following basic steps:

Application
Homestudy
Compliance with immigration/naturalization requirements
Referral
Placement
Post-placement supervision

ADDITIONAL PROGRAMS/SERVICES

The Alliance for children provides counseling services for birthparents and their families, foster care for newborns, support groups, and social activities.

BRANCH/NETWORK OFFICES

None

LICENSE/ACCREDITATION/PROFESSIONAL AFFILIATIONS

The Alliance for Children, Inc. is licensed by the Commonwealth of Massachusetts Council of Human Service Providers, Open Door Society, Alliance for Young Families, and International Concerns Committee for Children.

THE BERKSHIRE CENTER FOR FAMILIES AND CHILDREN

472 West Street
Pittsfield, MA 01201
(413) 448–8281
Program director: Claudia L. Finck, ACSW, LICSW, Adoption Coordinator

THE PROGRAM

The Berkshire Center for Families and Children (BCFC) is a nonprofit social service agency, serving residents of Massachusetts who either live or work in Berkshire County. Providing services for children for over a hundred years, BCFC has changed over the years in response to national trends, offering several adoption programs, including traditional adoptions, designated adoptions, and international adoptions. Traditional adoptions involve the matching of an infant who has been surrendered to the agency to a couple whose homestudy has been approved by the agency. Designated adoptions involve a situation in which prospective adoptive parents have become aware of a specific couple who are willing to specify the adoption of their child by those parents. BCFC places approximately 6 children annually through these programs. Through its international program, BCFC places children from India. Because the international program is relatively new, the agency is unable to give an accurate estimate of the annual number of placements. In all of its adoption programs, BCFC's primary purpose is "to assure a permanent family for each child and to promote the optimal growth and individual development of all persons receiving its services."

THE COST

The agency's fee is 8% of the family's gross income, plus an application fee of $200, with a maximum fee of $4,500. The fee includes the homestudy, placement, post-placement services, legal costs, and finalization. Fees for counseling sessions prior to acceptance for homestudy are based on family size and income.

For designated adoptions, prospective adoptive parents should also anticipate financial responsibility for legal and medical costs. For international adoptions, applicants should anticipate additional expenses for filing, copying, and authenticating required documents, long-distance telephone calls, overseas legal and agency fees, and airfare to bring the child from India to the United States.

THE WAIT

The time from application for acceptance into the program to the homecoming of the adoptive child varies with a range of 1 to 5 years.

THE CHILDREN

BCFC places infants from the United States (primarily Caucasian) and India.

THE REQUIREMENTS

Age: No requirement.
Health: Applicants must be in reasonably good health. Applicants with health problems or handicaps are given individual consideration.
Religion: No requirement.
Financial status: No requirement, but must demonstrate financial stability.
Marital status: No requirement, but married couples must have been married for at least 2 years.
Family size: Applicants may have no more than 1 child currently in the family. Exceptions may be made for applicants pursuing international adoption.
Racial, ethnic or cultural origin: No requirement.

THE PROCEDURE

Participation in BCFC adoption programs entails the following basic steps:
Individual orientation/counseling sessions
Application
Homestudy (either individual or group)
Compliance with immigration/naturalization requirements
   (international adoptions only)
Placement
Post-placement supervision
Finalization

ADDITIONAL PROGRAMS/SERVICES

BCFC provides counseling to families, couples, and individuals of all ages. In addition, the agency offers special services to young parents and adolescents, operates a licensed day care center, and sponsors educational programs to meet the needs of adoptive families.

BRANCH/NETWORK OFFICES

None.

LICENSE/ACCREDITATION/PROFESSIONAL AFFILIATIONS

The Berkshire Center for Families and Children is licensed by the Commonwealth of Massachusetts Office for Children.

BETHANY CHRISTIAN SERVICES

62 Foundry Street
Wakefield, MA 01880
(616) 246–1890
Program director: James K. Haveman, Jr., Executive Director

THE PROGRAM

For a full description of programs and services, refer to Michigan listing:
Bethany Christian Services
901 Eastern Avenue, N.E.
Grand Rapids, MI 49503–1295
(616) 459–6273

BOSTON CHILDREN'S SERVICE ASSOCIATION

867 Boylston Street
Boston, MA 02116
(617) 267–3700
Program director: Mary C. Byrne, Assistant Executive Director

THE PROGRAM

Boston Children's Service Association (BCSA) was formed through the merger of Children's Aid Association and Boston Children's Friend Society in 1960. It is, however, the successor to six agencies under different names dating back to 1800 and is consequently the oldest child welfare agency in the United States. BCSA is a voluntary, nonprofit, multi-service agency which provides assistance for children of all ages, races and ethnic backgrounds from their prenatal days through infancy, childhood, and adolescence. Based on the philosophy that the family is the basic structure for the physical and emotional nurturing of every child, all BCSA services and every possible community resource are made available to support and enrich family life. In the event of a breakdown of the family unit, BCSA stands ready with an alternative plan "to assure every child the chance to develop in a safe, secure, and loving environment." Serving the greater Boston area (Suffolk, Norfolk, Middlesex and Essex Counties), BCSA places between 25 and 40 children annually.

THE COST

The agency fee is based on a sliding scale and currently ranges from $100 to $3,500. (However, applicants should note that the fee schedule is pending revision.) Services covered by the fee include application and screening interview, educational series (6 sessions), home assessment, placement, post-placement services, legalization, and support groups.

THE WAIT

The time from application for acceptance into the program to the placement of the adoptive child varies depending on the circumstances of each case. The wait for a Caucasian, healthy, legally free infant is indeterminate. For the legal risk program (older, minority, and special-needs children and sibling groups), the wait ranges from 6 months to 3 years.

THE CHILDREN

BCSA places both healthy and special-needs children, ranging in age from birth to 15 years, of all racial backgrounds. Countries of origin include U.S. and Hong Kong.

THE REQUIREMENTS

Age: No requirement.

Health: Applicants must be in good health. Infertility documentation is required for legally free infants. Applicants with health problems or handicaps are given individual consideration.

Religion: No requirement.

Financial status: Applicants must demonstrate financial stability.

Marital status: No requirement.

Family size: No requirement for legal risk placement. For legally free Caucasian infant, applicants may have no more than 1 child currently in the family.

Racial, ethnic or cultural origin: No requirement, but preference for placing children in families of similar origin.

THE PROCEDURE

Participation in BCSA's adoption programs entails the following basic steps:
Orientation meeting
Application
Screening interview
Group education series
Homestudy
Placement

ADDITIONAL PROGRAMS/SERVICES

BCSA offers a wide range of support services including individual and group counseling; services to expectant mothers and single parents; protective services to children reported to be neglected or abused and their families; foster care services; specialized home care program for mentally retarded children and adults; after school program for children of non-English speaking Asian parents; a short-term residential treatment center for teenage boys (Baird Center); a small mental health center (Center for Therapy); training and advocacy programs.

BRANCH/NETWORK OFFICES

None.

LICENSE/ACCREDITATION/PROFESSIONAL AFFILIATIONS

Boston Children's Service Association is licensed by the Commonwealth of Massachusetts Office for Children, is accredited by the Council on Accreditation of Services for Families and Children and is a member of the Child Welfare League of America.

BRIGHTSIDE FOR FAMILIES AND CHILDREN

2112 Riverdale Street
West Springfield, MA 01089
(413) 788–7366
Program director: Joan B. Kagan, ACSW, LICSW, Supervisor; Judy Lavinski, ACSW, LICSW, Supervisor

THE PROGRAM

Our Lady of Providence Children's Center, known as Brightside, is a nonprofit multi-service agency serving families who live in the 4 western counties of Massachusetts and northern Connecticut. Founded in 18881 by the Sisters of Providence out of "a commitment to family as the cornerstone of life, growth, and development," the agency has evolved in response to the changing needs of the community and today provides services ranging from residential care for children and adolescents experiencing social, emotional or behavioral problems to community education and outreach. Through its adoption program, the agency provides domestic and international placement services and places approximately 125 children annually. Working directly with birthmothers, with private and public agencies throughout the state, and with regional exchange programs, the agency places both healthy and special-needs infants and older children born in the U.S. Working directly with child welfare institutions abroad and working cooperatively with other U.S. agencies which maintain international programs, the agency places foreign-born children from many countries in American families. In addition, the agency provides homestudy and supervisory services for applicants pursuing inter-agency adoption (domestic or international, designated or identified adoptions, and relative adoptions.

THE COST

The agency's fee for adoption services of non-special-needs children is based on a sliding scale and averages $2,500. Services covered by the fee include homestudy, placement, and post-placement supervision. Applicants pursuing international adoption should anticipate fees to the foreign or cooperating agency, possible travel expenses, immigration and naturalization fees, and related costs. Applicants pursuing designated or identified adoption should anticipate financial responsibility or certain expenses of the birthmother and child (i.e., medical, counseling). For all programs, applicants are responsible for legal fees connected with finalization.

THE WAIT

The time from application to placement varies depending on the program. For a traditional agency adoption of a healthy infant, the wait may be 6 years or more. For special-needs adoption, there is little or no wait after completion of the homestudy. For international adoption, the wait varies depending on the country of origin or the cooperating agency.

THE CHILDREN

Brightside places both healthy and special-needs children, ranging in age from birth to 16 years, of all racial backgrounds. Countries of origin include U.S., Bolivia, Chile, and (in cooperation with other U.S. agencies) many other countries.

THE REQUIREMENTS

Age: Applicants must be at least 21.

Health: Applicants with health problems or handicaps are given individual consideration. Exploration of medical reasons for infertility is recommended for the adoption of a healthy infant.

Religion: No requirement. However, by law, the preferences of the birthmother are honored if she designates a preference.

Financial status: No requirement.

Marital status: Preference is given to married couples. Single applicants will be considered on a case-by-case basis.

Family size: For healthy infant adoption, applicants must be childless. For other programs, the requirement varies depending on the needs of the child.

Racial, ethnic or cultural origin: Preference for placing children in families of similar origins. The agency strives to maintain a balance between the child's needs for permanency and his/her racial identity needs. The requirement varies depending on the availability of racially and culturally relevant families.

THE PROCEDURE

Participation in Brightside's adoption program entails the following steps:

Inquiry

Orientation meeting (held monthly)

Registration

Registration interview

Application

Group training sessions

Homestudy

Compliance with immigration/naturalization requirements (international adoptions only)

Placement

Post-placement supervision

ADDITIONAL PROGRAMS/SERVICES

Brightside provides a wide range of services including diagnostic services for children ages 6–16 with social, emotional, or behavioral problems; group home; special needs day treatment program; temporary, specialized, and permanent foster care; pregnant and parenting services; individual, family, and group therapy; community education and advocacy (including the "Brightside Series," conferences featuring internationally known experts in human service fields); post-legal adoption services.

BRANCH/NETWORK OFFICES

None

LICENSE/ACCREDITATION/PROFESSIONAL AFFILIATIONS

Brightside for Families and Children is licensed by the Commonwealth of Massachusetts Office for Children and the Department of Public Health and is accredited by the Council on Accreditation of Services for Families and Children. The agency is a member of the Child Welfare League of America, Catholic Charities USA, and Providence Systems.

CAMBRIDGE ADOPTION AND COUNSELING ASSOCIATES, INC.

Mailing address: P.O. Box 190
Cambridge, MA 02142
Office address: 80 Mt. Auburn Street
Watertown, MA
(617) 923–0370

Program director: Madeline Daniels (MSW, ACSW, LICSW), Executive Director

THE PROGRAM

Incorporated in 1980, Cambridge Adoption and Counseling Associates is a nonprofit adoption agency serving the state of Massachusetts and placing under 100 children annually. The agency is committed "to finding and approving adoptive homes where children without permanent families may find security in a normal, loving atmosphere." The agency offers several domestic and foreign adoption programs. The domestic adoption programs include traditional and identified U.S. adoptions. A traditional adoption involves the matching of an infant who has been surrendered to the agency to a couple whose homestudy has been approved by the agency. An identified adoption refers to a situation in which prospective adoptive parents have become aware of a specific pregnant woman who is willing to specify the adoption of her child by those parents. The foreign adoption programs include agency-mediated adoptions and parent-initiated adoptions. In an agency- mediated adoption, Cambridge Adoption and Counseling Associates works with sources it has identified abroad and/or with several U.S.-based licensed child placement agencies which operate programs in foreign countries. "Parent- initiated" foreign adoptions are those in which prospective adoptive parents have themselves, through familial or diplomatic contacts, made initial arrangements for an overseas adoption. The agency will work with properly accredited agencies or individuals in any country (including the U.S.) on a case-by-case basis, subject to U.S. Department of State approval of the integrity of the source.

THE COST

The fee varies depending on the program selected and the services given. The basic fee schedule is as follows:

Application fee	$50.00
Homestudy and pre-placement services	$950.00
Post-placement counseling and preparation of reports for finalization	$550.00

For foreign adoptions, prospective adoptive parents should also anticipate financial responsibility for legal fees here and abroad, child care and medical costs, travel expenses, document and translation costs, possibly a donation to an orphanage, and processing fees for agencies in both countries. Currently, the total cost of an intercountry adoption ranges between $9,000 and $13,000.

For domestic traditional and identified adoptions, a placement fee is charged on a sliding scale. In addition, prospective adoptive parents should anticipate financial responsibility for maternity costs, legal fees, and additional costs for travel time and mileage for those living outside the Boston metropolitan area.

THE WAIT

The average time from application for acceptance into the program to the homecoming of the adoptive child is usually 1 year or less.

THE CHILDREN

Cambridge Adoption and Counseling Associates places infants to toddlers of all racial backgrounds. Countries of origin include Chile, Thailand, Colombia, El Salvador, Guatemala, Honduras, Peru, Paraguay, Philippines, Taiwan, India, Poland, and U.S.

THE REQUIREMENTS

Age: Applicants must be at least 25 and no more than 55 years of age. In foreign adoption programs, requirements may vary depending on the country.
Health: Applicants must be in reasonably good health.
Religion: No requirement.
Financial status: Applicants must demonstrate financial stability.
Marital status: The requirement varies depending on the program selected.
Family size: No requirement.
Racial, ethnic or cultural origin: No requirement.

THE PROCEDURE

Participation in Cambridge Adoption and Counseling Associates' programs entails the following basic steps:
Orientation meeting
Application
Individual or group counseling sessions
Homestudy
Compliance with immigration/naturalization requirements (foreign adoptions only)
Referral
Placement
Post-placement supervision

ADDITIONAL PROGRAMS/SERVICES

Cambridge Adoption and Counseling Associates offers adoption readiness counseling and personal counseling throughout the adoption process and the adjustment period. This is a small agency with the capacity for individual attention to its clients.

BRANCH/NETWORK OFFICES

Inquiries and applications are processed through the main office. Cases in outlying areas are assigned by the main office to local representatives.

LICENSE/ACCREDITATION/PROFESSIONAL AFFILIATIONS

Cambridge Adoption and Counseling Associates is licensed by the Commonwealth of Massachusetts Office for Children. All social workers are licensed by the Commonwealth of Massachusetts and are members of the National Association of Social Work. The agency is a member of the Massachusetts Council of Human Service Providers.

CAMBRIDGE FAMILY AND CHILDREN'S SERVICE

99 Bishop Allen Drive
Cambridge, MA 02139
(617) 876–4210
Program director: Adoption Program Director

THE PROGRAM

Cambridge Family and Children's Service (CFCS) is a nonprofit multi-service agency serving primarily Middlesex County and neighboring communities and placing approximately 20 children annually through its adoption program. Founded in 1870 as Avon Home, the agency has evolved in response to the changing needs of the community and today provides a wide range of services "to support and strengthen the individual's and family's ability to function in an effective and emotionally healthy manner." The agency was the first agency in Massachusetts to be contracted by the state to provide special-needs adoption services. Through the One Church, One Child program, the agency addresses the needs of minority children waiting for adoptive families. In addition, the agency provides identified adoption services. An identified adoption is one in which the prospective adoptive parents locate a birthmother who is willing to specify the adoption of her child by those parents. The prospective adoptive parents then refer the birthmother to the agency. The agency provides counseling of both parties, social work services, foster care, and legal services required to complete the adoption process.

THE COST

As of October 1988, the agency's fee for identified adoption services is $4,800. Services covered by the fee include all phases of the adoption process. For the One Church, One Child program, services are provided at no cost to the applicant.

THE WAIT

For infant adoption, the time from application to placement averages 2 years. For special-needs adoption, the wait ranges from 6 months to 2 years.

THE CHILDREN

CFCS places both healthy and special-needs children, ranging in age from birth to 18 years, of all racial backgrounds, born in the U.S.

THE REQUIREMENTS

Age: Applicants must be at least 21 years of age.
Health: Applicants must be in reasonably good health. Applicants with health problems or handicaps are given individual consideration.
Religion: No requirement.
Financial status: Applicants must demonstrate the ability to provide adequately for the family.
Marital status: Applicants may be either married or single.
Family size: The requirement varies depending on the needs of the child.

Racial, ethnic or cultural origin: The requirement varies depending on the needs of the child. The agency seeks to place the child in a family which will best provide the child an opportunity to develop a sense of identity.

THE PROCEDURE

Participation in the adoption program of CFCS entails the following basic steps:
Orientation meeting and consultation interview
Application
Group counseling sessions
Individual counseling sessions
Homestudy
Placement
Post-placement supervision
Finalization
Post legalization services

ADDITIONAL PROGRAMS/SERVICES

CFCS provides foster care; adoption counseling; support groups for adults and for children.

BRANCH/NETWORK OFFICES

None.

LICENSE/ACCREDITATION/PROFESSIONAL AFFILIATIONS

Cambridge Family and Children's Services is licensed by the Commonwealth of Massachusetts Office for Children. The agency is a member of Family Service America, Child Welfare League of America, and the State Adoption Committee.

CATHOLIC CHARITIES CENTRE OF OLD COLONY AREA

686 North Main Street
Brockton, MA 02401
(617) 587–0815
Program director: Diane L. Carlson, MSW, LICSW

THE PROGRAM

Catholic Charities Centre of Old Colony Area is a non-profit agency which has placed children in adoptive homes since 1916. Catholic Charities Centre serves the following towns: Abington, Avon, the Bridgewaters, Brockton, Carver, Duxbury, Halifax, Hanson, Holbrook, Kingston, Lakeville, Marshfield, Middleboro, Norwell, Pembroke, Plymouth, Plympton, Rochester, Rockland, Scituate, Stoughton, and Whitman. In 1986, Catholic Charities Centre placed 11 children.

THE COST

The agency's fee is based on a sliding scale. For applicants with a combined income of under $15,000, the fee is 5% of the gross income; for applicants with an income between $15,000 and $30,000, the fee is 7 1/2% of the gross income; for applicants with an income over $30,000, the fee is 10% of the gross income, with a maximum fee of $5,000. Services covered by the fee include informational meetings, pre-homestudy discussion group, homestudy, and post-placement supervision. Fees are adjusted or waived for special-needs adoptions.

In addition, prospective adoptive parents should anticipate financial responsibility for legal fees related to finalization (approximately $100) and foster care fees (approximately $300).

THE WAIT

For a healthy Caucasian infant, the time from application for acceptance into the program to the homecoming of the adoptive child ranges from 5 to 8 years. There is no wait for special-needs adoptions.

THE CHILDREN

Catholic Charities Centre places both special-needs and healthy children, ranging in age from birth to 4 years, from all racial backgrounds. Children placed by Catholic Charities Centre are born in the United States.

THE REQUIREMENTS

Age: No requirement.
Health: Applicants must be in reasonably good health. Applicants with health problems or handicaps are given individual consideration. Infertility documentation is required for healthy Caucasian infant adoption.
Religion: No requirement.
Financial status: No requirement.
Marital status: In most cases, applicants must be married couples who have been married for at least 1 year. However, single applicants are accepted for adoptions involving older children.
Family size: For healthy Caucasian infant adoption, applicants must be childless. No requirement for special-needs adoptions.
Racial, ethnic or cultural origin: No requirement, but preference for placing children in families of similar origins.

THE PROCEDURE

Participation in Catholic Charities Centre adoption programs entails the following basic steps:
Application
Orientation meeting
Group counseling sessions
Homestudy
Placement
Post-placement supervision

ADDITIONAL PROGRAMS/SERVICES

Catholic Charities Centre sponsors workshops on adoption, offers post-legalization services to adoptive parents, birthparents, and adoptees.

BRANCH/NETWORK OFFICES

Catholic Charities Centre is a branch office of Catholic Charities, Archdiocese of Boston (49 Franklin Street, Boston, MA 02110).

Catholic Charities Centre of Old Colony Area is licensed by the Commonwealth of Massachusetts Office for Children.

CATHOLIC FAMILY SERVICES

55 Lynn Shore Drive
Lynn, MA 01902
(617) 593–2312
Program director: Jane Lovett, Director of Placement Services; Katie Anno, Adoption Program Director

THE PROGRAM

Catholic Family Services is a nonprofit multi-service child and family agency serving residents of 10 communities in Essex and Middlesex Counties on a non-sectarian basis. Founded in 1919, the mission of the Catholic Family Services is "to provide caring, professional support to help people of all ages, economic status, race and/or religion achieve increasingly independent functioning through traditional and innovative social services provides educational, medical, and social services to pregnant women and new mothers. The goal of this program is to assist young women who are unprepared for the responsibilities of parenthood "to acquire the knowledge and skills needed to provide a nurturing, safe environment for their children." The agency places infants for adoption when birthmothers in the agency's program elect adoptive placement as the best plan for their child. The agency is also actively involved in recruiting families for special-needs and/or legal risk adoptions. Through these programs, the agency placed 5 children for adoption in 1987. In addition, the agency will provide homestudy and post-placement supervision for applicants pursuing domestic inter-agency adoption.

THE COST

The agency's fee for adoption services is based on a sliding scale with an average fee of $3,000 and a maximum fee of $5,000. Services covered by the fee include all phases of the adoption process (homestudy through finalization).

THE WAIT

The time from application to placement varies depending on the program. For healthy Caucasian legally free infant adoptions, the wait ranges from 4 to 5 years. For special-needs and/or legal risk placements, the wait averages 2 years or less.

THE CHILDREN

Catholic Family Services places both healthy and special-needs children, ranging in age from birth to 14 years, of Caucasian, Hispanic, Black, and bi-racial backgrounds, born in the U.S.

THE REQUIREMENTS

Age: The requirement varies depending on the age of the child being considered for placement.
Health: Applicants should be in reasonably good health.
Applicants with health problems or handicaps are given individual consideration. Infertility documentation is preferred if that is applicant's reason for seeking adoption.
Religion: No requirement
Financial status: Applicants must have a stable income with adequate financial resources to provide for family members.
Marital status: Married couples and single parents are welcome to apply.
Family size: For healthy Caucasian legally free infant adoptions, applicants must be childless. No requirement for special needs/legal risk program.
Racial, ethnic or cultural origin: No requirement, but preference for placing children in families of similar racial origins if possible.

THE PROCEDURE

Participation in the adoption program of Catholic Family Services entails the following basic steps:
   Application
   Homestudy (including 3 group educational sessions, counseling sessions with the couple, and individual counseling sessions)
   Referral
   Placement
   Post-placement supervision
   Finalization by Catholic Family Services attorney

ADDITIONAL PROGRAMS/SERVICES

Catholic Family Services provides a wide range of services to the community including protective services for children; parent aide program; Project PREPARE; transitional housing for young families; foster care; Christ Child Day Care Center; Family day care; mental health services; residence for developmentally disabled women; parish and community training and consultation services.

BRANCH/NETWORK OFFICES

6 Salem Street
Reading, MA 01867
(617) 942–0690

LICENSE/ACCREDITATION/PROFESSIONAL AFFILIATIONS

Catholic Family Services is licensed by the commonwealth of Massachusetts Office for Children and is accredited by the Council on Accreditation of Services for Families and Children. The agency is a member of the Child Welfare League of America and is a United Way affiliate.

CATHOLIC SOCIAL SERVICES OF FALL RIVER

783 Slade Street
P.O. Box M—South Station
Fall River, Massachusetts 02724
(617) 674–4681
Program director: Mary Lou Mancini

The Program

Catholic Social Services of Fall River is a nonprofit organization serving legal residents of the Diocese of Fall River and placing approximately 20 children annually. Services are offered to all persons regardless of race, nationality, or religious affiliation. The agency places infants for adoption when birthparents in the agency's unmarried parents program decide that the best interests of the infant will be served by adoptive placement. The agency also occasionally places foreign-born children and special-needs children. The agency's purpose is to find families "who can meet the individual needs of a particular child and who can provide the conditions and opportunities favorable to healthy personality growth through the development of individual potentialities."

The Cost

The agency's fee for adoption services is based on a sliding scale of 10% of the family's gross annual income with a maximum fee of $5000. The adoption fee includes all phases of the adoption process. In addition to the fee, adopting couples should expect financial responsibility for legal costs connected with legalization of the adoption. Ability to pay a fee is not a criterion of acceptance.

The Wait

The average wait is from 2 to 4 years following approval of the application. The wait is affected by the number of applicants and the availability of the children.

The Children

Catholic Social Services of Fall River places primarily healthy Caucasian children who range in age from birth to 1 year. On occasion, special-needs children, older children, or foreign-born children are also placed.

The Requirements

Age: Applicants must be 21 years of age or older. Generally, the difference in age between the adoptive parents and child should not exceed 40 years.

Health: Applicants should be in reasonably good health; those applicants with health problems or handicaps are given individual consideration. Infertility documentation is required.

Religion: Applicants must be practising members of an organized church.

Financial status: Applicants must demonstrate financial stability.

Marital status: Applicants must be married. The length of the marriage must be at least 3 years.

Family size: Applicants must be childless.

Racial, ethnic or cultural origin: Preference for placing children in families of similar origins.

The Procedure

Participation in Catholic Social Services' adoption programs entails the following basic steps:

Application
Wait listing
Orientation meeting
Individual counseling sessions
Home visit
Compliance with immigration/naturalization laws (foreign-born children only)
Referral
Placement
Post-placement supervision

Additional Programs/Services

Catholic Social Services of Fall River provides individual, marital, and family counseling; pregnancy counseling services; foster care of newborns; refugee resettlement; information and referral services.

Branch/Network Offices

CSS of Attleboro
10 Maple Street
Attleboro, MA 02703
(617)226–4780

CSS of Cape Cod
261 South Street
Hyannis, MA 02601
(617)771–6771

CSS of New Bedford
59 Rockland Street
New Bedford, MA 02740
(617) 997–7337

License/Accreditation/Professional Affiliations

Catholic Social Services of Fall River is licensed by the Commonwealth of Massachusetts Office for Children.

Children's Aid and Family Service of Hampshire County, Inc.

8 Trumbull Road
Northampton, MA 01060
(413) 584–5690
Program director: Priscilla Deane Freund, MSW

The Program

Children's Aid and Family Service (CAFS) is a nonprofit family agency serving 4 western counties of Massachusetts for infant adoptions and the entire state and occasionally bordering states for special-needs adoptions. Founded in 1910, the agency sponsored a home for children for a number of years. Since World War II, however, children have been placed in adoptive homes directly from the hospital after birth, from foster homes, or from birthparents' homes. For the past 13 years, CAFS has developed a strong and innovative placement program for children with special needs and is affiliated with Project IMPACT (see Project IMPACT listing for complete description of program). CAFS believes that all children need and deserve permanent loving families and seeks families for children who cannot remain with or readily return to their biological families. The agency is "concerned with the well-being of birth and adoptive parents, yet sees the child as central to the process and goals of adoption. CAFS regards the child's special needs as a challenge rather than as an insurmountable barrier to the nurturing experience of family connection." CAFS places 8 to 10 infants and 8 to 12 special-needs children annually. CAFS will also provide homestudy and supervisory services for applicants pursuing international adoption, subject to state approval of the integrity of the source.

THE COST

The agency's fee for adoption services varies depending on the program. There is no fee for special-needs adoptions which are funded through state contracts. For infant adoptions, the fee is 10% of the applicants' adjusted gross income. Services covered by the fee include family preparation, homestudy, placement, post-placement supervision and legalization services. For designated infant adoptions, applicants should anticipate possible medical and/or foster care expenses for the birthmother and child, possible transportation expenses, and possible legal expenses for interstate adoptions.

THE WAIT

The time from application to the homecoming of the adoptive child varies depending on the program. For healthy Caucasian infant adoption, the wait ranges from 3 to 5 years. For special-needs adoptions, the length of the wait depends on the flexibility of the applicants and their willingness to accept a "waiting" child or children.

THE CHILDREN

CAFS places both healthy and special-needs children, ranging in age from birth to 18 years. CAFS serves children of all racial backgrounds, but most children placed are Caucasian and are born in the U.S. CAFS will provide homestudy and supervisory services for applicants pursuing international adoption, subject to state approval of the integrity of the source.

THE REQUIREMENTS

Age: No firm requirement, but may vary depending on the health, energy, and individual circumstances of the applicants.

Health: For infant adoptions, infertility documentation is required. Applicants with health problems or handicaps are given individual consideration regarding ability to meet the child's needs.

Religion: No requirement.

Financial status: No requirement. Massachusetts subsidy may be available depending on the special needs of the child.

Marital status: For undesignated infant adoptions, applicants must be married, and the length of the marriage is usually at least 2 years. For special-needs adoption, the requirement varies depending on the needs of the child.

Family size: For undesignated infant adoptions, applicants may have no more than 1 previously adopted child and no biological children of both parents. No requirement for special-needs adoptions, but may vary depending on the needs of the child.

Racial, ethnic or cultural origin: Preference for placing children in families of similar origins whenever possible. If a search for a match through the agency's infant or special needs programs or nearby resources is not successful, the agency will cross racial/ethnic lines.

THE PROCEDURE

Participation in CAFS' adoption programs entails the following basic steps:
    Orientation meeting
    Application
    Group preparation
    Homestudy
    Placement
    Post-placement supervision and support
    Post-legalization services

ADDITIONAL PROGRAMS/SERVICES

Children's Aid and Family Service provides young parent services (counseling, support groups, respite care, individual or group childbirth preparation); foster care; parent aide program; counseling; workshops; consultation services; post legalization services to adoptees, birthparents, and adoptive families.

BRANCH/NETWORK OFFICES

CAFS has no branch offices but is a member of the Project IMPACT network:

Project IMPACT, Inc.
25 West Street
Boston, MA 02111–1213
(617) 451–1472

LICENSE/ACCREDITATION/PROFESSIONAL AFFILIATIONS

Children's Aid and Family Service is licensed by the Commonwealth of Massachusetts Office for Children and is accredited by the Council on Accreditation of Services for Families and Children. CAFS is a member of the Project IMPACT Network, the Child Welfare League of America, and the Hampshire County United Way.

DARE FAMILY SERVICES

3 Monument Square
Beverly, MA 01915
(617) 927–1674
Program director: Janet Lee

THE PROGRAM

DARE Family Services is a program operated by DARE, Inc., a private nonprofit child welfare agency serving eastern Massachusetts and placing 10–15 children annually. Funded by the Massachusetts Department of Social Services, DARE was initially established as a foster care program and has evolved over the past ten years into a foster care and adoption program. Dedicated to the belief that "every child is entitled to the security of a loving family," DARE's mission is to provide adoption preparation, placement, and post-placement support to older children (10+ years), emotionally disturbed children under the age of 10, and sibling groups.

THE COST

There is no fee for the adoption of DARE children.

THE WAIT

The time from application for acceptance into the program to the homecoming of the adoptive child varies depending on the applicant's interests. The wait is shorter (6 months to 1 year) for applicants who wish to adopt older children.

THE CHILDREN

Children placed by DARE are primarily Caucasian, ranging in age from birth to 16 years. Most children placed by DARE are physically healthy, but emotionally disturbed, often with a history of neglect and/or abuse.

THE REQUIREMENTS

Age: Applicants must be at least 21 years of age.
Health: Applicants must be in reasonably good health.
Religion: No requirement.
Financial status: No requirement.
Marital status: No requirement.
Family size: No requirement.
Racial, ethnic or cultural origin: No requirement.

THE PROCEDURE

Participation in DARE's adoption program entails the following basic steps:
Application
Orientation/Training (6 sessions)
Homestudy
Placement
Post-placement supervision

ADDITIONAL PROGRAMS/SERVICES

DARE provides foster care and foster parent training, mentor care (an individualized and specialized foster care program), an emergency mentor program for young people "in crisis," twenty-four hour support services.

BRANCH/NETWORK OFFICES

Boston Region
55 Dimock Street
Roxbury, MA 02119
(617) 427-7346

LICENSE/ACCREDITATION/PROFESSIONAL AFFILIATIONS

DARE is licensed by the Commonwealth of Massachusetts Office for Children.

DOWNEY SIDE, INC.

999 Liberty Street
Springfield, MA 01104
(413) 781-2123
Program director: Richard Koslowski

THE PROGRAM

Downey Side is a nonprofit adoption agency serving New England, with the principal area of service being western and central Massachusetts. Downey Side is the only adoption agency in the United States specifically designed to provide permanent placement for homeless adolescents. Founded in 1967 by Father Paul Engel, a Capuchin priest, the agency has been successful in placing "the older youth" (10–17 years) in adoptive homes. Guided by Father Engel's conviction that "there need be no homeless children," the agency places approximately 12 children annually.

THE COST

There is no fee for the adoption of Downey Side children except for a nominal fee ($50–$75) to cover the cost of the training classes. Services offered by the agency to adoptive families include the following:
Exploring Adoption classes (8 sessions)
Homestudy
Placement
Adoption and court fees

THE WAIT

The time from application to the homecoming of the adoptive child varies. Applicants must first attend Downey Side's eight-week training classes and then they identify their own child. Consequently, the length of the wait depends on the applicants themselves. Placement can occur at any time after the completion of the training session, with finalization of the adoption taking place 12 to 15 months after placement.

THE CHILDREN

Downey Side places both special needs and healthy children, ranging in age from 10 to 17 years.

THE REQUIREMENTS

Age: Applicants must be at least 18 years old.
Health: Applicants must be in reasonably good health. Applicants with health problems or handicaps are given individual consideration.
Religion: No requirement.
Financial status: No requirement.
Marital status: No requirement.
Family size: No requirement.
Racial, ethnic or cultural origin: No requirement.

THE PROCEDURE

Participation in Downey Side's adoption program entails the following basic steps:
Application
Orientation meeting
Adoption training classes (8 sessions)
Homestudy
Placement
Individual and group counseling sessions

ADDITIONAL PROGRAMS/SERVICES

Downey Side provides a family life advocate for each family, a therapist on duty for counseling, 24–hour emergency services, and family life support group meetings.

Downey Side
Southgate Tower, Hudson Room
371 7th Avenue
New York, N.Y. 10001–3984
(212) 629–8599

LICENSE/ACCREDITATION/PROFESSIONAL AFFILIATIONS

Downey Side, Inc. is licensed by the Commonwealth of Massachusetts Office for Children. Downey Side is a member of the North American Council on Adoptable Children and of the Massachusetts Council of Human Service Providers.

FAMILY AND CHILDREN SERVICES OF CATHOLIC CHARITIES, WORCESTER

15 Ripley Street
Worcester, Massachusetts
(617) 798–0191
Program director: Rachel T. Renaud, ACSW, LICSW

THE PROGRAM

Family and Children Services (F&CS) is a nonprofit multiservice organization serving the county of Worcester, and residents of Marlboro, Hudson, Ashby, Townsend, and the military families at Fort Devens and placing approximately 12 children annually. Established in 1950 to serve those in need, the agency's mission is "to promote the gift and sacredness of life from the first moment of conception through all stages of human growth and development." F&CS places infants for adoption when birthmothers in the agency's pregnancy services program decide that the best interests of the infant will be served by adoptive placement. At the present time, F&CS' waiting list fro adoption services is closed.

THE COST

The agency's fee for adoption services is based on a sliding scale of 15% of the gross family income (Maximum fee $9,000). Services covered by the fee include interviews, homestudy, consultation, formal review and selection process, placement, post-placement supervision, and completion of all legal documents required by the court. In addition, the fee includes partial payment for the medical and living expenses of the birthmother and child prior to placement.

THE WAIT

The time from application for acceptance into the program to the homecoming of the adoptive child ranges from 1 to 2 years. However, applicants should note that F&CS's waiting list is currently closed.

THE CHILDREN

F&CS places primarily healthy Caucasian children ranging in age from birth to nine months. On occasion, the agency also places special-needs children.

THE REQUIREMENTS

Age: Primary consideration for infant adoption is given to couples under 45 years of age.

Health: Applicants must be in reasonably good health, although applicants with health problems or handicaps are given individual consideration. Infertility documentation is required.

Religion: Applicants must be practicing members of an organized church.

Financial status: Applicants must demonstrate financial stability.

Marital status: Applicants must be married. The length of the marriage must be at least 3 years.

Family size: Applicants may have no more than 1 child currently in the family. Priority is given to applicants who are childless.

Racial, ethnic or cultural origin: No requirement, but preference for placing children in families of similar origin.

THE PROCEDURE

Participation in F&CS's adoption program entails the following basic steps:
Referral
Orientation meeting
Individual counseling sessions (as needed)
Application
Home study (individual or group)
Placement
Post-placement supervision
Post-adoption services

ADDITIONAL PROGRAMS/SERVICES

F&CS provides a wide range of services including counseling for individuals, couples, and families; support groups; neighborhood services; temporary emergency residence; pregnancy services' refugee services.

BRANCH/NETWORK OFFICES

53 Highland Avenue
Fitchburg, MA 01420
(617) 343–4879/422–6918

203 Union Street
Clinton, MA 01510
(617) 365–7391

838 West Broadway
Gardner, MA 01440
(617) 632–3968/939–2011/874–0469

12 Riverbend Street
Athol, MA 01331
(617) 249–4563

79 Elm Street
Southbridge, MA 01550
(617) 765–5936/987–0424

16 Main Street
Uxbridge, MA 01569
(617) 278–2424/278–2106

171 Main Street
North Brookfield, MA 01535
(617) 867–8000

LICENSE/ACCREDITATION/PROFESSIONAL AFFILIATIONS

Family and Children Services is licensed by the Commonwealth of Massachusetts Office for Children and is accredited by the Council on Accreditation of Services for Families and Children.

FLORENCE CRITTENTON LEAGUE OF LOWELL, INC.

119 Hall Street
Lowell, MA 01854
(508) 452–9671
Program director: Ilze Keegan, Executive Director

THE PROGRAM

The Florence Crittenton League of Lowell is a nonprofit agency serving residents of Massachusetts. Incorporated in 1907, the agency has historically provided counseling services to birthparents and adoption services for infants. The agency annually places a small number of domestic infants through this program. In 1972, the agency began working with FANA, an orphanage in Bogota, Colombia, to place Colombian children in Massachusetts families. In addition, the agency will provide homestudy and supervisory services for applicants pursuing domestic or international interagency adoption.

THE COST

As of October 1988, the agency's fee for adoption through Colombia includes a $2,500 fee to Florence Crittenton League (for the homestudy, placement, supervision, and legal services) and a $4,000 donation to the orphanage in Colombia. In addition, applicants should anticipate expenses related to travel to Colombia to pick up the child and accommodations for 1 week to 10 days. For domestic infant adoptions, the agency's fee is based on a sliding scale in accordance with the applicants' income.

THE WAIT

The time from application to the homecoming of the adoptive child averages 1 year.

THE CHILDREN

The Florence Crittenton League places healthy infants of Caucasian and Hispanic racial backgrounds. Countries of origin include Colombia and the U.S.

THE REQUIREMENTS

Age: Applicants must be at least 25 and no more than 40 years of age.
Health: Applicants must be in reasonably good health.
Religion: No requirement.
Financial status: Applicants must have sufficient income to provide for the needs of the family.
Marital status: Applicants must be married couples; the length of the marriage must be at least 3 years.
Family size: Applicants may have no more than 2 children currently in the family.
Racial, ethnic or cultural origin: No requirement.

THE PROCEDURE

Participation in the adoption program of the Florence Crittenton League entails the following basic steps:
Orientation meeting
Application
Homestudy
Compliance with immigration/naturalization requirements (international adoptions only)
Placement
Group counseling sessions
Post-placement supervision

ADDITIONAL PROGRAMS/SERVICES

Florence Crittenton League provides counseling free of charge to birthparents; foster care for infants awaiting placement; education and training for foster parents.

BRANCH/NETWORK OFFICES

None.

LICENSE/ACCREDITATION/PROFESSIONAL AFFILIATIONS

Florence Crittenton League of Lowell, Inc. is licensed by the Commonwealth of Massachusetts Office for Children and is a member of the Child Welfare League of America.

INTERNATIONAL ADOPTIONS, INC.

282 Moody Street
Waltham, MA 02154
(617) 894–5330
Program director: Phyllis Loewenstein, Executive Director; Vicki Peterson, Director of Program and Administration

THE PROGRAM

Founded in 1973 to provide for homeless Vietnamese children, International Adoptions is a nonprofit child-welfare agency serving the states of Massachusetts, Connecticut, Rhode Island, Vermont, New Hampshire, and New York. Working on behalf of children in many countries, International Adoptions seeks to "find and prepare the best possible homes for children who need homes" by aiding prospective parents to prepare themselves, supporting overseas agencies which help families stay together, counseling pregnant women, and caring for children whether or not they are "adoptable." International Adoptions places approximately 335 children annually. In addition, International Adoptions will provide homestudy and supervisory services for applicants pursuing parent-initiated adoption in any country, subject to approval of the integrity of the source.

THE COST

The agency fee is based on a sliding scale and ranges from $1,000 to $5,000. Services covered by the fee include homestudy, individual and family preparation group, cultural education, networking, program information, presentation of referral, post-placement supervision and counseling, preparation of legal documents, social events, newsletter, and program maintenance.

In addition, prospective adoptive parents should anticipate financial responsibility for overseas program fees, transportation, immigration and naturalization fees, overseas travel expenses, and legal fees (in New York only).

THE WAIT

The time from application for acceptance into the program to the homecoming of the adoptive child ranges from 1 to 2 years.

THE CHILDREN

International Adoptions places both healthy and special-needs children, ranging in age from birth to 15 years, of all racial backgrounds. Countries of origin include U.S., South Korea, India, Taiwan, Hong Kong, Thailand, the Philippines, Guatemala, Honduras, Colombia, El Salvador and others as relationships are established. In addition, the agency will provide homestudy and supervisory services for applicants pursuing parent-initiated adoptions in any country subject to approval of the integrity of the source.

THE REQUIREMENTS

Age: The requirement varies depending on the age of the child, the health of the parents, financial and other support systems.

Health: Applicants with health problems or handicaps are given individual consideration.

Religion: No requirement.

Financial status: No requirement.

Marital status: No requirement. If married, applicants should be married for at least 2 years unless circumstances are unusual.

Family size: No firm requirement, but may vary depending on the child's country of origin.

Racial, ethnic or cultural origin: No requirement.

THE PROCEDURE

Participation in International Adoptions, Inc. program entails the following basic steps:
Orientation meeting
Application
Individual counseling sessions
Group counseling sessions
Homestudy
Compliance with immigration/naturalization requirements
Culture education
Referral
Placement
Post-placement supervision
Legalization of the adoption
Naturalization of the child

ADDITIONAL PROGRAMS/SERVICES

International Adoptions sponsors workshops, seminars, and support groups; provides foster care, birth-parent counseling, post-legalization counseling, and in-service training at mental health facilities; facilitates parent-initiated adoptions.

BRANCH/NETWORK OFFICES:

IAI—New Hampshire
5 South State Street
Concord, NH 03301
(603) 224–5174

IAI—Connecticut
99 W. Main Street
New Britain, CT 06050
(203) 223–6172

IAI—Vermont
66 North Avenue
P.O. Box 3115
Burlington, VT 05402
(802) 658–0249

IAI—New York
7 Elmwood Drive
New City, NY 10956
(914) 634–5809

IAI—New York
22 Yerk Avenue
Ronkonkoma, NY 11779
(516) 585–1008

LICENSE/ACCREDITATION/PROFESSIONAL AFFILIATIONS

International Adoptions is licensed by the appropriate state department in each of the following states: Massachusetts, New Hampshire, New York, Connecticut, Rhode Island, and Vermont. International Adoptions is a member of the Joint Council on International Children's Services and is an associate member of the Child Welfare League of America.

JEWISH FAMILY AND CHILDREN'S SERVICE

31 New Chardon Street
Boston, MA 02114
(617) 227–6641
Program director: Alma Orchinik, Director of Children's Service; Judith Kasser, Executive Director

THE PROGRAM

Serving the metropolitan Boston area, Jewish Family and Children's Service (JF&CS) is a private nonprofit agency whose purpose is "to preserve and enhance the lives of Jewish families" by providing a wide range of family services. The adoption services provided by JF&CS include a traditional adoption program and a designated adoption program. In the traditional adoption program, prospective adoptive families wait until a child becomes available for adoption through

JF&CS. In the designated adoption program, the adoptive family locates a birthmother who chooses to specify the placement of her child with that family. The agency also provides services to the birthparents in its adoption programs. JF&CS places 20 to 28 children annually.

THE COST

The agency fee ranges from $2,000 to $5,400. The fee for a traditional adoption is based on a sliding scale; the agency charges a flat fee for a designated adoption. Services covered by the fee include the homestudy and other pre-placement services, placement services, post-placement and post-legalization services. In addition to agency fees, prospective adoptive parents should anticipate financial responsibility for foster care as well as legal and medical expenses for the birthparents.

THE WAIT

The time from application to the homecoming of the adoptive child varies depending on the program. The average wait in the traditional program is 4 to 5 years. In the designated program, the length of time ranges from 9 to 18 months, depending on the adoptive parents' degree of assertiveness.

THE CHILDREN

Children placed by JF&CS are healthy, Caucasian infants born in the U.S.

THE REQUIREMENTS

Age: Applicants must be at least 22 and no more than 40 years old.
Health: Applicants must be in reasonably good health.
Religion: The requirement varies depending on the program.
Financial status: Applicants must have demonstrated capacity for financial stability.
Marital status: Applicants must be married and must have been married for at least 3 years.
Family size: The requirement varies depending on the program.
Racial, ethnic or cultural origin: The requirement varies depending on the program.

THE PROCEDURE

Participation in JF&CS adoption programs entails the following basic steps:
Orientation meeting
Application
Homestudy
Placement services
Post-placement services

ADDITIONAL PROGRAMS/SERVICES

JF&CS provides a wide range of services including services for older persons; community outreach and family life programs; mental health and family counseling; services for children; home health services; relinquishment counseling for birthparents.

BRANCH/NETWORK OFFICES

The JF&CS adoption programs are located at 31 New Chardon Street in Boston. However, the staff will travel to the branch offices listed below:

616 Pleasant Street
Brockton, MA 02401
(617) 588–7324
637 Washington Street
Brookline, MA 02146
(617) 566–5716
One Salem Street
Malden, MA 02148
(617) 322–4766
Grosman Community Campus
4333 Nahanton Street
Newton, MA 02159
(617) 965–6890
1 Highland Avenue
Randolph, MA 02368
(617) 986–4850

LICENSE/ACCREDITATION/PROFESSIONAL AFFILIATIONS

Jewish Family and Children's Service is licensed by the Commonwealth of Massachusetts Office for Children, is accredited by the Council on Accreditation of Services for Families and Children, and is affiliated with the Child Welfare League of America and with the Association of Jewish Family and Children's Agencies.

JEWISH FAMILY SERVICE OF GREATER FRAMINGHAM

14 Vernon Street
Framingham, MA 01701
(617) 875–3100
Program director: Candace Mandel, Executive Director; Paul Dubroff, Director of Adoption Services

THE PROGRAM

Jewish Family Service of Greater Framingham is a non-profit multi-service agency providing statewide adoption services and placing approximately 30 children annually through its adoption program. The agency provides "a range of high quality services for children and adolescents and their families who are experiencing emotional and social problems." Such services are provided without limitation with respect to race or religion with the belief that, whenever possible, it is desirable to keep families together while counseling and offering treatment services to the child and parents. Through its adoption program, the agency provides both traditional and identified adoption services. Traditional adoption involves the matching of an infant who has been surrendered to the agency to a couple whose homestudy has been approved by the agency. In an identified adoption, the applicants locate a specific pregnant woman who is willing to specify the adoption of her child by those parents. In addition, the agency will provide homestudy and supervisory services for applicants pursuing interagency adoption.

The Cost

The agency's fee for adoption services is based on a sliding scale and ranges from $2,550 to $5,750. Services covered by the fee include counseling services to the birthparents and adoption services to the applicants (homestudy, placement, post-placement services, and assistance with finalization). In addition, applicants can expect to pay legal fees (average legal costs in Massachusetts are $1,500) and the medical expenses of the birthmother and child (average medical expenses are $4,000).

For applicants pursuing interagency adoption, the agency's fee for homestudy and supervisory services ranges from $2,550 to $5,750.

The Wait

For applicants pursuing identified adoption, the time from application to placement averages 1 year.

The Children

Jewish Family Service places primarily healthy infants of Caucasian and bi-racial backgrounds, born in the U.S In addition, the agency will provide homestudy and supervisory services for applicants pursuing interagency adoption of children of any age, race, or national origin.

The Requirements

Age: Applicants should be within the limits of child-bearing age. The requirement may vary depending on the age of the child.

Health: Applicants must be in reasonably good health. Applicants with health problems or handicaps are given individual consideration.

Religion: No requirement.

Financial status: No requirement.

Marital status: If married, the length of the marriage must be at least 3 years. Single applicants are considered.

Family size: No requirement.

Racial, ethnic or cultural origin: No requirement.

The Procedure

Participation in the adoption program of Jewish Family Service entails the following basic steps:

Individual counseling sessions
Group counseling sessions
Application
Homestudy
Placement
Post-placement supervision

Additional Programs/Services

Jewish Family Service provides counseling services for children and families; consultations concerning identified adoption; workshops on open adoption and other adoption issues.

Branch/Network Offices

None

License/Accreditation/Professional Affiliations

Jewish Family Service of Greater Framingham is licensed by the Commonwealth of Massachusetts Office for Children.

JEWISH FAMILY SERVICE OF GREATER SPRINGFIELD

15 Lenox Street
Springfield, MA 01108
(413) 737–2601
Program director: Harriet Elish, ACSW

The Program

Serving the community for over seventy years, the Jewish Family Service of Greater Springfield is a private nonprofit agency which provides services on a non-sectarian basis to the Springfield community, neighboring towns, and the Commonwealth of Massachusetts. The adoption services provided by Jewish Family Service include 2 programs—the traditional program and the designated program (interstate and intrastate). In both of these programs, the principal role of the agency is to act as a coordinator, working with the birthparents, the adoptive couple, and the referring physician or attorney. In the traditional program, the prospective adoptive family makes a telephone inquiry, is placed on a waiting list, and waits for a birthparent to request services from the agency without a specific adoptive family in mind. In the designated program, the birthmother specifies the adoptive placement of her child to a particular family. A designated adoption may be intrastate (the adoption of a child born in Massachusetts) or interstate (the adoption of a child born in any other state). Finding the potential birthmother is the responsibility of the prospective adoptive family, though the agency provides advice and support in this process. The agency places 4 to 6 children annually through the traditional program and 8 to 15 children through the designated program.

The Cost

The agency fee is based on a sliding scale and includes the following services:

consultation in identifying options and resources available in adoption

assistance in developing an adoption plan

assistance in identifying and locating potential source of infants for interstate adoption

homestudy evaluation and recommendation

support and advice in evaluating the risks of a designated adoption

referrals to legal and medical consultants planning for the adoptive infant

placement services (traditional program)

post-placement supervision

finalization services

pre and post adoption support groups

In addition to the agency fee, prospective adoptive parents should anticipate financial responsibility for all direct costs of the birthmother and child; all legal fees related to the surrender and subsequent freedom of the child for adoptive purposes; all medical, foster home care, and transportation costs for the child.

THE WAIT

In the traditional program, the time from initial inquiry to the homecoming of the adoptive child is 3 to 5 years. In the designated program, the time from inquiry to homecoming is 1 year.

THE CHILDREN

Most children placed by Jewish Family Services are healthy Caucasian infants born in the United States. However, children of other races are also available, and JFS will assist in the interstate adoption of healthy or special-needs children of all races and ages.

THE REQUIREMENTS

Age: No requirement.
Health: Infertility documentation is required. A medical evaluation and report are required.
Religion: No requirement.
Financial status: No requirement.
Marital status: No requirement.
Family size: Applicants may have no more than 1 child currently in the family for placement through the traditional program; no requirement for the designated program.
Racial, ethnic or cultural origin: No requirement.

THE PROCEDURE

Participation in the adoption programs offered by Jewish Family Service entails the following basic steps:
Application
Orientation meeting
Individual counseling sessions
Homestudy
Post-placement supervision

ADDITIONAL PROGRAMS/SERVICES

Jewish Family Service provides a wide range of services, offered on a non-sectarian basis, including older adult services (in-home mental health services, counseling, referrals to community resources, guardianship program); family counseling services (evaluation and referrals, support groups, counseling); consultation and education service; family life workshops; resettlement services.

BRANCH/NETWORK OFFICES

None.

LICENSE/ACCREDITATION/PROFESSIONAL AFFILIATIONS

Jewish Family Service is licensed by the Commonwealth of Massachusetts Office for Children.

JEWISH FAMILY SERVICE OF THE NORTH SHORE, INC.

564 Loring Avenue
Salem, MA 01970
(617) 745–9760
Program director: David Colten

THE PROGRAM

Jewish Family Service of the North Shore is a nonprofit agency serving residents of eastern Massachusetts and placing approximately 12 children annually through its adoption program. Founded over 90 years ago, the agency's mission is the "strengthening of family life." The agency provides services to birthparents and places infants for adoption when birthparents elect adoptive placement as the best plan for their child. In addition, the agency will provide homestudy and supervisory services for applicants pursuing independent or interagency adoption.

THE COST

The agency's fee for adoption services is based on a sliding scale and ranges from $1,200 to $4,000. Services covered by the fee include the homestudy, placement, and post-placement supervision. Additional expenses which applicants should anticipate include legal fees and medical expenses of the birthmother and child.

THE WAIT

The time from application to the homecoming of the adoptive child averages 1 year.

THE CHILDREN

Jewish Family Service places healthy infants, born in the U.S.

THE REQUIREMENTS

Age: The age requirement is evaluated on a case-by-case basis.
Health: Applicants should be in reasonably good health. Infertility documentation is required.
Religion: No requirement.
Financial status: Applicants must demonstrate financial stability.
Marital status: Applicants must be married couples who have been married for at least 2 years.
Family size: No requirement.
Racial, ethnic or cultural origin: No requirement.

THE PROCEDURE

Participation in the adoption program of Jewish Family Service entails the following basic steps:
Orientation
Application
Homestudy
Referral
Placement
Post-placement supervision

ADDITIONAL PROGRAMS/;SERVICES

Jewish Family Service provides a range of family and community services including individual, marital, and family counseling; services to birthparents; services to single parents; services to the elderly; resettlement services; foster care.

BRANCH/NETWORK OFFICES

147 Washington Street
Lynn, MA 01902
(617) 592–2331

LICENSE/ACCREDITATION/PROFESSIONAL AFFILIATIONS

Jewish Family Service of the North Shore, Inc. is licensed by the Commonwealth of Massachusetts Office for Children and is accredited by the Council on Accreditation of Services for Families and Children. The agency is a member of the Association of Jewish Family Service Agencies and the United Way.

LA ALIANZA HISPANA, INC.

409 Dudley Street
Roxbury, MA 02119
(617) 427–7175
Program director: Arnaldo A. Solis

THE PROGRAM

La Alianza Hispana is a community-based, nonprofit agency organized to provide Hispanics necessary or desirable social services and "dedicated to combating the effects of poverty, discrimination, and the stresses of migration." Initiated in 1984, the agency's adoption and foster care program (Te Quiero) strives "to unite Hispanic children who need a permanent home with Hispanic families who wish to adopt." Working in cooperation with the Department of Social Services, La Alianza Hispana places approximately 3 children annually.

THE COST

Adoption services are provided at no cost to the adoptive family.

THE WAIT

The time from application for acceptance into the program to the homecoming of the adoptive child varies depending on the number of children referred by the Department of Social Services for placement.

THE CHILDREN

La Alianza Hispana places both healthy and special needs Hispanic children, ranging in age from birth to 17 years. Countries of origin include the U.S. and Puerto Rico.

THE REQUIREMENTS

Age: No requirement.
Health: Applicants must be in reasonably good health.
Religion: No requirement.
Financial status: No requirement.
Marital status: No requirement.
Family size: No requirement.
Racial, ethnic or cultural origin: Applicants must be Hispanic.

THE PROCEDURE

Participation in La Alianza Hispana's adoption program entails the following basic steps:
  Referral
  Application
  Orientation meeting
  MAPP Training (Massachusetts Approach to Partnership in Parenting)
  Individual counseling sessions
  Homestudy
  Submission of required documents (medical exam, references)
  Placement
  Post-placement supervision

ADDITIONAL PROGRAMS/SERVICES

La Alianza Hispana provides a wide range of community services including counseling and advocacy; social services; substance abuse programs; elderly service center; housing assistance; adult education programs; drug prevention/education/recreation programs; after school day care; community development and revitalization programs.

BRANCH/NETWORK OFFICES

None.

LICENSE/ACCREDITATION/PROFESSIONAL AFFILIATIONS

La Alianza Hispana, Inc. is licensed by the Commonwealth of Massachusetts Office for Children and is a member of the Project IMPACT network.

LOVE THE CHILDREN OF MASSACHUSETTS

P.O. Box 334
Cambridge, MA 02238
(617) 576–2115
Program director: Theresa Weisberger

THE PROGRAM

For a full description of programs and services, refer to Pennsylvania listing:
  Love the Children
  221 West Broad Street
  Quakertown, PA 18951
  (215) 536–4180

MASSACHUSETTS ADOPTION RESOURCE EXCHANGE, INC.

867 Boylston Street
Boston, MA 02116
(617) 536–0362
Program director: Phyllis P. Tourse

THE PROGRAM

MARE is a private, nonprofit organization, founded in 1957 and serving all of New England. MARE works as an adoption information and referral service and as a photo-listing and recruitment center. Working with the public and private adoption agencies, MARE helps find permanent adoptive families for older and special-needs children, facilitating the placement of 120–125 children annually. MARE's various recruitment methods, including the nationally renowned "Wednesday's Child" series, have proven tremendously successful in special-needs adoptions. In addition, MARE offers a support center for adoptive parents and adolescents, quarterly adoption parties, training programs for agency professionals and adoptive families, and a quarterly newsletter.

THE COST

MARE does not charge a fee for its services.

THE WAIT

The average time from child registration to pre-placement with an adoptive family is approximately 6–8 months.

THE CHILDREN

MARE assists in the placement of children of all ages with physical, intellectual and emotional special needs; healthy children age 7 and older; sibling groups. Children registered with MARE are born in the U.S. of Caucasian, Black, Hispanic and mixed racial backgrounds.

THE REQUIREMENTS

Age: No requirement
Health: No requirement.
Religion: No requirement.
Financial status: No requirement.
Marital status: No requirement.
Family size: No requirement.
Racial, ethnic or cultural origin: No requirement.

THE PROCEDURE

MARE is an indirect service agency whose primary purpose is to link waiting children with permanent families. Older and special-needs children for whom homes are being sought are registered with MARE by their social workers if their agencies have no suitable homes available. Similarly, all appropriate waiting families who have been approved for adoption are registered by their social workers. In addition, appropriate studied families may register themselves with MARE six months after completion of their home-study. When a child becomes registered with MARE, the agency first tries to match the child with one of its registered families. The agency then refers all suitable families to the child's social worker, who then pursues those families for a potential match.

ADDITIONAL PROGRAMS/SERVICES

In addition to its Match/Referral service, MARE is actively involved in numerous programs relating to adoption. MARE has a highly successful recruitment program, provides a photo-listing service, sponsors adoption parties, promotes interagency communications, hosts three large training workshops annually, and works closely with a network of adoptive parent support groups.

BRANCH/NETWORK OFFICES

MARE—Springfield Office
(413) 781–0323, Ext. 46

LICENSE/ACCREDITATION/PROFESSIONAL AFFILIATIONS

MARE is licensed by the Commonwealth of Massachusetts Office for Children and is funded primarily by the Massachusetts Department of Social Services through a purchase of service contract.

MERRIMACK VALLEY CATHOLIC CHARITIES

430 North Canal Street
Lawrence, MA 01840
(617) 685–5930
Program director: Maureen K. Brown

THE PROGRAM

Merrimack Valley Catholic Charities (MVCC) is a private, nonprofit agency serving Greater Haverhill, Lawrence, Lowell, and numerous neighboring towns. The mission of MVCC is "to provide service to those most in need, to advocate for justice and to convene the Church and other people of good will to do the same." MVCC assists birthparents in making permanent plans for their infant children and, if appropriate, to facilitate adoption by childless couples. In addition to its infant program, MVCC is a member of the Project IMPACT network through which the agency facilitates the placement of special-needs children (refer to Project IMPACT, Inc. for a full description of programs and services).

THE COST

The agency's fee is based on a sliding scale. If the family's total income is over $30,000, the agency fee is 10%, with a maximum of $5,000. If the family's total income is under $30,000, the agency fee is 7 1/2%. The fee includes homestudy, pre-placement planning, placement, post-placement supervision, legal consultation, and adoption legalization. There is no fee for the adoption of special-needs children through Project IMPACT.

THE WAIT

For the past three years, MVCC's waiting list has been closed. MVCC is now re-opening its waiting list, but is currently unable to predict accurately the average time from application for acceptance into the program to the homecoming of the adoptive child. Prior to re-opening, couples on the list waited 3 to 4 years.

THE CHILDREN

MVCC places healthy infants and toddlers of Caucasian, Black, and Hispanic racial backgrounds, born in the U.S. Through its participation in Project IMPACT, the agency also places children with severe physical, emotional, and developmental needs, of all ages and racial backgrounds.

THE REQUIREMENTS

Age: At the time of application, applicants must be at least 23 and preferably under 40 years of age. No requirement for Project Impact placements.

Health: Applicants must be in reasonably good health. Physician's report on fertility status of husband and wife is required.

Religion: The requirement varies depending on the birthmother's designation.

Financial status: No requirement.

Marital status: Applicants must be married couples who have been married for at least 3 years. No requirement for Project Impact placements.

Family size: Applicants must be childless. No requirement for Project Impact placements.

Racial, ethnic or cultural origin: Preference for placing children in families of similar origins.

THE PROCEDURE

Participation in MVCC adoption programs entails the following basic steps:
Orientation meeting
Application
Group counseling sessions
Homestudy
Pre-placement visit
Placement
Post-placement supervision
Legalization of the adoption

ADDITIONAL PROGRAMS/SERVICES

MVCC provides infant foster care, services to birthparents, and special-needs adoptions through Project IMPACT. In addition, MVCC operates a mental health clinic.

BRANCH/NETWORK OFFICES

Merrimack Valley Area offices
Lowell Catholic Charities
70 Lawrence Street
Lowell, MA 01852
(617) 452–1421
Haverhill Catholic Charities
52–54 Merrimack Street
Haverhill, MA 01830
(617) 372–1031

Cambridge-Somerville Area offices
Catholic Charities of Cambridge and Somerville
270 Washington Street
P.O. Box 457
Somerville, MA 02143
(617) 625–1920
99 Bishop Richard Allen Drive
Cambridge, MA 02139
(617) 547–9566
40 Belmont Street
Watertown, MA 02127
(617) 625–1920

Greater Lynn Area offices
Catholic Family Services of Greater Lynn
55 Lynn Shore Drive
Lynn, MA 01902
(617) 593–2312
6 Salem Street
Reading, MA 01867
(617) 942–0690

North Shore and Cape Ann Area office
North Shore Catholic Charities Center
3 Margin Street
Peabody, MA 01540
(617) 532–3600

Archdiocese of Boston office
Catholic Charitable Bureau of the Archdiocese of Boston, Inc.
49 Franklin Street
Boston, MA 02110
(617) 523–5165

Project IMPACT, Inc.
25 West Street
Boston, MA 02111
(617) 451–1472

LICENSE/ACCREDITATION/PROFESSIONAL AFFILIATIONS

Merrimack Valley Catholic Charities is licensed by the Commonwealth of Massachusetts Office for Children and is accredited by the Council on Accreditation of Services for Families and Children.

NEW BEDFORD CHILD AND FAMILY SERVICE

1061 Pleasant Street
New Bedford, MA 02740
(508) 996–8572
Program director: Jane Reilly

THE PROGRAM

New Bedford Child and Family Service is a nonprofit agency serving residents of southeastern Massachusetts and placing approximately 15 to 20 children annually. Providing adoption and foster care services since 1843, the agency's mission is "to provide a permanent placement for children who can no longer live with their biological families." Working directly with birthparents, with other licensed agencies, with the public agency, and with national and regional exchange programs, the agency places both healthy and special-needs children born in the U.S. Working in cooperation with other U.S. agencies which maintain international programs, the agency aids in the placement of foreign-born children in Massachusetts families. In addition, the agency provides homestudy and supervisory services for applicants pursuing interagency adoption (domestic or international).

THE COST

As of October 1988, the agency's fee for adoption services is $3,500. Services covered by the fee include the homestudy, placement, and post-placement supervision. Applicants pursuing interagency adoption should anticipate fees to the cooperating agency. Applicants pursuing international adoption should anticipate possible expenses related to travel, immigration and naturalization, and the like. There are no fees for the adoption of children in the custody of the state.

THE WAIT

The time from application to placement varies depending on the type of adoption. For healthy infant adoption, the time from application to placement ranges from 1 to 3 years or longer.

THE CHILDREN

New Bedford Child and Family Services places both healthy and special-needs children, ranging in age from birth to 16 years, of all racial backgrounds. Various countries of origin are represented.

THE REQUIREMENTS

Age: No requirement.
Health: Applicants must be in reasonably good health. The requirement varies depending on the age of the child and the child's needs.
Religion: No requirement.
Financial status: No requirement.
Marital status: Applicants may be married or single. If married, the length of the marriage must be at least 3 years.
Family size: No requirement.
Racial, ethnic or cultural origin: No requirement.

THE PROCEDURE

Participation in the adoption program of New Bedford Child and Family Service entails the following basic steps:
Adoption information form
Screening interview
Educational series
Homestudy
Compliance with immigration/naturalization requirements
   (international adoptions only)
Referral
Placement
Post-placement supervision
Legalization

ADDITIONAL PROGRAMS/SERVICES

New Bedford Child and Family Service provides short term foster care.

BRANCH/NETWORK OFFICES

None.

LICENSE/ACCREDITATION/PROFESSIONAL AFFILIATIONS

New Bedford Child and Family Service is licensed by the Commonwealth of Massachusetts Office for Children and is accredited by the Council on Accreditation of Services for Families and Children. The agency is a member of the Child Welfare League of America.

NEW ENGLAND HOME FOR LITTLE WANDERERS

161 South Huntington Avenue
Boston, MA 02130
(617) 232–8600
Program director: Marilyn Sneden, LCSW

THE PROGRAM

Originally founded as an orphanage 123 years ago, New England Home for Little Wanderers (NEH) is today a multi-service, private, nonprofit child welfare agency serving eastern Massachusetts. Serving approximately 1,000 children annually through a wide range of educational, residential, and day treatment programs, the agency's focus is "to provide quality care, through a strong team of multi-disciplined professionals, and to work toward the establishment of a healthy home environment and the opportunity for the child to eventually become a self-sufficient adult." When a child in the agency's program is ready for family life but unable to return to his/her biological family, NEH works to find a permanent adoptive family for the child or long-term foster care for children who are not legally free for adoption. The agency places primarily older children, but also younger children referred to the agency by the Department of Social Services.

THE COST

The agency's fee for adoption services is based on a sliding scale and ranges from $500 to $3,500. Services covered by the fee include all phases of the adoption process (pre-placement services through post legalization).

THE WAIT

The time from application to the homecoming of the adoptive child varies depending on the applicant's flexibility and willingness to accept the special needs of the child. The wait ranges from 6 months to 3 years.

THE CHILDREN

NEH places both healthy and special-needs children, ranging in age from infancy to 16 years, of Black, Caucasian, Hispanic and bi-racial backgrounds. NEH describes its "typical" child as "emotionally abandoned, often having wandered from family to family, institution to institution. Though born normal, home abuse and neglect have produced problems larger than he or she is capable of handling." Approximately half are minorities, and almost 40% are teenagers, though younger children are also available through referral from the Department of Social Services.

THE REQUIREMENTS

Age: No requirement, but the agency will not place a child with a parent who could not have borne a child of that age.

Health: Applicants with health problems or handicaps are given individual consideration.

Religion: No requirement.

Financial status: No requirement.

Marital status: No requirement.

Family size: No requirement.

Racial, ethnic or cultural origin: Preference for placing children in families of similar origins.

THE PROCEDURE

Participation in NEH's adoption program entails the following basic steps:
  Orientation meeting
  Group training sessions
  Application
  Homestudy
  Referral
  Placement
  Post-placement supervision

ADDITIONAL PROGRAMS/SERVICES

NEH provides a wide range of services including residential care, educational programs, day treatment programs, family life and individual counseling, foster care services, training services for foster and adoptive families, parent support groups. In addition, NEH is in the process of developing a formal post- adoption services program.

BRANCH/NETWORK OFFICES

None.

LICENSE/ACCREDITATION/PROFESSIONAL AFFILIATIONS

New England Home for Little Wanderers is licensed by the Commonwealth of Massachusetts Office for Children and is accredited by the Council on Accreditation of Services for Families and Children. NEH is a member of the following national, state, and local organizations: National Council on Social Welfare, National Foster Parents' Association, The New England Association for Child Care, Massachusetts Council of Voluntary Child Care Agencies, Massachusetts Council of Human Service Providers, Massachusetts Foster Parents Association, and the United Way of Massachusetts Bay.

NORTH SHORE CATHOLIC CHARITIES

3 Margin Street
Peabody, MA 01960
(617) 532–3600
Program director: Louise Plesha, Adoption Coordinator; Mary Byrne, Director of Professional Services

THE PROGRAM

North Shore Catholic Charities is a nonprofit multi-service agency serving residents of the North Shore area of Massachusetts and placing approximately 9 to 10 children annually through its adoption program. Founded to provide adoption services in 1893, the agency has expanded over the years to include many other community services designed "to encourage and strengthen the integrity of the family and the well-being of its children." The agency provides services to birthparents and places infants for adoption when birthparents elect adoptive placement as the best plan for their child. In addition, the agency will provide homestudy and supervisory services for applicants pursuing domestic interagency adoption.

THE COST

The agency's fee for adoption services is based on a sliding scale and ranges from $1,000 to $7,000. Services covered by the fee include all phases of the adoption process (homestudy through finalization). For homestudy only or any other combination of services, the fee is pro-rated. In special circumstances, the fee may be waived.

THE WAIT

The time from application for acceptance into the program to the homecoming of the adoptive child ranges from 3 to 4 years.

THE CHILDREN

North Shore Catholic Charities places healthy infants (birth to 12 months), primarily of Caucasian but also of bi-racial backgrounds, born in the U.S.

THE REQUIREMENTS

Age: No requirement.

Health: Applicants with health problems or handicaps are given individual consideration.

Religion: No requirement.

Financial status: Applicants must demonstrate financial stability.

Marital status: No requirement.

Family size: Applicant must be childless.

Residence: Applicants must be residents of towns on the North Shore and Cape Ann.

Racial, ethnic or cultural origin: No requirement.

THE PROCEDURE

Participation in the adoption program of North Shore Catholic Charities entails the following basic steps:
  Application
  Orientation meeting

Group counseling sessions
Homestudy
Placement
Post-placement supervision

ADDITIONAL PROGRAMS/SERVICES

North Shore Catholic Charities provides services to young parents (teen pregnancy program); mental health clinic (counseling services); foster care; day care; protective services; community services (food bank, economic assistance).

BRANCH/NETWORK OFFICES

North Shore Catholic Charities is affiliated with other Catholic social service agencies under the jurisdiction of the Archdiocese of Boston.

LICENSE/ACCREDITATION/PROFESSIONAL AFFILIATIONS

North Shore Catholic Charities is licensed by the Commonwealth of Massachusetts Office for Children and is accredited by the Council on Accreditation of Services for Families and Children.

PARSONS CHILD AND FAMILY CENTER

66 Lake Buel Road
Great Barrington, MA 02130
(413) 528–5727/2749
Program director: Deborah McCurdy

THE PROGRAM

For a full description of programs and services, refer to New York listing:
Parsons Child and Family Center
845 Central Avenue
Albany, NY 12206
(518) 438–4571

PROJECT IMPACT, INC.

25 West Street, 3rd Floor
Boston, MA 02111–1213
(617) 451–1472
Program director: Juliet Askenase

THE PROGRAM

Project IMPACT is a private nonprofit adoption agency which specializes in the permanent placement of children with severe special needs who are in the care of the Commonwealth of Massachusetts. Project IMPACT is funded by purchase of service by the Massachusetts Department of Social Services and by private and federal grants. The project was initiated in 1976 to address the needs of children who are traditionally considered hard-to-place, children with severe emotional and/or developmental handicaps. Working with the Massachusetts Department of Social Services and with a network of six private agencies, Project IMPACT places 30–40 children annually. Its purpose is to find the most appropriate family for each child and to ensure the permanence and stability of the placement.

THE COST

There is no fee for the adoption of IMPACT children. Adoption subsidy is available through the Department of Social Services to parents based on the child's special need.

THE WAIT

The time from initial inquiry to the homecoming of the adoptive child varies to meet the needs of the child as well as the family. Generally, the child moves into his/her new family's home in 1 to 6 months from the initial visit with the child.

THE CHILDREN

Children referred to IMPACT by the Massachusetts Department of Social Services may be of any race or ethnic background and range in age from birth to 22 years. They have special emotional, physical, and intellectual needs and are considered the most difficult to place of the "waiting children" of Massachusetts.

THE REQUIREMENTS

Age: No requirement.
Health: Applicants must be in reasonably good health; the requirement may vary depending on the child's needs.
Religion: No requirement, but may vary depending on the child's wishes.
Financial status: No requirement.
Marital status: No requirement, but may vary depending on the child's needs and desires.
Family size: No requirement.
Racial, ethnic or cultural origin: No requirement, but may vary depending on the child's needs and wishes.

THE PROCEDURE

Participation in Project IMPACT entails the following basic steps:
Inquiry
Family registration
Social worker contact
Introductory session
Family preparation
Placement
Post-placement services
Post-adoption services

ADDITIONAL PROGRAMS/SERVICES

Project IMPACT conducts workshops and training seminars for adoptive families; offers a crisis intervention service; pilots a family resource program at The Hogan Regional Center; runs a specialized foster care program; provides post-placement and post-adoption services.

BRANCH/NETWORK OFFICES

Project IMPACT is a member of the Family Builder Network, a national association of agencies dedicated to the adoption of children with special needs. The Project IM-

PACT Network includes the following private agencies, located throughout the state of Massachusetts:

Merrimack Valley Catholic Charities
430 No. Canal Street
Lawrence, MA 01840
(617) 685–5930

New Bedford Child and Family Service
1061 Pleasant Street
New Bedford, MA 02740
(617) 996–8572

Children's Aid and Family Service of Hampshire Co., Inc.
8 Trumbull Road
Northampton, MA 01060
(413) 586–3509

Protestant Social Service Bureau
776 Hancock Street
Quincy, MA 02170
(617) 773–6203

Roxbury Children's Service
22 Elm Hill Avenue
Roxbury, MA 02119
(617) 445–6655

La Alianza Hispana, Inc.
409 Dudley Street
Roxbury, MA 02119
(617) 427–7175

LICENSE/ACCREDITATION/PROFESSIONAL AFFILIATIONS

Project IMPACT is licensed by the Commonwealth of Massachusetts Office for Children and is a member of the Family Builder Network and the Project IMPACT Network.

PROTESTANT SOCIAL SERVICE BUREAU, INC.

776 Hancock Street
Wollaston, MA 02170
(617) 773–6203
Program director: Robert Taylor, ACSW, Executive Director; Phyllis Speciale, LICSW, Child Placement Coordinator

THE PROGRAM

Protestant Social Service Bureau (PSSB) is a nonprofit social service agency and a cooperative effort of South Shore Protestant churches whose mission is "to strengthen family life, provide substitute temporary (foster) and permanent (adoptive) families for some children and adolescents in need of them and to provide help in times of crisis to individuals and families." PSSB serves residents of South Shore and Cape Cod and places approximately 10 special-needs children annually through its adoption program. Since the adoption program began in 1974, the agency's focus has been special-needs adoption. Working cooperatively with public agencies and with national and regional exchange programs, the agency facilitates the placement of older children, sibling groups, children with intellectual, physical, or emotional handicaps, and "legal risk" children. Through the One Church–One Child program, the agency recruits, studies, and supervises Black families who wish to adopt Black children. The agency is open to the possibility of intercountry special-needs adoption; however, the agency's involvement at this point is minimal. In addition, the agency will provide homestudy and supervisory services for applicants pursuing interagency adoption (domestic or international).

THE COST

For the placement of children referred to the agency by the State, adoption services are provided at no cost to the adoptive family. For other placements, the agency's fee is based on a sliding scale, ranging from $540 to $4,000. Services covered by the fee include all phases of the adoption process (educational group series, homestudy, child identification, placement supervision, services to facilitate legalization, and post-adoptive services). Applicants pursuing interagency international adoption should anticipate fees to the cooperating agency, possible travel and other expenses related to international adoption.

THE WAIT

The time from application to acceptance and placement is dependent on several factors including (1) the family's commitment to a block of time to begin the homestudy process, (2) the availability of time on the part of the agency's social workers, and (3) the special needs of the child(ren). For a "child specific" recruitment, the time averages 6 to 9 months.

THE CHILDREN

PSSB facilitates the placement of special-needs children, ranging in age from 6 to 16 years, of all racial backgrounds, born in the U.S. In addition, PSSB provides homestudy and supervisory services to facilitate the interagency placement of children of any age, race, or national origin.

THE REQUIREMENTS

Age: The requirement varies depending on the needs of the child, the applicant's health and ability to parent.
Health: Applicants must be in sufficiently good health to carry out anticipated parenting tasks.
Religion: No requirement; however, applicants must agree to provide medical services for the adopted child.
Financial status: No requirement.
Marital status: No requirement.
Family size: No requirement.
Racial, ethnic or cultural origin: Preference for placing children in families of similar racial and ethnic origins.

THE PROCEDURE

Participation in the adoption program of PSSB entails the following basic steps:
Orientation meeting
Screening interview
Application
Educational group series
Homestudy (including individual, couple, and family interviews)

Placement
Post-placement supervision
Finalization
Post-adoptive services

ADDITIONAL PROGRAMS/SERVICES

PSSB provides individual, marital, family, and group counseling; foster care services for children from birth to 18 years of age; services to the elderly (shared living, equity conversion counseling, home sharing); post-adoptive services.

BRANCH/NETWORK OFFICES

None

LICENSE/ACCREDITATION/PROFESSIONAL AFFILIATIONS

Protestant Social Service Bureau, Inc. is licensed by the Commonwealth of Massachusetts Office for Children. All social work staff are licensed by the Commonwealth of Massachusetts, and the majority of social work staff have advanced degrees in social work.

ROXBURY CHILDREN'S SERVICE, INC.

22 Elm Hill Avenue
Dorchester, MA 02121
(617) 445–6655
Program director: Dorothy Cox, MSW, Acting Director

THE PROGRAM

Founded in 1974, Roxbury Children's Service (RCS) is a nonprofit social service agency serving primarily the Commonwealth of Massachusetts but also occasionally neighboring states as well and placing 12–15 children annually. During its decade of service, RCS has expanded from three programs to a comprehensive community-based system that provides for varied needs of the predominantly Black community of greater Boston. Providing services without regard to race, color, creed, marital status, or ability to pay, the agency's mission is "to provide preventive, ameliorative and rehabilitative intervention in the many and complex problems in community service." To that end, the agency provides adoption services, day care services, and community health services and maintains a mental health clinic.

THE COST

The agency's fee for adoption services is based on a sliding scale and ranges from $400 to $3,500. Services covered by the fee include all phases of the adoption process (pre-placement services through legalization). Through a contract with the Commonwealth of Massachusetts, the agency studies minority families at no cost to the applicants. However, minority applicants should anticipate a fee of $750 to cover supervision of placement and legal fees if the agency provides post-placement services.

THE WAIT

The time from application for acceptance into the program to the homecoming of the adoptive child ranges from 3 to 18 months.

THE CHILDREN

Roxbury Children's Service places both healthy and special-needs children, ranging in age from birth to 16 years, of Black and bi-racial backgrounds, born in the U.S.

THE REQUIREMENTS

Age: Applicants must be at least 21 years of age.
Health: No requirement.
Religion: No requirement.
Financial status: No requirement.
Marital status: No requirement.
Family size: No requirement.
Racial, ethnic or cultural origin: Preference for placing children in families of similar origins. Applicants must be Black (single or married) or interracial couples.

THE PROCEDURE

Participation in RCS' adoption program entails the following basic steps:
Application
Individual counseling sessions
Homestudy
Referral
Placement
Post-placement supervision
In addition, applicants are encouraged to participate in an 8–week training program (one evening per week) sponsored by Massachusetts Adoption Resource Exchange (MARE).

ADDITIONAL PROGRAMS/SERVICES

RCS provides protective services and teen counseling; provides services to court-referred youths; provides parent aide program; maintains a family day care center; maintains a mental health clinic; provides early intervention program; provides foster care services; operates Madison Park Collaborative (counseling program in a local high school).

BRANCH/NETWORK OFFICES

Adoption, Day Care, Parent Aide Programs
347 Washington Street
Dorchester, MA 02124
(617) 436–3564
Mental Health and Early Intervention Programs
185 Dudley Street
Roxbury, MA 02119
(617) 442–3167
Madison Park Collaborative
Madison Park High School
Roxbury, MA 02119
(617) 442–8412

LICENSE/ACCREDITATION/PROFESSIONAL AFFILIATIONS

Roxbury Children's Service is licensed by the Commonwealth of Massachusetts Office for Children. RCS is a member of the Child Welfare League of America and of the Project IMPACT Network.

WORCESTER CHILDREN'S FRIEND SOCIETY

21 Cedar Street
Worcester, MA 01609
(508) 753–5425
Program director: Carol R. Epstein

THE PROGRAM

Worcester Children's Friend Society (WCFS) is a nonprofit agency serving residents of southern Worcester County and placing approximately 6 to 8 children annually through its adoption program. Established in 1848, the Society's purpose is "to serve the needs of children by providing a comprehensive system of child welfare and mental health services and to be an advocate for their interests, rights, and welfare." The agency provides services to birthparents and places a small number of infants annually when birthparents elect adoptive placement as the best plan for their child. Working in cooperation with MARE (Massachusetts Adoption Resource Exchange), the Society provides homestudy and supervisory services for applicants pursuing special-needs adoption.

THE COST

As of October 1988, the agency's fee for adoption services is based on a sliding scale, with a maximum fee of $4,500. Services covered by the fee include all phases of the adoption process. In addition, applicants can expect to pay a $10 fee at the time of registration.

THE WAIT

Prospective applicants register with the agency and then receive an application from the agency. The agency does not send out applications until they believe that placement can occur within 12 months. Couples are registered up to 3 years before receiving an application.

THE CHILDREN

WCFS directly places both healthy and special-needs infants (usually under 12 months), of all racial backgrounds, born in the U.S. In cooperation with MARE, WCFS facilitates the placement of special-needs children.

THE REQUIREMENTS

Age: The general guideline is that, in the normal course of events, applicants should expect to live until the child reaches adulthood.
Health: Applicants with health problems or handicaps are given individual consideration. Applicants' general health should indicate normal life expectancy.
Religion: If the applicants profess a religion, the agency expects them to be practicing members of that religion. The preferences of the birthparents are honored.
Financial status: Applicants must demonstrate the ability to manage financial resources.

Marital status: For healthy infant adoption, applicants must be married couples. Single applicants are considered for special needs placements.*Family size*: For healthy infant adoption, applicants must be childless. The requirement varies for special needs placements.

Racial, ethnic or cultural origin: The agency believes that a child is entitled to permanency; if a home of the same ethnicity appears unlikely, the agency will place across ethnic lines.

THE PROCEDURE

Participation in the adoption program of WCFS entails the following basic steps:
   Application
   Homestudy (including orientation, group discussions, and individual interviews)
   Placement
   Post-placement supervision
   Post-legalization services (upon request)

ADDITIONAL PROGRAMS/SERVICES

WCFS provides counseling services; foster care; post-legalization services including information, brief casework help, psychotherapy, and search services for adoptees of the agency.

BRANCH/NETWORK OFFICES

None.

LICENSE/ACCREDITATION/PROFESSIONAL AFFILIATIONS

Worcester Children's Friend Society is licensed by the Commonwealth of Massachusetts Office for Children and is accredited by the Council on Accreditation of Services for Families and Children. The agency is a member of the Child Welfare League of America.

WORLD ADOPTION SERVICES, INC.

49 Lexington Street
Newton, MA 02165
(617) 332–3307
Program director: Suzanne Burke

THE PROGRAM

World Adoption Services, Inc., is a nonprofit adoption agency that serves Massachusetts and New Hampshire and places approximately 60 children annually. Established in 1978 by adoptive parents and professionals, the agency provides homestudy and post-placement supervision for its clients and works cooperatively with other U.S.-based licensed agencies and programs to place foreign-born and domestic-born children in American families. In addition, the agency provides nationwide services free of charge to birthparents who are considering the adoption alternative.

THE COST

The agency's fee for homestudy and supervisory services is based on a sliding scale and ranges from $500 to $1,200. There is also a $75 application fee. In addition, applicants can expect to pay placement fees to the cooperating agency or program through which World Adoption Services arranges the adoption.

THE WAIT

The average time from application to the homecoming of the adoptive child ranges from 6 months to 2 years (with an average wait of 11 months).

THE CHILDREN

World Adoption Services places both healthy and special-needs children who range in age from birth through school age, from all racial backgrounds. Places of origin include the U.S., Latin America, Asia, and India.

THE REQUIREMENTS

Age: The requirement varies depending on the age and needs of the adoptive child.

Health: Applicants should be in good health.

Religion: The requirement varies depending on the program chosen.

Financial status: Applicants must demonstrate financial stability.

Marital status: The requirement varies depending on the program chosen. Couples must be married at least 2 years.

Family size: No requirement.

Racial, ethnic or cultural origin: The requirement varies depending on the needs of the adoptive families and children.

THE PROCEDURE

Participation in World Adoption Services' adoption program entails the following basic steps:

Orientation meeting (optional)
Application
Individual counseling sessions
Homestudy
Compliance with immigration/naturalization requirements
Placement
Post-placement group sessions
Post-placement supervision
Finalization in local probate court

ADDITIONAL PROGRAMS/SERVICES

Other services that World Adoption Services, Inc., offers include foster care and counseling, and free services to birthparents considering the adoption alternative.

BRANCH/NETWORK OFFICES

All adoption inquiries are processed through the main office in Newton, MA.

LICENSE/ACCREDITATION/PROFESSIONAL AFFILIATIONS

World Adoption Services, Inc. is licensed by the Commonwealth of Massachusetts Office for Children and by the State of New Hampshire Department of Health and Human Services.

Michigan

PUBLIC ADOPTION PROGRAM/ COMMUNITY RESOURCES

Department of Social Services
Office of Children and Youth Services
300 South Capitol Avenue
P.O. Box 30037
Lansing, MI 48909
(517) 373-3513
Adoption specialist: Richard Hoekstra

THE PROGRAM

Public adoption services in Michigan are provided by the Department of Social Services, Office of Children and Youth Services (DSS/ OCYS) through branch offices located in each county. The focus of the DSS/OCYS Adoption Program is to recruit and prepare families who are interested in special-needs adoption. Children in DSS custody who are available for adoption through DSS/OCYS are primarily older, minority, and handicapped children and sibling groups.

STATE EXCHANGE

Michigan Adoption Resource Exchange. For information, contact the Office of Children and Youth Services (above).

STATE ADOPTION REUNION REGISTRY

None.

STATE SUBSIDY

Adoption Subsidy Program. For information, contact the Office of Children and Youth Services (above).

NACAC REPRESENTATIVE

Jerry Hewitt
11311 Old Bridge Road
Grand Blanc, MI 48439
(313) 694-2926

GENERAL ADOPTION RESOURCES

The following list of resources was compiled by Mary E. Parks for the Children's Charter of the Courts of Michigan (115 W. Allegan, Suite 500, Lansing, MI 48933), an organization which provides community education, training, technical assistance, and advocacy on child welfare issues.

Addition by Adoption (ABA)
20608 Westhaven
Southfield, MI 48075
Contact: Tony Holbrook
(313) 355-0094

Adoptive Parents and Children (APAC)
1025 State St.
Brighton, MI 48116
Contact: Brian and Becky Martin
(313) 227-1235

Adoptive Parents Outreach
10014 Grandville Ave.
Detroit, MI 48228
Contact: Lillo Greer
(313) 835-9642

The Adoption Option
P.O. Box 7052
Huntington Woods, MI 48070-7052
Contact: Don Marengere
(313) 737-0267

All Doing Our Part Together (ADOPT)
6939 Shields Ct.
Saginaw, MI 48603
Contact: Jim and Maxine Berden
(517) 781-2089

Citizens for Handicapped, Adopted and Needy Children (CHANC)
2441 Flintridge Ave.
Pontiac, MI 48055
Contact: Mary Ann Van Trease
(313) 391-1048 (evenings)

Families For Children (FFC)
26615 Monticello Ave.
Inkster, MI 48141
Contact: Mary Lou Bosworts
(313) 544-9930

Families For International Children
2124 College, SE
Grand Rapids, MI 49507
Contact: Eric and Charlene Longman
(616) 245-1705

Families Through Adoption
31157 Applewood Ln.
Farmington Hills, MI 48018
Contact: Lynne Moffitt
(313) 476-7345

Lenawee Families of Adoptive Foreign Children
5315 Whig Highway
Clayton, MI 49235
Contact: Lesley Jones
(517) 436-3290

Macomb Assn. of Adoptive Families
29659 MacKenzie Circle
Warren, MI 48089
Contact: Linda Legate
(313) 751-2433

MI Assn. of Single Adoptive Parents
2830 Old Plank Rd.
Milford, MI 48042
Contact: Betty Bonathan
(313) 732-7493

MI Foster and Adoptive Parent Assn.
22075 Koths
Taylor, MI 48180
(313) 295-0257

OURS of Greater Ann Arbor Area
6727 Heatheridge Dr.
Saline, MI 48176
Contact: Derexa Grindatti
(313) 429-7097

OURS of Greater Lansing
  4036 Dell Rd.
  Lansing, MI 48910
  Contact: Suzanne Dickerson
  (517) 394–2580

OURS of Michiana
  2835 Cook St.
  Niles, MI 49120
  Contact: Kurt and Mary Ann Traxler
  (219) 277–2246

OURS of Southwestern Michigan
  562 Columbus Ave.
  Benton Harbor, MI 49022
  Contact: Mary Muday
  (616) 925–0387

OURS of Flint
  9339 Hilda Ln.
  Flushing, MI 48433
  Contact: Judy Lichnovzky
  (313) 659–7641

People Adopting Children Everywhere
  94 W. 18th St.
  Holland, MI 49423
  Contact: Dave & Vicki Carothers
  (616) 392–6764

Parents Adopting Children Everywhere
  10503 Croswell
  W. Olive, MI 49460
  Contact: Jerry and Kathy Hertel
  (616) 399–3569

Parents for International Adoptions
  5503 W. Baseline Rd.
  Weidman, MI 48893
  Contact: Marsha Huzzey
  (517) 644–3685

Singles for Adoption
  619 Norton Dr.
  Kalamazoo, MI 49001
  Contact: Carol Powell
  (616) 381–2581

SPECIAL-NEEDS ADOPTION RESOURCES

National Resource Center for Special-needs Adoption
  Spaulding for Children
  P.O. Box 337
  Chelsea, MI 48118
  (313) 475–8693

OUT-OF-STATE AGENCIES

AGENCY

  Christian Family Service, Kansas

SEE APPENDIX A

  Agencies Providing Nationwide Services

ADVENTIST ADOPTION & FAMILY SERVICES

P.O. Box C
125 College Avenue
Berrien Springs, MI 49103
(616) 471–2221
Program director: Fern Ringering, MSW

THE PROGRAM

For a full description of programs and services, refer to Oregon listing:

Adventist Adoption & Family Services
  6040 S.E. Belmont Street
  Portland, OR 97215
  (503) 232–1211

AMERICANS FOR INTERNATIONAL AID AND ADOPTION

877 S. Adams
Birmingham, MI 48011
(313) 645–2211
Program director: Nancy M. Fox, Agency Director; Moti Irani, Director of Social Services/Indian Coordinator; Elizabeth Gorning, Korean "Waiting Children's" Coordinator

THE PROGRAM

Americans for International Aid and Adoption (AIAA) is a nonprofit adoption and aid organization providing nationwide service (offices in Michigan, New York, and Washington) and placing approximately 350 children annually. Dedicated to helping children in need overseas, the agency's principal focus is the children who wait—because of age, racial background, or physical condition. Founded in 1975 by three couples who adopted Vietnamese children, the agency has expanded to include programs for the adoption of children from India, and Korea. In addition to adoption services, the agency is committed to providing the essentials of life for the well-being of children throughout the world through the provision of food, clothing and medical supplies; overseas family assistance program (which allows children to remain with their own families); educational scholarships (for high school students in orphanages or poor families); contributions to facilities which provide care and treatment for children; escorting services for children coming to the U.S. for specialized medical care or adoption; and sponsor family coordination for Amerasian youth and young adults.

THE COST

For Michigan, New York, and Washington residents, the agency's fee for adoption services is based on a sliding scale and ranges from $5,000 to $7,000 depending on the program. Applicants from other states arrange for a licensed agency in their home state to provide homestudy and supervisory services. In addition, all applicants should anticipate overseas processing fees; foster care, medical, and legal fees in the country of origin; immigration and legal fees connected with finalization in the U.S.

THE WAIT

The time from application to the homecoming of the adoptive child varies depending on the program, but generally occurs within 1 1/2 years.

THE CHILDREN

AIAA places both healthy and special-needs children, ranging in age from birth to 16 years, of all racial backgrounds. Countries of origin include India and Korea.

THE REQUIREMENTS

Age: The requirement varies depending on the program. The general guideline is that the applicants should theoretically have been able to give birth to the child.

Health: Applicants should be in reasonably good health. Applicants with health problems or handicaps are given individual consideration.

Religion: No requirement, but may vary depending on the request of the biological parent or child care facility.

Financial status: The requirement is assessed on an individual basis and may vary depending on the requirements of the overseas agency.

Marital status: The requirements vary depending on the program. For Korean adoption, applicants must be couples who have been married for at least 3 years. Single applicants are accepted for Indian adoption.

Family size: The requirement varies depending on the program and the type of child being requested.

Racial, ethnic or cultural origin: No requirement, but preference for placing children in families of similar origins.

THE PROCEDURE

Participation in AIAA's adoption program entails the following basic steps:
Questionnaire
Application
Homestudy
Compliance with immigration/naturalization requirements
Referral
Court procedure (Michigan residents)
Interstate compact procedure (out-of-state families)
Placement
Post-placement supervision
Finalization
Naturalization and notification of agency

ADDITIONAL PROGRAMS/SERVICES

AIAA works closely with parent groups in providing support systems, cultural experiences, and workshops. The agency provides foster care services and counseling on an individual basis. The agency conducts fund-raising activities for sponsorships, aid and supplies to be donated to overseas child welfare organizations.

BRANCH/NETWORK OFFICES

AIAA/New York State
8199 Wheaton Rd.

Baldwinsville, NY 13027
(315) 638–4669
Administrator: Bruce Baehr

AIAA/Washington State
P.O. Box 6051
Spokane, WA 99207–0901
(509) 489–2015
Administrator: Carol Hollar

LICENSE/ACCREDITATION/PROFESSIONAL AFFILIATIONS

AIAA is licensed by the State of Michigan Department of Social Services and by the State of Washington Department of Social and Health Services and is approved for placement in New York State. The agency is a member of Joint Council on International Children's Services of North America, North American Council on Adoptable Children, and Michigan Association of Children's Agencies.

BETHANY CHRISTIAN SERVICES

901 Eastern Avenue, N.E.
Grand Rapids, MI 49503
(616) 459–6273
Program director: James K. Haveman, Jr.,Executive Director

THE PROGRAM

Bethany Christian Services is a nonprofit, multi-service child placement agency with offices in over 40 communities nationwide. Bethany Christian Services places approximately 1,000 children annually through its various adoption programs. Bethany's adoption programs include domestic healthy infant, international children, and older and special-needs children (Michigan only). Bethany's mission is "to express the love of God by providing excellent social services that protect and enhance the lives of children, young people and their families."

THE COST

Agency fees vary according to the applicant's state of residence and financial situation.

THE WAIT

The time from application for acceptance into the program to the homecoming of the adoptive child varies according to the applicant's state of residence.

THE CHILDREN

Bethany Christian Services places both healthy and special-needs children, ranging in age from birth to 15 years, of all racial backgrounds. Countries of origin include U.S., Korea, India, and various South American countries.

THE REQUIREMENTS

Age: Applicants must be between 25 and 38 years of age.
Health: Infertility documentation is required for domestic healthy infant program.

Religion: No requirement for international adoption. For other programs, applicants must be active members of an evangelical church.

Financial status: : Applicants must demonstrate financial stability.

Marital status: Applicants must be married and must have been married for at least 3 years.

Family size: For domestic infant adoption, applicants may have no more than 1 child currently in the family.

Racial, ethnic or cultural origin: No requirement, but preference for placing children in families of similar origins.

Residence: Applicants must be residents of a state in which Bethany Christian Services is licensed to place children.

THE PROCEDURE

The adoption procedure varies depending on the applicant's state of residence.

ADDITIONAL PROGRAMS/SERVICES

Bethany Christian Services offers a wide range of services including Crisis Pregnancy Services (1–800–B-E-T-H-A-N-Y, toll-free national 24–hour crisis pregnancy hot line); 3 maternity homes across the U.S.; Foster Care Program; bimonthly newsletters (Bethany's Rainbow Connection and Grafting). In Michigan, additional services include Refugee Foster Care Program; Marital and Individual Counseling; Residential Treatment Program for adolescent boys; Day Care Center.

BRANCH/NETWORK OFFICES

Bethany Christian Services has offices throughout the United States. Refer to appropriate state listings for addresses and telephone numbers of local Bethany offices. Branch offices located in Michigan are as follows:

Corporate Office
901 Eastern Ave., N.E.
Grand Rapids, MI 49504
(616) 459–6273

135 North State St.
Holland, MI
(616) 396–0623

6995 W. 48th St.
P.O. Box 173
Fremont, MI
(616) 924–3390

32500 Concord, Suite 353–West
Madison Heights, MI
(313) 588–9400

LICENSE/ACCREDITATION/PROFESSIONAL AFFILIATIONS

Bethany Christian Services is licensed by the appropriate state department in each of the states in which the agency maintains a branch office. The agency is a member of the National Committee For Adoption, the Michigan Federation of Private Child and Family Agencies, and the Evangelical Council for Financial Accountability.

CATHOLIC FAMILY SERVICES

1819 Gull Road
Kalamazoo, MI 49001
(616) 381–9800
Program director: Mrs. Frances Denny, ACSW

THE PROGRAM

Catholic Family Services is a nonprofit agency serving couples in Kalamazoo and Allegan Counties regardless of their religious preferences and serving Roman Catholic couples in Allegan, Berrien, Cass, Calhoun, Kalamazoo, Branch, Barry, Van Buren and St. Joseph Counties. The agency was founded in 1915 through the Sisters of St. Joseph to provide services to women experiencing unplanned pregnancies. Today, the agency provides residential care for pregnant women in group home, foster home, or independent living settings. The agency places primarily infants (but occasionally older children as well) when birthparents in the agency's program elect adoptive placement as the best plan for their child. The agency places approximately 10 to 20 children annually. In addition, the agency provides homestudy and supervisory services for applicants pursuing independent or interagency adoption.

THE COST

The agency's fee for adoption services is based on a sliding scale according to income and currently ranges from $0 to $4,198. Services covered by the fee include the homestudy, placement, and post-placement supervision and services. In addition, applicants can expect to pay a $20 court filing fee at the time of finalization.

THE WAIT

The time from application to the homecoming of the adoptive child averages 4 to 5 years.

THE CHILDREN

Catholic Family Services places both healthy and special-needs infants (newborn to 1 year), of all racial backgrounds, born in the U.S. The agency also occasionally places older children.

THE REQUIREMENTS

Age: Applicants should be no more than 40 years of age. However, the requirement varies depending on the needs of the child.

Health: Applicants with health problems or handicaps are given individual consideration. Infertility documentation is required for healthy Caucasian infant adoption.

Religion: No requirement for residents of Kalamazoo and Allegan Counties. For other counties (see "Program"), applicants must be practicing Roman Catholics.

Financial status: : Applicants must demonstrate the ability to live within their income.

Marital status: Applicants must be married; the length of the marriage must be at least 2 years.

Family size: For healthy Caucasian infant adoption, applicants must be childless. The requirement is flexible for special needs or minority placements.

Racial, ethnic or cultural origin: Preference for placing children in families of similar origins.

THE PROCEDURE

Participation in the adoption program of Catholic Family Services entails the following basic steps:
Orientation meeting
Application
Homestudy (either individual or group format)
Placement
Post-placement supervision

ADDITIONAL PROGRAMS/SERVICES

Catholic Family Services provides a wide range of services including family counseling; foster care; pregnancy counseling; residential programs for unmarried teen mothers and pregnant women; residential program and counseling for runaway teens; senior citizen home; legalization services for illegal aliens.

BRANCH/NETWORK OFFICES

None.

LICENSE/ACCREDITATION/PROFESSIONAL AFFILIATIONS

Catholic Family Services is licensed by the State of Michigan Department of Social Services and is accredited by the Council on Accreditation of Services for Families and Children. The agency is a member of the Michigan Federation of Private Child and Family Agencies.

CATHOLIC FAMILY SERVICE OF BAY CITY

Diocese of Saginaw
1008 South Wenona
Bay City, MI 48706
(517) 892–2504
Program director: Thomas Gaybrick

THE PROGRAM

Catholic Family Service of the Diocese of Saginaw is a nonprofit agency serving residents of the Diocese of Saginaw (11 counties) and placing approximately 30 children annually. In existence for nearly 50 years, child welfare issues have always been the focal point of the agency's program. The agency provides services to birthparents and places infants for adoption when birthparents in the agency's counseling program elect adoptive placement as the best plan for their child. The agency also actively recruits families for special-needs children.

THE COST

For infant adoption, the agency's fee is based on a sliding scale and ranges from $1,500 to $4,100. Services covered by the fee include all phases of the adoption process (application, homestudy, preparation of legal documents, post-placement supervision) and counseling services to the birthparents. The only additional expenses which applicants need

anticipate are court filing fees ($20–$40) and the fee for a new birth certificate ($20). For special-needs adoption, services are provided at no cost to the adoptive family.

THE WAIT

For infant adoption, the time from application to the homecoming of the adoptive child averages 4 years. For older child or special-needs adoption, the wait ranges from 1 to 3 years, depending on the type of child the family wishes to adopt.

THE CHILDREN

Catholic Family Service places both healthy and special-needs children, infants and older children, of all racial backgrounds, born in the U.S.

THE REQUIREMENTS

Age: For infant adoption, applicants must be at least 21 and no more than 40 years of age. For special-needs adoption, the rule of thumb is that there should be no more than 40 years difference between the child and the youngest parent.

Health: Applicants should be in reasonably good health. Applicants with health problems or handicaps are given individual consideration. Infertility documentation is required for infant adoption.

Religion: No requirement. However, for infant adoption, the preferences of the birthmother are honored. For older child and special-needs adoption, if the child is a practicing member of a specific faith, the agency will seek a family that will honor that faith.

Financial status: Applicants must demonstrate the ability to live within their means and to support an additional family member.

Marital status: For infant adoption, applicants must be married, and the length of the marriage must be at least 2 years. For special-needs adoption, single applicants are considered.

Family size: For infant adoption, applicants may have no more than 1 child currently in the family. For special-needs adoption, there is no specific requirement, but all family members must agree to the plan of adoption.

Racial, ethnic or cultural origin: Preference for placing children in families of similar origins. Transracial placements may be made if the prospective adoptive family is able to demonstrate their ability to honor the race of the child and to ensure acceptance within the family and the community.

THE PROCEDURE

Participation in Catholic Family Service's adoption program entails the following basic steps:
Pre-adoptive inquiry
Yearly letters verifying interest
Orientation meeting
Individual and group counseling sessions (as needed)
Homestudy
Application
Referral
Placement
Post-placement supervision

ADDITIONAL PROGRAMS/SERVICES

Catholic Family Service provides foster care, pregnancy counseling, intensive probation program, and counseling services.

BRANCH/NETWORK OFFICES

710 N. Michigan
Saginaw, MI 48602
(517) 753–8446

4805 N. Jefferson
Midland, MI 48640
(517) 631–4711

LICENSE/ACCREDITATION/PROFESSIONAL AFFILIATIONS

Catholic Family Service is licensed by the State of Michigan Department of Social Services and is accredited by the Council on Accreditation of Services for Families and Children. Catholic Family Service workers are part of the District V Adoption Council which is instrumental in educating the public on adoption issues through group workshops.

CATHOLIC SOCIAL SERVICES

347 Rock Street
Marquette, MI 49855
(906) 228–8630
Program director: Gerard Kedzierzawski

THE PROGRAM

Catholic Social Services is a nonprofit agency serving residents of Upper Michigan and placing approximately 11 children annually through its adoption program. Serving families and individuals of the Upper Peninsula since 1952, the agency's mission is to provide services which reflect "a sense of the worth and dignity of each person, a conviction that each person has the capacity to grow and change, a belief that each person is responsible for his/her behavior, and a dedication to the concept that love and respect help people to grow and change, to be healed and reconciled, to love." Working directly with birthparents, with other private and public agencies, and with national and regional exchange programs, the agency places infants and special-needs children for adoption. In addition, the agency will provide homestudy and supervisory services for applicants pursuing interagency adoption (domestic or international).

THE COST

The agency's fee for adoption services is $3,000. Services covered by the fee include all phases of the adoption process.

THE WAIT

The time from application to placement averages 8 to 10 years.

THE CHILDREN

Catholic Social Services places both healthy and special-needs children, ranging in age from birth to 2 years, of Caucasian backgrounds.

THE REQUIREMENTS

Age: Applicants must be at least 20 and no more than 35 years of age.
Health: Applicants should be in reasonably good health. Applicants with health problems or handicaps are given individual consideration.
Religion: Applicants should be practicing members of a Christian faith.
Financial status: : Applicants must demonstrate financial stability.
Marital status: No requirement.
Family size: Applicants must be childless.
Racial, ethnic or cultural origin: Preference for placing children in families of similar origins.

THE PROCEDURE

Participation in the adoption program of Catholic Social Services entails the following basic steps:
Inquiry
Orientation meeting
Application
Individual counseling sessions
Group counseling sessions
Homestudy
Placement
Post-placement supervision

ADDITIONAL PROGRAMS/SERVICES

Catholic Social Services provides pre-marital, marital, and family counseling; foster care, problem pregnancy counseling.

BRANCH/NETWORK OFFICES

Catholic Social Services maintains branch offices in Sault Saint Marie, Escanaba, Iron Mountain, and Houghton.

LICENSE/ACCREDITATION/PROFESSIONAL AFFILIATIONS

Catholic Social Services is licensed by the State of Michigan Department of Social Services and is affiliated with the National Association of Social Workers and the American Association of Counseling Development.

CATHOLIC SOCIAL SERVICES OF FLINT

202 E. Boulevard Drive, Suite 210
Flint, MI 48503–1893
(313) 232–9950
Program director: Yvonne Butler, ACSW, Program Supervisor

THE PROGRAM

Catholic Social Services is a nonprofit multi-service agency serving residents of Genesee County, Michigan, and placing approximately 12 children annually through its adoption program. The agency's purpose is "the enhancement of family life and the amelioration of suffering in the social, psychological and emotional realms." Accordingly, the agency provides "a range of services aimed at the promotion of healthy individual, family and community functioning and the treatment of relationship problems, mental illness, and situational adversity." Catholic Social Services has provided adoption and foster care services since 1956. The agency provides services to birthparents and places both healthy and special-needs infants for adoption when birthparents elect adoptive placement as the best plan for their child. Recent changes in the adoption process include the availability of more cooperative (open) placement procedures. In addition to traditional adoption services, the agency will provide homestudy and supervisory services for applicants pursuing domestic interagency adoption.

THE COST

The agency's fee for adoption services is $1,800. Services covered by the fee include the homestudy, placement, post-placement supervision for 1 year, and additional post-placement support as needed. In addition, applicants can expect to pay filing costs at the time of placement.

THE WAIT

The time from application to the homecoming of the adoptive child averages 3 years.

THE CHILDREN

Catholic Social Services places both healthy and special-needs children, ranging in age from birth to 2 years, of all racial backgrounds, born in the U.S.

THE REQUIREMENTS

Age: Applicants must be at least 25 and no more than 37 at the time of application. The requirement may be waived for the placement of a special-needs infant.

Health: Applicants should be in reasonably good health. Applicants with health problems or handicaps are given individual consideration. Infertility documentation is required (but may be waived for the placement of special-needs infants).

Religion: No requirement. However, the preferences of the birthparents are honored whenever possible.

Financial status: : Applicants must demonstrate financial stability.

Marital status: Applicants must be married, and the length of the marriage must be at least 3 years. The length of the marriage requirement is flexible for special needs placements, and single applicants are considered.

Family size: Applicants must be childless. The requirement may be waived for the placement of a special-needs infant.

Racial, ethnic or cultural origin: Preference for placing children in families of similar origins.

THE PROCEDURE

Participation in the adoption program of Catholic Social Services entails the following basic steps:
Orientation meeting
Application
Homestudy (group format)
Individual counseling sessions (if needed)

Placement
Post-placement supervision

ADDITIONAL PROGRAMS/SERVICES

Catholic Social Services provides seminars on pregnancy prevention; pregnancy counseling; foster care for infants; foster care for pregnant teens, teen mothers and their infants; individual, family, and group therapy; marital counseling.

BRANCH/NETWORK OFFICES

None.

LICENSE/ACCREDITATION/PROFESSIONAL AFFILIATIONS

Catholic Social Services is licensed by the State of Michigan Department of Social Services. The agency is a member of the Child Welfare League of America and the Michigan Federation of Private Child and Family Agencies.

CATHOLIC SOCIAL SERVICES OF ST. CLAIR COUNTY

2601 13th Street
Port Huron, MI 48060
(313) 987–9100
Program director: Liz Lamb

THE PROGRAM

Founded in 1947, Catholic Social Services is a nonprofit multi-service child and family agency serving residents of St. Clair County and placing approximately 7 children annually through its adoption program. The primary purpose of the agency's adoption service is "to help children who would not otherwise have a home of their own, and who can benefit by family life, to become members of a family which can give them the love, care, protection, and opportunities essential for their healthy personality growth and development. The agency provides services to birthparents and places infants for adoption when birthparents in the agency's counseling program elect adoptive placement as the best plan for their child. The agency maintains a current list of couples requesting infant adoptions and holds periodic orientation meetings to accept applications as the number of approved families is diminished through placements.

THE COST

The agency's fee for adoption services is $2,000. Services covered by the fee include all phases of the adoption process. The only additional expense which applicants need anticipate is a $40 court fee to cover the costs of filing of the adoption petition and obtaining a revised birth certificate.

THE WAIT

For infant adoptions, the time from application to the homecoming of the adoptive child ranges from 2 to 5 years.

THE CHILDREN

Catholic Social Services places primarily healthy infants, born in the U.S.

THE REQUIREMENTS

Age: For infant adoption, applicants may be no more than 40 years of age. For older/harder to place adoptions, the requirement is flexible.

Health: Applicants should be in reasonably good health. Infertility documentation is required for infant adoption.

Religion: Applicants must be practicing members of a Christian religion.

Financial status: : Applicants must demonstrate financial stability.

Marital status: For infant adoption, applicants must be married (first marriage preferred), and the length of the marriage must be at least 3 years.

Family size: For infant adoption, applicants may have no more than 1 child currently in the family.

Racial, ethnic or cultural origin: Preference for placing children in families of similar origins.

THE PROCEDURE

Participation in Catholic Social Services' adoption program entails the following basic steps:
   Orientation meeting
   Application
   Homestudy (including individual and group sessions)
   Placement
   Post-placement supervision

ADDITIONAL PROGRAMS/SERVICES

Catholic Social Services provides counseling and support services on many family issues including alcoholism, depression, neglect or abuse, aging, divorce, illness, unemployment, unplanned pregnancy, and pre-marital or marital problems. The agency provides free pregnancy testing, unmarried parent counseling services, and foster care.

BRANCH/NETWORK OFFICES

None.

LICENSE/ACCREDITATION/PROFESSIONAL AFFILIATIONS

Catholic Social Services of St. Clair County is licensed by the State of Michigan Department of Social Services and Department of Public Health and is accredited by the Council on Accreditation of Services for Families and Children. The agency is affiliated with the United Way, the Child Welfare League of America, and the Michigan Federation of Private Child and Family Agencies.

CATHOLIC SOCIAL SERVICES OF WASHTENAW COUNTY

117 N. Division St.
Ann Arbor, MI 48104
(313) 662–4534
Program director: John Martin, Executive Director

THE PROGRAM

Catholic Social Services of Washtenaw County is a non-profit multi-service agency serving residents of Washtenaw County and placing approximately 15–20 children annually through its adoption program. Founded in 1959, the agency provides a wide range of services to residents of Washtenaw County regardless of religious beliefs, race, handicap, age, sex, or income level. The agency provides services to birth-parents and places infants for adoption when birthparents in the agency's counseling program elect adoptive placement as the best plan for their child. The agency offers options of various degrees of openness in the adoption process, and birthparents participate in the selection of the adoptive family. In all of its programs, the agency's mission is "to advocate for the poor, the powerless, and the oppressed; to prevent deterioration of individual and family life; and to enhance and improve the quality of life for individuals and families."

THE COST

The agency's fee for adoption services is based on a sliding scale and ranges from $500 to $2,250. Services covered by the fee include all phases of the adoption process (educational services through post-placement supervision). In addition, applicants can expect to pay a court filing fee ($10) and a birth certificate fee ($10).

THE WAIT

The time from application until acceptance into the program averages 5 years; the time from acceptance into the program to the homecoming of the adoptive child ranges from 6 months to 2 years.

THE CHILDREN

Catholic Social Services places both healthy and special-needs infants (1 week to 12 months old), primarily of Caucasian, Black, and bi- racial backgrounds, born in the U.S.

THE REQUIREMENTS

Age: Applicants must be at least 25 and no more than 45 years of age.

Health: Applicants must be in reasonably good health. Applicants with health problems or handicaps are given individual consideration.

Religion: No requirement.

Financial status: : Applicants must be above poverty level.

Marital status: Applicants must be married couples.

Residence: Applicants must live or work in Washtenaw County, Michigan.

Family size: For healthy Caucasian infant adoption, applicants may have no more than 1 child currently in the family. Exceptions are made for minority infants and special-needs infants.

Racial, ethnic or cultural origin: Preference for placing children in families of similar origins.

THE PROCEDURE

Participation in Catholic Social Services' adoption program entails the following basic steps:
   Orientation meeting
   Individual counseling sessions
   Application
   Group counseling and educational sessions
   Homestudy
   Placement
   Post-placement supervision

ADDITIONAL PROGRAMS/SERVICES

Catholic Social Services provides a wide range of community services including counseling (outpatient mental health counseling; outpatient substance abuse counseling; pre- and post-adoption counseling; prevention of child abuse); parent aide programs; pregnancy counseling; short term foster care; emergency food program; older adult outreach; family life enrichment.

BRANCH/NETWORK OFFICES

220 Pearl Street
Ypsilanti, MI 48197
(313) 484-1260

LICENSE/ACCREDITATION/PROFESSIONAL AFFILIATIONS

Catholic Social Services of Washtenaw County is licensed by the State of Michigan Department of Social Services and is accredited by the Council on Accreditation of Services for Families and Children. The agency is a member of the United Way, Catholic Charities U.S.A., and the Michigan Federation of Family and Children's Agencies.

CATHOLIC SOCIAL SERVICES OF WAYNE COUNTY

9851 Hamilton Avenue
Detroit, MI 48202
(313) 883-2100
Program director: Carol Quilliam, Acting Supervisor

THE PROGRAM

Catholic Social Services of Wayne County is a nonprofit multi-service agency. Through its adoption program, the agency serves residents of Wayne County for healthy Caucasian infants and residents of Wayne, Oakland, and Macomb Counties for healthy Black infants and special-needs children. Serving the community for more than a quarter century, the agency places approximately 75 children annually.

THE COST

The agency's fee for adoption services is based on a sliding scale and ranges from $0 to $2,000. Services covered by the fee include individual and group studies, home visits, parenting classes, post-placement supervision, and filing of petitions. Applicants assume responsibility for petition filing fee ($20 per child) and birth certificate fee ($20 per child).

THE WAIT

The time from application to the homecoming of the adoptive child varies depending on the program. For healthy Caucasian infant, first placement, the wait averages 3 1/2 years; healthy Caucasian infant, second placement, 2 1/2 years; healthy Black infant, 3 to 6 months. For special needs placements, the wait varies depending on the availability of children, their ages, and the nature of their physical or emotional handicaps.

THE CHILDREN

Catholic Social Services places both healthy and special-needs children, ranging in age from infancy to adolescence, of Black, Caucasian, and bi-racial backgrounds, born in the U.S.

THE REQUIREMENTS

Age: For all programs, applicants must be at least 25 years of age. For healthy Caucasian infant, neither applicant can be over 36 at the time of the first application or over 38 at the time of the 2nd application. No maximum age requirement for healthy Black infant or special-needs adoption.

Health: Applicants with health problems or handicaps are given individual consideration. Infertility documentation is required for healthy Caucasian infant adoption.

Religion: Applicants must be practicing members of a Christian religion.

Financial status: : The requirement is assessed on an individual basis.

Marital status: For healthy Caucasian infant adoption, applicants must be married and the length of the marriage must be at least 3 years. For special needs and healthy Black infant adoptions, single applicants are accepted. If married, the length of the marriage must be at least 1 year.

Family size: The requirement is assessed on an individual basis.

Racial, ethnic or cultural origin: Preference for placing children in families of similar origins, but transracial placements are made when in the best interests of the child.

THE PROCEDURE

Participation in Catholic Social Services' adoption program entails the following basic steps:
Orientation meeting
Application
Group counseling sessions
Individual counseling sessions
Homestudy
Adoptive parenting classes (for couples adopting first healthy Caucasian infant)
Child referral
Placement
Post-placement supervision

ADDITIONAL PROGRAMS/SERVICES

Catholic Social Services provides a wide range of programs including pregnancy counseling; adoption search assistance; family reunification; foster care services; individual, marital, and family counseling; foster grandparents program; retired senior volunteer program; senior companion program; communication around prevention of substance abuse; Hispanic outreach program; substance abuse counseling.

BRANCH/NETWORK OFFICES

Eastside Office
19653 Mack Ave.
Grosse Pointe Woods, MI 48236
(313) 881-6645

Northwest Office
17332 Farmington Rd.
Livonia, MI 48152
(313) 421–3730

Out-County Office
24331 Van Born Rd.
Taylor, MI 48180
(313) 292–5690

Downriver Human Svcs. Ctr.
19101 Inkster
Romulus, MI 48174
(313) 782–4244

NorWayne Counseling Ctr.
32715 Dorsey
Westland, MI 48185
(313) 326–4262
Southwest Outreach
Holy Redeemer CC
1721 Junction
(313) 843–1045

LICENSE/ACCREDITATION/PROFESSIONAL AFFILIATIONS

Catholic Social Services of Wayne County is licensed by the State of Michigan Department of Social Services and is accredited by the Council on Accreditation of Services for Families and Children. The agency is a member of the Family Assignment System.

CATHOLIC SOCIAL SERVICE/ST. VINCENT HOME FOR CHILDREN, INC.

2800 W. Willow Street
Lansing, MI 48917
(517) 323–4734
Program director: Douglas Miller, Director, Child Welfare

THE PROGRAM

Catholic Social Service/St. Vincent Home for Children is a nonprofit multi-service agency serving residents of Jackson, Shiawassee, Ingham, Eaton, and Clinton Counties. Through its adoption program, the agency places approximately 14–15 children annually. In April of 1985, Catholic Social Services of Lansing (founded 1948) and St. Vincent Home for Children (founded 1952) merged into one agency. This merger enabled the development of a continuum of service for families and children, from birth to senior years. The agency's mission is "to provide a network of services which promote and support the social and emotional well-being of individuals and families of all beliefs, carried out in accordance with the social principles of the Catholic Church." The agency provides services for infant as well as special-needs adoptions.

THE COST

The agency's fee for infant adoption services is $2,500. For adoption of special-needs children, costs will vary. Services covered by the fee include adoption study, parenting classes, adoption supervision, workshops and training programs. Prospective adoptive parents should also anticipate financial responsibility for court filing fees connected with finalization.

THE WAIT

For infant adoption, the time from application to the homecoming of the adoptive child averages 5 to 6 years. For special-needs adoption, the wait varies.

THE CHILDREN

The agency places both healthy and special-needs children, ranging in age from birth to 18 years, of all racial backgrounds.

THE REQUIREMENTS

Age: The requirement varies depending on the needs and age of the child.
Health: Applicants with health problems or handicaps are given individual consideration. Infertility documentation is required for infant adoptions.
Religion: No requirement.
Financial status: : No requirement.
Marital status: For infant adoptions, applicants must be married couples. No requirement for other programs.
Family size: For infant adoptions, applicants may have no more than 1 child currently in the family. No requirement for other programs.
Racial, ethnic or cultural origin: No requirement.

THE PROCEDURE

Participation in the adoption program of Catholic Social Service/St. Vincent Home for Children entails the following basic steps:
Orientation meeting
Application
Homestudy
Placement
Post-placement supervision

ADDITIONAL PROGRAMS/SERVICES

The agency provides a wide range of services including foster grandparent program; senior day time center; senior companion program; family counseling center; refugee services; pregnancy counseling; foster care and specialized foster care programs; residential treatment for children.

BRANCH/NETWORK OFFICES

None.

LICENSE/ACCREDITATION/PROFESSIONAL AFFILIATIONS

Catholic Social Service/St. Vincent Home for Children, Inc. is licensed by the State of Michigan Department of Social Services and is accredited by the Council on Accreditation of Services for Families and Children. The agency is a member of the Michigan Federation of Private Family and Child Agencies, Michigan Association of Children's Alliance, and Child Welfare League of America.

CHILD AND FAMILY SERVICE OF BAY COUNTY

904 Sixth Street
Bay City, MI 48708
(517) 895–5932
Program director: Richard R. Lilliefors

THE PROGRAM

Child and Family Service of Bay County is a nonprofit agency serving residents of Bay County and placing approximately 2 to 4 children annually through its adoption program. The agency provides services to birthparents and places infants for adoption when birthparents elect adoptive placement as the best plan for their child. Working cooperatively with the public agency, the agency facilitates the placement of special-needs children.

THE COST

The agency's fee for adoption services is based on a sliding scale and ranges from $900 to $2,500. Services covered by the fee include all phases of the adoption process.

THE WAIT

The time from application for acceptance into the program to the homecoming of the adoptive child varies depending on the program. For infant adoption, the wait is indeterminate.

THE CHILDREN

Child and Family Service places both healthy and special-needs children, ranging in age from birth to 14 years, of all racial backgrounds.

THE REQUIREMENTS

Age: Applicants may be no more than 40 years of age.
Health: Applicants must be in reasonably good health. Infertility documentation is required for infant adoption.
Religion: No requirement.
Financial status: : Applicants must have sufficient income to provide for an additional family member.
Marital status: Applicants must be married; the length of the marriage must be at least 2 years.
Family size: For the adoption of an infant or a child under the age of 5, applicants must be childless.
Racial, ethnic or cultural origin: No requirement, but preference for placing children in families of similar origins.

THE PROCEDURE

Participation in the adoption program of Child and Family Service entails the following basic steps:
Orientation meeting
Application
Group study sessions
Homestudy
Placement
Post-placement supervision

ADDITIONAL PROGRAMS/SERVICES

Child and Family Service of Bay County provides foster care, family counseling, pregnancy counseling.

BRANCH/NETWORK OFFICES

None.

LICENSE/ACCREDITATION/PROFESSIONAL AFFILIATIONS

Child and Family Service of Bay County is licensed by the State of Michigan Department of Social Services.

CHILD AND FAMILY SERVICES OF MICHIGAN, INC.

Central Office
2157 University Park Drive
Box 348
Okemos, MI 48864
(517) 349–6226
Program director: Vern C. Dahlquist, Executive Director

THE PROGRAM

Founded in 1891, Child and Family Services of Michigan evolved from an agency which housed homeless children in a small institution to a statewide network of 14 direct service member agencies and a central office delivering a range of services for persons from infancy to old age, including foster care, adoption, pregnancy counseling, residential care, services to older adults, and family and individual therapy. In all of its programs, the mission of the organization is "to enhance the quality of life for the citizens of Michigan." Each member agency is independent and functions separately, with policies, fees, and the like set by its local board. Working directly with birthparents, with other private and public agencies, and with national and regional exchange programs, member agencies place both healthy and special-needs children in Michigan families.

THE COST

Fees for adoption services vary depending on the member agency. Services covered by the fee generally include all phases of the adoption process, excluding court filing fees required for finalization.

THE WAIT

The time from application to placement varies depending on the location of the member agency and the availability of children in need of adoptive families.

THE CHILDREN

Child and Family Services of Michigan places both healthy and special-needs children, ranging in age from birth to 18, of all racial backgrounds, born in the U.S.

THE REQUIREMENTS

Age: Applicants must be at least 21 years of age. The requirement varies depending on the age and needs of the child being considered for placement.

Health: Applicants should be in reasonably good health. Applicants with health problems or handicaps are evaluated on an individual basis.

Religion: No requirement.

Financial status: Applicants must have sufficient income to provide adequately for the family.

Marital status: Applicants may be married or single. The requirement may vary depending on the type of adoption.

Family size: For healthy infant adoption, applicants may have no more than 1 child currently in the family. For special-needs adoption, the requirement varies depending on the age and needs of the child.

Racial, ethnic or cultural origin: No requirement, but preference for placing children in families of similar origins. The requirement varies depending on the needs of the child.

THE PROCEDURE

The process of assessment and adoption preparation varies from one member agency to another. In general, applicants can expect the following basic procedure:

Orientation meeting
Application
Homestudy (including individual and group counseling sessions)
Placement
Post-placement supervision

ADDITIONAL PROGRAMS/SERVICES

Child and Family Services of Michigan provides a wide range of services including individual, marital, and family counseling; pregnancy counseling; short and long-term foster care; residential services for children and adults; parent aide services; homemaking services; educational groups; workshops and seminars.

BRANCH/NETWORK OFFICES

Family Counseling & Children's Svcs. of Lenawee Co.
213 Toledo St.
Adrian, MI 49221
(517) 265–5352

Child & Family Svcs. of Michigan
1044 US 23 N., P.O. Box 516
Alpena, MI 49707
(517) 356–4567

Family & Children's Svc. of Calhoun Co.
182 W. Van Buren St.
Battle Creek, MI 49017
(616) 965–3247

Child & Family Svcs. of Michigan
202 E. Boulevard Dr., Suite 220
Flint, MI 48503
(313) 234–3671

Child & Family Svcs. of Michigan
412 Century Ln.
Holland, MI 49423
(616) 396–2301

Child & Family Svcs. of Michigan
3075 E. Grand River, Suite 140
Howell, MI 48843

(517) 546–7530

Family Svc. & Children's Aid of Jackson Co.
906 W. Monroe, P.O. Box 6128
Jackson, MI 49204–6128
(517) 787–7920

Family & Children Svcs. of the Kalamazoo Area
1608 Lake St.
Kalamazoo, MI 49001
(616) 344–0202

Child & Family Svcs. of Michigan, Inc., Capitol Area
300 N. Washington, Suite 102
Lansing, MI 48933
(517) 484–4455

Child & Family Svcs. of the U.P.
109 Harlow Block, P.O. Box 706
Marquette, MI 49855–0706
(906) 226–2516

Family & Children's Svc. of Midland
116 Harold St., P.O. Box 2086
Midland, MI 48641–2086
(517) 631–5390]

Child & Family Svcs. of Michigan
1002 10th Ave., P.O. Box 611363
Port Huron, MI 48061–1363
(313) 984–2647

Child & Family Svcs. of Michigan
2000 S. State St.
St. Joseph, MI 49085
(616) 983–5545

Child & Family Svcs. of Michigan
3785 N. Townhall Rd.
Traverse City, MI 49684
(616) 946–8975

LICENSE/ACCREDITATION/PROFESSIONAL AFFILIATIONS

All Child and Family Services of Michigan, Inc. member agencies are licensed by the State of Michigan Department of Social Services and are members of the Child Welfare League of America. Some are accredited by the Council on Accreditation of Services for Families and Children, and some are also members of Family Service America.

CHILD AND FAMILY SERVICES OF MICHIGAN, INC., CAPITOL AREA

300 N. Washington, Suite 102
Lansing, MI 48933
(517) 484–4455
Program director: Lee M. Moss

THE PROGRAM

Child and Family Services of Michigan, Inc. Capitol Area is a nonsectarian social service agency which is part of a statewide network of community human services (Child and Family Services of Michigan, Inc.). Serving residents of Clinton, Eaton, Ingham, and Shiawassee Counties, the agency's purposes are "to contribute to harmonious family relationships, to strengthen the positive values in family life and to promote healthy personality development and satisfactory social functioning of various family members" with emphasis on enrichment, prevention, and treatment. The agency provides pregnancy counseling services and places infants for adoption when birthparents in the agency's counseling program decide that the best interests of their child will be met by adoptive placement. However, applicants should note that the agency's intake list for healthy Caucasian infant adoptions is currently closed. The agency is also actively involved in recruiting families for special-needs children (older children, children of minority race, and children with special emotional, mental, or physical needs).

THE COST

The agency's fee for adoption services is $3,000. Fees may be waived partially or in total, and financial assistance may be available for some children with special needs. Services covered by the fee include all phases of the adoption process, excluding legal fees connected with finalization of the adoption.

THE WAIT

For infant adoption (intake currently closed), the time from application to the homecoming of the adoptive child averages 7 years. For special-needs adoption, the wait varies according to the range of special needs the prospective adoptive family can accept.

THE CHILDREN

Child and Family Services places both healthy and special-needs children, ranging in age from infancy through adolescence, of all racial backgrounds, born in the U.S.

THE REQUIREMENTS

Age: The requirement is evaluated on an individual basis. Applicants should be within "normal" parenting age for infant adoptions.

Health: Applicants should be in reasonably good health. Applicants with health problems or handicaps are given individual consideration.

Religion: Applicants are served regardless of religious preference.

Financial status: : Applicants must have adequate income to meet the everyday expenses of the family.

Marital status: The requirement is evaluated on an individual basis.

Family size: The requirement is evaluated on an individual basis.

Racial, ethnic or cultural origin: Preference for placing children in families of similar origins, although transracial placements are made when in the best interests of the child.

THE PROCEDURE

Participation in Child and Family Services' adoption program entails the following basic steps:
Intake interview (intake currently closed)
Application
Homestudy (including individual and group sessions)
Child referral
Transitional visits (older and special needs)
Placement
Post-placement supervision

ADDITIONAL PROGRAMS/SERVICES

Child and Family Services provides a wide range of community services including individual and family counseling; foster care; pregnancy counseling; residential treatment facilities and intensive foster care for youth; group homes for mentally retarded adults; personal care and homemaker services for the aged; shelter for abuse victims.

BRANCH/NETWORK OFFICES

Child and Family Services of Michigan, Inc., Capitol Area is a member agency of a statewide network of community human services.

Child and Family Services of Michigan, Inc. Central Office
2157 University Park Drive
Okemos, MI 48864
(517) 349–6226

LICENSE/ACCREDITATION/PROFESSIONAL AFFILIATIONS

Child and Family Services of Michigan, Inc., Capitol Area is licensed by the State of Michigan Department of Social Services and is accredited by the Council on Accreditation of Services for Families and Children. The agency is a member of the Michigan Federation of Private Child and Family Agencies and the Capital Area United Way.

CHILD AND FAMILY SERVICE OF SAGINAW COUNTY

1226 N. Michigan Avenue
Saginaw, MI 48602
(517) 753–8491
Program director: Jack W. Frye, ACSW

THE PROGRAM

Child and Family Service of Saginaw County (CFS) is a nonprofit nonsectarian multi-service agency serving residents of Saginaw, Bay, Midland, Gratiot, and Tuscola Counties and placing approximately 11 children annually through its adoption program. Originally founded as an orphanage in 1870, CFS has evolved in response to the changing needs of the community and has continuously "assisted in maintaining and raising the stability of family living in the community." Working with birthparents, with public and private agencies, and with national and regional exchange programs, the agency places both healthy and special-needs children born in the U.S. Working directly with child welfare institutions abroad and in cooperation with other U.S. agencies which maintain international programs, the agency facilitates the placement of children from various foreign countries in Michigan families.

THE COST

The agency's fee for adoption services is $2,000. Services

covered by the fee include all phases of the adoption process. Applicants pursuing international adoption should also anticipate fees to the cooperating agency (U.S. or foreign), possible travel expenses, and related costs.

THE WAIT

The time from application to the homecoming of the adoptive child varies depending on the program. For healthy domestic infant adoption, the wait averages 5 to 7 years. For international adoption, the wait varies depending on the cooperating agency and ranges from 6 months to 1 year.

THE CHILDREN

CFS places both healthy and special-needs children, ranging in age from infancy to adolescence, of all racial backgrounds. Various countries of origin are represented.

THE REQUIREMENTS

Age: The age requirement is evaluated on a case-by-case basis.

Health: Applicants should be in reasonably good health. Applicants with health problems or handicaps are given individual consideration. Infertility documentation is required for healthy domestic infant adoptions.

Religion: No requirement.

Financial status: : Applicants must have sufficient resources to provide adequately for an additional family member.

Marital status: Married applicants must have been married for at least 2 years. Some options are available to single parents.

Family size: For healthy domestic infant adoptions, applicants must be childless. For international or special needs placements, family size is evaluated on a case-by-case basis.

Racial, ethnic or cultural origin: No requirement.

THE PROCEDURE

Participation in CFS' adoption program entails the following basic steps:

Orientation meeting
Application
Homestudy
Compliance with immigration/naturalization requirements
    (international adoptions only)
Referral
Placement
Post-placement supervision

ADDITIONAL PROGRAMS/SERVICES

CFS provides a wide range of services including individual, marital and family counseling; long term, short term, and crisis intervention counseling to victims of sexual assault; problem pregnancy counseling; foster home care.

BRANCH/NETWORK OFFICES

None.

LICENSE/ACCREDITATION/PROFESSIONAL AFFILIATIONS

Child and Family Service of Saginaw County is licensed by the State of Michigan Department of Social Services and is accredited by the Council on Accreditation of Services for Families and Children. The agency is a member of the Child Welfare League of America, Family Service America, Michigan Federation of Private Child and Family Agencies, and the United Way of Saginaw County.

CHRISTIAN FAMILY SERVICES/ PROTESTANT YOUTH ORGANIZATION

17105 W. 12 Mile Road
Southfield, MI 48076
(313) 557–8390
Program director: Mr. M. Lee Gardner

THE PROGRAM

Christian Family Services is a nonprofit agency serving residents of southeastern Michigan (outskirts of Detroit) and placing approximately 12 to 15 children annually. The agency began in 1948 when a group of area Christian business leaders set about correcting some of the juvenile delinquency problems in Detroit. Through counseling these youths and their families, the agency perceived a need for foster care and adoption services and consequently established a program to address these needs. The agency's mission is "to provide support services to mothers finding themselves in a crisis pregnancy situation, to provide an alternative to abortion, and to provide adoptive Christian homes for infants and children in need."

THE COST

The agency's fee for adoption services is based on a sliding scale and ranges from $1,500 to 8% of the applicants' annual gross income. Services covered by the fee include all phases of the adoption process (homestudy through court representation) as well as all services to the biological mother and child.

THE WAIT

The time from application for acceptance into the program to the homecoming of the adoptive child averages 2 years.

THE CHILDREN

Christian Family Services places both healthy and special-needs children, ranging in age from birth to 3 years, of Caucasian, Black, and bi- racial backgrounds, born in the U.S.

THE REQUIREMENTS

Age: The requirement varies depending on the needs of the child.

Health: Applicants must be in reasonably good health. Infertility documentation is required.

Religion: Applicants must be practicing members of a Fundamental Evangelical Church.

Financial status: Applicants must have sufficient income to support the family.

Marital status: Applicants must be married and the length of the marriage must be at least 3 years.

Family size: Applicants may have no more than 1 child currently in the family. The requirement is more flexible for special-needs adoption.

Racial, ethnic or cultural origin: Preference for placing children in families of similar origins.

THE PROCEDURE

Participation in Christian Family Services' adoption program entails the following basic steps:
Initial contact
Preliminary information form
Psychological testing
Application
Orientation meeting (group)
Individual and group counseling (as needed)
Homestudy
Placement
Post-placement supervision

ADDITIONAL PROGRAMS/SERVICES

Christian Family Services provides professional counseling services (psychiatric and psychological) and adoption support group (Christian Adoptive Parents Fellowship).

BRANCH/NETWORK OFFICES

None.

LICENSE/ACCREDITATION/PROFESSIONAL AFFILIATIONS

Christian Family Services is licensed by the State of Michigan Department of Social Services.

D.A. BLODGETT SERVICES FOR CHILDREN AND FAMILIES

805 Leonard Street, N.E.
Grand Rapids, MI 49503
(616) 451–2021
Program director: Eileen Knaus Cronin, M.A., Program Supervisor

THE PROGRAM

D.A. Blodgett Services for Children and Families is a nonprofit agency serving families who live within an hour's drive from Grand Rapids and placing approximately 50 children annually. The agency's Special-needs adoption Program was established to meet the unique needs of older children, sibling groups, and children of all ages with disabilities and to provide services for families pursuing special-needs adoption. In January 1986, after receiving funding from private foundations, the program became operational and received the benefit of expert consultation from Spaulding for Children, a nationally recognized special needs program. Since its beginning, the program has expanded, and over 100 children have been placed in adoptive homes. The agency's mission is "to enhance the well-being of children and their families by providing traditional and innovative programs that will assure them the best opportunity to realize their potential as human beings."

THE COST

Adoption services are provided at no cost to the adoptive family.

THE WAIT

The agency advises applicants to anticipate a wait of approximately 1 year, although for some it is a matter of months, and for others the wait is longer. Much depends on the types and ages of children the family feel they can accept. The agency maintains a list of approximately 10 waiting families at any given time so that a variety of resources are available for waiting children.

THE CHILDREN

D.A. Blodgett Services for Children and Families places special-needs children (both those who are physically healthy and those who have special developmental needs), ranging in age from birth to 17 years, of all racial backgrounds. Most children are born in the U.S., but the agency does service foreign-born children who have experienced adoption disruptions.

THE REQUIREMENTS

All of the following requirements are discussed and considered on an individual basis.

Age: No specific requirement, but applicants are generally expected to be between 22 and 55 years of age. The age factor will be reviewed with the applicant and will impact upon the age of the child considered for placement.

Health: Applicants should be in reasonably good health. Applicants with health problems or handicaps are given individual consideration.

Religion: No requirement.

Financial status: No specific requirement. Applicants should feel that adding a child to the family will not place them in a financially stressful situation. Adoption support subsidy is also available for some children.

Marital status: No requirement.

Family size: No requirement.

Racial, ethnic or cultural origin: No requirement.

THE PROCEDURE

Participation in the agency's adoption program entails the following basic steps:
Orientation meeting
Application
Homestudy and group preparation/training sessions
Placement
Post-placement supervision
Adoptive parent support group

ADDITIONAL PROGRAMS/SERVICES

D.A. Blodgett Services for Children and Families works closely with adoptive parents on preparation and training and also provides support through close follow-up and monthly parent support group meetings. The agency has ready access to psychological testing and therapists in the community, available to families upon referral. The agency is also in the process of developing post-finalization services in addition to its post-placement services program.

None.

LICENSE/ACCREDITATION/PROFESSIONAL AFFILIATIONS

D.A. Blodgett Services for Children and Families is licensed by the State of Michigan Department of Social Services. The agency is a member of Michigan Federation of Private Child and Family Agencies and is supported in part by Kent County United Way.

FAMILY COUNSELING AND CHILDREN'S SERVICES OF LENAWEE COUNTY

213 Toledo Street
Adrian, MI 49221
(517) 265–5352
Program director: Cam Vozar, MSW

THE PROGRAM

Family Counseling and Children's Services (FCCS) is a nonprofit family service agency providing services to residents of Lenawee County and placing approximately 8 children annually through its adoption program. Founded in 1969 and providing adoption services since 1971, the agency's mission is "to strengthen family relationships, promote healthy personality development and social functioning of individuals and families, and to achieve permanence for children." Working directly with birthparents, with other private and public agencies, and with national and regional exchange programs, FCCS places both healthy and special-needs children. In addition, the agency will provide homestudy and supervisory services for applicants pursuing inter- agency adoption (domestic or international) or independent adoption.

THE COST

The agency's fee for adoption services is based on a sliding scale and ranges from $750 to $3,000. Services covered by the fee include the homestudy, training sessions, court services, placement services, and post- placement supervision and services. In addition, applicants can expect to pay a court filing fee of $20 and a birth certificate fee of $20.

THE WAIT

The time from application to the homecoming of the adoptive child varies depending on the program. For older child placements, the wait ranges from 1 to 3 years. For infant placements, the wait is 5 years or more.

THE CHILDREN

FCCS places both healthy and special-needs children, ranging in age from birth to 13 years, of all racial backgrounds, born in the U.S.

THE REQUIREMENTS

Age: No specific requirement. The requirement varies depending on the individual's health and resources.

Health: Applicants should be in reasonably good health.

Religion: No requirement.

Financial status: Applicants must be self supporting.

Marital status: For infant adoption, applicants must be married. Single parents are considered for older child placements. All married couples must have been married for at least 2 years.

Family size: For infant adoption, applicants may have no more than 1 child currently in the family. The requirement is flexible for older child and special needs placements.

Racial, ethnic or cultural origin: Preference for placing children in families of similar origins.

THE PROCEDURE

Participation in the adoption program of FCCS entails the following basic steps:
Inquiry
Orientation meeting
Application
Training classes
Homestudy
Placement
Post-placement supervision
Post-placement services (on-going training and counseling as needed)

ADDITIONAL PROGRAMS/SERVICES

FCCS provides individual, marital and family counseling; pregnancy counseling; Healthy Moms/Happy Babies program; parent advisory counsel; foster care; intensive foster care; foster care for developmentally disabled children; community baby shower; annual workshop for area professionals.

BRANCH/NETWORK OFFICES

FCCS is a member agency of a statewide network of community human services.

Child and Family Services of Michigan, Inc.
Central Office
2157 University Park Drive
Okemos, MI 48864
(517) 349–6226

LICENSE/ACCREDITATION/PROFESSIONAL AFFILIATIONS

Family Counseling and Children's Services of Lenawee County is licensed by the State of Michigan Department of Social Services.

FAMILY SERVICE DIVISION- CATHOLIC SOCIAL SERVICES OF MONROE COUNTY

16 E. Fifth Street
Monroe, MI 48161
(313) 242–3800
Program director: Agency Executive Director

The Program

Family Service Division-Catholic Social Services of Monroe County is a nonprofit multi-service agency serving residents of Monroe County and placing approximately 6 to 12 children annually through its adoption program. Founded in 1952, the agency has evolved in response to the changing needs of the community and today provides a wide range of services on a non-sectarian basis to individuals and families. Working directly with birthparents, with other private and public agencies, and with national regional exchange programs Family Service Division places both healthy and special-needs children. In addition, the agency will provide homestudy and supervisory services for applicants pursuing interagency adoption (domestic or international). Post-adoption services provided by the agency include support groups for birthparents; support groups for adoptive parents; counseling and search assistance for adult adoptees.

The Cost

The agency's fee for adoption services is based on a sliding scale and ranges from $1,200 to $2,000. Services covered by the fee include all phases of the adoption process (homestudy through finalization). Applicants are responsible for court fees related to filing of the adoption petition and the new birth certificate.

The Wait

The time from application to the homecoming of the adoptive child averages 3 to 5 years.

The Children

Family Service Division places both healthy and special-needs children, ranging in age from infancy to adolescence, predominantly of Caucasian but also of bi-racial backgrounds, born in the U.S.

The Requirements

Age: Applicants' age is evaluated in relation to the age of the child being considered for placement.

Health: Applicants should be in reasonably good health. Infertility documentation is required for healthy infant adoption.

Religion: No requirement.

Financial status: Applicants should have sufficient income to provide for an additional member.

Marital status: For healthy infant adoption, applicants must be married. Single applicants are considered for special-needs adoption. For both programs, the length of the marriage must be at least 3 years for married couples.

Family size: The requirement varies depending on the age of the child being considered for placement. For infants and pre-school aged children, applicants must be childless. For older or special-needs children, no requirement.

Racial, ethnic or cultural origin: Preference for placing children in families of similar origins.

The Procedure

Participation in the adoption program of Family Service Division entails the following basic steps:

Orientation meeting
Application
Homestudy
Referral
Placement
Post-placement supervision

Additional Programs/Services

Family Service Division provides a wide range of services including individual, marital, family and group counseling; counseling on specific issues (divorce adjustment, child behavior, single parent); pregnancy counseling ; older adult services; educational workshops; runaway services; transition and education for teenage parents.

Branch/ Network Offices

Adoption services are provided through the main office in Monroe.

License/Accreditation/Professional Affiliations

Family Service Division-Catholic Social Services of Monroe County is licensed by the State of Michigan Department of Social Services and is accredited by the Council on Accreditation of Services for Families and Children. The agency is a member of Michigan Federation of Private Child and Family Agencies and the United Way of Monroe County.

HOMES FOR BLACK CHILDREN

2340 Calvert
Detroit, MI 48206
(313) 869–2316
Program director: Sydney Duncan

The Program

Homes for Black Children is a nonprofit agency serving the metropolitan Detroit area and placing approximately 30 children annually. Founded in 1969, Homes for Black Children specializes in the placement of Black and bi-racial children of all ages. Before the agency opened in 1969, Black children accounted for 1 adoption in 15, although 58% of out-of-wedlock births were to Black mothers. Within two years of its founding, Homes for Black Children had placed 272 children and had approved homes waiting, demonstrating to other agencies that Black families do adopt. The success of the agency in recruiting Black families for the adoption of Black children is attributed to the innovative efforts of its director, Sydney Duncan, a young Black woman with no previous child welfare experience, and to the decision to house the agency in a Black community, rather than in the office of an existing White agency.

The Cost

Adoption services are provided at no cost to the adoptive family.

The Wait

The time from application to the homecoming of the adoptive child averages 1 year.

THE CHILDREN

Homes for Black Children places both healthy and special needs Black and bi-racial children of all ages, born in the U.S.

THE REQUIREMENTS

Age: The requirement varies depending on the age of the child.

Health: Applicants should be in reasonably good health. Applicants with health problems or handicaps are given individual consideration.

Religion: No requirement.

Financial status: : Applicants must have the ability to meet their own financial needs.

Marital status: No requirement, but if married, the length of the marriage must be at least 2 years.

Family size: No requirement.

Racial, ethnic or cultural origin: Applicants must be either Black or bi-racial couples.

THE PROCEDURE

Participation in the adoption program of Homes for Black Children entails the following basic steps:

Orientation meeting (individual)
Application
Homestudy
Placement
Post-placement supervision

ADDITIONAL PROGRAMS/SERVICES

Homes for Black Children provides pregnancy counseling, family counseling, and foster care services.

BRANCH/NETWORK OFFICES

None.

LICENSE/ACCREDITATION/PROFESSIONAL AFFILIATIONS

Homes for Black Children is licensed by the State of Michigan Department of Social Services. The agency is a member of the Michigan Federation of Child Placing Agencies and the Child Welfare League of America.

JEWISH FAMILY SERVICE

24123 Greenfield
Southfield, MI 48075
(313) 559–1500
Program director: Eleanor Keys, MSW

THE PROGRAM

Jewish Family Service is a nonprofit agency serving residents of Wayne, Oakland and Macomb counties. The agency provides services to birthparents and places infants for adoption when birthparents in the agency's counseling program elect adoptive placement as the best plan for their child. The agency also provides homestudy and supervisory services for applicants pursuing interstate adoption.

THE COST

The agency's fee for adoption services is based on the applicant's ability to pay as established by the Probate Courts. Each county has different fee scales. Services covered by the fee include all phases of the adoption process.

THE WAIT

The time from application to placement averages 3 to 4 years.

THE CHILDREN

Jewish Family Service places (primarily) healthy Caucasian infants. Occasionally there is an older child available for adoption.

THE REQUIREMENTS

Age: The requirement is evaluated on an individual basis.
Health: Infertility documentation is required.
Religion: Applicants must be Jewish.
Financial status: : No requirement.
Marital status: Applicants must be married, and the length of the marriage must be at least 3 years.
Family size: Applicants must be childless and unable to have their own children.
Racial, ethnic or cultural origin: The requirement is evaluated on an individual basis.

THE PROCEDURE

Participation in the adoption program of Jewish Family Service entails the following basic steps:

Application
Individual counseling sessions
Homestudy
Placement
Post-placement supervision
Finalization

ADDITIONAL PROGRAMS/SERVICES

Jewish Family Service provides a wide range of community services including foster care; foster parent training; individual, marital, and family counseling; parent education; respite care; homemaker services; Kosher Meals on Wheels; housing relocation services; volunteer services; advocacy; group homes for the elderly.

BRANCH/NETWORK OFFICES

None.

LICENSE/ACCREDITATION/PROFESSIONAL AFFILIATIONS

Jewish Family Service is licensed by the State of Michigan Department of Social Services and is accredited by the Council on Accreditation of Services for Families and Children. The agency's affiliations include the Child Welfare League of America, Association of Jewish Family and Children's Agencies, Family Service America, Area Agency on Aging, Jewish Welfare Federation, and United Foundation.

LDS SOCIAL SERVICES

37634 Enterprise Court
Farmington Hills, MI 48018
(313) 533–0902
Program director: Leland R. Hardy

THE PROGRAM

For a full description of programs and services, refer to Utah listing
LDS Social Services
50 East North Temple Street
Salt Lake City, UT 84150

LUTHERAN ADOPTION SERVICE

8131 E. Jefferson Avenue
Detroit, MI 48214
(313) 822–8546
Program director: Jim Lewis

THE PROGRAM

Lutheran Adoption Service is a nonprofit agency serving residents of the Lower Peninsula of Michigan and placing approximately 100 children annually. A joint venture of Lutheran Social Service of Michigan and Lutheran Child and Family Service of Michigan, the agency provides services for non-special needs and special-needs children. However, the agency's focus is "to provide permanent homes for Michigan's special-needs children." The agency provides extensive post-finalization services (search, reunion and aftermath counseling and support for all triad members; community education programs, panel presentations and workshops for triad members and professionals; resource library; professional training and consultation) through the Post Adoption Resources Center.

THE COST

If the child is in the custody of the State, there is no fee for adoption services. For the adoption of children who are not State wards, the agency's fee for adoption services is based on a sliding scale and ranges from $1,000 to $3,500. Services covered by the fee include all phases of the adoption process, excluding court filing fees ($20).

THE WAIT

The time from application to the homecoming of the adoptive child ranges from 2 to 3 years for Caucasian infants and from 9 months to 2 years for special-needs children.

THE CHILDREN

Lutheran Adoption Service places both healthy and special-needs children, ranging in age from birth to 15 years, of Caucasian, Black, and bi- racial backgrounds, born in the U.S.

THE REQUIREMENTS

Age: The requirement varies depending on the race and age of the child and the applicant's maturity.

Health: Applicants must be in reasonably good health. Applicants with health problems or handicaps are given individual consideration.

Religion: No requirement for special-needs adoption. For Caucasian infant adoption, applicants must be practicing members of a Protestant faith.

Financial status: Applicants must demonstrate financial stability.

Marital status: For Caucasian infant adoption, applicants must be married, and the length of the marriage must be at least 2 years. Single applicants are accepted for special-needs adoption.

Family size: No requirement for special-needs adoption. For Caucasian infant adoption, applicants must be childless.

Racial, ethnic or cultural origin: Preference for placing children in families of similar origins.

THE PROCEDURE

Participation in Lutheran Adoption Service's program entails the following basic steps:
   Application
   Orientation meeting
   Homestudy
   Placement
   Post-placement supervision
   Post-finalization services

ADDITIONAL PROGRAMS/SERVICES

Lutheran Adoption Service provides short-term foster care in conjunction with the Department of Mental Health. The agency also maintains Post Adoption Resources Center which provides education, consultation, counseling and support to all involved in the adoption process (adoptive parents, adoptees, birthparents, and professionals), including a library of books, audio and video materials for education and training purposes.

BRANCH/NETWORK OFFICES

Bay City Office
6019 W. Side Saginaw Road
Bay City, MI 48707
(517) 686–3170

LICENSE/ACCREDITATION/PROFESSIONAL AFFILIATIONS

Lutheran Adoption Service is licensed by the State of Michigan Department of Social Services and is accredited by the Council on Accreditation of Services for Families and Children. The agency is a member of the Child Welfare League of America.

LUTHERAN SOCIAL SERVICES

3200 W. Highland Boulevard
Box 08520
Milwaukee, WI 53208
(414) 342–7175
Program director: Michael Short, Adoption Coordinator

THE PROGRAM

Lutheran Social Services maintains branch offices throughout the Upper Peninsula in Michigan. For current addresses and telephone numbers of Michigan branch offices, contact the main office in Milwaukee (above).

METHODIST CHILDREN'S HOME SOCIETY

26645 West Six Mile Road
Detroit, MI 48240
(313) 531–4060
Program director: Isla Mitchell, Placement Department Supervisor

THE PROGRAM

The Methodist Children's Home Society is a nonprofit agency serving residents of Michigan and placing approximately 15–25 children annually. Founded in 1917 by the United Methodist Church as a haven for homeless and needy children, the agency has evolved in response to the changing needs of the community and now provides residential treatment for emotionally impaired children on a large campus which includes a school, chapel, medical facilities, and 9 cottage units. Additional services include adoption (infant, older child, and special needs), foster care, and single parent counseling. The agency's mission is "to provide an environment of love and understanding in which children can develop normally; to meet the physical, emotional and spiritual needs of the children in its care; and to develop and support those family and community relationships which will contribute to normal developmental opportunities for the children."

THE COST

The agency's fee for adoption services is based on a sliding scale and ranges from $0 to $2,000. Services covered by the fee include all phases of the adoption process. The only additional fees which applicants need anticipate are court filing fees and birth certificate fees.

THE WAIT

The time from application to the homecoming of the adoptive child varies depending on the type of child the applicants wish to adopt. There is almost immediate placement for some special-needs children. For healthy young children, on the other hand, the wait may be up to 2 1/2 years.

THE CHILDREN

Methodist Children's Home Society places both healthy and special-needs children, ranging in age from birth to 17 years, of Caucasian and Black racial backgrounds, born in the U.S.

THE REQUIREMENTS

Age: The requirement varies depending on the age of the child being considered for placement.
Health: Applicants should be in reasonably good health.

Applicants with health problems or handicaps are given individual consideration.
Religion: No requirement.
Financial status: : No requirement.
Marital status: No requirement. Each case is given individual consideration.
Family size: No requirement.
Racial, ethnic or cultural origin: Preference for placing children in families of similar origins. Each case is given individual consideration.

THE PROCEDURE

Participation in the adoption program of the Methodist Children's Home Society entails the following basic steps:
Random selection intake process
Orientation meeting
Application
Homestudy
Placement
Post-placement supervision

ADDITIONAL PROGRAMS/SERVICES

Methodist Children's Home Society provides residential treatment; day treatment school program; single parent counseling; generic foster care; intensive treatment foster care; summer camp for emotionally impaired children (Camp Knight of the Pines).

BRANCH/NETWORK OFFICES

None.

LICENSE/ACCREDITATION/PROFESSIONAL AFFILIATIONS

Methodist Children's Home Society is licensed by the State of Michigan Department of Social Services and is accredited by the Council on Accreditation of Services for Families and Children. The agency's affiliations include the National Association of Social Workers, Health and Welfare Certification Council of the United Methodist Church, the Child Welfare League of America, the United Foundation of Metropolitan Detroit, United Community Services of Metropolitan Detroit, Michigan Association of Children's Agencies, and Michigan Federation of Private Child and Family Agencies.

OAKLAND FAMILY SERVICES

50 Wayne Street
Pontiac, MI 48058
(313) 332–8352
Program director: MaryJane Clark, MSW, ACSW, Director, Children Services

THE PROGRAM

Oakland Family Services is a private, nonprofit agency serving residents of Oakland County for infant adoptions and residents of Oakland, Wayne, and Macomb for special-needs adoptions. The agency places approximately 20 children annually. In 1972, Michigan Children's Aid and Adoption (founded 1893) merged with Oakland Family Services. The agency's mission is "to develop, provide and promote superior services to individuals, couples and families so that their lives and relationships are improved, and the quality of community life is enhanced."

THE COST

The agency's fee for adoption services is 8% of the primary wage earner's annual gross income. (Fees are set by Oakland County Court.) Services covered by the fee include all phases of the adoption process, excluding a $40 petition filing fee (which includes the fee for a new birth certificate).

THE WAIT

For infant placement, the time from application to the homecoming of the adoptive child averages 5 to 6 years.

THE CHILDREN

Oakland Family Services places both healthy and special-needs children of all ages and all races, born in the U.S.

THE REQUIREMENTS

Age: No age restrictions for special needs placements. For infant adoption, applicants may be no more than 42 years old at the time of placement.

Health: Applicants must be in reasonably good health. Applicants with health problems or handicaps are given individual consideration. Infertility documentation is required for infant adoption.

Religion: No requirement.

Financial status: Applicants must demonstrate financial stability.

Marital status: For infant adoption, applicants must be married, and the length of the marriage must be at least 2 years at the time of application. Single applicants are accepted for special needs placements.

Family size: For infant adoption, applicants may have no more than 1 child currently in the family. The requirement is flexible for special needs placements.

Racial, ethnic or cultural origin: No requirement, but preference for placing children in families of similar origins.

THE PROCEDURE

Participation in Oakland Family Services' adoption program entails the following basic steps:
Orientation meeting
Application
Individual counseling sessions (as needed)
Homestudy
Placement
Post-placement supervision

ADDITIONAL PROGRAMS/SERVICES

Oakland Family Services provides a wide range of services including individual, family, and group counseling; substance abuse counseling; pregnancy counseling; sexual abuse treatment unit; foster care services; workshops and seminars.

BRANCH/NETWORK OFFICES

2351 12 Mile Road
Berkley, MI 48072
(313) 544–4004

50 Wayne St.
Pontiac, MI 48058
(313) 332–8352

2085 W. Maple Rd.
Walled Lake, MI 48088
(313) 624–3811]

5886 Dixie Highway
Waterford, MI 48095
(313) 623–6988

Family Center
132 Franklin Blvd.
Pontiac, MI 48053
(313) 858–7766

LICENSE/ACCREDITATION/PROFESSIONAL AFFILIATIONS

Oakland Family Services is licensed by the State of Michigan Department of Social Services and is accredited by the Council on Accreditation of Services for Families and Children. The agency is a member of the Child Welfare League of America, Family Service America, and Michigan Federation of Private Child and Family Agencies.

ORCHARDS CHILDREN'S SERVICES

30233 Southfield Road, Suite 118
Southfield, MI 48076
(313) 258–0440
Program director: Gerald Levin

THE PROGRAM

Orchards Children's Services is a nonprofit multi-service agency serving residents of Wayne and Oakland Counties and placing approximately 25 special-needs children annually. Established in 1962, the agency "is dedicated to providing professional help to children who are unable to function within their day-to-day environment. The agency is committed to establishing innovative programs that respond to children and families who are experiencing emotional problems that place the family unit in jeopardy." The agency's adoption program began in 1986 as an outgrowth of its foster care program. Adoptive placement is sought as a permanent resource when a child is unable to return to his or her family of origin and when the parental rights of the birthparents have been terminated by the courts.

THE COST

As of October 1988, the agency's fee for adoption services is $3,700. Services covered by the fee include all phases of the adoption process.

THE WAIT

The time from application to placement averages 9 months.

THE CHILDREN

Orchards Children's Services places special-needs children, ranging in age from birth to 16 years, of all racial backgrounds, from Wayne and Oakland Counties.

THE REQUIREMENTS

Age: No requirement.
Health: No requirement.
Religion: No requirement.
Financial status: No requirement.
Marital status: No requirement.
Family size: No requirement.
Racial, ethnic or cultural origin: No requirement.

THE PROCEDURE

Participation in the adoption program of Orchards Children's Services entails the following basic steps:
Orientation meeting
Application
Group counseling sessions
Homestudy
Referral
Placement
Post-placement supervision

ADDITIONAL PROGRAMS/SERVICES

Orchards Children's Services provides a wide range of services for children and families including community-based residences for children; family foster care and specialized foster care; day camp; family life education; child development library; community services.

BRANCH/NETWORK OFFICES

None.

LICENSE/ACCREDITATION/PROFESSIONAL AFFILIATIONS

Orchards Children's Services is licensed by the State of Michigan Department of Social Services and is a member of the Child Welfare League of America.

SPAULDING FOR CHILDREN ADMINISTRATION

P.O. Box 337
Chelsea, MI 48118
(313) 475–8693
Program director: Judith K. McKenzie, Executive Director; Natalie Thompson, Program Director

THE PROGRAM

Spaulding for Children is a nonprofit agency, established in 1968, serving the metropolitan Detroit area and placing approximately 25 children annually. Spaulding for Children "is committed to serve children with special needs who are waiting for permanent families." The majority are Black children and teenagers who have been abused and neglected. Many have serious developmental and emotional problems. Prior to being referred to Spaulding, they have been in temporary care for most of their lives. These children bring unique challenges to their new families. In response to these challenges, Spaulding provides support services that help to preserve new families as they adjust to their changing roles. In addition to direct services for children and families, Spaulding for Children maintains a National Resource Center for Special-needs adoption and provides training programs for adoption, child welfare, and mental health professionals.

THE COST

Adoption services are provided at no cost to the adoptive family.

THE WAIT

The time from application to the homecoming of the adoptive child varies depending on the needs of the child and on the types and ages of children the adoptive family can accept.

THE CHILDREN

Spaulding for Children places special-needs children (8 years or age and older) and sibling groups, of all racial backgrounds.

THE REQUIREMENTS

Age: No requirement.
Health: Applicants should be in reasonably good health.
Religion: No requirement.
Financial status: : No requirement.
Marital status: No requirement.
Family size: No requirement.
Racial, ethnic or cultural origin: The requirement varies depending on the needs of the child being considered for placement.

THE PROCEDURE

Participation in the adoption program of Spaulding for Children entails the following basic steps:
Orientation meeting
Application
Individual and group counseling sessions (as needed)
Homestudy
Placement
Post-placement supervision
Post-placement services
Post-legalization services

ADDITIONAL PROGRAMS/SERVICES

Adoption support services provided by Spaulding for Children include individualized permanency planning consultation, goal specific short-term foster care, post-adoption outreach services, parent and adolescent support groups, family and child therapy, and parenting skills training. Training and leadership services provided by the agency include the National Resource Center for Special-needs adoption, training programs for adoption, child welfare and mental health professionals, and nationwide recruitment and training of new leaders in special-needs adoption and related services.

BRANCH/NETWORK OFFICES

Spaulding for Children Direct Services
800 Livernois
Detroit, MI 48220
(313) 544–0850
Director: Natalie Thompson

LICENSE/ACCREDITATION/PROFESSIONAL AFFILIATIONS

Spaulding for Children is licensed by the State of Michigan Department of Social Services.

SUNNY RIDGE FAMILY CENTER

Fairview Professional Building
5675 Fairview Avenue
Stevensville, MI 49127
(616) 429–2757
Program director: Larry G. Betts, President

THE PROGRAM

For a full description of programs and services, refer to Illinois listing:
Sunny Ridge Family Center
2 S 426 Orchard Road
Wheaton, IL 60187
(312) 668–5117

Minnesota

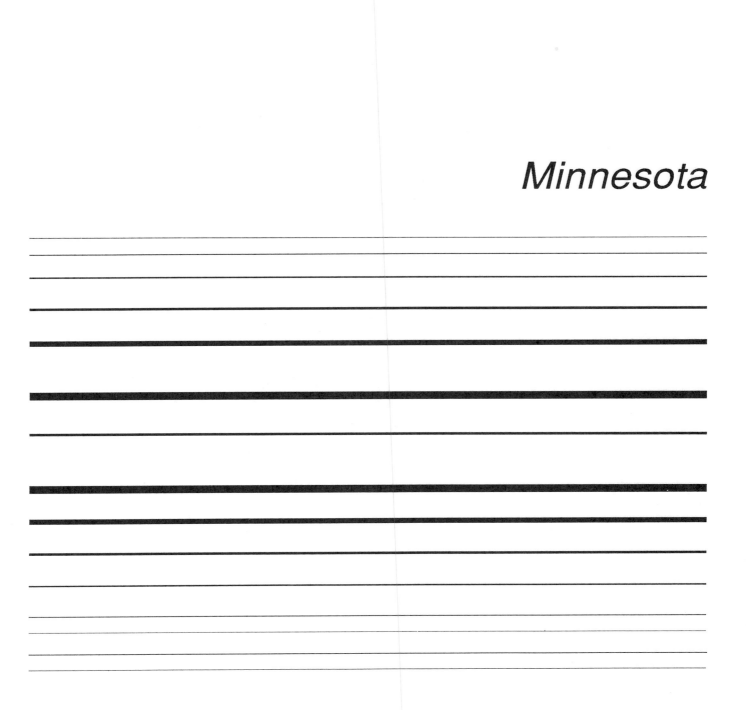

PUBLIC ADOPTION PROGRAM/ COMMUNITY RESOURCES

Department of Human Services
Adoption and Guardianship Section
444 Lafayette Road
St. Paul, MN 55155–3831
(612) 296–0584
Adoption specialist: Sandra Erickson, Acting Supervisor

THE PROGRAM

Adoption services in Minnesota are provided through social services agencies located in each county and by licensed child placing agencies. The focus of the Adoption and Guardianship Section is to ensure the recruitment and preparation of families for children with special needs and to supervise services to children with special needs (primarily older, minority, and handicapped children and sibling groups) who are under the guardianship of the State of Minnesota.

STATE EXCHANGE

State Adoption Exchange is a photographic exchange used by local social service and licensed child placing agencies. Agencies in other states may register children and families approved to adopt children with special needs. Agencies may contact the Adoption Exchange by writing to the Adoption and Guardianship Section (above).

STATE ADOPTION REUNION REGISTRY

Minnesota does not operate a state registry. Post-adoption services are available through the appropriate local social service or licensed child placing agency. Adult adoptees or birthparents may also inquire about the original birth certificate at the following:
Minnesota Department of Health
Section of Vital Statistics
717 Delaware Southeast
Minneapolis, MN 55440
(612) 623–5128

STATE SUBSIDY

Children with special needs under agency guardianship may qualify for a subsidized adoption and medical assistance. The program is administered by the Adoption and Guardianship Section (above).

NACAC REPRESENTATIVE

Judith Anderson
9125 W. Bush Lake Road
Bloomington, MN 55438
(612) 941–5146

GENERAL ADOPTION RESOURCES

Adoption Option Committee, Inc.
P.O. Box 24132
Minneapolis, MN 55424
(612) 944–0866

OURS, Inc.
3307 Hwy. 100 N., Suite 203
Minneapolis, MN 55422
(612) 535–4829
Citizens Coalition on Permanence for Children
9155 W. Bush Lake Road
Minneapolis, MN 55438
(612) 941–7047

SPECIAL-NEEDS ADOPTION RESOURCES

The Possibility Handbook: Adoptive Parent's Guide to Community Resources, by Bennetta E. Harrington (Adoption Unit, Minnesota Department of Human Services, 1986) is an important resource for families adopting children with special-needs in Minnesota. The handbook answers questions about children with special needs, the adoption process, and financial assistance and includes a directory of local, state, and national resources for health, educational, vocational, and social services for children with special needs. The handbook is available from the Adoption and Guardianship Section (above).

OUT-OF-STATE AGENCIES

AGENCY

Christian Family Life Services, North Dakota

SEE APPENDIX A

Agencies Providing Nationwide Services

BETHANY CHRISTIAN SERVICES

421 South Main
Stillwater, MN 55082–5127
(612) 439–9603
Program director: James K. Haveman, Jr., Executive Director

THE PROGRAM

International adoptions only. For a full description of programs and services, refer to Michigan listing:
Bethany Christian Services
901 Eastern Avenue, N.E.
Grand Rapids, MI 49503–1295
(616) 459–6273

BUILDING FAMILIES THROUGH ADOPTION

P.O. Box 550, 7th and Chestnut
Dawson, MN 56232
(612) 769–2933
Program director: Mary Carpenter and Therese Giesen

THE PROGRAM

Building Families through Adoption is a nonprofit agency serving families in Minnesota, North and South Dakota, Iowa, and Wisconsin and specializing in "waiting" child adoption. After adopting 6 special-needs children, Roger and Pamela Reinert founded BFTA, encouraged by inquiries and support from professionals in the field of social welfare, government officials, and many families interested in adopting "waiting" children. Today, with outreach offices in over 30 locations throughout the five-state area, BFTA places approximately 200 children (domestic and foreign) annually.

THE COST

The agency's fee for adoption services is based on a sliding scale and ranges between $1,000 and $2,500. Services covered by the fee include pre-adoptive training, educational classes, homestudy investigation, child find, placement, post-placement services, and post-legalization services. For foreign adoptions, prospective adoptive parents should anticipate immigration/naturalization fees, foreign source fees, and travel expenses. In addition, applicants assume responsibility for legal fees connected with finalization of the adoption.

THE WAIT

The average time from application for acceptance into the program to the homecoming of the adoptive child is 12 months.

THE CHILDREN

BFTA places both healthy and special-needs children, ranging in age from birth to 17 years, of all racial backgrounds. Countries of origin include U.S., Mexico, Brazil, Chili, Taiwan, Sri Lanka, Haiti, and Jamaica.

THE REQUIREMENTS

Age: No requirement, but may vary for foreign program depending on child's country of origin.
Health: Applicants with health problems or handicaps are given individual consideration. The requirement may vary for foreign program depending on the child's country of origin.
Religion: No requirement, but may vary for foreign program depending on the child's country of origin.
Financial status: No requirement, but may vary for foreign program depending on the child's country of origin.
Marital status: No requirement, but may vary for foreign program depending on the child's country of origin. Single applicants are accepted for several programs.
Family size: No requirement, but may vary for foreign program depending on the child's country of origin.
Racial, ethnic or cultural origin: No requirement, but may vary depending on child's state or country of origin.

THE PROCEDURE

Participation in BFTA's adoption programs entails the following basic steps:
Orientation meeting
Pre-application
Educational training
Application
Group and individual counseling sessions
Homestudy
Compliance with immigration/naturalization requirements (foreign adoptions only)
Referral
Placement
Post-placement supervision
Post-legalization services

ADDITIONAL PROGRAMS/SERVICES

BFTA provides consultation and counseling services; parent and child support groups; referral services to child advocacy organizations and local support groups; cultural activities and materials which preserve the child's contact with his/her culture of origin; annual publications; clothing and supply drives as well as fund-raising events to benefit international projects.

BRANCH/NETWORK OFFICES

BFTA has branch offices throughout Minnesota, Iowa, Wisconsin, North and South Dakota. Interested persons are asked to call the main office (612–769–2933) for information concerning the nearest informational meeting, current program information, and addresses and telephone numbers of branch offices.

LICENSE/ACCREDITATION/PROFESSIONAL AFFILIATIONS

BFTA is licensed by the Department of Human Services to provide services in each of the states in which it operates and meets the standards required for approval by the Minnesota Charities Review Council.

CATHOLIC CHARITIES, INC.

1200 Memorial Drive, Box 610
Crookston, MN 56716
(218) 281–4224
Program director: Gerry Bryant
Program coordinator: Karen Myszkowski

THE PROGRAM

Catholic Charities is a nonprofit agency serving residents of 14 counties in Minnesota within the Diocese of Crookston and placing approximately 6 children annually. Incorporated in 1947, the agency provides services to birthparents and places infants for adoption when birthparents in the agency's program elect adoptive placement as the best plan for their child.

THE COST

The agency's fee for adoption services is based on a sliding scale and averages $2,500. Services covered by the fee include homestudy, placement, post-placement supervision, and preparation of documents for finalization. In addition, applicants should anticipate legal fees connected with finalization of the adoption.

THE WAIT

The time from application for acceptance into the program to the homecoming of the adoptive child averages 5 to 6 years.

THE CHILDREN

Catholic Charities places primarily healthy Caucasian infants (birth to 1 year), but occasionally bi-racial children as well, born in the U.S.

THE REQUIREMENTS

Age: Applicants may be no more than 38 years old at the time of inquiry and 45 years old at the time of placement.

Health: Applicants must be in reasonably good health. Infertility documentation is required.

Religion: Applicants must be practicing members of a Christian church.

Financial status: Applicants must have adequate income, housing, health and life insurance.

Marital status: Applicants must be married couples. The length of the marriage must be at least 3 years by the time of the homestudy.

Family size: Applicants may have no more than 1 child currently in the family.

Racial, ethnic or cultural origin: Preference for placing children in families of similar origins, according to State law.

THE PROCEDURE

Participation in Catholic Charities' adoption program entails the following basic steps:
Letter of inquiry
Application
Homestudy
Workshop
Placement
Post-placement supervision

ADDITIONAL PROGRAMS/SERVICES

Catholic Charities provides adoption workshops; foster care services; unwed parent counseling; referral and search services for birthparents and adult adoptees; post- abortion counseling.

BRANCH/NETWORK OFFICES

None.

LICENSE/ACCREDITATION/PROFESSIONAL AFFILIATIONS

Catholic Charities is licensed by the State of Minnesota Department of Human Services.

CATHOLIC CHARITIES OF THE ARCHDIOCESE OF ST. PAUL AND MINNEAPOLIS

215 Old Sixth Street
St. Paul, MN 55102
(612) 222-3001
Program director: Robert B. Denardo, ACSW

THE PROGRAM

Catholic Charities is a nonprofit agency serving residents of the Archdiocese of St. Paul and Minneapolis and placing approximately 130 children annually through its adoption programs. Founded in 1859, child welfare services have been a major component of Catholic Charities' program throughout its history. Catholic Charities believes "that adoption exists to meet the needs of the child. The agency's commitment to the sanctity of all human life and to the sanctity of the family as the basic unit of society mandates the maintenance of an active and viable adoption program." Currently, the agency offers extensive services to birthparents and places both healthy and special-needs children (infants to toddlers) when birthparents elect adoptive placement as the best plan for their child. Working with child welfare institutions abroad, Catholic Charities places Korean and Latin American children. In addition, the agency will provide homestudy and supervisory services for applicants pursuing interagency adoption (domestic or international).

THE COST

The agency's fee for adoption services varies depending on the program. For domestic adoptions, the agency's fee is $3,050 plus $950 for foster care. For international adoptions, the agency's fee is $2,100. In addition, applicants interested in the international program should anticipate a fee to the overseas agency and miscellaneous costs (minimal) related to foreign adoption. For both programs, applicants are responsible for legal costs connected with finalization of the adoption ($100 or less without an attorney; $175 to $300 with an attorney).

THE WAIT

For domestic adoptions, applicants can expect to be on a waiting list for 1 1/2 to 2 years prior to the initiation of the homestudy. The time from completion of the homestudy to placement averages 1 year. For international adoptions, the time from application to placement averages 14 to 18 months.

THE CHILDREN

Catholic Charities places both healthy and special-needs children (domestic, infants to toddlers; international, infants to adolescents), of all racial backgrounds. Countries of origin include U.S., Korea, and some Latin American countries.

THE REQUIREMENTS

Age: No requirement for domestic adoptions. For Korean adoptions, applicants must be at least 25 and no more than 45 years of age.

Health: Applicants should be in reasonably good health. Applicants with health problems or handicaps are given individual consideration.

Religion: Applicants must be in a valid Catholic marriage, and one partner must be a practicing Catholic.

Financial status: No requirement for domestic adoptions. For Korean adoptions, applicants must have an income of at least $20,000.

Marital status: Applicants must be married, and the length of the marriage must be at least 3 years.

Family size: For Korean adoption, applicants may have no

more than 4 children currently in the family. For domestic adoption, applicants must be childless, but the requirement may vary depending on the situation.

Racial, ethnic or cultural origin: No requirement, but preference for placing children in families of similar origins in accordance with state and federal legislation.

THE PROCEDURE

Participation in Catholic Charities' adoption program entails the following basic steps:
Orientation meeting
Application
Homestudy (including individual and group counseling sessions)
Compliance with immigration/naturalization requirements (international adoptions only)
Referral
Placement
Post-placement supervision

ADDITIONAL PROGRAMS/SERVICES

Catholic Charities develops short term groups and presentations of a supportive or educational nature. Programs offered include presentations on infertility, building positive family relations, adoption triad meetings, living the Korean adoption experience, and the evolution of families built through adoption.

BRANCH/NETWORK OFFICES

None.

LICENSE/ACCREDITATION/PROFESSIONAL AFFILIATIONS

Catholic Charities of the Archdiocese of St. Paul and Minneapolis is licensed by the State of Minnesota Department of Human Services and is accredited by the Council on Accreditation of Services for Families and Children. The agency is a member of Catholic Charities USA.

CATHOLIC SOCIAL SERVICES, DIOCESE OF WINONA, INC.

55 W. Sanborn Street
Box 588
Winona, MN 55987
(507) 454–4643
Program director: Francis Landwehr

THE PROGRAM

Catholic Social Services is a nonprofit agency serving residents of southern Minnesota and placing approximately 38 children annually. Founded as an orphanage in the early 1900s, today the agency provides a range of services to the community. Working directly with birthparents, with other private and public agencies, and with national and regional exchange programs, the agency places both healthy and special-needs children. Working cooperatively with other U.S. agencies which maintain international programs, the agency facilitates the placement of Korean children in Min-

nesota families. In addition, the agency will provide homestudy and supervisory services for applicants pursuing interagency adoption (domestic or international).

THE COST

The agency's fee for adoption services varies depending on the program. For infant adoption, the agency's fee ranges from $0 to $4,000. For special-needs adoption, the agency's fee ranges from $0 to $2,000. For Korean adoption, the agency's fee is $1,700. In addition, applicants pursuing Korean adoption should anticipate financial responsibility for fees to the cooperating U.S. agency and the Korean agency, air fare, and legal costs (totaling approximately $3,300).

THE WAIT

The time from application to placement varies depending on the program. For infant adoption, the wait averages 1 to 3 years. For special-needs adoption, the wait averages 1 to 3 years. For Korean adoption, the wait averages 6 months.

THE CHILDREN

Catholic Social Services places both healthy and special-needs children, ranging in age from birth to 6 years, of all racial backgrounds. Countries of origin include U.S. and Korea.

THE REQUIREMENTS

Age: Applicants must be at least 25 and no more than 37 years of age.
Health: Applicants should be in reasonably good health. Applicants with health problems or handicaps are given individual consideration. Infertility documentation is required for infant adoption.
Religion: Applicants must be practicing Catholics.
Financial status: Applicants must have sufficient income to provide for an additional family member.
Marital status: Applicants must be married; the length of the marriage must be at least 3 years.
Family size: For infant adoption, applicants may have no more than 1 child currently in the family.
Racial, ethnic or cultural origin: No requirement.

THE PROCEDURE

Participation in the adoption program of Catholic Social Services entails the following basic steps:
Application
Orientation meeting
Group counseling sessions
Homestudy
Compliance with immigration/naturalization requirements (international adoptions only)
Placement
Post-placement supervision

ADDITIONAL PROGRAMS/SERVICES

Catholic Social Services provides marital and family counseling; foster care; refugee resettlement; migrant workers ministry; natural family planning.

111 Riverfront
Winona, MN 55987
(507) 454–2270

903 West Center Street
Rochester, MN 55902
(507) 287–2047

423 W. 7th
Mankato, MN 56001
(507) 387–5586

1118 Oxford St.
Worthington, MN 56187
(507) 376–9757

LICENSE/ACCREDITATION/PROFESSIONAL AFFILIATIONS

Catholic Social Services, Diocese of Winona, Inc. is licensed by the State of Minnesota Department of Human Services.

CHILDREN'S HOME SOCIETY OF MINNESOTA

2230 Como Avenue
St. Paul, MN 55108
(612) 646–6393

Program director: Margie Mereen, Director of Adoption Programs and Permanency Planning; Virginia McDermott, Ph.D., American Special Needs Supervisor; David Pilgrim, International Adoption Supervisor

THE PROGRAM

Children's Home Society of Minnesota is a nonprofit agency serving the state of Minnesota. The agency also works cooperatively with licensed agencies in other states to place waiting international children. The agency began in 1889 in response to the "Orphan Train," bringing homeless children from New York City to the Midwest for adoption. From serving American infants in the early and mid 20th century, the agency expanded in the 1970s to include an International Adoption Program and an American Waiting Child Program. Placing approximately 600 children annually, the agency's focus today is the placement of American and foreign-born special-needs children. In all of its programs, the agency's mission is "to provide quality human services to children and families enabling them to realize their potential and helping them improve their own well-being."

THE COST

The agency's fee for adoption services is based on a sliding scale and varies depending on the program. The basic fee schedule is as follows:

International Adoption $600.00–$2,400.00
American Infant Adoption $800.00–$3,200.00
    plus $800 child care for normal-needs child
American Waiting Child Adoption $0.00–$600.00
    refundable if reimbursed by State subsidy

In addition, applicants interested in pursuing international adoption should anticipate international agency fees and travel costs. For all programs, applicants assume financial responsibility for legal fees connected with finalization of the adoption. Services covered by the fee include homestudy, placement, post-placement supervision, and court reporting. In the American Waiting Child program (which concentrates on children from Minnesota) continuing services are provided without additional charge after finalization, typically for a period of 5 to 6 years.

THE WAIT

The time from application to the homecoming of the adoptive child varies depending on the program. The wait for a foreign-born child ranges from 10 to 30 months, depending on the age and special needs of the child being considered for placement. The wait for an American infant ranges from 1 to 3 years, if the applicant is selected from the family resource list. A family adopting an American special-needs child may wait 6 months to 2 years.

THE CHILDREN

Children's Home Society of Minnesota places both healthy and special-needs children, ranging in age from birth to 17 years, of all racial backgrounds. Countries of origin include U.S., Korea, Latin America, Hong Kong, and India.

THE REQUIREMENTS

Age: Applicants must be at least 22 years old. In international adoptions, applicants must be at least 23 and no more than 40 years of age for adoption of an infant. Some international programs have more restrictive age policies, while the American Special Needs Program has no upper age limits.

Health: Applicants must be in reasonably good health. Applicants with health problems or handicaps are given individual consideration. The requirement may vary depending on the policies of the agency which has custody of the child.

Religion: No requirement, but may vary depending on the requirements of the agency which has custody of the child and, for older child adoptions, the wishes of the child.

Financial status: No requirement, but may vary depending on the requirements of the agency which has custody of the child. Management of funds is more important than income level.

Marital status: The requirement varies depending on the requirements of the agency which has custody of the child, the child's country of origin, and the special needs of the child. In the majority of cases, applicants must be married couples, and the length of the marriage ranges from 2 to 5 years. For international adoption, the requirement is typically 3 years.

Family size: The requirement may vary depending on the requirements of the agency which has custody of the child, country of origin, and special needs of the child.

Racial, ethnic or cultural origin: Preference for placing children in families of similar origins.

THE PROCEDURE

Participation in Children's Home Society of Minnesota's adoption programs entails the following basic steps:
  Orientation meeting
  Registration
  Application
  Group counseling sessions
  Individual counseling sessions
  Homestudy
  Compliance with immigration/naturalization requirements (international adoptions only)
  Referral
  Placement
  Post-placement supervision (extensive services)
  Finalization
  Naturalization (international adoptions only)
Because the needs of American Waiting Children are varied and extensive, families are recruited, prepared, and supported following placement by an adoption team which utilizes guidelines and practices which may differ from those set out here.

ADDITIONAL PROGRAMS/SERVICES

Children's Home Society of Minnesota provides post-legal adoption services (counseling, support groups, workshops); unplanned pregnancy counseling services; foster care; child day care; crisis nurseries; young parent program; group lifebook/identity counseling for older foster/adoptive children.

BRANCH/NETWORK OFFICES

None.

LICENSE/ACCREDITATION/PROFESSIONAL AFFILIATIONS

Children's Home Society is licensed by the Minnesota Department of Human Services and is accredited by the Council on Accreditation of Services for Families and Children. Children's Home Society is a member of the Child Welfare League of America and the United Way.

CROSSROADS, INC.

4640 W. 77th St.
Minneapolis, MN 55435
(612) 831–5707
Program director: Myrna Otte

THE PROGRAM

Crossroads, Inc. is a nonprofit agency serving the state of Minnesota and placing approximately 125 children annually. In locating, bringing together, and supporting children and parents after placement, Crossroads strives "to work with each parent and child as an individual with unique potential and needs, and to accord each of them dignified, caring assistance." Approximately half the children placed by the agency are from the U.S. and are placed through both public and private U.S. agencies. Over the past 11 years, Crossroads has placed children from 26 different countries. Current

sources include India, Korea, the Philippines, Honduras, Chile, and El Salvador.

THE COST

The agency's fee for adoption services is based on a sliding scale (family's gross income) and ranges from $1,250 to $2,150. The referral fee for out-of-state families when the homestudy and post-placement services are not provided by Crossroads is currently $350. Current approximate totals, not including Crossroads' fee, are as follows:

U.S. (plus travel)	$0.00–$6000.00
India (including travel)	$4000.00
The Philippines (including travel)	$2950.00–$3150.00
Chile (plus travel, documentation and translation expenses)	$3200.00
El Salvador (plus escort or travel)	$5,000.00

In addition, prospective adoptive parents should anticipate financial responsibility for legal fees connected with finalization of the adoption (generally under $100 for a Minnesota adoption).

THE WAIT

The time from application for acceptance into the program to the homecoming of the adoptive child varies depending on the child's country of origin and the kind of child being considered for placement. In most cases, families have a child in their home within 12 to 18 months following completion of the homestudy.

THE CHILDREN

Crossroads places U.S. children, primarily minority (Black and bi-racial) infants and school-aged children of all racial backgrounds. Older children usually have some special needs (physical, intellectual, or emotional). Crossroads places children of all ages from many different countries, including Chile, Korea, India, the Philippines, Honduras, and El Salvador. Crossroads will provide homestudy and supervisory services for Minnesota applicants pursuing parent-initiated adoptions of children from any country, subject to state approval of the integrity of the source.

THE REQUIREMENTS

Age: No specific requirement, but may vary depending on the child's country of origin.
Health: No specific requirement, but may vary depending on the child's country of origin.
Religion: No specific requirement, but may vary depending on the child's country of origin.
Financial status: No specific requirement, but may vary depending on the child's country of origin.
Marital status: No specific requirement, but may vary depending on the child's country of origin.
Family size: No specific requirement, but may vary depending on the child's country of origin.
Racial, ethnic or cultural origin: No specific requirement, but may vary depending on the child's country of origin.

THE PROCEDURE

Participation in Crossroads' adoption program entails the following basic steps:
  Inquiry

Orientation meeting
Application
Group education sessions
Individual/family counseling sessions
Homestudy
Child search and referral
Compliance with immigration/naturalization requirements
    (foreign adoptions only)
Placement
Post-placement supervision
Finalization
Naturalization
Reapplication

ADDITIONAL PROGRAMS/SERVICES

Crossroads sponsors support groups, conferences, and workshops on adoption issues; hosts an annual picnic for adoptive families; conducts supply drives for overseas projects; publishes a quarterly newsletter (Crossings).

BRANCH/NETWORK OFFICES

None.

LICENSE/ACCREDITATION/PROFESSIONAL AFFILIATIONS

Crossroads, Inc. is licensed by the State of Minnesota Department of Human Services.

HOPE INTERNATIONAL FAMILY SERVICES, INC.

421 South Main
Stillwater, MN 55082
(612) 439–2446
Program director: Anne McManus

THE PROGRAM

HOPE (Helping Others with a Personal Emphasis) International Family Services, Inc., is a nonprofit agency serving residents of Minnesota (counties of Anoka, Carver, Chisago, Dakota, Hennepin, Isanti, Ramsey, Scott, Washington, and Wright) and Wisconsin (Polk, St. Croix, Pierce, and Dunn Counties) and adjoining counties by special arrangement. While HOPE does not usually take guardianship of children, the agency facilitates approximately 120 adoptions annually. Founded in 1978, HOPE provides adoption information and referral services as well as homestudy and supervisory services, working cooperatively with U.S-based and international agencies to facilitate the placement of children from the U.S. and other countries. The agency's "Buddy System" helps new clients adjust to adoption by assigning experienced adoptive families who can offer support and practical advice. HOPE strives to offer all its clients "assistance given in a personal, confidential, supportive way."

THE COST

The agency charges a flat fee of $1,500. Services covered by the fee include the homestudy, adoption assistance, and post-placement supervision. The fee also includes a $300 non-refundable application fee. The fee for subsequent adoptions is $1,300. In addition, applicants can expect to pay fees to the cooperating placement agency, possible travel expenses, and legal fees connected with finalization.

THE WAIT

Not applicable.

THE CHILDREN

HOPE provides homestudy and supervisory services to facilitate the adoption of both healthy and special-needs children of all ages, races, and countries of origin.

THE REQUIREMENTS

Age: Applicants must be at least 21 years of age.
Health: Applicants should be in reasonably good health.
Religion: No requirement.
Financial status: Applicants must demonstrate financial stability.
Marital status: No requirement.
Family size: No requirement.
Racial, ethnic or cultural origin: No requirement.

THE PROCEDURE

Participation in HOPE's adoption program entails the following basic steps:
Informational meeting
Application
Homestudy (including individual counseling sessions)
Group educational meetings
Buddy family support system
Compliance with immigration/naturalization requirements
Placement (by cooperating agency)
Post-placement supervision

ADDITIONAL PROGRAMS/SERVICES

HOPE offers pre-adoptive counseling for couples and single people; provides information and referral services; provides assistance with immigration requirements and legalization of the adoption in the U.S.

BRANCH/NETWORK OFFICES

None.

LICENSE/ACCREDITATION/PROFESSIONAL AFFILIATIONS

HOPE International Family Services, Inc. is licensed by the State of Minnesota Department of Human Services and by the State of Wisconsin Department of Health and Social Services.

LUTHERAN SOCIAL SERVICE OF MINNESOTA

2414 Park Avenue
Minneapolis, MN 55404
(612) 871–0221/MN WATS (800) 582–5260
Program director: Patricia Eldridge, ACSW

THE PROGRAM

Lutheran Social Service of Minnesota (LSS) is a nonprofit agency providing statewide service and placing approximately 200 children in Evangelical Christian homes annually. LSS provides domestic and foreign adoption services and works with several U.S.-based licensed agencies which operate programs in foreign countries to place Korean, Filipino, and Latin American children in American families. The agency is also actively involved in the recruitment of families for special-needs children. In all of its programs, the agency's mission is "to enable individuals, families, congregations, communities and other institutions of society to achieve healthier and more satisfying social and spiritual relationships through the process of healing, reconciliation, growth and development."

THE COST

The agency's fee schedule for adoption services is as follows:

American-born child without special needs	$2,600.00
Foreign-born child	$2,125.00

Services covered by the fee include pre-adoptive counseling, homestudy, and post-placement services. For American-born children, applicants should anticipate cooperating agency fees and possible travel expenses for out-of-state children. For foreign-born children, applicants should anticipate foreign agency fees and travel expenses. In both programs, applicants assume responsibility for legal fees connected with finalization of the adoption.

Applicants offering homes to waiting children with special needs will be eligible for greatly reduced pre-adoptive counseling fees and at times will have all of their expenses paid through the subsidized adoption program.

THE WAIT

The time from registration to the homecoming of the adoptive child varies depending on the program. For special-needs adoptions, the time from registration to placement ranges from 1 to 2 years. For foreign adoptions, the time from registration to placement ranges from 1 to 2 years.

THE CHILDREN

Lutheran Social Service of Minnesota facilitates the placement of both healthy and special-needs children, ranging in age from infancy to adolescence, of all racial backgrounds. Countries of origin include U.S., Korea, the Philippines, and Central and South America.

THE REQUIREMENTS

Age: Applicants must be at least 21 years of age. The maximum age limit varies depending on the requirements of the cooperating agency.

Health: Applicants with health problems or handicaps are given individual consideration.

Religion: Applicants must be practicing members of an evangelical Christian church.

Financial status: Applicants must demonstrate ability to provide for the child with security and stability.

Marital status: For Korean adoption, applicants must be married. For other programs, the requirement varies depending on the requirements of the cooperating agency.

Family size: Priority is given to childless couples and couples with no more than 1 child in the family. For Korean adoption, applicants may have no more than 5 children currently in the family.

Racial, ethnic or cultural origin: Preference for placing children in families of similar origins whenever possible.

THE PROCEDURE

Participation in LSS' adoption program entails the following basic steps:

Inquiry/Information packet
Orientation meeting
Application
Homestudy (including individual and group counseling)
Cross-cultural workshop (if appropriate)
Compliance with immigration/naturalization requirements (foreign adoptions only)
Referral
Placement
Post-placement supervision

ADDITIONAL PROGRAMS/SERVICES

LSS provides workshops and seminars; post-legal adoption services; quarterly newsletter; child care services; refugee resettlement services; unaccompanied minors program; individual, marital, and family counseling; volunteer opportunities.

BRANCH/NETWORK OFFICES

All adoption inquiries are processed through the main office.

LICENSE/ACCREDITATION/PROFESSIONAL AFFILIATIONS

Lutheran Social Service of Minnesota is licensed by the State of Minnesota Department of Human Services and is a member of the United Way.

NEW LIFE HOMES AND FAMILY SERVICES

3361 Republic Avenue
St. Louis Park, MN 55426
(612) 920–8117
Program director: Jeanette Vought, Executive Director

THE PROGRAM

New Life Homes and Family Services is a nonprofit social service agency serving communities within a 25 mile radius of Minneapolis, Rochester, and Coon Rapids, Minnesota and placing approximately 30 children annually. Established as a ministry of Greater Minneapolis Association of Evangelicals in 1973 to provide adolescent group homes, the agency has expanded to provide crisis pregnancy, foster care, and adoption services. The mission of the New Life Crisis Pregnancy Center is "to provide Christ-centered, personal, and practical assistance to persons faced with a pregnancy that demands difficult and crucial decisions. The intent of the Center is to take positive action to protect the sanctity of life and to make information, counseling, and practical assistance available in an atmosphere of Christian love." New Life Homes places infants for adoption when birthmothers in the agency's crisis pregnancy program decide that the best interests of the infant will be served by adoptive placement.

THE COST

The agency requests that prospective adoptive parents make a contribution, based on a sliding scale to help cover the cost of services provided. Costs generally equal $3,500 per adoption. These costs originate from the following services: counseling, clerical support, homestudy, legal fees connected with termination of parental rights, foster care of the infant until placement, supervision of placement, and finalization reports. In addition, applicants should anticipate financial responsibility for legal fees connected with finalization of the adoption.

THE WAIT

The average time from screening of applicants to the homecoming of the adoptive child is 3 years.

THE CHILDREN

New Life Homes primarily places healthy Caucasian infants. However, the agency also occasionally places infants of Hispanic/Caucasian, Asian/Caucasian, and Black/Caucasian backgrounds.

THE REQUIREMENTS

Age: Applicants must be at least 21 and no more than 39 years of age at the time their names are placed on the waiting list.

Health: Applicants must be infertile, unable to carry a pregnancy to term, or have hereditary, genetic factor causing biological children to be high risk if conceived. Applicants with other health problems or handicap are given individual consideration.

Religion: While applicants may be of any Christian denomination, they must have an understanding and personal acceptance of salvation in Jesus Christ.

Financial status: Applicants must demonstrate ability to live responsibly and comfortably within their income.

Marital status: Applicants must be married and must have been married for at least 2 years.

Family size: Applicants may have no more than 1 child currently in the family. Requirement may vary for applicants who are open to accept an older, handicapped, or bi-racial child.

Racial, ethnic or cultural origin: Preference for placing children in families of similar origins.

THE PROCEDURE

Participation in New Life Homes' adoption program entails the following basic steps:
Preliminary Information Sheet (screening)
Waiting list (approximately 2 years)
Information meeting
Application
Homestudy (including individual/couple counseling sessions)
Referral (non-identifying adoptive summary shown to birthmothers)
Placement
Post-placement supervision

ADDITIONAL PROGRAMS/SERVICES

New Life Homes and Family Services operates crisis pregnancy centers at all four locations; operates Judith Place (a rule #8 group home for adolescent girls with emotional and adjustment problems); provides foster care and family counseling; sponsors Becomers (a recovery program for those experiencing past childhood sexual abuse), Conquerors (a post-abortion support group), Quest (an infertility support group), and Uphold (a support group for women who have placed a child for adoption).

BRANCH/NETWORK OFFICES

435 Aldine, Suite 201
St. Paul, MN 55104
Office: (612) 641–5595
Hotline: (612) 920–1006

2525 Coon Rapids Blvd.
Coon Rapids, MN 55432
Office: (612) 421–0155
Hotline: (612) 920–1006

814 N. Broadway
Rochester, MN 55904
Office: (507) 282–3377
Hotline: (507) 282–1111

LICENSE/ACCREDITATION/PROFESSIONAL AFFILIATIONS

New Life Homes and Family Services is licensed by the State of Minnesota Department of Human Services.

Mississippi

PUBLIC ADOPTION PROGRAM/ COMMUNITY RESOURCES

Department of Public Welfare
Placement and Prevention Department, Adoption Unit
P.O. Box 352
Jackson, MS 39205
(601) 354–0341
Adoption specialist: Patricia P. Jones and Mary Ann Everett

THE PROGRAM

Public adoption in Mississippi is provided by the Department of Public Welfare through branch offices located in each area. DPW has a relatively small infant placement service. Placement of children with special needs (older, minority, and handicapped children and sibling groups) is the primary focus of the adoption program.

STATE EXCHANGE

Mississippi Adoption Resource Exchange. For information, contact the Adoption Unit (above).

STATE ADOPTION REUNION REGISTRY

None.

STATE SUBSIDY

Adoption Subsidy Program. For information, contact the Adoption Unit (above).

NACAC REPRESENTATIVE

Linda West
1801 N. West Street
Jackson, MS 39202
(601) 352–7784

GENERAL ADOPTION RESOURCES

Adoption support services in Mississippi are normally provided by private adoption agencies as a service to their clients. Contact private adoption agencies in Mississippi (see Mississippi listing) for information on support services in your area.

SPECIAL-NEEDS ADOPTION RESOURCES

For information concerning special-needs adoption resources, contact the Adoption Unit (above).

OUT-OF-STATE AGENCIES

AGENCY

Holt International Children's Services, Tennessee branch
Smithlawn Maternity Home, Texas (special-needs and minority placements)

SEE APPENDIX A

Agencies Providing Nationwide Services

BETHANY CHRISTIAN SERVICES

3000 Old Canton Road, Room 360
Woodland Hills Building
Jackson, MS 39216
(601) 366–4282
Program director: James K. Haveman, Jr., Executive Director

THE PROGRAM

For a full description of programs and services, refer to Michigan listing:
Bethany Christian Services
901 Eastern Avenue, N.E.
Grand Rapids, MI 49503–1295
(616) 459–6273

BRANCH OFFICES

Bethany Christian Services/Mississippi:
Crisis Pregnancy Center
100 N. 33rd Ave.
Hattiesburg, MS 39401–9641
(601) 264–2648

CATHOLIC CHARITIES, INC.

748 North President Street
P.O. Box 2248
Jackson, MS 39225–2248
(601) 355–8634
Program director: Dollie Hambrick, ACSW

THE PROGRAM

Catholic Charities, Inc., is a nonprofit social service organization that serves 65 counties in the state of Mississippi and places approximately 27 children annually. Established in 1963, Catholic Charities provides a number of social and community services and through its adoption program strives "to place each child committed into our care in the best possible home for permanent adoption." Dedicated to the belief that "every child has a right to a permanent, loving family," Catholic Charities emphasizes services to others, advocacy and increased public awareness to community needs.

THE COST

The agency's fee for adoption is based on a sliding scale that ranges from $400 to $6,300, based on the applicants income. Services covered by the fee include the homestudy, supervisory services, placement, post-placement, and other agency expenses. In addition, the agency charges a $300 legal fee associated with the finalization of the adoption. Exceptions are made for families adopting special-needs children.

THE WAIT

The average time from application for acceptance into the program to the homecoming of the adoptive child ranges from 3 1/2 to 4 years. The time from application to placement is much shorter for families adopting special-needs children.

THE CHILDREN

Catholic Charities places both healthy and special-needs children who range in age form birth to 18 years, of Black, Caucasian, and bi-racial backgrounds. Children placed by Catholic Charities are born in the U.S.

THE REQUIREMENTS

Age: Applicants should be between 25 and 40 years of age, although exceptions are made for cases involving special-needs children.

Health: Applicants should be in reasonably good health.

Religion: Applicants should be practicing members of a church.

Financial status: Applicants must demonstrate financial stability.

Marital status: Preference is given to married applicants with a stable marriage of at least 3 years. However, applications from single people and from couples married less than 3 years are accepted.

Family size: No requirement.

Racial, ethnic or cultural origin: No requirement.

THE PROCEDURE

Participation in Catholic Charities' adoption program entails the following basic steps:

Orientation
Application
Submission of references, police checks, child abuse register checks
Group meetings for new applicants
Homestudy (including individual and joint interviews)
Approval or rejection
Placement
Post-placement supervision
Finalization

ADDITIONAL PROGRAMS/SERVICES

Catholic Charities offers a variety of social services and programs including special-needs foster care and post-adoption services.

BRANCH/NETWORK OFFICES

Sr. Clare Hogan, M.S.W., Director
Catholic Charities
Box 74 Natchex, MS 39120
(601) 442–4579

LICENSE/ACCREDITATION/PROFESSIONAL AFFILIATIONS

Catholic Charities is licensed by the State of Mississippi Department of Public Welfare.

CATHOLIC SOCIAL AND COMMUNITY SERVICES, INC.

198 Reynoir Street
P.O. Box 1457
Biloxi, MS 39533
(601) 374–8316
Program director: Rev. George E. Murphy

THE PROGRAM

Catholic Social and Community Services is a nonprofit multi-service agency serving residents of the 17 southern-most counties in Mississippi (Hancock, Harrison, Jackson, George, Stone, Pearl River, Walthall, Marion, Lamar, Forrest, Perry, Greene, Wayne, Jones, Covington, Jefferson Davis, and Lawrence) and placing between 13 and 20 children annually. Founded in 1977, the agency's primary mission is "to meet the needs of those children placed for adoption by their birthparents. While the primary consideration is given to the needs of the infant, the agency feels a strong responsibility in educating and evaluating prospective adoptive parents to prepare them for the special challenges that adoption brings." In addition to full-service infant adoptions, the agency provides homestudy and supervisory services for applicants pursuing interagency adoption.

THE COST

The agency's fee for adoption services is currently $4,500 and includes homestudy, placement preparation, placement, post-placement supervision, and finalization. For applicants pursuing interagency adoption, the agency's fee schedule is as follows:

Homestudy only	$500.00
Homestudy, post-placement supervision, finalization	$1,000.00
Home visits (coast families) (per visit)	$35.00
Home visits (outlying families) (per visit)	$40.00

THE WAIT

The time from application to the homecoming of the adoptive child ranges from 2 to 5 years.

THE CHILDREN

Catholic Social and Community Services places both healthy and special-needs infants, of Black, Caucasian, Vietnamese, and bi-racial backgrounds, born in the U.S.

THE REQUIREMENTS

Age: Applicants must be at least 25 and no more than 40 years of age. The requirement may vary depending on the current need for adoptive families.

Health: Applicants should be in reasonably good health. Applicants with health problems or handicaps are given individual consideration.

Religion: Applicants must be active participants in their chosen religion.

Financial status: Applicants must demonstrate financial stability.

Marital status: Applicants must be married; the length of the marriage must be at least 5 years. The requirement may vary depending on the current need for adoptive families.

Family size: Applicants may have no more than 1 child currently in the family.

Racial, ethnic or cultural origin: Preference for placing children in families of similar origins.

THE PROCEDURE

Participation in the adoption program of Catholic Social and Community Services entails the following basic steps:

Referral

Preliminary inquiry
Application
Orientation meeting
Group counseling sessions
Individual counseling sessions
Homestudy
Placement
Post-placement supervision

ADDITIONAL PROGRAMS/SERVICES

Catholic Social and Community Services provides a wide range of services to individuals and families including Adoptive Families Together (support group); pre-adoptive foster care; post-adoption services; individual, marital, and family counseling; maternity services; refugee resettlement; emergency/disaster assistance; family life programs; parish and community organization services.

BRANCH/NETWORK OFFICES

All adoption inquiries are processed through the Biloxi office.

LICENSE/ACCREDITATION/PROFESSIONAL AFFILIATIONS

Catholic Social and Community Services, Inc. is licensed by the State of Mississippi Department of Public Welfare.

MISSISSIPPI CHILDREN'S HOME SOCIETY AND FAMILY SERVICE ASSOCIATION

P.O. Box 1078
Jackson, MS 39205
(601) 352–7784
Program director: Betti Watters, MSW

THE PROGRAM

Mississippi Children's Home Society and Family Service Association (MCHS) is a nonprofit multi-service agency providing statewide services and placing approximately 40 children annually. Founded in 1912, the agency provides services on a non-sectarian basis, striving to find "a permanent, loving family for every child." The agency provides services to birthparents and places infants for adoption when birthparents in the agency's counseling program decide that the best interests of the child will be served by adoptive placement. The agency is also actively involved in the placement of special-needs children and will provide homestudy and supervisory services for applicants pursuing open or identified adoptions.

THE COST

The agency's fee for adoption services is based on a sliding scale. Fees for special-needs placements range from no fee to $3,000. Fees for infant placements range from $6,000 to $10,000. Services covered by the fee include adoption study, placement, and post-placement supervision. Applicants assume responsibility for legal fees connected with finalization of the adoption and the fee for a new birth certificate.

THE WAIT

The time from application for acceptance into the program to the homecoming of the adoptive child averages 6 to 12 months.

THE CHILDREN

MCHS places both healthy and special-needs children, ranging in age from birth to 18 years, of all racial backgrounds.

THE REQUIREMENTS

Age: Applicants must be at least 21 years of age and may be no more than 40 years older than the child being considered for placement. The requirement may vary depending on the needs of the child.

Health: Applicants with health problems or handicaps are given individual consideration.

Religion: No requirement.

Financial status: Applicants are evaluated individually on the basis of their ability to manage financial resources adequately.

Marital status: Preference is given to married couples who have been married for at least 3 years, but the requirement may vary depending on the needs of the child.

Family size: The requirement varies depending on the needs of the child.

Racial, ethnic or cultural origin: Preference for placing children in families of similar origins, but varies depending on the needs of the child.

THE PROCEDURE

Participation in MCHS' adoption program entails the following basic steps:
Orientation meeting
Application
Group counseling sessions
Individual counseling sessions
Homestudy
Placement
Post-placement supervision
Finalization
Post-legal adoption services

ADDITIONAL PROGRAMS/SERVICES

MCHS provides individual, marital, and family counseling; services to birthparents; services to runaway youth; residential services for chemically dependent youth; residential services for young women experiencing emotional and/or behavioral problems; public awareness and education services; birth searches for adult adoptees.

BRANCH/NETWORK OFFICES

None.

LICENSE/ACCREDITATION/PROFESSIONAL AFFILIATIONS

Mississippi Children's Home Society and Family Service Association is licensed by the State of Mississippi Department of Public Welfare and is accredited by the Council on Accreditation of Services for Families and Children. The agency's professional affiliations include the Child Welfare League of America, Southeastern Network of Youth and Family Services, National Council on Adoptable Children, Governor's Task Force on Children and Youth, Juvenile Justice Task Force, Human Resources Coalition, Task Force on Adolescent Pregnancy, and the United Way.

Missouri

Public Adoption Program/ Community Resources

Department of Social Services
Division of Family Services
P.O. Box 88
Jefferson City, MO 65103
1–800–554–2222 (Adopt-line; toll free in Missouri)
Adoption specialist: Doris Lindsey

The Program

Public adoption services in Missouri are provided by the Department of Social Services, Division of Family Services through regional offices located throughout the state. The focus of the DFS adoption program is to recruit and prepare families and supervise the placement of special-needs children (older, minority, and handicapped children and sibling groups).

State Exchange

The Adoption Exchange of Missouri
P.O. Box 88
Jefferson City, MO 65103
1–800–554–2222

State Adoption Reunion Registry

None.

State Subsidy

Adoption Subsidy Program. For information, contact the Department of Social Services, Division of Family Services (above).

NACAC Representative

Laurie Johnson
8711 Bridgeport
Brentwood, MO 63144
(314) 968–5239

General Adoption Resources

Adoption support services in Missouri are normally provided by private adoption agencies as a service to their clients. Contact private agencies in Missouri (see Missouri listing) for support services in your area.

Special-Needs Adoption Resources

See General Adoption Resources (above).

Out-of-State Agencies

Agency

Universal Family, Colorado

See Appendix A

Agencies Providing Nationwide Services

The Adams Center

9200 Ward Parkway, Suite 655
Kansas City, MO 64114
(816) 444–4545
Program director: Patti Glass

The Program

Opened in January 1985, the Adams Center is a nonprofit agency that serves the metropolitan Kansas City area in both Missouri and Kansas. The founders of the Adams Center wanted an agency that could provide services, support, and advocacy to pregnant women whether they decided to place their infants for adoption or parent their infants. The agency is dedicated to "the prevention of unwanted pregnancies" and seeks "to improve the health and well being of both relinquishing and non-relinquishing young women and their children through supportive services." Providing services on a non-sectarian basis, the agency is committed to serving all members of the adoption triad.

The Cost

The Adams Center charges a flat fee of $7,000. Services covered by the fee include the homestudy, counseling for birthparents, group education for the adopting parents, medical and legal expenses of the birthmother and infant, and post-placement supervision. The adopting family should expect to pay their own attorney's fees (approximately $500) for finalization of the adoption.

The Wait

The wait varies greatly depending on the availability of the children.

The Children

The Adams Center places both healthy and special-needs children, (primarily newborn American infants) of all racial backgrounds.

The Requirements

Age: Applicants must be at least 25 and no more than 45 years of age.
Health: Applicants should be in reasonably good health; individual consideration is given to those with health problems or a handicap.
Religion: No requirement.
Financial status: Applicants must be financially stable and able to meet the daily expenses incurred by raising a child.
Marital status: Applicants must be married. The length of the marriage must be at least 3 years.
Family size: Applicants may have no more than 1 child currently in the family.
Residence: Applicants must reside within 1 hour travel time of metropolitan Kansas City.
Racial, ethnic or cultural origin: No requirement.

The Procedure

Participation in the Adams Center adoption program entails the following basic steps:
Application
Orientation meeting

Homestudy
Group counseling sessions
Placement
Post-placement supervision

ADDITIONAL PROGRAMS/SERVICES

The Adams Center provides counseling to pregnant women considering adoption or planning to raise their own children.

BRANCH/NETWORK OFFICES

None.

LICENSE/ACCREDITATION/PROFESSIONAL AFFILIATIONS

The Adams Center is licensed by the State of Kansas Department of Social Rehabilitative Services and by the State of Missouri Department of Social Services.

ADOPTION RESOURCE CENTER

R & R Health Services, Inc.
2207 Park Avenue
St. Louis, MO 63104
(314) 664–2942
Program director: Carolyn J. Riske, MA, MSW

THE PROGRAM

Adoption Resource Center is a for-profit agency serving primarily residents of Missouri (but working cooperatively with other agencies throughout the U.S. as well). In 1987, 39 children were placed. Begun four years ago to provide domestic and international adoption services, the mission of the Adoption Resource Center is "to provide high quality services for families seeking adoption with a focus on Latin American resources, but not overlooking hard-to-place children in the U.S." Working with birthparents, with other private and public agencies, and with national and regional exchange programs, the agency places both healthy and special-needs children born in the U.S. Working with other U.S. agencies which maintain international programs and working directly with foreign sources, the agency places children from Central and South American families in Missouri families. In addition, the agency will provide homestudy and supervisory services for applicants pursuing interagency adoption (domestic or international) or independent adoption. Educational preparation of prospective adoptive parents and cost-containment for families are high priorities for the Adoption Resource Center.

THE COST

The agency estimates that the total cost for adoption from Latin America is approximately $8,000. Services covered by the estimate include the homestudy, foreign source fees or cooperating agency fees, travel expenses (excluding food), foster and medical care for the child, Immigration and Naturalization Service fees, visa and passport for the child, U.S. attorney and court costs for a recognition of the adoption. The estimate does not include post-placement supervision (when required). Applicants should note that fees vary and are subject to change.

THE WAIT

The time from completion of the homestudy and submission of the dossier to placement of the child is less than 1 year.

THE CHILDREN

Adoption Resource Center places both healthy and special-needs children, ranging in age from birth to 16 years, of all racial backgrounds. At this time, the agency is not accepting sex specifications for children up to the age of 6 years. Countries of origin include U.S., Columbia, Peru, Paraguay, El Salvador, Guatemala, Chile, Honduras, Costa Rica, Mexico, and Bolivia.

THE REQUIREMENTS

Age: Applicants must be at least 21 and no more than 69. Specific requirements vary depending on the requirements of the source or the cooperating agency.
Health: Applicants should be in reasonably good health. Applicants with health problems or handicaps are given individual consideration.
Religion: No requirement.
Financial status: No requirement.
Marital status: No requirement.
Family size: No requirement.
Racial, ethnic or cultural origin: No requirement.

THE PROCEDURE

Participation in the adoption program of the Adoption Resource Center entails the following basic steps:
Inquiry (extensive information packet)
Application
Educational sessions
Homestudy
Compliance with immigration/naturalization requirements (international adoptions only)
Referral
Placement
Post-placement supervision (required only for domestic adoptions and adoption through Chile)

ADDITIONAL PROGRAMS/SERVICES

Adoption Resource Center provides counseling services, foster care, and social work training.

BRANCH/NETWORK OFFICES

None.

LICENSE/ACCREDITATION/PROFESSIONAL AFFILIATIONS

Adoption Resource Center is licensed by the State of Missouri Department of Social Services.

BETHANY CHRISTIAN SERVICES

7750 Clayton Road
St. Louis, MO 63117
(314) 644–3535
Program director: James K. Haveman, Jr., Executive Director

THE PROGRAM

For a full description of programs and services, refer to Michigan listing:

Bethany Christian Services
901 Eastern Avenue, N.E.
Grand Rapids, MI 49503–1295
(616) 459–6273

CATHOLIC CHARITIES OF KANSAS CITY-ST. JOSEPH, INC.

1112 Broadway
Kansas City, MO 64105
(816) 221–4377
Program director: Martha Norris, DSW

THE PROGRAM

Catholic Charities is a nonprofit multi-service agency whose mission is "to witness to and carry out the social teachings of the Gospels as revealed by God and lived out in the life of his son, Jesus Christ." Placing children for adoption since before 1900, the agency provides services to residents of Missouri for Caucasian infant adoptions and services for Black and bi-racial infant adoptions through agency and regional exchange programs. The agency provides services to birthparents and places infants for adoption when birthparents elect adoptive placement as the best plan for their child. Catholic Charities places approximately 50 children annually.

THE COST

For Caucasian infant adoption, the agency's fee is $7,500 and includes all phases of the adoption process, excluding legal and court fees connected with finalization. For special needs or minority placements, the agency's fee is based on a sliding scale, ranges from $250 to $7,500, and includes all services except legal and court fees connected with finalization. Missouri subsidy is available for some special-needs infants.

THE WAIT

For Caucasian infant adoption, the time from application to placement ranges from 2 to 4 years. For special needs or minority placements, the wait ranges from 6 months to 1 year.

THE CHILDREN

Catholic Charities places primarily healthy infants (birth to 6 months) of all racial backgrounds, born in the U.S.

THE REQUIREMENTS

Age: For Caucasian infant adoption, applicants must be at least 25 and no more than 39 years of age. No requirement for special needs or minority placements.
Health: Applicants should be in good health.
Religion: Applicants must be either Catholic or Protestant and must have a pastoral reference.
Financial status: Applicants must demonstrate financial stability.

Marital status: Applicants must be married; the length of the marriage must be at least 2 years.
Family size: For Caucasian infant adoption, applicants may have no more than 1 child currently in the family. No requirement for special needs or minority placements.
Racial, ethnic or cultural origin: No requirement.

THE PROCEDURE

Participation in the adoption program of Catholic Charities entails the following basic steps:
Pre-application waiting list
Application
Orientation meeting
Homestudy
Placement
Post-placement supervision

ADDITIONAL PROGRAMS/SERVICES

Catholic Charities provides a range of community services including foster care; homemaking; emergency counseling; refugee services; farm crisis initiative; adult literacy program; assistance and parish social ministry; comprehensive mental health services; criminal and victim services; services to the elderly.

BRANCH/NETWORK OFFICES

1302 Faraon
St. Joseph, MO 64501
(816) 232–2885
123 Ming
Warrensburg, MO 64093
(816) 747–2241

LICENSE/ACCREDITATION/PROFESSIONAL AFFILIATIONS

Catholic Charities of Kansas City-St. Joseph, Inc. is licensed by the State of Missouri Department of Social Services and by the State of Kansas Department of Social and Rehabilitation Services. The agency is accredited by the Council on Accreditation of Services for Families and Children.

CATHOLIC SERVICES FOR CHILDREN AND YOUTH

4140 Lindell Boulevard
St. Louis, MO 63108
(314) 371–4980
Program director: Kathie Schiffler

THE PROGRAM

Catholic Services for Children and Youth is a nonprofit multi-service agency serving residents of the Archdiocese of St. Louis and placing approximately 45 children annually through its adoption program. The agency's mission is "to bring together Catholic family tradition and the professional skills of the human sciences in a multi-service ministry for children, youth, and their families in the Archdiocese of St. Louis." The agency provides services to birthparents and places infants for adoption when birthparents elect adoptive placement as the best plan for their child. Working cooperatively with other private and public agencies and with national and regional exchange programs, the agency facilitates the placement of special-needs children.

THE COST

The agency's fee for adoption services is based on a sliding scale according to income and ranges from $2,000 to $7,000. Services covered by the fee include all phases of the adoption process, excluding pre-adoptive foster care (which varies annually) and legal fees connected with finalization. Fees can be waived for special needs and minority adoptions.

THE WAIT

For healthy Caucasian infant adoption, the time from application to placement is approximately 6–7 years. For special-needs adoption, the time from application to placement varies depending on the current need for adoptive families and on the range of special needs the adoptive family can accept.

THE CHILDREN

Catholic Services for Children and Youth places both healthy and special-needs children, ranging in age from infancy to adolescence, of all racial backgrounds, born in the U.S.

THE REQUIREMENTS

Age: For the adoption of a first child, applicants must be under the age of 35 at the time of application. For a second child, applicants must be under the age of 38 at the time of application. The age requirement is flexible for special needs and minority adoptions.

Health: Applicants must be in good health with no life threatening illnesses.

Religion: One spouse must be a practicing Catholic and registered in a parish. The couple must have a valid Catholic marriage certificate and must be committed to religious practice. This requirement is waived for couples adopting special-needs children as well as for those adopting children of a minority race.

Financial status: Applicants must have adequate income to provide for the needs of the child with a reasonable degree of security.

Marital status: Applicants must be married.

Family size: Applicants may have no more than 1 child currently in the family for infant adoption. The requirement is flexible for special-needs adoption and for the adoption of minority race children.

Racial, ethnic or cultural origin: Preference for placing children in families of similar origins.

THE PROCEDURE

Participation in the adoption program of Catholic Services for Children and Youth entails the following basic steps:
Registration
Homestudy
Placement
Post-placement supervision

ADDITIONAL PROGRAMS/SERVICES

Catholic Services for Children and Youth provides pregnancy counseling; short term foster care; outreach counseling; residential placement; independent living group home; shelter for abused women.

BRANCH/NETWORK OFFICES

None.

LICENSE/ACCREDITATION/PROFESSIONAL AFFILIATIONS

Catholic Services for Children and Youth is licensed by the State of Missouri Department of Social Services and is accredited by the Council on Accreditation of Services for Families and Children. The agency is a member of Catholic Charities of Saint Louis and the United Way.

CENTRAL BAPTIST FAMILY SERVICES

7750 Clayton Road, Suite 204
St. Louis, MO 63117
(314) 644-4548
Program director: Lisa Middleman, ACSW

THE PROGRAM

Central Baptist Family Services (CBFS) is a nonprofit child welfare agency serving residents of Missouri. Although CBFS maintains a child placing license, the agency does not offer a full range of adoption services. However, the agency will provide homestudy and post-placement supervision for families pursuing independent or interagency adoption.

THE COST

The agency charges a fee of $1,000 for completion of a homestudy and $500 for post-placement supervision.

THE WAIT

Not applicable.

THE CHILDREN

Not applicable.

THE REQUIREMENTS

Age: No requirement.
Health: No requirement.
Religion: No requirement.
Financial status: No requirement.
Marital status: No requirement.
Family size: No requirement.

Racial, ethnic or cultural origin: No requirement.

THE PROCEDURE

Families pursuing independent or interagency adoption are invited to contact CBFS to arrange for homestudy and/or post-placement services.

ADDITIONAL PROGRAMS/SERVICES

CBFS provides family therapy and counseling services.

BRANCH/NETWORK OFFICES

CBFS Illinois office provides a full range of adoption services.

Central Baptist Family Services
1803 Ramada Boulevard
Collinsville, IL 62234
(618) 345–9644

LICENSE/ACCREDITATION/PROFESSIONAL AFFILIATIONS

Central Baptist Family Services is licensed by the State of Missouri Department of Social Services and is accredited by the Council on Accreditation of Services for Families and Children. The agency is a member of the Child Welfare League of America and is a United Way affiliate.

CHILD PLACEMENT SERVICES, INC.

201 W. Lexington, Suite 304
Independence, MO 64050
(816) 461–3488
Program director: Nancy P. Chapman, Executive Director

THE PROGRAM

Child Placement Services is a nonprofit agency providing services for adoptive applicants within a 120–mile radius of Kansas City and nationwide services for members of RLDS Church (Reorganized Church of the Latter Day Saints). Established 17 years ago, the agency receives support from RLDS Church but works with families and birthmothers of all religious affiliations. The agency provides extensive counseling services for birthmothers, involves birthmothers in the family selection process, and encourages on-going communication (agency-mediated) between the birthmother and the adoptive family. Child Placement Services places approximately 14 children annually.

THE COST

The agency's fee for adoption services is $6,700. Services covered by the fee include orientation, adoptive parent education, homestudy, placement, post-placement supervision, and post-legalization services. In addition, applicants should anticipate financial responsibility for legal fees connected with temporary custody hearing and finalization.

THE WAIT

Applicants should anticipate being wait-listed for approximately 6 to 8 months before initiation of the homestudy. The time from the initiation of the homestudy to the homecoming of the adoptive child averages 2 to 3 years; however, applicants should note that the time varies greatly due to the birthmother's extensive involvement in the selection process.

THE CHILDREN

Child Placement Services places primarily healthy infants of Caucasian and bi-racial backgrounds, born in the U.S.

THE REQUIREMENTS

Age: At the time of placement of a first child, applicants must be at least 22 and no more than 40 years of age. For placement of a second child, the maximum age limit is 45 years.

Health: Applicants must be in reasonably good health. Infertility documentation is required.

Religion: Applicants of all religious backgrounds are accepted. However, applicants must have reached an agreement as to the religious denomination in which the child will be raised.

Financial status: Applicants must have adequate income to provide for the needs of the family.

Marital status: Applicants must be married couples. The length of the marriage must be 2 years for a first marriage and 4 years for a second marriage.

Family size: Applicants may have no more than 1 child currently in the family.

Racial, ethnic or cultural origin: No requirement.

THE PROCEDURE

Participation in Child Placement Services' adoption program entails the following basic steps:
Pre-application (wait-listing)
Orientation meeting
Application
Homestudy (including education for adoptive parenting)
Placement (temporary custody)
Post-placement supervision
Finalization

ADDITIONAL PROGRAMS/SERVICES

Child Placement Services provides foster care services; support services, on-going educational services, and social activities for adoptive and waiting families; on-going support group for birthmothers.

BRANCH/NETWORK OFFICES

None.

LICENSE/ACCREDITATION/PROFESSIONAL AFFILIATIONS

Child Placement Services is licensed by the State of Kansas Department of Social and Rehabilitative Services and by the State of Missouri Department of Social Services.

CHRISTIAN FAMILY SERVICES, INC.

8039 Watson Road, Suite 120
Webster Groves, MO 63119
(314) 968–2216
Program director: Kent Coffel

THE PROGRAM

Christian Family Services, a nonprofit agency, was established in 1973 by members of the Churches of Christ in the St. Louis area. Their major concern was to serve the interests of children who were in need of temporary care outside their own homes. Since that time, the goals of the agency have expanded to include permanent adoptive care for children and counseling for families. The agency's mission is "to reach out to the community, bringing them the love of God in ways that touch their lives." The agency provides services to birthparents and places infants for adoption in Church of Christ families when birthparents in the agency's counseling program elect adoptive placement as the best plan for their child. Working cooperatively with the public agency, Christian Family Services also recruits families for special-needs children. Licensed in Missouri and Illinois (and making some placements in other states as well), the agency places approximately 12 children annually. In addition, the agency will provide homestudy and supervisory services for Church of Christ families pursuing independent or interagency adoption.

THE COST

The agency's fee for adoption services is 12% of the applicants' adjusted gross income, with a minimum fee of $3,000 and a maximum of $7,000. Services covered by the fee include all phases of the adoption process and services (counseling and medical) to the birthmother and child. Applicants need anticipate no additional expenses.

THE WAIT

The time from submission of an application to acceptance of the application is 5 months. The time from acceptance of the application to the homecoming of the adoptive child averages 2 years.

THE CHILDREN

Christian Family Services places both healthy and special-needs children, ranging in age from birth to 18 years, of all racial backgrounds, born in the U.S.

THE REQUIREMENTS

Age: Applicants may be no more than 45 years older than the child being considered for placement.
Health: Applicants should be in reasonably good health. Applicants with health problems or handicaps are given individual consideration. Infertility documentation is required for infant adoptions.
Religion: Applicants must be practicing members of the Churches of Christ.
Financial status: Applicants must demonstrate sufficient income to adopt and provide for an additional family member.
Marital status: For infant adoption, applicants must be married, and the length of the marriage must be at least 3 years. Single parents are considered for special-needs adoption.
Family size: For Missouri and Illinois families, applicants may have no more than 2 children currently in the family. For out-of-state families, applicants may have no more than 1 child currently in the family.

Racial, ethnic or cultural origin: Preference for placing children in families of similar origins.

THE PROCEDURE

Participation in the adoption program of Christian Family Services entails the following basic steps:
Letter of inquiry, expressing interest in adoption
Application
Submission of references and medical reports
Psychological tests
Homestudy
Meeting with agency psychologist
Placement
Post-placement supervision

ADDITIONAL PROGRAMS/SERVICES

Christian Family Services provides foster care; counseling to individuals, couples, and families; services to expectant mothers.

BRANCH/NETWORK OFFICES

None.

LICENSE/ACCREDITATION/PROFESSIONAL AFFILIATIONS

Christian Family Services, Inc. is licensed by the State of Missouri Department of Social Services and by the State of Illinois Department of Children and Family Services.

CHRISTIAN FAMILY SERVICES OF THE MIDWEST, INC.

6000 Blue Ridge Boulevard
Raytown, MO 64133
(913) 491–6751
Program director: Douglas L. Mead

THE PROGRAM

For a full description of programs and services, refer to Kansas listing:
Christian Family Services of the Midwest, Inc.
10901 Granada Lane, Suite 102
Overland Park, KS 66211
(913) 491–6751

FAMILY ADOPTION AND COUNSELING SERVICES, INC.

9378 Olive Street Road, Suite 320
St. Louis, MO 63132
(314) 567–0707
Program director: Luke W. Leonard, MSW

THE PROGRAM

Family Adoption and Counseling Services (FACS) is a not-for-profit agency serving primarily residents of Missouri (but residents of other states as well for international placements) and placing approximately 50–60 children annually. Founded in 1979 by Luke and Georgia Leonard "to serve the orphan, those in emotional crisis, and adoptive families," the agency provides domestic and international adoption services. The agency provides services to birthparents and places infants for adoption when birthparents elect adoptive placement as the best plan for their child. Working cooperatively with public agencies and with regional and national exchange programs, the agency facilitates the placement of special-needs children. Working directly with international sources and with other U.S. agencies which maintain international programs, the agency places children from Asia, India, and Latin America in American families.

THE COST

The agency's fee for domestic adoption services is about $7,000. Services covered by the fee include services to the adoptive parents (homestudy, placement, and post-placement supervision) and services to the birthparents and child (medical and legal expenses, foster care, and counseling). Applicants pursuing international adoption should anticipate possible travel and other expenses related to adopting from overseas, with total costs ranging from $10,000 to $12,000.

THE WAIT

For domestic adoptions, the time from application to placement averages 5 to 6 years. For international adoptions, the time from application to placement averages 1 to 2 years.

THE CHILDREN

FACS places both healthy and special-needs children, ranging in age from birth to 10 years, of all racial backgrounds. Countries of origin include U.S., India, and several Asian and Latin American countries.

THE REQUIREMENTS

Age: Applicants must be at least 25 and no more than 45 years of age. The requirement may vary depending on the country of origin.
Health: Applicants should be in reasonably good health. Applicants with health problems or handicaps are given individual consideration.
Religion: No requirement. The agency is ecumenically based.
Financial status: No requirement other than adequate income to support an additional family member and insurance coverage.
Marital status: For domestic infant adoption, applicants must be married couples who have been married for at least 3 years. Single applicants are accepted for some international programs.
Family size: No requirement.
Racial, ethnic or cultural origin: No requirement.

THE PROCEDURE

Participation in the adoption program of FACS entails the following basic steps:
Orientation meeting or telephone screening
Application
Individual and group counseling sessions
Homestudy

Compliance with immigration/naturalization requirements (international adoptions only)
Referral
Placement
Post-placement supervision

ADDITIONAL PROGRAMS/SERVICES

FACS provides foster care and counseling services.

BRANCH/NETWORK OFFICES

811 Cherry Street
Columbia, MO 65201
(314) 449–3231

LICENSE/ACCREDITATION/PROFESSIONAL AFFILIATIONS

Family Adoption and Counseling Services, Inc. is licensed by the State of Missouri Department of Social Services.

HEART OF AMERICA FAMILY SERVICES

3217 Broadway
Kansas City, MO 64111
(816) 753–5280
Program director: Margaret McCorkendale

THE PROGRAM

Heart of America Family Services is a nonprofit multi-service agency serving residents of Missouri and Kansas and placing between 80 and 100 children annually through its adoption program. Founded in 1880 by pioneer community leaders, the agency has evolved in response to the changing needs of the community and today provides a wide range of services to individuals and families. The agency's mission is "to strengthen the lives of families and individuals throughout the family life cycle and to foster a community environment that promotes social responsibility." Heart of America Family Services provides domestic and international adoption services. The agency provides services to birthparents and places infants for adoption when birthparents decide that the child's best interests will be met through adoptive placement. Working cooperatively with public agencies and with the Metropolitan Kansas City exchange program, the agency facilitates the placement of special-needs children. Working directly with child welfare institutions in Korea and Paraguay, the agency places both healthy and special needs foreign-born children in American families. In addition, the agency will provide homestudy and supervisory services for applicants pursuing interagency adoption (domestic or international) or independent adoption.

THE COST

The agency's fee for the homestudy is $1,200. Post-placement supervision fees range from $1,000 to $2,000. In addition, applicants pursuing international adoption can expect to pay fees to the agency in the child's country of origin, travel expenses, immigration and naturalization fees, and related costs. Applicants are responsible for legal fees connected with finalization.

The Wait

For adoption through Korea, the time from application to placement is approximately 3 to 4 years. For adoption through Paraguay, the time from application to placement is approximately 1 year.

The Children

Heart of America Family Services places both healthy and special-needs children, ranging in age from birth to 10 years, primarily of Asian and Hispanic racial backgrounds. Countries of origin include U.S., Korea, and Paraguay.

The Requirements

Age: For adoption through Korea, applicants must be at least 25 and no more than 45. For adoption through Paraguay, applicants must be at least 30 and no more than 60.

Health: Applicants should be in reasonably good health.

Religion: No requirement.

Financial status: Applicants must demonstrate financial stability.

Marital status: Applicants must be married.

Family size: Applicants may have no more than 4 children currently in the family.

Racial, ethnic or cultural origin: No requirement.

The Procedure

Participation in the adoption program of Heart of America Family Services entails the following basic steps:

Application
Group counseling sessions
Individual counseling sessions
Homestudy
Compliance with immigration/naturalization requirements
Referral
Placement
Post-placement supervision

Additional Programs/Services

Heart of America Family Services provides a wide range of services to individuals and families including individual, marital, and family counseling; stress management; substance abuse services; family violence and abuse counseling; family life education programs; employee services; older adult services; post-adoption counseling.

Branch/Network Offices

While the agency maintains 8 branch offices serving Kansas and Missouri, all adoption inquiries are processed through the midtown office in Kansas City, Missouri.

License/Accreditation/Professional Affiliations

Heart of America Family Services is licensed by the State of Missouri Department of Social Services and by the State of Kansas Department of Social and Rehabilitative Services. The agency is accredited by the Council on Accreditation of Services for Families and Children. The agency is a member of the Child Welfare League of America and the Joint Council on International Children's Services.

Highlands Child Placement Service

5506 Cambridge Avenue
Kansas City, MO 64132
(816) 924–6565
Program director: Rev. Vernon Cooper, ACSW

The Program

Highlands Child Placement Service is a nonprofit agency which was founded 21 years ago "to offer an alternative to abortion to young women pregnant out of wedlock and to place children into Christian homes across America." The agency provides services to birthparents of all racial and religious backgrounds and places infants for adoption with Assembly of God families when birthparents elect adoptive placement as the best plan for their child. Working cooperatively with other U.S. agencies which maintain international programs, Highlands facilitates the placement of foreign-born children in Assembly of God families through the provision of homestudy and supervisory services. In addition, the agency will provide homestudy and supervisory services for applicants pursuing independent adoption. Highlands directly places approximately 18–20 children annually.

The Cost

The agency's fee for adoption services is $4,000. Services covered by the fee include homestudy, placement, and post-placement supervision. Applicants pursuing international adoption should anticipate fees to the cooperating agency, possible travel and related expenses. Applicants assume responsibility for legal fees connected with finalization.

The Wait

The time from application to the homecoming of the adoptive child averages 4 years.

The Children

Highlands places primarily healthy (but also occasionally special needs) children, ranging in age from birth to 12 years, of all racial backgrounds, born in the U.S. Working cooperatively with other U.S. agencies, Highlands facilitates the placement of children from several foreign countries.

The Requirements

Age: For infant adoption, applicants must be at least 21 and no more than 40 years of age.

Health: Applicants should be in reasonably good health. Applicants with health problems or handicaps are given individual consideration.

Religion: Applicants must be practicing members of the Assemblies of God.

Financial status: Applicants are evaluated on the basis of income, indebtedness, and ability to manage income.

Marital status: Applicants must be married; the length of the marriage must be at least 3 years.

Family size: Applicants may have no more than 1 child currently in the family.

Racial, ethnic or cultural origin: Preference for placing children in families of similar origins.

THE PROCEDURE

Participation in Highlands' adoption program entails the following basic steps:
- Referral
- Application
- Individual counseling sessions
- Group counseling sessions
- Homestudy
- Placement
- Post-placement supervision
- Finalization

ADDITIONAL PROGRAMS/SERVICES

None.

BRANCH/NETWORK OFFICES

None.

LICENSE/ACCREDITATION/PROFESSIONAL AFFILIATIONS

Highlands Child Placement Service is licensed by the appropriate state departments in Arkansas, Kansas, and Missouri.

JEWISH FAMILY CHILDREN'S SERVICE

9385 Olive Boulevard
St. Louis, MO 63132
(314) 993–1000
Program director: Kathleen Doyle

THE PROGRAM

Jewish Family Children's Service is a nonprofit agency serving residents of the metropolitan St. Louis area and placing approximately 3 children annually through its adoption program. Established approximately 25 years ago, the adoption program is designed "to help Jewish couples become adoptive parents" and to assist couples in exploring their motivation for adoption and their fears, wishes, and attitudes about adoption. The agency provides services to birthparents and places both healthy and special-needs infants for adoption when birthparents elect adoptive placement as the best plan for their child. In addition, the agency will provide homestudy and supervisory services for applicants pursuing interagency adoption.

THE COST

The agency's fee for adoption services is based on a sliding scale, with a maximum fee of $9,000. Services covered by the fee include all phases of the adoption process, including legal fees connected with finalization of the adoption.

THE WAIT

The time from application to the homecoming of the adoptive child ranges from 2 to 4 years.

THE CHILDREN

Jewish Family Children's Service places both healthy and special-needs infants (2 to 5 months), of Caucasian and biracial backgrounds, born in the U.S.

THE REQUIREMENTS

Age: No requirement.
Health: Applicants with health problems or handicaps are given individual consideration. Infertility documentation is required.
Religion: Applicants must be Jewish.
Financial status: Applicants must be financially stable and must have sufficient income to provide adequately for the child.
Marital status: Applicants must be married.
Family size: Applicants may have no more than 1 child currently in the family.
Racial, ethnic or cultural origin: Preference for placing children in families of similar origins.

THE PROCEDURE

Participation in the adoption program of Jewish Family Children's Service entails the following basic steps:
- Referral
- Application
- Individual counseling sessions
- Homestudy
- Placement
- Post-placement supervision

ADDITIONAL PROGRAMS/SERVICES

Jewish Family Children's Service provides counseling services and birthparent counseling.

BRANCH/NETWORK OFFICES

None.

LICENSE/ACCREDITATION/PROFESSIONAL AFFILIATIONS

Jewish Family Children's Service is licensed by the State of Missouri Department of Social Services.

KANSAS CHILDREN'S SERVICE LEAGUE

Black Adoption Program and Services
1601 E. 18th Street, Suite 227
Kansas City, MO 64127
(816) 283–3596
Program director: Janice Greene

THE PROGRAM

For a full description of programs and services, refer to Kansas listing:

Kansas Children's Service League
Black Adoption Program and Services
710 Minnesota
Kansas City, KS 66101
(913) 621–2016

LDS SOCIAL SERVICES

517 West Walnut
Independence, MO 64050
(816) 461–5512
Program director: W. Jay Leak

THE PROGRAM

For a full description of programs and services, refer to Utah listing:

LDS Social Services
50 East North Temple Street
Salt Lake City, UT 84150

BRANCH OFFICES

LDS Social Services/Missouri:
12483 Pennridge Dr.
Bridgeton, MO 63044
(314) 344–0048

LOVE BASKET, INC.

8965 Old Lemay Ferry Road
Hillsboro, MO 63050
(314) 789–4100
Program director: Frank R. Block, ACSW, LCSW, Executive Director

THE PROGRAM

Love Basket is a nonprofit agency which places approximately 12 to 20 children annually in Christian homes. The agency provides nationwide placement services for the adoption of children from India and statewide services for residents of Missouri and Illinois for domestic adoptions and for the adoption of children from Guatemala and Colombia. Love Basket was founded in 1979 and licensed in 1982 by two missionary families who traveled extensively in India and who adopted internationally. The agency considers itself "a bridge between children needing families and Christians desiring to add to their family through adoption." Working directly with birthparents, with public agencies, and with national and regional exchange programs, the agency places both healthy and special-needs children born in the U.S. Working directly with child welfare institutions in India, the agency places children from India in American families. Working in cooperation with other U.S. agencies which maintain international programs, the agency facilitates the placement of children from Guatemala and Colombia. In addition, the agency will provide homestudy and post-placement services for Missouri and Illinois residents pursuing interagency adoption (domestic or international) or private adoption.

THE COST

For domestic adoption, the agency's fee is based on a sliding scale with a minimum fee of $3,500 and a maximum fee of $9,000. Fee consideration may be given for special needs or hard-to-place domestic children. Medical and foster care costs of the birthmother and child are billed in addition to the agency's fee. Foreign adoption costs range from $4,900 to $6,000 for an adoption from India, and from $6,000 to $9,000 for adoption from Colombia and Guatemala and include the homestudy (for Missouri and Illinois residents), stateside and overseas processing, and travel/escort expenses. Out-of-state applicants should anticipate fees to a licensed agency in their home state for the homestudy and post-placement services. For all programs, applicants are responsible for legal fees connected with finalization of the adoption.

THE WAIT

For both domestic and foreign adoption, the time from application to the homecoming of the adoptive child ranges from 1 to 3 years.

THE CHILDREN

Love Basket places both healthy and special-needs children (domestic, infants to toddlers; foreign, infants to 10 years) of all racial backgrounds. Countries of origin include U.S., India, Haiti, Guatemala, and Colombia.

THE REQUIREMENTS

Age: Married applicants must be between the ages of 23 and 50. Single applicants must be at least 26 years of age. The maximum age permissible varies depending on the age of the child.
Health: Applicants should be in reasonably good health. Infertility documentation is required for domestic adoption.
Religion: Applicants must be practicing members of a Christian church.
Financial status: No requirement.
Marital status: For domestic adoption, applicants must be married, and the length of the marriage must be at least 3 years. Single applicants are accepted for some domestic and foreign programs. Specific requirements for foreign adoption vary depending on the country.
Family size: For domestic adoptions, applicants may have no more than 1 child currently in the family. For foreign adoption, the requirement varies depending on the country.
Racial, ethnic or cultural origin: No requirement, but preference for placing children in families of similar origins.

THE PROCEDURE

Participation in the adoption program of Love Basket entails the following basic steps:
   Application
   Orientation meeting (for domestic adoption applicants)
   Homestudy
   Referral
   Compliance with immigration/naturalization requirements
      (international adoptions only)
   Placement
   Post-placement supervision
   Submission of progress reports for international adoptions
      (if required)

ADDITIONAL PROGRAMS/SERVICES

Love Basket provides birthparent counseling, birthmother support group, labor coaching, foster care.

BRANCH/NETWORK OFFICES

Love Basket is affiliated with Covenant Children in Bismarck, North Dakota.

LICENSE/ACCREDITATION/PROFESSIONAL AFFILIATIONS

Love Basket, Inc. is licensed by the State of Missouri Department of Social Services. The agency is a member of the Community Adoption Council, the Joint Council on International Children's Services, and the Evangelical Council for Financial Accountability.

LUTHERAN FAMILY AND CHILDREN'S SERVICES OF MISSOURI

4625 Lindell Boulevard, Suite 501
St. Louis, MO 63108
(314) 361–2121
Program director: Paulette Foerster

THE PROGRAM

Lutheran Family and Children's Services is a nonprofit agency providing statewide services and placing approximately 25 children annually. Founded as an orphanage in 1868, the agency's mission is "to counsel, educate and support families, children and individuals, and to be an advocate on behalf of those in need." The agency provides services to birthparents and places infants and children (healthy and special needs) for adoption when birthparents in the agency's program elect adoptive placement as the best plan for their child. Working cooperatively with U.S.-based agencies, Lutheran Family and Children's Services facilitates the placement of children from several foreign countries including Thailand, India, and Korea. In addition, the agency provides homestudy and supervisory services for applicants pursuing interagency adoption (domestic or international) or independent adoption.

THE COST

The agency's fee schedule is as follows:
Domestic Program: The fee is 12% of the applicants' combined adjusted gross income, with a minimum fee of $4,000 and a maximum fee of $6,500. Services covered by the fee include homestudy, placement, and post-placement services. Applicants reimburse the agency for legal/court costs incurred in the termination of parental rights (generally $100–$300).
Special-Needs Program: The fee is 3% of the applicants' combined adjusted gross income, not to exceed $1,500. For families applying for a second child and requiring an updated homestudy, the normal fee will be reduced by 1/3 (maximum reduction of $500). Services covered by the fee include homestudy, placement, and post-placement services. Applicants reimburse the agency for legal/court costs incurred in the termination of parental rights (generally $100–$300).
Foreign Adoption Program: The fee is 5% of the appli-

cants' combined adjusted gross income, with a minimum fee of $1,200 and a maximum fee of $2,000. For families applying for a second child and requiring an updated home study, the normal fee will be reduced to 3%. Services covered by the fee include homestudy and post-placement services. Applicants should anticipate responsibility for fees to the cooperating agency, travel or escort expenses, and related costs.

For all programs, applicants reimburse the agency for travel costs of the social worker if they live beyond a 50 mile radius of the St. Louis office. In addition, applicants are responsible for legal fees connected with finalization of the adoption (ranging from $300 to $800).

THE WAIT

For Caucasian infant adoption, the time from application to the homecoming of the adoptive child ranges from 1 to 3 years. For minority or special-needs adoptions, placement usually occurs within 1 year. For international adoption, the wait varies depending on the child's country of origin.

THE CHILDREN

Through its domestic program, Lutheran Family and Children's Services places both healthy and special-needs children, ranging in age from birth to 3 years, of all racial backgrounds. Through its international program, the agency works cooperatively with other U.S.-based agencies to facilitate the placement of children from Thailand, India, and Korea.

THE REQUIREMENTS

Age: For Caucasian infant adoption, applicants must be at least 23 and no more than 40 years of age. For special-needs adoption, the requirement is flexible. For international adoption, the requirement varies depending on the country of origin.
Health: Applicants should be in reasonably good health. Applicants with health problems or handicaps are given individual consideration. For Caucasian infant adoption, infertility documentation is required.
Religion: For Caucasian infant adoption, preference is given to Protestant Christians. No requirement for special needs or international adoption.
Financial status: Applicants must demonstrate adequate income to support an additional family member.
Marital status: For Caucasian infant adoption, applicants must be married. Single applicants are accepted for minority, special needs, and international adoptions.
Family size: For Caucasian infant adoption, applicants may have no more than 1 child currently in the family. For minority and special-needs adoptions, the requirement is assessed on an individual basis. For international adoptions, the requirement varies depending on the country of origin.
Racial, ethnic or cultural origin: No specific requirement, but preference for placing children in families of similar origins. Transracial placements are made when in the best interests of the child.

THE PROCEDURE

Participation in the adoption program of Lutheran Family and Children's Services entails the following basic steps:

Orientation meeting
Application
Homestudy
Individual counseling sessions
Group workshop
Compliance with immigration/naturalization requirements
   (international adoptions only)
Placement
Post-placement supervision

ADDITIONAL PROGRAMS/SERVICES

Lutheran Family and Children's Services provides counseling services for single expectant parents and workshops for adoptive parents.

BRANCH/NETWORK OFFICES

833 Broadway
Cape Girardeau, MO 63701
(314) 334–5866

LICENSE/ACCREDITATION/PROFESSIONAL AFFILIATIONS

Lutheran Family and Children's Services of Missouri is licensed by the State of Missouri Department of Social Services and is accredited by the Council on Accreditation of Services for Families and Children.

MISSOURI BAPTIST CHILDREN'S HOME

11300 St. Charles Rock Road
Bridgeton, MO 63044
(314) 739–6811
Program director: Raymond R. Kenison, Executive Director; Jim Furgerson, Program Administrator

THE PROGRAM

Founded in 1886 as an orphanage, Missouri Baptist Children's Home is a nonprofit multi-service child welfare organization providing statewide services and placing approximately 10 infants and 2–3 older children annually in Southern Baptist families. The agency's mission is "to provide care for children, and to provide preventive and redemptive services for children, parents, and family." The agency provides residential services for school age youth, independent living skills program (group living experience) for older teenagers, foster/adoptive program, and biological parents program. The agency places infants for adoption when birthparents in the agency's biological parents program elect adoptive placement as the best plan for their child. Through the foster/adoptive program, the agency recruits families for children of all ages, including minority children and children with special physical, emotional, and/or behavioral needs. Children are placed in the foster home in the hope that they will become legally free for adoption. In all of its programs, the agency serves "as a family finding agency for children, not a child-finding agency for families."

THE COST

The agency's fee for adoption services is based on a sliding scale and varies depending on the program. For infant adoption, the agency's fee ranges from $3,500 to $7,000. Services covered by the fee include all phases of the adoption process (excluding legal services connected with finalization of the adoption) as well as services to the birthmother and child. For adoption through the foster/adoptive program, services are provided at no cost to the foster/adoptive family.

THE WAIT

For infant adoption, the time from application to the homecoming of the adoptive child ranges from 3 to 5 years. For the foster/adoptive program, the time from application to foster placement varies depending on the number of children currently in need of foster/adoptive families.

THE CHILDREN

Missouri Baptist Children's Home places both healthy and special-needs children, ranging in age from birth to 2 years, of Caucasian, Black, and bi-racial backgrounds, born in the U.S. Through the foster/adoptive program, the agency places both healthy and special-needs children of all ages (but predominantly older children) and all racial backgrounds.

THE REQUIREMENTS

Age: For infant adoption, applicants must be at least 21 and no more than 40 years of age. The requirements for the foster/adoptive program are more flexible.
Health: Applicants with health problems or handicaps are given individual consideration.
Religion: Applicants must be practicing members of a Southern Baptist Church.
Financial status: No requirement.
Marital status: Applicants must be married, and the length of the marriage must be at least 3 years.
Family size: For infant adoption, applicants must be childless. For the foster/adoptive program, family size is evaluated on an individual basis.
Racial, ethnic or cultural origin: Preference for placing children in families of similar origins.

THE PROCEDURE

Participation in the adoption program of Missouri Baptist Children's Home entails the following basic steps:
Orientation meeting
Application
Group counseling sessions
Individual counseling sessions
Homestudy
Placement
Post-placement supervision

ADDITIONAL PROGRAMS/SERVICES

Missouri Baptist Children's Home provides residential treatment programs; biological parent (unwed mothers) program; counseling services; parent training programs; long term foster care.

BRANCH/NETWORK OFFICES

Hutchens Campus
Box 568
Mt. Vernon, MO 65712
(417) 466–7844

Byrne Campus
  Box 447
  Peculiar, MO 64078
  (816) 758–5173

LICENSE/ACCREDITATION/PROFESSIONAL AFFILIATIONS

Missouri Baptist Children's Home is licensed by the State of Missouri Department of Social Services and is accredited by the National Association of Homes for Children. The agency is affiliated with the Missouri Child Care Association.

M.O.M., INC. (MISSIONS OF MERCY)

6978 Chippewa, Suite 2
St. Louis, MO 63109
(314) 351–1541
Program director: Ms. Bernie Egly, ACSW

THE PROGRAM

MOM (Missions of Mercy) is a nonprofit agency providing nationwide placement services and placing approximately 25 children annually. The program was organized in 1983 (and licensed in 1985) by Leigh S. Yocius as a humanitarian effort in Honduras to provide homes for abandoned children. "Pledged to the welfare of children throughout the world," the agency now provides domestic and international adoption services. Working directly with birthparents, with public and private agencies, and with national and regional exchange programs, the agency places domestic infants and special-needs children. Working with various international sources, the agency places infants, older children, and special-needs children from Honduras, Mexico, and Guatemala. In addition, the agency will provide homestudy and supervisory services for applicants pursuing interagency adoption (domestic or international).

THE COST

The agency's fee schedule for adoption services is as follows:

Foreign Adoption
  Base fee (application, processing, agency fee) $7,600.00
  Out-of-state applicant fee $1,000.00

Caucasian Infant Adoption
  Base fee (application, processing, agency fee) $8,600.00
  Out-of-state applicant fee $1,000.00

Black Infant Adoption
  Base fee (application, processing, agency fee) $5,100.00

Bi-racial Infant Adoption
  Base fee (application, processing, agency fee) $5,600.00

For all programs, Missouri applicants can expect to pay the agency additional fees for personality profile, homestudy, and parenting classes ($950 for single applicants, $1,200 for couples). Out-of-state applicants arrange with an agency in their home state to provide adoption preparation, homestudy, and supervisory services. For all domestic adoptions, applicants are responsible for legal fees connected with finalization.

Additional expenses for applicants pursuing foreign adoption may include travel costs, visa and passport fees, translation fees, possible medical and foster care expenses. For foreign adoption, finalization of the adoption takes place in Honduras, and foreign legal fees connected with adoption finalization are included in the agency's base fee.

THE WAIT

For domestic Caucasian infant adoption, the time from application to the homecoming of the adoptive child averages 6 months to 1 year. For international adoptions, the wait averages 6 months to 2 years.

THE CHILDREN

MOM places both healthy and special-needs children, ranging in age from birth to 12 years, of Caucasian, Black, Hispanic, and bi-racial backgrounds. Countries of origin include Honduras, Mexico, Guatemala, and the U.S.

THE REQUIREMENTS

Age: The age requirement is assessed on a case-by-case basis.
Health: Applicants should be in reasonably good health.
Religion: No requirement.
Financial status: Applicants must have sufficient income to support an additional family member.
Marital status: The marital requirement is assessed on a case-by-case basis. Some options are available to single parents.
Family size: For domestic Caucasian infant adoption, applicants must be childless or have no more than 1 child currently in the family. For international adoption, couples with children are encouraged to apply.
Racial, ethnic or cultural origin: The requirement is assessed on a case-by-case basis.

THE PROCEDURE

Participation in MOM's adoption program entails the following basic steps:
  Application
  Homestudy
  Approval of homestudy
  Orientation meeting
  Group and individual counseling sessions
  Compliance with immigration/naturalization requirements
    (international adoptions only)
  Referral
  Placement
  Post-placement supervision

ADDITIONAL PROGRAMS/SERVICES

MOM provides counseling services for birthparents and adoptive parents, foster care services, and parenting classes.

BRANCH/NETWORK OFFICES

None.

MOM, Inc. is licensed by the State of Missouri Department of Social Services and is a member of the Christian Child Care Conference.

WORLDWIDE LOVE FOR CHILDREN, INC.

1221 East Republic Road
Springfield, MO 65807
(417) 881–1044
Program director: Barbara Monroe

THE PROGRAM

Worldwide Love For Children (WLFC) is a nonprofit agency serving residents of Missouri and placing approximately 50 children annually. Working directly with birthparents, other private and public agencies, and national and regional exchange programs, the agency places both healthy and special-needs children, born in the U.S. Working with child welfare institutions abroad and with other U.S. agencies which maintain international programs, the agency places children from various countries in Missouri families. In addition, the agency will provide homestudy and supervisory services for applicants pursuing interagency adoption (domestic or international).

THE COST

The agency's fee for adoption services varies depending on the program and ranges from $1,000 to $6,000. Services covered by the fee include all phases of the adoption process, excluding legal fees connected with the finalization of the adoption.

THE WAIT

The time from application to placement averages 1 year for infant adoptions, 18 months for foreign adoptions, and 1 year for special-needs adoptions.

THE CHILDREN

WLFC places both healthy and special-needs children, ranging in age from birth to 17 years, of all racial backgrounds. Countries of origin include Hong Kong, Israel, Brazil, Colombia, India, the Philippines, Korea, Japan, Thailand, and the U.S.

THE REQUIREMENTS

Age: Applicants must be at least 25 and no more than 45 years of age. However, the requirement may vary depending on the program and the age of the child.
Health: Applicants with health problems or handicaps are given individual consideration. Infertility documentation is required for Caucasian infant adoption.
Religion: Applicants must be practicing members of a Christian faith.
Financial status: Applicants must demonstrate financial stability.

Marital status: For Caucasian infant adoption, applicants must be married, and the length of the marriage must be at least 5 years. Some options are available to single applicants.
Family size: For Caucasian infant adoption, applicants may have no more than 1 child currently in the family. For other programs, applicants may have no more than 6 children currently in the family.
Racial, ethnic or cultural origin: Preference for placing children in families of similar origins, but will consider transracial placements if culturally and racially relevant families are not available.

THE PROCEDURE

Participation in the adoption program of WLFC entails the following basic steps:
Registration application
Group counseling sessions
Formal application
Individual counseling sessions
Homestudy
Compliance with immigration/naturalization requirements (international adoptions only)
Placement
Post-placement supervision
Post-finalization meetings

ADDITIONAL PROGRAMS/SERVICES

WLFC provides workshops, newsletter, speakers bureau, foster care, and counseling for birthparents and adoptive parents.

BRANCH/NETWORK OFFICES

None.

LICENSE/ACCREDITATION/PROFESSIONAL AFFILIATIONS

Worldwide Love For Children, Inc. is licensed by the State of Missouri Department of Social Services. The agency is a member of the Joint Council on International Children's Services, the Child Welfare League of America, Governor's Task Force on Adoption, Springfield Child Welfare League, North American Council on Adoptable Children, Child Advocacy Council of Southwest Missouri, Missouri Adoptive and Foster Parents, Adoptive Parents of Ozarks, and International Concerns Committee for Children.

Montana

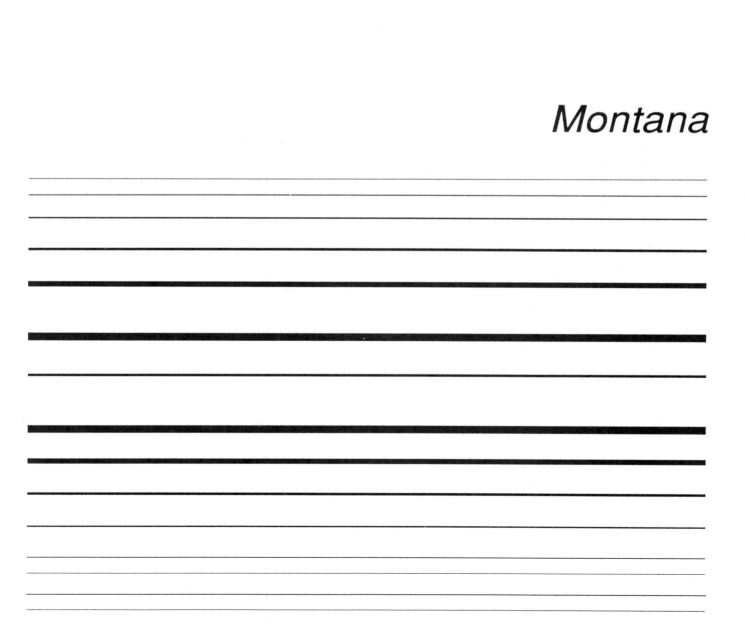

PUBLIC ADOPTION PROGRAM/ COMMUNITY RESOURCES

Department of Social and Rehabilitative Services
Department of Family Services
48 N. Last Chance Gulch
P.O. Box 8005
Helena, MT 59604
(406) 444-5900
Adoption specialist: Betty Bay

THE PROGRAM

Public adoption services in Montana are provided by district offices of the Department of Family Services, located throughout the state. Services provided by the public adoption program include recruitment, preparation, and supervision of families pursuing adoption of infants as well as special-needs children (older, minority, and handicapped children and sibling groups) who are in the custody of the State of Montana.

STATE EXCHANGE

None.

STATE ADOPTION REUNION REGISTRY

None.

STATE SUBSIDY

For information contact the Department of Family Services (above).

NACAC REPRESENTATIVE

Mel and Lois Jones
1408 West Third
Anaconda, MT 59711
(406) 563-5077

GENERAL ADOPTION RESOURCES

Families for Adoptable Children
Wilma and Bill McDonald
1251 W. Platinum
Butte, MT 59701
(406) 782-3090

Citizens Concerned about Adoption
Pam Moritz
1 S. Montana
Conrad, MT 59425
(406) 278-5445

Foster/Adoptive Circle Encouraging Teamwork (FACET)
Kari Bloom
1209 10th Ave., NW
Great Falls, MT 59404
(406) 727-5497

Together Let's Care
Mark and Judy Mozer
1804 Dry Gulch
Helena, MT 59601
(406) 442-9446

Billings Adoptive Parent Group
Bonnie and Allen Teda
3126 Turnberry Circle
Billings, MT 59101
(406) 256-5592

Havre Adoptive Parent Group
Donna Hilliard
425 1st Ave.
Havre, MT 59501
(406) 265-9009

Bozeman Adoptive Parent Group
Ed Newman
20 E. Olive 1-D
Bozeman, MT 59715
(406) 587-1894

The Greater Billings Adoptive Parent Support Group
Norma Johnson
715 Wyoming
Laurel, MT 59044
(406) 628-4284 or (406) 656-5692

Rod and Ada Baker
3907 Columbia Falls Stage
Columbia Falls, MT 59912
(406) 892-2890

Bruce and Susan Sharbono
1212 N. River Ave.
Glendive, MT 59330
(406) 365-8790

SPECIAL-NEEDS ADOPTION RESOURCES

Dr. Paul Crellin
The Children's Clinic, PC
Child Study Center
P.O. Box 2000
Billings, MT 59103
(406) 252-6601

OUT-OF-STATE AGENCIES

SEE APPENDIX A

Agencies Providing Nationwide Services

LDS SOCIAL SERVICES

2001 Eleventh Avenue
Helena, MT 59601
(406) 443-1660
Program director: D. Mark Ricks

THE PROGRAM

For a full description of programs and services, refer to Utah listing:

LDS Social Services
50 East North Temple Street
Salt Lake City, UT 84150

LUTHERAN SOCIAL SERVICES OF MONTANA

501 Central Plaza
P.O. Box 1345
Great Falls, MT 59403
(406) 761–4341
Program director: Kenneth Gjerde

THE PROGRAM

Lutheran Social Services of Montana (LSS/MT) is a private, non profit social service agency owned and operated by the Lutheran churches in Montana and serving people in the state of Montana without regard to race, religion, or country of origin. LSS/MT was founded in 1954 by the Lutheran congregations in Montana to provide child welfare services consisting of adoption, pregnancy counseling, and infant foster care. Since that time, the agency has expanded to provide a wide range of counseling and support services, striving "to combine Christian love with service and to enable individuals, couples and families to live more abundant lives." LSS/MT places approximately 30 children annually.

THE COST

The agency's fee for adoption services is based on a sliding scale and ranges from $2500 to $6000. In addition, prospective adoptive parents are asked to contribute $900 to the birthparents' fund. (This fund provides some financial assistance for medical expenses to relinquishing birthparents who do not have insurance or Medicaid coverage.) The agency's fee includes all adoption preparation work and post-placement services up to the time of finalization of the adoption which occurs about 6 months after placement. In addition, prospective adoptive parents should anticipate financial responsibility for legal fees connected with finalization of the adoption, legal fees in the event that the placement is contested, and medical expenses of the child during the 6 months between placement and finalization.

THE WAIT

The time from registration for adoptive study to the placement of the adoptive child is approximately 2 years.

THE CHILDREN

LSS/MT places primarily healthy infants born in the U.S. Most children placed by the agency are Caucasian; some are bi-racial (Native American, Hispanic, Black).

THE REQUIREMENTS

Age: Applicants may be no more than 40 years of age.
Health: Infertility documentation is required. Applicants with health problems or handicaps are given individual consideration.
Religion: Applicants must have an active affiliation with a Christian congregation which subscribes to one of the three ancient Christian creeds (Nicean, Apostles or Athanasian).
Financial status: Applicants must demonstrate financial stability.
Marital status: Applicants must be married and must have been married for at least 3 years.
Family size: Applicants may have no more than 1 child currently in the family.
Racial, ethnic or cultural origin: No requirement.

THE PROCEDURE

Participation in LSS/MT's adoption program entails the following basic steps:
- Orientation meeting
- Application
- Submission of autobiographical materials prepared by applicants
- Submission of medical reports on couple and child, if any, currently in the home
- Submission of 4 letters of reference (including one from the applicants' pastor or minister)
- Homestudy
- Individual counseling sessions
- Group counseling sessions
- Placement
- Post-placement supervision

ADDITIONAL PROGRAMS/SERVICES

In addition to its adoption program, the agency provides a wide range of services including counseling (individual marital, family, infertility, and unplanned pregnancy counseling), an unaccompanied refugee minors program, chaplaincy, educational workshops and seminars, and consultation services.

BRANCH/NETWORK OFFICES

100 24th Street West, Suite C
Billings, MT 59102
(406) 652–1310
Sargent & Riverview Ave.
Box 850
Glendive, MT 59330
(406) 365–8486
202 Brooks
Missoula, MT 59801
(406) 549–0147

LICENSE/ACCREDITATION/PROFESSIONAL AFFILIATIONS

Lutheran Social Services of Montana is licensed by the State of Montana Department of Family Services. The agency is a member of The Evangelical Lutheran Church of America and The Lutheran Church, Missouri Synod.

MONTANA CHILDREN'S HOME/ SHODAIR CHILDREN'S SPECIALTY SERVICES

Box 5539
840 Helena Avenue
Helena, MT 59604
(406) 442–1980
Program director: Mrs. Rebecca "Becci" M. Jones

THE PROGRAM

Montana Children's Home is a non-profit agency serving residents of the state of Montana and placing approximately 12 children annually. Since 1897, the agency has provided adoption and foster care services to Montana families.The agency provides services to birthparents and places infants for adoption when birthparents in the agency's counseling program elect adoptive placement as the best plan for their child. The agency also occasionally places older children. In all its programs, the agency's mission is "to help individuals and families develop into healthy entities through optional counseling and services."

THE COST

The agency's fee for adoption services is $2,000. Services covered by the fee include pre-adoption counseling, homestudy, anticipatory placement counseling, post-placement counseling and services. In addition, applicants may be requested to assist with medical expenses incurred in behalf of the birthmother.

THE WAIT

The time from application for acceptance into the program to the homecoming of the adoptive child ranges from 4 months to 2 years.

THE CHILDREN

Montana Children's Home places primarily healthy Caucasian infants but also occasionally special-needs, older, and minority children as well.

THE REQUIREMENTS

Age: Applicants must be at least 20 years of age and no more than 40 years older than the child being considered for placement. The requirement may vary depending on the specific circumstances of the case.

Health: Applicants must be in reasonably good health (doctor's recommendation is required). Applicants with health problems or handicaps are given individual consideration. Infertility documentation is required.

Religion: No requirement.

Financial status: No requirement other than the ability to support an additional family member.

Marital status: Applicants must be married couples, and the length of the marriage must be at least 3 years.

Family size: For infant adoption, applicants may have no more than 1 child currently in the family.

Racial, ethnic or cultural origin: No requirement, but varies depending on the specific circumstances of the case.

THE PROCEDURE

Participation in Montana Children's Home's adoption program entails the following basic steps:

Orientation
Application
Individual counseling sessions
Homestudy
References
Placement
Post-placement supervision

ADDITIONAL PROGRAMS/SERVICES

Montana Children's Home provides services to birthparents and counseling services to individuals and families.

BRANCH/NETWORK OFFICES

None

LICENSE/ACCREDITATION/PROFESSIONAL AFFILIATIONS

Montana Children's Home/Shodair Children's Specialty Services is licensed by the State of Montana Department of Family Services.

Nebraska

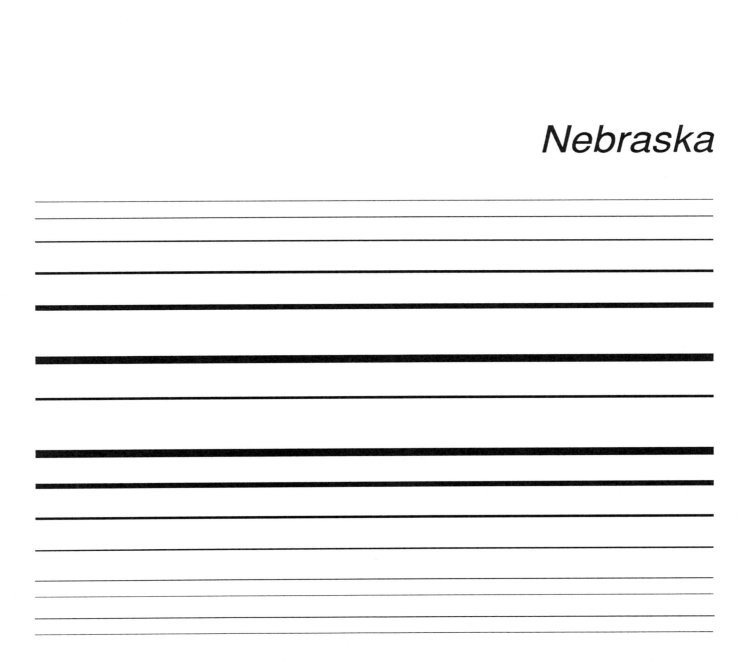

PUBLIC ADOPTION PROGRAM/ COMMUNITY RESOURCES

Department of Social Services
Adoption Program
P.O. Box 95026
Lincoln, NE 68509
(402) 471–3121
Adoption Specialist: Alreta Fritts

THE PROGRAM

Public adoption services in Nebraska are provided by the Department of Social Services through district offices located throughout the state. The Department's adoption program focuses on children who are older (8–18), need to be placed with one or more siblings, are of a minority race, or have a behavioral, emotional, or physical handicap.

STATE EXCHANGE

Nebraska Adoption Agencies Association Adoption Exchange
Department of Social Services
501 Centennial Mall South, 5th Floor
Lincoln, NE 68509
(402) 471–9331

STATE ADOPTION REUNION REGISTRY

None.

STATE SUBSIDY

For information, contact Nebraska Adoption Agencies Association Adoption Exchange (above).

NACAC REPRESENTATIVE

Kathy Moore, Executive Director
Voices for Children in Nebraska
5005 South 181 Plaza
Omaha, NE 68135
(402) 895–5971

GENERAL ADOPTION RESOURCES

Adoption support services in Nebraska are normally provided by private adoption agencies as a service to their clients. Contact private agencies in Nebraska (see Nebraska listing) for support services in your area.

SPECIAL-NEEDS ADOPTION RESOURCES

For information concerning special-needs adoption resources, contact the Department of Social Services, Adoption Program (above).

OUT-OF-STATE AGENCIES

AGENCY

Christian Family Service, Kansas

SEE APPENDIX A

Agencies Providing Nationwide Services

CATHOLIC SOCIAL SERVICE BUREAU, INC.

215 Centennial Mall South, Room 212
Lincoln, NE 68508
(402) 474–1600
Program director: Aline M. Gamache, BSW

THE PROGRAM

Catholic Social Service Bureau (CSSB) is a nonprofit multi-service agency serving residents of Lincoln and outlying communities and placing approximately 15 children annually. The agency's mission is "to strengthen family life and provide support services which enable individuals to achieve their potential and enrich their lives." CSSB provides services to birthparents and places infants for adoption when birthparents in the agency's counseling program elect adoptive placement as the best plan for their child. The agency is also actively involved in recruiting families for special-needs children.

THE COST

The agency's fee for the homestudy is $75. The placement fee is based on the adjusted gross income and ranges from $1,000 to $4,500. In addition, applicants pursuing infant adoption should anticipate financial responsibility for the medical costs of the birthmother and child. In all programs, applicants are responsible for legal fees connected with finalization of the adoption.

THE WAIT

The time from application to the homecoming of the adoptive child varies depending on the program. The wait for a healthy Caucasian infant ranges from 2 months to 2 years. The wait for minority or special-needs children ranges from 2 months to 1 year.

THE CHILDREN

CSSB places primarily infants, both healthy and special needs, of all racial backgrounds.

THE REQUIREMENTS

Age: For infant adoption, applicants must be at least 21 and no more than 40 years of age.
Health: For infant adoption, a recent medical report together with a medical diagnosis for inability to conceive is required.
Religion: No requirement, but the preference of the birthmother is honored.
Financial status: Applicants must demonstrate financial stability.
Marital status: For infant adoption, applicants must be married, and the length of the marriage must be at least 3 years.
Family size: Preference is given to childless couples for infant adoptions.
Racial, ethnic or cultural origin: No requirement.

THE PROCEDURE

Participation in CSSB's adoption program entails the following basic steps:

Letter of inquiry
Application
Homestudy (including individual counseling sessions)
Homestudy review and recommendation
Placement
Post-placement supervision
Finalization

ADDITIONAL PROGRAMS/SERVICES

CSSB provides individual, marital, and family counseling; psychiatric evaluation, diagnosis, and therapy; services to older adults; refugee resettlement services; marriage preparation course; pregnancy counseling; foster care services.

BRANCH/NETWORK OFFICES

Community Social Service
303 West 4th
Hastings, NE 68901
(402) 463–2112

LICENSE/ACCREDITATION/PROFESSIONAL AFFILIATIONS

Catholic Social Service Bureau, Inc. is licensed by the State of Nebraska Department of Social Services and is a member of the Adoption Task Force of Catholic Charities USA.

CHILD SAVING INSTITUTE

115 S. 46th Street
Omaha, NE 68132
(402) 553–6000
Program director: Donna Tubach-Davis, Executive Director; Marcia Blum, Supervisor Family Services

THE PROGRAM

Child Saving Institute (CSI) is a nonprofit agency serving residents of the state of Nebraska and placing approximately 30–35 children annually. Since 1892, Child Saving Institute has provided pregnancy counseling and adoption services. CSI places infants for adoption when birthparents in the agency's program elect adoptive placement as the best plan for their child. In addition, in conjunction with the State Department of Social Services, the agency sponsors Black Homes for Black Children, a program designed to recruit Black and interracial families for adoptive placement of Black and bi-racial children.

THE COST

The agency's fee for infant adoption services is $5,000. Services covered by the fee include all phases of the adoption process (pre-placement counseling through post-placement supervision), excluding legal fees connected with finalization of the adoption. In addition, fees help to underwrite the cost of services to birthparents (counseling, medical/hospital expenses, and foster care). Fees for Black Homes for Black Children are greatly reduced, and in some cases children are eligible for subsidy.

THE WAIT

The time from application for acceptance into the program to the homecoming of the adoptive child averages 3 to 4 years. For Black Homes for Black Children program, the wait ranges from 2 to 9 months.

THE CHILDREN

CSI places primarily healthy infants (birth to 2 years), of Caucasian, Hispanic, Asian, and Indian racial backgrounds, born in the U.S. Through Black Homes for Black Children, the agency places Black and bi-racial children, both healthy and special needs, of all ages.

THE REQUIREMENTS

Age: Applicants must be at least 21 and no more than 43 years of age, but the requirement may vary depending on the best interests of the child.
Health: Applicants must be in reasonably good health. Applicants with health problems or handicaps are given individual consideration.
Religion: No requirement, but the preference of the birthparents is honored.
Financial status: Applicants must demonstrate financial stability and must have sufficient income to support an additional family member.
Marital status: Single applicants are accepted for Black Homes for Black Children. For other programs, applicants must be married, and the length of the marriage must be at least 2 years.
Family size: No requirement.
Racial, ethnic or cultural origin: Preference for placing children in families of similar origins.

THE PROCEDURE

Participation in CSI's adoption program entails the following basic steps:
Pre-adoption interview
Preliminary waiting list
Homestudy (orientation group meeting, application, individual counseling sessions, approval)
Placement
Post-placement supervision

ADDITIONAL PROGRAMS/SERVICES

CSI provides a wide range of family support services including parent education classes (S.T.E.P.); temporary emergency shelter for children up to 12 years of age; developmental day care; short term foster care; short term family counseling; single parent support group; parent aide program (trained volunteers assisting parents in need of support); referral and support on family issues (Parent Assistance Line).

BRANCH/NETWORK OFFICES

None.

LICENSE/ACCREDITATION/PROFESSIONAL AFFILIATIONS

Child Saving Institute is licensed by the State of Nebraska Department of Social Services. All social workers have B.A.

or M.A. degrees and are supervised by a licensed social worker with an M.S.W.

HOLT INTERNATIONAL CHILDREN'S SERVICES, INC.

P.O. Box 12153
(8702 N. 30th St., Suite 6)
Omaha, NE 68112(402) 457–6323
Program director: David H. Kim, Executive Director

THE PROGRAM

Holt International Children's Services in Omaha serves residents of Nebraska, Wyoming, and South Dakota. For a full description of programs and services, refer to Oregon listing:

Holt International Children's Services, Inc.
P.O. Box 2880
1195 City View
Eugene, OR 97402
(503) 687–2202

JEWISH FAMILY SERVICE

333 South 132nd Street
Omaha, NE 68154
(402) 330–2024
Program director: Alice Weiss

THE PROGRAM

Jewish Family Service (JFS) is a nonprofit multi-service agency that serves Nebraska families and places approximately 1 child annually through its adoption program. While general programs (see Additional Programs/Services Available through Agency) are available to the community at large, the adoption program is open to Jewish couples only. JFS provides services to birthparents and places infants for adoption when birthparents elect adoptive placement as the best plan for their child. The goal of the agency's adoption program is "to place adoptable infants and children with Jewish families who can best provide the love, nurturing and guidance for the care and raising of a child."

THE COST

The agency's fee for adoption services is $4,500 and includes all phases of the adoption process (social services to adoptive parents; counseling and medical expenses for birthparents and child), excluding legal fees connected with finalization. In addition, if the actual medical costs of the birthmother and child exceed $4,000, applicants assume responsibility for these additional costs.

THE WAIT

The time from application for acceptance into the program to home- coming of the adoptive child ranges from 6 months to 4 years.

THE CHILDREN

Jewish Family Service places healthy children who range in age from birth to 13 months, primarily of Caucasian racial background, born in the U.S.

THE REQUIREMENTS

Age: Applicants must be at least 21 years old and no more than 40 years old.
Health: Applicants should be in reasonably good health, although applicants with health problems or handicaps are given individual consideration. Infertility documentation is required.
Religion: Applicants must be practicing members of Judaism.
Financial status: Applicants must demonstrate financial stability.
Marital status: Applicants must be married. The length of the marriage must be at least 2 1/2 years at the time of the application.
Family size: Applicants may have no more than 1 child currently in the family.
Racial, ethnic or cultural origin: No requirement.

THE PROCEDURE

Participation in Jewish Family Service's adoption program entails the following basic steps:
Orientation meeting
Application
Individual counseling sessions
Homestudy
Placement
Post-placement supervision

ADDITIONAL PROGRAMS/SERVICES

Jewish Family Service offers a variety of family and social programs including family, individual, and marital counseling, pregnancy counseling, family life education, financial planning and aid, social casework services, and consultation.

BRANCH/NETWORK OFFICES

None.

LICENSE/ACCREDITATION/PROFESSIONAL AFFILIATIONS

Jewish Family Service is licensed by the State of Nebraska Department of Social Services and is a member of the United Way of the Midlands and the Jewish Federation of Omaha.

LUTHERAN FAMILY SERVICES OF NEBRASKA

120 South 24th Street
Omaha, NE 68102(402) 342–7007
Program director: Ruth Rexin, Executive Director; Marti Wilson, Children's Services Program Director

THE PROGRAM

Lutheran Family Services is a nonprofit agency serving the state of Nebraska and placing between 35 and 60 children annually. The agency has been in existence since 1892 and has evolved into a multi-service agency providing a wide range of programs (counseling, partial care alcoholism treatment, domestic violence and sexual assault counseling, foster care services, pregnancy counseling services, mental health clinic services, and family life enrichment programs) in addition to its adoption programs. In all of its programs, the agency's mission is "to enable individuals, families, groups and institutions of society to experience, understand, and positively participate in God's plan for harmony, wholeness and mutual caring between all portions of God's human family." Lutheran Family Services places infants for adoption when birthparents in the agency's pregnancy counseling program decide that the best interests of the child will be served by adoptive placement. The agency also facilitates the placement of special-needs children. Lutheran Family Services will provide homestudy and supervisory services for applicants pursuing independent adoption or international adoption, subject to state approval of the integrity of the source.

THE COST

The agency's fee for adoption services varies depending on the program. The fee for the adoption of an infant is $4,700 (including social services, foster care, and medical expenses of the birthmother and child). The fee for special-needs adoptions is based on a sliding scale and ranges from $425 to $1,625. The fee for homestudy and supervisory services for private or international adoption is $1,500. (Applicants pursuing international adoption should anticipate foreign agency fees and travel expenses which vary from country to country). In addition, all prospective adoptive parents assume responsibility for legal fees connected with finalization. Services covered by the fee include all phases of the adoption process provided by Lutheran Family Services staff.

THE WAIT

The time from application for acceptance into the program to the homecoming of the adoptive child varies depending on the program. For infant adoption, if the application is accepted, the wait ranges from 9 to 18 months. For special-needs adoptions, the wait ranges from 6 months to 2 years. For a bi-racial infant adoption, the wait is 1 year. For international adoptions, the wait varies depending on the country and can range from 6 months to 2 years.

THE CHILDREN

Lutheran Family Services places both healthy and special-needs children, ranging in age from birth to 15 years, of all racial backgrounds born in the U.S. The agency will also provide homestudy and supervisory services for applicants pursuing international adoption, subject to state approval of the integrity of the source.

THE REQUIREMENTS

Age: For infant adoption, applicants must be at least 21 and no more than 45 years of age. For other programs, the requirement varies depending on the needs of the child.

Health: Applicants must be in reasonably good health. Applicants with health problems or handicaps are given individual consideration.

Religion: Applicants must be practicing members of a Christian faith.

Financial status: Applicants must demonstrate financial stability.

Marital status: Applicants may be either married or single. If married, the length of the marriage must be at least 2 years. Programs open to single applicants include special needs and international adoptions.

Family size: For Caucasian infant adoption, applicants may have no more than 1 child currently in the family. For other programs, requirement varies depending on the needs of the child.

Racial,, ethnic or, cultural origin: No requirement, but preference for placing children in families of similar origins.

THE PROCEDURE

Participation in Lutheran Family Services' adoption programs entails the following basic steps:
 Orientation meeting
 Application
 Individual counseling sessions
 Homestudy
 Group counseling sessions
 Compliance with immigration/naturalization requirements
  (foreign adoptions only)
 Placement
 Post-placement supervision

ADDITIONAL PROGRAMS/SERVICES

Lutheran Family Services provides individual, family, and group counseling; alcoholism treatment; domestic violence and sexual assault counseling and support groups; mental health clinic; foster care services; alternative family homes for unwed mothers; home-based counseling services; family life enrichment workshops.

BRANCH/NETWORK OFFICES

1912 Hancock
Bellevue, NE 68005
(402) 291–6065

4620 Randolph
Lincoln, NE 68510
(402) 489–7744

6th & Washington
Beatrice, NE 68310
(402) 223–5268

2204 14th Street
Columbus, NE 68601
(402) 564–1616

411 East 6th
McCook, NE 69001
(308) 532–0587

123 N. 4th
Norfolk, NE 68901
(402) 371–7535

302 West "B"
Ogallala, NE 69153
(308) 532–0587

1515 N. Webb Rd.
Grand Island, NE 68801
(308) 382–0476

1300 E. 4th St.
North Platte, NE 69101
(308) 532–0587

250 Main Street
Chadron, NE 69337
(308) 432–5929

205 E. 7th Street
Lexington, NE 68850
(308) 532–0587

937 Jackson Street
Sidney, NE 69162
(308) 848–2803

Route 1, Box 76
Arnold, NE 69120
(308) 848–2803

LICENSE/ACCREDITATION/PROFESSIONAL AFFILIATIONS

Lutheran Family Services of Nebraska is licensed by the State of Nebraska Department of Social Services.

NEBRASKA CHILDREN'S HOME SOCIETY

3549 Fontenelle Boulevard
Omaha, NE 68104
(402) 451–0787
Program director: Harris Van Oort, Executive Director

THE PROGRAM

Nebraska Children's Home Society (NCHS) is a nonprofit child welfare agency serving residents of the state of Nebraska and placing approximately 125 children annually. Committed to helping children and youth in need since 1893, the agency provides emergency shelter care for adolescents, long and short term foster care, services to birthparents, and adoption services. The agency places infants for adoption when birthparents in the agency's counseling program elect adoptive placement as the best plan for their child. The agency is also actively involved in recruiting families for special-needs children. In all of its programs, the agency's "first concern is always the welfare of the child and the placement of each child in the home that seems most suitable for that particular youngster."

THE COST

The agency does not charge a fee for adoption services. Adoptive parents are asked to contribute to the agency's support voluntarily and in accordance with their ability. Applicants assume responsibility for legal fees connected with finalization of the adoption.

THE WAIT

The time from application for acceptance into the program to the homecoming of the adoptive child varies greatly. The agency does not make placements on the basis of the length of time the applicants have waited but on the basis of the child's best interests. In addition, waiting time is increasingly difficult to predict because of the birthparents' involvement in the selection process. However, placement usually occurs within 2 years.

THE CHILDREN

NCHS places both healthy and special-needs children, ranging in age from infancy to adolescence, of all racial backgrounds, born in the U.S.

THE REQUIREMENTS

Age: The agency's guideline is that the age difference between either parent and the child should be no more than 40 years.

Health: Applicants with health problems or handicaps are given individual consideration. The agency believes it to be advisable for a couple to explore their infertility medically prior to exploring adoption.

Religion: Preference is given to couples who share a common faith which they regularly practice together.

Financial status: Applicants should have sufficient resources to provide adequately for the needs of the child or children.

Marital status: Applicants must be married, and the agency recommends that couples be married at least a few years before exploring adoption.

Family size: For the adoption of healthy Caucasian infants, preference is given to childless couples. For special-needs adoptions, families of all sizes may apply.

Racial,, ethnic or, cultural origin: No requirement, but preference for placing children in families of similar origins.

THE PROCEDURE

Participation in NCHS' adoption program entails the following basic steps:

Letter of inquiry and introduction
Informational meeting
Intake interview and application
Group counseling sessions
Individual counseling sessions
Adoption committee review and recommendation
Placement
Post-placement supervision

ADDITIONAL PROGRAMS/SERVICES

NCHS provides foster care services; emergency shelter care for adolescents; counseling and planning services for single pregnant women.

BRANCH/NETWORK OFFICES

All initial adoptive inquiries are handled through the Omaha office.

P.O. Box 146
Whitney, NE 69367
(308) 667–1913

1916 West "F" Street
North Platte, NE 69101
(308) 534–3250

908 N. Howard Ave., #107
Grand Island, NE 68803
(308) 381–0568

The Doctors Building
Norfolk, NE 68701
(402) 379–3378

4600 Valley Rd., #304
Lincoln, NE 68510
(402) 483–7879

LICENSE/ACCREDITATION/PROFESSIONAL AFFILIATIONS

Nebraska Children's Home Society is licensed by the State of Nebraska Department of Social Services. The agency is a member of the National Committee For Adoption.

Nevada

PUBLIC ADOPTION PROGRAM/ COMMUNITY RESOURCES

Department of Human Resources
Welfare Division
2527 North Carson Street
Carson City, NV 89710
(702) 885–3023
Adoption specialist: Rota Rosaschi

THE PROGRAM

Public adoption services in Nevada are provided by the Welfare Division of the Department of Human Resources through district offices located throughout the state. While services are provided to birthparents, children, and adoptive parents, the Division's focus is to address the needs of Nevada's waiting children.

STATE EXCHANGE

For information, contact the Welfare Division (above).

STATE ADOPTION REUNION REGISTRY

None.

STATE SUBSIDY

For information, contact the Welfare Division (above).

NACAC REPRESENTATIVE

None at this time.

GENERAL ADOPTION RESOURCES:

Members and Advocates for Minority Adoptions (MAMA)
P.O. Box 4767
Las Vegas, NV 89106
Contact: Katerina Holand, President
(702) 486–5000

SPECIAL-NEEDS ADOPTION RESOURCES

Department of Human Resources
505 E. King St., Capitol Complex
Carson City, NV 89710
Bureau of Community Health
Services
(702) 885–4885
Special Children's Clinic
(702) 789–0341 (Reno)
(702) 486–5223 (Las Vegas)
Mental Health and Mental
Retardation Div.
(702) 885–5943
Bureau of Services to the Blind
(702) 885–4444
Bureau of Vocational Rehabilitation
(702) 885–4470
Bureau of Child Care Services
(702) 885–5911
State Department of Education
Special Education
400 E. King St., Capitol Complex
Carson City, NV 89710

(702) 885–3140
1–800–992–0900, Ext. 3140
Developmental Disabilities Advocates Office
Protection and Advocacy
2105 Capurro Way, Suite B
Sparks, NV 89431
(702) 789–0233
1–800–992–5715
Nevada Specially Trained Effective Parents
3015 Heights Dr.
Reno, NV 89503
Contact: Phil or Debbie Davis
(702) 747–5110
Nevada Assn. for the Handicapped
6200 W. Oakey Blvd.
Las Vegas, NV 89101
(702) 870–7050
Northern NV Center for Independent Living
624 E. 4th
Reno, NV 89512
(702) 322–6046
Direction Service of Nevada
Project Director: Debbie Davis
(702) 747–5392
Project Assistant: Deidre Hammon
(702) 747–3395
Coalition for Handicapped Children's Education (CHANCE)
Chair Person: Dale Loftis
(702) 878–7756
Regional Vice Chair: Deidre Hammon
(702) 747–3395
Regional Vice Chair: Billy Rogerson
(702) 878–3560
Easter Seals Society
5400 Equity Ave.
Reno, NV 89502
(702) 322–6262

1455 E. Tropicana, Suite 600
Las Vegas, NV 89119
(702) 739–7771

OUT-OF-STATE AGENCIES

SEE APPENDIX A

Agencies Providing Nationwide Services

CATHOLIC COMMUNITY SERVICES OF NEVADA—SOUTH

P.O. Box 1926
Las Vegas, NV 89125
(702) 385–2662
Program director: Sr. Marilyn Ingram

The Program

Catholic Community Services of Nevada began receiving children for placement in permanent homes in 1940 and now places from 30 to 35 children annually. The agency is a nonprofit adoption agency, serving southern Nevada and providing support services to unwed mothers. The mission of Catholic Community Services is "to create a supportive community for young women experiencing a problem pregnancy" and to "provide...assistance throughout her entire pregnancy" as well as to "provide a loving permanent home for the child who has been relinquished for adoption."

The Cost

The adoption fee is based on a sliding scale from no payment to $5,000, depending on the ability of the adopting family to pay. Services covered by the fee include all phases of the adoption process; medical costs for the birthmother and baby; living expenses as needed by the mother and child prior to placement; legal costs to the agency; foster care of the baby; salaries and administrative costs. Applicants should also expect to pay legal fees connected with finalization of the adoption.

The Wait

Applicants are placed on a waiting list before beginning pre-adoptive screening. The average time on the waiting list is 4 years. After the couple's homestudy is approved, they can expect a wait of 6 months to 1 year before the child is placed in the home.

The Children

Catholic Community Services places primarily healthy infants of all racial backgrounds born in the U.S. However, the agency also occasionally places special needs children. Catholic Community Services will provide homestudy and supervisory services for applicants considering adoption of a child from a foreign source.

The Requirements

Age: Applicants must be at least 21 and no more than 40 years old.

Health: Applicants should be in reasonably good health. Those with health problems or a handicap are given individual consideration. Infertility documentation is required.

Religion: Applicants must be practicing Catholics, Jews, or mainstream Protestants.

Financial status: The requirement varies depending on the ability of the adopting family to adequately provide for the child's needs.

Marital status: Applicants must be married. The length of the marriage must be at least 3 years.

Family size: Generally, applicants may have no more than 1 child currently in the family; however, consideration is given to those families willing to accept a special needs or "hard to place" child.

Racial, ethnic or cultural origin: Preference for placing children in families of similar origins.

The Procedure

Participation in the Catholic Community Services of Nevada adoption program entails the following basic steps:
Placement on the waiting list
Application
Individual counseling sessions
Homestudy
Placement
Post-placement supervision

Additional Programs/Services

Catholic Community Services of Nevada also provides counseling for unwed mothers, residential accommodations, for unwed mothers who plan to relinquish their children for adoption, and temporary foster care for those children waiting for adoption.

Branch/Network Offices

Catholic Community Services of Nevada—North
P.O. Box 5415
Reno, NV 89513
(702) 322-7073

License/Accreditation/Professional Affiliations

Catholic Community Services of Nevada is licensed by the State of Nevada Department of Human Resources and is affiliated with Catholic Charities USA.

LDS Social Services

1906 Santa Paula Drive
Las Vegas, NV 89104
(702) 735–1072
Program director: O. Pat Barney

The Program

For a full description of programs and services, refer to Utah listing:
LDS Social Services
50 East North Temple Street
Salt Lake City, UT 84150

Branch Offices

LDS Social Services/Nevada
507 Casazza Dr., #C
Reno, NV 89502
(702) 323–7376
Director: Tom Bunch

New Hampshire

PUBLIC ADOPTION PROGRAM/ COMMUNITY RESOURCES

Department of Health and Human Services
Division for Children and Youth Services
6 Hazen Drive
Concord, NH 03301
(603) 271–4457
Adoption specialist: Glenna Law

THE PROGRAM

Public adoption services in New Hampshire are centralized, and all inquiries about adoption should be directed to the Division for Children and Youth Services, Adoption Unit. The Adoption Unit provides complete adoption services (except for international and private adoptions) to New Hampshire families. The Adoption Unit distributes a quarterly newsletter and provides training for parents.

STATE EXCHANGE

Maine/Vermont/New Hampshire Exchange. For information, contact the Division for Children and Youth Services (above).

STATE ADOPTION REUNION REGISTRY

None.

STATE SUBSIDY

Adoption Subsidy
Program Specialist: Glenna Law
6 Hazen Drive
Concord, NH 03301
(603) 271–4706

NACAC REPRESENTATIVE

Karen Needham
347 Candia Road
Chester, NH 03036
(617) 967–4648

GENERAL ADOPTION RESOURCES

Adoption support services in New Hampshire are normally provided by private adoption agencies as a service to their clients. Contact private agencies in New Hampshire (see New Hampshire listing) for information about support services in your area.

SPECIAL-NEEDS ADOPTION RESOURCES

For information, contact the Division for Children and Youth Services (above).

OUT-OF-STATE AGENCIES

AGENCY

World Adoption Services, Massachusetts
Vermont Children's Aid Society (Grafton and Sullivan Counties), Vermont

SEE APPENDIX A

Agencies Providing Nationwide Services

ADOPTIVE FAMILIES FOR CHILDREN

26 Fairview Street
Keene, NH 03431
(603) 357–4456
Program director: Ardith A. Lee, MS

THE PROGRAM

Adoptive Families For Children is a for-profit agency serving adoptive families in New Hampshire and birthparents and children in New England and placing approximately 15 to 20 children annually. Licensed by the State of New Hampshire and in operation for 4 years, the agency's mission is "to provide adoption services on a voluntary basis for children, birthparents, and adoptive families as needed and requested." The agency provides services to birthparents and places infants for adoption when birthparents elect adoptive placement as the best plan for their child. In addition, the agency will provide homestudy and supervisory services for applicants pursuing inter- agency adoption (domestic or international) or private adoption.

THE COST

The agency's fee for adoption services is $4,250. Services to adoptive parents covered by the fee include the homestudy, placement, post- placement supervision, court reports, and finalization. Fees also help to underwrite the cost of counseling services to birthparents. In addition, applicants should anticipate financial responsibility in some cases for medical expenses of the child, foster care (minimal), and occasional legal fees.

THE WAIT

For healthy Caucasian infant adoption, the time from application to placement is approximately 5 years.

THE CHILDREN

Adoptive Families For Children places primarily healthy Caucasian infants (but also some older children, special-needs children, and children of Black, Asian, and bi-racial backgrounds) born in the U.S.

THE REQUIREMENTS

Age: For healthy Caucasian infant adoption, applicants must be at least 21 and no more than 45. The requirement may vary depending on the needs of the child.
Health: Applicants should be in reasonably good health. Applicants with health problems or handicaps are given individual consideration.
Religion: No requirement.
Financial status: Applicants must have sufficient income to provide adequately for the needs of the child.
Marital status: For healthy Caucasian infant adoption, applicants must be married and the length of the marriage

must be at least 2 years. The requirement may vary depending on the needs of the child.

Family size: For healthy Caucasian infant adoption, applicants must be childless. The requirement may vary depending on the needs of the child.

Racial ethnic, or cultural origin: No requirement, but preference for placing children in families of similar origins.

THE PROCEDURE

Participation in the adoption program of Adoptive Families For Children entails the following basic steps:
Application
Homestudy (including counseling sessions)
Referral
Placement
Post-placement supervision

ADDITIONAL PROGRAMS/SERVICES

Adoptive Families For Children provides temporary foster care for infants.

BRANCH/NETWORK OFFICES

None.

LICENSE/ACCREDITATION/PROFESSIONAL AFFILIATIONS

Adoptive Families For Children is licensed by the State of New Hampshire Division for Children and Youth Services.

BETHANY CHRISTIAN SERVICES

Box 395
Hancock, NH 03449–0395
(603) 525–4923
Program director: James K. Haveman, Jr.—Executive Director

THE PROGRAM

For a full description of programs and services, refer to Michigan listing
Bethany Christian Services
901 Eastern Avenue, N.E.
Grand Rapids, MI 49503–1295
(616) 459–6273

CHILD AND FAMILY SERVICES OF NEW HAMPSHIRE

99 Hanover Street
Manchester, NH 03105
(603) 668–1920
1–800–642–6486 (in New Hampshire)
Program director: Walker T. Brown, Ph.D., ACSW

THE PROGRAM

Child and Family Services is a nonprofit child welfare agency serving residents of the state of New Hampshire and placing approximately 16 children annually. Founded in 1850, the agency provides a wide range of services to children and youth including counseling, residential care, and child advocacy programs. The agency sponsors an education and community service program aimed at increasing awareness of adoption as a positive outcome of unplanned pregnancy and provides extensive pregnancy counseling services. The agency places infants for adoption when birthmothers in the agency's program elect adoptive placement as the best plan for their children. Since most special needs placements are now supervised by the state, the agency does not study families for special-needs adoptions. However, the agency will provide homestudy and supervisory services for applicants pursuing independent adoption.

THE COST

The agency's fee for adoption services is based on a sliding scale, with an average fee of $3,000 and a maximum fee of $6,000. Services covered by the fee include all phases of the adoption process (pre-placement counseling through finalization). Fees help to underwrite the cost of services to birthparents (legal and medical expenses). In addition, applicants should anticipate a $25 waiting list registration fee.

THE WAIT

The time from wait-listing to formal application is approximately 5 years, and the time from formal application to placement is approximately 1 1/2 years.

THE CHILDREN

Child and Family Services places primarily healthy Caucasian infants, born in the U.S. In addition, the agency will provide homestudy and supervisory services for applicants pursuing independent adoption of children of any age, race, or nationality.

THE REQUIREMENTS

Age: Applicants for agency infant program must be at least 21 and no more than 40 years of age.
Health: Applicants with health problems or handicaps are given individual consideration.
Religion: No requirement.
Financial status: No requirement.
Marital status: For infant adoptions, applicants must be married couples.
Family size: For agency infant adoptions, applicants must be childless. No requirement for independent adoptions.
Racial, ethnic or cultural origin: No requirement, but preference for placing children in families of similar origins.

THE PROCEDURE

Participation in Child and Family Services' adoption program entails the following basic steps:
Registration/wait-listing
Application
Orientation meeting
Group counseling sessions
Homestudy
Referral
Placement
Post-placement supervision

ADDITIONAL PROGRAMS/SERVICES

Child and Family Services provides extensive pregnancy counseling/adoption awareness programs; foster care services; counseling for families and children; drug abuse prevention programs; homemaker program; runaway and homeless youth program; child advocacy program.

BRANCH/NETWORK OFFICES

1 Thompson St.
Concord, NH 03301
(603) 224–7479

LICENSE/ACCREDITATION/PROFESSIONAL AFFILIATIONS

Child and Family Services of New Hampshire is licensed by the State of New Hampshire Department of Health and Human Services and is accredited by the Council on Accreditation of Services for Families and Children. The agency is a member of the Child Welfare League of America, the New Hampshire Association for Mental Health, the New Hampshire Social Welfare Council, and the New Hampshire Group Home Association. The agency is affiliated with the United Way.

INTERNATIONAL ADOPTIONS, INC.

5 South State Street
Concord, NH 03301
(603) 224–5174
Program director:

THE PROGRAM

For a full description of programs and services, refer to Massachusetts listing:

International Adoptions, Inc.
282 Moody Street
Waltham, MA 02154
(617) 894–5330

LDS SOCIAL SERVICES

131 Route 101A
Amherst Plaza, #204
Amherst, NH 03031(603) 889–0148
Program director: Byron N. Ray

THE PROGRAM

For a full description of programs and services, refer to Utah listing

LDS Social Services
50 East North Temple Street
Salt Lake City, UT 84150

NEW HAMPSHIRE CATHOLIC CHARITIES, INC.

215 Myrtle Street
Manchester, NH 03104
(603) 669–3030
NH toll free (800) 562–5249
Program director: Suzanne R. Foye

THE PROGRAM

New Hampshire Catholic Charities (NHCC) is a nonprofit multi-service agency serving residents of the state of New Hampshire and placing approximately 15–25 children annually. Founded in 1945, NHCC provides services without regard to age, race, or economic status. NHCC provides services to birthparents and places infants for adoption when birthparents in the agency's counseling program decide that the best interests of the child will be served by adoptive placement.

THE COST

The agency's fee for adoption services is based on a sliding scale with a maximum fee of $4,000. Services covered by the fee include all phases of the adoption process (pre-placement counseling through finalization). In addition, fees help to underwrite the cost of services to birthparents and child (counseling, medical and legal expenses, and foster care).

THE WAIT

The time from application for acceptance into the program to the homecoming of the adoptive ranges from 3 to 4 years.

THE CHILDREN

NHCC places primarily healthy Caucasian infants (birth to 2 years), but also special-needs children, born in the U.S.

THE REQUIREMENTS

Age: No specific requirement. Each case is evaluated individually.
Health: Applicants must be in reasonably good health. Applicants with health problems or handicaps are given individual consideration. Infertility documentation is required for healthy Caucasian infant adoption.
Religion: Applicants must be practicing Catholics.
Financial status: No requirement.
Marital status: Applicants must be married couples, and the length of the marriage must be at least 3 years.
Family size: Applicants must be childless.
Racial, ethnic or cultural origin: Preference for placing children in families of similar origins.

THE PROCEDURE

Participation in NHCC's adoption program entails the following basic steps:
Orientation meeting
Application
Individual counseling sessions
Homestudy
Placement
Post-placement supervision

ADDITIONAL PROGRAMS/SERVICES

NHCC provides individual and family counseling; information and referral services; maternity services; migration and refugee services; parent education workshops; services to people with disabilities; services to the elderly; couples communications workshops.

BRANCH/NETWORK OFFICES

52 Gilbert St.
Berlin, NH 03570
(603) 752–1325

72 S. Main St.
Concord, NH 03301
(603) 228–1108

17 Gilford Ave.
Laconia, NH 03246
(603) 528–3035

215 Myrtle St.
Manchester, NH 03105
(603) 669–3030

40 Mechanic St., Rm 225
Keene, NH 03431
(603) 357–3093

265 Lake St.
Nashua, NH 03060
(603) 889–9431

Commercial Bldg., Suite 11
Lebanon, NH 03766
(603) 448–5151

16 Cottage St., Box 323
Littleton, NH 03561
(603) 444–7727

215 Main St.
Salem, NH 03079
(603) 893–1971

23 Grant St.
Rochester, NH 03867
(603) 332–7701

LICENSE/ACCREDITATION/PROFESSIONAL AFFILIATIONS

New Hampshire Catholic Charities, Inc. is licensed by the State of New Hampshire Department of Health and Human Services.

New Jersey

PUBLIC ADOPTION PROGRAM/ COMMUNITY RESOURCES

Department of Human Services
Division of Youth and Family Services, Adoption Unit
1 South Montgomery Street, CN 717
Trenton, NJ 08625
(609) 633–3991
Adoption specialist: Mary Lou Sweeney

THE PROGRAM

Public adoption services in New Jersey are provided by the Division of Youth and Family Services through regional adoption resource centers located throughout the state. The primary focus of the DYFS adoption program is to recruit and prepare families and to identify and prepare children for adoption, including healthy and special-needs children (older, minority, and handicapped children and sibling groups) who are in the custody of the Department of Human Services.

STATE EXCHANGE

New Jersey Adoption Exchange. For information, contact the Division of Youth and Family Services (609–984–8199)

STATE ADOPTION REUNION REGISTRY

For information, contact the Division of Youth and Family Services (609–292–8816)

STATE SUBSIDY

For information, contact the Division of Youth and Family Services (609–633–3991).

NACAC REPRESENTATIVE

None at this time.

GENERAL ADOPTION RESOURCES

Concerned Persons for Adoption
P.O. Box 179
Whippany, NJ 07981

Latin America Parents Association (LAPA)
P.O. Box 631
Maple Shade, NJ 08052

SPECIAL-NEEDS ADOPTION RESOURCES

SNAP of New Jersey, Inc.
Special-Needs Adoptive Parents of New Jersey
80 Dakota Trail
Browns Mills, NJ 08015
(609) 893–7875

OUT-OF-STATE AGENCIES

AGENCY

Harlem-Dowling Children's Services, New York
New Beginnings Family and Children's Services, New York
Child and Home Study Associates, Pennsylvania
The Adoption Agency, Pennsylvania

Jewish Family and Children's Services, Pennsylvania
Love the Children, Pennsylvania
Tabor Home for Children, Pennsylvania
Welcome House for Adoption Services, Pennsylvania
The Edna Gladney Center, Texas
Rainbow Christian Services, Virginia

SEE APPENDIX A

Agencies Providing Nationwide Services

ADOPTION PLACEMENT SERVICES, INC.

RD 2, 375 Fergeson Avenue
Franklinville, NJ 08322
(609) 728–8744
Program director: Lois E. Deveney-Harrop, MSW

THE PROGRAM

Founded in 1984, Adoption Placement Services is a non-profit agency serving residents of southern New Jersey and placing approximately 3 to 7 children annually. Working directly with birthparents, with other private and public agencies, and with national and regional exchange programs, the agency places both healthy and special-needs children born in the U.S. In addition, the agency will provide homestudy and supervisory services for applicants pursuing inter-agency adoption (domestic or international) or private adoption.

THE COST

The agency's fee for adoption services is based on a sliding scale (10 to 14% of the applicant's annual gross income), with a maximum fee of $4,500. Services covered by the fee include the homestudy, placement, and post-placement supervision. In addition, applicants can expect to pay a $25 application fee and legal fees connected with finalization of the adoption.

THE WAIT

The time from application for acceptance into the program to the homecoming of the adoptive child averages 3 years.

THE CHILDREN

Adoption Placement Services places both healthy and special-needs children, ranging in age from birth to 18 years, of all racial backgrounds, born in the U.S.

THE REQUIREMENTS

Age: Applicants may be no more than 40 years of age for infant adoption. The requirement may vary depending on the age of the child.
Health: Applicants should be in reasonably good health. Applicants with health problems or handicaps are given individual consideration.
Religion: No requirement, but the preference of the birthparents is honored.
Financial status: No requirement.

Marital status: Applicants must be married; the length of the marriage must be at least 3 years.

Family size: Applicants must be childless for infant adoption.

Racial, ethnic or cultural origin: No requirement.

THE PROCEDURE

Participation in the adoption program of Adoption Placement Services entails the following basic steps:
Application
Homestudy
Placement
Post-placement supervision
Post-placement counseling

ADDITIONAL PROGRAMS/SERVICES

Adoption Placement Services provides counseling and foster care services.

BRANCH/NETWORK OFFICES

None.

LICENSE/ACCREDITATION/PROFESSIONAL AFFILIATIONS

Adoption Placement Services, Inc. is licensed by the State of New Jersey Department of Human Services.

ASSOCIATED CATHOLIC CHARITIES/CATHOLIC COMMUNITY SERVICES

17 Mulberry Street
Newark, NJ 07102
(201) 596–3958
Program director: Loretta T. Alfano

THE PROGRAM

Catholic Community Services is a nonprofit agency serving residents of Essex, Hudson, Union, and Bergen Counties and placing approximately 25 to 30 children annually through its adoption program. An adoption and child caring agency of the Archdiocese of Newark since 1904, the agency's mission is "to provide the ways and means by which children will be reared with permanent stable families and will become independent men and women who have healthy self images." The agency provides services to birthparents and places both healthy and special-needs infants for adoption when birthparents elect adoptive placement as the best plan for their child. In addition, the agency will provide homestudy and supervisory services for applicants pursuing interagency adoption (domestic or international) or independent adoption.

THE COST

The agency's fee for adoption services is 12% of the applicants' combined annual gross income and includes all phases of the adoption process, excluding legal fees connected with finalization of the adoption.

THE WAIT

The time from application to placement averages 18 months.

THE CHILDREN

Catholic Community Services places both healthy and special-needs children, ranging in age from birth to 1 year, of all racial backgrounds.

THE REQUIREMENTS

Age: The requirement is evaluated on a case-by-case basis.
Health: Applicants should be in reasonably good health.
Religion: Applicants must be practicing members of an established religion.
Financial status: Applicants must demonstrate the ability to maintain and provide for family needs.
Marital status: Applicants must be married.
Family size: Applicants must be childless.
Racial, ethnic or cultural origin: The requirement is evaluated on a case-by-case basis.

THE PROCEDURE

Participation in the adoption program of Catholic Community Services entails the following basic steps:
Orientation meeting
Application
Individual counseling sessions
Homestudy
Referral
Placement
Post-placement supervision

ADDITIONAL PROGRAMS/SERVICES

Catholic Community Services provides foster care, counseling services, alternative living arrangement for birthmothers, and medical planning services for birthmothers.

BRANCH/NETWORK OFFICES

None.

LICENSE/ACCREDITATION/PROFESSIONAL AFFILIATIONS

Associated Catholic Charities/Catholic Community Services is licensed by the State of New Jersey Department of Human Services and is a member of Catholic Charities USA.

BETHANY CHRISTIAN SERVICES

475 High Mountain Road
North Haledon, NJ 07508
(201) 427–2566
Program director: James K. Haveman, Jr.—Executive Director

THE PROGRAM

For a full description of programs and services, refer to Michigan listing
Bethany Christian Services
901 Eastern Avenue, N.E.
Grand Rapids, MI 49503–1295
(616) 459–6273

BRANCH OFFICES

Bethany Christian Services/New Jersey
3142 Hiawatha
Point Pleasant, NJ 08742
(201) 899–0403

BETTER LIVING SERVICES, INC.

317 Washington Street
P.O. Box 759
Hackettstown, NJ 07840(201) 850–0947
Program director: George Van Meter

THE PROGRAM

Better Living Services, Inc. is a nonprofit social service organization that provides homestudy and supervisory services for New Jersey families pursuing adoption through an agency or source outside of the state of New Jersey. Although Better Living Services does not directly place children for adoption, the agency facilitated the placement of over 300 children in 1986. In 1988, Better Living Services plans to offer an identified adoption program to families who have identified a birthmother who is willing to surrender her child for adoption. Better Living Services also provides homestudy and supervisory services for private adoptions through the New Jersey courts.

THE COST

The agency's fee for adoption services is as follows: (1) $350 for the homestudy; (2) variable rate for supervisory services.

THE WAIT

Not applicable.

THE CHILDREN

Better Living Services, Inc. provides homestudy and supervisory services for applicants pursuing the adoption of children of any age, race, or national origin.

THE REQUIREMENTS

Age: No requirement.
Health: Applicants should be in reasonably good health.
Religion: No requirement.
Financial status: No requirement.
Marital status: No requirement.
Family size: No requirement.
Racial, ethnic or cultural origin: No requirement.

THE PROCEDURE

Applicants pursuing adoption through an agency or source outside of the state of New Jersey who are in need of homestudy and supervisory services are invited to contact the agency directly to arrange for an interview.

ADDITIONAL PROGRAMS/SERVICES

Better Living Services, Inc. provides counseling for adoptive parents and birthparents and offers seminars on the adoption process and options.

BRANCH/NETWORK OFFICES

None. However, the agency's services are available to all New Jersey residents.

LICENSE/ACCREDITATION/PROFESSIONAL AFFILIATIONS

Better Living Services, Inc. is licensed by the State of New Jersey Department of Human Services and certified through the State's Division of Youth and Family Services.

CATHOLIC CHARITIES, DIOCESE OF TRENTON

47 N. Clinton Avenue
Trenton, NJ 08607
(609) 394–5181
Program director: Faye M. Cheeseman

THE PROGRAM

Catholic Charities of the Diocese of Trenton is a nonprofit agency serving residents of Burlington, Mercer, Monmouth, and Ocean Counties and placing approximately 40 children annually through its adoption program. Maternity and adoption services have been an integral component of Catholic Charities since the early 1900s. Catholic Charities "offers to any person or persons in a crisis pregnancy a comprehensive program of both pragmatic and therapeutic value. During this process, decision making that meets not only the best interest of the unborn child, but also the nuclear family is encouraged and supported." When birthparents in the agency's program decide that the best interests of the child will be served by adoptive placement, infants are placed immediately with adoptive parents who have been studied, evaluated, and approved by the agency. In addition, the agency will provide homestudy and supervisory services for applicants pursuing interagency adoption (domestic or international) or private adoption.

THE COST

The agency's fee for adoption services is based on a sliding scale, with an average fee of $4,800. Services covered by the fee include all phases of the adoption process, excluding legal fees connected with finalization of the adoption.

THE WAIT

The time from application to the homecoming of the adoptive child ranges from 2 to 4 years.

THE CHILDREN

Catholic Charities places both healthy and special-needs infants (4 to 12 weeks old) of all racial backgrounds, born in the U.S.

THE REQUIREMENTS

Age: For healthy Caucasian infant adoption, applicants may be no more than 41 years of age.
Health: Applicants should be in reasonably good health. Applicants with health problems or handicaps are given individual consideration. Infertility documentation is required.

Religion: Applicants must be practicing members of an organized church.

Financial status: The requirement is evaluated on a case-by-case basis.

Marital status: For healthy Caucasian infant adoption, applicants must be married. Single applicants are accepted for special needs placements.

Family size: The requirement varies depending on the type of child applicants wish to adopt.

Racial, ethnic or cultural origin: Preference for placing children in families of similar origins.

THE PROCEDURE

Participation in the adoption program of Catholic Charities entails the following basic steps:

Preliminary application
Group counseling sessions
Orientation meeting
Formal application
Homestudy
Individual counseling sessions
Placement
Post-placement supervision

ADDITIONAL PROGRAMS/SERVICES

Catholic Charities provides foster care; residential and medical care for birthmothers; pre- birthing classes; individual and group therapy; open adoption; adult adoptee research program.

BRANCH/NETWORK OFFICES

Burlington County
115 W. Pearl Street
Burlington, NJ 08016
(201) 747–9660

Monmouth and Ocean Counties
145 Maple Avenue
Red Bank, NJ 07701
(609) 386–7331

LICENSE/ACCREDITATION/PROFESSIONAL AFFILIATIONS

Catholic Charities, Diocese of Trenton, is licensed by the State of New Jersey Department of Human Services and is accredited by the Council on Accreditation of Services for Families and Children. the agency is a member of the Child Welfare League of America, Adoption Resource Exchange, and Interagency Adoption Council.

CATHOLIC FAMILY AND COMMUNITY SERVICES

476 17th Avenue
Paterson, NJ 07504
(201) 523–2666
Program director: Betty S. Borresen, ACSW

THE PROGRAM

Catholic Family and Community Services is a nonprofit agency serving residents of Passaic, Morris, and Sussex Counties. The agency currently places so few infants that they have not accepted new applications for the past 4 years, and the agency does not anticipate re-opening its waiting list in the foreseeable future. However, the agency will provide homestudy and supervisory services for families pursuing international adoption, subject to state approval of the integrity of the source.

THE COST

The agency's fee schedule for homestudy and supervisory services is as follows:

Homestudy (without supervision)	$500 plus travel
Homestudy (with supervision)	$800 plus travel
Homestudy for Immigration Visa	$500 plus travel

THE WAIT

Not applicable.

THE CHILDREN

Not applicable.

THE REQUIREMENTS

The following are the agency's requirements for applicants pursuing international adoption and requesting homestudy and supervisory services.

Age: No agency requirement, but may vary depending on the child's country of origin.

Health: Applicants must be in reasonably good health.

Religion: No requirement.

Financial status: No requirement.

Marital status: No agency requirement, but may vary depending on the child's country of origin.

Family size: No requirement.

Racial, ethnic or cultural origin: No requirement.

THE PROCEDURE

Applicants pursuing international adoption through another legitimate source are invited to contact Catholic Family and Community Services to arrange for homestudy and supervisory services.

ADDITIONAL PROGRAMS/SERVICES

Catholic Family and Community Services provides a range of support services, including marital and family counseling, pre- and post- adoption counseling, and pregnancy counseling.

BRANCH/NETWORK OFFICES

None.

LICENSE/ACCREDITATION/PROFESSIONAL AFFILIATIONS

Catholic Family and Community Services is licensed by the State of New Jersey Department of Human Services.

CATHOLIC SOCIAL SERVICES

1845 Haddon Avenue
Camden, NJ 08103
(609) 756–7945
Program director: Ann Gallagher, ACSW, Adoption Supervisor

THE PROGRAM

Catholic Social Services is a nonprofit agency serving residents of the Diocese of Camden (Atlantic, Camden, Cumberland, Cape May, Gloucester, and Salem Counties) and placing approximately 23 infants annually through its adoption program. "Believing that every human life is sacred and deserving of respect, Catholic Social Services of the Diocese of Camden commits itself to a comprehensive program of services whereby it seeks to secure dignity for every human life—born or unborn." Accordingly, the agency provides services to birthparents (regardless of race, religion, ethnic group, legal residence, economic status, or marital status) and places both healthy and special-needs infants for adoption when birthparents elect adoptive placement as the best plan for their child. In addition, the agency will provide homestudy and supervisory services for applicants pursuing interagency adoption (domestic or international) or private adoption.

THE COST

The agency's fee for adoption services is based on a sliding scale and ranges from $1,000 to $8,000. Services covered by the fee include all phases of the adoption process, excluding legal fees connected with finalization of the adoption.

THE WAIT

The time from acceptance into the program to the homecoming of the adoptive child ranges from 6 months to 1 1/2 years.

THE CHILDREN

Catholic Social Services places both healthy and special-needs infants (birth to 6 months) of all racial backgrounds.

THE REQUIREMENTS

Age: Applicants must be at least 23 and no more than 37 years of age. The requirement may vary depending on the type of child being considered for placement.
Health: Applicants should be in reasonably good health. Applicants with health problems or handicaps are given individual consideration.
Religion: At least 1 spouse must be a practicing member of the Catholic Church.
Financial status: Applicants must demonstrate financial stability.
Marital status: Applicants must be married, and the length of the marriage must be at least 3 years.
Family size: The requirement varies depending on the type of child being considered for placement.
Racial, ethnic or cultural origin: No requirement.

THE PROCEDURE

Participation in the adoption program of Catholic Social Services entails the following basic steps:
　Orientation meeting
　Application
　Individual counseling sessions
　Homestudy
　Placement
　Post-placement supervision

ADDITIONAL PROGRAMS/SERVICES

Catholic Social Services provides counseling and foster care.

BRANCH/NETWORK OFFICES

25 N. Massachusetts Ave.
Atlantic City, NJ 08401
(609) 345–3448

El Centro
1035 Mechanic St.
Camden, NJ 08104
(609) 964–2133

3808 S. Shore Rd.
Rio Grande, NJ 08242
(609) 886–2662

236 E. Commerce St.
Bridgeton, NJ 08302
(609) 451–1319

De Paul Center
810 Montrose St.
Vineland, NJ 08360
(609) 691–1841

8 Greene Ave.
Woodbury, NJ 08096
(609) 845–9200

21 W. Main St.
Penns Grove, NJ 08069
(609) 299–1296

LICENSE/ACCREDITATION/PROFESSIONAL AFFILIATIONS

Catholic Social Services is licensed by the State of New Jersey Department of Human Services.

CHILDREN'S AID AND ADOPTION SOCIETY OF NEW JERSEY

360 Larch Avenue
Bogota, NJ 07603
(201) 487–2022
Program director: Grace W. Sisto, Executive Director

THE PROGRAM

Children's Aid and Adoption Society of New Jersey (CAAS), founded in 1899, is the state's largest private, nonprofit, non-sectarian child service organization. Originally founded to protect abused and homeless children, the agency has broadened over the years to provide the full range of child welfare services. The adoption program serves Bergen, Essex, Morris, Passaic, and Hudson Counties and places approximately 40 children annually. The agency's mission is "to find the home where each child is most suited, where each has the best chance of growing up happy and secure." CAAS places infants for adoption when birthparents in the agency's pregnancy counseling program decide that the best interests of the child will be served by adoptive placement. The agency also facilitates the adoption of minority and special-needs children who are in the custody of the State of New Jersey Department of Human Services. CAAS will provide homestudy and supervisory services for applicants pursuing international adoption, subject to state approval of the integrity of the source.

THE COST

The agency's fee for adoption services is based on a sliding scale. The fee is 10% of the annual gross income for applicants with an income of $35,000 and under; $5,000 for applicants with an income of $35,000 to $49,999; $6,000 for applicants with an income of $50,000 to $74,999; $7,000 for applicants with an income of $75,000 or over. Fees are adjusted or waived for families adopting hard-to-place children. Services covered by the fee include all phases of the adoption process. In addition, applicants assume responsibility for legal fees connected with finalization of the adoption.

THE WAIT

The time from application for acceptance into the program to the homecoming of the adoptive child varies depending on the type of child being considered for placement.

THE CHILDREN

Children's Aid and Adoption Society places both healthy and special-needs children, ranging in age from birth to adolescence, of all racial backgrounds, born in the U.S. The agency will provide homestudy and supervisory services for international adoptions, subject to state approval of the integrity of the source.

THE REQUIREMENTS

Age: Married applicants must be at least 18 years old. If single, applicants must be at least 25 years old.
Health: Applicants must be in reasonably good health and have normal life expectancy.
Religion: No requirement.
Financial status: Applicants must demonstrate financial stability.
Marital status: Applicants may be either married or single. If married, applicants must have been married long enough to evaluate the relationship.
Family size: The requirement varies depending on caseworker's evaluation.
Racial, ethnic or cultural origin: No requirement.

THE PROCEDURE

Participation in CAAS' adoption program entails the following basic steps:
Inquiry
Orientation meeting
Application
Homestudy
Placement
Post-placement supervision

ADDITIONAL PROGRAMS/SERVICES

CAAS provides services to birthparents, foster care services, and post-adoption counseling services.

BRANCH/NETWORK OFFICES

439 Main Street
Orange, NJ 07050
(201) 673–6454
34 Elm Street
Morristown, NJ 07960
(201) 285–0165

LICENSE/ACCREDITATION/PROFESSIONAL AFFILIATIONS

Children's Aid and Adoption Society is licensed by the State of New Jersey Department of Human Services.

CHILDREN OF THE WORLD, INC.

855 Bloomfield Avenue
Glen Ridge, NJ 07028
(201) 429–0045
Program director: Veronica Serio, M.A., Executive Director

THE PROGRAM

Children of the World is a nonprofit organization that specializes in international adoption. Founded in 1985, Children of the World works with approximately 100 applicants annually.

THE COST

Children of the World charges a flat fee of $500 that covers the homestudy. Prospective adoptive parents should anticipate a total cost ranging from $5,000 to about $10,000 or $12,000.

THE WAIT

The average time from the homestudy to homecoming of the adoptive child is 6 months to 1 year depending on the source agency.

THE CHILDREN

Children of the World works with a number of international agencies to place healthy and special-needs children who range in age from birth to 16 years. Countries of origin include India, Colombia, Guatemala, and others in Central and South America.

THE REQUIREMENTS

Age: No requirement.
Health: Applicants with health problems or handicaps are given individual consideration.
Religion: No requirement.

Financial status: Applicants must demonstrate financial stability.

Marital status: No requirement; however, married couples should be married for at least 3 years.

Family size: No requirement.

Racial, ethnic or cultural origin: No requirement.

THE PROCEDURE

Participation in Children of the World's program entails the following basic steps:

Orientation

Application

Referral to source agency

Homestudy

Compliance with immigration/naturalization requirements

Post-placement supervision

ADDITIONAL PROGRAMS/SERVICES

Children of the World also performs adoption court investigations.

BRANCH/NETWORK OFFICES

None.

LICENSE/ACCREDITATION/PROFESSIONAL AFFILIATIONS

Children of the World is licensed by the State of New Jersey Department of Human Services

CHILDREN'S HOME SOCIETY OF NEW JERSEY

929 Parkside Avenue
Trenton, NJ 08618
(609) 695–6274
Program director: Joan Rimer

THE PROGRAM

Established in 1894, children's Home Society of New Jersey is a nonprofit, non-sectarian agency serving residents of the state of New Jersey and Bucks County, Pennsylvania. Placing approximately 34 children annually, the agency's mission is "to promote stable, nurturing family life for children through the use of quality human services to families and through adoption placement."

THE COST

For Caucasian infant adoption, the agency's fee is 10% of the applicants' annual gross income, with a maximum fee of $7,000. Services covered by the fee include all phases of the adoption process excluding legal fees connected with finalization of the adoption. For "waiting child" adoptions, services are provided at no cost to the adoptive family. In some cases, subsidies are available.

THE WAIT

For Caucasian infant adoptions, the time from application to the homecoming of the adoptive child ranges up to 2 years. For "waiting child" adoptions, placement may occur at any time after approval of the homestudy, and the length of the wait depends on the family's flexibility.

THE CHILDREN

Children's Home Society of New Jersey places both healthy and special-needs children, ranging in age from birth to 18 years, of all racial backgrounds.

THE REQUIREMENTS

Age: The age requirement is evaluated on an individual basis.

Health: Applicants must be in reasonably good health. Applicants with health problems or handicaps are considered on an individual basis.

Religion: No requirement.

Financial status: No requirement.

Marital status: No requirement.

Family size: No requirement.

Racial, ethnic or cultural origin: No requirement.

THE PROCEDURE

Participation in Children's Home Society adoption program entails the following basic steps:

Orientation meeting

Application

Homestudy

Placement

Post-placement supervision

Finalization

Post-adoption services

ADDITIONAL PROGRAMS/SERVICES

Children's Home Society of New Jersey provides counseling for expectant parents, foster care for pregnant adolescents, foster care for infants and toddlers family day care, individual and family counseling, support groups, educational meetings and workshops, post-adoption services.

BRANCH/NETWORK OFFICES

Rt. 47
Westville, NJ 08093
(609) 853–6490

121 Shelley Dr., Suite 2A
Hackesttstown, NJ 07840
(201) 852–5825

LICENSE/ACCREDITATION/ PROFESSIONAL AFFILIATIONS

Children's Home Society of New Jersey is licensed by the State of New Jersey Department of Human Services and is accredited by the Council on Accreditation of Services for Families and children. The agency is a charter member of the Child Welfare League of America.

CHRISTIAN HOMES FOR CHILDREN

275 State Street
Hackensack, NJ 07601(201) 342–4235
Program director: Dr. Sharon S. Ulrich

THE PROGRAM

Christian Homes for Children is a nonprofit, multi-service agency serving the states of New Jersey and New York and placing approximately 14 children annually. Founded in 1900 to provide residential services to children of all ages, Christian Homes for Children has evolved through the years in response to the changing needs of the community. The Child Placement Program (including foster care, birthparent counseling, and adoption services) was initiated in 1982. The agency's mission is "to provide for the spiritual, emotional, social, and physical welfare of children born and unborn and their families."

THE COST

The agency's fee is based on a sliding scale and ranges from $2,000 to $6,500. For the first placement, the agency's fee is 10% of the family's gross annual income. For the second placement, the agency's fee is 8% of the family's gross annual income. Financial adjustments are made for the placement of special-needs children. Services covered by the fee include homestudy, supervision, pre- and post-adoptive group meetings, interviews, consultations, and record maintenance. In addition, prospective adoptive parents should anticipate financial responsibility for legal fees connected with finalization of the adoption.

THE WAIT

The time from application for acceptance into the program to the homecoming of the adoptive child varies depending on the type of child being considered for placement. For a healthy child, the waiting period ranges up to 3 years. For a special-needs child, the waiting period is much shorter.

THE CHILDREN

Christian Homes for Children places both healthy and special-needs children, ranging in age from infancy to adolescence, of all racial backgrounds. Children placed by the agency are born in the U.S.

THE REQUIREMENTS

Age: The age requirement varies depending on the age of the child being considered for placement. For a healthy Caucasian infant, the combined age of the couple may not exceed 80.

Health: Applicants must be in reasonably good health. For healthy Caucasian infant adoption, infertility documentation is required.

Religion: Applicants must be practicing members of an evangelical church. Applicants must be born-again Christians and active members of their church.

Financial status: Applicants must demonstrate financial stability.

Marital status: For health Caucasian infant adoption, applicants must be married and must have been married for at least 2 years. Single applicants may be considered for special-needs adoptions.

Family size: For healthy Caucasian infant adoption, applicants must be childless or must have adopted their first child through the agency. Requirement may vary for special-needs adoptions.

Racial, ethnic or cultural origin: Preference for placing children in families of similar origins.

THE PROCEDURE

Participation in Christian Homes for Children's adoption program entails the following basic steps:
Inquiry
Preliminary application and statement of faith
Pre-adoptive application group meeting
Formal application
Joint interview at the agency with applicants
Submission of references
Submission of autobiographical materials
Homestudy
Agency evaluation and recommendation
Placement
Post-placement supervision

ADDITIONAL PROGRAMS/SERVICES

Christian Homes for Children provides a range of services including counseling for situations involving children, born or unborn; foster care; distribution of material goods to children and families in need; educational services; birthparent services.

BRANCH/NETWORK OFFICES

None.

LICENSE/ACCREDITATION/PROFESSIONAL AFFILIATIONS

Christian Homes for Children is licensed by the State of New Jersey Department of Human Services and by the State of New York Department of Social Services. The agency is affiliated with 16 national and local organizations. Among those are Association for Children of New Jersey, Concerned Persons for Adoption, Evangelical Free Church of America, Interagency Adoption Council of New Jersey, and the National Committee for Adoption.

THE FAMILY AND CHILDREN'S COUNSELING AND TESTING CENTER

40–52 North Avenue
Elizabeth, NJ 07207
(201) 352–7474
Program director: Ellen M. Clark, Ph.D., Executive Director

THE PROGRAM

The Family and Children's Counseling and Testing Center (FCCTC) is a nonprofit, non-sectarian family service agency providing statewide services and placing approximately 9 American infants annually through its adoption program. Additionally, approximately 50 homestudies are completed annually, and children are placed through various other sources. Founded in 1893 and providing adoption services since 1946, the agency's goal is "to maintain a comprehensive mental health facility for Union county residents and to provide comprehensive adoption services and temporary foster care services for residents of the State of New Jersey." The agency provides extensive psychotherapy and counseling services (individual, family, marital, and parent-child counseling). the agency provides services to birthparents and places infants for adoption when birthparents elect adoptive placement as the best plan for their child. The agency maintains a small waiting list for adoptive applicants interested in this program. Working cooperatively with other licensed agencies which maintain international programs, the agency facilitates the placement of foreign-born children in New Jersey families.

THE COST

The agency's fees vary depending on the program and the services provided. For applicants pursuing international adoption, the agency's fee for the homestudy is $600. Services associated with this fee include the homestudy, immigration processing, administrative work with the cooperating agency, information and guidance throughout the process. Applicants pursuing international adoption should also anticipate fees to the cooperating agency, travel/escort fees, and related expenses payable directly to that agency.

For applicants pursuing domestic infant adoption, the agency's fee is $7,000 and includes all phases of the adoption process, excluding psychiatric/psychological assessment (if requested). For all programs, applicants are responsible for legal fees connected with finalization of the adoption.

THE WAIT

For domestic adoption, the time from application to the homecoming of the adoptive child is indefinite, depending on when and if a child becomes available. For international adoption, the wait varies depending on the cooperating agency.

THE CHILDREN

FCCTC places and facilitates the placement of both healthy and special-needs children, ranging from infancy to adolescence, of all racial backgrounds. Countries of origin include U.S., India, and various Asian, South and Central American countries.

THE REQUIREMENTS

Age: The requirement varies depending on the child's country of origin and the requirements of the cooperating agency.

Health: The requirement varies depending on the child's country of origin and the requirements of the cooperating agency.

Religion: No requirement, but may vary depending on the child's country of origin and the requirements of the cooperating agency.

Financial status: No requirement.

Marital status: The requirement varies depending on the child's country of origin and the requirements of the cooperating agency.

Family size: The requirement varies depending on the child's country of origin and the requirements of the cooperating agency.

Racial, ethnic or cultural origin: No requirement.

THE PROCEDURE

Participation in the adoption program of FCCTC entails the following basic steps:
  Application
  Orientation
  Homestudy
  Compliance with immigration/naturalization requirements
    (international adoptions only)
  Individual counseling sessions (when possible)
  Referral
  Compliance with specific requests of the country of origin
  Placement
  Post-placement supervision

ADDITIONAL PROGRAMS/SERVICES

FCCTC provides a wide range of services to children and families including individual psychotherapy; counseling relating to parent-child relationships and child behavior; family therapy; group therapy (children, adolescents and adults); couple therapy; separation/divorce mediation therapy; art therapy; psychological testing (adults and children); psychiatric consultation; specialized vocational and aptitude testing; in-service workshops for staff development and training; services to birthparents; foster care for infants.

BRANCH/NETWORK OFFICES

While all telephone inquiries are processed through the main office (201)352–7474), the agency maintains the following branch office (by appointment only).
  628 Wood Avenue
  Linden, NJ 07036

LICENSE/ACCREDITATION/PROFESSIONAL AFFILIATIONS

The Family and Children's Counseling and Testing Center is licensed by the State of New Jersey Department of Human Services.

GOLDEN CRADLE

Executive Offices
2201 Route 38, 8th Floor
Cherry Hill, NJ 08002
(609) 667–2229
Birthmother Hotline: (800) 327–2229
Program director: Marlene Piasecki, Executive Director

THE PROGRAM

Golden Cradle is a nonprofit, non-sectarian adoption and maternity services agency serving residents of New Jersey, Pennsylvania (Delaware, Bucks, Montgomery, and Philadelphia Counties), and Delaware (New Castle County) and placing approximately 85 to 120 children annually. Golden Cradle was founded in 1980 by Arty Elgart, a Philadelphia businessman who, together with his wife, sought adoption of a baby for nearly five years. Believing that there must be "a way that would fill the needs of pregnant women in crisis and make infant adoption possible for infertile, married couples, Mr. Elgart began an advertising campaign designed to present adoption as a healthy, viable option. His unique approach turned Golden Cradle into a highly successful, nationally recognized and reputable adoption agency. Golden Cradle's mission is "to provide adoption as an option to birthparents with unplanned pregnancies, infertile couples seeking to enlarge their families by raising children, and the children who are conceived from unplanned pregnancies whose birthparents wish to use adoption as a future permanent plan for the child." Golden Cradle views the child as the primary client and strives to act, serve, and advocate in the best interests of the child.

THE COST

The agency's fee for adoption services is $12,500. Applicants should note that the fee is subject to change. Services covered by the fee include services to birthparents (medical and hospital expenses, counseling, housing, and transportation), services to adoptive couples (group meetings. group seminars, and placement services), and post-legal adoption services. In addition, applicants can expect to pay fees to a local licensed agency in their area for the homestudy and post-placement supervision. Applicants are also responsible for expenses related to transportation at the time of placement and at the time of finalization as well as legal fees connected with finalization of the adoption.

THE WAIT

The time from approval of the homestudy by Golden Cradle to placement is approximately 1 year to 18 months.

THE CHILDREN

Golden Cradle places both healthy and special-needs infants (including infants born with medical problems), of Caucasian and bi-racial backgrounds, born in the U.S.

THE REQUIREMENTS

Age: Applicants must be at least 25 and no more than 40 years of age.
Health: Infertility documentation is required (even if infertility is "unexplained or inconclusive").
Religion: No requirement.
Financial status: Applicants must be able to pay the fee and the costs involved and must be able to provide adequately for the child's needs.
Marital status: Applicants must be married for at least 3 years.
Family size: Childless applicants and applicants who adopted their first child through Golden Cradle are eligible.
Racial, ethnic or cultural origin: No requirement, but preference for placing children in families of similar origins.

THE PROCEDURE

Participation in the adoption program of Golden Cradle entails the following basic steps:
Application
Orientation meeting and program meetings
Panel discussion by birthparents and adult adoptees
Presentation by an attorney on legal issues
Presentation by ob/gyn physician on relevant issues
Presentation by neo-natalogist pediatrician
Presentation by geneticist

Group counseling sessions
Homestudy (provided by cooperating licensed agency)
Placement
Post-placement supervision (provided by cooperating licensed agency)

ADDITIONAL PROGRAMS/SERVICES

Golden Cradle provides extensive services to birthparents free of charge, including food, clothing, shelter, and pre- and post-natal medical care, educational assistance, emotional support, and extensive counseling by master-level social workers. Golden Cradle sponsors prospective adoptive grandparent groups, infant C.P.R. classes, and Proud Parent Organization.

BRANCH/NETWORK OFFICES

None.

LICENSE/ACCREDITATION/PROFESSIONAL AFFILIATIONS

Golden Cradle is licensed by the State of New Jersey Department of Human Services. The agency is a member of the Child Welfare League of America, Delaware Valley Adoption Council, Interagency Adoption Council in New Jersey, and the North American Council on Adoptable Children.

HOMESTUDIES, INC.

405 Cedar Lane, Suite #3
Teaneck, NJ 07666
(201) 836–2874
Program director: Marie Shukaitis, ACSW

THE PROGRAM

Homestudies, Inc. is a nonprofit organization serving the states of New Jersey and New York which provides homestudy and post-placement supervisory services for families pursuing adoption through another domestic or foreign childplacing source. The agency also provides adoption complaint investigations and counseling services related to adoption.

THE COST

The agency's fee schedule is as follows:

Homestudy (without post-placement supervision)	$500.00
Homestudy (with post-placement supervision) plus $75 per visit	$500.00
Homestudy for Immigration Visa	$500.00
Update studies	$25.00

THE WAIT

Not applicable.

THE CHILDREN

Not applicable.

THE REQUIREMENTS

Age: Applicants must be at least 21 and no more than 55

years of age. Requirement may vary depending on individual case circumstances.

Health: Applicants must be in reasonably good health.

Religion: No requirement.

Financial status: Applicants must demonstrate financial stability.

Marital status: No requirement.

Family size: No requirement.

Racial, ethnic or cultural origin: No requirement

THE PROCEDURE

Applicants pursuing adoption through another domestic or foreign source may contact Homestudies to arrange for homestudy and/or post- placement supervision.

ADDITIONAL PROGRAMS/SERVICES

Homestudies investigates adoption complaints and provides counseling services related to adoption.

BRANCH/NETWORK OFFICES

N.Y. Office
190 Lathrop Ave.
Staten Island, NY 10314
(201) 720–1642

LICENSE/ACCREDITATION/PROFESSIONAL AFFILIATIONS

Homestudies, Inc. is licensed by the State of New Jersey Department of Human Services.

HOLT INTERNATIONAL CHILDREN'S SERVICES, INC.

2490 Pennington Road (Rt. 31)
Trenton, NJ 08638
(609) 737–7710
Program director: David H. Kim, Executive Director

THE PROGRAM

Holt International Children's Services in Trenton serves residents of New Jersey. For a full description of programs and services, refer to Oregon listing:

Holt International Children's Services, Inc.
P.O. Box 2880
1195 City View
Eugene, OR 97402
(503) 687–2202

LUTHERAN SOCIAL SERVICES OF NEW JERSEY

P.O. Box 30
Trenton, NJ 08601
(609) 393–3440
Program director: John Weinbach

THE PROGRAM

Lutheran Social Services of New Jersey is a nonprofit agency providing statewide service and placing approximately 20 children annually. Providing services on a nonsectarian basis, the mission of the agency's adoption program is "to match available children, both domestically and internationally, with families seeking to adopt." The agency has several adoption programs, including infant adoptions, special-needs adoptions, and international adoptions.

THE COST

The agency's fee is based on a sliding scale and ranges from $500 to $7,500. Services covered by the fee include services to birthparents, homestudy, child matching, assistance with preparation of documents (international adoptions), placement supervision, and assistance with legalization. In addition, prospective adoptive parents should anticipate financial responsibility for legal fees connected with finalization of the adoption and, for international adoptions, overseas agency fees and related costs.

THE WAIT

The time from application to the homecoming of the adoptive child varies depending on the program. For the adoption of a Caucasian infant, the waiting period before application is 4 to 6 years, and the time from application to homecoming is 1 to 2 years. For the adoption of minority children, the wait ranges from 4 to 9 months. For the adoption of special-needs children, the wait ranges from 4 to 12 months. For the adoption of a child from Latin America, the wait ranges from 12 to 18 months.

THE CHILDREN

Lutheran Social Services places both healthy and special-needs children, ranging in age from birth to adolescence, of all racial backgrounds. Countries of origin include U.S. and Latin America.

THE REQUIREMENTS

Age: No specific requirement. The requirement may vary depending on the program and on the age of the child being considered for placement.

Health: The requirement varies depending on the program.

Religion: No requirement.

Financial status: The requirement varies depending on the program.

Marital status: The requirement varies depending on the program.

Family size: The requirement varies depending on the program.

Racial, ethnic or cultural origin: No requirement.

THE PROCEDURE

Participation in Lutheran Social Services' adoption program entails the following basic steps:

Individual counseling sessions

Application

Homestudy

Compliance with immigration/naturalization requirements (international adoptions only)

Referral
Placement
Finalization
Naturalization (international adoptions only)
Post-adoption services (if requested)

ADDITIONAL PROGRAMS/SERVICES

Lutheran Social Services provides counseling and other services for birthparents, conducts searches if requested by adult adoptees or birthparents, and facilitates reunions if all parties agree.

BRANCH/NETWORK OFFICES

None.

LICENSE/ACCREDITATION/PROFESSIONAL AFFILIATIONS

Lutheran Social Services is licensed by the State of New Jersey Department of Human Services.

SPAULDING FOR CHILDREN

36 Prospect Street
Westfield, NJ 07090
(201) 233–2282
Program director: Phyllis Gold

THE PROGRAM

Spaulding for Children is a nonprofit agency serving families that reside in New Jersey and placing from 40 to 50 children annually. The agency was founded in 1971 by adoptive parents who believed that there was a need for a specialized adoption agency for "waiting children." The agency's purpose is "to find permanent adoptive homes" for "waiting children" in the U.S.

THE COST

Adoption services are provided by Spaulding for Children at no cost to the adoptive parents.

THE WAIT

The average time from completion of preparation for placement to the homecoming of the adoptive child is 9 months.

THE CHILDREN

Spaulding for Children places teenage children of all races (occasionally a sibling group, usually with more boys than girls); Black and bi-racial children age 7 and older; children with exceptional needs (physical, emotional, and/or educational) of all ages and racial backgrounds; pre-school Caucasian children who are either retarded or multi-handicapped. All children placed by Spaulding are born in the U.S.

THE REQUIREMENTS

Age: Applicants must be at least of legal age and, by New Jersey law, at least 10 years older than the child being considered for placement.
Health: Applicants with health problem or handicap are given individual consideration.

Religion: No requirement.
Financial status: No requirement.
Marital status: No requirement. If the applicants are married, the marriage should have had time to stabilize.
Family size: No requirement.
Racial, ethnic or cultural origin: No requirement.

THE PROCEDURE

Participation in Spaulding for Children's adoption program entails the following basic steps:
Orientation meeting
Educational adoption course
Application
Home visits
Referral
Placement
Post-placement services

ADDITIONAL PROGRAMS/SERVICES

Spaulding for Children provides post-finalization services.

BRANCH/NETWORK OFFICES

6 Kings Highway East
Haddonfield, NJ 08033
(609) 428–2667
230 Park Avenue
East Orange, NJ 07017
(201) 678–4975

LICENSE/ACCREDITATION/PROFESSIONAL AFFILIATIONS

Spaulding for Children is licensed by the State of New Jersey Department of Human Services and is a member of Family Builders, Inc.

UNITED FAMILY AND CHILDREN'S SOCIETY

305 W. 7th Street
Plainfield, NJ 07060
(201) 755–4848
Program director: Ralph R. Perrone

THE PROGRAM

United Family and Children's Society is a nonprofit agency serving residents of central New Jersey and placing approximately 12 to 15 children annually. Providing adoption services since 1942, the agency's mission is "to strengthen family life through varied counseling services and to provide foster care and adoption services to infants needing such care." The agency provides services to birthparents and places both healthy and special-needs infants for adoption when birthparents elect adoptive placement as the best plan for their child. In addition, the agency will provide homestudy and post-placement services to applicants pursuing interagency adoption (domestic or international) or independent adoption.

THE COST

The agency's fee for adoption services is based on a sliding scale with an average cost of $6,000. Services covered by the fee include services to birthparents, foster care for infants, and adoption study and supervision. Applicants are responsible for legal fees connected with finalization of the adoption.

THE WAIT

The time from application for acceptance into the program to the homecoming of the adoptive child ranges from 1 to 3 years.

THE CHILDREN

United Family and Children's Society places both healthy and special-needs infants (2 to 9 months of age), of all racial backgrounds.

THE REQUIREMENTS

Age: Applicants may be no more than 38 years of age.

Health: Applicants should be in reasonably good health. Applicants with health problems or handicaps are given individual consideration. Infertility documentation is required.

Religion: No requirement.

Financial status: No requirement other than the ability to meet the needs of an additional family member.

Marital status: For married applicants, the length of the marriage must be at least 5 years. Single applicants are considered for special needs placements.

Family size: The requirement varies depending on the needs of the child.

Racial, ethnic or cultural origin: No requirement, but preference for placing children in families of similar origins.

THE PROCEDURE

Participation in the adoption program of United Family and Children's Society entails the following basic steps:

Orientation meeting
Application
Homestudy
Placement
Post-placement supervision

ADDITIONAL PROGRAMS/SERVICES

United Family and Children's Society provides foster care, counseling, and a support program for deinstitutionalized persons.

BRANCH/NETWORK OFFICES

None.

LICENSE/ACCREDITATION/PROFESSIONAL AFFILIATIONS

United Family and Children's Society is licensed by the State of New Jersey Department of Human Services.

New Mexico

PUBLIC ADOPTION PROGRAM/ COMMUNITY RESOURCES

Human Services Department
Social Services Division, Adoption Unit
P.O. Box 2348
Santa Fe, NM 87504–2348
(505) 827–4109
1–800–432–2075 (toll-free in New Mexico)
Adoption specialist: Patricia Shannon, Adoption Manager

THE PROGRAM

Public adoption services in New Mexico are provided by the Social Services Division, Adoption Unit, through several district offices.

STATE EXCHANGE

New Mexico Adoption Exchange. For information, contact the Adoption Unit (above).

STATE ADOPTION REUNION REGISTRY

None.

STATE SUBSIDY

For information, contact the Adoption Unit (above).

NACAC REPRESENTATIVE

Larry Schreiber
P.O. Box 42
San Cristobal, NM 87564
(505) 776–8158

GENERAL ADOPTION RESOURCES

Adoptive parent support groups vary from area to area. For a current list of support groups in your area, contact the SSD Adoption Unit in your county. Adoptive Parent Support Organization
ACT (Alliance for Children Today)
    Contact: Cindy Eldred
    208 W. Ash
    Bloomfield, NM 87413
Birthparent/Adoptee Search Organization
    Operation Identity
    Contact: Sally File
    13101 Blackstone, N.E.
    Albuquerque, NM 87111
    (505) 293–3144

SPECIAL-NEEDS ADOPTION RESOURCES

PRO (Parents Reaching Out)
1–800–524–5176 (toll-free in New Mexico)

OUT-OF-STATE AGENCIES

AGENCY

Universal Family, Colorado
Adams Center, Missouri
Child Placement Services, Missouri
Methodist Home, Texas

Smithlawn Maternity Home, Texas (special-needs and minority placements

SEE APPENDIX A

Agencies Providing Nationwide Services

CATHOLIC SOCIAL SERVICES OF SANTA FE, INC.

P.O. Box 443
Santa Fe, NM 87501
(505) 982–0441
Program director: C.F. Lucero

THE PROGRAM

Catholic Social Services of Santa Fe is a nonprofit multi-service agency serving residents of New Mexico. Providing adoption services since 1958, the agency "takes pride in the tradition of high quality, professional unplanned pregnancy services which have been offered in the past and is committed to further developing and refining such services in the future." The agency provides services to birthparents and places both healthy and special-needs infants for adoption when birthparents elect adoptive placement as the best plan for their child. Working cooperatively with other U.S. agencies which maintain international programs, the agency facilitates the placement of children from various other countries in New Mexico families. In addition, the agency will provide homestudy and supervisory services for applicants pursuing interagency adoption (domestic or international).

THE COST

The agency's fee for adoption services is $5,000 and includes all phases of the adoption process, excluding legal fees connected with finalization of the adoption.

THE WAIT

No reliable estimate of the time from application to the homecoming of the adoptive child is available.

THE CHILDREN

Catholic Social Services places both healthy and special-needs infants of all racial backgrounds. Working cooperatively with other U.S. agencies, Catholic Social Services facilitates the placement of foreign-born children from various countries.

THE REQUIREMENTS

Age: The requirement is evaluated on a case-by-case basis.
Health: Applicants should be in reasonably good health.
Religion: Applicants must be practicing members of a church.
Financial status: Applicants must demonstrate financial stability.
Marital status: The requirement varies depending on the needs of the child.
Family size: The requirement varies depending on the needs of the child.
Racial, ethnic or cultural origin: No requirement.

THE PROCEDURE

Participation in the adoption program of Catholic Social Services entails the following basic steps:
Application
Individual counseling sessions
Homestudy
Placement
Post-placement supervision

ADDITIONAL PROGRAMS/SERVICES

Catholic Social Services provides a wide range of counseling services including individual, marital, and family counseling; pre-marriage counseling; divorce counseling; grief counseling; counseling for women in transition; referral services.

BRANCH/NETWORK OFFICES

Catholic Social Services maintains branch offices in Albuquerque, Clovis, Milan, and Las Cruces.

LICENSE/ACCREDITATION/PROFESSIONAL AFFILIATIONS

Catholic Social Services of Santa Fe, Inc. is licensed by the State of New Mexico Department of Human Services. The agency is a member of New Mexico Adoption Services Providers and Catholic Charities USA.

CHRISTIAN CHILD PLACEMENT SERVICES

West Star Route, Box 48
Portales, NM 88130
(505) 356–4232
Program director: Charles Anderson

THE PROGRAM

Christian Child Placement Services is a nonprofit agency serving New Mexico and western Texas and placing approximately 12–15 children annually. A division of the New Mexico Christian Children's Home, the agency has provided adoption services since 1979 and in addition offers group care, "single again" parent program, and counseling programs. The agency places infants for adoption when birthparents in the agency's pregnancy counseling program decide that the best interests of the child will be served by adoptive placement. The agency also places older and special-needs children.

THE COST

The agency's fee for adoption services is based on a sliding scale and ranges from $3,700 to $5,000. Services covered by the fee include pre- placement services, placement, and post-placement supervision as well as medical expenses for the birthmother, legal expenses involved in freeing the child for adoption, and travel expenses for social workers. In addition, applicants should anticipate financial responsibility for legal fees connected with finalization of the adoption.

THE WAIT

The time from application for acceptance into the program to the homecoming of the adoptive child ranges from 1 to 3 years.

THE CHILDREN

Christian Child Placement Services places both healthy and special-needs children, ranging in age from birth to adolescence, of Caucasian, Black, and Hispanic racial backgrounds. Children placed by the agency are born in the U.S.

THE REQUIREMENTS

Age: For infant adoption, applicants must be at least 25 and no more than 42 years of age. For older child or special-needs adoption, the requirement varies depending on the age of the child being considered for placement.
Health: Applicants must be in reasonably good health. Applicants with health problem or handicap are given individual consideration.
Religion: Applicants must be practicing members of Churches of Christ. Requirement may be waived for special-needs adoption.
Financial status: Applicants must demonstrate financial stability.
Marital status: For infant adoption, applicants must be married. Requirement may be waived for special-needs adoption.
Family size: Requirement varies depending on agency's assessment of family dynamics and preference of the birthparents.
Racial, ethnic or cultural origin: Preference for placing children in families of similar origins.

THE PROCEDURE

Participation in Christian Child Placement Service's adoption program entails the following basic steps:
Application
Orientation meeting
Group adoptive couple seminar
Homestudy
Presentation of homestudy evaluation to screening committee
Placement
Post-placement supervision

ADDITIONAL PROGRAMS/SERVICES

Christian Child Placement Service provides foster care services, counseling services, and "single again" parent program.

BRANCH/NETWORK OFFICES

1441 Mesa
Las Cruces, NM 88001
(505) 522–8103

LICENSE/ACCREDITATION/PROFESSIONAL AFFILIATIONS

Christian Child Placement Service is licensed by the State of New Mexico Department of Human Services. The agency is a charter member of the New Mexico Alliance of Adoption Service Providers and a member of the Christian Adoption Resource Exchange.

FAMILIES FOR CHILDREN—A DIVISION OF NEW MEXICO BOYS RANCH

920 Ortiz, N.E.
Albuquerque, NM 87108
(505) 266–8282
Program director: Mrs. Billye N. Coey

THE PROGRAM

Families for Children is a nonprofit agency providing statewide services and placing approximately 10–15 children annually in Christian homes. New Mexico Boys Ranch began actively working in 1977 to move toward a foster care/ adoption program and to support legislation (passed in 1981) necessary to allow private agencies to exist and function in New Mexico. Families for Children was licensed in 1982 and has been in continuous operation since, providing "a ministry of love and service through temporary or permanent Christian care for children and their families."

THE COST

The agency's fee for adoption services ranges from $3,700 to $5,500, varying in accordance with the applicants' income. For older child adoptions, fees are reduced or waived. Services covered by the fee include all phases of the adoption process (adoptive parent training through post-placement support services), excluding legal fees connected with finalization of the adoption.

THE WAIT

The time from application for acceptance into the program to the homecoming of the adoptive child ranges from 6 months to 2 years, depending on the availability of children, the motivation of the couple, and caseworker work load.

THE CHILDREN

Families for Children places both healthy and special-needs children (limited to mild needs), ranging in age from birth through adolescence, of all racial backgrounds, born in the U.S.

THE REQUIREMENTS

Age: For infant adoption, applicants must be at least 22 and no more than 45 years of age. The requirement is flexible for older child adoptions.

Health: For infant adoption, preference is given to infertile couples. Applicants must be in reasonably good health. Applicants with health problems or handicaps are given individual consideration.

Religion: Applicants must be practicing members of mainstream Protestant or Catholic Christian churches.

Financial status: Applicants must demonstrate financial stability.

Marital status: Preference is given to married couples who have been married for at least 3 years. Single parents are occasionally accepted if they have an adequate support system.

Family size: The requirement varies depending on the age of the child applicants wish to parent and the number of children available.

Racial, ethnic or cultural origin: The requirement varies depending on the needs of the prospective adoptive parents and the child. Children and parents are racially matched when possible.

THE PROCEDURE

Participation in Families for Children's adoption program entails the following basic steps:
Orientation meeting
Application
Individual counseling sessions
Homestudy
Adoptive parent training seminar (20 classroom hours)
Adoptive parent service league (support group)
Placement
Post-placement supervision

ADDITIONAL PROGRAMS/SERVICES

Families for Children provides extensive counseling and support to birthparents; training for foster parents; complete foster care program for children of all ages; extensive assistance and support to adoptive and foster parents; intermediary services in open adoptions.

BRANCH/NETWORK OFFICES

All adoption inquiries are processed through the main office in Albuquerque.

LICENSE/ACCREDITATION/PROFESSIONAL AFFILIATIONS

Families for Children is licensed by the State of New Mexico Department of Human Services. The agency is a member of the Rocky Mountain Adoption Exchange, the New Mexico Christian Child Care Association, and the New Mexico Alliance for Adoption Service Providers.

LDS SOCIAL SERVICES

3811 Atrisco N.W.
Albuquerque, NM 87120
(505) 836–5947
Program director: Charles I. Bradshaw

THE PROGRAM

For a full description of programs and services, refer to Utah listing:
LDS Social Services
50 East North Temple Street
Salt Lake City, UT 84150

BRANCH OFFICES

LDS Social Services/New Mexico
925 West L.E. Murray Thruway
Farmington, MN 87401
(505) 327–6123
Director: Steven A. Sunday

RAINBOW HOUSE/F.C.V.N.

19676 Highway 85
Belen, NM 87002
(505) 865-5550
Program director: Cheryl Markson, Executive Director

THE PROGRAM

For a full description of programs and services, refer to Colorado listing:
Friends of Children of Various Nations
600 Gilpin Street
Denver, CO 80218
(303) 321-8251

TRIAD ADOPTION SERVICES, INC.

500 Oak, N.E., Suite 111
Albuquerque, NM 87106
(505) 764-9656
Program director: Vonda C. Cheshire, President; Shirley Van Haren, Executive Director of Social Program

THE PROGRAM

Triad Adoption Services is a nonprofit organization serving the state of New Mexico. The organization was founded in 1986 by Vonda Cheshire to promote and provide for open adoption in New Mexico. The organization promotes open adoption by facilitating the exchange of non-identifying information between birthparents and adoptive parents and by facilitating the meeting of all parties involved in the adoption process, using first names only. Program operation began in January of 1987, and Triad placed 8 children as of August, 1987. In addition, Triad will provide counseling, homestudy, and supervisory services for applicants pursuing private adoption.

THE COST

The agency's fee schedule for adoption services is as follows:

Orientation/Educational Class	$ 50.00
Homestudy	$ 750.00
(If applicants have a homestudy, the agency charges $200 for review and update.)	
Placement	$6,250.00

Medical expense for the birthmother and child are covered from the placement fee up to $2,500.00. Medical expenses in excess of this amount are to be paid by applicants. In addition, applicants assume responsibility for legal fees connected with finalization of the adoption.

THE WAIT

Because birthparents are involved in the selection process, the waiting time for placement may vary considerably. 22 families approved for placement will be kept on file. The agency's goal is to achieve placement for studied families in less than 2 years.

THE CHILDREN

Triad places infants of Caucasian, Hispanic, Black, or bi-racial (Caucasian/Hispanic, Black/Hispanic, Caucasian/Black) backgrounds, born in the U.S.

THE REQUIREMENTS

Age: No requirement. Birthparents' preferences are honored.
Health: Applicants must be in reasonably good health.
Religion: No requirement. Birthparents' preferences are honored.
Financial status: No base requirement, but applicant must be financially able to provide for an additional family member.
Marital status: If married, applicants must have been married for at least 2 years. As birthparents' preferences are honored, it is unlikely that a single applicant would be selected.
Family size: No requirement. Birthparents' preferences are honored.
Racial, ethnic or cultural origin: No requirement. Birthparents' preferences are honored.

THE PROCEDURE

Participation in Triad's adoption program entails the following basic steps:
Orientation meeting
Application
Homestudy
Preparation of non-identifying file
Review of non-identifying file by birthparents of social worker's choice
Optional personal meeting between birthparents and applicants at agency office
Placement
Post-placement supervision

ADDITIONAL PROGRAMS/SERVICES

Triad will provide counseling, homestudy, intermediary, and supervisory services for applicants pursuing private adoption.

BRANCH/NETWORK OFFICES

None.

LICENSE/ACCREDITATION/PROFESSIONAL AFFILIATIONS

Triad Adoption Services, Inc. is licensed by the State of New Mexico Department of Human Services. Professional staff are all members of AACD (American Association for Counseling and Development).

New York

PUBLIC ADOPTION PROGRAM/ COMMUNITY RESOURCES

Department of Social Services
New York State Adoption Services
40 North Pearl Street
Albany, NY 12243
(518) 474–2868
1–800–342–3715 (toll-free in New York)
Adoption specialist: Peter Winkler

THE PROGRAM

Public adoption services in New York are provided by New York State Adoption Services (NYSAS) through Department of Social Services branch offices located in each county. The focus of NYSAS is to recruit and prepare families and to supervise the placement of special-needs children (older, minority, and handicapped children and sibling groups) who are in the custody of the State of New York. New York State's Waiting Children is a multi-volume photo-listing with individual descriptions of approximately 800 children who are awaiting permanent adoptive homes. It is published by the Department of Social Services and is available at public and private adoption agencies and many other locations across the state. For information about adoption in New York, contact NYSAS at:
(800) 342–3715 (from New York State)
(518) 473–1509 (from outside New York State)
Interested persons may also contact Department of Social Services' regional adoption specialists at:

New York City
Metropolitan Regional Office
80 Maiden Ln., 6th Fl.
New York, NY 10038
(212) 804–1192/1193

Albany
Eastern Regional Office
40 N. South Pearl Street
Albany, NY 12243
(518) 432–2782 or (800) 342–3715, Ext. 2–2782

Rochester
Western Regional Office
259 Monroe Avenue
Monroe Square
Rochester, NY 14609
(716) 238–8197

Buffalo
Buffalo Regional Office
125 Main Street
Buffalo, NY 14203
(716) 847–3145

Materials available upon request include adoption regulations, subsidy information, lists of adoption agencies and adoptive parent groups, and locations where New York State's Waiting Children (also known as the "Blue Books") is available for viewing.

STATE EXCHANGE

None

STATE ADOPTION REUNION REGISTRY

For information, contact New York State Adoption Services (above).

STATE SUBSIDY

For information, contact New York State Adoption Services (above).

NACAC REPRESENTATIVE

Judith Ashton
105 McIntyre Place
Ithaca, NY 14850
(607) 257–7903

GENERAL ADOPTION RESOURCES

The following list represents selected adoptive support organizations and general adoption resources in New York. For a complete and current list of adoptive parent groups, contact Department of Social Services regional adoption specialists (above).

Adoptive Parents Committee-Long Island
Lt. R. Steinberg
368 Hickory St.
Massapequa, NY 11758
(516) 541–9536

APC-New York City
Larry Gellerstein
1889 East 7th Street
Brooklyn, NY 11223
(718) 376–0716

APC-New York State
Ed Speer
1962 Cynthia Lane
Merrick, NY 11566
(516) 223–9494

APC-Westchester/Rockland
Allan Speigelman
80 Bischoff Ave.
Chappaqua, NY 10514
(914) 238–5268

Council on Adoptable Children-Rockland
Marian DeGennaro
86 Kings Highway
New City, NY 10956
(914) 634–8922

Council on Adoptable Children
Ernesto Loperena
666 Broadway, 8th Floor
New York, NY 10012
(212) 475–0222

Council of Adoptive Parents
Dolores Jones
110 Flint Hill Rd.
Mumford, NY 14511
(716) 538–6523

Latin America Parents Assn. (LAPA)
P.O. Box 72
Seaford, NY 11783
(516) 752–0086

Niagra Co. Minority Recruitment Assn.
 Emma Holley
 1317 Niagara St.
 Niagara Falls, NY 14305
 (716) 282–4471

OURS through Adoption
 Phillip Pawlowski and Ada Manke
 73 Quincy Street
 Buffalo, NY 14212
 (716) 894–4802

OURS-Long Island Chapter
 Joan Goetschius
 26 Crystal Beach Blvd.
 Moriches, NY 11955
 (516) 878–1806

Rockland County OURS
 Elaine and Steve Horowitz
 33 Halley Drive
 Pomona, NY 10970
 (914) 354–3888

OURS of Greater Utica/Rome
 Chris and Tom Riley
 247 Main St.
 Whitesboro, NY 13492
 (315) 736–2421

Parents and Children Together (PACT)
 Kathy Stumph
 P.O. Box 243
 Ghent, NY 12075
 (518) 392–2618

Parents and Children Together (PACT)
 Martin Gershowitz
 9 Arnold Road
 Poughkeepsie, NY 12601
 (914) 473–4123

Single Parents for Adoption
 Nancy Kresge
 7 Tarkington
 Tonawanda, NY 14150
 (716) 873–4173

Single People for the Adoption of Children Everywhere
 Philip Lalonda
 P.O. Box 942
 Albany, NY 12201
 (518) 465–6763

Birthparent, Adoptee, and Adoptive Parent Organization

Adoption Circle
 (support group/search assistance)
 Joseph M. Soll
 401 East 74th Street, Suite 17D
 New York, NY 10021
 (212) 988–0110

Special-Needs Adoption Resources

New York State provides a wide range of resources for special-needs children and their adoptive families. Speci-
ficinformation about these services should be requested from the nearest regional adoption specialist or the licensed adoption agency with which the family has worked.

Out-of-State Agencies

Agency

Universal Family, Colorado
International Alliance for Children, Connecticut
Christian Homes for Children, New Jersey
The Edna Gladney Center, Texas
Rainbow Christian Services, Virginia

See Appendix A

Agencies Providing Nationwide Services

Adoption and Counseling Services, Inc.

One Fayette Park
Syracuse, NY 13202
(315) 471–0109
Program director: Mary Louise Hartenstein; Mary T. Honey

The Program

Adoption and Counseling Services is a nonprofit agency serving residents of central New York and facilitating the placement of approximately 20–25 children annually. Incorporated in 1984, the agency's mission is "to enhance individual and family life" by providing a complete range of adoption services. Since the agency rarely assumes guardianship of children needing adoptive homes, most placements are made in cooperation with other licensed agencies, including several which operate programs in foreign countries to place Asian and Latin American children in American families. In addition, the agency will provide homestudy and supervisory services for applicants pursuing parent-initiated adoptions.

The Cost

For cooperative adoptions, the agency's fee for homestudy and supervisory services is $1,500. For adoptions in which the agency takes guardianship through voluntary surrender, the fee is based on the costs related to the placement. These usually include pregnancy counseling, medical expenses not covered by Medicaid or insurance, foster home care, legal fees and professional services to the adopting family.

The Wait

The time from application to the homecoming of the adoptive child ranges from 6 months to 2 years.

The Children

Adoption and Counseling Services facilitates the adoption of both healthy and special-needs children, ranging in age from infancy to adolescence, of Caucasian, Asian, Black, and bi-racial backgrounds. Countries of origin include U.S., Korea, and Latin America.

THE REQUIREMENTS

Age: Applicants must be at least 20 years of age. Maximum age requirement varies depending on the requirements of the cooperating agency.

Health: Applicants must be in reasonably good health.

Religion: No requirement.

Financial status: Applicants must have adequate income to support the family, must demonstrate sound financial management, and must have health and life insurance.

Marital status: No requirement.

Family size: No requirement.

Racial, ethnic or cultural origin: No requirement.

THE PROCEDURE

Participation in Adoption and Counseling Services' adoption program entails the following basic steps:

Orientation interview

Application

Homestudy (including individual counseling sessions)

Compliance with immigration/naturalization requirements (foreign adoptions only)

Placement

Post-placement supervision

Preparation of documents for finalization

Assistance with naturalization (as needed)

ADDITIONAL PROGRAMS/SERVICES

Adoption and Counseling Services provides foster care services, counseling services, and workshops.

BRANCH/NETWORK OFFICES

None.

LICENSE/ACCREDITATION/PROFESSIONAL AFFILIATIONS

Adoption and Counseling Services, Inc. is licensed by the State of New York Department of Social Services. Both directors are members of the National Association of Social Workers.

AMERICANS FOR INTERNATIONAL AID AND ADOPTION

8199 Wheaton Road
Baldwinsville, NY 13027
(315) 638–4669
Program director: Bruce Baehr

THE PROGRAM

For a full description of programs and services, refer to Michigan listing:

Americans for International Aid and Adoption 877 S. Adams

Birmingham, MI 48011

(313) 645–2211

BROOKWOOD CHILD CARE

363 Adelphi Street
Brooklyn, NY 11238
(718) 783–2610
Program director: Beryle Hartman

THE PROGRAM

Brookwood Child Care is a nonprofit multi-service child welfare agency serving residents of New York City and placing approximately 55 to 80 children annually. The adoption program began in 1970 to provide adoptive placement as a permanent resource for children in the agency's foster care program who cannot return to their biological families. Today, working directly with birthparents, with other private and public agencies, with Special Services for Children in New York City, and with the Council on Adoptable Children, the agency places both healthy and special-needs children, born in the U.S. In addition, the agency provides homestudy and supervisory services for applicants pursuing either international adoption or domestic interagency adoption.

THE COST

As of October 1988, the agency's fee for adoption services is based on a sliding scale, with an average cost of $600 for the homestudy and $2,000 for placement and supervision. Services covered by the fee include all phases of the adoption process, excluding legal fees connected with finalization (approximately $600).

THE WAIT

The time from application to placement varies depending on the type of adoption. Most placements made by the agency originate as foster placements which become adoptive placements when the child's birthparents relinquish their parental rights.

THE CHILDREN

Brookwood Child Care places both healthy and special-needs children, ranging in age from birth to 18 years, of all racial backgrounds, born in the U.S.

THE REQUIREMENTS

Age: No requirement.

Health: No requirement.

Religion: No requirement.

Financial status: No requirement.

Marital status: No requirement.

Family size: Applicants may have no more than 6 children currently in the family (as per New York State regulations).

Racial, ethnic or cultural origin: Preference for placing children in families of similar origins.

THE PROCEDURE

Participation in the adoption program of Brookwood Child Care entails the following basic steps:

Orientation meeting

Application

Individual counseling sessions

Homestudy

Placement
Post-placement supervision

ADDITIONAL PROGRAMS/SERVICES

Brookwood Child Care provides a range of services including workshops and seminars; foster care; counseling; family day care; group home for adolescents.

BRANCH/NETWORK OFFICES

None.

LICENSE/ACCREDITATION/PROFESSIONAL AFFILIATIONS

Brookwood Child Care is licensed by the State of New York Department of Social Services and is accredited by the Council on Accreditation of Services for Families and Children. The agency is a member of the Child Welfare League of America.

CATHOLIC CHARITIES

1654 W. Onondaga Street
Syracuse, NY 13204
(315) 424–1871
Program director: Carol Downs

THE PROGRAM

Catholic Charities is a nonprofit agency which offers a wide range of services to individuals and families in the counties of Onondaga, Oswego, Cortland, and Madison. The goal of the agency's adoption program is "to help children freed for adoption become part of a permanent family, to assist parents in creating a stable family life—one which enhances the social emotional, spiritual and physical dimensions of each family—and to increase the community's awareness of the needs of children waiting for adoption families." The adoption program has three components: the infant program, possible risk/minority infant program, and waiting child program. The infant program usually involves the placement of a normal healthy Caucasian infant after the legal surrender of the child by its birth parents to Catholic Charities. The possible risk/minority infant program involves the placement of infants and young children (under the age of 2) who may represent a degree of risk (known or unknown) because of their birthparents' medical history, psychiatric history, use of drugs during pregnancy, legal complications in the surrendering process, the child's prematurity or other birth problems. The waiting child program involves the placement of children with diverse special needs who are currently in foster or institutional care. Through these programs, Catholic Charities places 20 to 25 children annually.

THE COST

The adoption fee ($130–$6,000) is determined by a sliding scale based on services provided, the applicant's yearly gross income, and in the waiting child and possible risk programs, on the number of people in the family. The fee covers adoption home study, costs related to placement, supervision of placement and completion of documents for finalization, and post-adoptive counseling. Prospective adoptive parents should anticipate financial responsibility for legal fees in connection with finalization.

THE WAIT

After attending an information meeting and completing an inquiry form, people are placed on waiting lists by program. Infant and possible risk waiting lists are processed in chronological order. Waiting child inquiries are prioritized according to the availability of the type of child the family is interested in adopting. The average time on the waiting list before the applicant is scheduled for an adoption study is 6 to 7 years for the infant program, 3 years for the possible risk program, and less than 6 months for the waiting child program.

THE CHILDREN

Catholic Charities places both healthy and special-needs children of all ages and all racial backgrounds. All children placed by the agency are born in the U.S.

THE REQUIREMENTS

Age: No requirement.
Health: No requirement. Applicants with health problems or handicaps are given individual consideration.
Religion: No requirement.
Financial status: No requirement.
Marital status: No requirement, but preference given to married, childless couples for Infant Program. Married couples must have been married for at least one year prior to application.
Family size: No requirement, but preference given to married, childless couples for Infant Program.
Racial, ethnic or cultural origin: Preference for placing children in families of similar origins.

THE PROCEDURE

Participation in Catholic Charities' adoption programs entails the following basic steps:
Orientation meeting
Placement on waiting list for appropriate program
Application
Home study (including group and individual counseling)
Placement
Post-placement supervision
Finalization

ADDITIONAL PROGRAMS/SERVICES

Catholic Charities provides a wide range of community services including Child and Elder Abuse services; individual, marital and family counseling; expectant parent services; emergency assistance services; neighborhood services (nutritional, educational, recreational, and residential programs).

BRANCH/NETWORK OFFICES

None.

LICENSE/ACCREDITATION/PROFESSIONAL AFFILIATIONS

Catholic Charities is licensed by the State of New York Department of Social Services.

CATHOLIC CHARITIES OF THE DIOCESE OF OGDENSBURG

716 Caroline Street
Ogdensburg, NY 13669
(315) 393-2660
Program director: Rev. Stephen H. Gratto

THE PROGRAM

Catholic Charities of the Diocese of Ogdensburg is a nonprofit agency serving the counties of Clinton, Essex, Franklin, Jefferson, Lewis, St. Lawrence, and part of Hamilton County and placing approximately 8–16 children annually. Incorporated in 1917 to provide institutional care for children and the elderly, Catholic Charities has evolved in response to the changing needs of the community and is now a multi-service agency providing a wide range of services to communities, families, and children without regard to race, religion, sex, or level of income. The agency provides services for unmarried parents and places infants for adoption when birthparents in the agency's pregnancy counseling program decide that the best interest of the child will be served by adoptive placement.

THE COST

The agency's fee for adoption services is based on a sliding scale and ranges from $550 to $6,000. Services covered by the fee include homestudy and supervision of placement. In addition, prospective adoptive parents should anticipate financial responsibility for legal fees connected with finalization of the adoption (usually between $250 and $350).

THE WAIT

The time from application for acceptance into the program to the homecoming of the adoptive child ranges from 2 to 5 years.

THE CHILDREN

Catholic Charities places both healthy and special-needs children, usually Caucasian infants but occasionally Black or bi-racial infants as well. Children placed by Catholic Charities are born in the U.S.

THE REQUIREMENTS

Age: The age requirement varies. The general guideline is that applicants should be at least 21 and within child-bearing age range.
Health: Applicants must be in reasonably good health. Applicants with health problems or handicaps are given individual consideration.
Religion: Applicants must be practicing members of their faith.
Financial status: No requirement.
Marital status: Applicants must be married. The length of the marriage must be at least 2 years.
Family size: Preference is given to childless couples.
Racial, ethnic or cultural origin: No requirement.

THE PROCEDURE

Participation in Catholic Charities of the Diocese of Ogdensburg's adoption program entails the following basic steps:
   Orientation meeting
   Application
   Homestudy
   Group counseling sessions
   Placement
   Post-placement supervision

ADDITIONAL PROGRAMS/SERVICES

Catholic Charities provides a wide range of services including individual, marital, and family counseling; maternity and early childhood services; services for unmarried parents; foster care services; support groups for separated or divorced persons; counseling for veterans; life skills groups for children and youth.

BRANCH/NETWORK OFFICES

57 East Main St.
Malone, NY 12953
(518) 483-1460

151 South Catherine St.
Plattsburgh, NY 12901
(518) 561-0470

380 Arlington St.
Watertown, NY 13601
(315) 788-4330

LICENSE/ACCREDITATION/PROFESSIONAL AFFILIATIONS

Catholic Charities of the Diocese of Ogdensburg is licensed by the State of New York Department of Social Services. The agency is a member of Catholic Charities USA.

CATHOLIC FAMILY CENTER

50 Chestnut Street
Rochester, NY 14604
(716) 546-7220
Program director: Mary Jo Crimi, Supervisor

THE PROGRAM

Catholic Family Center is a nonprofit multi-service agency serving residents of the Diocese of Rochester and placing approximately 70 children annually. Providing adoption services since 1917, Catholic Family Center's mission is "to alleviate human suffering, eradicate the cause, and promote growth." The agency provides services to birthparents and places infants for adoption when birthparents in the agency's counseling program decide that the best interests of the child will be served by adoptive placement. The agency is also actively involved in the placement of minority and special-needs children. In addition, the agency will provide homestudy and supervisory services for applicants pursuing foreign adoption.

THE COST

The agency's fee for adoption services is based on a sliding scale and ranges from no fee to $3,829. Services covered by the fee include all phases of the adoption process (adoption study through post-placement supervision), excluding legal fees connected with finalization of the adoption.

THE WAIT

The time from application to the homecoming of the adoptive child varies depending on the program. For healthy Caucasian infants, the wait ranges up to 4 years. For minority or special-needs adoptions, the wait ranges up to 1 year.

THE CHILDREN

Catholic Family Center places both healthy and special-needs children, ranging in age from infancy to adolescence, of all racial backgrounds. In addition, the agency will provide homestudy and supervisory services for applicants pursuing foreign adoption of children of any age, race, or national origin.

THE REQUIREMENTS

Age: Applicants must be at least 21 years of age. Maximum age requirement varies depending on the needs of the child.

Health: Applicants with health problems or handicaps are given individual consideration.

Religion: No specific requirement, but varies depending on the preference of the birthmother or the needs of the child.

Financial status: Applicants must demonstrate financial stability.

Marital status: The requirement varies depending on the needs of the child.

Family size: The requirement varies depending on the needs of the child.

Racial, ethnic or cultural origin: Preference for placing children in families of similar origins.

THE PROCEDURE

Participation in Catholic Family Center's adoption program entails the following basic steps:

Orientation meeting

Application

Homestudy (including individual counseling sessions)

Compliance with immigration/naturalization requirements (foreign adoptions only)

Group counseling sessions

Placement

Post-placement services

ADDITIONAL PROGRAMS/SERVICES

Catholic Family Center provides services to birthparents; foster care services; individual, marital, and family counseling.

BRANCH/NETWORK OFFICES

All adoption inquiries are processed through the main office.

LICENSE/ACCREDITATION/PROFESSIONAL AFFILIATIONS

Catholic Family Center is licensed by the State of New York Department of Social Services and is accredited by the Council on Accreditation of Services for Families and Children. The agency is a member of Catholic Charities USA and Family Service America.

CATHOLIC SOCIAL SERVICES OF BROOME COUNTY

232 Main St.
Binghamton, NY 13905
(607) 729–9166
Program director: Patricia Glazier, CSW, Supervisor of Casework

THE PROGRAM

Catholic Social Services of Broome County (CSS) is a nonprofit social service agency founded in 1937 which offers a wide range of services. The mission of the agency is to "embody Christ's teaching by advocacy for and service to people, along with convening people around social issues to develop just responses." In its adoption program, CSS serves Broome and adjacent New York State counties, placing between 8 and 15 children annually. CSS places infants for adoption when birthparents in the agency's unmarried parent program decide that the best interests of their children will be served through adoptive placement. Via participation in New York State's Waiting Child Program, the agency can place special-needs children. The agency also facilitates the placement of foreign-born children through cooperation with various international agencies.

THE COST

The adoption fee is based on a sliding scale from $500 to $4,400 for regular adoptions and $2,000 for international adoptions. The fee covers application costs, homestudy, placement, post-placement supervision, and legalization services. Applicants should also expect to pay lawyer's fees for finalization, and in the case of international adoptions, fees to the international agency and transportation costs.

THE WAIT

The agency is child-centered, selecting the best possible home for each child to be placed. Thus, every approved and waiting family is considered for every child, but families can generally expect a wait of 1 1/2 to 3 years.

THE CHILDREN

CSS places primarily infants, but can also place children with special needs and older children of all racial backgrounds. Countries of origin are determined by the international agencies with which adoptive applicants are working concurrently.

THE REQUIREMENTS

Age: The minimum age for an applicant is 18 according to New York law. Requirement varies depending on the age of the child being considered for placement.

Health: Applicants must be in reasonably good health. Applicants with health problems or a handicap are given individual consideration. Infertility exploration is strongly recommended.

Religion: No requirement unless a preference is specified by the birthparents who have the legal right to make this choice.

Financial status: Applicants must demonstrate financial stability.

Marital status: No requirement for special-needs children. For healthy infant adoption, married couples are preferred because of the preferences of the birthparents which CSS honors whenever possible. The length of the marriage must be at least 1 year.

Family size: No requirement.

Racial, ethnic or cultural origin: No requirement.

THE PROCEDURE

Participation in the CSS' adoption program entails the following basic steps:

Orientation meeting

Application

Homestudy (including individual counseling sessions as needed)

Compliance with immigration and naturalization requirements (foreign adoptions only)

Placement

Post-placement

ADDITIONAL PROGRAMS/SERVICES

CSS also provides a teenage pregnancy prevention program, unmarried parent services, newborn foster care, individual and group therapy, emergency assistance, information and referral services, and social action.

BRANCH/NETWORK OFFICES

Catholic Social Services of Broome County is one of the agencies under Catholic Charities of the Roman Catholic Diocese of Syracuse, New York. The main office is in Syracuse, New York, and several branches can be found throughout central New York.

LICENSE/ACCREDITATION/PROFESSIONAL AFFILIATIONS

Catholic Social Services of Broome County is licensed by the State of New York Department of Social Services. The agency is a member of Catholic Charities USA, New York State Association for Human Services, and United Way of Broome County.

CENTER FOR COUNSELING

12 South Lake Avenue
Albany, NY 12203
(518) 462–6531
Program director: Susan Abagnale, Executive Director

THE PROGRAM

Center for Counseling is a nonprofit agency providing services within a 75 mile radius of Albany. Founded in the early 1800s, the agency is the originator of many Albany area human services (Visiting Nurses Association, the Widowed Person's Service) and has as its purpose "to provide professional human services to Capital District area residents designed to enable families to deal successfully with the continuing changes and challenges incurred within personal relationships, in the workforce and throughout the family life cycle." Currently, the agency places so few infants that it is not accepting new applications and does not anticipate reopening its waiting list in the foreseeable future. However, the agency will provide homestudy and supervisory services for families pursuing private adoption or international adoption (subject to state approval of the integrity of the source). The agency also provides specialized adoption counseling pertaining to infertility, adjustment problems, disruption, and all other issues involving biological parents, adoptees, and adoptive families.

THE COST

The agency's fee for homestudy and all other adoption services (updating a homestudy, preparing documents for finalization and immigration, post-placement supervision, travel, etc.) is $50 per hour plus travel and long distance telephone expenses. The average cost of an initial homestudy is approximately $600.

THE WAIT

Not applicable.

THE CHILDREN

Not applicable.

THE REQUIREMENTS

The Center will work within the established framework of requirements of the placing agency.

Age: No additional requirement.

Health: Applicants must provide a recent medical evaluation.

Religion: No additional requirement.

Financial status: No additional requirement.

Marital status: No additional requirement.

Family size: No additional requirement.

Racial, ethnic or cultural origin: No additional requirement.

THE PROCEDURE

Applicants pursuing private adoption or international adoption through another source are invited to contact Center for Counseling to arrange for homestudy and supervisory services.

ADDITIONAL PROGRAMS/SERVICES

Center for Counseling provides family counseling services and operates an employee assistance program.

BRANCH/NETWORK OFFICES

All telephone inquiries are processed through the main office. Center for Counseling maintains branch offices at the following locations:

480 Broadway
Saratoga, NY 12866

1789 Route 9
Clifton Park, NY 12065
1807 Ninth St.
Rensselaer, NY 12144

LICENSE/ACCREDITATION/PROFESSIONAL AFFILIATIONS

Center for Counseling is licensed by the State of New York Department of Social Services and is accredited by the Council on Accreditation of Services for Families and Children. The Center is a member of ALMACA (Association of Labor-Management Administrators and Consultants on Alcoholism, Inc.) and Family Service America.

CHILD AND FAMILY SERVICES

330 Delaware Avenue
Buffalo, NY 14202
(716) 842–2750
Program director: Marjorie Connors, Adoption Services

THE PROGRAM

Child and Family Services is a multi-function, nonprofit agency that provides direct services to families and children at various locations throughout Erie County. Providing services without regard to race, creed, color, national origin, or economic status, the agency's mission is "to support family life through coordinated services, education for family enrichment, and advocacy." The agency's adoption program is part of the Children's Services Department whose major function is foster care placement. The agency places infants for adoption (approximately 5 annually) when birthparents in the agency's program for single parents decide that the best interests of the child will be met through adoptive placement. Through its specialized adoption program, the agency places older and special-needs children (approximately 10–15 annually).

THE COST

The agency's fee for placement of children 2 years of age and under is based on a sliding scale and ranges from no charge to $3,500. The fee covers homestudy, placement, post-placement services, and preparation of agency documents for legalization as well as medical services for the birthmother and infant, counseling for the birthparents, and short-term foster care of the infant. There are no agency fees for placement of children over 2 years of age. In addition, prospective adoptive parents should anticipate financial responsibility for legal fees connected with finalization.

THE WAIT

The time from application to the homecoming of the adoptive child is from 6 months to 2 years for a Black infant; 4 to 6 years for a Caucasian infant; and from 6 months to 3 years for older children.

THE CHILDREN

Child and Family Services places both healthy and special-needs children, ranging in age from birth to adolescence, of Caucasian, Black, Asian, and Indian racial backgrounds. All children placed by the agency are born in the U.S.

THE REQUIREMENTS

Age: Applicants must be at least 21 and no more than 38 years old. The requirement may vary for older child and special-needs adoptions.
Health: Applicants with a health problem or a handicap are given individual consideration.
Religion: No requirement.
Financial status: Applicants must demonstrate financial stability.
Marital status: The requirement may vary depending on the needs of the child being considered for placement. If married, applicants must have been married for at least 2 years.
Family size: For infant adoption, applicants may have no more than 1 child currently in the family. For older child or special-needs adoption, no requirement.
Residence: Applicants must reside in Erie County.
Racial, ethnic or cultural origin: Preference for placing children in families of similar origins.

THE PROCEDURE

Participation in Child and Family Services' adoption program entails the following basic steps:
Orientation meeting
Application
Individual counseling sessions
Group counseling sessions
Homestudy
Placement
Post-placement supervision

ADDITIONAL PROGRAMS/SERVICES

Child and Family Services provides a wide range of services including family counseling and family advocacy; single parent services; emergency child protection services; residential treatment centers (Conners Children's Center, Morey House, and Haven House); West Side Services for Native Americans and Spanish-speaking citizens of Erie County; Reach-out Program for Buffalo's East Side; services for senior citizens; family life education programs; travelers aid; employee assistance program; Cathedral Park counseling services.

BRANCH/NETWORK OFFICES

Amherst Regional Office
5449 Main Street
Williamsville, NY 14221
(716) 532–5500
North Regional Office
3407 Delaware Avenue
Kenmore, NY 14217
(716) 876–8174
East Regional Office
45 Anderson Road
Cheektowaga, NY 14225
(716) 896–7485
South Regional Office
585 Ridge Road
Lackawanna, NY 14218
(716) 823–2531

Child and Family Services is licensed by the State of New York Department of Social Services and is accredited by Family Service America, the Child Welfare League of America, the Council on Accreditation of Services for Families and Children, and the Travelers Aid Association of America. The agency is a member of the United Way of Erie County.

THE CHILDREN'S AID SOCIETY

150 East 45th Street
New York, NY 10017
(212) 949–4800
Program director: Ann McCabe

THE PROGRAM

Founded in 1853, The Children's Aid Society is a non-profit multi-service agency serving residents of the New York metropolitan area. Originally founded to provide care for orphaned and destitute children, the agency's "historical and practicing mission to strengthen family life is based on the premise of its founder, Charles Loring Brace, that every child needs family and community life conducive to the development of his potential as a physically, socially, and emotionally healthy adult." The focus of the Adoption and Foster Home Division today is to provide waiting children with the services essential to their best development through foster and adoptive placements, casework and auxiliary services, and counseling services. The majority of the children placed by the agency are adopted by their foster families. Adoptive families are recruited for older minority children and sibling groups. In addition, the agency will provide homestudy and supervisory services for applicants pursuing interagency adoption of New York State waiting children (generally older special needs minority children).

THE COST

Adoption services are provided at no cost to adoptive families. The only fees which applicants need anticipate are legal fees connected with finalization of the adoption.

THE WAIT

The time from application to the completion of the homestudy is 4 months. The time from completion of the homestudy to placement varies according to the availability of the type of child requested.

THE CHILDREN

The Children's Aid Society places both healthy and special-needs children, ranging in age from 5 to 14 years, primarily of Black and Hispanic racial backgrounds, born in the U.S. Most available children have some emotional or behavioral problems.

THE REQUIREMENTS

Age: Applicants must be at least 18 years of age.
Health: Applicants must be in reasonably good health.

Applicants with health problems or handicaps are given individual consideration.
Religion: No requirement.
Financial status: The requirement varies depending on the applicant's ability to support the existing family. Applicants must have some source of income through employment, Public Assistance, or other benefits.
Marital status: Applicants may be single or married. If married, the length of the marriage must be at least 1 year.
Family size: No requirement.
Racial, ethnic or cultural origin: Preference for placing children in families of similar origins.

THE PROCEDURE

Participation in the adoption program of The Children's Aid Society entails the following basic steps:
Orientation meeting
Application
Homestudy
Individual counseling sessions
Referral
Group counseling sessions
Placement
Post-placement supervision

ADDITIONAL PROGRAMS/SERVICES

The Children's Aid Society provides a range of community services including foster care; preventive services; homemaker services; PINS mediation; community centers for recreation, medical/dental care, tutoring, Head Start program, sports activities, and mental health services.

BRANCH/NETWORK OFFICES

None.

LICENSE/ACCREDITATION/PROFESSIONAL AFFILIATIONS

The Children's Aid Society is licensed by the State of New York Department of Social Services and is accredited by the Council on Accreditation of Services for Families and Children. The agency is a member of the Child Welfare League of America and the Council of Family and Child Caring Agencies.

THE CHILDREN'S HOME OF KINGSTON

26 Grove Street
Kingston, NY 12401
(914) 331–1448

Program director: Wendy Rothe, MA

THE PROGRAM

The Children's Home of Kingston is a nonprofit agency serving the Hudson Valley region, specializing in residential and foster care for adolescent boys. The Children's Home is a relatively small, highly personalized, multi-service treatment center created to meet the needs of adolescent males (aged 10–17) who are experiencing difficulty at home, in school, or in the community. First known as the Industrial Home of Kingston, the agency became incorporated by a group of concerned citizens in 1876. Through its doors, orphans and other dependent children found a home. In the 1960s, the agency evolved into a treatment center to meet the residential, clinical, and educational needs of its residents. The agency now operates a residential treatment center, a day treatment program, H.A.L.T. (an outpatient family treatment program), an on-campus school, and foster care services. The Children's Home does not provide adoption services. However, if a foster family is interested in adoption, the Home attempts to arrange a match between them and a boy in the agency's care who has been freed for adoption. After 6 months, the case can then be referred to the Department of Social Services for adoption proceedings.

THE COST

When a boy in The Children's Home is freed for adoption, adoption services are provided by the Department of Social Services at no cost to the adoptive family. Foster parents and pre-adoptive parents receive financial support ($24.56/day plus clothing allowance) for the child's care.

THE WAIT

The time from application for acceptance into the program as a foster parent to the placement of the foster child averages approximately 2 months, but may vary depending on the age preference of the foster family.

THE CHILDREN

The Children's Home of Kingston serves physically healthy adolescent males (10–17 years) who are experiencing emotional difficulty, of Caucasian, Black, and Hispanic racial backgrounds, born in the U.S.

THE REQUIREMENTS

The following are the agency's requirements for applicants who are interested in becoming foster parents:

Age: Applicants must be at least 21 and no more than 60 years of age.

Health: Applicants must be in reasonably good health, must have had a recent physical examination, and must be free of communicable diseases.

Religion: No requirement.

Financial status: No requirement, but applicants must be able to meet the needs of the child without aid by public assistance.

Marital status: No requirement.

Family size: No requirement.

Racial, ethnic or cultural origin: No requirement.

THE PROCEDURE

Participation in The Children's Home of Kingston's foster care program entails the following basic steps:

Application
Orientation meeting
Individual counseling sessions
Homestudy
Meeting with children/staff team
Referral

Weekend visits with child to ease transition
Placement
Post-placement supervision and counseling
Assistance with adoption process

ADDITIONAL PROGRAMS/SERVICES

The Children's Home of Kingston operates a residential treatment center and a day treatment program; provides group home and foster home care; provides H.A.L.T. (outpatient family therapy); provides opportunities for volunteer services.

BRANCH/NETWORK OFFICES

None.

LICENSE/ACCREDITATION/PROFESSIONAL AFFILIATIONS

The Children's Home of Kingston is licensed by the State of New York Department of Social Services.

THE CHILDREN'S VILLAGE

Dobbs Ferry, NY 10522
(914) 693–0600, Ext. 264
Program director: Brian Scholl

THE PROGRAM

The Children's Village is a private, nonprofit agency which serves the counties of Westchester, Rockland, Putnam, Orange, Dutchess, Sullivan, Ulster, and New York City. Most of the children placed by The Children's Village come from the agency's residential treatment program for older boys (10–16 years old). The agency places approximately 6 children annually.

THE COST

There is no fee for the adoption of The Children's Village boys. The only fee which prospective adoptive families should anticipate is the cost of a physical examination.

THE WAIT

The average time from application to the homecoming of the adoptive child is 6 months (including a 2–month visiting period).

THE CHILDREN

The Children's Village places boys between the ages of 10 and 16 who have special emotional needs. The majority are Black.

THE REQUIREMENTS

Age: No requirement.

Health: Applicants with health problems or handicaps are given individual consideration.

Religion: No requirement.

Financial status: No requirement.

Marital status: No requirement.

Family size: No requirement.

Racial, ethnic or cultural origin: Preference for placing children in families of similar origins.

THE PROCEDURE

Participation in The Children's Village adoption program entails the following basic steps:
Orientation meeting
Application
Homestudy
Group counseling sessions
Two-month visiting period
Placement

ADDITIONAL PROGRAMS/SERVICES

The Children's Village operates a residential treatment program, group homes, and a foster care program.

BRANCH/NETWORK OFFICES

None.

LICENSE/ACCREDITATION/PROFESSIONAL AFFILIATIONS

The Children's Village is licensed by the New York State Department of Social Services and the New York State Office of Mental Health. It is accredited by the Council on Accreditation for Families and Children, the Joint Commission on Accreditation of Hospitals, and the American Association of Psychiatric Services for Children.

COMMUNITY MATERNITY SERVICES

27 North Main Avenue
Albany, NY 12203
(518) 482–8836
Program director: Mary G. Creighton

THE PROGRAM

Community Maternity Services is a nonprofit agency serving the Diocese of Albany (14 counties) and placing approximately 40 children annually. In 1971, the Board of Trustees of Catholic Charities of the Diocese of Albany committed themselves to improve services to pregnant women through the establishment of Community Maternity Services (CMS), a comprehensive network of innovative and effective programs, designed to meet the needs of pregnant adolescents and young parents within the Diocese. Through extensive counseling and support, CMS "assists the adolescent person to explore female/male relationships, the dignity of each individual, and hopefully allows them to realize their own self worth." Adoption and foster care are decisions which rest with the birthparents. When birthparents elect adoptive placement as the best plan for their child, the agency provides placement services. Services to birthparents and to adoptive parents are provided without regard to race, religion, sex, or level of income. In addition, the agency will provide homestudy and supervisory services for applicants pursuing special needs or foreign adoption, subject to state approval of the integrity of the source.

THE COST

The agency's fee for adoption services is 9% of the applicants' combined annual gross income, not to exceed $10,000. Services covered by the fee include all phases of the adoption process (adoption preparation, post-placement supervision through finalization), excluding legal fees connected with finalization. In addition, fees help to underwrite the cost of services to birthparents and child (medical and foster care).

THE WAIT

The time from application for acceptance into the program to the homecoming of the adoptive child ranges from 3 to 5 years.

THE CHILDREN

CMS places primarily healthy infants of all racial backgrounds. In addition, CMS will provide homestudy and supervisory services for applicants pursuing special needs or foreign adoption of children of any age, race, or national origin.

THE REQUIREMENTS

Age: For healthy Caucasian infant, applicants must be at least 21 and no more than 40 years of age. For foreign or special-needs adoptions, the requirement varies depending on the placing source.
Health: Applicants must be in reasonably good health. Applicants with health problems or handicaps are given individual consideration. Medical exploration of infertility status is required for healthy Caucasian infant adoption.
Religion: Applicants must be practicing members of a religious faith.
Financial status: Applicants are evaluated individually on the basis of their ability to manage financial resources adequately.
Marital status: For healthy Caucasian infant adoption, applicants must be married couples, and the length of the marriage must be at least 3 years. The requirement for foreign or special-needs adoptions varies depending on the placing source.
Family size: For healthy Caucasian infant adoption, applicants must be childless. The requirement for foreign or special-needs adoptions varies depending on the placing source.
Racial, ethnic or cultural origin: Preference for placing children in families of similar origins.

THE PROCEDURE

Participation in CMS' adoption program entails the following basic steps:
Application
Orientation meeting
Homestudy (including individual and group counseling sessions)
Compliance with immigration/naturalization requirements (foreign adoptions only)
Placement
Post-placement supervision
Finalization
Post-adoption services (counseling; adoption search)

ADDITIONAL PROGRAMS/SERVICES

CMS provides extensive maternity services for young pregnant women; counseling services to single parents and their families; infant and adolescent foster care; infant health assessment; parenting education for adolescents and their families; family life education (prevention services); adoption search services.

BRANCH/NETWORK OFFICES

Schoharie County
41 W. Main St.
Cobleskill, NY 12043
(518) 234–3541

Otsego County
39 Walnut St.
Oneonta, NY 13820
(607) 432–3920

Herkimer County
216 Henry St.
Herkimer, NY 13350
(315) 866–5171

Warren County
Lower Amherst St.
Lake George, NY 12845
(518) 668–3167

Washington County
19 Bulkley Ave.
Granville, NY 12832
(518) 642–1471

Fulton County
208 W. State St.
Johnstown, NY 12095
(518) 762–8313

Montgomery County
1 Kimball St.
Amsterdam, NY
(518) 842–4202

Rensselaer County
240 Second St.
12010 Troy, NY 12180
(518) 274–9245

LICENSE/ACCREDITATION/PROFESSIONAL AFFILIATIONS

Community Maternity Services is licensed by the State of New York Department of Social Services. The agency is a member of the National Committee for Adoption, Catholic Charities USA, New York State Council of Child Caring Agencies, and National Organization on Adolescent Pregnancy and Parenting.

EVANGELICAL ADOPTION AND FAMILY SERVICE, INC.

201 South Main Street
North Syracuse, NY 13212
(315) 458–1415

Program director: Larry D. Taylor, CSW, Executive Director

THE PROGRAM

Evangelical Adoption and Family Service, Inc. (EAFS) is a nonprofit agency providing statewide service and placing approximately 60 children annually. Offering services since 1965 on a non-sectarian, non-denominational basis, the agency's purpose is "to work with individuals and couples who love children, have a sincere desire to adopt, and demonstrate the capacity to respond appropriately to the individual needs of the child." EAFS offers several adoption programs, including infant adoptions, "waiting child" adoptions, and international adoptions. Through its infant adoption program, the agency places infants when birthparents in the agency's pregnancy counseling program decide that the best interests of the child will be served by adoptive placement. At the present time, the agency accepts 25–30 applications for Caucasian infant adoptions annually. Through its "waiting child" program, the agency provides homestudy and supervisory services to applicants who wish to adopt a special-needs child who is in the custody either of a cooperating agency or New York State. Through its international program, the agency provides homestudy and supervisory services to applicants interested in adopting a foreign-born child.

THE COST

The agency's fee for adoption services varies depending on the program. The basic fee schedule is as follows:

Domestic infant adoption	$5,100.00
International adoption	
Homestudy (without supervision)	$ 900.00
Homestudy (with supervision)	$1,500.00
Placement supervision only	$ 900.00
International Mission of Hope adoption	$4,960.00–$5,560.00
International adoption w/ independent consultant	$2,500.00
Waiting child adoption	$1,000.00

Applicants interested in pursuing international adoption with an independent consultant should anticipate additional expenses related to travel, document translation, and the like. In all programs, applicants assume responsibility for legal fees connected with finalization. Services covered by the fee vary depending on the program and/or services requested. Applicants should note that fees are approximate and subject to change.

THE WAIT

The time from application to the homecoming of the adoptive child varies depending on the program.

THE CHILDREN

Evangelical Adoption and Family Service directly places Caucasian children surrendered to the agency by the birthparents, ranging in age from birth to 5 years. The agency facilitates "waiting child" and international adoptions of both healthy and special-needs children of all ages, races, and countries of origin.

THE REQUIREMENTS

Age: Applicants must be at least 21 years old. Some international programs have a maximum age limit.

Health: Applicants must be in reasonably good health and must submit a report from a physician.

Religion: For infant adoption, the preferences of the birth-parents are honored. As the majority of the birthparents served by the agency have an evangelical faith, the preference of the birthparents is usually that the child be placed in an evangelical family. No requirement for "waiting child" or international adoptions.

Financial status: Applicants must demonstrate financial stability.

Marital status: For infant adoption, applicants must be married. The length of the marriage must be at least 1 year. Single applicants are eligible for "waiting child" and international adoptions.

Family size: For infant adoption, applicants must be childless or have no more than 1 child currently in the family. No requirement for "waiting child" and international adoptions.

Racial, ethnic or cultural origin: Preference for placing children in families of similar origins.

THE PROCEDURE

Participation in EAFS' adoption programs entails the following basic steps:
Intake interview
Application
Individual/group educational sessions
Homestudy
Placement
Post-placement supervision
Finalization
Post-finalization services

ADDITIONAL PROGRAMS/SERVICES

EAFS provides services to birthparents; provides individual, marital, and family counseling; publishes a quarterly newsletter (Keepin' In Touch).

BRANCH/NETWORK OFFICES

EAFS has satellite workers throughout New York State.

Western New York
Sue E. Vosburgh
7882 York Rd.
Pavillion, NY 14525
(716) 584-3668

Western New York
Wendy R. Baxter
4220 Sowerby Rd.
Silver Springs, NY 14550
(716) 237-6320

Southern Tier
Gary Short
RD#2, Box 67
Mitchellsville Rd.
Bath, NY 14810
(607) 776-7844

Mid-Hudson Valley

Kathryn Weiss
70 Old Ford Rd.
New Paltz, NY 12561
(914) 255-6502

Long Island
Paul Williams
8 Laurel Ave.
East Islip, NY 11730
(516) 581-3092

LICENSE/ACCREDITATION/PROFESSIONAL AFFILIATIONS

Evangelical Adoption and Family Service, Inc. is licensed by the State of New York Department of Social Services. The agency is a member of the Evangelical Council for Financial Accountability, North American Council on Adoptable Children, and North American Association of Christians in Social Work.

FAMILY AND CHILDREN'S SERVICE

204 N. Cayuga Street
Ithaca, NY 14850
(607) 273-7494
Program director: Janet H. Burton, MSW

THE PROGRAM

Family and Children's Service (F&CS) is a nonprofit multi-service agency that serves Tompkins and adjacent counties in central New York and places approximately 4 to 8 children annually. F&CS focuses on infant and international adoptions and works cooperatively with other U.S.-based licensed placement agencies, providing homestudy and supervisory services. Applicants should note that a homestudy conducted by F&CS must include post-placement supervision. F&CS has been providing adoption services for over fifty years.

THE COST

The agency's fees are as follows:
Nonrefundable homestudy application fee $50.00
Hourly homestudy rate (average/hour) $40.00-$55.00
    (about 15 to 20 hours including support service time)
Hourly rate for post-placement supervision fee $40.00-$55.00
    (20 hours)
Placement fee $1,500.00–$3,000.00
In addition, applicants can expect to pay legal fees involved with finalization of the adoption.

THE WAIT

The time from inquiry to initiation of the homestudy is 3 years. The homestudy takes about 4 to 6 months, with placement occurring within a year after completion of the homestudy.

THE CHILDREN

F&CS places infants, of all racial backgrounds. Countries of origin include the U.S. and many foreign countries.

THE REQUIREMENTS

Age: No requirement.

Health: Applicants should be in reasonably good health. Applicants with health problems or handicaps are given individual consideration.

Religion: No requirement.

Financial status: No requirement.

Marital status: No requirement.

Family size: Applicants can have no more than 1 child currently in the family. F&CS can place only 2 children per family.

Racial, ethnic or cultural origin: No requirement.

THE PROCEDURE

Participation in F&CS's adoption program entails the following basic steps:

Referral from waiting list

Application

Individual counseling sessions

Homestudy

Placement

Post-placement supervision

Post-legal services

ADDITIONAL PROGRAMS/SERVICES

Family and Children's Service offers a full-range counseling program for families, individuals, and children; pregnancy counseling; post-adoption services for all members of the adoption triad.

BRANCH/NETWORK OFFICES

None.

LICENSE/ACCREDITATION/PROFESSIONAL AFFILIATIONS

Family and Children's Services is licensed by the State of New York Department of Social Services.

FAMILY RESOURCES ADOPTION PROGRAM

226 N. Highland Avenue
Ossining, NY 10562
(914) 762–6550
Program director: Bernard H. McNamara

THE PROGRAM

Family Resources is an innovative, nonprofit agency serving northern New York City, Westchester, Putnam, Rockland, Dutchess, and Orange Counties. The agency directly places approximately 20–30 special-needs children annually and facilitates (through referral and by helping children and families connect) an additional 30 placements annually. Founded by a dedicated group of adoptive families and community members to find "permanent, loving families for the children waiting for adoptive homes," Family Resources is a specialized program that works cooperatively with all adoption programs in the state of New York and across the country to place children for whom local agencies have no available resources. Family Resources actively recruits families who are willing to commit themselves to a waiting child and then intensively prepares families for the challenges of raising a child who may have been abandoned, abused, or neglected before being released for adoption. Family Resources has an innovative post-placement services program (including counseling, intensive therapy, 24–hour hotline, teen and pre-teen rap groups, Buddy Family volunteer support system) which has dramatically reduced high-risk adoption disruptions by enabling children and parents to grow together as a family. Family Resources also developed SAFE (Sex Abuse Family Education), the first U.S. prevention and treatment program for adoptive families.

THE COST

The agency's fee for adoption services is based on a sliding scale and is set by the prospective adoptive parents themselves. The suggested fee of 5% of the annual gross income is adjusted by the family for needs such as high medical expenses or large family size, and a comfortable plan for payment after placement, usually monthly, is arranged by the family. The majority of children placed for adoption come with a monthly adoption subsidy, usually $150–$250 per month, which the family receives until the child is 18 or 21. Some children and families are also eligible to receive subsidies for legal costs, expenses related to visiting before adoption, medical expenses, or other needs. All fees and expenses related to adoption up to $1,500 are tax deductible according to federal legislation on special-needs adoption, and all donations are tax deductible. The only additional fees which applicants should anticipate are legal fees connected with finalization of the adoption ($300–$500).

THE WAIT

The time from application to the homecoming of the adoptive child ranges from 8 weeks to 2 1/2 years, with an average wait of 1 year.

THE CHILDREN

Family Resources directly places and facilitates the placement of special-needs children of all ages and racial backgrounds.

THE REQUIREMENTS

Age: No requirement.

Health: No requirement.

Religion: No requirement.

Marital status: No requirement.

Family size: No requirement.

Racial, ethnic or cultural origin: No requirement.

THE PROCEDURE

Participation in Family Resources' adoption program entails the following basic steps:

Inquiry

Informational meeting

Parent preparation (Intensive preparation for special-needs adoption; TEAM approach; Buddy Family Support

Network; pre- placement therapy; SAFE—Sex Abuse Family Education.)

Referral (Family reviews adoption exchange books and Family Resources listings and referrals; Family Resources sends family's adoption study to referring agencies and pursues all possible placements.)

Compliance with Interstate Compact requirements (Out-of-state children only.)

Placement

Post-placement services (Weekly therapy beginning immediately after placement; family support meetings; Buddy Family contacts; single parent support groups; social activities; seminars; workshops.)

Finalization

Post-finalization services (On-going support services and continuation of post-placement services listed above.)

ADDITIONAL PROGRAMS/SERVICES

In addition to extensive parent preparation and post-placement services, Family Resources hosts social activities (picnics, potlucks, parties, campouts); publishes a quarterly newsletter; provides professional training services; provides information and referral services. Family Resources Director Bernard H. McNamara and Associate Director Joan McNamara are co-authors of *The Special Child Handbook* (Hawthorne Books, Inc., 1977). Joan McNamara is also the author of *The Adoption Advisor* (Hawthorne Books, Inc., 1975). Other publications available through Family Resources include Families, The Ordinary Miracle, SAFE Kids, and Tangled Feelings.

BRANCH/NETWORK OFFICES

None.

LICENSE/ACCREDITATION/PROFESSIONAL AFFILIATIONS

Family Resources Adoption Program is licensed by the State of New York Department of Social Services, is incorporated as a not-for-profit organization, and is federally tax-exempt.

GRAHAM WINDHAM

33 Irving Place
New York, NY 10003
(212) 529–6445
Program director: Ray Hall

THE PROGRAM

Graham Windham is a nonprofit child welfare agency serving greater New York City and placing approximately 40 children annually. Founded in 1806 by Ms. Graham and Mrs. Alexander Hamilton as an orphanage, Graham Windham is one of the oldest non-sectarian child welfare agencies in the nation. The agency is principally a foster care agency which provides foster homes, group homes, and residential care to children whose biological families are unable to care for them. When children in the foster or residential care program become legally free for adoption, the agency works to find permanent families for them.

THE COST

Adoption services are provided at no cost to the adoptive family. The only fees which prospective adoptive parents should anticipate are legal fees connected with finalization of the adoption.

THE WAIT

The time from application to the homecoming of the adoptive child ranges from 3 months to 2 years.

THE CHILDREN

Graham Windham places both healthy and special-needs children, ranging in age from birth to 18 years, of all (but primarily Black) racial backgrounds, born in the U.S.

THE REQUIREMENTS

Age: Applicants must be at least 21 years of age. The maximum age requirement varies depending on the age of the child and the health of the parents.

Health: Applicants with health problems or handicaps are given individual consideration.

Religion: No requirement.

Financial status: Applicants must demonstrate ability to support themselves and the child.

Marital status: No requirement.

Family size: No requirement.

Racial, ethnic or cultural origin: Preference for placing children in families of similar origins.

THE PROCEDURE

Participation in Graham Windham's adoption program entails the following basic steps:
Orientation meeting
Application
Individual counseling sessions
Homestudy
Referral
Placement
Post-placement supervision

ADDITIONAL PROGRAMS/SERVICES

Graham Windham provides foster care, group home care, and residential care.

BRANCH/NETWORK OFFICES

None.

LICENSE/ACCREDITATION/PROFESSIONAL AFFILIATIONS

Graham Windham is licensed by the State of New York Department of Social Services and is accredited by the Council on Accreditation of Services for Families and Children.

HARLEM-DOWLING CHILDREN'S SERVICES

2090 Adam Clayton Powell Jr. Boulevard
New York, NY 10027
(212) 749–3656
Program director: Steve Stitt, CSW

THE PROGRAM

Harlem-Dowling Children's Services is a nonprofit agency serving residents of the New York metropolitan area, New Jersey and Connecticut and placing approximately 45 children annually through its adoption program. Founded in 1969 under the auspices of Spence-Chapin, Harlem-Dowling became an autonomous agency in 1980. "Committed to keeping families together," Harlem-Dowling was the first licensed, community-based,, comprehensive child welfare agency specifically serving the Black and Hispanic community in New York City. Clients are provided with a wide range of services and programs including individual, family, and group counseling; medical care; crisis intervention; legal counseling; preventive services; mental health care; emergency placements; foster care and adoption. Working directly with birthparents, with other licensed agencies, and with national and regional exchange programs, Harlem-Dowling works to find permanent homes for Black and Hispanic children who are in need of adoptive families. In addition, the agency will provide homestudy and supervisory services for children pursuing interagency adoption (domestic or international) or independent adoption.

THE COST

The agency's fee for private adoption services is $2,000. Services covered by the fee include all phases of the adoption process.

THE WAIT

The time from application to the homecoming of the adoptive child averages 6 months for healthy infant placements and 12 to 18 months for children between the ages of 2 and 5. The wait for older child placements varies depending on the number of children currently in need of adoptive families.

THE REQUIREMENTS

Age: The requirement is evaluated on a case-by-case basis.
Health: Applicants should be in reasonably good health.
Religion: No requirement.
Financial status: Applicants should have sufficient income to provide adequately for an additional family member.
Marital status: No requirement.
Family size: No requirement.
Racial, ethnic or cultural origin: Preference for placing children in families of similar origins.

THE PROCEDURE

Participation in the adoption program of Harlem-Dowling Children's Services entails the following basic steps:
Orientation meeting
Application
Homestudy
Referral
Placement
Post-placement supervision

ADDITIONAL PROGRAMS/SERVICES

Harlem-Dowling provides individual, family, and group counseling; medical care; crisis intervention; legal counseling; preventive services; mental health care; emergency placements; foster care; post-adoption counseling and referrals.

BRANCH/NETWORK OFFICES

None.

LICENSE/ACCREDITATION/PROFESSIONAL AFFILIATIONS

Harlem-Dowling Children's Services is licensed by the State of New York Department of Social Services and is approved for placement by the State of New Jersey Department of Human Services and the State of Connecticut Department of Children and Youth Services.

HILLSIDE CHILDREN'S CENTER

150 Floverton Street
Rochester, NY 14610
(716) 482–3992
Program director: Marjorie Stevens, Director of Adoption

THE PROGRAM

Founded 150 years ago, Hillside Children's Center is a not-for- profit, non-sectarian comprehensive child welfare, social service and mental health agency for children, youth and their families, serving residents of the greater Rochester area. The agency is "dedicated to strengthening families and promoting, restoring and sustaining the functioning of children at their optimum potential through an array of 29 services," including preventive and adoption services, education and day treatment services, short term emergency shelter and crisis counseling, and long term care and treatment. The agency has 3 adoption programs. The Northaven Adoption Program provides services to birthparents and places infants for adoption when birthparents elect adoptive placement as the best plan for their child. The Hillside Adoption Program serves children with special needs (Caucasian children, aged 12 and older; minority children, aged 7 and older; children of all ages with serious physical, mental, and emotional needs). Through its International Program, the agency provides referral, homestudy, and post-placement services to facilitate the placement of foreign-born children. Through these programs, the agency directly places and facilitates the placement of approximately 71 children annually. In addition, the agency will provide homestudy and supervisory services for applicants pursuing private or interagency adoption.

THE COST

For infant and international adoption, the agency's fee is based on a sliding scale in accordance with the applicant's income. As of October 1988, fees for infant adoption range from $1,760 to $5,500 (includes homestudy, placement, and post-placement services); fees for international adoption range from $880 to $2,750 (includes homestudy and post-placement services). Applicants pursuing international adoption should anticipate additional costs which vary depending on the country of origin or the cooperating agency. For special-needs adoption, services are provided at no cost to the applicant. For all programs, applicants are responsible for legal fees connected with finalization.

THE WAIT

The time from application to placement varies depending on the program. For special-needs adoption, the wait is approximately 1 year. For domestic infant adoption, the wait ranges from 1 to 5 years. For international adoption, the wait ranges from 1 to 2 years.

THE CHILDREN

Hillside Children's Center places both healthy and special-needs children, ranging in age from infancy to adolescence, of all racial backgrounds, born in the U.S. In addition, the agency facilitates the placement of foreign-born children from various countries.

THE REQUIREMENTS

Age: No requirement for Hillside. For international adoption, applicants must meet the requirements of the cooperating agency or source.

Health: No requirement for Hillside. For international adoption, applicants must meet the requirements of the cooperating agency or source.

Religion: No requirement for Hillside. For international adoption, applicants must meet the requirements of the cooperating agency or source.

Financial status: Applicants must be self-supporting. For international adoption, applicants must meet the requirements of the cooperating agency or source.

Marital status: No requirement for Hillside. For international adoption, applicants must meet the requirements of the cooperating agency or source.

Family size: No requirement for Hillside. For international adoption, applicants must meet the requirements of the cooperating agency or source.

Racial, ethnic or cultural origin: Preference for placing children in families of similar origins. The requirement varies depending on the needs of the child.

THE PROCEDURE

Participation in the adoption program of Hillside Children's Center entails the following basic steps:
Orientation meeting
Application
Individual counseling sessions
Homestudy (group format)
Compliance with immigration/naturalization requirements (international adoptions only)
Referral
Placement
Post-placement supervision
Family support group

ADDITIONAL PROGRAMS/SERVICES

In addition to its adoption programs, Hillside Children's Center provides a wide range of services including preventive services (intensive family support, preservation, and counseling programs; programs for pregnant and parenting teens; outreach and life skills training programs for independent youth); education and day treatment programs (campus school; resource classrooms; day treatment; family life education); short term care (emergency crisis counseling; residential group care; foster family care; group emergency and diagnostic assessment); long term care and treatment (residential treatment center; community based group care; transitional living group home; cluster and therapeutic foster family care).

BRANCH/NETWORK OFFICES

While Hillside maintains satellite offices at several locations, all adoption inquiries are processed by the Floverton Street office.

LICENSE/ACCREDITATION/PROFESSIONAL AFFILIATIONS

Hillside Children's Center is licensed by the State of New York Department of Social Services. The agency is accredited by the Joint Commission on Accreditation of Healthcare Organizations, Council on Accreditation of Services for Families and Children, and Division of Accreditation of the American Association of Psychiatric Services for Children. The agency holds membership in numerous social welfare organizations, including the American Association of Children's Residential Centers, Child Welfare League of America, Council of Family and Child Caring Agencies, and others.

INTERNATIONAL ADOPTIONS,

7 Elmwood Drive
New City, NY 10956
(914) 634–5809
Program director:

THE PROGRAM

For a full description of programs and services, refer to Massachusetts listing:
International Adoptions, Inc.
282 Moody Street
Waltham, MA 02154
(617) 894–5330

BRANCH OFFICE

International Adoptions/New York
22 Yerk Avenue
Ronkonkoma, NY 11779
Telephone: (516) 585–1008

Jewish Child Care Association

575 Lexington Avenue
New York, NY 10022
(212) 371–1313
Program director: Paula R. Ainsley

The Program

Jewish Child Care Association (JCCA) is a nonprofit child welfare agency serving the state of New York and placing approximately 20 children annually. Founded in 1822 "to ameliorate the condition of the unfortunate," JCCA has evolved in response to the changing needs of the community and today provides a wide range of services for children including residential treatment centers, foster home care, and preventive/mental health/support services. The agency's adoption focus is to serve older, special needs, and minority children. When children in the agency's foster care program become legally free for adoption, the agency works to find permanent families for them. In addition, through its Networking Adoption Program, the agency provides counseling, homestudy, and supervisory services to applicants pursuing non-traditional adoptions.

The Cost

Adoption services are provided at no cost to the adoptive family. The Networking Adoption Program has a sliding scale fee.

The Wait

The time from application for acceptance into the program to the homecoming of the adoptive child varies depending on the applicant's openness to the special needs of the child.

The Children

JCCA places special-needs children, usually between the ages of 10 and 17, of Black, Hispanic and bi-racial backgrounds, born in the U.S.

The Requirements

Age: Applicants must be at least 21 years of age.
Health: Applicants with health problems or handicaps are given individual consideration.
Religion: The requirement varies depending on the needs of the child.
Financial status: No requirement.
Marital status: No requirement.
Family size: Applicants may have no more than 4 children currently in the family.
Racial, ethnic or cultural origin: The requirement varies depending on the needs of the child and the family.

The Procedure

Participation in JCCA's adoption program entails the following basic steps:
Orientation meeting
Application
Individual counseling sessions
Homestudy
Placement
Post-placement supervision

Additional Programs/Services

JCCA provides a wide range of services including residential treatment, foster care services, information and referral services, preventive/mental health/support services. In addition, through The Networking Adoption Program, the agency provides professional support, information, and counseling throughout the adoption process as a resource for parents to gain the skills they need to be successful adoptive parents. Networking Adoption Program is a fee for service program.

Branch/Network Offices

All inquiries are processed through the main office.

License/Accreditation/Professional Affiliations

Jewish Child Care Association is licensed by the State of New York Department of Social Services and is a member of the Federation of Jewish Philanthropies of New York and the United Way.

Jewish Family Service of Buffalo and Erie County

70 Barker Street
Buffalo, NY 14209
(716) 883–1914
Program director: David M. Gersh, Ph.D.

The Program

Jewish Family Service of Buffalo and Erie County is a nonprofit agency serving residents of western New York. While Jewish Family Service is licensed to provide child-placement services, the agency has not handled domestic adoptions directly for the past 5 years. However, the agency does provide homestudy and supervisory services for applicants pursuing independent adoption or international adoption through a cooperating agency. The agency's plans for the future include a network of services to address problems relating to infertility and to post-adoption adjustment.

The Cost

The agency's fee for services is based on a sliding scale and ranges from $5 to $60 per hour. Services available include individual counseling, group therapy, homestudy and supervisory services, and professional consultation.

The Wait

Not applicable.

The Children

Jewish Family Service will provide homestudy and supervisory services for applicants pursuing independent or international adoption of children of any age, race, or country of origin.

THE REQUIREMENTS

Age: No requirement.
Health: No requirement.
Religion: Services are provided primarily to members of the Jewish community.
Financial status: No requirement.
Family size: No requirement.
Racial, ethnic or cultural origin: No requirement.

THE PROCEDURE

Applicants pursuing independent or international adoption who are in need of homestudy and supervisory services are invited to contact the agency directly to arrange for an interview.

ADDITIONAL PROGRAMS/SERVICES

Jewish Family Service provides an active Family Life Education Program (workshops and seminars on a variety of topics). The agency also provides counseling to individuals, couples, families, and groups.

BRANCH/NETWORK OFFICES

None.

LICENSE/ACCREDITATION/PROFESSIONAL AFFILIATIONS

Jewish Family Service of Buffalo and Erie County is licensed by the State of New York Department of Social Services.

LDS SOCIAL SERVICES

105 Main Street
Fishkill, NY 12524
(914) 896–8266
Program director: Ed M. Axford

THE PROGRAM

For a full description of programs and services, refer to Utah listing:

LDS Social Services
50 East North Temple Street
Salt Lake City, UT 84150

LITTLE FLOWER CHILDREN'S SERVICES

Adoption Department
186 Joralemon Street
Brooklyn, NY 11201
(718) 260–8840
Program director: Camille Swift

THE PROGRAM

Little Flower Children's Services is a voluntary, nonprofit agency serving adoptable children of New York State for placement nationwide, placing approximately 85 children annually. Providing care for children for 60 years and adoption services since 1971, the philosophy of Little Flower is that "children grow best in families." The agency's primary goal is to provide permanency for each child by reuniting families that have been broken as a result of illness, poverty, death, or other tragedies of today's society. When reunification is impossible, efforts are intensified to create a new family through adoption. The agency believes that "a family is a child's most precious possession!" Working in cooperation with the New York State Department of Social Services, Little Flower places both healthy and special-needs children.

THE COST

Adoption services are provided at no cost to applicants. If the child does not qualify for subsidy, applicants are responsible for legal fees connected with finalization.

THE WAIT

The time from application to placement varies depending on the type of adoption. For a healthy Caucasian child, ranging in age from birth to 5 years, the wait is approximately 6 years. For a minority special-needs child, the wait is 6 months.

THE CHILDREN

Little Flower places both healthy and special-needs children, ranging in age from birth to 21 years, of all racial backgrounds, born in the U.S.

THE REQUIREMENTS

Age: Applicants must be at least 21 years of age.
Health: Applicants must be in reasonably good health. Applicants with health problems or handicaps are given individual consideration.
Religion: No requirement.
Financial status: Applicants must have sufficient income to provide for an additional family member. Applicants may be on Public Assistance.
Marital status: Applicants may be married, single, or divorced. Applicants who are separated but not divorced are not accepted.
Family size: No requirement.
Racial, ethnic or cultural origin: No requirement.

THE PROCEDURE

Participation in the adoption program of Little Flower entails the following basic steps:
Orientation meeting
Application
Homestudy
Adoption training
Licensing by state
Individual counseling sessions as needed
Referral
Placement
Post-placement supervision

ADDITIONAL PROGRAMS/SERVICES

Little Flower Children's Services provides a wide range of services including foster boarding homes; residential treatment center and shelter school (grades 1 to 8); group home program for adolescents; agency operated boarding homes; intermediate care facilities for developmentally disabled; "Boarder Baby" rescue operation.

BRANCH/NETWORK OFFICES

In addition to its New York City office, Little Flower maintains a branch office in Wading River, New York (Long Island).

LICENSE/ACCREDITATION/PROFESSIONAL AFFILIATIONS

Little Flower Children's Services is licensed by the State of New York Department of Social Services and by the State of New Jersey Department of Human Services. The agency is a member of the Child Welfare League of America, National Adoption Exchange, National Adoption Network, National Association of Foster and Adoptive Parents, Bi-County Exchange (Nassau/Suffolk), and Council of Family and Child Care Agencies.

LOUISE WISE SERVICES

12 East 94th Street
New York, NY 10128
(212) 876–3050
Program director: Morton S. Rogers, Executive Director

THE PROGRAM

Louise Wise Services is a nonprofit agency serving metropolitan New York City and placing approximately 40 children annually through its adoption program. Working directly with birthparents, with other private and public agencies, and with national and regional exchange programs, the agency places both healthy and special-needs children. The agency believes that "there is a permanent adoptive home for every child in need of one."

THE COST

The agency's fee for adoption services is 10% of the applicants' annual gross income with a maximum fee of $3,000. For children who are in the custody of the State of New York, adoption services are provided at no cost to the adoptive family. Services covered by the fee include all phases of the adoption process, excluding legal fees connected with finalization of the adoption.

THE WAIT

The time from application to the homecoming of the adoptive child ranges from 1 to 12 months for the adoption of a Black child and from 3 to 5 years for the adoption of a Caucasian child.

THE CHILDREN

Louise Wise Services places both healthy and special-needs children, ranging in age from birth to 16 years. Most children available for adoption are Black, some are Hispanic, and few are Caucasian.

THE REQUIREMENTS

Age: Applicants must be at least 18 years of age (in accordance with statute).

Health: Applicants should be in reasonably good health.
Religion: No requirement.
Financial status: No requirement.
Marital status: No requirement.
Family size: No requirement.
Racial, ethnic or cultural origin: No requirement.

THE PROCEDURE

Participation in the adoption program of Louise Wise Services entails the following basic steps:
    Orientation meeting
    Application
    Individual counseling sessions
    Homestudy
    Referral
    Placement
    Post-placement supervision
    Post-adoption counseling

ADDITIONAL PROGRAMS/SERVICES

Louise Wise Services provides a range of services including foster care and emergency foster care; maternity residence; mother/baby residence; residence for retarded children; preventive services; refugee assistance program for unaccompanied minors.

BRANCH/NETWORK OFFICES

None.

LICENSE/ACCREDITATION/PROFESSIONAL AFFILIATIONS

Louise Wise Services is licensed by the State of New York Department of Social Services and the State of New Jersey Department of Human Services. The agency is a member of the Child Welfare League of America.

LOVE THE CHILDREN

28 Foxboro Lane
Fairport, NY
(716) 223–1868
Program director: Mary L. Graves

THE PROGRAM

For a full description of programs and services, refer to Pennsylvania listing:
Love the Children
    221 W. Broad Street
    Quakertown, PA 18951
    (215) 536–4180

BRANCH OFFICES

LTC-Syracuse, NY
    8199 Wheaton Road
    Baldwinsville, NY
    (315) 638–9449
LTC-Buffalo, NY
    118 N. Ellicott Creek Road
    Tonawanda, NY
    (716) 691–5166

LUTHERAN COMMUNITY SERVICES, INC.

33 Worth Street
New York, NY 10013
(212) 431–7470
Program director: Helen S. Okun

THE PROGRAM

Lutheran Community Services is a nonprofit agency serving residents of New York City, Long Island, Rockland, Orange, Ulster, Dutchess, and Putnam Counties and placing approximately 20 children annually through its Outreach Adoption Program. Outreach Adoption Program (contracted by the City of New York, Department of Social Services) is a specialized program within Lutheran Community Services which seeks to find adoptive homes for New York State's waiting children (children who are legally free for adoption, living in foster care, in need of a permanent adoptive home). The agency will also provide homestudy and supervisory services to applicants pursuing interagency adoption (domestic or international) or private adoption.

THE COST

Adoption services for New York waiting children are provided at no cost to the adoptive family. For applicants pursuing international or private adoption, the agency's fees are based on a sliding scale with a maximum fee of $600 for the homestudy and a maximum fee of $200 for post-placement supervision and report.

THE WAIT

The time from application to placement varies depending on the range of special needs the prospective adoptive family can accept.

THE CHILDREN

Lutheran Community Services places primarily special-needs children (ranging from mildly to severely physically or emotionally handicapped), ranging in age from birth to 21 years, primarily of Black, Hispanic, and bi-racial backgrounds. The agency makes a limited number of Caucasian placements.

THE REQUIREMENTS

Age: Applicants must be at least 18. The requirement varies depending on the applicant's health and resources.
Health: Applicants should be in reasonably good health. Applicants with health problems or handicaps are given individual consideration.
Religion: No requirement.
Financial status: Applicants must be able to document their source of income and the extent of their expenses. Applicants must demonstrate sufficient resources to provide adequately for the family's needs.
Marital status: Applicants may be married, single, legally separated, or legally divorced (documentation required). If married, the length of the marriage must be at least 1 year.
Family size: No requirement. If applicants have other children, they must be able to demonstrate that they have the space and the time to meet the needs of an additional child.
Racial, ethnic or cultural origin: Preference for placing children in families of similar origins.

THE PROCEDURE

Participation in the adoption program of Lutheran Community Services entails the following basic steps:
Orientation meeting
Application
Homestudy
Referral
Placement
Application for subsidy (for New York waiting children)
Post-placement supervision
Finalization

ADDITIONAL PROGRAMS/SERVICES

Lutheran Community Services provides foster home care for children from infancy to 18 or 21 years of age, foster group care for boys and girls, and foster group care for the mentally retarded.

BRANCH/NETWORK OFFICES

All adoption inquiries are processed through the main office.

LICENSE/ACCREDITATION/PROFESSIONAL AFFILIATIONS

Lutheran Community Services, Inc. is licensed by the State of New York Department of Social Services and is affiliated with the United Way.

NEW BEGINNINGS FAMILY AND CHILDREN'S SERVICES

141 Willis Avenue
Mineola, NY 11501
(516) 747–2204
Program director: Pooja Park, MSW, Director of Social Services

THE PROGRAM

New Beginnings Family and Children's Services is a nonprofit agency serving residents of New York, New Jersey, and Connecticut and placing approximately 200 children annually through its adoption program. Providing services since 1984, the mission of the agency's adoption program is to seek an adoptive family for each child deprived of a permanent home "in which he may have the opportunity for growth and development through loving care, parental guidance, and the security of a permanent home." Working directly with birthparents, with other private and public agencies, and with national and regional exchange programs, New Beginnings places both healthy and special-needs children born in the U.S. Working directly with birthparents, with intermediaries, and with child welfare institutions abroad, the agency places children from Asia and Latin America in American families. In addition, the agency will provide homestudy and post-placement services for applicants pursuing interagency adoption (domestic or international) or independent adoption.

THE COST

'The agency's fee for adoption services varies greatly depending on the program and ranges from $0 to $8,000. Services covered by the fee include all phases of the adoption process, excluding legal fees connected with finalization of the adoption and excluding travel reimbursement or travel expenses when required.

THE WAIT

The time from application to the homecoming of the adoptive child varies depending on the program and ranges from 6 months to 2 years.

THE CHILDREN

New Beginnings places both healthy and special-needs children, ranging in age from birth to 14 years, of all racial backgrounds. Places of origin include Asia, Latin America, and U.S.

THE REQUIREMENTS

Age: The age requirement varies depending on the country of origin.
Health: The requirement varies depending on the country of origin.
Religion: The requirement varies depending on the child's religion.
Financial status: The requirement varies depending on the country of origin.
Marital status: The requirement varies depending on the country of origin.
Family size: Applicants may have no more than 3 children currently in the family.
Racial, ethnic or cultural origin: The requirement varies depending on the child's needs.

THE PROCEDURE

Participation in the program of New Beginnings entails the following steps:
Pre-application screening
Application
Orientation meeting
Individual and group counseling sessions
Homestudy
Compliance with immigration/naturalization requirements (international adoptions only)
Placement
Post-placement supervision

ADDITIONAL PROGRAMS/SERVICES

New Beginnings provides a wide range of services including post-legal adoption services (individual and/or family enrichment, problem solving, supportive services); individual, family, and group counseling; advocacy; speakers bureau workshops and seminars in key localities; culture exchanges; extensive recruitment of minority families through "one health center one child" and "one church one child" campaigns.

BRANCH/NETWORK OFFICES

None.

LICENSE/ACCREDITATION/PROFESSIONAL AFFILIATIONS

New Beginnings Family and Children's Services is licensed by the appropriate state department in New York, New Jersey, and Connecticut.

NEW YORK CATHOLIC GUARDIAN SOCIETY

1011 First Avenue
New York, NY 10022
(212) 371–1000, Ext. 2340
Program director: Barbara Peck, Administrative Supervisor; Kathleen Holahan, Program Director

THE PROGRAM

New York Catholic Guardian Society (NYCGS) is a nonprofit voluntary agency whose services are principally (but not exclusively) directed to residents of the greater New York metropolitan area. "Dedicated to providing care for children and adults who in their distress turn to the agency for comfort and support," the agency's adoption program is focused on finding permanent homes for older children (10+) who are in need of adoptive families. However, the agency is primarily focused on providing foster homes. The agency's mission is "to provide an environment that recognizes physical, emotional, educational, and social as well as spiritual needs."

THE COST

Adoption services are provided at no cost to the adoptive family. The only expenses which prospective adoptive parents should anticipate are possible legal fees connected with finalization of the adoption.

THE WAIT

The time from application to the homecoming of the adoptive child varies greatly.

THE CHILDREN

NYCGS places primarily older children (10+), both healthy and special needs, of all racial backgrounds. Most children placed by the agency are born in the U.S.

THE REQUIREMENTS

Age: Applicants must be at least 18 years of age.
Health: Applicants should be in reasonably good health. Applicants with health problems or handicaps are given individual consideration.
Religion: No requirement.
Financial status: Applicant's financial status is evaluated individually, but there is no minimum income requirement.
Marital status: Applicants may be either married couples or single parents with defined legal status.

Family size: No requirement.

Racial, ethnic or cultural origin: Preference for placing children in families of similar origins.

THE PROCEDURE

Participation in NYCGS adoption program entails the following basic steps:

Orientation meeting

Application

Individual counseling sessions

Homestudy

Referral

Placement

Post-placement supervision

ADDITIONAL PROGRAMS/SERVICES

NYCGS provides foster care services and training for foster parents, group homes, and individual training for adoptive parents.

BRANCH/NETWORK OFFICES

None.

LICENSE/ACCREDITATION/PROFESSIONAL AFFILIATIONS

New York Catholic Guardian Society is licensed by the State of New York Department of Social Services.

NEW YORK SPAULDING FOR CHILDREN

121 West 27th Street, 6th Floor
New York, NY 10001
(212) 645–7610

Program director: Sarah B. Greenblatt

THE PROGRAM

Founded in 1977, New York Spaulding for Children is a nonprofit special-needs adoption agency serving children in New York City and adoptive families in New York City, Westchester County, and Long Island. The agency's mission is "to place older, handicapped and minority children with adoptive families, to support new families created, and to provide training to other agencies in special-needs adoption."

THE COST

Adoption services are provided at no cost to the adoptive parents.

THE WAIT

The time from application to placement ranges from 3 to 6 months.

THE CHILDREN

New York Spaulding for Children places special-needs children, usually over the age of 6, of all racial backgrounds, born in the U.S.

THE REQUIREMENTS

Age: Applicants must be at least 21 years of age. The maximum age requirement varies depending on the special needs of the child and the applicant's support system.

Health: Applicants should be in reasonably good health. Applicants with health problems or handicaps are given individual consideration and may be accepted if the health problem or handicap does not interfere with their ability to parent a special-needs child.

Religion: No requirement.

Financial status: Applicants must demonstrate the ability to manage their financial resources.

Marital status: No requirement.

Family size: No requirement.

Racial, ethnic or cultural origin: Preference for placing children in families of similar origins.

THE PROCEDURE

Participation in the adoption program of New York Spaulding for Children entails the following basic steps:

Orientation meeting

Application

Adoptive parent training

Homestudy

Visiting period

Placement

Post-placement supervision

Post-finalization support services

ADDITIONAL PROGRAMS/SERVICES

New York Spaulding for Children provides training in special-needs adoption services for other adoption agencies and social workers.

BRANCH/NETWORK OFFICES

None.

LICENSE/ACCREDITATION/PROFESSIONAL AFFILIATIONS

New York Spaulding for Children is licensed by the State of New York Department of Social Services. The agency is a member of the Child Welfare League of America.

OHEL CHILDREN'S HOME AND FAMILY SERVICES

4423 16th Avenue
Brooklyn, NY 11204
(718) 815–6300

Program director: Samuel Frankel, CSW

THE PROGRAM

Ohel Children's Home and Family Services is a nonprofit multi- service agency serving residents of the New York metropolitan area and placing approximately 25 children annually. Founded 18 years ago, the agency's mission is "to provide a Jewish family for any Jewish child in need of foster care or adoption." Working directly with birthparents, with other private and public agencies, and with national and regional exchange programs, Ohel Children's Home places both healthy and special needs Jewish children.

THE COST

The agency's fees vary depending on the services provided. As of October 1988, adoption fees range from $1,500 to $2,500. Applicants are responsible for legal fees connected with finalization of the adoption.

THE WAIT

The time from application to placement ranges from 1 to 2 years.

THE CHILDREN

Ohel Children's Home places both healthy and special-needs children, ranging from birth to 18 years of age, of Jewish ethnic background.

THE REQUIREMENTS

Age: No requirement.
Health: Applicants must be in reasonably good health. Applicants with health problems or handicaps are given individual consideration.
Religion: Applicants must be practicing members of the Jewish religion.
Financial status: No requirement.
Marital status: No requirement.
Family size: No requirement.
Racial, ethnic or cultural origin: Children are placed in families of Jewish ethnic and cultural backgrounds.

THE PROCEDURE

Participation in the adoption program of Ohel Children's Home and Family Services entails the following basic steps:
Orientation meeting
Application
Individual counseling sessions
Homestudy
Referral
Placement
Post-placement supervision

ADDITIONAL PROGRAMS/SERVICES

Ohel Children's Home and Family Services provides foster care; residential programs for emotionally and mentally handicapped children; preventive care services.

BRANCH/NETWORK OFFICES

None.

LICENSE/ACCREDITATION/PROFESSIONAL AFFILIATIONS

Ohel Children's Home and Family Services is licensed by the State of New York Department of Social Services and is a member of the Child Welfare League of America.

PRACA

853 Broadway, 5th Floor
New York, NY 10003
(212) 673-7320
Program director: Carmen Olan, MSW

THE PROGRAM

PRACA (Puerto Rican Association for Community Affairs, Inc.) is a nonprofit community membership organization established in 1952 to provide advocacy and service to the Puerto Rican/Hispanic community. PRACA's guiding principle is "that the needs and development of Hispanic children are best attended in an Hispanic family environment where the retention of Spanish and Hispanic cultural experiences is assured." In 1977, Criemos los Nuestros foster care and adoption program was established to address the specific needs of Puerto Rican and Hispanic children. The primary goal of the program is to facilitate the return of the child to his biological family. If this is not possible, Criemos los Nuestros develops an alternate plan of foster care and/or adoption to provide stability and permanency for the child.

THE COST

Adoption services are provided at no cost to the applicant. If the child being considered for placement is not eligible for subsidy, applicants are responsible for legal fees connected with finalization of the adoption.

THE WAIT

The time from application to placement averages approximately 1 to 1 1/2 years.

THE CHILDREN

Criemos los Nuestros places both healthy and special-needs children, ranging in age from infancy to adolescence, of Puerto Rican or Hispanic backgrounds.

THE REQUIREMENTS

Age: Applicants must be at least 18 years of age.
Health: Applicants must be in reasonably good health.
Religion: No requirement.
Financial status: Applicants may receive Public Assistance.
Marital status: Applicants may be either single or married.
Family size: No requirement.
Racial, ethnic or cultural origin: Preference for placing children in families of similar origins. Non-Hispanic applicants who speak Spanish fluently and who exhibit sensitivity to Hispanic culture are considered.

THE PROCEDURE

Participation in PRACA's adoption program entails the following basic steps:
Orientation meeting
Application
Group counseling sessions
Individual counseling sessions
Homestudy
Placement
Post-placement supervision

ADDITIONAL PROGRAMS/SERVICES

PRACA provides a wide range of services to the Hispanic community including extensive counseling services; psychological assessment and therapy; foster care; workshops and seminars on a range of topics.

BRANCH/NETWORK OFFICES

All adoption inquiries are processed through the main office.

LICENSE/ACCREDITATION/PROFESSIONAL AFFILIATIONS

PRACA is licensed by the State of New York Department of Social Services and is a member of the Child Welfare League of America.

PARSONS CHILD AND FAMILY CENTER

845 Central Avenue
Albany, NY 12206
(518) 438–4571
Program director: Mary Louise Baum

THE PROGRAM

Parsons Child and Family Center is a nonprofit agency serving children and families. Founded in 1829 as a shelter for homeless children, Parsons has evolved in response to the changing needs of the community and today provides a wide range of services including residential, educational and clinical services for youth who may be emotionally troubled, developmentally disabled, and/or in need of a home through foster care or adoption. Parsons has 3 adoption programs. Through the Older Child Program and the Minority Adoption Program, the agency places older, minority, and special-needs children with families in central and upstate New York. Through the International Adoption Program, the agency places Korean infants and children in American families. The International Adoption Program serves residents of central and upstate New York, western Massachusetts, and Vermont. Placing over 150 children annually, the agency's mission is "to provide a continuum of child welfare, educational, clinical and child care services to children, youth, and their families."

THE COST

The agency's fee for adoption services is based on a sliding scale and varies depending on the program. For the Older Child Program, the fee for a homestudy is $375, plus a $25 registration fee. If the child is adopted through Parsons, the homestudy fee is reimbursed. For the Minority Program, there is no cost to prospective parents. For the International Adoption Program, the fee ranges from $4,600 to $7,000. Services covered by the fee include all phases of the adoption process, excluding legal fees connected with finalization of the adoption.

THE WAIT

The time from application to the placement of the adoptive child varies depending on the program. For the older and minority programs, the wait can be from 3 to 6 months. For the international program, the wait can be 10 to 16 months.

THE CHILDREN

Parsons Child and Family Center places both healthy and special-needs children, ranging in age from birth to 18 years, of all racial origins. Countries of origin include U.S. and Korea.

THE REQUIREMENTS

Age: The age requirements vary according to the program.
Health: Applicants must be in reasonably good health. Applicants with health problems or handicaps will be given special consideration.
Religion: No requirement.
Financial status: No requirement.
Marital status: No requirement for older, minority, and special-needs adoptions. For Korean adoption, applicants must be married, and the length of the marriage must be at least 3 years.
Family size: No requirement for older, minority, and special-needs adoptions. For Korean adoption, applicants may have no more than 4 children currently in the family.
Racial, ethnic or cultural origin: Preference for placing children in families of similar origins.

THE PROCEDURE

Participation in Parsons Child and Family Center's adoption programs entails the following basic steps:
Orientation meeting
Application
Individual counseling sessions
Group counseling sessions
Homestudy
Compliance with immigration/naturalization requirements (Korean adoptions only)
Referral
Placement
Post-placement supervision
Finalization
Post-legalization services (provided directly or through referral, if requested)

ADDITIONAL PROGRAMS/SERVICES

Parsons Child and Family Center sponsors workshops, seminars, and culture camps to strengthen the cultural identity of Korean children adopted by American families; provides educational, clinical, and residential programs; hosts an annual picnic for adoptive families; conducts fund-raising activities to support child welfare programs in Korea; works closely with Korean-American Families (KAF), a support group.

BRANCH/NETWORK OFFICES

Parsons Child and Family Center serves residents of western Vermont, central and upstate New York through the Albany office. Residents of western Massachusetts are invited to

contact Parsons' branch office in Massachusetts:
66 Lake Buel Road
Great Barrington, MA 01230
(413) 528–2749

LICENSE/ACCREDITATION/PROFESSIONAL AFFILIATIONS

Parsons Child and Family Center is licensed by the appropriate state departments in New York, Vermont, and Massachusetts. The agency is accredited by the Joint Commission on Accreditation of Health Care Organizations (JCAH) and by the Council on Accreditation of Services for Families and Children.

THE SALVATION ARMY SOCIAL SERVICES FOR CHILDREN

233 East 17th Street
New York, NY 10003
(212) 505–4200
Program director: Robert H. Gutheil

THE PROGRAM

The Salvation Army Social Services for Children (SASSC) is a nonprofit child welfare agency serving greater New York City. Founded in London, England in 1865, The Salvation Army came to the U.S. in 1880. The Social Services for Children began as a nursery program and then expanded to include foster care and adoption services. Today, the agency is principally a foster care agency which provides foster homes, group homes, and residential care to children whose biological families are unable to care for them. When children in the foster or residential care program become legally free for adoption, the agency works to find permanent families for them. In addition, the agency will provide homestudy and supervisory services for families interested in adopting children photolisted in New York State's Waiting Children. The agency is committed "to serving children with special needs and their families, utilizing the full range of professional and community resources in order to enable each child in its care to realize his or her full human potential."

THE COST

Adoption services are provided at no cost to the adoptive family. The only expenses which applicants should anticipate are legal fees connected with finalization of the adoption.

THE WAIT

The time from application to completion of the homestudy is 2 to 3 months. The agency will study only those families interested in adopting a child in the agency's care or children photolisted in New York State's Waiting Children.

THE CHILDREN

SASSC places both healthy and special-needs children, ranging in age from birth to 18 years, primarily of Black and Hispanic racial backgrounds, born in the U.S.

THE REQUIREMENTS

Age: Applicants must be at least 21 years of age. The maximum age limit varies depending on each child's situation and needs.

Health: Applicants must be in reasonably good health. Applicants with health problems or handicaps are given individual consideration.

Religion: No requirement.

Financial status: Applicants must demonstrate ability to provide for the needs of the family.

Marital status: No requirement.

Family size: No specific requirement, but applicants are evaluated individually on the basis of the adequacy of housing space in relation to the number of children in the family and the ability to care for an additional child.

Racial, ethnic or cultural origin: Preference for placing children in families of similar origins.

THE PROCEDURE

Participation in SASSC's adoption program entails the following basic steps:
Orientation
Application
Individual counseling sessions
Homestudy
Referral
Clearance with State Child Abuse Registry
Placement
Post-placement supervision

ADDITIONAL PROGRAMS/SERVICES

SASSC provides extensive foster care services and foster parent training; preventive services; day care services; community residences for the mentally retarded.

BRANCH/NETWORK OFFICES

None.

LICENSE/ACCREDITATION/PROFESSIONAL AFFILIATIONS

The Salvation Army Social Services for Children is licensed by the State of New York Department of Social Services and is accredited by the Council on Accreditation of Services for Families and Children. Affiliations include the Child Welfare League of America, New York State Council of Family and Child Caring Agencies, and United Way.

SPENCE-CHAPIN SERVICES TO FAMILIES AND CHILDREN

6 East 94th Street
New York, NY 10128
(212) 369–0300
Program director: Jane D. Edwards, ACSW

THE PROGRAM

Spence-Chapin is a nonprofit, non-sectarian social service agency serving residents of the state of New York and other states as well and placing in adoption approximately 350 children annually. Since the turn of the century, the agency's mission has been to "place out infants and children who need families with parents who need and want children." Responding to societal needs, the agency provides domestic and foreign adoption programs. The agency provides extensive services to birthparents and places infants for adoption when birthparents elect adoptive placement as the best plan for their child. The agency is also actively involved in recruiting families for special-needs children. Working with a child welfare agency in Korea, Spence-Chapin places Korean children in American families for adoption.

THE COST

The agency's fee for adoption services is based on a sliding scale of approximately 10% of the applicants' annual gross income. Total cost estimates (excluding legal fees connected with finalization) for each program are as follows:

Domestic infant adoption	$ 6,000.00–$10,000.00
Domestic special-needs adoption	$0.00–$10,000.00
Korean adoption	$ 3,000.00–$ 7,000.00

Services covered by the fee include all phases of the adoption process (services to birthparents, adoptive parents, and child care services).

THE WAIT

The time from application to the homecoming of the adoptive child varies depending on the program. The wait for domestic infant adoption ranges from 6 months to 1 1/2 years; for domestic special needs, 0 to 1 year; for Korean adoption, 6 months to 1 year.

THE CHILDREN

Spence-Chapin places both healthy and special-needs infants of all racial backgrounds. Countries of origin include U.S., Korea, and South America.

THE REQUIREMENTS

Age: The ages of adoptive parents are considered on an individual basis.

Health: Applicants must be in reasonably good health.

Religion: The agency is non-sectarian. By law, for all adoptions the preferences of the birthparents are honored.

Financial status: Applicants must demonstrate financial stability.

Marital status: Married couples and single individuals may apply.

Family size: The size of the family is a consideration depending on the program.

Racial, ethnic or cultural origin: The agency places children within ethnic and cultural lines where practicable.

THE PROCEDURE

Participation in Spence-Chapin's adoption program entails the following basic steps:

Inquiry
Orientation meeting
Application/intake interview
Homestudy (preparation for parenthood)
Compliance with immigration/naturalization requirements (intercountry adoptions only)

Child referral
Placement
Post-placement supervision
Finalization
Post-legal services

ADDITIONAL PROGRAMS/SERVICES

Spence-Chapin provides extensive services to birthparents and services for families and individuals involved in the adoptive experience (ACT) who are having some problems.

BRANCH/NETWORK OFFICES

All adoption inquiries are processed through the main office.

LICENSE/ACCREDITATION/PROFESSIONAL AFFILIATIONS

Spence-Chapin Services to Families and Children is licensed by the State of New York Department of Social Services. Spence-Chapin is a member agency of the United Way, the Child Welfare League of America, the National Committee for Adoption, the National Conference on Social Welfare, the Interagency Mental Health Council, and the New York State Council of Family and Child Caring Agencies.

ST. JOSEPH CHILDREN'S SERVICES

345 Adams Street, 6th Floor
Brooklyn, NY 11201
(718) 858–8700
Program director: Carol Ann Yeaple

THE PROGRAM

St. Joseph Children's Services is a nonprofit agency serving residents of Brooklyn, Queens, and the surrounding areas. Originally founded by the Sisters of Charity in 1826 to care for the orphaned girls left by Irish immigrants, St. Joseph's is today a multi-service child and family agency caring for over 2,000 children daily in Brooklyn and Queens through a range of programs which include foster boarding homes, emergency foster boarding homes, adoption, family day care, diagnostic services, group homes and residential programs, and community based programs. When a child in foster or residential care cannot be reunited with his or her family of origin, St. Joseph's works to find a permanent adoptive family for the child. Often the child is adopted by his or her foster parents; most parents who adopt through St. Joseph's begin as foster parents. Through this program, St. Joseph's places approximately 38 children annually in adoptive families. In all of its programs, St. Joseph Children's Services "maintains as its highest aspiration the generation of a society of caring people who will nurture the future by prioritizing the children of today."

THE COST

Adoption services are provided at no cost to the adoptive family.

The Wait

Most parents who adopt a child through St. Joseph's begin as foster parents. It takes approximately 3 months to become licensed as a foster parent. Once licensed as a foster parent, the wait varies from nothing to a few months.

The Children

Children available for adoption through St. Joseph's are in the custody of the Commissioner of Social Services of the City of New York. St. Joseph's places both healthy and special-needs children, ranging in age from birth to 18 years of age, primarily of Black and Hispanic racial backgrounds.

The Requirements

Age: No requirement.
Health: No requirement.
Religion: No requirement.
Financial status: No requirement.
Marital status: Applicants may be married, single, divorced, or legally separated.
Family size: No requirement.
Racial, ethnic or cultural origin: No requirement.

The Procedure

Participation in the adoption program of St. Joseph Children's Services entails the following basic steps:
Orientation meeting
Application
Homestudy
Individual counseling sessions
Placement
Periodic training sessions
Post-placement supervision and support

Additional Programs/Services

St. Joseph Children's Services provides a wide range of services including foster boarding homes; emergency foster boarding homes; family day care; diagnostic services; residential program; group homes and agency operated boarding homes; community based preventive services; supportive services; post-adoption legalization services.

Branch/Network Offices

All inquiries concerning adoption and foster care are processed through the main office.

License/Accreditation/Professional Affiliations

St. Joseph Children's Services is licensed by the State of New York Department of Social Services. The agency is affiliated with Catholic Child Care Society, Council of Family and Child Caring Agencies, Child Welfare League of America, National Association of Social Workers, New York State Foster and Adoptive Parent Association, North American Council on Adoptable Children, and Adoption Action Network of New York State.

Voice for International and Domestic Adoptions, Inc. (V.I.D.A.)

354 Allen Street
Hudson, N.Y. 12534
(518) 828–4527
Program director: DeGuerre A. Blackburn, Ph.D., ACSW

The Program

VIDA is a nonprofit agency providing nationwide service and placing 40 children annually. The mission of the agency is "to facilitate domestic and international adoptions (South and Central America) and to establish and maintain physical and mental rehabilitation programs in both South and Central America." The rehabilitation program has been in place since 1980. The adoption program, an outgrowth of the rehabilitation program, was established in 1985.

The Cost

The agency's fees are based on a sliding scale. The average fee is $5,300 to VIDA, the U.S.-based agency, and a donation of $1,000–$3,500 to the overseas agency. Services covered by the fee include initial interview session, pre-adoption counseling, homestudy, processing of Immigration pre-adoption requirements, full coordination with overseas agency, translations, authentications, post-adoption counseling, and two-year follow-up. In addition, prospective adoptive parents should anticipate financial responsibility for transportation and stay overseas as well as visa/exit permits.

The Wait

The average time from application for acceptance into the program to the homecoming of the adoptive child is 6 months.

The Children

VIDA places children (newborns to adolescents) both individually and in sibling groups. Many of the children come from Central and South American countries. Children with special needs are placed through cooperation with the New York State Blue Books and various intercountry exchanges.

The Requirements

Age: Applicants must be over 21, and there must be a reasonable age difference between parents and child.
Health: Applicants with health problems or handicaps are given individual consideration.
Religion: No specific requirement.
Financial status: No specific requirement.
Marital status: No requirement.
Family size: No requirement.
Racial, ethnic or cultural origin: No requirement.

The Procedure

Participation in VIDA's adoption program entails the following basic steps:
Application
Orientation meeting

Individual counseling sessions
Psychological examination
Homestudy
Compliance with immigration/naturalization requirements
Placement
Post-placement supervision, 2 years (required by agreement with overseas agencies)

ADDITIONAL PROGRAMS/SERVICES

In addition to its adoption program, VIDA provides foster care, psychological services, and various rehabilitation programs.

BRANCH/NETWORK OFFICES

None. Staff members travel, when appropriate, to all parts of the U.S. as well as overseas.

LICENSE/ACCREDITATION/PROFESSIONAL AFFILIATIONS

VIDA is licensed by the State of New York Department of Social Services, State of New Jersey Department of Human Services, and State of Connecticut Department of Children and Youth Services. All VIDA social workers are licensed by the State of New York.

North Carolina

PUBLIC ADOPTION PROGRAM/ COMMUNITY RESOURCES

Department of Human Resources
Social Services Division
325 North Salisbury Street
Raleigh, NC 27611
(919) 733–3801
Adoption specialist: Robin Peacock

THE PROGRAM

Public adoption services in North Carolina are provided by the Department of Human Resources, Social Services Division (DHR/SSD) through county departments of social services. While there are some infants and toddlers available for adoption through county departments of social services, the focus of the program is to recruit and prepare families and to supervise the placement of special-needs children (older, minority, and handicapped children and sibling groups) who are in the custody of the State of North Carolina.

STATE EXCHANGE

North Carolina Adoption Resource Exchange
Exchange Coordinator: Janice Williams
325 North Salisbury Street
Raleigh, NC 27611
(919) 733–3801

STATE ADOPTION REUNION REGISTRY

None.

STATE SUBSIDY

For information, contact the Social Services Division (above).

NACAC REPRESENTATIVE

Nan Poplin
5102 Ellenwood Drive
Greensboro, NC 27410
(919) 855–8006

GENERAL ADOPTION RESOURCES

Adoptive Parents Together (APT)
Contact: Peggy Southerland
107 Glenwood Trail
Southern Pines, NC 28387
(919) 692–5321

Southern Piedmont OURS
Contact: Louise Bingham
P.O. Box 221946
Charlotte, NC 28222–1946
(704) 563–9646

Triangle OURS Through Adoption
Contact: Judy Holland
54 Newton Dr.
Durham, NC 27707
(919) 489–9809 or 929–1979

Western Carolina OURS
Contact: Paula Wells

29 Griffing Blvd.
Asheville, NC 28804

SPECIAL-NEEDS ADOPTION RESOURCES

For information on special-needs resources, contact the Social Services Division (above).

OUT-OF-STATE AGENCIES

AGENCY

Adoption Service Information Agency, District of Columbia
World Child, District of Columbia
Catholic Charities of Richmond, Virginia

SEE APPENDIX A

Agencies Providing Nationwide Services

BETHANY CHRISTIAN SERVICES

25 Reed Street
P.O. Box 15569
Asheville, NC 28813(704) 274–7146
Program director: James K. Haveman, Jr.—Executive Director

THE PROGRAM

For a full description of programs and services, refer to Michigan listing:
Bethany Christian Services
901 Eastern Avenue, N.E.
Grand Rapids, MI 49503–1295
(616) 459–6273

BRANCH OFFICES

Bethany Christian Services/North Carolina
East Main St.
P.O. Box 1614
P.O. Box 999
(704) 369–6188
Murphy, NC 28906–0999
Franklin, NC 28734–1614
(704) 837–8261
410 Oberlin Rd., Suite 402
P.O. Box 12094
Raleigh, NC 27605–2094
(919) 828–6281

CATHOLIC SOCIAL MINISTRIES OF THE DIOCESE OF RALEIGH, INC.

Executive Office
300 Cardinal Gibbons Dr.
Raleigh, NC 27606

Adoption Administrator
400 Oberlin Rd., Suite 350
Raleigh, NC 27605
(919) 832–0225
Program director: Roderick B. O'Connor

THE PROGRAM

Catholic Social Ministries is a nonprofit multi-service child and family agency serving residents of the eastern half of North Carolina and placing approximately 7 to 12 children annually through its adoption program. Founded on the belief "in the basic worth and inherent dignity of human life at all stages from conception to natural death," the agency is committed "not only to defend each person's right to life, but to strive to help them enhance the quality of that life." Catholic Social Ministries provides services to birthparents and places infants for adoption in Catholic families when birthparents elect adoptive placement as the best plan for their child. In addition, the agency will provide homestudy and supervisory services for applicants pursuing either foreign or domestic interagency adoption.

THE COST

The agency's fee for adoption services is 10% of the gross income of the principal wage earner, with a maximum fee of $3,600. Services covered by the fee include the homestudy, placement, and post-placement supervision. For applicants pursuing either foreign or domestic interagency adoption, the agency's fee is $800 for the homestudy and $690 for supervision.

THE WAIT

The time from application to the homecoming of the adoptive child ranges from 2 to 2 1/2 years.

THE CHILDREN

Catholic Social Ministries places healthy newborn infants of all racial backgrounds, born in the U.S.

THE REQUIREMENTS

Age: Applicants must be at least 25 and no more than 45 years of age.

Health: Applicants must be in reasonably good health. Applicants with health problems or handicaps are given individual consideration. Infertility documentation is required.

Religion: At least 1 spouse must be a practicing Roman Catholic.

Financial status: No requirement.

Marital status: Applicants must be married couples who have been married for at least 3 years. Single parents are considered in exceptional situations.

Family size: Applicants may have no more than 1 child currently in the family.

Racial, ethnic or cultural origin: No requirement, but preference for placing children in families of similar origins.

THE PROCEDURE

Participation in the adoption program of Catholic Social Ministries entails the following basic steps:

Application

Individual counseling sessions
Group counseling sessions (for applicants pursuing foreign interagency adoption)
Homestudy
Placement
Post-placement supervision

ADDITIONAL PROGRAMS/SERVICES

Catholic Social Ministries provides a wide range of community services including crisis pregnancy program; emergency assistance referral; group home (preparation for independent living); infant study homes; legalization of undocumented aliens; individual and marital counseling; pregnancy testing; post-abortion counseling.

BRANCH/NETWORK OFFICES

While Catholic Social Ministries maintains branch offices in 6 locations, all inquiries about adoption are processed through the adoption administration office (above).

LICENSE/ACCREDITATION/PROFESSIONAL AFFILIATIONS

Catholic Social Ministries of the Diocese of Raleigh, Inc. is licensed by the State of North Carolina Department of Human Resources. The agency is a member of the North Carolina Child Care Association and Catholic Charities USA.

CATHOLIC SOCIAL SERVICES OF THE DIOCESE OF CHARLOTTE, INC.

Office Address
116 East First Street
Charlotte, NC 28202
(704) 333–9954
Mailing Address
P.O. Box 35523
Charlotte, NC 28235–5523
Program director: Elizabeth K. Thurbee, ACSW

THE PROGRAM

Catholic Social Services of the Diocese of Charlotte is a nonprofit multi-service agency serving residents of the geographic Diocese of Charlotte (46 counties) and placing approximately 20 children annually through its adoption program. Catholic Social Services has been providing pregnancy support and adoption services for 40 years. Working with birthparents, with other private and public agencies, and occasionally with national and regional exchange programs, the agency places both healthy and special-needs children (primarily infants and young children). Catholic Social Services provides extensive counseling and support services for pregnant women who decide to parent their children as well as those who elect adoptive placement as the best plan for their children. In addition, Catholic Social Services will provide homestudy and supervisory services for applicants pursuing inter- agency adoption (both domestic and international). In all of its programs, the mission of Catholic Social Services is "to work toward the liberation of all people on behalf of justice and the transformation of the world as reflection of the love of the Triune God for people and for an expression of our love for one another."

The Cost

The agency's fee for adoption services (as of 3/88) is 10% of the annual gross income of the highest wage earner. Services covered by the fee include all phases of the adoption process, excluding legal fees connected with finalization of the adoption. The agency is willing to negotiate fees in cases where regular rates would work a hardship. For applicants pursuing interagency adoption (domestic or international), the agency's fee for homestudy and supervisory services is based on an hourly rate for services rendered.

The Wait

No applicants have waited longer than 2 1/2 years for placement, and placement usually occurs sooner.

The Children

Catholic Social Services places both healthy and special-needs children (but primarily healthy), ranging in age from birth to 2 years, of Caucasian, Black, and bi-racial backgrounds, born in the U.S.

The Requirements

Age: Applicants must be at least 21 years old. The maximum age requirement is evaluated on a case-by-case basis.

Health: Applicants should be in reasonably good health. Applicants with health problems or handicaps are given individual consideration. Infertility documentation is required for families requesting healthy Caucasian infants.

Religion: Applicants must be practicing members of a Christian denomination.

Financial status: Applicants should be self-sufficient and financially stable.

Marital status: Single applicants are accepted for special needs and minority placements. For Caucasian infant adoption, applicants must be married, and the length of the marriage must be at least 3 years.

Family size: Applicants may have no more than 1 child currently in the family for Caucasian infant adoption. No requirement for special needs and minority placements.

Racial, ethnic or cultural origin: Preference for placing children in families of similar origins. The agency will consider Caucasian or Black families for the placement of bi-racial children.

The Procedure

Participation in the adoption program of Catholic Social Services entails the following basic steps:

Intake interview
Application
Individual counseling sessions
Homestudy
Group counseling sessions
Placement
Post-placement supervision

Additional Programs/Services

Catholic Social Services provides a full range of counseling services including individual, marital, and family counseling; substance abuse counseling; substance abuse intervention; crisis counseling. The agency also provides financial assistance programs; foster care for pregnant teens and infants; free pregnancy testing; assistance in securing a medical referral; mediation between significant others to insure necessary supports during and after pregnancy.

Branch/Network Offices

75 Blue Ridge Avenue
Asheville, NC 28806
(704) 255–0146
P.O. Box 10962
Winston-Salem, NC 10962
(919) 727–0705

License/Accreditation/Professional Affiliations

Catholic Social Services of the Diocese of Charlotte, Inc. is licensed by the State of North Carolina Department of Human Resources.

THE CHILDREN'S HOME SOCIETY OF NORTH CAROLINA, INC.

Administrative Office
Greensboro, NC 27405
(919) 274–1538
740 Chestnut Street
Mailing Address
P.O. Box 14608
Greensboro, NC 27415
Program director: Ruth McCracken, Executive Director; Kathleen Hasty, Director of Professional Services

The Program

Founded in 1902, The Children's Home Society of North Carolina is the only private, statewide, non-sectarian adoption agency in North Carolina. Through 8 district offices, the agency provides problem pregnancy counseling services, adoption services, direct foster care for infants and pre-school age children awaiting placement, post-placement services, and post-legal adoption counseling services. The agency provides services to birthparents and places both healthy and special-needs children for adoption (traditional placement program) when birthparents in the agency's counseling program elect adoptive placement as the best plan for their child. Through the interagency placement program, the agency recruits, studies, and makes available adoptive homes for children referred from other agencies, both public and private. Children placed through the interagency program are often of minority heritage, generally are of school age, often come as sibling groups who need to stay together in adoption, and often have physical, emotional, or intellectual problems.

Children referred through the interagency program remain in the care of the referring agency until The Children's Home Society can offer an appropriate adoptive home. The agency will accept referral of any child at any time from both North Carolina agencies and out-of-state agencies. The agency places approximately 205 children annually.

The Cost

The agency does not charge a fee for adoption services. The agency is heavily dependent on voluntary contributions from adoptive parents who are encouraged to contribute in accordance with their ability to do so. A fee of $25 for filing of the adoption petition is paid directly to the Court.

The Wait

For healthy Caucasian infant adoptions, the agency averages approximately 3 years from the time of application to the placement of the child. For special-needs children and children referred through the inter- agency placement program, the wait is generally much shorter.

The Children

The Children's Home Society places both healthy and special-needs children. Infants and pre-school age children are placed from direct care. Children of all ages are placed, upon referral, through the inter- agency placement program. Any child of any racial heritage or country of origin is accepted into either program.

The Requirements

Age: For infant adoption, applicants must be at least 26; the maximum age for the wife is 35 years, and for the husband, 39 years. For older child and special-needs adoption, the requirement is flexible and varies depending on the age of the child being considered for placement.

Health: Applicants should be in reasonably good health. Applicants with health problems or handicaps are given individual consideration. Infertility documentation is required for Caucasian infant adoption.

Religion: No requirement. However, the agency asks that the child be given the choice regarding church attendance when the child is old enough to make a choice.

Financial status: No requirement other than the ability to support a child without undue financial burden.

Marital status: For Caucasian infant adoption, applicants must be married, and the length of the marriage must be at least 3 years. Single applicants are accepted for older child and special-needs adoptions.

Family size: For Caucasian infant adoption, applicants must be childless. No requirement for older child and special-needs adoptions.

Racial, ethnic or cultural origin: No requirement, but preference for placing children in families of similar origins. Placements are made across racial, ethnic, and cultural lines when in the child's best interests.

The Procedure

Participation in the adoption program of The Children's Home Society entails the following basic steps:
Orientation meeting
Application
Individual counseling sessions
Homestudy
Placement
Post-placement supervision

Additional Programs/Services

The Children's Home Society provides short term foster care for children awaiting placement; sponsors workshops and seminars, generally focusing on problem pregnancy; provides post-legal adoption counseling services to birthparents, adoptive parents, and adoptees whose lives have been touched through the services of the agency.

Branch/Network Offices

Asheville District Office
528 Biltmore Ave.
Asheville, NC 28801
(704) 258–1661

Charlotte District Office
2129 E. Seventh St.
Charlotte, NC 28204
(704) 334–2854

Fayetteville District Office
Suite 202, Cumberland Community Foundation Center
Fayetteville, NC 28302
(919) 483–8913

Greenville District Office
Wilcar Building
223 W. 10th St.
Greenville, NC 27834
(919) 752–5847

Jacksonville District Office
NCNB Building
New River Shopping Center
Jacksonville, NC 28540
(919) 347–7262

Raleigh District Office
Suite 203, 4904 Professional Ct.
Raleigh, NC 27609
(919) 872–1848

Wilmington District Office
Oak Park Suite B-3
4801 Wrightsville Ave.
Wilmington, NC 28403
(919) 799–0655

License/Accreditation/Professional Affiliations

The Children's Home Society of North Carolina is licensed by the State of North Carolina Department of Social Services and is accredited by the Council on Accreditation of Services for Families and Children. The agency is a member of the Child Welfare League of America, the North Carolina Child Care Association, and the North Carolina Child Advocacy Institute.

FAMILY SERVICES, INC.

610 Coliseum Drive
Winston-Salem, NC 27106
(919) 722–8173
Program director: Sarah Y. Austin, President

THE PROGRAM

Family Services is a nonprofit multi-service agency serving residents of Forsyth County, North Carolina, and placing between 5 and 15 children annually through its adoption program. Striving "to strengthen the well being of families," the agency provides a wide range of services to children and families (see Additional Programs/Services Available through Agency). Working with birthparents, with other public and private agencies, and with national and regional exchange programs, Family Services places both healthy and special-needs children. The agency's current focus is to provide more comprehensive post-placement adoption services. In addition, the agency will provide homestudy and supervisory services for applicants pursuing international adoption.

THE COST

The agency's fee for adoption services is 7% of the applicants' annual gross income. Services covered by the fee include all phases of the adoption process, excluding legal fees connected with finalization of the adoption.

THE WAIT

For Caucasian infant adoption, the time from application to the homecoming of the adoptive child ranges from 2 1/2 to 4 1/2 years. For special-needs adoption, the wait varies depending on the range of special needs the prospective adoptive family can accept.

THE CHILDREN

Family Services places both healthy and special-needs children, ranging in age from infancy to adolescence, of all racial backgrounds, born in the U.S.

THE REQUIREMENTS

Age: Applicants must be at least 25 years of age. The maximum age requirement varies depending on the age of the child and individual family circumstances.
Health: Applicants should be in reasonably good health. Applicants with health problems or handicaps are given individual consideration.
Religion: No requirement.
Financial status: Applicants must demonstrate sound financial management.
Marital status: For Caucasian infant adoption, applicants must be married, and the length of the marriage must be at least 3 years. Single applicants are considered for special needs placements.
Family size: For Caucasian infant adoption, applicants must be childless. No requirement for special needs placements.
Racial, ethnic or cultural origin: Preference for placing children in families of similar origins.

THE PROCEDURE

Participation in the adoption program of Family Services entails the following basic steps:
Orientation meeting
Application
Group educational meetings
Homestudy
Referral
Placement
Post-placement supervision

ADDITIONAL PROGRAMS/SERVICES

Family Services provides a wide range of services including individual, marital, and family therapy; group therapy; Headstart program; battered women's shelter; rape counseling; therapy program for abusive men; pregnancy counseling services; foster care.

BRANCH/NETWORK OFFICES

None.

LICENSE/ACCREDITATION/PROFESSIONAL AFFILIATIONS

Family Services, Inc. is licensed by the State of North Carolina Department of Social Services and is accredited by the Council on Accreditation of Services for Families and Children.

LDS SOCIAL SERVICES

5624 Executive Center Drive, #109
Charlotte, NC 28212
(704) 535–2436
Program director: J. Richard Fletcher

THE PROGRAM

For a full description of programs and services, refer to Utah listing:
LDS Social Services
50 East North Temple Street
Salt Lake City, UT 84150

LUTHERAN FAMILY SERVICES IN NORTH CAROLINA, INC.

P.O. Box 12287
Raleigh, NC 27605
(919) 832–2620
Program director: Joyce Gourley

THE PROGRAM

Lutheran Family Services is a nonprofit agency serving residents of North Carolina and facilitating the placement of approximately 25 children annually. Lutheran Family Services was licensed in 1986 to conduct adoptive homestudies and provide post-placement supervision to adoptive families. Working cooperatively with U.S. agencies which maintain international programs (notably World Child in Washington, D.C. and Los Ninos in Texas), Lutheran Family Services facilitates the placement of foreign-born children in North Carolina families. In addition, the agency provides homestudy and supervisory services for applicants pursuing inter-agency adoption (domestic or international) in cooperation with any licensed and reputable child-placing agency outside the state of North Carolina.

THE COST

The agency's fee for homestudy and post-placement supervision is $1,500. In addition, applicants should anticipate fees to the cooperating agency, fees to the foreign agency, possible travel expenses to the child's country of origin (if travel is required), and legal fees connected with finalization of the adoption.

THE WAIT

The time from application to initiation of the homestudy is 2 to 4 months. The homestudy takes 3 to 4 months, plus typing and processing. After the homestudy is forwarded to the placing agency, applicants can expect to wait 6 to 18 months for placement, depending on the placing agency.

THE CHILDREN

Lutheran Family Services facilitates the placement of both healthy and special-needs children, ranging in age from infancy to 9 years. Countries of origin include Korea, Guatemala, El Salvador, Paraguay, Chili, Colombia, Peru, and Ecuador.

THE REQUIREMENTS

The following are Lutheran Family Services requirements. In addition, applicants must comply with the requirements of the cooperating agency, which vary depending on the child's country of origin.

Age: Preference is given to applicants who are at least 28 and no more than 45 years of age.

Health: No requirement other than normal life expectancy.

Religion: No requirement.

Financial status: No requirement.

Marital status: Preference is given to married couples who have been married for at least 5 years.

Family size: No requirement.

Residence: Applicants must be residents of North Carolina, and residency must be at least 6 months prior to application.

Racial, ethnic or cultural origin: No requirement.

THE PROCEDURE

Participation in the adoption program of Lutheran Family Services entails the following basic steps:

Inquiry (telephone)
Application
Group session
Homestudy
Compliance with immigration/naturalization requirements
  Referral
Placement
Post-placement supervision

ADDITIONAL PROGRAMS/SERVICES

Lutheran Family Services provides a range of services to individuals and families.

BRANCH/NETWORK OFFICES

While the agency maintains contract social workers throughout the state, all adoption inquiries are processed by the main office.

LICENSE/ACCREDITATION/PROFESSIONAL AFFILIATIONS

Lutheran Family Services in North Carolina, Inc. is licensed by the State of North Carolina Department of Human Resources and is accredited by the Council on Accreditation of Services for Families and Children. The agency is a member of the Child Welfare League of America and the North American Council on Adoptable Children.

North Dakota

PUBLIC ADOPTION PROGRAM/ COMMUNITY RESOURCES

Department of Human Services
Children and Family Services
Bismark, ND 58505
(701) 224–2316
Adoption specialist: Virginia Petersen

THE PROGRAM

Adoption services in North Dakota are provided only by private licensed child-placing agencies. The Department of Human Services contracts with North Dakota private adoption agencies to provide services for special-needs children in the custody of the State who are in need of adoptive families.

STATE EXCHANGE

None.

STATE ADOPTION REUNION REGISTRY

None.

STATE SUBSIDY

For information concerning the state and federal (IV-E) subsidy programs, contact the Department of Human Services (above).

NACAC REPRESENTATIVE

None at this time.

GENERAL ADOPTION RESOURCES

Adoptive parent support services in North Dakota are normally provided by private adoption agencies as a service to their clients. Contact private adoption agencies in North Dakota (see North Dakota listing) for information on support services in your area.

SPECIAL-NEEDS ADOPTION RESOURCES

See General Adoption Resources (above).

OUT-OF-STATE AGENCIES

SEE APPENDIX A

Agencies Providing Nationwide Services

BUILDING FAMILIES THROUGH ADOPTION/ND

P.O. Box 550, 7th and Chestnut
Dawson, MN 56232
(612) 769–2933
Program director: Mary Carpenter and Therese Giesen

THE PROGRAM

For current address and telephone number of BFTA North Dakota branch offices, contact BFTA main office (listed above). For a full description of BFTA programs and services, refer to Minnesota listing for Building Families Through Adoption.

CATHOLIC FAMILY SERVICE

3003 S. 11th Street
Fargo, ND 58103
(701) 235–4457
Program director: Verne Aaker, LCSW, Supervisor of Child Welfare

THE PROGRAM

Catholic Family Service is a nonprofit agency serving the state of North Dakota and placing approximately 30 children annually. Incorporated in 1926 to serve unmarried mothers and to provide adoption services, the agency's mission is "to liberate individuals and groups from their oppression, whether this oppression shall be self-inflicted or external, whether it be physical, social, emotional, economic or spiritual." The agency places infants for adoption upon referral or when birthparents in the agency's pregnancy counseling program decide that the best interests of the child will be served by adoptive placement. The agency places special-needs children referred to the agency by the Department of Human Services or out-of-state agencies.

THE COST

The agency's fee for adoption services is $3,200. A reduction of the fee will be considered if it is a barrier to placement. Services covered by the fee include pre-placement, placement, and post-placement services to the adoptive family. In addition, applicants assume responsibility for legal fees connected with finalization of the adoption. The State of North Dakota has a subsidized adoption program available for special-needs children.

THE WAIT

The time from application for acceptance into the program to the homecoming of the adoptive child varies depending on the type of child the applicants wish to adopt. The wait for a healthy Caucasian infant is 5 to 6 years. The wait for a special-needs child depends on the needs of waiting children and the current availability of adoptive homes.

THE CHILDREN

Catholic Family Service places both healthy and special-needs children, ranging in age from birth to adolescence, of all racial backgrounds. Children placed by the agency are born in the U.S.

THE REQUIREMENTS

Age: The age difference between the applicant and the child being considered for placement must be 40 years of less. Exceptions are made for special-needs adoptions.

Health: Infertility documentation is required. Exceptions are made for special-needs adoptions. Applicants with health problem or handicap are given individual consideration.

Religion: Applicants must be practicing members of the Catholic faith. Married applicants must have a valid Catholic marriage. Exceptions are made for special-needs adoptions.

Financial status: Applicants' income must be adequate to meet the needs of the child.

Marital status: Married applicants are preferred, but single applicants are accepted.

Family size: Applicants may have no more than 2 children currently in the family. Exceptions are made for special-needs adoptions.

Racial, ethnic or cultural origin: Preference for placing children in families of similar origins, but exceptions are made for special-needs adoptions.

THE PROCEDURE

Participation in Catholic Family Service's adoption program entails the following basic steps:
Orientation meeting
Pre-application
Application
Individual counseling sessions
Group counseling sessions
Homestudy
Placement
Post-placement services
Post-legalization services (as requested)

ADDITIONAL PROGRAMS/SERVICES

Catholic Family Service provides foster care services for children; unmarried parent services; family life program; corporate guardianship services for the developmentally disabled.

BRANCH/NETWORK OFFICES

30 Avenue A West
P.O. Box 1734
Bismarck, ND 58502
(701) 255–1793

221 4 Street South
Grand Forks, ND 58201
(701) 775–4196

400 22nd Avenue, N.W.
Minot, ND 58701
(701) 852–2854

LICENSE/ACCREDITATION/PROFESSIONAL AFFILIATIONS

Catholic Family Service is licensed by the State of North Dakota Department of Human Services and is a member agency of seven United Ways in North Dakota. All professional staff are licensed by the State of North Dakota, and the program supervisor is a member of the Academy of Certified Social Workers (ACSW).

CHRISTIAN FAMILY LIFE SERVICES

15 South 10th Street
Fargo, ND 58103
(701) 241–8520
Program director: Andrew Vanyo, MSW, LCSW

THE PROGRAM

Christian Family Life Services is a nonprofit agency serving the states of North Dakota and Minnesota and placing 15 to 20 children annually. Founded in 1985, the agency's mission is based on "the gospel commission to love one another as He (God) has loved us." The agency provides counseling services and a residential facility for unwed birthmothers and places infants for adoption when birthmothers in the agency's program decide that the best interests of the child will be served by adoptive placement. The agency also facilitates the placement of special-needs children. In its adoption program, the agency is guided by the belief that "those children in need of proper care and nurture are entitled to a home and parents who can provide this."

THE COST

The agency's fee for adoption services is based on a sliding scale and averages $4,000 plus legal termination fee. Reduction of fees will be considered depending on the circumstances of any given case. Services to adoptive parents covered by the fee include pre-placement services, homestudy, placement, supervision, post-placement services. The fee also helps to underwrite services to birthmothers and servicing of foster homes. In addition, prospective adoptive parents should anticipate financial responsibility for legal fees connected with finalization of the adoption and the fee for an amended birth certificate.

THE WAIT

The time from application for acceptance into the program to the homecoming of the adoptive child currently averages approximately 2 years.

THE CHILDREN

Christian Family Life Services places primarily healthy Caucasian infants, but also special needs and older children of all racial backgrounds. Children placed by the agency are born in the U.S.

THE REQUIREMENTS

Age: Applicants should be no more than 40 years of age. In general, the age difference between the applicants and the child should not exceed 40 years.

Health: Applicants must be in reasonably good health. Report on infertility status is required.

Religion: Applicants must be practicing members of a Christian church and must recognize salvation through Jesus Christ. A personal commitment is necessary.

Financial status: Applicants must demonstrate ability to provide adequately for the child.

Marital status: Applicants must be married. The length of the marriage must be at least 3 years.

Family size: Applicants may have no more than 2 children currently in the family. Exceptions are made for special-needs adoptions.

Racial, ethnic or cultural origin: No requirement.

THE PROCEDURE

Participation in Christian Family Life Services' adoption program entails the following basic steps:

Application
Orientation meeting
Individual counseling sessions
Homestudy
Placement
Post-placement supervision

ADDITIONAL PROGRAMS/SERVICES

Christian Family Life Services is a subsidiary agency under the auspices of Help & Caring Ministries. Other services provided by the agency include individual, marital, and credit counseling; residential facility for unwed mothers (The Perry Center); counseling services for unwed mothers (Women's Help & Caring Connection); foster care services.

BRANCH/NETWORK OFFICES

None.

LICENSE/ACCREDITATION/PROFESSIONAL AFFILIATIONS

Christian Family Life Services is licensed by the State of North Dakota Department of Human Services and by the State of Minnesota Department of Human Services. The agency director is licensed by the State of North Dakota and is a member of the National Association of Christian Counselors.

COVENANT CHILDREN

P.O. Box 2344
Bismarck, ND 58502–2344
(701) 222–3960
Program director: Ruth and Steve Lester, Outreach Directors

THE PROGRAM

Covenant Children is a nonprofit organization founded in 1974 by a group of Christians to make "a tangible difference in the lives of many children through adoption, sponsorship, medical and spiritual outreach." Covenant Children provides direct services for North Dakota residents and nationwide adoption placement services through the Interstate Compact for applicants working with licensed agencies in their home state who will provide homestudy, preparation for placement, and supervisory services. Covenant Children works with foreign government child welfare and private agencies in locating and placing abandoned children, primarily from Latin America. Covenant Children places approximately 40 children annually in Christian homes.

THE COST

The total cost for adoption through Covenant Children varies depending on the circumstances of each case. Generally, however, the cost ranges from $5,000 to $8,000. Agency services covered by the fee include pre- placement services, placement, and post-placement supervision. In addition, applicants should anticipate financial responsibility for legal fees connected with finalization.

THE WAIT

The time from inquiry to the homecoming of the adoptive child varies depending on the circumstances of each case. Requests for children above 5 years old, mentally or physically limited, Black or bi-racial, and/or sibling groups are subject to a shorter waiting period (4 to 12 months). The waiting period for healthy children under 6 years of age is between 12 and 36 months.

THE CHILDREN

Covenant Children places both healthy and special-needs children, ranging in age from birth to adolescence. The racial identity of the Latin American children placed by the agency is Spanish, Latin American Indian, Black or a mixture of these races.

THE REQUIREMENTS

Age: Applicants must be at least 22 and no more than 55 years of age. The requirement may vary depending on the age of the child being considered for placement and the requirements of the child's country of origin.

Health: No agency requirement, but may vary depending on the requirements of the child's country of origin.

Religion: Applicants must be practicing Christians.

Financial status: No agency requirement, but may vary depending on the requirements of the child's country of origin.

Marital status: Applicants must be married. The length of the marriage must be at least 2 years. The requirement may be more restrictive depending on the child's country of origin.

Family size: No agency requirement, but may vary depending on the requirements of the child's country of origin.

Racial, ethnic or cultural origin: No requirement.

THE PROCEDURE

Participation in Covenant Children's adoption program entails the following basic steps:

Inquiry
Registration/Application
Orientation meeting
Group counseling sessions
Homestudy
Placement
Post-placement supervision
Finalization
Naturalization

ADDITIONAL PROGRAMS/SERVICES

Covenant Children provides sponsorship, medical, and spiritual outreach programs.

LICENSE/ACCREDITATION/PROFESSIONAL AFFILIATIONS

Covenant Children is licensed by the State of North Dakota Department of Human Services.

LUTHERAN SOCIAL SERVICES OF NORTH DAKOTA

1325 S. 11th Street
P.O. Box 389
Fargo, ND 58107(701) 235–7341
Program director: Kay Johnson, LSW

THE PROGRAM

Lutheran Social Services is a nonprofit agency serving the state of North Dakota and placing approximately 20 to 30 children annually. Providing adoption services for over 50 years, the primary goal of the agency's adoption program is "to help children who would otherwise not have a home of their own to become members of families that can give them the love, protection, nurturing, and opportunities essential for healthy personal growth and development." The agency places both healthy and special-needs children. However, applicants should note that the agency's registration list for healthy Caucasian infants has been closed since 1985. The agency anticipates re-opening the registration list in 1988 to accept a limited number of registrants. The requirements described below may be subject to change at that time.

THE COST

The agency's fee for adoption services is $3,000. Services covered by the fee include pre-placement, placement, post-placement and post- legalization services. In addition, applicants assume responsibility for legal fees connected with finalization of the adoption.

THE WAIT

The time from inquiry to the homecoming of the adoptive child varies depending on the type of child the applicants wish to adopt. For a healthy Caucasian infant, applicants wait 4 to 5 years on the registration list and 1 year from application approval (adoption study) to adoptive placement.

THE CHILDREN

Lutheran Social Services places both healthy and special-needs children, ranging in age from birth to adolescence, primarily of Caucasian but also of mixed (Native American, Black, or Iranian/Caucasian) racial backgrounds. Children placed by the agency are born in the U.S.

THE REQUIREMENTS

Age: No requirement, but varies depending on the age of the child being considered for placement.

Health: Applicants must be in reasonably good health. Applicants with health problem or handicap are given individual consideration.

Religion: No requirement, but most applicants are of Lutheran or other Protestant faith.

Financial status: Applicants must have sufficient income to assure financial stability and security, to meet expenses involved in the daily care of the child, and to make reasonable provision for the future.

Marital status: Families are selected in which a husband and a wife are living together and the marriage has been of sufficient duration to give evidence of stability.

Family size: No requirement at this time.

Racial, ethnic or cultural origin: No requirement, but preference for placing children in families of similar origins.

THE PROCEDURE

Participation in Lutheran Social Services' adoption program entails the following basic steps:
Orientation meeting
Registration
Application
Individual counseling sessions
Homestudy
Group counseling sessions
Referral
Placement
Post-placement supervision

ADDITIONAL PROGRAMS/SERVICES

Lutheran Social Services provides a wide range of programs including residential treatment for adolescent females; residential treatment for developmentally disabled adults; an educational, recreational and social facility for socially and mentally handicapped adults; food bank; Native American outreach services; counseling; foster care; volunteer senior companion services; support groups; refugee resettlement; job development; refugee sponsorship for children who have escaped their homeland without parents or families.

BRANCH/NETWORK OFFICES

Northwest Region
400 2nd Ave., NW
Minot, ND 58701
(701) 838–7800
Southwest Region
418 E. Rosser Ave.
Bismarck, ND 58501
(701) 223–1510
Northeast Region
3012 University Ave.
Grand Forks, ND 58201
(701) 772–7577

LICENSE/ACCREDITATION/PROFESSIONAL AFFILIATIONS

Lutheran Social Services is licensed by the State of North Dakota Department of Human Services.

NEW HORIZONS FOREIGN ADOPTION SERVICES, INC.

2876 Woodland Place
Bismarck, ND 58501
(701) 258–8650
Program director: Nancy Kleingartner, MSW, Executive
Director

THE PROGRAM

New Horizons Foreign Adoption Services is a nonprofit
agency serving North Dakota and placing approximately 40
children annually. New Horizons specializes in foreign
adoption and is currently placing children from 12 foreign
countries. New Horizons also facilitates a limited number of
domestic special needs, Black, or bi-racial adoptions and will
provide homestudy and supervisory services for applicants
pursuing identified adoption (in which applicants locate a
birthparent who wishes to place his/her child with them) or
parent-initiated foreign adoption (in which applicants have
themselves, through familial or diplomatic contacts, made
initial arrangements for a foreign adoption), subject to state
approval of the integrity of the source.

THE COST

Costs vary greatly from country to country. The total cost
for foreign adoption services ranges from $5,500 to $12,000,
with most adoptions falling in the $5,500–$7,000 range. Cost
estimates include all agency services (pre-placement through
post-placement), legal fees, translation and document authentication costs, and travel expenses.

For domestic special needs, Black, or bi-racial adoptions,
the cost ranges from $3,000 to $8,000, excluding travel
within the U.S. For identified adoptions, total costs are
approximately $2,500 to $3,000, plus possible medical costs
of the birthmother and child.

THE WAIT

The time from completion of the homestudy to the placement of the adoptive child ranges from 6 to 18 months.

THE CHILDREN

New Horizons places both healthy and special-needs children, ranging in age from birth to adolescence, of all racial
backgrounds. Countries of origin include Bolivia, Colombia,
Ecuador, El Salvador, Guatemala, Honduras, Panama, Peru,
Hong Kong, India, Korea, Philippines, Thailand, Taiwan,
and U.S.

THE REQUIREMENTS

Age: Applicants must be at least 22 years of age. Other
specific requirements vary depending on the child's country
of origin.
Health: No specific requirement, but may vary depending
on the child's country of origin.
Religion: No specific requirement, but may vary depending on the child's country of origin.
Financial status: No specific requirement, but may vary
depending on the child's country of origin.

Marital status: No specific requirement, but may vary
depending on the child's country of origin.
Family size: No specific requirement, but may vary depending on the child's country of origin.
Racial, ethnic or cultural origin: No requirement.

THE PROCEDURE

Participation in New Horizon's adoption program entails
the following basic steps:
  Inquiry
  Registration
  Orientation meeting
  Application
  Homestudy
  Referral
  Placement
  Post-placement supervision
  Finalization
  Naturalization

ADDITIONAL PROGRAMS/SERVICES

New Horizons provides counseling services for birthparents, post-legal adoption counseling, and cultural programs
for international families.

BRANCH/NETWORK OFFICES

None.

LICENSE/ACCREDITATION/PROFESSIONAL AFFILIATIONS

New Horizons Foreign Adoption Services, Inc. is licensed
by the State of North Dakota Department of Human Services.

THE VILLAGE FAMILY SERVICE CENTER

P.O. Box 7398
Fargo, ND 58109–7398
(701) 235–6433/3328
Program director: Sharon Maier

THE PROGRAM

The Village Family Service Center is a nonprofit, multi-
service agency serving the State of North Dakota and placing
approximately 60 children annually. Working with families
and children since 1891, the Village has evolved over the
years in response to the changing needs of the community,
providing a wide range of community programs. The agency
sponsors an infant adoption program and a special-needs
adoption program. The agency places infants for adoption
when birthparents in the agency's pregnancy counseling
program decide that the best interests of the child will be
served by adoptive placement. The agency promotes open
adoption through the exchange of non- identifying information between birthparents and adoptive parents and through
the supervision of meetings (in which only first names are
used) between birthparents and adoptive parents. The Village
also actively promotes the adoption of special-needs chil-

dren, including older children, sibling groups of all ages, children with mental or physical handicaps, and children of mixed racial backgrounds.

THE COST

The agency's fee for adoption services varies depending on the program. For healthy Caucasian infant adoptions, the agency's fee is $3,100. The fee for special-needs adoptions is adjusted according to the applicant's ability to contribute. Services covered by the fee include all phases of the adoption process (pre-placement through post-placement services). In addition, applicants assume responsibility for legal fees connected with finalization of the adoption.

THE WAIT

The time from application to the homecoming of the adoptive child varies depending on the program. For healthy Caucasian infants, the wait averages 5 years. For special-needs adoptions, the waiting period varies depending on the type of child the applicants wish to adopt.

THE CHILDREN

The Village places both healthy and special-needs children, ranging in age from birth to adolescence, of Caucasian, Black, and mixed racial backgrounds.

THE REQUIREMENTS

Age: The general requirement for infant adoptions is that applicants should be no more than 40 years of age at the time of placement. The requirement is flexible for special-needs adoptions.

Health: Applicants must be in reasonably good health. For healthy Caucasian infant adoption, infertility documentation is required.

Religion: No requirement.

Financial status: Applicants must demonstrate financial stability.

Marital status: For Caucasian infant adoption, applicants must be married. Single applicants are eligible for special-needs adoptions. Couples applying for special-needs adoption must be married for 3 years at the time of the homestudy.

Family size: For Caucasian infant adoption, applicants may have no more than 1 child currently in the family. No requirement for special-needs adoption.

Racial, ethnic or cultural origin: No requirement.

THE PROCEDURE

Participation in The Village's adoption program entails the following basic steps:

Application
Group education sessions
Homestudy
Placement
Post-placement supervision

ADDITIONAL PROGRAMS/SERVICES

The Village provides a wide range of services including family and individual counseling; problem pregnancy services; consumer credit counseling service; big brother/big sister program; retired senior volunteer program; adopt-a-grandparent program; family therapy.

BRANCH/NETWORK OFFICES

415 East Avenue A
Bismarck, ND 58501–4051
(701) 255–1165/3328
1610 South Washington
Grand Forks, ND
58201–6334
(701) 746–4584–8060
400 22nd Ave., NW
Minot, ND 58701–3120
(701) 852–3328
P.O. Box 1029
Williston, ND 58802–1029
1–800–732–4475

LICENSE/ACCREDITATION/PROFESSIONAL AFFILIATIONS

The Village Family Service Center is licensed by the State of North Dakota Department of Human Services and is accredited by the Council on Accreditation of Services for Families and Children and the National Foundation for Consumer Credit, Inc. The agency is a member of the Child Welfare League of America.

Ohio

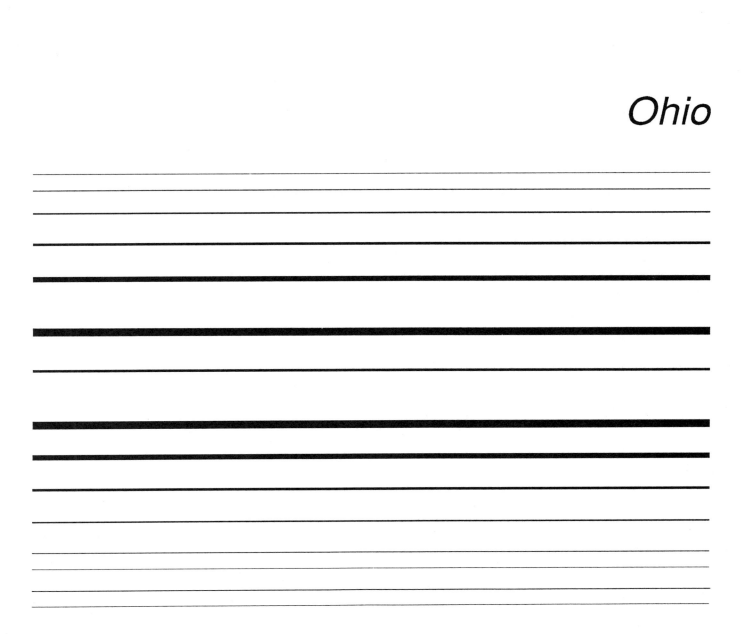

PUBLIC ADOPTION PROGRAM/ COMMUNITY RESOURCES

Department of Human Services
Bureau of Service Operations
30 East Broad Street, 32nd Floor
Columbus, OH 43266–0423
(614) 466–8520
Adoption specialist: Kenneth Kotch

THE PROGRAM

Public adoption services in Ohio are provided by the Department of Human Services (DHS) through county DHS branch offices and through Children Services Boards located in each county. The focus of the DHS program is to recruit and prepare families and to supervise the placement of special-needs children (older, minority, and handicapped children and sibling groups) who are in the custody of the State of Ohio.

STATE EXCHANGE

Ohio Adoption Resource Exchange
30 East Broad Street, 30th Floor
Columbus, OH 43215
(614) 466–8520

STATE ADOPTION REUNION REGISTRY

Ohio Department of Health
Bureau of Vital Statistics
65 S. Front St.
Columbus, OH 43215
(614) 466–2533

STATE SUBSIDY

For information, contact the Bureau of Service Operations at (614) 466–6176.

NACAC REPRESENTATIVE

Beth Frank
518 Carrol Avenue
Sandusky, OH 44870
(419) 625–6149

GENERAL ADOPTION RESOURCES

Adoption Listing Service of Ohio (ALSO)
3737 Lander Rd.
Cleveland, OH 44124
(216) 929–2670

SPECIAL-NEEDS ADOPTION RESOURCES

For information about special-needs adoption resources in Ohio, contact Spaulding for Children—Beech Brook (refer to Ohio listing).

OUT-OF-STATE AGENCIES

AGENCY

Smithlawn Maternity Home , Texas (special-needs and minority placements)

SEE APPENDIX A

Agencies Providing Nationwide Services

THE BAIR FOUNDATION

P.O. Box 168
Brookfield, OH 44403
(216) 448–0244
Program director: Alice Clapper

THE PROGRAM

For a full description of programs and services, refer to Pennsylvania listing:
The Bair Foundation
241 High Street
New Wilmington, PA 16142
(412) 946–8711

BAPTIST CHILDREN'S HOME AND FAMILY MINISTRIES INC.

2150 S. Center Boulevard
Springfield, OH 45506
(513) 324–2352
Program director: Dr. Donald E. Worch, President; Charles S. Monroe, Executive Director

THE PROGRAM

Baptist Children's Home and Family Ministries, Inc. (BCH) is a nonprofit family service agency that serves residents of Ohio and places approximately 9 children annually through its adoption program. BCH also has offices in Indiana, Iowa, and Michigan. Initiated in 1979, the Ohio agency provides services to birthparents and places infants with Baptist families committed to spiritual growth when birthparents elect adoptive placement as the best plan for their child. The goal of BCH is "to receive and care for homeless boys and girls and unwed mothers, and to offer assistance to families in counseling, group home, foster care and adoptive placement."

THE COST

The agency's fee for adoption services is based on a sliding scale with an average fee of $4,050. Services covered by the fee include all phases of the adoption process (social services to adoptive parents; counseling, residential, and medical care to birthmothers) excluding legal fees connected with finalization of the adoption.

THE WAIT

The time from application for acceptance into the program to home- coming of the adoptive child is about 3 1/2 to 4 years for Caucasian infants. For older and special-needs children, the wait varies depending on the availability of children and on the current need for adoptive families.

THE CHILDREN

BCH places both healthy and special-needs children who range in age from birth to 17 years old, of all racial backgrounds. Children are born in the U.S.

THE REQUIREMENTS

Age: There should be no more than 40 years difference between the age of the child and the age of the youngest adoptive parent.

Health: Applicants should be in reasonably good health; however, individual consideration is given to applicants with handicaps or health problems. The requirement may vary depending on the needs of the child.

Religion: Applicants must be practicing members of the Independent Fundamental Baptistic and Separatist Church.

Financial status: Applicants must demonstrate financial stability.

Marital status: Applicants must be married.

Family size: The requirement varies depending on the ability of the family to provide for the child's emotional, physical, and spiritual needs.

Racial, ethnic or cultural origin: Preference for placing children in families of similar origins.

THE PROCEDURE

Participation in BCH's adoption program entails the following basic steps:

Application
Church association
Orientation meeting
Individual counseling sessions
Homestudy
Placement
Post-placement supervision
Finalization

ADDITIONAL PROGRAMS/SERVICES

The Baptist Children's Home and Family Ministries in Ohio offers a range of services including individual and family counseling; services to unwed mothers (maternity foster homes, obstetric care, individual and family counseling); foster care.

BRANCH/NETWORK OFFICES

BCH adoption services for families who reside in states other than Indiana, Iowa, Michigan, and Ohio are provided by the Indiana Office through BCH's interstate adoption program.

Indiana Office
354 West St.
Valparaiso, IN 46383
(219) 462–4111
Director: Wayne Yoccum

Iowa Office
224 1/2 Northwest Abilene
Ankeny, IA 50021
(515) 964–0986
Director: Kevin Thomas

Michigan Office
214–216 Mill St.
St. Louis, MI 48880
(517) 681–2171
Director: Bill McCurdy

LICENSE/ACCREDITATION/PROFESSIONAL AFFILIATIONS

Baptist Children's Home and Family Ministries, Inc. is licensed by the appropriate state department in each of the states in which a branch office is located.

BETHANY CHRISTIAN SERVICES

1655 West Market Street
Suite 340
Akron, OH 44313
(216) 867–2362
Program director: James K. Haveman, Jr., Executive Director

THE PROGRAM

For a full description of programs and services, refer to Michigan listing:
Bethany Christian Services
901 Eastern Avenue, N.E.
Grand Rapids, MI 49503–1295
(616) 459–6273

CATHOLIC SERVICE BUREAU

Lake/Geauga Adoption Services
#455 AmeriTrust Building
8 N. State Street
Painesville, OH 44077
(216) 352–6191, 946–7264
Program director: Beth Brindo, Adoption Specialist

THE PROGRAM

Catholic Service Bureau is a nonprofit agency serving residents of northeast Ohio. The agency's mission is "to provide the highest level of quality service in meeting the mental health and social service needs of children, birthparents, and adoptive families." The agency provides services to birthparents and places infants for adoption when birthparents in the agency's counseling program elect adoptive placement as the best plan for their child. Working with birthparents, with the public agency, and with national and regional exchange programs, the agency places older, minority, and special-needs children. Working in cooperation with other licensed agencies which have international programs, the agency facilitates the placement of infants and special-needs children from several foreign countries. In addition, the agency will provide homestudy and supervisory services for applicants pursuing interagency adoption (domestic and international) and independent adoption.

THE COST

The agency's fee for adoption services is based on a sliding scale and ranges from $410 to $4,600. Services covered by the fee include all phases of the adoption process, excluding occasional medical expenses related to infant adoption. Applicants pursuing international adoption can expect to pay fees to the cooperating agency, travel costs, and related expenses.

THE WAIT

The time from application to the homecoming of the adoptive child ranges from 1 to 2 years.

THE CHILDREN

Catholic Service Bureau places both healthy and special-needs children, ranging in age from birth to 17 years, of all racial and religious backgrounds. Countries of origin vary depending on the cooperating agency.

THE REQUIREMENTS

Age: Applicants must be at least 21 years of age. The maximum preferred age difference between the child and the mother is 40 years.

Health: Applicants with health problems or handicaps are given individual consideration.

Religion: No requirement. However, for infant adoptions, the religious preferences of the birthparents are given strong consideration.

Financial status: Applicants must demonstrate economic stability.

Marital status: No requirement. However, if married, the length of the marriage must be at least 1 year.

Family size: No requirement. However, for infant adoptions, the request of the birthparents is honored.

Racial, ethnic or cultural origin: Preference for placing children in families of similar origins, but the requirement varies depending on the needs of the child.

THE PROCEDURE

Participation in the adoption program of Catholic Service Bureau entails the following basic steps:
Orientation meeting
Application
Individual and group homestudy training and preparation
Home visit
Homestudy
Referral
Compliance with immigration/naturalization requirements (international adoptions only)
Placement
Post-placement supervision
Finalization
Post-legal support group (optional)

ADDITIONAL PROGRAMS/SERVICES

Catholic Service Bureau provides birthparent counseling; foster care; adoptive and foster parent training and support groups; counseling for adoptive families and children with mental health professionals specializing in adoption issues.

BRANCH/NETWORK OFFICES

10771 Mayfield Rd.
Chardon, OH 44024
(216) 285–3537

LICENSE/ACCREDITATION/PROFESSIONAL AFFILIATIONS

Catholic Service Bureau is licensed by the State of Ohio Department of Human Services. The agency is a member of the North American Council on Adoptable Children and Catholic Charities U.S.A.

CATHOLIC SERVICE LEAGUE, INC. OF ASHTABULA COUNTY

2905 Donahoe Drive, P.O. Drawer 1338
Ashtabula, OH 44004
(216) 992–2121
Program director: John A. Hudak, Acting Director

THE PROGRAM

Catholic Service League, Inc. of Ashtabula County is a nonprofit agency serving residents of Ashtabula County since 1944 and providing a range of family and child welfare services. The agency provides a full range of adoption services including infant adoption, special-needs adoption, and international adoption in cooperation with other U.S. agencies which maintain international programs.

THE COST

The agency's fee for adoption services is based on a sliding scale and varies depending on the program. For infant adoption, the agency's fee ranges from $1,400 to $2,500 and includes all phases of the adoption process. Adoption services for special-needs placements are provided at no cost to the adoptive family. For international adoption, the agency's fee for homestudy and supervisory services is $500. Applicants pursuing international adoption should also expect to pay fees to the cooperating agency, travel expenses, and related costs.

THE WAIT

The time from application to the homecoming of the adoptive child varies depending on the program. For infant adoption, the wait ranges from 2 to 7 years. For special-needs adoption, the wait ranges from 1 to 3 years. For international adoption, the wait varies depending on the child's country of origin and may range from 1 to 3 years.

THE CHILDREN

Catholic Service League places both healthy and special-needs children, ranging in age from birth to 15 years, of all racial backgrounds. Catholic Service League facilitates the placement of foreign-born children from Korea, South America, and Taiwan.

THE REQUIREMENTS

Age: Applicants must be at least 21 and no more than 40

years of age. The requirement is flexible for special-needs adoptions.

Health: Applicants with health problems or handicaps are given individual consideration. Infertility exploration is suggested for applicants pursuing infant adoption.

Religion: No requirement, but the preference of the birthparents is honored. Catholic families are given preference.

Financial status: No requirement.

Marital status: Applicants must be married, and the length of the marriage must be at least 3 years.

Family size: No requirement.

Racial, ethnic or cultural origin: The requirement is evaluated on a case-by-case basis.

THE PROCEDURE

Participation in the adoption program of the Catholic Service League entails the following basic steps:
Adoption inquiry interview
Homestudy
Group orientation
Compliance with immigration/naturalization requirements (international adoptions only)
Placement
Post-placement supervision
Finalization
Post-adoption services

ADDITIONAL PROGRAMS/SERVICES

Catholic Service League provides a wide range of community services including unwed parent services; foster home care; casework with children in their own homes; information and referral services; individual, marital, parent-child, and family counseling; financial assistance; support groups; consumer credit counseling; retired senior volunteer program; protective services for the elderly.

BRANCH/NETWORK OFFICES

None.

LICENSE/ACCREDITATION/PROFESSIONAL AFFILIATIONS

Catholic Service League, Inc. of Ashtabula County is licensed by the State of Ohio Department of Human Services.

CATHOLIC SERVICE LEAGUE OF SUMMIT COUNTY, INC.

640 N. Main Street
Akron, OH 44310
(216) 762–7481
Program director: Nancy Clemens

THE PROGRAM

Catholic Service league of Summit County is a nonprofit agency serving residents of Summit County since 1920. The agency provides services to birthparents and places both healthy and special-needs infants for adoption when birthparents in the agency's counseling program elect adoptive placement as the best plan for their child. The agency also works cooperatively with the public agency and with national and regional exchange programs to recruit families for special-needs children. In addition, the agency will provide homestudy and supervisory services for applicants pursuing private adoption.

THE COST

The agency's fee for adoption services is based on a sliding scale and varies depending on the program. For agency regular infant adoptions, the fee ranges from $4,900 to $7,900 and includes all phases of the adoption process. For special-needs adoptions, the fee is $3,000 and includes all phases of the adoption process. For agency assisted private adoptions, the agency's fee for homestudy and supervisory services is $3,000.

THE WAIT

The time from application to the homecoming of the adoptive child averages 2 years.

THE CHILDREN

Catholic Service League places both healthy and special-needs infants of all racial backgrounds, born in the U.S.

THE REQUIREMENTS

Age: Applicants must be at least 21 and no more than 37 years of age.

Health: Applicants must be in reasonably good health. Exploration of infertility must be documented for non-special-needs adoptions.

Religion: Applicants must be practicing members of the Catholic faith. Exceptions are made for special needs and independent placements.

Financial status: No requirement.

Marital status: Applicants must be married, and the length of the marriage must be at least 3 years in accordance with state law.

Family size: For non-special-needs adoptions, preference is given to childless couples, and applicants may have no more than 1 child currently in the family. Exceptions are made for special-needs placements.

Racial, ethnic or cultural origin: No requirement.

THE PROCEDURE

Participation in the adoption program of Catholic Service League entails the following basic steps:
Orientation meeting
Application
Homestudy
Placement
Post-placement supervision

ADDITIONAL PROGRAMS/SERVICES

Catholic Service League provides counseling services, services to unmarried parents, and seminars for foster parents.

BRANCH/NETWORK OFFICES

480 W. Tuscarawas, Suite 203
Barberton, OH 44203
(216) 745–3197

480 W. Aurora Rd.
Northfield, OH 44067
(216) 467–4888

LICENSE/ACCREDITATION/PROFESSIONAL AFFILIATIONS

Catholic Service League of Summit County, Inc. is licensed by the State of Ohio Department of Human Services and is accredited by the Council on Accreditation of Services for Families and Children. The agency is a member of the Child Welfare League of America and Family Service America.

CATHOLIC SERVICE LEAGUE OF WESTERN STARK COUNTY

1807 Lincoln Way East
Massillon, OH 44646
(216) 833–8516
Program director: Anita R. Drda

THE PROGRAM

Catholic Service League of Western Stark County is a nonprofit agency serving families in Western Stark County. Founded in 1922, the mission of the adoption program is "to help children who would not otherwise have a stable home to become members of families who can give them love, care, protection and opportunities essential for healthy growth and development." The agency provides services to birthparents and places infants for adoption when birthparents in the agency's counseling program elect adoptive placement as the best plan for their child.

THE COST

The agency's fee for adoption services is $2,200. Services covered by the fee include all phases of the adoption process. Additional costs may occur in instances where special medical attention is required.

THE WAIT

The time from application to the homecoming of the adoptive child averages 3 years but varies depending on the availability of newborn infants and the number of families currently waiting for placement.

THE CHILDREN

Catholic Service League places healthy infants of all racial backgrounds, born in the U.S.

THE REQUIREMENTS

Age: The prospective adoptive mothers' average age is 40 years. The prospective adoptive fathers' average age is 45 years.
Health: Applicants must be in reasonably good health. Medical information concerning infertility status is requested.
Religion: Applicants must be practicing members of the Catholic Church.
Financial status: Applicants must demonstrate job security, budget management, and adequate income to provide for the child's needs.
Marital status: Applicants must be married, and the length of the marriage must be at least 3 years.
Family size: Family size is evaluated on a case-by-case basis.
Racial, ethnic or cultural origin: Preference for placing children in families of similar origins.

THE PROCEDURE

Participation in Catholic Service League's adoption program entails the following basic steps:
Orientation meeting
Application
Individual counseling sessions
Homestudy
Submission of references and medical information
Group counseling sessions
Waiting period
Pre-placement interview
Foster or adoptive parents meeting
Placement
Post-placement supervision

ADDITIONAL PROGRAMS/SERVICES

Catholic Service League provides counseling for individuals, children, adolescents, families, and couples.

BRANCH/NETWORK OFFICES

None.

LICENSE/ACCREDITATION/PROFESSIONAL AFFILIATIONS

Catholic Service League of Western Stark County is licensed by the State of Ohio Department of Human Services. The agency is a member of the Ohio Association of Child Care Workers, National Conference of Catholic Charities, and United Way of Western Stark County.

CATHOLIC SOCIAL SERVICES, DIOCESE OF TOLEDO

1933 Spielbusch Avenue
Toledo, OH 43624
(419) 244–6711
Program director: Kathleen Donnellan, Diocesan Director

THE PROGRAM

Providing adoption services since 1915, Catholic Social Services is a nonprofit agency serving residents of 19 counties in northwestern Ohio and placing approximately 18 children annually through its adoption program. The agency's mission is "to serve those in need, following the example of Jesus who fed the hungry, visited the sick, and cared for the poor with compassion." While the agency provides services to birthparents and places both healthy and special-needs children, the agency's current focus is the placement of special-needs children. Working cooperatively with other U.S. agencies which maintain international programs, the agency facilitates the placement of children from various countries in Ohio families. In addition, the agency will provide homestudy and post-placement supervision for applicants pursuing interagency adoption (domestic or international).

THE COST

The agency's fee for adoption services is $3,000 and includes all phases of the adoption process, excluding legal fees connected with finalization of the adoption. Applicants pursuing international adoption should also anticipate fees to the cooperating agency, possible travel expenses, and other costs related to adoption from abroad.

THE WAIT

For healthy infant adoption, the time from application to placement averages 7 years. For special-needs placements, the wait varies depending on the number of children currently in need of adoptive families and the range of special needs the prospective family can accept. For international placements, the wait varies depending on the cooperating agency.

THE CHILDREN

Catholic Social Services places both healthy and special-needs children, ranging in age from birth to 2 years, of Caucasian, Black, Hispanic, and bi-racial backgrounds, born in the U.S. In addition, the agency facilitates the adoption of foreign-born children, working cooperatively with international agencies.

THE REQUIREMENTS

Age: The requirement varies depending on the needs of the child.

Health: Applicants should be in reasonably good health. Applicants with health problems or handicaps are given individual consideration.

Religion: Applicants must be practicing Catholics.

Financial status: Applicants must demonstrate financial stability.

Marital status: For healthy infant adoption, applicants must be married.

Family size: The requirement varies depending on the needs of the child.

Racial, ethnic or cultural origin: Preference for placing children in families of similar origins.

THE PROCEDURE

Participation in the adoption program of Catholic Social Services entails the following basic steps:
Orientation meeting
Application
Group counseling sessions
Individual counseling sessions
Homestudy
Placement
Post-placement supervision

ADDITIONAL PROGRAMS/SERVICES

Catholic Social Services provides pregnancy counseling; foster family care; special-needs adoption seminars.

BRANCH/NETWORK OFFICES

Western Region
1012 Ralston Ave.
Defiance, OH 43512
(419) 782–4933
Southern Region
117 Pierce St.
Lima, OH 45801
(419) 222–8110
Eastern Region
249 W. Main St.
Norwalk, OH 44897
(419)668–3073

LICENSE/ACCREDITATION/PROFESSIONAL AFFILIATIONS

Catholic Social Services, Diocese of Toledo, is licensed by the State of Ohio Department of Human Services and is accredited by the Council on Accreditation of Services for Families and Children.

CHILDREN'S HOME INC. OF CINCINNATI

5051 Duck Creek Road
Cincinnati, OH 45227
(513) 272–2800
Program director: P. Jeane Goings; Margo McKaig

THE PROGRAM

Children's Home of Cincinnati is a nonprofit multi-service child welfare agency serving residents of Hamilton and Clermount Counties and placing approximately 40 to 50 infants annually through its adoption program. Founded in 1864, the agency's mission is "to be the agent through which children become permanent members of a family that can provide them with love, physical care, and protection; encourage their mental health; and provide assurance of a productive future." Working directly with birthparents, with other licensed agencies, with the public agency, and with national and regional exchange programs, the agency places both healthy and special-needs infants. In addition, the agency will provide homestudy and supervisory services for applicants pursuing interagency adoption (domestic or international).

THE COST

For special needs and minority adoptions, adoption services are provided at no cost to the adoptive family. As of October 1988, the agency's fee for applicants adopting healthy Caucasian infants is based on a sliding scale, ranging from $1,500 to $9,300. Services covered by the fee include all phases of the adoption process, excluding legal and court costs (minimal) connected with finalization of the adoption.

THE WAIT

The time from application to placement averages 2 years.

THE CHILDREN

Children's Home of Cincinnati places healthy and special-needs infants, ranging in age from birth to 1 year, of Caucasian, Black, and bi- racial backgrounds, born in the U.S.

THE REQUIREMENTS

Age: For healthy Caucasian infant adoption, applicants must be at least 25 and no more than 37 years of age. The requirement is flexible for special needs and minority adoptions.

Health: Applicants must be in reasonably good health. Infertility documentation is required for healthy Caucasian infant adoption.

Religion: No requirement.

Financial status: Applicants must demonstrate the ability to provide adequately for the family's needs.

Marital status: For healthy Caucasian infant adoption, applicants must be married and the length of the marriage must be at least 3 years. For special needs or minority adoptions, applicants may be married or single. If married, the length of the marriage must be at least 2 years.

Family size: Applicants may have no more than 1 child currently in the family for healthy Caucasian infant adoption. The requirement is flexible for special needs or minority adoptions.

Racial, ethnic or cultural origin: Preference for placing children in families of similar origins.

THE PROCEDURE

Participation in the adoption program of Children's Home of Cincinnati entails the following basic steps:

Orientation meeting
Application
Group counseling sessions
Individual counseling sessions
Homestudy
Placement
Post-placement supervision

ADDITIONAL PROGRAMS/SERVICES

Children's Home of Cincinnati provides foster care; residential treatment; post adoption counseling; post adoption workshops.

BRANCH/NETWORK OFFICES

None.

LICENSE/ACCREDITATION/PROFESSIONAL AFFILIATIONS

Children's Home of Cincinnati is licensed by the State of Ohio Department of Human Services and is accredited by the Council on Accreditation of Services for Families and Children. The agency is a member of the Child Welfare League of America, the Association of Child Caring Agencies, the United Way and Community Chest.

CHILDREN'S SERVICES OF CLEVELAND

1001 Euclid Avenue
Cleveland, OH 44115
(216) 781–2043
Program director: Kathryn A. Pearson, ACSW, LISW

THE PROGRAM

Children's Services of Cleveland is a nonprofit, nonsectarian child welfare agency providing a wide range of services to children and families in the greater Cleveland area (Cuyahoga, Lake, and Geauga Counties) without regard to race, creed, national origin, religion, or income. Since its founding in 1876, the agency "has demonstrated a strong commitment to caring for children and families in need." The agency provides services to birthparents and places infants for adoption when birthparents in the agency's counseling program elect adoptive placement as the best plan for their child. The agency also occasionally places older children who are released to the agency for adoption. In addition, the agency will provide homestudy and supervisory services for applicants pursuing interstate, international, and court approved private adoptions. The agency places approximately 30 children annually.

THE COST

The agency's fee for adoption services is based on a sliding scale and ranges from $600 (for applicants with annual gross income of $10,000) to $3,500 (for applicants with annual gross income of $26,000 and up). Services covered by the fee include all phases of the adoption process, excluding legal fees connected with finalization of the adoption and new birth certificate.

THE WAIT

The time from application to the homecoming of the adoptive child ranges from 1 month to 6 months for Black infants and from 4 years to 10 years for Caucasian infants.

THE CHILDREN

Children's Services places both healthy and special-needs children. In addition, the agency will provide homestudy and supervisory services for applicants pursuing interstate, international, and court approved private adoptions.

THE REQUIREMENTS

Age: Applicants must be at least 22 and no more than 38 years of age. Exceptions are made for special-needs adoptions (minority or handicapped children).

Health: Applicants with health problems or handicaps are given individual consideration. Medical exploration of infertility is required for Caucasian infant adoption.

Religion: No requirement.

Financial status: Applicants must be employed and must have sufficient income to support an additional family member.

Marital status: For Caucasian infant adoption, applicants must be married, and the length of the marriage must be at least 2 years. The requirement is flexible for special-needs adoptions (minority or handicapped children).

Family size: For Caucasian infant adoption, applicants must be childless. The requirement is flexible for special-needs adoptions (minority or handicapped children).

Racial, ethnic or cultural origin: Preference for placing children in families of similar origins.

THE PROCEDURE

Participation in Children's Services' adoption program entails the following basic steps:
    Intake (telephone inquiry)
    Orientation meeting
    Homestudy
    Application
    Individual counseling sessions (as needed)
    Referral
    Placement
    Post-placement supervision

ADDITIONAL PROGRAMS/SERVICES

Children's Services provides a wide range of services to children and families including services to troubled children in their own homes; emergency child care; family day care; services for the learning disabled; aid to single and teen-age mothers; foster care programs; residential care and treatment for troubled children.

BRANCH/NETWORK OFFICES

None.

LICENSE/ACCREDITATION/PROFESSIONAL AFFILIATIONS

Children's Services of Cleveland is licensed by the State of Ohio Department of Human Services and is accredited by the Council on Accreditation of Services for Families and Children. The agency is a member of United Way Services, Federation for Community Planning, Ohio Welfare Conference, the Ohio Association of Child Caring Agencies, and a charter member of the Child Welfare League of America.

FAMILY AND COMMUNITY SERVICES OF CATHOLIC CHARITIES

302 N. Depeyster Street
Kent, OH 44240
(216) 678–3911
Program director: Donald P. Finn, LISW, Executive Director; Eileen Daly, Program Coordinator

THE PROGRAM

Family and Community Services is a nonprofit multi-service agency providing a wide range of services to residents of Portage County and placing 4 to 6 children annually through its adoption program. Established in 1941, the original purpose of the agency's child welfare program was to provide adoption and foster care services. Services to birthparents and infant adoption remain an important focus of the agency. This agency encourages and supports openness in the adoption process to a degree which is comfortable for all parties involved. The agency will also recruit families for special-needs children as the need arises. In addition, the agency will provide homestudy and supervisory services for applicants pursuing inter- agency adoption. In all of its programs, the agency's mission is "to support and encourage the dignity and responsibility of each person while attempting to eliminate oppressive and dehumanizing situations."

THE COST

The agency's fee for adoption services is $3,500 (as of February, 1988). Applicants should note that adjustments can be made and that the fee schedule is arranged so that applicants may "pay as they go." Services covered by the fee include all phases of the adoption process, excluding legal fees connected with finalization (court costs, new birth certificate, attorney's fees).

THE WAIT

The time from application to the homecoming of the adoptive child ranges from 3 to 7 years.

THE CHILDREN

Family and Community Services places primarily healthy infants (birth to 6 weeks old), of Caucasian and bi-racial backgrounds, born in the U.S. However, the agency also occasionally places special-needs children of all racial backgrounds.

THE REQUIREMENTS

Age: In accordance with state law, the maximum permissible age is 40 years for the prospective adoptive mother and 50 years for the prospective adoptive father.

Health: Applicants should be in reasonably good health. Applicants with health problems or handicaps are given individual consideration. Infertility documentation is required.

Religion: The agency will place infants from all faiths in families of all faiths. However, the agency does require that infants born of Catholic mothers be placed in Catholic adoptive homes.

Financial status: Applicants must have sufficient income to adequately provide for the child.

Marital status: Applicants must be married, and the length of the marriage must be at least 5 years.

Family size: Applicants may have no more than 1 child currently in the family. Exceptions are made for special-needs placements.

Racial, ethnic or cultural origin: Preference for placing children in families of similar origins. The requirement may vary depending on the request of the birthparents.

THE PROCEDURE

Participation in the adoption program of Family and Community Services entails the following basic steps:
    Orientation meeting
    Individual counseling sessions
    Homestudy
    Group counseling sessions
    Application
    Placement
    Post-placement supervision

ADDITIONAL PROGRAMS/SERVICES

The agency provides a wide range of community services including individual, marital, and family counseling; problem pregnancy counseling; foster care; support groups for adult children of alcoholics; support groups and shelter for abused women; consumer credit counseling; career counseling; emergency financial assistance; retired senior volunteer program.

BRANCH/NETWORK OFFICES

None.

LICENSE/ACCREDITATION/PROFESSIONAL AFFILIATIONS

Family and Community Services of Catholic Charities is licensed by the State of Ohio Departments of Human Services and Mental Health and is accredited by the Council on Accreditation of Services for Families and Children. The agency is affiliated with Catholic Charities of the Diocese of Youngstown and is a member of the United Way.

FAMILY COUNSELING & CRITTENTON SERVICES, INC.

1229 Sunbury Road
Columbus, OH 43219
(614) 252–5229
Program director: Sue Marsh

THE PROGRAM

Family Counseling and Crittenton Services is a nonprofit family and children's service facility as well as a mental health service facility serving residents of Franklin County and placing approximately 20 children annually through its adoption program. The agency is the result of the merger of two nonprofit corporations (Associated Charities of Columbus and the Florence Crittenton Home of Columbus) whose history of service dates back to the turn of the century. The agency's mission is "to promote, establish, and maintain family, children, and out-of-wedlock pregnancy services in order to aid families and individuals to achieve a sense of life mastery, well-being, quality family living, and positive human relationships." The agency provides services to birthparents and places infants for adoption when birthparents elect adoptive placement as the best plan for their child. In addition, the agency provides homestudy and post-placement services for applicants either pursuing interagency adoption (international and domestic) or private adoption.

THE COST

As of October 1988, the agency's fee for adoption services is based on a sliding scale and ranges from $3,000 to $6,010. Services covered by the fee include all phases of the adoption process (excluding legal and court costs connected with finalization) and services to the birthparents and the child (counseling, medical expenses).

THE WAIT

The time from application to placement ranges from 3 to 5 years.

THE CHILDREN

Family Counseling and Crittenton Services places primarily healthy but also special-needs children, ranging in age from birth to 1 year, of all racial backgrounds, born in the U.S.

THE REQUIREMENTS

Age: Applicants must be at least 21 and no more than 40 years of age.
Health: Applicants must be in reasonably good health.
Religion: No requirement.
Financial status: Applicants must demonstrate financial stability.
Marital status: No requirement.
Family size: Family size is evaluated on a case-by-case basis.
Racial, ethnic or cultural origin: Preference for placing children in families of similar origins.

THE PROCEDURE

Participation in the adoption program of Family Counseling and Crittenton Services entails the following basic steps:
Waiting list
Orientation meeting
Application
Homestudy
Individual counseling sessions
Placement
Post-placement supervision

ADDITIONAL PROGRAMS/SERVICES

Family Counseling and Crittenton Services provides mental health counseling to families and individuals; family life education; parenting education; Crittenton Maternity Home for residential care during pregnancy.

BRANCH/NETWORK OFFICES

While the agency maintains 5 service facilities in Franklin County, all adoption inquiries are processed through the Sunbury Road office.

LICENSE/ACCREDITATION/PROFESSIONAL AFFILIATIONS

Family Counseling and Crittenton Services, Inc. is licensed by the State of Ohio Department of Human Services and is accredited by the Council on Accreditation of Services for Families and Children. The agency is a member of the Child Welfare League of America.

FAMILY SERVICE AGENCY

535 Marmion Avenue
Youngstown, OH 44502
(216) 782–5664
Program director: Michael Reichart/Joann Marlier

THE PROGRAM

Family Service Agency is a nonprofit multi-service agency placing approximately 4 children annually through its adoption program and serving residents of the following: Mahoning County, Columbiana County, Liberty Township, Girard, Hubbard, and Niles. Providing adoption services for over 50 years, the agency views the child as the primary client. Accordingly, the primary goal of the adoption program is "to find the best home for each child placed for adoption, not to provide childless couples with children." The agency provides services to birthparents and places infants for adoption when birthparents elect adoptive placement as the best plan for their child. Increasingly, birthparents participate in the selection of adoptive homes. In addition, the agency provides homestudy and supervisory services for applicants pursuing interagency adoption (domestic or international) or private adoption.

THE COST

The agency's fee for adoption services is based on a sliding scale and ranges from $1,500 to $2,500 and includes the homestudy and post-placement supervision. Applicants are responsible for legal fees connected with finalization of the adoption.

THE WAIT

The time from initial inquiry to the initiation of the homestudy averages 6 to 8 years.

THE CHILDREN

Family Service Agency places healthy infants (but will accept children up to the age of 2 for placement) of all racial backgrounds, born in the U.S.

THE REQUIREMENTS

Age: Applicants must be at least 24 and no more than 45 years of age.

Health: Applicants should be in reasonably good health. Applicants with health problems or handicaps are given individual consideration. Infertility documentation is required.

Religion: No requirement.

Financial status: Applicants must have an annual income of at least $15,000, must demonstrate financial stability and the ability to provide for an additional family member.

Marital status: Applicants must be married; the length of the marriage must be at least 3 years.

Family size: Applicants must be childless. (The agency's waiting list for 2nd placements is presently closed.)

Racial, ethnic or cultural origin: Preference for placing children in families of similar racial origins.

THE PROCEDURE

Participation in the adoption program of Family Service Agency entails the following basic steps:
Initial inquiry (name placed on inquiry list)
Application
Homestudy
Group counseling sessions
Placement
Post-placement supervision

ADDITIONAL PROGRAMS/SERVICES

Family Service Agency provides a wide range of services including individual, marital, and family counseling; rape information and counseling; consumer credit counseling; services to unmarried parents/problem pregnancy counseling; runaway shelter; host homes; short term infant foster care.

BRANCH/NETWORK OFFICES

None.

LICENSE/ACCREDITATION/PROFESSIONAL AFFILIATIONS

Family Service Agency is licensed by the State of Ohio Department of Human Services and is accredited by the Council on Accreditation of Services for Families and Children. The agency is affiliated with the Child Welfare League of America and Family Service America.

FAMILY SERVICE ASSOCIATION OF TRUMBULL COUNTY

1704 North Road, S.E.
Warren, OH 44484
(216) 856–2907 or 530–0395
Program director: Barbara Glaize, LISW, ACSW

THE PROGRAM

Family Service Association (FSA) is a nonprofit multiservice agency serving residents of Trumbull County and placing approximately 1 to 5 children annually through its adoption program. Originally founded in 1924 as the Family Service Bureau to administer relief services, the agency has evolved in response to the changing needs of the community and today provides a wide range of services to individuals and families. In 1984, FSA and Northeast Ohio Adoption Services (NOAS) entered into a state approved contract to work in the infant adoption program. Couples interested in adoption contact FSA and are referred to NOAS for a home evaluation. FSA counsels with the birthparents. When a baby is surrendered for adoption, FSA and NOAS mutually place the baby in an approved adoptive home. In addition to infant adoption services, the agency will provide homestudy and supervisory services for applicants pursuing interagency adoption (domestic or international).

THE COST

The agency's fee for adoption services is based on a sliding scale according to income, with a maximum fee of approximately $4,000. Services covered by the fee include the homestudy, placement, and post-placement supervision. In addition, applicants should anticipate possible financial responsibility for the medical expenses of the birthmother ad well as legal fees connected with finalization. Homestudies and post-placement supervision for applicants pursuing interagency adoption (domestic or international) are provided on an hourly fee-for-service basis ($68 per hour).

THE WAIT

The time from application to the homecoming of the adoptive child ranges from 3 months to 6 years.

THE CHILDREN

FSA places both healthy and special-needs infants of all racial backgrounds, born in the U.S. In addition, FSA will provide homestudy and supervisory services to facilitate the interagency placement of a child of any age, race, or country of origin.

THE REQUIREMENTS

Age: Applicants must be at least 21 and no more than 50 years of age.
Health: Applicants should be in reasonably good health.
Religion: No requirement.
Financial status: Applicants must demonstrate financial stability.
Marital status: Applicants must be married; the length of the marriage must be at least 1 year.
Family size: No requirement.
Racial, ethnic or cultural origin: Preference for placing children in families of similar origins.

THE PROCEDURE

Participation in the adoption program of FSA entails the following basic steps:
Application
Homestudy (by NOAS)
Placement
Post-placement supervision

ADDITIONAL PROGRAMS/SERVICES

FSA provides a wide range of services including individual, marital, and family counseling; consumer credit counseling; employee assistance services; services to birthparents; foster care; educational programs.

BRANCH/NETWORK OFFICES

None.

LICENSE/ACCREDITATION/PROFESSIONAL AFFILIATIONS

Family Service Association of Trumbull County is licensed by the State of Ohio Department of Human Services and is accredited by the Council on Accreditation of Services for Families and Children. The agency is a member of Family Service America and the United Way.

FAMILY SERVICES OF SUMMIT COUNTY

212 East Exchange Street
Akron, OH 44304
(216) 376–9494
Program director: Judy Joyce, ACSW, LISW

THE PROGRAM

Family Services of Summit County is a not-for-profit family service agency serving residents of Summit County for healthy Caucasian infant adoptions and residents of the entire state for healthy minority infant adoptions. Providing services for well over 60 years, the agency's mission is "to maintain and stabilize family relationships for the benefit of families themselves as well as for the good of the community." The agency provides services to birthparents and places infants for adoption when birthparents in the agency's counseling program elect adoptive placement as the best plan for their child. Through its adoption program, the agency places approximately 20 children annually.

THE COST

The agency's fee for adoption services is based on a sliding scale and ranges from $1,000 to $3,700. Services covered by the fee include all phases of the adoption process, excluding legal fees connected with finalization of the adoption. In addition, applicants can expect to pay $1,500 to the medical fund to assist birthparents who lack insurance or public support for medical expenses.

THE WAIT

The time from application to the homecoming of the adoptive child averages 2 years.

THE CHILDREN

Family Services places both healthy and special-needs children, ranging in age from birth to 2 years, of all racial backgrounds, born in the U.S.

THE REQUIREMENTS

Age: Applicants must be at least 25 and no more than 38 years of age. Exceptions can be made depending upon the needs of the child.
Health: Applicants should be in reasonably good health. Applicants with health problems or handicaps are given individual consideration. For Caucasian infant adoption, infertility documentation or documentation indicating that a pregnancy would be injurious to the health of the mother is required.
Religion: No requirement.
Financial status: Applicants must have an income of at least $15,000.
Marital status: Applicants must be married, and the length of the marriage must be at least 3 years. Single applicants are considered depending on the needs of the child.
Family size: For Caucasian infant adoption, applicants may have no more than 1 child currently in the family. Minority applicants with more than 1 child currently in the home are accepted.
Racial, ethnic or cultural origin: Preference for placing children in families of similar origins.

THE PROCEDURE

Participation in the adoption program of Family Services entails the following basic steps:
Orientation meeting
Application

Homestudy (including individual/joint sessions)
Placement
Post-placement supervision
Finalization/post-placement services

ADDITIONAL PROGRAMS/SERVICES

Family Services provides a wide range of services including individual, marital, and family counseling; education for family living; consumer credit counseling; community services for the deaf; teenage parents center; foster care; family advocacy; volunteer programs.

BRANCH/NETWORK OFFICES

South Summit Office
480 N. Tuscarawas #101
Barberton, OH 44203
(216) 753–3064

North Summit Office
2057 E. Aurora
Twinsburg, OH 44087
(216) 425–7825 or 657–2389

Teenage Parents Center
220 S. Broadway
Akron, OH 44308
(216) 535–3117 or 376–9351

LICENSE/ACCREDITATION/PROFESSIONAL AFFILIATIONS

Family Services of Summit County is licensed by the State of Ohio Department of Human Services and is accredited by the Council on Accreditation of Services for Families and Children. The agency is a member of Rehabilitation Services Commission of Ohio, Family Service America, Child Welfare League of America, and an affiliated agency of the United Way of Summit County.

GENTLE CARE ADOPTION SERVICES, INC.

48 West Whittier Street
Columbus, OH 43206
(614) 443–2229
Program director: Kimberlee A. Brown, Executive Director

THE PROGRAM

Gentle Care Adoption Services is a nonprofit, non-sectarian agency serving primarily residents of Ohio (but making some out-of-state placements as well). Founded in 1985, Gentle Care strives "to place children in the best possible homes, to provide birthmothers with as many supportive services as possible throughout the pregnancy and beyond, and to aid adopting couples in the adoption process." Gentle Care provides services to birthmothers and places both healthy and special-needs infants for adoption when birthmothers in the agency's counseling program elect adoptive placement as the best plan for their children. Working cooperatively with the Ohio Adoption Resource Exchange, the agency also places minority and special-needs children available for adoption in Ohio. As a network affiliate of Los Ninos International Adoption Center in Texas, Gentle Care facilitates the placement of children from various foreign countries, providing coordination, homestudy, and post-placement services. In addition, the agency will provide homestudy and supervisory services for applicants pursuing independent adoption.

THE COST

The agency's fee schedule for its various programs is as follows:
Domestic Infant Adoption
$8,500 in-state placements
$8,750 out-of-state placements
Out-of-state applicants can also expect to pay fees to a licensed agency in their home state for homestudy and supervisory services.
Minority and Special-Needs Adoption
$1,700 plus medical and miscellaneous expenses if necessary.
Foreign Adoption
$1,750 homestudy and post-placement supervision fee
$5,000–$10,000 cooperating agency fees, travel, and related expenses, varying depending on the country of origin.
Bi-Racial Adoption
$3,000 plus medical and miscellaneous expenses if necessary.
Identified (Targeted) Adoption
$2,850 plus medical and miscellaneous expenses if necessary. If the homestudy must be completed within 25 days of first contact, applicants pay an additional $300 at the time of placement. If the placement is inter-state, applicants pay an additional $400 at the time of placement.
For all programs, applicants are responsible for legal fees and court costs related to finalization of the adoption. Applicants should note that fees are subject to change without notice.

THE WAIT

The time from application to the homecoming of the adoptive child varies depending on the program, with an average of 2 years.

THE CHILDREN

Gentle Care Adoption Services directly places healthy and special-needs infants, of Black, Caucasian, and bi-racial backgrounds. Working cooperatively with regional exchange programs and with U.S.-based agencies which maintain foreign programs, the agency facilitates the placement of healthy and special-needs children of all ages and all racial backgrounds. Places of origin include U.S., Central and South America.

THE REQUIREMENTS

Age: Applicants must be at least 21; the prospective adoptive mother may be no more than 40, and the prospective adoptive father may be no more than 45. The requirement may vary depending on the child's race, health status, age, and country of origin.

Health: Applicants should be in reasonably good health. Applicants with health problems or handicaps are given individual consideration. Infertility documentation is required for healthy Caucasian infant adoption.

Religion: No requirement other than the intention of raising the child with moral and religious values.

Financial status: Applicants should have sufficient income to support an additional family member.

Marital status: For healthy Caucasian infant adoption, applicants must be married, and the length of the marriage must be at least 3 years. Single applicants are accepted for other programs.

Family size: Applicants may have 1 other child currently in the family. However, the agency will place no more than 2 children in a family.

Racial, ethnic or cultural origin: No requirement.

THE PROCEDURE

Participation in the adoption program of Gentle Care Adoption Services entails the following basic steps:
Pre-application
Acceptance/rejection of pre-application
Orientation meeting
Application and group counseling session
Individual counseling sessions
Homestudy
Placement
Post-placement supervision

ADDITIONAL PROGRAMS/SERVICES

Gentle Care provides counseling and assistance to birth-parents.

BRANCH/NETWORK OFFICES

None.

LICENSE/ACCREDITATION/PROFESSIONAL AFFILIATIONS

Gentle Care Adoption Services is licensed by the State of Ohio Department of Human Services. The agency is a member of the Child Welfare League of America and the National Committee For Adoption.

HARAMBEE: SERVICES TO BLACK FAMILIES

1468 East 55th Street
Cleveland, OH 44103
(216) 391–7044
Program director: L. Ione Willis-Hancock, Executive Director; Mary E. Pope, Director of Social Services

THE PROGRAM

HARAMBEE: Services to Black Families is a nonprofit agency serving residents of the greater Cleveland area, Cuyahoga County, Northeast Ohio and facilitating the placement of approximately 20 Black and bi-racial children annually. Founded in 1979 by members of the Cleveland Chapter of the National Association of Black Social Workers, the agency's initial and continuing concern is to address the needs of Black children in temporary and permanent custody who need permanent adoptive homes. HARAMBEE actively recruits, studies, and trains prospective adoptive families and works cooperatively with private and public custodial agencies to facilitate and supervise the placement of Black children in Black adoptive families. While HARAMBEE does not have custody of the children, the agency works closely with the custodial agencies to provide match/referral services. In addition to adoption services, the agency sponsors The Family Program (a series of activities which enhance family life by improving communication between parents and children through educational and recreational activities) and provides short-term family counseling services. In all of its programs, the agency's mission is "to preserve and strengthen the Black family through a variety of services and programs."

THE COST

The agency's fee for adoption services is based on a sliding scale and ranges from $0 to $1,250. Services covered by the fee include all phases of the adoption process, excluding minimal court costs connected with finalization of the adoption.

THE WAIT

The time from application to the homecoming of the adoptive child ranges from 8 weeks to 1 1/2 years (with an average wait of 6 months) and varies depending on the availability of the type of child applicants wish to adopt.

THE CHILDREN

HARAMBEE places both healthy and special-needs children, ranging in age from birth to 18 years, of Black and bi-racial backgrounds, born in the U.S.

THE REQUIREMENTS

Age: Applicants must be at least 21 years of age.

Health: Applicants should be in reasonably good health. Applicants with health problems or handicaps are given individual consideration.

Religion: No requirement.

Financial status: Applicants should have adequate income for themselves and the child.

Marital status: No requirement. If married, the length of the marriage must be at least 1 year.

Family size: No requirement.

Racial, ethnic or cultural origin: Applicants may be either Black or bi-racial individuals or couples or inter-racial couples.

THE PROCEDURE

Participation in HARAMBEE's adoption program entails the following basic steps:
Orientation meeting
Application
Homestudy
Adoption training program
Placement
Post-placement supervision
Finalization

ADDITIONAL PROGRAMS/SERVICES

HARAMBEE provides family counseling services; family programs; adoption support groups; adoption training program; recruitment and public education programs.

BRANCH/NETWORK OFFICES

None.

LICENSE/ACCREDITATION/PROFESSIONAL AFFILIATIONS

HARAMBEE: Services to Black Families is licensed by the State of Ohio Department of Human Services. The agency is a member of the National Black Child Development Institute, Northeastern Ohio Adoption Resource Exchange-Urban Coalition, and ALSO (Adoption Listing Services of Ohio).

JEWISH CHILDREN'S BUREAU

22001 Fairmount Boulevard
Shaker Heights, OH 44118
(216) 932–2800
Program director: Dr. Amnon Shai, Director of Clinical Services

THE PROGRAM

Jewish Children's Bureau is a nonprofit child welfare agency serving Jewish families in Cleveland and surrounding areas and placing approximately 7 children annually through its adoption program. Originally an orphanage for Jewish orphans of the Civil War, the Bureau "provides comprehensive child care service to children," including a wide range of residential placement options, treatment programs, and community services. The agency provides traditional and cooperative adoption programs for domestic adoptions. A traditional adoption involves the matching of an infant who has been surrendered to the agency to a couple whose homestudy has been approved by the agency. In a cooperative adoption, the agency assists couples in the adoption of a child whose birthmother was referred to the agency by other responsible parties in the community (clinics, hospitals, private medical practitioners, attorneys, and clergy). Jewish Children's Bureau has recently expanded its program to include an international component, working cooperatively with other U.S. agencies which maintain international programs to place foreign-born children in Cleveland families. In addition, the agency will provide homestudy and supervisory services for applicants pursuing inter-agency adoption (domestic or international) or independent adoption.

THE COST

For traditional adoption services, the agency's fee is $4,485 and includes all phases of the adoption process. For cooperative adoption services, individual fee contracts are prepared, identifying the anticipated number of hours of service and the rate (currently $65 per hour). Contracts rarely exceed $5,200. In addition, applicants pursuing cooperative adoption should anticipate financial responsibility for services to the birthmother and child (counseling, medical, and foster care,

if required) and legal fees connected with finalization. For applicants pursuing international adoption, homestudy and supervisory services are billed at $65 per hour. International applicants should anticipate fees to the cooperating agency, possible travel expenses, and other costs related to international adoption.

THE WAIT

The time from application for acceptance into the program to the homecoming of the adoptive child averages 3 years.

THE CHILDREN

Jewish Children's Bureau places primarily healthy infants (and occasionally special-needs children as well), of Caucasian, Hispanic, and bi-racial backgrounds, born in the U.S. In addition, the agency will provide homestudy and supervisory services to facilitate international adoptions.

THE REQUIREMENTS

Age: For traditional adoption, females must be between the ages of 24 and 37, and males must be between the ages of 25 and 45. No requirement for cooperative adoption. For international adoption, the requirement varies depending on the cooperating agency.

Health: Applicants should be in reasonably good health. Infertility documentation is required for traditional adoption.

Religion: For traditional adoption, applicants must be practicing members of the Jewish religion. No requirement for cooperative or international adoptions.

Financial status: No requirement other than the ability to provide adequately for the child.

Marital status: Applicants must be married; the length of the marriage must be at least 2 years.

Family size: For traditional adoption, applicants must be childless. No requirement for cooperative or international adoptions.

Racial, ethnic or cultural origin: No requirement.

THE PROCEDURE

Participation in the adoption program of Jewish Children's Bureau entails the following basic steps:
Orientation meeting
Application
Group counseling sessions
Homestudy
Individual counseling sessions
Placement
Post-placement supervision
Finalization

ADDITIONAL PROGRAMS/SERVICES

Jewish Children's Bureau provides a wide range of services including adoptive parent support groups; post-placement services (mother-infant play group, educational programs, support meetings); psychological evaluation and testing; information and referral; counseling for individuals, families and groups; parent guidance; substance abuse; services to unwed parents; big brother/big sister outreach; community education; consultation to agencies; foster care and specialized foster care; group homes; group residence; emergency shelter; family in-home day care; preschool and kindergarten day care; residential treatment; day treatment; special education; research.

BRANCH/NETWORK OFFICES

None.

LICENSE/ACCREDITATION/PROFESSIONAL AFFILIATIONS

Jewish Children's Bureau is licensed by the State of Ohio Department of Human Services and is accredited by the Council on Accreditation of Services for Families and Children. The agency is affiliated with Bellefaire, Child Welfare League of America, Jewish Community Federation of Cleveland, National Conference on Social Welfare, Ohio Association of Child Caring Agencies, and United Way Services of Greater Cleveland.

JEWISH FAMILY SERVICE

1710 Section Road
Cincinnati, OH 45237
(513) 351–3680
Program director: Phyllis Tobias

THE PROGRAM

Jewish Family Service is a nonprofit agency serving residents of Hamilton County, surrounding counties, and northern Kentucky. Providing adoption services since 1943, the agency believes "that each child thrives best in a family of its own and that some couples will need the agency's help in becoming parents. The agency's role is to serve the child, birthparents, and adoptive parents, each in the way that can best encourage their mental health and productive future." Working directly with birthparents, with other licensed agencies, with the public agency, and with national and regional exchange programs, the agency places both healthy and special-needs children (but primarily infants) in families which maintain a Jewish home. Jewish Family Service places approximately 6 children annually through its adoption program.

THE COST

The agency's fee for adoption services is based on a sliding scale in accordance with the applicants' income, with a maximum fee of $6,000 as of October, 1988. There is some flexibility regarding fees for applicants in special circumstances. Services covered by the fee include the homestudy, placement, and post-placement supervision. In addition, applicants can expect to pay a $100 application fee.

THE WAIT

The time from application to placement varies tremendously, with placement frequently occurring before 2 years.

THE CHILDREN

Jewish Family Service places both healthy and special-needs children (but primarily infants) of all racial backgrounds (but primarily Caucasian), born in the U.S.

THE REQUIREMENTS

Age: For the adoption of a first child, the wife may be no more than 38 and the husband may be no more than 40 years of age.

Health: Applicants with health problems or handicaps are given individual consideration.

Religion: Applicants must have a Jewish home.

Financial status: The requirement is assessed on a case-by-case basis.

Marital status: Applicants must be married; the length of the marriage must be at least 3 years.

Family size: Applicants may have no more than 1 child currently in the family.

Racial, ethnic or cultural origin: Preference for placing children in families of similar origins

THE PROCEDURE

Participation in the adoption program of Jewish Family Service entails the following basic steps:
Orientation meeting
Application
Homestudy (including individual and group counseling)
Placement
Post-placement supervision

ADDITIONAL PROGRAMS/SERVICES

Jewish Family Service provides individual and family counseling; early child development program; foster care; family life education; services to the aging and their families.

BRANCH/NETWORK OFFICES

7770 Cooper
Montgomery, OH 45242
(513) 891–6535

LICENSE/ACCREDITATION/PROFESSIONAL AFFILIATIONS

Jewish Family Service is licensed by the State of Ohio Department of Human Services. The agency is a member of the Child Welfare League of America and Family Service America.

JEWISH FAMILY SERVICE

4501 Denlinger Road
Dayton, OH 45426–2395
(513) 854–2944
Program director: Sheldon W. Switkin, ACSW, LISW, Executive Director; Lois Zeidman, ACSW, LISW, Clinical Social Worker

THE PROGRAM

Jewish Family Service (JFS) is a nonprofit multi-service agency serving residents of the Miami Valley of Ohio. JFS has provided adoption services to the community for over 70 years. In its early history, JFS was fairly active in adoption; however, over the past 20 years, there have been few agency adoptions (less than 1 per year in which JFS has custody of the child). At present, JFS works with prospective adoptive parents to provide information and referral services about other options (waiting children, private adoption, international adoption) and to provide homestudy and supervisory services to applicants interested in pursuing these options.

THE COST

For agency adoptions in which JFS has custody of the child, the fee for services is based on a sliding scale with an average cost of $4,000. Services covered by the fee include all phases of the adoption process, excluding legal fees connected with finalization of the adoption and excluding the medical expenses of the birthmother and child.

For applicants interested in pursuing waiting child, private, or international adoption, the agency's fee for the homestudy is $750 (and slightly higher if applicants reside outside Montgomery, Preble, or Greene Counties). There is an additional fee for the supervisory visits following placement. In waiting child, private, or international adoptions, applicants should anticipate expenses which may include fees to the custodial agency, medical expenses of the birthmother and child, legal fees connected with finalization, and related expenses.

THE WAIT

For agency adoptions in which JFS has custody of the child, no reliable estimates of the time from application to placement are available. For applicants pursuing waiting child, private, or international adoptions, the wait varies depending on factors which are beyond the agency's control.

THE CHILDREN

JFS directly places healthy infants (on a very limited basis). JFS provides homestudy and supervisory services to facilitate the placement of both healthy and special-needs children of any age, race, or country of origin.

THE REQUIREMENTS

Age: The general guideline is to maintain normal family age spans.

Health: Applicants should be in reasonably good health.

Religion: No requirement for applicants requesting homestudy and supervisory services in connection with waiting child, private, or international adoption. For direct placements through JFS, applicants must be Jewish.

Residence: Applicants must have lived in the Miami Valley for a minimum of 1 year.

Financial status: Applicants must have sufficient income to maintain the family.

Marital status: No requirement for applicants requesting homestudy and supervisory services in connection with waiting child, private, or international adoption. For direct placements through JFS, applicants must be married, and the length of the marriage must be at least 2 years.

Family size: No requirement.

Racial, ethnic or cultural origin: The requirement may vary depending on the requirements of the custodial agency.

THE PROCEDURE

Participation in the adoption program of JFS entails the following basic steps:

Orientation meeting

Application
Homestudy
Individual counseling sessions
Adoptive parent preparation class
Placement
Post-placement supervision

Applicants interested in pursuing waiting child, private, or international adoption are invited to contact the agency to arrange for information/referral services and homestudy and supervisory services.

ADDITIONAL PROGRAMS/SERVICES

JFS provides a wide range of services including individual, marital, and family counseling; services to children and youth; foster care; vocational assessment; educational guidance; information/referral; homemaker service referrals; refugee resettlement and acculturation; family life education; counseling for birthparents, adoptive parents, and adoptees.

BRANCH/NETWORK OFFICES

None.

LICENSE/ACCREDITATION/PROFESSIONAL AFFILIATIONS

Jewish Family Service is licensed by the State of Ohio Department of Human Services. The agency is a member of the Association of Jewish Family and Children's Agencies and the Miami Valley Adoption Coalition.

JEWISH FAMILY SERVICE

6525 Sylvania Avenue
P.O. Box 507
Sylvania, OH 43560
(419) 885–2561
Program director: L. Louis Albert, ACSW, LISW, Executive Director

THE PROGRAM

Jewish Family Service is a nonprofit family service agency serving residents of northwest Ohio (primarily Lucas, Wood, Fulton and Ottawa Counties). The agency's purpose is "to conserve, develop and promote healthy family life in the Jewish community of Toledo, Ohio and the nearby communities." The agency provides services to birthparents and places infants for adoption in Jewish families when birthparents in the agency's counseling program elect adoptive placement as the best plan for their child. Through this program which has been operative since 1970, the agency places approximately 3 children annually. In addition, the agency provides homestudy and supervisory services to both Jewish and non-Jewish clients who are pursuing private, international, and special-needs adoption. Through this program, the agency facilitates the placement of approximately 25 children annually.

THE COST

For infant placement with Jewish parents, the agency's fee is based on a sliding scale and ranges from $2,125 to $3,700.

Services covered by the fee include all phases of the adoption process and post-adoptive counseling, excluding legal fees connected with finalization of the adoption.

For Jewish and non-Jewish applicants pursuing private, international, or special-needs adoption, the agency's fees are based on a sliding scale according to gross family income. The fee for homestudy ranges from $325 to $500. Fees for updates of previously completed homestudies which have expired range from a minimum of $54.00, plus $110 for the first hour and $27 to $55 for each additional hour required to complete the homestudy update. Post- placement fees are based on the amount of time required for supervising the different types of adoption. International post-adoptive placement services range from $810 to $1,650; special needs post-adoptive placement services range from $1,080 to $2,200; independent post-adoptive placement services range from $540 to $1,100.

Applicants pursuing international adoption should anticipate fees to the international source agency. Applicants pursuing independent adoption should anticipate medical expenses for the birthmother and child. For all programs, applicants assume responsibility for legal fees connected with finalization.

The Wait

For infant placement with Jewish parents, the time from approval of the homestudy to the homecoming of the adoptive child ranges from 1 to 3 years.

The Children

Jewish Family Service directly places healthy Caucasian infants (birth to 1 year), born in the U.S. The agency also provides homestudy and supervisory services to facilitate the placement of healthy and special-needs children of any age, race, or national origin.

The Requirements

Age: Applicants must be at least 21 and no more than 45 years of age.

Health: Applicants should be in reasonably good health. Applicants with health problems or handicaps are given individual consideration. For infant placement with Jewish parents, infertility documentation is required.

Religion: For infant placement, applicants must be Jewish. No requirement for applicants requesting assistance with international, independent, or special-needs adoption.

Financial status: Applicants must have an annual income of at least $15,000.

Marital status: For infant placement with Jewish parents, applicants may be either married or single. Assistance is provided for both single and married parents pursuing international, independent, or special-needs adoption.

Family size: For infant placement with Jewish parents, applicants may have no more than 1 child currently in the family.

Racial, ethnic or cultural origin: No requirement.

The Procedure

Participation in the adoption program of Jewish Family Service entails the following basic steps:

Application

Homestudy (including individual counseling sessions)

Compliance with immigration/naturalization requirements (international adoptions only)

Referral

Placement

Post-placement supervision (6 to 12 months)

Additional Programs/Services

Jewish Family Service provides support groups for adoptive parents; counseling and financial assistance for birthparents; foster care for infants; family life education programs about adoption issues.

Branch/Network Offices

None.

License/Accreditation/Professional Affiliations

Jewish Family Service is licensed by the State of Ohio Department of Human Services and is accredited by the Council on Accreditation of Services for Families and Children. All social workers are licensed by the State of Ohio Counselor and Social Worker Board.

LDS Social Services∘

P.O. Box 367
4431 Marketing Place
Groveport, OH 43125 (614) 836–2466
Program director: Wayne A. Tolman

The Program

For a full description of programs and services, refer to Utah listing:

LDS Social Services
50 East North Temple Street
Salt Lake City, UT 84150

Lutheran Children's Aid and Family Services

4100 Franklin Boulevard
Cleveland, OH 44113
(216) 281–2500
Program director: Rev. John K. Wisch, ACSW, LISW, Executive Director

The Program

Lutheran Children's Aid and Family Services (LCAFS) is a nonprofit multi-service agency serving residents of northeastern Ohio and placing approximately 35 to 40 children annually through its adoption program. Serving both the Lutheran and non-Lutheran communities for 85 years, LCAFS is an agency "vitally concerned with the well-being of children and families" whose mission is "to give expression of our faith in the reconciling work of God through Jesus Christ by providing a full range of social services and counsel designed to enable each child and family to develop in Christian love." Working directly with birthparents, with other private and public agencies, and with national and regional exchange programs, the agency places both healthy and special-needs children born in the U.S. Working in cooperation with other U.S. agencies which maintain international programs, the agency facilitates the placement of foreign-born children in Ohio families. In addition, the agency provides homestudy and supervisory services for applicants pursuing interagency adoption (domestic or international) or private adoption (referred to the agency by the Probate Court).

THE COST

As of October 1988, the agency's fee for adoption services is based on a sliding scale and ranges from $2,100 to $5,300. Services covered by the fee include the homestudy, foster care for the child pending placement, placement, post-placement supervision, and finalization of the adoption. Applicants pursuing international adoption should also anticipate fees to the cooperating agency and other miscellaneous expenses related to adoption from abroad.

THE WAIT

The time from application to placement varies depending on the type of adoption, with a range of 3 to 5 years.

THE CHILDREN

LCAFS places both healthy and special-needs children, ranging in age from birth to 6 years, of all racial backgrounds. Countries of origin include U.S., Korea, Thailand, Vietnam, and South America.

THE REQUIREMENTS

Age: The requirement varies depending on the age of the child being considered for placement.

Health: Applicants should be in reasonably good health. Applicants with health problems or handicaps are given individual consideration.

Religion: The requirement varies depending on the program. For infant adoptions in which the agency has custody of the child, applicants must be practicing Lutherans. For private adoption, the preferences of the birth- parents are honored. There are no restrictions for special needs or international adoptions.

Financial status: Applicants must have sufficient financial resources to provide adequately for the child. *Marital status*: Applicants may be either married or single. If married, the length of the marriage must be at least 2 years.

Family size: For healthy Caucasian infant adoption, applicants may have no more than 1 child currently in the family. For other programs, the requirement varies.

Racial, ethnic or cultural origin: Preference for placing children in families of similar origins. The preferences of the birthparents are honored.

THE PROCEDURE

Participation in the adoption program of LCAFS entails the following basic steps:
Orientation meeting
Application

Group counseling sessions
Individual counseling sessions
Homestudy
Compliance with immigration/naturalization requirements (international adoptions only)
Placement
Post-placement supervision
Finalization

ADDITIONAL PROGRAMS/SERVICES

LCAFS provides a wide range of services including counseling services to birthparents; foster care; family life education; counseling for individuals, children, and families; counseling for adoptees.

BRANCH/NETWORK OFFICES

None.

LICENSE/ACCREDITATION/PROFESSIONAL AFFILIATIONS

Lutheran Children's Aid and Family Services is licensed by the State of Ohio Department of Human Services and is accredited by the Council on Accreditation of Services for Families and Children. The agency is affiliated with The Evangelical Lutheran Church in America and recognized by the Lutheran Church-Missouri Synod. The agency is a member of the Child Welfare League of America and the United Way.

LUTHERAN SOCIAL SERVICES OF CENTRAL OHIO

57 East Main Street
Columbus, OH 43215
(614) 228–5209
Program director: Salvatore Piazza, Director, Family & Children's Svcs.

THE PROGRAM

Lutheran Social Services of Central Ohio is a nonprofit agency serving residents of central and southeast Ohio and placing approximately 65 children annually. The agency's adoption program began in 1969 with a placement program for healthy Caucasian infants and has expanded over the years to include international adoptions, special-needs adoptions, and Black adoptions.

THE COST

The agency's fee for adoption services varies depending on the program. For healthy Caucasian infant adoptions, the agency's fee is $2,750 which includes all phases of the adoption process. For international adoptions, the agency charges $55 per hour for services rendered. For both programs, applicants are responsible for legal fees (attorney's fees, court costs, birth certificate fees). For international adoptions, applicants should anticipate fees to the cooperating agency, immigration/naturalization fees, and possible travel expenses. For Black adoption and special-needs adoption, the agency's fee is based on a sliding scale and ranges from $170 to $1,560. The only additional fees which applicants need anticipate are legal fees connected with finalization of the adoption.

THE WAIT

The time from application to the homecoming of the adoptive child varies depending on the program. For Caucasian infant adoption, the wait averages 2 years. For international adoption, the wait ranges from 6 months to 3 years. For Black adoption, the wait ranges from 3 to 6 months. For special-needs adoption, the wait varies depending on the range of special needs the adoptive family feels they can accept and on the needs of the child.

THE CHILDREN

Lutheran Social Services places both healthy and special-needs children, ranging in age from infancy to adolescence, of all racial backgrounds. Countries of origin include U.S., Korea, Central America, India and some European countries.

THE REQUIREMENTS

Age: For Caucasian infant adoption, applicants must be at least 21 and no more than 37 years of age. For other programs, the requirement varies depending on the needs of the child and the requirements of the child's country of origin.

Health: Applicants should be in reasonably good health.

Religion: No requirement.

Financial status: Applicants must demonstrate the ability to manage financial resources responsibly.

Marital status: For Caucasian infant adoption, applicants must be married, and the length of the marriage must be at least 2 years. No requirement for Black adoption program. For international adoption, the requirement varies depending on the country of origin. For special-needs adoption, the requirement varies depending on the needs of the child.

Family size: No requirement for Black adoption or special-needs adoption. For Caucasian infant adoption, applicants must be childless. For international adoption, the requirement varies depending on the country of origin.

Racial, ethnic or cultural origin: No requirement, but preference for placing children in families of similar origins.

THE PROCEDURE

Participation in the adoption program of Lutheran Social Services entails the following basic steps:

Orientation meeting
Application
Group counseling sessions
Individual counseling sessions
Compliance with immigration/naturalization requirements international adoptions only)
Placement
Post-placement visit
Finalization
Post-finalization services

ADDITIONAL PROGRAMS/SERVICES

Lutheran Social Services provides family life education programs; counseling services; foster care services.

BRANCH/NETWORK OFFICES

None.

LICENSE/ACCREDITATION/PROFESSIONAL AFFILIATIONS

Lutheran Social Services of Central Ohio is licensed by the State of Ohio Department of Human Services.

LUTHERAN SOCIAL SERVICES OF THE MIAMI VALLEY

P.O. Box 506
Dayton, OH 45405
(513) 278–9617
Program director: Ed Petry

THE PROGRAM

Lutheran Social Services of the Miami Valley is a non-profit agency serving residents of southwest Ohio and placing approximately 15–20 children annually. The agency's mission is "to enable people to manage change and achieve dignity and wholeness in relationship with God, family and community by providing opportunities to experience growth, reconciliation, and fullness of life, and to encourage partnerships within the Church and community in promoting concern for changing conditions and human needs." The agency began its adoption program in 1967. The agency provides services to birthparents and places infants for adoption when birthparents in the agency's counseling program decide that the best interests of the child will be met through adoptive placement. In addition, the agency provides complete adoption services for applicants pursuing identified adoption and provides homestudy, referral and post-placement services for applicants pursuing international adoption.

THE COST

For Caucasian infant adoption, the agency's fee for services is based on a sliding scale and ranges from $2,500 to $4,000. Services covered by the fee include all phases of the adoption process, excluding court costs and legal fees connected with finalization. For other programs, fees are based on the actual cost of services and on the applicants' ability to pay.

THE WAIT

The time from application to the homecoming of the adoptive child averages 3 years for Caucasian infant adoptions and 4 months for Black infant adoptions.

THE CHILDREN

Lutheran Social Services places both healthy and special-needs infants (3 days to 3 months old), of Caucasian and Black racial backgrounds, born in the U.S. In addition, the agency will provide homestudy, supervisory, and related services for applicants pursuing identified or international adoption.

THE REQUIREMENTS

Age: For Caucasian infant adoption, applicants must be at least 22 and no more than 37 years of age. The requirement is flexible for other programs.

Health: Applicants should be in reasonably good health. Applicants with health problems or handicaps are given individual consideration.

Religion: For Caucasian infant adoption, applicants should be practicing members of the Lutheran Church or Protestant couples residing in Montgomery County. The requirement is flexible for other programs.

Financial status: Applicants must have sufficient income to provide adequately for an additional family member.

Marital status: For Caucasian infant adoption, applicants must be married, and the length of the marriage must be at least 2 years. The requirement is flexible for other programs.

Family size: For Caucasian infant adoption, applicants may have no more than 1 child currently in the family. The requirement is flexible for other programs.

Racial, ethnic or cultural origin: Preference for placing children in families of similar origins.

THE PROCEDURE

Participation in Lutheran Social Services' adoption program entails the following basic steps:
Orientation meeting
Application
Group counseling sessions
Individual counseling sessions
Homestudy
Placement
Post-placement supervision

ADDITIONAL PROGRAMS/SERVICES

Lutheran Social Services provides services to birthparents and foster care for newborn infants.

BRANCH/NETWORK OFFICES

233 A Northland Blvd.
Cincinnati, OH 45246
(513) 771–3322

LICENSE/ACCREDITATION/PROFESSIONAL AFFILIATIONS

Lutheran Social Services is licensed by the State of Ohio Department of Human Services.

LUTHERAN SOCIAL SERVICES OF NORTHWESTERN OHIO, INC.

2149 Collingwood Boulevard
Toledo, OH 43620
(419) 243–9178
Program director: Reverend A. Armond Simone, M. Div., MS, LISW

THE PROGRAM

Lutheran Social Services of Northwestern Ohio is a nonprofit agency serving residents of 23 counties in northwest-ern Ohio and southeastern Michigan. The agency's mission is "to provide professional services to assist clients seeking mental, spiritual, and social adjustments so that such persons may function to their highest level for independent living." Providing adoption services since 1927, the agency offers services to birthparents and places infants (Caucasian, bi-racial, and high risk) for adoption when birthparents elect adoptive placement as the best plan for their child. In addition, the agency provides homestudy and supervisory services for applicants pursuing interagency adoption (domestic and international).

THE COST

The agency's fee for adoption services is based on a sliding scale in accordance with the applicants' income. As of October 1988, the agency's fee schedule is as follows:
Healthy infant adoption
$2,600.00–$6,800.00
Special needs/bi-racial adoption
$500.00–$1,600.00
International adoption (homestudy,
supervision, and finalization report)
$1,200.00–$3,000.00
In addition, applicants pursuing domestic infant adoption should anticipate possible medical expenses for the birthmother. For all programs, applicants are responsible for legal and court costs related to finalization of the adoption.

THE WAIT

The time from application to placement varies depending on the type of adoption and the availability of children. Generally, the wait ranges from 18 to 30 months.

THE CHILDREN

Lutheran Social Services places both healthy and special-needs infants of all racial backgrounds, born in the U.S.

THE REQUIREMENTS

Age: Applicants must be at least 21 and no more than 40 years of age. The requirement may vary for special-needs adoptions.

Health: Applicants must be in reasonably good health. Infertility documentation is required.

Religion: Applicants must be practicing members of the same Lutheran church. The requirement may vary for special-needs adoptions.

Financial status: Applicants must have sufficient income to provide for the needs of the family. *Marital status*: Applicants must be married; the length of the marriage must be at least 2, and preferably 3, years.

Family size: Applicants may have no more than 1 child currently in the family. The requirement may vary for special-needs adoptions.

Racial, ethnic or cultural origin: Preference for placing children in families of similar origins. The requirement may vary for special-needs adoptions.

THE PROCEDURE

Participation in the adoption program of Lutheran Social Services entails the following basic steps:
Application

Orientation meeting
Homestudy
Approval of the homestudy
Placement
Post-placement supervision
Finalization

ADDITIONAL PROGRAMS/SERVICES

Lutheran Social Services is licensed to investigate and license foster homes. The agency provides counseling to birthparents.

BRANCH/NETWORK OFFICES

Lutheran Social Services maintains regional offices throughout northwestern Ohio.

LICENSE/ACCREDITATION/PROFESSIONAL AFFILIATIONS

Lutheran Social Services of Northwestern Ohio, Inc. is licensed by the State of Ohio Department of Human Services and is accredited by the Council on Accreditation of Services for Families and Children. The agency is a member of seven United Ways and the Child Welfare League of America.

NORTHEAST OHIO ADOPTION SERVICES

8029 E. Market Street
Warren, OH 44484
(216) 856–5582
Program director: Barbara L. Roberts, Executive Director

THE PROGRAM

Northeast Ohio Adoption Services (NOAS) is a nonprofit agency serving residents of northeast Ohio and placing approximately 35–40 children annually. NOAS began in 1975 as a federally funded demonstration project to place children with special needs for adoption. NOAS has been operating as a private agency since 1978, with service purchased by participating public child welfare agencies. NOAS is predicated on the belief "that every child has a right to grow up in a permanent nurturing family regardless of age, race, medical, physical, or mental condition."

THE COST

Adoption services are provided at no cost to the adoptive family. The adoptive family is, however, responsible for legal fees connected with finalization of the adoption.

THE WAIT

The time from application to placement ranges from 2 months to several years, depending on the range of special needs the adoptive family is able to accept.

THE CHILDREN

NOAS places children of all racial backgrounds who range in age from birth to 18 years (primarily 10 and older), born in the U.S. Most children placed by NOAS have special-needs

in the areas of emotional/behavioral functioning; some have developmental or physical disabilities; some are part of sibling groups to be placed together.

THE REQUIREMENTS

Age: The requirement varies depending on the special needs and age of child(ren) being considered for placement.
Health: Applicants with health problems or handicaps are given individual consideration.
Religion: No requirement.
Financial status: No requirement.
Marital status: No requirement.
Family size: No requirement.
Racial, ethnic or cultural origin: No requirement, but preference for placing children in families of similar origins.

THE PROCEDURE

Participation in the adoption program of NOAS entails the following basic steps:
Intake interview
Orientation meeting
Educative group sessions
Application
Homestudy
Placement
Post-placement services
These steps are flexible and may vary depending on family circumstances and the needs of the child(ren).

ADDITIONAL PROGRAMS/SERVICES

NOAS provides supportive services and post-legalization services.

BRANCH/NETWORK OFFICES

None.

LICENSE/ACCREDITATION/PROFESSIONAL AFFILIATIONS

Northeast Ohio Adoption Services is licensed by the State of Ohio Department of Human Services. The agency is an associate member of the Child Welfare League of America.

SPAULDING FOR CHILDREN— BEECH BROOK

3737 Lander Road
Cleveland, OH 44124
(216) 464–4445
Program director: John C. Cowles, ACSW

THE PROGRAM

Spaulding for Children is a nonprofit agency serving families in northeast Ohio and placing approximately 15 special-needs children annually. Beech Brook, a multi-service psychiatric center for children, was founded in 1846. The Spaulding for Children program was founded in 1976 by a group of adoptive parents who were concerned about the needs of waiting children. Spaulding for Children is committed exclusively to finding families for children with special needs.

The Cost

Adoption services are provided at no cost to the adoptive family. The only fees which applicants need anticipate are court costs related to finalization of the adoption.

The Wait

The time from application to the homecoming of the adoptive child varies depending on the number of children in need of adoptive families and on the range of special needs which the adoptive family can accept.

The Children

Spaulding for Children places special-needs children up to the age of 17 (the average age of children placed is 11 years) of all racial backgrounds, born in the U.S.

The Requirements

Age: No requirement.
Health: No requirement. Applicants with health problems of handicaps are given individual consideration.
Religion: No requirement.
Financial status: No requirement.
Marital status: No requirement.
Family size: No requirement.
Racial, ethnic or cultural origin: No requirement.

The Procedure

Participation in the adoption program of Spaulding for Children entails the following basic steps:
Orientation meeting
Group counseling sessions
Application
Individual counseling sessions
Homestudy
Placement
Post-placement supervision

Additional Programs/Services

Spaulding for Children—Beech Brook provides a range of services including adoption counseling; bonding program; weekend residential services; post-placement support services. The agency is developing a Foster to Adoption program for older children.

Branch/Network Offices

None.

License/Accreditation/Professional Affiliations

Spaulding for Children—Beech Brook is licensed by the State of Ohio Department of Human Services. The agency is a member of Family Builders, Inc. and the Child Welfare League of America.

Oklahoma

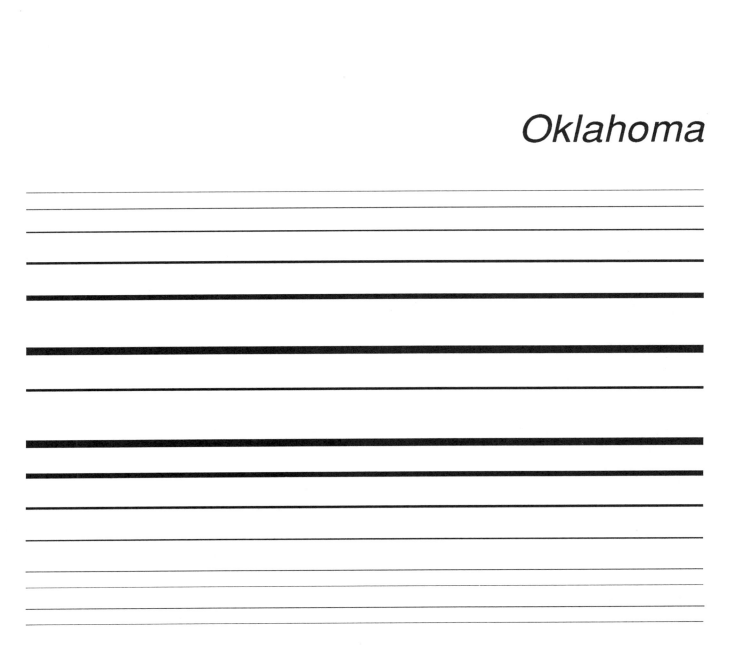

PUBLIC ADOPTION PROGRAM/ COMMUNITY RESOURCES

Department of Human Services
Adoption Program
P.O. Box 25352
Oklahoma City, OK 73125
(405) 521–4373
Adoption specialist: James Bohanon, Child Welfare Supervisor; Jane Conner, Adoption Specialist

THE PROGRAM

Public adoption services in Oklahoma are provided by the Department of Human Services through branch offices located in each county. The focus of the DHS Adoption Program is to recruit and prepare families and to supervise the placement of special-needs children (older, minority, and handicapped children and sibling groups) who are wards of the State of Oklahoma.

STATE EXCHANGE

Oklahoma Children's Adoption Resource Exchange (OK CARE)
P.O. Box 60934
Oklahoma City, OK 73146
(405) 239–2832

STATE ADOPTION REUNION REGISTRY

Voluntary Adoption Reunion Registry. For information, contact the Department of Human Services, Adoption Program (above).

STATE SUBSIDY

Adoption Subsidy Program. For information, contact the Department of Human Services, Adoption Program (above).

NACAC REPRESENTATIVE

Dwe Williams
2609 Northwest 38th Street
Oklahoma City, OK 73112
(405) 942–0810

GENERAL ADOPTION RESOURCES

Adoption support services in Oklahoma are normally provided by private adoption agencies as a service to their clients. Contact private agencies in Oklahoma (see Oklahoma listing) for support services in your area.

Adult Adoptee Search Assistance
Loretta Reynolds
717 W. Joplin
Tulsa, OK

Lynda Reed
8220 N.W. 114th St.
Oklahoma City, OK 73132

SPECIAL-NEEDS ADOPTION RESOURCES

For information on Oklahoma resources for children with special needs, contact the Department of Human Services, Adoption Program (above).

OUT-OF-STATE AGENCIES

AGENCY

Christian Family Services, Kansas
The Edna Gladney Center, Texas
Smithlawn Maternity Home, Texas (special-needs and minority placements)

SEE APPENDIX A

Agencies Providing Nationwide Services

THE ADOPTION CENTER OF NORTHEAST OKLAHOMA

Mailing address
P.O. Box 595
Bartlesville, OK 74005
Office address
1824 S.E. Hillcrest
Bartlesville, OK 74003
(918) 336–1827
Program director: Suzanne Joyce

THE PROGRAM

The Adoption Center of Northeast Oklahoma is a non-profit agency providing statewide services and placing approximately 40 children annually. Licensed in 1986, the agency's mission is "to locate permanent, loving families for both American and foreign-born children in need of homes and to support those placements for their continued success." Working directly with birthparents, in cooperation with other licensed agencies, and with national and regional exchange programs, the agency places and facilitates the placement of domestic and international infants and special-needs children. In addition, the agency provides homestudy and supervisory services for applicants pursuing interagency adoption (domestic and international) and independent adoption.

THE COST

The agency's fee for adoption services is $1,325. Services covered by the fee include the homestudy, assistance in locating a child, facilitation of placement, post-placement supervision, and court reports required for finalization. Applicants pursuing international adoption can expect to pay fees to the cooperating agency (in the U.S. or overseas), travel costs, and related expenses. For all programs, applicants pay legal fees connected with finalization. Post-placement counseling is provided on a fee-for-service basis.

THE WAIT

The time from application to the homecoming of the adoptive child averages 1 year.

THE CHILDREN

The Adoption Center places both healthy and special-needs children, ranging in age from birth to 17 years, of all racial backgrounds. Countries of origin include India, Korea, South, Central and Latin America, and the U.S.

THE REQUIREMENTS

Age: For international adoption, applicants must be at least 25 years of age. For domestic special-needs adoption, the requirement varies according to the needs of the child.

Health: Applicants with health problems or handicaps are given individual consideration.

Religion: No requirement.

Financial status: Applicants must have sufficient income to support an additional family member.

Marital status: No requirement.

Family size: For international adoption, the requirement varies depending on the country of origin. For domestic special-needs adoption, the requirement varies according to the needs of the child.

Racial, ethnic or cultural origin: No requirement.

THE PROCEDURE

Participation in The Adoption Center's adoption program entails the following basic steps:
Orientation meeting
Application
Parent adoptive preparation education workshop
Homestudy
Compliance with immigration/naturalization requirements (international adoptions only)
Referral
Placement
Post-placement supervision

ADDITIONAL PROGRAMS/SERVICES

The Adoption Center provides foster care, workshops, and counseling services. Post-placement services include preteen adoption clarification group, adolescent group, workshops for prospective parents, educational and cultural programs, and social activities.

BRANCH/NETWORK OFFICES

None.

LICENSE/ACCREDITATION/PROFESSIONAL AFFILIATIONS

The Adoption Center of Northeast Oklahoma is licensed by the State of Oklahoma Department of Human Services.

CATHOLIC CHARITIES

739 North Denver
Tulsa, OK 74106
(918) 585–8167
Program director: Dr. Edward Maillet, Agency Director; Rita E. Wilson, ACSW, Adoption Supervisor

THE PROGRAM

Catholic Charities is a nonprofit agency serving residents of Tulsa and the surrounding communities and placing approximately 6–10 children annually. Since its inception in 1951, the agency has provided services to birthparents and adoption services. The agency places infants for adoption when birthparents in the agency's counseling program elect adoptive placement as the best plan for their child.

THE COST

The agency's fee for adoption services is $3,500. Services covered by the fee include all phases of the adoption process, excluding legal fees connected with finalization of the adoption. The fee also includes the medical costs of the birthmother and child. However, in the event that the medical expenses exceed the allotment, the additional costs must be paid by the adoptive couple.

THE WAIT

The time from application to the homecoming of the adoptive child ranges from 2 to 3 years.

THE CHILDREN

Catholic Charities places newborns (birth to 3 months), both healthy and special needs, of all racial backgrounds, born in the U.S.

THE REQUIREMENTS

Age: Applicants may be no more than 45 years of age.

Health: Applicants must be in reasonably good health. Applicants with health problems or handicaps are given individual consideration. Infertility documentation is required.

Religion: At least one spouse must be a practicing member of the Catholic faith.

Financial status: Applicants must demonstrate the ability to meet the child's needs.

Marital status: Applicants must be married couples who have been married for at least 5 years.

Family size: Applicants may have no more than 1 child currently in the family.

Racial, ethnic or cultural origin: No requirement.

THE PROCEDURE

Participation in Catholic Charities' adoption program entails the following basic steps:
Referral
Application
Individual counseling sessions
Homestudy
Placement
Post-placement supervision

ADDITIONAL PROGRAMS/SERVICES

Catholic Charities provides a wide range of services including foster care services; counseling services; migration and refugee services; emergency aid; legalization services; legal assistance; housing for families in need (St. Elizabeth's Lodge); residential services for unwed adults who are pregnant or have young children (Madonna House); residential services for AIDS victims (St. Joseph's Residence).

BRANCH/NETWORK OFFICES

None.

LICENSE/ACCREDITATION/PROFESSIONAL AFFILIATIONS

Catholic Charities is licensed by the State of Oklahoma Department of Human Services.

CATHOLIC SOCIAL MINISTRIES

425 N.W. 7th Street
P.O. Box 1516
Oklahoma City, OK 73101
(405) 232–8514
1–800–522–4003 (toll free in Oklahoma)
Program director: Jeanette Davis, LSW, ACSW

THE PROGRAM

Catholic Social Ministries is a nonprofit agency serving residents of the Archdiocese of Oklahoma City and placing approximately 6 to 10 children annually through its adoption program. Adoption/foster care services and services to unwed mothers have been a vital part of Catholic Charities programs since the early 1900s. De-emphasizing the institutional aspect which was characteristic of such services in the past, current programs focus on holistic maternity counseling and support services. The agency's mission is "to enhance the human condition so that Christian life may flourish."

THE COST

The agency's fee for adoption services is $4,750 and includes services to the birthparents and child (counseling, legal, medical, and foster care) and services to the applicants (homestudy, placement, and post-placement supervision). Applicants are responsible for legal fees connected with finalization of the adoption.

THE WAIT

The time from application for acceptance into the program to the homecoming of the adoptive child ranges from 1 to 2 years.

THE CHILDREN

Catholic Social Ministries places both healthy and special-needs infants (birth to 4 months) of all racial backgrounds, born in the U.S.

THE REQUIREMENTS

Age: For healthy infant adoption, applicants must be at least 21 and no more than 40 years of age. The requirement is flexible for special-needs adoption.

Health: Applicants should be in reasonably good health. Applicants with health problems of handicaps are given individual consideration. Infertility documentation is required.

Religion: Applicants must be practicing members of the Christian faith. Priority is given to childless Catholic couples.

Financial status: No requirement.

Marital status: Applicants must be married; the length of the marriage must be at least 3 years.

Family size: Applicants may have no more than 1 child currently in the family. The requirement is flexible for special-needs placements.

Racial, ethnic or cultural origin: For the placement of Black children, Black adoptive families are preferred, but the requirement varies depending on the availability of appropriate families and geographic location.

THE PROCEDURE

Participation in Catholic Social Ministries' adoption program entails the following basic steps:
Application
Individual counseling sessions
Homestudy
Placement
Post-placement supervision

ADDITIONAL PROGRAMS/SERVICES

Catholic Social Ministries provides maternity counseling; infant foster care; outreach to the elderly; outreach to the Hispanic community; immigration and amnesty services; parish social ministry development; residential services to the elderly; counseling; advocacy for social justice.

BRANCH/NETWORK OFFICES

None.

LICENSE/ACCREDITATION/PROFESSIONAL AFFILIATIONS

Catholic Social Ministries is licensed by the State of Oklahoma Department of Human Services.

DEACONESS HOME

5401 N. Portland
Oklahoma City, OK 73112
(405) 942–5001
Program director: Betty Hollingshead

THE PROGRAM

The Deaconess Home is a nonprofit organization that provides services for unwed mothers and has placed over 10,500 infants for adoption since it was established in 1900. The Deaconess Home is a ministry of the Free Methodist Church of North America and provides counsel and support for birthmothers and adoption services to families throughout the United States, who can offer the children a loving Christian home. The mission of the Deaconess Home is to "serve the needs of the unwed mother regardless of race, creed or color with compassion and love in a Christian environment."

THE COST

The agency's fee for casework is $350. In addition, the Deaconess Home requests that adoptive parents pay for actual medical and other expenses of the birthmother and child. Additional non-agency fees include legal fees connected with finalization of the adoption.

THE WAIT

The average time from application for acceptance into the program to homecoming of the adoptive child is 2 years.

THE CHILDREN

The Deaconess Home places both healthy and special needs American infants of all races.

THE REQUIREMENTS

Age: Applicants must be at least 21 and no more than 40 years of age.

Health: Applicants should be in reasonably good health.

Religion: Applicants must be a practicing member of a Protestant mainline faith.

Financial status: Applicants must demonstrate financial stability.

Marital status: Applicants must be married. The length of the marriage must be at least 3 years.

Family size: Applicants must have no more than 1 child currently in the family.

Racial, ethnic or cultural origin: No requirement, but preference for placing children in families of similar origin.

The Procedure

Participation in the Deaconess House's adoption program entails the following basic steps:

Inquiry
Orientation meeting
Group and individual counseling sessions
Homestudy
Placement
Post-placement supervision

Additional Programs/Services

Deaconess Home provides extensive services to birthmothers (residential, spiritual, educational, medical, legal, and counseling services).

Branch/Network Offices

None.

License/Accreditation/Professional Affiliations

Deaconess Home is licensed by the State of Oklahoma Department of Human Services.

Dillon International, Dillon Children's Services, Inc.

7615 E. 63rd Place South
Tulsa, OK 74133
(918) 250–1561
Program director: Deniese Dillon

The Program

Dillon Children's Services, Inc., is a multi-service adoption agency and part of Dillon International, Inc., a nonprofit corporation founded in 1978 to serve the needs of children and families in developing countries. Dillon Children's Services (DCS) was founded in 1972 and works with the Eastern Child Welfare Society in Korea to place Korean children with families living in Texas and Oklahoma. DCS has placed over 3,400 children since its founding and annually places about 120 Korean children. The mission of DCS is "to insure sound adoption safeguards through the successful placement of each child and to make suitable provisions for the child should placement for any reason fail."

The Cost

The agency's fee for adoption services is $4,095 for the first sibling and $3,965 for the second sibling. The fee includes services in Korea such as medical and living expenses for the child, Korean court and legal fees, visa and passport costs, scheduling transportation and securing escorts for the child, and airfare to the U.S. The fee also covers U.S. services such as processing the application, cooperative services of caseworkers involved in the homestudy and supervision, processing family documents, training seminars for adoptive parents, and replacement services for an unsuccessful placement. In addition, adoptive parents can expect to pay $600 for the homestudy. Non- agency fees adoptive parents should anticipate include legal fees connected with the finalization of the adoption.

The Wait

The time from application for acceptance into the program to home- coming of the adoptive child is about 1 year.

The Children

DCS places healthy and special-needs Korean children who range in age from birth to 13 months. The primary country of origin is Korea, although the agency has placed children from the U.S., El Salvador, and India.

The Requirements

Age: Applicants must be at least 25 and no more than 45 years of age.

Health: Applicants with health problems or handicaps are given individual consideration.

Religion: Applicants must be practicing members of a Judeo-Christian faith.

Financial status: Applicants must demonstrate financial stability.

Marital status: Applicants must be married. The length of the marriage must be at least 3 years.

Family size: Applicants may have no more than 4 children currently in the family.

Racial, ethnic or cultural origin: No requirement.

The Procedure

Participation in Dillon Children Service's adoption program entails the following basic steps:

Pre-application
Application
Orientation meeting
Homestudy
Group counseling sessions
Individual counseling sessions
Referral
Compliance with immigration/naturalization requirements
Placement
Post-placement supervision until finalization
Continuing counseling services

Additional Programs/Services

Dillon Children Services provides parenting workshops, seminars with guest speakers for families and professionals, day camp for parents and children, and counseling services for adoptive parents and children. Every two years the agency holds a children's day (Mungungwha Day) for adoptive families to get a chance to acquaint themselves with Korean culture.

None.

LICENSE/ACCREDITATION/PROFESSIONAL AFFILIATIONS

Dillon Children's Services, Inc., is licensed by the State of Oklahoma Department of Human Services and by the State of Texas Department of Human Services. The agency is a member of the Joint Council on International Children's Services and is affiliated with Eastern Child Welfare Society of Korea.

LDS SOCIAL SERVICES

2017 S. Elm Place, Suite 107
Broken Arrow, OK 74012
(918) 451–3090
Program director: Lyle J. Burrup

THE PROGRAM

For a full description of programs and services, refer to Utah listing:
LDS Social Services
50 East North Temple Street
Salt Lake City, UT 84150

LUTHERAN SOCIAL SERVICE

2901 N. Classen
Oklahoma City, OK 73106
(405) 528–3124
Program director: Virginia Rodman, LSCSW, ACSW

THE PROGRAM

For a full description of programs and services, refer to Kansas listing:
Lutheran Social Service of Kansas and Oklahoma
1855 N. Hillside
Wichita, KS 67214
(316) 686–6645

METROCENTER FOR FAMILY MINISTRIES, INC.

P.O. Box 2380
Edmond, OK 73083
(495) 359–1400
Program director: Ken Pearce, Ph.D.

THE PROGRAM

Metrocenter for Family Ministries, Inc, (METRO), is a nonprofit multi-service agency that places primarily infants in Oklahoma and other states (through Interstate Compact). METRO serves the needs of unwed mothers and places about 20 children annually. Established in 1984, METRO strives "to provide life for unborn babies and hope for their mothers."

THE COST

The agency's fee for adoptions services is as follows:
Adoption application $100.00
Homestudy $300.00
If the child is placed, adoptive parents should expect to pay $4,000 in administrative costs, $300 for counseling of birth parents, and medical and living expenses (average 5 month stay of $2,400) for the birthmother and child. Additional fees that the prospective adoptive parents should anticipate include social worker visits (1 to 3) if the family lives over 50 miles from the agency and legal fees connected with finalization of the adoption.

THE WAIT

The time from application to approval is 2 to 6 months. From approval to the homecoming of the adoptive child, the wait ranges from 1 to 2 years.

THE CHILDREN

METRO places both healthy and special-needs children who range in age from birth to pre-school age, of all races. Children placed by METRO are born in the U.S.

THE REQUIREMENTS

Age: Applicants must be at least 24 years old. The median maximum age for both adoptive parents is 40 years of age.
Health: Applicants must be in reasonably good health. Infertility documentation is generally required but the agency may consider couples who do not have a reason for infertility but whose physician recommends adoption.
Religion: Both applicants must be practicing Christians in the same local church.
Financial status: Applicants must demonstrate financial stability (two financial statements required).
Marital status: Applicants must be married. The length of the marriage must be at least 3 years.
Family size: Applicants may have no more than 2 children currently in the family.
Racial, ethnic or cultural origin: Preference for placing children in family of similar origins.

THE PROCEDURE

Participation in METRO's adoption program entails the following basic steps:
Application
Approval for initial eligibility
Group counseling sessions (on-site workshop)
Individual counseling sessions (on-site workshops)
Home visits
Final approval
Placement
Post-placement supervision

ADDITIONAL PROGRAMS/SERVICES

Metrocenter for Family Ministries, Inc., offers foster care, individual and group counseling for expectant parents, housing, and other social services to expectant parents.

BRANCH/NETWORK OFFICES

None.

LICENSE/ACCREDITATION/PROFESSIONAL AFFILIATIONS

Metrocenter for Family Ministries is licensed by the State of Oklahoma Department of Human Services.

PROJECT ADOPT

1613 N. Broadway
Oklahoma City, OK 73103
(405) 236–1839
Program director: Carole Patten

THE PROGRAM

Project Adopt is a nonprofit adoption agency that helps place primarily special-needs children throughout the United States. Licensed in 1980, Project Adopt works with a number of national and international agencies in placing about 30 children annually. Designed to serve the needs of those families who want to adopt the special-needs child, Project Adopt strives "to find permanent, loving homes for hard-to-place children."

THE COST

The agency's fee for adoption services is based on a sliding scale and ranges from $0 to $5,000, with an average cost of $3,500. Services include the adoption study, searching and placement, and post-placement supervision and counseling. Additional non-agency fees that prospective adoptive parents should anticipate include legal fees for finalization.

THE WAIT

The time from application for acceptance into the program to the homecoming of the adoptive child ranges from 1 to 2 years.

THE CHILDREN

Project Adopt places both healthy and special-needs children, ranging in age from birth to 18 years, of all racial backgrounds. Numerous countries of origin are represented.

THE REQUIREMENTS

Age: Applicants must be at least 21 years of age.
Health: Applicants should be in reasonably good health. Applicants with health problems or handicaps are given individual consideration.
Religion: No requirement.
Financial status: No requirement.
Marital status: The length of marriage for married couples must be at least 2 years.
Family size: No requirement.
Racial, ethnic or cultural origin: No requirement.

THE PROCEDURE

Participation in Project Adopt's adoption program entails the following basic steps:
Telephone inquiry, letter, or visit to agency
Application
Group and individual counseling as requested
Homestudy
Approval
Search for child
Referral
Exchange of information between agency and family (with a pre-placement visit if required)
Compliance with immigration/naturalization requirements
Placement
Post-placement supervision

ADDITIONAL PROGRAMS/SERVICES

Project Adopt offers workshops for adoptive parents and social work professionals, foster care and training for foster parents.

BRANCH/NETWORK OFFICES

None.

LICENSE/ACCREDITATION/PROFESSIONAL AFFILIATIONS

Project Adopt is licensed by the State of Oklahoma Department of Human Services.

SMALL MIRACLES INTERNATIONAL, INC.

7430 Southeast 15th Street
Midwest City, OK 73110
(405) 732–7295
Program director: Margaret Orr, Director; Debra Pinkerton, Administrator

THE PROGRAM

Small Miracles International is a nonprofit agency providing nationwide and international services (homestudies for Oklahoma families only) and placing approximately 50 children annually. Licensed to provide adoption services in 1985, the agency's mission is "to unite homeless children with loving adoptive families and to support and assist those children waiting for a home." The agency provides services to birthparents and places infants for adoption when birthparents elect adoptive placement as the best plan for their child. Working directly with private attorneys and child welfare institutions in Guatemala, the agency places children from Guatemala in U.S. families. Out-of-state families arrange for a licensed agency in their home state to provide homestudy and supervisory services. The agency will also work with U.S. families living abroad. In addition, for Oklahoma families, the agency will provide homestudy and supervisory services for applicants pursuing inter- agency adoption (domestic or international), parent-initiated international adoption, or private adoption.

THE COST

The agency's fee for adoption services varies depending on the program and the applicant's place of residence. For Oklahoma applicants, the average fee for adoption through Guatemala is $7,500 plus travel. For Oklahoma applicants, the fee for domestic infant adoption ranges from $1,500 to $8,500. For Oklahoma applicants pursuing interagency, parent-initiated, or private adoption, the agency's fee for homestudy and post-placement services is $1,500.

For out-of-state applicants, the agency's placement fee for adoption through Guatemala is $7,300. For domestic infant adoption, the placement fee varies depending on the circumstances. In addition, out-of-state applicants should anticipate fees to an agency in their home state for homestudy and supervisory services. Out-of-state applicants pursuing adoption through Guatemala should also anticipate miscellaneous fees related to international adoption (fingerprinting; immigration and naturalization fees; certification, verification, authentication and translation of documents; travel; courier and telephone bills; etc.).

For all programs, applicants are responsible for legal fees connected with finalization of the adoption.

THE WAIT

The time from application to the homecoming of the adoptive child ranges from 9 to 12 months.

THE CHILDREN

Small Miracles International places primarily healthy (but also some special needs) children, ranging in age from birth to 16 years, of all racial backgrounds. Countries of origin include U.S. and Guatemala and, in cooperation with other agencies, Korea and other Asian and Central American countries.

THE REQUIREMENTS

Age: Applicants must be at least 25 and no more than 55 years of age. The requirement varies depending on the circumstances and on the age of the child.

Health: Applicants should be in reasonably good health. Applicants with health problems or handicaps are given individual consideration.

Religion: No requirement, but may vary depending on the program.

Financial status: No requirement.

Marital status: For married applicants, the length of the marriage must be at least 2 years. Single applicants are accepted.

Family size: No requirement, but may vary depending on the program.

Racial, ethnic or cultural origin: No requirement.

THE PROCEDURE

Participation in the adoption program of Small Miracles International entails the following basic steps:
Application
Orientation meeting (for Oklahoma families only)
Homestudy
Compliance with immigration/naturalization requirements (international adoptions only)
Referral
Placement
Post-placement supervision
Out-of-state applicants arrange for a licensed agency in their home state to provide homestudy and supervisory services.

ADDITIONAL PROGRAMS/SERVICES

Small Miracles International provides workshops and seminars, adoptive parent support group, and counseling on an as-needed basis. The agency created and maintains (jointly with the United Church of Guatemala) a day care facility in Guatemala City which provides day care, basic education, medical services, nutritional aid and counseling, and family counseling services. This facility makes employment possible for many single parent families, thereby providing them the opportunity to remain intact if that is their desire.

BRANCH/NETWORK OFFICES

None.

LICENSE/ACCREDITATION/PROFESSIONAL AFFILIATIONS

Small Miracles International, Inc. is licensed by the State of Oklahoma Department of Human Services. The agency is a member of the Joint Council on International Children's Services and the North American Council on Adoptable Children.

UNITED METHODIST COUNSELING SERVICES

1720 N.W. 27th, #1
Oklahoma City, OK 73106
(405) 528–1906
Program director: Karen Hope, MSW

THE PROGRAM

United Methodist Counseling Services is a nonprofit agency serving residents of Oklahoma and placing approximately 15 children annually through its adoption program. Founded 15 years ago and funded by Children, Youth and Family Services of Oklahoma Conference of the United Methodist Church, the agency's mission is "to serve all Oklahoma residents and provide ministry to birth and adoptive parents." The agency provides services to birthparents and places both healthy and special-needs children when birthparents elect adoptive placement as the best plan for their child. In addition, the agency will provide homestudy and supervisory services for applicants pursuing interagency adoption (domestic or international) or private adoption.

THE COST

As of October 1988, the agency's fee schedule for adoption services is as follows:

Application fee	$90.00
Office visit fee	$75.00
Homestudy fee	$350.00
Placement fee	$7,500.00
Post-placement supervision fee	$150.00

Services covered by the placement fee include all expenses of the birthmother and child (medical care; food, clothing, and shelter; foster care; legal fees).

THE WAIT

The time from application to placement averages 1 to 1 1/2 years.

THE CHILDREN

United Methodist Counseling Services places both healthy and special-needs children, ranging in age from birth to 2 years, of all racial backgrounds, born in the U.S.

THE REQUIREMENTS

Age: Applicants must be at least 21 and no more than 40 years of age.

Health: Applicants should be in reasonably good health. Applicants with handicaps are given individual consideration. Infertility documentation is required.

Religion: Applicants must be practicing members of the same Christian church.

Financial status: Applicants must have sufficient income to provide for an additional family member.

Marital status: Applicants must be married; the length of the marriage must be at least 3 years.*Family size*: Applicants may have no more than 3 children currently in the family.

Racial, ethnic or cultural origin: Preference for placing children in families of similar origins.

THE PROCEDURE

Participation in the adoption program of United Methodist Counseling Center entails the following basic steps:

Application
Individual counseling sessions
Homestudy
Orientation meeting
Referral
Group counseling sessions
Placement
Post-placement supervision

ADDITIONAL PROGRAMS/SERVICES

United Methodist Counseling Center provides a full range of counseling services (drug and alcohol abuse, marital and family counseling, speech pathology, psychological testing, IQ testing); foster care; workshops on a range of topics including teenage pregnancy, AIDS, teenage suicide, and adoption.

BRANCH/NETWORK OFFICES

None.

LICENSE/ACCREDITATION/PROFESSIONAL AFFILIATIONS

United Methodist Counseling Center is licensed by the State of Oklahoma Department of Human Services and is a member of the Child Welfare League of America.

Oregon

PUBLIC ADOPTION PROGRAM/ COMMUNITY RESOURCES

Department of Human Resources
Children's Services Division
198 Commercial Street, S.E.
Salem, OR 97310–0450
(503) 378–4452
Adoption specialist: Fred Stock, Adoption Services Manager

THE PROGRAM

Public adoption services in Oregon are provided by the Department of Human Resources, Children's Services Division. Services provided by the Division include adoption counseling and planning; services to birthparents; homestudy, placement, and post-placement supervision of adoptive families; maintenance of state adoption registry; and processing of adoption subsidies. The Division contracts for the necessary investigations related to independent adoptions and contracts with private licensed agencies in Oregon for adoption services to hard-to-place children.

STATE EXCHANGE

None.

STATE ADOPTION REUNION REGISTRY

For information, contact the Children's Services Division (above).

STATE SUBSIDY

For information, contact the Children's Services Division (above).

NACAC REPRESENTATIVE

None at this time.

GENERAL ADOPTION RESOURCES

Adoption support services in Oregon are normally provided by private adoption agencies as a service to their clients. Contact private agencies in Oregon (see Oregon listing) for information about support services in your area.

SPECIAL-NEEDS ADOPTION RESOURCES

See General Adoption Resources (above).

OUT-OF-STATE AGENCIES

SEE APPENDIX A

Agencies Providing Nationwide Services

ADVENTIST ADOPTION & FAMILY SERVICES

6040 S.E. Belmont Street
Portland, OR 97215
(503) 232–1211
Program director: Fern Ringering, MSW

THE PROGRAM

Adventist Adoption & Family Services (AAFS) is a non-profit agency providing nationwide service and placing approximately 40 children annually. Originally founded to assist Christian birthparents in locating Christian adoptive families, the agency today provides services on a non-sectarian basis with regional offices in Washington and Michigan. The agency offers adoption placement services to birthparents who have selected adoption as the plan for their infants. The agency also facilitates the placement of special-needs children and foreign-born children (principally from Central America).

THE COST

The agency's fee for newborn infant placement services ranges up from $5,000 and varies depending on the actual expenses. Services covered by the fee include legal relinquishment, medical expenses, other related services provided to birthparents and the adoptive family. In addition, applicants assume financial responsibility for homestudy (completed by a licensed child-placing agency in their home area) and legal fees connected with finalization of the adoption.

THE WAIT

The time from application for acceptance into the program to the homecoming of the adoptive child ranges from 1 to 3 years.

THE CHILDREN

AAFS places both healthy and special-needs children, ranging in age from birth to 18 years, of all racial backgrounds. Countries of origin include Central America and U.S.

THE REQUIREMENTS

Age: For infant adoptions, applicants may be no more than 40 years of age. The requirement may vary depending on the special needs of the child.
Health: Applicants must be in reasonably good health. Infertility documentation is required for infant adoption. The requirement may vary depending on the special needs of the child.
Religion: No requirement.
Financial status: No requirement.
Marital status: For infant adoption, applicants must be married, and the length of the marriage must be at least 3 years. The requirement may vary depending on the special needs of the child.
Family size: For infant adoption, applicants may have no more than 1 child currently in the family. The requirement may vary depending on the special needs of the child.
Racial, ethnic or cultural origin: No requirement, but preference for placing children in families of similar origins.

THE PROCEDURE

Participation in AAFS' adoption program entails the following basic steps:
Application
Homestudy

Compliance with Interstate Compact regulations
Compliance with immigration/naturalization requirements
   (foreign adoptions only)
Placement

ADDITIONAL PROGRAMS/SERVICES

None.

BRANCH/NETWORK OFFICES

Michigan AAFS
   P.O. Box C
   125 College Ave.
   Berrien Springs, MI 49103
   (616) 471–2221

Washington AAFS
   P.O. Box 3838
   816 N.E. 87th Ave., Suite 101
   Vancouver, WA 98664
   (206) 892–1572

LICENSE/ACCREDITATION/PROFESSIONAL AFFILIATIONS

Adventist Adoption & Family Services is licensed by the appropriate state department in Oregon, Washington, Michigan, Colorado, and Connecticut.

ALBERTINA KERR CENTERS FOR CHILDREN

424 N.E. 22nd Avenue
Portland, OR 97232
(503) 239–8101
Program director: Herbert Hansen

THE PROGRAM

Serving children and families in Oregon for over 80 years, Albertina Kerr Centers for Children is a nonprofit child welfare agency providing statewide services and placing approximately 30 to 50 children annually through its adoption programs. Originally founded as the Albertina Kerr Nursery in 1912, the agency has grown to become a multifaceted children's services agency with 3 major service components: Kerr Center for Maternity, Adoption and Foster Care Services, Kerr Youth and Family Center (a treatment and respite center for children who have been sexually or emotionally abused), and Kerr Developmental Disabilities Services (a residential habilitation and training center and group homes for severely and multiply-handicapped children and youth). The Kerr Center for Maternity, Adoption and Foster Care Services continues Albertina Kerr's mission "of finding loving homes for needy children." Although the program continues to place healthy babies, the emphasis today is the adoptive and foster care placement of "hard-to-place" children (school-aged children; handicapped children of all ages; minority children; school-aged sibling groups). The Center also provides assistance (homestudy and post-placement supervision) for interstate and intercountry adoptions, but the placement of Oregon children is the highest priority.

THE COST

The agency's fee for adoption services varies depending on the program. For special-needs adoption of Oregon children, services are provided at no cost to the adoptive family. For healthy infant, interstate, and intercountry placements, the fee schedule is as follows:

Application	$50.00
Homestudy	$550.00
Interagency coordination fee (interstate and intercountry placements) (maximum)	$850.00
Placement fee	
Infant adoption	$3,000.00–$5,000.00
Interstate adoption	3–6% of gross income

Applicants pursuing intercountry adoption can also expect to pay between $3,000 and $8,000 to the cooperating agency. Services covered by the fee include all phases of the adoption process (pre-study through post-legal services), excluding legal fees connected with finalization of the adoption.

THE WAIT

The time from application to the homecoming of the adoptive child varies depending on the program and ranges from 6 months to 3 years.

THE CHILDREN

Albertina Kerr Centers for Children places both healthy and special-needs children, ranging in age from birth to 16 years, of all racial backgrounds.

THE REQUIREMENTS

Age: The requirement is evaluated on a case-by-case basis.
Health: Applicants should be in reasonably good health. Applicants with health problems or handicaps are given individual consideration.
Religion: No requirement.
Financial status: Applicants must have sufficient income to provide for an additional family member. In some instances, adoption subsidy may be available to mitigate this requirement.
Marital status: No requirement.
Family size: No requirement.
Racial, ethnic or cultural origin: Preference for placing children in families of similar origins. The requirement varies depending on the availability of racially and culturally relevant families and on the needs of the child.

THE PROCEDURE

Participation in the adoption program of Albertina Kerr Centers for Children entails the following basic steps:
   Orientation meeting
   Application
   Individual counseling sessions
   Homestudy
   Compliance with immigration/naturalization requirements
      (intercountry adoptions only)
   Referral
   Placement
   Post-placement supervision
   Post-adoption services

Additional Programs/Services

Albertina Kerr Centers for Children provides a wide range of services for families and children through the Kerr Center for Maternity, Adoption and Foster Care (pregnancy counseling, foster care, adoption); Kerr Youth and Family Center (residential treatment, day treatment, out-patient clinic for family counseling, on-site school and chapel); Kerr Developmental Disabilities Services (physical, speech, and occupational therapies, counseling, independent living skills training).

Branch/Network Offices

None.

License/Accreditation/Professional Affiliations

Albertina Kerr Centers for Children is licensed by the State of Oregon Department of Human Resources. The agency is an associate member of the Child Welfare League of America.

The Boys and Girls Aid Society of Oregon

2301 N.W. Glisan Street
Portland, OR 97210
(503) 222–9661
Program director: James R. Wheeler, MSW, ACSW, RCSW, Associate State Director

The Program

The Boys and Girls Aid Society of Oregon is a nonprofit child welfare agency serving residents of the state of Oregon and southwest Washington and placing approximately 80 children annually. Founded in 1885, the purpose of the Society is "to promote the welfare of children" by providing educational, preventive, treatment, and residential care programs. The agency provides assistance to birthparents and places infants for adoption when birthparents in the agency's program decide that the best interests of the child will be served by adoptive placement. The agency encourages openness in adoption placements through the exchange of non-identifying information between birthparents and adoptive parents. In addition, the agency is actively involved in recruiting families for minority and bi-racial children, sibling groups, physically and emotionally handicapped and older children.

The Cost

The agency's fee for adoption services is based on a sliding scale and ranges from $4,000 to $6,000. However, fees may be reduced or waived when in the best interest of the child. Services covered by the fee include all phases of the adoption process (homestudy through post-placement services for 1 year), excluding pre-adoption classes and legal fees connected with finalization of the adoption. Fees help to underwrite the cost of services to birthparents (counseling, medical, and residential). Adoption services for special-needs children (age 8–18) are provided at no cost to the adoptive family.

The Wait

The time from application for acceptance into the program to the homecoming of the adoptive child ranges from 6 to 18 months.

The Children

The Society places both healthy and special-needs children, primarily infants but older children as well, primarily Caucasian but of minority and bi-racial backgrounds as well, born in the U.S.

The Requirements

Age: For infant adoption, it is preferred that applicants be no more than 40 years of age. The requirement is flexible for special-needs adoptions.
Health: Applicants with health problems or handicaps are given individual consideration.
Religion: No requirement.
Financial status: No requirement.
Marital status: For infant adoption, preference is given to married couples who have been married for at least 2 years. Some options are available to single parents.
Family size: No requirement.
Racial, ethnic or cultural origin: Preference for placing children in families of similar origins.

The Procedure

Participation in the Society's adoption program entails the following basic steps:
   Orientation meeting
   Application
   Pre-adoption classes
   Homestudy
   Placement
   Post-placement supervision

Additional Programs/Services

The Boys and Girls Aid Society of Oregon provides a wide range of services to families and children including individual and group counseling; foster care; group care; residential treatment program; maternity services; crisis intervention; support groups; diversion services; family preservation program; post-legal adoption services (counseling, support groups, registry); information and referral services.

Branch/Network Offices

P.O. Box 3490
660 Francis Lane
Ashland, OR 97520
(503) 482–8895

License/Accreditation/Professional Affiliations

The Boys and Girls Aid Society of Oregon is licensed by the State of Oregon Department of Human Services and is accredited by the Council on Accreditation of Services for Families and Children.

CATHOLIC SERVICES FOR CHILDREN

814 Spaulding Building
319 S.W. Washington Street
Portland, OR 97204
(503) 228–6531
Program director: Millie Susnjara

THE PROGRAM

Catholic Services for Children is a nonprofit agency serving residents of the state or Oregon and placing approximately 10 children annually. In operation for 72 years, the agency's mission is "to provide a program of care for the religious, moral, social, educational, and physical well being of children and to operate a program according to the principles of Christian charity and within the letter and statutes of the State of Oregon." The agency provides services to birthparents and places infants for adoption when birthparents elect adoptive placement as the best plan for their child. Working cooperatively with private and public agencies (both in and out-of- state) and with national and regional exchange programs, the agency places U.S. special-needs children. Working cooperatively with other U.S. agencies which maintain international programs, the agency facilitates the placement of children from various countries. In addition, the agency will provide homestudy and supervisory services for applicants pursuing parent-initiated foreign adoption, interagency adoption (domestic or international), and private adoption.

THE COST

The contribution to the agency for adoption services is $3,500 for placements in which Catholic Services for Children has custody of the child. Services covered by the contribution include all phases of the adoption process, excluding legal fees connected with finalization. For applicants pursuing parent-initiated foreign adoption, interagency adoption, or private adoption, the agency's fee for homestudy and supervisory services is $800.

THE WAIT

The time from application to placement averages 1 1/2 to 2 years.

THE CHILDREN

Catholic Services for Children directly places both healthy and special-needs children (primarily infants) of all racial backgrounds. In addition, the agency will provide homestudy and supervisory services to facilitate the placement of children of any age, race, or country of origin.

THE REQUIREMENTS

Age: The requirement is evaluated on a case-by-case basis.
Health: Applicants with health problems or handicaps are given individual consideration.
Religion: The preferences of the birthmother are honored.
Financial status: The requirement is evaluated on a case-by-case basis.
Marital status: Applicants must be married; the length of the marriage must be at least 2 years.

Family size: The requirement is evaluated on a case-by-case basis.
Racial, ethnic or cultural origin: The requirement is evaluated on a case-by-case basis.

THE PROCEDURE

Participation in the adoption program of Catholic Services for Children entails the following basic steps:
   Application
   Homestudy
   Compliance with immigration/naturalization requirements (international adoptions only)
   Referral
   Placement
   Post-placement supervision
   Individual/family post-placement counseling (as needed)

ADDITIONAL PROGRAMS/SERVICES

Catholic Services for Children provides two group homes for mentally retarded/developmentally disabled children; resettlement program; maternity home; workshops for foster parents and group home parents.

BRANCH/NETWORK OFFICES

Catholic Services for Children maintains branch offices in Baker and Medford.

LICENSE/ACCREDITATION/PROFESSIONAL AFFILIATIONS

Catholic Services for Children is licensed by the State of Oregon Department of Human Resources and is accredited by the Council on Accreditation of Services for Families and Children. The agency is a member of Catholic Charities USA.

HOLT INTERNATIONAL CHILDREN'S SERVICES, INC.

P.O. Box 2880, 1195 City View
Eugene, OR 97402
(503) 687–2202
Program director: David H. Kim, Executive Director

THE PROGRAM

Holt International Children's Services is a nonprofit international adoption and child caring agency serving homeless children in Korea, Thailand, the Philippines, India, Hong Kong and Latin America. Holt serves 50 states and places approximately 1,000 children annually. Holt began in 1955 when Harry and Bertha Holt, moved by the plight of thousands of homeless children left in the wake of the Korean War, founded the agency "in order to help unite homeless children with families who would love them as their own." Holt's work is based on the following goals: (1) to enable the biological family to stay together, (2) if the child cannot be kept in his biological family, to place him in a permanent adoptive family in his birth country, (3) if the child cannot be placed in an adoptive family in his birth country, to find an adoptive family for him in another country.

The Cost

Holt charges a flat fee which varies depending on the child's country of origin. The average fee is $5,000 and includes the home study, U.S. processing fee, overseas processing fee, transportation, and post-placement supervision. In addition, prospective adoptive parents should anticipate financial responsibility for naturalization fees ($30) and legal fees in connection with finalization of the adoption.

The Wait

The time from application to the homecoming of the adoptive child ranges from 18 to 24 months.

The Children

Holt places children of Asian, Caucasian, and mixed racial backgrounds, ranging in age from 6 months to 16 years. Holt places both healthy and special-needs children. Countries of origin include Korea, Thailand, Philippines, India, Hong Kong, and Latin America.

The Requirements

Age: The requirement varies depending on the requirements of the child's birth country.
Health: The requirement varies depending on the requirements of the child's birth country.
Religion: No requirement.
Financial status: The requirement varies depending on the requirements of the child's birth country.
Marital status: The requirement varies depending on the requirements of the child's birth country.
Family size: The requirement varies depending on the requirements of the child's birth country.
Racial, ethnic or cultural origin: The requirement varies depending on the requirements of the child's birth country.

The Procedure

Participation in Holt's adoption program entails the following basic steps:
Application
Homestudy
Compliance with immigration/naturalization requirements
Referral
Placement
Post-placement supervision

Additional Programs/Services

Holt offers a sponsorship program which provides financial support for homeless children; sponsors a special friends program designed to provide special medical treatment for homeless children; provides pregnancy counseling; sponsors heritage camps and tours to birth countries; publishes Hi Families!, a bimonthly magazine (an annual donation of $10.00 is required to cover the cost of publishing and mailing).

Branch/Network Offices

Northern California Office
(serving Bay area and Sacramento)
14895 East 14th, Suite 350
San Leandro, CA 94578
(415) 351-4996

Southern California Office
(serving ten southern counties)
5230 Clark Ave., Suite 32
Lakewood, CA 90713
(213) 925-0933

Iowa Office
(serving Iowa)
2175 N.W. 86th St., Suite 10
Des Moines, IA 50322
(515) 253-0622

Kentucky Office
(serving Kentucky)
4229 Bardstown Rd., Suite 234
Chrysler Building
Louisville, KY 40218-0266
(502) 499-1562

Nebraska Office
(serving NE, WY, and SD)
P.O. Box 12153
(8702 N. 30th St., Suite 6)
Omaha, NE 68112
(402) 457-6323

New Jersey Office
(serving New Jersey)
2490 Pennington Rd. (Rt. 31)
Trenton, NJ 08638
(609) 737-7710

Tennessee Office
(serving TN, MS, and AR)
5347 Flowering Peach
Memphis, TN 38115
(901) 794-6082

License/Accreditation/Professional Affiliations

Holt is licensed as a child placing agency in the states of New Jersey, Iowa, Mississippi, Tennessee, Arkansas, Kentucky, Nebraska, Oregon, Wyoming and parts of California. Holt is a member of the North American Council on Adoptable Children and a Cooperating Agency with the American Council of Voluntary Agencies for Foreign Service. Holt is also registered as a Private Voluntary Organization with the United States Agency for International Development. Holt is a member of the Evangelical Council for Financial Accountability.

LDS Social Services

3000 Market Street, N.E., #268
Salem, OR 97301
(503) 581-7483
Program director: Alvin W. Morgan, Jr.

The Program

For a full description of programs and services, refer to Utah listing:

LDS Social Services
50 East North Temple Street
Salt Lake City, UT 84150

BRANCH OFFICES

LDS Social Services/Oregon
7575 Pacific Ave.
White City, OR 97503
(503) 826–5633

OPEN ADOPTION & FAMILY SERVICES

239 E. 14th Avenue
Eugene, OR 97401
(503) 343–4825
Program director: Jeanne Etter

THE PROGRAM

Open Adoption & Family Services is a nonprofit agency serving residents of the state of Oregon and placing approximately 50 children annually. Founded in 1985, the agency offers "a compassionate choice to women faced with untimely pregnancies and real hope to families wanting to adopt." The agency believes that birthparents, adoptive parents, and children benefit from the honesty of open adoption. Through professional counseling and mediation, the agency guides all parties through the process and facilitates an ongoing channel of communication which may include letters, phone calls, or visits, agreed upon by both parties. Confidentiality can be guaranteed, if desired. At the time of placement, the adoptive parents become the sole legal parents of the child, and the agency stresses that "open adoptions through licensed agencies are as permanent and binding as any other type of adoption."

THE COST

The agency's fee for adoption services ranges from $2,400 to $2,700. Services covered by the fee include pre-adoption classes and support group, homestudy, adoption counseling and mediation (for birthparents and adoptive parents), placement, post-placement supervision, and birthparent counseling. In addition, applicants should anticipate financial responsibility for the medical expenses of the birthmother and child and legal fees connected with finalization of the adoption.

THE WAIT

The average time from application for acceptance into the program to the homecoming of the adoptive child is 10 months.

THE CHILDREN

Open Adoption & Family Services places healthy children, ranging in age from birth to 3 years, of all racial backgrounds, born in the U.S.

THE REQUIREMENTS

Age: No requirement. Birthparents' preferences are honored.

Health: Applicants with health problem or handicap are given individual consideration.

Religion: No requirement. Birthparents' preferences are honored.

Financial status: Applicants must demonstrate financial stability.*Marital status*: No requirement. Birthparents' preferences are honored.

Family size: No requirement. Birthparents' preferences are honored.

Racial, ethnic or cultural origin: No requirement. Birthparents' preferences are honored.

THE PROCEDURE

Participation in Open Adoption & Family Services' adoption program entails the following basic steps:
Orientation meeting
Application
Group counseling sessions
Individual counseling sessions
Homestudy
Mediation with birthparents
Placement
Post-placement supervision

ADDITIONAL PROGRAMS/SERVICES

The agency sponsors workshops related to open adoption and transracial adoption.

BRANCH/NETWORK OFFICES

Open Adoption & Family Services
529 S.E. Grand Avenue
Portland, OR 97214
(503) 233–9660

LICENSE/ACCREDITATION/PROFESSIONAL AFFILIATIONS

Open Adoption & Family Services, Inc. is licensed by the State of Oregon, Children's Services Division. The agency is affiliated with the Oregon Council of Adoption Agencies, Oregon Mediation Association, and Academy of Family Mediators.

PLAN LOVING ADOPTIONS NOW, INC. (PLAN)

P.O. Box 667
McMinnville, OR 97128
(503) 472–8452
Program director: Ann Scott, Executive Director; Nancy Stohl, U.S. Program Director; Julie Eagleson, Latin American Program Director; Delores Lauben, Asian Program Director

THE PROGRAM

Plan Loving Adoptions Now (PLAN) is a nonprofit agency serving the state of Oregon and placing approximately 130 children annually. An outgrowth of an adoptive parent support group, PLAN was licensed in 1975 to facilitate adoptions of homeless children, with emphasis on special-needs children. The agency has several domestic and international adoption programs. PLAN provides services to birthparents and places infants for adoption when birthparents in the agency's pregnancy counseling program (Loving Options) decide that the best interests of the child will be served by adoptive placement. The agency works with private and public state-approved foreign agencies to place foreign-born children from various countries and is currently working with sources in ten countries. The agency will work with out-of-state families for the placement of sibling groups or children over 7 years of age.

THE COST

PLAN's fee for adoption services is based on a sliding scale and ranges from $900 to $1,500. Services covered by the basic agency fee include pre-adoption classes, application, processing, adoption study, coordination with child-placing agency, post-placement services and court report for finalization. In addition, for foreign adoption, applicants should anticipate from $3,000 to $5,000 additional expenses for immigration fees, document translation, foreign agency fees, and travel. In all programs, applicants assume responsibility for legal fees connected with finalization.

THE WAIT

The time from application for acceptance into the program to the homecoming of the adoptive child varies according to the program and/or the child's country of origin. Most placements occur within 12 months, with almost immediate placement for boys and a longer wait for girls.

THE CHILDREN

PLAN places both healthy and special-needs children, ranging in age from birth to adolescence, of all racial backgrounds. Countries of origin include Guatemala, India, Colombia, Brazil, Korea, Philippines, Hong Kong, Taiwan, Costa Rica, and U.S.

THE REQUIREMENTS

Age: The requirement varies depending on the child's country of origin. Generally, the age difference between the applicant and the child being considered for placement should not exceed 40 years.

Health: Applicants must be in reasonably good health. Applicants with health problems or handicaps are given individual consideration.

Religion: No requirement.

Financial status: The requirement varies depending on child's country of origin.

Marital status: The requirement varies depending on the child's country of origin. Some options are available for single parents. If married, applicants must be married for at least 1 year.

Family size: No requirement, but may vary depending on the child's country of origin.

Racial, ethnic or cultural origin: The requirement varies depending on the child's country of origin.

THE PROCEDURE

Participation in PLAN's adoption program entails the following basic steps:

Orientation meeting
Group counseling sessions
Application
Homestudy
Referral
Compliance with immigration/naturalization requirements (foreign adoptions only)
Placement
Post-placement supervision
Court report for finalization
Post-legalization support services

ADDITIONAL PROGRAMS/SERVICES

PLAN provides parent education support groups (5 sessions) for families wishing to adopt through PLAN or other agencies; sponsors workshops and conferences for adoptive parents, para-professionals, and social workers; provides counseling services; provides foster care for young pregnant women and short-term foster care for infants waiting placement.

BRANCH/NETWORK OFFICES

None.

LICENSE/ACCREDITATION/PROFESSIONAL AFFILIATIONS

PLAN is licensed by the State of Oregon Department of Human Services.

Pennsylvania

PUBLIC ADOPTION PROGRAM/ COMMUNITY RESOURCES

Department of Public Welfare
Office of Children, Youth and Families
P.O. Box 2675
Harrisburg, PA 17105–2675
(717) 787–7756
Adoption specialist: Robert Gioffre

THE PROGRAM

Public adoption agencies in Pennsylvania are county Children and Youth Services agencies under the supervision of the Department of Public Welfare, Office of Children, Youth and Families. County Children and Youth Services agencies recruit and prepare families and supervise the placement of special-needs children (older, minority, and handicapped children and sibling groups) who are in the custody of the county.

STATE EXCHANGE

Pennsylvania Adoption Exchange
Lanco Lodge, Second Floor
P.O. Box 2675
Harrisburg, PA 17105–2675
(717) 257–7015
(800) 227–0225 (toll-free in Pennsylvania)

STATE ADOPTION REUNION REGISTRY

Pennsylvania Department of Health
Division of Vital Records
P.O. Box 1528
New Castle, PA 16103
(412) 656–3100

STATE SUBSIDY

The adoption subsidy program is supervised by county Children and Youth Services agencies. Contact the agency in your county for information.

NACAC REPRESENTATIVE

Pam Grabe
127 E. Wayne St.
Butler, PA 16001
(412) 283–1971

GENERAL ADOPTION RESOURCES

The following list represents selected adoptive parent groups and adoption resources in Pennsylvania. For a complete and current list, contact Pennsylvania Adoption Exchange (above).

Adoptive Parents International
13223 Buena Vista Road
Waynesboro, PA 17268
(717) 794–2035

Audobon Adoption Referral Service
715 Pondview Drive
Audobon, PA 19403
(215) 631–1057

Council on Adoptable Children (COAC) Armstrong & Indiana Counties
Contact: Mr. and Mrs. Walt Slomski
RD #2, Box 13–A
Marion Center, PA 15759

COAC of Southwestern Pennsylvania
Contact: Mike Anderson
224 South Aiken Avenue
Pittsburgh, PA 15206
(412) 361–4419

Northwestern Pennsylvania COAC
Contact: Janet Staley
327 Joliette Avenue
Erie, PA 16511
(814) 899–3517

COAC of Chester County, Inc.
Contact: Sharon Ames
114 Governors Circle
Downingtown, PA 19335
(215) 269–7094

Families for Adoptable Children Everywhere
Contact: Amy Hutton
127 South Fairmont Avenue
Pittsburgh, PA 15206
(412) 661–0176

FCVN/Open Door Society
Contact: Pat Sexton
1835 Troxell Street
Allentown, PA 18103

Parents of Adopted Children Organization (PACO)
Tressler Lutheran Service Assoc.
25 W. Springettsbury Avenue
York, PA 17403
(717) 815–9113

PACO of Lancaster County
Contact: Inez Tomlinson
60 North Hazel Street
Manheim, PA 17545
(717) 665–4561

PACO West
Contact: Wendy Pingor
One Lou Anne Lane
Delmont, PA 15626
(412) 795–5912

PACO Midwest
Contact: Kathy Hamilton
RD 6, Winters Road
Butler, PA 16001

PACO Lawrence County
Contact: Gina Williams
419 Sumner Avenue
New Castle, PA 16101
(412) 658–8308

PACO Mercer County
Contact: Violet Brown
RD #7, Box 7092
Mercer, PA 16137

PACO of North Central Pennsylvania
  Contact: Rosemary Bailey
  1029 Rural Avenue
  Williamsport, PA 17701

PACO Washington County
  Contact: Rebecca Tomasiak
  551 McCrea Avenue
  Donora, PA 15033

Parents of Overseas Adoption
  Contact: David Jones
  8571 Lake Pleasant Road
  Erie, PA 16509
  (814) 866–6280

Together for Adoptive Children
  Contact: Mr. and Mrs. Barry Heverly
  307 Church Street
  Phoenixville, PA 19460

SPECIAL-NEEDS ADOPTION RESOURCES

For information on Pennsylvania resources for children with special needs, contact COAC (see General Adoption Resources above).

OUT-OF-STATE AGENCIES

AGENCY

World Child, Washington, DC
Children's Home Society of New Jersey, New Jersey (Bucks County)
The Edna Gladney Center, Texas

SEE APPENDIX A

Agencies Providing Nationwide Services

AID FOR CHILDREN INTERNATIONAL, LTD

118 W. Walnut Street
Marietta, PA 17547
(717) 426–4331
Program director: Vicki Armstrong and Beverly Garber

THE PROGRAM

Aid for Children International is a nonprofit agency serving residents who live within a 75 mile radius (approximately) of Lancaster City and facilitating the placement of approximately 8 to 10 children annually. Founded in 1983 by several members of the Glah family, the agency "has a 'heart' for the homeless and special-needs child and works in loving behalf of homeless children to provide permanent homes and families." The agency emphasizes personal, one-to-one assistance and enjoys the benefits of working with a closely associated group of families. Working with other private and public agencies and with national and regional exchange programs, the agency facilitates the placement of domestic special-needs infants and children. Working cooperatively with other U.S. agencies which maintain international programs, the agency facilitates the placement of foreign-born children in Pennsylvania families.

THE COST

The agency's fee for adoption services is 3% of the applicants' annual gross income with an average fee of $1,000 (minimum fee, $700; maximum fee, $1,500). Services covered by the fee include the homestudy process, post-placement supervision, and the finalization process. In addition, applicants should anticipate (when applicable) fees to the cooperating agency, foster care or orphanage fees, travel or escort fees, translation fees, and related costs. Applicants are responsible for legal fees connected with finalization of the adoption.

THE WAIT

The time from application acceptance to the homecoming of the adoptive child averages 1 year.

THE CHILDREN

Aid for Children International facilitates the placement of both healthy and special-needs children, ranging in age from birth to 16 years, of all racial backgrounds. Countries of origin vary depending on the cooperating agency.

THE REQUIREMENTS

Age: Applicants must be at least 25 years of age. The maximum age requirement varies depending on the country of origin and the cooperating agency.
Health: Applicants should be in reasonably good health. Applicants with health problems or handicaps are given individual consideration. The requirement may vary depending on the country of origin and the cooperating agency.
Religion: Applicants must be practicing members of the Christian faith and must attend a house of worship.
Financial status: No requirement other than the requirements of the country of origin or the cooperating agency.
Marital status: The marital requirement varies depending on the country of origin and the cooperating agency. Married applicants must have been married for at least 2 years.
Family size: No requirement other than the requirements of the country of origin or the cooperating agency.
Racial, ethnic or cultural origin: No requirement, but preference for placing children in families of similar origins.

THE PROCEDURE

Participation in the adoption program of Aid for Children International entails the following basic steps:
  Inquiry
  Registration
  Application
  Homestudy
  Compliance with immigration/naturalization requirements
    (international adoptions only)
  Referral
  Placement
  Post-placement supervision

ADDITIONAL PROGRAMS/SERVICES
  None.

BRANCH/NETWORK OFFICES

None.

LICENSE/ACCREDITATION/PROFESSIONAL AFFILIATIONS

Aid for Children International is licensed by the Commonwealth of Pennsylvania Department of Public Welfare.

THE ADOPTION AGENCY

76 Rittenhouse Place
Ardmore, PA 19003
(215) 642–7200
Program director: Maxine G. Chalker, MSW

THE PROGRAM

The Adoption Agency is a nonprofit agency, founded by Maxine G. Chalker in 1984, currently serving residents of Pennsylvania and New Jersey (within a 90 mile radius of the Philadelphia area) and residents of Delaware. Placing approximately 50 children annually, the primary goal of The Adoption Agency is "to provide adoption services to clients in a humane, intimate manner that respects individual rights and encourages responsibility of all parties to their child." The agency offers a range of adoption services including an open adoption placement program, a minority recruitment program, special-needs adoption program, and foreign adoption program. In open adoption, the birthparents select the adoptive parents for their child by reviewing profiles and pictures of the couples. They then have the option of meeting the couple and can receive on-going information as the child grows. To insure privacy, meetings between adoptive parents and birthparents are conducted using first names only. After placement, communications about the child are handled through the agency. Through its minority recruitment program, the agency actively seeks families to adopt minority and bi-racial children. Through its special-needs adoption program, the agency works with the National Adoption Exchange, P.A.C.E. and Three Rivers Adoption Exchange to facilitate the adoption of older or special-needs children. Through its foreign adoption program, the agency works to facilitate direct adoptions in Colombia, South America, and India (in the future).

THE COST

The Adoption Agency's fee schedule is as follows:

Open Adoption Program (direct placement of infants and toddlers)

Application fee	$35.00
Homestudy fee	$550.00
Update of previous homestudy	$100.00–$300.00
Yearly participation fee	$100.00
Pre-placement fee (per hour)	$50.00
Placement fee (includes post-placement visit and report)	$5,500.00
Termination of parental rights	$300.00–$450.00

In addition, prospective adoptive parents applying for open adoption program should anticipate financial responsibility for possible medical costs of the birthmother and legal costs involved in finalization of the adoption.

Special-needs adoption Program

Application, homestudy, and pre-placement fees as indicated above.

Placement fee for Caucasian child	$1,500
Post-placement visits and report	$75/visit
Placement fee for minority children (direct placement) $1,500*	
Placement fee for minority children (in the custody of another agency)	$1,000*

*Includes post-placement visit and report

Foreign Adoption Program

Application, homestudy as indicated above.

Foreign adoption assistance fee (referral and assistance) $500.00

India (children escorted)	pending
Bogota, Colombia* (parents must travel) plus travel	$6,300.00

*Includes 1 post-placement visit and report

Applicants should note that foreign adoption program fees are subject to change.

THE WAIT

In the agency's open adoption placement program, birthparents select adoptive parents. Consequently, an adoptive family may be selected as soon as 1 month after completion of the homestudy or may wait an undetermined length of time. In the agency's other adoption programs, the length of time from application to the homecoming of the adoptive child varies depending on the child's country of origin and availability of children through the adoption exchanges.

THE CHILDREN

The Adoption Agency places healthy and special-needs children of all racial backgrounds, ranging in age from birth to 18 years. Countries of origin include U.S., Colombia, and India in the future.

THE REQUIREMENTS

The agency's requirements are flexible. However, applicants should note that, in the open adoption placement program, the birthparents' preferences with regard to the following requirements are honored.

Age: Applicants must be at least 21 years old. Maximum age varies depending on the preference of the birthparents. For adoption of a child from Colombia, applicants must be under 40 years of age.

Health: Applicants must be in reasonably good health with normal life expectancy.

Religion: No requirement.

Financial status: Applicants must demonstrate financial stability.

Marital status: No requirement.

Family size: No requirement.

Racial, ethnic or cultural origin: No requirement, but preference for placing children in families of similar origins.

THE PROCEDURE

Participation in The Adoption Agency's programs entails the following basic steps:
Application
Homestudy (including group and individual counseling sessions)
Placement
Post-placement supervision

ADDITIONAL PROGRAMS/SERVICES

The Adoption Agency provides a wide range of services including intermediary services for assistance with private adoptions; birthparent support group; child birth education classes for pregnant women; infant care education classes for adoptive parents; post-placement seminars for adoptive parents; social activities.

BRANCH/NETWORK OFFICES

Applicants should note that the Lancaster office provides services for birthparents only. Adoptive applicants should contact either the Ardmore or the Wilmington office.

Ardmore Office
P.O. Box 5432
Lancaster, PA 17601
(717) 299–9999

Wilmington Office
1308 Delaware Ave.
Wilmington, DE 19806
(302) 658–8883

LICENSE/ACCREDITATION/PROFESSIONAL AFFILIATIONS

The Adoption Agency is licensed by the Commonwealth of Pennsylvania Department of Public Welfare, the State of New Jersey Department of Human Services, and the State of Delaware Department of Services for Children, Youth and Their Families. The agency is a member of the Delaware Valley Adoption Council.

ADOPTION SERVICE, INC.

115 South St. Johns Dr.
Camp Hill, PA 17055
(717) 737–3960
Program director: Dr. Vincent Berger

THE PROGRAM

First licensed in February 1985, Adoption Services, Inc., is a nonprofit adoption agency serving Pennsylvania and neighboring states. The agency places approximately 10–20 children annually. Adoption Services provides extensive services to birthparents and places infants for adoption when birthparents in the agency's counseling program decide that the best interests of the child will be served through adoptive placement. Through its specialized programs, Adoption Services facilitates the adoption process by helping to eliminate many of the doubts and concerns birthmothers might have regarding placement. The agency also provides homes-tudy and supervisory services for applicants pursuing interstate, international, or private adoption.

THE COST

The agency's fee for adoption services varies depending on the services requested. The basic fee schedule is as follows:

Registration fee (non-refundable)	$95.00
Application fee (refundable if application is denied)	$200.00
Homestudy fee (plus travel)	$1,200.00
Agency service fee (support services, post-placement services, preparation submission of documents to the court, and court appearance)	$2,700.00

Applicants assume responsibility for legal fees connected with termination of parental rights and with finalization of the adoption. Applicants pursuing international adoption should anticipate foreign agency/source fees, possible overseas legal fees, possible fees for document translation and authentication, travel expenses, and related costs. Applicants pursuing adoption of American-born infants should anticipate legal fees connected with termination of birthparents' rights, medical and foster care services to the birthmother and child, and possible travel expenses.

THE WAIT

The time from application to completion of a homestudy ranges from 3 weeks to 3 months. The time from application for acceptance into the program to homecoming of the adoptive child ranges from 1 to 3 years.

THE CHILDREN

Adoption Services, Inc. places primarily healthy infants (newborn to 2 years), of all racial and ethnic backgrounds. In addition, the agency will provide homestudy and supervisory services for the adoption of children of any age, race, or nationality.

THE REQUIREMENTS

Age: No requirement.
Health: Applicants must be able to physically care for the child.
Religion: No requirement.
Financial status: No requirement.
Marital status: No requirement.
Family size: No requirement.
Racial, ethnic or cultural origin: No requirement.

THE PROCEDURE

Participation in Adoption Services' program entails the following basic steps:
Registration
Application
Homestudy
Compliance with immigration/naturalization requirements (foreign adoptions only)
Referral
Placement
Supervisory visits

ADDITIONAL PROGRAMS/SERVICES

Adoption Services, Inc., provides counseling, support programs for birthparents and community education programs.

BRANCH/NETWORK OFFICES

None.

LICENSE/ACCREDITATION/PROFESSIONAL AFFILIATIONS

Adoption Services, Inc. is licensed by the Commonwealth of Pennsylvania Department of Public Welfare.

ADOPTION UNLIMITED

2770 Weston Road
Lancaster, PA 17603
(717) 872–1340
Program director: Mary E. Murphy, M.Ed.

THE PROGRAM

Adoption Unlimited is a for-profit agency serving residents of eastern and central Pennsylvania and anticipating cooperative placement of approximately 20 to 30 children annually. Adoption Unlimited is a new agency (licensed in 1988) which works cooperatively with public agencies, national and regional exchange programs, and other U.S. agencies which maintain international programs to place both healthy and special-needs children from the U.S. and abroad in central and eastern Pennsylvania families. The agency gives special attention "to parents over the age of 35 and singles who are often refused by 'traditional' agencies but who are eligible to adopt children from Latin America." In addition, the agency will provide homestudy and post-placement supervision for applicants pursuing interagency adoption (domestic or international) or private adoption.

THE COST

The agency's fee for adoption services is $500 for the homestudy, $500 for referral to the cooperating custodial agency, and $75 per post-placement supervisory visit (usually 3 visits). In addition, applicants can expect to pay between $2,000 and $12,000 to the cooperating agency (the fee varies depending on the program and the country), immigration fees ($50), passport and visa fees for the child ($150), and legal fees connected with finalization of the adoption.

THE WAIT

The agency anticipates that the time from application to placement will average less than 1 year.

THE CHILDREN

Adoption Unlimited facilitates the placement of both healthy and special-needs children, newborn and older, of Hispanic, Black, Caucasian (older children), and bi-racial backgrounds. Countries of origin include India, Sri Lanka, Taiwan, Mexico, Haiti, Puerto Rico, and various countries in Central and South America.

THE REQUIREMENTS

Age: No requirement, but may vary depending on the requirements of the cooperating agency.
Health: Applicants should be in reasonably good health.
Religion: No requirement, but may vary depending on the requirements of the cooperating agency.
Financial status: No requirement, but may vary depending on the requirements of the cooperating agency.
Marital status: No requirement, but may vary depending on the requirements of the cooperating agency.
Family size: No requirement, but may vary depending on the requirements of the cooperating agency.
Racial, ethnic or cultural origin: No requirement.

THE PROCEDURE

Participation in the adoption program of Adoption Unlimited entails the following basic steps:
Application
Homestudy (including group counseling sessions)
Compliance with immigration/naturalization requirements (international adoptions only)
Referral
Placement
Post-placement supervision (if required)

ADDITIONAL PROGRAMS/SERVICES

Adoption Unlimited provides pre-adoption counseling, counseling for adoptive parents and children, infertility counseling, and speakers on international adoption. For applicants pursuing international adoption, the agency provides assistance with immigration procedures and guidance in planning the adoption trip to the child's country of origin.

BRANCH/NETWORK OFFICES

None.

LICENSE/ACCREDITATION/PROFESSIONAL AFFILIATIONS

Adoption Unlimited is licensed by the Commonwealth of Pennsylvania Department of Public Welfare.

THE BAIR FOUNDATION

241 High Street
New Wilmington, PA 16142
(412) 946–8711
Program director: Alice Clapper

THE PROGRAM

Licensed in 1980, the Bair Foundation is a nonprofit agency that serves the residents of western Pennsylvania in placing primarily special-needs children and some infants for adoption. Since 1980, the Bair Foundation has placed 112 children and annually places from 10 to 15 children with adoptive families. The Bair Foundation is committed to Christian family values and considers as its primary purpose in placing for adoption those children "who would not otherwise have a home of their own, and who can benefit from families that can give them the love, care, protection, and opportunities essential for their healthy personal growth and development."

THE COST

The agency charges a flat fee of $3,500. Services covered by the fee include parent training, homestudy, pre-adoptive counseling, placement supervision, post-adoption counseling, and administrative costs

THE WAIT

The average time from application for acceptance into the program to the homecoming of the adoptive child is 2 years for a special-needs child and 5 years for an infant.

THE CHILDREN

The Bair Foundation places American children who range in age from birth to 17 years. The agency places healthy and special-needs children of all races.

THE REQUIREMENTS

Age: Applicants must be at least 25 and no more than 40 years of age.

Health: Applicants must be in reasonably good health. Infertility documentation is required for infant adoption.

Religion: Applicants must be a practicing member of a Christian church.

Financial status: Applicants must demonstrate financial stability.

Marital status: Applicants for infant adoption must be married. The length of the marriage must be at least 5 years. No requirement for special-needs adoption.

Family size: Applicants for infant adoption may not have more than one child. For special-needs adoptions, applicants may have no more than 6 children currently living in the home and no more than 3 special-needs children in the family.

Racial, ethnic or cultural origin: No requirement.

THE PROCEDURE

Participation in the Bair Foundation's adoption program entails the following basic steps:
Registration
Orientation meeting
Application
Homestudy (includes group training and counseling)
Individual counseling sessions
Referral
Placement
Post-placement supervision (minimum of 6 months)
Finalization

ADDITIONAL PROGRAMS/SERVICES

The Bair Foundation offers family services that include EXODUS (Experiential Development of Opportunities for Unity and Success) and the Annual Family Life Convention, day treatment services, L.I.F.E. Academy, and foster care services.

BRANCH/NETWORK OFFICES

Bair Foundation Ohio
P.O. Box 168
Brookfield, OH 44403
(216) 448–0244

The Bair Foundation
1401 N. Vine Street
Middletown, PA 17057
(717) 944–1674

LICENSE/ACCREDITATION/PROFESSIONAL AFFILIATIONS

The Bair Foundation is licensed by the Commonwealth of Pennsylvania Department of Public Welfare and by the State of Ohio Department of Human Services. The agency is affiliated with SPAN (Specialized Pennsylvania Adoption Network), Pennsylvania Council of Children's Services, and Pennsylvania State Foster Parent Association.

BETHANY CHRISTIAN SERVICES

1107 Bethlehem Pike, Suite #210
Flourtown, PA 19031–1919
(215) 233–4626
Program director: James K. Haveman, Jr., Executive Director

THE PROGRAM

For a full description of programs and services, refer to Michigan listing:
Bethany Christian Services
901 Eastern Avenue, N.E.
Grand Rapids, MI 49503–1295
(616) 459–6273

BRANCH OFFICES

Bethany Christian Services/Pennsylvania
224 Manor Ave.
Millersville, PA 17551–0417
(717) 872–0945
694 Lincoln Ave.
Pittsburgh, PA 15202–3477
(412) 734–2662

CATHOLIC CHARITIES

115 Vannear Avenue
Greensburg, PA 15601
(412) 837–1840
Program director: Sr. Joanne Marie Stank

THE PROGRAM

Catholic Charities of the Diocese of Greensburg is a nonprofit multi-service agency serving residents of the Diocese of Greensburg (Indiana, Armstrong, Westmoreland, and Fayette Counties) and placing approximately 12 children annually through its adoption program. For over 30 years, Catholic Charities has provided services to birthparents, adoptive parents, and children in need of adoptive families. Prior to 1986, infant adoptions were the focus of Catholic Charities. Today, the agency also provides services for applicants pursuing special needs, minority, and Korean adoption.

In all of its programs, Catholic Charities is guided by the belief that the dignity and sanctity of human life "is best nurtured and preserved within the framework of a strong and healthy family life."

THE COST

The agency's fee for adoption services is $65.00 per service hour, with a total of approximately 20 hours. Services include individual and group sessions, homestudy, matching and placement, three supervisory visits, and pre-legal services and agency representation in court. Applicants pursuing domestic infant adoption should also anticipate responsibility for birthparents' voluntary relinquishment fees. Applicants pursuing Korean adoption should anticipate foreign agency fees, travel/escort costs, and immigration and naturalization fees. For all programs, applicants are responsible for legal fees connected with finalization.

THE WAIT

The average time from application for acceptance into the program to homecoming of the adoptive child is 5 to 8 years for a healthy Caucasian infant, 6 to 12 months for a minority or bi-racial infant, and 12 to 18 months for a Korean infant.

THE CHILDREN

Catholic Charities places both healthy and special-needs children, ranging in age from birth to 7 years and up, of all racial backgrounds. Countries of origin include the U.S. and Korea.

THE REQUIREMENTS

Age: The maximum age for adoptive parents of infants is 40 years. For non-infants, age requirements vary depending on the age of the child. Generally, there should not be more than 40 years between the adoptive parent and child.

Health: Applicants should be in reasonably good health. Applicants with health problems or handicaps are given individual consideration. For healthy Caucasian infants, infertility documentation is required.

Religion: Applicants should be practicing members of a religious faith.

Financial status: Applicants should have sufficient financial resources to provide for an additional family member.

Marital status: The marital requirement varies depending on the program and on the specific requests of the birthparents.

Family size: For healthy Caucasian infant adoption, applicants may have no more than 1 child currently in the family. The requirement is flexible for other programs.

Racial, ethnic or cultural origin: Preference for placing children in families of similar origins. However, the agency does place Korean children with Caucasian families.

THE PROCEDURE

Participation in Catholic Charities' adoption program entails the following basic steps:

Orientation meeting
Application
Individual counseling sessions
Group counseling sessions
Homestudy
Referral
Compliance with immigration/naturalization requirements (Korean adoptions only)
Placement
Post-placement supervision

ADDITIONAL PROGRAMS/SERVICES

Catholic Charities provides a wide range of services including services to birthparents and host homes for pregnant women; foster care; post-adoption services and social activities; services to the elderly; friendly visitor/respite care program; marriage preparation; widows and widowers program; program for the separated and divorced; individual, marital, and family counseling.

BRANCH/NETWORK OFFICES

3040 Leechburg Road
Lower Burrell, PA 15068
(412) 335–5551

Indiana Theatre Building
637 Philadelphia Street
Indiana, PA 15701
(412) 463–8806

92 East Main Street
Uniontown, PA 15401
(412) 439–3531

Old Post Office
212 State Street
Belle Vernon, PA 15012
(412) 929–4699

LICENSE/ACCREDITATION/PROFESSIONAL AFFILIATIONS

Catholic Charities is licensed by the Commonwealth of Pennsylvania Department of Public Welfare. The agency is a member of the Pennsylvania Catholic Conference, Catholic Charities USA, and the United Way.

CATHOLIC CHARITIES OF THE DIOCESE OF PITTSBURGH, INC.

307 Fourth Avenue, Suite 300
Pittsburgh, PA 15222
(412) 471–1120
Program director: Director of Family Services, Allegheny County

THE PROGRAM

Catholic Charities of the Diocese of Pittsburgh, Inc. (CCDP), is a nonprofit organization that places approximately 15 to 20 children annually in homes throughout the Diocese of Pittsburgh (Allegheny, Beaver, Butler, Greene, Lawrence, and Washington counties). The mission of CCDP is to provide family and social services to those in need and foster understanding and "concern about health and welfare services and human rights." The agency strives to provide adoptive children homes that can give them "the love, care, protection, and opportunities essential for their healthy growth and development." The agency has domestic and foreign adoption programs.

THE COST

The agency charges a flat fee of $3,500 that includes all phases of the adoption process (pre-adoption counseling through post-placement supervision), excluding legal fees connected with finalization. Fees help to underwrite medical, legal, and foster care services.

THE WAIT

The time from application for acceptance into the program to homecoming of the adoptive child ranges from 2 to 5 years. Placement usually occurs from several months to one year after the homestudy has been completed. CCDP has an open (and consequently lengthy) waiting list.

THE CHILDREN

CCDP places both healthy and special-needs children, ranging in age from birth to 1 year. Caucasian, Black, and Korean children are available. Countries of origin include the U.S. and Korea.

THE REQUIREMENTS

Age: Applicants must be at least 21 years old and no more than 42 years.
Health: Applicants should be in reasonably good health.
Religion: Applicants should be practicing members of a religious faith.
Financial status: Applicants should demonstrate financial stability.
Marital status: The length of marriage for married couples must be at least 3 years. CCDP accepts single applicants depending on the kind of adoption.
Family size: No requirement.
Racial, ethnic or cultural origin: No requirement.

THE PROCEDURE

Participation in the adoption program of Catholic Charities of the Diocese of Pittsburgh entails the following basic steps:
Application (telephone inquiry)
Orientation meeting
Group counseling sessions
Individual counseling sessions
Home visit
Placement
Post-placement supervision

ADDITIONAL PROGRAMS/SERVICES

Catholic Charities of the Diocese of Pittsburgh, Inc., offers a number of community and family programs including community education about the agency, family day care, family and individual counseling, foster care for infants, and services for pregnant women and single parents offered through the Rosalia Center.

BRANCH/NETWORK OFFICES

Allegheny County Neighborhood Based Services
P.O. Box 40200
Pittsburgh, PA 15201
(412) 687–6683

Allegheny County Rosalia Center
624 Clyde Street
Pittsburgh, PA 15213
(412) 682–4410
Beaver County
1260 N. Brodhead
Monaca, PA 15061
(412) 775–0758
Butler County
300 S. Washington Street
Butler, PA 16001
(412) 287–4011
Greene County
195 E. High Street
Waynesburg, PA 15370
(412) 627–6410
Lawrence County Family Services
20 S. Mercer Street
New Castle, PA 16101
(412) 658–5526
Lawrence County Area Agency on Aging
20 S. Mercer Street
New Castle, PA 16101
(412) 658–5661
Washington County
12 W. Pike Street
Cannonsburg, PA 15317
(412) 745–4800

LICENSE/ACCREDITATION/PROFESSIONAL AFFILIATIONS

Catholic Charities of the Diocese of Pittsburgh is licensed by the Commonwealth of Pennsylvania Department of Public Welfare and is accredited by the Council on Accreditation of Services for Families and Children. The agency is a member of Catholic Charities USA and the Child Welfare League of America.

CATHOLIC SOCIAL AGENCY

928 Union Boulevard
Allentown, PA 18103(215) 435–1541
Program director: Lynne Shampain, ACSW

THE PROGRAM

Catholic Social Agency (CSA) is a nonprofit agency that provides adoption services for Lehigh, Northampton, Berks, Schuylkill, and Carbon Counties. Founded in 1954 as part of the Archdiocese of Philadelphia, CSA was incorporated under the Diocese of Allentown in 1961. CSA places American and Korean-born infants and annually places for adoption 25 children. Part of the mission of CSA is "to enrich and strengthen the family, to enhance the stability of family life," and "to promote respect for human life" through its social service programs and pregnancy support services.

THE COST

The agency fees for adoption services range from $550 to $4,800. Services covered by the fee include homestudy, placement and supervision, court representation, and services to birthmother and child (foster care, medical care, and legal relinquishment). Additional non-agency fees that adoptive parents should anticipate include legal finalization of the adoption; foreign or source agency fees, travel, and related expenses for foreign adoptions; and fees for state required clearances for child abuse and criminal history.

THE WAIT

The time from application for acceptance into the program to homecoming of the adoptive child averages 5 years for a healthy Caucasian infant; 3 to 5 years for a Korean infant; and 1 to 2 years for a bi-racial infant or infant with a significant health problem.

THE CHILDREN

CSA places healthy Caucasian, Black, and Hispanic American-born infants, a limited number of Korean-born infants, and special-needs infants.

THE REQUIREMENTS

Age: The minimum age for an applicant is 21 for an American-born infant, and 25 for a Korean infant; the maximum age is 35 for the younger adoptive parent of an American-born infant, and 40 for a Korean infant.
Health: Applicants should be in reasonably good health. Applicants with health problems or handicaps are given individual consideration. Infertiliy documentation is required for Caucasian infant.
Religion: Applicants must be practicing members of an organized church.
Financial status: Applicants are evaluated individually on the basis of their ability to effectively utilize financial resources.
Marital status: For healthy Caucasian or Korean infant, applicants must be married. The length of the marriage must be at least 2 years for adoptive parents of Caucasian infants and 3 years for Korean infants. No requirement for special needs, other race, or bi-racial infants.
Family size: For healthy Caucasian infant, applicants must be childless. For other infants, the requirements vary according to the state or country of origin of the birthmother and child.
Racial, ethnic or cultural origin: No requirement, but CSA tries to place children in families of similar origins.

THE PROCEDURE

Participation in Catholic Social Agency's adoption program entails the following basic steps:
Telephone inquiry
Letter of request
Submission of inquiry form
Submission of application and references
Homestudy (performed only by the main branch of CSA)
Approval of homestudy
Placement
Post-placement supervision
Post-adoption services

ADDITIONAL PROGRAMS/SERVICES

Catholic Social Agency provides a range of social services including professional counseling and therapy, foster care, pregnancy support, migration assistance, retired senior volunteer program, and an adoptive and pre-adoptive parent support group.

BRANCH/NETWORK OFFICES

Catholic Social Agency
c/o St. Francis Center
900 W. Market Street
Orwigsburg, PA 17961
(717) 366–1403
Catholic Social Agency
138 N. 9th Street
Reading, PA 19601
(215) 374–4891

LICENSE/ACCREDITATION/PROFESSIONAL AFFILIATIONS

Catholic Social Agency is licensed by the Commonwealth of Pennsylvania Department of Public Welfare. The agency is a member of Catholic Charities USA, the Pennsylvania Council of Children's Services, and the Pennsylvania Catholic Conference.

CATHOLIC SOCIAL SERVICES

(Central Office)
222 N. 17th Street
Philadelphia, PA 19103
(215) 587–3900
Program director: Sr. M. Bartholomew, MSBT, ACSW, Administrator, Pregnancy Services and Adoption Assistance Department

THE PROGRAM

Catholic Social Services is a nonprofit multi-service agency serving residents of the Archdiocese of Philadelphia (Philadelphia, Bucks, Chester, Delaware, and Montgomery Counties) and placing approximately 200 children annually through its adoption program. Providing adoption services for more than 50 years, the agency believes "that family life is critically important in fostering and developing the dignity of every person." The agency provides services to birthparents (counseling and maternity residence) and places infants for adoption when birthparents elect adoptive placement as the best plan for their child. Working cooperatively with the public agency and with national and regional exchange programs, the agency facilitates the placement of special-needs children. Working directly with child welfare institutions abroad and in cooperation with other U.S. agencies which maintain international programs, the agency places children from Korea and India in Pennsylvania families. In addition, the agency will provide homestudy and supervisory services for applicants pursuing interagency adoption (domestic or international) or, occasionally, relative adoption. In 1975, the agency instituted a post-adoption services program, providing search counseling and assistance for adult adoptees and birthparents.

The Cost

The agency's fee for adoption services varies depending on the program. For special-needs adoption, there is no fee if subsidy is available. For Caucasian infant adoption, the fee is $3,500; Black infant adoption, $2,000; Korean adoption, $1,200; Indian adoption, $1,200. Services covered by the fee include the homestudy, placement, and post-placement supervision. In addition, applicants pursuing international adoption can expect a fee to the overseas agency (Korea, $3,480; India, $4,210). For all programs, applicants are responsible for criminal and child abuse clearances ($20) and legal fees connected with finalization of the adoption ($250–$350).

The Wait

The time from inquiry to placement varies depending on the program, as follows:

Program	Inquiry to Application	Application to Placement
Caucasian	2 years	2 years
Black/Bi-racial	1 to 2 months	8 to 16 months
Korea	4 months	16 months
India	6 months	2 years
Special Needs	1 to 2 months	Varies

The Children

Catholic Social Services places both healthy and special-needs children, ranging in age from infancy to adolescence (but predominantly healthy infants in all programs), of all racial backgrounds. Countries of origin include U.S., Korea, India, and occasionally the Philippines.

The Requirements

Age: Applicants must be at least 21 years of age. For Caucasian infant adoption, applicants may be no more than 36. For Korean adoption, applicants may be no more than 41. No requirement for Black, bi-racial, and special needs placements.

Health: Applicants should be in reasonably good health. Applicants with health problems or handicaps are given individual consideration. Infertility documentation is required for childless couples requesting healthy infants.

Religion: For Caucasian infant adoption, applicants must be Catholic couples or couples of mixed religion with blessed Catholic marriages. For other programs, applicants must be practicing Christians.

Financial status: Public assistance recipients are not eligible.

Marital status: For Caucasian infant adoption and Korean adoption, applicants must be married. Single applicants are accepted for all other programs. For all programs except Korea, married applicants must be married for at least 2 years. For Korean adoption, the length of the marriage must be at least 3 years.

Family size: For Caucasian infant adoption, applicants must be childless. For Korean adoption, applicants may have no more than 2 children currently in the family. No requirement for other programs.

Racial, ethnic or cultural origin: No requirement.

The Procedure

Participation in Catholic Social Services' adoption program entails the following basic steps:
  Orientation meeting
  Application
  Counseling sessions
  Homestudy
  Compliance with immigration/naturalization requirements (international adoptions only)
  Placement
  Post-placement supervision

Additional Programs/Services

Catholic Social Services provides a wide range of services including foster care; institutional services; counseling and guidance clinic; family services; day care; long-term care for the aging; information and referral; parish social ministry; senior adult services; criminal justice; migration and refugee resettlement; spiritual ministry; Vietnamese ministry; Hispanic apostolate; hospice and homeless programs.

Branch/Network Offices

Bucks County
  McGee Professional Bldg.
  Route 413 at Oakland Ave.
  Levittown, PA 19056
  (215) 945–2550

Upper Bucks County
  105 Franklin Bldg.
  16 N. Franklin St.
  Doylestown, PA 18901
  (215) 348–9820

Chester County
  320 N. Church St.
  West Chester, PA 19380
  (215) 692–1811

Delaware County
  600 N. Jackson St.
  Media, PA 19063
  (215) 565–5880

Montgomery County
  1339 Sandy St.
  Norristown, PA 19401
  (215) 279–7372

Chester Branch of Delaware County Office
  130 E. 7th St.
  Chester, PA 19013

LICENSE/ACCREDITATION/PROFESSIONAL AFFILIATIONS

Catholic Social Services is licensed by the Commonwealth of Pennsylvania Department of Public Welfare and by the State of New Jersey Department of Human Services. The agency is accredited by the Council on Accreditation of Services for Families and Children and is a member of the Child Welfare League of America and the Pennsylvania State Catholic Conference.

CHILD AND HOME STUDY ASSOCIATES

31 E. Franklin Street
Media, PA 19063
(215) 565–1544
Program director: Geraldine F. Carson and Helene Gumerman

THE PROGRAM

Child and Home Study Associates (C&HSA) is a nonprofit agency that works with a number of child placement entities to place American, Latin American, Korean, and Indian children. C&HSA serves Delaware, southeast Pennsylvania, and New Jersey and last year placed 92 children. Founded in 1979, C&HSA provides a variety of adoption services and has been responsible for the placement of over 400 children.

THE COST

The fee for adoption varies from $6,000 to $12,000 depending on the program and country of origin. In addition, C&HSA charges a $50 per hour adoption counseling fee as well as post-placement and supervisory fees that vary with the service required. Homestudy for adoptive parents within a 50 mile radius of C&HSA is $500. Additional non-agency fees include travel costs to the country of origin for adoptive parents of foreign children and living expenses they might incur while waiting to receive guardianship or finalize the adoption of the child.

THE WAIT

The time from application to the homecoming of the adoptive child varies but usually averages less than 1 year.

THE CHILDREN

C&HSA facilitates the placement of healthy children who range in age from 3 months to 8 years, of Caucasian, Hispanic, Caucasian/Indian, and Indian racial backgrounds. Countries of origin include U.S., Chile, Colombia, Ecuador, El Salvador, Guatemala, Bolivia, Honduras, Paraguay, Peru, India, and Korea.

THE REQUIREMENTS

Age: The requirement varies according to the age of the child.
Health: Applicants must be in reasonably good health.
Religion: No requirement.
Financial status: Applicants must demonstrate financial stability.

Marital status: The requirement varies depending on the requirements of the source agency.
Family size: The requirement varies depending on the requirements of the source agency.
Racial, ethnic or cultural origin: The requirement varies depending on the requirements of the source agency.

THE PROCEDURE

Participation in C&HSA's adoption programs entails the following basic steps:
  Counseling if requested
  Application
  Group counseling sessions
  Individual counseling sessions
  Homestudy
  Compliance with immigration/naturalization requirements
    (foreign adoptions only)
  Referral
  Placement
  Post-placement supervision

ADDITIONAL PROGRAMS/SERVICES

C&HSA offers pre- and post-adoption counseling.

BRANCH/NETWORK OFFICES

101 Stonecrop Road
Wilmington, DE 19810
(302) 475–5433

LICENSE/ACCREDITATION/PROFESSIONAL AFFILIATIONS

Child and Home Study Associates is licensed by the appropriate department in the states of Delaware, New Jersey, and the Commonwealth of Pennsylvania. The agency is a member of the Delaware Valley Adoption Council.

CHILDREN'S AID HOME AND SOCIETY OF SOMERSET COUNTY

574 E. Main Street
Somerset, PA 15501
(814) 443–1637
Program director: Patricia B. Stone, Executive Director

THE PROGRAM

Children's Aid Home and Society of Somerset County (CAHS) is a nonprofit multi-service agency serving residents of Somerset County and placing approximately 4 or 5 children annually through its adoption program. Established in 1889 and providing adoption services since 1921, the agency's adoption program is a small one in comparison to other agency programs but is viewed "as an essential service to provide permanent homes for children if the biological parents are unable to care for the children or cannot be helped to assume parental responsibilities." Working directly with birthparents, with other private and public agencies, and with national and regional exchange programs, the agency places both healthy and special-needs children. Working cooperatively with other U.S. agencies which maintain international programs, the agency facilitates the placement of children from India and Korea with families who live in Somerset County. In addition, the agency will provide homestudy and supervisory services for applicants pursuing interagency adoption (domestic or international) or private adoption.

THE COST

The agency's fee for adoption services is $500. Services covered by the fee include application, homestudy, placement and supervision. Applicants are responsible for legal fees connected with finalization of the adoption. Applicants pursuing international adoption should also anticipate fees to the cooperating agency and other fees related to international adoption.

THE WAIT

The time from application to placement varies depending on the number of children currently in need of adoptive families.

THE CHILDREN

CAHS places both healthy and special-needs children, ranging in age from birth to 13 years, of all racial backgrounds. Countries of origin include U.S. and, in cooperation with other U.S. agencies, India and Korea.

THE REQUIREMENTS

Age: No requirement.
Health: The requirement varies depending on the needs of the child.
Religion: No requirement.
Financial status: No requirement.
Marital status: Married couples are preferred. Some options are available to single applicants.
Family size: No requirement.
Racial, ethnic or cultural origin: No requirement.

THE PROCEDURE

Participation in the adoption program of CAHS entails the following basic steps:
Application
Orientation meeting
Act 33 Certification in PA
Individual counseling sessions
Group counseling sessions
Homestudy
Compliance with immigration/naturalization requirements (international adoptions only)
Referral
Placement
Post-placement supervision

ADDITIONAL PROGRAMS/SERVICES

CAHS provides community-based services which include emergency shelter services, residential services, foster family services, partial hospitalization program, and counseling/intervention services to families and children in their own homes.

BRANCH/NETWORK OFFICES

None.

LICENSE/ACCREDITATION/PROFESSIONAL AFFILIATIONS

Children's Aid Home and Society of Somerset County is licensed by the Commonwealth of Pennsylvania Department of Public Welfare. The agency is a member of the Pennsylvania Council of Child Care Services.

THE CHILDREN'S AID SOCIETY OF FRANKLIN COUNTY

P.O. Box 353
Chambersburg, PA 17201
(717) 263–4159
Program director: Jane R. Englerth, Adoption Caseworker;
Richard L. Aveni, Executive Director

THE PROGRAM

The Children's Aid Society of Franklin County is a non-profit organization that provides adoption and other social services for the residents of Franklin County and surrounding Pennsylvania counties. The Children's Aid Society works with other agencies (for example, the National Adoption Exchange, Holt, and Catholic Social Services in Philadelphia) to place available children from the U.S. and foreign countries and annually places from 5 to 10 children. Founded in 1884, the Children's Aid Society established a Children's Home and since its founding has helped place over 500 children for adoption. The Children's Aid Society assumes public responsibility for the children and administers residential facilities for adolescent children who have difficulty adjusting to their families or to foster care, or who have committed delinquent acts in the county. The philosophy of the Children's Aid Society is "to provide quality social services" in continuing programs of (1) foster care; (2) specialized foster care; (3) adoption; (4) problem pregnancy; (5) counseling; (6) emergency shelter; and (7) the Children's Home.

THE COST

The agency's fee for adoption services ranges from $900 to $1,100. Services covered by the fee include the application fee, study process, placement, and post-placement supervision. Non-agency fees that prospective adoptive parents should anticipate include legal finalization, travel fees and foreign agency fees for foreign adoptions.

THE WAIT

The average time from application for acceptance into the program to homecoming is 1 year or more depending on the child requested.

THE CHILDREN

The Children's Aid Society places Black, Caucasian, and bi-racial children, both healthy and special needs, who range from birth to adult age. For foreign adoptions, the Children's Aid Society works with other adoption agencies to place children from various countries.

THE REQUIREMENTS

Age: Applicants must be at least 21 years old. Generally, applicants may be no more than 40 years older than the child who is being placed with them.

Health: Applicants should be in reasonably good health. Applicants with health problems or handicaps are given individual consideration. For infant adoption, infertility documentation is requested.

Religion: No requirement

Financial status: Applicants must demonstrate ability to manage on income.

Marital status: For infant adoption, applicants must be married. The length of the marriage must be at least 3 years. For other adoptions, the requirements may vary depending on the wishes of the birthparents or the agency's study of the prospective applicants.

Family size: The requirement may vary depending on the wishes of the birthparents or on the agency's study of the prospective applicants.

Racial, ethnic or cultural origin: Preference for placing children in families of similar origins.

THE PROCEDURE

Participation in the Children Aid Society of Franklin County's adoption program entails the following basic steps:
Inquiry interview
Application
Individual counseling sessions and homestudy
Compliance with immigration/naturalization requirements (foreign adoptions only)
Referral
Placement
Post-placement supervision

ADDITIONAL PROGRAMS/SERVICES

The Children's Aid Society of Franklin County offers a wide range of social and family programs including a residential facility for adolescents (Children's Home); pregnancy counseling; marital and family counseling; foster care; specialized foster care; emergency shelter.

BRANCH/NETWORK OFFICES

225 Miller St.
Chambersburg, PA 17201
(717) 263-4159

LICENSE/ACCREDITATION/PROFESSIONAL AFFILIATIONS

The Children's Aid Society of Franklin County is licensed by the Commonwealth of Pennsylvania Department of Public Welfare. The agency is a member of the Pennsylvania Council of Children's Services.

CHILDREN'S AID SOCIETY OF MERCER COUNTY

P.O. Box 167
350 West Market Street
Mercer, PA 16137

(412) 662-4730
Program director: Paul D. Reitnauer

THE PROGRAM

Founded in 1889, Children's Aid Society of Mercer County is a nonprofit child welfare agency serving Mercer County and contiguous counties. Providing adoption services and counseling services for birthparents since its inception, the agency has evolved over the years to meet the changing needs of children, focusing today on providing assistance for special-needs children. The agency's goal is the "prevention and early intervention in the lives of children (and their families) who are in need because of dependency, neglect, the potential of either, or due to a family crisis." Children's Aid Society places 5 to 20 special-needs children annually.

THE COST

The agency's fee schedule is as follows:
Application process $150.00
Family summary (includes parent
    preparation sessions, summary completion,
    home visits, reference and clearance checks) $500.00
Child search (includes interagency contacts,
    dissemination of family summaries,
    follow-up) $288.00
Placement services (includes legalization process,
    presentation of adoption request to court,
    placement of child, supervisory visits) $750.00
Administrative services $150.00
Total fee (minimum estimate) $1,850.00
In addition, prospective adoptive parents should anticipate travel costs involved in pre-placement visits to the child as well as legal fees connected with finalization of the adoption.

THE WAIT

The average time from application for acceptance into the program to the homecoming of the adoptive child is 7 to 12 months. The time may vary depending on the acceptance of the homestudy by the agency which has custody of the child.

THE CHILDREN

Children's Aid Society places children of all ages and all racial backgrounds who have special physical, emotional, and developmental needs.

THE REQUIREMENTS

Age: For adoption of an infant, applicants must be at least 21 and no more than 40 years old. The requirement is flexible for the adoption of older special-needs children.

Health: Applicants must be in reasonably good health. Applicants with health problems or handicaps are given individual consideration.

Religion: No requirement.

Financial status: Applicants must demonstrate financial stability.

Marital status: No requirement, but if married, applicants must have been married for at least 3 years.

Family size: No requirement.

Racial, ethnic or cultural origin: Preference for placing children in families of similar origins.

THE PROCEDURE

Participation in Children's Aid Society's adoption program entails the following basic steps:
Orientation meeting
Application
Homestudy
Referral
Placement
Post-placement supervision

ADDITIONAL PROGRAMS/SERVICES

Children's Aid Society provides counseling for birthparents, adoptees, and adoptive parents; sponsors workshops on parenting; provides residential care, foster home care, and emergency shelter for children; provides preschool, Head Start, and other educational programs; operates satellite offices for Community Mental Health Center and for the Association of Children with Learning Disabilities; provides crisis intervention and emergency childline; publishes newsletters.

BRANCH/NETWORK OFFICES

None.

LICENSE/ACCREDITATION/PROFESSIONAL AFFILIATIONS

Children's Aid Society is licensed by the State of Pennsylvania Department of Public Welfare and is affiliated with the North American Council on Adoptable Children, the National Association of Homes for Children, Children's Defense Fund, Pennsylvania Charitable Organizations, United Way, Mercer County Human Services Council, and Mercer County Preschool Council.

THE CHILDREN'S HOME OF PITTSBURGH

3618 Kentucky Avenue
Pittsburgh, PA 15232
(412) 441-4884
Program director: Betty Musick, Director of Adoptions

THE PROGRAM

The Children's Home of Pittsburgh is a nonprofit agency serving families within a 50 mile radius of Pittsburgh and placing approximately 24 children annually. The Home was organized in 1893 as an orphanage and has evolved in response to the changing needs of the community, providing services without regard to race, nationality, or creed. The Home provides pregnancy counseling services and places healthy and special-needs infants for adoption when birthparents in the agency's program decide that the best interests of their child will be served by adoptive placement.

THE COST

The agency's fee for adoption services is $6,000. The fee is negotiable in cases of minority or medically handicapped babies. Services covered by the fee include legal services related to termination of parental rights; medical and foster care of birthmother and child; birthmother, birthfather and birthparent extended family counseling; pre-placement counseling, homestudy, and supervisory services for adoptive parents. Additional costs for the adoptive couple include their attorney's fees and filing fees for the adoption finalization.

THE WAIT

Intake for accepting names of new prospective adoptive couples interested in adopting healthy Caucasian infants takes place by telephone only, on dates which are set by the agency according to the anticipated need for applicants. In the recent past, the agency has scheduled an intake day about once per year and has accepted the names of approximately 40 couples each time. Applicants who wish to know when the next intake date is scheduled are invited to call the agency any Tuesday morning between 10:00 a.m. and 12:00 noon. Applicants interested in adopting a minority or special-needs infant need not wait for an intake day and may call at any time. The time from intake to the homecoming of the adoptive child ranges from 18 months to 2 years.

THE CHILDREN

The Children's Home of Pittsburgh places both healthy and special-needs infants (under the age of 1), of all racial backgrounds, born in the U.S.

THE REQUIREMENTS

Age: Applicants may be no more than 40 years of age.
Health: Applicants must be in reasonably good health. For healthy Caucasian infant adoption, infertility documentation is required.
Religion: No requirement.
Financial status: Applicants must demonstrate financial stability.
Marital status: Applicants must be married. If infertility is very definitive, the length of the marriage must be at least 3 years. If fertility status is still questionable, the length of the marriage must be at least 5 years. Infertility status is not a factor for special-needs adoptions.
Family size: For healthy Caucasian infant adoption, applicants must be childless. The requirement varies for special-needs adoptions.
Racial, ethnic or cultural origin: Strong preference for placing children in families of similar origins.
Residence: For healthy Caucasian infant adoption, applicants must live within a 50 mile radius of Pittsburgh. There is no geographic requirement for special-needs adoptions.

THE PROCEDURE

Participation in The Children's Home of Pittsburgh's adoption program entails the following basic steps:
Telephone inquiry on Intake Day
Orientation meeting
Filing application materials
Individual counseling sessions and homestudy
Placement
Post-placement supervision

ADDITIONAL PROGRAMS/SERVICES

The agency provides problem pregnancy counseling and referral services for women who elect other options than adoption; foster care services; guest speaker series on adoption issues.

BRANCH/NETWORK OFFICES

None.

LICENSE/ACCREDITATION/PROFESSIONAL AFFILIATIONS

The Children's Home of Pittsburgh is licensed by the Commonwealth of Pennsylvania Department of Public Welfare and is a member of the National Committee for Adoption.

CONCERN

One East Main Street
Fleetwood, PA 19522
(215) 944-0447 or 398-9220
Program director: Mary Beth Hughes

THE PROGRAM

CONCERN is a nonprofit agency that places infants, special-needs children, and foreign children with adoptive families living within a 50 mile radius of the Fleetwood area. Most of the children CONCERN places have been referred for adoption from various states, and the agency annually places about 60 children. The mission of CONCERN is "to meet the emotional needs of children for significant attachments and permanency."

THE COST

The charge for adoption is a flat fee that varies according to the program (infant, special needs, or foreign) and ranges from $300 to $5,500. Services covered by the fee include recruitment, preparation and assessment, pre- and post-placement services, professional reports, and intermediary/court work. In addition, non-agency fees that prospective applicants should anticipate include legal finalization, preparation of dossiers, and, for foreign adoptions, immigration/naturalization application fees, airfare, and foreign agency/attorney fees.

THE WAIT

The time from application for acceptance into the program to the homecoming of the adoptive child averages 2 to 5 years for a healthy Caucasian infant, 1 to 2 years for a foreign child, and 6 months to 2 years for a special need child.

THE CHILDREN

CONCERN places healthy and special-needs children who range in age from birth to 17 years. CONCERN places Caucasian, Black, Hispanic, Asian, and racially mixed children. Countries of origin include U.S., Korea, and various Central and Latin American and Asian countries.

THE REQUIREMENTS

Age: The requirement varies depending on the child's age and country of origin.
Health: Applicants should be in reasonably good health. Applicants with health problems or handicaps are given individual consideration. For foreign-born children, requirements may vary depending on the child's needs and country of origin.
Religion: No requirement for American-born children; for foreign-born children, requirements may vary depending on the child's country of origin.
Financial status: Applicants must demonstrate financial stability.
Marital status: The requirement varies depending on the country of origin.
Family size: The requirement varies depending on the country of origin.
Racial, ethnic or cultural origin: No requirement.

THE PROCEDURE

Participation in CONCERN's adoption program entails the following basic steps:
Informational meeting
Application
Group educational/supportive sessions
Individual sessions
Home visit
Compliance with immigration/naturalization requirements (foreign adoptions only)
Referral
Placement
Post-placement supervision
Adoption finalization

ADDITIONAL PROGRAMS/SERVICES

CONCERN offers a variety of programs and services that include foster care, community group homes, day care, private and unplanned pregnancy counseling.

BRANCH/NETWORK OFFICES

While CONCERN maintains branch offices in Lewisburg, Doylestown, and Pittston, all adoption inquiries and services are processed through the main office.

LICENSE/ACCREDITATION/PROFESSIONAL AFFILIATIONS

CONCERN is licensed by the Commonwealth of Pennsylvania Department of Public Welfare. The agency is a member of the Delaware Valley Adoption Council and the North American Council on Adoptable Children.

COUNCIL OF THREE RIVERS AMERICAN INDIAN CENTER

Native American Adoption Resource Exchange (NAARE)
200 Charles Street
Pittsburgh, PA 15238
(412) 782-4457
Program director: Mary Wood

THE PROGRAM

The Council of Three Rivers American Indian Center is a nonprofit organization that provides statewide direct adoption placement services for special-needs children of all ages and racial backgrounds and nationwide match/referral services to facilitate the placement of American Indian children in American Indian families. Funded by the Bureau of Indian Affairs (BIA), Native American Adoption Resource Exchange (NAARE) began as a regional exchange program which quickly expanded to provide national service. Fully staffed by American Indians, NAARE assists tribes and placement agencies in locating adoptive families for waiting Indian children. The agency recruits adoptive Indian families, registers adoptive Indian children and families, helps match children with families, and works as an advocate for Indian children and Indian rights. In accordance with the Indian Child Welfare Act, only Indian families are eligible to adopt children through NAARE. The agency directly places approximately 20 special-needs children annually and facilitates the placement of approximately 50 American Indian children through the exchange.

THE COST

The Council of Three Rivers American Indian Center charges a flat fee of $600 for its direct adoption placement services in Pennsylvania. Services covered by the fee include the homestudy, child search, and post- placement supervision. Additional non-agency fees that prospective adoptive parents should anticipate include travel costs and legal fees. NAARE charges an annual fee of $60 for exchange services.

THE WAIT

The time from application for acceptance into the direct adoption placement program to homecoming of the adoptive child is about 6 months.

THE CHILDREN

The Council of Three Rivers American Indian Center directly places healthy minority children and special-needs children of all races from the U.S. NAARE facilitates the placement of both healthy and special needs American Indian children who range in age from birth to 16 years.

THE REQUIREMENTS

Age: Applicants must be at least 18 years old.

Health: Applicants should be in reasonably good health, although individual consideration is given to applicants with health problems or handicaps.

Religion: No requirement.

Financial status: Varies.

Marital status: No requirement.

Family size: No requirement.

Racial, ethnic or cultural origin: For the direct adoption placement, program preference for placing children in families of similar origin

Financial status: Applicants are evaluated individually on the basis of their ability to effectively utilize financial resources.

Marital status: No requirement.

Family size: No requirement.

Racial, ethnic or cultural origin: No requirement, but preference for placing children in families of similar origins.

THE PROCEDURE

Participation in the Council of Three Rivers American Indian Center's direct adoption placement program entails the following basic steps:

Orientation meeting
Application
Group counseling sessions
Individual counseling sessions
Homestudy
Referral
Placement
Post-placement supervision

Participation in the NAARE exchange adoption program involves guidelines established by the Indian Child Welfare Act. Generally Indian families wanting to adopt an Indian child can expect the following:

Family registration with NAARE
Participation in the adoption awareness program
Referral to a local adoption agency for homestudy
Child search through NAARE match/referral service
Placement by local adoption agency
Post-placement supervision by local adoption agency

ADDITIONAL PROGRAMS/SERVICES

NAARE provides information services about its adoption exchange program, training and technical assistance for American Indians, and information about American Indian rights.

BRANCH/NETWORK OFFICES

None.

LICENSE/ACCREDITATION/PROFESSIONAL AFFILIATIONS

Council of Three Rivers American Indian Center is licensed by the Commonwealth of Pennsylvania Department of Public Welfare.

FAMILY SERVICE AND CHILDREN'S AID SOCIETY OF VENANGO COUNTY

716 East Second Street
Oil City, PA 16301
(814) 677–4005

Program director: Robert A. Carone, ACSW, Executive Director; Janet T. Schwabenbauer, Adoption Program Director

THE PROGRAM

Family Service and Children's Aid Society (FS&CAS) of Venango County is a nonprofit agency that provides adoption services to the residents of Venango County and adjacent counties in northwestern Pennsylvania. Celebrating 100 years of service, FS&CAS annually places 1 or 2 locally born infants and works with other placement agencies to assist in placing special needs and foreign children with its clients. While the adoption program of FS&CAS has grown, its commitment to family service remains the same as reflected in its mission statement, "Strength to Families."

THE COST

The agency fee is based on a sliding scale and averages $2,200. Services covered by the fee include the homestudy, counseling of birthparents, foster care of the child awaiting adoption placement, legal fees (relinquishment and court costs for adoption finalization), and placement supervision. Additional non-agency fees that prospective parents should anticipate include medical expenses for local birthmother without insurance and cooperating agency fees and travel costs for foreign adoptions.

THE WAIT

The average time from application for acceptance into the program to homecoming of the adoptive child is 2 years.

THE CHILDREN

FS&CAS places healthy children who range in age from birth to 1 year. The agency places Caucasian and bi-racial children. Working with cooperating agencies, FS&CAS also facilitates the placement of children from overseas. Most recent newcomers to Venango County have come from India, Korea, and Colombia.

THE REQUIREMENTS

Age: Applicants must be at least 25 and no more than 40 years of age.
Health: Applicants with health problems or handicaps are given special consideration.
Religion: No requirement.
Financial status: No requirement.
Marital status: For local infant adoption, applicants must be married. The length of the marriage must be at least 3 years. FS&CAS assists single applicants in adopting special needs or foreign-born children through other placement agencies.
Family size: For local infant adoption, applicants must be childless. FS&CAS assists families with children in adopting special needs or foreign-born children through other placement agencies.
Racial, ethnic or cultural origin: No requirement.

THE PROCEDURE

Participation in FS&CAS's adoption program entails the following basic steps:
   Orientation meeting
   Application
   Individual counseling sessions
   Homestudy
   Compliance with immigration/naturalization requirements (foreign adoptions only)
   Referral
   Placement
   Placement supervision
   International adoption post-placement supervision

ADDITIONAL PROGRAMS/SERVICES

FS&CAS provides a range of family and social services that include counseling, foster care, services for the developmentally delayed, victims of violent crime and sexual assault, and family life education.

BRANCH/NETWORK OFFICES

None.

LICENSE/ACCREDITATION/PROFESSIONAL AFFILIATIONS

Family Service and Children's Aid Society is licensed by the Commonwealth of Pennsylvania Department of Public Welfare.

JEWISH FAMILY AND CHILDREN'S SERVICE

8253 Bustleton Avenue
Philadelphia, PA 19152
(215) 342–6200
Program director: Shirley Sagin

THE PROGRAM

Jewish Family and Children's Service (JFCS) is a non-profit agency serving residents of Philadelphia, surrounding counties, and New Jersey communities near Philadelphia. Providing adoption services for over 100 years, the primary purpose of JFCS's adoption service is "to find the most suitable home for each adoptable child. While JFCS recognizes the interdependent needs of all parties to adoption, the needs of the child should take priority." The agency provides services to birthparents and places infants for adoption when birthparents elect adoptive placement as the best plan for their child. Working cooperatively with the public agency and with national and regional exchange programs, the agency places special-needs children. In addition, the agency provides homestudy and supervisory services, working cooperatively with other U.S. agencies, to facilitate the placement of foreign-born children and children born in other states. The agency will also provide homestudy and supervisory services for applicants pursuing private adoption. The agency directly places approximately 3 children annually and facilitates the placement of an additional 25 children annually.

THE COST

The agency's fee for adoptive placements in which JFCS has custody is $3,500. Services covered by the fee include all phases of the adoption process, excluding legal fees connected with finalization of the adoption. For applicants pursuing interagency or private adoption, the agency's fees are $500 for the homestudy and $200 for post-placement supervision. Applicants pursuing international adoption should anticipate fees to the cooperating agency or source, possible travel expenses, miscellaneous expenses related to international adoption, and legal fees.

The Wait

For adoptive placements in which JFCS has custody of the child, the time from application to placement ranges from 1 to 2 years. For cooperative and private placements, the wait is usually 6 months to 1 year.

The Children

JFCS directly places both healthy and special-needs children (primarily infants), of all racial backgrounds, born in the U.S. JFCS will provide homestudy and supervisory services to facilitate the placement of children of any age, race, or country of origin.

The Requirements

Age: For JFCS infant adoption, applicants may be no more than 40 years of age. For other programs, the requirement varies depending on the age and special needs of the child and/or the requirements of the cooperating agency.

Health: Applicants should be in reasonably good health. Applicants with health problems or handicaps are given individual attention. For JFCS infant adoption, infertility documentation is required.

Religion: For JFCS infant adoption, applicants must be Jewish. There is no religious requirement for other programs.

Financial status: Applicants must demonstrate financial stability and sufficient income to provide for an additional family member.

Marital status: For JFCS infant adoption, applicants must be married, and the length of the marriage must be at least 3 years. For other programs, the requirement varies depending on the needs of the child and the requirements of the cooperating agency or source.

Family size: For JFCS infant adoption, applicants must be childless. No requirement for other programs.

Racial, ethnic or cultural origin: Preference for placing children in families of similar origins.

The Procedure

Participation in JFCS' adoption program entails the following basic steps:
Application
Homestudy (including group counseling sessions)
Compliance with immigration/naturalization requirements (international adoptions only)
Referral
Placement
Post-placement supervision

Additional Programs/Services

JFCS provides a range of community services including family education workshops; foster care; specialized foster care; service to children in their own homes; counseling; services to older people; services to the deaf; homemaker service; refugee resettlement services; drug/alcohol counseling.

Branch/Network Offices

1610 Spruce St.
Philadelphia, PA 19103
(215) 545–3290

8900 Roosevelt Blvd.
Philadelphia, PA 19115
(215) 673–0100

6445 Castor Ave.
Philadelphia, PA 19149
(215) 533–0102

Benjamin Fox Pavilion
Jenkintown, PA 19046
(215) 844–0285

9 E. Athens Ave.
Ardmore, PA 19004
(215) 896–8180

License/Accreditation/Professional Affiliations

Jewish Family and Children's Service is licensed by the Commonwealth of Pennsylvania Department of Public Welfare and by the State of New Jersey Department of Human Services. The agency is accredited by the Council on Accreditation of Services for Families and Children and is affiliated with the Child Welfare League of America, Association of Jewish Family and Children's Agencies, Family Service America, Delaware Valley Adoption Council, and Child, Youth and Family Council of Delaware Valley.

LOVE THE CHILDREN

221 W. Broad Street
Quakertown, PA 18951
(215) 536–4180
Program director: Mary L. Graves

The Program

Love the Children is a nonprofit agency which provides adoption services in Pennsylvania, New Jersey, New York, and Massachusetts. Since its inception in 1978, Love the Children has worked closely with foreign child welfare agencies (and especially with Eastern Child Welfare Society in Korea) to provide for the adoption of foreign-born children in the United States and to support child welfare programs in the foreign countries from which these children come. Love the Children requests that prospective adoptive parents make a commitment not only to the child who will become a part of their family, but to the children who remain behind and to the foreign agencies which serve those children. Love the Children believes that "families who have received children...and find joy and fulfillment in seeing those children grow must open their hearts and minds and energies to aid the children and the agency which has made this joy possible."

The Cost

The agency's fee schedule is as follows:

Application fee (not refundable)	$100.00
Agency service fee	$2,200.00
Overseas agency fee	$2,500.00
Travel costs	$1,000.00
Courier fees (for each shipment of documents or information)	$57.00
Total	$5,357.00

The fee to Love the Children (agency service fee) covers the cost of the home-study, interviews with applicant and references, travel costs in studying and supervising the placement, and other procedures involved in study, approval and supervision. In addition, prospective adoptive parents should anticipate miscellaneous fees connected with immigration/naturalization processing and legal fees connected with finalization of the adoption.

THE WAIT

The average time from acceptance into the program to the homecoming of the adoptive child is 9 months to 1 year.

THE CHILDREN

Love the Children places both healthy and special-needs children, primarily infants from Korea.

THE REQUIREMENTS

Age: Applicants must be at least 25 and no more than 40 years of age. Applicants over 40 are considered for children who are not infants.

Health: Applicants must be in reasonably good health. If the wife becomes pregnant during the period of the adoption, proceedings must be suspended.*Religion*: Applicants must be practicing members of a religious faith.

Financial status: Applicants must have a minimum income of $5,000 per dependent per year.

Marital status: Applicants must be married and must have been married for at least 3 years.

Family size: Preference is given to families having no children or not more than 2 children.

Racial, ethnic or cultural origin: Preference for placing children in families of similar origins.

THE PROCEDURE

Participation in Love the Children's adoption program entails the following basic steps:
Inquiry (write or call for information screening)
Questionnaire
Compliance with immigration/naturalization requirements
Application
Orientation meeting
Group counseling sessions
Individual counseling sessions
Homestudy
Placement
Post-placement supervision

ADDITIONAL PROGRAMS/SERVICES

Love the Children provides counseling services, sponsors culture camps to strengthen the cultural identity of Korean children adopted by American families, and sponsors a network of parent support groups.

BRANCH/NETWORK OFFICES

LTC—Massachusetts
P.O. Box 334
Cambridge, MA 02238
(617) 576–2115

LTC—Rochester, NY
28 Foxboro Lane
Fairport, NY
(716) 223–1868

LTC—Syracuse, NY
8199 Wheaton Road
Baldwinsville, NY
(315) 638–9449

LTC—Buffalo, NY
118 N. Ellicott Creek Road
Tonawanda, NY
(716) 691–5166

LICENSE/ACCREDITATION/PROFESSIONAL AFFILIATIONS

Love the Children is licensed by the State of New York Department of Social Services, the Commonwealth of Massachusetts Office for Children, the Commonwealth of Pennsylvania Department of Public Welfare, and the State of New Jersey Department of Human Services. Love the Children is a member of the Agency Joint Council and the International Concerns Committee for Children. All Love the Children social workers are MSW and AACSW.

LUTHERAN CHILDREN AND FAMILY SERVICE OF EASTERN PENNSYLVANIA

2900 Queen Lane
Philadelphia, PA 19129–1093
(215) 951–6800
Program director: Freida A. Williams, MSW, Adoption Supervisor

THE PROGRAM

Lutheran Children and Family Service (LCFS) is a non-profit agency serving residents of Philadelphia, Bucks, Montgomery, Delaware, and Chester Counties and placing approximately 40 children annually through its adoption program. In existence for over 66 years, the agency's mission is "to develop and provide specialized ministries of care, shelter, counseling, empowerment and education to children, youth, adults and families on behalf of the Lutheran Church in southeastern Pennsylvania, ministries which facilitate caring communities, which challenge and strengthen effectiveness of social institutions, and which support the Christian vision that Christ's victory over death has brought justice, peace and reconciliation to the world family." The agency provides birthparent option counseling and places infants for adoption when birthparents elect adoptive placement as the best plan for their child. Working cooperatively with the public agency and with national and regional exchange programs, the agency facilitates the placement of special-needs children (primarily Black and minority children). Working in cooperation with U.S. agencies which maintain international programs, the agency facilitates the placement of children from Asia and Latin America in

Pennsylvania families. In addition, the agency will provide homestudy and supervisory services for applicants pursuing interagency adoption (foreign).

THE COST

The agency's fee for adoption services ranges from $1,900 to $8,000 and includes application, homestudy, intermediary/child search, and post- placement services. Applicants can also expect additional fees which vary depending on the program and may include medical and foster care expenses, fees to a cooperating agency, travel expenses, miscellaneous fees related to international adoption, and legal fees connected with finalization of the adoption.

THE WAIT

The time from application to the homecoming of the adoptive child varies depending on the program, with a range of 6 months to 2 years.

THE CHILDREN

LCFS places both healthy and special-needs children, ranging in age from infancy to adolescence, of all racial backgrounds. Countries of origin include U.S., Korea, Thailand, and several Latin American countries.

THE REQUIREMENTS

Age: Applicants must be at least 21. For Caucasian infant adoption and for international adoption, applicants may be no more than 43. For other programs, the requirement varies depending on the age of the child.

Health: Applicants should be in reasonably good health. Applicants with health problems or handicaps are given individual consideration.

Religion: The requirement varies depending on the program. Some foreign countries require a specific religious denomination or a pastor's reference.

Financial status: The requirement may vary depending on the program. Applicants should have sufficient income to meet the needs of the family.

Marital status: Some options are available to single parents. The requirement for married applicants as to the length of the marriage varies depending on the program.

Family size: No requirement, but may vary depending on the program. Some foreign countries specify the number of children applicants may have.

Racial, ethnic or cultural origin: Preference for placing children in families of similar origins. Transracial placements may be made when in the child's best interests.

THE PROCEDURE

Participation in the adoption program of LCFS entails the following basic steps:
Orientation meeting
Application and group counseling sessions
Homestudy
Compliance with immigration/naturalization requirements (international adoptions only)
Referral
Placement
Post-placement supervision

ADDITIONAL PROGRAMS/SERVICES

LCFS provides a range of services to individuals and families including domestic foster care; refugee foster care; job readiness and job placement programs; migration and refugee program; literacy program; high school dropout prevention; day care; Lutheran International Children's Services.

BRANCH/NETWORK OFFICES

None.

LICENSE/ACCREDITATION/PROFESSIONAL AFFILIATIONS

Lutheran Children and Family Service of Eastern Pennsylvania is licensed by the Commonwealth of Pennsylvania Department of Public Welfare. The agency is a member of the Delaware Valley Adoption Council, Pennsylvania Council of Children and Youth Agencies, Children Youth and Family Council of Delaware Valley, Advocacy Advisory Committee (Department of Immigration and Refugee Services), and Pennsylvania Council of Voluntary Child Care Agencies.

THE LUTHERAN HOME

Topton, PA 19562
(215) 682–1504
Program director: Ann M. Karas, MA

THE PROGRAM

The Lutheran Home is a multi-service agency providing services to residents of 15 counties of the Northeast Pennsylvania Synod without regard to age, race, sex, creed, or social status. A charitable and benevolent agency related to the Evangelical Lutheran Church in America, The Lutheran Home provides a wide range of residential facilities to the elderly as well as human services designed to meet the physical, spiritual, and psychological needs of children, families, individuals, and the aging. These services include foster care, specialized foster care, day care, problem pregnancy, and adoption services. The agency provides services to birthparents and places infants for adoption when birthparents in the agency's counseling program elect adoptive placement as the best plan for their child. The agency also places older and special-needs children. In addition, the agency works in cooperation with other licensed child-placing agencies to provide homestudy and supervisory services for applicants pursuing foreign adoption. Through its adoption program, the agency places approximately 18 children annually. In all of its programs, the agency's mission is to provide "a healing ministry, involving the whole person, in the Name of Jesus Christ who calls us to serve our brothers and sisters in His name."

THE COST

The agency's fee for adoption services ranges from $250 to $4,500. Services covered by the fee include adoption study, social services, legal representation for relinquishment, post-placement supervision, and preparation of intermediary's report for finalization. In addition, applicants should anticipate possible birth, delivery, and pediatric care fees if the birthmother has no insurance. Applicants pursuing foreign adoption should anticipate immigration fees, fees to the placing agency, and possible travel expenses.

THE WAIT

The time from application to placement ranges form several weeks to several years.

THE CHILDREN

The Lutheran Home places both healthy and special-needs children, ranging in age from birth to 16 years, of Caucasian, Asian, and bi-racial backgrounds. In addition, the agency facilitates the adoption of children from other countries including Korea, India, and Ecuador.

THE REQUIREMENTS

Age: For infant adoptions, applicants must be at least 21 and no more than 40 years of age. For other programs, the requirement varies depending on the age of the child being considered for placement.

Health: Applicants must be in reasonably good health. Applicants with health problems or handicaps are given individual consideration.

Religion: Preference is given to couples with an active faith life.

Financial status: Applicants must have sufficient income to provide adequately for the adopted child.

Marital status: The requirement varies depending on the program. Married couples and single parents may apply. If married, the length of the marriage must be at least 2 years.

Family size: For infant adoption, applicants must be childless.

Racial, ethnic or cultural origin: No requirement.

THE PROCEDURE

Participation in The Lutheran Home adoption program entails the following basic steps:
Orientation meeting
Application
Homestudy
Compliance with immigration/naturalization requirements
Referral
Placement
Post-placement supervision
Finalization

ADDITIONAL PROGRAMS/SERVICES AVAILABLE

The Lutheran Home provides a wide range of services including residential facilities for the elderly; problem pregnancy services; foster care and specialized foster care; day care services; individual, marital, and family counseling.

BRANCH/NETWORK OFFICES

None.

LICENSE/ACCREDITATION/PROFESSIONAL AFFILIATIONS

The Lutheran Home is licensed by the Commonwealth of Pennsylvania Department of Public Welfare. The Lutheran Home is a member of the National Committee for Adoption, the Child Welfare League of America, and Pennsylvania Council of Children's Services.

LUTHERAN SERVICE SOCIETY OF WESTERN PENNSYLVANIA

11 Garden Center Drive
Greensberg, PA 15601
(412) 837–9385
Program director: Kirsti L. Adkins, MPH

THE PROGRAM

The Lutheran Service Society is a nonprofit organization that serves residents of nine counties in southwestern Pennsylvania and places about 30 children annually. The Lutheran Service Society is committed to provide a range of adoption services at a reasonable cost for families in southwestern Pennsylvania. The program as it exists today has been operating for about 10 years and includes training of families, placement of older children, and facilitation of the placement of foreign-born children. The agency does not take legal custody of the children they place for adoption but works cooperatively with other custodial agencies for matching, placement, and supervision.

THE COST

The agency's fees vary according to the service provided. For a homestudy, the fee is $500. For three supervisory visits, the fee is $300. For an older American child, the adoption fee ranges from $625 to $1,500. A portion of this fee may be paid by the agency that has legal custody of the child through purchase of service agreements. In addition, applicants can expect to pay fees to international agencies for foreign-born children and transportation costs.

THE WAIT

The time from application for acceptance into the program to homecoming of the adoptive child varies depending on the program. For an older American child, the wait can be less than 1 year. For foreign-born children the wait can be as long as 2 years.

THE CHILDREN

The Lutheran Service Society facilitates the placement of both healthy and special-needs children. American-born children range in age from 8 and up; foreign-born children range from newborn and up. The children are Caucasian, Asian, Black, and of mixed race. Countries of origin include the U.S., Korea, India, and several Latin American countries.

THE REQUIREMENTS

Age: The requirement varies depending on the requirements of the custodial agency, but common sense should prevail.

Health: Applicants should be in reasonably good health. Applicants with health problems or handicaps are given individual consideration. Again, common sense should prevail.

Religion: No requirement for the Lutheran Service Society but this may vary depending on the custodial agency's requirements.

Financial status: Applicants must demonstrate financial stability.

Marital status: No requirement for the Lutheran Service Society but this may vary depending on the custodial agency's requirements.

Family size: No requirement for the Lutheran Service Society but this may vary depending on the custodial agency's requirements.

Racial, ethnic or cultural origin: No requirement.

THE PROCEDURE

Participation in the Lutheran Service Society's adoption program entails the following basic steps:
Application
Group training sessions
Homestudy
Compliance with immigration/naturalization requirements (foreign adoptions only)
Referral
Placement (by custodial agency)
Supervision of placement
Finalization

ADDITIONAL PROGRAMS/SERVICES

The Lutheran Service Society offers counseling and adoptive family training programs.

BRANCH/NETWORK OFFICES

None.

LICENSE/ACCREDITATION/PROFESSIONAL AFFILIATIONS

The Lutheran Service Society is licensed by the Commonwealth of Pennsylvania Department of Public Welfare and is a member of the Three Rivers Adoption Council.

NATIONAL ADOPTION CENTER

1218 Chestnut Street
Philadelphia, PA 19107
(215) 925–0200
Program director: Carolyn Johnson

THE PROGRAM

The National Adoption Center is a nonprofit organization providing nationwide service and facilitating the placement of approximately 600 special-needs children annually. The National Adoption Center works as an adoption information and referral service and as a photo-listing and recruitment center. Working with public and private adoption agencies, the National Adoption Center helps find permanent adoptive families for older and special-needs children. The agency's various recruitment methods (including television, newspaper and magazine features, public service announcements, and print advertisements) maximize awareness and visibility of waiting children and increase the pool of prospective parents. The agency maintains a telecommunications system (National Adoption Network) which provides participating agencies with access to a national list of waiting children and approved families.

THE COST

The agency's fee for family registration is $15; the fee for family registration and match/referral services is $35.

THE WAIT

Not applicable.

THE CHILDREN

The National Adoption Center assists in the placement of children of all ages with physical, developmental, and emotional special needs; healthy children primarily age 10 and older; sibling groups. Children registered with the National Adoption Center are born in the U.S. of all racial backgrounds.

THE REQUIREMENTS

Age: No requirement.
Health: No requirement.
Religion: No requirement.
Financial status: No requirement.
Marital status: No requirement.
Family size: No requirement.
Racial, ethnic or cultural origin: No requirement.

THE PROCEDURE

The National Adoption Center is an indirect service agency whose primary purpose is to link waiting children with permanent families. Older and special-needs children for whom homes are being sought are registered with the Center by their social workers if their agencies have no suitable homes available. Similarly, all appropriate waiting families who have been approved for adoption are registered by their social workers. In addition, appropriately studied families may register themselves with the Center. When a child is registered with the Center, the agency first tries to match the child with one of its registered families. The agency then refers all suitable families to the child's social worker, who then pursues those families for a potential match.

ADDITIONAL PROGRAMS/SERVICES

In addition to the National Adoption Exchange and the Adoption Exchange of Delaware Valley, the National Adoption Center is actively involved in numerous programs relating to adoption and provides public education programs, information services, training and consultation.

BRANCH/NETWORK OFFICES

None.

LICENSE/ACCREDITATION/PROFESSIONAL AFFILIATIONS

The National Adoption Center is affiliated with Delaware Valley Adoption Council, Child Welfare League of America, National Black Child Development Institute, North American Council on Adoptable Children, Adoption Exchange Association, and Council for Exceptional Children.

Native American Adoption Resource Exchange (NAARE)

200 Charles Street
Pittsburgh, PA 15238
(412) 782–4457
Program director: Mary Wood

The Program

For a full description of NAARE's program, refer to Pennsylvania listing:

Council of Three Rivers American Indian Center
200 Charles Street
Pittsburgh, PA 15238
(412) 782–4457

The Pearl S. Buck Foundation, Inc.

Green Hills Farm
P.O. Box 181
Perkasie, PA 18944
(215) 249–0100
Program director: Grace C. K. Sum, Executive Director; Kala Lilani, Social Services Director

The Program

The Pearl S. Buck Foundation is a nonprofit child welfare agency historically dedicated to helping the displaced children of the world. The main thrust of the Foundation is to provide in-country services to Amerasian children in southeast Asia. Since its inception in 1964, the Foundation has provided adoption services on a case-by-case basis. In 1975 in Vietnam, the Pearl S. Buck Foundation participated in "Operation Babylift" and placed these Amerasian children in American families from 1975 to 1979. In an attempt to meet the needs of children in other parts of Asia, the Foundation has recently joined hands with a child welfare agency in India which provides shelter, food, education, medical services, job training and counseling to children of all ages. There is a small group of children (ranging in age from birth to 5 years) whose needs can best be met by placement in adoptive families. The Foundation is currently accepting applications for this program from prospective adoptive parents who live within an hour's commuting distance of the Foundation. The Foundation is also accepting applications from applicants interested in adopting older Amerasian children from Korea and Thailand. Other programs provided by the Foundation include the placement of teenage Amerasian children in sponsor homes in the U.S. under Amerasian Immigration Act, PL 97–359, of 1982; placement of U.S. special-needs children; homestudy and supervisory services for applicants pursuing interagency adoption (domestic or international) or independent adoption.

The Cost

The agency's fee for adoption services is $5,000. Services covered by the fee include application fee, homestudy and post-placement counseling, international processing fee, Indian agency fee, and travel cost for the child (parents do not have to travel). In addition, applicants should anticipate expenses related to authentication of documents, medical exams, child abuse/criminal records clearance, and legal fees connected with finalization of the adoption.

The Wait

The time from application to placement averages 1 1/2 to 2 years.

The Children

The Pearl S. Buck Foundation places both healthy and special-needs children (India, birth to 7 years old; Korea and Thailand, 13 to 22 years of age primarily) of Caucasian and Asian racial backgrounds. Countries of origin include India, Korea, and Thailand. The Foundation also places U.S. special-needs children of all ages and racial backgrounds.

The Requirements

The following are the requirements for the Foundation's adoption program and for the foster care/sponsorship program for teenage Amerasian children.

Age: For adoption from India, applicants must be at least 25 and no more than 42 years of age. For foster care/sponsorship program, the age difference between the child and the sponsor should not exceed 40 years.

Health: Applicants must be in reasonably good health. For adoption from India, infertility documentation is required.

Religion: No requirement.

Financial status: No requirement for adoption program. For foster care/sponsorship program, INS requires that the sponsor be able to support sponsored Amerasian at 125% of current poverty level guidelines.

Marital status: Applicants must be married for adoption program, and the length of the marriage must be at least 3 years. For foster care/sponsorship program, applicants may be either single or married.

Family size: For adoption from India, applicants may have no more than 1 child currently in the family. For foster care/sponsorship program, applicants may have no more than 5 children currently in the family.

Racial, ethnic or cultural origin: The requirement is evaluated on a case-by-case basis. Applicants of all backgrounds are welcome.

The Procedure

Participation in the Foundation's adoption program entails the following basic steps:
Application
Orientation meeting
Homestudy
Individual counseling sessions
Group counseling sessions
Compliance with immigration/naturalization requirements
Referral
Placement
Post-placement supervision

ADDITIONAL PROGRAMS/SERVICES

The Pearl S. Buck Foundation provides cross-cultural counseling; human search and unification (uniting fathers with children left behind in southeast Asia); foster care and sponsorship for Amerasian children (primarily teenagers).

BRANCH/NETWORK OFFICES

The Pearl S. Buck Foundation maintains offices for in-country support programs and Amerasian Immigration Act children in Thailand, Korea, Okinawa, Taiwan, and the Philippines. All adoption inquiries are processed by the Perkasie office.

LICENSE/ACCREDITATION/PROFESSIONAL AFFILIATIONS

The Pearl S. Buck Foundation is licensed by the Commonwealth of Pennsylvania Department of Public Welfare.

PROJECT S.T.A.R. (SPECIALIZED TRAINING FOR ADOPTION READINESS)

The Rehabilitation Institute of Pittsburgh
6301 Northumberland Street
Pittsburgh, PA 15217
(412) 521–9000 Ext. 396, 215
Program director: Susan Maczka

THE PROGRAM

Founded in 1985, Project STAR is a nonprofit organization funded by the Pennsylvania Developmental Disabilities Planning Council "to find permanent, loving homes for children with developmental disabilities who might otherwise spend their lives in institutions or foster homes." STAR parents receive specialized training which will assist them in effectively parenting a special child. Because of the specialized training STAR provides, parents should live within driving distance of the Pittsburgh area. STAR places approximately 16 children annually.

THE COST

Agency services are provided at no cost to adoptive parents. Agency services include group preparation sessions, individual meetings with social workers, final family study, matching, and placement. Applicants should anticipate financial responsibility for abuse/arrest record checks and legal fees connected with finalization. Most adoptive parents receive a monthly subsidy as well as medical assistance for their adopted child.

THE WAIT

The time from application for acceptance into the program to the homecoming of the adoptive child ranges from 4 months to 1 year.

THE CHILDREN

Project STAR places children with developmental disabilities, ranging in age from birth to adolescence, of all racial backgrounds, born in the U.S.

THE REQUIREMENTS

Age: No requirement.
Health: Applicants must be in reasonably good health.
Religion: No requirement.
Financial status: No requirement.
Marital status: No requirement.
Family size: No requirement. Families with more than 6 children currently in the family may require a waiver.
Racial, ethnic or cultural origin: Preference for placing children in families of similar origins.

THE PROCEDURE

Participation in Project STAR's adoption program entails the following basic steps:
   Orientation meeting
   Application
   Group and individual counseling sessions
   Homestudy
   Matching meeting
   Referral
   Transitional visits
   Placement
   Post-placement supervision and support

ADDITIONAL PROGRAMS/SERVICES

Project STAR sponsors parent support groups, conducts educational series (every other month), and provides behavioral consultation services.

BRANCH/NETWORK OFFICES

None.

LICENSE/ACCREDITATION/PROFESSIONAL AFFILIATIONS

Project STAR is licensed by the Commonwealth of Pennsylvania Department of Public Welfare and is sponsored by Allegheny County Children and Youth Services, Three Rivers Adoption Council, and The Rehabilitation Institute of Pittsburgh.

TABOR CHILDREN'S SERVICES, INC.

601 New Britain Road
Doylestown, PA 18901–2799
(215) 348–4071
Program director: Eve Gutnajer, MSW, Director of Adoption

THE PROGRAM

Tabor Children's Services, Inc. is a nonprofit, multi-service child welfare agency serving families in the Delaware Valley and New Jersey, within an hour's traveling time of either the Philadelphia or Doylestown office. Founded in 1907 to provide temporary shelter for orphaned youth, Tabor Children's Services has remained committed "to providing services to dependent and neglected children." Over the years these services have become diversified and expanded to include a diagnostic-evaluation unit, emergency shelter, foster family care, supervised independent living, services to children in their own homes, and adoption services. Providing services regardless of age, race, religion, or sex of the client, the primary objective of the adoption program is to find permanent adoptive homes for waiting children, particularly special needs and minority children. Working with public agencies as well as regional and national adoption exchange programs, Tabor places approximately 20 children annually. In addition, Tabor will provide homestudy and supervisory services for applicants pursuing private, out-of-state, or foreign adoptions, subject to state approval of the integrity of the source.

THE COST

The agency's basic fee schedule is as follows:

Application	$45.00
U.S. special-needs adoption	No charge*

All other U.S. children:

Homestudy	$400.00
Post-placement supervision	$400.00

Private and foreign adoption

Homestudy	$600.00
Post-placement supervision	$400.00
Update of Tabor homestudy after lapse of 1 year	$100.00

*This is dependent upon a purchase of service payment by the agency which has custody of the child to Tabor for placement and supervision. In addition, applicants assume responsibility for legal fees connected with finalization of the adoption.

THE WAIT

Because the number and kinds of children in Bucks County in need of adoptive placement varies each year, the agency is unable to predict accurately the time interval between homestudy and placement. The time interval has varied from as little as a few months to several years. Much depends on the flexibility of the family and the type of child whom they feel they can parent.

THE CHILDREN

Tabor Children's Services places special-needs children who are currently defined as children with severe physical handicaps, retardation, or pronounced medical problems; minority children of school age; children over the age of 12; sibling groups of 3 or more. In addition, Tabor will provide homestudy and supervisory services for applicants pursuing private, out-of- state, or foreign adoption of a child of any age or race.

THE REQUIREMENTS

Age: No requirement.
Health: Applicants must be in reasonably good health.
Religion: No requirement.
Financial status: No requirement.
Marital status: No requirement, but if married, applicants must demonstrate marital stability and marriage of at least 2 years duration.
Family size: No requirement.
Racial, ethnic or cultural origin: No requirement.

THE PROCEDURE

Participation in Tabor Children's Services' adoption program entails the following basic steps:
    Inquiry
    Application
    Individual or group counseling sessions
    Homestudy
    Match/referral
    Transitional visits
    Placement
    Post-placement supervision
    Finalization

ADDITIONAL PROGRAMS/SERVICES

Tabor provides diagnostic-evaluation services; emergency shelter; foster family care; supervised independent living; residential care; post legal adoption services.

BRANCH/NETWORK OFFICES

401 North 21st Street
Philadelphia, PA 19130
(215) 557–9915

LICENSE/ACCREDITATION/PROFESSIONAL AFFILIATIONS

Tabor Children's Services, Inc. is licensed by the Commonwealth of Pennsylvania Department of Public Welfare and by the State of New Jersey Department of Human Services. The agency maintains membership in the following organizations: Adoption Council of Delaware Valley; Better Business Bureau; Bucks County Chamber of Commerce; Children, Youth and Family Council of the Delaware Valley; National Network of Runaway and Youth Services, Inc.; Pennsylvania Foster Parent Association; Philadelphia Chamber of Commerce; United Way Donor Option Program; Youth Services Alliance of Pennsylvania.

TRESSLER-LUTHERAN SERVICES

25 W. Springettsbury
York, PA 17403
(717) 845–9113
Program director: Barb Tremitiere

THE PROGRAM

Since it was founded, Tressler-Lutheran Services has placed almost 2,000 children in adoptive families throughout central Pennsylvania. As of 1972, the agency places only special-needs children and provides education and support for adoptive parents of such children. Tressler-Lutheran Services annually places 100 to 150 special-needs children.

THE COST

The agency charges a flat fee of $1,000 that covers all phases of the adoption process (pre-adoptive education through post-placement family support services), excluding legal fees connected with finalization of the adoption (approximately $300).

THE WAIT

The wait depends on how selective the adoptive family is regarding the special needs of the child. The agency can place a child quickly if the adoptive family is "open" to the special needs of the child.

THE CHILDREN

Tressler-Lutheran Services places special-needs children, ranging in age from birth to 18 years, of all racial backgrounds, born in the U.S.

THE REQUIREMENTS

Age: No requirement.
Health: No requirement.
Religion: No requirement.
Financial status: Applicants must demonstrate financial stability.
Marital status: No requirement.
Family size: No requirement.
Racial, ethnic or cultural origin: No requirement.

THE PROCEDURE

Participation in Tressler-Lutheran Services' adoption program entails the following basic steps:
Application
Orientation meeting
Homestudy
Group counseling sessions
Referral
Placement
Post-placement supervision

ADDITIONAL PROGRAMS/SERVICES

Tressler-Lutheran Services offers family education and support programs to adoptive parents of special-needs children.

BRANCH/NETWORK OFFICES

All adoption inquiries are handled by the main office in York, Pennsylvania.

LICENSE/ACCREDITATION/PROFESSIONAL AFFILIATIONS

Tressler-Lutheran Services is licensed by the Commonwealth of Pennsylvania Department of Public Welfare.

WELCOME HOUSE ADOPTION SERVICES

P.O. Box 836
Doylestown, PA 18901
(215) 345–0430
Program director: Barbara B. Bird, Executive Director

THE PROGRAM

Welcome House was founded by renowned author Pearl S. Buck in 1949. It was the first United States adoption agency with the primary objective of finding families for Amerasian children born in the U.S. From this initial concern, Welcome House has expanded to include several intercountry and domestic adoption programs for many special children who might otherwise have difficulty finding homes, providing services without regard to race, national origin, handicap, or religion. Recently, additional emphasis has been placed on the U.S. special needs and Black family adoption programs. Serving the states of Pennsylvania, Delaware, Virginia, New Jersey, Maryland, and Washington, D.C., Welcome House places approximately 300 children annually.

THE COST

The agency's basic fee schedule for adoption services is as follows:

Application fee	$75.00
Welcome House service fee	
U.S. special-needs adoption	$1,500.00
Intercountry adoption	$2,500.00
Sibling group/supervision fee	$400.00

Services covered by the fee include family education and assessment services, placement services, post-placement supervision, and post-adoption services. Applicants interested in pursuing intercountry adoption should also anticipate overseas agency costs, transportation expenses, and immigration/naturalization fees. In addition, all applicants assume responsibility for legal fees connected with finalization of the adoption. Applicants should note that no fees are refundable once service has been rendered and all fees are subject to change.

THE WAIT

The time from application for acceptance into the program to the homecoming of the adoptive child varies depending on the program and the child's country of origin.

THE CHILDREN

Welcome House places both healthy and special-needs children, ranging in age from birth to adolescence, of all racial backgrounds. Countries of origin include Philippines, Korea, Hong Kong, India, and U.S.

THE REQUIREMENTS

Age: The general requirement is that the age difference between the applicant and the child being considered for placement should not exceed 40 years.
Health: Applicants with health problems or handicaps are given individual consideration.
Religion: No requirement.
Financial status: Applicants must demonstrate financial stability.
Marital status: Married applicants must have been married for at least 3 years. Some options are available to single applicants.
Family size: The requirement varies depending on the child's country of origin. Some require no more than 1 child currently in the family; others permit as many as 5 children currently in the family.
Racial, ethnic or cultural origin: No requirement.

THE PROCEDURE

Participation in Welcome House's adoption program entails the following basic steps:

Inquiry
Orientation meeting
Application
Homestudy (including group sessions)
Compliance with immigration/naturalization requirements
    (intercountry adoptions only)
Referral
Placement
Post-placement supervision
Court report for finalization
Finalization
Naturalization (intercountry adoptions only)

ADDITIONAL PROGRAMS/SERVICES

Welcome House utilizes a TEAM approach to adoption services in which experienced adoptive parents are actively involved with social work staff in preparing and supporting new adoptive parents in all phases of the adoption process. In addition, Welcome House sponsors adoptive parents support groups; hosts an annual picnic; conducts fund-raising activities to support overseas child welfare programs; publishes a quarterly newsletter; provides sponsorship programs; offers a range of post-finalization services including counseling, workshops, and groups.

BRANCH/NETWORK OFFICES

Administrative Office
    P.O. Box 836
    Rt. 202 & Beulah Rd.
    Doylestown, PA 18901
    (717) 532–8931

Philadelphia Branch
    Presidential Apts., D-109
    City Line Ave.
    Shippensburg, PA 17257
    (215) 345–0430

Central PA Branch
    403 Roxbury Rd.
    Philadelphia, PA 19131
    (215) 879–2594

Pittsburgh Branch
    120 Spring Ln.
    Delmont, PA 15626
    (412) 468–8193

Delaware Branch
    P.O. Box 1079
    Hockessin, DE 19707
    (302) 239–2102

Richmond, VA Branch
    5905 W. Broad St., #300
    Richmond, VA 23230
    (804) 288–3920

Roanoke, VA Branch
    P.O. Box 596
    Christiansburg, VA 24073
    (703) 382–5975

LICENSE/ACCREDITATION/PROFESSIONAL AFFILIATIONS

Welcome House Adoption Services is licensed by the appropriate state department in Pennsylvania, Delaware, and Virginia. The agency is affiliated with the Delaware Valley Adoption Council, Joint Council on International Children's Services, North American Council on Adoptable Children, Specialized Pennsylvania Adoption Network, and Virginia Association of Licensed Child Placement Agencies.

WILEY HOUSE

1650 Broadway
Bethlehem, PA 18015–3998
(215) 867–5051
800–346–7817 (Pennsylvania)
800–346–7827 (U.S.)
Program director: D. James Ezrow, ACSW, Foster Care and Adoption Supervisor

THE PROGRAM

Wiley House is a nonprofit, non-sectarian, private organization serving children, youth and families who exhibit dysfunctional behaviors. Wiley House provides a wide range of services and programs, including residential care, diagnostic shelter care, foster care, group home care, in- home sponsorship, educational services, specialized preschool program, child and family guidance centers, afternoon treatment programs, day treatment programs, and counseling institute program. Adoption Service (a program which began in 1984) is a subdivision of the Wiley House Professional Foster Care Program. Children accepted for adoption service have usually been involved in the Wiley House Foster Care Program. The goal of the Adoption Service program is "to pursue adoption as a permanent resource for a child who cannot return to his/her own home." Typically, the placement originates as a foster placement which becomes an adoptive placement when the child's birthparents relinquish their parental rights. Wiley House makes approximately 3 to 5 adoptive placements annually.

THE COST

There is no fee for adoption services if the placement is initially a foster placement. For placements in which the prospective adoptive parents are not the child's foster parents, the agency's fee for adoption services is $1,200. Services covered by the fee include all phases of the adoption process, excluding legal fees connected with finalization.

THE WAIT

The wait varies depending on the number of children currently in need of adoptive families.

THE CHILDREN

Wiley House places special needs and healthy children who range in age from birth to 17 of all racial backgrounds.

THE REQUIREMENTS

Age: Applicants must be at least 21 years of age.

Health: Applicants should be in reasonably good health.

Religion: No requirement.

Financial status: Applicants must demonstrate financial stability.

Marital status: No requirement.

Family size: In accordance with foster care regulations, applicants may have no more than 6 children currently in the home. However, a waiver may be granted by the Pennsylvania Department of Public Welfare in special circumstances.

Racial, ethnic or cultural origin: No requirement, but preference for placing children in families of similar origins.

THE PROCEDURE

Participation in Wiley House's adoption program entails the following basic steps:

Application

Orientation meeting

Homestudy (includes written evaluation, legal checks, child abuse checks, etc.)

Individual counseling sessions

Referral

Placement

Post-placement supervision

ADDITIONAL PROGRAMS/SERVICES

Wiley House offers a range of social welfare programs designed to help children and families. Programs include residential care, diagnostic shelter care, foster care, group home care, in-home sponsorship, educational services, specialized preschool program, child and family guidance centers, afternoon and day treatment programs, primary school age treatment program, and counseling institute program.

BRANCH/NETWORK OFFICES

Programs and Services Directory for Wiley House is available upon request.

LICENSE/ACCREDITATION/PROFESSIONAL AFFILIATIONS

Wiley House is licensed by the Commonwealth of Pennsylvania Department of Public Welfare and is a member of the Delaware Valley Adoption Council.

Rhode Island

PUBLIC ADOPTION PROGRAM/ COMMUNITY RESOURCES

Department for Children and Their Families
Division of Direct Services
Special-needs adoption Home Finding Unit
610 Mt. Pleasant Avenue
Providence, RI 02908
(401) 457-4545/4802/4548
Adoption specialist: Richard G. Prescott, Adoption Home-finder

THE PROGRAM

Public adoption services in Rhode Island are provided by the Department for Children and Their Families (DCF) through the special-needs adoption Home Finding Unit. The focus of the program is to recruit and prepare families and to supervise and support the placement of special-needs children (older, minority, and handicapped children and sibling groups) who are in the custody of the State of Rhode Island.

STATE EXCHANGE

Ocean State Adoption Resource Exchange (OSARE) is a private, nonprofit organization established in 1981 to promote the building of families through special-needs adoption. OSARE provides information/referral and listing/recruitment services for special-needs children (older children, minority children, children with emotional, intellectual, or physical special needs, and sibling groups).
500 Prospect Street
Pawtucket, RI 02860
(401) 724-1910
Director: Lisa K. Funaro

STATE ADOPTION REUNION REGISTRY

None.

STATE SUBSIDY

For information, contact the Division of Direct Services (401-457-4631).

NACAC REPRESENTATIVE

None at this time.

GENERAL ADOPTION RESOURCES

Adoptive Parent Support Groups
GIFT of Rhode Island (Getting International and Transcultural Families Together)
Providence, RI 02906
(401) 331-6197
Contact: Carol DesForge

SPACE (Single Parents Adopting Children Everywhere)
49 Harris Street
93 Lauriston St.
East Providence, RI 02914
(401) 433-1264
Contact: Wanda Mullen

The Black Adoptive Family Support Group
c/o Urban League of Rhode Island
246 Prairie Avenue
Providence, RI 02905
(401) 351-5000
Contact: Wilbur Jennings
Ocean State Foster and Adoptive Parent Assn.
8 Vale Ave.
Cranston, RI 02910
(401) 946-0968
Contact: Mr. and Mrs. Clifford
Search Assistance or Support
The Adoption Connection, Inc.
11 Peabody Square, #6
Peabody, MA 01960
(617) 532—1261
Parents and Adoptees Liberty Movement
861 Michell's Ln.
Middletown, RI 02840
Contact: Betty Angier

SPECIAL-NEEDS ADOPTION RESOURCES

Resource Adoptive Parents Group
OSARE
500 Prospect St.
Pawtucket, RI 02860
(401) 724-1910
One Church, One Child Program
c/o Urban League of Rhode Island
246 Prairie Ave.
Providence, RI 01905
(401) 351-5000
Contact: Edith Baptista

OUT-OF-STATE AGENCIES

AGENCY

International Adoptions, Massachusetts

SEE APPENDIX A

Agencies Providing Nationwide Services

CATHOLIC SOCIAL SERVICES

433 Elmwood Avenue
Providence, RI 02907
(401) 467-7200
Program director: Rev. George L. Frappier

THE PROGRAM

Catholic Social Services is a nonprofit agency serving residents of Rhode Island and placing approximately 30 children annually through its adoption program. Founded in 1926 by the Catholic Church in the Diocese of Providence, the agency's mission is 'to go in service to the needs of society and its members." The agency provides services to birthparents and places infants and young children for adoption when birthparents decide that the best interests of their child will be served by adoptive placement. In addition, the agency will provide homestudy and supervisory services for applicants pursuing interagency adoption (primarily domestic although occasionally international as well).

THE COST

The agency's fee for adoption services is based on a sliding scale, with a minimum fee of $2,500 and a maximum fee of $9,600. Services covered by the fee include the adoption study, placement, post-placement supervision, and legal finalization.

THE WAIT

The time from application to the homecoming of the adoptive child averages 1 1/2 to 2 years.

THE CHILDREN

Catholic Social Services places both healthy and special-needs children, ranging in age from birth to 2 years, of Caucasian, Black, Hispanic, and bi-racial backgrounds, born in the U.S.

THE REQUIREMENTS

Age: Applicants must be at least 25 and no more than 35 years of age. The requirement may vary depending on the needs of the child.

Health: Applicants should be in reasonably good health. Applicants with health problems or handicaps are given individual consideration. Verified infertility is not a prerequisite, but medical exploration of the causes of infertility is strongly recommended.

Religion: Applicants must be practicing Roman Catholics. The requirement may vary depending on the needs of the child.

Financial status: Applicants must have an annual gross income of at least $15,000.

Marital status: For infant adoption, applicants must be married, and the length of the marriage must be at least 3 years. The requirement may vary depending on the needs of the child.

Family size: For healthy infant adoption, applicants must be childless. The requirement may vary depending on the needs of the child.

Racial, ethnic or cultural origin: Preference for placing children in families of similar origins. The requirement varies depending on the availability of racially and culturally relevant families.

THE PROCEDURE

Participation in Catholic Social Services' adoption program entails the following basic steps:
Orientation meeting
Application
Homestudy
Placement
Post-placement supervision

ADDITIONAL PROGRAMS/SERVICES

Catholic Social Services provides counseling services for birthparents, foster care, marital counseling, and refugee resettlement services.

BRANCH/NETWORK OFFICES

None.

LICENSE/ACCREDITATION/PROFESSIONAL AFFILIATIONS

Catholic Social Services is licensed by the State of Rhode Island Department for Children and Their Families and is accredited by the Council on Accreditation of Services for Families and Children.

CHILDREN'S FRIEND AND SERVICE, INC.

2 Richmond Street
Providence, RI 02903
(401) 331–2900
Program director: Matthew F. DeChirico, Executive Director

THE PROGRAM

Children's Friend and Service, Inc. (CF&S) is a nonprofit child welfare agency that provides a range of social and mental health services to children and their families. CF&S was formed in 1942 as the result of the merger of the Children's Friend Society (founded in 1832) and the Rhode Island Child Service (originally founded in 1882 as the Rhode Island Society for the Prevention of Cruelty to Children). Between 1969 and 1981 CF&S offered a residential treatment program for emotionally disturbed children. Currently operating as a multi-service child welfare agency, CF&S has changed to meet the needs of the community and is licensed to place children for adoption throughout Rhode Island. CF&S places approximately 30 children annually in adoption. CF&S provides enrichment programs to strengthen family life, furthers the advocacy of children's welfare and family education programs, and offers training for social welfare professionals.

THE COST

CF&S's fee for adoption services is based on a sliding scale and ranges from $1,000 to $5,000. Services covered by the fee include a $100 application fee (nonrefundable), evaluation/approval, and post-placement and legal finalization of the adoption. The agency will provide assessments and supervisory services for applicants pursuing identified or relative adoptions. For evaluation services only, the fee is half the maximum fee; for evaluation and placement supervision, applicants will be charged the maximum fee. In addition, applicants can expect to pay possible legal fees connected with finalization of the adoption; however, a social worker can replace an attorney if the applicants wish.

THE WAIT

The time from application for acceptance into the program to home-coming of the adoptive child varies depending on the type of child the applicants wish to adopt.

THE CHILDREN

CF&S places both healthy and special-needs children of all races who range in age from infancy to adolescence.

THE REQUIREMENTS

Age: No requirement.

Health: Applicants should be in reasonably good health. Applicants with health problems or handicaps are given individual consideration.

Religion: No requirement.

Financial status: No requirement.

Marital status: No requirement for special-needs children.

Family size: No requirement for special-needs children. Applicants must be childless for healthy Caucasian infant adoption.

Racial, ethnic or cultural origin: No requirement, but preference for placing children in families of similar origin if placement is not delayed significantly.

THE PROCEDURE

Participation in CF&S's adoption program entails the following basic steps:

Orientation meeting
Registration
Application
Group counseling and education sessions
Individual counseling sessions
Assessment session
Placement
Post-placement counseling and education
Finalization
Post-legal adoption services

ADDITIONAL PROGRAMS/SERVICES

Children's Friend and Service provides clinical counseling for families, foster care, family day care, and family life enrichment programs.

BRANCH/NETWORK OFFICES

None.

LICENSE/ACCREDITATION/PROFESSIONAL AFFILIATIONS

Children's Friend and Service, Inc. is licensed by the State of Rhode Island, Department for Children and Their Families. It is accredited by the Council on Accreditation of Services for Families and Children and is a member of the Child Welfare League of America.

South Carolina

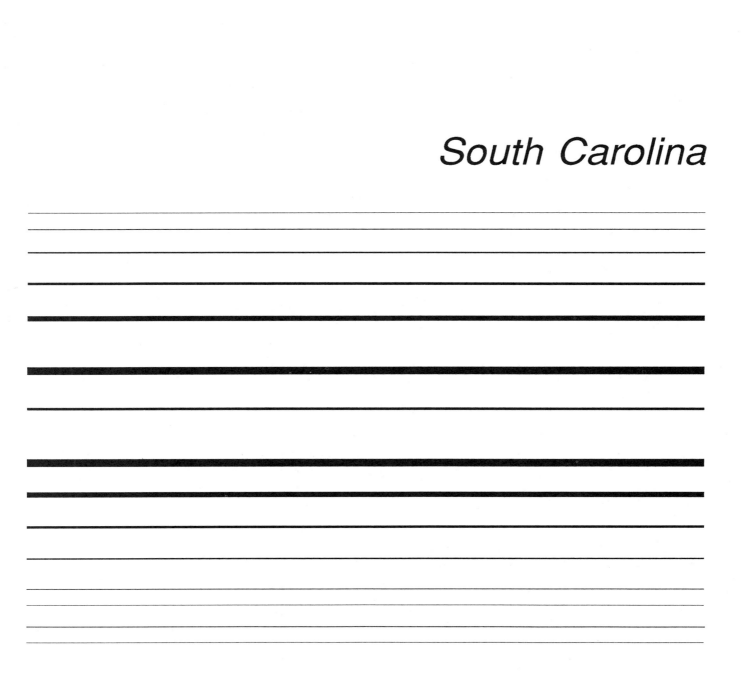

PUBLIC ADOPTION PROGRAM/ COMMUNITY RESOURCES

Department of Social Services
Office of Children, Family and Adult Services
Adoption and Birth Parent Services
P.O. Box 1520
Columbia, SC 29202–1520
(803) 734–6095
(803) 734–6095 (One Church, One Child Adoption Program)
Adoption specialist: Denise R. Cosby

THE PROGRAM

Public adoption services in South Carolina are provided by the Department of Social Services through branch offices located in six areas across the state. Adoption and Birth Parent Services provides a wide range of services including services to birthparents, children, and adoptive parents; general information concerning adoption; referral service to other agencies; information and referrals on intercountry and interstate adoptions; committees, workshops, conferences, and community education programs on child welfare and adoption issues. While the agency does place infants and young children, the focus of the DSS program is to address the needs of waiting children (older, minority, handicapped children and sibling groups). In an effort to meet the needs of these children, the South Carolina Department of Social Services has entered into a partnership (public-private) with the One Church, One Child Ministerial Association to facilitate the adoption of children with special needs. The One Church, One Child Program secures the participation of South Carolina congregations in finding adoptive families for special-needs children.

STATE EXCHANGE

South Carolina Seedlings is a looseleaf book containing photographs and biographical information about children waiting to be adopted which is available for viewing at public and private agencies, COAC meetings, many county libraries, and other appropriate locations. South Carolina Seedlings was begun in 1980 by members of the South Carolina Council on Adoptable Children and is staffed by parent volunteers.
Project coordinator: Linda R. Williams
Route 13, Box 298
Easley, SC 29640
(803) 269-7713

STATE ADOPTION REUNION REGISTRY

Adoption Reunion Register. Adoptees and biological siblings who are 21 years of age and birthparents may register. For information, contact the Department of Social Services (above).

STATE SUBSIDY

For information, contact Adoption and Birthparent Services (above).

NACAC REPRESENTATIVE

Joyce Thompson
1453 Hammond Pond Road
North Augusta, SC 29841
(803) 279–4184
Ellen Millard
112 Seminole Drive
Greenville, SC 29605
(803) 242–1913

GENERAL ADOPTION RESOURCES

Regional Adoption Exchange
SEE US (Southeastern Exchange of the United States)
P.O. Box 6647
Columbia, SC 29260–6647
(803) 782–0882
Adoptive Parent Association
South Carolina Council on Adoptable Children
Route #13, Box 298
Easley, SC 29640
(803) 269–7713

Search Assistance and Support
Triad
1725 Atascadero Drive
Columbia, SC 29206
(803) 787–3778
ABIS
P.O. Box 5551
West Columbia, SC 29171
(803) 796–4508

SPECIAL-NEEDS ADOPTION RESOURCES

For information on resources for children with specific special needs or handicapping conditions, contact South Carolina Council on Adoptable Children (above).

Boys Clubs of Greater Columbia
P.O. Box 123
Columbia, SC 29202
(803) 733–5490
Brothers and Sisters, Inc.
1800 Main St., 3rd Fl.
Columbia, SC 29201
(803) 733–5480
Children's Center
University of South Carolina
Booker T. Washington Complex
Early Childhood Development
Columbia, SC 29208
(803) 777–5733
Columbia Area Mental Health Center
1618 Sunset Dr.
Columbia, SC 29203
(803) 737–5550
Columbia Crippled Children's Clinic
P.O. Box 125
State Park, SC 29147
(803) 758–4406

Family Service Center
P.O. Box 7876
Columbia, SC 29202
(803) 733–5450
1–800–922–5651 (toll-free in SC)

Psychological Service Center
University of South Carolina
1819 Pendleton St.
Columbia, SC 29208
(803) 777–4864

Schools Intervention Program
Lexington/Richland Alcohol and Drug Abuse Council
134 N. Hospital Dr.
West Columbia, SC 29169

William S. Hall Psychiatric Institute
P.O. Box 202
Columbia, SC 29202
(803) 734–7041

OUT-OF-STATE AGENCIES

SEE APPENDIX A

Agencies Providing Nationwide Services

BETHANY CHRISTIAN SERVICES

300 University Ridge
Suite 114
Greenville, SC 29601(803) 235–2273
Program director: James K. Haveman, Jr., Executive Director

THE PROGRAM

For a full description of programs and services, refer to Michigan listing:
Bethany Christian Services
901 Eastern Avenue, N.E.
Grand Rapids, MI 49503–1295
(616) 459–6273

EPWORTH CHILDREN'S HOME

2900 Millwood Avenue
P.O. Box 50466
Columbia, SC 29250
(803) 256–7394
Program director: Charles A. Hutchins, President and Chief Executive Officer

THE PROGRAM

Epworth Children's Home is a nonprofit multi-service child and family agency affiliated with the South Carolina Conference of the United Methodist Church and serving residents of South Carolina. Founded in 1895 as a children's home, Epworth has evolved into "a therapeutic, redemptive community providing Christian training and services to children, youth and families, including (but not limited to) residential care, foster family care, family counseling, shelter care, adoptive placement, compensatory education, higher education, diagnostic and evaluation services, in-family aid, and a variety of programs to serve mentally retarded persons and their families." When children in the agency's residential or foster care program cannot return to their own homes, Epworth works to find permanent adoptive families. While most children placed by Epworth are school aged children (6 to 17 years old), the agency also provides services to birthparents and occasionally places infants for adoption when birthparents elect adoptive placement as the best plan for their child. In addition, the agency will provide homestudy and supervisory services for applicants pursuing interagency or independent adoption.

THE COST

The agency's fee for adoption services is based on the applicants' ability to pay. Services include all phases of the adoption process, excluding legal fees connected with finalization of the adoption.

THE WAIT

The time from application to placement varies depending on the current number of children in need of adoptive families and on the adoptive family's openness to the child's special needs.

THE CHILDREN

Epworth Children's Home places both healthy and special-needs children, primarily school aged (6 to 17 years old), of all racial backgrounds, born in the U.S.

THE REQUIREMENTS

Age: The age requirement is evaluated on a case-by-case basis.
Health: The health requirement is evaluated on a case-by-case basis.
Religion: Applicants must be practicing members of a Christian church. The requirement may vary depending on the child's needs.
Financial status: The financial requirement is evaluated on a case-by-case basis.
Marital status: Applicants must be married couples.
Family size: Family size is evaluated on a case-by-case basis.
Racial, ethnic or cultural origin: Preference for placing children in families of similar origins.

THE PROCEDURE

Participation in the adoption program of Epworth Children's Home entails the following basic steps:
Application
Individual counseling sessions
Group counseling sessions
Homestudy
Placement
Post-placement supervision

ADDITIONAL PROGRAMS/SERVICES

Epworth Children's Home provides a wide range of services including residential care, foster family care, family counseling, shelter care, adoptive placement, compensatory education, higher education, diagnostic and evaluation services, in-family aid, and a variety of programs to serve mentally retarded persons and their families.

BRANCH/NETWORK OFFICES

None.

LICENSE/ACCREDITATION/PROFESSIONAL AFFILIATIONS

Epworth Children's Home is licensed by the State of South Carolina Department of Social Services. The agency is accredited by the Council on Accreditation of Services for Families and Children and is a member of the Child Welfare League of America, the South Carolina Association of Homes for Children, the National Association of Homes for Children, Southeastern Child Care Association, and National Health and Welfare Ministries of The United Methodist Church.

LOVE LIFE MINISTRIES, INC.

P.O. Box 247
Florence, SC 29503
(803) 665-8473
Program director: John Craddock

THE PROGRAM

Love Life Ministries is a nonprofit agency providing statewide services and placing approximately 30 children annually. Founded in 1984 with the objective of providing an alternative to abortion, the agency's mission is "to change one life and save another through sharing the gospel of Jesus Christ." The agency provides services to birthparents and places both healthy and special-needs infants for adoption when birthparents in the agency's counseling program elect adoptive placement as the best plan for their child.

THE COST

The agency's fee for adoption services varies depending on the length of the birthmother's stay in the agency's maternity home. Services covered by the fee include all phases of the adoption process, excluding legal fees connected with finalization of the adoption.

THE WAIT

The time from application to the homecoming of the adoptive child varies depending on the availability of infants.

THE CHILDREN

Love Life Ministries places both healthy and special-needs infants of all racial backgrounds, born in the U.S.

THE REQUIREMENTS

Age: The age requirement is evaluated on a case-by-case basis.

Health: The health requirement is evaluated on a case-by-case basis.

Religion: Applicants must be practicing members of a Christian church.

Financial status: Applicants must have sufficient income to provide adequately for an additional family member.

Marital status: Applicants must be married, and the length of the marriage must be at least 5 years.

Family size: Applicants may have no more than 1 child currently in the family.

Racial, ethnic or cultural origin: Preference for placing children in families of similar origins.

THE PROCEDURE

Participation in the adoption program of Love Life Ministries entails the following basic steps:
Orientation meeting
Application
Group counseling sessions
Individual counseling sessions
Homestudy
Referral
Placement
Post-placement supervision

ADDITIONAL PROGRAMS/SERVICES

Love Life Ministries maintains a crisis pregnancy center and a maternity home and provides counseling services.

BRANCH/NETWORK OFFICES

None.

LICENSE/ACCREDITATION/PROFESSIONAL AFFILIATIONS

Love Life Ministries, Inc. is licensed by the State of South Carolina Department of Social Services.

SOUTHEASTERN CHILDREN'S HOME, INC.

825 Woods Chapel Road
Duncan, SC 29334
(803) 439-0259
Program director: Melissa Thigpen, MSW

THE PROGRAM

Southeastern Children's Home is a nonprofit agency serving residents of South Carolina and placing approximately 12 children annually. Founded in 1968, the agency provides care to needy children and families through group home care, foster care, maternity services, counseling, and adoption services. Southeastern Children's Home is committed "to improving the quality of life of individuals, families, and the community in which it exists."

THE COST

The agency's fee for adoption services is $4,500. Services covered by the fee include all phases of the adoption process, excluding legal fees connected with finalization of the adoption and travel expenses for visits to the agency and for bringing the child home.

THE WAIT

The time from application to the homecoming of the adoptive child averages 3 years for healthy Caucasian infants; 18 months for minority or special-needs children.

THE CHILDREN

Southeastern Children's Home places both healthy and special-needs children, ranging in age from birth to 15 years, of Caucasian, Black, and Hispanic racial backgrounds, born in the U.S.

THE REQUIREMENTS

Age: The requirement varies depending on the age of the child being considered for placement.

Health: Applicants with health problems or handicaps are given individual consideration. Infertility documentation is required for healthy Caucasian infant adoption.

Religion: Applicants must be practicing members of the Church of Christ.

Financial status: Applicants must demonstrate financial stability.

Marital status: Applicants must be married couples who have been married for at least 3 years.

Family size: No requirement.

Racial, ethnic or cultural origin: No requirement.

THE PROCEDURE

Participation in the adoption program of Southeastern Children's Home entails the following basic steps:
Application
Orientation meeting
Homestudy
Individual counseling sessions
Placement
Post-placement supervision

ADDITIONAL PROGRAMS/SERVICES

Southeastern Children's Home provides foster care, group home care, maternity services, counseling services, and parenting workshops.

BRANCH/NETWORK OFFICES

None.

LICENSE/ACCREDITATION/PROFESSIONAL AFFILIATIONS

Southeastern Children's Home is licensed by the State of South Carolina Department of Social Services. All employees are Certified Adoption Investigators.

South Dakota

PUBLIC ADOPTION PROGRAM/ COMMUNITY RESOURCES

Department of Social Services
Child Protection Services
700 Governors Drive
Pierre, SD 57501
(605) 773–3227
Adoption specialist: Patricia J. Stewart

THE PROGRAM

Public adoption services in South Dakota are provided by the Department of Social Services by regional adoption specialists located throughout the state. The focus of the Child Protection Services adoption program is to recruit, prepare, supervise, and support families who are interested in adopting special-needs children (older, minority, and handicapped children and sibling groups) who are in the custody of the State of South Dakota.

STATE EXCHANGE

None.

STATE ADOPTION REUNION REGISTRY

None.

STATE SUBSIDY

For information, contact the Department of Social Services (above).

NACAC REPRESENTATIVE

Carol Heltzel and Donna Bieber
Co-chairpersons, State Adoption Council)
P.O. Box 105
Philip, SD 57567
(605) 859–2039

GENERAL ADOPTION RESOURCES

Families through Adoption
P.O. Box 851
Sioux Falls, SD 57101
(605) 331–3570

State Adoption Council
P.O. Box 105
Philip, SD 57567
(605) 859–2039

SPECIAL-NEEDS ADOPTION RESOURCES

For information about resources for children with special needs, contact Child Protection Services or the State Adoption Council (above). In addition, information is available through the University of South Dakota School of Medicine/ UAF/CDD Helpline (a computerized resource list for parents of disabled children): (605) 677–5311.

OUT-OF-STATE AGENCIES

AGENCY

Holt International Children's Services, Tennessee Branch

SEE APPENDIX A

Agencies Providing Nationwide Services

BETHANY CHRISTIAN SERVICES

2009 Buena Vista
Rapid City, SD 57702–4371
(605) 343–3078
Program director: James K. Haveman, Jr.—Executive Director

THE PROGRAM

For a full description of programs and services, refer to Michigan listing:
Bethany Christian Services
901 Eastern Avenue, N.E.
Grand Rapids, MI 49503–1295
(616) 459–6273

BUILDING FAMILIES THROUGH ADOPTION

P.O. Box 550, 7th and Chestnut
Dawson, MN 56232
(612) 769–2933
Program director: Mary Carpenter and Therese Giesen

THE PROGRAM

For current address and telephone number of BFTA South Dakota branch offices, contact BFTA main office (listed above). For a full description of BFTA programs and services, refer to Minnesota listing for Building Families Through Adoption.

CATHOLIC FAMILY SERVICES

3100 W. 41st Street
Sioux Falls, SD 57105
(605) 333–3375
Program director: Mary Standaert, MSW

THE PROGRAM

Catholic Family Services is a nonprofit agency serving eastern South Dakota and placing approximately 12 to 20 children annually. Founded in 1961, the agency's primary purpose is to assist unwed parents with unplanned pregnancies and to facilitate adoption of infants into caring and nurturing families. The agency also provides homestudy and supervisory services for applicants pursuing special-needs adoption or foreign adoption, subject to state approval of the integrity of the source. In all of its programs, the agency's mission is to provide "direct and indirect service to those in need, and to address institutional and societal problems of injustice which deny or restrict human rights and the dignity of individuals and families."

THE COST

The agency's fee for adoption services is based on a sliding scale and averages $2,035. Services covered by the fee include homestudy, placement, and post-placement supervision. Applicants pursuing foreign adoption should anticipate additional fees including foreign agency fees, transportation and escort fees, and related costs. In all programs, applicants assume responsibility for legal fees connected with finalization of the adoption.

THE WAIT

The time from application for acceptance into the program to the homecoming of the adoptive child ranges from 1 1/2 to 2 1/2 years.

THE CHILDREN

Catholic Family Services places primarily healthy Caucasian infants, born in the U.S., but also occasionally infants of mixed racial backgrounds (Mulatto, Native American/Caucasian). In addition, the agency will provide homestudy and supervisory services for the adoption of special needs or foreign-born children.

THE REQUIREMENTS

Age: Applicants must be at least 21 and no more than 45 years of age.
Health: Applicants must be in reasonably good health. Applicants with health problems or handicaps are given individual consideration. Infertility documentation is required.
Religion: Either the husband or the wife must be a practicing member of the Catholic faith.
Financial status: No requirement.
Marital status: Applicants must be married couples.
Family size: Applicants may have no more than 2 children currently in the family.
Racial, ethnic or cultural origin: No requirement.

THE PROCEDURE

Participation in Catholic Family Services' adoption program entails the following basic steps:
Orientation meeting
Application
Group counseling sessions
Individual counseling sessions
Home visit
Compliance with immigration/naturalization requirements (foreign adoptions only)
Placement
Post-placement supervision
Finalization

ADDITIONAL PROGRAMS/SERVICES

Catholic Family Services provides a wide range of services including individual, marital, and family counseling;

annual parenting workshop for adoptive couples; foster care for unwed mothers and infants; on-going training for foster care team; post-adoption services; post-abortion counseling; divorced, widowed, separated support groups; Systematic Training for Effective Parenting; Community Church Crisis Fund.

BRANCH/NETWORK OFFICES

310 15th St., S.E.
Aberdeen, SD 57401
(605) 226–1304

LICENSE/ACCREDITATION/PROFESSIONAL AFFILIATIONS

Catholic Family Services is licensed by the State of South Dakota Department of Social Services. The agency is a member of Alternatives to Abortion International and the United Way.

CHRISTIAN COUNSELING SERVICES

231 S. Phillips Avenue, Suite 350
Sioux Falls, SD 57102
(605) 334–6556
Program director: Vinette Bomhoff

THE PROGRAM

Christian Counseling Services is a nonprofit agency serving residents of South Dakota and placing approximately 15 children annually in Christian families. Licensed 4 years ago and affiliated with the Baptist Churches of South Dakota, Christian Counseling Services "works for the well being of birthparents and their families, adoptive parents, and children." The agency provides services to birthparents and places infants for adoption when birthparents elect adoptive placement as the best plan for their child. In addition, the agency will provide homestudy and supervisory services for applicants pursuing interagency adoption or independent adoption.

THE COST

The agency's fee for adoption services is based on a sliding scale and ranges from $4,000 to $6,000. Services covered by the fee include all phases of the adoption program, excluding legal fees connected with finalization and sometimes the medical expenses of the birthmother and child.

THE WAIT

The time from application to the homecoming of the adoptive child averages 2 years.

THE CHILDREN

Christian Counseling Services places both healthy and special-needs infants.

THE REQUIREMENTS

Age: Applicants may be no more than 40 years of age.
Health: Infertility documentation is required.

Religion: Applicants must be practicing members of a Christian church.

Financial status: Applicants must demonstrate financial stability.

Marital status: Applicants must be married; the length of the marriage must be at least 3 years.

Family size: Applicants may have no more than 1 child currently in the family.

Racial, ethnic or cultural origin: No requirement, but preference for placing children in families of similar origins.

THE PROCEDURE

Participation in the adoption program of Christian Counseling Services entails the following basic steps:
Orientation meeting
Application
Individual counseling sessions
Homestudy
Referral
Placement
Post-placement supervision

ADDITIONAL PROGRAMS/SERVICES

Christian Counseling Services provides foster care and counseling services.

BRANCH/NETWORK OFFICES

None.

LICENSE/ACCREDITATION/PROFESSIONAL AFFILIATIONS

Christian Counseling Services is licensed by the State of South Dakota Department of Social Services.

LDS SOCIAL SERVICES

2525 West Main Street, #310
Rapid City, SD 57702
(605) 342–3500
Program director: Vernon J. Pearson

THE PROGRAM

For a full description of programs and services, refer to Utah listing:
LDS Social Services
50 East North Temple Street
Salt Lake City, UT 84150

LUTHERAN SOCIAL SERVICES OF SOUTH DAKOTA

600 West 12th Street
Sioux Falls, SD 57104
(605) 336–3347
Program director: Mrs. Ruby J. Dahl, CSW

THE PROGRAM

Lutheran Social Services is a nonprofit agency serving families who are legal residents of the state of South Dakota and placing approximately 15 to 25 children annually. Incorporated 68 years ago to provide services to people in crisis, the agency's mission is "to enable people to grow in intimacy with God, themselves, family and others by providing opportunities to experience wholeness, reconciliation, and fullness of life." The agency provides services to birthparents and places infants for adoption when birthparents in the agency's counseling program decide that the best interests of the child will be served by adoptive placement. The agency also provides homestudy and supervisory services for applicants pursuing special-needs adoption or foreign adoption, subject to state approval of the integrity of the source.

THE COST

The agency's fee for adoption services is adjusted annually according to the agency's cost of providing services. Services covered by the fee include pre-adoption services, family study, placement, post-placement supervision and services, assistance with legal completion (including required reports to court and Dept. of Social Services), birthparent counseling, and services to foster parents. In addition, applicants assume responsibility for legal fees connected with finalization of the adoption.

THE WAIT

The time from completion of the homestudy and approval of the family to placement of the child ranges from 18 to 24 months. For applicants pursuing foreign adoption, the wait varies depending on the child's country of origin.

THE CHILDREN

Lutheran Social Services places both healthy and special-needs infants (usually newborn to 3 months of age), primarily of Caucasian but also of mixed racial backgrounds, born in the U.S. The agency will also provide homestudy and supervisory services for the adoption of foreign-born children.

THE REQUIREMENTS

Age: Applicants may be no more than 42 years of age for the adoption of a domestic infant. For foreign adoptions, the requirement varies depending on the child's country of origin.

Health: Applicants must be in reasonably good health. Applicants with health problems or handicaps are given individual consideration. Infertility documentation is required for the adoption of a healthy Caucasian infant.

Religion: Applicants must be practicing members of a Christian faith.

Financial status: Applicants are evaluated individually on the basis of their utilization of financial resources.

Marital status: For domestic infant adoption, applicants must be married couples, and the length of the marriage must be at least 2 years. For foreign adoptions, the requirement varies depending on the child's country of origin.

Family size: For domestic infant adoption, applicants may have no more than 1 child currently in the family. For foreign adoptions, the requirement varies depending on the child's country of origin.

Racial, ethnic or cultural origin: Preference for placing children in families of similar origins.

THE PROCEDURE

Participation in Lutheran Social Services' adoption program entails the following basic steps:

Orientation meeting

Application

Homestudy (including group and individual counseling sessions)

Compliance with immigration/naturalization requirements (foreign adoptions only)

Referral

Placement

Post-placement supervision

Assistance with legal completion

ADDITIONAL PROGRAMS/SERVICES

Lutheran Social Services periodically conducts workshops for adoptive parents and children and for foster parents. The agency provides post-adoption counseling services as well as search/outreach services for adult adoptees.

BRANCH/NETWORK OFFICES

All adoption services are provided through the Sioux Falls office.

LICENSE/ACCREDITATION/PROFESSIONAL AFFILIATIONS

Lutheran Social Services is licensed by the State of South Dakota Department of Social Services.

Tennessee

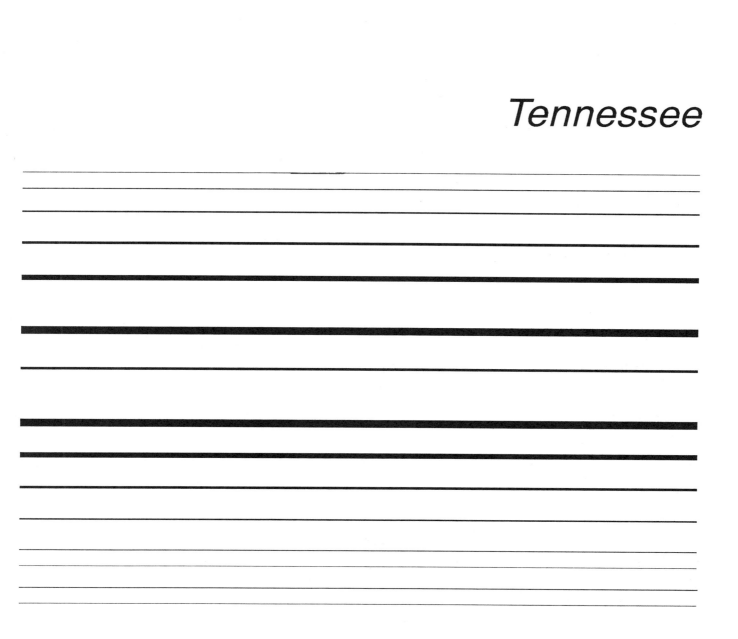

PUBLIC ADOPTION PROGRAM/ COMMUNITY RESOURCES

Department of Human Services
Adoption Unit
400 Deaderick Street
Citizens Plaza Building
Nashville, TN 37219
(615) 741–5935
Adoption specialist: Joyce N. Harris

THE PROGRAM

Public adoption services in Tennessee are provided by the Department of Human Services through district and county offices located throughout the state. The focus of the DHS adoption program is to recruit, prepare, supervise, and support families who are interested in adopting special-needs children (older, minority, and handicapped children and sibling groups) who are wards of the State of Tennessee. To provide on-going support for families adopting Black children, DHS assisted in the development of Friends of Black Children Councils (see General Adoption Resources below).

STATE EXCHANGE

Tennessee Adoption Resource Exchange. For information, contact the Adoption Unit (above).

STATE ADOPTION REUNION REGISTRY

Putative Father Registry. For information, contact the Adoption Unit (above).

State Subsidy: Adoption Subsidy is available for special-needs children placed by the state agency or by a private licensed child placing agency. For information, contact the Adoption Unit (above).

NACAC REPRESENTATIVE

Joyce Maxey
7630 Luscombe Drive
Knoxville, TN 37919
(615) 974–2287

GENERAL ADOPTION RESOURCES

PAPPOOS (Pre and Post Adoptive Parents Offering Ongoing Support)
   757 Darden Place
   Nashville, TN 37205
   Contact: Susan Levy

COAC (Council on Adoptable Children)
   P.O. Box 1787
   Knoxville, TN 37901

Friends of Black Children Councils
   Knoxville Friends of Black Children
   State Technical Institute
   P.O. Box 19802
   Knoxville, TN 37919
   Contact: Linda Calvert

   Knoxville Friends of Black Children
   1301 Chipwood Road
   Knoxville, TN 37932
   Contact: Linda Calvert

Memphis Friends of Black Children
2310 Sparks Road
Memphis, TN 38106
Contact: James Rogers

Chattanooga Friends of Black Children
5124 Lantana Lane
Chattanooga, TN 37416
Contact: Shirley Jackson

Nashville Friends of Black Children
929 Gale Lane
Nashville, TN 37204
Contact: Weslia Holloway

SPECIAL-NEEDS ADOPTION RESOURCES

For information about resources for children with special needs, contact the Adoption Unit (above) or private agencies in Tennessee specializing in special-needs adoption.

OUT-OF-STATE AGENCIES

AGENCY

Smithlawn Maternity Homes, Texas (special-needs and minority placements)

SEE APPENDIX A

Agencies Providing Nationwide Services

BETHANY CHRISTIAN SERVICES

4719 Brainerd Road
Chattanooga, TN 37411
(615) 622–7360
Program director: James K. Haveman, Jr., Executive Director

THE PROGRAM

For a full description of programs and services, refer to Michigan listing:
Bethany Christian Services
   901 Eastern Avenue, N.E.
   Grand Rapids, MI 49503–1295
   (616) 459–6273

BETHEL BIBLE VILLAGE

3001 Hamill Road
P.O. Box 5000
Hixson, TN 37343
(615) 842–5757
Program director: Ike Keay, Executive Director; Harry R. Jackson, M.Ed., Director of Family Services

THE PROGRAM

Bethel Bible Village is a nonprofit social welfare organization that provides foster care and group care for the children of men and women serving in prisons. Founded in June 1954 by an evangelist minister, Bethel Bible Village gives these children the spiritual, emotional, educational, and social guidance they need and strives to reunite the children with their families. If this goal is not possible, Bethel Bible Village can place the children for adoption or in other foster homes. The agency serves East Tennessee and places about 1 child annually. Bethel Bible Village is the only social agency in the United States established exclusively for the children of prisoners.

THE COST

The agency's fee for adoption is based on a sliding scale and ranges from $500 to $3,000, depending on the extent of office work, travel costs, and medical and court expenses involved. In addition, applicants should expect to pay hospital expenses of the birthmother and child and legal fees connected with the finalization of the adoption.

THE WAIT

The time from application for acceptance into the program to home- coming of the adoptive child averages 1 month depending on the availability of the child.

THE CHILDREN

Bethel Bible Village places both healthy and special-needs children of all racial backgrounds. Children placed by Bethel Bible Village are born in the U.S.

THE REQUIREMENTS

Age: Applicants are considered on an individual basis.
Health: Applicants must be in reasonably good health. Infertility documentation is required.
Religion: Applicants must be practicing members of a Christian faith.
Financial status: Applicants must demonstrate financial stability.
Marital status: Preference is given to married couples. However, single applicants are considered on an individual basis.
Family size: No requirement.
Racial, ethnic or cultural origin: No requirement.

THE PROCEDURE

Participation in Bethel Bible Village adoption program entails the following basic steps:
Application
Verification of marriage
Medical evaluation
Financial security evaluation
Group counseling sessions
Individual counseling sessions
Homestudy
Referral
Placement
Post-placement

ADDITIONAL PROGRAMS/SERVICES

Bethel Bible Village conducts workshops and counseling sessions.

BRANCH/NETWORK OFFICES

None.

LICENSE/ACCREDITATION/PROFESSIONAL AFFILIATIONS

Bethel Bible Village is licensed by the State of Tennessee Department of Human Services. The agency's professional affiliations include National Association of Homes for Children, Southeastern Group Child Care Association, Tennessee Association for Child Care, Tennessee Conference on Social Welfare, and Evangelical Council for Financial Accountability.

CATHOLIC CHARITIES OF TENNESSEE, INC.

30 White Bridge Road
Nashville, TN 37205
(615) 352–3087
Program director: Anne M. Cain

THE PROGRAM

Catholic Charities of Tennessee is a nonprofit agency serving residents of Tennessee east of the Tennessee River and residents of Georgia in the four counties immediately around Chattanooga, Tennessee. Licensed as a child placing agency since 1962, the agency promotes "programs and services which support the family unit." Catholic Charities provides services to birthparents and places infants for adoption when birthparents in the agency's program decide that the best interests of the child will be served by adoptive placement. The agency also places special-needs children and will provide homestudy and supervisory services for applicants pursuing foreign adoption, subject to state approval of the integrity of the source. Catholic Charities places an average of 25 children annually.

THE COST

The agency's fee for placement services is 10% of the applicants' annual gross income (with a minimum fee of $2,500) and $600 for homestudy evaluation. Services covered by the fee include pre-placement services, homestudy, placement, and post-placement supervision. In addition, fees help to underwrite the cost of medical services for the birthmother and child and legal fees involved in freeing the child for adoption. In addition, applicants assume responsibility for legal fees connected with finalization of the adoption.

THE WAIT

The average time from application to the homecoming of the adoptive child is approximately 3 years.

THE CHILDREN

Catholic Charities places both healthy and special-needs children, primarily infants though occasionally older children as well, born in the U.S., of all racial backgrounds. In addition, the agency provides homestudy and supervisory services for applicants pursuing foreign adoption.

THE REQUIREMENTS

Age: The general requirement is that the applicants may be no more than 42 years older than the child being considered for placement. The requirement is somewhat flexible.

Health: Applicants must be in reasonably good health. Priority is given to applicants who are unable to have their own child.

Religion: For healthy Caucasian infant adoption, either the husband or the wife must be a practicing Catholic. For minority and special-needs adoptions, the requirement is waived. For foreign adoptions, applicants must meet the requirements of the placing agency or the child's country of origin.

Financial status: Applicants must demonstrate financial stability.

Marital status: For healthy Caucasian infant adoption, applicants must be married couples, and the length of the marriage must be at least 3 years. Single applicants are accepted for minority or special-needs adoptions.

Family size: For healthy Caucasian infant adoption, applicants may have no more than 1 child currently in the family. For minority, special needs, or foreign adoptions, family size is evaluated on a case by case basis.

Racial, ethnic or cultural origin: Preference for placing children in families of similar origins.

THE PROCEDURE

Participation in Catholic Charities' adoption program entails the following basic steps:

Orientation meeting

Application

Homestudy (including group and individual counseling sessions)

Compliance with immigration/naturalization requirements (foreign adoptions only)

Placement

Post-placement supervision

ADDITIONAL PROGRAMS/SERVICES

Catholic Charities provides extensive pregnancy counseling services for young women who have a crisis pregnancy. The agency sponsors post-placement groups for women who decide to place their children for adoption and parenting groups for women who decide to parent their children.

BRANCH/NETWORK OFFICES

Catholic Social Services
119 Dameron
Knoxville, TN 37917
(615) 524–9896

Catholic Social Services
1018 Dallas Road
Chattanooga, TN 37405
(615) 267–1297

LICENSE/ACCREDITATION/PROFESSIONAL AFFILIATIONS

Catholic Charities of Tennessee, Inc. is licensed by the State of Tennessee Department of Human Services. The agency is a member of Catholic Charities USA.

CHILD AND FAMILY SERVICES

114 Dameron Avenue
Knoxville, TN 37917
(615) 524–7483
Program director: Mary Fietz, LCSW

THE PROGRAM

Child and Family Services is a nonprofit, multi-service agency serving families within a 100 mile radius of Knoxville and placing 2–10 infants and 10–24 special-needs children annually. Providing adoption services since its inception in 1929, the agency's mission is "to preserve and strengthen family life." The agency provides pregnancy counseling services and places infants for adoption when birthparents in the agency's program decide that the best interests of the child will be served by adoptive placement. The agency is also actively involved in the recruitment of adoptive families for special-needs children.

THE COST

The agency's fee for infant adoptions is based on a sliding scale and ranges from $3,500 to $8,000. For infant adoptions there is also a separate, non-refundable $500 fee for the homestudy. Services covered by the fee include pre-placement services, homestudy, placement, and monthly home or office visits for one year after placement. The agency provides adoption services for special-needs children at no cost to the adoptive family. Non-agency fees which applicants should anticipate include fees for medical exams, travel and other expenses for pre-placement visits with older and special-needs children, and legal fees connected with finalization of the adoption.

THE WAIT

The time from application for acceptance into the program to the homecoming of the adoptive child varies depending on the program. For infant adoption, the wait ranges from 3 to 5 years. For older child and special-needs adoptions, the wait ranges from 6 months to 2 years.

THE CHILDREN

Child and Family Services places healthy infants (up to 2 years of age), of Caucasian, Black, and bi-racial backgrounds, born in the U.S. The agency also places special-needs children, currently defined as older children (10 years of age or older); sibling groups of 3 or more; Black children age 3 and older; bi-racial children of any age; children with physical, emotional, or mental handicaps.

THE REQUIREMENTS

Age: For infant adoption, applicants must be at least 21 and no more than 38 years of age. For special-needs adoption, applicants must be at least 21 and no more than 65 years of age.

Health: Applicants must be in reasonably good health. Applicants with health problems or handicaps are given individual consideration. For infant adoption, infertility documentation is required.

Religion: No requirement.

Financial status: Applicants must demonstrate financial stability. For special-needs adoptions, applicants must have adequate financial resources to care for an additional child or children. Subsidies are available in some cases.

Marital status: For infant adoptions, applicants must be married couples. Single parents are accepted for older and special-needs children.

Family size: For infant adoptions, applicants must be childless. No requirement for special-needs adoptions.

Racial, ethnic or cultural origin: Preference for placing children in families of similar origins, but bi-racial children are placed with Black or Caucasian families.

THE PROCEDURE

Participation in Child and Family Services' adoption program entails the following basic steps:
  Orientation meeting
  Application
  Individual discussion sessions
  Group discussion sessions
  Homestudy
  Referrals
  Transitional visits (special-needs adoptions)
  Placement
  Post-placement supervision

ADDITIONAL PROGRAMS/SERVICES

Child and Family Services provides individual, marital, and family counseling services; family life enrichment programs; protective services counseling; independent living programs; self-sufficiency training for teen parents; companionship services; pregnancy counseling; foster care services; volunteer programs. In addition, the agency operates the Knoxville Institute for Sexual Abuse Treatment Training, group homes, a runaway shelter, and a family crisis center.

BRANCH/NETWORK OFFICES

Blount County C&FS
  309 Court St.
  Maryville, TN 37801
  (615) 983–9390

Cocke County C&FS
  c/o First Baptist Church
  212 E. Broadway
  Newport, TN 37821
  (615) 625–1238

Jefferson County C&FS
  c/o First Baptist Church
  King Street
  Jefferson City, TN 37760
  (615) 524–7483

Roane County C&FS
  c/o Bethel Presbyterian Church
  P.O. Box 10
  Kingston, TN 37763
  (615) 376–6354

LICENSE/ACCREDITATION/PROFESSIONAL AFFILIATIONS

Child and Family Services is licensed by the State of Tennessee Department of Human Services and is accredited by The Family Service Association of America. Child and Family Services is a member agency of the Child Welfare League of America and of the United Way.

CHRISTIAN COUNSELING SERVICES

515 Woodland Street
P.O. Box 60383
Nashville, TN 37206
(615) 254–8341
Program director: Michael Malloy, ACSW

THE PROGRAM

Christian Counseling Services (CCS) is a nonprofit agency serving residents of the state of Tennessee and placing approximately 8–10 children in Christian adoptive homes annually. CCS emphasizes that "the Christian homes must meet the requirements of CCS as well as be able to meet the needs of the children available for adoption." The agency provides services to birthparents and places infants for adoption when birthparents in the agency's program decide that the best interests of the child will be served by adoptive placement. The agency also places a limited number of older children. Working in cooperation with other U.S. agencies which maintain international programs, CCS facilitates the placement of foreign-born children in Tennessee families. Applicants of Catholic, Protestant, and Jewish religious affiliations are eligible for the international program.

THE COST

The agency's fee for domestic adoption services is 11% of the applicants' combined incomes, with a minimum of $3,500 and a maximum of $7,000. Services covered by the fee include pre-placement counseling, homestudy, placement, and post-placement supervision for 1 year. Fees also help to underwrite the medical expenses of the birthmother and child as well as foster care for the child prior to placement. For international adoption, the agency's fee is 5% of the applicants' combined incomes, with a minimum fee of $1,000 and a maximum fee of $2,500. Applicants pursuing international adoption should also anticipate fees to the international agency and other expenses related to international adoption. For both programs, applicants assume responsibility for court fees ($77.75) for finalization of the adoption.

THE WAIT

The time from application for acceptance into the program to the homecoming of the adoptive child ranges from 2 to 3 years for domestic adoptions. For international adoption, the wait varies depending on the cooperating agency.

THE CHILDREN

CCS directly places both healthy and special-needs infants (birth to 5 months), of Caucasian, Black, and bi-racial backgrounds, born in the U.S. Working in cooperation with other U.S. agencies, CSS facilitates the placement of children from various countries.

THE REQUIREMENTS

Age: Applicants must be at least 21 (in accordance with state law) and no more than 41 years of age. For special-needs adoptions, the maximum age requirement is 45 years. For international adoption, the requirement varies depending on the cooperating agency.

Health: For Caucasian infant adoption, infertility documentation is required. The requirement varies for special-needs adoptions. For international adoption, the requirement varies depending on the cooperating agency.

Religion: For domestic adoptions, applicants must be practicing members of a protestant church and must have a personal relationship with and a commitment to Jesus Christ. For international adoptions, applicants of Catholic, Protestant, and Jewish religious affiliations may apply.

Financial status: No requirement.

Marital status: For Caucasian infant adoption, applicants must be married couples, and the length of the marriage must be at least 5 years. The requirement varies for special-needs adoption. For international adoption, the requirement varies depending on the cooperating agency.

Family size: For Caucasian infant adoption, applicants may have no more than 1 child currently in the family. The requirement varies for special-needs adoption. For international adoption, the requirement varies depending on the cooperating agency.

Racial, ethnic or cultural origin: Preference for placing children in families of similar origins.

THE PROCEDURE

Participation in CSS' adoption program entails the following basic steps:
Application
Orientation meeting
Individual counseling sessions
Homestudy
Compliance with immigration/naturalization requirements
    (international adoptions only)
Placement
Post-placement supervision (1 year)
Finalization hearing in court

ADDITIONAL PROGRAMS/SERVICES

CSS provides individual and marital counseling; Promise Program (individual and group counseling for homosexuals); Conet Program (a support program for pastors and their families); birthparent services; foster care services; community services (workshops and seminars).

BRANCH/NETWORK OFFICES

None.

LICENSE/ACCREDITATION/PROFESSIONAL AFFILIATIONS

Christian Counseling Services is licensed by the State of Tennessee Department of Human Services.

FAMILY AND CHILDREN'S SERVICE

201 23rd Avenue, North
Nashville, Tennessee 37203
(615) 327–0833
Program director: Kathy Rogers

THE PROGRAM

Since its beginning in 1952, the adoption program of Family and Children's Services, a nonprofit organization, has had as its primary focus adoption of children 3 years or older. In 1977 the special needs only adoption program was started with the same commitment to "strengthening family life and improving the emotional well-being of children and adults." The agency is dedicated to "alleviating interpersonal, family, and individual psychological and social problems" and recognizes the family as "an essential institution encompassing a broad range of personal relationships, values, and cultural traditions." The agency serves the Nashville vicinity (within a 50 mile radius of the city), placing approximately 10 children annually. Children in the adoption program are in the guardianship of the Tennessee Department of Human Services and are referred to the agency for such service. Children with special emotional and medical needs are most often placed, and the agency emphasizes ongoing support for the adopting family.

THE COST

Family and Children's Services provides adoption service at no cost to the adoptive family as services are provided through contract with the Department of Human Services. The only expense which prospective adoptive parents should anticipate is the cost for filing an adoption petition and legalizing the adoption (approximately $250–$300). The Family and Children's Services recruits adoptive families in the Nashville area, prepares the child referred by the Tennessee Department of Human Services, places the child, and provides post-placement support and counseling to adopting families as well as post-legal counseling to families referred by the Tennessee Department of Human Services.

THE WAIT

The wait varies depending on the availability of the children and the kind of request from the adopting family. The time from application until completion of the adoptive parent preparation and home study is usually between 4 and 6 months.

THE CHILDREN

Family and Children's Services places special-needs children born in the U.S., including Black children from 3 years and older; Caucasian children from 10 years and older; handicapped children and sibling groups of all ages and racial backgrounds.

THE REQUIREMENTS

Age: Applicants must be 21 years or older.
Health: Applicants should be in reasonably good health.
Religion: No requirement, but may vary depending on the

needs of the child.

Financial status: No requirement other than the ability to meet the needs of an additional family member.

Marital status: No requirement.

Family size: No requirement.

Racial, ethnic or cultural origin: No requirement, but preference for placing children in families of similar origins.

THE PROCEDURE

Participation in the Family and Children's Services adoption program entails the following basic steps:
Recruitment of families for adoption by the agency
Orientation meeting
Application
Group/individual counseling sessions
Home study
Referral
Placement
Post placement services until finalization of the adoption (about 1 year)
Optional participation for families in Adoption Placement Group
Post-legal services

ADDITIONAL PROGRAMS/SERVICES

Family and Children's Services provides support groups for adoptive families; treatment groups for children; adoption preparation groups for children; post-finalization counseling; individual and family counseling; workshops on various topics including parenting, stages of adoption, parenting sexually abused children.

BRANCH/NETWORK OFFICES

All adoption inquiries are processed by the main office.

LICENSE/ACCREDITATION/PROFESSIONAL AFFILIATIONS

Family and Children's Services is licensed by the State of Tennessee Department of Human Services and is accredited by the Council on Accreditation of Services for Families and Children. Family and Children's Services is a member of the United Way and the Child Welfare League of America.

FAMILY AND CHILDREN'S SERVICES, INC.

323 High Street
Chattanooga, TN 37403
(615) 755–2800
Program director: Sandra C. Kesler, MSSW

THE PROGRAM

Family and Children's Services is a nonprofit agency serving residents of Hamilton County and placing approximately 4 to 10 children annually through its adoption program. Providing adoption services since 1942, the agency's mission is "to preserve and strengthen individual and family life, to create and promote conditions conducive to personal growth, and to alleviate and prevent human distress through appropriate community, social, and other services." The agency provides a full range of services to birthparents and places both healthy and special-needs infants for adoption when birthparents elect adoptive placement as the best plan for their child. In addition, the agency will provide homestudy and supervisory services for applicants pursuing interagency adoption (domestic) or independent adoption.

THE COST

The agency's fee for adoption services is 10% of the applicants' combined annual gross income (with an average fee of $4,000 to $5,000). Services covered by the fee include all services to the birthmother and child as well as services to the applicants, excluding legal fees connected with finalization.

THE WAIT

The time from application for acceptance into the program to the homecoming of the adoptive child averages 3 years.

THE CHILDREN

Family and Children's Services places both healthy and special-needs infants (2 to 3 months old), of Caucasian, Black, and bi-racial backgrounds.

THE REQUIREMENTS

Age: Applicants must be at least 25 and no more than 38 years of age. The requirement is flexible for special-needs adoptions.

Health: Applicants must be in good health. Applicants with health problems or handicaps are given individual consideration. Infertility documentation is required for Caucasian infant adoption.

Religion: No requirement.

Financial status: Applicants must demonstrate sound financial management.

Marital status: Applicants must be married couples; the length of the marriage must be at least 3 years.

Family size: Applicants must be childless for Caucasian infant adoption. The requirement is flexible for special-needs adoptions.

Racial, ethnic or cultural origin: Preference for placing children in families of similar origins.

THE PROCEDURE

Participation in the adoption program of Family and Children's Services entails the following basic steps:
Orientation meeting
Application
Individual counseling sessions
Homestudy
Placement
Post-placement supervision

ADDITIONAL PROGRAMS/SERVICES

Family and Children's Services provides a range of services including counseling; foster care; workshops and seminars; consumer credit counseling; prevention outreach; services to birthparents (including public school education during pregnancy).

BRANCH/NETWORK OFFICES

None.

LICENSE/ACCREDITATION/PROFESSIONAL AFFILIATIONS

Family and Children's Services is licensed by the State of Tennessee Department of Human Services. The agency is a member of Family Service America and the Child Welfare League of America.

HOLSTON UNITED METHODIST HOME FOR CHILDREN

P.O. Box 188
Holston Drive
Greeneville, TN 37743
(615) 638–4171
Program director: Carl Anderson, Director of Family Services; Arthur Masker, Program Administrator

THE PROGRAM

Holston United Methodist Home for Children is a non-profit, multi-service agency serving the state of Tennessee and 17 counties in southwestern Virginia and placing approximately 80–100 children annually. Originally founded as an orphanage by Elizabeth Wiley in 1895, the Home has evolved over the years, responding to current societal social service needs and guided by its mission "to provide preventive, supportive, and rehabilitative services to children and families" within its area of service. Today, the agency provides a wide range of services to children, including several domestic and foreign adoption programs. The agency provides services to birthparents and places infants for adoption when birthparents in the agency's program decide that the best interests of the child will be served by adoptive placement. Working with regional and national adoption exchange programs, Holston is also actively involved in the placement of special-needs children. For applicants interested in pursuing international adoption, Holston provides referral, homestudy, and supervisory services.

THE COST

The agency's fee for adoption services varies depending on the program. The basic fee schedule is as follows:
Caucasian infant adoption
The minimum fee is $5,000 for applicants with combined annual gross income of $26,000. For annual gross income above $26,000 the fee is a percentage of the applicants' gross income with a maximum fee of $6,500.
Black or bi-racial infant adoption
The fee is $2,000 or 10% of annual gross income, whichever is the least.
Foreign adoption
The fee is $1,000 for homestudy, information and referral, supervision, and court report.
Special-needs adoption
There is no fee for service. A donation is encouraged.

For foreign adoption, services covered by the fee are as stated. In addition, applicants should anticipate international agency fees, possible travel expenses, and related costs. For domestic adoption, services covered by the fee include pre-placement services, homestudy, placement, post-placement supervision, and court report. Representation by an attorney at the time of finalization is not required.

THE WAIT

The time from application to the homecoming of the adoptive child varies depending on the program. For healthy, Caucasian infant adoption, the wait averages 20 months; for special-needs adoption, 6 months; for foreign adoption, 14 months.

THE CHILDREN

Holston places both healthy and special-needs children, ranging in age from birth to 18 years, of all racial backgrounds. Children placed directly by Holston are born in the U.S. However, Holston facilitates foreign adoptions of children from Southeast Asia and South and Central America.

THE REQUIREMENTS

Age: For Caucasian infant adoption, applicants must be at least 23 and no more than 37 years of age. The requirement varies for special needs and foreign adoptions.
Health: Applicants must be in reasonably good health. For Caucasian infant adoption, infertility report is required.
Religion: No requirement. For Caucasian infant adoption, the preference of the birthmother is honored.
Financial status: Applicants must demonstrate financial stability.
Marital status: For healthy Caucasian infant, applicants must be married couples, and the length of the marriage must be at least 3 years. For healthy Black infant, applicants must be married couples, and the length of the marriage must be at least 2 years. No specific requirement for foreign or special-needs adoption, but may vary depending on the needs of the child or the requirements of the child's country of origin.
Family size: For Caucasian infant adoption, applicants must be childless. No requirement for special needs or foreign adoptions.
Racial, ethnic or cultural origin: Preference for placing children in families of similar origins.

THE PROCEDURE

Participation in Holston's adoption programs entails the following basic steps:
Inquiry/referral
Orientation meeting
Application
Group counseling sessions
Individual counseling sessions
Homestudy
Compliance with immigration/naturalization requirements
    (foreign adoptions only)
Placement
Post-placement supervision

ADDITIONAL PROGRAMS/SERVICES

Holston provides a wide range of services including foster

family care; problem pregnancy services; child day care; residential treatment; community-based group homes; services to developmentally disabled clients; individual and family counseling.

BRANCH/NETWORK OFFICES

Bristol Holston Home, VA Area Office
300 Moore St., Suite D
Kingsport, TN 37665
(615) 246–2888

Bristol-Kingsport, TN Area Office
1437 Plainview
Bristol, VA 24201
(703) 466–3883

Knoxville Area Office
1620 North Central St.
Knoxville, TN 37917
(615) 524–8659

Cleveland-Chattanooga, TN Area Office
1165 South Church St.
Cleveland, TN 37311
(615) 476–4504 (Cleveland)
(615) 624–1228 (Chattanooga)

LICENSE/ACCREDITATION/PROFESSIONAL AFFILIATIONS

Holston United Methodist Home for Children, Inc. is licensed by the State of Tennessee Department of Human Services and by the Commonwealth of Virginia Department of Public Welfare. Holston is a member of the National Association of Homes for Children and is affiliated with the Tennessee Conference Adoption Services and the United Methodist Adoption Services.

HOLT INTERNATIONAL CHILDREN'S SERVICES, INC.

5347 Flowering Peach
Memphis, TN 38115
(901) 794–6082
Program director: David H. Kim, Executive Director

THE PROGRAM

Holt International Children's Services in Memphis serves residents of Tennessee, Mississippi, and Arkansas. For a full description of programs and services, refer to Oregon listing:
Holt International Children's Services, Inc.
P.O. Box 2880
1195 City View
Eugene, OR 97402
(503) 687–2202

PORTER-LEATH CHILDREN'S CENTER

868 North Manassas Street
Memphis, TN 38107
(901) 526–3111
Program director: Lindee M. Wade, MSSW, ACSW

THE PROGRAM

Porter-Leath Children's Center is a nonprofit agency providing nationwide service and placing approximately 25–30 children annually. Founded in 1850 to care for Civil War orphans, the agency expanded during two Yellow Fever epidemics which decimated Memphis in 1900. Porter-Leath is the oldest child-placing agency in west Tennessee and has operated continuously for the past 137 years. Congruent with its mission "to serve children in need," the agency's current focus is to find permanent adoptive homes for healthy and special-needs Black infants.

THE COST

The agency's fee for adoption services is based on a sliding scale, ranging from $0 to $8,000, with an average fee of $2,000. Services covered by the fee include homestudy, placement, and post-placement supervision. In addition, fees help to underwrite counseling and medical services to the birthmother and child as well as foster care for the child prior to placement. In addition, applicants should anticipate transportation costs (if the placement is out of the area) and legal fees connected with finalization of the adoption.

THE WAIT

The time from application for acceptance into the program to the homecoming of the adoptive child averages 2 years.

THE CHILDREN

Porter-Leath places both healthy and special needs Black infants, born in the U.S.

THE REQUIREMENTS

Age: Applicants must be at least 24 and no more than 42 years of age.
Health: Applicants must be in reasonably good health.
Religion: No requirement.
Financial status: Applicants are evaluated individually on the basis of their utilization of financial resources.
Marital status: No requirement.
Family size: No requirement.
Racial, ethnic or cultural origin: Preference for placing children in families of similar origins.

THE PROCEDURE

Participation in Porter-Leath's adoption program entails the following basic steps:
Application
Homestudy
Referral
Clearance through Interstate Compact office (out-of-state placements only)
Placement
Post-placement supervision

ADDITIONAL PROGRAMS/SERVICES

Porter-Leath provides maternity counseling services, foster care services, family day care services, emergency shelter care, foster grandparents program, and after-school enrichment program.

BRANCH/NETWORK OFFICES

None.

LICENSE/ACCREDITATION/PROFESSIONAL AFFILIATIONS

Porter-Leath Children's Center is licensed by the State of Tennessee Department of Human Services. The agency is a member of the Child Welfare League of America.

SAINT PETER HOME FOR CHILDREN

1805 Poplar Avenue
Memphis, TN 38104
(901) 725–8240
Program director: Executive Director

THE PROGRAM

Saint Peter Home for Children is a nonprofit agency serving Catholic families in the Diocese of Memphis and protestant families in Shelby County and placing approximately 15 children annually. Established as an orphanage in 1852, the agency has provided adoption services since that time. The agency provides services to birthparents and places infants for adoption when birthparents in the agency's program elect adoptive placement as the best plan for their child.

THE COST

The agency's fee for adoption services is 10% of the applicants' annual gross income (maximum fee $6,500), plus a homestudy fee of $300. In addition, applicants can expect to pay legal fees in connection with the finalization of the adoption ($300–$500).

THE WAIT

The time from application to the homecoming of the adoptive child ranges from 4 to 5 years for Catholic applicants and from 6 to 7 years for Protestant applicants. While the agency accepts applications from members of any Christian denomination, most placements are made with Catholic families at the request of the birthmothers.

THE CHILDREN

Saint Peter Home for Children places both healthy and special-needs infants (birth to 4 months), primarily of Caucasian and Black racial backgrounds, born in the U.S.

THE REQUIREMENTS

Age: Applicants must be at least 26 and no more than 40 years of age. The requirement may vary depending on the needs of the child.
Health: Applicants must be in reasonably good health. Infertility documentation is required.

Religion: Applicants must be practicing members of a Christian church.
Financial status: Applicants must demonstrate financial stability.
Marital status: For healthy Caucasian infant adoption, applicants must be married couples. If infertility is documented, the length of the marriage must be at least 3 years. If no medical reason for childlessness can be established, the length of the marriage must be at least 5 years. Single applicants are accepted for special needs placements.
Family size: Applicants may have no more than 1 child currently in the family, and preference is given to childless couples.
Racial, ethnic or cultural origin: No requirement, but preference for placing children in families of similar origins.

THE PROCEDURE

Participation in the adoption program of Saint Peter Home for Children entails the following basic steps:
Orientation meeting
Group counseling sessions
Application
Individual counseling sessions
Homestudy
Placement
Post-placement supervision

ADDITIONAL PROGRAMS/SERVICES

Saint Peter Home for Children provides foster care and counseling services. In conjunction with the Memphis Council of Adoption Agencies, the agency sponsors workshops and seminars.

BRANCH/NETWORK OFFICES

None.

LICENSE/ACCREDITATION/PROFESSIONAL AFFILIATIONS

Saint Peter Home for Children is licensed by the State of Tennessee Department of Human Services and is a member of the Memphis Council of Adoption Agencies.

TENNESSEE BAPTIST CHILDREN'S HOMES, INC.

P.O. Box 728
205 Franklin Road
Brentwood, TN 37024(615) 373–5707
Program director: Dr. Gerald L. Stow

THE PROGRAM

Tennessee Baptist Children's Homes, Inc. is a nonprofit agency providing statewide service and placing approximately 24 children annually. Owned and operated by the churches of the Tennessee Baptist Convention, the agency's objective is "the ministry in the name of Jesus Christ to neglected, dependent, and abused children and their families while leading them to become whole persons in Christ." The agency provides counseling, housing, medical, and spiritual aid to birthmothers and places infants for adoption when birthmothers in the agency's program decide that the best interests of their children will be served by adoptive placement. The agency also places a limited number of older and special-needs children.

THE COST

The agency's fee for adoption services is $4,000. Services covered by the fee include pre-adoption counseling, homestudy, placement, and post-placement supervision and counseling. Fees also help to underwrite the medical costs of the birthmother and child. In addition, applicants assume responsibility for legal fees connected with finalization of the adoption.

THE WAIT

The time from initial application to approval of the homestudy is 2 to 3 years. The time from approval to placement is 6 months to 1 year.

THE CHILDREN

Tennessee Baptist Children's Homes place primarily infants (birth to 3 years) of all racial backgrounds, but also older children. Children placed by the agency are born in the U.S.

THE REQUIREMENTS

Age: For infant adoption, applicants must be under 41 years of age.

Health: For infant adoption, medical documentation of infertility is required.

Religion: Applicants must be practicing members of a Tennessee Baptist Church.

Financial status: Applicants must demonstrate financial stability.

Marital status: Applicants must be married couples in their first marriage (unless the first marriage was terminated by death), and the length of the marriage must be at least 5 years.

Family size: For infant adoption, applicants must be childless. Exceptions are made for the placement of older or special-needs children.

Racial, ethnic or cultural origin: Preference for placing children in families of similar origins.

THE PROCEDURE

Participation in Tennessee Baptist Children's Homes' adoption program entails the following basic steps:
Application
Orientation meeting
Individual counseling sessions
Homestudy
Referral
Placement
Post-placement supervision

ADDITIONAL PROGRAMS/SERVICES

The agency provides foster care, counseling services, emergency care, care for expectant mothers, and crisis intervention for emotionally troubled youth.

BRANCH/NETWORK OFFICES

East Tennessee Campus-TBCH
6623 Lee Highway
Chattanooga, TN 37421
(615) 892-2722

Middle Tennessee Campus-TBCH
P.O. Box 519
1310 Franklin Rd.
Franklin, TN 37065
(616) 377-6551

Johnson City Cottage-TBCH
P.O. Box 5206
209 1/2 University Pkwy.
Johnson City, TN 37601
(615) 929-8512

Alternative Home-TBCH
1212 S. Graycroft
Nashville, TN 37216
(615) 860-0426

Alternative Home-TBCH
212 North Irish St.
Greeneville, TN 37744
(615) 638-1913

West Tennessee Campus-TBCH
6896 Highway 70
Memphis, TN 38134
(901) 386-3961

TBCH at Burrville
Rt. 1, Box 109
Sunbright, TN 37872
(615) 628-5161

LICENSE/ACCREDITATION/PROFESSIONAL AFFILIATIONS

Tennessee Baptist Children's Homes, Inc. is licensed by the State of Tennessee Department of Human Services. The agency is a member of the National Association of Homes for Children and the Tennessee Association of Child Care.

TENNESSEE CONFERENCE ADOPTION SERVICE

900 Glendale Lane
Nashville, TN 37204
(615) 292-3500
Program director: Ariail Seshul

THE PROGRAM

Tennessee Conference Adoption Service (TCAS) is an outreach ministry of the Tennessee Conference of the United Methodist Church. In operation since 1984, TCAS serves residents of middle Tennessee on a non-profit, non-sectarian basis and places approximately 15 to 20 children annually through its adoption program. TCAS believes that "planning for children who need a good home and family stability is a concrete expression of concern for the welfare of children." The agency is committed to the placement of these children in homes where they can develop to their full potential. Working directly with birthparents, other private and public agencies, and national and regional exchange programs, TCAS places both healthy and special-needs children, born in the U.S. Working directly with child welfare institutions abroad and with other U.S. agencies which maintain international programs, the agency places foreign-born children in Tennessee families. In addition, the agency provides homestudy and supervisory services for applicants pursuing interagency adoption (domestic or international) or private adoption.

THE COST

As of October 1988, the agency's fee for adoption services is based on a sliding scale and ranges from $4,000 to $8,500. Special financial needs of the applicants may be taken into consideration. Services covered by the fee include all phases of the adoption process. In some cases, applicants should anticipate possible legal fees. For interagency adoptions and international adoptions, applicants should anticipate fees to the cooperating agency or the foreign child welfare institution.

THE WAIT

The time from application to placement ranges from 2 to 3 years.

THE CHILDREN

TCAS places both healthy and special-needs children, ranging in age from birth to 18 years, of all racial backgrounds. All children are served without regard to race, national origin, religious affiliation or handicap. Various countries of origin are represented.

THE REQUIREMENTS

Age: Applicants must be at least 25 years of age. For domestic infant adoption, applicants may be no more than 38 years of age. There is no maximum age limit for applicants pursuing international or special-needs adoption.

Health: Applicants should be in reasonably good health. Infertility documentation is required for domestic infant adoption.

Religion: Applicants are accepted without regard to religious affiliation.

Financial status: Applicants must demonstrate the ability to manage their income and to support an additional family member.*Marital status*: In general, applicants must be married, and the length of the marriage must be at least 3 years. Single applicants are considered for specific cases.

Family size: Family size is evaluated on a case-by-case basis. Preference is given to childless couples for a first placement.

Racial, ethnic or cultural origin: No requirement.

THE PROCEDURE

Participation in the adoption program of TCAS entails the following basic steps:
Application
Orientation meeting
Group counseling sessions
Individual counseling sessions
Homestudy
Compliance with immigration/naturalization requirements (international adoptions only)
Placement
Post-placement supervision

ADDITIONAL PROGRAMS/SERVICES

TCAS provides foster care and counseling services.

BRANCH/NETWORK OFFICES

None.

LICENSE/ACCREDITATION/PROFESSIONAL AFFILIATIONS

Tennessee Conference Adoption Service is licensed by the State of Tennessee Department of Human Services and is a member of the Child Welfare League of America.

WEST TENNESSEE AGAPE

1882 Union Avenue
Box 11411
Memphis, TN 38111
(901) 272–7339
Program director: Douglas A. Gauss, LCSW, Director of Social Services

THE PROGRAM

Founded in 1970, West Tennessee AGAPE is a nonprofit, multi-service child and family agency serving western Tennessee and placing approximately 10–12 children annually. Seeking "to strengthen families," AGAPE provides counseling and maternity services to birthmothers regardless of their religious or racial backgrounds. The agency places infants for adoption when birthparents in the agency's program decide that the best interests of the child will be served by adoptive placement. The agency also facilitates the placement of older and special-needs children. In addition, AGAPE provides family counseling, foster and group care.

THE COST

The agency's fee for adoption services is based on a sliding scale and ranges from $3,000 to $8,000. Services covered by the fee include pre- adoption counseling, placement, and post-placement supervision. In addition, prospective adoptive parents should anticipate financial responsibility for legal fees connected with finalization of the adoption.

THE WAIT

The time from application for acceptance into the program to the homecoming of the adoptive child ranges from 1 to 4 years.

THE CHILDREN

AGAPE places primarily healthy infants, but also some special-needs children. Children may be of Caucasian, Black, or mixed racial backgrounds.

THE REQUIREMENTS

Age: Applicants may be no more than 40 years older than the adoptive child. The requirement may vary for special-needs adoptions.

Health: Applicants must be in reasonably good health.

Religion: Applicants must be faithful members of the Church of Christ.

Financial status: Applicants must demonstrate financial stability.

Marital status: For adoption of a healthy Caucasian infant, applicants must be married couples. The requirement may vary for special-needs adoptions.

Family size: For adoption of a healthy Caucasian infant, applicants may have no more than 1 child currently in the family. The requirement may vary for special-needs adoptions.

Racial, ethnic or cultural origin: Preference for placing children in families of similar origins.

THE PROCEDURE

Participation in AGAPE's adoption program entails the following basic steps:

Application
Homestudy
Placement
Post-placement supervision

ADDITIONAL PROGRAMS/SERVICES

In addition to adoption services, AGAPE provides foster care services; counseling and foster care for birthmothers; individual, marital, and family counseling.

BRANCH/NETWORK OFFICES

None.

LICENSE/ACCREDITATION/PROFESSIONAL AFFILIATIONS

West Tennessee AGAPE is licensed by the State of Tennessee Department of Human Services and by the State of Mississippi Department of Public Welfare.

Texas

PUBLIC ADOPTION PROGRAM/ COMMUNITY RESOURCES

Department of Human Services
P.O. Box 2960
Austin, TX 78769
(512) 450–3302
Adoption specialist: Susan Klickman

THE PROGRAM

Public adoption services in Texas are provided by the Department of Human Services through regional offices located throughout the state. While DHS does place a limited number of infants and young children in adoptive homes, the focus of the DHS adoption program is to recruit, prepare, supervise, and support families who are interested in adopting special-needs children (older, minority, and handicapped children and sibling groups) who are wards of the State of Texas.

STATE EXCHANGE

Texas Adoption Resource Exchange. For information, contact the Department of Human Services (above).

STATE ADOPTION REUNION REGISTRY

For information, contact the Department of Human Services (512–450–3282).

STATE SUBSIDY

For information, contact the Department of Human Services (512–450–3362).

NACAC REPRESENTATIVE

Clara Flores
Route 2, Box 177F
Edinburg, TX 78539
(512) 383–2680

GENERAL ADOPTION RESOURCES:

Council on Adoptable Children of Texas, Inc. (COAC)
2709 Hunlac Trail
Round Rock, TX 78681
(512) 244–6288
Contact: Jody Casey

4317 Woodland Creek
Corpus Christi, TX 78410
(512) 241–9634
Contact: Sharon McBride

P.O. Box 141199, Dept. 366
Dallas, TX 75214
(214) 242–0236
Contact: Ted and Ellen Musantry

601 Harvard
Tyler, TX 75703
(214) 534–1221
Contact: Chris Smith

2102 Carmel Court
Arlington, TX 76012
(817) 265–3496
Contact: Mary Lou Mauldin

Box 894
Archer City, TX 76531
(817) 574–4041
Contact: Lynn Morgan

Ruth Barron
2209 Boyd
Midland, TX 79701
(915) 684–4655

Clara C. Flores
Rt. 2, Box 177–F
Edinburg, TX 78539
(512) 383–2680

Lois Wilson
P.O. Box 3472
San Angelo, TX 75902
(915) 949–1013

Additional Adoptive Parent Support Groups
Adoptive Parents of El Paso (APE)
458 Butchofsky
El Paso, TX 79907
Contact: Beverly Franklin

OURS
P.O. Box 56492
Houston, TX 77256
Contact: Ann Rayo

Adoptive Parents
Contact: Gleanor Gaudreau
Rt. 1, Box 363
Campbell, TX 75422

Latin American Families (LAF)
Phyllis Penny
8438 Waterwood
Dallas, TX 75217

SPECIAL -NEEDS ADOPTION RESOURCES

Council on Adoptable Children of Texas, Inc. (COAC)
P.O. Box 19432
Austin, TX 78761

OUT-OF-STATE AGENCIES

AGENCY

Christian Child Placement Services, New Mexico
Dillon Children's Services, Oklahoma
Metrocenter for Family Ministries, Oklahoma

SEE APPENDIX A

Agencies Providing Nationwide Services

ABC ADOPTION AGENCY

417 San Pedro
San Antonio, TX 78212
(512) 227–7820
Program director: Mrs. J.P. Mason

THE PROGRAM

ABC Adoption Agency is a nonprofit organization serving residents of Texas and placing approximately 20 children annually. ABC Adoption Agency provides counseling services to birthparents and places infants for adoption when birthparents in the agency's program decide that the best interests of the child will be served by adoptive placement. Licensed in 1986, the agency serves parents and adoptive children of all races and creeds.

THE COST

The agency's fee for adoption services averages $7,500. Services covered by the fee include homestudy, placement, post-placement supervision, and legal fees. In addition, applicants should anticipate financial responsibility for medical and foster care services to the birthmother and child.

THE WAIT

The time from application to the homecoming of the adoptive child varies depending on the type of placement and ranges from 6 months to 2 years.

THE CHILDREN

ABC Adoption Agency places both healthy and special-needs infants, primarily of Caucasian and Hispanic racial backgrounds, born in the U.S.

THE REQUIREMENTS

Age: Requirement varies depending on agency's evaluation of applicant.
Health: Applicants must be in reasonably good health.
Religion: No requirement.
Financial status: Applicants are evaluated individually on the basis of their ability to utilize financial resources effectively.
Marital status: Requirement varies depending on agency's evaluation of applicant.
Family size: Requirement varies depending on agency's evaluation of applicant.
Racial, ethnic or cultural origin: No requirement.

THE PROCEDURE

Participation in ABC Adoption Agency's program entails the following basic steps:
Initial interview
Application
Reference check
Homestudy
Individual counseling sessions
Placement
Post-placement supervision
Finalization

ADDITIONAL PROGRAMS/SERVICES

The agency provides counseling services to birthparents.

BRANCH/NETWORK OFFICES

The agency maintains branch offices in Laredo and Corpus Christi.

LICENSE/ACCREDITATION/PROFESSIONAL AFFILIATIONS

ABC Adoption Agency is licensed by the State of Texas Department of Human Services.

ADOPTION AGENCY OF MARK JORDAN SIEGEL

Dallas, TX 75219
(214) 520–0004
Program director: Mark J. Siegel; Vivian Y. George, Administrator

THE PROGRAM

The Adoption Agency of Mark Jordan Siegel is a nonprofit organization serving residents of the state of Texas and placing approximately 60 children annually. Licensed in 1985, the agency handles only private adoptions and places only healthy newborns with adoptive families. Mr. Siegel was the first attorney in north Texas licensed by the State to privately place children for adoption.

THE COST

The agency's fee for adoption services is $14,000. Services covered by the fee include all phases of the adoption process (application through finalization) and all legal and medical expenses of the birthmother and child. A $750 non-refundable fee (covers the homestudy) prior to acceptance is required.

THE WAIT

The time from application to the homecoming of the adoptive child averages 6 months. However, applicants should note that placement time is not guaranteed.

THE CHILDREN

The agency places healthy newborn infants biologically matched with the adoptive family.

THE REQUIREMENTS

Age: Applicants in good health up to the age of 55 are accepted.
Health: Applicants must free of commutable diseases, terminal illnesses, or conditions that would prevent them from raising a child to maturity.
Religion: Applicants of all demoninations may apply.
Financial status: Applicants must demonstrate financial stability and sufficient income to raise a child.
Marital status: Applicants must display a stable marriage.
Family size: No requirement.
Racial, ethnic or cultural origin: No requirement, but strong preference for placing children in families of similar origins.

THE PROCEDURE

Participation in the agency's adoption program entails the following basic steps:

Adoptive Family
  Application
  Homestudy/Follow-up
  Placement
  Legal representation
  Finalization
  Birth certificate
Birthmother
  Discussion/Contract
  Medical Expenses and care
  Counseling
  Transportation
  Pre- and post-natal care
  Legal representation

ADDITIONAL PROGRAMS/SERVICES

The agency provides services to the birthmother, including assistance in the selection of a doctor and hospital as well as living facilities, if desired, for birthmothers over 18 years of age.

BRANCH/NETWORK OFFICES

None.

LICENSE/ACCREDITATION/PROFESSIONAL AFFILIATIONS

The Adoption Agency of Mark Jordan Siegel is licensed by the State of Texas Department of Human Services.

ADOPTION RESOURCE CONSULTANTS OF NORTH TEXAS, INC.

P.O. Box 1224
Richardson, TX 75083
(214) 956–9901
Program director: Janie Gore Golan, MSSW, CSW; Cynthia Nitschke, CSW-ACSW

THE PROGRAM

Adoption Resource Consultants of North Texas is a for-profit agency serving residents of the state of Texas. The agency provides information, referral and consultation services to persons interested in adoption and provides homestudy and supervisory services to applicants pursuing domestic or international, agency-mediated or independent placements, subject to state approval of the integrity of the source. Adoption Resource Consultants facilitates the placement of approximately 40 children annually.

THE COST

The agency's fee for homestudy and supervisory services ranges from $800 to $1,200, depending on the extent of services provided.

THE WAIT

Not applicable.

THE CHILDREN

Adoption Resource Consultants will provide homestudy and supervisory services for applicants pursuing the adoption of children of any race, age, or national origin, subject to state approval of the integrity of the source.

THE REQUIREMENTS

Age: No agency requirement, but varies depending on the requirements of the placing source.
Health: No agency requirement, but varies depending on the requirements of the placing source.
Religion: No agency requirement, but varies depending on the requirements of the placing source.
Financial status: No agency requirement, but varies depending on the requirements of the placing source.
Marital status: No agency requirement, but varies depending on the requirements of the placing source.
Family size: No agency requirement, but varies depending on the requirements of the placing source.
Racial, ethnic or cultural origin: No agency requirement, but varies depending on the requirements of the placing source.

THE PROCEDURE

Applicants pursuing domestic or international, agency-mediated or independent adoption are invited to contact Adoption Resource Consultants to arrange for homestudy and supervisory services.

ADDITIONAL PROGRAMS/SERVICES

Adoption Resource Consultants provides information, referral and consultation services to persons interested in adoption and sponsors quarterly workshops on adoption issues.

BRANCH/NETWORK OFFICES

All adoption inquiries are processed through the main office.

LICENSE/ACCREDITATION/PROFESSIONAL AFFILIATIONS

Adoption Resource Consultants of North Texas, Inc. is licensed by the State of Texas Department of Human Services and is a member of the Dallas Interagency Adoption Council.

ADOPTION SERVICES ASSOCIATES

8703 Wurzbach Road
San Antonio, TX 78240
(512) 699–6088 or 1–800–648–1807
Program director: Linda Zuflacht, Executive Director

THE PROGRAM

Adoption Services Associates is a nonprofit non-denominational agency providing nationwide placement services and placing approximately 200 children annually. Founded by Linda Zuflacht, attorney, and James Timmens, MSW, Director of Social Services, in 1984, the agency's mission is "to provide excellent professional child placement services in accordance with the licensing requirements, with services to meet the needs of the best interests of the child, the biological parents, and the adoptive parents." The agency provides traditional and identified adoption programs. A traditional adoption involves the matching of an infant who has been surrendered to the agency to a couple whose homestudy has been approved by the agency. In an identified adoption, the applicants locate a specific pregnant woman who is willing to specify the adoption of her child by those parents. The agency promotes open adoption through the exchange of non-identifying information between the birth-parents and the adoptive parents. In addition, the agency will provide homestudy and supervisory services for applicants pursuing interagency adoption (domestic or international).

THE COST

The agency's fee for adoption services averages $10,000 to $14,000. Services covered by the fee include full counseling services, homestudy, medical expenses, reasonable maintenance expenses to the biological parents, all legal fees related to the adoption process, post-placement supervision, and post-placement support group activities for biological parents. Out-of- state applicants should anticipate fees to an agency in their home state for homestudy and supervisory services, the cost of transportation to San Antonio for placement and finalization (2 trips), and court filing fees ranging from $250 to $450.

THE WAIT

The application process normally takes a maximum of 2 months for documentation, homestudy, and interviews. Upon acceptance of the homestudy, applicants become "parents-in-waiting." For the traditional program, the maximum wait is 1 year (and may be less). For the identified program, the time from acceptance to actual placement can occur between 1 and 6 months, depending on a number of variables.

THE CHILDREN

Adoption Services Associates places primarily healthy infants (but occasionally special-needs children as well), 3 days to 2 weeks old, of Caucasian, Hispanic, or bi-racial backgrounds, born in the U.S.

THE REQUIREMENTS

Age: Applicants must be at least 25 years of age. One parent must be 45 years of age or younger. The requirement is flexible for special needs placements.

Health: Applicants should be in reasonably good health (medical report is required). Applicants with health problems or handicaps are given individual consideration. Infertility documentation is required.

Financial status: No specific requirement.

Marital status: Generally, applicants must be married, and the length of the marriage must be at least 3 years. The agency will consider exceptional single parents.

Family size: Applicants may have no more than 1 child currently in the family.

Racial, ethnic or cultural origin: No requirement.

THE PROCEDURE

Participation in the adoption program of Adoption Services Associates entails the following basic steps:
Inquiry form
Orientation meeting
Application
Individual counseling sessions
Homestudy
Placement
Post-placement supervision
Out-of-state applicants arrange for a licensed agency in their home state to provide homestudy and supervisory services.

ADDITIONAL PROGRAMS/SERVICES

Adoption Services Associates provides orientation seminars, foster care, support group for adoptive parents, and support group for biological parents.

BRANCH/NETWORK OFFICES

All inquiries are processed through the San Antonio office. However, the agency does have field staff representatives in some states who can conduct interviews and homestudies.

LICENSE/ACCREDITATION/PROFESSIONAL AFFILIATIONS

Adoption Services Associates is licensed by the State of Texas Department of Human Resources and by the State of New Jersey Department of Human Services. The agency is registered and approved by the State of Connecticut Department of Children and Youth Services. Professional social work staff are certified by the Texas Social Work Certification Board. The agency is a member of the San Antonio Adoption Council.

AGAPE SOCIAL SERVICES, INC.

7929 Brookriver, Suite 280
Dallas, TX 75247
(214) 871–7995
Program director: Linda K. Knight, CSW, ACSW, Executive Director

THE PROGRAM

AGAPE is a nonprofit agency serving the state of Texas and placing approximately 80 children annually. Founded in 1981, AGAPE's original purpose was to provide assistance to families adopting internationally. The agency expanded to include placement services for local handicapped and minority children, sibling groups, and older children. While the agency continues to provide homestudy and supervisory services for applicants pursuing international adoption, the agency's focus today is the placement of special-needs children. AGAPE places special-needs children both with Texas families and with out-of-state families. (Out-of-state families arrange for a licensed agency in their home state to provide homestudy and supervisory services.) In addition, AGAPE provides counseling and prenatal care for both relinquishing and non-relinquishing birthmothers and places infants for adoption when birthmothers in the agency's program decide that the best interests of the child will be served by adoptive placement. In all of its programs, AGAPE's mission is "to secure the best adoptive and foster care placement for children in need."

THE COST

The agency's fee for adoption services averages $6,000. Services covered by the fee include all phases of the adoption process (pre-adoption counseling through post-placement supervision), excluding legal fees connected with finalization of the adoption. Fees also help to underwrite the cost of services to the birthmother and child (medical, foster care, termination of parental rights).

THE WAIT

The time from application for acceptance into the program to the homecoming of the adoptive child averages 6 months.

THE CHILDREN

AGAPE places both healthy and special-needs children, ranging in age from birth to 17 years, of all racial backgrounds, born in the U.S. Most children placed with out-of-state families are of Black or bi-racial heritage. AGAPE also provides homestudy and supervisory services for applicants pursuing international adoption.

THE REQUIREMENTS

Age: For infant adoptions, applicants should be preferably no more than 40 years of age. No requirement for special needs placements.
 Health: No requirement.
 Religion: No requirement.
 Financial status: No requirement.
 Marital status: No requirement.
 Family size: No requirement.
 Racial, ethnic or cultural origin: No requirement.

THE PROCEDURE

Participation in AGAPE's adoption program entails the following basic steps:
 Application
 Orientation meeting (for Texas families)
 Homestudy
 Compliance with immigration/naturalization requirements (international adoptions only)
 Compliance with Interstate Compact procedures (out-of-state special needs placements only)
 Referral
 Placement
 Post-placement supervision
 Out-of-state families arrange for a licensed agency in their home state to provide the homestudy and post-placement supervision.

ADDITIONAL PROGRAMS/SERVICES

AGAPE sponsors support groups for relinquishing birth-parents and their families and support groups for adoptive parents.

BRANCH/NETWORK OFFICES

None.

LICENSE/ACCREDITATION/PROFESSIONAL AFFILIATIONS

AGAPE Social Services, Inc. is licensed by the State of Texas Department of Human Services. AGAPE is a member of the Interagency Adoption Council of Dallas. Staff members are affiliated with the National Committee for Adoption and the National Association of Social Workers.

THE CARE CONNECTION

400 Harvey Street
San Marcos, TX 78666
(512) 396–8111
Program director: Peggy J. Stamy, CSW; Pamela G. Cook

THE PROGRAM

The Care Connection is a nonprofit adoption agency that serves Texas residents and places 10 to 18 children annually. Founded in 1985 by one of the co-directors who had difficulty adopting her own child, the agency was established to serve atypical couples—over 40, of different races, different religions, in second marriages, blended families—who wish to adopt a child. The Care Connection is "searching for couples who want to parent, not for couples who want children who look like them."

THE COST

The agency's fee for adoption ranges from $4,500 for an older, hard- to-place child to $10,000 for an infant. Services covered by the fee include the homestudy, placement fee, supervision fee, and court-ordered social study fee. In addition, applicants should anticipate financial responsibility for foster care expenses and unusual medical or legal expenses.

THE WAIT

The time from completion of homestudy to the home coming of the adoptive child is 1 to 1 1/2 years.

THE CHILDREN

The Care Connection places both healthy and special-needs children, ranging in age from birth to 11 years of age, mainly of Hispanic, Hispanic/Caucasian and Black racial backgrounds, born in the U.S.

THE REQUIREMENTS

Age: No requirement.
 Health: Applicants with health problems or handicaps are given individual consideration.
 Religion: No requirement.
 Financial status: No requirement.
 Marital status: No requirement.
 Family size: No requirement.
 Racial, ethnic or cultural origin: No requirement.

THE PROCEDURE

Participation in the Care Connection's adoption program entails the following basic steps:
Orientation meeting
Group counseling sessions
Application
Individual counseling sessions
Homestudy
Referral
Placement
Post-placement supervision

ADDITIONAL PROGRAMS/SERVICES

The Care Connection offers on-going counseling programs for birthmothers and adoptive parents, foster care, and free pregnancy counseling.

BRANCH/NETWORK OFFICES

None.

LICENSE/ACCREDITATION/PROFESSIONAL AFFILIATIONS

The Care Connection is licensed by the State of Texas Department of Human Services and has a fully qualified professional staff (CSW and ACSW). The Care Connection is also a member of Search Line.

CHILD PLACEMENT CENTER OF TEXAS

501 Harris Avenue
Killeen, TX 76541
(817) 526–8872
Program director: Suzy B. Lackmeyer; Cecille Mooney, Director of Interstate Services

THE PROGRAM

Child Placement Center of Texas is a nonprofit agency serving the state of Texas for Caucasian infant adoptions and the U.S. for Black, bi- racial, or special-needs adoptions. The agency provides services to birthparents and places infants for adoption when birthparents in the agency's counseling program decide that the best interests of the child will be served by adoptive placement. Working with other agencies and with referrals from the Department of Human Services, the agency also places special-needs children.

THE COST

The agency's fee for adoption services is based on a sliding scale and ranges from $5,400 to $9,500 for out-of-state applicants. Texas applicants should contact the agency for a current fee schedule. Services covered by the fee include all phases of the adoption process (pre-adoption counseling through post-placement supervision), excluding legal fees connected with finalization of the adoption. Fees also help to underwrite the cost of services to the birthmother and child (including medical, legal, and foster care).

THE WAIT

The time from application to the homecoming of the adoptive child ranges from 6 to 18 months.

THE CHILDREN

Child Placement Center places both healthy and special-needs children, ranging in age from birth to 6 years, of all racial backgrounds. Children placed by the agency are born in the U.S.

THE REQUIREMENTS

Age: Applicants may be no more than 43 years of age. The requirement may be flexible depending on the needs of the child.
Health: Applicants with health problems or handicaps are given individual consideration.
Religion: No requirement.
Financial status: No requirement.
Marital status: No requirement. If married, the length of the marriage must be at least 5 years for a first marriage or 8 years for a second marriage for the adoption of a Caucasian child. All others are considered on a case-by-case basis.
Family size: No requirement.
Racial, ethnic or cultural origin: No requirement.

THE PROCEDURE

Participation in Child Placement Center's adoption program entails the following basic steps:
Inquiry
Preliminary information packet
Application
Homestudy
Placement
Post-placement supervision

ADDITIONAL PROGRAMS/SERVICES

None.

BRANCH/NETWORK OFFICES

505 University East, Suite 203
College Station, TX 77840
(409) 268–5577

1 Liberty Place, Suite 402
Waco, TX 76701

LICENSE/ACCREDITATION/PROFESSIONAL AFFILIATIONS

Child Placement Center of Texas is licensed by the State of Texas Department of Human Services.

CHILDREN'S SERVICE BUREAU

625 North Alamo Street
San Antonio, TX 78215
(512) 223–6281
Program director: Constance J. Hood

THE PROGRAM

The Children's Service Bureau is a nonprofit agency serving San Antonio and the surrounding communities and placing approximately 20 children annually. Founded in 1901 as a chapter of the National Humane Society to provide protective services to children, the agency has evolved through the years in response to the changing needs of the community. Today, the agency operates Holmgreen Memorial Children's Shelter (temporary residential group care for children), provides foster care services, adoption services, and services to birthparents. The agency places infants for adoption when birthparents in the agency's counseling program decide that the best interests of the child will be served by adoptive placement. The agency is also actively involved in the placement of special-needs children, working with private agencies throughout the state and with the Department of Human Services. In all of its programs, the agency is guided by the belief that "children have a right to the physical, emotional, intellectual, and spiritual nurturing essential to the development of healthy and responsible adults."

THE COST

The agency's fee for adoption services is based on the applicants' combined annual gross income and ranges from $1,400 to $6,000. Services covered by the fee include all phases of the adoption process (pre-adoption counseling through post-placement supervision), excluding legal fees connected with finalization. Children referred to the agency by the State of Texas Department of Human Services (usually older, special needs, or sibling groups) are placed at no charge to the adoptive family.

THE WAIT

The time from initial inquiry to the homecoming of the adoptive child averages 1 year. The wait varies depending on the children currently free for adoption, the applicant's readiness to move ahead, and available staff time.

THE CHILDREN

Children's Service Bureau places both healthy and special-needs children, ranging in age from birth to adolescence, of all racial backgrounds. Children placed by the agency are born in the U.S.

THE REQUIREMENTS

Age: Applicants must be at least 25 years of age. Maximum age limit varies depending on the age of the child being considered for placement.
Health: Applicants must be in reasonably good health.
Religion: No requirement.
Financial status: Applicants must demonstrate financial stability.
Marital status: Some options are available to single applicants.
Family size: No requirement.
Racial, ethnic or cultural origin: Preference for placing children in families of similar origins.

THE PROCEDURE

Participation in the Children's Service Bureau's adoption program entails the following basic steps:
Application
Orientation meeting
Individual counseling sessions
Homestudy
Placement
Post-placement supervision

ADDITIONAL PROGRAMS/SERVICES

Children's Service Bureau provides temporary residential group care for children in need of emergency shelter; foster care services; permanency planning services (birthparent counseling program).

BRANCH/NETWORK OFFICES

None.

LICENSE/ACCREDITATION/PROFESSIONAL AFFILIATIONS

Children's Service Bureau is licensed by the State of Texas Department of Human Services. The agency is a member of the United Way.

CHRISTIAN CHILD HELP FOUNDATION

4219 Richmond Avenue, Suite 100
Houston, TX 77027
(713) 850–9703
Program director: Michael D. Ross

THE PROGRAM

Christian Child Help Foundation (CCHF) is a nonprofit agency serving the Houston-Galveston metropolitan area and placing approximately 25–33 children annually. Founded in 1968 out of concern for neglected children, the agency provides a number of programs to help children and continues to develop innovative programs to meet the needs of the community. CCHF pioneered the use of community-based homes in Houston for emotionally disturbed children, pioneered techniques used statewide for assisting children through the Permanency Planning Project, and began the Spaulding for Children program (now a separate agency), providing specialized adoption services for handicapped and minority children. While the agency's focus is permanency planning (services to children who have been in foster care for an extended period of time), the agency also provides services to birthparents and places infants for adoption when birthparents in the agency's counseling program decide that the best interests of the child will be served by adoptive placement. In all of its programs, the agency is guided by the belief that "every child has a right to a permanent, loving Christian home."

THE COST

The agency's fee for adoption services is based on a sliding scale and ranges from $500 to $10,000. The fee structure is designed to meet actual program costs and to facilitate placement of special-needs children. Services covered by the fee include all phases of the adoption process (pre- adoption counseling through post-placement supervision), excluding legal fees connected with finalization of the adoption (approximately $400–$550).

THE WAIT

The time from application to the homecoming of the adoptive child varies depending on the type of child the applicants wish to parent and ranges from 1 month to 2 years.

THE CHILDREN

CCHF places both healthy and special-needs children and sibling groups, ranging in age from infancy to adolescence, of all racial backgrounds. Children placed by the agency may be American-born or immigrants.

THE REQUIREMENTS

Age: Applicants must be at least 21 and no more than 40 years older than the child to be adopted.

Health: Applicants must be in reasonably good health and must have a recommendation from a physician.

Religion: Applicants must be practicing members of a Christian congregation.

Financial status: Applicants are evaluated individually on the basis of their ability to manage financial resources.

Marital status: Applicants must be married couples. The length of the marriage must be at least 3 years.

Family size: No requirement, but may vary depending on agency's assessment of family dynamics and needs.

Racial, ethnic or cultural origin: Preference for placing children in families of similar origins.

THE PROCEDURE

Participation in CCHF's adoption program entails the following basic steps:
Telephone inquiry
Orientation meeting
Application
Homestudy
Placement
Post-placement supervision

ADDITIONAL PROGRAMS/SERVICES

CCHF provides services to birthparents; foster care services; individual and family counseling; workshops and seminars on a number of child welfare issues; publishes a quarterly newsletter (CCHF Update).

BRANCH/NETWORK OFFICES

None.

LICENSE/ACCREDITATION/PROFESSIONAL AFFILIATIONS

Christian Child Help Foundation is licensed by the State of Texas Department of Human Services.

THE EDNA GLADNEY CENTER

2300 Hemphill Street
Fort Worth, TX 76110
(817) 926–3304
Program director: Eleanor Tuck, Executive Director

THE PROGRAM

The Edna Gladney Center is a nonprofit agency primarily serving the states of Texas, Oklahoma, Louisiana, and Arkansas, with a limited number of placements in New York City with nearby Connecticut, New Jersey and Philadelphia areas included. Established in 1887 and chartered by the State of Texas as "The Texas Children's Home and Aid Society" in 1904, the agency's original purpose was to find permanent families for homeless children. Under the guidance of Mrs. Edna Gladney (superintendent from 1927–1960), the agency's focus shifted to provide maternity care for unwed mothers and placement services for birthmothers who elect adoptive placement as the best plan for their infants. While this continues to be the agency's focus, the agency also places a limited number of infants from Korea as well as older, special-needs children (aged 6–16). The Edna Gladney Center places approximately 250 U.S. infants, 25 Korean infants, and 60 older/special-needs children annually.

THE COST

The agency's fee for adoption services is based on a sliding scale and varies depending on the program. For infant adoption, the agency's fee ranges from $8,000 to $14,000, with an average of $10,000. Services covered by the fee include all phases of the adoption process (pre-placement counseling through post-placement supervision), excluding legal fees connected with finalization. Fees also help to underwrite the cost of services to birthmothers, including residential care, medical care, and educational programs. For Korean infant adoption, the average fee is $5,500. For special-needs adoptions, fees may be reduced or waived.

THE WAIT

For infant adoptions, applicants should anticipate waitlisting for 18 months to 2 1/2 years prior to formal application. The time from formal application to placement averages 1 year. For Korean infant adoption, the time from inquiry to placement averages 9 months to 1 year. For special-needs adoption, the time from inquiry to placement averages 6 months.

THE CHILDREN

The Edna Gladney Center places primarily healthy infants (3 to 6 months), of Caucasian, Black, and Hispanic backgrounds. The agency also places infants from Korea and special-needs children, ranging in age from 6 to 16 years, of all racial backgrounds.

THE REQUIREMENTS

Age: Applicants must be at least 24 and no more than 39 years of age. The requirement is flexible for older and special-needs children.

Health: Applicants must be in reasonably good health. Applicants with health problems or handicaps are given individual consideration. Infertility documentation is required for the adoption of a healthy Caucasian infant.

Religion: Applicants must have an affiliation with an organized religious faith.

Financial status: Applicants are evaluated individually on the basis of their ability to effectively utilize their financial resources.

Marital status: For infant adoption, applicants must be married couples, and the length of the marriage must be at least 3 years. A marriage of at least 2 years is desirable for those seeking to adopt a special-needs child. Single parents are considered for the placement of special-needs children.

Family size: For Caucasian infant adoptions, applicants may have no more than 1 child currently in the family. For Korean adoption, applicants may have no more than 4 children currently in the family. No requirement for older, special needs placements.

Racial, ethnic or cultural origin: Preference for placing children in families of similar origins. No requirement for Korean or for older, special needs placements.

THE PROCEDURE

Participation in The Edna Gladney Center's adoption program entails the following basic steps:

Inquiry and waitlisting
Orientation meeting
Application
Group and individual counseling sessions
Homestudy
Placement
Post-placement supervision

ADDITIONAL PROGRAMS/SERVICES

The Edna Gladney Center provides post-adoption services for birthparents, adoptive parents, and adult adoptees; workshops for auxiliary members (volunteer organizations); seminars on teen pregnancy; seminars on adoption counseling for professionals and volunteers. The agency sponsors 20 auxiliaries (volunteer organizations founded by adoptive parents and Center supporters) through which adoptive parents and couples seeking to adopt have an opportunity to meet.

BRANCH/NETWORK OFFICES

None.

LICENSE/ACCREDITATION/PROFESSIONAL AFFILIATIONS

The Edna Gladney Center is licensed by the State of Texas Department of Human Services and Department of Health and is accredited by the Joint Commission on Accreditation of Hospitals. The agency's affiliations with adoption organizations include the Texas Association Licensed Child Caring Services, Texas Foster Parent Association, Texas Council on Adoptable Children, National Conference on Social Welfare, Texas Committee for Adoption, National Committee for Adoption, and the National Association of Social Workers.

FAMILY JUNCTION—A CHILD PLACEMENT AGENCY

3317 Pecan Valley Drive
Temple, TX 76502
(817) 774–7332
Program director: Brenda A. Eckel

THE PROGRAM

Family Junction is a nonprofit agency serving residents of central Texas and placing 5–10 children annually. Family Junction provides extensive services to birthparents and places infants for adoption when birthparents in the agency's program decide that the best interests of the child will be served by adoptive placement. The agency promotes open adoption through the non-identifying exchange of information between birthparents and adoptive parents.

THE COST

The agency's fee for adoption services is based on a sliding scale and averages $6,500. Services covered by the fee include all phases of the adoption process (pre-adoption counseling through finalization of the adoption) as well as all medical and legal expenses of the birthmother and child. In some cases, applicants should anticipate partial responsibility for birthmother's living expenses (housing and utilities for a maximum of 3 months) prior to delivery.

THE WAIT

The time from application for acceptance into the program to the homecoming of the adoptive child averages 18 months.

THE CHILDREN

Family Junction places healthy infants, born in the U.S., of Caucasian and mixed racial backgrounds (Caucasian/Black, Caucasian/Hispanic, Caucasian/Asian).

THE REQUIREMENTS

Age: Applicants must be at least 25 and no more than 40 years of age. Requirement may vary depending on the applicant's health.

Health: Applicants must be in reasonably good health. Infertility documentation is required.

Religion: Applicants must be practicing members of a church.

Financial status: No requirement.

Marital status: If applicants are married, the length of the marriage must be at least 3 years for a first marriage and at least 5 years for a second marriage. Single applicants are accepted.

Family size: Applicants may have no more than 1 child currently in the family.

Racial, ethnic or cultural origin: Preference for placing children in families of similar origins. Requirement varies depending on the needs of the child and the ability of the adoptive family (and their extended family) to accept a child of another race.

THE PROCEDURE

Participation in Family Junction's adoption program entails the following basic steps:
Referral
Orientation meeting
Group counseling sessions
Application
Individual counseling sessions
Homestudy
Placement
Post-placement supervision
Finalization

ADDITIONAL PROGRAMS/SERVICES

Family Junction provides individual and group infertility counseling; group adoption counseling; birthparent counseling; foster care for birthmothers under 18 years of age and living arrangements for birthmothers over 18 years of age; referral services.

BRANCH/NETWORK OFFICES

None.

LICENSE/ACCREDITATION/PROFESSIONAL AFFILIATIONS

Family Junction is licensed by the State of Texas Department of Human Services.

GULF COAST PLACEMENT AGENCY, INC.

P.O. Box 1209
Alvin, TX 77512
(713) 331–2000/TX WATS
(800) 445–5269
Program director: Althea Ketchum, MSW, CSW-ACP

THE PROGRAM

Gulf Coast Placement Agency, Inc. is a nonprofit agency providing statewide services and placing approximately 50 children annually. The agency provides extensive services to birthparents (24–hour crisis services, counseling, housing, education, job training, and support services) and places infants for adoption when birthparents in the agency's program elect adoptive placement as the best plan for their child. Originally established to provide decentralized comprehensive services on a 24–hour basis, the agency is committed to the premise that "services should not be categorically denied to any person because of race, religion, age, marital status, size of family, or physical handicap" and that "each person is entitled to appropriate consideration of his or her unique abilities and needs."

THE COST

The agency's fee for adoption services ranges from $3,000 to $15,000. Services covered by the fee include all phases of the adoption process (pre-adoption counseling through post-placement services), excluding legal fees connected with finalization. Fees help to underwrite the cost of the agency's services to birthparents.

THE WAIT

The time from application for acceptance into the program to the homecoming of the adoptive child currently ranges from 3 months to 1 year.

THE CHILDREN

Gulf Coast Placement Agency places primarily healthy infants (but some older children as well), primarily of Caucasian but also of Black, Hispanic, and bi-racial backgrounds, born in the U.S.

THE REQUIREMENTS

Age: No categorical restrictions; requirement based on the needs of children served.
Health: No categorical restrictions; requirement based on the needs of children served.
Religion: No categorical restrictions; requirement based on the needs of children served.
Financial status: No categorical restrictions; requirement based on the needs of children served.
Marital status: No categorical restrictions; requirement based on the needs of children served.
Family size: No categorical restrictions; requirement based on the needs of children served.
Racial, ethnic or cultural origin: No categorical restrictions; requirement based on the needs of children served.

THE PROCEDURE

Participation in the Gulf Coast Placement Agency adoption program entails the following basic steps:
Inquiry
Orientation meeting
Application
Individual counseling sessions
Homestudy
Placement
Post-placement supervision and support services

ADDITIONAL PROGRAMS/SERVICES

Gulf Coast Placement Agency provides extensive services to birthparents; support services to adoptive parents; parent education groups; social activities; quarterly newsletter (The Beacon).

BRANCH/NETWORK OFFICES

All adoption inquiries are processed through the main office.

LICENSE/ACCREDITATION/PROFESSIONAL AFFILIATIONS

Gulf Coast Placement Agency is licensed by the State of Texas Department of Human Services.

LDS SOCIAL SERVICES

16333 Hafer Road
Houston, TX 77090
(713) 537–0211
Program director: Paul M. Ricks

THE PROGRAM

For a full description of programs and services, refer to Utah listing:

LDS Social Services
50 East North Temple Street
Salt Lake City, UT 84150

BRANCH OFFICES

LDS Social Services/Texas:
1100 W. Jackson Rd.
Carrollton, TX 75006
(214) 242–2182
Director: Gordon T. Foote

LEE & BEULAH MOOR CHILDREN'S HOME

1100 East Cliff Drive
El Paso, TX 79902
(915) 544–8777
Program director: Madge Watson, Executive Director; Cathy Dewey, MSW, CSW, Director of Adoptions

THE PROGRAM

Lee & Beulah Moor Children's Home is a nonprofit organization serving the El Paso area and placing between 13 and 25 children annually. Founded in 1959 as a facility for children who needed a place to live, the Home was a gift to the El Paso community from the late Lee Moor and continues to be privately funded through a trust. Serving children (infants through adolescents) of all racial, cultural, and religious backgrounds, the agency's original goal was "to provide a family setting for children with no home or for those who could not live with their families." The agency expanded in 1960 to provide adoption services and services to birthparents. The agency offers open adoption through the non-identifying exchange of information between birthparents and adoptive parents. Currently, the agency provides adoption services, an unplanned pregnancy program, foster family care, and ten residential group homes.

THE COST

The agency's fee for adoption services is based on a sliding scale and ranges from $150 to $7,000. Services covered by the fee include counseling, homestudy, placement, post-placement supervision, and post- adoption seminars. In addition, applicants should anticipate legal fees connected with finalization of the adoption (approximately $500).

THE WAIT

The time from application for acceptance into the program to the homecoming of the adoptive child ranges from 6 months to 18 months.

THE CHILDREN

The Children's Home places primarily healthy infants (birth to 1 year) of all racial backgrounds, born in the U.S.

THE REQUIREMENTS

Age: Applicants must be at least 21 and no more than 45 years of age.

Health: Applicants must be in reasonably good health. Applicants with health problems or handicaps are given individual consideration. Infertility documentation is required.

Religion: Applicants must be practicing members of a religion.

Financial status: No requirement.

Marital status: Applicants must be married couples (birthmother's preference). The length of the marriage must be at least 2 years for a first marriage and at least 3 years for a second marriage.

Residence: Applicants must reside in the El Paso geographical area.

Family size: No requirement.

Racial, ethnic or cultural origin: Preference for placing children in families of similar origins.

THE PROCEDURE

Participation in the Children's Home adoption program entails the following basic steps:
Application
Orientation meeting
Homestudy
Placement
Post-placement supervision

ADDITIONAL PROGRAMS/SERVICES

The agency provides a continuing education program (professional speakers on child rearing and adoption issues); post-adoption services; adoption registry (adult adoptees register to meet their birthparents).

BRANCH/NETWORK OFFICES

None.

LICENSE/ACCREDITATION/PROFESSIONAL AFFILIATIONS

Lee & Beulah Moor Children's Home is licensed by the State of Texas Department of Human Services. The agency's professional affiliations include the National Association of Homes for Children, Texas Association of Licensed Children's Services, and Southwest Childcare Association.

LIFE ANEW, INC.

2635 Loop 286 N.E.
Paris, TX 75460
(214) 785–7410
Program director: Sharon S. Schneider, Program Director; Pamela Russell, ACSW, CSW-ACP, Executive Director

THE PROGRAM

Life Anew, Inc. is a nonprofit agency serving residents of the state of Texas and some out-of-state applicants as well. Licensed in August, 1985, Life Anew is guided by the conviction that "every child deserves to find a loving family." The agency provides services to birthparents and places infants for adoption when birthparents in the agency's counseling program decide that the best interests of the child will be served by adoptive placement. The agency also places a limited number of older children in the state of Texas. The agency is particularly interested in working with Black couples or single women who wish to adopt bi-racial infants. In addition, the agency will provide homestudy and supervisory services for local residents pursuing foreign adoption.

THE COST

The agency's fee for adoption services is based on a sliding scale and ranges from $6,000 to $12,000. Services covered by the fee include application, adoption seminar, homestudy, placement, and post-placement supervision. The fee also helps to underwrite the cost of medical and related services to the birthparents and child. In addition, applicants assume responsibility for legal fees connected with finalization of the adoption (approximately $500) as well as travel expenses.

THE WAIT

The time from application to acceptance into the program is approximately 3 months. The time from acceptance to completion of the homestudy depends on the family's flexibility and may take as long as 1 year. The agency's goal from completion of the homestudy to placement is within 12 months.

THE CHILDREN

Life Anew places primarily healthy infants but also some special-needs children (up to 18 years of age) of all racial backgrounds, born in the U.S. In addition, the agency will provide homestudy and supervisory services for local applicants pursuing foreign adoption.

THE REQUIREMENTS

Age: Applicants must be at least 25 and no more than 42 years of age. The requirement may vary for special-needs adoptions.
Health: Applicants must be in reasonably good health.
Religion: Denominational preference is open.
Financial status: Applicants must be financially stable.
Marital status: If married, the length of the marriage must be at least 2 years. Single applicants are considered for hard-to-place children.
Family size: The requirement varies depending on the flexibility and the individual needs of the family.
Racial, ethnic or cultural origin: Applicants of all racial, ethnic, and cultural backgrounds are served.

THE PROCEDURE

Participation in Life Anew's adoption program entails the following basic steps:
Adoption seminar
Application
Homestudy
Placement
Post-placement supervision
Finalization

ADDITIONAL PROGRAMS/SERVICES

Life Anew provides services for birthmothers (including housing, educational/vocational opportunities, scholarship resources, medical/dental care, and extensive professional counseling). Counseling is also available for birthfathers and birthfamilies as needed.

BRANCH/NETWORK OFFICES

None.

LICENSE/ACCREDITATION/PROFESSIONAL AFFILIATIONS

Life Anew, Inc. is licensed by the State of Texas Department of Human Services.

LOS NINOS INTERNATIONAL ADOPTION CENTER (LNI)

1110 W. William Cannon, Suite 504
Austin, TX 78745–5460
(512) 443–2833
Program director: Jean Nelson-Erichsen, President and Supervisor of Social Work

THE PROGRAM

Los Ninos International (LNI) is a nonprofit agency providing statewide service for domestic adoptions, nationwide service for international adoptions, and placing approximately 120 children annually. LNI was founded by Jean and Heino Erichsen who "parent-initiated" the adoption of their daughters in South America in 1972 and who then worked as volunteers for OURS and several adoption agencies to assist families in the successful completion of adoption of children from many countries. Licensed as an adoption agency in Texas since 1982, LNI works with private and public state-approved sources to process the placement of foreign-born children in American families. LNI also provides services to birthparents and places domestic infants for adoption when birthparents in the agency's counseling program decide that the best interests of the child will be served by adoptive placement. In addition, the agency will provide homestudy and supervisory services for applicants pursuing interstate, international, or private adoption.

THE COST

The agency's fee for adoption services varies depending on the program. For Texas-born children, the fee is $8,600. The fees help to underwrite the cost of services to birthparents (medical, legal, and counseling) and services to the infant (medical and foster care).

The program fee for international adoptions ranges from $3,000 to $5,500. This fee includes international source fees; medical, foster care, and legal fees in the child's country of origin, and documents required for the child's U.S. Visa. In addition, applicants pursuing international adoption should anticipate an international processing fee, travel expenses (including hotel and meals for 1–4 weeks depending on the country), U.S. agency fees (for homestudy and supervisory services), legal fees connected with finalization, and immigration/naturalization fees.

THE WAIT

The time from the acceptance of a formal dossier for a program to the homecoming of the adoptive child ranges from 12 to 18 months.

THE CHILDREN

LNI places both healthy and special-needs children, ranging in age from birth to 15 years, of Hispanic, Asian, Black, and bi-racial backgrounds. Countries of origin are subject to change but currently include Bolivia, Chile, Colombia, Costa Rica, Ecuador, El Salvador, Guatemala, Honduras, Panama, Paraguay, Peoples Republic of China, Peru, Taiwan, and U.S. Programs in Japan, the Philippines, and Thailand are pending approval.

THE REQUIREMENTS

Age: Applicants must be at least 25 and no more than 55 years of age.
Health: Applicants with health problems or handicaps are given individual consideration.
Religion: No requirement.
Financial status: No requirement.
Marital status: Applicants may be couples with a formal marriage of 1 year or an informal marriage of 1 year, validated by a Declaration of Informal Marriage from the Courthouse.
Family size: No requirement.
Racial, ethnic or cultural origin: No requirement.

THE PROCEDURE

Participation in Los Ninos' adoption program entails the following basic steps:
  Orientation meeting
  Application
  Individual homestudy
  Submission of supporting documents
  Completion and approval of homestudy
  Compliance with immigration requirements
  Selection of adoption source and preparation of dossier of
    originals for court
  Referral
  Travel
  Obtain custody and U.S. Visa for child
  Post-placement supervision
  Finalization
  Citizenship or naturalization

ADDITIONAL PROGRAMS/SERVICES

LNI conducts adoption seminars every other month; provides short-term foster care for children; provides counseling for adoptive parents and birthparents; sponsors Amigos de los Ninos (adoptive parent support group led by volunteers in many major cities); publishes a monthly newsletter (News of Los Ninos), How to Adopt from Asia, Europe and the South Pacific, and How to Adopt from Latin America (available through the agency). In addition, the founders of LNI, Jean and Heino Erichsen, are the authors of Gamines: How to Adopt from Latin America, Dillon Press, 1982, the definitive work on Latin American adoptions, and both hold masters degrees in Human Development with specialization in international adoption sources and procedures.

BRANCH/NETWORK OFFICES

Current program information, registration, and initiation of pre- and post-placement services are provided by the main office in Austin. LNI social workers are available for homestudy and supervisory services in the following cities in Texas: Dallas/Ft. Worth, El Paso, Houston, Livingston, McAllen, Midland/Odessa, San Antonio/San Marcos.

LNI works with a network of agencies in 38 states who provide homestudy and supervisory services for out-of-state applicants pursuing international adoption through LNI. Contact LNI for a complete list of networking agencies.

LNI maintains overseas offices in Santiago, Chile; Kobe, Japan; Tokyo, Japan; Panama City, Panama.

LICENSE/ACCREDITATION/PROFESSIONAL AFFILIATIONS

Los Ninos International Adoption Center is licensed by the State of Texas Department of Human Services. LNI is a member of North American Council on Adoptable Children (NACAC), Council on Adoptable Children (COAC), International Concerns Committee for Children (ICCC), and OURS.

METHODIST HOME

1111 Herring Avenue
Waco, TX 76708
(817) 753–0181
Program director: Bobby Gilliam

THE PROGRAM

Methodist Home is a nonprofit multi-service agency serving residents of Texas and New Mexico and placing approximately 12 to 18 children annually through its adoption program. The agency's mission is to facilitate "normal growth and development with the goal of enabling children and their families to enhance their wholeness and freedom in order to achieve and to become more productive individuals of greater dignity and worth." The agency's adoption program was designed as an adjunct to the foster care program to provide adoption as a permanent resource for the child who cannot return to his or her family of origin. Typically, the placement originates as a foster placement which becomes an adoptive placement, if this is elected as the appropriate plan for the child.

THE COST

As of October 1988, the agency's fee for adoption services is based on a sliding scale with an average cost of $3,000. Services covered by the fee include all phases of the adoption process.

THE WAIT

The wait varies depending on the number of children currently in need of adoptive families.

THE CHILDREN

Methodist Home places both healthy and special-needs children, 2 years of age and older, of all racial backgrounds, born in the U.S.

The Requirements

Age: The requirement varies depending on the age of the child being considered for placement.

Health: Applicants must be in reasonably good health.

Religion: Applicants must be practicing members of the Christian faith.

Financial status: Applicants must have sufficient income to provide for an additional family member.

Marital status: Applicants must be married; the length of the marriage must be at least 3 years.

Family size: No requirement.

Racial, ethnic or cultural origin: No requirement.

The Procedure

Methodist Home adoptive placements originate as foster placements which become adoptive placements when the child's need for permanency is best served by the adoption plan. Consequently, applicants who wish to adopt through Methodist Home begin as licensed foster parents who may then become adoptive parents. The adoption procedure entails the following basic steps:

Application
Orientation meeting
Homestudy
Placement
Post-placement supervision

Additional Programs/Services

Methodist Home provides foster care and counseling services.

Branch/Network Offices:

4801 S. Austin
Amarillo, TX 79110
(806) 358–7095

1501 University
Lubbock, TX 79401
(806) 762–0130

P.O. Box 12186
4024 Caruth
Dallas, TX 75225
(214) 692–1361

3409 Mulberry
Houston, TX 77006
(713) 523–8534

1800 San Pedro, Suite 202
San Antonio, TX 78212
(512) 733–3904

8100 Mountain N.E., Suite 112
Albuquerque, NM 87110
(505) 255–8740

License/Accreditation/Professional Affiliations

Methodist Home is licensed by the State of Texas Department of Human Services and is accredited by the Council on Accreditation of Services for Families and Children. The agency is a member of the Child Welfare League of America.

NEW LIFE CHILDREN'S SERVICES

19911 Tomball Parkway (FM 149)
Houston, TX 77070
(713) 955–1001
Program director: Sara C. Black, MSW

The Program

New Life Children's Services is a nonprofit organization designed "to provide spiritual guidance, support and care for pregnant unwed mothers." Serving residents of the state of Texas, the agency provides shepherding homes, group and individual counseling, and childbirth classes for the unwed mothers in its program. The agency places infants for adoption when birthmothers in the agency's program decide that the best interests of their children will be served by adoptive placement. Each birthmother participates in the choosing of the adoptive family for her child. New Life Children's Services places approximately 20 children annually in two-parent Christian families.

The Cost

The agency's fee for adoption services is $9,000. Services covered by the fee include all phases of the adoption process (pre-adoption counseling through post-placement supervision), excluding legal fees connected with finalization of the adoption. Fees help to underwrite the cost of services to birthmothers.

The Wait

The time from application for acceptance into the program to the homecoming of the adoptive child ranges from 3 months to 1 1/2 years.

The Children

New Life Children's Services places primarily healthy, Caucasian infants, born in the U.S.

The Requirements

Age: Applicants must be at least 21 and no more than 39 years of age. Exceptions are made for the placement of special-needs infants.

Health: Applicants must be in reasonably good health. The agency requires medical reports indicating that all family members are in good health.

Religion: Applicants must be practicing Christians and must recognize Jesus Christ as Lord and Savior.

Financial status: Applicants must demonstrate financial stability and sufficient income to raise a child. A financial report is required.

Marital status: Applicants must be married couples. The length of the marriage must be at least 3 years.

Family size: The requirement is based on individual evaluation if the adoptive family has more than 1 child.

Racial, ethnic or cultural origin: The agency accepts applicants of all racial backgrounds.

The Procedure

Participation in New Life Children's Services' adoption program entails the following basic steps:

Telephone inquiry
Pre-adoption counseling
Application
Homestudy
Approval of homestudy
Waiting period
Placement
Post-placement supervision

ADDITIONAL PROGRAMS/SERVICES

New Life Children's Services provides extensive counseling services, residential care, and childbirth preparation for unwed mothers.

BRANCH/NETWORK OFFICES

None.

LICENSE/ACCREDITATION/PROFESSIONAL AFFILIATIONS

New Life Children's Services is licensed by the State of Texas Department of Human Services.

PRESBYTERIAN CHILDREN'S HOME AND SERVICE AGENCY

400 South Zang, Suite 1210
Dallas, TX 75208
(214) 942–8674
Program director: Bettie D. O'Brien, ACSW, CSW-ACP

THE PROGRAM

Presbyterian Children's Home and Service Agency (PCHSA) is a non-profit agency serving residents of the state of Texas and placing approximately 15 children annually. Since the inception of the adoption program in 1953, the agency's focus has been the placement of older, minority, and special-needs children and sibling groups. The agency's purpose is "to provide a variety of Christ-centered child care services which minister to the spiritual, physical, intellectual, emotional, and social needs of dependent, neglected and disturbed children and youth, together with their families."

THE COST

The agency's fee for adoption services is 10% of the applicants' combined annual gross income, not to exceed $6,000. Services covered by the fee include all phases of the adoption process (pre-adoption counseling through post-placement supervision), excluding legal fees connected with finalization of the adoption. In addition, out-of-area families should anticipate expenses related to coming to Dallas for a 1 1/2 day orientation seminar prior to homestudy.

THE WAIT

The time from application for acceptance into the program to the homecoming of the adoptive child averages 2 years.

THE CHILDREN

Presbyterian Children's Home & Service Agency places both healthy and special-needs children, 4 years old and older, of Caucasian, Black, Hispanic, and bi-racial backgrounds, born in the U.S.

THE REQUIREMENTS

Age: Applicants must be at least 25 and no more than 50 years of age.
Health: Applicants must be in reasonably good health. Applicants with health problems or handicaps are given individual consideration.
Religion: Applicants must be practicing members of a Christian church.
Financial status: Applicants must submit financial statement and previous year's IRS 1040 to demonstrate ability to provide for additional family member.
Marital status: For married applicants, the length of the marriage must be at least 3 years. Single applicants are accepted.
Family size: No requirement.
Racial, ethnic or cultural origin: Preference for placing children in families of similar origins.

THE PROCEDURE

Participation in PCHSA's adoption program entails the following basic steps:
Application
Orientation meeting
Group counseling sessions
Individual counseling sessions
Homestudy
Placement and placement ceremony
Post-placement supervision (6 months)
Court reports for finalization

ADDITIONAL PROGRAMS/SERVICES

PCHSA provides foster care services; post-adoption counseling for adoptees and their families; workshops on legal aspects of adoption and on adopting the sexually abused child.

BRANCH/NETWORK OFFICES

8000 Centre Park Dr., Suite 300
Austin, TX 78754
(512) 339–8888

LICENSE/ACCREDITATION/PROFESSIONAL AFFILIATIONS

Presbyterian Children's Home and Service Agency is licensed by the State of Texas Department of Human Services.

QUALITY OF LIFE, INC.

P.O. Box 781382
Dallas, TX 75378–13
(214) 350–1637
Program director: Dolores Delgadillo, ACSW, CSW-ACP

THE PROGRAM

Quality of Life is a nonprofit agency providing statewide service and placing approximately 5–12 children annually.

An out-growth of the pro-life movement, the agency's mission is to provide "a continuum of care from pregnancy to responsible parenting." The agency provides services to birthparents and places infants for adoption when birthparents in the agency's program decide that the best interests of the child will be served by adoptive placement. The agency also provides homestudies and post-placement supervision for applicants pursuing adoption through international programs.

THE COST

The agency's fee for adoption services is based on a sliding scale and ranges from no fee to approximately $12,000. Services covered by the fee include pre-adoption counseling, homestudy, placement, and supervisory services. In addition, fees help to underwrite the cost of legal, medical, and counseling services to birthparents and child. Applicants assume responsibility for legal fees connected with finalization of the adoption (approximately $450).

THE WAIT

The time from application for acceptance into the program to the homecoming of the adoptive child ranges from 2 months to 2 years.

THE CHILDREN

Quality of Life places primarily healthy infants (birth to 1 year) of all racial backgrounds, born in the U.S. Working cooperatively with out-of-state child placing agencies, Quality of Life facilitates the placement of children from South America and the Philippines through provision of homestudy and supervisory services.

THE REQUIREMENTS

Age: Applicants must be at least 25 and no more than 45 years of age.
Health: Applicants with health problems or handicaps are given individual consideration. Infertility studies are required for infant adoptions.
Religion: No requirement.
Financial status: No requirement.
Marital status: Applicants must be married couples.
Family size: No requirement.
Racial, ethnic or cultural origin: No requirement.

THE PROCEDURE

Participation in Quality of Life's adoption program entails the following basic steps:
Orientation meeting
Application
Homestudy
Individual counseling sessions
Family life enrichment sessions (in-home)
Compliance with immigration/naturalization requirements (international adoptions only)
Placement
Post-placement supervision

ADDITIONAL PROGRAMS/SERVICES

Quality of Life provides workshops, seminars, and counseling services, in conjunction with community resources.

BRANCH/NETWORK OFFICES

None.

LICENSE/ACCREDITATION/PROFESSIONAL AFFILIATIONS

Quality of Life, Inc. is licensed by the State of Texas Department of Human Services and is a member of the Interagency Adoption Council.

SMITHLAWN MATERNITY HOME AND ADOPTION AGENCY

P.O. Box 6451
Lubbock, TX 79493–6451(806) 745–2574
Program director: Howard Hulett, ACSW, CSW-ACP

THE PROGRAM

Smithlawn Maternity Home and Adoption Agency is a nonprofit organization serving primarily Texas but also residents of other states and placing approximately 80–100 children annually. Founded in 1960 as a ministry of the Smithlawn Church of Christ, the organization's original focus was to minister to unmarried expectant mothers, providing counseling and residential services and striving "to enhance each bio-parent's feeling of self-worth." Smithlawn became a licensed child placing agency in 1968, thereby extending its services to infants and adoptive couples. Smithlawn places infants for adoption when birthmothers in the agency's program decide that the best interests of the child will be served by adoptive placement. Smithlawn continues to practice confidential adoption. However, birthparents and adoptive parents know pertinent (but non-identifying) information about each other.

THE COST

The agency's collection for adoption services is $7,000. Services covered by the fee include homestudy, placement, and post-placement supervision. In addition, applicants assume responsibility for travel expenses and legal fees connected with placement and finalization of the adoption. This collection is approximately half of the actual cost per infant. The balance is subsidized by contributions from churches, individuals, and foundations.

THE WAIT

The time from application for acceptance into the program to the homecoming of the adoptive child ranges from 6 to 12 months.

THE CHILDREN

Smithlawn places healthy infants (2 days to 2 months old) of all racial backgrounds. In most instances, infants are placed directly from the maternity home.

THE REQUIREMENTS

Age: Applicants must be at least 25 and no more than 44 years of age. The requirement is somewhat flexible.
Health: Applicants must be in reasonably good health.

Religion: Preference is given to members of the Church of Christ. The requirement may vary depending on the birthmother's religious affiliation.

Financial status: Applicants must demonstrate financial stability.

Marital status: Applicants must be married couples. Exceptions are made for babies with special needs.

Family size: No requirement.

Racial, ethnic or cultural origin: Smithlawn places children of all races, and applicants of all races are accepted. Smithlawn tries to find the best possible home for each child.

THE PROCEDURE

Participation in Smithlawn's adoption program entails the following basic steps:
Application
Orientation meeting
Homestudy
Approval of homestudy by screening committeePlacement
Post-placement supervision
Finalization

ADDITIONAL PROGRAMS/SERVICES

Smithlawn conducts seminars for prospective adoptive parents, provides post-legal adoption services, and sponsors Council of Adoptive Parents (a support group).

BRANCH/NETWORK OFFICES

Marla Pollan
Dallas, TX
(214) 467–6051

Gwen Gooch
Temple, TX
(817) 778–0898

Vicki Broom
San Antonio, TX
(512) 647–0325

Brenda Cothran
Houston, TX
(713) 476–0856

LICENSE/ACCREDITATION/PROFESSIONAL AFFILIATIONS

Smithlawn Maternity Home is licensed by the State of Texas Department of Health; Smithlawn Adoption Agency is licensed by the State of Texas Department of Human Services. All social work staff are certified by the State of Texas Department of Human Services. Smithlawn is affiliated with the Texas Association of Licensed Children's Services, National Association of Social Workers, National Committee For Adoption, Christian Adoption Resource Exchange, Christian Child Care Conference, and Texas Committee for Adoption.

SOUTHWEST MATERNITY CENTER

Methodist Mission Home
6487 Whitby Road
San Antonio, TX 78240
(512) 696–7021
1–800–292–5103 (toll free in Texas)
1–800–255–9612 (toll free, states other than Texas)
Program director: Bryce Hatch

THE PROGRAM

Southwest Maternity Center is a nonprofit agency serving residents of Texas, New Mexico, Colorado, and Louisiana and placing approximately 80 children annually through its adoption program. Founded in 1895, the agency has placed over 5,000 infants in permanent adoptive families. The agency provides services to birthparents and places both healthy and special-needs infants for adoption when birthparents elect adoptive placement as the best plan for their child. The agency began "openness practices in adoption" in 1982 and organized post-adoption services (including updated, non-identifying social medical histories and assistance with search and reunion) in 1986.

THE COST

The agency's fee for adoption services is $10,650. Services covered by the fee include all phases of the adoption process (services to birthparents as well as services to adoptive parents), excluding legal fees connected with finalization of the adoption. In addition, applicants should anticipate responsibility for travel expenses to and from the agency for educational meetings, interviews, placement, and finalization.

THE WAIT

The time from application for acceptance into the program to the homecoming of the adoptive child ranges from 14 to 24 months.

THE CHILDREN

Southwest Maternity Center places both healthy and special-needs infants (birth to 3 months), of Caucasian, Black, Hispanic, and bi-racial backgrounds, born in the U.S.

THE REQUIREMENTS

Age: For the adoption of a first child, applicants must be at least 24 and no more than 42 years of age.

Health: Applicants should be in reasonably good health.

Religion: Applicants must be practicing members of a main-line religious organization or church.

Financial status: Applicants must demonstrate financial responsibility and must have sufficient income to support an additional family member.

Marital status: Applicants must be married; the length of the marriage must be at least 3 years.

Family size: Applicants may have no more than 1 child currently in the family.

Racial, ethnic or cultural origin: Preference for placing children in families of similar origins.

THE PROCEDURE

Participation in the adoption program of Southwest Maternity Center entails the following basic steps:
Preliminary information form
Orientation meeting
Submission of clergy reference
Application
Group counseling sessions
Individual counseling sessions
Home visit
Approval and fee commitment
Placement
Post-placement supervision

ADDITIONAL PROGRAMS/SERVICES

Southwest Maternity Center provides a support group for adoptive families (MAPLE, Inc.) which sponsors annual seminars, post-relinquishment support groups for birthparents, foster care, and training for foster parents.

BRANCH/NETWORK OFFICES

Southwest Maternity Center maintains field workers throughout the state of Texas and in Colorado and Louisiana. Adoption inquiries are processed through the main office in San Antonio.

LICENSE/ACCREDITATION/PROFESSIONAL AFFILIATIONS

Southwest Maternity Center, Methodist Mission Home is licensed by the State of Texas Department of Human Services and by the State of Colorado Department of Social Services. The agency is a member of San Antonio Adoption Council and Texas Association of Licensed Children's Services.

SPAULDING FOR CHILDREN

4219 Richmond, Suite 100
Houston, TX 77027
(713) 850–9707
Program director: Kitty Clement

THE PROGRAM

Spaulding for Children is a nonprofit agency serving the greater Houston area and placing approximately 30 children annually. Founded in 1977 as Spaulding Southwest, a division of Christian Child Help Foundation, and funded by the Edna McConnell Clark Foundation, the agency became a separate legal entity in April, 1980, and in 1983 the name of the agency was changed to Spaulding for Children. The agency is committed to "finding permanent, caring families for children with special needs."

THE COST

Adoption services are provided at no cost to adoptive parents. The only fees which adoptive parents should anticipate are legal fees connected with finalization of the adoption.

THE WAIT

The time form application to the homecoming of the adoptive child ranges from 2 to 12 months.

THE CHILDREN

Spaulding for Children places special-needs children, ranging in age from 2 to 17 years of all racial backgrounds, born in the U.S.

THE REQUIREMENTS

Age: No requirement.
Health: Applicants must be in reasonably good health. Applicants with health problems or handicaps are given individual consideration.
Religion: No requirement.
Financial status: No requirement
Family size: No requirement.
Racial, ethnic or cultural origin: Preference for placing children in families of similar origins.

THE PROCEDURE

Participation in the Spaulding for Children adoption program entails the following basic steps:
Intake interview
Application
Homestudy (including individual counseling sessions)
Group counseling sessions (may be concurrent or prior to homestudy)
Pre-placement visits
Placement
Post-placement supervision and services

ADDITIONAL PROGRAMS/SERVICES

Spaulding for Children provides workshops and seminars on issues related to special-needs adoption and offers post-placement counseling.

BRANCH/NETWORK OFFICES

None.

LICENSE/ACCREDITATION/PROFESSIONAL AFFILIATIONS

Spaulding for Children is licensed by the State of Texas Department of Human Services and is a member of Family Builders, Inc.

THE TEXAS CRADLE SOCIETY

221 W. Poplar
San Antonio, TX 78212
(512) 225–5151
Program director: Dorothy Barkley, ACSW

THE PROGRAM

The Texas Cradle Society is a nonprofit agency providing services to residents of Texas for healthy domestic infant adoptions and nationwide services for special-needs adoptions. Founded in 1936 by Mrs. Jennie Furlow, the agency's mission is "to promote the welfare of children, birthparents and adoptive families through its maternity option counseling program, its adoptive placement program, and its post adoption services program." Since its founding, the agency has served thousands of children by providing care and counseling for birthmothers and, if desired, adoptive placement planning for their children. The agency annually places approximately 30 children. In addition, the agency will provide homestudy and supervisory services for applicants pursuing interagency adoption (domestic or international) or private adoption.

THE COST

The agency's fee for adoption services is based on a sliding scale and ranges from $7,000 to $10,000. Services covered by the fee include all phases of the adoption process, excluding legal fees connected with finalization of the adoption ($500 to $600).

THE WAIT

The time from application for acceptance into the program to the homecoming of the adoptive child ranges from 1 to 3 years.

THE CHILDREN

The Texas Cradle Society places both healthy and special-needs infants, of Hispanic, Black, Caucasian, and bi-racial backgrounds, born in the U.S.

THE REQUIREMENTS

Age: For first child placement, applicants must be at least 25 and no more than 38 years of age. For second child placement, the maximum age is 43. Exceptions may be made for special-needs infants.

Health: Applicants should be in reasonably good health. Infertility documentation is required.

Religion: No requirement.

Financial status: Applicants must demonstrate financial stability.

Marital status: Applicants must be married; the length of the marriage must be at least 3 years.

Family size: Applicants may have no more than 1 child currently in the family.

Racial, ethnic or cultural origin: No requirement.

THE PROCEDURE

Participation in the adoption program of The Texas Cradle Society entails the following basic steps:
Pre-application inquiry form
Orientation meeting
Application
Individual interview
Joint interviews
Homestudy
Placement
Post-placement supervision

ADDITIONAL PROGRAMS/SERVICES

The Texas Cradle Society provides birthmothers option counseling and foster care for infants pending placement. The Society sponsors The Post Adoption Center of the Southwest which provides adoption education workshops, post-adoptive parent education seminars, latency-age adoptee workshops, and post-adoptive counseling for all members of the adoption triad.

BRANCH/NETWORK OFFICES

None.

LICENSE/ACCREDITATION/PROFESSIONAL AFFILIATIONS

The Texas Cradle Society is licensed by the State of Texas Department of Human Services and by the State of New Jersey Department of Human Services. the agency is a member of the National Committee For Adoption and the San Antonio Adoption Council.

Utah

PUBLIC ADOPTION PROGRAM/ COMMUNITY RESOURCES

Department of Social Services Adoptions Unit
2835 South Main Street
P.O. Box 15729
Salt Lake City, UT 84115
(801) 487–8000
Adoption specialist: Mary Lines

THE PROGRAM

Public adoption services in Utah are provided by Department of Social Services through Family Services branch offices located throughout the state. The focus of the Department of Social Services adoption program is to recruit, prepare, supervise, and support families interested in adopting special-needs children (older, minority, and handicapped children and sibling groups) who are in the custody of the State of Utah.

STATE EXCHANGE

None.

STATE ADOPTION REUNION REGISTRY

Adoption Reunion Registry
Department of Health
Vital Statistics
288 N. 1460 W.
Salt Lake City, UT
(801) 538–6105

STATE SUBSIDY

For information, contact the Department of Social Services (above).

NACAC REPRESENTATIVE

Suzanna Stott
1219 South Windsor
Salt Lake City, UT 84105
(801) 487–3916

GENERAL ADOPTION RESOURCES

Families Involved in Adoption
P.O. Box 16477
Salt Lake City, UT 84116

H.O.P.E. of Utah Inc.
P.O. Box 1146
Provo, UT 84601

Families of Adopted Children Together
P.O. Box 9162
Ogden, UT 84409

Adoptive Support Group of Utah
2835 S. Main
Salt Lake City, UT 84115

SPECIAL-NEEDS ADOPTION RESOURCES

For information on special-needs resources, contact the Department of Social Services (above).

OUT-OF-STATE AGENCIES

AGENCY

Smithlawn Maternity Home, Texas (special-needs and minority placements)

SEE APPENDIX A

Agencies Providing Nationwide Services

ADOPTION SERVICES OF WACAP

2290 E. 4500 South
Salt Lake City, UT 84117
(801) 272–8459
Program director: Janice Neilson, Executive Director

THE PROGRAM

For a full description of programs and services, refer to Washington listing:

Adoption Services of WACAP
P.O. Box 88948
Seattle, WA 98138
(206) 575–4550

CHILDREN'S AID SOCIETY OF UTAH

652 26th Street
Ogden, UT 84401
(801) 393–8671
Program director: Colleen R. Burnham

THE PROGRAM

Children's Aid Society of Utah is a nonprofit, non-denominational agency providing statewide services and placing approximately 25 to 30 children annually through its adoption program. Organized by a group of concerned Ogden women in 1910, Children's Aid Society's mission is "to foster and promote the welfare and happiness of children in the State of Utah and the welfare of the family unit in society." The agency provides extensive counseling and support services to both relinquishing and non-relinquishing birthparents. Healthy and special-needs infants are placed for adoption when birthparents elect adoptive placement as the best plan for their child. Birthparents are given the opportunity to participate in the selection of the adoptive family through the review of non-identifying information about prospective families. Working directly with sources in Guatemala, Children's Aid Society places several Guatemalan children annually in Utah families. In addition, the agency will provide homestudy and supervisory services for applicants pursuing interagency adoption (domestic or international) or private adoption.

THE COST

As of October 1988, the agency's fee for adoption services is 15% of the applicants' annual gross income for the previous year, with a minimum fee of $4,000. Services covered by the fee include all phases of the adoption process, excluding legal fees connected with finalization of the adoption.

THE WAIT

The time from application to placement ranges from 1 to 2 1/2 years.

THE CHILDREN

Children's Aid Society places both healthy and special-needs children (but primarily infants), of all racial backgrounds. Countries of origin include the U.S., Guatemala, and others on request through cooperating agencies.

THE REQUIREMENTS

Age: For infant adoption, applicants must be at least 23 and no more than 38 years of age. The requirement varies depending on the age of the child being considered for placement.

Health: Applicants must be in reasonably good health. Applicants with health problems or handicaps are given individual consideration. Infertility documentation is required for infant adoption.

Religion: No requirement.

Financial status: Applicants must have sufficient income to afford the cost of the adoption and to provide for an additional family member.

Marital status: Applicants must be married. The length of the marriage must be at least 2 1/2 years.*Family size*: Applicants may have no more than 1 child currently in the family.

Racial, ethnic or cultural origin: No requirement, but preference for placing children in families of similar origins. The requirement varies depending on the availability of ethnically and culturally relevant families.

THE PROCEDURE

Participation in the adoption program of Children's Aid Society of Utah entails the following basic steps:
Orientation meeting
Application
Parenting seminar
Homestudy
Individual counseling sessions
Compliance with immigration/naturalization requirements (international adoptions only)
Placement
Post-placement supervision

ADDITIONAL PROGRAMS/SERVICES

Children's Aid Society provides a range of services including parenting programs and parenting support services for adoptive parents and for birthparents who elect to parent their children; children's developmental group; counseling services.

BRANCH/NETWORK OFFICES

2520 S. State, Suite 117
Salt Lake City, UT 84115
(801) 533–5558

15 W. 400 North
Provo, UT 84601
(801) 374–2135

LICENSE/ACCREDITATION/PROFESSIONAL AFFILIATIONS

Children's Aid Society of Utah is licensed by the State of Utah Department of Social Services. The agency is a member of the Utah Adoption Council and the Child Welfare League of America.

CHILDREN'S HOUSE INTERNATIONAL

P.O. Box 2321, 3614 Hillside Lane
Salt Lake City, Utah 84109
(801) 272–4822
Program director: Ric Oddone

THE PROGRAM

Children's House International is a nonprofit agency serving western Utah and placing approximately 12–15 children annually. For the past 14 years, the agency has worked with private and public state-approved sources to place children from India with American Christian families.

THE COST

The agency's fee for adoption services is $5,000. The fee covers all phases of the adoption process (pre-adoption counseling through post- placement supervision, excluding legal fees connected with finalization of the adoption), source agency fees, and transportation costs.

THE WAIT

The time from application for acceptance into the program to the homecoming of the adoptive child ranges from 9 to 14 months.

THE CHILDREN

Children's House International places healthy infants (4–11 months), born in India.

THE REQUIREMENTS

Age: Applicants must be at least 21 and no more than 40 years of age.

Health: Applicants must be in reasonably good health. Infertility documentation is required.

Religion: Applicants must be practicing members of a Christian faith.

Financial status: No requirement.

Marital status: Applicants must be married couples.

Family size: Applicants must be childless.

Racial, ethnic or cultural origin: No requirement.

THE PROCEDURE

Participation in Children's House International adoption program entails the following basic steps:
Application
Orientation meeting

Individual counseling sessions
Group counseling sessions
Homestudy
Compliance with immigration/naturalization requirements
Placement
Post-placement supervision

ADDITIONAL PROGRAMS/SERVICES

None.

BRANCH/NETWORK OFFICES

None.

LICENSE/ACCREDITATION/PROFESSIONAL AFFILIATIONS

Children's House International is licensed by the State of Utah Department of Social Services.

CHILDREN'S SERVICE SOCIETY OF UTAH

576 East South Temple
Salt Lake City, UT 84102
(801) 355-7444
Program director: Sandra L. Dreis, Executive Director; Jolene Millard-Farley, Adoption Counselor

THE PROGRAM

Children's Service Society of Utah is a nonprofit agency serving residents of the state of Utah and placing 15 to 20 special-needs children and 5 to 10 infants annually. Founded in 1884, the agency's original purpose was "to provide assistance and relief to destitute children and to obtain such temporary and permanent homes as may be practicable." Since that time, the agency has evolved from a day care/ orphanage to a full-service adoption agency. The agency provides services to birthparents and places infants for adoption when birthparents in the agency's counseling program decide that the best interests of the child will be served by adoptive placement. The agency is also actively involved in advocacy for and placement of special-needs children. In addition, the agency will provide homestudy and supervisory services for applicants pursuing independent or foreign adoptions.

THE COST

The agency's fee for adoption services varies depending on the program. For special-needs adoptions, the fee ranges from $200 to $1,200. For infant adoptions, the fee ranges from $2,200 to $6,000. Services covered by the fee include all phases of the adoption process (orientation through post-placement supervision), excluding legal fees connected with finalization of the adoption and travel expenses to visit out-of-state children (when applicable).

THE WAIT

The time from application to the homecoming of the adoptive child varies depending on the program. For infant adoptions, the wait averages 3 years. For special-needs adoptions, the wait ranges from 6 months to 1 year.

THE CHILDREN

The Children's Service Society of Utah places both healthy and special-needs children, ranging in age from birth to 18 years, of all racial backgrounds, born in the U.S. In addition, the agency provides homestudy and supervisory services for applicants pursuing independent or foreign adoptions.

THE REQUIREMENTS

Age: For infant adoptions, applicants must be at least 24 and no more than 38 years of age. For special-needs adoptions, applicants must be at least 10 years older and no more than 40 years older than the child being considered for placement.
Health: Applicants must be in reasonably good health.
Religion: No requirement.
Financial status: No requirement except the ability to financially sustain an additional child or children.
Marital status: For infant adoptions, applicants must be married couples who have been married for at least 3 years with no more than 1 divorce each. For special-needs adoptions, applicants may be single or married. If married, the length of the marriage must be at least 3 years with no more than 1 divorce each.
Family size: For infant adoptions, applicants may have no more than 1 child currently in the family. No requirement for special-needs adoptions.
Racial, ethnic or cultural origin: Preference for placing children in families of similar origins.

THE PROCEDURE

Participation in The Children's Service Society's adoption program entails the following basic steps:
Infant Adoptions
 Orientation meeting
 Application
 Homestudy
 Placement
 Post-placement supervision
Special-needs adoptions
 8–week training group
 Application
 Homestudy
 Referral
 Placement
 Post-placement supervision

ADDITIONAL PROGRAMS/SERVICES

The Children's Service Society provides pregnancy counseling services; support groups; child care resource and referral services (Child Care Connection).

BRANCH/NETWORK OFFICES

None.

LICENSE/ACCREDITATION/PROFESSIONAL AFFILIATIONS

The Children's Service Society of Utah is licensed by the State of Utah Department of Social Services.

LDS SOCIAL SERVICES

50 East North Temple Street
Seventh Floor
Salt Lake City, UT 84150
(800) 453–3860
Program director: Harold C. Brown

THE PROGRAM

Licensed to provide adoption services since 1921, LDS Social Services is a nonprofit organization serving the U.S., Canada, England, Australia, and New Zealand and placing approximately 500 children annually. The agency's purpose is to provide adoption, foster care, and clinical services (consultation and therapy) to members of the Church of Jesus Christ of Latter-day Saints.

THE COST

The agency's fee is $4,000 for healthy newborn placements and approximately $1,000 for special needs placements. Services to adoptive parents include study, placement, and supervisory services. Services to birthparents include pre-natal counseling, foster care, assistance in making arrangements for medical and hospital care relating to the birth, medical expenses and foster care for the infant prior to placement. In addition, prospective adoptive parents should anticipate financial responsibility for legal fees connected with finalization of the adoption.

THE WAIT

The time from application for acceptance into the program to the homecoming of the adoptive child averages 2 years.

THE CHILDREN

LDS Social Services places both healthy and special-needs children ranging in age from birth to 17 years of all racial backgrounds. Most children placed by LDS are Caucasian infants.

THE REQUIREMENTS

Age: Generally, applicants may be no more than 40 years older than the child who is being placed with them.
Health: Applicants must be in reasonably good health. Applicants with health problems or handicaps are given individual consideration. Infertility documentation is required for the adoption of a healthy infant.
Religion: Applicants must be practicing members of the Church of Jesus Christ of Latter-day Saints (Mormon).
Financial status: Applicants must demonstrate ability to manage on income.
Marital status: Applicants must be married and must have been married for at least 2 years.
Family size: For the adoption of a healthy infant or child under 5 years of age, applicants may have no more than 1 child currently in the family.
Racial, ethnic or cultural origin: Preference for placing children in families of similar origins.

THE PROCEDURE

Participation in LDS Social Services adoption program entails the following basic steps:

Orientation meeting
Application
Individual counseling sessions
Homestudy
Placement
Post-placement supervision

ADDITIONAL PROGRAMS/SERVICES

LDS Social Services provides services to unwed birthparents, foster care, family and individual counseling, and parent-child classes.

BRANCH/NETWORK OFFICES

LDS Social Services has branch offices throughout the United States. Refer to appropriate state listings for addresses and telephone numbers of local LDS offices. Branch offices located in Utah are as follows:

350 East 300 North, Suite B
American Fork, UT 84003
(801) 756–5217

110 West 535 South
Cedar City, UT 84720
(801) 586–4479

281 South Main
Centerville, UT 84014
(801) 298–5700

95 West 100 South, #340
Logan, UT 84321
(801) 752–5302

349 12th Street
Ogden, UT 84404
(801) 621–6510

85 East 400 North
Price, UT 84501
(801) 637–2991

1190 North 900 East
Provo, UT 84604
(801) 378–7620

P.O. Box 817, 55 North 100 West
Richfield, UT 84701
(801) 896–6446

780 West 800 South
Salt Lake City, UT 84104
(801) 537–7900

625 East 8400 South
Sandy, UT 84070
(801) 566–2556

LICENSE/ACCREDITATION/PROFESSIONAL AFFILIATIONS

LDS Social Services is licensed by the appropriate state department in each of the states in which it has a branch office and in most adjoining states.

Vermont

PUBLIC ADOPTION PROGRAM/ COMMUNITY RESOURCES

Department of Social and Rehabilitation Services
Division of Social Services, Adoption Unit
103 South Main Street
Waterbury, VT 05676
(802) 241–2131
Adoption specialist: Cindy Walcott

THE PROGRAM

Public adoption services in Vermont are provided by the Division of Social Services Adoption Unit through district offices located throughout the state. The focus of the Division of Social Services adoption program is to recruit, prepare, supervise, and support families who are interested in adopting special-needs children (older, minority, and handicapped children and sibling groups) who are in the custody of the State of Vermont.

STATE EXCHANGE

Maine/Vermont/New Hampshire Exchange. Contact the Adoption Unit (above) for information.

STATE ADOPTION REUNION REGISTRY

None.

STATE SUBSIDY

Contact the Adoption Unit (above) for information.

NACAC REPRESENTATIVE

Susan and Hector Badeau
AASK Northeast
Box 197
Cabot, VT 05647
(802) 479–2197

GENERAL ADOPTION RESOURCES

Room for One More
Contact: Pam Kay
36 Bellwood Avenue
Colchester, VT 05446
(803) 862–6976

SPECIAL-NEEDS ADOPTION RESOURCES

For information about resources for children with special needs, contact Susan and Hector Badeau, NACAC representatives (above).

OUT-OF-STATE AGENCIES

AGENCY

Parsons Child and Family Center, New York

SEE APPENDIX A

Agencies Providing Nationwide Services

THE ELIZABETH LUND HOME

76 Glen Road
P.O. Box 4009
Burlington, VT 05401
(802) 864–7467
Program director: Coizie Bettinger, Adoption Coordinator

THE PROGRAM

The Elizabeth Lund Home is a nonprofit agency serving residents of Vermont and New York residents along the Vermont border. Dedicated "to uniting families who want children with children in Vermont, the U.S., and the world who need permanent homes," the Lund Home believes that there are children available for families through many types of adoption and works with families to find the right children for them. The agency has been placing infants relinquished through its maternity residence for 98 years. The agency has recently expanded its services to include out-of-state infant adoption, international adoption, private adoption, and waiting child adoption. Working with other U.S. agencies which maintain international programs, the agency facilitates the placement of children from various foreign countries in Vermont families. Working with other U.S. agencies, the Lund Home assists applicants in locating healthy infants (usually Black, Hispanic, or biracial) born out-of-state. In addition, the agency will provide homestudy and/or supervisory services for applicants pursuing domestic or international private adoption. Working with public agencies and with national and regional exchange programs, the agency facilitates the placement of U.S. waiting children (typically, school-age and older children, sibling groups, children with medical or emotional disabilities, and minority children). The Lund Home is committed to supporting adoptive families as their children grow and offers follow-up counseling, consultation, and referrals.

THE COST

For adoption services in which the Lund Home has custody of the infant, the agency's fee is based on a sliding scale, ranging from $5,000 to $10,000 (includes all phases of the adoption process). For interagency adoptions, the fee is based on a sliding scale and ranges from $1,000 to $2,500 (includes homestudy, help in locating child/program, post-placement supervision, finalization). For homestudy only, the agency's fee is $750. Applicants pursuing international adoption should also anticipate expenses which may include fees to the cooperating U.S. agency and to the foreign agency, immigration and naturalization fees, dossier preparation, possible travel and related expenses.

THE WAIT

For infant adoptions in which the Lund Home has custody, the time from application to placement may extend to 4 years. For other programs, the wait varies depending on the cooperating agency and the country of origin.

THE CHILDREN

The Lund Home directly places healthy infants, primarily Caucasian, born in Vermont. The agency will provide homestudy and supervisory services to facilitate the placement of a child of any age, race, or country of origin.

THE REQUIREMENTS

Applicants will be accepted on their ability to provide a stable, loving home to a child and on their sincere wish to be adoptive parents.

Age: Applicants must be at least 21 years of age.

Health: Applicants should be in good health. Applicants with disabilities are given equal consideration.

Religion: No requirement.

Financial status: No requirement.

Marital status: No requirement.

Family size: No requirement.

Racial, ethnic or cultural origin: No requirement.

THE PROCEDURE

Participation in the adoption program of the Lund Home entails the following basic steps:

Pre-application

Information meeting

Homestudy (including individual counseling sessions)

Compliance with immigration/naturalization requirements (international adoptions only)

Referral

Placement

Post-placement supervision

Extended post-placement services

ADDITIONAL PROGRAMS/SERVICES

The Lund Home provides workshops for people considering adoption and post-placement services including consultation, counseling, and referrals throughout the development of the child.

BRANCH/NETWORK OFFICES

None.

LICENSE/ACCREDITATION/PROFESSIONAL AFFILIATIONS

The Elizabeth Lund Home is licensed by the State of Vermont Department of Social and Rehabilitative Services.

INTERNATIONAL ADOPTIONS, INC.

66 North Avenue

P.O. Box 3115

Burlington, VT 05402 (802) 658–0249

Program director:

THE PROGRAM

For a full description of programs and services, refer to Massachusetts listing:

International Adoptions, Inc.

282 Moody Street

Waltham, MA 02154

(617) 894–5330

ROOTWINGS MINISTRIES, INC.

P.O. Box 614

Barre, VT 05641

(802) 479–2197

Program director: Susan Badeau

THE PROGRAM

Founded in 1985 by adoptive parents, Hector and Susan Badeau, Rootwings Ministries is a nonprofit agency serving adoptive families in Vermont and facilitating the placement of approximately 30 special-needs children annually. Rootwings' mission is "to 'cultivate' families for waiting children, to 'plant' children in families, to help these families help these children to grow: to give the children roots and wings." Rootwings works cooperatively with the public agency, with other licensed private agencies, and with national and regional exchange programs to recruit and prepare families for special-needs adoptions and to support families after placement. Rootwings also provides homestudy and supervisory services for applicants pursuing interagency adoption (domestic or international) or independent adoption.

THE COST

Rootwings does not charge fees to parents adopting special-needs children. However, parents reimburse Rootwings for costs incurred by the agency in providing adoption services (approximately $50 for class materials, long-distance telephone calls, postage, copying, etc.). In addition, Rootwings advises parents to budget approximately $200 for adoption related costs (court finalization filing fee, medical exams, travel to parent preparation classes, travel for pre-placement visits with the child, etc.).

For applicants pursuing interagency adoption (domestic or international) or independent adoption, Rootwings fee schedule is as follows:

Homestudy	$750.00
Homestudy update	$350.00
Matching services	$50.00
Placement services (per hour)	$20.00
Placement supervision (per hour)	$20.00
Finalization service	$150.00
Post-finalization support services (as needed) (per hour)	$20.00

Applicants pursuing interagency adoption should anticipate fees to the custodial agency, possible travel expenses, and related costs. Applicants pursuing independent adoption should anticipate financial responsibility for the legal and medical expenses of the birthmother and child.

THE WAIT

The time from application to the homecoming of the adoptive child varies depending on the range of special needs which the adoptive family feels they can accept and on the needs of the child being considered for placement.

THE CHILDREN

Rootwings' primary purpose is to facilitate the placement of special-needs children (Caucasian children over the age of 10; minority children over the age of 5; children of all ages and racial backgrounds that have significant mental, physical, or emotional disabilities; sibling groups). Rootwings will also provide homestudy and supervisory services to facilitate interagency or private placement of children of any age, race, or national origin.

THE REQUIREMENTS

Age: No requirement.
Health: No requirement.
Religion: No requirement.
Financial status: No requirement.
Marital status: No requirement.
Family size: No requirement.
Racial, ethnic or cultural origin: No requirement.

THE PROCEDURE

Participation in Rootwings' adoption program entails the following basic steps:
Orientation meeting
Parent preparation classes
Application
Homestudy
Placement
Post-placement supervision

ADDITIONAL PROGRAMS/SERVICES

Rootwings provides a family support network (a clearing house of information and services available to help parents deal effectively with the challenges of parenting); information and referral (resources for birthparents, adult adoptees, and prospective adoptive parents on a wide range of adoption issues); advocacy and public awareness; training workshops for parents and professionals in cooperation with SPARK, Inc.; newsletter (News & Notes).

BRANCH/NETWORK OFFICES

None.

LICENSE/ACCREDITATION/PROFESSIONAL AFFILIATIONS

Rootwings Ministries, Inc. is licensed by the State of Vermont Department of Social and Rehabilitative Services. Rootwings is the Vermont affiliate of AASK (Aid to Adoption of Special Kids).

VERMONT CATHOLIC CHARITIES, INC.

351 North Avenue
Burlington, VT 05401
(802) 658–6110, Ext. 230
Program director: Rev. Roland Rivord, Executive Director

THE PROGRAM

Vermont Catholic Charities is a nonprofit social service agency providing statewide services and placing approximately 2 to 7 children annually through its adoption program. The agency's mission is "to provide professional services that will foster human growth and development in all stages of human life." Working directly with birthparents, with other private and public agencies, and with national exchange programs, the agency places both healthy and special-needs children (but predominantly healthy infants). In addition, the agency will provide homestudy and supervisory services for applicants pursuing interagency adoption (domestic or international) or private adoption.

THE COST

The agency's fee for adoption services is 9% of the applicants' annual gross income. Services covered include homestudy, placement, and post-placement supervision.

THE WAIT

The time from application to placement ranges from 1 to 2 years.

THE CHILDREN

Vermont Catholic Charities places primarily healthy infants (but also special-needs children), born in the U.S. The agency will also provide homestudy and supervisory services for applicants pursuing international adoption.

THE REQUIREMENTS

Age: Applicants must be at least 18 and no more than 38 years of age.
Health: Applicants must be in reasonably good health. Infertility documentation is required.
Religion: If the child being considered for placement is of a Catholic religious background, applicants must be practicing members of the Catholic Church.
Financial status: Applicants must be financially stable.
Marital status: Applicants must be married, and the length of the marriage must be at least 3 years. (However, the agency will provide homestudies for single applicants pursuing international adoption.)
Family size: Applicants must be childless.
Racial, ethnic or cultural origin: Preference for placing children in families of similar origins.

THE PROCEDURE

Participation in the adoption program of Vermont Catholic Charities entails the following basic steps:
Orientation meeting
Application
Individual counseling sessions
Homestudy
Compliance with immigration/naturalization requirements (international adoptions only)
Placement
Post-placement supervision
Finalization

ADDITIONAL PROGRAMS/SERVICES

Vermont Catholic Charities provides a range of community services including foster care; unwed parent, individual, marital, and family counseling; refugee resettlement; parish outreach; family enrichment; residential facilities for children; residential facilities for the well aging; natural family planning; family life education; marriage preparation.

BRANCH/NETWORK OFFICES

24 1/2 Center St.
Rutland, VT 05701
(802) 773-3379

Vermont Catholic Charities, Inc. is licensed by the State of Vermont Department of Social and Rehabilitation Services and is accredited by the Council on Accreditation of Services for Families and Children. The agency is a member of Catholic Charities USA.

VERMONT CHILDREN'S AID SOCIETY, INC.

79 Weaver Street
P.O. Box 127
Winooski, VT 05404–0127
(802) 655–0006
Program director: Maurine Gelley, Director of Professional Services

THE PROGRAM

Vermont Children's Aid Society is a nonprofit agency serving residents of Vermont and residents of Grafton and Sullivan Counties in New Hampshire and placing approximately 50 to 75 children annually. In existence since 1919, the agency offers several adoption programs. The agency provides services to birthparents and places infants for adoption when birthparents elect adoptive placement as the best plan for their child. Working with public agencies and with national and regional exchange programs through the Interstate Compact, the agency facilitates the placement of special-needs children (notably Black and bi-racial children). In 1983, the agency began a program for applicants pursuing parent-initiated foreign adoption. In addition, the agency will provide homestudy and post-placement services for applicants pursuing interagency adoption (domestic or international) or private adoption.

THE COST

The agency's fee for agency arranged domestic adoption is based on a sliding scale and varies depending on the program. Services covered by the fee include all phases of the adoption process from inquiry through finalization (with the exception of possible medical and pregnancy-related costs of the birthmother for agency arranged domestic adoptions). As of October 1988, the agency's fee schedule is as follows:

Agency placement (healthy infant) $3,000.00–$6,000.00
Interstate placement (usually
   Black/bi-racial) $1,000.00–$2,500.00
International placement $1,000.00–$2,500.00

For applicants pursuing private adoption, the agency's fee is $700 for the homestudy and $400 for post-placement supervision (optional). Applicants pursuing interagency adoption (domestic or international) should also anticipate fees for the cooperating agency.

THE WAIT

The time from application to placement varies depending on the program. For healthy Caucasian infant adoption, the wait ranges from 3 to 5 years. For international or interstate (usually special-needs or Black/bi-racial) adoptions, the wait ranges from 12 to 18 months.

THE CHILDREN

Vermont Children's Aid Society directly places healthy infants and facilitates the placement of both healthy and special-needs children, ranging in age from infancy to adolescence, of all racial backgrounds. Through the parent-initiated foreign adoption program, the agency facilitates the placement of children from various countries.

THE REQUIREMENTS

Age: The requirement varies depending on the age of the child.
Health: Applicants should be in reasonably good health. Applicants with health problems or handicaps are given individual consideration. Infertility documentation is required for infant adoption.
Religion: No requirement.
Financial status: Applicants must demonstrate financial stability.
Marital status: For healthy Caucasian infant adoption, applicants must be married. For interstate or international adoptions, applicants may be married or single.
Family size: No requirement for special-needs placements. For healthy Caucasian infant adoptions, applicants may have no more than 1 child in the family.
Racial, ethnic or cultural origin: No requirement.

THE PROCEDURE

Participation in the adoption program of Vermont Children's Aid Society entails the following basic steps:
Orientation meeting
Application
Homestudy
Compliance with immigration/naturalization requirements
   (parent-initiated foreign adoptions only)
Placement
Post-placement supervision

ADDITIONAL PROGRAMS/SERVICES

Vermont Children's Aid Society provides counseling for troubled families and children; pregnancy counseling and single parent services, including support services for mothers who elect to parent their children themselves; temporary foster care; post-adoption counseling with individual families as requested.

BRANCH/NETWORK OFFICES

While the agency maintains branch offices in Woodstock and Rutland, all adoption inquiries are processed by the main office in Winooski.

LICENSE/ACCREDITATION/PROFESSIONAL AFFILIATIONS

Vermont Children's Aid Society is licensed by the State of Vermont Department of Social and Rehabilitation Services and by the State of New Hampshire Department of Health and Human Services. The agency is accredited by the Council on Accreditation of Services for Families and Children and is a charter member of the Child Welfare League of America.

Virginia

PUBLIC ADOPTION PROGRAM/ COMMUNITY RESOURCES

Department of Social Services
Bureau of Child Welfare Services
Blair Building
8007 Discovery Drive
Richmond, VA 23229–8699
(804) 662–9819
Adoption specialist: Lynne Edwards

THE PROGRAM

Public adoption services in Virginia are provided by the Department of Social Services through branch offices located in each county. The primary focus of the DSS adoption program is to recruit and prepare families and to supervise the placement of special-needs children (older and/or minority children; children with physical, intellectual, or emotional handicaps; sibling groups) who are in the custody of local departments of Social Services.

STATE EXCHANGE

Adoption Resource Exchange of Virginia
8007 Discovery Drive
Richmond, VA 23288
(804) 663–9151

STATE ADOPTION REUNION REGISTRY

None.

STATE SUBSIDY

For information, contact the Bureau of Child Welfare Services (above).

NACAC REPRESENTATIVE

Sharon Richardson
3407 Hawthorne Avenue
Richmond, VA 23227
(804) 321–2590

GENERAL ADOPTION RESOURCES

For a current list of adoptive parent support groups, contact Adoption Resource Exchange of Virginia (above).
OURS, Inc.
Families through Adoption
Contact: Mary Ann Sparrow
1224 Wivenhoe Ct.
Virginia Beach, VA 23454
(804) 481–1202
Prince William COAC
Contact: Marcia Bower
7578 Remington Rd.
Manassas, VA 22110
People for Adoption of Children
Contact: Sharon Richardson
3407 Hawthorne Ave.
Richmond, VA 23222
(804) 329–7276

F.A.C.E.
Contact: Laura Armitage
277 Windover Ave., NW
Vienna, VA 22180

SPECIAL-NEEDS ADOPTION RESOURCES

For information on special-needs adoption resources contact COAC (see General Adoption Resources above) or Adoption Resource Exchange of Virginia (see State Exchange above).

OUT-OF-STATE AGENCIES

AGENCY

Adoption Service Information Agency, District of Columbia

The Barker Foundation, District of Columbia
Lutheran Social Services, District of Columbia

SEE APPENDIX A

Agencies Providing Nationwide Services

BETHANY CHRISTIAN SERVICES

246 Maple Avenue, E.
Vienna, VA 22180
(703) 255–4775
Program director: James K. Haveman, Jr., Executive Director

THE PROGRAM

For a full description of programs and services, refer to Michigan listing:
Bethany Christian Services
901 Eastern Avenue, N.E.
Grand Rapids, MI 49503–1295
(616) 459–6273

BRANCH OFFICES

Bethany Christian Services/Virginia:
433 Bridgewater St.
Fredericksburg, VA 22401–3347
(703) 371–4630

CATHOLIC CHARITIES OF RICHMOND, INC.

4206 Chamberlayne Avenue
Richmond, VA 23227
(804) 264–2778
Program director: Jane Hotchkiss

THE PROGRAM

Catholic Charities of Richmond is a nonprofit agency serving residents of Virginia, Maryland, North Carolina, and Washington, D.C., and placing approximately 22 American-born and 14 foreign-born children annually. Providing services to the community since 1923, the agency's mission is "to provide social services, as its resources permit, to any person who applies regardless of race, color, creed or national origin, and to assist them in the development of their own capacities to live lives of dignity and meaning." The agency provides services to birthparents and places infants for adoption when birthparents in the agency's counseling program decide that the best interests of the child will be served by adoptive placement. Working cooperatively with other U.S.-based agencies and directly with foreign sources, the agency facilitates the placement of foreign-born children in American families.

THE COST

The agency's fee for adoption services varies depending on the program. For domestic adoptions, the agency's fee is 10% of the applicants' annual gross income, with a minimum of $3,000 and a maximum of $7,500. Services covered by the fee include all phases of the adoption process (adoptive parent preparation through finalization). Fees also help to underwrite the cost of services (legal, medical, and foster care) to birthmother and child. For international adoptions, the agency's fee for homestudy and supervisory services is $1,850. In addition, applicants are responsible for caseworker travel expenses (if family is beyond a 25 mile radius of Richmond) and all calls outside of the Continental U.S. Applicants pursuing international adoption should also anticipate foreign agency fees (ranging from $500–$5,500) and travel/escort expenses.

THE WAIT

The time from application for acceptance into the program to the homecoming of the adoptive child varies depending on the program and ranges from 1 to 4 years.

THE CHILDREN

Catholic Charities places both healthy and special-needs children of all racial backgrounds. American-born children are typically infants. Foreign-born children range in age from 2 months to 14 years. Countries of origin include U.S., Chile, Panama, Guatemala, Honduras, Colombia, Brazil, El Salvador, Hong Kong, India, Korea, the Philippines, and Taiwan.

THE REQUIREMENTS

Age: For domestic adoptions, applicants must be at least 25 and 1 member of the couple must be no more than 40 years old at the time of placement. For international adoptions, the requirement varies depending on the country of origin.
Health: Applicants with health problems or handicaps are given individual consideration.
Religion: For domestic infant adoptions, the birthmother's preference is honored. No requirement for foreign adoptions.
Financial status: No requirement.
Marital status: For domestic infant adoptions, applicants must be married couples. For foreign adoptions, the requirement varies depending on the child's country of origin. Some programs are available to single applicants.
Family size: For domestic infant adoptions, applicants may have no more than 1 child currently in the family. For foreign adoptions, the requirement varies depending on the child's country of origin.

Racial, ethnic or cultural origin: No requirement, but may vary depending on the needs of the child and the birthmother's preference.

THE PROCEDURE

Participation in Catholic Charities' adoption program entails the following basic steps:
Registration
Group counseling sessions
Application
Individual counseling sessions
Homestudy
Compliance with immigration/naturalization requirements (foreign adoptions only)
Referral and placement
Post-placement supervision

ADDITIONAL PROGRAMS/SERVICES

Catholic Charities of Richmond provides counseling and residential services to birthmothers; foster care services for infants; elderly/handicapped services; individual, marital, and family counseling; emergency financial assistance; family life education programs; refugee unaccompanied minors program; foster care for foreign youths; specialized foster care for special-needs children; independent living skills training; cross cultural counseling; volunteer opportunities.

BRANCH/NETWORK OFFICES

None.

LICENSE/ACCREDITATION/PROFESSIONAL AFFILIATIONS

Catholic Charities of Richmond, Inc. is licensed by the Commonwealth of Virginia Department of Social Services and is accredited by the Council on Accreditation of Services for Families and Children.

CATHOLIC FAMILY AND CHILDREN'S SERVICES

820 Campbell Avenue, S.W.
Roanoke, VA 24016(703) 344–5107
Program director: Anne Brooke Carpenter

THE PROGRAM

Catholic Family and Children's Services (CF&CS) is a nonprofit agency serving southwestern Virginia (Harrisonburg to Bristol, Appomattox to Grundy) and placing between 10 and 30 children annually. The agency provides extensive services to birthparents and places infants for adoption when birthparents in the agency's program decide that the best interests of the child will be served by adoptive placement. The agency also maintains an Intercountry Adoption Program, placing children from Central and South American, India, and Korea.

THE COST

The agency's fee for domestic adoption services is as follows:

Application fee $50.00
Homestudy fee $800.00
Placement and supervision fee is 10% of gross income for preceding year with a maximum fee of $8,500.00

Fees for the Intercountry Program vary depending on the country and range from $6,000 to $14,000.

Fees cover all phases of the adoption process, excluding legal fees connected with finalization of the adoption. Services are provided free of charge to birthmothers, and agency fees help to underwrite the cost of these services.

THE WAIT

The time from application for acceptance into the domestic program to the homecoming of the adoptive child ranges from 5 to 7 years. For intercountry adoption, the wait is approximately 2 years from the completion of the homestudy.

THE CHILDREN

CF&CS places newborn infants of Caucasian, Black, and bi-racial backgrounds, born in the U.S. The agency also places children from Central and South America, India, and Korea.

THE REQUIREMENTS

Age: Applicants must be 40 years or under to be wait listed for a healthy Caucasian infant.

Health: Applicants must be in reasonably good health. Applicants with health problems or handicaps are given individual consideration.

Religion: No requirement.

Financial status: No requirement for the domestic program other than the ability to support an additional family member. For intercountry adoption, substantial income is required by some countries.

Marital status: For healthy Caucasian infant, applicants must be married couples. Single applicants are considered for Black or bi-racial infants and for intercountry adoption.

Family size: For healthy Caucasian infant, applicants must be childless or have no more than 1 child. No requirement for Black or bi-racial infant adoption. For intercountry adoption, the requirement varies depending on the country.

Racial, ethnic or cultural origin: No requirement.

THE PROCEDURE

Participation in CF&CS' adoption program entails the following basic steps:
Application
Homestudy
Placement
Post-placement supervision

ADDITIONAL PROGRAMS/SERVICES

CF&CS provides comprehensive pregnancy counseling; individual, marital, and family counseling; foster care for infants awaiting placement and pregnant minor teens; outreach services to the elderly.

BRANCH/NETWORK OFFICES

St. Mary's Catholic Church
706 Harding Rd.
Blacksburg, VA 24060

LICENSE/ACCREDITATION/PROFESSIONAL AFFILIATIONS

Catholic Family and Children's Services is licensed by the Commonwealth of Virginia Department of Social Services and is a member of Catholic Charities USA. The agency is currently undergoing accreditation through the Council on Accreditation of Services for Families and Children.

CATHOLIC FAMILY SERVICES

1809 Airline Boulevard
Portsmouth, VA 23707
(804) 393–0043
Program director: Ted Burk, Executive Director; Catherine DeLapp, MSW, Adoption Supervisor

THE PROGRAM

Catholic Family Services is a nonprofit agency serving the Tidewater area (including Suffolk and the Isle of Wight) and placing approximately 5–10 children annually. Providing continuous service since 1945, Catholic Family Services seeks "to foster the development of family life, to promote the well being of families, and the health of its individual members." The agency provides services to birthparents and places infants for adoption when birthparents in the agency's program decide that the best interests of the child will be met by adoptive placement. The purpose of the adoption program is "to ensure the best possible home for each child entrusted to the agency's care."

THE COST

The agency's fee for adoption services is based on a sliding scale and ranges from $0 to 12% of the applicants' annual gross income. Services covered by the fee include all phases of the adoption process (homestudy through post-placement supervision), excluding legal fees connected with finalization of the adoption. Fees also help to underwrite the cost of services to the birthmother and child (legal, medical, and foster care). Applicants should note that fees for the placement of "hard-to-place" infants (including healthy, Black infants) are negotiable.

THE WAIT

The time from application to the homecoming of the adoptive child varies depending on the type of child the applicants wish to parent. For healthy, Caucasian infants, applicants typically wait 2 to 3 years for the homestudy to begin and 1 to 12 months for placement after approval of the homestudy. For "hard-to-place" children, the time from application to placement ranges from 1 to 12 months.

THE CHILDREN

Catholic Family Services places primarily healthy children, ranging in age from birth to 6 years, of all racial backgrounds, born in the U.S.

THE REQUIREMENTS

Age: For healthy, Caucasian infant, applicants must be at least 25 and no more than 40 years of age. For "hard-to-place" children, the requirement is more flexible.

Health: Applicants must be in reasonably good health. Applicants with health problems or handicaps are given individual consideration.

Religion: No requirement.

Financial status: Applicants must meet a minimum income requirement of 80% of the median income for a family of four.

Marital status: Applicants must be married. The length of the marriage must be at least 3 years.

Family size: Applicants may have no more than 1 child currently in the family.

Racial, ethnic or cultural origin: No requirement, but preference for placing children in families of similar origins.

THE PROCEDURE

Participation in Catholic Family Services' adoption program entails the following basic steps:

Wait listing
Orientation meeting
Application
Homestudy
Referral
Placement
Post-placement supervision

ADDITIONAL PROGRAMS/SERVICES

Catholic Family Services provides individual, marital, and family counseling; problem pregnancy counseling; foster care services; community education programs.

BRANCH/NETWORK OFFICES

Suffolk Branch Office
202 S. Broad Street
Suffolk, VA 23234
(804) 934–1188

LICENSE/ACCREDITATION/PROFESSIONAL AFFILIATIONS

Catholic Family Services is licensed by the Commonwealth of Virginia Department of Social Services. The agency is a member of the Virginia Association of Licensed Child Placing Agencies, Catholic Charities USA, Family Service Council of Virginia, and the United Way.

CHILDREN'S HOME SOCIETY OF VIRGINIA

4200 Fitzhugh Avenue
Richmond, VA 23230
(804) 353–0191
Program director: Peter M. Pufki

THE PROGRAM

The Children's Home Society of Virginia is a nonprofit agency serving residents of the state of Virginia and placing approximately 50–60 children annually. Founded in 1900 by a group of concerned citizens, the agency's original purpose was "to find family homes for homeless, indigent, or dependent poor children in the State of Virginia." The agency has evolved to meet the changing needs of the community, and today the agency's mission is "to find homes for children and to provide professional counseling on issues and problems related to untimely pregnancy and the adoption process." The agency provides services to birthparents and places infants for adoption when birthparents in the agency's program decide that the best interests of the child will be served by adoptive placement. The agency is also actively involved in the placement of special-needs children (Black or bi-racial children, older Caucasian children, sibling groups, and children with physical and/or mental handicaps).

THE COST

The agency's fee for adoption services is based on a sliding scale and ranges from $200 to $6,000. Services covered by the fee include counseling, homestudy, child search, placement, and post-placement supervision. Fees also help to underwrite the cost of services to birthparents (counseling, foster care, and medical care). Applicants assume responsibility for legal fees connected with finalization of the adoption.

THE WAIT

The time from application to placement varies depending on the type of child the applicants wish to parent. For healthy Caucasian infant adoption, the time from wait listing to placement is 3 to 7 years. For special needs placements, the wait varies depending on the family's flexibility and openness to the child's special needs. For Black and bi- racial children of all ages, the wait is approximately 6 months. For older Caucasian children, the wait is approximately 1 year.

THE CHILDREN

Children's Home Society places both healthy and special-needs children, ranging in age from infancy to adolescence, of all racial backgrounds, born in the U.S.

THE REQUIREMENTS

Age: For healthy, Caucasian infant adoption, applicants must be between the ages of 25 and 40. For special-needs adoptions, applicants must be at least 25 and no more than 45 years older than the child.

Health: Applicants with health problems or handicaps are given individual consideration.

Religion: No requirement.

Financial status: No requirement.

Marital status: For Caucasian infant adoption, applicants must be married, and the length of the marriage must be at least 3 years. Single applicants are accepted for older child and special-needs adoption.

Family size: For Caucasian infant adoption, applicants may have no more than 1 child currently in the family. No requirement for other programs.

Racial, ethnic or cultural origin: Preference for placing children in families of similar origins.

THE PROCEDURE

Participation in Children's Home Society's adoption program entails the following basic steps:

Orientation meeting
Application
Homestudy
Referral

Placement
Post-placement supervision

ADDITIONAL PROGRAMS/SERVICES

Children's Home Society provides pregnancy counseling services and foster care services for pregnant teens and infants.

BRANCH/NETWORK OFFICES

Southwestern Virginia Branch Office
1620 Fifth St.
Roanoke, VA 24016
(703) 344-9281

LICENSE/ACCREDITATION/PROFESSIONAL AFFILIATIONS

Children's Home Society of Virginia is licensed by the Commonwealth of Virginia Department of Social Services and is a member of the United Way.

CHILDREN'S SERVICES OF CATHOLIC CHARITIES

Diocese of Arlington
3838 North Cathedral Lane
Arlington, VA 22203
(703) 841-2531
Program director: Helen Patricia Mudd, ACSW

THE PROGRAM

Children's Services of Catholic Charities is a nonprofit multi-service agency serving 21 counties in northern Virginia and placing approximately 50 children annually. Since 1948, Children's Services has provided service to the community, regardless of the age, race, creed, or marital status of those requesting assistance. The agency provides pregnancy counseling and assistance to relinquishing and non-relinquishing birthmothers and places infants for adoption when birthmothers in the agency's pregnancy counseling program decide that the best interests of the child will be served by adoptive placement. The agency also provides homestudy and supervisory services for applicants who are pursuing international or special-needs adoption through another source, subject to state approval of the integrity of the source. In all its programs, the agency is guided by the belief in "the right of people to the development of their full potential."

THE COST

The agency's fee for complete adoption services is based on a sliding scale and ranges from $4,000 to $8,000. Services covered by the fee include all phases of the adoption process (homestudy through post-placement services), excluding legal fees connected with finalization of the adoption. The agency's fee for homestudy only is $850.

THE WAIT

The time from application for acceptance into the program to the homecoming of the adoptive child ranges from 18 months to 2+ years.

THE CHILDREN

Children's Services of Catholic Charities places both healthy and special-needs children, predominantly infants (1 month to 1 year) but also occasionally toddlers or pre-school children. The children are predominantly Caucasian but also occasionally Black, Hispanic, Asian, and bi-racial.

THE REQUIREMENTS

Age: Applicants must be at least 21 years of age. The upper age limit varies depending on whether it is a first or second adoption and whether it is an international or special-needs adoption.
Health: Applicants must be in reasonably good health and must have normal life expectancy. For Caucasian infant adoption, infertility documentation is required.
Religion: The requirement varies depending on the religious preference of the birthmother. For Catholic infants, at least 1 parent must be a practicing Catholic, and there must be a valid Catholic marriage.
Financial status: Applicants must demonstrate ability to manage on their income.
Marital status: Single applicants are accepted for international and special-needs adoptions. Married applicants must have been married for at least 3 years.
Family size: The requirement varies depending on the program.
Racial, ethnic or cultural origin: Preference for placing children in families of similar origins, but varies depending on the needs of the children in the agency's care.

THE PROCEDURE

Participation in Children's Services of Catholic Charities' adoption program entails the following basic steps:
Telephone screening for preliminary eligibility
Referral (if appropriate)
Orientation meeting
Application
Pre-adoption group sessions
Homestudy (including individual sessions)
Compliance with immigration/naturalization requirements (foreign adoptions only)
Placement
Post-placement supervision

ADDITIONAL PROGRAMS/SERVICES

Children's Services of Catholic Charities provides foster care services for birthmothers and infants; operates a residential facility in cooperation with a local Catholic parish; offers special childbirth preparation courses for single birthmothers; sponsors workshops and seminars on adoption and foster care; sponsors Friends of Children's Services (FOCS), an adoption support group; provides post-adoption services for adoptees, adoptive parents and birthparents.

BRANCH/NETWORK OFFICES

5294 Lyngate Court
Burke, VA 22015
(703) 425-0100
131 S. West Street
Alexandria, VA 22314
(703) 548-4227

10 W. Boscawen St.
Winchester, VA 22601
(703) 549–8644

LICENSE/ACCREDITATION/PROFESSIONAL AFFILIATIONS

Children's Services of Catholic Charities is licensed by the Commonwealth of Virginia Department of Social Services and is affiliated with Catholic Charities USA, United Way of the National Capital Area, the Virginia Association of Licensed Child-Placing Agencies, and the Virginia Council of Social Welfare.

FAMILY LIFE SERVICES

Box 27000
Lynchburg, VA 24506(804) 847–6806
Program director: Dr. Richard H. Morrison, ACSW

THE PROGRAM

Family Life Services is a nonprofit agency providing nationwide service. Founded 5 years ago, the agency "is designed to offer to young women an alternative to abortion." The agency operates a pregnancy crisis center and a maternity home and provides child placement services when birthmothers in the agency's program decide that the best interests of their children will be served by adoptive placement.

THE COST

The agency's fee is based on a sliding scale and ranges from $1,500 to $7,000. Services covered by the fee include all phases of the adoption process (pre-adoption counseling through post-placement supervision), excluding legal fees connected with finalization of the adoption, physician's fee for medical examination and report, and police record fees (minimal). In addition, fees help to underwrite the cost of services to the birthmother (social, medical, and residential).

THE WAIT

The average wait for acceptance into the program is 3 months. The time from acceptance to initiation of the homestudy is approximately 1 to 1 1/2 years. The time from completion of the homestudy to placement is approximately 1 year. Applicants should note that these estimates are approximate and subject to considerable variation.

THE CHILDREN

Family Life Services places primarily healthy infants (birth to 6 months), of Caucasian or Black racial backgrounds.

THE REQUIREMENTS

Age: Applicants must be at least 21 and no more than 40 years of age.
Health: Applicants must be in reasonably good health. Applicants with health problems or handicaps are given individual consideration.
Religion: Applicants must have a personal commitment to Jesus Christ as Savior and Lord as a demonstration of ongoing spiritual growth.
Financial status: Applicants must have an annual income of at least $10,000–$11,000.
Marital status: For healthy infant adoptions, applicants must be married couples. The length of the marriage must be at least 4 years. Single applicants might be considered for special-needs adoptions.
Family size: Applicants may have no more than 1 child currently in the family.
Racial, ethnic or cultural origin: Preference for placing children in families of similar origins.

THE PROCEDURE

Participation in Family Life Services' adoption program entails the following basic steps:
Application
Orientation meeting
Individual counseling sessions
Homestudy
Group counseling sessions
Referral
Placement
Post-placement supervision

ADDITIONAL PROGRAMS/SERVICES

Family Life Services provides extensive services to birthmothers; workshops and seminars on parenting and adoption; foster care services; counseling services.

BRANCH/NETWORK OFFICES

None.

LICENSE/ACCREDITATION/PROFESSIONAL AFFILIATIONS

Family Life Services is licensed by the Commonwealth of Virginia Department of Social Services. All social workers are MSW.

HOLSTON UNITED METHODIST HOME FOR CHILDREN

300 Moore Street, Suite D
Bristol, VA 24201
(703) 466–3883
Program director: Carl Anderson, Director of Family Services; Arthur Masker, Program Administrator

THE PROGRAM

Holston United Methodist Home for Children in Bristol serves residents of 17 counties in southwestern Virginia. For a full description of programs and services, refer to Tennessee listing:

Holston United Methodist Home for Children
P.O. Box 188
Holston Drive
Greeneville, TN 37743
(615) 638–4171

JEWISH FAMILY SERVICES, INC.

7027 Three Chopt Road
Richmond, VA 23226
(804) 282–5644
Program director: Ruth Loube Kershner, MSW

THE PROGRAM

Jewish Family Services is a nonprofit social service agency serving Richmond and the surrounding area. Providing service to the community since 1849, the agency's primary goals are "to contribute to harmonious family interrelationships, to strengthen the positive values in family life, and to promote healthy personality development and satisfactory social functioning of various family members." The agency places primarily healthy infants (birth to 2 years) in Jewish families. The agency will also provide homestudy and supervisory services to applicants pursuing private, interstate, or foreign adoptions, subject to state approval of the integrity of the source. In reviewing the policy descriptions which follow, applicants should note that policies are applied with flexibility and with exceptions made in the interest of each child. In all cases, the child's needs must be the deciding factor in a decision to move toward adoptive placement.

THE COST

The agency's fee for homestudy and supervisory services is $60 per interview session. The placement fee is 10% of the adoptive family's annual gross income plus the medical costs of the birthmother and infant, with a maximum of $15,000. In addition, applicants assume responsibility for legal fees connected with finalization.

THE WAIT

The time from application to the homecoming of the adoptive child ranges from 1 to 10 years.

THE CHILDREN

Jewish Family Services places primarily healthy infants (birth to 2 years) and will place infants of any racial background. In addition, the agency will provide homestudy and supervisory services for applicants pursuing private, interstate, or international adoption.

THE REQUIREMENTS

Age: Applicants must be at least 25 and no more than 45 years of age. The requirement may vary depending on the age of the child.
Health: Applicants must be in reasonably good health. Infertility documentation is required.
Religion: Applicants must be practicing members of the Jewish faith.
Financial status: Applicants are evaluated individually on the basis of their ability to manage financial resources effectively.
Marital status: Married couples and single applicants are accepted. If married, the length of the marriage must be at least 3 years.
Family size: Applicants may have no more than 1 child currently in the family.
Racial, ethnic or cultural origin: No requirement.

THE PROCEDURE

Participation in Jewish Family Services' adoption program entails the following basic steps:
Application
Homestudy
Individual counseling sessions
Referral
Placement
Post-placement supervision

ADDITIONAL PROGRAMS/SERVICES

Jewish Family Services provides information and referral services and counseling services to couples, biological parents and their families, and adoptees.

BRANCH/NETWORK OFFICES

None.

LICENSE/ACCREDITATION/PROFESSIONAL AFFILIATIONS

Jewish Family Services is licensed by the Commonwealth of Virginia Department of Social Services and is accredited by the Council on Accreditation of Services for Families and Children. The agency is a member of the Association of Jewish Family and Children's Agencies and the Virginia Council on Social Welfare.

JEWISH FAMILY SERVICE OF TIDEWATER, INC.

7300 Newport Avenue
Norfolk, VA 23507
(804) 489–3111
Program director: Susan J. Rubenstein, LCSW

THE PROGRAM

Jewish Family Service of Tidewater is a nonprofit agency serving residents of the Tidewater area and placing 1 child annually.

THE COST

The agency's fee for adoption services is based on a sliding scale and ranges up to $7,000. Services covered by the fee include counseling, homestudy, placement, post-placement supervision, and preparation of reports for submission to the court. In addition, applicants should anticipate legal fees connected with finalization of the adoption.

THE WAIT

The time from application for acceptance into the program to the homecoming of the adoptive child varies greatly.

THE CHILDREN

Jewish Family Service places primarily healthy infants of Caucasian and bi-racial backgrounds, born in the U.S.

THE REQUIREMENTS

Age: Applicants may be no more than 40 years of age.
Health: Applicants must be in reasonably good health.

Religion: Applicants must be Jewish and must have a valid Jewish marriage certificate.

Financial status: No requirement.

Marital status: Married couples and single applicants are accepted. If married, the length of the marriage must be at least 3 years.

Family size: Applicants may have no more than 2 children currently in the family.

Racial, ethnic or cultural origin: No requirement.

THE PROCEDURE

Participation in Jewish Family Service's adoption program entails the following basic steps:
Orientation meeting
Application
Homestudy
Placement
Post-placement supervision

ADDITIONAL PROGRAMS/SERVICES

Jewish Family Service provides counseling services, homemaking services, and services to senior adults.

BRANCH/NETWORK OFFICES

Adoption inquiries are processed through the Norfolk office.

LICENSE/ACCREDITATION/PROFESSIONAL AFFILIATIONS

Jewish Family Service of Tidewater is licensed by the Commonwealth of Virginia Department of Social Services.

JEWISH SOCIAL SERVICE AGENCY OF METROPOLITAN WASHINGTON

8822 Little River Turnpike
Fairfax, VA 22031
(301) 881–3700
(703) 323–1668
Program director: Agency Executive Director

THE PROGRAM

For a full description of programs and services, refer to Maryland listing:

Jewish Social Service Agency of Metropolitan Washington
6123 Montrose Road
Rockville, MD 20852
(301) 881–3700

LDS SOCIAL SERVICES

P.O. Box 34361
Richmond, VA 23234
(804) 743–0727
Program director: Grant H. Taylor

THE PROGRAM

For a full description of programs and services, refer to Utah listing:

LDS Social Services
50 East North Temple Street
Salt Lake City, UT 84150

PAN AMERICAN ADOPTION AGENCY, INC.

12604 Kahns Road
Manassas, VA 22111
(703) 791–3260
Program director: Nancy Croteau, Executive Director

THE PROGRAM

Pan American Adoption Agency is a for-profit agency providing nationwide services and placing approximately 40 children annually. Founded 7 years ago by 2 attorneys, Nancy Croteau and Dr. Raymond Croteau, Jr., who practice only adoption law and staffed by qualified social workers, the agency provides domestic and international placement services and specializes in the placement of healthy infants. Guided by the belief that "there is no one formula for a happy family," the agency has successfully placed younger children with older couples, single parents, and many other types of applicants who have been led to believe that adoption of young children was not possible for them.

THE COST

The agency's fee for adoption services is based on a sliding scale and ranges from $0 to $5,000. Services covered by the fee include all phases of the adoption process with the exception of the homestudy, if provided by Pan American. Pan American will provide the homestudy for residents of Washington, D.C. and for Maryland and Virginia residents who live close to D.C. (with fees ranging from $650 to $1,000). Out-of-state clients and clients who live outside the D.C. metropolitan area arrange for a local agency to provide homestudy and supervisory services, and Pan American Adoption Agency provides placement services ($1,500–$3,000). In addition, applicants pursuing foreign adoption should anticipate variable fees, depending on the child's country of origin, which may include overseas legal fees; foster care and medical expenses; orphanage contribution; immigration expenses; transportation for escort and child. In general, the total cost for an international adoption ranges from $8,000 to $10,500.

THE WAIT

Applicants who have been accepted into the program, have completed the homestudy, and have prepared and submitted the documents required for international adoption can usually expect to bring their adoptive child home within a range of 2 to 8 months. 98% of the agency's clients bring their child home within a year.

THE CHILDREN

Pan American Adoption Agency places primarily healthy

infants (but also some older children) from El Salvador, Paraguay, Mexico, and the U.S.

THE REQUIREMENTS

Age: Applicants must be at least 25 and no more than 55 years of age.

Health: Applicants must be in reasonably good health.

Religion: No requirement.

Financial status: No requirement.

Marital status: No requirement.

Family size: Applicants may have no more than 4 children currently in the family.

Racial, ethnic or cultural origin: No requirement.

THE PROCEDURE

Participation in Pan American Adoption Agency's program entails the following basic steps:
Application
Homestudy
Compliance with immigration/naturalization requirements
Referral
Placement
Post-placement supervision
Finalization
Naturalization

ADDITIONAL PROGRAMS/SERVICES

The agency provides homestudy and supervisory services for applicants in Virginia, Maryland, and Washington, D.C.

BRANCH/NETWORK OFFICES

3325 Garfield St. N.W.
Washington, D.C. 20008
(202) 690–3079

LICENSE/ACCREDITATION/PROFESSIONAL AFFILIATIONS

Pan American Adoption Agency, Inc. is licensed by the appropriate state department in New York, Maryland, Virginia, and Washington, D.C.

RAINBOW CHRISTIAN SERVICES

Box 9
Gainesville, VA 22065
(703) 754–8516
Program director: Philip M. Higgins, Jr.

THE PROGRAM

Rainbow Christian Services is a nonprofit agency providing service from New York to the North Carolina/Virginia state line. The agency places approximately 10 children annually in the homes of Church of Christ families.

THE COST

The agency's fee for adoption services is based on a sliding scale and ranges from $500 to $7,500. Services covered by the fee include pre-and post-placement counseling, homestudy, placement, and supervision as required by statute. In addition, applicants should anticipate legal fees connected with finalization and travel expenses (out-of-state applicants).

THE WAIT

The time from application to the homecoming of the adoptive child averages 18 months or more.

THE CHILDREN

Rainbow Christian Services places healthy and special-needs children, ranging in age from infancy to 17 years, of Caucasian, Black, and bi-racial backgrounds.

THE REQUIREMENTS

Age: Applicants must be at least 21 years of age.

Health: Applicants with health problems or handicaps are given individual consideration.

Religion: Applicants must be practicing members of the Church of Christ.

Financial status: Applicants are evaluated individually on the basis of their ability to utilize financial resources effectively.

Marital status: If applicants are living together, they must be married, and the length of the marriage must be at least 3 years. Single applicants are accepted.

Family size: No requirement, but may vary depending on the age and number of children the applicants wish to parent.

Racial, ethnic or cultural origin: Preference for placing children in families of similar origins, but interracial placements are considered.

THE PROCEDURE

Participation in Rainbow Christian Services' adoption program entails the following basic steps:
Referral
Application
Orientation meeting
Homestudy
Individual counseling sessions
Placement
Post-placement supervision

ADDITIONAL PROGRAMS/SERVICES

Rainbow Christian Services sponsors quarterly group meetings for adoptive parents which include discussion and presentation of topics by professional speakers. The agency hosts an annual picnic for adoptive families.

BRANCH/NETWORK OFFICES

None.

LICENSE/ACCREDITATION/PROFESSIONAL AFFILIATIONS

Rainbow Christian Services is licensed by the Commonwealth of Virginia Department of Social Services.

United Methodist Family Services

3900 West Broad Street
Richmond, VA 23230
(804) 353–4461
Program director: Kay L. Herrell

The Program

United Methodist Family Services is a nonprofit agency providing statewide service and placing approximately 25 children annually. Founded in 1902 as an orphanage, the agency has evolved in response to the changing needs of the community. Believing that "every child has the right to have a family to call his/her own," the agency provides a range of services to support families and children. The agency offers pregnancy counseling services and places infants for adoption when birthmothers in the agency's program decide that the best interests of their children will be served by adoptive placement. The agency is also actively involved in the placement of special-needs children.

The Cost

The agency's fee for infant adoption services is based on a sliding scale (4% of income for homestudy fee and 4% for placement fee). Services covered by the fee include all phases of the adoption process, excluding legal fees connected with finalization. The agency does not charge a fee for special needs placements.

The Wait

The time from application to the homecoming of the adoptive child varies depending on the age of the child the applicants wish to parent. For Caucasian infant adoptions, applicants wait 2 to 5 years before the homestudy begins. For older child adoptions, there is a short wait for the homestudy to begin, but the time from homestudy to placement varies depending on the applicants' flexibility and openness to the special needs of the child.

The Children

United Methodist Family Services places healthy and special-needs children of all ages and all racial backgrounds, born in the U.S.

The Requirements

Age: For infant adoptions, applicants must be at least 25 and no more than 45 years of age. For older child adoptions, there is no specified upper age limit.
Health: Applicants must be in reasonably good health.
Religion: No requirement.
Financial status: Applicants are evaluated individually on the basis of their ability to utilize financial resources effectively.
Marital status: For Caucasian infant adoptions, applicants must be married, and the length of the marriage must be at least 3 years. Single applicants are accepted for older child or special-needs adoptions.
Family size: For Caucasian infant adoptions, applicants may have no more than 1 child currently in the family. No requirement for older or special-needs adoptions.
Racial, ethnic or cultural origin: Preference for placing children in families of similar origins, but may vary depending on the child's needs.

The Procedure

Participation in United Methodist Family Services' adoption program entails the following basic steps:
Orientation meeting
Application
Homestudy group
Placement
Post-placement supervision
Post-adoption supervision

Additional Programs/Services

United Methodist Family Services provides a residential treatment program for teenagers; specialized foster care; counseling services; pregnancy counseling.

Branch/Network Offices

Tidewater Regional Center
(pregnancy counseling/special-needs adoptions)
5441 Virginia Beach Blvd., Suite 109
Virginia Beach, VA 23462
(804) 490–9791
Northern Virginia Regional Center
(pregnancy counseling
2315 South Grant St.
Arlington, VA 22202
(703) 486–8080

License/Accreditation/Professional Affiliations

United Methodist Family Services is licensed by the Commonwealth of Virginia Department of Social Services.

Virginia Baptist Children's Home and Family Services

P.O. Box 849
Salem, VA 24153–0849
(703) 389–5468
Program director: David G. Dillon, MSW, Director of Family Services

The Program

Virginia Baptist Children's Home and Family Services (VBCH) is a nonprofit agency providing statewide services and placing approximately 3–5 children annually. Providing care to children in need since 1890, the agency provides a wide range of services for children including campus-based group care, foster family care, emergency shelter, and counseling. Through the agency's adoption program, a few infants and young children are placed annually with qualified couples who are childless and unable to conceive.

The Cost

The agency's fee for adoption services is $4,500. Services covered by the fee include application, homestudy, placement, and post-placement supervision. Fees also help to underwrite the cost of medical services to the birthmother and child, and applicants should note that fees are subject to change. In addition, applicants assume responsibility for legal fees connected with finalization of the adoption.

THE WAIT

The time from application for acceptance into the program to the homecoming of the adoptive child averages 3 to 4 years.

THE CHILDREN

VBCH places primarily healthy Caucasian children, ranging in age from birth to 10 years, born in the U.S.

THE REQUIREMENTS

Age: For infant adoption, applicants may not be over 40 years of age at the time of placement. The age limit is flexible for school age children.

Health: Applicants must be in reasonably good health. Applicants with health problems or handicaps are given individual consideration. Infertility documentation is required for Caucasian infant adoptions.

Religion: For Caucasian infant adoptions, applicants must be practicing members of a Virginia Southern Baptist church. For adoption of a school age child, applicants must be active members of a traditional Christian denomination.

Financial status: Applicants are evaluated individually on the basis of their ability to manage financial resources.

Marital status: Applicants must be married couples, and the length of the marriage must be at least 3 years.

Family size: For Caucasian infant adoption, applicants must be childless. No requirement for the adoption of a school age child.

Racial, ethnic or cultural origin: Preference for placing children in families of similar origins.

THE PROCEDURE

Participation in VBCH's adoption program entails the following basic steps:
Referral
Submission of letter of interest for inquiry file
Application
Orientation meeting
Homestudy (including individual counseling sessions)
Placement
Post-placement supervision

ADDITIONAL PROGRAMS/SERVICES

VBCH provides a wide range of services including information and referral; campus-based group care; foster family care; emergency care shelter; family assistance; family and pregnancy counseling.

BRANCH/NETWORK OFFICES

VBCH operates branch offices throughout Virginia. However, adoption inquiries are processed only through the Salem office.

LICENSE/ACCREDITATION/PROFESSIONAL AFFILIATIONS

Virginia Baptist Children's Home and Family Services is licensed by the Commonwealth of Virginia Department of Social Services. The agency is affiliated with the National Association of Homes for Children, the Virginia Association of Children's Homes, the Southeastern Child Care Association, the Virginia Association of Licensed Child Placing Agencies, and the Virginia Council on Social Welfare.

WELCOME HOUSE ADOPTION SERVICES

5905 W. Broad Street, #300
Richmond, VA 23230
(804) 288–3920
Program director: Barbara B. Bird, Executive Director

THE PROGRAM

For a full description of programs and services, refer to Pennsylvania listing:
Welcome House Adoption Services
P.O. Box 836
Doylestown, PA 18901
(215) 345–0430

Washington

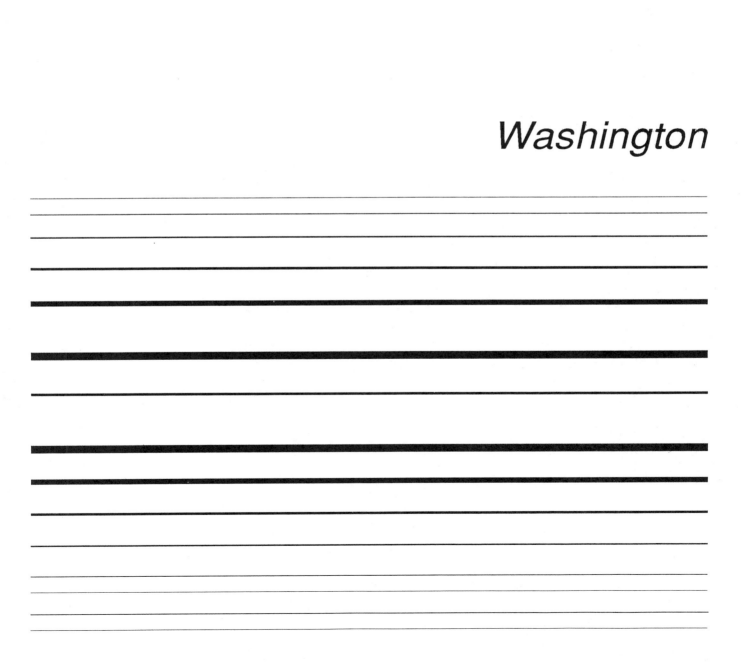

PUBLIC ADOPTION PROGRAM/ COMMUNITY RESOURCES

Department of Social and Health Services
Division of Children and Family Services
Adoption Program MS OB 41–C
Olympia, WA 98504
(206) 753–2178/0965
1–800–562–5682 (toll-free in Washington)
Adoption specialist: Pennie Oliver and Patrick Weber

THE PROGRAM

Public adoption services in Washington are provided by the Department of Social and Health Services (DSHS) through regional Children and Family Services offices located throughout the state. Working cooperatively with the Washington Adoption Resource Exchange (WARE), DSHS recruits and prepares families and supervises the placement of special-needs children (older and/or minority children; children with physical, intellectual, and emotional special needs; sibling groups) who are in the custody of the State of Washington. When out-of-state placement is a possibility, waiting children are also listed with the Northwest Adoption Exchange (NWAE, 909 N.E. 43rd, Suite 208, Seattle Washington 98105), a regional exchange program which includes Washington, Oregon, Idaho, Utah, Nevada, and Alaska. Information concerning adoption in Washington State can be obtained through the Adoption Information Service (a tax-exempt nonprofit organization of adoptive parents committed to making information about adoption available to the community) at the following address:

Adoption Information Service
P.O. Box 22640
Seattle, WA 98122–0640
(206) 325–9500

STATE EXCHANGE

Washington Adoption Resource Exchange. For information, contact the Division of Children and Family Services (above).

STATE ADOPTION REUNION REGISTRY

For information, contact the Division of Children and Family Services (above).

STATE SUBSIDY

Adoption Support Program
OB41–C
Olympia, WA 98504
(206) 753–7010
1–800–562–5682

NACAC REPRESENTATIVE

Jacqueline Erholm
1229 Cornwall Avenue, Suite 202
Bellingham, WA 98225
(206) 676–5437

GENERAL ADOPTION RESOURCES

For a complete and current list of adoption resources, contact Adoption Information Service (see Program above).

GENERAL ADOPTION RESOURCES

ABC (The Adoption of Black Children Committee)
P.O. Box 22831
Seattle, WA 98122
(206) 329–7877

Adoption Resource Center
Children's Home Society of Washington
Northwest Branch
3300 N.E. 65th Street
Seattle, WA 98115
(206) 524–6020

Advocates of Single Adoptive Parents/Northwest
2201 East Roanoke
Seattle, WA 98112
(206) 325–2506/725–4980/347–3937

Becoming Adoptive Parents
c/o Childbirth Education Association
14310 Greenwood Avenue N.
Seattle, WA 98133
(206) 367–2327

Birth and Life Bookstore
7001 Alonzo N.W.
P.O. Box 70625
Seattle, WA 98107
(206) 789–4444

Forever Families
c/o Shannon Wainscott
3215 177th Avenue N.E.
Redmond, WA 98052
(206) 885–3477

KIDS (Korean Identity Development Society)
503 N. 190th Street
Seattle, WA 98133
(206) 542–8646

KIN/OURS Adoptive Family Group
P.O. Box 5459
Everett, WA 98206
(206) 743–3049

Northwest Resource Center for Children, Youth, and Families
University of Washington
School of Social Work JH-30
4101 15th Avenue N.E.
Seattle, WA 98195
(206) 543–1517

Parents Supporting Adoptions from India (PSAI)
P.O. Box 1168
Bothell, WA 98041
(206) 481–4223

South Puget Sound Adoptive Parents
c/o Rita Foss
1224 Eldorado
Tacoma, WA 98466
(206) 564–2316

Information and Support Services for Infertile Couples
Infertility Counseling Center
University Place Offices

4705 16th Avenue N.E.
Seattle, WA 98105
(206) 527–0725

Resolve of Puget Sound
P.O. Box 31231
Seattle, WA 98103–1231
(206) 587–7234

Search Assistance and Support Services

Washington Adoptees Rights Movement (WARM)
c/o Pat Cunliffe-Owen
5960 6th Ave., S., Suite 107
Seattle, WA 98108
(206) 767–9510

SPECIAL-NEEDS ADOPTION RESOURCES

For information about resources for children with special needs, contact Adoption Information Service or the Division of Children and Family Services (above).

OUT-OF-STATE AGENCIES

AGENCY

Boys and Girls Aids Society of Oregon, Oregon (southwest Washington)

SEE APPENDIX A

Agencies Providing Nationwide Services

ADOPTION ADVOCATES INTERNATIONAL

658 Black Diamond Road
Port Angeles, WA 98362
(206) 452–4777
Program director: Merrily Ripley, Executive Director

THE PROGRAM

Adoption Advocates International is a nonprofit agency providing nationwide placement services (homestudy and supervisory services in Washington and Alaska only) and placing approximately 150 children annually. Founded in 1983, the agency's mission is to "provide adoption services to meet the needs of foreign children not generally served by other agencies, i.e. older children, handicapped children, children with medical problems or sibling groups." The agency has a commitment to children not yet adopted or who may never be adopted, and sends medicines, clothing, toys, school supplies and other infant and children's items to make life more comfortable for children without families. Adoptive parents are asked to help in this effort in some way. Finally, the agency also provides homestudy and supervisory services for applicants pursuing domestic special-needs adoption or foreign adoption through an independent source.

THE COST

The agency's fee for adoption services is based on the applicants' annual gross income.

Application	$36.00
Homestudy and post-placement supervision	$450.00–$850.00
Homestudy review (if homestudy is conducted by another agency)	$150.00
Processing	$450.00–$850.00

In addition, applicants should anticipate foreign agency fees and transportation costs ranging from $3,400 to $8,000 as well as legal fees connected with finalization.

THE WAIT

The time from application for acceptance into the program to the homecoming of the adoptive child(ren) is usually less than 1 year.

THE CHILDREN

Adoption Advocates International places primarily special-needs children (older children, children with special developmental needs, handicapped children, and sibling groups), ranging in age from birth to 16 years. Countries of origin include India, Taiwan, Korean, and Mexico. The agency also provides homestudy and supervisory services for applicants pursuing domestic special-needs adoption or foreign adoption through an independent source.

THE REQUIREMENTS

Age: No requirement, but may vary in some cases depending on the requirements of the country of origin.

Health: Applicants should be in reasonably good health. Applicants with health problems or handicaps are given individual consideration. Infertility documentation is required for some programs.

Religion: No requirement.

Financial status: No requirement. However, medical insurance for the adopted child is required.

Marital status: No requirement.

Family size: No requirement, but may vary in some cases depending on the requirements of the country of origin.

Racial, ethnic or cultural origin: No requirement.

THE PROCEDURE

Participation in Adoption Advocates International's adoption program entails the following basic steps:
Application
Homestudy
Compliance with immigration/naturalization requirements
Referral
Placement
Post-placement supervision

ADDITIONAL PROGRAMS/SERVICES

The agency provides opportunities for sponsorship (for people who are interested in sponsoring a child in a foreign country) and for direct aid (for people who are willing to collect supplies to be sent to orphanages abroad). The agency publishes a newsletter, The Adoption Advocate ($5.00 annual subscription).

BRANCH/NETWORK OFFICES

None.

LICENSE/ACCREDITATION/PROFESSIONAL AFFILIATIONS

Adoption Advocates International is licensed by the State of Washington Department of Social and Health Services. The agency is a member of the North American Council on Adoptable Children, the Joint Council on International Children Services, and International Council on Social Welfare.

ADOPTION SERVICES OF WACAP

P.O. Box 88948
Seattle, WA 98138
(206) 575-4550
Program director: Janice Neilson, Executive Director

THE PROGRAM

Adoption Services of WACAP (Western Association of Concerned Adoptive Parents) is a nonprofit agency providing nationwide services (homestudies for Washington, Alaska, Idaho, and Utah residents only) and placing approximately 450 children annually. WACAP began as a parent initiated, grass roots child placement agency in 1976. WACAP staff now includes 30 staff members and 45 volunteer adoptive parent groups with over 1500 volunteers working for the agency on a regular basis. While the agency is today one of the largest in the U.S., WACAP strives "to provide unique and personal service to each family and to maintain an attitude of openness and flexibility." WACAP's initial and continuing focus is to find families for waiting children. In addition, WACAP provides services to birthparents (Options for Pregnancy) and places infants for adoption when birthparents elect adoptive placement as the best plan for their child. Working directly with child welfare institutions abroad, WACAP places children from various countries in American families. In addition, the agency will provide homestudy and supervisory services for Washington, Alaska, Idaho or Utah residents pursuing interagency adoption (domestic or international) or independent adoption.

THE COST

The agency's fee for adoption services varies depending on the program and ranges from $1,500 to $5,000. Services included in the fee also vary depending on the program. Out-of-state applicants can expect to pay a licensed agency in their home state for homestudy and supervisory services. For all programs, applicants are responsible for legal fees connected with finalization of the adoption.

THE WAIT

The time from application to the homecoming of the adoptive child ranges from 6 months to 2 years.

THE CHILDREN

Adoption Services of WACAP places both healthy and special-needs children, ranging in age from birth to 17 years, of all racial backgrounds. Countries of origin include the Philippines, Korea, India, Thailand, Colombia, and U.S.

THE REQUIREMENTS

Age: No WACAP requirement, but may vary depending on the requirements of the cooperating agency or country (if applicable).

Health: No WACAP requirement, but may vary depending on the requirements of the cooperating agency or country (if applicable).

Religion: No WACAP requirement, but may vary depending on the requirements of the cooperating agency or country (if applicable).

Financial status: No WACAP requirement, but may vary depending on the requirements of the cooperating agency or country (if applicable).

Marital status: No WACAP requirement, but may vary depending on the requirements of the cooperating agency or country (if applicable).

Family size: No WACAP requirement, but may vary depending on the requirements of the cooperating agency or country (if applicable).

Racial, ethnic or cultural origin: No WACAP requirement, but may vary depending on the requirements of the cooperating agency or country (if applicable).

THE PROCEDURE

Participation in the adoption program of WACAP entails the following basic steps:
  Application
  Orientation
  Homestudy
  Compliance with immigration/naturalization requirements (international adoptions only)
  Referral
  Placement
  Post-placement supervision
Out-of-state applicants arrange with a licensed agency in their home state to provide homestudy and supervisory services.

ADDITIONAL PROGRAMS/SERVICES

WACAP provides foster care, pregnancy counseling, adoptive parent support groups, and a speakers' bureau.

BRANCH/NETWORK OFFICES

2290 E. 4500 S.
Salt Lake City, UT 84111
(801) 272-8459

P.O. Box 240741
Anchorage, AK 99524
(907) 278-3574

LICENSE/ACCREDITATION/PROFESSIONAL AFFILIATIONS

Adoption Services of WACAP is licensed by the appropriate state department in Alaska, Idaho, Utah, and Washington. The agency is an associate member of the Child Welfare League of America and the Joint Council on International Children's Services.

ADVENTIST ADOPTION & FAMILY SERVICES

P.O. Box 3838
816 N.E. 87th Avenue, Suite 101
Vancouver, WA 98664(206) 892-1572
Program director: Fern Ringering, MSW

THE PROGRAM

For a full description of programs and services, refer to
Oregon listing:
Adventist Adoption & Family Services
6040 S.E. Belmont Street
Portland, OR 97215
(503) 232-1211

AMERICANS FOR INTERNATIONAL AID AND ADOPTION

Washington State Branch
P.O. Box 6051
Spokane, WA 99207-0901
(509) 484-0206
Program director: Carol Ann Hollar

THE PROGRAM

For a complete description of programs and services, refer
to Michigan listing:
Americans for International Aid and Adoption
887 S. Adams
Birmingham, MI 48013
(313) 645-2211

BETHANY CHRISTIAN SERVICES

103 E. Holly Street, #316
Bellingham National Bank Bldg.
Bellingham, WA 98225(206) 733-6042
Program director: James K. Haveman, Jr., Executive
Director

THE PROGRAM

For a full description of programs and services, refer to
Michigan listing:
Bethany Christian Services
901 Eastern Avenue, N.E.
Grand Rapids, MI 49503-1295
(616) 459-6273

CATHOLIC COMMUNITY SERVICES

1715 East Cherry
P.O. Box 22608
Seattle, WA 98122
(206) 323-6336
Program director: Agency Executive Director

THE PROGRAM

Catholic Community Services is a nonprofit multi-service
agency serving residents of King County and placing approximately 120 children annually through its adoption programs. In all of its programs, the agency's mission is "to
minister to children, families, individuals and elderly of any
creed or color who are poor, troubled, or otherwise in need of
caring human services." The agency provides services to
birthparents and places infants for adoption when birthparents in the agency's counseling program elect adoptive
placement as the best plan for their child. Birthparents who
decide to make an adoption plan are offered the opportunity
to select and meet the adoptive family, the option of receiving
yearly progress reports for the first few years of the child's
life, and the opportunity to leave a letter, a personal family
history, or a gift for their child. Working cooperatively with
other private and public agencies and with national and
regional exchange programs, the agency locates children of
all races for couples and single parents who wish to adopt
school-age youngsters, handicapped children of all ages, or
sibling groups. Working cooperatively with child welfare
institutions in Korea and Japan, the agency places Korean and
Japanese infants and older children in American families.
Applicants should note that residency in King County is
required for all programs except for the Korean program. For
the Korean program, only Washington State residents are
eligible.

THE COST

The agency's fee for adoption services varies depending
on the program. For domestic infant adoptions, the agency's
fee is $5,500. This fee represents reimbursement to the
agency for medical/hospital/legal expenses of the birthmother
and child and payment for services to the adoptive family and
to the birthparents.

For special-needs adoptions, the agency's fee is $1,000.
Services covered by the fee include the homestudy, list and
search fee, placement, and post- placement supervision. If a
child from another area is available for placement, the adoptive parents meet travel and visiting costs.

For adoption from Japan, the fee ranges from $1,300 to
$1,500 and includes the homestudy, matching and placement
services, and document fees in Japan. At least 1 member of
the couple must travel to Japan to meet the child and escort
him/her to the U.S. In addition, applicants should anticipate
immigration/naturalization fees (minimal).

For adoption from Korea, the fee for King County families
is $4,750. An additional fee, ranging from $200 to $400, will
be assessed for families who live outside of King County but
have their studies and post-placement services provided by
the Seattle staff. Applicants should anticipate immigration/
naturalization fees (minimal).

Applicants should note that fees are subject to change and
that applicants assume responsibility for legal fees connected
with finalization of the adoption.

THE WAIT

The time from application to the homecoming of the
adoptive child varies depending on the program. For domestic infant adoption, the wait is generally 1 1/2 to 2 years. For

special-needs adoption, the wait is ordinarily 6 months to 1 year. For adoption through Korea, the wait is ordinarily 6 to 8 months, and through Japan, 1 to 2 years.

THE CHILDREN

Catholic Community Services places both healthy and special-needs children, ranging in age from infancy to adolescence, of all racial backgrounds. Countries of origin include U.S., Korea, and Japan.

THE REQUIREMENTS

Age: For Korean adoption, applicants must be between the ages of 25 and 45. For special-needs adoption, the requirement varies depending on the needs of the child. For domestic infant adoption, couples should not be much over 40.

Health: Applicants should be in good health. For domestic infant adoption, medical exploration of infertility status is required.

Religion: For domestic infant adoption, at least one spouse should be a practicing Catholic. For special-needs adoption, the requirement varies depending on the needs of the child. No requirement for other programs.

Financial status: Applicants must demonstrate financial stability.

Marital status: Single applicants are accepted for special-needs adoption. For other programs, applicants must be married and must demonstrate marital stability. For Korean adoption, the length of the marriage must be at least 3 years; for domestic infant adoption, 2 years.

Family size: For Korean adoption, applicants may have no more than 4 children in the family; for domestic infant adoption, no more than 3 children currently in the family. For special-needs adoption, the requirement varies depending on the needs of the child.

Racial, ethnic or cultural origin: No requirement.

THE PROCEDURE

Participation in Catholic Community Services adoption programs entails the following basic steps:
Orientation meeting
Application
Homestudy
Compliance with immigration/naturalization requirements (international adoptions only)
Placement
Post-placement supervision

ADDITIONAL PROGRAMS/SERVICES

Catholic Community Services provides a wide range of services including maternity services; foster care; family life education; services to the elderly; individual, marital, and family counseling; alcohol counseling; crisis intervention counseling; referral services.

BRANCH/NETWORK OFFICES

South King County Branch Office
232 S. Second Ave., Suite 200
Kent, WA 98031
(206) 854–0077

East King County Branch Office
14023 N.E. 8th

P.O. Box 6188
Bellevue, WA 98008–0188
(206) 643–1937

LICENSE/ACCREDITATION/PROFESSIONAL AFFILIATIONS

Catholic Community Services is licensed by the State of Washington Department of Social and Health Services and is accredited by the Council on Accreditation of Services for Families and Children. The agency is a member of the United Way.

CATHOLIC COMMUNITY SERVICES

5410 N. 44th Street
Tacoma, WA 98407
(206) 752–2455
Program director: Pat Ditter

THE PROGRAM

Catholic Community Services is a nonprofit multi-service agency serving residents of Pierce and Kitsap Counties and placing approximately 18 children annually through its adoption program. Providing services in Pierce County since the early 1920s, the agency's mission is "to preserve and strengthen families and individuals in the community through a thoughtfully conceived and carefully implemented program of social service, advocacy and convening." Working directly with birthparents, with other private and public agencies, and with national and regional exchange programs, the agency places both healthy and special-needs children. Working cooperatively with other U.S. agencies which maintain international programs, the agency places Korean children. In addition, the agency will provide homestudy and supervisory services for applicants pursuing interagency adoption (domestic or international) or private adoption.

THE COST

The agency's fee for adoption services is $3,000. Services covered by the fee include the homestudy, placement, and post-placement services. For domestic infant adoption, applicants occasionally pay medical expenses of the birthmother and child. For international adoption, applicants should anticipate fees to the cooperating agency. For both programs, applicants are responsible for legal fees connected with finalization of the adoption.

THE WAIT

The time from application for acceptance into the program to the homecoming of the adoptive child ranges from 2 months to 5 years.

THE CHILDREN

Catholic Community Services places both healthy and special-needs children, ranging in age from birth to 10 years, of Caucasian, Asian, and bi-racial backgrounds. Countries of origin include U.S. and Korea.

THE REQUIREMENTS

Age: Applicants must be at least 23 and no more than 40 years of age.

Health: Applicants should be in reasonably good health. Applicants with health problems or handicaps are given individual consideration.

Religion: No requirement.

Financial status: Applicants must demonstrate financial stability.

Marital status: Applicants must be married; the length of the marriage must be at least 2 years.

Family size: For domestic infant adoption, applicants may have no more than 1 child in the family. For Korean adoption, applicants may have up to 4 children currently in the family.

Racial, ethnic or cultural origin: No requirement, but preference for placing children in families of similar origins.

THE PROCEDURE

Participation in the adoption program of Catholic Community Services entails the following basic steps:

Pre-application
Orientation meeting
Application
Compliance with immigration/naturalization requirements (Korean adoptions only)
Homestudy
Placement
Post-placement supervision

ADDITIONAL PROGRAMS/SERVICES

Catholic Community Services provides infant care classes for adoptive families; adoptive parent support meetings and social activities; foster care; counseling.

BRANCH/NETWORK OFFICES

None.

LICENSE/ACCREDITATION/PROFESSIONAL AFFILIATIONS

Catholic Community Services is licensed by the State of Washington Department of Social and Health Services.

CATHOLIC COMMUNITY SERVICES OF SNOHOMISH COUNTY

1410 Broadway
Everett, WA 98201
(206) 259–9188
Program director: Carol Steckler

THE PROGRAM

Catholic Community Services is a nonprofit social service agency serving residents of Snohomish County. Through its adoption program, the agency places approximately 4–6 children annually. Providing adoption services for 45 years, the program has historically included independent adoptions, overseas adoptions, and healthy infant adoptions. Currently, the agency is directly placing only healthy infants born in the U.S. through its adoption program. Special-needs infants and children (ranging in age from 6 months to 10 years) are placed through the agency's foster care program. In all of its programs, the agency's mission is "to minister to children, families, individuals, and elderly of any creed or color who are poor, troubled, or…in need of caring human services."

THE COST

The agency's fee for healthy infant adoption is as follows:
Application/psychological evaluation $150.00
Homestudy $700.00
Placement $4,500.00–$5,350.00

The fee for special needs older child adoptions varies, with an average cost of $1,000. For all programs, applicants assume responsibility for legal fees connected with finalization of the adoption (approximately $500).

THE WAIT

The time from application for acceptance into the program to the homecoming of the adoptive child ranges from 12 to 32 months.

THE CHILDREN

Catholic Community Services places both healthy and special-needs children, ranging in age from birth to 10 years, of all racial backgrounds, born in the U.S.

THE REQUIREMENTS

Age: The age requirement is evaluated on an individual basis.

Health: Applicants should be in reasonably good health. Applicants with health problems or handicaps are given individual consideration. Infertility documentation is required for healthy infant adoptions.

Religion: No requirement.

Financial status: The agency looks for adoptive parents who have a history of living within their own resources without accumulating large debts. The amount of the resources is not relevant.

Marital status: Married couples who have been married at least 3 years and single parents are eligible. Divorces are taken into consideration and evaluated as to the patterns of an individual's relationship.

Family size: For infant adoptions, applicants may have no more than 1 child currently in the family. For applicants pursuing special needs or older child adoption through the foster program, there is no specific limit on the number of children currently in the family.

Racial, ethnic or cultural origin: Preference for placing children in families of similar origins.

THE PROCEDURE

Participation in Catholic Community Services' adoption program entails the following basic steps:

Application
Psychological evaluation
Individual counseling sessions (if appropriate)
Homestudy
Placement
Post-placement supervision

ADDITIONAL PROGRAMS/SERVICES

Catholic Community Services provides a wide range of community services including counseling; foster care; maternity services; pregnancy aide program; home-based services; volunteer chore services; independent living program; alcohol program; anger management program.

BRANCH/NETWORK OFFICES

None.

LICENSE/ACCREDITATION/PROFESSIONAL AFFILIATIONS

Catholic Community Services of Snohomish County is licensed by the State of Washington Department of Social and Health Services. The agency is a member of the Alliance for Family, Youth and Children and the National Catholic Charities Network.

CHILDREN'S HOME SOCIETY

201 S. 34th Street
Tacoma, WA 98408
(206) 472-3355
Program director: Roy Beams

THE PROGRAM

Children's Home Society is a nonprofit agency serving residents of Washington State and placing approximately 20 children annually through its adoption program. While the agency provides services to birthparents and occasionally places infants for adoption, the primary focus of the program is to recruit, prepare, supervise, and support families adopting special-needs children. The agency provides educational programs on issues facing adoptive families (a 6 week class as well as several 1 day workshops) and sponsors a parent support group.

THE COST

The agency's fee for adoption services ranges from $1,500 to $3,000. Services covered by the fee include all phases of the adoption process, excluding legal fees connected with finalization of the adoption.

THE WAIT

The time from application to placement averages 18 months.

THE CHILDREN

Most children placed by the Children's Home Society have been abused and many have special needs resulting from that experience. The children range in age from 7 to 13 and are of Caucasian, Black, and bi-racial backgrounds.

THE REQUIREMENTS

Age: Applicants must be at least 21 years of age.
Health: Applicants with health problems or handicaps are given individual consideration.
Religion: No requirement.
Financial status: The requirement varies depending on the number of individuals in the family and the family's ability to successfully manage their expenses.

Marital status: Married couples and single parents may apply. If married, the length of the marriage must be at least 2 years.
Family size: No requirement.
Racial, ethnic or cultural origin: Preference for placing children in families of similar origins.

THE PROCEDURE

Participation in the adoption program of the Children's Home Society entails the following basic steps:
Application
Group counseling sessions
Homestudy (group format)
Referral
Placement
Post-placement supervision

ADDITIONAL PROGRAMS/SERVICES

Children's Home Society provides foster care; family counseling; parent aide program; support group for single parents; group for sexually abused grade school girls.

BRANCH/NETWORK OFFICES

Adoption inquiries are processed by the Tacoma office.

LICENSE/ACCREDITATION/PROFESSIONAL AFFILIATIONS

Children's Home Society is licensed by the State of Washington Department of Social and Health Services.

CHILDREN'S HOME SOCIETY OF WASHINGTON

(Northwest Branch)
3300 N.E. 65th Street
P.O. Box 15190
Seattle, WA 98115-0190
(206) 524-6020
Program director: Chris Ingersoll, Placement Services; Randy Perin, Adoption Resource Center

THE PROGRAM

Children's Home Society of Washington is a nonprofit agency serving residents of King County and the Puget Sound region and placing between 5 and 10 children annually. Striving "to strengthen and support families," the agency's adoption program was developed to find permanent homes for boys residing in the residential treatment center, either through foster care guardianship or adoption. The agency accepts no outside referrals of children, placing only those children who are served by the agency's residential treatment program. In addition, the agency maintains the Adoption Resource Center to address the on-going needs of all members of the adoption triad and to serve as a resource to professionals in their work with triad members. Services provided through the Adoption Resource Center include support groups; family, individual, and group therapy; classes and workshops; extensive library of adoption related material.

The Cost

Adoption services are provided at no cost to the adoptive family. The only expenses which applicants need anticipate are legal fees connected with finalization of the adoption.

The Wait

The time from application to the homecoming of the adoptive child is approximately 1 year. This includes a lengthy visitation process of 3 to 9 months, depending on the child's needs. Children currently in residential treatment may or may not be ready to leave at the time of meeting the adoptive family, but may nevertheless need family involvement during this transitional stage.

The Children

Children's Home Society places healthy children who may be either emotionally or behaviorally troubled, ranging in age from 10 to 15 years, primarily of Caucasian but also of biracial backgrounds, born in the U.S.

The Requirements

Age: Applicants must be at least 21 years of age.
Health: Applicants should be in reasonably good health. Applicants with health problems or handicaps are given individual consideration.
Religion: No requirement.
Financial status: No requirement.
Marital status: No requirement.
Family size: No requirement.
Racial, ethnic or cultural origin: Preference for placing children in families of similar origins.

The Procedure

Participation in the adoption program of the Children's Home Society entails the following basic steps:
Orientation meeting
Application
Homestudy
Adoptive parent training
Referral
Placement
Post-placement supervision and services

Additional Programs/Services

Children's Home Society provides permanent foster care; long term treatment foster care; residential treatment; counseling; individual and group treatment; respite care; support groups. Through The Adoption Resource Center, the agency provides a variety of services to the Triad community including counseling/therapy, workshops, classes, advocacy, support groups, genetic histories, and a resource room. Services are based on the philosophy that "adoption is a life-long process and services must be made available to all individuals connected with adoption."

Branch/Network Offices

Tacoma Office
202 S. 34th St.
Tacoma, WA 98408
(206) 472-3355

Applicants should note that program offerings of the Tacoma office are separate and distinct from those offered by the Seattle office.

License/Accreditation/Professional Affiliations

Children's Home Society of Washington is licensed by the State of Washington Department of Social and Health Services and is a member of the Child Welfare League of America.

Church of Christ Homes for Children

30012 Military Road, S.
Federal Way, WA 98003
(206) 839-2755
Program director: Barbara Grimm

The Program

Church of Christ Homes for Children is a nonprofit agency providing nationwide services and placing approximately 12 infants annually. Founded almost 20 years ago, the agency's mission is "to provide permanent Christian homes for children." The agency provides services to birthmothers and places infants for adoption when birthmothers in the agency's counseling program elect adoptive placement as the best plan for their children. The agency also provides homestudy and supervisory services for applicants pursuing independent adoption.

The Cost

The agency's fee for adoption services varies depending on the actual cost of services to the birthmother and child and ranges from $3,000 to $7,000. Services covered by the fee include all phases of the adoption process.

The Wait

The time from application to the homecoming of the adoptive child averages 2 years.

The Children

Church of Christ Homes for Children places primarily healthy children, ranging in age from birth to 5 years, of all racial backgrounds, born in the U.S.

The Requirements

Age: Applicants may be no more than 40 years of age.
Health: Applicants must be in good health. Infertility documentation is preferred but not required.
Religion: Applicants must be active members of the Church of Christ.
Financial status: Applicants must have a stable financial history.
Marital status: Applicants must be married couples who have been married for at least 3 years.
Family size: Applicants may have no more than 1 child currently in the family.
Racial, ethnic or cultural origin: Preference for placing children in families of similar origins.

THE PROCEDURE

Participation in the Church of Christ Homes for Children adoption program entails the following basic steps:
Application
Individual counseling sessions
Homestudy
Placement
Post-placement supervision

ADDITIONAL PROGRAMS/SERVICES

The agency provides counseling services for birthparents; homestudy and supervisory services for applicants pursuing independent adoption.

BRANCH/NETWORK OFFICES

None.

LICENSE/ACCREDITATION/PROFESSIONAL AFFILIATIONS

Church of Christ Homes for Children is licensed by the State of Washington Department of Social and Health Services.

THE FAMILY FOUNDATION

1229 Cornwall Avenue, Suite 202
Bellingham, WA 98225
(206) 676–5437 (KIDS)
Program director: Jacqueline R. Erholm, Executive Director

THE PROGRAM

The Family Foundation is a nonprofit agency serving residents of the state of Washington (primarily Region III) and facilitating the placement of approximately 25 special-needs children annually. The agency was founded in 1985 by Jaqueline Erholm (Executive Director, author of *Adoptive Parent Preparation Training*, and mother of 10 children—two "home-grown," two long-term foreign exchange students, and six adopted children) to increase public awareness of the needs of waiting children and to facilitate the placement of special-needs children. The agency does not have custody of the children but works in cooperation with custodial agencies throughout the U.S. to provide placement services. The agency's focus is on recruiting, training, and supporting individuals, couples, and families willing to adopt waiting children. In addition, the agency will provide homestudy and supervisory services for applicants pursuing inter-agency adoption (domestic or international) or independent adoption, upon request of an attorney.

THE COST

The agency's fee for adoption services is $1,450. Services covered by the fee include application, adoptive parent preparation training (APPT), pre-placement report, placement and post-placement supervision and services. The only additional fees which applicants need anticipate are legal fees connected with finalization of the adoption (approximately $250–$350) and occasionally travel expenses (if the child is out of the area or out-of- state).

THE WAIT

The time from application to the homecoming of the adoptive child averages 9 months.

THE CHILDREN

The Family Foundation facilitates the placement of waiting children, ranging in age from infancy to adolescence, primarily of Caucasian, Black, and bi-racial backgrounds, born in the U.S.

THE REQUIREMENTS

Age: Applicants must be at least 21 years of age.
Health: Applicants with health problems or handicaps are given individual consideration.
Religion: No requirement.
Financial status: No requirement other than the ability to provide adequately for an additional family member.
Marital status: No requirement.
Family size: No requirement.
Racial, ethnic or cultural origin: No requirement.

THE PROCEDURE

Participation in the adoption program of The Family Foundation entails the following basic steps:
Orientation meeting
Application
Adoptive Parent Preparation Training (group format; 3 full days over 2 weekends)
Homestudy
Child search/referral
Placement
Post-placement supervision and services
Parents and Kids Support Night (required, once a month)
Transition counseling (required)

ADDITIONAL PROGRAMS/SERVICES

The Family Foundation provides specialized recruitment programs; speakers regarding special-needs adoption; on-going support services.

BRANCH/NETWORK OFFICES

None.

LICENSE/ACCREDITATION/PROFESSIONAL AFFILIATIONS

The Family Foundation is licensed by the State of Washington Department of Social and Health Services.

HOPE SERVICES/DIVISION OF BURDEN BEARERS

424 North 130th Street
Seattle, WA 98133
(206) 367–4606
Program director: Mary Struck

THE PROGRAM

Hope Services is a nondenominational, Christian, nonprofit, child-placing program providing pregnancy and adoption counseling services throughout Washington State. Burden Bearers was founded in 1964 by Hegge Iverson as a nondenominational Christian counseling center which later expanded services to include the placement of infants and children in Christian homes. The program's purpose is "to assist young women of all ages facing an unplanned pregnancy, helping them explore all of their options, while providing counsel, care and support for their individual needs." Couples are carefully prepared for adoption parenthood through a series of orientation meetings and the homestudy. Adoption is viewed as a shared, flexible, and open experience; birthparents select families from picture profiles, and both parties have an opportunity to meet each other before the birth. After placement, birthparents can receive pictures and progress reports. Working cooperatively with national and regional exchange programs, the program recruits families for older/special-needs children. In addition, the program will provide homestudy services for applicants pursuing international or independent adoptions if the couple meets program criteria. Out-of-state applicants are given consideration on a case-by-case basis. Washington State couples are given priority.

THE COST

The agency's fees are adjusted annually in accordance with the cost of providing services.

THE WAIT

The time from approval to placement is usually 1 year for infants.

THE CHILDREN

Hope Services places both healthy and special-needs children, ranging in age from birth to 17 years, of all racial backgrounds, born in the U.S.

THE REQUIREMENTS

Age: Applicants are generally expected to be between mid-twenties and mid-thirties, with some flexibility for older couples.

Health: Applicants should be in reasonably good health. Applicants with health problems or handicaps are given individual consideration. Reasonable evidence of infertility is required for infant adoption.

Religion: Applicants must be actively practicing Christians who attend church.

Financial status: Applicants must have sufficient income to provide for an additional family member.

Marital status: Applicants must be married, and the length of the marriage must be at least 2 years.

Family size: Applicants may have no more than 2 children currently in the family.

Racial, ethnic or cultural origin: No requirement.

THE PROCEDURE

Participation in the adoption program of Hope Services entails the following basic steps:
Request for application
Submission of application for review and approval
Orientation meeting for couples who reside near agency
Completion of homestudy
Selection by birthparent

Placement of child
Post-placement supervision

ADDITIONAL PROGRAMS/SERVICES

Hope Services provides counseling services to birthparents.

BRANCH/NETWORK OFFICES

Hope Services has trained pregnancy and adoption counselors throughout the state. All inquiries are processed through the main office.

LICENSE/ACCREDITATION/PROFESSIONAL AFFILIATIONS

Hope Services is licensed by the State of Washington Department of Social and Health Services.

JEWISH FAMILY SERVICE

1214 Boylston Avenue
Seattle, WA 98101
(206) 461–3240
Program director: Patti Gorman

THE PROGRAM

Jewish Family Service is a nonprofit social service agency serving Jewish families in the greater Seattle area. The agency maintains a small adoption program and directly places, on the average, 1 child annually. In addition, the agency will provide homestudy and supervisory services for applicants pursuing foreign or domestic adoption through another licensed custodial agency.

THE COST

For complete adoption services (when JFS has custody of the child), the agency's fee is $2,000. Services covered by the fee include all phases of the adoption process, excluding legal fees connected with finalization of the adoption. For specific services, the agency's fee schedule is as follows:

Homestudy	$650.00
Evaluation of previous homestudy	$50.00
Homestudy update	$300.00
Post-placement services	$300.00
"Next Friend" report for court	$300.00

THE WAIT

The agency maintains a file of 3 studied applicants for direct placement at any given time. The time from application to initiation of the homestudy can be several years. The time from completion of the homestudy to placement is much shorter. For interagency placements, the time from application to the initiation of the homestudy is almost immediate; the time from completion of the homestudy to placement varies depending on the cooperating agency.

THE CHILDREN

JFS directly places primarily healthy Caucasian infants, born in the U.S. JFS will provide homestudy and supervisory services for applicants pursuing the adoption of healthy or special-needs children of any age, race, or country of origin through a cooperating custodial agency.

THE REQUIREMENTS

Age: Applicants may be no more than 45 years of age.
Health: Applicants should be in reasonably good health.
Religion: Applicants must be members of the Jewish faith.
Financial status: No requirement.
Marital status: No requirement.
Family size: No requirement.
Racial, ethnic or cultural origin: No requirement.

THE PROCEDURE

Participation in the adoption program of JFS entails the following basic steps:
Application
Homestudy
Placement
Post-placement supervision
Applicants pursuing placement through another licensed custodial agency who need homestudy and supervisory services are invited to contact JFS to arrange for services.

ADDITIONAL PROGRAMS/SERVICES

JFS provides a range of community services including foster care; counseling; support services (food bank, direct aid); programs for the elderly; Big Pal program.

BRANCH/NETWORK OFFICES

11101 N.E. 8th
Bellevue, WA 98004
(206) 451-8512

LICENSE/ACCREDITATION/PROFESSIONAL AFFILIATIONS

Jewish Family Service is licensed by the State of Washington Department of Social and Health Services. The Agency is supported by the United Way and the Jewish Federation.

LDS SOCIAL SERVICES

North 606 Pines Road
Spokane, WA 99216
(509) 926-6581
Program director: Dennis D. Ashton

THE PROGRAM

For a full description of programs and services, refer to Utah listing:
LDS Social Services
50 East North Temple Street
Salt Lake City, UT 84150

BRANCH OFFICES

LDS Social Services/Washington
220 S. Third Place
Renton, WA 98055
(206) 624-3393
Director: Fred M. Riley

6500-B W. Deschutes
Kennewick, WA 99336
(509) 735-8406

LUTHERAN SOCIAL SERVICES OF WASHINGTON

19230 Forest Park Drive, N.E.
Seattle, WA 98155
(206) 365-2700
Program director: Linda Katz; Norma Spoonemore, Social Worker

THE PROGRAM

Lutheran Social Services of Washington is a nonprofit social service agency. The Northwest area office serves residents of King and Snohomish County and places approximately 8 to 10 children annually through its infant adoption program. The agency provides services to birthparents and places infants for adoption when birthparents in the agency's pregnancy counseling program elect adoptive placement as the best plan for their child. The agency offers an open adoption program which provides a number of options (options, not requirements) designed to increase knowledge and communication between birthparents and adoptive parents. Most birthparents select adoptive families from non-identifying autobiographical letters; most meet and share first names. All adoptive parents send pictures and information through the agency to birthparents at designated times each year from the time of placement until a child reaches age 18.

The agency also has a Permanency Planning Program through which individual children or sibling groups under the age of 9 are placed in homes of parents who have been licensed as foster parents but who are willing to become adoptive parents if the child or children placed in their home become legally free.

THE COST

The agency's fee for infant adoption services includes a $250 fee for a 6-week infant adoption preparation group (to learn about birthparents, how infertility affects adoption, needs of adoptees, and how parenting a child by adoption is different from parenting a child by birth) and a service fee ranging from $4,000 to $8,000. The service fee covers all phases of the adoption process (excluding legal fees connected with finalization) and all legal, medical, and counseling expenses of the birthparents.

Applicants interested in the Permanency Planning Program pay $250 for the 8-week preparation group. Families who then choose to continue on toward placement are charged 3% of their annual gross income. The first 1% is due at the completion of individual and/or family meetings with the caseworker. When a child is placed, families are reimbursed monthly by the State for the cost of caring for the child until the child becomes legally free, at which time the 2% portion of the fee becomes due.

THE WAIT

The agency's infant adoption program keeps a small pool of waiting families from whom birthparents select for placement of their baby. Some families receive placement within 2 months of completing the preparation process; others wait 2 years, depending on birthparents' requests. For the Permanency Planning Program, placement may occur at any time after completion of preparation and foster family licensing.

THE CHILDREN

Lutheran Social Services' infant adoption program places healthy Caucasian infants (birth to 3 months), born in the U.S. Through the Permanency Planning Program, the agency places older children and sibling groups who are not legally free for adoption but who may become free. Often, these children have been neglected, physically or sexually abused.

THE REQUIREMENTS

Age: For infant adoption, applicants must be at least 23 and no more than 39 years of age. No requirement for Permanency Planning Program.

Health: Applicants must be in reasonably good health. For infant adoption, infertility documentation is not required, but applicants must be seeking adoption because a pregnancy is either impossible or medically unwise.

Religion: No agency requirement, but birthparents often request practicing Lutheran or Christian families.

Financial status: No requirement.

Marital status: For infant adoption, applicants must be married couples who have been married for at least 3 years. No requirement for Permanency Planning Program other than the ability to provide a stable, nurturing family for a troubled child.

Family size: For infant adoption, applicants may have no more than 1 child currently in the family. No requirement for Permanency Planning Program.

Racial, ethnic or cultural origin: Preference for placing children in families of similar origins.

THE PROCEDURE

Participation in Lutheran Social Services' Adoption Program and Permanency Planning Program entails the following basic steps:

Adoption Program
Orientation meeting
Application
Adoption preparation group (6 weeks)
Homestudy (with individual counseling sessions)
Submission of open adoption options sheet and letter to birthparents
Referral
Placement
Post-placement supervision and services

Permanency Planning Program
Orientation meeting
Intake interview
Preparation group (8 weeks)
Foster family licensing
Placement
Post-placement supervision and services

ADDITIONAL PROGRAMS/SERVICES

Lutheran Social Services provides ongoing support through individual and family counseling, foster parent support groups, social gatherings for adoptive families, newsletters, and information and referral to community resources.

BRANCH/NETWORK OFFICES

Northeast Area Office
North 1226 Howard St.

Spokane, WA 99201
(509) 327-7761

Southeast Area Office
Plaza I, Suite 700
320 North Johnson St.
Kennewick, WA 99336
(509) 735-6446

Applicants should note that area offices also provide services for infant adoption. Permanency Planning Program is offered only through the Seattle office.

LICENSE/ACCREDITATION/PROFESSIONAL AFFILIATIONS

Lutheran Social Services of Washington is licensed by the State of Washington Department of Social and Health Services. All caseworkers are MSW and ACSW and members of the National Association of Social Workers.

MEDINA CHILDREN'S SERVICE

P.O. Box 22638
Seattle, WA 98122
(206) 324-9470

Program director: Donald V. Pearson, Executive Director; Marge Boothe, Director of Adoptions/Pregnancy Counseling

THE PROGRAM

Medina Children's Service is a nonprofit child welfare agency serving primarily residents of King County (within an hour's driving time of the agency) and placing approximately 50–60 children annually. Founded in 1921 as Medina Baby Home, an institution where babies were cared for prior to adoption, the agency has expanded in response to the changing needs of the community and today provides a wide range of services including foster care, pregnancy counseling (with an emphasis on minority clients), teenage pregnancy and parenting program (TAPP), and healthy infant and special-needs adoption. The agency's mission is "to support the community through the development and maintenance of resources and programs for the enhancement of family well being."

THE COST

The agency's fee for adoption services is based on a sliding scale which varies according to the program and ranges from $0 to $6,000. Fees are waived for some families who adopt certain children with special needs. Services covered by the fee include all phases of the adoption process (excluding legal fees connected with finalization, approximately $200–$300).

THE WAIT

The time from application to the homecoming of the adoptive child varies depending on the program. For a healthy Caucasian infant, the wait ranges from 1 to 2 years; for healthy minority infants, a few weeks to 1 year or more; for special-needs children, a few weeks to 1 year or more.

THE CHILDREN

Medina Children's Service places special-needs children (with significant non-correctable disabilities) ranging in age from birth to 18 years, of all racial backgrounds; healthy minority infants, ranging in age from birth to 10 months, primarily of Black and bi-racial backgrounds; healthy Caucasian infants, ranging in age from birth to 10 months. All children placed by the agency were born in the U.S.

THE REQUIREMENTS

Age: For a healthy Caucasian infant, both spouses may be no more than 38 years of age at the time of application. For a healthy minority infant, there is no requirement, but applicants are more likely to be selected by birthparents if they are under the age of 40. No requirement for special-needs adoption.

Health: Applicants should be in reasonably good health. Applicants with special health circumstances will be considered on a case-by-case basis. Infertility documentation is required for healthy Caucasian infant adoption.

Religion: No requirement.

Financial status: No requirement other than basic financial stability.

Marital status: For a healthy Caucasian infant, applicants must be married couples who have been married for at least 2 years. For healthy minority infant, married couples are strongly preferred. Single applicants are accepted for special-needs adoption.

Family size: For a healthy Caucasian infant, applicants may have no more than 1 child currently in the family. No requirement for other programs.

Racial, ethnic or cultural origin: Healthy minority infants are placed with racially and culturally relevant families. In all programs, the agency prefers to place children in families of similar origins.

THE PROCEDURE

Participation in the Medina Children's Service adoption program entails the following basic steps:

Pre-application interview

Application

Adoption education group (4–week program for families requesting healthy infants)

Adoption preparation group (8–week program for families requesting children with special needs)

Homestudy (2–3 interviews which are usually held after completion of education/preparation group)

Child referral

Placement

Post-placement supervision

ADDITIONAL PROGRAMS/SERVICES

Medina Children's Service provides counseling for pregnant clients and other parents considering relinquishment; temporary foster care for newborns pending legal freedom; post adoption services including community resource referral, search, parent support through special events; teenage pregnancy and parenting program (an interagency program to provide educational, health, and employment services to pregnant and parenting teens).

BRANCH/NETWORK OFFICES

None.

LICENSE/ACCREDITATION/PROFESSIONAL AFFILIATIONS

Medina Children's Service is licensed by the State of Washington Department of Social and Health Services. The agency is a member of the Alliance for Children, Youth, and Families and of Family Builders Network, Inc.

NEW HOPE OF WASHINGTON

2611 N.E. 125th, Suite 146
Seattle, WA 98125
(206) 363–1800
Program director: Agnes Y. Havlis

THE PROGRAM

New Hope of Washington is a nonprofit agency serving residents of the state of Washington (and occasionally residents of other states) and placing approximately 60 children annually in Christian adoptive homes. Incorporated in 1984, the agency provides services to birthparents and places infants for adoption when birthparents elect adoptive placement as the best plan for their child. The agency also sponsors a foster/adopt program for children who are free for adoption but need intensive services prior to adoption and for children who are not free for adoption, but may be relinquished if their biological parents are unable or unwilling to resume parental responsibilities. Children in the foster/adopt program may be in the custody either of the State of Washington or New Hope of Washington. In addition, the agency will provide homestudy and supervisory services for applicants pursuing private adoption.

THE COST

The agency's fee for adoption services of healthy newborns is based on a sliding scale, ranging from $5,500 to $6,500, and includes medical and legal expenses of the birthmother and all phases of the adoption process, excluding legal fees connected with finalization of the adoption (approximately $250 to $300).

THE WAIT

The time from completion of the homestudy to placement ranges from 6 to 18 months.

THE CHILDREN

New Hope of Washington places both healthy and special-needs children, ranging in age from infancy to adolescence, of Caucasian and bi- racial backgrounds, born in the U.S.

THE REQUIREMENTS

Age: The requirement varies depending on the preference of the birthparents.

Health: Infertility documentation is required.

Religion: Applicants must be committed members of the Christian faith.

Financial status: Applicants must demonstrate financial stability.

Marital status: Applicants must be married; the length of the marriage must be at least 2 years.

Family size: For healthy infant adoption, applicants may have no more than 1 child currently in the family. For special needs placements, the requirement varies depending on the needs of the child.

Racial, ethnic or cultural origin: No requirement, but preference for placing children in families of similar origins.

THE PROCEDURE

Participation in the adoption program of New Hope of Washington entails the following basic steps:
Application
Orientation meeting
Homestudy
Placement
Post-placement supervision

ADDITIONAL PROGRAMS/SERVICES

New Hope of Washington provides services to birthparents, seminars, and foster care.

BRANCH/NETWORK OFFICES

New Hope of Washington maintains branch offices in Tacoma and Spokane.

LICENSE/ACCREDITATION/PROFESSIONAL AFFILIATIONS

New Hope of Washington is licensed by the State of Washington Department of Social and Health Services.

REGULAR BAPTIST CHILD PLACEMENT AGENCY

P.O. Box 16353
Seattle, WA 98116
(206) 938–1487

Program director: Robert L. Van Alstine

THE PROGRAM

Regular Baptist Child Placement Agency (RBCPA) is a nonprofit agency primarily serving residents of Washington (but other states as well). The agency's focus is child-oriented rather than applicant-oriented, and the agency's primary emphasis is on foster care, with services to birthmothers and adoption services playing a lesser role. Through its adoption program, the agency places approximately 10 children annually in the homes of families actively involved in churches affiliated with the General Association of Regular Baptist Churches.

THE COST

The agency's fee for adoption services is based on the applicants' annual gross income with a minimum fee of $1,200 and a maximum of $2,000. Services covered by the fee include all phases of the adoption process, excluding legal fees connected with finalization and medical and transportation costs of the birthmother and child. Out-of-state appli-

cants can expect a reduction of $500 (the homestudy fee), as they will be required to arrange for homestudy and supervisory services by a licensed agency in their home state.

THE WAIT

The time from application to the homecoming of the adoptive child is approximately 3 years for healthy infant placements.

THE CHILDREN

The agency places both healthy and special-needs children, ranging in age from infancy through adolescence, of Caucasian and bi-racial backgrounds, born in the U.S.

THE REQUIREMENTS

Age: No requirement.
Health: Applicants must be in reasonably good health.
Religion: Applicants must be actively involved in a church affiliated with the General Association of Regular Baptist Churches.
Financial status: No requirement.
Marital status: Applicants must be married couples.
Family size: No requirement.
Racial, ethnic or cultural origin: No requirement.

THE PROCEDURE

Participation in RBCPA's adoption program entails the following basic steps:
Application
Orientation meeting
Homestudy
Placement
Post-placement supervision

ADDITIONAL PROGRAMS/SERVICES

RBCPA provides foster care for children as well as unwed mothers; counseling and assistance to unwed mothers.

BRANCH/NETWORK OFFICES

None.

LICENSE/ACCREDITATION/PROFESSIONAL AFFILIATIONS

Regular Baptist Child Placement Agency is licensed by the State of Washington Department of Social and Health Services and is affiliated with the General Association of Regular Baptist Churches.

SEATTLE INDIAN CENTER

Family Services
2222 Second Avenue
Seattle, WA 98121
(206) 728–8700
Program director: Arnold Troeh, Director

THE PROGRAM

Seattle Indian Center is a nonprofit organization serving residents of King County and placing between 10 and 15 children annually through its adoption program. The program has been in place for more than 10 years and strives "to provide all necessary family services for the Indian community and others, including foster home placements and adoptions."

THE COST

Adoption services are provided at no cost to the adoptive parents. However, adoptive parents may be asked to pay medical expenses incurred by the birthmother and child and may wish to make a donation to help cover agency costs. Adoptive parents are responsible for legal fees connected with finalization.

THE WAIT

The time from application to placement varies greatly. The law requires that Indian children be placed, in order of statutory priority, with (1) members of the extended family; (2) members of the child's tribe; (3) an Indian family. A match can be made very quickly or may take a considerable amount of time, depending on the factors involved in each case.

THE CHILDREN

Seattle Indian Center places both healthy and special needs American Indian children, ranging in age from birth to 18 years. Countries of origin include the U.S. and Canada.

THE REQUIREMENTS

Age: No requirement.
Health: No requirement.
Religion: No requirement.
Financial status: No requirement.
Marital status: No requirement.
Family size: No requirement.
Racial, ethnic or cultural origin: Children are placed in families of similar origin, as required by statute.

THE PROCEDURE

Participation in the adoption program of Seattle Indian Center entails the following basic steps:
Intake screening interview
Application
Homestudy
Referral
Placement
Post-placement supervision

ADDITIONAL PROGRAMS/SERVICES

Seattle Indian Center provides full family services including long-term care, planning for child welfare, counseling, and foster care services.

BRANCH/NETWORK OFFICES

None.

LICENSE/ACCREDITATION/PROFESSIONAL AFFILIATIONS

Seattle Indian Center is licensed by the State of Washington Department of Social and Health Services.

TRAVELERS AID ADOPTION SERVICE

909 Fourth Avenue, Room 630
Seattle, WA 98104
(206) 461–3888

Program director: Mary C. Curtis, ACSW

THE PROGRAM

Travelers Aid Adoption Service is a nonprofit non-sectarian agency providing statewide placement services and placing approximately 80–90 children (primarily from Korea) annually. Founded in 1921, the agency has been involved in intercountry adoption since 1974. Working cooperatively with the Social Welfare Society in Korea, the agency places Korean children in American families. The agency also places children (primarily older children) from Colombia, Japan, and Hong Kong. The agency's mission is "to offer professional social work services to prospective adoptive families with the goal of helping the family to be a functional interracial or intercultural family." The agency encourages families to integrate the child's cultural of origin into family life.

THE COST

The agency's fee for adoption services is $2,455 and includes the application, homestudy, placement and post-placement services. In addition, applicants pay $2,430 to Social Welfare Society in Korea and an escort fee of $800 (if applicants do not travel to Korea themselves). Applicants are responsible for legal fees connected with finalization of the adoption.

THE WAIT

The time from application to the homecoming of the adoptive child ranges from 4 months to 1 1/2 years, with an average wait of 6 to 8 months.

THE CHILDREN

Travelers Aid Adoption Service places both healthy and special-needs children, ranging in age from 3 months to 16 years, primarily of Asian but also of Mestizo racial backgrounds. 99% of the children placed are from Korea. Other countries of origin include Colombia, Japan, and Hong Kong.

THE REQUIREMENTS

Age: For Korean adoption, applicants must be at least 25 and no more than 44 years of age. The age requirement for other programs varies depending on the country.
Health: Applicants should be in reasonably good health. Applicants with health problems or handicaps are given individual consideration.
Religion: No requirement.
Financial status: Applicants must have an income of at least $20,000 (required by Korean government).
Marital status: For Korean adoption, applicants must be married, and the length of the marriage must be at least 3 years.
Family size: Applicants may have no more than 4 children currently in the family.

Racial, ethnic or cultural origin: No requirement.

THE PROCEDURE

Participation in the adoption program of Travelers Aid Adoption Service entails the following basic steps:

Application
Orientation meeting
Homestudy (assessment/educational sessions with the adoptive couple, including a home visit)
Compliance with immigration/naturalization requirements
Referral
Placement
Post-placement visits and interviews.

ADDITIONAL PROGRAMS/SERVICES

Travelers Aid Adoption Service provides parent support group meetings, social activities (potluck suppers, picnics, etc.), and newsletters.

BRANCH/NETWORK OFFICES

None.

LICENSE/ACCREDITATION/PROFESSIONAL AFFILIATIONS

Travelers Aid Adoption Service is licensed by the State of Washington Department of Social and Health Services.

West Virginia

PUBLIC ADOPTION PROGRAM/ COMMUNITY RESOURCES

Department of Human Services
1900 Washington Street, East
Charleston, WV 25305
(304) 348–7980
Adoption specialist: None at this time.

THE PROGRAM

Public adoption services in West Virginia are provided by the Department of Human Services (DHS) through area offices located throughout the state. Working cooperatively with the West Virginia Adoption Exchange (operated by the Children's Home Society of West Virginia and funded through a purchase-of-service contract by DHS), DHS recruits and prepares families and supervises the placement of special-needs children (older and/or minority children; children with physical, intellectual, and emotional special needs; sibling groups) who are in the custody of the State of West Virginia.

STATE EXCHANGE

West Virginia Adoption Exchange
Exchange director: Rebecca Shumate
1118 Kanawha Boulevard, E.
P.O. Box 2942
Charleston, WV 25330–2942
(304) 346–1062

STATE ADOPTION REUNION REGISTRY

None.

STATE SUBSIDY

For information, contact the Department of Human Services (above).

NACAC REPRESENTATIVE

Rebecca Shumate (see State Exchange above).

GENERAL ADOPTION RESOURCES

Appalachian Families for Adoption
P.O. Box 2775
Charleston, WV 25330

Parkersburg Adoptive Parent Assn.
P.O. Box 108
Parkersburg, WV 26102

SPECIAL-NEEDS ADOPTION RESOURCES

West Virginia Adoption Exchange
1118 Kanawha Blvd., E.
P.O. Box 2942
Charleston, WV 25330–2942
(304) 346–1062

State Developmental Disabilities Planning Council
625 D Street
South Charleston, WV 25303
(304) 348–0416

OUT-OF-STATE AGENCIES

SEE APPENDIX A

Agencies Providing Nationwide Services

THE CHILDREN'S HOME SOCIETY OF WEST VIRGINIA

P.O. Box 2942
(1118 Kanawha Blvd., E.)
Charleston, WV 25330
(304) 346–0795
Program director: Dennis Sutton, Executive Director; Rebecca C. Shumate, Director of Adoption Services

THE PROGRAM

The Children's Home Society of West Virginia is a non-profit child welfare organization which provides a wide range of services to children and families in West Virginia. Founded in 1896 with the mission of "finding homes for homeless and dependent children," the agency has evolved in response to the changing needs of the community and today provides shelters for short-term and emergency care for youth in crisis; child protective services; counseling services for birthparents; adoption counseling; and adoption services. The agency's adoption programs include infant adoption, international adoption (in cooperation with other U.S.-based licensed agencies which maintain international adoption programs), and special-needs adoption (through various regional and national exchange programs). Through these programs, the agency places between 10 and 20 children annually.

THE COST

The agency's fee for adoption services is based on a sliding scale and varies depending on the program. For domestic infant adoption, the agency's fee is 15% of the family's annual gross income with a maximum fee of $6,000. For special-needs adoption, the agency's fee is 5% of the applicants' annual gross income with a maximum fee of $5,000. For international adoption, the agency's fee is 5% of the applicants' annual gross income, with a minimum of $1,500 and a maximum of $5,000. Services covered by the fee include all phases of the adoption process, excluding legal fees connected with finalization of the adoption (approximately $300). Applicants pursuing international adoption should also anticipate fees to the cooperating agency, possible travel or escort expenses, and related costs.

THE WAIT

The time from completion of the Registration of Interest to the homecoming of the adoptive child varies depending on the program. For domestic infant adoption, the process from beginning to end may take 3 to 6 years. For international adoption, the wait varies depending on the cooperating agency. For special-needs adoption, the wait varies depending on the number of children in need of adoptive families and the range of special needs the family can accept.

The Children

The Children's Home Society places both healthy and special-needs children, ranging in age from birth to 18 years, of Caucasian, Black, and bi-racial backgrounds. The agency also facilitates the placement of children from many foreign countries, working with cooperating U.S.-based licensed agencies.

The Requirements

Age: For healthy Caucasian infant adoption, applicants may be no more than 40 years of age when the homestudy is initiated. No requirement for special-needs adoption. For international adoption, the requirement varies depending on the requirements of the cooperating agency.

Health: Applicants should be in reasonably good health. Applicants with health problems or handicaps are given individual consideration. For healthy Caucasian infant adoption, couples must be unable to have a healthy baby.

Religion: No requirement.

Financial status: No requirement other than the ability to provide for the child's needs.

Marital status: For healthy Caucasian infant adoption, applicants must be married couples. No requirement for special-needs adoption. For international adoption, the requirement varies depending on the requirements of the cooperating agency.

Family size: No requirement.

Racial, ethnic or cultural origin: Preference for placing children in families of similar origins, but varies depending on the needs of the child.

The Procedure

Participation in the adoption program of The Children's Society entails the following basic steps:

Orientation meeting or intake interview (for special needs applicants)
Registration of interest
Application
Homestudy (either individual or group format)
Compliance with immigration/naturalization requirements (international adoptions only)
Placement
Post-placement supervision
Finalization

Additional Programs/Services

The Children's Home Society provides a wide range of services for children and families including six emergency youth shelters; child protective services; volunteer program for victims of abuse and neglect; court-ordered homestudies; parenting support services. The Children's Home Society also operates the West Virginia Adoption Exchange to provide information and referral services for children waiting for homes and parents wanting to build their families through special-needs adoption.

Branch/Network Offices

1000 Van Voorhis Road
Morgantown, WV 26505
(304) 559–6505

First Tyler Bank Building
Sistersville, WV 26175
(304) 652–2800

License/Accreditation/Professional Affiliations

The Children's Home Society of West Virginia is licensed by the State of West Virginia Department of Human Services. The agency is a member of Families and Children Together (FACT); West Virginia Child Care Association; West Virginia Human Resources Association; Community Council of Kanawha Valley; and National Association of Homes for Children.

United Methodist Child Placement Services

4013 Teays Valley Road
Scott Depot, WV 25560
(304) 757–9127
Program director: Donna Chandler

The Program

United Methodist Child Placement Services (UMCPS) is a nonprofit agency serving residents of West Virginia and placing between 10 and 15 domestic and foreign-born children annually. Founded in 1956 as part of a group home facility, UMCPS became an independent ministry in 1969, held its first meeting with an organized board of directors in 1971, and became incorporated in 1978. The purpose of UMCPS is to provide counseling to birthparents regarding their options whenever an unintended pregnancy occurs and to provide services to adoptive parents. The agency places infants for adoption when birthparents elect adoptive placement as the best plan for their child. Working cooperatively with public agencies and with national and regional exchange programs, the agency facilitates the placement of special-needs children. Working with other U.S. licensed agencies which maintain international programs, the agency facilitates the placement of children from various foreign countries. In addition, the agency will provide homestudy and supervisory services for applicants pursuing interagency adoption (domestic or international) or independent adoption.

The Cost

The agency's fee schedule is as follows:
Homestudy $650 plus travel costs
Post-placement supervision $1,500 plus travel costs
Placement (through UMCPS)12% of applicants' annual gross income

Applicants pursuing international adoption should anticipate fees to the cooperating agency, possible travel expenses, document certification fees, and related costs. For all programs, applicants assume responsibility for legal fees connected with finalization of the adoption.

The Wait

For adoptions in which UMCPS has custody of the child,

the time from completion of the homestudy to placement ranges from 1 to 4 years.

THE CHILDREN

UMCPS directly places both healthy and special-needs children (primarily infants) of all racial backgrounds, born in the U.S. Working cooperatively with public and private agencies, UMCPS facilitates the placement of both healthy and special-needs children of all ages and racial backgrounds and of any country of origin.

THE REQUIREMENTS

The following are requirements for UMCPS placement. For interagency adoptions, UMCPS will work within the framework of the requirements of the cooperating agency.

Age: Applicants must be at least 23 and no more than 40 years of age.

Health: Applicants should be in reasonably good health. Applicants with health problems or handicaps are given individual consideration. For UMCPS placements, preference is given to childless couples for homestudy initiation.

Religion: No requirement.

Financial status: No requirement.

Marital status: No requirement. If married, the length of the marriage must be at least 3 years.

Family size: For UMCPS placements, preference is given to childless couples for initiation of the homestudy.

Racial, ethnic or cultural origin: No requirement.

THE PROCEDURE

Participation in the adoption program of UMCPS entails the following basic steps:

Application
Adoption training workshop
Homestudy
Individual counseling sessions (if needed)
Compliance with immigration/naturalization requirements
    (international adoptions only)
Referral
Placement
Post-placement supervision

ADDITIONAL PROGRAMS/SERVICES

UMCPS provides workshops for persons pursuing adoption and counseling services for birthparents.

BRANCH/NETWORK OFFICES

None.

LICENSE/ACCREDITATION/PROFESSIONAL AFFILIATIONS

United Methodist Child Placement Services is licensed by the State of West Virginia Department of Human Services.

Wisconsin

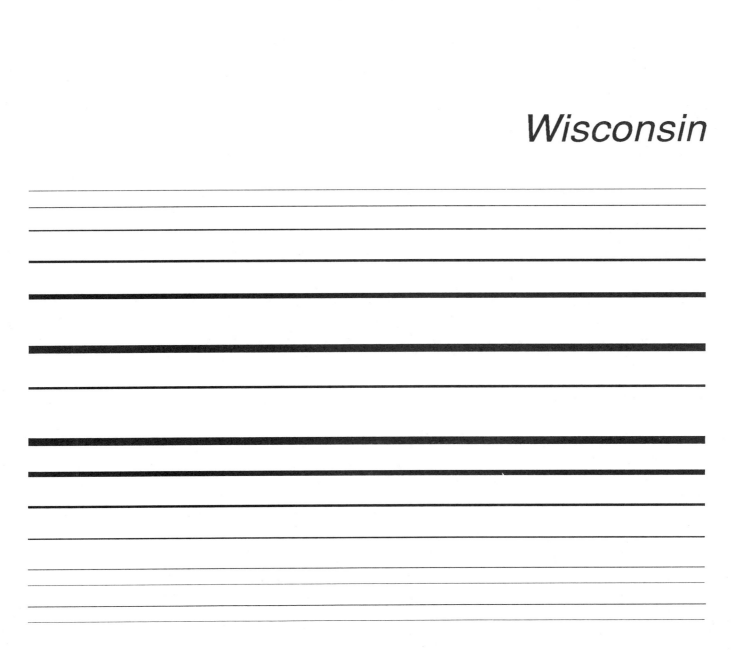

PUBLIC ADOPTION PROGRAM/ COMMUNITY RESOURCES

Department of Health and Social Services
Division of Community Services
Bureau for Children, Youth and Families
P.O. Box 7851
Madison, WI 53707
(608) 266–0690
Adoption specialist: Karen Oghalai

THE PROGRAM

Public adoption services in Wisconsin are provided by the Department of Health and Social Services (DHSS) through regional Community Services offices. Working cooperatively with the Adoption Exchange of Wisconsin (a project operated by the Coalition for Children in Families, Inc. and funded by the State of Wisconsin), DHSS recruits and prepares families and supervises the placement of special-needs children (older and/or minority children; children with physical, intellectual, and emotional special needs; sibling groups) who are under the guardianship of the State of Wisconsin.

Information about adoption in Wisconsin is provided by the Adoption Information Center, a state-funded service providing extensive information and referral services. For information, contact:

Adoption Information Center
1212 South 70th Street
West Allis, WI 53214
1–800–522–6882
(414) 453–0403 (Milwaukee)

STATE EXCHANGE

Adoption Exchange of Wisconsin
Coalition for Children in Families, Inc.
P.O. Box 10176
Milwaukee, WI 53210–0990
(414) 475–1246

STATE ADOPTION REUNION REGISTRY

Adoption Search Program
Adoption Search Coordinator
P.O. Box 7851
Madison, WI 53707
(608) 266–7163

STATE SUBSIDY

For information, contact the Bureau for Children, Youth and Families (above).

NACAC REPRESENTATIVE

Colleen Ellingson
Coalition for Children in Families
P.O. Box 10176
Milwaukee, WI 53210–0990
(414) 475–1246

GENERAL ADOPTION RESOURCES

Adoptive Parent Support Groups
Adoptive Parent Group of Superior
  Contact: Ron Gustafson
  201 E. 7th Street
  Superior, WI 54880
Adoption Support Group
  Contact: Peggy Schultz
  Children's Service Society
  1212 S. 70th St.
  West Allis, WI 53214
  (414) 453–1400
Adoptive Parent Group of Southern Wisconsin
  Contact: Marilyn Holshuh
  1408 Vilas Avenue
  Madison, WI 53711
  (608) 251–0736
Adoptive Parent Assn. of Greater Milwaukee
  Contact: Michelle Collins
  2760 Almesbury Avenue
  Brookfield, WI 53005
  (414) 797–8820
Adoptive Parents of Western Wisconsin
  Contact: Deborah Timmerman
  433 N. Wasson Lane
  River Falls, WI 54022
  (715) 425–7825
Adoption Insights
  Contact: Barbara Bache-Wiig
  800 Main Street
  Pewaukee, WI 53072
  (414) 547–9014
Brown County Adoptive Parents
  Contact: Connie Thirion
  1251 Doblon Street
  Green Bay, WI 54302
Central Wisconsin Adoption Support Group
  Contact: Karen Toepel
  134 Ash Street
  Montello, WI 53949
Families By Adoption, Inc.
  Contact: Mary Westerhaus
  231 N. 22nd
  LaCrosse, WI 54601
Families By Adoption of South Central Wisconsin
  P.O. Box 2544
  Madison, WI 53701–2544
Fox Lake Adoptive Parents
  Contact: Diane Davis
  RR 1, Box 296
  Berlin, WI 54923
Fox Valley Adoption Support Group
  Contact: Joan Moericke
  2606 N. Lisa Street
  Appleton, WI 54914
H.E.A.R.T.
  Contact: Margaret Grundeen
  4630 Springwood Drive

Wisconsin Rapids, WI 54494
(715) 421–4414

International Families
Contact: Janice Pezoldt
820 Illinois St.
Racine, WI 53405

Inter-Racial Families Network
Family Enhancement Program
605 Spruce St.
Madison, WI 53705

Love Through Adoption
Contact: Tom and Sue Kulhanek
4640 11th St., S.
Wisconsin Rapids, WI 54494
(715) 421–4414

OURS Through Adoption of NE Wisconsin
Contact: Linda Troyer
133 Appletree Court
Green Bay, WI 54302
(414) 465–0818

OURS of Greater Milwaukee
Contact: Cindi Bohman
10607 W. Lancaster
Milwaukee, WI 53225
(414) 527–0936

OURS of Greater Milwaukee
Contact: Sue Blazek
W28611 Hawthorne Road
Hartland, WI 53028
(414) 367–6226

Single Parent Adoptive Support Groups
Wisconsin Single Parents of Adopted Children
Contact: Anne Handschke
403 Vilas Avenue
Nekoosa, WI 54457
(715) 886–5572

Wisconsin Assn. of Single Adoptive Parents
Contact: Mary Cissoko
2111 Barton Avenue, #3
West Bend, WI 53095
(414) 338–2603

HOPE Network
P.O. Box 531
Menomonee Falls, WI 53051
(414) 251–7333

Wisconsin Single Parents of Adopted Children
Contact: Diane Karrow
127 St. Louis Dr.
Prairie du Chien, WI 53821

Infertility Support Group
Resolve
Contact: Debbie Bailey
P.O. Box 23406
Milwaukee, WI 53223–0406
(414) 354–7483

Birthparent Support Groups
P.A.S.T. (Post Adoption Support Through Time)
Contact: Pam Cira
3375 N. Dousman
Milwaukee, WI 53212
(414) 332–3423/276–CARE

Adoption Support Group
Contact: Peggy Schulz
Children's Service Society
1212 S. 70th Street
West Allis, WI 53214
(414) 453–1400/962–8859 (PM)

Adoption Triad Support Groups for Search and Support
Adoption Information and Direction
P.O. Box 8162
Eau Claire, WI 54703–8162
(715) 835–6695

Adoption Information and Direction
P.O. Box 7371
Madison, WI 53707–7371
(608) 592–5374

Adoption Information and Direction
1140 Cherry St.
Green Bay, WI 54301

Adoption Information and Direction
P.O. Box 23764
Milwaukee, WI 53224
(414) 543–4206

Adoption Information and Direction
P.O. Box 2043
Oshkosh, WI 54903–2043
(414) 233–6487

Adoption Information and Direction
2117 Clark Street
Stevens Point, WI 54481
(715) 345–1290

Adoption Information and Direction
P.O. Box 1522
LaCrosse, WI 54601

SPECIAL-NEEDS ADOPTION RESOURCES

Coalition for Children in Families
Contact: Colleen Ellingson
P.O. Box 10176
Milwaukee, WI 53210–0990
(414) 475–1246

Friends of Adoption
Contact: Rod and Brenda Schloneger
Route 1, Box 67
Shell Lake, WI 54871
(715) 468–2881

Rock County Adoptive Parent Group
Contact: Richard and Marian McFall
845 Nakoma Court
Beloit, WI 53511
(608) 365–9279

Open Door Society—Milwaukee
  Contact: Jackie Omdahl
  3253 N. Hackett Avenue
  Milwaukee, WI 53211
  (414) 963–1377

Open Door Society—Western Wisconsin
  Contact: Tony and Anne Millkamp
  Rt. 1, Box 92
  Chippewa Falls, WI 53729

S.N.A.P. (Special-Needs Adoptive Parents)
  Contact: Dave and Cara Leitner
  Rt. 1, Box 230C
  Scandinavia, WI 54977

OUT-OF-STATE AGENCIES

AGENCY

HOPE International Family Services, Minnesota

SEE APPENDIX A

Agencies Providing Nationwide Services

ADOPTION CHOICE, INC.

2542 N. Terrace Avenue
Milwaukee, WI 53211
(414) 332–7732
Program director: Co-directors: Jill Gerlach and Melinda Randa, ACSW

THE PROGRAM

Adoption Choice is a for-profit agency serving residents of Wisconsin and surrounding states and placing approximately 35 children annually. Initiated in 1986 by an adoptive mother/social worker and a supervisor of birthparent counseling, the agency provides a comprehensive program for adoptive parents and birthparents, characterized by "non-judgmental, open counseling."

THE COST

The agency's fee schedule for adoption services is as follows:

Birthparent counseling fee (paid by adoptive applicant)	$950.00
Homestudy fee	$1,500.00
Agency placement fee	$950.00
Post-placement supervision fee	$400.00

In addition, applicants should anticipate financial responsibility for medical expenses of the birthmother (if she does not have insurance) and legal fees connected with finalization of the adoption.

THE WAIT

The time from application for acceptance into the program to the homecoming of the adoptive child averages 18 to 24 months.

THE CHILDREN

Adoption Choice places primarily healthy infants (birth to 2 years), of Caucasian, Hispanic, and bi-racial backgrounds, born in the U.S.

THE REQUIREMENTS

Age: Applicants must be at least 23 and no more than 45 years of age.
Health: Applicants with health problems or handicaps are given individual consideration. Infertility documentation is required.
Religion: No requirement.
Financial status: No requirement.
Marital status: Married couples and single persons may apply. If married, the length of the marriage must be at least 3 years.
Family size: Applicants must be childless.
Racial, ethnic or cultural origin: No requirement.

THE PROCEDURE

Participation in the Adoption Choice program entails the following basic steps:
  Application
  Individual counseling sessions
  Homestudy
  Referral
  Placement
  Post-placement supervision

ADDITIONAL PROGRAMS/SERVICES

Adoption Choice provides extensive birthparent counseling services and participates in greater Milwaukee adoption seminars.

BRANCH/NETWORK OFFICES

None.

LICENSE/ACCREDITATION/PROFESSIONAL AFFILIATIONS

Adoption Choice, Inc. is licensed by the State of Wisconsin Department of Health and Social Services.

THE ADOPTION OPTION, INC.

1804 Chapman Drive
Waukesha, WI 53186
(414) 544–4278
Program director: Roberta Fries, ACSW

THE PROGRAM

The Adoption Option is a for-profit agency serving residents of the state of Wisconsin and facilitating the placement of approximately 25 children annually. Founded in 1985, the agency's mission is "to match parents who need children with children who need parents." The agency's primary focus is to provide homestudy and supervisory services to applicants pursuing foreign, independent, step-parent, or interagency adoption. However, the agency also provides counseling services to birthparents and places infants for adoption when birthparents in the agency's program decide that the best interests of the child will be served by adoptive placement. The agency promotes open adoption through the non-identifying exchange of information between birthparents and adoptive parents, and the agency will facilitate on-going communication, if so requested by all parties concerned.

THE COST

The agency's fee for adoption services ranges from $1,600 to $2,000. Services covered by the fee include homestudy, post-placement supervision, completion of court reports, and finalization of the adoption. Applicants pursuing foreign adoption should anticipate a total cost ranging from $6,000 to $8,000 (including The Adoption Option fee, foreign agency fee, travel costs, immigration fees, and legal fees). Applicants pursuing independent or agency-mediated domestic adoption should anticipate possible medical and foster care expenses for birthmother and child as well as a placement fee (agency-mediated adoption).

THE WAIT

The time from application to the homecoming of the adoptive child ranges from 9 months to 2 years, with an average of approximately 13 months.

THE CHILDREN

The Adoption Option facilitates the placement of both healthy and special-needs children, ranging in age from birth to 18 years, of all racial backgrounds. Places of origin include the Orient, Latin America, India, and the U.S.

THE REQUIREMENTS

Age: No agency requirement. The requirement may vary depending on the child's country of origin.
Health: Applicants must be in reasonably good health.
Religion: No requirement.
Financial status: No requirement.
Marital status: No requirement. If married, the length of the marriage must be at least 2 years.
Family size: No requirement.
Racial, ethnic or cultural origin: No requirement.

THE PROCEDURE

Participation in The Adoption Option's program entails the following basic steps:
Application
Joint and individual interviews
Home visit
Compliance with immigration/naturalization requirements (foreign adoptions only)
Compliance with State of Wisconsin requirements
Child referral
Placement
Post-placement supervision
Finalization

ADDITIONAL PROGRAMS/SERVICES

The Adoption Option provides foster care services for children and counseling services for birthparents.

BRANCH/NETWORK OFFICES

None.

LICENSE/ACCREDITATION/PROFESSIONAL AFFILIATIONS

The Adoption Option is licensed by the State of Wisconsin Department of Health and Social Services and is a member of the North American Council on Adoptable Children and the Wisconsin Coalition for Children in Families, Inc.

ADOPTION SERVICES OF GREEN BAY

529 S. Jefferson St.
Room 105
Green Bay, WI 54301
(414) 432–2030
Program director: Muriel H. McDermott, ACSW

THE PROGRAM

Adoption Services of Green Bay is a for-profit agency serving residents who live within 200 miles of Green Bay and placing approximately 25 children annually. Licensed in 1983, the agency originally provided services for step-parent adoption and then gradually expanded to include additional domestic adoption programs (independent and agency-mediated) and an international adoption program. The agency provides informational pre- adoption workshops, homestudy and supervisory services, and post-legal adoption services.

THE COST

The agency's fee for homestudy and post-placement supervision is $1,500. Fees for adoption counseling are $70 per hour. Workshop fees vary. Applicants pursuing international adoption should anticipate additional fees to the international placing agency, travel/escort expenses, and related costs. Applicants pursuing independent adoption should anticipate additional expenses for medical and foster care for the birthmother and child. In all programs, applicants assume responsibility for legal fees connected with finalization of the adoption.

THE WAIT

The time from the completion of the homestudy to the homecoming of the adoptive child ranges from 6 months to 2 years.

THE CHILDREN

Adoption Services of Green Bay facilitates the placement of both healthy and special-needs children, ranging in age from birth to 18 years, of Caucasian, Black, Asian, Hispanic and bi-racial backgrounds. Countries of origin include Central and South America, Philippines, Thailand, India, Korea, Hong Kong, and Taiwan. In addition, "waiting" children are available from most of these countries and in the U.S. through various regional and national exchange programs.

THE REQUIREMENTS

Age: No agency requirement. The requirement varies depending on the child's country of origin.
Health: Applicants must be in reasonably good health. Specific requirements vary depending on the child's country of origin.

Religion: No requirement.
Financial status: Applicants must demonstrate financial stability and independence.
Marital status: No requirement.
Family size: No requirement.*Racial, ethnic or cultural origin*: No requirement.

THE PROCEDURE

Participation in Adoption Services of Green Bay's adoption program entails the following basic steps:
Application
Individual counseling sessions
Homestudy
Compliance with immigration/naturalization requirements (international adoptions only)
Referral
Placement
Post-placement supervision

ADDITIONAL PROGRAMS/SERVICES

Adoption Services of Green Bay provides pre-adoption and post-legal adoption workshops as well as family and individual counseling.

BRANCH/NETWORK OFFICES

None.

LICENSE/ACCREDITATION/PROFESSIONAL AFFILIATIONS

Adoption Services of Green Bay is licensed by the State of Wisconsin Department of Health and Social Services and is a member of the International Concerns Committee for Children.

BETHANY CHRISTIAN SERVICES

W255 N477 Grandview Blvd.
Suite 207
Waukesha, WI 53188(414) 547–6557
Program director: James K. Haveman, Jr., Executive Director

THE PROGRAM

For a full description of programs and services, refer to Michigan listing:
Bethany Christian Services
901 Eastern Avenue, N.E.
Grand Rapids, MI 49503–1295
(616) 459–6273

BUILDING FAMILIES THROUGH ADOPTION

P.O. Box 550, 7th and Chestnut
Dawson, MN 56232
(612) 769–2933
Program director: Mary Carpenter and Therese Giesen

THE PROGRAM

For current address and telephone number of BFTA Wisconsin branch offices, contact BFTA main office (listed above). For a full description of BFTA programs and services, refer to Minnesota listing for Building Families Through Adoption.

CATHOLIC CHARITIES, INC.

Diocese of La Crosse
128 South 6th Street, P.O. Box 266
La Crosse, WI 54602–0266
(608) 784–5323
Program director: Warren W. Bjorge

THE PROGRAM

Catholic Charities is a nonprofit agency serving residents of the Diocese of La Crosse (19 counties) and placing approximately 30 children annually. Licensed since 1932, the agency's adoption program is based on the principle that "every child, created in God's image, has a need for and a right to the love and guidance of parents." The agency's goal is to find the most appropriate permanent home for each child in accordance with his needs and to provide support services to help the child and the adoptive family realize a satisfying adjustment. The agency provides services to birthparents and places infants for adoption when birthparents in the agency's program decide that the best interests of the child will be served by adoptive placement. The agency is also actively involved in the placement of special-needs children.

THE COST

The agency's fee for adoption services is $4,000 for a first adoption and $3,000 for a second adoption. Services covered by the fee include pre-adoptive counseling, placement, and post-placement services. Applicants assume responsibility for legal fees connected with finalization of the adoption.

THE WAIT

The time from application for acceptance into the program to the homecoming of the adoptive child averages 2 years.

THE CHILDREN

Catholic Charities places primarily infants (birth to 1 year), both healthy and special needs, of all racial backgrounds, born in the U.S.

THE REQUIREMENTS

Age: Applicants may be no more than 35 years of age for a first adoption of a healthy infant. The requirement is flexible for special-needs adoptions.
Health: Applicants must be in reasonably good health. Applicants need to have explored the causes of their infertility with their physician.
Religion: Applicants must be practicing members of a church community.
Financial status: Applicants must demonstrate financial stability.
Marital status: For healthy infant adoption, applicants

must be married couples. The requirement is flexible for special-needs adoptions.

Family size: For healthy infant adoption, applicants may have no more than 1 child currently in the family. The requirement is flexible for special-needs adoptions.

Racial, ethnic or cultural origin: No requirement.

THE PROCEDURE

Participation in Catholic Charities' adoption program entails the following basic steps:
Orientation meeting
Application
Individual counseling sessions
Group counseling sessions
Homestudy
Placement
Post-placement supervision

ADDITIONAL PROGRAMS/SERVICES

Catholic Charities provides counseling services for birthparents and their families and foster care for infants prior to implementation of permanent plans. The agency co- sponsors workshops on adoption issues.

BRANCH/NETWORK OFFICES

1107 Regis Court, Box 715
Eau Claire, WI 54702–0715
(715) 832–3483

1502 Main Street, Box 428
Stevens Point, WI 54482–0428
(715) 344–2500

903 Second Street, Box 1443
Wausau, WI 54602–1443
(715) 842–9011

230 South Second Street, Box 1102
Wisconsin Rapids, WI 54495–1102
(715) 423–9540

LICENSE/ACCREDITATION/PROFESSIONAL AFFILIATIONS

Catholic Charities, Inc. is licensed by the State of Wisconsin Department of Health and Social Services.

CATHOLIC SOCIAL SERVICES

Diocese of Green Bay
1825 Riverside Drive
P.O. Box 1825
Green Bay, WI 54305–5825
(414) 437–7531
Program director: Ruth M. Bruha

THE PROGRAM

Catholic Social Services is a nonprofit agency serving residents of the Diocese of Green Bay (16 counties) and placing approximately 15–30 children annually. Since its founding in 1918, the agency has provided services based on Christian values to individuals and families. The agency promotes open adoption, recognizing that "adoption is a lifelong process involving the adoptee, birthparents, and adoptive parents" and that "an adoptee, although relinquished and a full member of his/her adoptive family, nevertheless remains connected to his/her birth family." With full identifying information exchanged between adoptive parents and birthparents, they are able to establish and maintain open avenues of communication (letters, phone calls, visits) agreed upon by both parties.

THE COST

The agency's fee for adoption services is based on combined gross annual income (the previous 12 months' salary) of prospective adoptive couple and ranges between $1,500 and $3,000. Services from the time of application to the time of legal adoption are covered by the fee. In addition, applicants are responsible for legal fees connected with finalization.

THE WAIT

The time from application to placement is dependent upon the number of children available for placement. The agency maintains a bank of prospective homes, gauged according to the number of children placed the previous year.

THE CHILDREN

Catholic Social Services places primarily healthy Caucasian infants in the Diocese of Green Bay.

THE REQUIREMENTS

Age: A maximum differential of 38 years between the child placed and the adoptive parents is maintained.

Health: Applicants must be in reasonably good health. It is expected that applicants will have fully explored their infertility and reached resolution of their feelings.

Religion: One of the couple must be a practicing Catholic.

Financial status: Applicants must demonstrate financial stability.

Marital status: Because most birthparents who make placement plans for their children want a two-parent family, single applicants are not accepted.

Family size: No requirement.

Racial, ethnic or cultural origin: No requirement. Birthparents' preferences are honored.

THE PROCEDURE

Participation in Catholic Social Services' Open Placement program entails the following basic steps:
Application
Adoption group counseling
Adoption placement planning
Homestudy
Meeting between birthparents and adoptive parents (Full disclosure of identifying information required; meetings optional for birthparents.)
Placement
Post-placement and post-adoption services

ADDITIONAL PROGRAMS/SERVICES

Catholic Social Services provides a wide range of services including counseling (family, marriage, individual, pre-marriage, divorce, pregnancy, financial, grief, domestic abuse, and sexual abuse), services to the aging, foster care, adoption, adoption search, and stepparent adoption services.

BRANCH/NETWORK OFFICES

921 Midway Road, P.O. Box 256
Menasha, WI 54952
(414) 734-2601

201 Ceape Ave.
Oshkosh, WI 54901
(414) 235-6002

1203 N. 16th St., P.O. Box 398
Manitowoc, WI 54220
(414) 684-6651

903 Pierce Ave., P.O. Box 112
Marinette, WI 54143
(715) 735-7802/3539

LICENSE/ACCREDITATION/PROFESSIONAL AFFILIATIONS

Catholic Social Services is licensed by the State of Wisconsin Department of Health and Social Services. The agency is a member of the United Way.

CATHOLIC SOCIAL SERVICE

Diocese of Madison
4905 Schofield Street
Madison, WI 53716
(608) 221-2000
Program director: Robert G. Hintz

THE PROGRAM

Catholic Social Service is a nonprofit agency serving the Diocese of Madison (11 southwestern counties of Wisconsin) and placing approximately 30–35 children annually. The agency's adoption program, ANGELS (Adoptables Needing Good, Eligible, Loving Surroundings), was initiated in 1968 to recruit adoptive parents who have the special love and skills necessary to parent the special-needs child. Believing that "never has a child been born who should be loved less than another," the agency strives to meet the needs of minority and bi-racial children, older children, sibling groups, and children with physical, intellectual, or emotional handicaps.

THE COST

The agency's fee for adoption services is 7% of the applicants' annual gross income, with a maximum fee of $3,600. For families with children currently in the family, $1,000 per child is deducted from the gross annual income to determine the basis for the fee. Services include orientation to the special needs program, homestudy, placement, post-placement services, preparation of agency reports for finalization, and post-adoptive services. In addition, applicants assume responsibility for legal fees connected with finalization and the fee for a certified amended birth certificate.

THE WAIT

The time from application to the homecoming of the adoptive child varies greatly depending on the range of special needs the adoptive parents can accept. The average time from application to placement is 18 months.

THE CHILDREN

Catholic Social Service places both healthy and special-needs children, ranging in age from infancy to adolescence, of Caucasian, Black, and bi-racial backgrounds, born in the U.S.

THE REQUIREMENTS

Age: No requirement, but may vary depending on the child's needs.

Health: Applicants must be in reasonably good health. Applicants with health problems or handicaps are given individual consideration.

Religion: Preference is given to applicants who are practicing members of a church or a synagogue, but the requirement may be waived depending on the child's needs.

Financial status: Applicants are evaluated individually on the basis of their ability to manage financial resources effectively.

Marital status: Preference is give to married couples, but single applicants are accepted for some placements.

Family size: No requirement.

Racial, ethnic or cultural origin: No requirement.

THE PROCEDURE

Participation in Catholic Social Service's adoption program entails the following basic steps:
Orientation meeting
Application
Individual counseling sessions
Group counseling sessions
Home visit
Referral
Placement
Post-placement services

ADDITIONAL PROGRAMS/SERVICES

Catholic Social Service provides a wide range of services including a psychotherapy clinic; counseling services for birthparents (New Lives Program); infant foster care; developmental disability counseling; services to the aging; refugee resettlement; alcoholism and drug abuse services.

BRANCH/NETWORK OFFICES

25 S. Hancock St.
Madison, WI 53703
(608) 256-2358

2243 Prairie Ave.
Beloit, WI 53511
(608) 365-3665

23–25 W. Milwaukee, Suite 206/207
Janesville, WI 53545
(608) 752-4906

LICENSE/ACCREDITATION/PROFESSIONAL AFFILIATIONS

Catholic Social Service is licensed by the State of Wisconsin Department of Health and Social Services. The agency is a member of Wisconsin Advocates for Adoption, Catholic Charities USA, and the Wisconsin Association of Family and Children's Agencies.

Catholic Social Services

2021 N. 60th Street
Milwaukee, WI 53208
(414) 771–2881
Program director: Cecilia Braam, MSW, ACSW, Coordinator

The Program

Catholic Social Services (CSS) is a nonprofit agency serving residents of the Archdiocese of Milwaukee and placing approximately 40 children annually. CSS believes "that every child has a God-given right to grow up with the security, stability and caring of a permanent family." The agency provides services to birthparents and places infants for adoption when birthparents in the agency's counseling program elect adoptive placement as the best plan for their child. Birthparents participate in the selection of adoptive parents based on non-identifying information. The agency also places special-needs children (older children, minority children, children with major medical problems). CSS also provides homestudy and supervisory services for step-parent and relative adoptions and for independent adoptions.

The Cost

The agency's fee for a first adoption from CSS is 9% of the family's annual gross income (minimum, $1,500; maximum, $4,500). The fee for a second adoption from CSS is 7% of the family's annual gross income (minimum $1,500; maximum, $4,500). In addition, applicants pay a $25 filing fee (to list applicant's name for contact for a group information meeting) and a $45 fee for attendance at the group meeting. Services covered by the fee include all phases of the adoption process, excluding legal fees connected with finalization of the adoption.

The Wait

The time from application to the homecoming of the adoptive child varies depending on the flexibility of the adoptive family, the availability of children for placement, and birthparent selection. For infant adoption, the wait ranges from 30 to 48 months. For special-needs adoption, the wait ranges from 4 to 24 months.

The Children

CSS places both healthy and special need infants and young children of all racial backgrounds.

The Requirements

Age: For infant adoption, neither spouse may be more than 37 years old at the time of application for a first child, or 40 years old for a second child. The requirement is flexible for special-needs adoption.
Health: Applicants should be in reasonably good health. Infertility evaluation is required for infant adoption.
Religion: Applicants must be practicing Roman Catholics with intent to raise the child as Catholic. If only one spouse is Catholic, he or she must be a practicing Catholic.
Financial status: Applicants must have sufficient income and financial resources to provide adequately for an additional family member.

Marital status: Applicants should be married at least 2 years and must be in a valid Catholic marriage.
Family size: Applicants should be childless or have no more than 1 child currently in the home by birth or adoption. The requirement is flexible for special-needs adoption.
Racial, ethnic or cultural origin: Preference for placing children in families of similar origins.

The Procedure

Participation in the adoption program of CSS entails the following basic steps:
Inquiry/intake interview (telephone)
Application
Group informational meeting
Homestudy (foster home licensing)
Placement
Post-placement supervision

Additional Programs/Services

Catholic Social Services provides a range of services for individuals and families.

Branch/Network Offices

91–A S. Main St.
Fon du Lac, WI 54935
(414) 923–2550
503 Wisconsin Ave.
Sheboygan, WI 53081
(414) 458–5726
5820 3rd Ave.
Kenosha, WI 53140
(414) 658–2088
840 N. Grand Ave.
Waukesha, WI 53186
(414) 547–2463
2711 19th St.
Racine, WI 53403
(414) 637–8888
141 N. Main St.
West Bend, WI 53095
(414) 334–0886

License/Accreditation/Professional Affiliations

Catholic Social Services is licensed by the State of Wisconsin Department of Health and Social Services. The agency is a member of the Child Welfare League of America and Catholic Charities USA.

Children's Service Society of Wisconsin

1212 South 70th Street
West Allis, WI 53214
(414) 453–1400
Program director: Patricia Wendt, Adoption Supervisor

The Program

Children's Service Society of Wisconsin is a nonprofit,

non-sectarian agency providing statewide services and placing approximately 70 children annually. Providing adoption services since 1889, the agency has evolved in response to the changing needs of the community and today provides a wide range of "quality human services to Wisconsin children, youth and their families without regard to race, religion, or economic circumstances." The agency provides services to birthparents and places infants for adoption when birthparents in the agency's counseling program decide that the best interests of their child will be met by adoptive placement. The agency is also actively involved in recruiting families for special-needs children, provides homestudy and supervisory services for applicants pursuing independent adoption, and provides foreign adoption services.

THE COST

For infant adoption, the agency's fee is based on a sliding scale and ranges from $1,500 to $4,500. Services covered by the fee include all phases of the adoption process and all services to the birthmother and child. For special-needs adoption, fees may be waived or reduced. For independent adoption, fees are approximately $1,600, plus associated costs. For foreign adoptions, the agency's fees are approximately $1,500. Applicants pursuing foreign adoption should anticipate fees to the cooperating agency, possible travel expenses, and related costs.

THE WAIT

The agency uses an annual random selection process to choose applicants for the infant adoption list. Once on the list, studied, and approved, applicants may wait from several weeks to approximately 2 years for placement. The waiting time in special-needs adoption depends on the children awaiting placement and the specific desires of the adoptive family.

THE CHILDREN

Children's Service Society places both healthy and special-needs children, ranging in age from birth to 17 years, of all racial backgrounds, born in the U.S. In addition, the agency facilitates independent and foreign adoptions.

THE REQUIREMENTS

Age: The requirement varies depending on the type of adoption.
Health: Applicants should be in reasonably good health. Infertility documentation is required for infant adoption.
Religion: No requirement.
Financial status: No requirement.
Marital status: The requirement varies depending on the type of adoption.
Family size: The requirement varies depending on the type of adoption.
Racial, ethnic or cultural origin: No requirement.

THE PROCEDURE

Participation in the adoption program of Children's Service Society entails the following basic steps:
Orientation meeting
Application
Group counseling sessions

Individual counseling sessions
Homestudy
Placement
Post-placement supervision

ADDITIONAL PROGRAMS/SERVICES

In addition to adoption services, standard agency programs include counseling for children and their families; pregnancy counseling; foster care; intensive in-home services. Local offices provide various programs including Parents Anonymous; groups for bereaved parents; divorce adjustment groups; parenting classes; mentor programs; respite programs; Parent's Place; day care center. In addition, the agency contracts with the State of Wisconsin to operate the statewide Adoption Information Center.

BRANCH/NETWORK OFFICES

While the Children's Service Society of Wisconsin has numerous offices located throughout the state, the following branch offices house adoption workers who provide services to families throughout the state.
513 South Barstow
Eau Claire, WI 54701
(715) 835–5915

818 Sixth Ave.
Racine, WI 53403
(414) 633–3591

4915 Monona Dr.
Madison, WI 53716
(608) 249–8506

1212 S. 70th St.
West Allis, WI 53214
(414) 453–1400

201 Ceape Ave.
Oshkosh, WI 54901
(414) 235–1002

480 E. Grand Ave., #3
Wisconsin Rapids, WI 54494
(715) 421–0480

LICENSE/ACCREDITATION/PROFESSIONAL AFFILIATIONS

Children's Service Society of Wisconsin is licensed by the State of Wisconsin Department of Health and Social Services as a child placing agency and is accredited by the Council on Accreditation of Services for Families and Children. The agency is a founding member of the Child Welfare League of America and a member of the Wisconsin Association of Family and Children's Agencies. The agency is certified by the State of Wisconsin as an outpatient psychotherapy clinic.

COMMUNITY ADOPTION CENTER, INC.

115 E. Waldo Boulevard
Manitowoc, WI 54220
(414) 682–9211
Program director: Deanne Vollendorf

THE PROGRAM

Community Adoption Center is a for-profit agency serving residents in 40 southern and eastern counties of Wisconsin and anticipating placement of approximately 50 children annually. Founded in 1987 with a commitment "to provide quality and effective service to persons of all races and religions," Community Adoption Center works with foreign state-approved sources and with cooperating agencies in the U.S. to facilitate the placement of children from various countries with Wisconsin families. The agency provides homestudy and supervisory services for applicants pursuing independent adoption and step-parent adoptions. The agency also provides counseling services to birthparents and places infants for adoption when birthparents in the agency's program elect adoptive placement as the best plan for their infants.

THE COST

The agency's fee schedule for homestudy and supervisory services is as follows:

Foreign adoption study	$2,000.00
Foreign special-needs adoption study	$1,700.00
Independent adoption study	$1,600.00
Domestic special-needs program	$3,500.00
Healthy Caucasian infant program	$5,000.00

For foreign adoptions, services covered by the fee include homestudy, help in locating a child, and post-placement services. In addition, applicants pursuing foreign adoptions should anticipate between $2,000 and $6,000 in foreign agency fees, travel or escort costs, and related expenses.

For domestic adoptions (independent, special needs, and healthy Caucasian infant adoptions), applicants should anticipate responsibility for legal, medical, and foster care for the birthmother and child. For domestic special needs program and healthy Caucasian infant program, the agency's fee includes placement.

In all programs, applicants assume responsibility for legal fees connected with finalization of the adoption.

THE WAIT

The time from application to the homecoming of the adoptive child varies depending on the program and the type of child the applicants wish to parent. The agency's goal is to achieve placement for studied families within 1 year.

THE CHILDREN

Community Adoption Center facilitates the placement of both healthy and special-needs children, ranging in age from infancy to adolescence, of all racial backgrounds. Places of origin include U.S., Asia, India, South or Central America.

THE REQUIREMENTS

Age: No agency requirement, but may vary depending on the program.
Health: No agency requirement, but may vary depending on the program.
Religion: No requirement.
Financial status: No requirement.
Marital status: No agency requirement, but may vary depending on the program.
Family size: No agency requirement, but may vary depending on the program.
Racial, ethnic or cultural origin: No requirement.

THE PROCEDURE

Participation in Community Adoption Center's program entails the following basic steps:
Informational meeting
Application
Homestudy
Compliance with immigration/naturalization requirements (foreign adoptions only)
Referral
Placement
Post-placement services

ADDITIONAL PROGRAMS/SERVICES

Community Adoption Center provides adoptive parent support experiences, parenting classes, and adoptive parenting sharing.

BRANCH/NETWORK OFFICES

101 E. Milwaukee
Janesville, WI 53545
(608) 756–0405

7818 Big Sky Drive
Madison, WI 53719
(608) 833–5881

LICENSE/ACCREDITATION/PROFESSIONAL AFFILIATIONS

Community Adoption Center, Inc. is licensed by the State of Wisconsin Department of Health and Social Services.

EVANGELICAL CHILD AND FAMILY AGENCY

2401 N. Mayfair Road
Milwaukee, WI 53226
(414) 476–9550
Program director: Beverly M. Ozinga, ACSW

THE PROGRAM

Evangelical Child and Family Agency in Milwaukee provides services for residents of designated counties in Wisconsin (within a 50–mile radius of the agency's office). For a full description of programs and services, refer to Illinois listing:

Evangelical Child and Family Agency
1530 N. Main Street
Wheaton, IL 60187
(312) 653–6400

Lutheran Counseling and Family Services

Mail: P.O. Box 13367
Wauwatosa, WI 53213
Office: 3515 N. 124th Street
Brookfield, WI 53005
(414) 783–4564
Program director: Carol H. Bennett

The Program

Lutheran Counseling and Family Services is a nonprofit agency serving residents of the state of Wisconsin and placing approximately 15 children annually. The agency's mission is "to enable people served to grow and develop in self-worth through the assurance of God's saving grace in Jesus Christ." The agency provides services to birthparents and places infants for adoption when birthparents in the agency's program decide that the best interests of the child will be served by adoptive placement.

The Cost

The agency's fee for adoption services is 7% of the applicants' combined annual gross income, with a maximum of $5,000 plus a medical subsidy fee. Services covered by the fee include all phases of the adoption process, excluding legal fees connected with finalization of the adoption. In addition, applicants should anticipate the cost of a physical examination.

The Wait

The time from application for acceptance into the program to the homecoming of the adoptive child ranges from 4 to 5 years.

The Children

Lutheran Counseling and Family Services places primarily healthy infants, born in the U.S., but also occasionally special-needs children.

The Requirements

Age: Applicants must be at least 21 and no more than 40 years of age.
Health: Applicants must be in reasonably good health. Infertility documentation is required.
Religion: Applicants must be practicing members of the Lutheran Church, Missouri Synod.
Financial status: Applicants are evaluated individually on the basis of their ability to manage financial resources effectively.
Marital status: Applicants must be married couples. The length of the marriage must be at least 2 years.
Family size: Applicants may have no more than 1 child currently in the family.
Residence: Applicants must be residents of the state of Wisconsin.
Racial, ethnic or cultural origin: Preference for placing children in families of similar origins.

The Procedure

Participation in Lutheran Counseling and Family Services' adoption program entails the following basic steps:
Orientation meeting
Application
Homestudy
Placement
Post-placement services
Post-legal services

Additional Programs/Services

Lutheran Counseling and Family Services hosts an annual dinner for adoptive parents; conducts searches for adult adoptees; provides family and individual counseling, unwed parents counseling, and infant foster care.

Branch/Network Offices

611 N. Lynndale Dr.
Appleton, WI 54914
(414) 731–5651

3821 Kohler Memorial Dr.
Sheboygan, WI 53081
(414) 457–4011

2728 Mall Dr., Suite 4
Eau Claire, WI 54701
(715) 832–7615

c/o St. James Lutheran Church
336 S. Andrews
Shawano, WI 54166
(715) 524–4840

503 1/2 Jefferson St., Suite D
Wausau, WI 54401
(715) 845–6289

License/Accreditation/Professional Affiliations

Lutheran Counseling and Family Services is licensed by the State of Wisconsin Department of Health and Social Services. The agency is a member of the Council on Accreditation of Services for Families and Children.

Lutheran Social Services

3200 W. Highland Boulevard
P.O. Box 08520
Milwaukee, WI 53208(414) 342–7175
Program director: Michael Short, Adoption Coordinator

The Program

Lutheran Social Services is a nonprofit multi-service agency serving residents of Wisconsin and Upper Michigan and placing approximately 250 children annually. Founded in 1882, the agency's mission is "to help children, youth, adults and families improve the quality of their lives." Providing services to anyone in need, regardless of religion, race, age, or income, the agency offers domestic and international adoption programs for both healthy and special-needs children. The agency provides services to birthparents and places infants for adoption when birthparents elect adoptive placement as the best plan for their child. Working with birthparents, private and public agencies, and national and regional exchange programs, the agency places domestic special-needs children. Working directly with child welfare organizations overseas and cooperatively with other U.S. licensed agencies, Lutheran Social Services places children from various countries in Wisconsin and Michigan families. In addition, the agency will provide homestudy and supervisory services for applicants pursuing interagency adoption (domestic or international) or independent adoption.

THE COST

The agency's fee for homestudy and supervisory services averages $1,900. Other fees vary depending on the program and range from $4,000 to $8,000, including medical expenses for the birthmother and child for domestic adoptions, and including foreign agency fees, travel or escort expenses, and related costs for international adoptions. For all programs, applicants assume responsibility for legal fees connected with finalization.

THE WAIT

The time from application to the homecoming of the adoptive child varies depending on the program. For Korean adoptions, the time from inquiry to homecoming averages 18 months.

THE CHILDREN

Lutheran Social Services places both healthy and special-needs children, ranging in age from infancy to adolescence, of all racial backgrounds. Countries of origin include U.S., Korea, Philippines, Taiwan, Japan, and several Central and South American countries.

THE REQUIREMENTS

The requirements vary depending on the program. General guidelines are as follows:

Age: The rule of thumb is that there should be no more than 40 years difference between the adoptive parents and the child.

Health: Applicants should be in good health. Infertility documentation is required for some programs. There is some flexibility for special needs placements.

Religion: If the agency has legal guardianship of the child, applicants must be practicing Christians.

Financial status: Applicants must demonstrate financial stability.

Marital status: The requirement varies depending on the program. Some options are available to single parents. If married, the length of the marriage must be at least 2 years.

Family size: The requirement varies depending on the program.

Racial, ethnic or cultural origin: No requirement.

THE PROCEDURE

Participation in Lutheran Social Services' adoption program entails the following basic steps:
Application
Homestudy
Compliance with immigration/naturalization requirements (foreign adoptions only)

Placement
Post-placement supervision
Finalization
Naturalization (foreign adoptions only)

ADDITIONAL PROGRAMS/SERVICES

Lutheran Social Services provides a wide range of community services including individual, marital, and family counseling; residential care and foster care; services to the developmentally disabled; services for the elderly; refugee resettlement; alcohol or drug abuse intervention program; family life enrichment; volunteer opportunities.

BRANCH/NETWORK OFFICES

Lutheran Social Services maintains offices throughout Wisconsin and in Upper Michigan. Contact the main office in Milwaukee for a current list of locations and telephone numbers.

LICENSE/ACCREDITATION/PROFESSIONAL AFFILIATIONS

Lutheran Social Services is licensed by the State of Wisconsin Department of Health and Social Services and by the State of Michigan Department of Social Services. The agency is accredited by the Council on Accreditation of Services for Families and Children and is a member of Family Service America.

PAUQUETTE CHILDREN'S SERVICES

315 West Conant Street
P.O. Box 162
Portage, WI 53901
(608) 742–8004
Program director: Brian J. Tool, MSW

THE PROGRAM

Pauquette Children's Services is a for-profit agency serving residents of Wisconsin for foreign, independent, and interagency adoptions and a limited number of out-of-state residents for interstate private adoptions (those in which out-of-state couples locate a Wisconsin child or in which Wisconsin couples locate a child in another state). The agency works with private and public state-approved foreign sources to place children from various countries in American families. The agency also works with several cooperating agencies in the U.S. to place Black and bi-racial infants. Occasionally, infants with medical risks or physical challenges and older children are also available. In addition, the agency will provide homestudy and supervisory services for applicants pursuing independent or parent-initiated adoptions (domestic or foreign). Pauquette Children's Services facilitates the placement of approximately 150–200 children annually.

THE COST

The agency's fee for homestudy and supervisory services is $1,650 for foreign or domestic adoptions and $1,450 for independent adoptions. For foreign adoptions, applicants should anticipate a total cost ranging from $4,800 to $10,600 and varying depending on the child's country of origin. For domestic Black or bi-racial infant adoptions, applicants should anticipate a total cost of approximately $7,550 plus travel or escort expenses. For independent adoptions, applicants should anticipate responsibility for medical, foster care, and legal expenses of the birthmother and child. In all programs, applicants assume responsibility for legal fees connected with finalization.

THE WAIT

The time from application to the homecoming of the adoptive child varies greatly depending on the child's country of origin and the type of child the applicants wish to parent. For Black or bi-racial infant adoptions, the wait is approximately 3 to 6 months. For foreign adoptions, the wait ranges from 6 months to 2 years, with an average of 12 months.

THE CHILDREN

Pauquette Children's Services facilitates the placement of both healthy and special-needs children, ranging in age from infancy to adolescence, of all racial backgrounds. Countries of origin include Chile, Colombia, Mexico, Ecuador, Guatemala, India, the Philippines, Korea, Hong Kong, Thailand, Taiwan, and the U.S.

THE REQUIREMENTS

Age: Couples between the ages of 21 and 55 and single applicants between the ages of 25 and 55 may apply.
Health: Applicants must be in reasonably good health.
Religion: No requirement.
Financial status: Applicants must demonstrate financial stability.
Marital status: No requirement. If married, the length of the marriage must be at least 1 year.
Family size: No requirement.
Racial, ethnic or cultural origin: No requirement.

THE PROCEDURE

Participation in Pauquette Children's Services' adoption program entails the following basic steps:
  Informational meeting
  Homestudy (including individual counseling sessions)
  Compliance with immigration/naturalization requirements
    (foreign adoptions only)
  Compliance with Interstate Compact requirements (interstate adoptions only)
  Placement
  Post-placement supervision

ADDITIONAL PROGRAMS/SERVICES

Pauquette Children's Services provides counseling services to birthparents and to adoptive parents.

BRANCH/NETWORK OFFICES

None.

LICENSE/ACCREDITATION/PROFESSIONAL AFFILIATIONS

Pauquette Children's Services is licensed by the State of Wisconsin Department of Health and Social Services.

SEVEN SORROWS OF OUR SORROWFUL MOTHER INFANTS' HOME, INC.

Box 905
Necedah, WI 54646
(608) 565-2417
Program director: Mary C. Bulcher, R.N.

THE PROGRAM

Seven Sorrows of Our Sorrowful Mother Infants' Home is a nonprofit agency providing nationwide services to birthparents and statewide services to adoptive parents. Founded in 1972, the agency's mission is "to save the lives of the unborn" through the provision of counseling, medical, educational, and residential services to birthmothers. All services to birthmothers are provided free of charge and regardless of race, color, creed, or nationality. The agency places infants for adoption when a birthmother in the agency's program decides that the best interests of the child will be served by adoptive placement. However, the agency has a long waiting list, and the intake list is currently closed.

THE COST

Adoption services are provided at no charge to the adoptive couple. However, the agency will accept a donation after the placement of the child.

THE WAIT

The agency's intake list is currently closed. However, applicants who are currently wait listed can anticipate a wait of approximately 7 years before the homestudy is initiated, and a wait of approximately 2 years from completion of the homestudy to placement.

THE CHILDREN

Seven Sorrows of Our Sorrowful Mother Infants' Home places primarily infants, of all racial backgrounds, born in the U.S.

THE REQUIREMENTS

Age: Applicants must be at least 21 and no more than 40 years of age.
Health: Applicants must be in reasonably good health.
Religion: At least one parent must be a baptized practicing Catholic.
Financial status: Applicants must demonstrate financial stability.
Marital status: Applicants must be married couples. The length of the marriage must be at least 3 years.
Family size: For healthy infant adoption, applicants must be childless or have no more than 1 child currently in the family. For special-needs infants, the requirement may be waived.
Racial, ethnic or cultural origin: No requirement.

THE PROCEDURE

Participation in the agency's adoption program entails the following basic steps:

Intake inquiry (intake list currently closed)
Wait listing
Group informational meeting
Application
Homestudy
Placement
Post-placement supervision

ADDITIONAL PROGRAMS/SERVICES

The agency provides extensive services to birthmothers (counseling, residential care, medical care, and educational services), foster care for infants, residential care for children (from birth through age 10) who have severe physical, mental, or emotional handicaps.

BRANCH/NETWORK OFFICES

None.

LICENSE/ACCREDITATION/PROFESSIONAL AFFILIATIONS

Seven Sorrows of Our Sorrowful Mother Infants' Home, Inc. is licensed by the State of Wisconsin Department of Health and Social Services.

SUNNY RIDGE FAMILY CENTER

c/o Bethel Baptist Church
1601 Libal
Green Bay, WI 54301(414) 437–4437
Program director: Larry G. Betts, President

THE PROGRAM

For a full description of programs and services, refer to Illinois listing:
Sunny Ridge Family Center
2 S 426 Orchard Road
Wheaton, IL 60187
(312) 668–5117

WISCONSIN LUTHERAN CHILD AND FAMILY SERVICE

6800 N. 76th Street
P.O. Box 23980
Milwaukee, WI 53223
(414) 353–5000
Program director: Donna J. Gliniecki

THE PROGRAM

Wisconsin Lutheran Child and Family Service (WLCFS) is a nonprofit multi-service agency serving residents of the state of Wisconsin and placing approximately 10 to 15 children annually through its adoption program. Founded in 1965, the agency's mission is "to reflect the healing and helping ministry of Jesus Christ by serving God's children of all ages in their special needs, strengthening Christian faith and building Christian lives in a sinful and troubling world."

The agency provides services to birthparents and places infants for adoption when birthparents elect adoptive placement as the best plan for their child. Working cooperatively with the public agency in Wisconsin and with national and regional exchange programs, the agency facilitates the placement of special-needs children. In addition, the agency will provide homestudy and supervisory services for applicants pursuing inter- agency adoption (international).

THE COST

The agency's fee for adoption services varies depending on the program. For the Healthy White Infant Program, the agency's fee ranges from $2,500 to $4,000. For the Special Needs Program, the fee ranges from $1,000 to $2,500. Services covered by the fee include all phases of the adoption process, excluding the cost of a new birth certificate.

THE WAIT

For the Healthy White Infant Program, adoptive applicants can anticipate a 5 year wait before the homestudy is begun. Once the homestudy is completed, placement may occur at any time, with the goal of placement occurring within 1 year. For the Special Needs Program, the wait varies depending on the range of special needs the prospective adoptive family can accept.

THE CHILDREN

WLCFS places both healthy and special-needs children, ranging in age from birth to 17 years, of Caucasian and bi-racial backgrounds, born in the U.S.

THE REQUIREMENTS

Age: For the Healthy White Infant Program, applicants must be under the age of 40 at the time of placement. The Special Needs Program requires that there be no more than 40 years age difference between the parents and the child to be adopted.
Health: Applicants should be in reasonably good health. Applicants with health problems or handicaps are given individual consideration. Infertility documentation is required.
Religion: Applicants must be practicing members of Wisconsin Synod Evangelical Lutheran (WELS or affiliated synods).
Financial status: No requirement.
Marital status: Applicants must be married; the length of the marriage must be at least 2 years.
Family size: For the Healthy White Infant Program, applicants may have no more than 1 child currently in the family. The requirement is flexible for the Special Needs Program.
Racial, ethnic or cultural origin: No requirement.

THE PROCEDURE

Participation in the adoption program of WLCFS entails the following basic steps:
Submission of inquiry form
Orientation meeting
Application
Homestudy
Placement
Post-placement supervision

ADDITIONAL PROGRAMS/SERVICES

WLCFS provides a full range of services including foster care; services to unmarried parents; family counseling; alcoholism awareness; services to the mentally retarded; educational services; stewardship and health care services to the elderly.

BRANCH/NETWORK OFFICES

WLCFS/Appleton
225 N. Richmond
Appleton, WI 54911
(414) 731–9798

WLCFS/LaCrosse
1601 Caledonia St.
LaCrosse, WI 54602
(608) 781–5522

WLCFS/Eau Claire
1725 Westgate Rd.
Eau Claire, WI 54703
(715) 832–1678

WLCFS/Wausau
1725 Westgate Rd.
Wausau, WI 54401
(715) 842–5802

WLCFS/Morton Grove
6214 Capulina Ave.
Morton Grove, IL 60053
(312) 965–1330

WLCFS/Fort Atkinson
407 S. Main St.
Fort Atkinson, WI 53538
(414) 563–8680

LICENSE/ACCREDITATION/PROFESSIONAL AFFILIATIONS

Wisconsin Lutheran Child and Family Services is licensed by the State of Wisconsin Department of Health and Social Services. The agency is a member of the Child Welfare League of America, Wisconsin Association of Family and Children's Agencies, and Wisconsin Advocates for Adoption.

Wyoming

PUBLIC ADOPTION PROGRAM/ COMMUNITY RESOURCES

Department of Health and Social Services
Division of Public Assistance and Social Services
Family Services Unit
Hathaway Building
Cheyenne, WY 82002–0710
(307) 777–6789
Adoption specialist: Patricia McDaniel

THE PROGRAM

The Family Services Unit does not provide homestudy or supervisory services except pursuant to a court order or ICPC. When a child in the custody of the State of Wyoming is available for adoption, the Family Services Unit uses private Wyoming adoption agencies and the Rocky Mountain Adoption Exchange as a placement resource.

STATE EXCHANGE

Rocky Mountain Adoption Exchange (Regional)
5350 Leetsdale Drive, #10
Denver, CO 82200
(303) 333–0845

STATE ADOPTION REUNION REGISTRY

None.

STATE SUBSIDY

For information, contact the Division of Public Assistance and Social Services (above).

NACAC REPRESENTATIVE

Beverly Craig.
632 23rd Street
Cody, WY 82414
(307) 587–2494

GENERAL ADOPTION RESOURCES

Adoption support services in Wyoming are provided by private adoption agencies as a service to their clients and by the Division of Public Assistance and Social Services. In addition, the following organizations provide information and support services:

Wyoming OURS, Inc.
  Contact: Mary Patrick
  1654 Bellaire Drive
  Casper, WY 82601
  (307) 235–8163

Wyoming Adoption Council
  Contact: Barbara Shaw
  Wyoming Children's Society
  P.O. Box 105
  Cheyenne, WY 82003
  (307) 632–7619

SPECIAL-NEEDS ADOPTION RESOURCES

For information on resources for children with special needs, contact the Division of Public Assistance and Social Services (above).

OUT-OF-STATE AGENCIES

AGENCY

Holt International Children's Services, Tennessee branch

SEE APPENDIX A

Agencies Providing Nationwide Services

CATHOLIC SOCIAL SERVICES OF WYOMING, INC.

623 S. Wolcott
P.O. Box 2247
Casper, WY 82602–2247
(307) 237–2723
1–800–442–3278 (toll-free in Wyoming)
Program director: Tom Cotterill; Jan Cobb, Adoption Supervisor

THE PROGRAM

Established in 1964 to meet the needs of the orphaned child, Catholic Social Services of Wyoming is a nonprofit agency providing statewide services and placing approximately 25 children annually. The agency's mission is "to live Christ's compassion, to establish and facilitate services to those in need, and to advocate a Christian resolution to social injustices." The agency's services are open to all, regardless of religion, race or creed. The agency provides services to birthparents and places infants for adoption when birthparents decide that the child's best interests will be met by adoptive placement. Working cooperatively with the public agency and with national and regional exchange programs, the agency recruits families and facilitates the placement of special-needs children. Working cooperatively with U.S. agencies which maintain international programs, the agency facilitates the placement of children from several foreign countries. In addition, the agency will provide homestudy and supervisory services for applicants pursuing interagency adoption (domestic or international).

THE COST

The agency's fee schedule for infant adoption services is as follows:

Application fee	$150.00
Homestudy fee	$150.00

Placement fee is10% of the primary wage-earner's gross annual income with a minimum fee of $2,500

For special-needs adoptions, there is no placement fee. However, applicants can anticipate a supervisory fee of $200. For homestudy and supervisory services connected with interagency adoption, the agency's fee is $500. For all programs, applicants assume responsibility for legal fees connected with finalization.

THE WAIT

The time from application to the homecoming of the

adoptive child varies depending on the program. For infant adoption, the wait ranges from 1 1/2 to 2 1/2 years.

THE CHILDREN

Catholic Social Services directly places primarily healthy infants but will work with families who wish to adopt special-needs children of any age or racial background and with families pursuing international adoption.

THE REQUIREMENTS

Age: Applicants must be at least 21 years of age. The maximum age requirement varies depending on the age of the child being considered for placement.

Health: Applicants with health problems or handicaps are given individual consideration. Infertility documentation is required for infant adoptions.

Religion: Applicants must be practicing members of their faith.

Financial status: No requirement.

Marital status: For infant adoption, applicants must be married.

Family size: For infant adoption, applicants may have no more than 1 child currently in the family. The requirement is flexible for special-needs adoptions.

Racial, ethnic or cultural origin: No requirement.

THE PROCEDURE

Participation in the adoption program of Catholic Social Services entails the following basic steps:
Orientation meeting
Application
Individual counseling sessions
Homestudy
Compliance with immigration/naturalization requirements (international adoptions only)
Referral
Placement
Post-placement supervision

ADDITIONAL PROGRAMS/SERVICES

Catholic Social Services provides alternative care for birthmothers and babies, using individual family homes.

BRANCH/NETWORK OFFICES

Catholic Social Services maintains case workers throughout the state. All inquiries about adoption services are processed through the main office (1–800–442–3278, toll-free in Wyoming).

LICENSE/ACCREDITATION/PROFESSIONAL AFFILIATIONS

Catholic Social Services of Wyoming, Inc. is licensed by the State of Wyoming Department of Health and Social Services.

WYOMING CHILDREN'S SOCIETY

Mailing: P.O. Box 105
Cheyenne, WY 82003
Office: 716 Randall

Cheyenne, WY 82001
(307) 632–7619
Program director: Barbara Shaw

THE PROGRAM

Wyoming Children's Society is a nonprofit agency serving residents of the state of Wyoming and placing approximately 12 children annually. Founded in 1911 to provide care and housing for orphans, birthmothers, and infants, Wyoming Children's Society is the state's oldest adoption agency. Today, the agency has 12 casework consultants throughout the state and provides a range of services including pregnancy counseling, pre-and post-relinquishment counseling to birthparents, pre- and post-placement counseling to adoptive parents, and post-legal support services to adoptive families. The agency places infants for adoption when birthparents in the agency's counseling program elect adoptive placement as the best plan for their child. Working with various national and regional exchange programs, the agency facilitates the placement of special-needs children. The agency also provides homestudy and supervisory services for applicants pursuing private, interagency, or intercountry adoption.

THE COST

The agency's fee schedule for adoption services is as follows:

Application fee	$75.00
Homestudy fee (WCS placement)	$300.00
Homestudy fee (private, interagency or intercountry placement)	$500.00
Placement fee (infant adoption) is 10% of principal wage earner's annual gross income	
Placement fee (special-needs adoption)	None

In addition, applicants should anticipate financial responsibility for legal fees connected with finalization of the adoption (approximately $200–$500).

THE WAIT

For infant adoption, no accurate prediction of the time from application to placement is available. For special-needs adoption, the time from application to the homecoming of the adoptive child is at least 9–12 months.

THE CHILDREN

Wyoming Children's Society places both healthy and special-needs children, ranging in age from infancy to adolescence, of all racial backgrounds, born in the U.S. In addition, the agency provides homestudy and supervisory services for applicants pursuing intercountry adoption.

THE REQUIREMENTS

Age: Applicants must be at least 21 years of age.

Health: Applicants must be in reasonably good health. Applicants with health problems or handicaps are given individual consideration.

Religion: No requirement.

Financial status: No requirement.

Marital status: For infant adoption, applicants must be married couples. No requirement for special-needs adoption.

Family size: Family size is evaluated on an individual basis.

Racial, ethnic or cultural origin: No requirement, but preference for placing children in families of similar origins when possible.

THE PROCEDURE

Participation in Wyoming Children's Society's adoption program entails the following basic steps:
Inquiry
Application
Homestudy
Individual counseling sessions (as needed)
Placement
Referral to supportive services (as needed)
Post-placement supervision and support

ADDITIONAL PROGRAMS/SERVICES

Wyoming Children's Society works with several adoption support groups; provides counseling services to birthparents; provides pre- and post-placement as well as post- legal adoption counseling.

BRANCH/NETWORK OFFICES

Wyoming Children's Society has 12 casework consultants located throughout the state. However, all adoption inquiries are processed through the Cheyenne office.

LICENSE/ACCREDITATION/PROFESSIONAL AFFILIATIONS

Wyoming Children's Society is licensed by the State of Wyoming Department of Health and Social Services.

WYOMING PARENTING SOCIETY

P.O. Box 1483
Jackson, WY 83001
(307) 733–6357
Program director: Marilee Enright, MSW

THE PROGRAM

Wyoming Parenting Society is a nonprofit agency serving residents of Wyoming only and placing 2 to 3 children annually. Wyoming Parenting Society provides services to birthparents and places infants for adoption when birthparents in the agency's program elect adoptive placement as the best plan for their child. The agency also provides homestudy and supervisory services for applicants pursuing special-needs adoption.

THE COST

The agency's fee for adoption services is $500 for the homestudy and $1,500 for placement. Applicants are responsible for the medical costs of the birthmother and child and legal fees connected with finalization.

THE WAIT

The time from application to the homecoming of the adoptive child averages 1 to 2 years.

THE CHILDREN

Wyoming Parenting Society places primarily healthy Caucasian infants, born in the U.S. The agency will also provide homestudy and supervisory services for applicants pursuing special-needs adoption.

THE REQUIREMENTS

Age: No requirement.
Health: Applicants should be in reasonably good health.
Religion: No requirement.
Financial status: No requirement.
Marital status: For infant adoption, applicants must be married couples.
Family size: No requirement.
Racial, ethnic or cultural origin: No requirement.

THE PROCEDURE

Participation in the adoption program of Wyoming Parenting Society entails the following basic steps:
Application
Group counseling sessions
Individual counseling sessions
Homestudy
Placement
Post-placement supervision

ADDITIONAL PROGRAMS/SERVICES

Wyoming Parenting Society provides pregnancy counseling services; housing and foster care for birthmothers and babies; adoption support groups; new mothers groups.

BRANCH/NETWORK OFFICES

None.

LICENSE/ACCREDITATION/PROFESSIONAL AFFILIATIONS

Wyoming Parenting Society is licensed by the State of Wyoming Department of Health and Social Services.

Private Agency Summary

ALABAMA				Types of Adoption Services							
Agency	**Area Served**	**Age**	**Religion**	Single	Traditional	Identified	Open	Foreign	US Special Needs	Home Study/	Post-Placement
AGAPE of Central Alabama	Central AL	Varies with age of child	Church of Christ		Y				Y		
AGAPE of South Alabama	South AL	Varies with age of child	Church of Christ		Y				Y		
Catholic Family Services	Diocese of Birmingham	21–37	Catholic or Protestant		Y					Y	
Catholic Social Services	Central and Southeast AL	25—40	Christian	Y	Y				Y	Y	
Children's Aid Society	Jefferson, Shelby, Walker & Blount Cos.	Min. 24	Faith of choice	Y	Y			Y	Y		
ALASKA											
Adoption Services of WACAP	AK (National)	Varies with program	Varies with program	Y	Y			Y	Y	Y	
Catholic Social Services	AK	25—45	None		Y				Y	Y	
Fairbanks Counseling & Adoption	Northern AK	Varies	None	Y	Y			Y	Y	Y	
LDS Social Services	AK (National)	Varies with age of child	Mormon		Y				Y		
ARIZONA											
Arizona Children's Home Association	Tucson and surrounds	Varies with age of child	None	Y	Y				Y		
Catholic Family and Community Services	Diocese of Phoenix	25—45	Varies	Y	Y				Y	Y	
Christian Family Care Agency	AZ	Varies with age of child	Christian		Y				Y		
Dillon Southwest	AZ	Varies	Faith of choice				Y			Y	
Family Service Agency	Maricopa Co.	Min. 23	None		Y					Y	
Globe International Adoption	National	Varies with program	Christian	Y	Y			Y			
House of Samuel Children's Services	AZ	23—45	Evangelical	Y	Y			Y	Y		
LDS Social Services	AZ (National)	Varies with age of child	Mormon		Y				Y		
Southwest Adoption Center	National	None	None		Y						

ARKANSAS

Agency	Area Served	Age	Religion	Single	Traditional	Identified	Open	Foreign	US Special Needs	Home Study/Post-Placement
Bethany Christian Services	AR (National)	25—38	Evangelical		Y				Y	
For the Love of Children	AR	Min. 25	None	Y	Y				Y	

CALIFORNIA

Agency	Area Served	Age	Religion	Single	Traditional	Identified	Open	Foreign	US Special Needs	Home Study/Post-Placement
Aask Northern California	Northern CA	Min 21	None	Y					Y	
Adopt	San Francisco Bay Area	Varies with program	Varies with program					Y		Y
Adoption Horizon	Northern CA (4 counties)	Varies with program	None	Y				Y	Y	
Adoption Services International	CA	Varies with program	None	Y				Y		
Adoptions Unlimited	CA (5 counties)	Min. 25 (varies with program)	Varies with program	Y				Y	Y	Y
Bal Jagat Children's World	CA (5 counties)	Varies with program	None	Y				Y		Y
Bay Area Adoption Service	San Francisco area	Varies with program	None	Y				Y		
Bethany Christian Services	CA (National)	25—38	Evangelical		Y				Y	
Catholic Charities of San Francisco	Greater San Francisco Bay Area	Varies	Varies	Y	Y			Y	Y	
Catholic Community Services	Diocese of San Diego	Varies	Varies	Y						
Children's Home Society of California	CA	None	None	Y	Y		Y	Y	Y	Y
Children's Services Center	Monterey and San Benito Counties	None	None	Y	Y			Y	Y	Y
Christian Children's Services	Southern CA (10 counties)	Varies with age of child	Church of Christ		Y				Y	Y
Chrysalis House	CA (6 counties)	Varies	Varies	Y	Y			Y	Y	Y
Family Connections	CA	Varies with program	None	Y	Y			Y	Y	
Future Families	CA (5 counties)	None	None	Y					Y	
Holt International Children's Services	CA (National)	Varies with program	None	Y				Y		
Holy Family Services	Los Angeles and Orange Cos.	Varies with age of child	Faith of choice		Y		Y		Y	

| CALIFORNIA | | | | Types of Adoption Services | | | | | | |
Agency	Area Served	Age	Religion	Single	Traditional	Identified	Open	Foreign	US Special Needs	Home Study/Post-Placement
Jewish Family and Children's Services	San Francisco Bay Area	None	None	Y		Y				
LDS Social Services	CA (National)	Varies with age of child	Mormon		Y			Y		
Life Adoption Services	CA (5 counties)	Varies with program	None	Y				Y		Y
Partners for Adoption	CA (6 counties)	None	None	Y	Y			Y	Y	Y
Sierra Adoption Services	CA (9 counties)	Min. 21	None	Y			Y		Y	Y
Vista Del Mar	Los Angeles, Ventura, & Orange Cos.	None	None	Y	Y	Y	Y			Y
COLORADO										
Adoption Connection	CO	Varies with program	Varies with program	Y	Y					
Adoption Option	CO	Min. 25	None	Y	Y	Y			Y	
Bethany Christian Services	CO (National)	25–38	Varies with program		Y			Y	Y	
Catholic Social Services	Southern CO	Min. 21	None	Y	Y				Y	Y
Colorado Christian Services	CO	21–40	Church of Christ		Y				Y	
Friends of Children of Various Nations	CO (NM)	Varies with the program	None	Y				Y	Y	Y
Hand in Hand International Adoption Agency	National (except for GA, NJ, OH)	Varies with age of child	Christian or Jewish					Y		
LDS Social Services	CO (National)	Varies with age of child	Mormon		Y				Y	
Universal Family	CO, CA, NY, KS, MO	30–45	None	Y					Y	Y
CONNECTICUT										
Bethany Christian Services	CT (National)	25–38	Evangelical		Y				Y	

CONNECTICUT — Types of Adoption Services

Agency	Area Served	Age	Religion	Single	Traditional	Identified	Open	Foreign	US Special Needs	Home Study/ Post-Placement
Catholic Charities/ Catholic Family Services (Norwich)	Diocese of Norwich	None	Christian		Y			Y		
Catholic Charities Catholic Family Services (Hartford)	Hartford, New Haven, Litchfield Cos.	None	Varies	Y	Y	Y		Y		
Catholic Family and Social Service	Fairfield Co.	Min. 25	Varies	Y	Y			Y	Y	
Child and Family Services	CT	None	None	Y				Y		
Child and Family Agency	New London, Middlesex Cos.	Varies with program	None	Y	Y			Y	Y	
Children's Center	CT	Varies with program	Varies	Y	Y			Y	Y	
Curtis Home Children's Program	CT	None	None	Y				Y		
Family & Children's Aid of Greater Norwalk	CT	Varies with program	None			Y	Y		Y	
Hall Neighborhood House	Greater Bridgeport	Min. 18	None	Y	Y			Y		
Highland Heights	Greater New Haven	Varies with age of child	None	Y				Y		
International Alliance for Children	CT, NY	25–45	None					Y		
Jewish Family Service Infertility Center	CT	Varies	Varies with program		Y	Y				Y
Jewish Family Service	Greater Bridgeport	Varies	None	Y		Y				Y
Jewish Family Service of New Haven	South Central CT	Varies with age of child	Varies with program	Y	Y	Y		Y	Y	Y
Lutheran Child & Family Services	CT	Min. 25 (varies with age of child)	None	Y		Y		Y	Y	Y

DELAWARE				Types of Adoption Services						
Agency	**Area Served**	**Age**	**Religion**	Single	Traditional	Identified	Open	Foreign	US Special Needs	Home Study/ Post-Placement
Adoption Agency	DE (PA, NJ)	Min. 21 (varies with program)	None	Y			Y	Y	Y	Y
Catholic Social Services	DE	Varies with age of child	Faith of choice	Y	Y				Y	
Child and Home Study Associates	DE (PA, NJ)	Varies with age of child	None	Y	Y			Y		Y
Welcome House	DE (MD, NJ, PA, VA, DC)	Varies with age of child	None	Y				Y	Y	
DISTRICT OF COLUMBIA										
Adoption Service Information Agency	DC, MD, VA, NC	25–44	None		Y			Y		
American Adoption Agency	National	25–50 (varies with program)	None	Y				Y		Y
Associated Catholic Charities	DC, MD	Varies with program	Varies	Y	Y			Y	Y	
Barker Foundation	DC metropolitan area	Varies with age of child	None		Y			Y		
Homes for Black Children	DC metropolitan area	Varies with age of child	None	Y	Y				Y	
Jewish Social Service Agency	DC metropolitan area	Max. 40	Jewish		Y				Y	Y
Lutheran Social Service Agency	DC, VA, MD	Min. 25 (varies with age of child)	Faith of choice	Y	Y			Y	Y	
Pan American Adoption Agency	National	25–55	None	Y	Y			Y		Y
Saint Sophia Greek Orthodox Adoption Service	DC	None	None							Y
World Child	DC (NC, CT, PA)	Min. 25 (max. varies)	None	Y				Y		

| FLORIDA | | | | Types of Adoption Services | | | | | | |
Agency	**Area Served**	**Age**	**Religion**	Single	Traditional	Identified	Open	Foreign	US Special Needs	Home Study/Post-Placement
Adoption Centre	FL	Varies with program	None	Y	Y			Y	Y	
Catholic Charities Bureau (Jacksonville)	Diocese of St. Augustine	Varies with program	None	Y	Y				Y	
Catholic Charities Bureau (St. Augustine)	St. Johns Flagler, & Putnum Cos.	Varies with age of child	None	Y	Y				Y	Y
Catholic Social Services (Naples)	Diocese of Venice	20—40	Faith of choice		Y				Y	
Catholic Social Service (Orlando)	Central FL	Max. 40	Faith of choice		Y				Y	
Catholic Social Services (Pensacola)	Diocese of Pensacola	25—40	Varies		Y	Y			Y	
Catholic Social Services (Tampa)	Greater Tampa (4 counties)	21—45	Varies	Y	Y				Y	
Catholic Social Services (St. Petersburg)	Pinellas Co.	25—39	None	Y	Y				Y	Y
Children's Home Society of Florida	FL	Min. 23	Varies	Y	Y				Y	
Family Service Centers/Project CAN	West-central Florida	Varies with child's needs	None	Y					Y	
Florida Baptist Children's Home	FL	Varies with age of child	Christian		Y	Y			Y	
Jewish Family and Community Services	Northeastern FL	None	Varies		Y					
LDS Social Services	FL (National)	Varies with age of child	Mormon		Y				Y	
Shepherd Care Christian Adoption Services	FL	25—45	Evangelical		Y				Y	
St. Vincent Maternity & Adoption Center	Dade Co.	Varies with program	Faith of choice	Y	Y			Y	Y	Y
Suncoast International Adoptions	FL	Min. 25 (varies with age of child)	None	Y				Y		Y

Agency	Area Served	Age	Religion	Single	Traditional	Identified	Open	Foreign	US Special Needs	Home Study/ Post-Placement
Bethany Christian Services	GA (National)	25—38	Evangelical		Y				Y	
Catholic Social Services	Greater Atlanta	Max. 37	None		Y					Y
Children's Services International	National	Varies with program	Varies with program	Y	Y			Y	Y	Y
Families First	GA	None	None	Y	Y				Y	Y
Georgia Baptist Children's Home	Southwest GA	Min. 25 (varies with age of child)	Varies						Y	Y
Homes for Children International	National	Varies with program	None	Y				Y		Y
Illien Adoptions International	National	Varies with program	None	Y	Y			Y	Y	Y
Jewish Family Services	Greater Atlanta	None	Jewish		Y					Y
LDS Social Services	GA (National)	Varies with age of child	Mormon		Y				Y	
Lutheran Ministries of Georgia	GA	Varies with age of child	Faith of choice	Y	Y			Y	Y	
New Beginnings Adoption & Counseling Agency	GA	Min. 25	Christian		Y	Y	Y		Y	Y
Open Door Adoption Agency	GA (National for special needs)	Varies with program	Judeo-Christian	Y	Y		Y		Y	
Parent and Child Development	GA (National for special needs)	25—45	None	Y	Y				Y	

Agency	Area Served	Age	Religion	Single	Traditional	Identified	Open	Foreign	US Special Needs	Home Study/ Post-Placement
Catholic Services to Families	HI	Varies with program	None		Y			Y	Y	Y
Child & Family Services	HI	None	None		Y			Y	Y	Y
Hawaii International Child Placement	HI	Varies with program	Varies with program	Y	Y			Y	Y	Y
LDS Social Services	HI (National)	Varies with age of child	Mormon		Y				Y	
Queen Lili'ukolani Children's Center	HI	Varies with age of child	None	Y	Y				Y	

IDAHO				Single	Traditional	Identified	Open	Foreign	US Special Needs	Home Study/ Post-Placement
Agency	**Area Served**	**Age**	**Religion**							
Catholic Counseling Services	ID	Max. 45	None	Y	Y					Y
Christian Counseling Services of ID	ID	Max. 40	Varies			Y				
Idaho Youth Ranch Adoption Services	Central and southern ID	21—45	None		Y					Y
LDS Social Services	ID (National)	Varies with age of child	Mormon		Y				Y	
ILLINOIS										
Baby Fold	Central IL	24—38	None	Y	Y				Y	
Bensensville Home Society	IL	Varies with program	None	Y				Y	Y	
Bethany Christian Services	IL (National)	25—38	Varies with program		Y			Y	Y	
Bethany Home	IL (IA)	21—35	None	Y	Y				Y	
Catholic Charities (Springfield)	Diocese of Springfield	Min. 21	Faith of choice		Y			Y	Y	Y
Catholic Charities of Lake County	Lake Co.	Min. 23 (varies with program)	None	Y	Y				Y	
Catholic Charities of the Archdiocese of Chicago	Cook Co.	Varies with program	Varies		Y		Y		Y	Y
Catholic Social Service (Belleville)	Diocese of Belleville (28 counties)	Min. 21	Faith of choice	Y	Y			Y	Y	
Catholic Social Service (Peoria)	Central IL	Varies with program	Varies	Y	Y			Y	Y	
Catholic Social Services (Rockford)	Diocese of Rockford	21—40	Christian		Y			Y	Y	Y
Chicago Child Care Society	Cood Co.	Varies with age of child	None	Y	Y				Y	Y
Children's Home and Aid Society of Illinois	Chicago, Rockford, Champaign-Urbana, Alton-East St. Louis areas	Varies with age of child	None	Y	Y			Y	Y	Y
Counseling and Family Service	IL	Min. 25	None	Y	Y			Y	Y	Y
Evangelical Child and Family Agency	IL (WI)	Varies with age of child	Evangelical	Y	Y				Y	
Family Care Services	IL	Varies	Varies	Y	Y				Y	

| ILLINOIS | | | | Types of Adoption Services | | | | | | | |
Agency	Area Served	Age	Religion	Single	Traditional	Identified	Open	Foreign	US Special Needs	Home Study/ Post-Placement	
Family Counseling Clinic	Northeastern IL	Varies with program	None	Y	Y				Y	Y	
Family Service Agency	IL	Varies with age of child	Varies	Y	Y			Y	Y		
Family Service of Decatur	IL (7 counties)	Varies	None	Y	Y			Y	Y		
Family Service Center of Sangamon Co.	Sangamon Co.	Min. 21	None		Y				Y	Y	
Jewish Children's Bureau of Chicago	Greater Chicago	Varies with program	Jewish		Y	Y				Y	
LDS Social Services	IL (National)	Varies with age of child	Mormon		Y				Y		
Lutheran Child and Family Services	IL	Varies with program	Varies with program	Y	Y				Y		
St. Mary's Services	Cook, Lake, DuPage Cos.	Max. 39	Christian		Y						
Sunny Ridge Family Center	IL (WI, IN, MI)	Varies with program	Varies with program	Y	Y	Y		Y	Y	Y	
INDIANA											
Adoption Resource Service	IN	Min. 28	None		Y						
Bethany Christian Services	IN (National)	25—38	Varies with program		Y			Y	Y		
Catholic Charities Bureau	Diocese of Evansville (12 counties)	Min. 24	Varies with program	Y	Y				Y	Y	
Catholic Social Services (Ft. Wayne)	IN (9 counties)	Min. 21	None	Y	Y				Y	Y	
Catholic Social Service (South Bend)	St. Joseph Co.	Varies with program	None	Y	Y				Y		
Childplace	IN (KY)	21—40	Church of Christ		Y				Y	Y	
Children's Bureau of Indianapolis	Greater Indianapolis	None	None	Y	Y				Y		
Chosen Children Adoption Services	IN (National)	Min. 23	None		Y					Y	
Coleman Adoption Services	IN	Varies with program	None	Y	Y				Y	Y	
LDS Social Services	IN (National)	Varies with age of child	Mormon		Y				Y		

INDIANA

Agency	Area Served	Age	Religion	Single	Traditional	Identified	Open	Foreign	US Special Needs	Home Study/Post-Placement
Lutheran Child & Family Services	IN	Varies with program	None	Y	Y				Y	Y
Lutheran Family Services of NW Indiana	Northwest Indiana	Varies	Faith of choice	Y	Y				Y	Y
Lutheran Social Services	Northeastern IN	Varies with program	None		Y			Y	Y	Y
St. Elizabeth's Home	IN	Varies with program	None	Y	Y			Y	Y	Y
Sunny Ridge Family Center	IN (IL, MI, WI)	Varies with program	Varies with program	Y	Y			Y	Y	Y
Villages of Indiana	IN	Min. 21	None	Y					Y	

IOWA

Agency	Area Served	Age	Religion	Single	Traditional	Identified	Open	Foreign	US Special Needs	Home Study/Post-Placement
American Home Finding Association	IA	18—36	Faith of choice		Y				Y	
Bethany Christian Services	IA (National)	25—38	Evangelical		Y				Y	
Bethany Home	IA (IL)	21—35	None	Y	Y				Y	
Building Families Through Adoption	IA (MN, SD, ND, WI)	Varies with program	Varies with program	Y				Y	Y	
Catholic Charities (Dubuque)	Archdiocese of Dubuque	Max. 40	Protestant or Catholic		Y			Y	Y	
Catholic Charities (Sioux City)	Northwest IA	Max. 40	Faith of choice		Y					
Catholic Council for Social Concern	Diocese of Des Moines	Max. 35	Faith of choice		Y				Y	
Hillcrest Family Services	IA	Varies with program	None	Y	Y			Y		Y
Holt International Children's Services	IA (National)	Varies with program	None	Y				Y		
Iowa Children's & Family Services	Des Moines and surrounds	Min. 21 Varies with child	No specific requirement	Y					Y	
Lutheran Family Service	IA	Max. 36	Lutheran		Y					
Lutheran Social Service of Iowa	IA	Max. 34	Christian	Y	Y				Y	Y
Young House Family Services	Southeast IA	None	None	Y						Y

KANSAS				Types of Adoption Services						
Agency	**Area Served**	**Age**	**Religion**	Single	Traditional	Identified	Open	Foreign	US Special Needs	Home Study/Post-Placement
Baumann, Powell & Stonestreet Independent Adoptions	KS	Max. 50	None	Y			Y		Y	
Catholic Charities	Diocese of Salina	22—40	Catholic or Protestant		Y					
Catholic Social Services (Great Bend)	West KS	Varies	Catholic or Protestant		Y				Y	Y
Catholic Social Service (Kansas City)	Archdiocese of Kansas City	Max. 40	Faith of choice		Y		Y			
Christian Family Services of the Midwest	KS, MO, OK, NE, IA	Varies	Church of Christ		Y				Y	
Family Life Services Adoption Agency	KS	Max. 43	Christian		Y				Y	
Gentle Shepherd Child Placement Services	National	21—40	Christian		Y			Y	Y	
Heart of America Family Services	KS (MO)	Varies with program	None		Y			Y	Y	Y
INSERCO	KS	Varies	Varies	Y						Y
Kansas Children's Service League/ Black Adoption Program	Greater Kansas City	Min. 21	None	Y	Y				Y	
LDS Social Services	KS (National)	Varies with age of child	Mormon		Y				Y	
Lutheran Social Services of Kansas and Oklahoma	KS (OK)	Varies with age of child	Christian	Y	Y		Y		Y	
Villages	KS	Min. 21	None						Y	
Wyandotte House	KS	Min. 18	None	Y	Y				Y	Y
KENTUCKY										
Catholic Social Service Bureau	Diocese of Covington	23—38	None		Y					Y
Childplace	KY (IN)	21—40	Church of Christ		Y				Y	Y
Chosen Children Adoption Services	National	Min. 23	None		Y					Y
Holt International Children's Services	KY (National)	Varies with program	None	Y				Y		

LOUISIANA

Agency	Area Served	Age	Religion	Single	Traditional	Identified	Open	Foreign	US Special Needs	Home Study/Post-Placement
Catholic Community Services	Diocese of Baton Rouge	21—38	Faith of choice		Y				Y	Y
Catholic Social Services (Lafayette)	LA	25—37	Faith of choice		Y					
Catholic Social Services (Houma)	Terrebonne, Lafourche, St. Mary Parishes	21—35	Catholic		Y					Y
Children's Bureau of New Orleans	Greater New Orleans	21—45/50	None	Y	Y			Y	Y	Y
Christian Homes	LA (National for special needs)	Min. 25	Church of Christ		Y				Y	Y
Jewish Children's Regional Service	LA, AL, AR, MS, OK, TN, TX	Varies with age of child	Jewish							Y
LDS Social Services	LA (National)	Varies with age of child	Mormon		Y			Y		
Sellers Baptist Home & Adoption center	National	Varies with program	Varies with program		Y				Y	Y
Caring Alternatives-Volunteers of America	Central and southern LA	25—45/50	None	Y	Y				Y	Y

MAINE

Agency	Area Served	Age	Religion	Single	Traditional	Identified	Open	Foreign	US Special Needs	Home Study/Post-Placement
Coastal Adoption Placement Service	ME	Min. 21	None	Y					Y	
Community Counseling Center	Greater Portland	23—45	None	Y	Y		Y			Y
Good Samaritan Agency	ME	Varies with program	None	Y	Y			Y	Y	Y
Growing Through Adoption	ME	Min. 21	None	Y				Y	Y	Y
International Christian Adoption Agency	National	Min. 25 (varies with program)	Christian	Y				Y		
Maine Adoption Placement Service	ME	24—45	None	Y	Y			Y	Y	Y
Maine Children's Home for Little Wanderers	ME	Min. 21 (varies with age of child)	Varies	Y	Y				Y	
St. Andre Home	ME	22—38	Christian		Y					

Maryland

Types of Adoption Services

Agency	Area Served	Age	Religion	Single	Traditional	Identified	Open	Foreign	US Special Needs	Home Study/Post-Placement
Bethany Christian Services	MD (National)	25-38	Evangelical		Y			Y		
Family and Children's Services	Central Maryland	Min. 21	None	Y	Y			Y	Y	
Jewish Family Services	Greater Baltimore	Varies	Jewish		Y	Y			Y	
Jewish Social Service Agency of Metropolitan Washington	MD (DC, VA)	Max. 40	Jewish		Y			Y	Y	
LDS Social Services	MD (National)	Varies with age of child	Mormon		Y			Y		

Massachusetts

Agency	Area Served	Age	Religion	Single	Traditional	Identified	Open	Foreign	US Special Needs	Home Study/Post-Placement
Alliance for Children	MA (excluding Western MA)	25—45	Varies	Y		Y		Y		Y
Berkshire Center for Families & Children	Berkshire Co.	None	None	Y	Y	Y		Y		
Bethany Christian Services	MA (National)	25—38	Evangelical		Y			Y		
Boston Children's Service Association	Greater Boston	None	None	Y	Y			Y	Y	
Brightside for Families and Children	Western MA, Northern CT	Min. 21	None	Y	Y	Y		Y	Y	Y
Cambridge Adoption & Counseling Associates	MA	25—55	None	Y	Y	Y		Y		Y
Cambridge Family and Children's Service	Middlesex Co. and surrounds	Min. 21	None	Y		Y		Y		
Catholic Charities Centre/Old Colony Area	Old Colony area	None	None	Y	Y			Y		
Catholic Family Services	Essex and Middlesex Cos.	Varies with age of child	None	Y	Y			Y	Y	
Catholic Social Services of Fall River	Diocese of Fall River	Min. 21 (varies with age of child)	Faith of choice		Y			Y	Y	
Children's Aid & Family Service/Hampshire Co.	Western MA (4 counties)	Varies	None	Y	Y			Y	Y	
Dare Family Services	Eastern MA	Min. 21	None	Y				Y		

Agency	Area Served	Age	Religion	Single	Traditional	Identified	Open	Foreign	US Special Needs	Home Study/ Post-Placement
Downey Side	MA	Min. 18	None	Y				Y		
Family and Children's Services/ Catholic Charities	Worcester and surrounds	Under 45 preferred	Faith of choice		Y			Y		
Florence Crittenton League	MA	25–40	None		Y			Y		Y
International Adoptions	MA, RI (VT, NH, NY, CT)	Varies	None	Y	Y			Y	Y	Y
Jewish Family Service of the North Shore	Eastern MA	Varies	None		Y					Y
Jewish Family & Children's Service	Greater Boston	22—40	Varies		Y	Y				
Jewish Family Service of Greater Springfield	MA	None	None	Y	Y	Y				Y
Jewish Family Service of Greater Framingham	MA	Varies	None	Y	Y	Y				Y
La Alianza Hispana	MA	None	None	Y	Y			Y		
Love the Children	MA (PA, NJ, NY)	25—40	Faith of choice				Y			
Massachusetts Adoption Resource Exchange (MARE)	New England	None	None					Y***		
Merrimack Valley Catholic Charities	Haverhill, Lawrence, Lowell and surrounds	23—40 preferred	Varies	Y	Y			Y		
New Bedford Child and Family Service	MA	None	None	Y	Y			Y	Y	Y
New England Home for Little Wanderers	Eastern MA	Varies with age of child	None	Y	Y			Y		
North Shore Catholic Charities	North Shore area	None	None	Y	Y					Y
Parsons Child and Family Center	MA (NY, VT)	Varies with program	None				Y			
Project IMPACT	MA	None	None	Y				Y		
Protestant Social Service Bureau	South Shore, Cape Cod	Varies with age of child	None	Y					Y	Y
Roxbury Children's Service	MA	Min. 21	None	Y	Y			Y		
Worcester Children's Friend Society	Southern Worcester Co.	Varies with age of child	Varies	Y	Y			Y	Y	Y

Note: ***match-referral

| MASSACHUSETTS | | | | Types of Adoption Services | | | | | | |
Agency	Area Served	Age	Religion	Single	Traditional	Identified	Open	Foreign	US Special Needs	Home Study/ Post-Placement
World Adoption Services	MA, NH	Varies with age of child	Varies	Y	Y			Y	Y	Y
MICHIGAN										
Adventist Adoption & Family Services	MI (National)	Varies with age of child	None	Y	Y			Y	Y	
Americans for International Aid and Adoption	National	Varies with the program	Varies	Y				Y		
Bethany Christian Services	MI (National)	25—38	Varies with program		Y			Y	Y	
Catholic Family Service (Bay City)	Diocese of Saginaw	Varies with age of child	Varies	Y	Y				Y	
Catholic Family Services (Kalamazoo)	MI (9 counties)	Max. 40	Varies		Y				Y	Y
Catholic Social Services (Flint)	Genesee Co.	25—37	Varies	Y	Y		Y		Y	Y
Catholic Social Services (Port Huron)	St. Claire Co.	Max. 40	Christian		Y					
Catholic Social Services (Ann Arbor)	Washtenaw Co.	25—45	None		Y		Y		Y	
Catholic Social Services (Detroit)	Wayne, Oakland, Macomb Cos.	Min. 25 (Varies with program)	Christian	Y	Y				Y	
Catholic Social Services (Marquette)	Upper Peninsula	20—35	Christian	Y	Y				Y	Y
Catholic Social Service/St. Vincent Home	MI (5 counties)	Varies with age of child	None	Y	Y				Y	
Child and Family Service (Bay City)	Bay Co.	Ma.x 40	None		Y				Y	
Child and Family Service (Saginaw)	Saginaw	Varies	None	Y	Y			Y	Y	
Child and Family Services (Lansing)	Capitol area	Varies with age of child	Faith of choice	Y	Y				Y	
Child and Family Services of Michigan	MI	Min. 21	None	Y	Y				Y	
Christian Family Services	Southeast MI	Varies with child's needs	Evangelical		Y				Y	

| MICHIGAN | | | | Types of Adoption Services | | | | | | | |
Agency	Area Served	Age	Religion	Single	Traditional	Identified	Open	Foreign	US Special Needs	Home Study/ Post-Placement	
D.A. Blodgett Services for Children & Families	Greater Grand Rapids	Varies with age of child	None					Y			
Family Counseling and Children's Services	Lenawee Co.	Varies	None	Y	Y			Y	Y		
Family Service Division-Catholic Social Services	Monroe Co.	Varies with age of child	None	Y	Y			Y	Y		
Homes for Black Children	Greater Detroit	Varies with age of child	None	Y	Y			Y			
Jewish Family Service	Wayne, Oakland, Macomb Cos.	Varies	Jewish		Y				Y		
LDS Social Services	MI (National)	Varies with age of child	Mormon		Y			Y			
Lutheran Adoption Service	Lower Peninsula	Varies	Varies with program	Y	Y			Y			
Lutheran Social Services	Upper Peninsula	Varies with age of child	Varies with program		Y			Y	Y	Y	
Methodist Children's Home Society	MI	Varies with age of child	None	Y	Y			Y			
Oakland Family Services	Oakland, Wayne, Macomb Cos.	Varies with program	None	Y	Y			Y			
Orchards Children's Services	Oakland, Wayne Cos.	None	None	Y				Y			
Spaulding for Children	Greater Detroit	None	None	Y				Y			
Sunny Ridge Family Center	MI (IL, IN, WI)	Varies with program	Varies with program	Y	Y	Y		Y	Y	Y	
MINNESOTA											
Bethany Christian Services	MN (National)	25—38	Varies with program					Y			
Building Families Through Adoption	MN (IA, WI, ND, SD)	Varies with program	Varies with program	Y				Y	Y		
Catholic Charities (St. Paul)	Archdiocese of St. Paul & Minneapolis	Varies with program	Catholic		Y			Y	Y	Y	
Catholic Charities (Crookston)	Diocese of Crookston	Max. 38	Christian		Y						
Catholic Social Services (Winona)	South MN	25—37	Catholic		Y			Y	Y	Y	
Children's Home Society	MN	Varies with program	Varies		Y			Y	Y		

| MINNESOTA | | | | Types of Adoption Services | | | | | | |
Agency	Area Served	Age	Religion	Single	Traditional	Identified	Open	Foreign	US Special Needs	Home Study/Post-Placement
Crossroads	MN	Varies with program	Varies	Y				Y	Y	Y
Hope International Family Services	MN, WI	Min. 21	None	Y	Y			Y	Y	Y
LDS Social Services	MN (National)	Varies with age of child	Mormon		Y			Y		
Lutheran Social Service	MN	Min. 21	Evangelical	Y	Y			Y	Y	
New Life Homes and Family Services	Minneapolis, Rochester and Coon Rapids	21—39	Christian		Y					
MISSISSIPPI										
Bethany Christian Services	MS	25—38	Evangelical		Y				Y	
Catholic Charities	MS (65 counties)	25—40	Faith of choice	Y	Y				Y	
Catholic Social and Community Services	South MS (17 counties)	25—40	Faith of choice		Y				Y	Y
Mississippi Children's Home Society	MS	Varies with age of child	None		Y				Y	Y
MISSOURI										
Adams Center	Greater Kansas City (MO and KS)	25—45	None		Y				Y	
Adoption Resource Center	MO	21—69	None	Y	Y			Y	Y	Y
Bethany Christian Services	MO (National)	25—38	Evangelical		Y				Y	
Catholic Charities	MO	Varies with program	Catholic or Protestant		Y					
Catholic Services for Children and Youth	Archdiocese of St. Louis	Varies with program	Varies with program		Y				Y	
Central Baptist Family Service	MO	None	None							Y
Child Placement Services	Greater Kansas City (National for RCLDS)	22—40	Faith of choice		Y	Y				
Christian Family Services	MO, IL	Varies with age of child	Church of Christ	Y	Y				Y	Y
Family Adoption and Counseling Services	National	22—45	Faith of choice	Y	Y			Y	Y	

MISSOURI				Types of Adoption Services						
Agency	Area Served	Age	Religion	Single	Traditional	Identified	Open	Foreign	US Special Needs	Home Study/ Post-Placement
Heart of America Family Services	MO (KS)	Varies with program	None		Y		Y	Y	Y	
Highlands Child Placement Service	National	21—40	Assembly of God		Y		Y		Y	
Jewish Family Children's Service	Greater St. Louis	None	Jewish		Y				Y	Y
Love Basket	National	23—50	Christian	Y	Y		Y	Y	Y	
Lutheran Family and Children's Services	MO	Varies with program	Varies with program	Y	Y		Y	Y	Y	
MOM (Missions of Mercy)	National	Varies	None	Y	Y		Y	Y	Y	
Missouri Baptist Children's Home	MO	21—40	Southern Baptist		Y			Y		
Worldwide Love for Children	MO	25—45	Christian	Y	Y		Y	Y	Y	
MONTANA										
LDS Social Services	MT (National)	Varies with age of child	Mormon		Y			Y		
Lutheran Social Services	MT	Max. 40	Christian		Y					
Montana Children's Home (Shodair)	MT	Varies with age of child	None		Y			Y		
NEBRASKA										
Catholic Social Services Bureau	Greater Lincoln	21—40	Varies		Y				Y	
Child Saving Institute	NE	21—43	Varies	Y	Y				Y	
Holt International Children's Services	NE, WY, SD (National)	Varies with program	None	Y				Y		
Jewish Family Service	NE	21—40	Jewish		Y					
Lutheran Family Services of Nebraska	NE	21—45	Christian	Y	Y				Y	Y
Nebraska Children's Home Society	NE	Varies with age of child	Faith of choice		Y				Y	

Agency	Area Served	Age	Religion	Single	Traditional	Identified	Open	Foreign	US Special Needs	Home Study/ Post-Placement
Catholic Community Services	NV	21—40	Faith of choice		Y				Y	Y
LDS Social Services	NV	Varies with age of child	Mormon		Y				Y	
NEW HAMPSHIRE										
Adoptive Families for Children	NH	21—45	None		Y				Y	Y
Bethany Christian Services	NH (National)	25—38	Evangelical		Y				Y	
Child and Family Services of New Hampshire	NH	21—40	None		Y					Y
LDS Social Services	NH (National)	Varies with age of child	Mormon		Y				Y	
New Hampshire Catholic Charities	NH	Varies	Catholic		Y				Y	
NEW JERSEY										
Adoption Placement Services	South NJ	Varies with age of child	Varies		Y				Y	Y
Associated Catholic Charities/Catholic Community Services	Essex, Hudson, Bergen, Union Cos.	Varies	Faith of choice		Y				Y	Y
Bethany Christian Services	NJ (National)	25—38	Evangelical		Y				Y	
Better Living Services	NJ	None	None	Y						Y
Catholic Charities	NJ (4 counties)	Max. 41	Faith of choice	Y	Y				Y	Y
Catholic Family and Community Services	Passaic, Morris, Sussex Cos.	None	None	Y						Y
Catholic Social Services	Diocese of Camden	23–37	Catholic		Y				Y	Y
Children of the World	NJ	None	None	Y				Y		
Children's Aid & Adoption Society	NJ (5 counties)	Min. 18	None	Y	Y				Y	Y
Children's Home Society of New Jersey	NJ, PA (Bucks County)	Varies	None	Y	Y				Y	
Christian Homes for Children	NJ, NY	Varies with age of child	Evangelical	Y	Y				Y	

| NEW JERSEY | | | | Types of Adoption Services | | | | | | | |
| | | | | Single | Traditional | Identified | Open | Foreign | US Special Needs | Home Study/ Post-Placement | |
Agency	Area Served	Age	Religion								
Family & Children's Counseling & Testing Center	NJ	Varies with program	Varies with program	Y	Y			Y		Y	
Golden Cradle	NJ, PA, DE	25–40	None		Y				Y		
Holt International Children's Services	NJ (National)	Varies with program	None	Y				Y			
Homestudies	NJ, NY	21–55	None	Y						Y	
Lutheran Social Services	NJ	Varies with age of child	None	Y	Y			Y	Y		
Spaulding for Children	NJ	Varies with age of child	None	Y					Y		
United Family & Children's Society	Central NJ	Max. 38	None	Y	Y				Y	Y	
NEW MEXICO											
Catholic Social Services of Santa Fe	NM	Varies	Faith of choice		Y			Y	Y	Y	
Christian Child Placement Services	NM, TX	Varies with age of child	Church of Christ		Y				Y		
Families for Children	NM	22–45	Protestant or Catholic	Y	Y				Y		
LDS Social Services	NM (National)	Varies with age of child	Mormon		Y				Y		
Rainbow House	NM (CO)	Varies with program	None	Y				Y	Y	Y	
Triad Adoption Services	NM	Varies	Varies				Y			Y	
NEW YORK											
Adoption and Counseling Services	Central NY	Min. 20	None	Y	Y			Y	Y	Y	
Americans for International Aid and Adoption	National	Varies with program	None	Y				Y			
Brookwood Child Care	New York City	None	None	Y	Y				Y	Y	
Catholic Charities (Syracuse)	Upstate NY (4 counties)	None	None	Y	Y				Y		
Catholic Charities (Ogdensburg)	Upstate NY (7 counties)	Varies with age of child	Faith of choice		Y				Y		
Catholic Family Center	Diocese of Rochester	Min. 21	Varies		Y				Y	Y	

Agency	**Area Served**	**Age**	**Religion**	Single	Traditional	Identified	Open	Foreign	US Special Needs	Home Study	Post-Placement
Catholic Social Services	Broome County	Min. 18	Varies	Y	Y				Y	Y	
Center for Counseling	Greater Albany	None	None	Y						Y	
Child and Family Services	Erie County	21–38	None	Y	Y					Y	
Children's Aid Society	Metropolitan NYC	Min. 18	None	Y					Y	Y	
Children's Home of Kingston	Hudson Valley	21–60	None	Y						Y	
Children's Village	NY (8 counties)	None	None	Y						Y	
Community Maternity Services	Diocese of Albany	Varies with program	Faith of choice	Y	Y					Y	
Evangelical Adoption & Family Service	NY	Min. 21	Varies with program	Y	Y			Y	Y	Y	
Family and Children's Service	Central NY	None	None	Y	Y			Y		Y	
Family Resources Adoption Program	Southern NY (6 counties)	None	None	Y						Y	
Graham Windham	Greater NYC	Min. 21	None	Y						Y	
Harlem Dowling Children's Services	NY, NJ, CT	Varies	None	Y	Y				Y	Y	
Hillside Children's Center	Greater Rochester	None	None	Y	Y				Y	Y	
International Adoptions	NY (MA, CT, RI, VT, NH)	Varies with age of child	None	Y	Y			Y		Y	
Jewish Child Care Association	NY	Min. 21	Varies with child's needs	Y					Y	Y	
Jewish Family Service	West NY	None	Jewish	Y						Y	
LDS Social Services	NY (National)	Varies with age of child	Mormon		Y					Y	
Little Flower Children's Services	National	Min. 21	None	Y	Y					Y	
Louise Wise Services	Greater NYC	Min. 18	None	Y	Y					Y	
Love the Children	NY (PA, NJ, MA)	25–40	Faith of choice					Y			
Lutheran Community Services	NY	Min. 18	None	Y					Y	Y	

Agency	Area Served	Age	Religion	Single	Traditional	Identified	Open	Foreign	US Special Needs	Home Study/ Post-Placement
New Beginnings Family & Children's Services	NY, NJ, CT	Varies with program	Varies with program	Y	Y			Y	Y	Y
New York Catholic Guardian Society	Greater NYC	Min. 18	None	Y					Y	
New York Spaulding for Children	New York City, Long Island, Westchester Co.	Min. 21	None	Y					Y	
Ohel Children's Home and Family Services	Metropolitan NYC	None	Jewish	Y	Y				Y	
Parsons Child and Family Center	NY, VT (MA)	Varies with program	None	Y				Y	Y	
PRACA	New York City	Min. 18	None	Y	Y				Y	
Salvation Army Social Services for Children	Greater NYC	Min. 21	None	Y					Y	Y
Spence-Chapin Services to Families & Children	NY	Varies	Varies	Y	Y			Y	Y	
St. Joseph Children's Services	Brooklyn, Queens & surrounds	None	None	Y					Y	
VIDA	National	Min. 21 (varies with age of child)	None	Y				Y	Y	

Agency	Area Served	Age	Religion	Single	Traditional	Identified	Open	Foreign	US Special Needs	Home Study/ Post-Placement
Bethany Christian Services	NC (National)	25–38	Varies with program		Y			Y	Y	
Catholic Social Services	Diocese of Charlotte	Min. 21	Christian	Y	Y				Y	Y
Catholic Social Ministries	Eastern NC	25–45	Catholic		Y					Y
Children's Home Society	NC	26–35/39	None	Y	Y				Y	
Family Services	Forsyth Co.	Min. 25 (varies with age of child)	None	Y	Y				Y	Y
LDS Social Services	NC (National)	Varies with age of child	Mormon		Y				Y	
Lutheran Family Services	NC	28–45	None					Y		Y

NORTH DAKOTA				Single	Traditional	Identified	Open	Foreign	US Special Needs	Home Study/Post-Placement
Agency	**Area Served**	**Age**	**Religion**							
Building Families Through Adoption	ND (SD, MN, IA, WI)	Varies with program	Varies with program	Y				Y	Y	
Catholic Family Services	ND	Varies with age of child	Catholic	Y	Y				Y	
Christian Family Life Services	ND, MN	Varies with age of child	Christian		Y				Y	
Covenant Children	National	22–55	Christian					Y		
Lutheran Social Services	ND	Varies with age of child	None		Y				Y	
New Horizons Foreign Adoption Services	ND	Min. 22	Varies with program	Y		Y		Y	Y	Y
Village Family Service Center	ND	Max. 40	None	Y	Y		Y		Y	
OHIO										
Bair Foundation	OH (PA)	25–40	Christian	Y	Y				Y	
Baptist Children's Home & Family Ministries	OH	Varies with age of child	Baptist		Y				Y	
Bethany Christian Services	OH (National)	25–38	Varies with program					Y		
Catholic Service League of Ashtabula County	Ashtabula County	21–40	Varies		Y			Y	Y	
Catholic Service Bureau	Northeast OH	Varies with age of child	Varies	Y	Y			Y	Y	Y
Catholic Social Services	Northwest OH	Varies with child's needs	Catholic		Y			Y	Y	Y
Catholic Social Service League of Summit Co.	Summit Co.	21–37	Varies with program		Y				Y	Y
Catholic Social Service League/ Western Stark Co.	Western Stark Co.	Varies	Catholic		Y					
Children's Home of Cincinnati	Hamilton Co., Clermount Co.	23–37	None	Y	Y				Y	Y
Children's Services of Cleveland	Greater Cleveland	22–38	None		Y				Y	
Family and Community Services of Catholic Charities	Portage Co.	Max 40/50	Varies		Y		Y		Y	Y

Agency	Area Served	Age	Religion	Single	Traditional	Identified	Open	Foreign	US Special Needs	Home Study/Post-Placement
Family Counseling & Crittenton Services	Franklin Co.	21–40	None	Y	Y			Y	Y	
Family Services of Summit County	OH	25–38	None	Y	Y			Y		
Family Service Agency	OH	24–45	None		Y				Y	
Family Service Association of Trumbull Co.	Trumbull Co.	21–50	None		Y				Y	Y
Gentle Care Adoption Services	OH	21–40/45	Faith of choice	Y	Y	Y		Y	Y	Y
HARAMBEE: Services to Black Families	Northeast OH	Min. 21	None	Y	Y			Y		
Jewish Children's Bureau	Greater Cleveland	Varies with program	Varies with program		Y	Y		Y	Y	Y
Jewish Family Service	Hamilton Co. and surrounds	Max. 40	Varies		Y			Y		
Jewish Family Service (Dayton)	Miami Valley	Varies with age of child	Varies with program	Y	Y					Y
Jewish Family Service (Sylvania)	Northwest OH	21–45	Varies with program	Y	Y					Y
LDS Social Services	OH (National)	Varies with age of child	Mormon		Y			Y		
Lutheran Children's Aid & Family Services	Northeastern Ohio	Varies with age of child	Varies with program	Y	Y			Y	Y	Y
Lutheran Social Services of Central Ohio	Central, Southeast OH	Varies with program	None	Y	Y			Y	Y	
Lutheran Social Services of NW Ohio	Northwestern Ohio	21–40	Lutheran		Y				Y	Y
Lutheran Social Services of the Miami Valley	Southwest OH	22–37	Varies with program		Y				Y	Y
Northeast Ohio Adoption Services	Northeast OH	Varies with age of child	None	Y					Y	
Spaulding for Children/Beech Brook	Northeast OH	None	None	Y					Y	

| OKLAHOMA | | | | Types of Adoption Services | | | | | | |
Agency	**Area Served**	**Age**	**Religion**	Single	Traditional	Identified	Open	Foreign	US Special Needs	Home Study/Post-Placement
Adoption Center of Northeast Oklahoma	OK	Varies with the program	None	Y	Y			Y	Y	Y
Catholic Charities	Greater Tulsa	Max. 45	Catholic		Y			Y		
Catholic Social Ministries	Archdiocese of Oklahoma City	21–40	Christian		Y			Y		
Deaconess Home	National	21–40	Protestant		Y			Y		
Dillon Children's Services	OK, TX	25–45	Judeo-Christian				Y			
LDS Social Services	OK (National)	Varies with age of child	Mormon		Y			Y		
Lutheran Social Service	OK (KS)	Varies with age of child	Christian	Y	Y		Y	Y		
Metrocenter for Family Ministries	OK, TX	Min. 24	Christian		Y			Y		
Project Adopt	National	Min. 21	None		Y			Y	Y	
Small Miracles International	National	25–55	None	Y	Y			Y		Y
United Methodist Counseling Services	Oklahoma	21–40	Christian		Y				Y	Y
OREGON										
Adventist Adoption & Family Services	National	Max. 40	None		Y			Y	Y	
Albertina Kerr Centers for Children	OR	Varies	None	Y	Y				Y	Y
Boys and Girls Aid Society	OR	Under 40 preferred	None	Y	Y		Y		Y	
Catholic Services for Children	OR	Varies	Varies		Y			Y	Y	Y
Holt International Children's Services	National	Varies with program	None	Y				Y		
LDS Social Services	OR (National)	Varies with age of child	Mormon		Y			Y		
Open Adoption & Family Service	OR	Varies	Varies	Y			Y			
Plan Loving Adoptions Now	OR	Varies with age of child	None	Y	Y			Y	Y	

Agency	Area Served	Age	Religion	Single	Traditional	Identified	Open	Foreign	US Special Needs	Home Study/ Post-Placement
Adoption Agency	PA, NJ (DE)	Varies with program	None	Y			Y	Y	Y	
Adoption Service	National	None	None	Y	Y					Y
Adoption Unlimited	Eastern & central PA	Varies with program	Varies with program	Y				Y	Y	Y
Aid for Children International	Lancaster City & surrounds	Min. 25 (varies with program)	Christian					Y	Y	
Bair Foundation	Western PA (OH)	25–40	Christian	Y	Y				Y	
Bethany Christian Services	PA (National)	25–38	Evangelical		Y				Y	
Catholic Charities of Greensburg	Diocese of Greensburg	Varies with age of child	Faith of choice		Y			Y	Y	
Catholic Charities/ Diocese of Pittsburgh	Diocese of Pittsburgh	21–42	Faith of choice	Y	Y			Y	Y	
Catholic Social Services	Archdiocese of Philadelphia	Min. 21 (varies with program)	Varies with program	Y	Y			Y	Y	Y
Catholic Social Agency	PA (5 counties)	Varies with program	Faith of choice	Y	Y			Y	Y	
Child and Home Study Associates	PA, NJ (DE)	Varies with age of child	None	Y	Y			Y		Y
Children's Aid Society of Franklin County	Franklin Co. & surrounds	Varies with age of child	None		Y			Y	Y	
Children's Aid Society of Mercer Co.	Mercer Co. & surrounds	21–40	None	Y					Y	
Children's Home of Pittsburgh	Pittsburgh and surrounds	Max. 40	None		Y				Y	
Children's Aid Home & Society of Somerset Co.	Somerset Co.	None	None	Y	Y			Y	Y	Y
CONCERN	Fleetwood & surrounds	Varies with age of child	Varies with program	Y	Y			Y	Y	Y
Council of Three Rivers American Indian Center	PA	Min. 18	None	Y					Y	
Family Service and Children's Aid Society	Venango Co. & surrounds	25–40	None	Y	Y			Y	Y	
Jewish Family and Children's Service	Philadelphia and surrounds	Varies with child	Varies with program		Y			Y	Y	Y
Love the Children	PA, NJ, (NY, MA)	25–40	Faith of choice					Y		

| PENNSYLVANIA | | | | Types of Adoption Services | | | | | | | |
Agency	Area Served	Age	Religion	Single	Traditional	Identified	Open	Foreign	US Special Needs	Home Study/ Post Placement	
Lutheran Children & Family Service	Eastern PA	21–43	Varies with program	Y	Y			Y	Y	Y	
Lutheran Home	Northeast PA	Varies with age of child	Faith of choice	Y	Y			Y	Y		
Lutheran Service Society of Western PA	Southwest PA	Varies with program	Varies with program	Y				Y	Y		
National Adoption Center	National	None	None	Y					Y***		
Native American Adoption Resource Exchange (NAARE)	National	None	None	Y					Y***		
Pearl S. Buck Foundation	Perkasie & surrounds	25–42	None					Y	Y	Y	
Project STAR	Pittsburgh and surrounds	None	None	Y					Y		
Tabor Children's Services	PA, NJ	None	None	Y					Y	Y	
Tressler Lutheran Services	Central PA	None	None	Y					Y		
Welcome House Adoption Services	PA, NJ (DE, MD, VA, DC)	Varies with age of child	None	Y				Y	Y		
Wiley House	PA	Min. 21	None	Y					Y		
RHODE ISLAND											
Catholic Social Services	RI	25–35	Catholic		Y				Y	Y	
Children's Friend and Service	RI	None	None	Y	Y				Y		
SOUTH CAROLINA											
Bethany Christian Services	SC (National)	25–38	Varies with program		Y			Y	Y		
Epworth Children's Home	SC	Varies	Christian						Y	Y	
Love Life Ministries	SC	Varies	Christian		Y				Y		
Southeastern Children's Home	SC	Varies with age of child	Church of Christ		Y				Y		

Note: ***match-referral

SOUTH DAKOTA — Types of Adoption Services

Agency	Area Served	Age	Religion	Single	Traditional	Identified	Open	Foreign	US Special Needs	Home Study/ Post-Placement
Bethany Christian Services	SD (National)	25–38	Evangelical		Y			Y		
Building Families Through Adoption	SD (ND, MN, IA, WI)	Varies with program	Varies with program	Y			Y	Y		
Catholic Family Services	Eastern SD	21–45	Catholic		Y				Y	
Christian Counseling Services	SD	Max. 40	Christian		Y			Y	Y	
LDS Social Services	SD	Varies with age of child	Mormon		Y			Y		
Lutheran Social Services	SD	Max. 42	Christian		Y			Y	Y	

TENNESSEE

Agency	Area Served	Age	Religion	Single	Traditional	Identified	Open	Foreign	US Special Needs	Home Study/ Post-Placement
AGAPE	Central TN	Varies with age of child	Church of Christ	Y	Y			Y		
Bethany Christian Services	TN (National)	25–38	Evangelical		Y			Y		
Bethel Bible Village	East TN	Varies	Christian	Y	Y			Y		
Catholic Charities of Tennessee	East TN & GA (4 counties)	Varies with age of child	Varies with program	Y	Y			Y	Y	
Child and Family Services	Knoxville & surrounds	Varies with program	None	Y	Y			Y		
Christian Counseling Services	TN	Varies with program	Varies with program	Y	Y		Y	Y		
Church of God Home for children	National	25–40	Christian		Y			Y	Y	
Family and Children's Services (Chattanooga)	Hamilton County	25–38	None	Y			Y	Y		
Family and Children's Service (Nashville)	Nashville and surrounds	Min. 21	Varies with child's needs	Y				Y		
Holston United Methodist Home for Children	TN (VA)	Varies with program	Varies	Y	Y			Y	Y	Y
Holt International Children's Services	TN, MS, AR (National)	Varies with program	None	Y				Y		
Porter-Leith Children's Center	National	24–42	None	Y	Y			Y		
Saint Peter Home for Children	Diocese of Memphis	26–40	Christian	Y	Y			Y		

Agency	Area Served	Age	Religion	Single	Traditional	Identified	Open	Foreign	US Special Needs	Home Study/ Post-Placement
Tennessee Baptist Children's Home	TN	Max. 41	Baptist		Y				Y	
Tennessee Conference Adoption Service	Middle Tennessee	Min. 23	Faith of choice	Y	Y			Y	Y	Y
West Tennessee AGAPE	West TN	Varies with program	Church of Christ		Y				Y	
TEXAS										
ABC Adoption	TX	Varies	None		Y				Y	
Adoption Agency of Mark Jordan Siegel	TX	Max. 55	Faith of choice		Y					
Adoption Resource Consultants of North Texas	TX	Varies	Varies	Y						Y
Adoption Services Associates	National	25–45	None		Y	Y	Y		Y	Y
AGAPE Social Services	TX (National for special needs)	Varies with program	None	Y	Y				Y	Y
Care Connection	TX	None	None	Y	Y				Y	
Child Placement Center of Texas	TX (National for special needs)	Max. 43	None	Y	Y				Y	
Children's Service Bureau	San Antonio and surrounds	Min. 25	None	Y	Y				Y	
Christian Child Help Foundation	Houston-Galveston metropolitan area	Varies with age of child	Christian		Y				Y	
Edna Gladney Center	TX, OK, LA, AR, NY, CT, NJ, PA	24–39	Faith of choice	Y	Y			Y	Y	
Family Junction	Central TX	25–40	Faith of choice	Y	Y		Y			
New Life Children's Services	TX	21–39	Christian		Y		Y			
Presbyterian Children's Home and Service Agency	TX	25–50	Christian	Y					Y	
Quality of Life	TX	25–45	None		Y			Y		Y
Smithlawn Maternity Home & Adoption Agency	TX (other states for special needs)	25–44	Church of Christ preferred		Y				Y	
Southwest Maternity Center/ Methodist Mission Home	TX, NM, CO, LA	24–42	Faith of choice		Y		Y		Y	

TEXAS

Agency	Area Served	Age	Religion	Single	Traditional	Identified	Open	Foreign	US Special Needs	Home Study	Post-Placement
Gulf Coast Placement Center	TX	Varies with child's needs	Varies with child's needs	Y	Y			Y			
LDS Social Services	TX (National)	Varies with age of child	Mormon		Y			Y			
Lee & Beulah Moor Children's Home	Greater El Paso	21–45	Faith of choice		Y	Y					
Life Anew	TX	25–42	Faith of choice	Y	Y				Y	Y	
Los Ninos International Adoption Center	National	25–55	None		Y			Y		Y	
Methodist Home	Texas, New Mexico	Varies with age of child	Christian						Y		
Spaulding for Children	Greater Houston	None	None	Y					Y		
Texas Cradle Society	TX (National for special needs)	Varies	None		Y			Y	Y		

UTAH

Agency	Area Served	Age	Religion	Single	Traditional	Identified	Open	Foreign	US Special Needs	Home Study	Post-Placement
Adoption Services of WACAP	UT (National)	Varies with program	Varies with program	Y	Y			Y	Y	Y	
Catholic Community Services of Utah	UT	Varies with program	None	Y	Y				Y		
Children's Aid Society of Utah	UT	23–38	None		Y		Y	Y	Y	Y	
Children's Service Society of Utah	UT	Varies with program	None	Y	Y				Y	Y	
Children's House International	Western UT	21–40	Christian					Y			
LDS Social Services	National	Varies with age of child	Mormon		Y				Y		

VERMONT

Agency	Area Served	Age	Religion	Single	Traditional	Identified	Open	Foreign	US Special Needs	Home Study	Post-Placement
Elizabeth Lund Home	VT, NY	Min. 21	None	Y	Y			Y	Y	Y	
International Adoptions	VT, NH, (MA, RI, CT, NY)	Varies with age of child	None	Y	Y			Y		Y	
Rootwings Ministries	VT	None	None	Y					Y	Y	
Vermont Catholic Charities	VT	18–38	Varies with child's needs	Y	Y				Y	Y	

| VERMONT | | | | Types of Adoption Services | | | | | | |
Agency	Area Served	Age	Religion	Single	Traditional	Identified	Open	Foreign	US Special Needs	Home Study/ Post-Placement
Vermont Children's Aid Society	VT, NH (Grafton & Sullivan Cos.)	Varies with age of child	None	Y	Y			Y	Y	Y

VIRGINIA										
Bethany Christian Services	VA (National)	25–38	Evangelical		Y			Y		
Catholic Charities of Richmond	VA, MD, NC, DC	Varies with program	Varies	Y	Y			Y	Y	
Catholic Family and Children's Services	Southeast VA	Max. 40	None	Y	Y			Y		
Catholic Family Services	Tidewater area	25–40	None		Y			Y		
Children's Services of Catholic Charities	Northern VA	Min. 21 (varies with age of child)	Varies	Y	Y				Y	Y
Children's Home Society for Virginia	VA	Varies with age of child	None	Y	Y			Y		
Family Life Services	National	21–40	Christian		Y					
Family Services of Tidewater	Tidewater area	25–40	None		Y			Y	Y	Y
Holston United Methodist Home for Children	Southwest VA (TN)	Varies with program	None	Y	Y			Y	Y	Y
Jewish Family Services	Richmond & surrounds	25–45	Jewish	Y	Y					Y
Jewish Family Service of Tidewater	Tidewater area	Max. 40	Jewish	Y	Y					
Jewish Social Service Agency	VA,DC (MD)	Max. 40	Jewish		Y				Y	Y
LDS Social Services	VA (National)	Varies with age of child	Mormon		Y			Y		
Pan American Adoption Agency	National	25–55	None	Y	Y			Y		Y
Rainbow Christian Services	NY, NJ, DE, MD, DC, VA	Min. 21	Church of Christ	Y	Y			Y		
United Methodist Family Services	VA	25–45	None	Y	Y			Y		
Virginia Baptist Children's Home and Family	VA	Max. 40	Varies with program		Y			Y		
Welcome House Adoption Services	VA, MD, DC (PA, DE, NJ)	Varies with age of child	None	Y				Y	Y	

Agency	Area Served	Age	Religion	Single	Traditional	Identified	Open	Foreign	US Special Needs	Home Study/Post-Placement
Adoption Advocates International	National	Varies with program	None	Y				Y	Y	
Adoption Services of WACAP	National	Varies with program	Varies with program	Y	Y			Y	Y	Y
Adventist Adoption & Family Services	WA (National)	Varies with program	None	Y	Y			Y	Y	
Americans for International Aid and Adoption	WA (National	Varies with program	Varies	Y				Y		
Bethany Christian Services	WA (National)	25–38	Evangelical		Y				Y	
Catholic Community Services (Seattle)	King Co./WA	Varies with program	Varies with program	Y	Y		Y	Y	Y	
Catholic Community Services (Tacoma)	Pierce and Kitsap Cos.	23–40	None		Y			Y	Y	Y
Catholic Community Services of Snohomish Co.	Snohomish Co.	Varies	None	Y	Y				Y	
Children's Home Society	WA	Min. 21	None	Y					Y	
Children's Home Society (Northwest Branch)	King Co., Puget Sound	Min. 21	None	Y					Y	
Church of Christ Homes for Children	National	Max. 40	Church of Christ		Y					Y
Family Foundation	WA	Min. 21	None	Y					Y	Y
Hope Services Division of Burden Bearers	WA	Varies	Christian		Y		Y		Y	Y
Jewish Family Services	Greater Seattle	Max. 45	Jewish	Y	Y					Y
LDS Social Services	WA (National)	Varies with age of child	Mormon	Y					Y	
Lutheran Social Services of Washington	King and Snohomish Cos.	23–39	Varies	Y	Y		Y		Y	
Medina Children's Service	King Co.	Varies with program	None	Y	Y				Y	
New Hope of Washington	WA	Varies	Christian		Y				Y	Y
Regular Baptist Child Placement Agency	WA	None	Regular Baptist		Y				Y	

WASHINGTON				Types of Adoption Services						
Agency	Area Served	Age	Religion	Single	Traditional	Identified	Open	Foreign	US Special Needs	Home Study/Post-Placement
Seattle Indian Center/Family Services	King Co.	None	None	Y	Y			Y		
Travelers Aid Adoption Service	WA	Varies with program	None					Y		
WEST VIRGINIA										
Children's Home Society of West Virginia	WV	Varies with program	None	Y	Y			Y	Y	Y
United Methodist Child Placement Services	WV	23–40	None	Y	Y			Y	Y	Y
WISCONSIN										
Adoption Choice	WI and other states	23–45	None	Y	Y		Y			
Adoption Option	WI	Varies with program	None	Y	Y		Y	Y	Y	Y
Adoption Services of Green Bay	WI	Varies with program	None	Y		Y		Y	Y	Y
Bethany Christian Services	WI (National)	25–38	Varies with program		Y			Y	Y	
Building Families Through Adoption	WI (ND, SD, MN, IA)	Varies with program	Varies with program	Y				Y	Y	
Catholic Charities	Diocese of La Crosse	Max. 35	Faith of choice		Y				Y	
Catholic Social Service (Madison)	Diocese of Madison	Varies with child's needs	Faith of choice	Y					Y	
Catholic Social Services (Green Bay)	Diocese of Green Bay	Varies with age of child	Catholic				Y			
Catholic Social Services (Milwaukee)	Archdiocese of Milwaukee	Max. 37/40	Catholic		Y		Y		Y	Y
Children's Service Society of Wisconsin	WI	Varies with program	None		Y				Y	Y
Community Adoption Center	Southeast WI	Varies with program	None	Y	Y			Y	Y	Y
Evangelical Child and Family Agency	WI (IL)	Varies with age of child	Evangelical	Y	Y				Y	
Lutheran Counseling & Family Services	WI	21–40	Lutheran		Y				Y	

| WISCONSIN | | | | Types of Adoption Services | | | | | | | |
Agency	Area Served	Age	Religion	Single	Traditional	Identified	Open	Foreign	US Special Needs	Home Study/ Post-Placement	
Lutheran Social Services	WI, Upper MI	Varies with age of child	Varies with program	Y	Y			Y	Y	Y	
Pauquette Children's Services	WI	21–55	None	Y		Y		Y	Y	Y	
Seven Sorrows of Our Sorrowful Mother Infant's Home	WI	21–40	Catholic		Y						
Sunny Ridge Family Center	WI (IL, IN, MI)	Varies with program	Varies with program	Y	Y	Y		Y	Y	Y	
Wisconsin Lutheran Child & Family Service	WI	Varies with program	Evangelical Lutheran (WELS)		Y				Y	Y	

WYOMING											
Catholic Social Services of Wyoming	WY	Min. 21 (varies with age of child)	Faith of choice		Y			Y	Y	Y	
Wyoming Children's Society	WY	Min. 21	None	Y	Y				Y	Y	
Wyoming Parenting Society	WY	None	None		Y					Y	

National Child Welfare and Triad Support Organizations

AASK AMERICA

Aid to Adoption of Special Kids
450 Sansome Street, Suite 210
San Francisco, CA 94111
(415) 543–2275
Director: John D. Badger, Executive Vice President

THE PROGRAM

Aask America, Aid to Adoption of Special Kids, is a national non-profit organization founded in 1973 by Robert and Dorothy DeBolt (parents of 20 children, 14 of whom are adopted) to provide specialized services for special-needs children. Since its inception in 1973, the organization has placed over 5,000 special-needs children in permanent adoptive families and has evolved from a parent-led special-needs adoption agency into a multi-faceted national program providing match-referral services, training and consultation services, and advocacy. The purposes of Aask America are:
1. To place special-needs children in adoptive homes without fees to adopting families.
2. To assist and encourage other licensed adoption agencies to place special-needs children through Aask America's national referral and regional adoption exchanges.
3. To enable traditional and non-traditional families to successfully adopt a special-needs child.
4. To provide national leadership to the adoption field.

Aask America develops and tests innovative program models for national replication, addressing such issues as minority parent recruitment, computerization of adoption records, technical assistance to local and national organizations and affiliates, and, most recently, identification and placement of AIDS infants. Aask America believes "that handicaps or other 'special' conditions do not lessen a child's need for the love and security of a permanent family and that the success of Aask America over the years demonstrates that special-needs children are indeed adoptable." In recognition of their outstanding contribution to the field of special-needs adoption, the DeBolts were recently named to the prestigious Adoption Hall of Fame by the National Committee for Adoption.

SERVICES

The Aask America program includes the following components:

Match-Referral Service: Aask America provides a computerized information system which monitors the nationwide placement of special-needs children through the Aask network and other public and private agencies nationally. Families interested in adopting a special-needs child register with Aask America (call or write for the registration form). Licensed agencies register special-needs children in their custody in need of adoptive families. Aask America serves as an intermediary by making a preliminary "match" of families and children and notifying the families' and children's agencies.

National Consultation Services: Aask America provides technical assistance to branches and affiliates and other adoption agencies in order to increase their capacities to place special-needs children.

Placement Services: Aask America branch offices (Aask Northern California, Aask Southern California, Aask Northeast Region/Rootwings) are full-service adoption agencies providing adoption preparation, placement, and post-placement services to families adopting special-needs children.

Multi-Year Resource Campaign: Aask America coordinates the national fundraising campaign and provides branches and affiliates with a coordinated fundraising approach through grantsmanship procedures and public relations support.

BRANCH/NETWORK OFFICES

Aask Northern California
3530 Grand Avenue
Oakland, CA 94610
(415) 451–1748
Services: match/referral, placement, advocacy

Aask Southern California
2081 Business Center Drive, #164
Irvine, CA 92715
(714) 752–8305
Services: match/referral, placement, advocacy

Aask Northeast/Rootwings
P.O. Box 614
Barre, VT 05641
(802) 479–2197 or (802) 563–2042
Services: match/referral, placement, advocacy

Aask Texas Branch
325 N. St. Paul, Suite #3900
Dallas, TX 75201
(214) 747–2275
Services: match/referral, advocacy

AASK AMERICA AFFILIATES

Aask America Devocion Chapter, Inc.
2061 Carolwood Drive
Arcadia, CA 91006
(818) 355–7313
Services: parent recruitment and fundraising program

Aask Midwest
1605 Holland Road, Suite A5
Maume, OH 43537
(419) 891–0327
Services: regional exchange serving Ohio, Michigan, Indiana, and Illinois

Aask Arizona
234 N. Central Ave., Suite #127
Phoenix, AZ 85004
(602) 254–2275
Services: match/referral, placement, advocacy

FUNDING

Aask America is funded through individual and corporate contributions, foundation grants, fees for services, and fundraising events.

PROFESSIONAL AFFILIATIONS

Aask America is a member of the National Committee For Adoption, North American Conference on Adoptable Children, the National Adoption Exchange, and the Adoption Exchange Association.

AMERICAN ADOPTION CONGRESS

Cherokee Station
P.O. Box 20137
New York, NY 10028–0051
AAC Search Hotline: (505) 296–2198
Other Business: (212) 988–0110
Director: Kate Burke

THE PROGRAM

American Adoption Congress (AAC) is a nonprofit international educational network "dedicated to promoting openness and honesty in adoption." Established in 1978 to provide a national forum for search and support groups, AAC is involved in many endeavors to educate the general public and the adoption community to the needs for adoption reform. AAC members include birthparents, adoptees, adoptive parents, adoption agencies, and professionals in related fields.

SERVICES

AAC's program includes the following components:

AAC Search Hotline: Any interested person may call AAC's Search Hotline (505–296–2198) to receive referrals for search assistance in the U.S., Canada, or overseas. The hotline also provides information on other AAC services, such as the speakers' bureau, conferences, and membership.

Conferences: AAC sponsors an annual national conference and many regional conferences each year.

Newsletter: AAC members receive The Decree, a national newsletter which provides an overview of current trends in the adoption movement.

Speakers' Bureau: AAC provides speakers for adoption agencies, maternity homes, prospective adoptive parent groups, or any group interested in adoption.

Study and Publication Bibliography: AAC maintains a bibliography of all adoption-related studies and publications.

Legislative Guides: AAC distributes legislative guides which provide information on how to write a bill, how a bill is passed through a two house legislative body, and how to testify at a legislative hearing.

International Soundex Reunion Registry: ISRR is the only reunion registry sanctioned by AAC. ISRR is staffed by volunteers, and services are provided free of charge. A reunion will be effected when voluntary registrations from both parties are received (birthparent, adoptee, siblings or adoptive parents).

Independent Search Consultants: ISC is a professional association providing certification services for individuals assisting in search/reunion. Other ISC activities include publishing, public speaking, and training in search techniques.

FUNDING

ACC is supported through individual, organization, and agency membership dues as well as revenue generated from conferences and publications. Organizational and individual memberships are $25 annually (lifetime individual membership, $200; lifetime organization membership, $300). Agency memberships are $50 annually (lifetime agency membership, $500).

PROFESSIONAL AFFILIATIONS

None.

CHILD WELFARE LEAGUE OF AMERICA

440 First Street, N.W., Suite 310
Washington, DC 20001–2085
(202) 638–2952
Director: David S. Liederman, Executive Director

THE PROGRAM

The Child Welfare League of America (CWLA) is the largest privately supported, nonprofit organization in North America "devoting its efforts to helping deprived, neglected and abused children and their families." Founded in 1920 on the recommendation of the first White House Conference on Children, called by President Theodore Roosevelt in 1910, CWLA has historically played a crucial role in the formulation of public policy relating to the welfare of children and in setting high standards for social work practice. CWLA's history of innovative and distinguished service includes pioneering achievements in foster care, day care, services to adolescent parents, child welfare legislation, and professional accreditation. Supported by a network of more than 500 member agencies and 1,000 affiliates throughout the U.S. and Canada, CWLA today provides consultation and training services, sponsors conferences, conducts research, publishes books and pamphlets, and advocates in Congress on behalf of children. CWLA's current priorities include adolescent pregnancy, day care, child abuse and neglect, out-of-home care, adoption, and family support.

SERVICES

CWLA's program components include the following:

Legislative advocacy: CWLA addresses the need for congressional legislation on priority issues by conducting regional hearings, drafting legislation, testifying at congressional hearings, collaborating with other national groups, and lobbying for adequate funding and standards for child welfare programs.

Consultation and training: CWLA works closely with member agencies through regional representatives on a day-to-day basis to provide assistance and advice. CWLA sponsors training institutes to address specific needs, supports program development targeting priority issues, and solicits member participation in regional conferences, task forces, and committees.

Conferences: CWLA sponsors and co-sponsors national and regional conferences on child welfare issues. In 1987, CWLA's two national and six regional conferences drew 5,300 participants, addressing issues ranging from teen pregnancy prevention to the prevention of child abuse.

Research: Through its Research Department, CWLA conducts studies on a range of issues for use by CWLA and member agencies to improve practice and to lobby for proposed legislation.

Task Forces: CWLA sponsors task forces, made up only of CWLA members, to prepare recommendations for action in the areas of public policy, research, training, and program development. 1987 task forces addressed the following issues: children and AIDS, out-of-home care, adoption, day care, and board organization and mobilization.

Publications: CWLA is the largest publisher in North

America of child welfare and social work practice materials. The Publications Department publishes books and monographs in addition to CWLA's newsletter, *Children's VOICE*, and CWLA's bi-monthly professional journal, *Child Welfare*. CWLA's publications' distribution reaches over 200,000 professionals.

Library/Information Service: CWLA's library contains one of the most complete collections of material related to child welfare in North America. The library responds annually to thousands of requests for information and assistance from advocates, practitioners, and policymakers.

Standards of Practice: Since its founding in 1920, CWLA has published internationally recognized standards for child welfare practice. As child welfare practice evolves, CWLA develops new standards and revises existing standards. In addition, CWLA co-founded and co-sponsors the Council on Accreditation of Services for Families and Children which provides accreditation services for the mental health and social service fields.

FUNDING

CWLA is supported by membership dues, contributions, investments, grants, revenue from publications, and fees for service.

PROFESSIONAL AFFILIATIONS

CWLA's membership includes more than 500 member agencies and 1,000 affiliates in the U.S. and Canada.

COMMITTEE FOR SINGLE ADOPTIVE PARENTS, INC.

P.O. Box 15084
Chevy Chase, MD 20815
Mail inquiries only.
Directors: Hope Marindin, Betsy Burch, Margaret Collrin, James Forderer, Kathie Hutcheson, Mary Ryan, Kathy Sreedhar, Diane Veith, and Lorene Wedeking

THE PROGRAM

Founded in 1973 to provide information and referral services to both prospective and actual single adoptive parents, the Committee for Single Adoptive Parents strives to meet the following goals:
"To support the right of adoptable children to loving families, regardless of any difference in race, creed, color, or national origin, or of any handicap the children may have.
To serve members with information and assistance.
To inform public and private agencies of legislation and research applying to single-person adoption."
Membership is open to single individuals and agencies, and the Committee has member-subscribers across the U.S. and Canada.

SERVICES

The membership term is 24 months, and the fee is $15.00. Members receive the Source List and its updates, listing agencies and direct sources of adoptable children in the U.S.

and abroad who will accept single applicants. The Source List briefly describes cost, estimated time, and type of children available. The Source List does not endorse any source. Periodic updates also include other information of interest to single adoptive parents (support groups, recommended reading, adoption announcements). In addition, members may request (with SASE) a list of the names of prospective and actual single adoptive parents in their state.

The Committee publishes and distributes *The Handbook for Single Adoptive Parents*, compiled and edited by Hope Marindin, for $8.00. The book includes a description of the adoption process (for both domestic and foreign adoptions) in the U.S. and Canada, practical advice on single parenthood, actual adoption experiences described by five single adoptive parents, and recent research findings on single parent adoption.

FUNDING

The Committee for Single Adoptive Parents is supported by member-subscriptions to the Source List and by sales of The Handbook for Single Adoptive Parents.

PROFESSIONAL AFFILIATIONS

None.

COUNCIL ON ACCREDITATION OF SERVICES FOR FAMILIES AND CHILDREN, INC.

520 8th Avenue, Suite 2202B
New York, NY 10018
(212) 714–9399
Director: David Shover, Executive Director

THE PROGRAM

The Council on Accreditation of Services for Families and Children (COA) is a nonprofit organization which was established in 1978 by the Child Welfare League of America and Family Service America to develop and provide an accreditation process for the mental health and social service fields. COA is sponsored by 7 national organizations (Child Welfare League of America, Family Service America, Catholic Charities USA, Association of Jewish Family and Children's Agencies, Lutheran Social Service System, National Committee For Adoption, and National Association of Homes for Children) and currently accredits 550 agencies throughout the U.S. COA accreditation entails agency compliance (through objective, measurable standards) with professional requirements for organization and practice.

SERVICES

Accreditation is a private voluntary form of quality control which examines total agency operation against standards which exceed the minimum requirements of state or provincial licensing. Any agency which provides one or more of the 40 services for which COA has accreditation requirements may apply for accreditation. Services for which COA has accreditation requirements include the following:

Community Organization Service/Social Advocacy Service

Access Services: Information and Referral Service/Crisis Intervention Service/Emergency Telephone Response System

Emergency Shelter Service for Abused and Neglected Children/Emergency Shelter Service for Homeless Individuals and Families

Domestic Violence and/or Rape Crisis Service

Service for Runaway and Homeless Youth and Their Families

Resettlement Service

Immigration and Citizenship Assistance Service

Child Day Care Service/Early Childhood Education Service/Family and Group Day Care Home Service

Volunteer Friendship Service

Group Service for Social Development and Enrichment

Family Life Education Service

Financial Management Service/Credit Counseling Service

Supportive Service to the Aging/Supportive Service to Adults with Special Needs

Home Care Service/Homemaker Service for Children/ Homemaker-Home Health Aid Service

Protective Service for Adults

Day Care Service for the Aging

Day Treatment Service/Social Adjustment Service/Treatment-Oriented Day Care Service

Counseling Services: Family and Individual Counseling/ Service to Children in Their Own Homes/Mental Health Service to Families and Individuals/ Employee Assistance Program or Service

Substance Abuse Service/Chemical Dependency Service/ Transitional Residential Service

Protective Service for Children

Foster Family Care

Therapeutic Foster Care

Foster or Group Care for Unaccompanied Minor Entrants or Refugees

Group Home Service/Residential Center Service for Children and Youth

Residential Treatment Center for Children and Youth

Pregnancy Counseling and Supportive Service

Adoption Service

FUNDING

COA is supported primarily by fees for service but also by sale of COA publications.

PROFESSIONAL AFFILIATIONS

COA is sponsored by 7 national mental health and social services organizations (see Program above).

CUB (CONCERNED UNITED BIRTHPARENTS, INC.)

2000 Walker Street
Des Moines, IA 50317
(515) 262–9120
Director: Carole Anderson, President

THE PROGRAM

CUB (Concerned United Birthparents, Inc.) is a nonprofit organization originally founded in 1976 to provide mutual support for birthparents, men and women who have surrendered children to adoption. Today, CUB has branch offices and representatives in many states and CUB members include birthparents, adoptees, adoptive parents, and professionals. CUB's purposes are "providing mutual support for coping with the ongoing pains and problems of adoption, working for adoption reforms in law and social policy, preventing unnecessary family separations, assisting adoption separated relatives in searching for family members, and educating the public about adoption issues and realities."

SERVICES

CUB provides the following services:

Mutual Support: CUB provides monthly meetings, a monthly newsletter, correspondence and phone calls which help members cope with adoption difficulties and feelings.

Adoption Reform: Many CUB members work to promote legislative and social policy changes to assist birthparents in keeping their families together and, when adoption is necessary, to encourage a humane, open approach to adoption.

Prevention: CUB works to prevent unnecessary separations by providing temporary support, counseling, and information to people experiencing an unplanned pregnancy.

Search: CUB members provide one-to-one assistance and emotional support during search; CUB branches hold search workshops for members; CUB has a reunion registry.

Education: CUB distributes and produces literature concerning adoption; CUB members and leaders speak to community groups about issues relating to family separation and adoption.

Membership dues are $35 annually for new members and $25 annually for renewals. Membership includes a subscription to the Communicator (newsletter) and to The Family Advocate (semi-annual publication).

FUNDING

CUB is supported by membership dues and by receipts from the sale of CUB publications.

PROFESSIONAL AFFILIATIONS

CUB is a member of the American Adoption Congress.

FAMILY SERVICE AMERICA

11700 West Lake Park Drive
Milwaukee, WI 53224
(414) 359–2111
Director: Geneva B. Johnson, President and Chief Executive Officer

THE PROGRAM

Family Service America (FSA) is a nonprofit organization "dedicated to helping families in and out of crisis." Founded in 1911, the FSA network consists of 290 member agencies located throughout the United States and Canada. FSA member agencies are nonprofit, voluntary organizations which offer a wide range of services to support and strengthen family life.

Specific programs developed by member agencies vary depending on the needs of the local community and may include individual, marital, and family counseling; family advocacy; crisis intervention; parent education; services to the elderly; divorce mediation; adoption services; foster care; teen pregnancy and parenting programs; domestic violence programs; employee assistance programs; substance abuse programs; emergency assistance; information and referral services. Member agencies must meet standards set by the Council on Accreditation of Services for Families and Children.

SERVICES

FSA supports member agencies with the following services:

Technical assistance to member agencies in program development, clinical and management practices.

National Service to Industry Program to aid national corporations in developing employee assistance programs.

National Information Center (national clearinghouse on "state of the art" services to families).

Research on societal trends and their effects on family and community life.

National representation before government agencies to present FSA network interests and concerns.

Publication of professional journal, Social Casework.

National and regional training programs, conferences, and seminars for professional and volunteer leadership through FSA National Training Center in Milwaukee.

REGIONAL OFFICES

Requests for information should be directed to the national headquarters in Milwaukee.

Office on Governmental Affairs
1319 F. Street, N.W., Suite 606
Washington, D.C. 20004
(202) 347–1124

New York City
254 West 31st St.
New York, N.Y. 10001
(212) 967–2740

Oakland
445 30th Street
Oakland, CA 94609
(415) 836–2448

Raleigh:
1100 Navajo Drive
Raleigh, NC 27609
(919) 878–9203

FUNDING

FSA is privately supported through public contributions, contracts and grants from industries and foundations, member agency dues, and the sale of its publications.

PROFESSIONAL AFFILIATIONS

Family Service America is governed by an international volunteer Board of Directors composed of corporate, professional, and community leaders from the United States and Canada. FSA's network consists of 290 member agencies located throughout the United States and Canada.

INTERNATIONAL CONCERNS COMMITTEE FOR CHILDREN

911 Cypress Drive
Boulder, CO 80303
(303) 494–8333
Directors: Betty K. Laning, Anna Marie Merrill, Pat Sexton

THE PROGRAM

International Concerns Committee for Children (ICCC) is a non-profit charitable and educational organization which was founded in 1979 to provide nationwide services (information, advocacy, and referral) to interested citizens, prospective adoptive parents, and adoption agencies. ICCC is "a resource that has as its concern the welfare of children in foreign countries as well as those in the United States." The organization's mission is threefold: "(1) to acquaint the concerned public and prospective adoptive parents with the various ways to provide assistance to homeless children—sponsorship, fostering, and adoption, (2) to educate those interested on the personal and professional level about the adoption process, and (3) to inform prospective adoptive parents on the availability of 'waiting children' in foreign countries and in the United States."

SERVICES

Services provided by the International Concerns Committee for Children include:

Information Service about the availability of adoptable domestic and foreign children.

Publication of an annual *Report on Foreign Adoption* with monthly updates.

Personal adoption counseling by experienced adoptive parents for all interested parents and professionals.

Listing Service for foreign children in the United States whose adoptions have been disrupted and who need new adoptive parents in this country and for foreign "waiting children."

Family Register for prospective adoptive families seeking to adopt foreign-born children of a particular age, sex, or race.

Coordination with adoptive parent groups to obtain current information on personal support and adoption counseling.

Distribution of pertinent information by recognized experts in adoption.

The *Report on Foreign Adoption* contains a wealth of current information, including a country-by-country directory of U.S.-based and foreign agencies (children available, cost, wait, requirements), articles and practical advice relating to intercountry adoption, reading list, and information concerning sponsorship. The report (including monthly updates) is available by mail for a $15.00 donation.

ICCC Listing Service ($20.00 annual donation) photolists "waiting children" still living overseas as well as foreign-born children involved in U.S. adoption disruptions. The listing is distributed quarterly and includes a picture and description of each child, the name and address of the child's social worker or foreign representative to contact for further information. (Prospective parents and their adoption workers are solely responsible for pursuing a possible match.)

ICCC Listing Service and Family Register ($22.50 annual donation) lists prospective adoptive families seeking to adopt foreign-born children of a particular age, sex, and race. The listing includes information concerning the family's willingness to accept certain handicaps. Prospective adoptive parents register complete (but non-identifying) information about themselves which is then distributed with ICCC's Listing Service packet to U.S. and foreign agencies. Agencies interested in pursuing a possible match then contact ICCC by mail for specific information on registered families.

FUNDING

ICCC's only funding is derived from public contributions. There are no fees for services other than nominal charges for related expenses.

PROFESSIONAL AFFILIATIONS

ICCC's affiliations include the Open Door Society of Massachusetts and Colorado Parents for All Children.

INTERNATIONAL SOUNDEX REUNION REGISTRY (ISRR)

P.O. Box 2312
Carson City, NV 89702
(702) 882–6270
Director: Emma May Vilardi

THE PROGRAM

International Soundex Reunion Registry (ISRR) is a nonprofit, humanitarian service incorporated in 1981 "to serve and promote, through the Reunion Registry, the interests of any adult persons desiring and seeking a reunion with next-of-kin by birth." ISRR began as a supportive system primarily concerned with the needs of people whose lives are touched by adoption and has expanded to encompass the needs of all persons separated from family members by divorce, foster care, and acts of war. ISRR provides a confidential and voluntary identification system on a national and international scale and provides services to users free of charge.

SERVICES

ISRR is strictly a Reunion Registry and does not perform a search service or provide search assistance to its registrants. ISRR provides the following services:

Reunion Registry: An ISRR registrant may be any adult person 18 years of age or older, desiring and seeking reunion with next-of-kin by birth through voluntary registration in the ISRR (i.e., a birthmother searching for her child, an adoptee searching for birthfamily members, siblings in search of each other). Registrants complete and submit ISRR registration form which remains in force without further renewal unless the registrant requests that the registration be inactivated or notifies the registrar that his/her search has been concluded. When a match occurs, registrants are notified by a telephone call from the ISRR Registrar. ISRR services are provided free of charge to registrants.

Medical Alert System: In response to appeals from adult adoptees and from adoptive parents of children still in minority, ISRR has devised a medical alert system in order to remedy situations where lack of access to family pedigrees of two or more generations denies treatments that could prevent progressive damage and/or death.

Post-Match Consultant Service: ISRR provides assistance to adult adoptees and their extended families who are matched through the Registry and who need professional assistance as relationships are established.

FUNDING

ISRR is funded entirely through individual and affiliate contributions.

PROFESSIONAL AFFILIATIONS

ISRR cooperates with, and serves by affiliation, public and private institutions, adoption agencies, departments of social services, organizations, groups and associations across the country and abroad.

LATIN AMERICA PARENTS ASSOCIATION (LAPA)

New York Chapter of LAPA
P.O. Box 72
Seaford, NY 11783
(718) 236–8689
Director: LAPA Staff

THE PROGRAM

Latin America Parents Association (LAPA) is a not-for-profit organization with regional chapters in many states which provides assistance and moral support to prospective adoptive parents who are interested in adopting children from Latin America. Founded by a group of parents who adopted their children from Latin America, the organization's primary goals are "to assist prospective parents in their quest for a child, to aid the orphanages in Latin America by providing clothing toys and medical supplies, and to provide support for adoptive families after they bring their children home."

SERVICES

LAPA sponsors open meetings which feature programs of interest to parents who have adopted or are interested in adopting children from Latin America. LAPA gathers and disseminates information on current trends and policies relating to adoption from Latin America and on current sources of adoption. (For information packet, send a self-addressed, stamped envelope to the nearest regional office, listed below.) LAPA invites interested individuals to become members for an annual membership fee of $20, which includes a subscription to LAPA's newsletter and notices of upcoming meetings or social events. Membership fees help to underwrite the cost of such necessities as telephone, postage, and printing expenses.

CHAPTERS

Chapters are independent and should be contacted by letter with an enclosed self-addressed stamped envelope.

New Jersey State Chapter
P.O. Box 2013
Brick, NJ 08723
(201) 572–2509

Maryland-National Capitol Region
P.O. Box 4403
Silver Spring, MD 20904
(301) 384–7467

Northern New Jersey Chapter
P.O. Box 77
Emerson, NJ 07630
(201) 385–6278

Connecticut State Chapter
P.O. Box 523
Unionville, CT 06085–0523

FUNDING

LAPA is supported by voluntary contributions from interested individuals and by membership fees.

PROFESSIONAL AFFILIATIONS

None.

NATIONAL ASSOCIATION OF HOMES FOR CHILDREN

P.O. Box 1459
Millbrook, NY 12545
(914) 677–3283 (in New York State) (800) 843–6242 (outside of New York State)
Director: Mr. Arlin E. Ness, President

THE PROGRAM

Founded in 1975 as a voice for not-for-profit agencies providing out-of-home care for children (group residential care, child placement, adoption and/or foster family care services), the National Association of Homes for Children (NAHC) is a not-for-profit organization supported by a network of member agencies located throughout the U.S. Early in its history, NAHC adopted a Code of Ethics and instituted a system of accreditation for child care agencies. In 1987, NAHC became a major sponsor of the Council on Accreditation of Services for Families and Children. NAHC members are eligible to apply for COA accreditation, an evaluation of the total child care program. NAHC provides a range of services to member agencies (see Services below) designed to achieve the following goals:

1. To promote and protect the care of children.
2. To work toward the improvement of group residential care and related services for children and their families.
3. To provide the member homes and agencies with a means of identifying and solving problems of mutual concern and to coordinate their efforts.
4. To work together, in the public interest, with other voluntary and governmental organizations and agencies concerned with the care of children.

SERVICES

NAHC services to member agencies include:

Accreditation through the Council on Accreditation of Services for Families and Children.

Information on government laws and regulations affecting children and child care agencies through bi-monthly newsletter(Public Affairs Bulletin).

Quarterly publication (Caring) containing articles relevant to the child care field.

Public relations materials available to members for use within their own communities.

Annual conference (held in September) for the exchange of pertinent views.

National and regional workshops dealing with such issues as permanency, family linkage, meeting the special needs of minority youths, and the handling of crisis situations.

FUNDING

NAHC is funded by membership dues. Dues are nominal and are based either on the type of service provided by the member agency or on the number of children in the agency's care. Application and detailed information on the annual dues structure are available upon request.

PROFESSIONAL AFFILIATIONS

The National Association of Homes for Children is affiliated as a major sponsor with the Council on Accreditation of Services for Children and Families.

NATIONAL COMMITTEE FOR ADOPTION

P.O. Box 33366
Washington, D.C. 20033
(202) 638–0466
Director: Dr. William L. Pierce, President

THE PROGRAM

The National Committee For Adoption is a nonprofit organization which was founded in 1980 "to strengthen adoption and related services." NCFA's membership includes over 140 adoption or maternity services agencies located throughout the U.S., individual and family supporters, corporate supporters, and "friends of adoption." The organization provides extensive information and referral services, advocacy in state and federal legislatures, public awareness and education programs, and research on current adoption practices. The primary goal of the National Committee For Adoption is "to promote adoption as a positive option for young, single or troubled parents." NCFA strives to meet this goal in the following ways:

1. NCFA promotes coordination and cooperation among many national groups and local service providers.
2. NCFA collects and publishes accurate, current and useful information about the adoption process, laws, and services.
3. NCFA supports better funding for maternity homes.
4. NCFA encourages Federal policy revisions, tax law deductions for adoption expenses, and deductions for parental expenses incurred in providing a daughter with comprehensive services related to her unmarried pregnancy.

5. NCFA endorses provision of services in a discrete fashion and in a comprehensive setting.
6. NCFA encourages more research on the 'Adoption Option'.
7. NCFA encourages the Federal government, as well as national organizations, to work together to support efforts at the State and local level which support education and promotion of the positive option of adoption.
8. NCFA encourages professional standards through its sponsorship, with six other national organizations, of the Council on Accreditation of Services for Families and Children, Inc."

SERVICES

NCFA provides a wide range of services to individuals, families, agencies, and organizations involved in adoption issues. Services include:

National Adoption Hotline (202–638–0469) to provide information and referral on maternity services, adoption resources, and infertility support groups in the caller's area.

Newsletters and bulletins on adoption, services to unmarried parents, and help for infertile couples.

NCFA publications (brochures, directories, manuals, research findings) on adoption issues.

NCFA model legislation series.

NCFA book store (including materials, books, and resources published by NCFA and others available by mail order).

Consultation and training for member agencies and social workers.

Sponsorship of conferences on maternity services and adoption services.

Maintenance of the International Clearinghouse and Library on Adoption.

FUNDING

NCFA is supported by membership dues from individuals, families, agencies, foundations and corporations.

PROFESSIONAL AFFILIATIONS

NCFA's membership includes more than 140 licensed, not-for-profit agencies which provide maternity and/or adoption services, located throughout the U.S. For a complete list of member agencies, send a self-addressed, stamped envelope to NCFA headquarters in Washington, D.C.

NATIONAL RESOURCE CENTER FOR SPECIAL-NEEDS ADOPTION

3660 Waltrous Road
P.O. Box 337
Chelsea, MI 48118
(313) 475–8693
Director: Drenda S. Lakin, ACSW

THE PROGRAM

The National Resource Center for Special-Needs adoption was established in 1985 as a division of Spaulding for Children, a nationally known special-needs adoption agency founded in 1968. Spaulding was founded—and continues—

to serve those children with special needs not served by other adoption agencies in Michigan, "believing that all children whose families of birth cannot care for them have the right to quality adoption services and the opportunity to grow up in permanent families." As the agency developed innovative practice methods, those methods were shared with others through books, papers, and on-site training. Continuing this tradition, the National Resource Center for Special-needs adoption provides leadership, advocacy, training, technical assistance, and consultation in special-needs adoption. These services are provided to adoptive parent groups, child welfare, adoption, mental health, juvenile justice, and educational professionals throughout the U.S. In its 20 year history, Spaulding for Children/National Resource Center for Special-needs adoption has trained over 20,000 individuals from every state in the U.S., Puerto Rico, the Virgin Islands, Canada, Great Britain, and Australia.

SERVICES

The National Resource Center for Special-Needs Adoption provides training and consultation programs, delivered throughout the U.S. by nationally known trainers and consultants. Center services include the following:

Permanency Planning Program: Training and consultation in permanency planning for children with developmental disabilities, focusing on the specific needs of these children and their families. Specific assessment and community resource issues are examined.

Special-needs adoption/Post-Adoption Services: Training and consultation in special-needs adoption/post-adoption services, including training on preparation and assessment of children and families, preventive counseling and crisis intervention services designed to keep adoptive families intact.

Leadership Institute: Identification, recruitment, training, and mentoring of emerging leaders from metropolitan areas throughout the nation where large numbers of children wait in the foster care system, with special emphasis on developing minority and female leaders in public child welfare systems.

Publications: Quarterly journal, The Roundtable (international circulation of 9,000); National Resource Center for Special-needs adoption Book Catalog (informational and educational materials developed by special-needs adoption organizations throughout the country).

FUNDING

Spaulding for Children and the National Resource Center for Special-needs adoption are funded through federal and foundation grants, contracts with various states, and private child welfare, developmental disability, and mental health agencies, as well as fees for training, consultation, technical assistance, and educational materials.

PROFESSIONAL AFFILIATIONS

Spaulding for Children and the National Resource Center for Special-needs adoption are participating members of the Child Welfare League of America, Family Builders Network of Adoption Agencies, Michigan Federation of Private Child and Family Agencies, Michigan Alliance of Children's Agencies, Kinship/Detroit Area Adoption Agencies, and National Society of Fund Raising Executives, Michigan Chapter.

NORTH AMERICAN COUNCIL ON ADOPTABLE CHILDREN

1821 University Avenue, Suite S-275
St. Paul, MN 55104
(612) 644–3036
Director: Joe Kroll, Executive Director

THE PROGRAM

North American Council on Adoptable Children (NACAC) is a non-profit coalition of adoptive parent support groups in the United States and Canada which began as a small but determined "grass-roots" initiative in 1974 and has evolved into a national organization which addresses the needs of waiting children. The purpose of the Council is "to advocate the right of every child to a permanent, continuous and nurturing family, and to press for the legal adoptive placement of any child denied that right." NACAC monitors legislative activity and policy interpretation at the national level, assists in the formation of parent support groups across the U.S. and in Canada, trains advocates across the U.S., distributes a wide range of materials and resources, and provides the largest annual training conference on adoption issues in North America. Currently, NACAC's 3 major areas of organization concentration are "(1) placement of homeless children, particularly Black, Hispanic, and Native American children; (2) assurance of full implementation of Public Law 96–272 (the Adoption Assistance and Child Welfare Act of 1980) at the state level, especially adoption assistance programs; and (3) availability of pre and post-adoption services to families."

In addition to parent group and individual memberships, NACAC has a representative in each state or province who serves as a resource person in the state, providing information on special-needs adoption and advocating for waiting children on the state level.

SERVICES

NACAC's program includes the following components:

Annual Training Conference: NACAC holds an annual training conference in late summer which attracts approximately 1000 participants, including professionals, adoptive parents, and adoptees. It is the largest adoption-related conference in North America.

Adoptalk: NACAC publishes a quarterly newsletter distributed to 4,000 readers which includes legislative updates, news of conferences, resources, research, policy, current trends, and other information for all members of the adoption community.

National Adoption Week: Held by Congressional proclamation during Thanksgiving Week each year, NACAC produces materials for distribution and helps coordinate a wide variety of events and commemorations throughout the U.S. and Canada.

Support/Technical Assistance/Funding for Adoptive Parent Groups: NACAC provides support for local adoptive parent groups through funding for specific projects, technical assistance, and information exchange.

Advocacy: NACAC members are kept abreast of legislative activity and policy interpretation at a national level and are urged to take an active role in local issues such as monitoring proper implementation of PL 96–272.

Individual and family membership in NACAC is $25 per year. Adoptive parent organizations are encouraged to join as member groups, and organizations as affiliates. Citizen adoption group membership is $25 and organizational affiliation is $50 per year. Adoptalk subscription is included in membership.

FUNDING

Current funding is provided through parent group, agency, and individual memberships, a federal grant, and private foundation grants.

PROFESSIONAL AFFILIATIONS

NACAC's membership includes adoptive parent groups, agencies, and organizations located throughout the U.S. and Canada.

OURS, INC.

3307 Highway 100 North, Suite 203
Minneapolis, MN 55422
(612) 535–4829
Director: Susan Freivalds, Executive Director

THE PROGRAM

OURS, Inc. is a private, nonprofit membership organization of families and individuals that "provides problem-solving assistance and information about the challenges of adoption to adoptive and prospective adoptive families." OURS, Inc. began in 1967 with six families who met at the airport while awaiting the arrival of their children from Korea. Realizing that they had something very important in common, they arranged to meet again in a month. The agency that had placed this first organized group of Korean children in Minnesota began to refer prospective adoptive parents to the group for education about parenting adopted foreign-born children. Under the leadership of the founding president, Betty Kramer, the group grew locally, and then at the state and national levels. The first newsletter of OURS, Inc. has evolved into OURS: The magazine of adoptive families, the only national magazine by and for adoptive families. As membership grew, the focus expanded to include all types of adoptive families (families adopting same-race newborns, families adopting foreign-born children, families adopting older and/or special-needs children). As the umbrella organization for over 100 adoptive parent support groups around the country, OURS, Inc. provides technical and financial assistance to support the groups' local programs. Current membership includes 12,000 individuals and families and 100 groups.

SERVICES

OURS, Inc. provides the following services:

Information: Prospective adoptive parents are provided free-of-charge an information packet explaining the adoption process and listing agencies for potential placements.

Education: OURS, Inc. has available for purchase a variety of adoption and cultural parenting resource materials (including books for children and adults about adoption and about the various cultural heritages of our children, ethnic dolls appropriate for Asian, Black, Hispanic, and Indian children, language tools, and activities for family sharing).

Publication: OURS: The magazine of adoptive families is a bi-monthly publication which contains articles by professionals, stories written by adoptive parents, current adoption information, and practical advice on adoptive parenting. Receipt of the magazine is a benefit of membership in OURS, Inc. A free "Highlights" issue is available upon request.

Support: OURS, Inc. maintains a Family Support Network Listing, a current registration of families willing to support other families in crisis or simply to provide local information. A 24–hour "Helpline" for families in crisis is staffed by trained volunteers. A nationwide Adoptive Parent Support Group Listing helps families find local support and information.

Services to Adoptive Parent Support Groups: OURS, Inc. provides technical, financial, and programming assistance to over 100 adoptive parent support groups throughout the country through program grants, a quarterly newsletter for group leaders, a video-tape lending library, and referral of prospective new members.

Aid to Programs Working for Children without Permanent Families: OURS, Inc. provides substantial grants to aid both domestic and overseas programs working for children in need of permanence.

Current dues for U.S. members are $16.00 for a 1–year membership, $30.00 for a 2–year membership, and $45.00 for a 3 year membership. Canadian dues are U.S. $26.00 annually; others please write for current rates.

FUNDING

OURS, Inc. is funded primarily through membership dues, the sale of parenting resource materials, advertising revenue from OURS: The magazine of adoptive families, and donations.

PROFESSIONAL AFFILIATIONS

OURS, Inc. is a member of the Child Welfare League of America and the Joint Council on International Children's Services.

TRIADOPTION® LIBRARY, INC.

P.O. Box 638
Westminster, CA 92684
(714) 892–4098
Director: TRIADOPTION® Staff

THE PROGRAM

TRIADOPTION® Library is a nonprofit organization which began in 1978 "to respond to a great need for information about adoption and family separation/reunion issues." An ancillary service to search groups and reunion registries, TRIADOPTION® networks internationally with 493 search and support groups, consultants, and research/support organizations around the world. TRIADOPTION® provides

information and referral services on search issues and on cooperative adoption to over 4,000 people annually, believing that "access to information will provide people with the tools to make the best choices for their lives and relationships."

SERVICES

Services provided by TRIADOPTION® Library include:

TRIADOPTION® Publications: TRIADOPTION® publishes and distributes a number of books (including "how-to" books on search), booklets, and audio cassette tapes. Send a business size SASE for a current catalog and order form.

TRIADOPTION® Surname and Birthdate Search: TRIADOPTION® maintains a surname and birthdate index which cross-references all the names and dates listed in group newsletters since the early 1970s, some public records, individuals who have contacted TRIADOPTION® and other group memberships. Contributors receive a Birthdate Card to fill out and return to TRIADOPTION® with $5.00 per surname to be researched and $5.00 per date/state/country to be researched. TRIADOPTION® then forwards any pertinent information to the contributor.

TRIADOPTION® International Referral Service: TRIADOPTION® networks with 493 organizations and individuals all over the world who will help with search, support, reunion, and cooperative adoption. Listings are available at $2.00 per state (or foreign country), printed out by geographic area of service.

TRIADOPTION® Membership: A contribution of $75.00 or more entitles the contributor to lifetime membership, permanent recording of the contributor's information in TRIADOPTION®'s Birthdate and Surname Index, International Soundex Reunion Registry's free registration form and information on other reunion registries, TLContributors Package (including "how-to" publications, audio cassette tapes, and International Referral Service listings), and periodic mailings about important events, book offerings, research and surveys.

TRIADOPTION® Conference: TRIADOPTION® sponsors conferences on search, reunion, cooperative adoption, and other adoption issues.

FUNDING

TRIADOPTION® Library, Inc. is supported by membership contributions, fees for services, and revenue generated from sale of TRIADOPTION® publications.

PROFESSIONAL AFFILIATIONS

TRIADOPTION® Library, Inc. is a member of American Adoption Congress.

Appendix A

STATE	AGENCY	PROGRAM
California	Aask America	Nationwide match-referral services for children with special needs. For description, refer to "National Child Welfare and Triad Support Organizations."
Washington	Adoption Advocates International	Nationwide placement services for special needs children from India, Taiwan, Korea, and Mexico. Applicants may be married or single.There is no specific religious requirement.
Pennsylvania	Adoption Service	Nationwide placement services for domestic infant adoptions. Applicants may be married or single. There is no specific religious requirement.
Texas	Adoption Services Associates	Nationwide placement services for healthy infants (and occasionally special needs children as well). Generally, applicants must be married, but the agency will consider exceptional single parents. There is no specific religious requirement.
Washington	Adoption Services of WACAP	Nationwide placement services for healthy and special needs children from the U.S., Asia, and Latin America. Applicants may be married or single. There is no specific religious requirement.
Oregon	Adventist Adoption and Family Services	Nationwide placement services for domestic and international children, both healthy and special needs. Some options are available to single parents. There is no specific religious requirement.
Texas	AGAPE Texas Social Services	Nationwide placement services for children of minority race and children with special needs Applicants may be married or single. There is no specific religious requirement.
District of Columbia	American Adoption Agency	Nationwide placement services for healthy and special needs children from India and Latin America. There is no specific religious requirement.

Michigan	Americans for International Aid and Adoption	Nationwide placement services for children from India and Korea. The marital and religious requirements are flexible, but may vary depending on the program.
Michigan	Bethany Christian Services	Branch offices in many states provide placement services for domestic infant and special needs adoption and (in some states) international adoption. For domestic programs, applicants must be practicing members of an Evangelical Christian church. There is no specific religious requirement for the international program. Applicants must be married.
Missouri	Child Placement Services	Nationwide placement services for domestic infant adoptions for members of RLDS Church (Reorganized Church of the Latter Day Saints). Applicants must be married.
Texas	Child Placement Center of Texas	Nationwide placement services for Black and bi-racial children and children with special needs. Applicants may be married or single. There is no specific religious requirement.
Georgia	Children's Services International	Nationwide placement services for children from Latin America. There is no specific religious requirement. The marital status requirement varies depending on the country.
Kentucky	Chosen Children Adoption Services	Placement services for Caucasian infant adoptions for residents of Kentucky, Indiana, Tennessee, New York, New Jersey, and Connecticut. Placement services for Black and bi-racial infants for residents of all states except Michigan. Applicants must be married. There is no specific religious requirement.
Louisiana	Christian Homes	Nationwide placement services for special needs adoptions. Marital and religious requirements are flexible for this program.
Tennessee	Church of God Home for Children	Nationwide placement services for healthy and special needs infants. Applicants must be practicing Christians. Applicants must be married.

Washington	Church of Christ Homes for Children	Nationwide placement services for healthy infants and young children. Applicants must be active members of the Church of Christ. Applicants must be married.
North Dakota	Covenant Children	Nationwide placement services for children from Latin America. Applicants must be married. Applicants must be practicing Christians.
Oklahoma	Deaconess	Nationwide placement services Home for healthy and special needs infants. Applicants must be Protestants. Applicants must be married.
Missouri	Family Adoption and Counseling Services	Nationwide placement services for U.S. children with special needs and for children from El Salvador, Guatemala, India, and Thailand. Applicants may be married or single. There is no specific religious requirement.
Virginia	Family Life Services	Nationwide placement services for domestic infant adoptions. Generally, applicants must be married. Applicants must be practicing Christians.
Colorado	Friends of Children of Various Nations	Nationwide placement services for children from India. There is no specific religious requirement. Some options are available to single parents.
Kansas	Gentle Shepherd Child Placement Services	Nationwide placement services for domestic and international adoptions. Applicants must be married. Applicants must be practicing Christians.
Arizona	Globe International Adoption	Nationwide placement services for healthy and special needs children from Colombia, El Salvador, the Philippines, Taiwan, and India. Applicants must be Christian. Some options are available to single parents.
Colorado	Hand In Hand International Adoption Agency	Nationwide placement services (except for residents of Georgia, Ohio, and New Jersey) for healthy and special needs children from the Philippines. Applicants may be Jewish or Christian. Applicants must be married.

Missouri	Highlands Child Placement Service	Nationwide placement services for domestic healthy and special needs children. Applicants must be married. Applicants must be practicing members of the Assemblies of God.
Oregon	Holt International Children's Services	Branch offices in many states provide placement services for children from Asia and Latin America. Some options are available to single parents. There is no specific religious requirement.
Georgia	Homes for Children International	Nationwide placement services for children from Latin America. Some options are available to single parents. There is no specific religious requirement.
Georgia	Illien Adoptions International	Nationwide placement services for domestic and international adoptions. Applicants may be single or married. There is no specific religious requirement.
Maine	International Christian Adoption Agency	Nationwide placement services for children from Latin America, Asia, and the Middle East. Applicants must be practicing Christians. Applicants may be married or single.
Utah	LDS Social Services	Branch offices in most states provide placement services for healthy and special needs children. Applicants must be members of the Church of Jesus Christ of Latter-day Saints. Applicants must be married.
New York	Little Flower Children's Services	Nationwide placement services for waiting children in the custody of New York State Department of Social Services. Applicants may be married or single. There is no specific religions requirement.
Texas	Los Ninos International Adoption Center	Nationwide placement services for children from Asia and Latin America. There is no specific religious requirement.
Missouri	Love Basket	Nationwide placement services for children from India. Some options are available to single parents. Applicants must be practicing Christians.

Missouri	MOM (Missions of Mercy)	Nationwide placement services for Caucasian infant adoptions, Black and bi-racial infant adoptions, and international adoptions. Some options are available to single parents. There is no specific religious requirement.
Pennsylvania	National Adoption Center	Nationwide match-referral services for special needs children.
Pennsylvania	Native American Adoption Resource Exchange (NAARE)	Operated by the Council of Three Rivers American Indian Center, NAARE provides nationwide match-referral services for waiting American Indian children. Only American Indian families are eligible for match-referral services through NAARE.
Georgia	Open Door Adoption Agency	Nationwide placement services for special needs infants. Applicants may be married or single. Applicants may be Christian or Jewish.
Virginia	Pan American Adoption Agency	Nationwide placement services for domestic and international adoptions. Applicants may be married or single. There is no specific religious requirement.
Georgia	Parent and Child Development Services	Nationwide placement services for minority and special needs children. Applicants may be married or single. There is no specific religious requirement.
Tennessee	Porter-Leath Children's Center	Nationwide placement services for healthy and special needs Black infants. Applicants may be married or single. There is no specific religious requirement.
Oklahoma	Project Adopt	Nationwide placement services for domestic and international special needs children. Applicants may be married or single. There is no specific religious requirement.
Louisiana	Sellers Baptist Home and Adoption Center	Nationwide placement services for domestic healthy and special needs infants. Applicants must be married. For Caucasian infant adoption, applicants must be Southern Baptists. For minority or special needs infant adoption, applicants must be Christians.

Oklahoma	Small Miracles International	Nationwide placement services for children from Guatemala. Applicants may be married or single. There is no specific religious requirement.
Arizona	Southwest Adoption Center	Nationwide placement services for healthy infants and young children (up to 2 years of age). Applicants must be married. There is no specific religious requirement.
New York	Spence-Chapin Services to Families and Children	Nationwide placement services for minority children and for children with special needs. Applicants may be married or single. There is no specific religious requirement.
Texas	Texas Cradle Society	Nationwide placement services for children with special needs. Applicants must be married. There is no specific religious requirement.
New York	Voice for International and Domestic Adoptions (VIDA)	Nationwide placement services for children from Central and South America. Applicants may be married or single. There is no specific religious requirement.